THE OFFICIAL

AMERICA ONLINE

FOR MACINTOSH TOUR GUIDE

THIRD EDITION

COVERS VERSION THREE

THE OFFICIAL

AMERICA ONLINE

FOR MACINTOSH TOUR GUIDE

THIRD EDITION

COVERS VERSION THREE

Everything You Need to Begin Enjoying the Nation's Most Exciting Online Service

Tom Lichty

VENTANA

The Official America Online for Macintosh Tour Guide, Third Edition

Library of Congress Cataloging-in-Publication Data

96-062099

Third Edition 9 8 7 6 5 4 3 2 1

Printed in the United States of America

Ventana Communications Group, Inc.
P.O. Box 13964
Research Triangle Park, NC 27709-3964
919.544.9404
FAX 919.544.9472
http://www.vmedia.com

Limits of Liability & Disclaimer of Warranty

The author and publisher of this book have used their best efforts in preparing the book and the programs contained in it. These efforts include the development, research, and testing of the theories and programs to determine their effectiveness. The author and publisher make no warranty of any kind, expressed or implied, with regard to these programs or the documentation contained in this book.

The author and publisher shall not be liable in the event of incidental or consequential damages in connection with, or arising out of, the furnishing, performance or use of the programs, associated instructions and/or claims of productivity gains.

Trademarks

Trademarked names appear throughout this book, and on the accompanying compact disk. Rather than list the names and entities that own the trademarks or insert a trademark symbol with each mention of the trademarked name, the publisher states that it is using the names only for editorial purposes and to the benefit of the trademark owner with no intention of infringing upon that trademark.

Chief Executive Officer
Josef Woodman

Vice President of Content Development
Karen A. Bluestein

Managing Editor
Lois J. Principe

Production Manager
John Cotterman

Technology Operations Manager
Kerry L. B. Foster

Product Marketing Manager
Scott S. Johnson

America Online Marketing Account Manager
Marisa A. Paley

Acquisitions Editor
Neweleen A. Trebnik

Project Editor
Jessica A. Ryan

Copy Editor
Marion Laird

Technical Reviewer
Brian Little, Imagination Workshop

Desktop Publisher
Kristin Miller

Proofreader
Thomas Collins

Indexer
Ann Norcross

Cover Design
Image Communications of Vienna, VA

About the Author

Tom Lichty writes computer and design books from his home in Damascus, Oregon, where he's accompanied by two dogs and five computers in a tiny studio overlooking Mount Hood. He has been trying to retire for four years now, but never quite finds the time to get around to it.

About the Coauthor

Jennifer Watson is an online pioneer, writing books oriented toward the online community. She is also the founder and coordinator of the online training academy for community leaders and partners. Jennifer has the good fortune to lead an amazing team and help thousands learn new skills, all from her home in Ann Arbor, Michigan.

Acknowledgments

A book like this could never be the work of one person. Hundreds of AOL in-house staff and community leaders have contributed to its genesis. Marisa, Matt, Thea, Lisa, Jill, Jay, Bill, Ellen, Serge, Katherine, Randy, Julia, Clarisse, Tim, Maura, David, Dave, Chris, Walt, Daye, Jon, Sarah, Tom, Charlie, Teach, Mary, and (of course) Steve: We thank you all for your benevolence.

Keeping our eye on the details were Howard, who answered our questions no matter how odd, and Brian, who deftly cross-checked and re-verified our ramblings.

Even the writing process was a group effort. Jim and Michael: We thank you for your wordsmithery.

Somehow holding it all together, the people at Ventana Communications served as our bedrock. Scott, Neweleen, Jessica, Pam, Marion, Karen, and John: bless you for your patience.

Kudos to Matt, Bill, and Maureen at Waterside Productions for the arbitration for which you're renowned.

Namaste to Leonard, for providing continuity in MajorTom's patchwork life.

Offering generous support, wise advice, and devilish distraction when most needed: George, thank you for your contributions, the least of which were to the glossary.

Most of all, we thank you, the readers of *The Official America Online for Macintosh Tour Guide*. We have received thousands of suggestions for improvements to this book and many of them are reflected in this edition.

Throughout this book we refer to AOL as a community. As you can see, the *Tour Guide* is, perhaps, the consummate community effort.

Tom Lichty and Jennifer Watson
January 1997

Acknowledgments

[illegible]

Contents

Foreword

I first got interested in online services in the early 1980s. I didn't know much about them then, but I knew enough to realize that they had a lot of potential. So when I bought my first personal computer in 1982, I decided to buy a modem and get online. This proved to be a very frustrating experience. It took me several months before I had all the equipment properly configured and was able to connect for the first time. Once I got connected, I found the services themselves hard to use and expensive. Nevertheless, despite all the hassles and shortcomings, I thought it was amazing that such a wealth of information and services were out there, waiting to be tapped into.

That was more than a decade ago. When we founded America Online, Inc., our objective was simple: to make online services more accessible, more affordable, more useful, and more fun for people like you and me. America Online now serves more than a million customers and is the nation's fastest-growing online service.

Our success has been driven by a constant focus on making the power of online services accessible to everyone. In designing America Online, we worked hard to make it very easy to use. We didn't want people to have to read a book in order to get connected, so we made the software easy to install and easy to use. As a result, people are usually up and running with America Online in less than 15 minutes.

Although we've done a good job of making the process of connecting to America Online hassle-free, we still have a problem: once you're connected, what do you do? America Online has grown so quickly, and now contains so many different services, finding the services that best meet your specific needs can be a bit of a challenge.

That's where this book comes in. Think of it as your personal tour guide, helping you get the most out of America Online. It highlights a wide range of useful and fun services, so you can begin enjoying America Online immediately. After you're comfortable with the basics, it will take you to the next step by explaining some of the more advanced capabilities that are built into the service.

When Ventana Communications first contacted us about publishing an America Online book, we thought it was a great idea. Our members had been asking for a book for some time, so we knew there was interest. And we felt that by working with an independent publisher, we'd end up with a better book than if we tried to write it ourselves.

Ventana's choice of Tom Lichty as the author was inspired. Tom had written a number of popular computer books, so he knew how to communicate information in an interesting and humorous manner. (A lot of computer books are deathly dull; Tom's are funny and engaging.) And since Tom was a novice user of online services, we felt his insightful observations as a novice would help others get the most out of America Online.

When the first edition of this Tour Guide was published in 1992, it got raves from readers, so this new, third edition is certain to be even more popular.

As you'll soon discover, America Online is more than easy-to-use software and a collection of useful and fun services. It's a living, breathing "electronic community" that comes alive because thousands of people all across the country don't just passively read the information that scrolls by on their screens, they get involved and participate, exchanging ideas on hundreds of topics. We provide the basic framework; beyond that, America Online is shaped by the collective imagination of its participants.

A new interactive communications medium is emerging, and it will change the way we inform, educate, work, and play. America Online is at the forefront of this exciting revolution. Come join us, as we work together to shape this new medium.

Steve Case, President, America Online, Inc.
AOL E-Mail Address: SteveCase

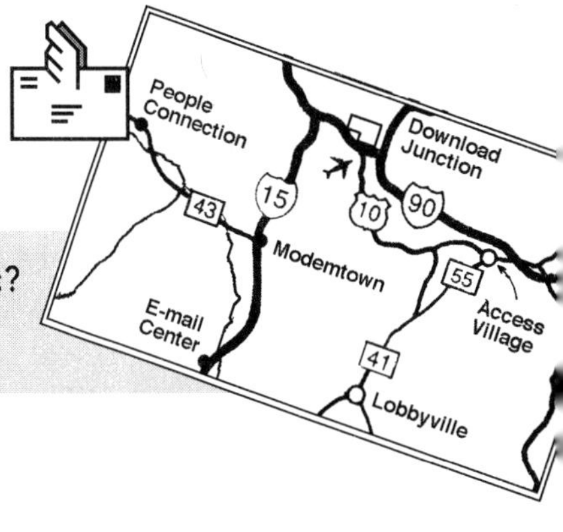
People Connection
Download Junction
43
15
10
90
Modemtown
55
Access Village
E-mail Center
41
Lobbyville

CHAPTER 1

Starting the Tour

- What Is America Online?
- How to Use This Book

We stood just inside the doorway, the auditorium walls dramatically curving away from us on either side. A soft susurration filled the air: a chorus of muffin fans, droning in the deserted expanse, melancholic, as only the sounds in an empty auditorium can be.

It was October 30. All day, I had seen America Online staffers roaming the halls, dressed in various degrees of whimsy. Even Steve Case was in costume. Now they had all gathered upstairs on the third floor for an after-hours Halloween fest, leaving us alone in a room built to accommodate hundreds—just Matt Korn and me . . .

. . . and 75,000 others, invisible and silent, ethereal as shadows.

Instant Gratification

Empowerment. That's what this book is all about. My mandate is to make you feel empowered by reading the Tour Guide. Thus, the following snippet of transcendental reward:

Sign on and stop at the Welcome screen. Move your cursor around on that screen and notice how the cursor changes. Passing over a button, for example, it becomes a pointing hand, ready to issue a command should you choose to click the mouse button.

Sometimes the cursor changes even when it is *not* over a button. This is not unique to the Welcome screen. When it changes unexpectedly like this, you should always experiment. This is no place for timidity.

Yes, there's a secret place within the Welcome window. It's intentional, and it changes every day.

Only you and I know about the Arcanum of the Welcome window; it's our little secret. Be empowered by this knowledge. But don't tell anyone.

Korn extended his hand to a switch on the wall and suddenly the room was a moonless night, black as a Halloween cat, aswirl in the breeze from the fans.

"Hold still a moment," he said. "Let your eyes adjust."

Slowly, flickering lights began to appear in the darkness. As my eyes adjusted, thousands of them became visible, winking randomly across the expanse of the auditorium. It was as if we were descending from a night flight, emerging from the cloud cover above a midnight city.

In time, the random flickers resolved into a pattern, revealing clusters of lights arranged in columns, miniature office buildings twinkling in the dark. I was later to learn that we were watching hundreds of *session controllers*: machines about the size of a VCR, each catering to the commands and caprices of AOL members.

The ability to accommodate capricious chaos is one of America Online's founding virtues. Members often leave multiple windows open on their screens—chat windows, Internet windows, library windows—and switch among those windows at will. Linearity isn't mandated by the software: there's no need to return to some kind of main menu before following another path. If a destination is visible on the screen, clicking its window takes you there. AOL's visionaries refer to this as their *modeless strategy*. For many of us who use AOL, following our impulses is as natural as respiration, and like respiration, we're unaware of the underlying "system" that makes it possible—unless, for some reason, it's withheld from us.

The electronic session controllers sense the members' clicks, determine where they want to go, and route them to the AOL computer that's appropriate for that task. Each session controller routes the commands of up to 64 members; cabinets the size of refrigerators each hold 4 to 7 session controllers. That evening, there were perhaps 300 cabinets in operation: around 75,000 people were logged on.

The lights were busy: it was Friday night; the members were playing. The lights wouldn't have been as active that afternoon when most people were working. Play is capricious; work tends to be more linear. On Friday night, most of those signed on were playing.

"That's New York," said Matt, pointing to a vertical array of lights. "That's Columbus, and Dallas, and Philadelphia. Los Angeles is over there; Seattle, Miami, Nashville . . ."

An auditorium of lights reflected people clicking mice all over the country. I felt like a voyeur. And I was mesmerized by what I saw.

Matt Korn

Matt Korn joined the firm in the early 1990s. He is a senior member of AOL's technical staff (Vice President of Operations, to be specific). Matt represents the median employee demographic: young, a participant in the employee stock-option plan, well educated, intelligent, and monomaniacally dedicated to his job: he had arrived at work around 8:00 this morning; it was now 7:30 in the evening and he still had a couple of hours of work ahead before going home. He seemed to be just getting his second wind. I wondered if he was married.

Soon after he arrived at AOL, Matt Korn became coordinator of the project that converted the auditorium into AOL's second computer room. A defense contractor had occupied the lower floor of the building before AOL purchased it; the auditorium served as the theater for extravagant presentations to the military—millions of public dollars riding on 10-minute productions! Though high technology still permeates the building, the fact that it's private telecommunications rather than public defense provides a microcosmic reflection of contemporary societal priorities.

What Is America Online?

I hope I haven't given you the wrong impression with this introduction. AOL is many things other than an auditorium-sized room filled with machines and wires.

A term like "America Online" doesn't give many clues as to its composition. We can safely deduce its country of origin (it's in America, all right: Dulles, Virginia, to be exact—just outside Washington, DC). But what's this "online" business? You won't even find the word in your dictionary if it's an older edition.

A definition is in order, and I am going to pursue that definition not only in terms of features and functions but also in relation to the "community" we join when we become AOL members. Over the next few pages, we'll allow America Online's technological capabilities to dazzle us, but by the end of this chapter you'll see that the true rewards are found in the *people* who await us on AOL.

It's One Big Thunder-Lizard Computer

One way of defining AOL is by describing its hardware. Coordinating thousands of simultaneous phone calls and storing tens of thousands of files requires one Thunder Lizard of a computer complex. No little Stegosaurus will do. We're talking Brontosaurus here, a beastie who relocates continents whenever he gets the urge to sneeze. Forget prefixes like *kilo* and *mega*. Think *giga* and *tera*. When they turn on the power to this thing, lights dim along the entire Eastern seaboard.

Open Architecture

I hate to disappoint you, but America Online isn't a single Brontosaurus-sized mainframe; it is, in fact, a number of refrigerator-sized computers, each having more in common with the adaptable Velociraptor than a leviathan as benign as the Brontosaurus.

Figure 1-1: A few of the many systems that are the heartbeat of America Online. A number of manufacturers are represented here, each product selected on the basis of suitability to a specific task. The homogenization factor is open architecture, which allows all of these diverse systems to work in concert.

Perhaps the best way to tackle this technologically complex subject is to return to that darkened room where we were standing a few pages back.

Our eyes fully adjusted now, Matt Korn and I walk among the session controllers as he continues his litany of cities: "Boston, Portland, Atlanta . . . " Each cabinet is labeled, though Korn has them memorized.

One thing strikes me as peculiar about these cabinets: the equipment mounted in them carries a variety of brand names. This isn't a place where a single manufacturer's equipment monotonously dominates the scene. I expected everything to say IBM or DEC on it, with matching colors and shapes like a model kitchen. Instead, what's inside of Korn's cabinets is a mélange of electronic diversity, more akin to a customized home entertainment system. AOL's cabinets hold equipment from a variety of manufacturers. IBM is there all right, but so are Hewlett-Packard, Cisco, Tandem, Silicon Graphics, Stratus, and a few others.

Using equipment from a single manufacturer, and connecting it with proprietary cables and communications protocols—so-called *closed systems*—used to be commonplace in mainframe computer installations. Today, however, closed systems are no more tolerated there than they are in home music systems. In my living room I have a Pioneer receiver, a TEAC tape deck, and a Sony CD player. Each had the features I wanted when I bought it, and the price was right. I was able to plug them all together using standardized cables, with never a worry that they might not work together properly.

In the computer business, this is called *open architecture*, and it's almost a mantra at AOL. Because of the common standard (TCP/IP—or *Transmission Control Protocol/Internet Protocol*, for those of you who care about those things), Korn can now buy mainframe components much as we buy components for our stereo systems: the best one for each job, at the best price.

All of which is to say that from a mechanical perspective, AOL is a diversity of computer systems interconnected with TCP/IP open architecture. Most of this hardware resides in that cavernous auditorium in Northern Virginia, about 20 miles from downtown Washington, DC.

Hosts & Clients

Let's define a couple of terms up front. You'll encounter them often, and without clarification they'll seem like that much more technobabble—and we all know how irritating that can be.

AOL's computer complex in Virginia is often referred to as *the host.* There are millions of us and only one AOL; we all "visit" AOL when we sign on; AOL's machines attend to our needs: these are the kinds of hostlike things that provoke the term.

Our computers—and the AOL software running on them—are the *clients.* Clients are served by the host; clients are numerable; and in this case, clients are patrons.

Client/host terminology is common in the networking industry, and when you think about it, AOL *is* a network. The meanings behind the terms aren't complex. Don't let the dweebs intimidate you.

Common Carriers

There's more to the technology of AOL than computers, however. There's also the nagging little problem of delivering the signal from your location to Vienna. Again, an analogy is in order.

If you wanted to get a package to a friend who lives across the country, you could probably hop in your car and drive it there yourself. But compared to the alternatives, driving across the country would be impractical, to say the least.

More likely, you'd hire a *common carrier*—a service such as United Parcel Service or FedEx—to deliver the package for you. For a fraction of what it would cost you to do the job yourself, common carriers can do it more reliably, less expensively, and much more conveniently.

AOLnet

In the early 1990s, when AOL was experiencing almost meteoric growth, even the largest common carriers couldn't keep up. It was as if you and I and everyone we know were to call FedEx for a pickup every 15 minutes. The common carriers clogged up, connections with AOL were difficult to establish during peak usage periods, and when connections were made, they were often sluggish.

Taking matters into its own hands, AOL established its own private network, *AOLnet.* AOLnet is your best choice of all the carriers because all of AOLnet's access numbers are high speed, and AOLnet's backbones—the transcontinental lines that run from city to city—are state of the art. For more information about AOLnet, sign on, press Command-K (for "keyword," AOL's navigational shortcut system), enter the keyword: **AOLnet**, and read the information you find there.

Figure 1-2: High-speed tele-communications equipment in use at America Online headquarters.

For much the same reason, AOL hires common carriers to deliver goods to its members. And, typical of AOL, it hires multiple common carriers, to ensure reliability. There's SprintNet, a service of US Sprint, and there's DataPac, a subsidiary of Bell Canada, for Canadian members. There are others. These common carriers offer *nodes*—local telephone numbers—in most cities in North America. They charge AOL for phone calls (placed or received) just as FedEx would charge you to deliver a package.

AOL is quickly installing AOLnet nodes in as many cities as possible, but for those cities that AOLnet doesn't serve, SprintNet or DataPac are used. No matter which carrier you use, the important thing to understand is that the carrier is as much a part of the AOL network as are the machines in Virginia.

It's a Telecommunications Service

Now *there's* a polysyllabic mouthful: *telecommunications*. As the term is used here, the word *telecommunications* refers to two-way communications via telephone lines. A phone call, in other words, is a form of telecommunicating. Telephone lines are good for things other than phone calls. Fax machines use telephone lines to transfer documents; video phones use them to transmit pictures; and modems use them to transfer computer data (the term *modem*—as well as many other terms—is defined in the Glossary at the back of this book). I'm not talking about expensive dedicated telephone lines here—I'm talking about the very same telephone lines that are already in our homes and offices.

Now we're getting somewhere. If you have a computer and I have a computer and we each have a modem, we can use our existing telephone lines to connect our computers to one another. Once connected this way, our computers can exchange data: text, graphics, sounds, animation—even programs.

Of course, you have to be at your computer and I have to be at mine—at the same time—and we have to know how to make our computers talk to one another, and we have to check for errors encountered in the transmission, and I'm just me and you're just you, and there's only so much computer data two people can exchange with one another before the whole thing gets to be pretty dull.

What we need is a *service* that will store our data so that we don't have to be at our computers at the same time. Instead of calling your computer, I have my computer call the service and store my data and messages there. When you're ready for that data, you can instruct your computer to call the service and retrieve the data at your convenience.

As long as we're imagining a service, we might imagine it to automate all the electronic technicalities as well. If we imagine it right, the service can mediate communications between the two computers, check for errors (and fix them when they're encountered), and even dial the telephone.

And who's to say that you and I should have the service all to ourselves? We can let everyone else with a computer in on it as well, regardless of the type of computer they own. Carried to its extreme, this scenario might result in hundreds of thousands—millions, actually—of people using the service, exchanging and storing thousands of computer files. Most of this data can be public rather than private, so the exchange becomes multilateral.

Which is precisely what telecommunications services—and AOL—are: a vast network of "members," each of whom uses a computer, a modem, and a telephone line to connect with a common destination—to "go online." Members can exchange public and private files; they can send and receive e-mail; and members who are online at the same time can "chat" in real time. They can even play online games with one another.

And what does this service cost? The economies of scale allow expenses to be distributed among the members. Moreover, even though AOL is near Washington, DC, very few members pay for long-distance calls. America Online has local telephone numbers in nearly every city in the contiguous United States. Even if you live in "the sticks," chances are you'll find a local number you can call—or one that's a "short" long-distance call away. If that's too expensive, there's always AOL's 800 number. (To find out more about access to AOL via the toll-free 800 number, sign on and use the keyword: **Access**.)

It's Software Installed in Your Computer

Conceptualizing AOL as nodes and mainframe computers isn't very comforting. For many of us, America Online is much more parochial than that: AOL is software in our computers—software on a disk bundled with the computer, ordered from a magazine ad, or provided in the *Official America Online Membership Kit*.

AMERICA
Online

Figure 1-3: America Online's logo appears whenever you run the software installed on your computer.

That's more like it. The software you use on your computer to sign on to AOL more accurately represents the personality of the service than anything we've discussed so far. It makes friendly noises, it's resplendent with windows and icons, and it automates tasks and procedures that only a few years ago used to exclude most semi-normal people from using telecommunications systems.

Here's what I mean. Nearly every telecommunications program assumes you know how to set certain arcane but necessary attributes and protocols, such as data bits, stop bits, parity, and flow. Frankly, though I've used telecommunications software for years and have adjusted my data bits and parity, I have no idea what they are, and I have always been kind of nervous about shooting in the dark like that. America Online, on the other hand, uses its own custom software at both ends of the line. After you install the software on your computer (a simple process I describe in Appendix A, "Making the Connection"), all the technicalities are coordinated by the host computer and your machine. They simply talk things over and make adjustments as required. This is as it should be.

We're getting closer to the mark. The phrase "user-friendly" is properly used to describe this service. America Online's new Macintosh software is familiar, predictable, and comfortable for the Macintosh user. The File menu says Open, Save, Close, and Quit. Its windows have title bars and close buttons.

Another unique aspect of the AOL software is its interface and communication strategy. The software is highly graphical, and transferring graphics online takes time (much more time than transferring text, for instance), which could make the service as sluggish as a hound in July. However, this should not cause problems because most of AOL's graphical components are transferred to your machine only once, then they're stored on your hard disk. After that, text is the primary information that flows between you and AOL, and text travels very quickly.

Tools on Demand

Occasionally, you'll encounter a message from AOL indicating that a change needs to be made to your application—the AOL client software running on your computer—and that an update needs to take place (see Figure 1-4).

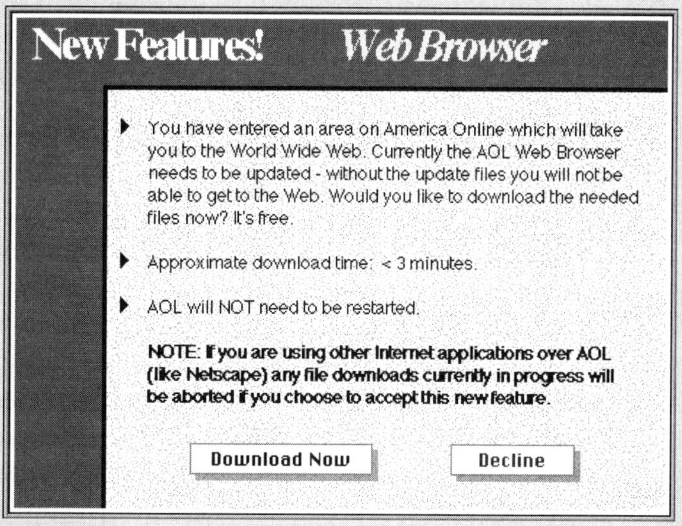
New Features! Web Browser
You have entered an area on America Online which will take you to the World Wide Web. Currently the AOL Web Browser needs to be updated - without the update files you will not be able to get to the Web. Would you like to download the needed files now? It's free.
Approximate download time: < 3 minutes.
AOL will NOT need to be restarted.
NOTE: If you are using other Internet applications over AOL (like Netscape) any file downloads currently in progress will be aborted if you choose to accept this new feature.
Download Now
Decline

Figure 1-4: A Tool on Demand download in progress.

Updates such as this usually amount to nothing more than the download of a few graphical elements—special artwork is being downloaded in Figure 1-4—that keep your software up to date. The download can amount to much more: AOL can add major features to your software this way, or update those that require updating.

AOL calls this feature *Tools on Demand.* The demand originates with your client, which, comparing notes with the host, makes note of outdated AOL software on your computer and requests new software to replace it.

Regardless of the complexity of the download, updates are free—you won't be billed for the time other than any long-distance or 800-number charges you're incurring.

AOL's multimedia interface is constantly changing. That's part of what makes AOL so exciting. AOL uses its own medium to distribute these updates, as well it should. Best of all: they're automatic and free of connect-time charges. More of life should be like this.

Here's the point: AOL is an advanced and progressive telecommunications service that grows daily and contains the features necessary to accommodate that growth. The software features I describe here reflect a progressive attitude, and that attitude is a better way of defining AOL.

It's a Resource

News, sports, weather—sure you can get them on radio and television, but not necessarily when you need or want them. You can get them in a newspaper, too, but it's going to cost the environment a tree or two, the pictures are fuzzy, and about all you can do with a newspaper you've read is throw it away (consult the Environmental Forum at keyword: **Environment** for recycling information). America Online offers the news, sports, and weather as well—available at your convenience and without sacrificing any trees. It's in electronic form, so you can file it, search it, and include it in documents of your own.

On an average day, I begin by reading the latest news and weather (discussed in Chapter 10, "Staying Informed"); then I check up on the investments in my modest portfolio (discussed in Chapter 12, "Personal Finance") and read my mail (discussed in Chapter 3, "Electronic Mail & the Personal Filing Cabinet"). Not long ago I researched the purchase of a new hard disk for my computer (see Chapter 15, "Buying & Selling"), and I often make my travel plans using AOL's airline reservation system. I constantly search the online video reviews before I rent a tape (the airline reservation system and video reviews are discussed in Chapter 11, "Divertissements"). Past issues of *Macworld, WIRED,* and *Smithsonian* are online for my review, as is *Compton's Encyclopedia, The Merriam-Webster Dictionary,* and "the Gray Lady": *The New York Times* (see Chapter 14, "Reference"). As a professional member of the desktop publishing community, I constantly collect graphics, fonts, and utilities (AOL has tens of thousands of such files online—described in Chapter 5, "Transferring Files").

In other words, I could describe AOL as a resource of almost infinite potential. You don't have to drive anywhere to use it; it's continuously maintained and updated; and it's all electronic—available for any use you can imagine. Many members find the resource potential alone ample justification for signing on to AOL, but to limit your participation this way would be a disservice to AOL and to yourself. Above all, AOL is people: friends, associates, consultants—even lovers. It's a resource, all right, but it's also a community. And therein lies its greatest value.

It's a Community

I've taken the easy way out. Yes, AOL is a telecommunications service. Yes, it's the host computer. Yes, it's client software in your computer. And yes, it's a resource. But that's like saying that Christmas is just another day of the year. There's much more to it than that. Christmas is reverence and good things; but for many of us, Christmas means people: family, friends, and community. AOL, too, is best defined by its people. America Online is a *community*. My dictionary defines community as "a social group sharing common characteristics or interests," and that is the best definition I can imagine for AOL.

As members, we have common interests, we all have computers, and we love to share. *That's* what AOL is all about. After a few weeks, the novelty of interconnection and graphical images wears off. After a few weeks, we stop wondering about the host computer and data bits. After a few weeks, we all discover the true soul of AOL, and that soul is its people.

Futuring

This is certainly a medium for futuring—for envisaging, musing, and aspiring. I future with nearly everyone I meet at AOL: they're the people who are shaping the future of telecommunications, and they're always a couple of years ahead of the rest of us. Fascinating discourse.

Steve Case is President of America Online. He is paid to future, and he loves his job. On this spectacular fall afternoon, sitting in his office with Virginia's autumnal splendor outside the window, Steve talks of what lies ahead for telecommunications.

Not even 9 percent of American homes were online in the fall of 1995 when we talked. Steve compares this to television in the late 1940s: "No one remembers television then. It was in less than 10 percent of American homes. It was an emerging technology, a curiosity, and the things television did in the '40s are all but forgotten."

He goes on to cite television's emergent moment, which he feels was the 1960 Presidential election. We couldn't help but take notice of television after that: the debates, after all, could very well have swayed the election.

Steve Case futures about the online medium in 10 years, when it has reached the same point along its developmental curve. Will the candidates appear in an online Rotunda of some sort, debating issues and answering questions from members? Will they offer an e-mail address and respond to all queries? Steve suspects that the online industry might very well influence the viability of a third political party in this country. What medium is better prepared to develop a party of the people? The online medium is the embodiment of the elusive flat playing field, where everyone is equally empowered and there is little cause for class, race, gender, or age discrimination. In an era where political candidates are perceived as media stars—inaccessible, almost chimerical—we're primed for a candidate who seems to be one of us, and the online medium is where such a creature might best be nurtured.

I never asked Steve Case if he thought he might ever be President. I doubt that he would take the job. He's having too much fun being Steve Case.

When I first agreed to write this book, community was the last thing on my mind. I have been a telecommunicator for years. I thought I'd seen it all. Now, however, I spend as much of my online time corresponding with friends—new friends in every part of the country—as I do conducting research. In Chapter 3, I admit to getting despondent if I don't hear the familiar mail notification when the Welcome screen comes up. Throughout this book, I'll offer little tips on how to make friends online. Follow these tips, and you'll become as much a part of this community as I am.

You really couldn't do much better.

Tom Lichty

Allow me to introduce myself. My name is Tom Lichty (say *lick'-tee*). I'm a full-time writer, living on a small farm in rural Oregon, where the air is clear and the politics are liberal. I often ply the waters of the Pacific Northwest and Alaska aboard Pick Pocket, my Spartan little aquatic cruiser. If you ever happen to be in Desolation Sound on a peaceful July evening and notice a small boat with a fellow bent over the keyboard of his laptop computer, it's probably me.

I'd be flattered if you'd check out my home page on the World Wide Web (the Web is discussed in Chapter 4, "Using the Internet"). Sign on to AOL, press Command-K and type **http://members.aol.com/majortom/private/index.html**. Be sure to type it exactly as shown, then click the Go button.

Here at my virtual side is Jennifer Watson, literary colleague and Macintosh guru. The Windows 95 and Macintosh editions of the Tour Guide face near-simultaneous deadlines, so while I'm working on the Windows 95 book, she's translating it into the Mac edition. Though you'll meet Jennifer again in Chapter 8, "The Community," you might want to check out her home page now, at **http://members.aol.com/jennifer/**.

The people at America Online have an uncommonly altruistic attitude toward the documentation for their service. *The Official America Online Tour Guide* is a book, not a manual. I'm an independent author, not a staff technical writer. And AOL chose a traditional publisher—Ventana Communications Group—to produce and distribute this book. It's not an AOL production. I therefore have the autonomy and elbow room to explore the subject with you independently, thoroughly, and candidly. The people at AOL are to be commended for their courage in choosing this path. It could be perilous. Confidence in their product, however, emboldens them, and rightfully so.

About AOL's Pricing

In December 1996, AOL inaugurated a new pricing structure. Most of the pricing plans now available are of the unlimited variety: there are no hourly fees. You can stay online as long as you want, enjoy all the news, information, entertainment, and shopping available on America Online, and surf the Web to your heart's delight with the comfort of knowing your monthly price in advance.

All pricing options assume you can reach AOL via a local number, without having to incur toll charges for the call. If AOL doesn't offer a local number in your area, there's an 800 (toll-free) number you can call to access AOL. There is a surcharge for use of this number. Use the keyword: **Access** to search for a local number and to learn more about AOL's 800-number access.

The **Standard Monthly Plan** is the default. Quite simply, it provides for unlimited use of AOL—including AOL's access to the Internet—for $19.95 a month. You can reduce this charge by paying in advance. Advance renewal rates are $14.95 per month if you pay in advance for two years; $17.95 per month if you pay in advance for one year. Advance payments are nonrefundable.

The **Bring Your Own Access** program is intended for people who use a local Internet provider to access AOL. If you subscribe to the services provided by a local Internet provider, you can access AOL through that account. Accessing AOL via another provider, again on an unlimited-use basis, is only $9.95 a month. Use the keyword: **Access** (and click the How to Connect button) to find out more about this method of accessing AOL.

Some people prefer to go online primarily for access to e-mail. Managed properly, e-mail doesn't require much time online. You can probably accomplish all of your e-mail activities in three hours a month of online time, especially if you use Automatic AOL (see Chapter 6, "Automatic AOL & the Download Manager"). If three hours a month is adequate for you, the **Light-Usage Program** is just $4.95, with additional time priced at $2.50 an hour.

All of these programs are described at keyword: **Pricing**. Use the keyword: **Billing** if you would like to change your pricing structure.

How to Use This Book

I suppose this book is the documentation—the "user's manual"—for America Online. You no doubt already know that documentation can be dull. Few people take a software manual to the hammock for a lazy afternoon of reading. As you might guess from the title, this is not your typical prosaic how-to instruction manual; you will find no inscrutable "technobabble." I hope you'll find it more of an odyssey—a pleasant journey of discovery—to the interesting places and people in America Online's virtual universe. Nonetheless, as your guide to all the diverse experiences AOL has to offer, I've included organizational and reference tools that will help you find your way around.

Finding Answers

I want you to be able to turn to *The Official America Online for Macintosh Tour Guide* whenever you have a question about AOL. I want you to be able to find the answer to your question with a minimum of effort, no matter how many different places the subject may appear in the book. Pursuant to that, a number of tools are at your disposal:

- The *table of contents* lists titles, section heads, and subheads for every chapter. When you need information on a specific subject, turn first to the table of contents. Nine times out of ten, it will be all you need.
- A thorough *index* appears at the end of the book, with references to subjects, procedures, and departments. If the subject you're after doesn't appear in the table of contents, turn to the index.
- A *listing of keywords* appears in Appendix B. Keywords are the interstate highway system at AOL. If you want to get somewhere in a hurry, use a keyword. As you discover places that appeal to you, add them to your list of favorite places in your Personal Filing Cabinet (described in Chapter 3).
- A *glossary* of terms used in the book follows the appendices. The glossary is especially thorough in its inclusion of telecommunications terminology that is unique to AOL. People often talk in shorthand when they're online—typing is so *slow*—and the glossary offers the necessary translations.

Activity Listings

With the exception of the first and last chapters, I've organized this book according to the way people use AOL. Chapters 2 through 15 each describe a typical online activity and how that activity is best pursued.

- Chapter 2, "The Abecedarium," comes up next. AOL is a big place. Lots of things are going on here, and when you first sign on it's like your first day on a new job: everyone seems to know what to do except you. Chapter 2 is like a neighborly coworker—showing you an *orderly, effective* approach for getting to know AOL and spending your time there productively. This chapter also defines the word *abecedarium.*

- Chapter 3, "Electronic Mail & the Personal Filing Cabinet," describes AOL's most popular feature: e-mail. You can communicate with people all over the world—not just fellow AOL members but anyone with e-mail access to the Internet—using AOL's mail filing system, which is second to none.
- Chapter 4, "Using the Internet," briefly introduces the Internet and AOL's tools for using it. I say "briefly" because AOL offers exceptional online help for this rapidly changing telecommunications Wunderkind. Just use the keywords: **Internet Questions** or the keyword: **Answerman** to find out more.
- Chapter 5, "Transferring Files," focuses on tricks and techniques for downloading and uploading files from and to AOL.
- Chapter 6, "Automatic AOL & the Download Manager," shows you how to read and write your mail offline, when you're not paying AOL for the time. You can also instruct your computer to perform your downloads automatically and unattended, in the middle of the night if you want, when the load on the system is minimal.
- Chapter 7, "Computing," explores AOL's computing resources: programs, drivers, and utilities, and offers commiseration and advice.
- Chapter 8, "The Community," introduces you to chat rooms and Instant Messages, where conversations occur in real time and strangers rarely remain strangers for long. This chapter also discusses the people who comprise that community: kids, seniors, and everyone in between.
- Chapter 9, "Boards & Forums," opens the doors to AOL's clubhouses, where people of similar interests gather to exchange wisdom and develop communities.
- Chapter 10, "Staying Informed," describes AOL's profound informational resources, including news, sports, and weather.
- Chapter 11, "Divertissements," makes an effort to acquaint you with the spectrum of interesting things you can do online. Though it's by no means comprehensive, this chapter includes online games; book,

film, and television reviews; ABC, MTV, and Entertainment Weekly; the comics; and travel, including Preview Travel, the Independent Traveler, Travelers' Corner, and Preview Travel Vacations.

- Chapter 12, "Personal Finance," offers a mini-primer on the subject of online finance. Not only can you buy and sell publicly traded issues with AOL, but you can also maintain a detailed portfolio, chart its performance, and consult the wisdom of experts when transactions must be made.
- Chapter 13, "Learning & Culture," explores learning opportunities for the student and teacher, Online Campus, the Nature Conservancy, Book Central, the Smithsonian, and the Odyssey Project.
- Chapter 14, "Reference," spotlights one of the online medium's most unique benefits: information retrieval. Encyclopedias, cookbooks, dictionaries—they're all electronically searchable, continually updated, and eminently quotable.
- Chapter 15, "Buying & Selling," runs the gamut from the classifieds to real estate. The online medium has become fertile ground for commerce—you can't beat it for convenience, after all—and AOL offers scores of ways to participate.
- Chapter 16, "Ten Best," offers my ten best ten-best lists—the ten best tips for using AOL, the ten questions most frequently asked of the AOL customer support team, the ten best files for downloading—that kind of thing. No fair reading this one first!

Moving On

Our lights-out experience in the auditorium concluded, Matt Korn sits in his office. The sounds of nocturnal revelry downstairs still sift through the building, but Matt has better things to do. He talks of an online future that incites the imagination. Virtual realities, video chat, personal agents—things that require new vocabularies to comprehend. I feel honored to be among his *beau monde*.

I'm honored, too, to share this extraordinary resource with you. Matt may be enamored with AOL's future—that's his job, after all—but I'm dazzled enough with its present. You will be too. Turn the page. A remarkable journey is about to begin.

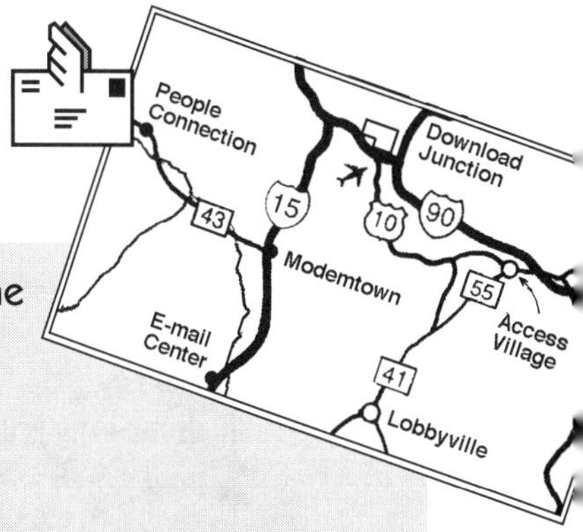

People Connection
Download Junction
43
15
10
90
Modemtown
55
Access Village
E-mail Center
41
Lobbyville

CHAPTER 2

The Abecedarium

- Discover America Online
- Road Trips
- Getting Help
- Guides
- My AOL
- Parental Controls
- Terms of Service (TOS)

Isn't that a *great* word? "Abecedarium." Pronounce the first three syllables as you would pronounce the first three letters in the alphabet: A-B-C, then add "darium" (it rhymes with "aquarium"). Indeed, the letters "ABC" are the root of the word, for in the original Medieval Latin, *abecedarium* meant "alphabet." Later the term was used to describe books for people who are learning the alphabet, and later still—as it is today—abecedarium was used to describe a primer on any subject. That's what we're doing with this chapter: presenting a primer for those of you who are new to this abecedary we call online telecommunications.

The Newbies, the Ditzels & the Dummies

In the fall of 1995, a long-term discussion broke out on the staff message boards at AOL: what term do we use to describe people who are new to online telecommunicating? "Dummy" is popular, but it's not a very flattering term. Its success as a book title, I suspect, relates more to a person's self perception, not to the person's status among others. "Ditzel" is perhaps too colloquial a term, and even less flattering than dummy.

The consensus among the staff was that "newbie" would have to do, though it wasn't a unanimous sentiment. The term is often used derisively, in spite of its original intent.

I like "abecedarian." No word with that many syllables can be derisive. No word that appears to be so confoundedly unpronounceable can possibly be colloquial. And its meaning is understood by so few that it will never be used unflatteringly—it's hardly used at all.

Perfect. We'll call ourselves abecedarians and perplex them all with our pedantic pedagogy. They're all a bunch of dweebs anyway. ;-)

Discover America Online

Somewhere, the Godiva people must have a chocolate warehouse. I'll bet it's huge. Imagine standing just inside of the door, confronted by shelves of chocolates, stacked to the ceiling in a warehouse that's measured in acres. Your host just told you to "Eat whatever you want." *Holy confections*! Where to begin?

Once the stupefaction wears off, most AOL abecedarians wander around aimlessly for their first few weeks, biting their nails and cultivating futility. This is no more productive a method of exploring AOL than it is of exploring Godiva's warehouse. We need some direction here: something or someone to show us where the best stuff is so we can get down to the business of prodigal consumption.

I don't know about Godiva, but AOL offers such a place, and it's right on the menu. To get there, use the keywords: **Discover AOL**. This will take you to the *Discover America Online* area, where all of AOL's new member help is consolidated, and there's a wealth of it.

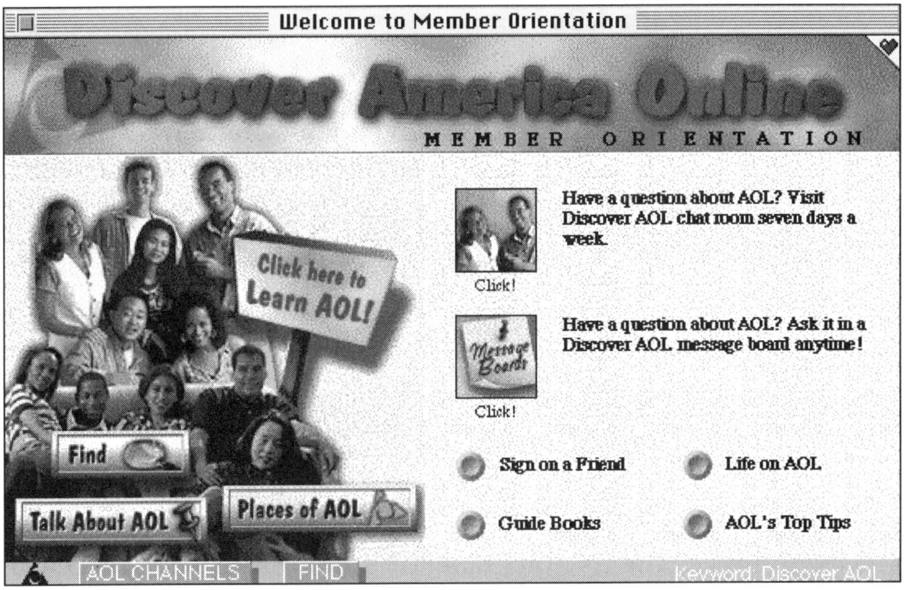
Welcome to Member Orientation
Discover America Online
MEMBER ORIENTATION
Click here to Learn AOL!
Have a question about AOL? Visit Discover AOL chat room seven days a week.
Click!
Message Boards
Have a question about AOL? Ask it in a Discover AOL message board anytime!
Click!
Find
Sign on a Friend
Life on AOL
Talk About AOL
Places of AOL
Guide Books
AOL's Top Tips
AOL CHANNELS
FIND
Keyword: Discover AOL

Figure 2-1: Discover America Online is the best way to learn about the service.

Keywords

I mentioned *keywords* in the previous chapter and I just mentioned them again, but more emphasis is appropriate. Keywords are shortcuts to specific destinations within AOL. Without keywords, accessing Family PC Online, for example, via menus and windows requires that I click the Computing button on the Main Menu, click the ZD Net button, click the Explore icon, and finally click the Family PC button. *Whew*! That's a lot of button-pushing, and I had to know which buttons to push. There's gotta be a better way.

And there is: keywords. The keyword(s) for Family PC Online is **Family PC**. Once I know the keyword, all I have to do is choose Keyword from the Go To menu (or click the Keyword button on the toolbar, or press Command-K) and enter **Family PC** into the area provided. Instantly, AOL takes me directly to Family PC Online, bypassing all the steps in between.

A list of keywords is available in Appendix B of this book and online at keyword: **KEYWORDS**. Keywords are also available within the Directory of Services (discussed later), which you can search right in the Keyword window. Just enter your criterion where the keyword would normally go and click the Search button.

A final note: Keywords are not case sensitive. **FAMILY PC** works just the same as **family pc**. You can leave out spaces too: **Family PC** works no better than **FamilyPC**.

Learn AOL

Remember the "hidden" area on the Welcome screen, the one we discussed in Chapter 1? You might recall that you discovered it by moving the cursor around on the screen, watching for changes.

The same is true of the Discover America Online screen. As you move the cursor over the "Click here to learn AOL" placard, it changes to a pointing hand. Beneath that placard is the area we'll call "Learn AOL."

As much as I like to think of this book as the perfect mechanism for learning about America Online, it does have its flaws. It's a single medium. It's not in 24-bit color. Its pictures don't move. It's difficult to change.

On the other hand, AOL offers the perfect medium for learning: fluidic, multimedia, and compelling. AOL is aware of this advantage, of course, and employs it well in the "Learn AOL" area that's under that placard.

There's a programmed learning area here: a dozen or so step-by-step lessons you can browse, each with colorful graphics and insight into the AOL experience. If you're new to the service, this is the place to begin.

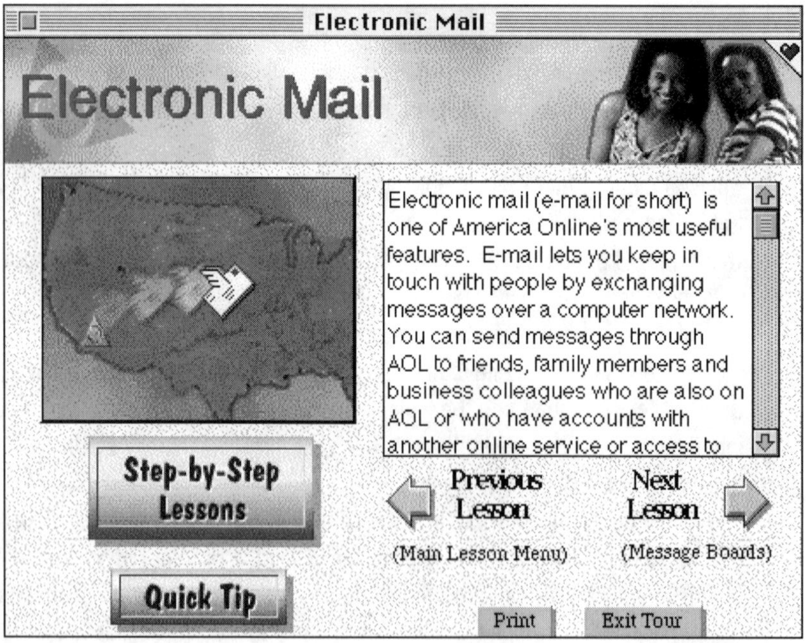
Electronic Mail
Electronic Mail
Electronic mail (e-mail for short) is one of America Online's most useful features. E-mail lets you keep in touch with people by exchanging messages over a computer network. You can send messages through AOL to friends, family members and business colleagues who are also on AOL or who have accounts with another online service or access to
Step-by-Step Lessons
Previous Lesson
(Main Lesson Menu)
Next Lesson
(Message Boards)
Quick Tip
Print
Exit Tour

Figure 2-2: The Electronic Mail tutorial is just one of many "lessons" designed to make the use of AOL easy and fun.

Find

AOL is a vast and glorious place. It's easy to lose sight of the forest while you're looking at the trees. There are hundreds—perhaps thousands—of places you might miss if you don't know where they are. You're probably not even aware that they exist.

How do you discover places like this? How would I find all of the places that had to do with chocolate, for example, when the only place I know of for chocolates is the refrigerator? It's easy. Use Find.

Find is not only available within the Discover America Online window, it's on the toolbar as well, where it's available regardless of where you are on the service. You can use Find to find people, events, and places and things. It searches not only AOL, but the Internet as well.

AOL Find
Find It On AOL!
Type what you're looking for and click "Search."
Search
OR, click on a tab below for suggested areas.
Places & Things
People
Events
AOL Directory
AOL Access Numbers
AOL Classifieds
AOL Homepage
Internet Newsgroups
Search for Software
Search the Internet
The Essentials
Browse Channels
Find Help

Figure 2-3: Here's the best way to explore AOL's universe: Find. It's available at Discover America Online, and its button is always available on the toolbar.

Using Find today, I found almost 4,000 places that had to do with chocolate, including Godiva Chocolatier (at keyword: **Godiva**) and even a chocolate pizza Web site. I may never resort to the refrigerator again.

Top Tips

Discover AOL offers lots of other opportunities to become familiar with the service, and I'll conclude with one you won't want to miss: AOL Top Tips. This is a place you will want to visit every week or so. It changes frequently, and the tips are invaluable. If you want to get the very most out of America Online, visit Top Tips regularly (see Figure 2-4).

AOL Top Tips
AOL Top Tips
Keyword: Top Tips
~~TODAY'S TIP~~
November 24, 1996
A QUICK REPLY TO EVERYONE
Most members think America Online's e-mail is easy to use, but most folks don't realize how powerful it can be (of course, if they did, they wouldn't need these tips). One the special features of AOL's e-mail is the ability to reply to just one
AOL Store
Billing Information
AOL's Online Safety For Kids
Check For Live Events
Check Out What's New on AOL
Creating Favorite Places
Directory of Services
Download the Latest Version...
Find Out The Latest About AOL
Game Information Exchange
Get Help With Your Homework
Send us your tip suggestions!
Learn AOL!
Want to learn more about how to use AOL? Click here.

Figure 2-4: Use the keywords: **Top Tips** at least once a week.

Road Trips

AOL's Road Trips are guided tours of the service. Virtually speaking, you climb aboard a bus (usually with 20 or so others) and take off on a magical adventure conducted by "tour guides"—people who know where they're going and identify features along the way (see Figure 2-5).

AOL Road Trips
TOUR SCHEDULE
Click for Tour Times
AOL
ROAD TRIP
Click here for Help
Create a Road Trip
Take a Road Trip

Figure 2-5: Road Trips are probably the best way to get to know AOL. Take the hand of an expert and participate in a methodical, revealing tour of America Online—and have fun along the way. Road Trips are available at the keywords: **Road Trip**.

Are You Current?

As is the case with many other areas in this book, the Road Trips discussion assumes you have the latest version of AOL's software. Do you? Here's how to find out:

1. Sign on and use the keyword: **Upgrade.**
2. Find the latest copy of AOL's software available for download in the upgrade area, then read its description to discover its version number.
3. Choose About America Online... from the Apple menu and note the number of the version you're now using.
4. If the versions don't match, you need to download the upgrade. Begin by printing the file's description that appears on your screen. *Don't neglect this step.*
5. Download the upgrade, then sign off.
6. Quit from the AOL software, then follow the directions in the description you have printed.

Road Trips aren't passive. At each stop, your tour guide will let you "off the bus" to explore the area for a while on your own. You can wander around in the Florida Wildflower Web page, for example (see Figure 2-6), and your tour guide will be at your side, ready to answer questions and point out features.

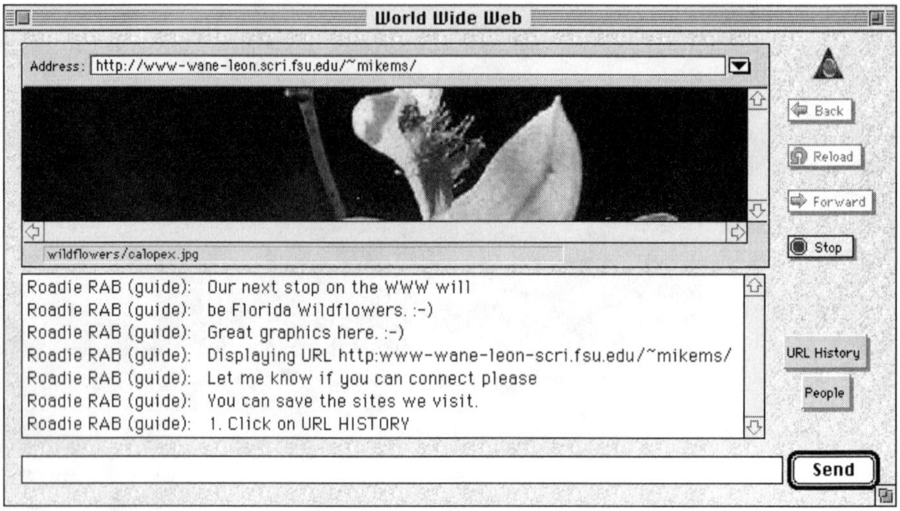
World Wide Web
Address: http://www-wane-leon.scri.fsu.edu/~mikems/
wildflowers/calopex.jpg
Back
Reload
Forward
Stop
Roadie RAB (guide): Our next stop on the WWW will
Roadie RAB (guide): be Florida Wildflowers. :-)
Roadie RAB (guide): Great graphics here. :-)
Roadie RAB (guide): Displaying URL http:www-wane-leon-scri.fsu.edu/~mikems/
Roadie RAB (guide): Let me know if you can connect please
Roadie RAB (guide): You can save the sites we visit.
Roadie RAB (guide): 1. Click on URL HISTORY
URL History
People
Send

Figure 2-6: The Florida Wildflower Web page invites my exploration in the top half of the Road Trip window. In the lower half, my tour guide is identifying features of the site. The very bottom of the window offers a text box where I can submit my questions and comments. The tour guide or anyone else on the bus can reply.

Road Trips aren't the exclusive purview of AOL's staff, by the way. Anyone can be a guide—even you. It's a great way to introduce friends to AOL, even if they're in another part of the country. It's really quite easy to prepare your own personal tour: press the Help button at keywords: **Road Trip** for more information.

Getting Help

Speaking of help, I'll never forget my first online experience. It was many years ago—long before America Online—and the service I subscribed to was a commercial service and the clock was running whenever I dialed their number. Anxiety had no finer ally.

In other words, I empathize with those of you whose fingers turn to cucumbers whenever you sign on—and so does America Online. Things have changed. Today there is help—plenty of help. Not only does AOL offer an abundance of help, it's most often free. I'd be five years younger today if the early days of the online industry had been that considerate.

Getting Help: A Methodical Approach

If you have a question about AOL and require help, *don't write to me!* I'm just one person, with one person's knowledge of the system. AOL offers an army of experts, each of them is thoroughly acquainted with the system, and each is trained in member assistance. To make effective use of them, I suggest you use the methods described below, in the order in which they appear. Most of the topics mentioned are explained in detail later in this chapter.

1. Look up the topic in the index of this book to see if your question is answered here. I'd like to think that most of your questions will be answered this way.
2. Run the AOL software (you don't need to sign on) and click the Help button on the Welcome window (the first window that appears after running the software). In this chapter I refer to this kind of help as *offline* help because it's available when you're offline (even though it's available online as well). Offline help offers an extensive searchable list of topics and will often answer your question, especially if it has to do with the most commonly asked AOL questions.
3. Sign on and click the question-mark button on the toolbar (the toolbar is that bar of icons just under the menu bar). Click the Yes button in response to the "Are you sure..." message. This will take you to AOL's Member Services, a particularly comprehensive (and free) resource. There's a Member Services button on each channel's screen as well.
4. Sign on and use the keyword: **Questions**. This will take you to the Quick Answers database, where you can review a slew of FAQs (Frequently Asked Questions) covering a wide variety of topics. From this keyword, you can also jump to a search of the Member Services answer database. This is an amazingly comprehensive collection of answers to almost any AOL- or Internet-related question you might have, and it's keyword-searchable.
5. Sign on and use the keyword: **MHM**. This will take you to AOL's Members Helping Members message board. Post your question in the appropriate folder there. Within a day or so you will have a response to your question from another member. Peer help is often the best help you can find.
6. Sign on and use the keywords: **Mac Help**. This will take you to the Mac Help Forum. They have a collection of *Frequently Asked Questions*, primers for uploading and downloading, and live help every weekday. The Mac Help Forum has message boards as well, where you can post questions about anything from Mac software to Mac AOL.

7. Sign on and use the keywords: **Tech Live**. This will take you to the Member Services department. Click the button labeled Contact Us, where you can consult AOL's Member Help Interactive service. This feature is free and available from roughly 7:00 AM. to 2:45 A.M., 7 days a week, except when the AOL system is down for maintenance.
8. Call Customer Support at 1-800-827-6364. They're open from 6 A.M. to 4 A.M. eastern time seven days a week. It's a toll-free call in the continental United States, and there's never any charge for support from AOL.

Altruistically, AOL offers both online and offline help. One set of help files resides on your hard disk and is available at any time regardless of whether you're online. I call this version AOL's *offline* help. The other version—*online* help—is always available online, without charge. We'll discuss both in this chapter.

Offline Help

Let's talk about offline help first. America Online's offline help is especially configured to answer the kind of questions you'll encounter when you're disconnected from the service. How do I connect when I'm away from my usual location? What's the Customer Support telephone number and when are they on duty? How do I sign up my friends?

AOL Guide

There are four ways to access AOL Guide, AOL's offline help. Perhaps the most obvious one is to click the Help button on the Welcome window before signing on. You can also access AOL Guide by pressing the Command-? keys or selecting AOL Guide from the question mark icon's pop-up menu on the right end of your menu bar. Finally, AOL Guide is also available through various windows within the AOL software, such as your Preferences or the Address Book. Regardless of how you access AOL Guide, the information that results is extensive, allowing you to look up by topic, through an index, or with a search. With System 7.5, the Mac introduced a new feature called Apple Guide and with it a policy that was new to the industry at the time: a Help application common to all programs. Help is a separate application that's called by other programs when the user wants help. When you click the Help button, AOL starts the Help application. When you ask for help with System 7.5 through Apple Guide, the same thing happens. The help files themselves are different, the Help application is the same (see Figure 2-7).

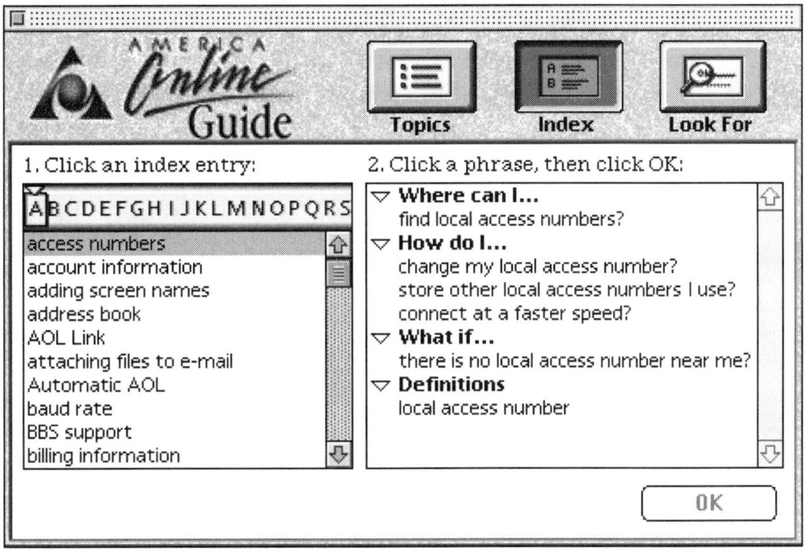
AMERICA
Online
Guide
Topics
Index
Look For
1. Click an index entry:
ABCDEFGHIJKLMNOPQRS
access numbers
account information
adding screen names
address book
AOL Link
attaching files to e-mail
Automatic AOL
baud rate
BBS support
billing information
2. Click a phrase, then click OK:
Where can I...
find local access numbers?
How do I...
change my local access number?
store other local access numbers I use?
connect at a faster speed?
What if...
there is no local access number near me?
Definitions
local access number
OK

Figure 2-7: A familiar face: AOL's Help utility looks and acts like the help utilities in other Mac programs.

America Online utilizes the Apple Guide application to its fullest. The AOL Guide help file is very large, and there are plenty of links to cross-reference help topics with one another. Any help topic can be searched and printed, and an extensive list of tips and tricks is available.

Help can be chosen at any time, whether you're online or off. These help topics are stored in a file on your hard disk, and so don't require that you go online to access them; you just need to launch the AOL program and click the Help button.

Look carefully at the list of help topics in Figures 2-7. Some of them are specifically for first-time users. Others are primarily for members on the road. The other help topics are oriented toward making the most out of your online experience: adding screen names, AOL Link, Automatic AOL, and more.

How to Use Help

The reason so many of the help topics relate to accessing AOL is because AOL's offline help is intended to serve you as you explore the software, well, offline. To access AOL Guide, click the Help button on the Welcome window, press Command-? (the command key is the one with a cloverleaf or Apple symbol), or select it from the Apple Guide icon at the far right of your menu bar. Wondering about your connection setup? From AOL Guide's Topic area, choose "The modem setup" in the scroll box on the left. Select the appropriate subtopic in the box at the right side of the window and click the OK button for further information (see Figure 2-8). (For a complete discussion of your connection setup, see Appendix A.)

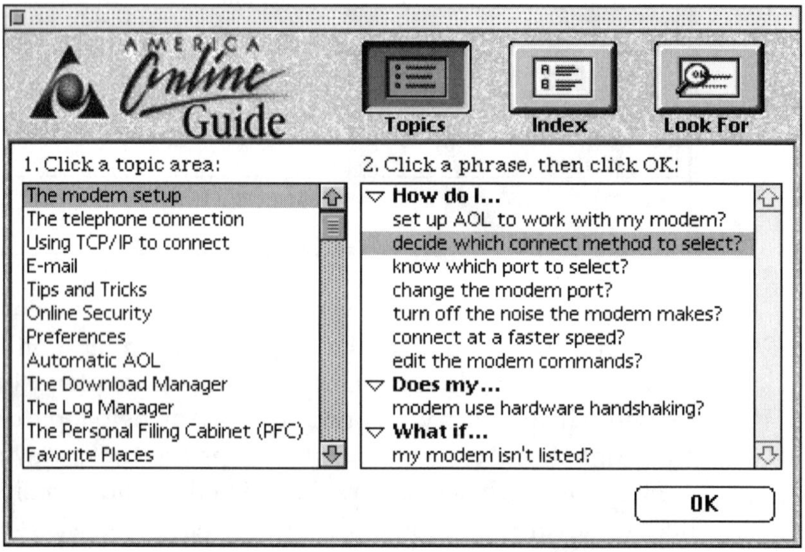
AMERICA Online Guide
Topics
Index
Look For
1. Click a topic area:
The modem setup
The telephone connection
Using TCP/IP to connect
E-mail
Tips and Tricks
Online Security
Preferences
Automatic AOL
The Download Manager
The Log Manager
The Personal Filing Cabinet (PFC)
Favorite Places
2. Click a phrase, then click OK:
How do I...
set up AOL to work with my modem?
decide which connect method to select?
know which port to select?
change the modem port?
turn off the noise the modem makes?
connect at a faster speed?
edit the modem commands?
Does my...
modem use hardware handshaking?
What if...
my modem isn't listed?
OK

Figure 2-8: Help with changing your setup is found under the modem setup topic.

Victoria, my wife, is a medical student. She learned a long time ago that it's impossible to memorize all of the things she has to know to become a successful practitioner. The sheer magnitude of the task was dragging her down until she realized that all she really had to know was where to look for information. She has a well-organized library and knows which books discuss which topics. When she needs assistance, she goes to her library and gets help.

You should do the same. Don't worry about memorizing all the petty details—for any computer program. Instead, learn how to use help. It will take 20 minutes and it will be the most productive 20 minutes you'll ever spend with your computer.

Online Help

America Online's online help is especially comprehensive. Moreover, because the online help files are stored on the host computer (and not on your hard disk) they can be updated quickly, whenever an update is required. In addition to the help you get using the online files, AOL staff and members stand ready to help you as well. This is world-class help, and its breadth is unique to AOL.

Member Services

AOL doesn't call their online help area "Online Help." In the true spirit of altruism, they call it *Member Services*. To access Member Services, choose Member Services from the Members menu, click the question mark icon on the toolbar (see Figure 2-9) or use the keyword: **Help**. You must be signed on for this: online help isn't stored on your hard disk. It's on AOL's host computer.

Just before you enter the Member Services area, AOL may flash the message pictured near the top of Figure 2-9. Unexpected dialog boxes like this often spell trouble, I know, but not this one. America Online is trying to say that you're about to pass through the "free curtain" (to use the AOL vernacular) and that you won't be charged for the time you're about to spend in Member Services. That's a comforting thought: online help is free of online charges. Of course, if you've elected the unlimited usage pricing plan, you will not see this dialog box nor need to worry that the area is free.

Once in the Member Services area, click the Quick Answers button to enter the Member Services answer database pictured at the bottom of Figure 2-9. Quick Answers is a great place to poke around, getting to know the service.

Random Acts of Help

The next time you sign on to AOL, click the toolbar's question mark icon and venture into the Quick Answers database. Once you're there, relax (the clock's not running) and explore this area casually. Poke around as you would at a flea market. Don't try to memorize anything. Get the feel of the place. Get to know what's there and where it's found. Consider this an exploratory mission without any particular agenda. After 20 minutes or so, move on to something else.

You will be amazed at what this kind of unstructured behavior can do for you. You will acquire a familiarity with the layout of the place, and you will gain confidence in the use of online help. Most important, the next time you need help, you won't hesitate to use the keyword. And that, in the long run, is perhaps the most productive attitude you can adopt toward the use of AOL.

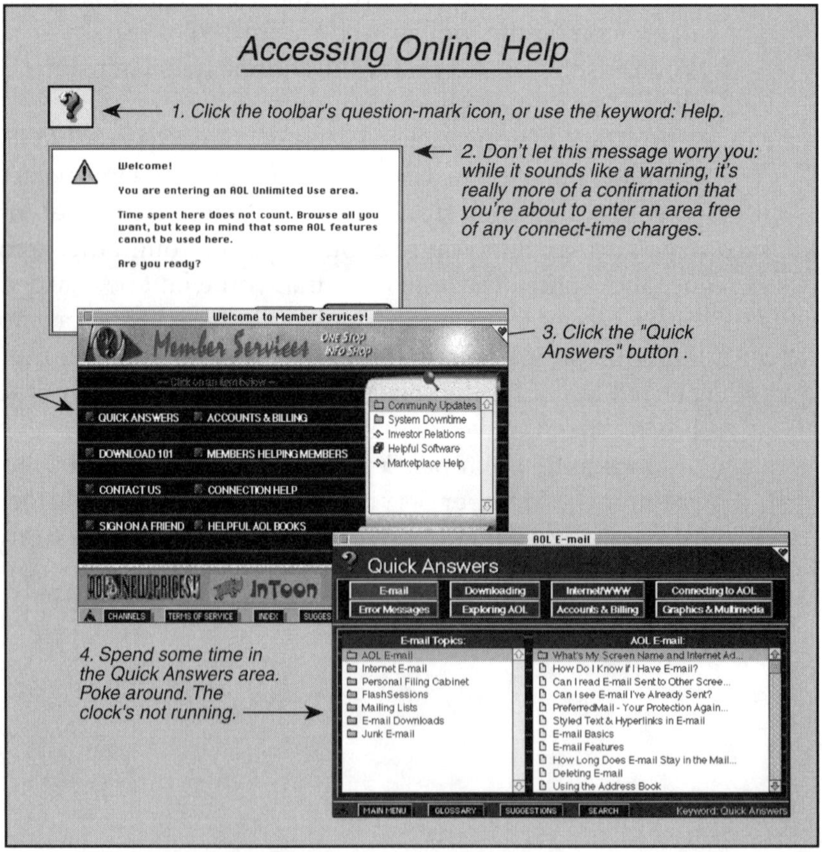
Accessing Online Help
1. Click the toolbar's question-mark icon, or use the keyword: Help.
Welcome!
You are entering an AOL Unlimited Use area.
Time spent here does not count. Browse all you want, but keep in mind that some AOL features cannot be used here.
Are you ready?
2. Don't let this message worry you: while it sounds like a warning, it's really more of a confirmation that you're about to enter an area free of any connect-time charges.
Welcome to Member Services!
Member Services
3. Click the "Quick Answers" button .
QUICK ANSWERS
ACCOUNTS & BILLING
DOWNLOAD 101
MEMBERS HELPING MEMBERS
CONTACT US
CONNECTION HELP
SIGN ON A FRIEND
HELPFUL AOL BOOKS
Community Updates
System Downtime
Investor Relations
Helpful Software
Marketplace Help
AOL E-mail
Quick Answers
E-mail
Downloading
Internet/WWW
Connecting to AOL
Error Messages
Exploring AOL
Accounts & Billing
Graphics & Multimedia
E-mail Topics:
AOL E-mail
Internet E-mail
Personal Filing Cabinet
FlashSessions
Mailing Lists
E-mail Downloads
Junk E-mail
AOL E-mail:
What's My Screen Name and Internet Ad...
How Do I Know If I Have E-mail?
Can I read E-mail Sent to Other Scree...
Can I see E-mail I've Already Sent?
PreferredMail - Your Protection Again...
Styled Text & Hyperlinks in E-mail
E-mail Basics
E-mail Features
How Long Does E-mail Stay in the Mail...
Deleting E-mail
Using the Address Book
MAIN MENU
GLOSSARY
SUGGESTIONS
SEARCH
Keyword: Quick Answers
4. Spend some time in the Quick Answers area. Poke around. The clock's not running.

Figure 2-9: Online help is available whenever you're online by clicking the question mark icon on the toolbar. The best part: it's absolutely free.

The subjects pictured in the Quick Answers window offer immediate answers for nearly anything you encounter while online. Each of these help topics can be saved, printed, or both. The list of topics is extensive, and the detail offered within each topic is bountiful (see Figure 2-10).

Figure 2-10: A few of the help topics available in the Quick Answers database.

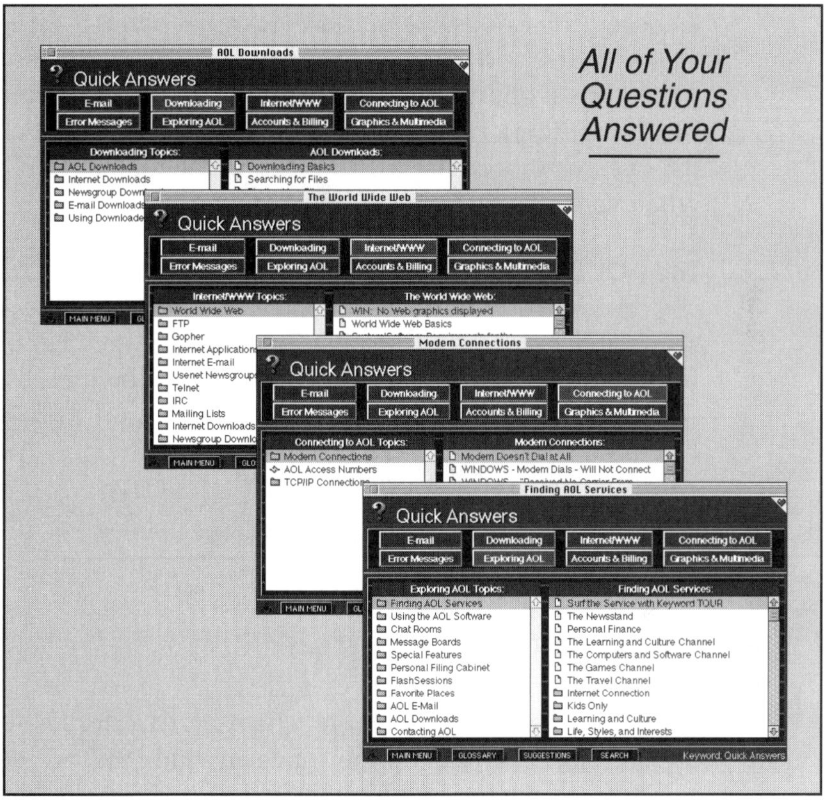
All of Your Questions Answered
AOL Downloads
Quick Answers
E-mail
Downloading
Internet/WWW
Connecting to AOL
Error Messages
Exploring AOL
Accounts & Billing
Graphics & Multimedia
Downloading Topics:
AOL Downloads:
AOL Downloads
Internet Downloads
Downloading Basics
Searching for Files
The World Wide Web
Internet/WWW Topics:
The World Wide Web:
World Wide Web
FTP
Gopher
Internet Applications
Internet E-mail
Usenet Newsgroups
Telnet
IRC
Mailing Lists
Internet Downloads
WIN: No Web graphics displayed
World Wide Web Basics
Modem Connections
Connecting to AOL Topics:
Modem Connections:
Modem Connections
AOL Access Numbers
TCP/IP Connections
Modem Doesn't Dial at All
WINDOWS - Modem Dials - Will Not Connect
Finding AOL Services
Exploring AOL Topics:
Finding AOL Services:
Finding AOL Services
Using the AOL Software
Chat Rooms
Message Boards
Special Features
Personal Filing Cabinet
FlashSessions
Favorite Places
AOL E-Mail
AOL Downloads
Contacting AOL
Surf the Service with Keyword TOUR
The Newsstand
Personal Finance
The Learning and Culture Channel
The Computers and Software Channel
The Games Channel
The Travel Channel
Internet Connection
Kids Only
Learning and Culture
Life, Styles, and Interests
MAIN MENU
GLOSSARY
SUGGESTIONS
SEARCH
Keyword: Quick Answers

To save an online help topic that's on your screen, simply choose Save (or Save As—they're the same command in this context) from the File menu. America Online asks you what you want to name the file and where you want to save it. Provide the information it needs, and that help topic will be stored on your disk, ready for any purpose you might have in mind. You can open the file containing the information you saved with a word processor or your AOL software: just choose Open from the File menu.

Printing Help More likely, you'll want to print a help topic for ready reference. As you might expect, all you have to do is choose Print from the File menu, or click the Print icon in the toolbar. Printing from AOL works like printing from any other Mac application. You'll receive the print dialog box associated with the printer you've selected via Chooser (the Chooser is under the Apple menu). Configure this dialog as you please and print. By the way, you can print just about any text file you read online, not just the online help files. If you run across a file description or news article you want to print, just choose Print from the File menu or click the Print icon in the toolbar—AOL will print whatever text is in the front-most (active) window.

The AOL Directory

Try the keyword: **Services**, which will take you to the AOL Directory, a searchable database of information on all the services available online. Information for each service includes the following:

- The service's name.
- Any keywords associated with that service.
- A menu path for access to that service.
- A description of that service.
- A button to take you there.

Searching the AOL Directory The AOL Directory is AOL's answer to the question: "I wonder if they have anything that addresses my interest in…" Are you interested in model airplanes? Search the AOL Directory. How about music, poetry, or fine food? Use the AOL Directory.

I was having trouble with Microsoft Word the other day. Couldn't get it to do things I knew it was capable of doing. What to do? Call five friends on the phone and get their voice mail? Call Microsoft long distance and wait as they play unendurable Microsoft deejayed music while I'm on hold?

None of the above. I simply signed on and consulted the Microsoft Knowledge Base. The Knowledge Base is the summation of nearly everything Microsoft knows about its products, including answers from their technical support staff. It's updated periodically and released on CD-ROM. You can subscribe if you wish (if you have a CD-ROM player)—it's only $295 a year.

Or you can use AOL. America Online offers a link to Microsoft's Knowledge Base Web page, complete with a search mechanism to find what you're after. If you forget Microsoft's keyword, use the Directory of Services to find it for you. That's just what I did the other day, and my question was answered within a few minutes (see Figure 2-11).

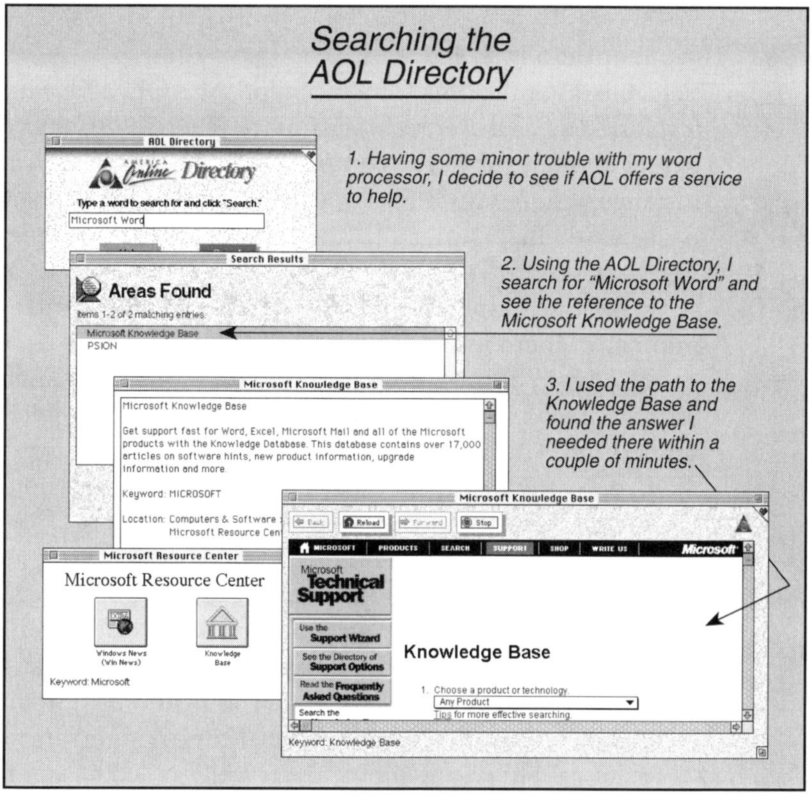
Searching the AOL Directory
1. Having some minor trouble with my word processor, I decide to see if AOL offers a service to help.
2. Using the AOL Directory, I search for "Microsoft Word" and see the reference to the Microsoft Knowledge Base.
3. I used the path to the Knowledge Base and found the answer I needed there within a couple of minutes.
AOL Directory
Type a word to search for and click "Search."
Microsoft Word
Search Results
Areas Found
Microsoft Knowledge Base
PSION
Microsoft Knowledge Base
Get support fast for Word, Excel, Microsoft Mail and all of the Microsoft products with the Knowledge Database. This database contains over 17,000 articles on software hints, new product information, upgrade information and more.
Keyword: MICROSOFT
Microsoft Resource Center
Keyword: Microsoft
Knowledge Base
Keyword: Knowledge Base

Figure 2-11: The AOL Directory found the Microsoft Knowledge Base for me, and the Knowledge Base had my answer.

Note that the middle window in Figure 2-11 offers the keyword(s) for the Knowledge Base, its location (the menu path that gets you there), and its description. If it isn't what I need, the description saves me the trouble of going there. If it is what I need, not only do the keyword and location tell me how to get there quickly, a Go button is provided at the bottom of the window. Clicking on it will take me there in a flash.

Locating the AOL Directory There are at least three ways to get to the AOL Directory. You can use the Find area (we discussed the Find area earlier in this chapter); click the Find button on the toolbar), or the keyword: **Services**, but you'll access the AOL Directory most often via the Keyword window. Type Command-K, enter your criterion, and click the Search button.

Member Help Interactive

Let's talk about rooms for a moment. At AOL, a *room* (you might hear it referred to as a *chat room*) is a place where a number of people gather to talk about a subject of common interest. There are classrooms, for instance, where you'll find a teacher and students (the Online Campus is discussed in Chapter 14, "Learning"). There's People Connection (the two heads button on the toolbar), where people go to mingle and meet other people. In fact, AOL offers scores of rooms, and we will explore a number of them in Chapter 8, "The Community."

Look again at the second window in Figure 2-9. There you'll see a button labeled Contact Us in the Member Services window. If you click that button, you'll discover a wide range of ways to get help from AOL, one of which is Member Help Interactive. Upon entering Member Help Interactive, you can choose from General Help or Technical Help. If you choose General Help, you will find yourself in a room with at least one AOL Representative and probably a number of other members, all with questions about the service. Conversations in the room are real-time: you don't have to wait for replies. This isn't mail, and it's not a message board. It's a room, and as in real rooms in real buildings, people there can hold real-time conversations.

Technical Help is available from roughly 7:00 A.M. to 2:45 A.M., eastern time. If you need an immediate response, this is the place to find it (see Figure 2-12).

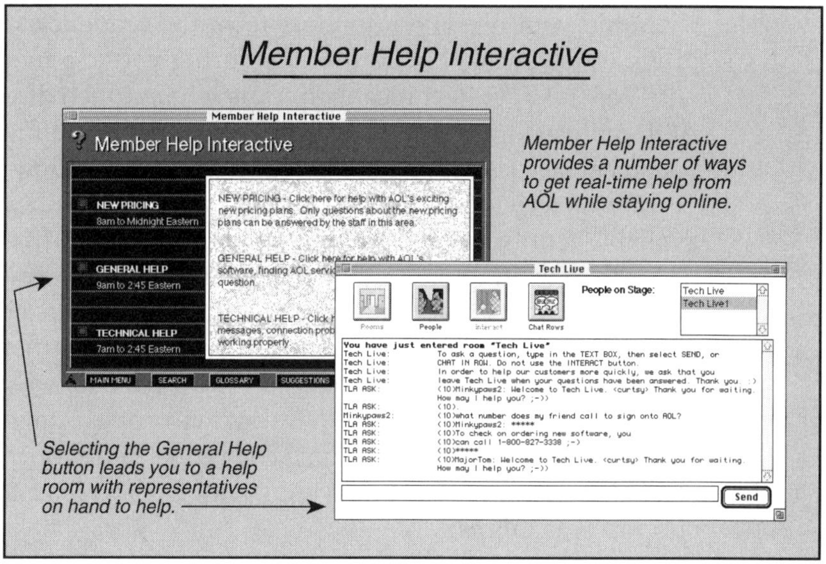

Member Help Interactive
Member Help Interactive
NEW PRICING
8am to Midnight Eastern
GENERAL HELP
9am to 2:45 Eastern
TECHNICAL HELP
7am to 2:45 Eastern
MAIN MENU
SEARCH
GLOSSARY
SUGGESTIONS
Member Help Interactive provides a number of ways to get real-time help from AOL while staying online.
Tech Live
People on Stage:
Tech Live
Tech Live1
Send
Selecting the General Help button leads you to a help room with representatives on hand to help.

Figure 2-12: A glimpse of general help in the Member Help Interactive service.

Take the Time

General Help, as you can imagine, is a popular place. At any one time, hundreds of members might be there, each asking questions to which they want answers *right now!*

Rather than toss everyone in the same "room" where they're forced to clamor for attention like reporters at a press conference, AOL arranges the General Help room in a series of "rows," each with its own representative, and each with a limited number of members. Of necessity, it's an elaborate structure with strict protocols—a structure that takes a bit of understanding in order to use.

As you pass into the General Help area, AOL offers a number of windows explaining the protocol and offering other methods of help you may wish to explore. When you make your first visit, take the time to read this information or search for a reply to a specific question. Once you get into the room and receive a prompt reply to an urgent question, you'll be glad you did.

Should your needs run to more technical tendencies, AOL also provides technical help. Rather than bring you to a room with others as with general help, technical help puts you in touch directly with an AOL representative for one-on-one help. When you first enter the Technical Help area, you are presented with a window explaining how Technical Help works and a countdown to let you know when the next available representative can help you (see Figure 2-13). This is much better than waiting on hold on the phone; you can explore the Member Services answer database while waiting and perhaps even find the answer on your own. The countdown will update automatically for you, so you'll always know how long you have to wait. When a representative is available, a small window will appear on your screen much like a private consultation room. The representative will ask how they can help you and you'll be on your way. I wish all customer service support was this easy.

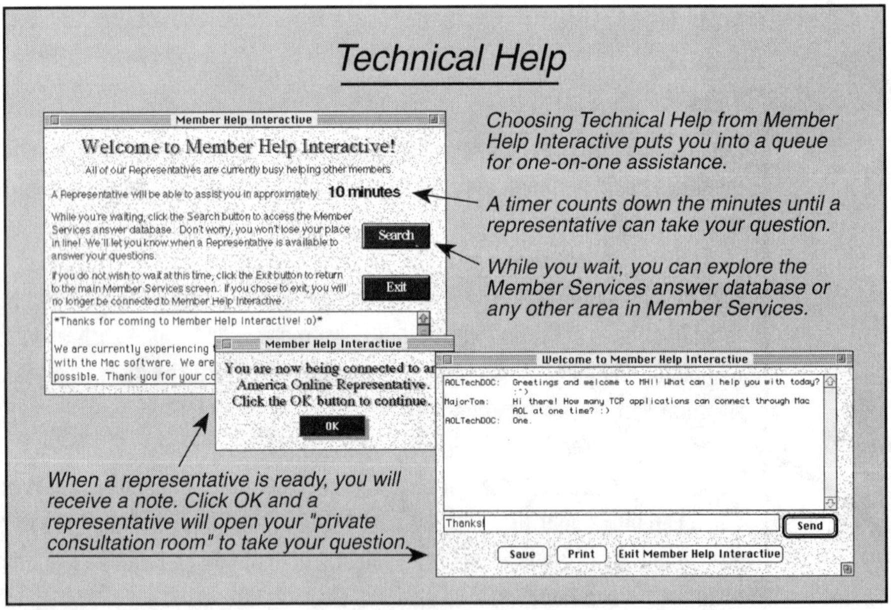
Technical Help
Member Help Interactive
Welcome to Member Help Interactive!
All of our Representatives are currently busy helping other members.
A Representative will be able to assist you in approximately 10 minutes
While you're waiting, click the Search button to access the Member Services answer database. Don't worry, you won't lose your place in line! We'll let you know when a Representative is available to answer your questions.
Search
If you do not wish to wait at this time, click the Exit button to return to the main Member Services screen. If you chose to exit, you will no longer be connected to Member Help Interactive.
Exit
Thanks for coming to Member Help Interactive! :o)
Choosing Technical Help from Member Help Interactive puts you into a queue for one-on-one assistance.
A timer counts down the minutes until a representative can take your question.
While you wait, you can explore the Member Services answer database or any other area in Member Services.
Member Help Interactive
America Online Representative.
Click the OK button to continue.
OK
Welcome to Member Help Interactive
AOLTechDOC: Greetings and welcome to MHI! What can I help you with today? :-)
MajorTom: Hi there! How many TCP applications can connect through Mac AOL at one time? :)
AOLTechDOC: One.
Thanks
Send
Save
Print
Exit Member Help Interactive
When a representative is ready, you will receive a note. Click OK and a representative will open your "private consultation room" to take your question.

Figure 2-13: Technical Help offers one-on-one help with a representative online.

The Help Rooms

Member Help Interactive is widely promoted and always free, and that often leads to a crowd. An alternative is the Help Room (more properly, the Help Rooms—there are usually more than one). The Help Rooms are chat rooms in the People Connection, and though they're not free, they're staffed by Guides and they're open every day from 3:00 P.M. eastern until 3 A.M. eastern. Read Chapter 8, "The Community," to learn about People Connection and chat rooms.

Members Helping Members

On my IRS 1040 form, right there next to the word Occupation, it says "educator." Though I've retired from the classroom, I still write books and do some consulting. As an educator, I attend a number of conferences. Most of these conferences are academic, each featuring a number of speakers and seminar leaders.

Reflecting back on those conferences, I must admit that the greatest benefit I receive from them is not from the speakers or the seminars, it's from the other people attending the conference. I get my education in the hallways and at lounge tables. People talking to people—peer to peer—that's where I find the Good Stuff.

America Online is no different. Some of the best help online is that received from other members. America Online knows that; that's why it provides Members Helping Members—a formalized version of peer support (Figure 2-14).

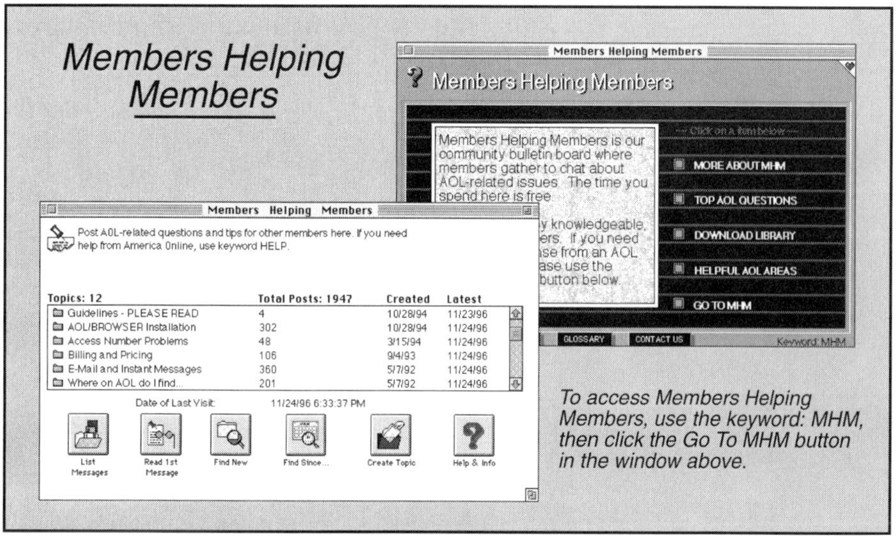
Members Helping Members
Members Helping Members
Members Helping Members is our community bulletin board where members gather to chat about AOL-related issues. The time you spend here is free
MORE ABOUT MHM
TOP AOL QUESTIONS
DOWNLOAD LIBRARY
HELPFUL AOL AREAS
GO TO MHM
GLOSSARY
CONTACT US
Keyword: MHM
Post AOL-related questions and tips for other members here. If you need help from America Online, use keyword HELP.
Topics: 12
Total Posts: 1947
Created
Latest
Guidelines - PLEASE READ 4 10/28/94 11/23/96
AOL/BROWSER Installation 302 10/28/94 11/24/96
Access Number Problems 48 3/15/94 11/24/96
Billing and Pricing 106 9/4/93 11/24/96
E-Mail and Instant Messages 360 5/7/92 11/24/96
Where on AOL do I find... 201 5/7/92 11/24/96
Date of Last Visit: 11/24/96 6:33:37 PM
List Messages
Read 1st Message
Find New
Find Since...
Create Topic
Help & Info
To access Members Helping Members, use the keyword: MHM, then click the Go To MHM button in the window above.

Figure 2-14: To access Members Helping Members, use the keyword: **MHM**.

Members Helping Members is a free feature at AOL. There's no cause for a rushed feeling while you're there.

Message Boards Members Helping Members is a *message board*. Though we'll discuss message boards in Chapter 9, "The Forums," the subject is worth a brief mention here as well.

Throughout AOL you'll see little pushpin icons. This is AOL's way of identifying message boards. A message board is analogous to the bulletin boards you see hanging in the halls of offices and academic institutions. People post things there for other people to see: postcards, lost mittens, announcements, and messages. America Online's message boards are exactly the same (though you might not see lost mittens on AOL's boards).

Look again at Figure 2-14. Note how AOL's boards are organized by using folders. The bulletin board analogy weakens a bit here, but AOL's boards get a lot of messages (the Members Helping Members board pictured in Figure 2-14 has 1,947). Unless they're organized in some fashion, 1,947 messages posted on a single board would be chaotic and overwhelming. The solution is folders.

You can read all the messages in a folder, browse through them (viewing only their subjects, rather than the messages themselves), or specify only those messages that have been posted since a specific date. This is a very convenient message-reading system and is described in detail in Chapter 9, "The Forums."

For the time being, let's select a folder and read its messages. I picked the AOL Hints & Tips folder and found the series of messages pictured in Figure 2-15.

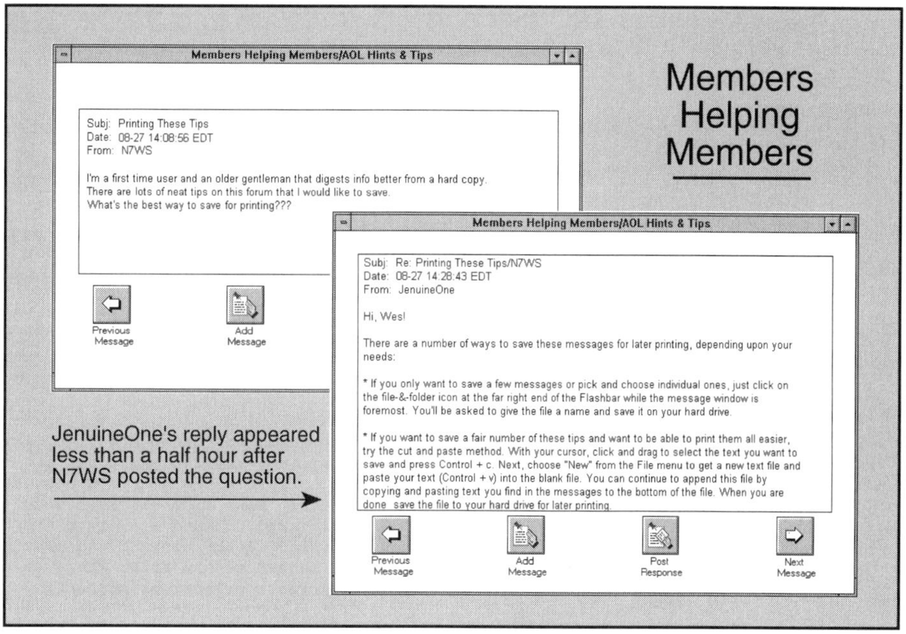
Members Helping Members/AOL Hints & Tips
Subj: Printing These Tips
Date: 08-27 14:08:56 EDT
From: N7WS
I'm a first time user and an older gentleman that digests info better from a hard copy. There are lots of neat tips on this forum that I would like to save. What's the best way to save for printing???
Previous Message
Add Message
Members Helping Members
Members Helping Members/AOL Hints & Tips
Subj: Re: Printing These Tips/N7WS
Date: 08-27 14:28:43 EDT
From: JenuineOne
Hi, Wes!
There are a number of ways to save these messages for later printing, depending upon your needs:
* If you only want to save a few messages or pick and choose individual ones, just click on the file-&-folder icon at the far right end of the Flashbar while the message window is foremost. You'll be asked to give the file a name and save it on your hard drive.
* If you want to save a fair number of these tips and want to be able to print them all easier, try the cut and paste method. With your cursor, click and drag to select the text you want to save and press Control + c. Next, choose "New" from the File menu to get a new text file and paste your text (Control + v) into the blank file. You can continue to append this file by copying and pasting text you find in the messages to the bottom of the file. When you are done, save the file to your hard drive for later printing.
Previous Message
Add Message
Post Response
Next Message
JenuineOne's reply appeared less than a half hour after N7WS posted the question.

Figure 2-15: N7WS needed help on saving messages for later printing. JenuineOne was there to help.

The Value of Member Help Look at the last message pictured in Figure 2-14. Not only does JenuineOne suggest three ideas for N7WS, she explains why and when each idea would work best. This is superb help, and it came from another member. The full text of the message from JenuineOne appears in Figure 2-16.

Figure 2-16: JenuineOne offers not one, but three solutions to a question.

JenuineOne's Message

Subj: Re: Printing These Tips/N7WS
Date: 8/27/96 9:47:40 AM
From: JenuineOne

Hi, Wes!

There are at least three ways to save these messages for later printing, depending upon your needs:

* If you only want to save a few messages or pick and choose individual ones, just click on the file-&-folder icon at the far right end of the toolbar while the message window is foremost. You'll be asked to give the file a name and save it on your hard drive.

* If you want to save a fair number of these tips and want to be able to print them all easier, try the cut and paste method. With your cursor, click and drag to select the text you want to save and press Command + c. Next, choose "New" from the File menu to get a new text file and paste your text (Command + v) into the blank file. You can continue to append this file by copying and pasting text you find in the messages to the bottom of the file. When you are done, save the file to your hard drive for later printing.

* If you want to save *all* the messages, use a log to capture everything. To open a log, select "Log Manager" from the "File" menu and open a System Log. Now all text you come across will be captured and saved in the log, whether you read it all or not! When you are done, go back to the Log Manager and close the log. You can read and print it right in AOL (if it isn't too big) or in a word processor.

* If you only want to print and not save, just click on the printer icon in the toolbar while the window you want to print is active.

I hope these ideas are helpful!

JenuineOne 0;>

Note another small detail: JenuineOne must have looked up N7WS's profile, as she addresses her message to "Wes." That's a nice touch. JenuineOne didn't have to do that, but it makes her message all the more personable. (How, you may wonder, do I know that JenuineOne is a she? *I* looked up *her* profile!) Profiles are discussed later in this chapter.

I'm reminded of community again. Visiting a big city a few months ago, I was struck by the isolation that seemed to surround everyone I passed on the street. Perhaps it's a defense mechanism for dealing with high population density, but it seemed that everyone was in a cocoon, oblivious to everyone else. No one smiled. No one ever looked anywhere but straight ahead. Thousands of people jostled together, yet no one was talking. An incredibly lonely place.

On the other hand, in Damascus—the little Oregon town closest to my home—there are no strangers. People stop on the street and say hello, swap some gossip, and perhaps offer advice.

America Online is more like Damascus. I spent years on other services and never felt like I belonged. I never got mail, I never contributed to a message board, and I never knew where to find help. It was like a big city to me, and I was always anxious to leave. At AOL I'm walking the street in a small town on a sunny day and everyone is smiling. The first day I arrived at AOL, I got a letter from Steve Case. People like JenuineOne go out of their way to offer assistance. This is my kind of place. I'm at home here.

Guides

I recall an art gallery I visited once in Amsterdam. There were a number of Rembrandts there, hanging on the wall just like any other picture. No glass cases or protective Lexan—just those radiant Rembrandts, emancipated and free. A gentleman in uniform stood near. He wasn't a guard; the uniform wasn't that severe. He was a guide. He was a volunteer. He got to spend his days in a room full of the Rembrandts he loved and at the same time share his interest with other people. He explained the Rembrandts to us in a fatherly way, exhibiting a proprietorial regard for his fellow countryman's legacy.

Which is precisely what AOL's *Guides* are. They're members just like the rest of us—experienced members, with particularly helpful online personalities—but members all the same. They remain politely in the background, leaving us to our own explorations, silent unless spoken to. If we need help, however, Guides are always nearby, ready with friendly advice and information. If you have a question—any question at all—about AOL, its services, or its policies, ask a Guide.

Like the guide in Amsterdam, you can identify Guides by their appearance: their screen names have the word "Guide" in them. If Figure 2-16's JenuineOne was to be a Guide (she should be), she would probably be "Guide JEN," or something like that.

Figure 2-17: A stop by the Lobby for some help from Guide MO.

A Night in the Lobby

MajorTom : Hi all!
Guide MO : Hey MajorTom :) ← *To help you follow what's going on, my part of the conversation appears in bold.*
Lthrneck : ::::getting out ostrich feather::::
Guide MO : Nononononono!!!
Lthrneck : ::::TICKLE, TICKLE:::::
Guide MO : ::giggling::
Guide MO : Hey Cantoni!! :)
Cantoni : Hi MO!
Guide MO : Hiya NyteMaire :)
NyteMaire : Hiya MO :)
CountStixx : Maire!!!! {}{}{}{}{}{} ← *These are hugs for a new arrival in the Lobby.*
NyteMaire : {{{{{{Count}}}}}}} **
LovlyVix : Nyte {}{}{}{}{}{}{}{}{}{}{}{}{}{}
NyteMaire : {{{Vix}}}}
LovlyVix : How are you Nyte?
NyteMaire : Getting crazy, and you? ;)
LovlyVix : Pretty good Nyte :)
MajorTom : Anybody know of a utility to convert JPEG to TIFF?
Guide MO : Let me check the libraries for you, T :) I always use Photoshop :)
PC Kate : <--trying to type while holding ice pack on face. :)
Lthrneck : ACK Kate, what happened?
Guide MO : Kate :(Dentist??
AFC Borg : Is the ice pack inside or outside the paper bag?
PC Kate : Lthr, had 3 hours of oral and sinus surgery yesterday. They say I should be able to eat again next Friday.
GWRepSteve : Alchemy would probably be the converter to use, MajorTom...
Lthrneck : Ouch! Kate!! {}{}{}{}{}{}{}{}
Lee123 : awww Kate. * to make it better..... ← *The asterisk is a kiss.*
LovlyVix : <--needs to go to dentist for Kates new diet :)
PC Kate : Vix, works real well... lost just under five pounds in 2 days. :)
LovlyVix : Perfect ...that would put me just where I want to be, Kate :)
Guide MO : MajorTom - I 'm sorry - I don't see what you need offhand, though I know we must have it here :/ ← *Chagrin.*
Guide MO : I'll check later and email you, if that's any help.
MajorTom : Thanks Guide. Appreciate it. I have a Plus. Can't run PhotoShop.
Guide MO : Ok - I just wrote a note to myself - I'll check for you when I get off shift at 9 and email you :)
MajorTom : Great! Thanks for the help. G'Night all! ← *I got an answer the next day.*
Guide MO : Night MajorTom :)

Figure 2-17 is a little hard to follow if you're not used to AOL's so-called chat rooms. Though chat rooms are discussed in Chapter 8, "The Community," a little explanation seems in order here as well. Twenty-one people were in the room when I visited. Many were just watching ("lurkers"), but others seemed to be old friends. The room was full of "smileys" (turn your head counterclockwise 90 degrees and :-) becomes a smile) and hugs. The entire illustration is a "chat log" (see your File menu for the Log Manager command).

Chat rooms can be intimidating to the first-time visitor. Don't be shy. Jump right in with a Hello, look for the Guide's name, and ask your question. More important, note that I received one immediate answer to my question (from GWRepSteve, a member) and another the next day from Guide MO. I got just what I needed (Alchemy worked perfectly, though now the AOL software handles conversion like this for me), and it only took 10 minutes.

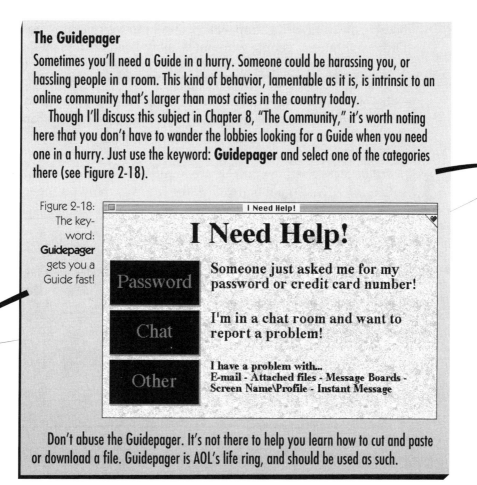

The Guidepager

Sometimes you'll need a Guide in a hurry. Someone could be harassing you, or hassling people in a room. This kind of behavior, lamentable as it is, is intrinsic to an online community that's larger than most cities in the country today.

Though I'll discuss this subject in Chapter 8, "The Community," it's worth noting here that you don't have to wander the lobbies looking for a Guide when you need one in a hurry. Just use the keyword: **Guidepager** and select one of the categories there (see Figure 2-18).

Figure 2-18: The keyword: **Guidepager** gets you a Guide fast!

I Need Help!
I Need Help!
Password
Someone just asked me for my password or credit card number!
Chat
I'm in a chat room and want to report a problem!
Other
I have a problem with...
E-mail - Attached files - Message Boards - Screen Name\Profile - Instant Message

Don't abuse the Guidepager. It's not there to help you learn how to cut and paste or download a file. Guidepager is AOL's life ring, and should be used as such.

Guides are on duty 24 hours a day, 7 days a week, 365 days a year. To find a Guide, click on the two heads button on the toolbar, or select the People Connection option from the Channels screen. Find the name of a room you like (Lobbies are good) and look for a Guide there. They're easy to spot: they all have the word "Guide" in their screen names.

My AOL

We're all guilty of a nesting instinct, some of us more than others. Faced with a new living space, many of us immediately turn to wallpaper samples and paint chips. A new office might sprout posters, bulletin boards, and a favorite lamp—all within minutes of taking possession. Or how about the people who put wobbly-head critters on the parcel shelf of a newly acquired automobile before they drive it off the lot? Regular robins in the spring, we are.

If you're a nester, you'll love the degree of personalization AOL offers. You can not only control AOL's environment, you can even control the way you're presented within that environment. AOL is a nester's Shangri-la.

All of these nesting controls are found at one location, appropriately called *My AOL*. To get there, click the My AOL icon on the toolbar.

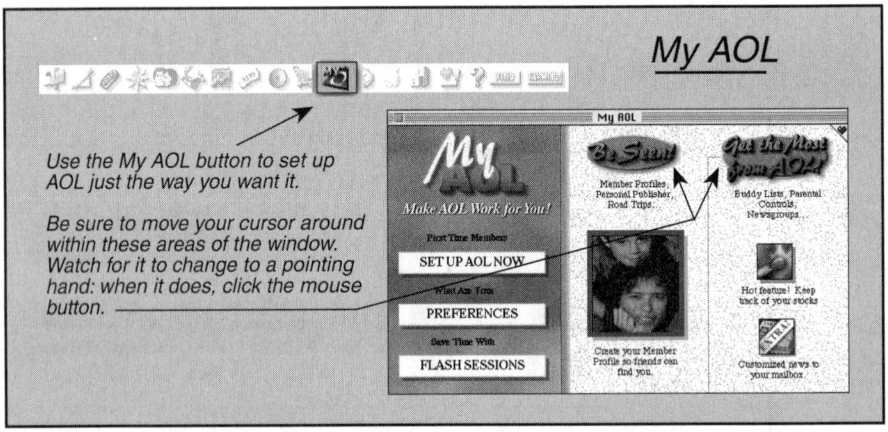
My AOL
Use the My AOL button to set up AOL just the way you want it.
Be sure to move your cursor around within these areas of the window. Watch for it to change to a pointing hand: when it does, click the mouse button.
My AOL
Make AOL Work for You!
SET UP AOL NOW
PREFERENCES
FLASH SESSIONS
Member Profiles, Personal Publisher, Road Trips...
Buddy Lists, Parental Controls, Newsgroups...
Hot feature! Keep track of your stocks
Create your Member Profile so friends can find you.
Customized news to your mailbox

Figure 2-19: The My AOL button on the toolbar allows you to configure your online environment exactly as you wish.

> **Changing Your Password**
>
> In the My AOL area, you will often be reminded that AOL staff will never ask for your password, and that you should change your password often.
>
> That's good advice, but how, exactly, *do* you change your password? None of the admonishments explain the process.
>
> It's easy: just use the keyword: **Password**, then follow the directions.

A number of the My AOL controls are so extensive that I've dedicated exclusive sections of the book to them. Others are best presented in contexts other than this one. Though I'll discuss many of the My AOL controls here, others are addressed elsewhere in the book:

- *Preferences* deserve an entire appendix, look for them in Appendix E.
- *Automatic AOL* is discussed in Chapter 6, "Automatic AOL & the Download Manager."
- The *Personal Filing Cabinet* is discussed in Chapter 3, "Electronic Mail & Personal Filing Cabinet."
- *Favorite Places* are discussed in Chapter 4, "Using the Internet."
- *Buddy Lists* are discussed in Chapter 8, "The Community."

There are a number of others features in the My AOL area, however, and we'll discuss them next.

Member Profiles

America Online offers you the opportunity to post a voluntary *member profile*. Profiles are the way AOL members describe themselves: hobbies, home towns, age, gender—that kind of stuff. It's all very enticing, but the operative term here is "voluntary." America Online values the individual's privacy, and if you wish to remain secluded in the online community, you may do so.

On the other hand, your profile is your opportunity to be anyone you want to be: if you've always wanted to be Jell-O Man, be Jell-O Man; if you have a fascination with wobbly-head critters, mention it in your profile and you'll probably meet some other wobbly heads online.

The Masquerade

The text mentions your profile, but be aware that you are by no means limited to a single one. Your AOL account provides for up to five account names, and each of those account names can have its own profile. Businesses might use these account names for individual employees and families might use them for individual family members, but most people use them as *nom de plumes*. At AOL, you never know whether you're talking to a real person or someone behind a mask. It's a regular masquerade here, for better or worse.

And that's my point: If you want to avoid the potential of meeting a misdirected personality concealed behind a mask, withhold any confidentialities until you're on reliably firm ground. Anonymity breeds impudence in some people, as does any mask; and like a mask, one's visage is not necessarily one's self. Contrary to Mother's adage, feel free to talk to strangers here. Just don't get in the car with them until you know who's driving and where the journey might go.

This masquerade is all part of the AOL community, which is discussed in Chapter 8.

As I mentioned a moment ago, member profiles are voluntary. If you elect not to complete a profile, however, you cut yourself out of a number of opportunities to become involved in the online community. If you elect to post a profile (or if you've already posted a profile and want to edit it), use the keyword: **Profile**. When you do, the Edit Your Online Profile window pictured in Figure 2-20 will appear.

Figure 2-20 reveals a secret that many of AOL's members don't know: You can complete as much or as little of the profile window as you wish. If you don't want people to know your name, put your screen name there, or your first name only. Many people include only their birth day and month, preferring to keep the year of their birth to themselves.

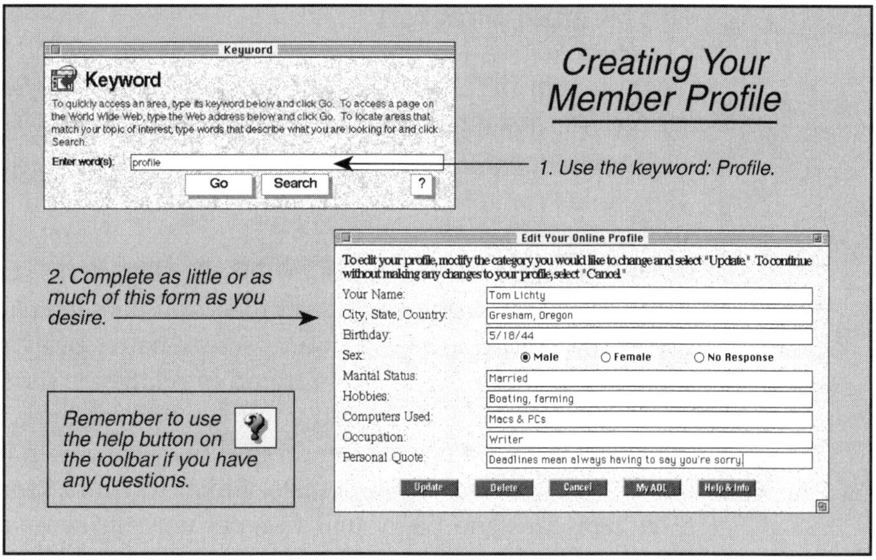
Keyword
Keyword
To quickly access an area, type its keyword below and click Go. To access a page on the World Wide Web, type the Web address below and click Go. To locate areas that match your topic of interest, type words that describe what you are looking for and click Search.
Enter word(s): profile
Go
Search
?
Creating Your Member Profile
1. Use the keyword: Profile.
2. Complete as little or as much of this form as you desire.
Edit Your Online Profile
To edit your profile, modify the category you would like to change and select "Update." To continue without making any changes to your profile, select "Cancel."
Your Name: Tom Lichty
City, State, Country: Gresham, Oregon
Birthday: 5/18/44
Sex: Male Female No Response
Marital Status: Married
Hobbies: Boating, farming
Computers Used: Macs & PCs
Occupation: Writer
Personal Quote: Deadlines mean always having to say you're sorry
Update
Delete
Cancel
My AOL
Help & Info
Remember to use the help button on the toolbar if you have any questions.

Figure 2-20: Be who you want to be: fill in as much or as little of this form as you wish.

In fact, here are a few profile secrets:

- If you include your birth day and month, people can send you birthday wishes via e-mail.
- If you include your first and last names *and* your city and state, people can use directory assistance to reach you by phone. Is that what you want them to do?
- You must be online to make any changes in your profile.
- Definitely do fill out a profile. You can't really participate in AOL's online community until you do.
- The Hobbies, Computers Used, and Occupation fields are often used by people looking for others with similar interests. If you enjoy quilting and you include quilting among your hobbies, there's a good chance you'll meet up with other quilters online.
- You're not committed to the information you include in your profile: you can add, modify, or delete it whenever you want—just use the keyword: **Profile**.

The Member Directory

There are two primary reasons for filling out a profile. Most often, someone will see your screen name online—in a chat room (chat rooms are discussed in Chapter 8, "The Community"), or in some e-mail—and they will want to know more about you. They'll choose Get a Member's Profile from the Members menu, enter your screen name, and your profile will be displayed.

The other use for profiles is the *Member Directory*. The Directory is AOL's database of everyone's profiles, and it's searchable. You can search for a member by real name, screen name, or by anything in their profile. You might wonder if a friend or relative is signed up with AOL: Search the directory and you'll know in seconds.

One of the more interesting things you can do with the directory is to search for people with interests similar to yours. Once you've found them, you can send them mail and, perhaps, strike up a friendship. It's all part of the electronic community.

I, for instance, enjoy cruising the waters of the Pacific Northwest. Thinking I might find someone to share my interest, I search the Member Directory for members with similar interests by specifying "cruising AND boat*" as my criteria (Figure 2-21).

Note that one of my criteria was "boat*" and that I use the Boolean function AND. The asterisk is a wildcard, and most Boolean functions are supported. Do terms like *wildcard* and *Boolean* make sense to you? Don't worry if they're mysteries, but if you plan to make much use of the Member Directory, you *will* want to learn about them: just click the Help & Info button pictured in Figure 2-21.

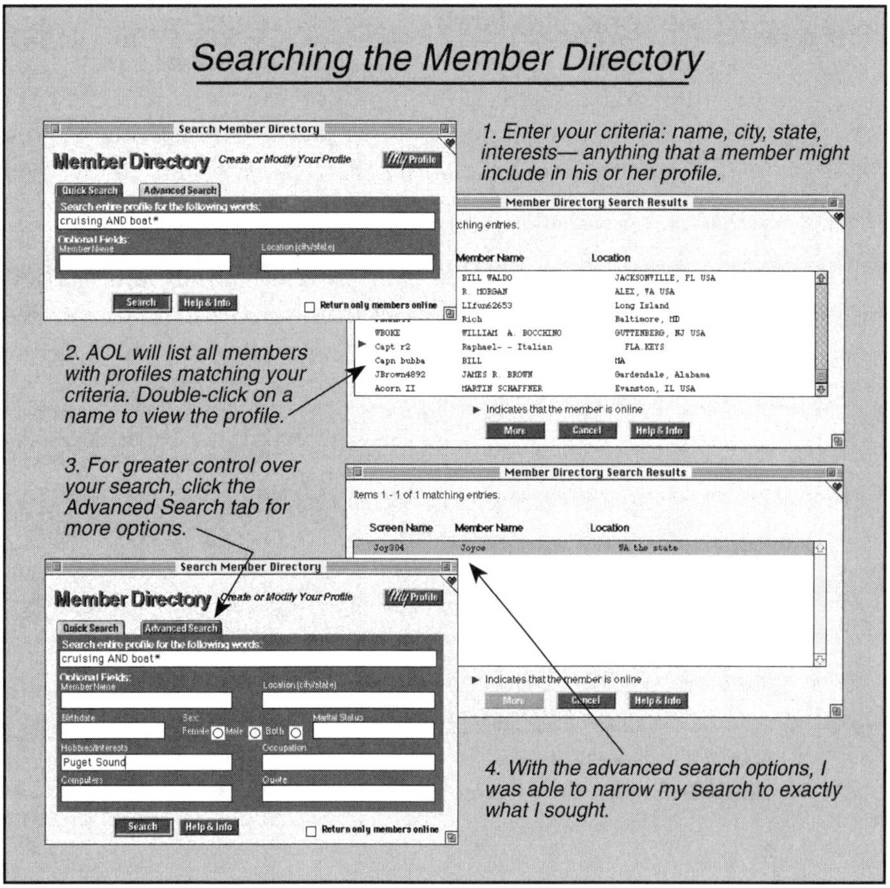
Searching the Member Directory
Search Member Directory
Member Directory Create or Modify Your Profile
Quick Search
Advanced Search
Search entire profile for the following words:
cruising AND boat*
Search
Help & Info
Return only members online
1. Enter your criteria: name, city, state, interests— anything that a member might include in his or her profile.
Member Directory Search Results
Member Name
Location
BILL WALDO
JACKSONVILLE, FL USA
R. MORGAN
ALEX, VA USA
LIfun62653
Long Island
Rich
Baltimore, MD
WBOKE
WILLIAM A. BOCCHINO
GUTTENBERG, NJ USA
Capt r2
Raphael- - Italian
FLA.KEYS
Capn bubba
BILL
MA
JBrown4892
JAMES R. BROWN
Gardendale, Alabama
Acorn II
MARTIN SCHAFFNER
Evanston, IL USA
Indicates that the member is online
More
Cancel
Help & Info
2. AOL will list all members with profiles matching your criteria. Double-click on a name to view the profile.
3. For greater control over your search, click the Advanced Search tab for more options.
Member Directory Search Results
Items 1 - 1 of 1 matching entries.
Screen Name
Member Name
Location
Joy304
Joyce
WA the state
Indicates that the member is online
More
Cancel
Help & Info
Search Member Directory
Member Directory Create or Modify Your Profile
Quick Search
Advanced Search
Search entire profile for the following words:
cruising AND boat*
Puget Sound
Search
Help & Info
Return only members online
4. With the advanced search options, I was able to narrow my search to exactly what I sought.

Figure 2-21: Much to my delight, there are lots of other aquatic cruisers on America Online.

The Member Directory offers both Quick Search and Advanced Search options. Quick Search (the default) is all most of us need, but if you really want to fine-tune your search, click the Advanced Search tab at the top of the first window in Figure 2-21. A full set of options will drop down for more in-depth searching. Using the Advanced Search feature, I was able to narrow down my search from 214 matching entries with Quick Search to just one match—exactly what I needed.

Personal Publisher

The Member Directory is searchable—quite a feat when you realize that AOL has over seven million members and each of them has five potential screen names—but that's its finest quality. It's textual, after all, and its fields are small. Most people can talk forever about themselves, and would love to post pictures of themselves, their dogs and cats, their cars and their families. They might even want to post the *sound* of their cat, or a short movie of their family. They might want to post this information in such a way that it's open to everyone—not just AOL's membership, but anyone with access to an online service or the Internet. You can't do that with the Member Directory. For that you need AOL's *Personal Publisher.*

> **The Gallery**
>
> If you want to know even more about a person, check out the Gallery (keyword: **Gallery**). Members can send their photographs to a scanning service and the electronic result is posted in the Gallery, or they can post scans of their own. There's a Search button, so you don't have to look through long listings. Steve Case is there; so am I. Printed gallery photos make great trading cards: "I'll trade you one Steve Case for two MajorToms..."

Personal Publisher

Personal Publisher is an area within AOL where you can create your own World Wide Web home page and post it online for others to see. (In fact, as I write this, AOL is beginning to call this area *My Home Page*, reflective of its purpose.) Though the World Wide Web is discussed in Chapter 4, "Using the Internet," you should know that a Web *page* is essentially a screenful of text and (optionally) graphics, sound, and video. A *home page* is typically a Web page describing a person or company. AOL has a home page: press Command-K, enter **http://www.aol.com/** in the space provided (type carefully!), then click the Go button (see Figure 2-22).

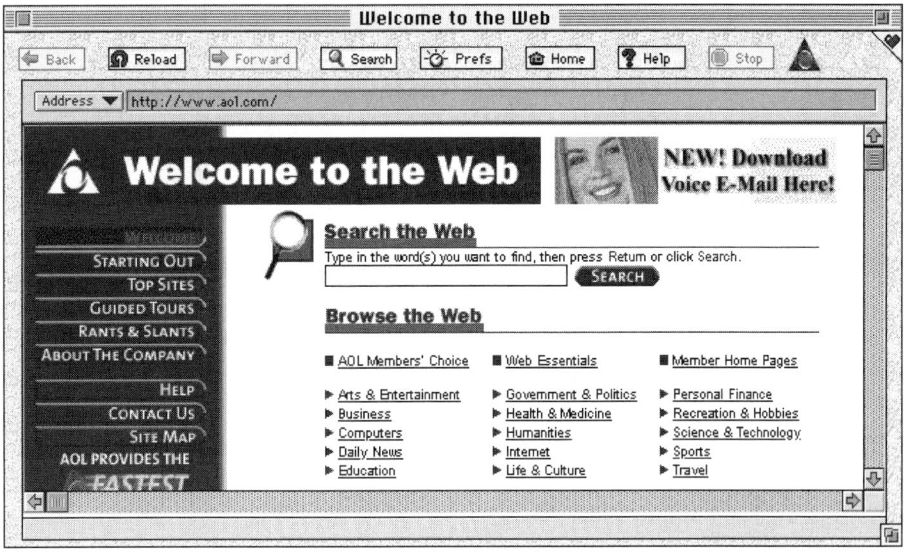
Welcome to the Web
Back
Reload
Forward
Search
Prefs
Home
Help
Stop
Address
http://www.aol.com/
Welcome to the Web
NEW! Download Voice E-Mail Here!
Welcome
Starting Out
Top Sites
Guided Tours
Rants & Slants
About The Company
Help
Contact Us
Site Map
AOL PROVIDES THE
FASTEST
Search the Web
Type in the word(s) you want to find, then press Return or click Search.
Search
Browse the Web
AOL Members' Choice
Web Essentials
Member Home Pages
Arts & Entertainment
Business
Computers
Daily News
Education
Government & Politics
Health & Medicine
Humanities
Internet
Life & Culture
Personal Finance
Recreation & Hobbies
Science & Technology
Sports
Travel

Figure 2-22: A portion of America Online's home page. You can make one of your own by using the keywords: **Personal Publisher**.

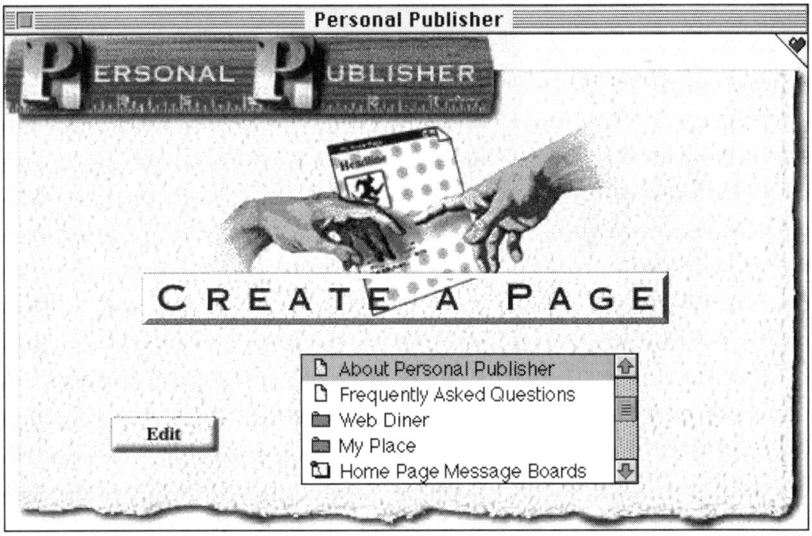
Personal Publisher
PERSONAL PUBLISHER
CREATE A PAGE
Edit
About Personal Publisher
Frequently Asked Questions
Web Diner
My Place
Home Page Message Boards

Figure 2-23: Personal Publisher offers templates, a Frequently Asked Questions file, and a message board for help.

This is not the chapter, nor is it even the book to detail the operation of AOL's Personal Publisher. Fortunately, there's no need to. The Personal Publisher window (see Figure 2-23) offers plenty of help on the subject, and the process itself is a sequential procedure, with explanatory messages almost every step of the way.

Scanners Optional

Your home page should really offer a picture or two. People expect to see a picture of you at least, and probably another one of your dog Spam.

Home page pictures, however, imply scanners, and a good color scanner is simply too expensive for most of us. What we need is a nice, friendly place where we can take our pictures and they'll scan them for us.

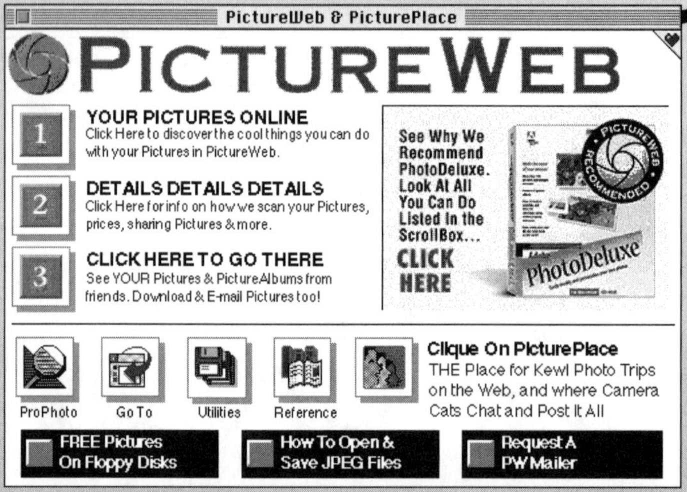
PictureWeb & PicturePlace
PICTUREWEB
1
YOUR PICTURES ONLINE
Click Here to discover the cool things you can do with your Pictures in PictureWeb.
2
DETAILS DETAILS DETAILS
Click Here for info on how we scan your Pictures, prices, sharing Pictures & more.
3
CLICK HERE TO GO THERE
See YOUR Pictures & PictureAlbums from friends. Download & E-mail Pictures too!
See Why We Recommend PhotoDeluxe. Look At All You Can Do Listed In the ScrollBox...
CLICK HERE
PhotoDeluxe
ProPhoto
Go To
Utilities
Reference
Clique On PicturePlace
THE Place for Kewl Photo Trips on the Web, and where Camera Cats Chat and Post It All
FREE Pictures On Floppy Disks
How To Open & Save JPEG Files
Request A PW Mailer

Figure 2-24: Send them your pictures, they send you files, at keyword: **PicturePlace**.

That place exists, it's remarkably inexpensive and fast: you send them your pictures (via the U.S. Mail), they scan them and post the resulting files online for you to download. They're called PicturePlace (see Figure 2-24) and they're waiting to tell you their story at keyword: **PicturePlace**.

How does Personal Publisher compare with the Member Directory? Pictures are the big difference: you can run rampant with graphics, whether they're photographs or graphics from AOL's own clip-art collection.

The Web Diner

Constructing and posting a personal home page is a complex task. You can spend a great deal of time trying to figure everything out and have nothing to show for your efforts. Errors in design, in function, in content—especially errors for all of the Internet to see—can be embarrassing or even devastating.

Unless you know all there is to know about the World Wide Web and home pages, become familiar with the Web Diner (see Figure 2-25). The Web Diner is where AOL has assembled all of its Web expertise and support services for its members. It's comprehensive, germane, and all at the keywords: **Web Diner**.

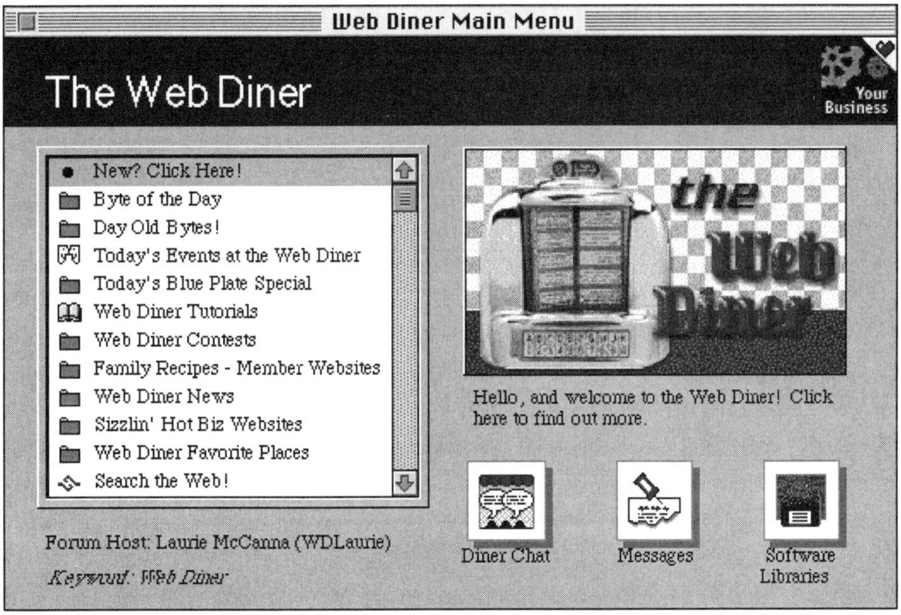
Web Diner Main Menu
The Web Diner
Your Business
New? Click Here!
Byte of the Day
Day Old Bytes!
Today's Events at the Web Diner
Today's Blue Plate Special
Web Diner Tutorials
Web Diner Contests
Family Recipes - Member Websites
Web Diner News
Sizzlin' Hot Biz Websites
Web Diner Favorite Places
Search the Web!
the Web Diner
Hello, and welcome to the Web Diner! Click here to find out more.
Forum Host: Laurie McCanna (WDLaurie)
Keyword: Web Diner
Diner Chat
Messages
Software Libraries

Figure 2-25: Tips, tours, tutorials, and more: the Web Diner is where to learn it all, at keywords: **Web Diner**.

Yes, MajorTom has a home page. You'll find it at **http://members.aol.com/majortom/private/index.html.** Sign on, press Command-K, and type that address into the space provided. Click the Go button and come by to say hello.

Parental Controls

In Chapter 1 I described AOL as a community. On a political level, communities range from socialism to anarchism. But in this country we think of something in between. There *is* a government, after all, but it's not authoritarian; people do pretty much as they please, within certain bounds.

Our politics are reflected in our families: We seek a balance between despotic authority and profligate anarchy. Parents struggle with this balance: Equanimity is elusive. Nowhere is this more evident than in matters of censure.

Every parent adopts a personal level of censorship: that's as it should be. Recently, however, the media have offered their assistance: all motion pictures are rated, many television cable companies offer selective channel blocking, a rating system is emerging for video games, and AOL offers a feature called *Parental Controls* (see Figure 2-26).

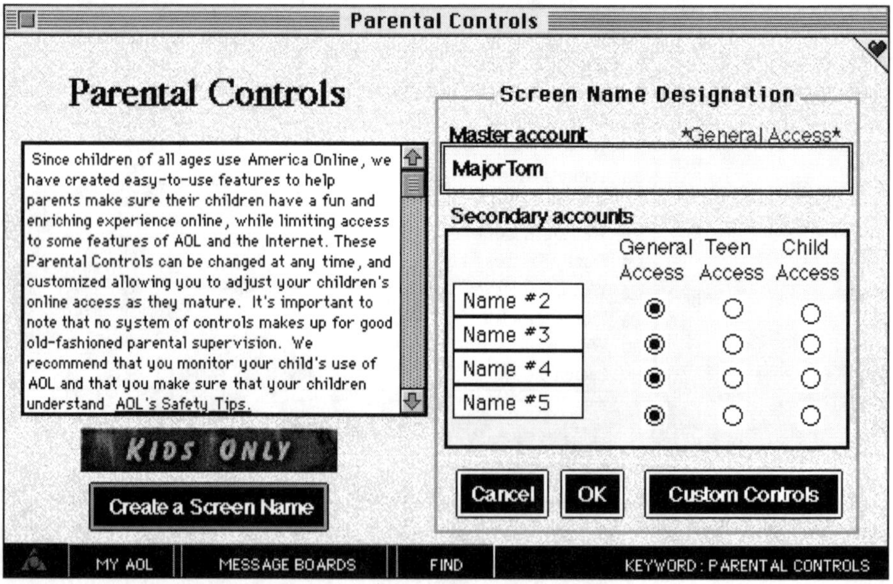
Parental Controls
Parental Controls
Since children of all ages use America Online, we have created easy-to-use features to help parents make sure their children have a fun and enriching experience online, while limiting access to some features of AOL and the Internet. These Parental Controls can be changed at any time, and customized allowing you to adjust your children's online access as they mature. It's important to note that no system of controls makes up for good old-fashioned parental supervision. We recommend that you monitor your child's use of AOL and that you make sure that your children understand AOL's Safety Tips.
KIDS ONLY
Create a Screen Name
Screen Name Designation
Master account
General Access
MajorTom
Secondary accounts
General Access
Teen Access
Child Access
Name #2
Name #3
Name #4
Name #5
Cancel
OK
Custom Controls
MY AOL
MESSAGE BOARDS
FIND
KEYWORD: PARENTAL CONTROLS

Figure 2-26: Parental Controls allow the master account holder to determine how much or how little of AOL's service is available to the screen names associated with the account.

Parental Controls can only be used by the master account. The master account is the permanent screen name that was created during your first sign-on to AOL. Parental Controls enable the master account holder to restrict—for other names on that account—access to certain areas and features available online. It can be set for one or all screen names on the account; and once it is set for a particular screen name, it is active each time that screen name signs on. Changes can be made only at the master account level, and therefore, only by the person who knows the master account's password. These restrictions are set at keywords: **Parental Controls**.

As shown in Figure 2-26, there are three account designation types used to control access to AOL: General, Teen, or Child. General access has no restrictions and is the default. Teen access restricts the screen name to World Wide Web sites selected for content appropriate to teens 13-16. Teen access is also blocked from newsgroups that allow file attachments. Child access only allows access to the Kids Only channel and World Wide Web sites appropriate to those under 12. Child access also restricts Instant Messages, Member Rooms, and file attachments on e-mail. These controls are particularly convenient if you are unfamiliar with all that AOL has to offer. If you prefer to tailor access, click the Custom Controls button for more specific options (see Figure 2-27).

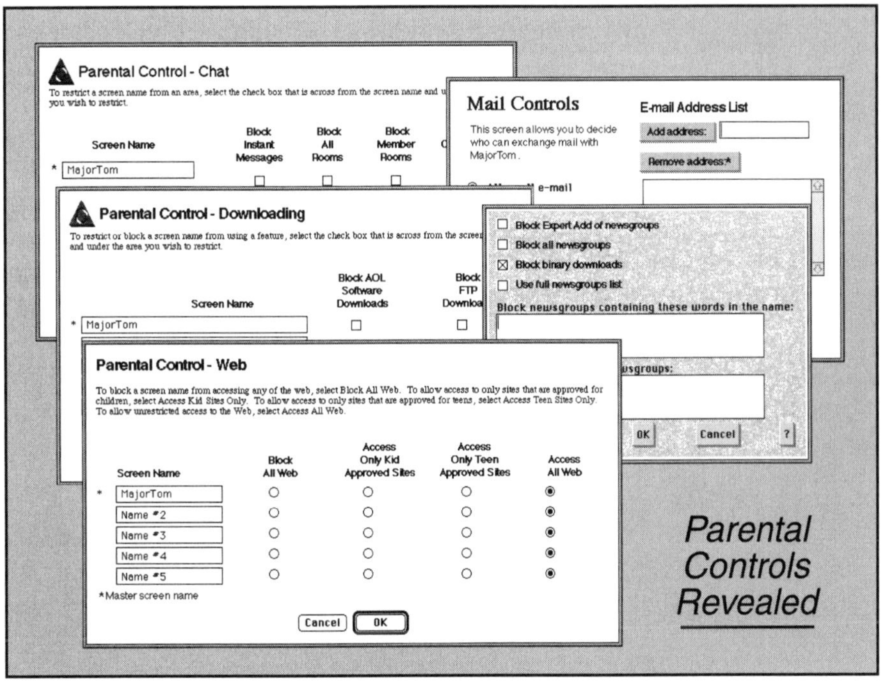
Parental Control - Chat
Screen Name
Block Instant Messages
Block All Rooms
Block Member Rooms
MajorTom
Mail Controls
E-mail Address List
This screen allows you to decide who can exchange mail with MajorTom.
Add address:
Remove address*
Parental Control - Downloading
Block AOL Software Downloads
Block FTP Downloa
Block Expert Add of newsgroups
Block all newsgroups
Block binary downloads
Use full newsgroups list
Block newsgroups containing these words in the name:
Parental Control - Web
To block a screen name from accessing any of the web, select Block All Web. To allow access to only sites that are approved for children, select Access Kid Sites Only. To allow access to only sites that are approved for teens, select Access Teen Sites Only. To allow unrestricted access to the Web, select Access All Web.
Screen Name
Block All Web
Access Only Kid Approved Sites
Access Only Teen Approved Sites
Access All Web
MajorTom
Name #2
Name #3
Name #4
Name #5
*Master screen name
Cancel
OK
Parental Controls Revealed

Figure 2-27: Using my master account I am able to customize access to certain areas within the service for all my other accounts.

Refer to Figure 2-27: the master account holder can set any or all of the following five Parental Control features:

- *Chat Controls* allow you to block all Instant Messages; block access to all rooms in the People Connection; block access to Member Rooms only; or block access to conference rooms found throughout AOL, such as the MTV Yack room in MTV Online.
- *Downloading Controls* allow you to block downloading of any data that's available on AOL, including programs, graphics, and multimedia (downloading is discussed in Chapter 5, "Transferring Files), as well as block FTP downloads, which are discussed in Chapter 4, "Using the Internet."
- *Web Controls* allow you to block all Web sites; allow only Web sites appropriate for children up to 12 years in age; allow only Web sites appropriate for teens; and allow all Web sites. The World Wide Web is discussed in Chapter 4.
- *Mail Controls* allow you to allow all e-mail (the default); block all e-mail; allow e-mail only from certain individuals; and block e-mail from certain addresses. Mail Controls are discussed in greater depth in Chapter 3, "Electronic Mail & the Personal Filing Cabinet."
- *Newsgroup Controls* allow you to block the ability to add newsgroups by typing in their newsgroup names; block access to all newsgroups regardless of their nature; and block the ability to download the Internet's so-called *binaries* (such as pictures, videos, and sounds). An additional control, *use full newsgroups list,* is *more* permissive when it's checked. Unless this option is checked, AOL's available list of newsgroups is abbreviated: the alt.sex.* groups don't appear on the list, for example. By listing all of the newsgroups on the Internet, members have access to a wider variety of options.

The Parental Controls feature is an elective, not an imperative. Use it if you want; ignore it if you wish. That's a level of intervention that accommodates any parental attitude, and that's the way most of us prefer to have it.

Terms of Service (TOS)

You're probably not aware of it, but you have a contract with AOL, and even though it's not a signed contract, you waived the need for your signature when you first signed on. The contract defines exactly what you can and cannot do online, and it defines exactly what AOL can do if it determines that you have violated the terms of contract.

The contract is called *Terms of Service*, or TOS for short. It's always available for review or downloading at keyword: **TOS** (see Figure 2-28). Time spent there is free of AOL's normal connect-time charges.

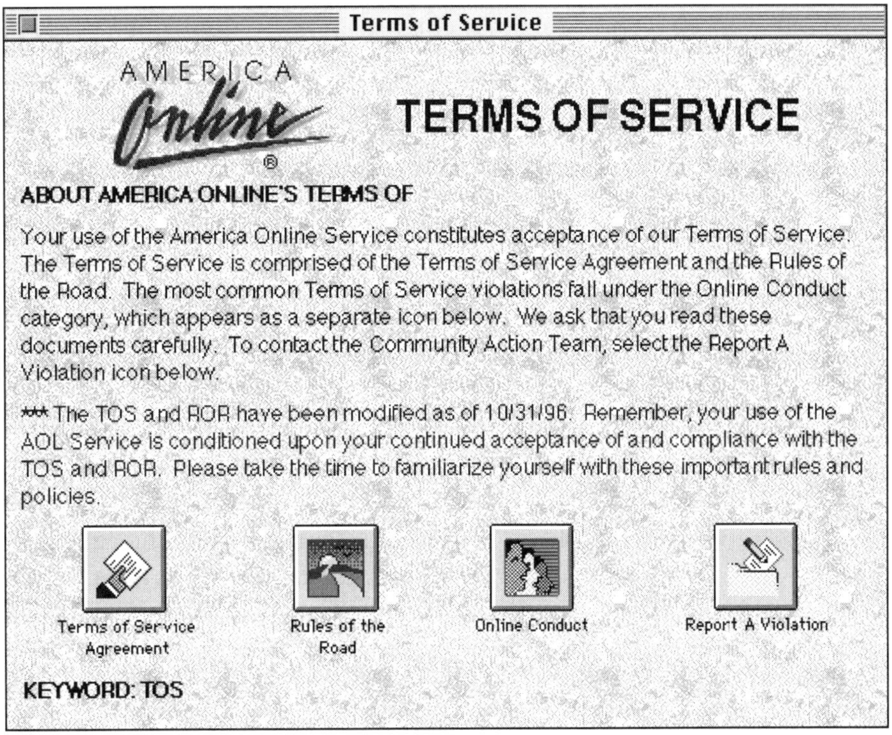
Terms of Service
AMERICA Online
TERMS OF SERVICE
ABOUT AMERICA ONLINE'S TERMS OF
Your use of the America Online Service constitutes acceptance of our Terms of Service. The Terms of Service is comprised of the Terms of Service Agreement and the Rules of the Road. The most common Terms of Service violations fall under the Online Conduct category, which appears as a separate icon below. We ask that you read these documents carefully. To contact the Community Action Team, select the Report A Violation icon below.
*** The TOS and ROR have been modified as of 10/31/96. Remember, your use of the AOL Service is conditioned upon your continued acceptance of and compliance with the TOS and ROR. Please take the time to familiarize yourself with these important rules and policies.
Terms of Service Agreement
Rules of the Road
Online Conduct
Report A Violation
KEYWORD: TOS

Figure 2-28: The contract that exists between all members and AOL is available at keyword: **TOS**.

Unless you have joined AOL with the specific intention of disrupting the service (snerts, phishers, and trolls are discussed in Chapter 8, "The Community"), TOS exists to protect you. Specifically, TOS describes violations such as offensive e-mail, impersonation of AOL staff, and online harassment. It also describes what you can do if you witness these violations. Look again at Figure 2-28: the Report a Violation button provides a number of ways for you to enforce your rights. Among other things, AOL's TOS team is the online "police," and they can take quick and conclusive action when provoked. I've seen it happen: it's not an experience soon forgotten.

TOS, like your local 911 service, exists to make the community a better and safer place to live. Like a 911 service, however, TOS can be abused—even by those with good intentions—by ignorance. If you think you might ever require TOS enforcement, read this information.

Here are some interesting TOS conditions:

- You agree that you are an individual, not a corporation.
- You agree that you are at least 18 years of age.
- You agree to notify AOL within 30 days if your billing information changes (e.g., your credit card is stolen).
- You are liable for all expenses incurred on your account—even if someone steals your password—until you notify AOL by telephone.
- AOL does not intentionally monitor or disclose any private electronic communications (such as e-mail or private chat rooms) unless required to do so by law.
- AOL *does* monitor public communication (public chat rooms, message board postings), though AOL "… has neither the practical capability, nor does it intend, to act in the role of 'Big Brother' by screening public communication in advance." (Quoting "Rules of the Road.")
- Unless you tell AOL otherwise (see Appendix E, "Preferences"), AOL has the right to distribute your name and address to third parties (for example, mailing lists). This right does not extend to your billing information, however.
- Both the Terms of Service agreement *and* the Rules of the Road (review Figure 2-28) constitute your contract with AOL. You should read them both.

I mention all of this not to infuse you with an Orwellian fear of AOL, but rather to offer a wake-up call: TOS has some very specific and significant conditions in it, conditions to which you have legally agreed. You should know your rights and know how to recognize others' wrongs. Read this agreement.

AOL's Voice

The male voice you hear when you sign on is that of Elwood Edwards, a professional announcer who, last I heard, works for Channel 50 in Washington, DC.

El's story is one of online romance made good. He was a member like the rest of us when, in the late 1980s, he met a female member online and began to chat with her. It turned out that the lady worked for AOL, where they were in the process of adding a voice to AOL's software. When she discovered El's profession, she asked him if he would like to record the voice tracks.

El and his newfound acquaintance met face-to-face for the recording session, discovered lots of things they had in common, and were married soon thereafter.

The voice tracks were recorded on a cassette recorder in 1989, and their quality isn't state of the art. El re-recorded his material digitally in late 1995 (including a fix for the grammatically incorrect "You've got mail"). To get the new tracks, use the keywords: **File Search**, click the PC Search button at the bottom, then search with the criteria: Edwards AND voice. If the file is still around, you'll see it as AOL_NEW.ZIP, available for downloading. Downloading is discussed in Chapter 5, "Transferring Files." The procedure for installing the new voice is discussed in the file's description.

Moving On

All of this talk about TOS notwithstanding, I hope this chapter has made you feel more comfortable and welcome at AOL. America Online offers more help—and more kinds of help—than any software I've known. It's online, it's offline, it's Tech Support Live, it's Members Helping Members, and it's Guides. Everyone at AOL—members included—helps someone else sooner or later. That's comforting. Not only is AOL a community, it's a *considerate* community, where no one remains a stranger for long.

Without a doubt, the mechanism that members most often use to communicate among themselves is electronic mail, or e-mail for short. AOL places notable emphasis on its e-mail features, and it shows. To see what I mean, turn the page....

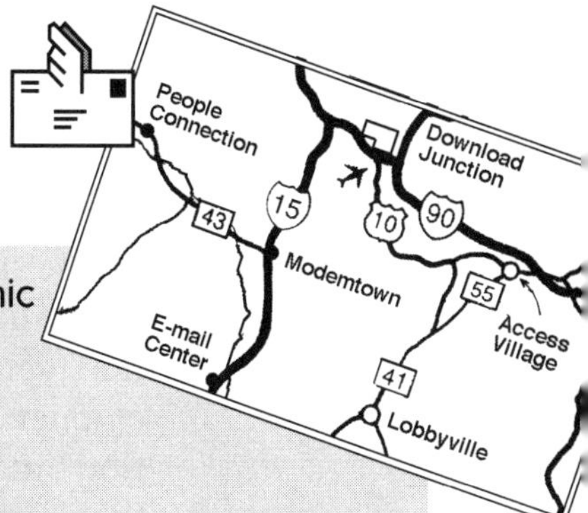
People Connection
Download Junction
Modemtown
E-mail Center
Access Village
Lobbyville
15
43
10
90
55
41

CHAPTER 3

Electronic Mail & the Personal Filing Cabinet

- What Exactly Is Electronic Mail?
- A Circular Exercise
- The Mail Menu
- Attaching Files to Messages
- Receiving Attached Files
- Internet Mail
- The Address Book
- The Personal Filing Cabinet
- Mail Controls

Cicero sent mail to his brother a hundred years before Christ was born. Pliny the Younger sent mail from Rome in the first century. Thoreau wrote from Walden, Louisa May Alcott wrote from the battlefield, and Emily Dickinson wrote from seclusion. As late as the 1950s, Anne Spencer Morrow Lindbergh used the mail to express her views on women's issues, but as a letter writer, she was by then in the dwindling minority. People used to spend hours every week composing lavish prose to one another, but by the middle of this century, letter writing was almost a forgotten art. The U.S. Postal Service had become a vehicle not for rhapsodic prose but for junk mail, magazines, and nasty little envelopes with glassine windows. When it comes to correspondence, most of us let our fingers do the walking.

A lamentable condition, that correspondence thing. People took time to search their souls when they corresponded via the mails—they reflected and introspected. They were exacting in choosing their words, reviewed what they wrote, and eagerly anticipated replies. It was a very considerate, unselfish, compassionate thing to do. And though it was common a century ago, by the 1950s it was as scarce as a 3-cent postage stamp is today.

There's cause for optimism, however. People are writing to each other again. There's a renaissance of correspondence, a revival of colloquy. Personal communication is no longer a phone call that interrupts dinner; it's a thoughtful process. And again the writer awaits a reply, expectant and hopeful as a bride.

The salvation, of course, is electronic mail. Electronic mail brings the convenience and immediacy of the telephone to written communication, yet it reflects contemplation, and retains—even encourages—the eloquence of the written word. It's a vehicle not only for communication but expression as well. And, significantly, not only the content but the costs of communication have rolled back to yesteryear.

What Exactly Is Electronic Mail?

Electronic mail (*e-mail* for short) is simply mail prepared on a computer and sent to another computer. There are lots of private e-mail networks—computers wired together and configured to send and receive mail. America Online is one of these. Many of these networks (including AOL) are connected to the Internet (discussed in Chapter 4, "Using the Internet"; Internet mail is discussed later in this chapter), and you can send mail to (and receive mail from) the people who are connected across these networks.

Most e-mail systems share common characteristics:

- Messages are composed of pure ASCII text. ASCII is an acronym (see the glossary in the back of this book), and even though the "AS" part stands for "American Standard," the standard is used around the world, on virtually every computer.
- Messages can thus be sent between dissimilar computers—PCs, Macintoshes, Amigas, personal digital assistants (such as Newtons)—even dumb terminals.
- The addressee must be known to the respective mail system.

Some of the features below are offered by some e-mail systems; AOL offers them all:

- Messages can be replied to by anyone or forwarded to anyone, including people connected to networks outside of AOL. This includes commercial services, such as Prodigy and CompuServe.
- Files—graphics, sounds, programs, spreadsheets—can be attached to messages, including those sent to Internet addresses outside of the AOL network.

- Messages can be addressed to multiple recipients. "Carbon copies" can be sent to people other than the addressee, and "blind" carbon copies (copies sent without the other addressees' knowledge) can be specified as well.
- Messages can contain textual formatting. Although most e-mail is composed of ASCII text (which offers no provision for textual formatting) using *HTML codes,* type size, color, background color, style, and paragraph alignment can be specified. (We'll discuss HTML codes later in this chapter.)
- Messages—both incoming and outgoing—can be filed in a hierarchical filing system similar to an office filing cabinet. Not surprisingly, AOL calls this feature your *Personal Filing Cabinet*. It's discussed later in this chapter.
- Messages need not be composed while you're online. Likewise, received messages need not be read while you're online. Any incoming message can be filed for later retrieval and read offline at your convenience. If you choose to reply, you can compose your reply offline as well. You need to sign on only to send and receive mail, a process that rarely consumes more than a couple of minutes online, and the process can even be automated—something we'll discuss in Chapter 6, "Automatic AOL & the Download Manager."

A Circular Exercise

Before we get to the details, here's a little exercise just to show you how e-mail works. This exercise is somewhat futile: sending mail to yourself is a bit pretentious and rarely productive. Nevertheless, do it just this once. Nobody's looking.

The Format Menu & Mini Toolbar

The Format menu allows you to change the font, size, style, color, and alignment of selected text in the mail window. A mini format toolbar can also be brought up, if you prefer, with the Show Text Format Toolbar option at the bottom of the Format menu or with the Format icon in a Compose Mail window (see bottom of Figure 3-1). Both the Format menu and the mini toolbar offer the same options; fiddle with them during this exercise. Select some text, then choose an option from the menu or the toolbar. See what happens.

1. With America Online up and running, sign on. Leave the Welcome screen showing, and choose Compose Mail from the Mail menu (or click the pen-and-paper button on the toolbar). An untitled Compose Mail form will appear (see Figure 3-1).

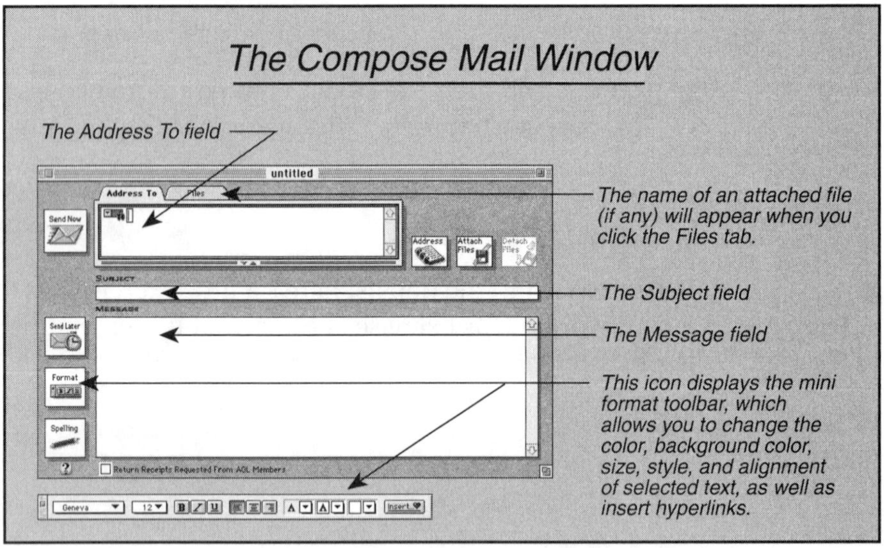
The Compose Mail Window
The Address To field
The name of an attached file (if any) will appear when you click the Files tab.
The Subject field
The Message field
This icon displays the mini format toolbar, which allows you to change the color, background color, size, style, and alignment of selected text, as well as insert hyperlinks.
untitled
Address To
Files
Send Now
Address
Attach Files
Detach Files
Send Later
Format
Spelling
Return Receipts Requested From AOL Members
Geneva
12
Insert

Figure 3-1: This window appears whenever you're about to compose some mail. AOL has already identified you as the sender; it's now waiting for you to identify the recipient.

2. The insertion point is now flashing in the Address To field, where you are required to enter the screen name of the recipient. Type in your own screen name. This is the futile part of the exercise—sending mail to yourself—but the rewards are immediate, and there will be no guessing as to whether the mail ever made it to the addressee.

3. In the Subject field, enter the word **Test**.

4. Type something into the Message field. Don't overdo it. People will talk.

5. Click the Send Now button.

If your Mac's sound is turned up, a voice instantly announces, "You've got mail!" Even if you don't hear anything, a tiny mailbox now flashes in the upper right corner of your screen. There's a particular comfort in that. Mail moves around the AOL circuit quite literally at the speed of light. You'll never wonder again if your mail will get to its destination by next Thursday. It gets there the instant you send it.

Note also that two things have happened: (1) the little mailbox icon is now flashing in the upper right corner; and (2) the You Have Mail icon on the Welcome screen is now active (Figure 3-2).

At the right end of your menu bar, a mailbox raises a tiny flag and blinks.
YOU HAVE MAIL
And in the Welcome window, another mailbox appears, stuffed with your mail.

Figure 3-2: *You have mail!* You get two doses of visual indication and one aural announcement every time mail is waiting for you at America Online.

6. By now, the Compose Mail window has closed and you're back at the Welcome screen. Click the You Have Mail button.

7. Your Online Mailbox window appears (see Figure 3-3). This window is a little redundant when you only have one piece of mail waiting, but soon you'll be a popular person, and dozens of entries will appear here every time you sign on.

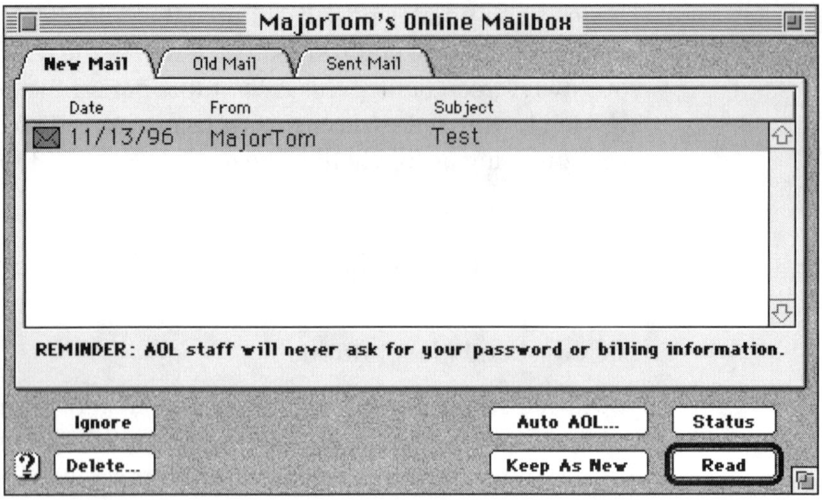
MajorTom's Online Mailbox
New Mail
Old Mail
Sent Mail
Date
From
Subject
11/13/96
MajorTom
Test
REMINDER: AOL staff will never ask for your password or billing information.
Ignore
Delete...
Auto AOL...
Status
Keep As New
Read

Figure 3-3: Your Online Mailbox window appears whenever you elect to read incoming mail.

8. Double-click the entry, which represents the mail you sent a moment ago.

9. The message window appears, with your "Test" message therein (see Figure 3-4).

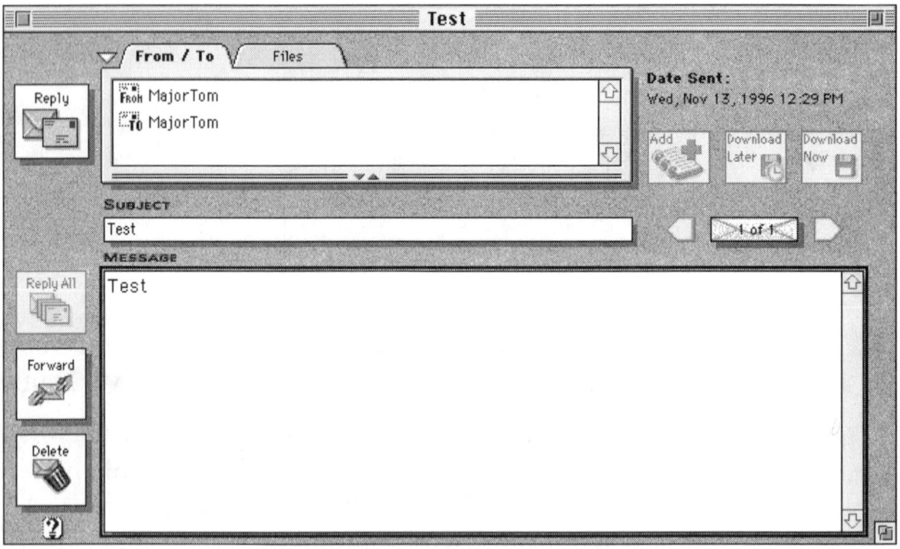
Test
From / To
Files
Reply
FROM MajorTom
TO MajorTom
Date Sent:
Wed, Nov 13, 1996 12:29 PM
Add
Download Later
Download Now
SUBJECT
Test
1 of 1
MESSAGE
Test
Reply All
Forward
Delete

Figure 3-4: The mail is received. Note that you can forward or reply to this mail by simply clicking the appropriate button.

It's probably best for you to toss this mail now, before anyone sees what you've been up to. To throw it away, double-click its Close button, or press Command-W. I just wanted you to see how simple, fast, and easy the process really is. That's the whole idea—above all, e-mail should be convenient, global, and inexpensive, and AOL certainly makes it so.

A Case for Exactitude

America Online is, perhaps, excessively lenient when it comes to e-mail addresses. At AOL, screen names are not case-sensitive. MajorTom works no better than majortom. Even spaces are ignored: mail addressed to Major Tom is always delivered to MajorTom.

On the Internet, however, the user name occasionally *is* case-sensitive, and spaces simply aren't tolerated.

Even if you don't know what the Internet is (you will if you read this chapter and the next), and even if you think you'll never exchange mail on the Internet, it's wise to develop the habit of entering e-mail addresses *exactly* as you encounter them. If your friend tells you that she's **JulAnnF**, send mail to **JulAnnF**. If she tells you that she's **julannf@umich.edu** (an Internet address—you can tell by the "@" sign), send mail to **julannf@umich.edu**. Many matters in life require adherence to rules. Like traffic lights, this is one of them.

The Mail Menu

Nearly all day-to-day mail activities are performed using the Mail menu (see Figure 3-5).

Mail
Compose Mail ⌘M
Read Mail ⌘R
Address Book
Read Offline Mail
Set Up Automatic AOL...
Run Automatic AOL...
Dictionary
Thesaurus
Mail Center
Mail Controls

Figure 3-5: The Mail menu handles most of your daily e-mail activities.

Composing Your Mail

The first option on the Mail menu is Compose Mail, which you choose whenever you want to send mail to someone. This option is available whether you're online or off; you can compose mail offline and send it later—a feature I'll discuss in Chapter 6, "Automatic AOL & the Download Manager."

When the Compose Mail command is issued, America Online responds with a blank, untitled piece of mail (review Figure 3-1). Note the position of the insertion point in Figure 3-1. It's located within the Address To field of the window. America Online, in other words, is waiting for you to provide the recipient's screen name. Type it in. (If you don't remember the screen name, use your Address Book, which I'll describe later in this chapter.)

You can type multiple addresses in the Address To field if you wish, starting subsequent names on a new line by pressing the Return key or typing a comma after the previous name, or simply clicking on the next blank line with your mouse. If you want to send mail to Steve Case and Tom Lichty, you could simply type **Steve Case,MajorTom** in this box and each name will appear on its own line automatically as you type. Note that the field is actually a scroll box. You can type as many addresses as you want.

To the left of each address is a small envelope icon that produces a pop-up menu when clicked. You can designate an address to receive a "carbon copy" of your mail by choosing the CC option in the pop-up menu. You can also begin the address with an open bracket: for example, typing **[MajorTom** will automatically designate this address as a carbon copy when complete without using the pop-up menu. Carbon copies (actually, they're called "courtesy copies" now—carbon paper isn't around much anymore) are really no different than originals. Whether a member receives an original or a copy is more a matter of protocol than anything else.

Blind Carbon Copies

As is the case with the traditional CC: (or cc:) at the bottom of a business letter, the addressee is made aware of any others who will receive an electronic carbon copy of the letter—a traditional courtesy.

On the other hand, you might want to send a copy of a message to someone without letting the addressee(s) know you have done so. This is known as a "blind" carbon copy, and at AOL it works whether you're mailing to another AOL member, an Internet address (I'll discuss Internet mail later in this chapter), or a combination of both. To address a blind carbon copy, choose the BCC option in the pop-up menu to the left of the address, available by clicking the envelope icon. You can also begin the address of the blind carbon copy recipient with an open parenthesis character, which will automatically trigger the BCC option without having to select it from the menu: for example, typing **(MajorTom** will designate this address as a blind carbon copy automatically without using the pop-up menu. No one but the recipient of the blind carbon copy will know what you've done. (The ethics of this feature are yours to ponder.)

Press the Tab key to move the insertion point to the Subject field, and enter a descriptive word or two. The Subject field can hold up to 182 characters, but I recommend you keep it below 80 characters so that recipients can read it in its entirety. **Note**: If the Subject field *is not* filled in, AOL will send the message with "No Subject" in the Subject field—not the best title to entice your reader.

Press the Tab key again. The insertion point moves to the Message field. Type your message there (see Figure 3-6). **Note**: If the Message field is *not* filled in, AOL will send the mail but without a message of any kind. This can be useful in certain cases, such as in sending requests to join Internet mailing lists (discussed in Chapter 4, "Using the Internet").

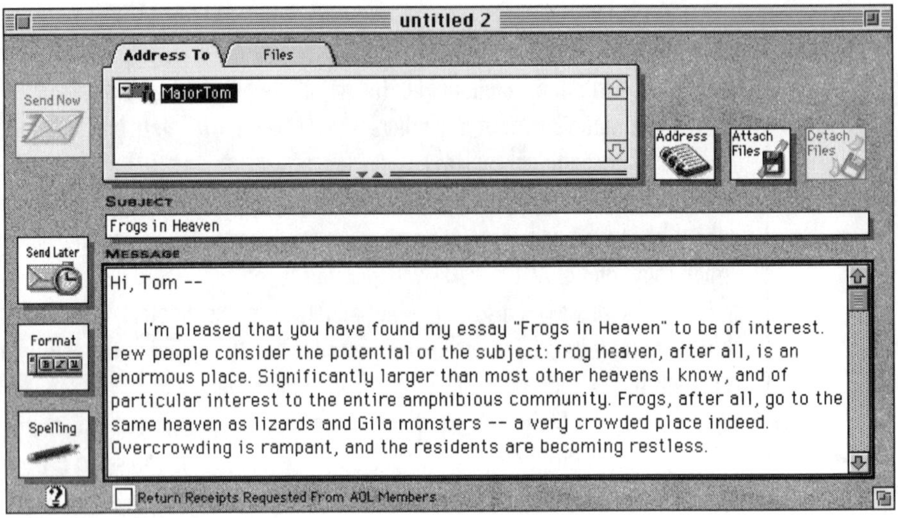
untitled 2
Address To
Files
Send Now
MajorTom
Address
Attach Files
Detach Files
Subject
Frogs in Heaven
Message
Send Later
Hi, Tom --
I'm pleased that you have found my essay "Frogs in Heaven" to be of interest. Few people consider the potential of the subject: frog heaven, after all, is an enormous place. Significantly larger than most other heavens I know, and of particular interest to the entire amphibious community. Frogs, after all, go to the same heaven as lizards and Gila monsters -- a very crowded place indeed. Overcrowding is rampant, and the residents are becoming restless.
Format
Spelling
Return Receipts Requested From AOL Members

Figure 3-6: The completed message is ready to send. Click the Send Now button (if you're online) or the Send Later button (if you're not online).

It's subtle, but note that the Send Now button in Figure 3-6 is dimmed: this message is being prepared offline (see the "Preparing Mail Offline" sidebar).

Preparing Mail Offline

Consider preparing mail when you're offline. You can linger over it that way, perfecting every word. When you complete a message, click the Send Later button. Next time you sign on, send the mail by choosing Read Offline Mail from the Mail menu, selecting the Mail Waiting To Be Sent tray (see Figure 3-7), then opening each to send them individually or clicking the Auto AOL button to send all of your messages.

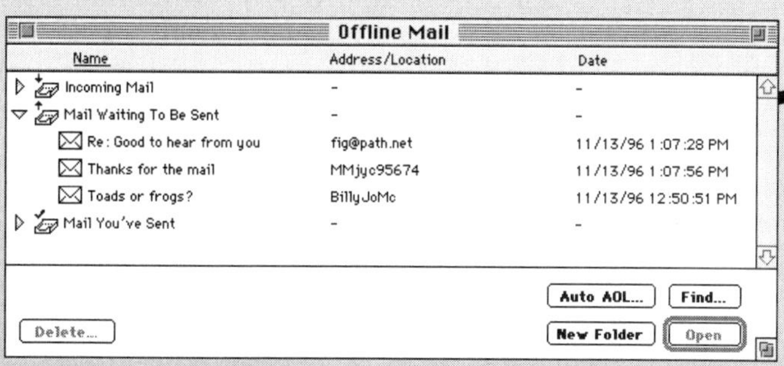
Offline Mail
Name
Address/Location
Date
Incoming Mail
Mail Waiting To Be Sent
Re: Good to hear from you
fig@path.net
11/13/96 1:07:28 PM
Thanks for the mail
MMjyc95674
11/13/96 1:07:56 PM
Toads or frogs?
BillyJoMc
11/13/96 12:50:51 PM
Mail You've Sent
Auto AOL...
Find...
Delete...
New Folder
Open

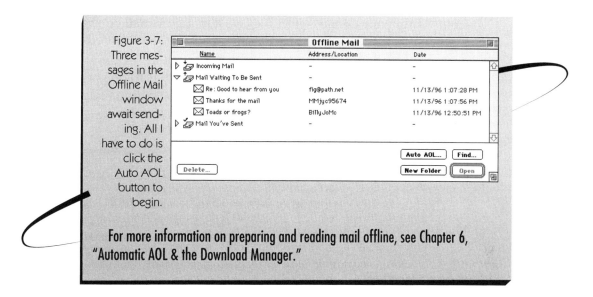

Figure 3-7: Three messages in the Offline Mail window await sending. All I have to do is click the Auto AOL button to begin.

For more information on preparing and reading mail offline, see Chapter 6, "Automatic AOL & the Download Manager."

Hyperlinks in E-Mail

Suppose your mother is an avid wrestling fan—you can't get her away from the TV when Hulk Hogan is hosting the bodyslammin' semifinals on Monday Night Raw—and you've just discovered the World Wrestling Federation Online on AOL.

Naturally, you want to tell her about it (and, naturally, she has an AOL account). Even better, you decide to *show* it to her, via e-mail.

Assuming you've added World Wrestling Federation Online to your list of Favorite Places (we'll discuss Favorite Places in Chapter 4), click the Favorite Places (heart-and-folder) icon on the toolbar to invoke the Favorite Places window. Move the Favorite Places window to the side of the screen so that the Compose Mail form is visible in the background. Now simply drag the WWF entry from your list of Favorite Places into the Compose Mail window's message field. A *hyperlink* will appear in the Compose Mail's message field, blue and underlined.

Let's say you're not a fan of World Wrestling Federation Online yourself and thus do not have it in your list of Favorite Places. You can still add it to your mother's message without first adding it to your own list. Just go to the area (in this case, keyword: **WWF**), click the heart icon in the upper right corner, and select the Copy it to the clipboard option. You can now use Command-V to paste the hyperlink right into the Compose Mail window. And if you haven't yet begun composing your e-mail, select the Use it in a new mail document option after clicking on the heart—this will automatically open a new Compose Mail window and place the hyperlink in it for you.

When your mother receives the mail, all she has to do is click the hyperlink. Assuming she's online, the World Wrestling Federation Online window will appear on her screen—automatically—and she's set for an afternoon of Wrestlemania.

You can establish hyperlinks in e-mail for anything with a Favorite Places icon in its corner, including references to pages on the World Wide Web.

The fine print: Your mother will have to be using AOL 3.0 or later. So will you.

Spell Checking

Not everyone was born with a dictionary in his or her head—for some of us, good spelling is as uncommon as, well, frogs in heaven. Fear not, though; AOL's built-in spell checker now gives us all the chance to fix our spelling and appear polished enough for even our high school English teachers. To use the spell checker, complete your message and, before you send it, click the Spelling button in the Compose Mail window. AOL's spelling and punctuation dictionaries will kick in and begin checking your text. When problems are detected, you will be prompted to skip or correct them. You can also teach the checker to "learn" the questionable word with the Learn button—this adds the word to your personal dictionary so use it only when appropriate.

Spell checking is not limited to e-mail text; you can check any text in AOL so long as it is in a Compose Mail window, a file document window, or a new, blank window (available by selecting New from the File menu). If you check your online spelling frequently, visit your Spelling Preferences and configure them to your liking (preferences are discussed in Appendix E).

Alternative Mail Sources

Occasionally you might want to send a text file via e-mail. Perhaps it's a file you have created with AOL's New command (File menu) or a text file you captured online. Regardless of the source, you can send a text file as mail (rather than as a file) by copying and pasting it into a Compose Mail window.

This feature is especially useful for those who prefer to use a word processor to compose messages. Word processors feature productivity tools that AOL's Compose Mail utility doesn't offer. If you prefer to use your word processor, here's how to do it:

- Prepare your message using your word processor. Don't bother with formatting details: see the "Stylized Text" sidebar.
- Select the portion of the message you wish to send, then copy it by choosing Copy from the word processor's Edit menu. This places a copy of the selected text on the clipboard, ready for transfer to any application.
- Assuming your AOL software is running, switch to it now. You can use the application menu in the upper right corner of your screen to switch between running programs quickly.
- Choose Compose Mail from AOL's Mail menu, click within the Message field of the Compose Mail form, then choose Paste from AOL's Edit menu.
- Supply the recipient's e-mail address in the Address To field and a subject in the Subject field. Sign on and send your mail on its way.

Stylized Text

If the recipient is using Version 3.0 (or later) of the AOL client software, you can embellish your mail with changes in size, color, style, alignment—even the background color. Prepare your mail normally, select the text you want to embellish, then click the Format icon on the Compose Mail window. The Format Text toolbar menu will appear, offering all of the choices mentioned here and more.

In fact, this feature will be correctly interpreted by any e-mail program that recognizes *HTML code*—the HyperText Markup Language that's common on the World Wide Web (the World Wide Web is discussed in Chapter 4, "Using the Internet"). Few e-mail programs are capable of interpreting HTML code at the moment, but their numbers are increasing every day. In other words, if the recipient is not an AOL member—that is, they receive their mail via the Internet—they might be able to see your fancy text. If you want to send formatted text to someone on the Internet, send them a test message: experimentation won't hurt. At the worst, they'll get some funny-looking codes in the middle of your message.

Reading New Mail

The second option on the Mail menu—Read Mail—gives you access to your online mailbox. I don't use this menu item. To me, mail is like Christmas morning: I can't wait to get to it. Immediately after hearing that I have mail, I click the You Have Mail button (see Figure 3-2) and start unwrapping my presents.

Night Mail

My passion for new mail is shared by plenty of others. In *Night Mail*, the poet W. H. Auden once wrote:

And none will hear the postman's knock
Without a quickening of the heart.
For who can bear to feel himself forgotten?

Perhaps that's e-mail's greatest virtue: it makes us feel appreciated. That little mailbox full of envelopes in the Welcome window says "Somebody's thinking of you," and there are few of us whose hearts don't quicken a bit when we see it.

Nonetheless, there are those who don't share my enthusiasm. That, I suppose, is why AOL provides this menu option. When it's chosen, America Online presents your Online Mailbox window (Figure 3-8).

Though Figure 3-8 shows only one unread piece of mail, a number of pieces may appear here. If more than one show up, they'll appear in the order in which they were received at America Online. The oldest mail will be at the top, the most recent at the bottom. In other words, to read your mail in chronological order from oldest to most recent, read your messages from top to bottom.

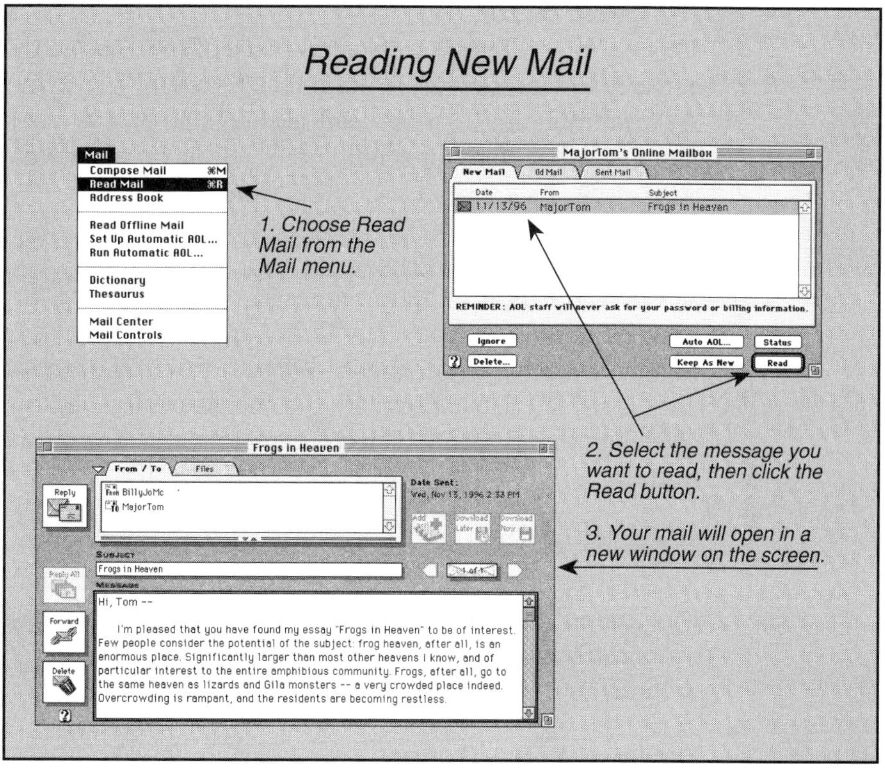
Reading New Mail
Mail
Compose Mail ⌘M
Read Mail ⌘R
Address Book
Read Offline Mail
Set Up Automatic AOL...
Run Automatic AOL...
Dictionary
Thesaurus
Mail Center
Mail Controls
1. Choose Read Mail from the Mail menu.
MajorTom's Online Mailbox
New Mail
Old Mail
Sent Mail
Date
From
Subject
11/13/96
MajorTom
Frogs in Heaven
REMINDER: AOL staff will never ask for your password or billing information.
Ignore
Delete...
Auto AOL...
Keep As New
Status
Read
Frogs in Heaven
From / To
Files
Reply
Date Sent:
Frogs in Heaven
Hi, Tom --
Forward
Delete
I'm pleased that you have found my essay "Frogs in Heaven" to be of interest. Few people consider the potential of the subject: frog heaven, after all, is an enormous place. Significantly larger than most other heavens I know, and of particular interest to the entire amphibious community. Frogs, after all, go to the same heaven as lizards and Gila monsters -- a very crowded place indeed. Overcrowding is rampant, and the residents are becoming restless.
2. Select the message you want to read, then click the Read button.
3. Your mail will open in a new window on the screen.

Figure 3-8: To read new mail, click the You Have Mail button in the Welcome window, press Command-R, click the leftmost icon on the toolbar, or choose Read Mail from the Mail menu.

Buttons in the Online Mailbox Window

A number of buttons appear across the bottom, as well as the top, of the Online Mailbox window pictured in Figure 3-8. They can be confusing at first; let's begin from the top:

The Mailbox Tabs

Across the top of the window are three buttons that look like tabs on file folders. The first tab is for New Mail, which is always selected when you first open your Online Mailbox. The second tab is for Old Mail, which when clicked will display the list of mail you've already read. The third tab is for Sent Mail, which lists mail you've sent recently. Old Mail and Sent Mail are discussed in more detail later.

The Ignore Button

This option will mark a selected piece of mail as read without your actually having to read it—in effect "ignoring" it. If the sender is an AOL member and issues a status check, he or she will see the word "Ignored" beside your screen name. Be sure that's what you want the addressee to see if you use this command.

The Delete Button

This feature allows you to remove a piece of mail permanently from your New Mail mailbox. It will not appear in the Old Mail list either nor will it appear in the Sent Mail window (I'll discuss the Old Mail and Sent Mail lists below). Status checks performed by other members on deleted mail say "Deleted." Compare this button with the Ignore button mentioned earlier.

The Auto AOL Button

This button is the equivalent of selecting Run Automatic AOL from the Mail menu. Click this button if you wish to collect or send your mail automatically. (Auto AOL is discussed in Chapter 6, "Automatic AOL & the Download Manager.")

The Keep As New Button

Clicking this button will return the selected piece of mail to your New Mail list, marking it as unread even though you have already read it. The mail is, however, still considered read as far as other members' status checks are concerned. In other words, if someone checks the status of a piece of mail that you read and then kept as new, they will see the time you read the mail, regardless of whether you kept it as new or not.

The Status Button

The Status button tells you when the mail was read by you or the other recipients (if the mail was sent to others as well). Though we'll talk about Internet mail later in this chapter, note that the Status button doesn't apply to Internet mail. AOL forwards Internet mail to the Internet within a few seconds after you press the Send button, but when is it actually "sent"? When it's posted? When it's routed to the recipient's country or mailbox? There are no answers to these questions. Thus, when you select a piece of Internet mail and click the Status button, AOL will display a dialog box informing you that you cannot check the status of Internet mail.

The Read Button

This button displays the selected piece of mail on the screen for reading. It's the default button: double-clicking an entry on the list does the same thing.

Checking Mail You've Read

We all forget things now and again: "What did I promise to get my mother for Valentine's Day?" That's why AOL provides the Old Mail option in the Online Mailbox window. When you click the Old Mail tab, AOL responds with the Old Mail list (see Figure 3-9).

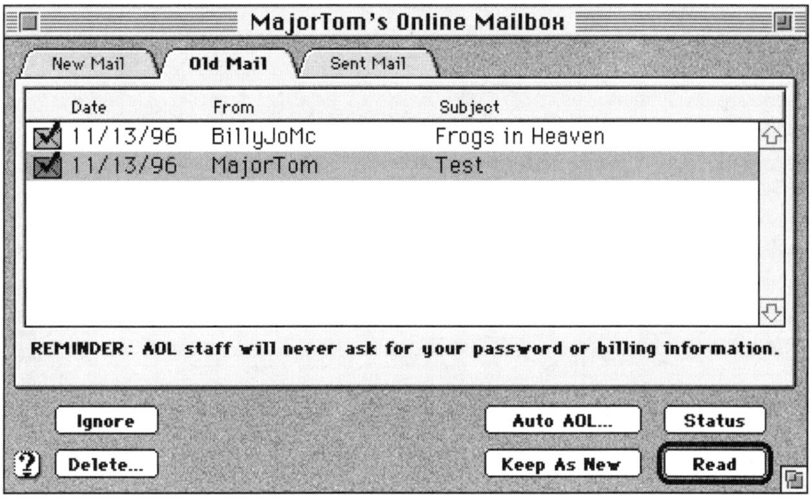
MajorTom's Online Mailbox
New Mail
Old Mail
Sent Mail
Date
From
Subject
11/13/96
BillyJoMc
Frogs in Heaven
11/13/96
MajorTom
Test
REMINDER: AOL staff will never ask for your password or billing information.
Ignore
Auto AOL...
Status
Delete...
Keep As New
Read

Figure 3-9: The Old Mail list displays the mail you have read, just in case you forget.

There are no surprises here. Double-click any message in the window to reread it. Mail that's been reread in this fashion can be forwarded and replied to just like any other mail.

The Old Mail list only shows the mail you've read that's available from AOL's machines in Vienna. AOL only holds mail for a few days (the exact period varies), and you have to be online to access this list. A superior method of checking mail you've read is to store it in and retrieve it from your Personal Filing Cabinet, which is filed on your hard disk—mail filed there remains there until you remove it. The Personal Filing Cabinet is discussed later in this chapter.

Checking Mail You've Sent

Occasionally you may want to review mail you've sent to others: "What exactly did I say to Billy Joe that caused him to visit the Tallahatchee Bridge last night?"

Even if you don't file your mail, AOL retains (for a few days) everything you send, and stores it on their hard disks in Vienna, just like your Old Mail list. You can review any sent mail by clicking the Sent Mail tab in the Online Mailbox window. AOL responds by displaying a listing of all the mail you've sent recently (see Figure 3-10). Choose the mail you want to know about from that list, then click the Read button to review what you've written.

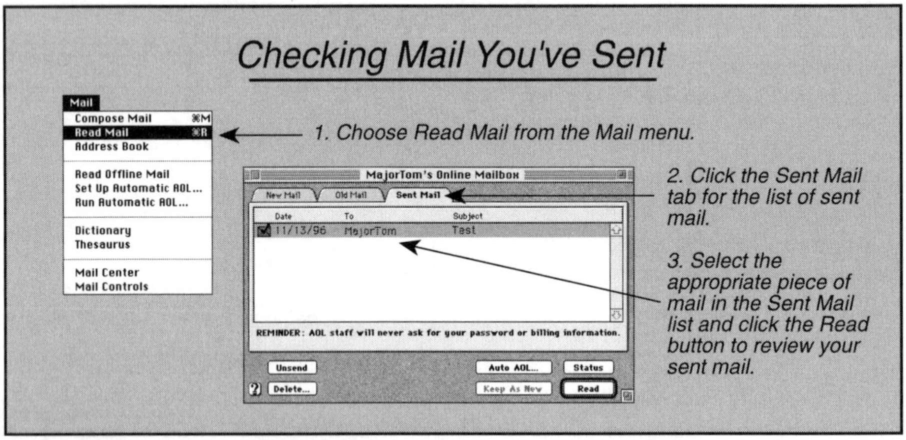
Checking Mail You've Sent
Mail
Compose Mail ⌘M
Read Mail ⌘R
Address Book
Read Offline Mail
Set Up Automatic AOL...
Run Automatic AOL...
Dictionary
Thesaurus
Mail Center
Mail Controls
1. Choose Read Mail from the Mail menu.
MajorTom's Online Mailbox
New Mail
Old Mail
Sent Mail
Date
To
Subject
11/13/96
MajorTom
Test
REMINDER: AOL staff will never ask for your password or billing information.
Unsend
Delete...
Auto AOL...
Status
Keep As New
Read
2. Click the Sent Mail tab for the list of sent mail.
3. Select the appropriate piece of mail in the Sent Mail list and click the Read button to review your sent mail.

Figure 3-10: You can reread any mail you've sent recently by clicking the Sent Mail tab when reading new mail.

As you're reading your sent mail, you can select and copy it, then paste it into other documents. This works especially well for reminder notices, clarifications, and nagging. It may save you some typing as well: you may need to send a message that's a near-duplicate of one you sent four days ago. Rather than retyping text from the old message, just reopen it using the Sent Mail button in the Online Mailbox window, copy the sections you need, and paste them into a new message window. Alternatively, you can forward the entire message (including its headers and any comments) by using the Forward button.

Buttons in the Sent Mail Window

Don't let the title of this window confuse you. You might interpret "Sent Mail" as meaning mail that is scheduled to be sent, as if it's queued in some sort of "out box." In this case, sent mail is mail you have *already* sent.

As with the other mailboxes, a number of buttons appear across the bottom of the Sent Mail window pictured in Figure 3-10; those buttons that differ in function are described here.

The Unsend Button

The Unsend button allows you to retrieve mail you have sent from the mailboxes of all recipients, as well as from your Sent Mail list. To unsend a piece of mail, highlight the mail you wish to unsend and click the Unsend button. This feature, however, will be disabled in the following circumstances:

- Any addressee was an Internet mail address.
- Any recipient has read that piece of mail (including you, if you were on the addressee list).

If you Unsend a piece of mail, it will be permanently deleted from the AOL archives. It won't show up on your Sent Mail list when you check it again. AOL will remind you of this when you click the Unsend button. If you want to modify or save an unsent message, open it while it still appears in the Sent Mail list, then either modify it (and resend it if you wish), or copy and paste it into some other document. Then you can Unsend it without fear of losing the original.

The Delete Button

This button simply removes the selected piece of mail from your Sent Mail list. It does not affect the message's destiny: AOL will still deliver it (and probably already has, by the time you find your way to this button). It's really a feature for people who get lots of mail and prefer to keep their Sent Mail lists short.

The Status Button

The Status button tells you when the mail was read by the recipient (or recipients, if the mail was sent to more than one address). Again, this doesn't apply to Internet mail.

Online Only

The Old Mail and the Sent Mail lists are available only when you're online. This mail is stored on AOL's machines, not yours; you have to be online to access data stored there.

Printing & Saving Mail

You can print or save any piece of mail that occupies the frontmost (active) window by choosing the appropriate command from the File menu or clicking the appropriate icon on the toolbar. If you choose Print, AOL displays the standard Mac dialog box identifying your default printer (as selected through the Chooser). Select any appropriate options, and click the Print button to print.

If you choose Save or Save As (in this context they're the same command), AOL responds with the traditional Mac Save As dialog box. Give your mail a name (use the pop-up menu at the bottom to select Text Only for maximum compatibility with other programs) and put it wherever you please. It will be saved as a standard text file (if you chose Text Only format) and you will be able to open it not only with AOL's software but with any word processor (or text editor such as SimpleText).

Alternatively, you can select and copy any text—mail included—appearing on your screen. Once it's copied, you can open any text file on your disk (or start a new one via the New command under the File menu) and paste your mail into that file. You can also paste copied AOL text into other Mac applications' files if you wish. You might want to do that to obtain more control over the appearance of the printed output.

Replying to Mail

You'll probably reply to mail more often than you forward it. Actually, all the Reply button does is call up a compose mail window with the Address To and Subject fields already filled in with the appropriate information (see Figure 3-11). Aside from these two features, a reply is no different from any other message. You can modify the addresses, if you wish, and discuss any subject that interests you in the message text. You can even change the Subject field or remove the original recipient's screen name from the Address To field, though this somewhat defeats the purpose.

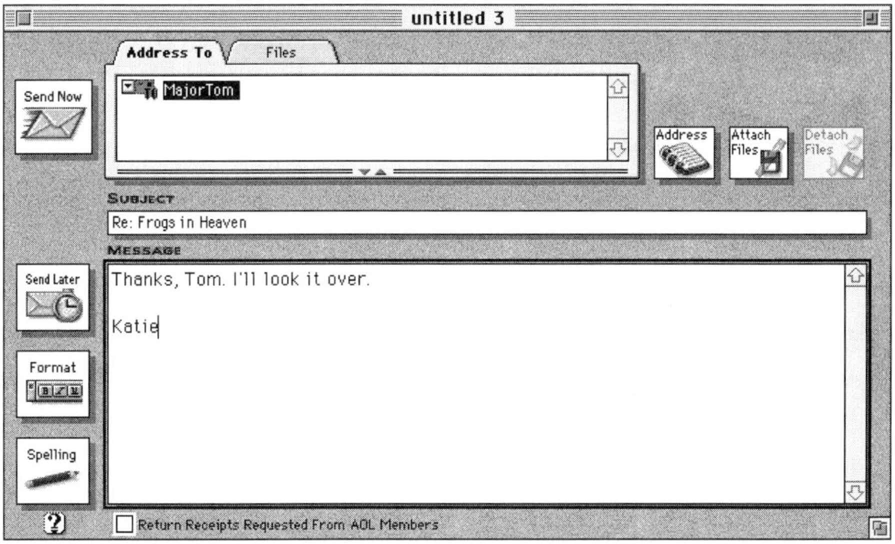
untitled 3
Address To
Files
Send Now
MajorTom
Address
Attach Files
Detach Files
Subject
Re: Frogs in Heaven
Message
Send Later
Thanks, Tom. I'll look it over.
Katie
Format
Spelling
Return Receipts Requested From AOL Members

Figure 3-11: The reply window. The Subject and Address To fields are already completed for you.

Replying to All

Look once again at the lower window in Figure 3-8. Note that there are two reply buttons, including one marked Reply to All. Reply to All allows you to reply to everyone who was sent a message, including any CC: addressees. In other words, you have your choice of replying only to the original sender (the Reply button) or to everyone who receives a message (the Reply to All button).

Like the Reply command, the Reply to All command really only completes a few fields of a New Mail form. You can add or delete recipients and change the Subject field if you want. This command is a convenience, not an imperative.

Replying to Blind Carbon Copies

The Reply to All button does not reply to blind CC: addressees. The rule here is this: Reply to All replies to all the addresses visible in the Mail window. If you don't see an address (which would be the case if someone received a blind carbon copy), that person will not receive your reply.

Quoting

Some people get mountains of mail and don't remember everything they've said. You might be responding to something someone e-mailed to you a week ago, and even though their message is right in front of you at the moment, it might be hundreds of messages in their past. If you respond with something like, "Yes. Next Thursday at 2:00 would be good," they might have to search laboriously through their mail filing system (assuming they have one) to discover what provoked your response.

To avoid such a situation, it's a common courtesy to quote the significant part(s) of the message to which you're replying. A typical quote might look like this: "In a message dated 1-12, you wrote <<Would you like to have lunch soon and discuss the contract?>>" Following that, your message, "Yes. Next Thursday at 2:00 would be good," makes a great deal more sense.

Those "chevron" brackets in the paragraph above (<< >>) indicate that you are *quoting*. Quoting can be tedious, but AOL's software makes it easy. Just select the portion of the message that you want to quote *before* you click the Reply button. There's no need to copy the selection. When you click the Reply button, AOL will automatically quote the selection in either the AOL style (which I'm using here as an example) or the Internet style (there's a preference command for this—see Appendix E in the back of this book). It works with forwarded mail, too.

Forwarding Mail

Once you have read your mail, you can forward it, reply to it, or throw it out. Each of these options is accomplished with a click of the mouse. To forward a piece of mail, click the Forward button pictured in the lower window of Figure 3-8. America Online will respond with the slightly modified compose mail window that appears at the center of Figure 3-12.

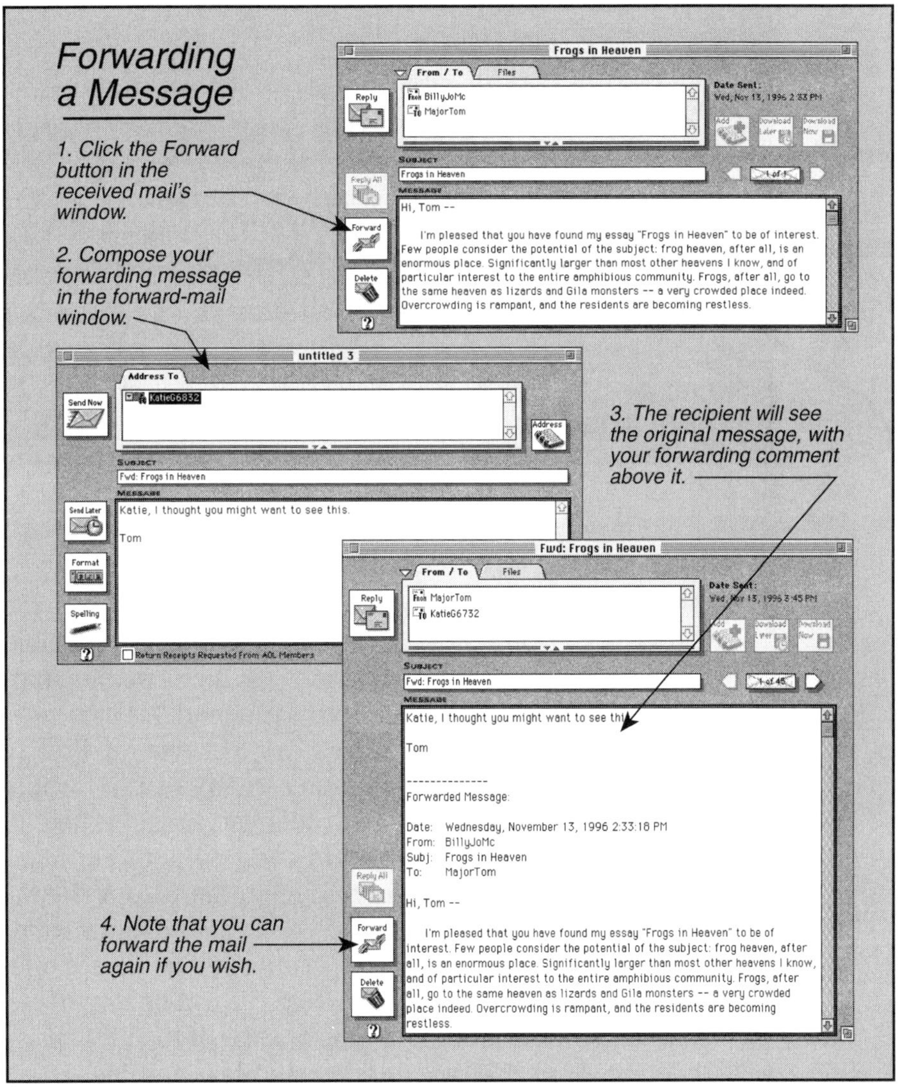
Forwarding a Message
1. Click the Forward button in the received mail's window.
2. Compose your forwarding message in the forward-mail window.
3. The recipient will see the original message, with your forwarding comment above it.
4. Note that you can forward the mail again if you wish.

Figure 3-12: Forwarding mail is as easy as clicking an icon, identifying the recipient, and typing your comments.

The center window pictured in Figure 3-12 is where you enter your forwarding comment and the address of the person who is to receive the forwarded mail. The new recipient then receives the mail with your comment preceding it. America Online clearly labels the mail as forwarded and identifies the person who forwarded it (see the bottom window in Figure 3-12).

There Are No Frogs in Heaven

This piece has appeared in several previous editions of the *Tour Guide*. Lots of people have read it and responded, asking me to send them a copy of "the 'Frogs in Heaven' essay" (pictured in Figure 3-12).

Perhaps there *are* frogs in heaven, but to the best of my knowledge there is no essay about them. Frogs in heaven? I've never heard a celestial croak—only choirs, harps, and the wispy fluttering of angels' wings. Surely frogs don't grow wings. (In reviewing this manuscript, my technical editor commented that if frogs *did* have wings, "they wouldn't bump their butts when they hop." Good point and typically well put, Brian.) It's improbable enough that they *un*grow their tails. Frogs in heaven: it's as implausible as metamorphosis.

Attaching Files to Messages

My contention that there are no frogs in heaven (see the "There Are No Frogs in Heaven" sidebar) could be wrong. It's possible that there *are* long-necked, winged amphibians up there, playing harps and singing in chorus. Stranger things have happened. If I *were* to write an essay on the subject, however, mere text would never do. I'd have to include pictures, sounds—perhaps even a video. And if I wanted to exchange this nontextual material with other esteemed herpetologists, I would need more than e-mail. I would need the ability to *attach files* to e-mail.

Understand that I'm not talking in the abstract here: files are files. Files can include text, graphics, data, sound, animation, even programs. Any of these files can be attached to a piece of e-mail using AOL's software, and any attached file can be downloaded in its native format (the format used by the creator of the file), ready for viewing, hearing, or (in the case of program files) running.

File transmission requires elaborate protocols and error checking. Not a single bit, nibble, or byte can be displaced. Other telecommunications services may require you to decide upon one of many protocols with cryptic names like XModem and Kermit. You also have to determine the number of data bits and stop bits, and the parity setting your system needs. All told, of the 50 or so potential configurations for file transfer, usually only one of them will work in a given situation.

Cheap Insurance

If your work involves travel and you take your laptop with you on the road, you can send e-mail to yourself, attaching important files you've constructed while away from the office. America Online will hold them for you. If something untoward should happen to your data while you're on the road, you can download your files when you return. It's cheap insurance.

Forget all of that. You need not become involved. America Online handles it all invisibly, efficiently, and reliably. If you want to send a file, all you have to do is click the Attach Files button (review Figure 3-1) and AOL takes care of it from there.

Use Attached Files Appropriately

Before the recipient can do anything with an attached file, it has to be downloaded, saved, and (usually) viewed with some kind of program other than AOL itself. This is something of a nuisance for the recipient. In other words, don't send attached files when a simple e-mail message will do.

You might be tempted, for instance, to send a word processing file instead of a conventional message to another member. Perhaps the message is long, or you just prefer your word processor over AOL's text editor. Resist the urge. No one expects fancy formatting when it comes to e-mail (if they do, AOL's HTML formatting should suffice—see the "Stylized Text" sidebar earlier in this chapter), and you can always send unformatted word processing files by copying them and pasting them into a Compose Mail window. Attached files should never be sent when simple messages will do.

Figure 3-13 follows a telecommunicated file from beginning to end. The journey spans half a continent—from Oregon to Mississippi—but only costs pennies.

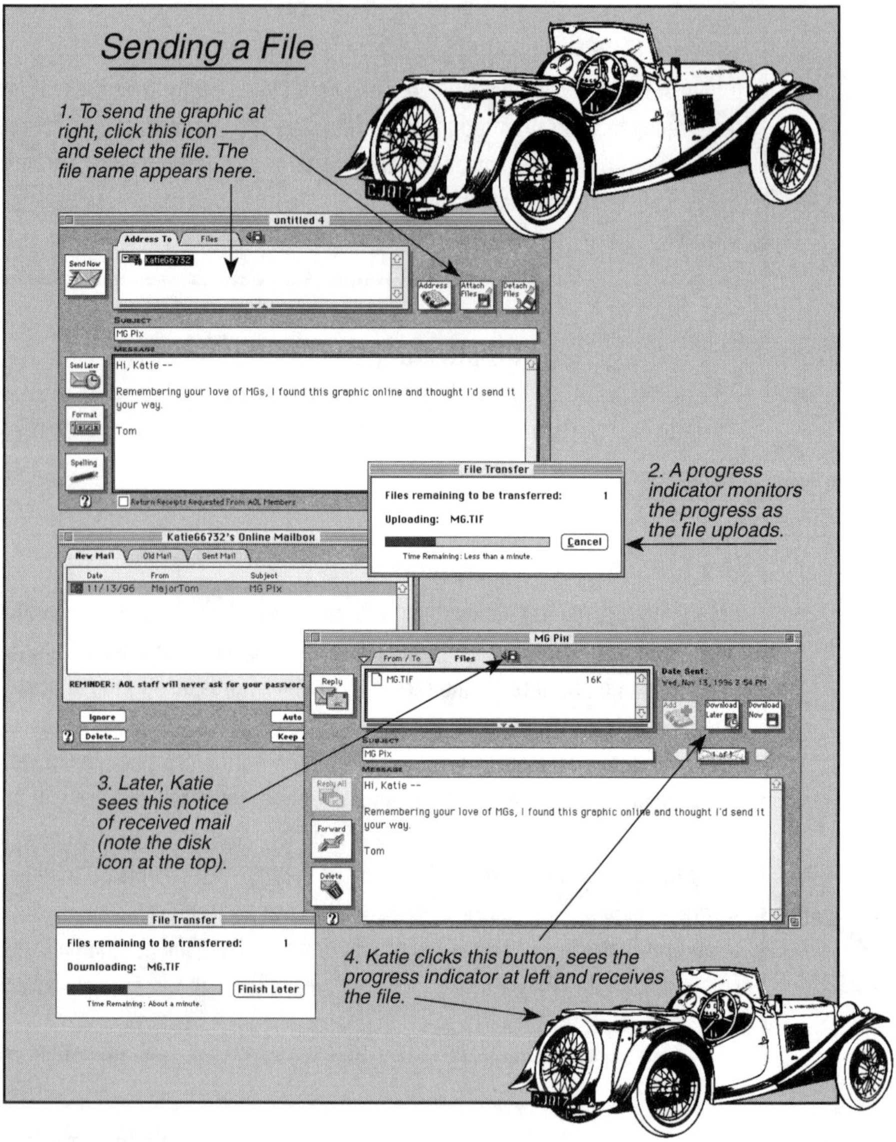
Sending a File
1. To send the graphic at right, click this icon and select the file. The file name appears here.
untitled 4
Address To
Files
KatieG6732
Send Now
Address
Attach Files
Detach Files
Subject
MG Pix
Message
Send Later
Format
Spelling
Hi, Katie --
Remembering your love of MGs, I found this graphic online and thought I'd send it your way.
Tom
Return Receipts Requested From AOL Members
File Transfer
Files remaining to be transferred: 1
Uploading: MG.TIF
Cancel
Time Remaining: Less than a minute.
2. A progress indicator monitors the progress as the file uploads.
KatieG6732's Online Mailbox
New Mail
Old Mail
Sent Mail
Date
From
Subject
11/13/96
MajorTom
MG Pix
Ignore
Delete...
MG Pix
From / To
Files
MG.TIF
16K
Reply
Date Sent:
Download Later
Download Now
MG Pix
Reply All
Forward
Delete
Hi, Katie --
Remembering your love of MGs, I found this graphic online and thought I'd send it your way.
Tom
3. Later, Katie sees this notice of received mail (note the disk icon at the top).
File Transfer
Files remaining to be transferred: 1
Downloading: MG.TIF
Finish Later
Time Remaining: About a minute.
4. Katie clicks this button, sees the progress indicator at left and receives the file.

Figure 3-13: Sending an MG across the country is as easy as clicking a mouse. (Illustration by Rich Wald.)

Note: The button marked Detach Files in the upper window of Figure 3-13 will be disabled until you actually attach a file. When you do, the Detach Files button will be available to remove attached files before they are sent.

Attaching a File

You can attach a file to any e-mail message by clicking the Attach Files button in the message's window. America Online will respond with the sequence of windows pictured in Figure 3-14.

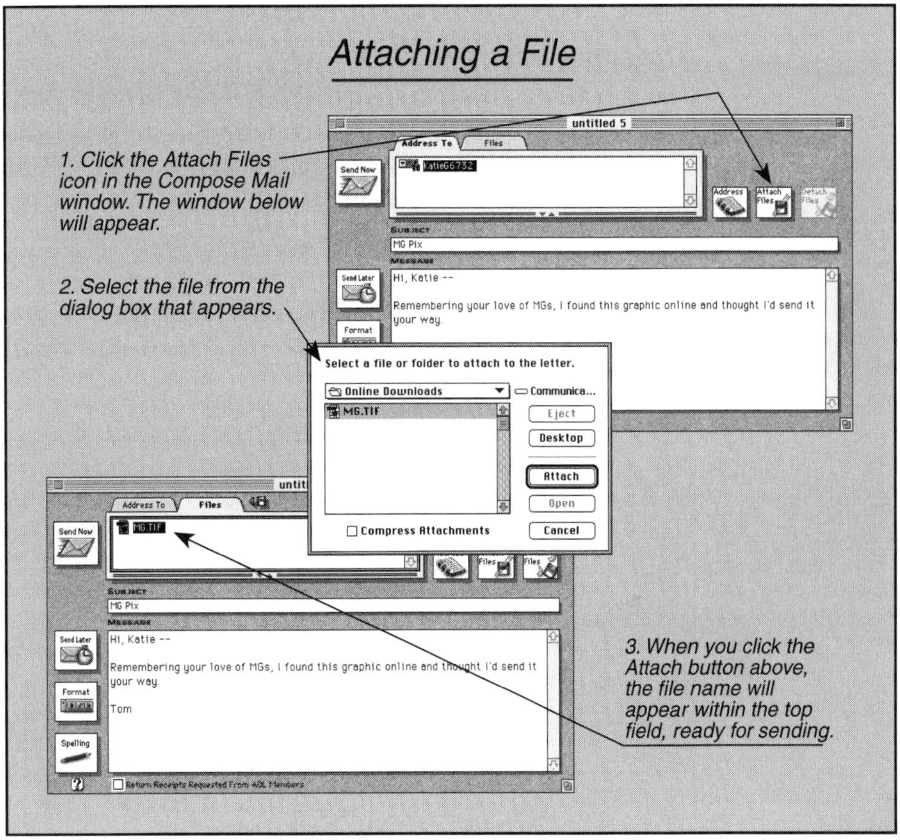
Attaching a File
1. Click the Attach Files icon in the Compose Mail window. The window below will appear.
2. Select the file from the dialog box that appears.
3. When you click the Attach button above, the file name will appear within the top field, ready for sending.
untitled 5
Send Now
Address To
Files
Address
Attach Files
Subject
MG Pix
Message
Send Later
Hi, Katie --
Remembering your love of MGs, I found this graphic online and thought I'd send it your way.
Format
Select a file or folder to attach to the letter.
Online Downloads
Communica...
MG.TIF
Eject
Desktop
Attach
Open
Compress Attachments
Cancel
Tom
Spelling

Figure 3-14: Attaching a file amounts to little more than clicking a button and locating the file on your disk.

When you click the Send Now button pictured in the bottom window of Figure 3-14, you trigger the sequence of events pictured in Figure 3-13. America Online will hold the mail and the file until the addressee is ready to read the mail and download the file. If you address the mail to multiple recipients—even if they're receiving carbon copies or blind carbon copies—each will be afforded the opportunity of downloading the file.

And downloading files attached to received mail *is* optional. Though the MG Pix window pictured in step 4 of Figure 3-13 offers both Download File and Download Later buttons, the recipient might elect to ignore them both. (Keep that in mind if you ever receive mail with attached files you don't want.)

Attaching Multiple Files

You can attach more than a single file to an e-mail message if you wish, in the form of a *StuffIt archive*. Though the subject is discussed in Chapter 7, "Computing," you should know that a StuffIt archive is often a collection of several files rolled into one. Typically, a StuffIt archive is compressed as it's compiled, streamlining the file-transfer process even further.

Your AOL software is capable of unstuffing files that have been compressed using StuffIt, and it's capable of stuffing files as well (see Figure 3-15).

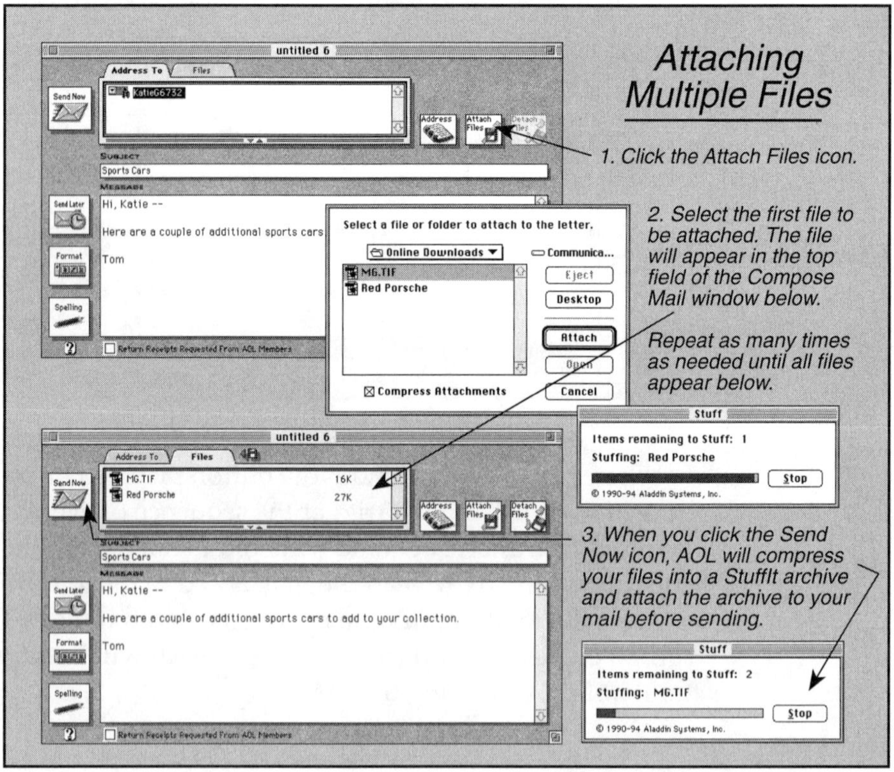
Attaching Multiple Files
1. Click the Attach Files icon.
2. Select the first file to be attached. The file will appear in the top field of the Compose Mail window below.
Repeat as many times as needed until all files appear below.
3. When you click the Send Now icon, AOL will compress your files into a StuffIt archive and attach the archive to your mail before sending.
untitled 6
Sports Cars
Hi, Katie --
Here are a couple of additional sports cars to add to your collection.
Tom
Select a file or folder to attach to the letter.
Online Downloads
MG.TIF
Red Porsche
Eject
Desktop
Attach
Cancel
Compress Attachments
Stuff
Items remaining to Stuff: 1
Stuffing: Red Porsche
Items remaining to Stuff: 2
Stuffing: MG.TIF
Stop
© 1990-94 Aladdin Systems, Inc.

Figure 3-15: AOL will stuff multiple files into a single archive when you attach them to mail.

The events pictured in Figure 3-15 all occur within the AOL software: you don't need additional software to create the archive or to unstuff it.

Not All Computers Are Macs

The feature that provides for the attachment of multiple files depends on StuffIt, which is Macintosh software. While StuffIt archives are commonplace in the Mac universe, they're black sheep everywhere else.

If the recipient isn't using a Mac, don't use the multiple-file compression feature, and don't compress single files. Send your files one at a time, without compression. This will take more effort and no doubt more online time. While you're waiting for the upload to conclude, use the time to reflect on your wisdom in choosing a Mac.

The important concept to understand is that your AOL software makes an intermediary file—the StuffIt archive (with the .sit extension) pictured in step 4 of Figure 3-15. Remember that StuffIt archives may contain multiple files. The archive is the (single) file that's actually sent; it isn't broken out into its individual components until the recipient downloads and unstuffs it. It's a bit like mailing a number of Christmas presents in a single box: when the recipient opens the box each present emerges independently, but until then it's a single package.

The AOL software unstuffs (decompresses) files attached to e-mail with the .sit filename extension automatically. The software usually makes a new folder, leaving the recipient with both the StuffIt archive and the folder on his or her disk.

This is much harder to explain than it is to do. Before you actually send multiple files to another member, find a couple of small (under 10K) files on your disk, attach them to a piece of mail, then send the mail to yourself. Participate in the process from start to finish, walking through the steps pictured in Figure 3-15. This will all make sense when you do.

You Can Stuff a Single File Too

If you look carefully in the second window of Figure 3-15, you'll note a little check box labeled "Compress Attachments." Though this box is automatically checked when you select multiple files, you might want to turn it on if you're selecting just one.

In fact, you should compress every file you send, unless it's very small—say, under 50K—or if it's headed for a machine that's not equipped to decompress it. Compressing files cuts down on uploading and downloading time. Compressing files not only benefits you but the recipient as well.

Receiving Attached Files

When you receive mail with an attached file, whether it's from another AOL member or someone on the Internet, two buttons will appear on the right side of the message, marked "Download Later" and "Download Now." (See Figure 3-16.)

Figure 3-16: Receiving attached files. Pay particular attention to the file-saving dialog box in the center window. Knowledge of where you saved the file and what you called it is required when you need to find it later.

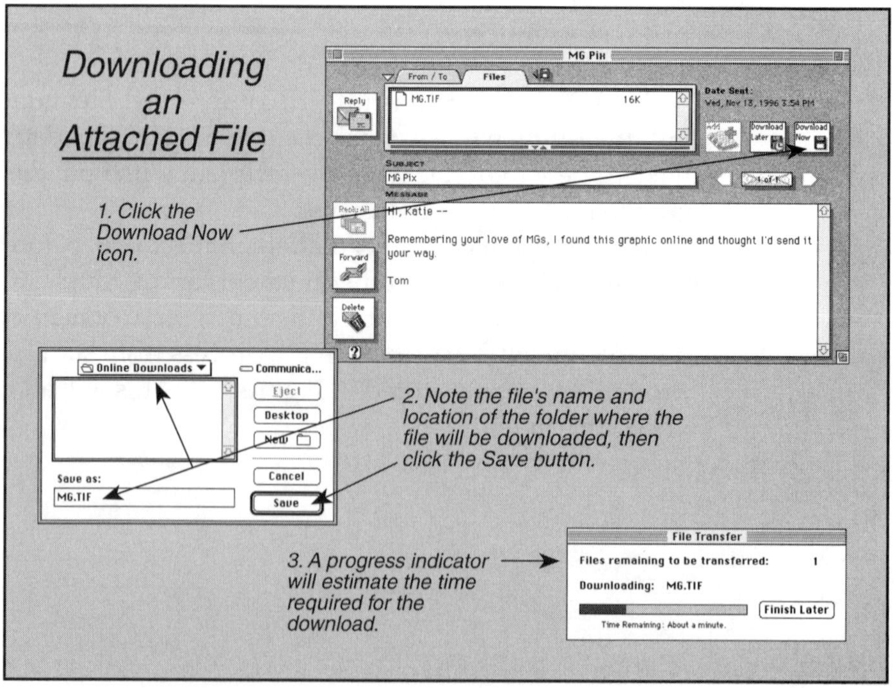
Downloading an Attached File
1. Click the Download Now icon.
2. Note the file's name and location of the folder where the file will be downloaded, then click the Save button.
3. A progress indicator will estimate the time required for the download.
MG Pix
From / To
Files
MG.TIF
16K
Date Sent:
Wed, Nov 13, 1996 3:54 PM
Reply
Download Later
Download Now
Subject
MG Pix
Message
Hi, Katie --
Remembering your love of MGs, I found this graphic online and thought I'd send it your way.
Tom
Forward
Delete
Online Downloads
Communica...
Eject
Desktop
New
Save as:
MG.TIF
Cancel
Save
File Transfer
Files remaining to be transferred: 1
Downloading: MG.TIF
Finish Later
Time Remaining: About a minute.

Sending Internet Mail

Internet e-mail is composed and sent conventionally. To address an Internet user, simply place the recipient's Internet address in the Address To field of the compose mail form (see Figure 3-17).

Figure 3-17: Sending mail via the Internet requires an entry in the Address To field. You can leave the Subject and/or Message field blank, but I don't recommend it.

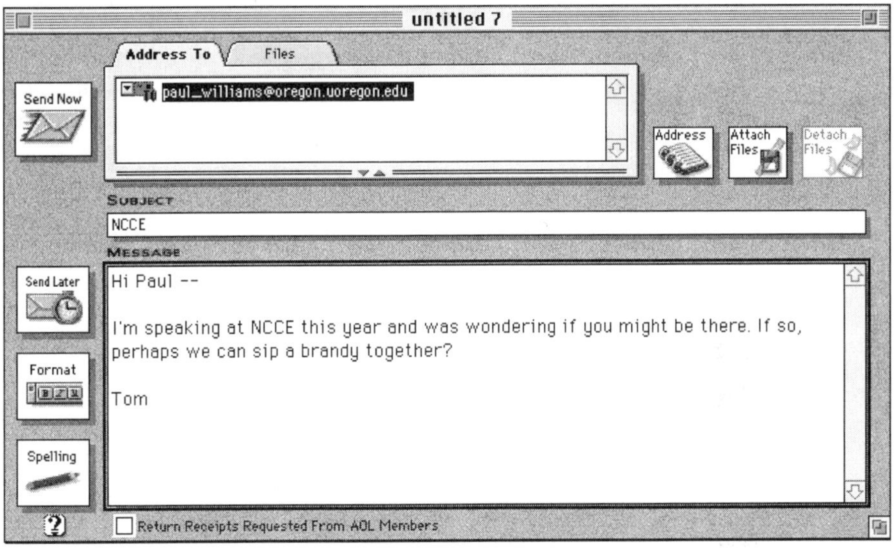
untitled 7
Address To
Files
Send Now
paul_williams@oregon.uoregon.edu
Address
Attach Files
Detach Files
SUBJECT
NCCE
MESSAGE
Send Later
Hi Paul --
I'm speaking at NCCE this year and was wondering if you might be there. If so, perhaps we can sip a brandy together?
Tom
Format
Spelling
Return Receipts Requested From AOL Members

Once you click the Send Now button (or once you run an Automatic AOL session containing outgoing Internet mail), your outgoing mail is immediately posted on the Internet. There's no waiting.

Undeliverable Internet Mail

Because Internet addresses are complex, you might occasionally misaddress a piece of Internet mail. Fortunately, your fallibility has been anticipated in the form of Internet "postmasters." Should you include a nonexistent domain or user name, the receiving site's postmaster will intercede and send the mail back to you. It's no problem, really, as the postmaster sends back the body of the message as well (shown in Figure 3-18). All you have to do is select and copy the message text, paste it into a new mail window, enter the proper address, and resend the mail. Your mail won't end up in some kind of Internet dead letter box: the Internet always delivers.

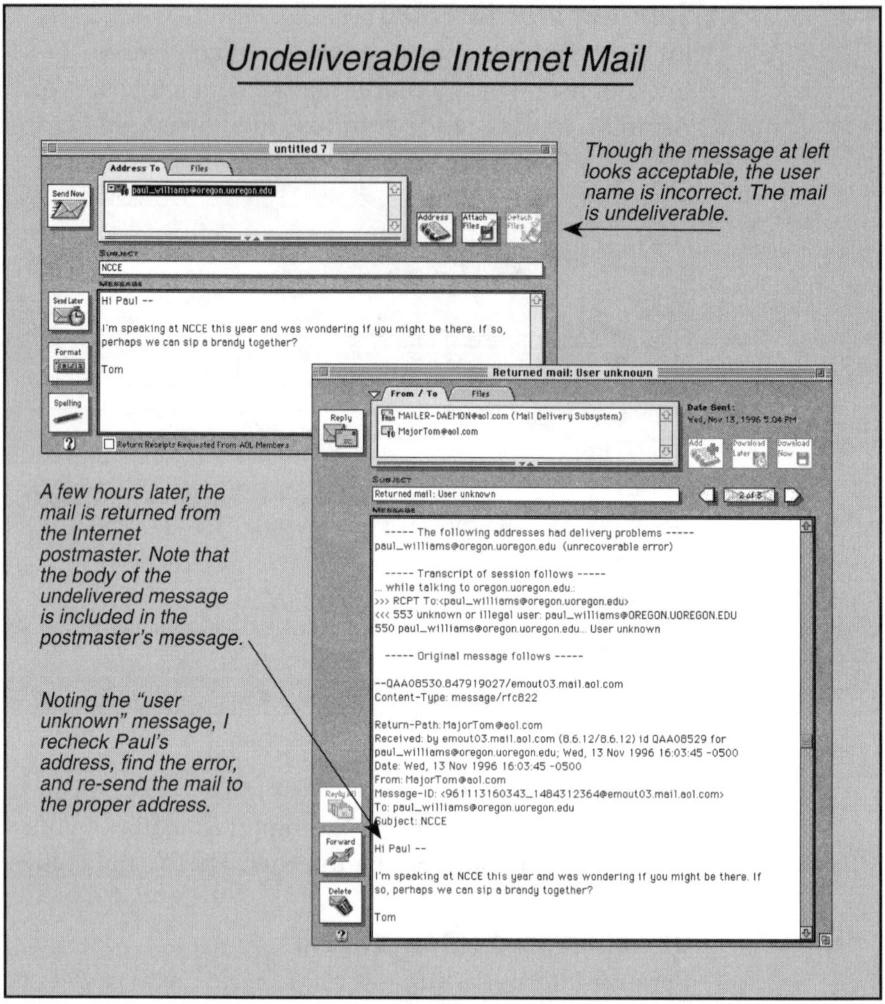

Undeliverable Internet Mail
untitled 7
Address To
Files
Send Now
paul_williams@oregon.uoregon.edu
Address
Attach Files
Detach Files
Subject
NCCE
Message
Send Later
Hi Paul --
I'm speaking at NCCE this year and was wondering if you might be there. If so, perhaps we can sip a brandy together?
Tom
Format
Spelling
Return Receipts Requested From AOL Members
Though the message at left looks acceptable, the user name is incorrect. The mail is undeliverable.
Returned mail: User unknown
From / To
Files
Reply
MAILER-DAEMON@aol.com (Mail Delivery Subsystem)
MajorTom@aol.com
Date Sent:
Returned mail: User unknown
----- The following addresses had delivery problems -----
paul_williams@oregon.uoregon.edu (unrecoverable error)
----- Transcript of session follows -----
... while talking to oregon.uoregon.edu.:
>>> RCPT To:<paul_williams@oregon.uoregon.edu>
<<< 553 unknown or illegal user: paul_williams@OREGON.UOREGON.EDU
550 paul_williams@oregon.uoregon.edu... User unknown
----- Original message follows -----
--QAA08530.847919027/emout03.mail.aol.com
Content-Type: message/rfc822
Return-Path: MajorTom@aol.com
Received: by emout03.mail.aol.com (8.6.12/8.6.12) id QAA08529 for paul_williams@oregon.uoregon.edu; Wed, 13 Nov 1996 16:03:45 -0500
Date: Wed, 13 Nov 1996 16:03:45 -0500
From: MajorTom@aol.com
Message-ID: <961113160343_1484312364@emout03.mail.aol.com>
To: paul_williams@oregon.uoregon.edu
Subject: NCCE
Hi Paul --
I'm speaking at NCCE this year and was wondering if you might be there. If so, perhaps we can sip a brandy together?
Tom
Forward
Delete
A few hours later, the mail is returned from the Internet postmaster. Note that the body of the undelivered message is included in the postmaster's message.
Noting the "user unknown" message, I recheck Paul's address, find the error, and re-send the mail to the proper address.

Figure 3-18: At top, a misaddressed Internet mail message looks as good as any other, but a few minutes later I receive the "User unknown" message pictured in the center window.

In Figure 3-18, note the inclusion of my message's text in the postmaster's message in the bottom window. When I later copy and paste the mail into a new mail window (and correct the address), the mail will be delivered satisfactorily.

Daemons

Look at the sender's address in Figure 3-18. Isn't that a vicious-sounding word: *daemon*? My dictionary defines the word as a "subordinate deity." In this context, however, a daemon is an innocuous little UNIX program—one that's usually transparent to the user—which is anything but a deity, subordinate or not. Macs have daemons, too (though we don't call them that). Perhaps the most familiar example is the PrintMonitor—the background program that spools the print output from your applications to your printer.

Sending Mail to Other Commercial Services

I'm going to fudge a bit here and refer you to an online resource. Addressing e-mail to CompuServe and some of the other commercial online services can be tricky. Moreover, the number and names of commercial online services is changing—it seems like every day.

Fortunately, AOL maintains a ready (and current) reference for Internet e-mail addressing techniques, including the instructions on how to address mail to the other online services. Use the keywords: **Mail Gateway** to access it.

Be aware of one thing: not all of the commercial online services are as lenient as AOL. Many of them charge their members for Internet mail. Before you send mail to a friend on another commercial online service, be sure they want to receive it.

Receiving Internet Mail

Internet mail is received like any other AOL mail: it's announced when you sign on, and you can read it by clicking the You Have Mail button on the Welcome screen. The only way you'll know it's Internet mail is by looking at the sender's address, which will contain an @ sign and a domain name. You'll also see the Internet "header" at the end of the message. Reading Internet headers is a little like reading the Bible in its original Hebrew: enlightening perhaps, but not requisite to effective use of the medium.

Internet Mail Conundrum

A perplexing mail question, frequently received at AOL, has to do with blind carbon copies and Internet mail. It's possible that you might receive a piece of Internet mail, yet your name will not appear in the header as a recipient. "Was the mail misdirected?" you'll ask.

Probably not. More than likely, you were sent a blind carbon copy (a "BCC"). When you are a recipient of BCC Internet mail, your name will not appear among the recipients in the header, yet you *will* receive the mail. If you think about it, it makes sense: if your name appeared in the header—or anywhere else for that matter—the BCC effort would be thwarted. It's confusing, I know, but comforting to know that your anonymity is assured.

A few notes regarding received Internet mail:

- If you want to give your Internet address to someone else (it's very impressive printed on your business cards), remove any spaces, change everything to lowercase, and follow it with @aol.com. As I mentioned earlier, my Internet address is majortom@aol.com. Steve Case's Internet address is stevecase@aol.com.
- America Online offers plenty of help with Internet e-mail, including a message board and an avenue for communication with the AOL Internet staff. Use the keywords: **Mail Gateway** to explore this feature.

Internet Mail Trivia

Actually, this isn't trivia at all. I was trying to attract your attention with a sidebar. If you're an Internet mail user, this is Really Important Stuff:

- Though AOL places no prohibitions on the length of e-mail messages, some other e-mail systems do. If you must send a message longer than about 20 pages (30K) via the Internet, cut your mail into smaller pieces, and mail the pieces independently. Identify your strategy in the Subject field: "Letter to Mom 1/2," and "Letter to Mom 2/2." This is common shorthand for split mail on the Internet.

➡

- **If you use a word processor to prepare outgoing Internet mail (and you copy and paste it into a new mail form as mentioned earlier in this chapter), all character and paragraph formatting will be removed from your message when you paste it.**
- **Don't use any special characters (such as copyright symbols or the "smart quotes" offered by some word processors) in Internet mail. The ASCII standard doesn't recognize them, therefore it's unlikely they'll make it to the destination. They might survive after you've pasted them into the Compose Mail window, but they'll never make it to the destination.**
- **America Online doesn't charge you anything extra for Internet mail, sent or received. If you're counting your blessings, add that to the list.**

Attaching Files to Internet Messages

Because there's no universal standard for attaching files to e-mail on the Internet, you can't directly send files (or receive them) via Internet mail. Internet mail, like most e-mail, is pure ASCII text, and most files take the form of binary data, not ASCII text. Don't worry if you can't define the term *binary data*; just understand that it's not ASCII text and therefore not native to e-mail.

With that said, it will seem contradictory when I tell you that you *can* attach a file to Internet mail, but it's true. A few comments follow:

- If you attach a file to Internet mail, AOL will convert it to text before it's sent. This may seem anachronistic: how can you send a picture of a frog (or the sound of a frog), for example, as text? Simple: use a program that converts binary data into ASCII text. AOL does this for you, via a technique called *MIME* (Multipurpose Internet Mail Extensions) *base64 encoding.*
- The recipient's e-mail program must understand MIME base64 encoding and be able to decode it. If that's not possible, the recipient will have to decode it manually. There are a number of programs that can do this, most notably a little shareware application called MPack. It's available in AOL's libraries. Downloading files from AOL's libraries is discussed in Chapter 5, "Transferring Files."

- There are other binary-to-text-and-back techniques for transferring files on the Internet—one called *uuencoding* comes to mind, and Macintosh users are fond of *BinHex*—and if someone sends an attached file to you, it might be encoded using one of these other techniques. If that happens, your AOL software will not be able to automatically decode the message and offer to download the file to your machine. You'll have to do this manually. A description of that process—a process that can take many forms depending on the encoding method used—is beyond the scope of this book; but again, you can find answers (and ask questions) by visiting the keywords: **Mail Gateway**.
- It should be apparent that file attachments to Internet mail are not universally supported, just barely standardized, and fraught with the potential for error. Both you and the intended recipient should be prepared for a period of experimentation and adjustment. The system doesn't always work the first time it's tried.

With all of the disclaimers out of the way, and though the convert-to-text-and-back process sounds a little bit like a sow's ear, it is in fact a technique that's been used for years on the Net. It works flawlessly when it works, and thousands of people do it every day. My friend Jim and I often exchange architectural drawings this way.

The Address Book

America Online provides an address book just like the address book next to your telephone. In effect, AOL's book is a cross-reference, listing people's real names and their corresponding e-mail addresses. My recommendation is that you use the Address Book, even if you only have a name or two to put there now. E-mail addresses (especially Internet addresses) are tricky; you're not going to want to type them very often. Typing them is too much work, and it's too easy to make mistakes.

Adding a Name to the Address Book

No one memorizes Internet addresses. Internet addresses are eccentric composites of alphabet, punctuation, and symbol characters—for example, speterman@lemming.uvm.edu. Addresses like this are eminently forgettable. AOL's addresses are less complex but, like most addresses, they too are forgettable. That's why America Online provides an Address Book.

Of course, before you can use the Address Book you have to put some addresses there. It's easy. Online or off, choose Address Book from the Mail menu and America Online will provide the Address Book editing window pictured in Figure 3-19.

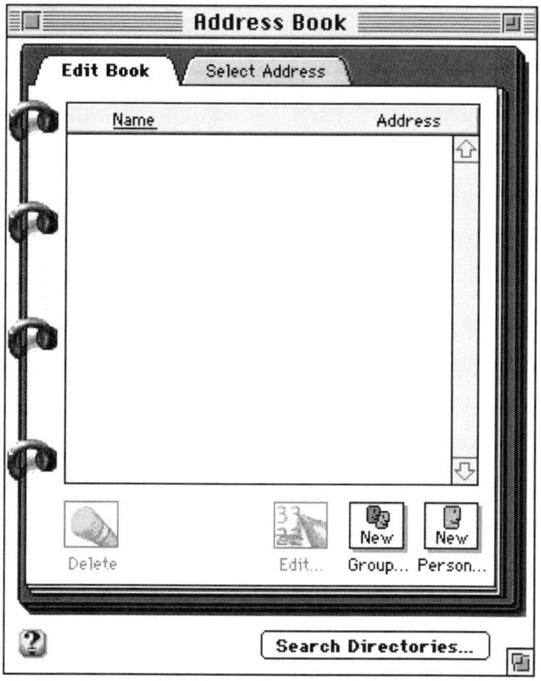
Address Book
Edit Book
Select Address
Name
Address
Delete
Edit...
New
Group...
New
Person...
Search Directories...

Figure 3-19: The Address Book window allows you to create, modify, and delete members' names and screen names, or to search for a specific member.

To add an entry to your Address Book, click the New Person... button. AOL provides the editing form pictured in Figure 3-20.

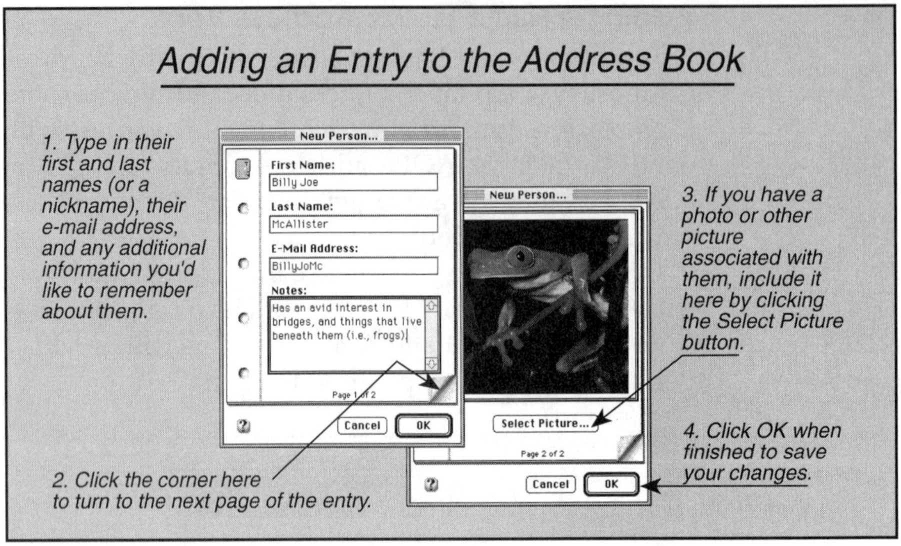
Adding an Entry to the Address Book
1. Type in their first and last names (or a nickname), their e-mail address, and any additional information you'd like to remember about them.
New Person...
First Name:
Billy Joe
Last Name:
McAllister
E-Mail Address:
BillyJoMc
Notes:
Has an avid interest in bridges, and things that live beneath them (i.e., frogs)
Page 1 of 2
Cancel
OK
New Person...
Select Picture...
Page 2 of 2
Cancel
OK
3. If you have a photo or other picture associated with them, include it here by clicking the Select Picture button.
4. Click OK when finished to save your changes.
2. Click the corner here to turn to the next page of the entry.

Figure 3-20: The New Person editing form.

Place the person's full real name, or a nickname you know them by, in the First Name and Last Name fields, then place their e-mail address in the E-Mail Address field. Finally, add any information you want to remember in the Notes field. If you have a photo or a graphic of them, you can add it to their entry by clicking the dog-eared corner and selecting a graphic file. The next time you choose Address Book from the Mail window, the new name will appear there (see Figure 3-21).

You can add group entries as well as individual ones. Imagine that you're participating in an online discourse on frog heaven with three other esteemed theologians. Nearly every piece of mail on the subject has to be sent to all three. In this situation, you can create a group entry called "Froggers" in your Address Book and list all three addresses. Just click the New Group... button and fill in the group name and all addresses you'd like in the group. The group entry will appear in your list with a small picture of two heads to the left of its name to help you differentiate it from individual entries. Once complete, all you have to do is select the Froggers entry from your Address Book to send mail to them all.

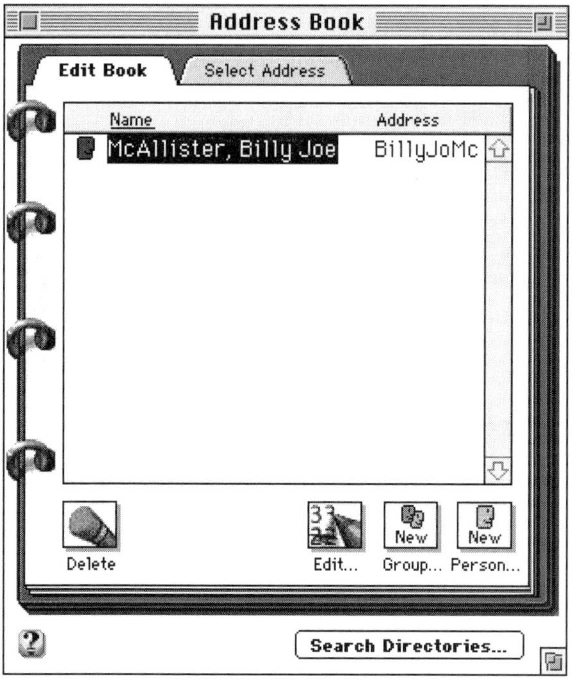
Address Book
Edit Book
Select Address
Name
Address
McAllister, Billy Joe
BillyJoMc
Delete
Edit...
New
Group...
New
Person...
Search Directories...

Figure 3-21: The Address Book now contains the new entry.

Now you are ready to use the Address Book whenever you prepare mail. Look again at Figure 3-1. Do you see the Address icon in the Compose Mail window? If your Address Book is current, you can use it to look up addresses and plug them into the address tab of the Compose Mail window. Whenever a Compose Mail Form is displayed on your screen, all you have to do is click that icon. From then on, it's only a matter of clicking the mouse.

The Personal Filing Cabinet

I have a number of friends who live far away, and I use e-mail to keep in touch with them. Jim, for example, lives on Whidbey Island in Washington state. I also do almost all my business via e-mail. When e-mail becomes something other than a casual dalliance, a system for filing it becomes strategic. Fortunately, such a system is included in your AOL software, and it's called the *Personal Filing Cabinet*.

Mail Preferences

Though preferences are discussed in detail in Appendix E at the back of this book, two mail preferences deserve mention here. Note the "Save the mail..." preferences pictured in Figure 3-22. These preferences are available by choosing Preferences from the Members menu, then clicking the Mail button.

When they're selected, the two "Save the mail..." preferences, shown in Figure 3-22, cause your local AOL software to save every piece of mail you send or read. This is a new feature, and it's truly a blessing.

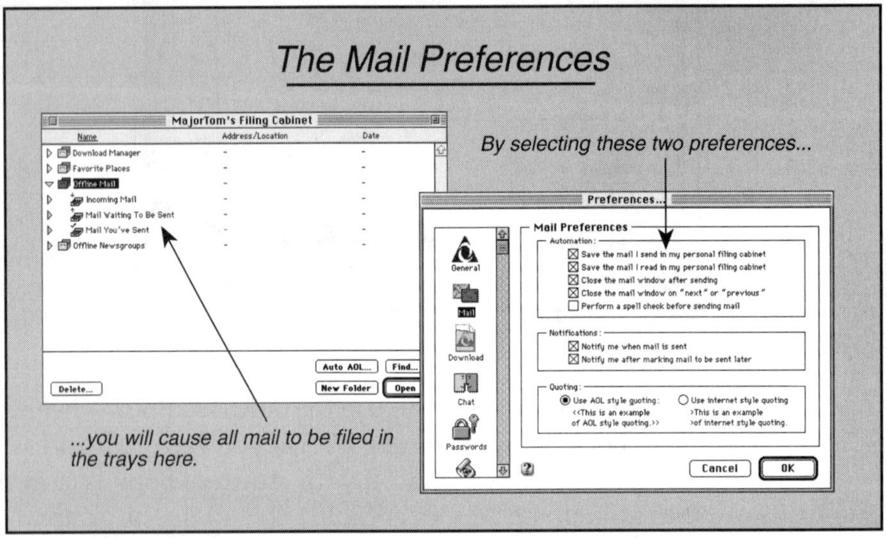
The Mail Preferences
MajorTom's Filing Cabinet
Download Manager
Favorite Places
Offline Mail
Incoming Mail
Mail Waiting To Be Sent
Mail You've Sent
Offline Newsgroups
Delete...
Auto AOL...
Find...
New Folder
Open
By selecting these two preferences...
...you will cause all mail to be filed in the trays here.
Preferences...
Mail Preferences
Save the mail I send in my personal filing cabinet
Save the mail I read in my personal filing cabinet
Close the mail window after sending
Perform a spell check before sending mail
Notify me when mail is sent
Notify me after marking mail to be sent later
Use AOL style quoting:
Use internet style quoting
Cancel
OK

Figure 3-22: When they're turned on, the two "Save the mail..." preferences, shown here in the "on" condition ("off" is the default), cause all of your mail to be saved automatically in the Personal Filing Cabinet on your hard disk.

When they're turned on, the "Save the mail..." preferences route all your mail—sent and read—to the Read Offline Mail folder pictured in Figure 3-22. Once the preferences are on, copies of all of your mail are retained locally for your review.

After an online session has concluded, when you're offline and the clock isn't running, you can choose Read Offline Mail from the Mail menu and sort through your mail leisurely, reading, replying, filing, and deleting. This is real mail, too; it's not just text. When you open a message, it appears in a mail window, complete with Forward and Reply buttons (see Figure 3-23). If you use mail as much as I do, this is one of the best features AOL has to offer—and lots of people aren't even aware of it!

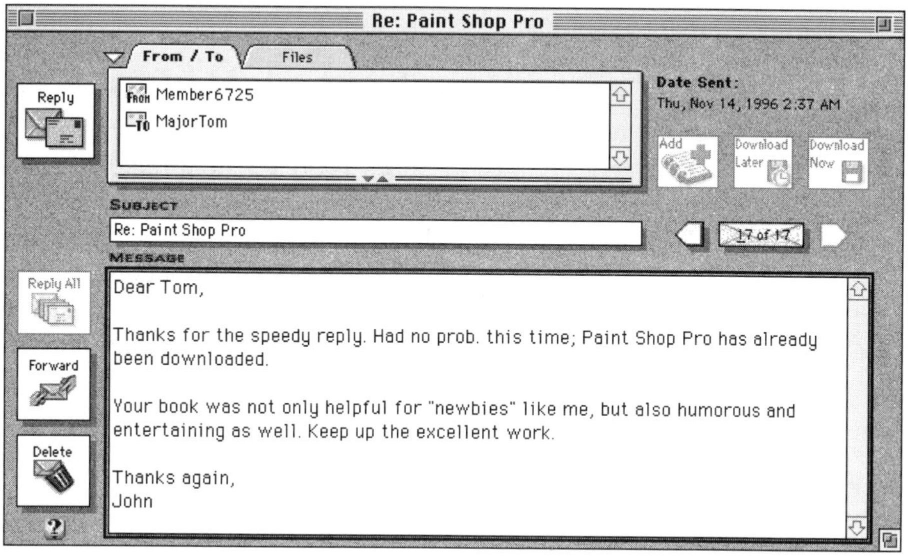
Re: Paint Shop Pro
From / To
Files
Reply
Member6725
MajorTom
Date Sent:
Thu, Nov 14, 1996 2:37 AM
Add
Download Later
Download Now
Subject
Re: Paint Shop Pro
17 of 17
Message
Reply All
Forward
Delete
Dear Tom,
Thanks for the speedy reply. Had no prob. this time; Paint Shop Pro has already been downloaded.
Your book was not only helpful for "newbies" like me, but also humorous and entertaining as well. Keep up the excellent work.
Thanks again,
John

Figure 3-23: Mail stored in your Personal Filing Cabinet isn't simply text, it's AOL mail. When it's opened, it appears in a mail window, complete with Forward and Reply buttons.

Keyword: Suggestions

The Save the mail... features described in the text are not only one of the best features AOL has to offer for avid e-mail users; it also represents an idea that came from a member. That member used the keyword: **Suggestions**, then proposed the feature. Not long after that, the feature appeared in the AOL client.

In other words, AOL listens. If you have a great idea that AOL could use, tell them about it. Like any community, this one functions better when people give back to the community whenever they can, and the keyword: **Suggestions** makes it easy.

Managing Your Mail

Leaving mail in your Incoming/Saved Mail and Mail You've Sent trays is not a good idea. Though it will accumulate there in alphabetical order, there will be no other organization whatsoever. Once a few dozen entries pile up, you will realize that you need some kind of filing system.

Filing Schemes

Filing schemes are very personal things. As you observe the illustrations in this section of the book, you'll note that I file my mail using folders with people's names on them. You may prefer to file by date, by project, or by geographical location. There are no limits. Filing schemes can be multilayered: you might have two primary folders—"Friends" and "Business," for example, in which items are filed by date. My friend Leonard gets so much mail that he has alphabetical sections—"A-F," "G-P," and "Q-Z"—and folders with people's names on them within each of those sections. Some people argue the merits of their particular system the way the boys down at the pub compare Fords and Chevys. It really doesn't make much difference how you set up your system; just pick one and do it. You can always reorganize later if you have to.

Back It Up!

Many of us configure our backup programs to back up only a portion of our hard disk—the portion that contains data. The portion that contains programs might not get backed up as often, or at all. This makes sense: why back up program files, which normally don't change and are stored already on floppies or CD-ROMs?

Although the theory is sound, the data we're discussing in this section—your Personal Filing Cabinet data—are stored in your Data folder, located in your America Online Preferences folder, inside your Preferences folder in your System Folder.

If you value the contents of your Personal Filing Cabinet, be sure to back it up. Ideally, back up your entire System folder and perform that backup regularly.

Making New Folders

No matter what kind of filing scheme you elect to use, it will be done with folders. Think of a real filing cabinet: to organize your stuff, you visit the stationery store and buy a box of tabbed folders. You label them according to your filing scheme, put them in the filing cabinet, and store papers inside them. You might even store folders inside of folders. That's the metaphor used in your Personal Filing Cabinet.

Making a new folder is better done if you open the folder (the "parent" folder) in which you want the new folder to appear before you click the New Folder button. In Figure 3-24, for example, note that I opened the Offline Mail folder before I made the Jim folder. Doing so causes my new folder to appear automatically within the Offline Mail folder. I don't have to drag it around once it has been created.

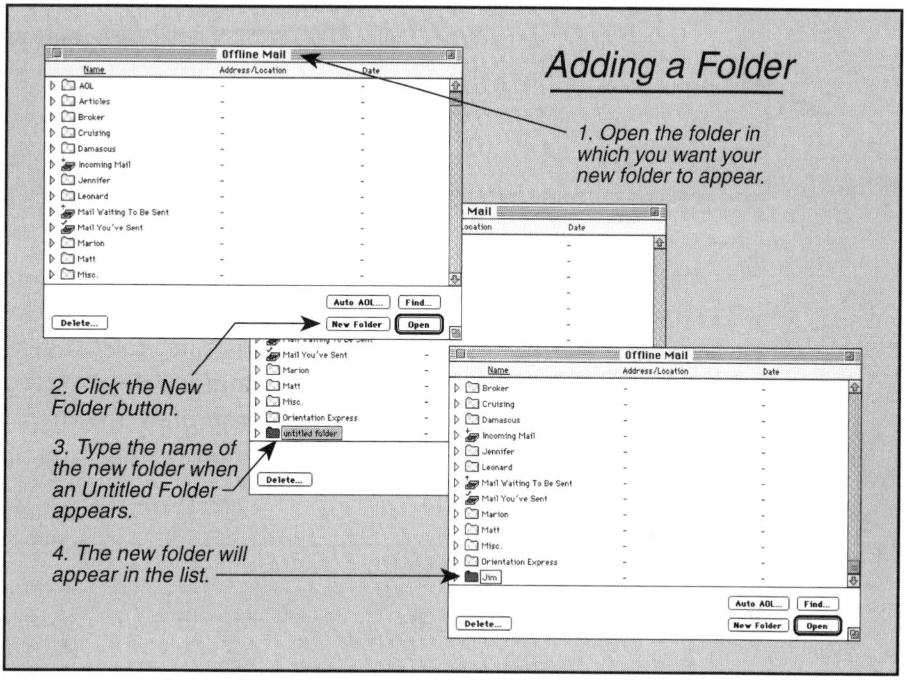
Adding a Folder
1. Open the folder in which you want your new folder to appear.
2. Click the New Folder button.
3. Type the name of the new folder when an Untitled Folder appears.
4. The new folder will appear in the list.
Offline Mail
Offline Mail

Figure 3-24: Open the intended parent folder before you click the New Folder button.

You can name a folder anything you choose. Folder names can include spaces and punctuation, and the limit of 23 characters is more than you'll ever need.

You can name a folder anything you choose. Folder names can include spaces and punctuation, and the limit of 23 characters is more than you'll ever need.

Your Data Folder

If there's a "flaw" in the Personal Filing Cabinet, it's that you're going to use it, and use it extensively. You'll save everything. Doing so, of course, implies storage considerations: if you store too much, your Filing Cabinet can become unwieldy.

This is significant. The contents of your Personal Filing Cabinet are stored on your hard disk, not on AOL's machines, in a file with your screen name on it. You'll find it in the Data folder in your America Online folder within your Preferences folder (located in your System Folder). You might find as many as five files there, one for each of your account names. Check them often (using Get Info or View By Name), and if matters get out of hand, start cleaning house.

Drag & Drop

To organize mail within folders, simply drag and drop it to and from folders. Figure 3-25, for example, illustrates the process of dragging a selected piece of mail from my Incoming/Saved Mail folder to my Leonard folder. You can drag and drop mail up, down, or across your hierarchy using this method. You can drag and drop folders as well.

Figure 3-25: To move mail from one folder to another, drag and drop it.

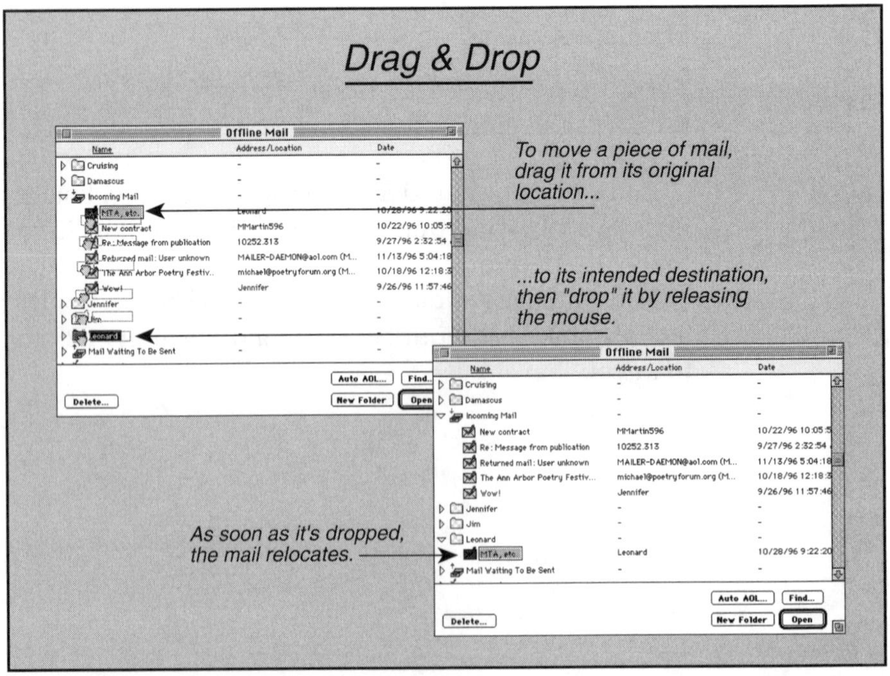
Drag & Drop
Offline Mail
To move a piece of mail, drag it from its original location...
...to its intended destination, then "drop" it by releasing the mouse.
Offline Mail
As soon as it's dropped, the mail relocates.

You can reorganize your folders using the same drag-and-drop method. If you have three folders named "Baker," "Charlie," and "Able," and you want to place them in a folder titled "Bridge Friends," just select and drag the three folders over the "Bridge Friends" folder and release the mouse. The three folders will appear in alphabetical order here, as they do elsewhere.

Deleting Mail

Earlier I mentioned the need for housecleaning. No matter how well it's organized, your Personal Filing Cabinet can become unwieldy if you don't clean it out now and then. I copy my Filing Cabinet to a floppy disk on the first day of each month, then go through it methodically and delete all mail that's more than a month old. On May 1, for example, I copy my Filing Cabinet to a floppy, then delete all the mail from March. This keeps the volume of mail in my Filing Cabinet at manageable levels. It also provides a comprehensive monthly backup, and if I have to refer to outdated mail, I can always restore my Filing Cabinet file from the floppy (making sure to back up my current Filing Cabinet first).

You can delete mail from your Personal Filing Cabinet either by opening it and pressing the Delete button pictured in Figure 3-23, or by selecting it and pressing the Delete button pictured in Figure 3-26. The three Routing Request messages selected in Figure 3-26, for example, will be deleted when I click the Delete button. The Delete key on your keyboard will do the same thing.

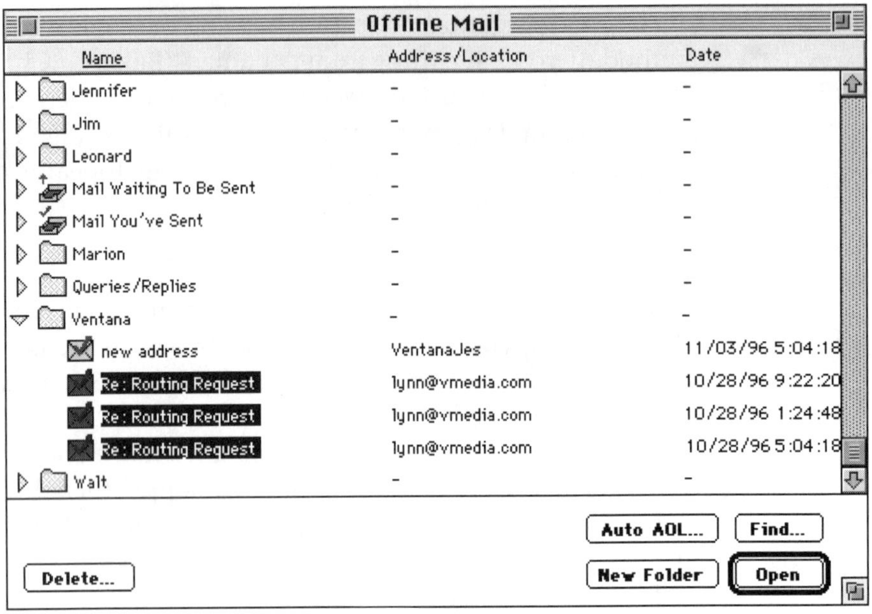
Offline Mail
Name
Address/Location
Date
Jennifer
Jim
Leonard
Mail Waiting To Be Sent
Mail You've Sent
Marion
Queries/Replies
Ventana
new address
VentanaJes
11/03/96 5:04:18
Re: Routing Request
lynn@vmedia.com
10/28/96 9:22:20
Re: Routing Request
lynn@vmedia.com
10/28/96 1:24:48
Re: Routing Request
lynn@vmedia.com
10/28/96 5:04:18
Walt
Auto AOL...
Find...
Delete...
New Folder
Open

Figure 3-26: Delete mail by first selecting it then pressing the Delete button in the Personal Filing Cabinet window.

Multiple Selections

You can select multiple messages or folders—or a combination of both—in the Personal Filing Cabinet by using the modifier keys used by many Mac applications today. The three contiguous files pictured in Figure 3-26 were selected by clicking on the top message, holding down the Shift key, then clicking on each of the other messages. This selects each message.

If I had preferred to select messages in *discontinuous* order, I would have pressed Shift+Option as I selected them. The Shift and Option keys also work for folder selection.

Once selected, multiple folders or messages can be moved or deleted as if they were one.

Searching Your Files

With all of the functionality described so far, the Personal Filing Cabinet offers even more, in the form of two elegant searching commands. Let's say I was engaged in a discourse with an associate on the subject of the Communications Decency Act, the so-called "Cyberspace Bill" that rocked the online community in the spring of 1995. I remember reading something about that bill in the "Computer Underground Digest," a mailing list I subscribe to.

But where did I see it? I save my back issues of the Digest for reference, but the "Digest" is a lengthy publication, and searching manually through several issues looking for a specific item can be tedious.

The solution is the Find button pictured in Figure 3-27. That button invokes the Find dialog box that's also pictured in Figure 3-27. All I need to do is fill it in and tell it to find for me.

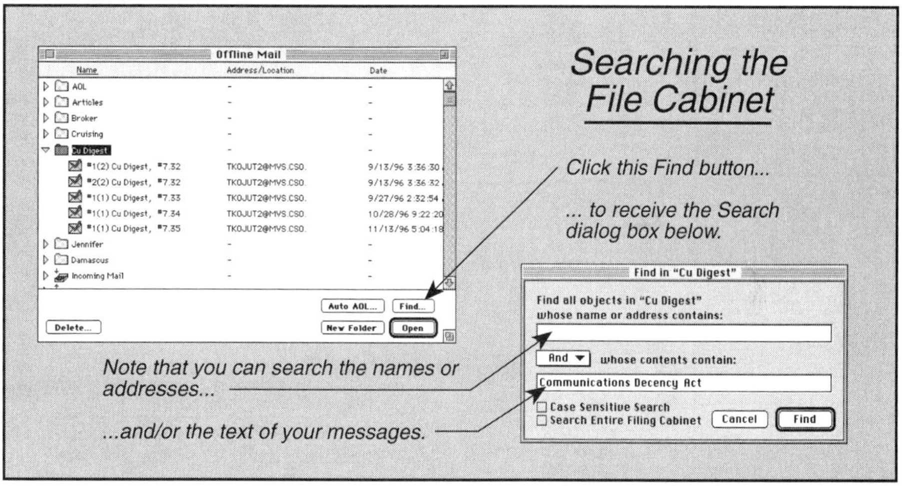
Searching the File Cabinet
Click this Find button...
... to receive the Search dialog box below.
Note that you can search the names or addresses...
...and/or the text of your messages.
Offline Mail
Find in "Cu Digest"
Find all objects in "Cu Digest" whose name or address contains:
And
whose contents contain:
Communications Decency Act
Case Sensitive Search
Search Entire Filing Cabinet
Cancel
Find

Figure 3-27: The Find button allows you to search your entire Personal Filing Cabinet, or portions of it, for either a specific message title or a string of characters in the message body.

Searching through your messages in this way is remarkably fast, and when AOL finds a match, it lists the message(s) containing the found text (see the top window in Figure 3-28). Selecting a message will show you its location within your Personal Filing Cabinet in the lower half of the window.

Finding the message containing the text is only half the task, however. The other half is finding the text itself. This is accomplished with the Find in Top Window command that's pictured in Figure 3-28. Once the Find command has found a message, open it and choose Find in Top Window from the Edit menu. You'll see the window pictured in Figure 3-28, and once it's completed, the matching text will be found in no time.

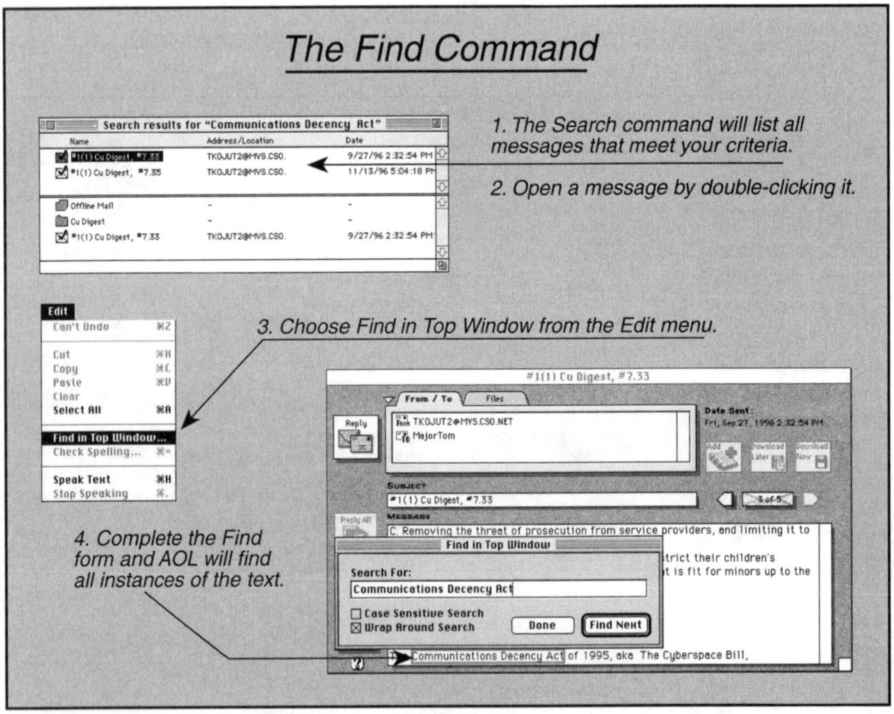
The Find Command
1. The Search command will list all messages that meet your criteria.
2. Open a message by double-clicking it.
3. Choose Find in Top Window from the Edit menu.
4. Complete the Find form and AOL will find all instances of the text.
Search results for "Communications Decency Act"
Find in Top Window
Search For:
Communications Decency Act
Case Sensitive Search
Wrap Around Search
Done
Find Next

Figure 3-28: The Find in Top Window command finishes the job of searching for specific information in your Personal Filing Cabinet.

The Find in Top Window command applies to any window, by the way, not just to those windows containing mail in your Personal Filing Cabinet. You can use it to find text in articles, newsgroup postings—any text file you can open with AOL's Open command.

Mail Center

Choosing the Mail Center option on the Mail menu takes you to the Mail Center, where AOL has gathered an arsenal of material to support you in your e-mail endeavors, no matter what they might be. If you ever have any questions about e-mail, visit the Mail Center first (see Figure 3-29).

The Mail Center
Mail Center
Are you new to E-mail? Learn to use AOL e-mail with free step-by-step
HELP TIPS
You'll never forget an important date with AOL's Gift Reminder!
Read New Mail
Compose Mail
More E-Mail Functions
Other things you can do with E-Mail
Thanksgiving Virtual Postcards
Online Newsletters
Remember important dates!
Keep in touch with friends
Find a new pen pal
Play a game!
Basic E-Mail Help
Message Exchange
Beyond the Basics
Ask the Mail Team
AOL CHANNELS
MEMBER SERVICES
FIND
MAIL CONTROLS
Keyword: Mail

Figure 3-29: The Mail Center should be your first stop when you have questions about e-mail.

Mail Controls

You may not be receiving a great deal of mail yet, but there may come a day when you receive much more, including the ubiquitous "junk e-mail." Luckily, AOL offers the option to regulate the mail you receive with Mail Controls, the last option on your Mail menu. Mail Controls are similar to Parental Controls (discussed in Chapter 2, "The Abecedarium") in that you can control mail for each individual screen name on your account using your master screen name.

Mail control options range from allowing all mail (the default) to blocking all mail (see the bottom window in Figure 3-30). For greater control, you can allow mail only from certain addresses and block all other mail, or block mail only from those addresses you do not wish to receive mail from and allow all others. You can also block attached files.

Figure 3-30: Mail Controls allow you to block and allow mail for each of your screen names.

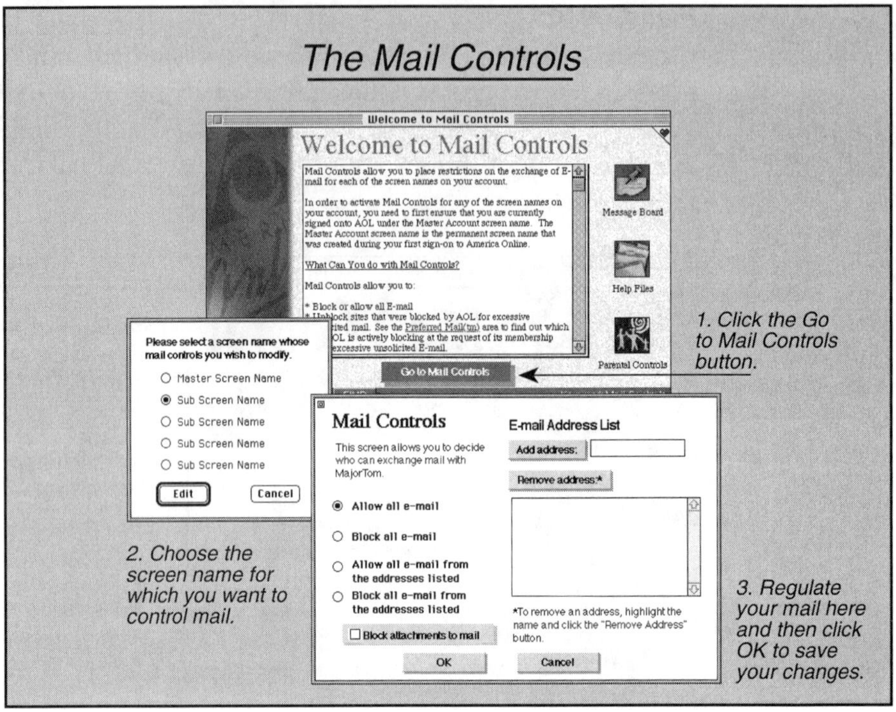
The Mail Controls
Welcome to Mail Controls
Welcome to Mail Controls
Mail Controls allow you to place restrictions on the exchange of E-mail for each of the screen names on your account.
In order to activate Mail Controls for any of the screen names on your account, you need to first ensure that you are currently signed onto AOL under the Master Account screen name. The Master Account screen name is the permanent screen name that was created during your first sign-on to America Online.
What Can You do with Mail Controls?
Mail Controls allow you to:
* Block or allow all E-mail
Message Board
Help Files
Parental Controls
Go to Mail Controls
1. Click the Go to Mail Controls button.
Please select a screen name whose mail controls you wish to modify.
Master Screen Name
Sub Screen Name
Sub Screen Name
Sub Screen Name
Sub Screen Name
Edit
Cancel
2. Choose the screen name for which you want to control mail.
Mail Controls
This screen allows you to decide who can exchange mail with MajorTom.
Allow all e-mail
Block all e-mail
Allow all e-mail from the addresses listed
Block all e-mail from the addresses listed
Block attachments to mail
E-mail Address List
Add address:
Remove address:*
*To remove an address, highlight the name and click the "Remove Address" button.
OK
Cancel
3. Regulate your mail here and then click OK to save your changes.

As for "junk e-mail," AOL automatically blocks unsolicited e-mail from addresses that the community has complained about in the past. If your mailbox seems a bit empty and you'd like to receive junk mail after all, use the keyword: **PreferredMail** and check the option to disable the block. You can also view the list of banned addresses here.

Moving On

As you can see, AOL's e-mail facility is effective and easy to use. It holds your mail for you, even after you've read it, and even if you don't file it yourself. It allows you to reply to and forward mail at the click of a button. It offers a filing system that's the best in the business. Perhaps best of all, it rarely costs you any more than your monthly AOL membership fee.

Very impressive indeed.

E-mail, however, is not a local thing. Just like U.S. Mail, you aren't limited to sending and receiving mail within your community (AOL) itself when you use AOL's mail feature. You can send e-mail to anyone who can receive it and vice-versa, regardless of the community—or even country—they live in. The tool for that is the Internet. I've mentioned the Net a number of times in this chapter; now's the time to get to know it better. Read on.

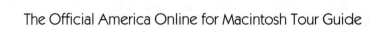

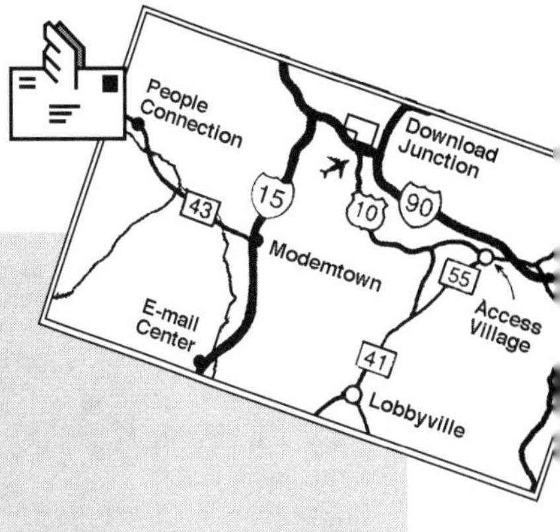
People Connection
Download Junction
Modemtown
E-mail Center
Access Village
Lobbyville
43
15
10
90
55
41

CHAPTER 4

Using the Internet

- A Superset of AOL
- Military Preparedness
- Academic Anarchy
- Internet Addresses
- The World Wide Web
- Mailing Lists
- Newsgroups
- Getting Help
- Gopher
- FTP
- Telnet
- AnswerMan

Most students of mathematics can recall that humbling moment when, with algebra mastered, and buoyed by an embryonic self-confidence, they opened a door marked *Calculus*—and stepped into an incalculable abyss. At that moment, pride of accomplishment turned to humility, confidence to catatonia. Everything learned prior to that event was reduced to insignificance in the shadow of this megalith, this inscrutable, unfathomable vastness.

And no small comfort came from the discovery soon after that this phoenix of fancy was developed in the 17th century, by people *in their twenties!!*

Welcome to the "calculus" of communications, the Internet. Like algebra, America Online is but a subset of an infinitely larger universe—a single star in a galaxy of telecommunications grandeur. And the galaxy, of course, is the Internet. While AOL counts members in the millions, the Internet counts them in the *tens* of millions—and like calculus, many of these people are in their youth, Newtons of the Net, Mozarts of the metaverse, Rembrandts of the right-of-way.

Jeff Stewart
Object01@aol.com
(C) 1995

Figure 4-1: "NET01," by Jeff Stewart, is the artist's conception of how the Internet might appear in virtual reality. Jeff has a number of images posted online. Click the disk-and-magnifier icon on the toolbar, then search for NET01.

Imagine connecting your computer not just to AOL, not just to computers outside of AOL, but to thousands of other computer *networks*, many with forums, e-mail, and thousands of files to download. It's not unlike the wonder you might feel while gazing at stars in a summer sky—each star itself a sun, many with planets—except that these stars are attainable. The Internet takes you there.

Three Years in Search of 75 Cents

Speaking of the stratosphere, meet Cliff Stoll, who is an astronomer. Since astronomers do a lot of computer modeling, Cliff is fairly adept at using computers. That's a good thing, because there *isn't* much work for astronomers, and there *is* for computer operators, especially at Cliff's level.

Which is how Cliff Stoll came to be involved with the Internet and Milnet, an Internet branch that ties together thousands of unclassified computers in the Army, Navy, and Air Force. When I asked Cliff to contribute to this book, he wrote:

"Hmmm . . . military computers on a network? A group of German programmers, adept at breaking into computers, decided to make money from their skills. For a year, they snuck into dozens of systems across the Milnet, copied data from them, and sold this information to the Soviet KGB. They were high-tech spies. With keyboards and modems, they exploited security holes in distant computers. Once on a system, they scanned for sensitive material, passwords, or pathways to other computers. For a year, they went undetected. Then they bumped into me.

"In August 1986, while managing an astronomy computer in Berkeley, California, I noticed a 75-cent accounting error. Someone had used a few minutes of computer time without a valid billing address. Curious . . . just nickels and dimes, but worth checking into. Zooks, but what I found! Using a printer and several PCs, I watched someone sneak through my system, onto the Milnet, and then steal information from military systems a thousand miles away.

"Instead of locking him out of my system, I let him prowl through it, quietly tracking him back to his roost. The trace took a year; but in the end, we proved that five guys were spying over the computer networks. They were convicted of espionage in 1990."

For the whole story, read Cliff's book, *The Cuckoo's Egg.* It's the true story of tracking a spy through the maze of computer espionage, and it ought to be required reading for any Internet user.

Cliff also has a new book called *Silicon Snake Oil.* Buy his books, read them, then send Cliff some e-mail telling him you heard about it here. His screen name: CliffStoll.

A Superset of AOL

The Internet, then, is a superset of AOL. It's everything AOL is—forums, mail, files to download, chats—only bigger. Much bigger. At the moment, AOL is more than seven million people in only five countries; the Internet is as many as 50 million people in more than 100 countries. No one owns it; it has no central facility; there are no Guides or Terms of Service. And there's no Steve Case. An advisory committee is at the helm; its concerns are primarily technical; and its members are all volunteers.

Now that I read the previous paragraph, I hasten to add that there's no "it" either. The Internet isn't a single entity. It comprises scores of independent networks—some military, some academic, some commercial—all interconnected. Indeed, these *inter*connected *net*works are the very basis of the Internet name.

Nouns & Adjectives

If you're going to live in the neighborhood, you're going to have to speak the language. Used as a noun, the Internet is referred to as "the Internet." One would never say, "Send me a message on Internet"; it would be, "Send me a message on *the* Internet."

Used as an adjective, the article is dropped. It's "Internet mail," not "the Internet mail."

If you really want to speak in the vernacular, just call it "the Net," and refer to yourself as a "netter." That'll keep 'em guessing.

Military Preparedness

The best way to define the Internet is to examine what it was: like democracy, the Internet is best understood by observing its past.

Most important, the Internet began as a military contrivance. Most Net users know this, but many have never grasped its significance. The Internet's early military credentials have more to do with what it is today than any other factor.

The Internet is a collection of an uncounted number of independent computers distributed worldwide. Most are networked (wired) together locally and connected to a hub of some sort—a server. These servers—and, in some cases, other independent computers—belong to a *domain*: a network that's connected to the Internet and listed in the Domain Name System (a name registry).

Using leased high-speed digital lines (not modems), each domain is wired to at least one other domain on the Net (often more). The slowest of these lines operates at 56 kbps—twice the speed of a 28.8 kbps modem. Many of these domains maintain a constant connection to the Net. They don't sign on and off as we do with AOL; they're online all the time.

A simplified map of this arrangement might look like that pictured in Figure 4-2.

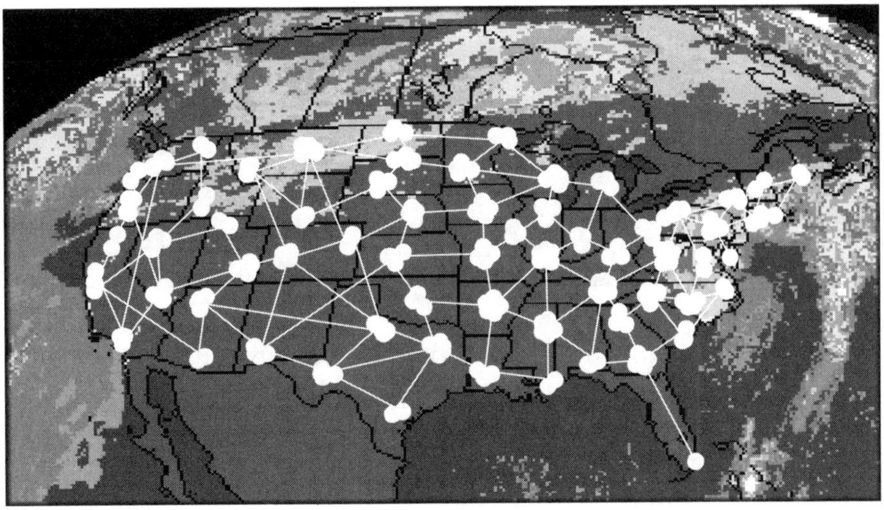

Figure 4-2: The Internet extends around the globe as a web of independent domains interconnected continuously, around the clock, by high-speed dedicated connections.

Don't interpret either Figure 4-2 or 4-3 literally. I drew the white lines, and they're not intended to represent actual Internet or AOL nodes (especially because all I've included is the U.S. mainland—a politicocentric decision if there ever was one). It would take a map the size of a picture window to display all these nodes. While there might be such maps somewhere, this isn't the place to present them. The image of the continent is from the GEOS satellite. Use the keyword: **Weather**, then investigate the weather maps there.

Compare the Internet's strategy with that of AOL. America Online consists of a host computer system (in Virginia) and thousands of client computers (our Macs). While the Internet strategy looks like a web, the AOL strategy looks more like a star (see Figure 4-3).

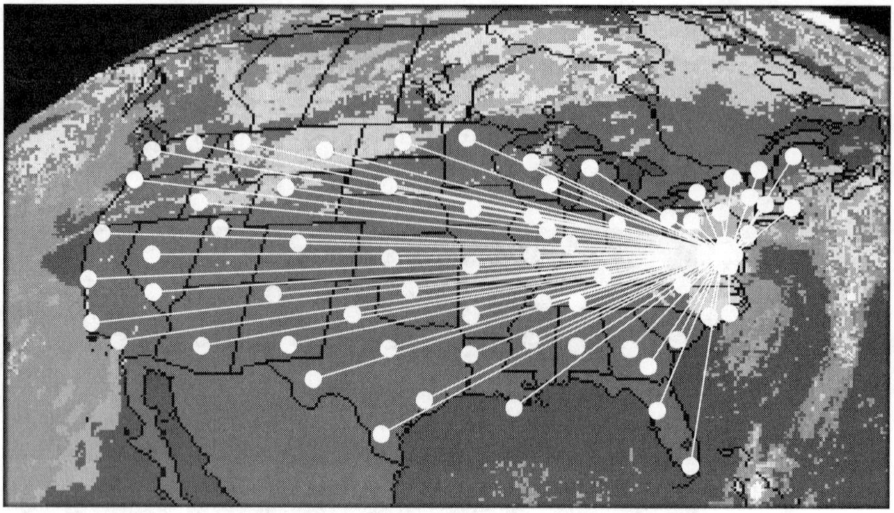

Figure 4-3: America Online's starlike network consists of a host computer and millions of intermittently connected clients.

Now the military part: look again at Figure 4-3. If Ace Excavation were to dig up a fiber-optic cable in Vienna, Virginia, most of us would be without AOL—an unpleasant prospect indeed. On the other hand, if a backhoe unplugged a domain in the Internet, communications would simply be routed around it. Indeed, a large percentage of the Net's domains could be eliminated and the Net would still function.

Forever prepared, the Defense Department commissioned the Advanced Research Projects Agency (ARPA) to configure a computer network that would accommodate just such a possibility. This plan was implemented in the late 1960s; the network was called the ARPANET.

Academic Anarchy

By the early 1980s, educators discovered the value of sharing research information and computing resources through interconnected computers—especially supercomputers, which are as precious as gold (literally—an older Cray-1 supercomputer has thousands of dollars worth of gold connectors in it). The educators weren't interested (primarily) in security; their interest was access. Their computers held vast amounts of data and, true to form, they wanted to share that information objectively, without bias, with anyone in the community who wanted access.

ARPANET was a possible answer, but there were—how shall I put it?—fundamental differences in the military and academic attitudes. The academic community elected instead to develop its own network, which it called NSFNET (named for the National Science Foundation, the academics' primary source of funding). Significantly, NSFNET used the same networking strategy ARPANET used: interconnected domains randomly distributed around the United States. The result could have been dysfunctional anarchy, but by definition a computer network implies some form of universal protocol—electronic standards that everyone agrees to observe. The result is best described as *consensual anarchy*, whereby everyone marches to his or her own drummer but all agree on a common route for the parade.

And that's how the Internet is today: an agglomeration of independent domains drawn from both ARPANET and NSFNET, each owned by organizations that are independent of one another, interconnected by high-speed data lines, and not subject to any form of central control. There's no central data storage, either. Data are scattered about the Net like dyed eggs on Easter Sunday, hidden in faraway places, awaiting discovery. It amazes me that the thing even exists—it's one of the few working models of functional anarchy today, and it works extremely well.

WIRED Magazine

WIRED is the "magazine of the digital generation"—covering interactive media, the networking community, and the toys of technology. Started in early 1993, *WIRED* has quickly advanced to the vanguard of the literary aristocracy. Its design is precocious, its content acerbic, its language always provocative (and often offensive to some). The information age has few perspectives that can match *WIRED*'s insight, candor, or irreverence, and none can match them all.

Best of all, *WIRED* is available online at AOL. Only past issues of *WIRED* are available—you'll have to visit your newsstand for the latest edition—but its focus isn't so myopic that its content becomes obsolete in a month or two. If this chapter interests you and you're not yet a *WIRED* devotee, read this magazine. Use the keyword: **WIRED**.

Until recently, military and academic users dominated the Internet community. It might have been an anarchistic community, but it was also very exclusive. Things have changed. Commercial accounts were allowed access in the early 1990s, opening the door to businesses as well as millions of everyday computer users like you and me. Now all of us with AOL accounts are offered Internet access. And there's no extra charge.

Internet Addresses

Before we go any further, we need to discuss Internet addresses. I touched on them briefly in Chapter 3, but they deserve more than that. They're really not much different from the addresses the U.S. Postal Service uses, though rather than being sent to you at your home, Internet mail is sent to your *domain*. Domain or domicile, they're the same thing: they're the places where you receive mail.

International Top-Level Domains

When my friend Kyoko writes to me from Japan, the address she places on the envelope goes from the specific to the general: she starts with my name and ends with "U.S.A.," in the *name/address/city/state/usa* format.

International Internet addresses are exactly the same. At the far right you'll find the name of the country. This is called the *top-level* domain. Well, *almost* always. The Net's an anarchy, after all. Figure 4-4 identifies the abbreviations for some common international top-level domains.

Figure 4-4: Country abbreviations are the top-level domain of international Internet addresses.

Abbreviation	Country
au	Australia
at	Austria
ca	Canada
dk	Denmark
fi	Finland
fr	France
de	Germany
it	Italy
jp	Japan
no	Norway
uk	United Kingdom
us	United States

Perhaps the best-known example of an international top-level domain is

username@well.sf.ca.us.

indicating a user on the Whole Earth 'Lectronic Link (the WELL) in San Francisco (sf), California (ca), U.S.A. (us).

Note that the segments of Internet addresses are separated by periods. It's always that way. (Well, here again, *almost* always. You occasionally will see other address formats. They're rare, however, and assuredly the exception to the rule.)

U.S. Top-Level Domains

At the risk of sounding politicocentric again, most domains are within the United States, and the *us* top-level domain is typically omitted from American domain names, just as it is on paper mail that's to stay within our borders. Instead, top domains for U.S. users typically identify the type of system they're using. Figure 4-5 identifies the common U.S. top-level domains.

Figure 4-5: U.S. top-level domains identify the nature of the user's affiliation.

Abbreviation	Affiliation
com	business and commercial
edu	educational institutions
gov	government institutions
mil	military installations
net	network resources
org	other (typically nonprofit)

My Internet address, as mentioned in Chapter 3, is **majortom@aol.com**. Anyone looking at my top-level domain can determine that I'm affiliated with a commercial organization—in this case, America Online.

Domain Names & Computer Names

Immediately to the left of the top-level domain is the location of the network that's actually connected to the Internet. Thus, a domain name such as **uoregon.edu** implies that there's a network named "uoregon" somewhere, and it has a direct line to the Internet.

Many institutions—especially educational ones—have more than one local area network (LAN). Most of my academic associates work at the University of Oregon, but the U of O has at least seven satellite networks connected to the university's central mainframe, which is connected to the Net. One of those networks is located within a building called Oregon Hall, and the users on that network add **oregon.uoregon.edu** to the string, which identifies the Oregon Hall (oregon) LAN, which is connected to the University of Oregon domain (uoregon), which is an educational institution (edu).

User Names

Most Internet activity takes the form of e-mail, and e-mail is sent to individuals. To identify an individual, the format **username@oregon.uoregon.edu** is used. Everything to the left of the at sign (@) in an Internet address is the user's name. Internet user names aren't subject to AOL's 10-character limit, so they can become quite elaborate.

Many people on the Net use their first initial and last name as their Internet name. This format is unique (at least to the domain), and it's not gender-specific (an issue that many Net users prefer to avoid). Spaces aren't allowed (so you'll often see underscores in their place: **fred_morgan@mit.edu**), and Internet addresses are usually not case-sensitive. None of this should make a whit of difference to you: your screen name (minus any spaces) automatically becomes your Internet user name. Your domain (sounds regal, doesn't it?) is **aol.com**.

The World Wide Web

Cultivated in UNIX and nurtured by computer professionals, the Internet became a patchwork of disjointed fragments: Usenet, FTP, Telnet, and e-mail. The Internet almost seemed to take pride in its incoherence. Now that the Net has evolved from its experimental stage, coherence, convenience—even hospitality—are not only appropriate but essential.

Apparently, the scientists at CERN—the European Particle Physics Laboratory in Geneva, Switzerland—agree: in 1989 they set out to take the Internet another step up the evolutionary ladder. The result—introduced in 1990—is the *World Wide Web*, which has become somewhat like a department store: a gathering of FTP, Gopher, WAIS gateways, e-mail, and newsgroups. The Web puts all these things under one roof, in familiar and convenient surroundings. If you can use a mouse, you can use the Web. Indeed, the Web is so obliging, it might become your only means of using the Internet (other than e-mail) from now on.

Hypermedia

The Web's cosmos consists of *hypermedia*. In my experience, the use of polysyllabic buzzwords usually indicates that the words' true meanings are obtuse and opaque. The word "hypermedia" is no exception, but it's the heart of the Web, and you must understand one to understand the other. Perhaps Figure 4-6 will help.

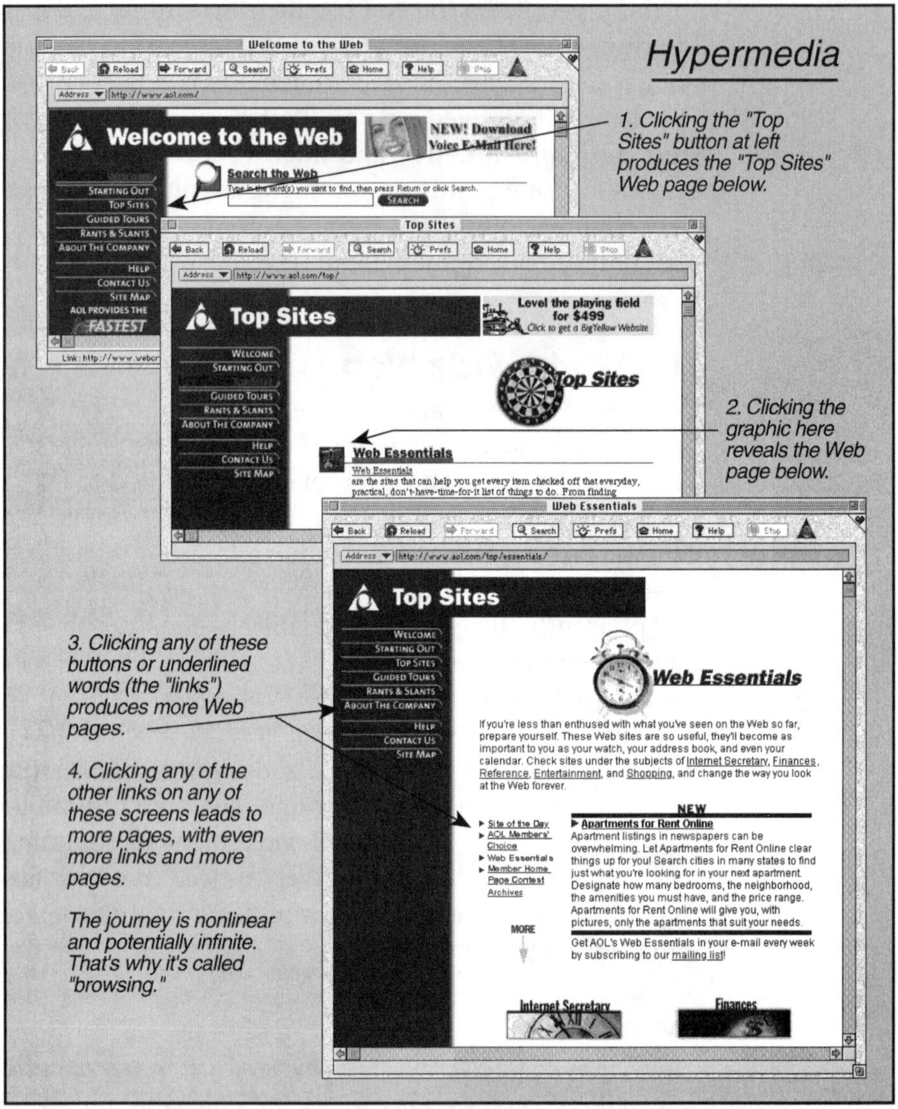
Hypermedia
1. Clicking the "Top Sites" button at left produces the "Top Sites" Web page below.
2. Clicking the graphic here reveals the Web page below.
3. Clicking any of these buttons or underlined words (the "links") produces more Web pages.
4. Clicking any of the other links on any of these screens leads to more pages, with even more links and more pages.
The journey is nonlinear and potentially infinite. That's why it's called "browsing."
Welcome to the Web
Top Sites
Web Essentials

Figure 4-6: Hypermedia provide a nonlinear pathway to the infinite potential of the World Wide Web.

Each Web *page* consists of text and graphics (and more—such as sound and video—if it's a really ambitious page), usually marked with *links* (*hyperlinks*, actually) or areas on the page that when clicked lead to something else. Links can lead you to more Web pages, graphics, sounds, or videos: there are no limits other than the capability of your hardware and the link designer's imagination. The path shown in

Figure 4-6 is only one of an infinite number of paths we could have explored. A click on the Community or What's Hot buttons on AOL's Welcome to the Web page would send you down other paths just as fertile and just as infinite as the one in the illustration. Indeed, the Web is a vast cosmos of resources, linked to related resources all over the world. This, perhaps, is why it's called the World Wide Web.

Nomenclature

So far, we've defined the *World Wide Web*, *page*, and *link*, but there are a few other terms that require interpretation before we continue.

A *Web browser* is software designed to access the World Wide Web—the Internet's graphical interface. Web access requires a hefty piece of software; you'll see Web browsers for sale at software stores and in mail order catalogs, and they're not cheap. You needn't fret: your AOL software contains a superb Web browser; there's nothing else to buy.

The *URL* is the Uniform Resource Locator, or the address for each article of text, and each graphic, sound, or video on the Web. There are millions of URLs, thus their addresses are lengthy and specific. They can be typed directly into the text field just below the toolbar in AOL's Web Browser window. They can be pasted there, too, which is probably a better idea.

HTTP stands for HyperText Transfer Protocol. Appearing at the left end of a URL, HTTP tells the browser to expect a hypertext Web document.

HTML is HyperText Markup Language, the scripting language that's used to create Web pages.

Favorite Places

As you explore the Web, you'll discover pages you'll want to return to. And when you return, you won't want or need to type URLs again from the keyboard. That's what the *Favorite Places* feature is for.

Most Web pages have a little heart-shaped icon in the upper right corner of the window. This icon serves as a bookmark: if you want to "mark" a page by adding it to your list of Favorite Places, simply click its little heart icon and select "Add it to my favorite places" (see Figure 4-7). You also have the option of using it as a hyperlink in e-mail (see Chapter 3, "Electronic Mail & the Personal Filing Cabinet") or simply copying it to your Clipboard to paste in a document later.

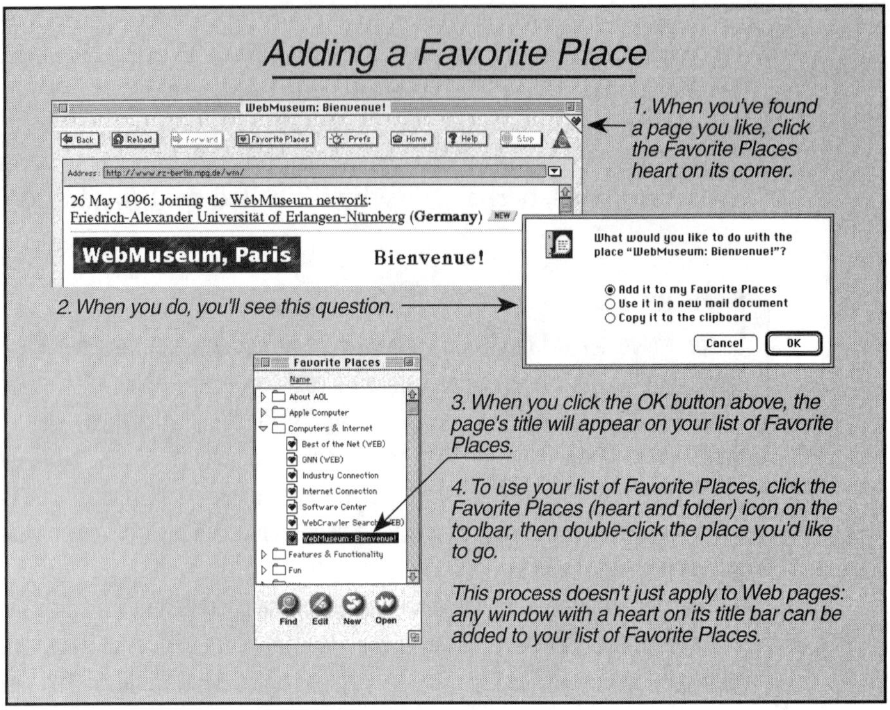
Adding a Favorite Place
WebMuseum: Bienvenue!
26 May 1996: Joining the WebMuseum network:
Friedrich-Alexander Universität of Erlangen-Nürnberg (Germany)
WebMuseum, Paris
Bienvenue!
1. When you've found a page you like, click the Favorite Places heart on its corner.
What would you like to do with the place "WebMuseum: Bienvenue!"?
Add it to my Favorite Places
Use it in a new mail document
Copy it to the clipboard
Cancel
OK
2. When you do, you'll see this question.
Favorite Places
About AOL
Apple Computer
Computers & Internet
Best of the Net (WEB)
GNN (WEB)
Industry Connection
Internet Connection
Software Center
WebMuseum: Bienvenue!
Features & Functionality
Fun
Find
Edit
New
Open
3. When you click the OK button above, the page's title will appear on your list of Favorite Places.
4. To use your list of Favorite Places, click the Favorite Places (heart and folder) icon on the toolbar, then double-click the place you'd like to go.
This process doesn't just apply to Web pages: any window with a heart on its title bar can be added to your list of Favorite Places.

Figure 4-7: Adding Favorite Places is as simple as click or drag.

This technique doesn't apply only to Web page windows: many areas within AOL offer a heart icon in their windows; whenever you see one you can use it to add your current location to your list of personal Favorite Places.

To open the Favorite Places window, click the Favorite Places icon on the toolbar at any time, whether you're online or off. To go to one of your favorite places, just double-click it in the Favorite Places window.

Finding Stuff on the Web

There are a number of Web pages that allow you to search the Web for a subject of interest. One of the more popular sites is *Webcrawler*, a technology now owned by AOL. I use it more than any other because it's so convenient: just use the keyword: **Webcrawler**. When you do, AOL will launch its Web browser and call up the Webcrawler page, automatically. All you have to do is specify what you're looking for and click the Search button.

Browsing

This is not a place to become mired in procedural details. As the AOL software presents it, the Web really requires no instructions. It's a place for leisurely browsing, like an art gallery (try the WebMuseum at **http://sunsite.unc.edu/wm/**) or the shelves of books in a public library (try the World Wide Web Virtual Library at **http://www.w3.org/hypertext/DataSources/bySubject/Overview.html**). Be prepared to wander and wonder at all the remarkable rewards the Web has to offer. Drag and drop bookmarks when you find places you want to return to, and surf the sea of the Internet the way the people at CERN intended. (The people at AOL hope you'll make extensive use of the Web too: look at Figure 4-8.) This is the Internet at its best; it will bring you back time after time.

Mailing Lists

Internet mailing lists are something of a cross between Ed McMahon and Rush Limbaugh (a vivid, if not particularly adept, analogy if there ever was one).

Mailing lists are like Ed McMahon in that they arrive in your mailbox frequently and seemingly unbidden. They're like Rush Limbaugh in that they accept material from listeners (subscribers in this case) and broadcast those contributions to everyone else on the list.

Think of AOL's message boards. Mailing lists, like boards, are where people discuss issues of common interest. There are thousands of lists, and the issues range from ablation to zymurgy.

Lists are sometimes called *reflectors*: mail you send to a list is broadcast (reflected) to everyone else who subscribes to the list. Conversely, you will automatically receive—as Internet mail—any message sent to the list by any other subscriber.

In that way, mailing lists are similar to the AOL Address Book feature. Using the Address Book, you can associate a number of screen names with a single address book entry; when you select that entry, multiple screen names are plugged into the Address To: field of an outgoing mail form. An Internet mailing list is much the same: mail sent to it is normally received by every subscriber to the list. One name represents many.

Figure 4-8: The World Wide Web is integrated throughout America Online. Look for "world" buttons or "WEB" selections.

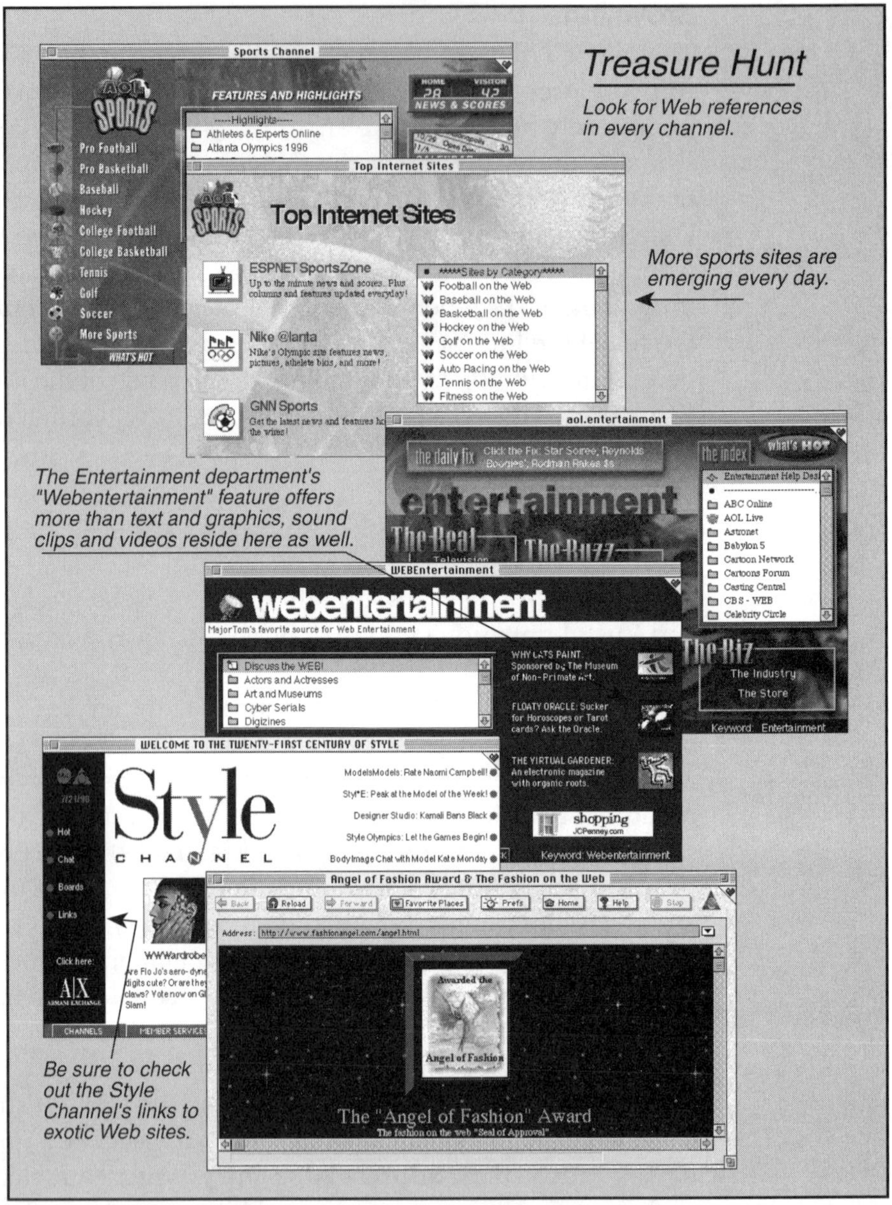
Treasure Hunt
Look for Web references in every channel.
More sports sites are emerging every day.
The Entertainment department's "Webentertainment" feature offers more than text and graphics, sound clips and videos reside here as well.
Be sure to check out the Style Channel's links to exotic Web sites.
Sports Channel
Top Internet Sites
aol.entertainment
WEBEntertainment
webentertainment
WELCOME TO THE TWENTY-FIRST CENTURY OF STYLE
Style
CHANNEL
Angel of Fashion Award & The Fashion on the Web
The "Angel of Fashion" Award

America Online offers a direct line to its Internet mailing list feature; just use the keywords: **Mailing Lists** (see Figure 4-9).

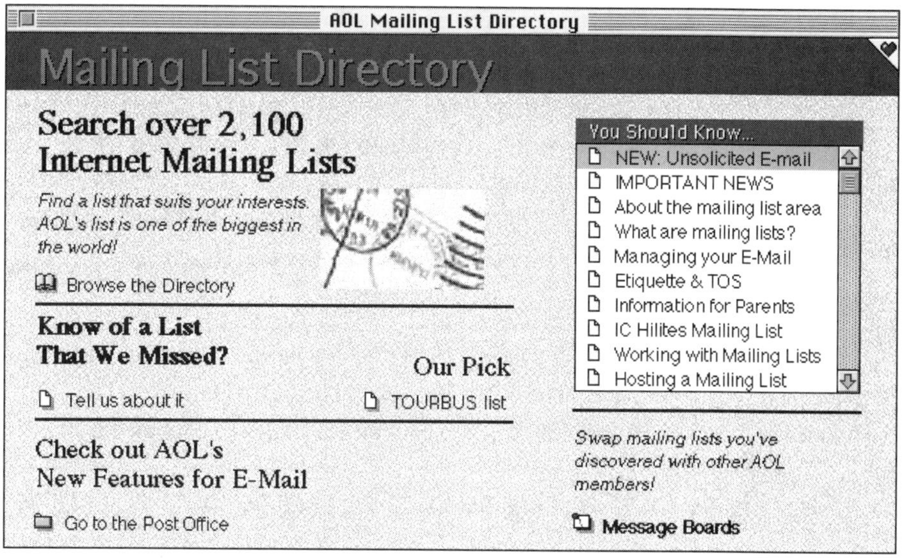
AOL Mailing List Directory
Mailing List Directory
Search over 2,100
Internet Mailing Lists
Find a list that suits your interests. AOL's list is one of the biggest in the world!
Browse the Directory
Know of a List
That We Missed?
Tell us about it
Our Pick
TOURBUS list
Check out AOL's
New Features for E-Mail
Go to the Post Office
You Should Know...
NEW: Unsolicited E-mail
IMPORTANT NEWS
About the mailing list area
What are mailing lists?
Managing your E-Mail
Etiquette & TOS
Information for Parents
IC Hilites Mailing List
Working with Mailing Lists
Hosting a Mailing List
Swap mailing lists you've discovered with other AOL members!
Message Boards

Figure 4-9: The keywords: **Mailing Lists** provide access to Internet mailing list information, including a searchable database of lists currently available.

Subscribing to a good mailing list can be entertaining, stimulating, enlightening—and overwhelming. You should subscribe to one just for the experience. Before you do, however, understand a few mailing list basics:

- It's not unusual for a list to generate a prodigious volume of mail. For this reason, it is important that you check on your mailbox often to avoid losing your mail. Your AOL mailbox—the one in Virginia, where your unread mail is held—is limited to 550 pieces of mail, including both read and unread mail. Unread mail disappears four weeks after the date it was sent. Mail you've read disappears one week after the date it was sent—even sooner when the mail load at AOL is heavy. If your total mailbox mail count (both read and unread) exceeds 550 pieces, the AOL system will start to delete excess mail, starting with read mail and then mail you've sent. AOL will not delete unread mail earlier than the four week limit, however. This means if you have more than 550 pieces of unread mail your mailbox will fill and anyone attempting to send you e-mail will be notified of this.
- Find out whether any mailing list you wish to join has a "digest" mode, which compiles all of the day's (or week's—it depends on volume) messages into a single mailing. You can usually spot a digest version of any particular mailing list by looking for the word *digest* in the list's name. If a digest is offered, subscribe to it.

- Don't subscribe to a mailing list unless you plan to read it.
- When reading a list's description, be sure to take note of how to "unsubscribe," in case you change your mind about receiving it. (Often, once you subscribe to a list, you'll be sent a confirming message that also explains how to unsubscribe—put this message in a safe place in case you need that information.)
- If you subscribe to any mailing lists, sign on regularly to read your mail and clear your mailbox.
- Some lists are "moderated"; some are not. Moderated lists are comparable to AOL's hosted chat rooms in that their content never strays too far off the subject and rarely becomes offensive. Lists that are not moderated embody the anarchistic nature of the Internet and can become quite idiosyncratic and immoderate.

America Online offers a searchable directory of lists (review Figure 4-9). Again, the keywords: **Mailing Lists** will take you there. Don't be surprised if the subject you have in mind isn't listed. Do spend some time exploring the directory: it searches the list descriptions by content rather than by keyword. A search using the criterion *flying*, for example, produces all the lists with the word *flying* in their descriptions, including high-flying and flying by the seat of your pants. While searches like this can drift off the subject quickly, you never know what gems you'll unearth.

Note: Because the Mailing List Directory is intended to be a resource for Internet users worldwide as well as AOL's members, it is available via a series of World Wide Web pages. You can also obtain the Directory via FTP; instructions are at keywords: **Mailing Lists**.

Newsgroups

Newsgroups are similar to mailing lists in that they provide forums for the free exchange of ideas, opinions, and comments, usually confined to a specific field of interest. You visit a newsgroup, read the messages you find there, reply to those that inspire a response, post new messages when you have a new topic to propose, and come back another day to see what responses you've provoked.

Unlike mailing lists, no mail is involved with newsgroups, and you needn't subscribe—all newsgroups are open to everyone. Most activity occurs while you're online, including reading and responding to postings. Thus, some will say that newsgroups are more immediate, more interactive, and more conversational than mailing lists. Newsgroups or mailing lists? For most it's a matter of preference. You probably will want to dabble in both for a while.

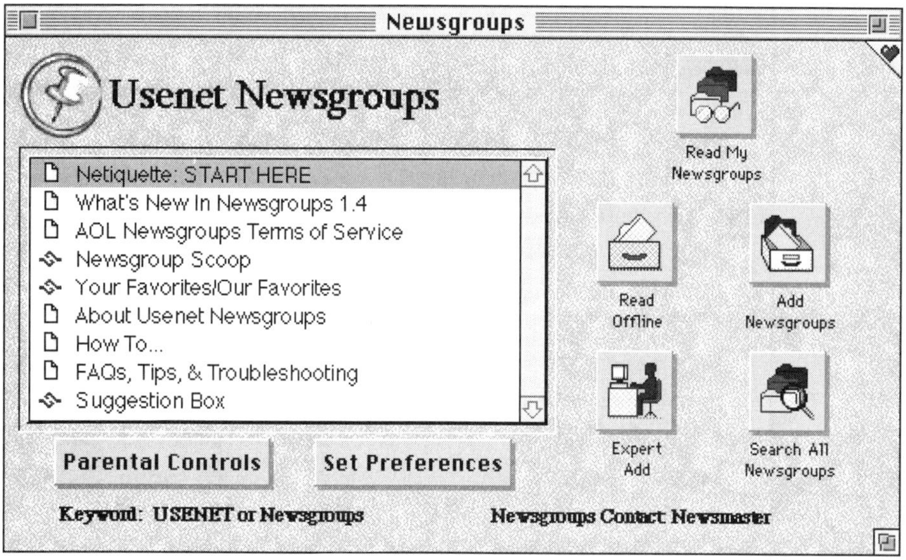
Newsgroups
Usenet Newsgroups
Netiquette: START HERE
What's New In Newsgroups 1.4
AOL Newsgroups Terms of Service
Newsgroup Scoop
Your Favorites/Our Favorites
About Usenet Newsgroups
How To...
FAQs, Tips, & Troubleshooting
Suggestion Box
Read My Newsgroups
Read Offline
Add Newsgroups
Expert Add
Search All Newsgroups
Parental Controls
Set Preferences
Keyword: USENET or Newsgroups
Newsgroups Contact Newsmaster

Figure 4-10: The America Online Newsgroups screen. To reach it, use the keyword: **Newsgroups**.

At the moment, more than 36,000 newsgroups flood the Internet. This figure is 9 times the 4,000 mentioned in Adam Engst's *Internet Starter Kit* (copyright 1993), which is in turn more than double the 1,500 mentioned in Ed Krol's *The Whole Internet* (first edition, copyright 1992). If the number of newsgroups keeps doubling and tripling every year, we'll have more than half a million of them by the turn of the century.

One thing's for sure: few newsgroups have anything to do with the news. Newsgroups aren't groups assembled to discuss *Washington Week in Review*. This is an anarchy: there are no restrictions whatsoever on newsgroup topics. That's why there are 20,000 of them.

The Internet doesn't have a monopoly on newsgroups. America Online has hundreds of them, though AOL prefers to call them message boards. CompuServe has "forums"; GEnie has "bulletin boards"; and Delphi has "round tables." They're all the same thing, and they all exist to satisfy our passion for discourse. Accordingly, newsgroups are arguably the most popular resource on the Internet.

Bizarre Talk

The Internet is a diverse place. Scientists exchange formulae for the creation of life. Programmers exchange code for the creation of daemons. And others exchange palaver in the newsgroup talk.bizarre. To wit, the following:

Subject: The Solbergs Do The Zoo
From: andsol@cml.rice.edu (Andrew Solberg)
Date: 17 Jul 1994 22:53:59 -0500
Message-ID: <9407180354.AA01851@cml.rice.edu>

Andy: Ah, the heady aroma of the zoo.
Dema: Buy me a Slushee.

-*-

Andy: Dema, are the moats around these critters meant to keep them in or little kids out?
Dema: I think they're actually meant to trap little kids. They fall down the steep walls and die there, kind of like pitcher plants.
Andy: I get it! The kids die and their bodies decompose into a thick, nutrient-rich mulch........
Dema: .....which plants grow in, which the elephants eat....
Andy: Oo! Oo! Let me say it!
Dema: Okay.
Andy: "....And Thus Is The Cycle Of Nature Renewed."
Dema: People are staring.

-*-

Dema: They don't have a meerkat!
Andy: A what?
Dema: A meerkat! Like in The Lion King!
Andy: Are you sure that's a real creature?
Dema: Of *course* it is! Disney wouldn't *dare* invent it!
Andy: I don't buy it.
Dema: Then buy me another Slushee.

Special thanks to Professor Andrew J. Solberg from the University of Oslo, Norway, for his wit and permission to display a bit of it here.

And they *are* an Internet resource, meaning they're outside of AOL's sphere of influence. No one polices the Internet. Newsgroup subject matter and use of language are appropriate to the Internet anarchy. In a way, AOL is performing a service similar to that of the telephone company when it comes to newsgroups: AOL is just the medium, not the message.

Because newsgroups are an Internet resource, AOL's own internal Terms of Service (TOS) don't apply. There are guidelines, however, and AOL's Usenet Newsgroups TOS is a codification of these guidelines. The Usenet TOS is always available in the list box at the keyword: **Newsgroups**, where it's called "AOL Newsgroups Terms of Service." Be sure to read it—it might save you considerable newsgroup face.

The Ringmaster Pub

The Ringmaster Pub and Deli is just up the street from AOL—an easy walk, even in the rain. It's inside the building that houses the offices of Ringling Brothers and Barnum & Bailey's Greatest Show on Earth. If you enter the wrong door on your way to the pub, you land in Barnum & Bailey's foyer surrounded by the stuffed remains of Gargantua the Gorilla and a magnificent wall mural, measuring perhaps 20 by 35 feet. It's an elaborate painting—exquisitely detailed—of a three-ring circus with clowns, tigers, and trapeze artists, all caught in midair.

AOLers don't frequent the Ringmaster Pub, preferring to walk another couple of yards uptown—figuratively and literally—to the American Cafe. I'm more of a pub guy and I try to visit the Ringmaster every time I travel to AOL. Gargantua and I are old friends.

It's appropriate that AOL and the circus occupy neighboring office buildings. Both services make a living by juggling balls in the air. Both services have their tigers and their clowns, and both services have amassed their fortunes a couple of dollars at a time. AOL could place that three-ring mural in its foyer and nothing would seem out of place.

Getting Help

Help is never far away when you're using AOL's Internet features. A number of methods are available for accessing help—from AOL, from other members, or from the Internet community at large.

Online Help

Nearly every Internet window on AOL offers a potential for online help. Figure 4-11 offers a sampling.

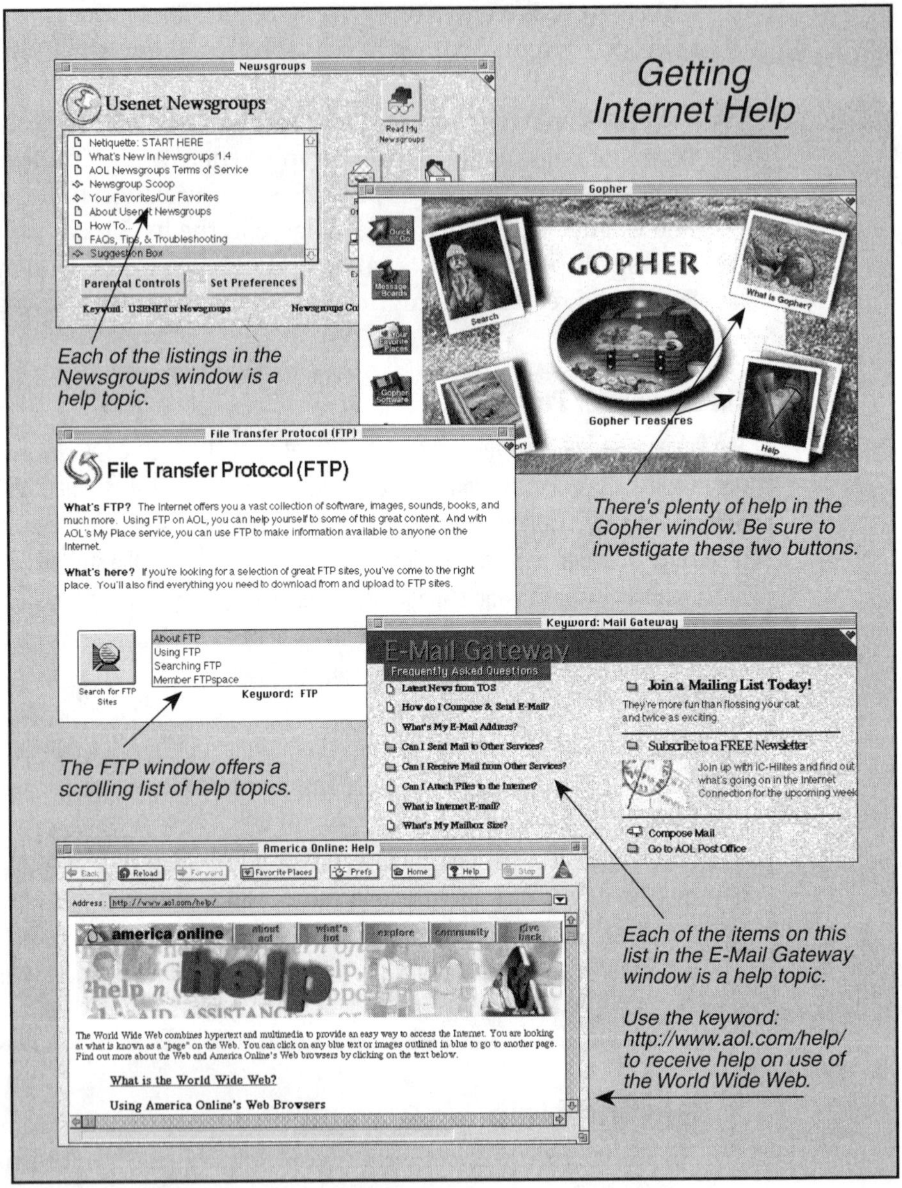
Getting Internet Help
Newsgroups
Usenet Newsgroups
Netiquette: START HERE
What's New in Newsgroups 1.4
AOL Newsgroups Terms of Service
Newsgroup Scoop
Your Favorites/Our Favorites
About Usenet Newsgroups
How To...
FAQs, Tips, & Troubleshooting
Suggestion Box
Parental Controls
Set Preferences
Keyword: USENET or Newsgroups
Read My Newsgroups
Each of the listings in the Newsgroups window is a help topic.
Gopher
GOPHER
Search
What is Gopher?
Gopher Treasures
Help
There's plenty of help in the Gopher window. Be sure to investigate these two buttons.
File Transfer Protocol (FTP)
File Transfer Protocol (FTP)
What's FTP? The Internet offers you a vast collection of software, images, sounds, books, and much more. Using FTP on AOL, you can help yourself to some of this great content. And with AOL's My Place service, you can use FTP to make information available to anyone on the Internet.
What's here? If you're looking for a selection of great FTP sites, you've come to the right place. You'll also find everything you need to download from and upload to FTP sites.
Search for FTP Sites
About FTP
Using FTP
Searching FTP
Member FTPspace
Keyword: FTP
The FTP window offers a scrolling list of help topics.
Keyword: Mail Gateway
E-Mail Gateway
Frequently Asked Questions
Latest News from TOS
How do I Compose & Send E-Mail?
What's My E-Mail Address?
Can I Send Mail to Other Services?
Can I Receive Mail from Other Services?
Can I Attach Files to the Internet?
What is Internet E-mail?
What's My Mailbox Size?
Join a Mailing List Today!
They're more fun than flossing your cat and twice as exciting.
Subscribe to a FREE Newsletter
Join up with IC-Hilites and find out what's going on in the Internet Connection for the upcoming week
Compose Mail
Go to AOL Post Office
America Online: Help
Back
Reload
Forward
Favorite Places
Prefs
Home
Help
Stop
Address: http://www.aol.com/help/
america online
about aol
what's hot
explore
community
give back
help
The World Wide Web combines hypertext and multimedia to provide an easy way to access the Internet. You are looking at what is known as a "page" on the Web. You can click on any blue text or images outlined in blue to go to another page. Find out more about the Web and America Online's Web browsers by clicking on the text below.
What is the World Wide Web?
Using America Online's Web Browsers
Each of the items on this list in the E-Mail Gateway window is a help topic.
Use the keyword: http://www.aol.com/help/ to receive help on use of the World Wide Web.

Figure 4-11: Help topics abound at the Internet Connection.

The good news is that because the newsgroup Help files are stored at AOL (and not on your hard disk), they can be changed whenever the Internet staff wants to change them. These Help files, in other words, always reflect changes made in response to suggestions from users as well as changes in the Net itself.

The bad news is that you have to be online to access them, and for that you pay.

Here's a tip: print 'em. Whenever a Help window is open, all you have to do is choose Print from the File menu, and you'll have a hardcopy of the online Help file that's currently open. You can print them all in this manner if you like.

Peer Assistance

I'm a firm believer in peer assistance. America Online members are usually your best source of help because they can empathize; they understand your needs. Experts often are too far removed from your situation (and have too many other things to do) to help the way other members can. In other words, if you have a question, ask around.

You might start with the Internet Connection message boards. Use the keyword: **Internet**, then double-click any of the Message Board listings in the main window. The Internet Connection's message boards provide places where you can post questions and receive replies from others who've experienced similar situations. Look for the Internet Exchange item in the Internet Connection window's list box.

An ambitious team of "CyberJockeys" patrols these boards as well, answering especially difficult questions. You can recognize CyberJockeys by the leading "CJ" in their screen names.

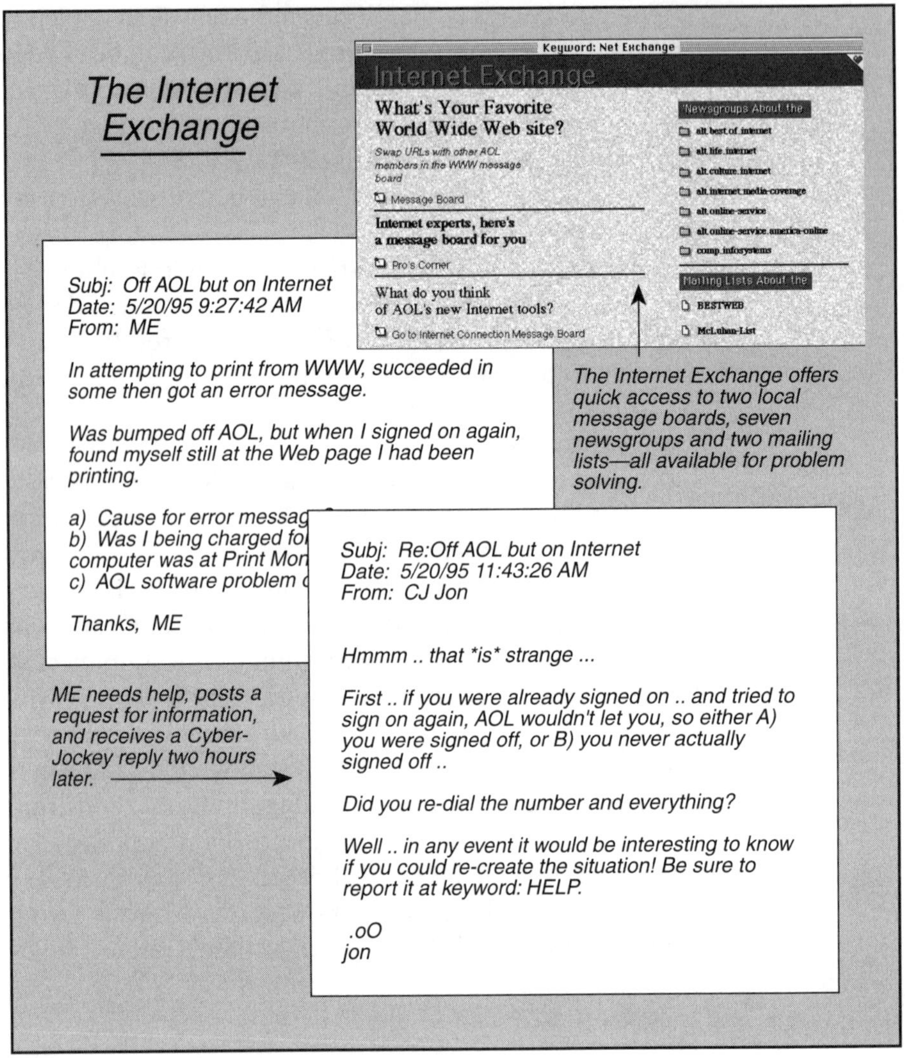
The Internet Exchange
Keyword: Net Exchange
Internet Exchange
What's Your Favorite World Wide Web site?
Swap URLs with other AOL members in the WWW message board
Message Board
Internet experts, here's a message board for you
Pro's Corner
What do you think of AOL's new Internet tools?
Go to Internet Connection Message Board
Newsgroups About the
alt.best.of.internet
alt.life.internet
alt.culture.internet
alt.internet.media-coverage
alt.online-service
alt.online-service.america-online
comp.infosystems
Mailing Lists About the
BESTWEB
McLuhan-List
Subj: Off AOL but on Internet
Date: 5/20/95 9:27:42 AM
From: ME
In attempting to print from WWW, succeeded in some then got an error message.
Was bumped off AOL, but when I signed on again, found myself still at the Web page I had been printing.
a) Cause for error messag
b) Was I being charged fo
computer was at Print Mon
c) AOL software problem
Thanks, ME
The Internet Exchange offers quick access to two local message boards, seven newsgroups and two mailing lists—all available for problem solving.
Subj: Re:Off AOL but on Internet
Date: 5/20/95 11:43:26 AM
From: CJ Jon
Hmmm .. that *is* strange ...
First .. if you were already signed on .. and tried to sign on again, AOL wouldn't let you, so either A) you were signed off, or B) you never actually signed off ..
Did you re-dial the number and everything?
Well .. in any event it would be interesting to know if you could re-create the situation! Be sure to report it at keyword: HELP.
.oO
jon
ME needs help, posts a request for information, and receives a Cyber-Jockey reply two hours later.

Figure 4-12: The Internet Exchange offers a comprehensive help compilation at keywords: **Net Exchange**.

aol.newsgroups.help

Finally, be sure to subscribe to the **aol.newsgroups.help** newsgroup (it is part of the default newsgroup subscription list—you're probably already subscribed). This is the most active location for newsgroup assistance, and it's not broadcast throughout the Internet—your questions are only seen by fellow AOL members, and your responses will come from fellow AOL members.

Netiquette

Nowhere is the etiquette of online conduct more critical (or more abused) than in newsgroups. Most *faux pas* are committed by newbies—people like you and me. The Internet is a community, after all: one with a particularly stalwart camaraderie and an intense adherence to a set of unwritten guidelines for interactions with others. Most specialized social organizations are that way, and to become a member of one without first becoming familiar with its catechism invites disgrace. A minicourse in Netiquette, then, might help:

- Having stung myself a number of times, I've taken to writing my missives and *waiting* for at least a couple of hours before posting them. I save them and recall them the next time I sign on. For some reason, this obliges me to read them again before I click the Post button—and it has often saved me considerable newsgroup face.
- There are real people on the other end of the line: people with emotions and feelings. Honor them.
- Honor yourself as well. You are known on the Net by what you write. Project the image you want others to see.
- Brevity is admirable; verbosity is disfavored (among other things, because it wastes time, disk space, and network bandwidth). Say what you have to say succinctly; your words will carry greater authority and impact.
- Read before writing. Add something to the conversation; don't simply repeat what's already been said. Subscribe to the **news.answers** newsgroup and read the Frequently Asked Questions file (FAQ) for your newsgroup before posting. By reading before you write you'll have a better sense of the tenor and conventions of the newsgroup to which you are posting.
- Quote the messages to which you're responding. Edit the quoted material for brevity (and indicate when you've done so); use the quoting fashion you see in other messages; and always acknowledge the person you're quoting. (Quoting is also discussed in Chapter 3, "Electronic Mail & the Personal Filing Cabinet.")

- Contribute something. Some people speak simply to be heard; these same people post mainly to see their material online. Don't contribute to the tedium: look for a new perspective, ask a probing question, make an insightful comment. If none come to mind, wait for another opportunity. There are plenty of opportunities on the Net; we all have something worthwhile to contribute eventually.
- Use Help. If the Help files described in this chapter don't answer your question, post a message in **aol.newsgroups.help**. Lots of people are willing to help you if you ask.

Emily Postnews

Brad Templeton originally created Emily Postnews a number of years ago; Steve Summit keeps her alive today. Emily is a satirical document, providing witty examples of what *not* to do when using newsgroups. Here's an example:

Q: What sort of tone should I take in my article?

A: Be as outrageous as possible. If you don't say outlandish things, and fill your article with libelous insults of net people, you may not stick out enough in the flood of articles to get a response. The more insane your posting looks, the more likely it is that you'll get lots of followups. The net is here, after all, so that you can get lots of attention. If your article is polite, reasoned and to the point, you may only get mailed replies. Yuck!"

Emily Postnews is posted every couple of months in the **news.answers** newsgroup. She might be satirical but she's effective at conveying the spirit of the newsgroup community without being condescending. Be sure to read her.

Gopher

Growth on the Internet is a stupendous thing. Most everyone agrees that it exceeds 100 percent a year; some contend that it's as high as 20 percent *per month.* Regardless of the figure, navigating the Net has become about as convenient as navigating the Atlantic Ocean: relatively easy if you have the right tools, but impractical—some might say perilous—if you don't.

One such tool is *Gopher*. Originating in 1991 at the University of Minnesota (where the school mascot is the Golden Gopher), Gopher is a system of sites containing amazing numbers of files (mostly text), all listed in hierarchical menus. All you have to do is keep choosing menu items until you find what you're after, then Gopher "goes for" (it's kind of a double pun: mascot and "gofer") your material on the Net.

People new to the Net tend to think of e-mail, Usenet, and the Web as the only resources available on the Internet. Those who do are doing themselves a lamentable disservice. The Gopher system has been around for over seven years now—nearly a third of the Internet's lifetime—and the amount of data that's stored there is extensive and for many Internet users, undiscovered (see Figure 4-13). And Gopher has a measurable advantage over many Web resources: it's fast. Most Gopher pages are textual, and a textual Gopher page transfers much more quickly than a Web page filled with graphics and links.

Gopher
Quick Go
Message Boards
Your Favorite Places
Gopher Software
About Gopher
GOPHER
Search
What is Gopher?
Gopher Treasures
Gopher Directory
Help

Figure 4-13: The keyword: **Gopher** takes you to AOL's Gopher service where vast—and often overlooked—Internet resources await your exploration.

The Gopher system is actually composed of a number of *Gopher servers* located around the world. Each server is like a good librarian: it organizes content for your convenience. (Librarians organize libraries with card files; Gophers organize the Internet's content with menus.) When you find what you're looking for, the Gopher retrieves the information for you. Better yet, Gophers reference other Gophers: AOL's Gopher, for example, offers access to hundreds of other Gophers. It's as if you were given access to a librarian's convention, and the librarians, every one, brought their card files with them.

Though there are a number of Gopher servers, you're rarely aware of them individually: AOL simply groups them all into one massive menu tree that you're free to peruse as you wish. In a way, that's too bad, because you're usually unaware of the vast distances you're traveling when you access the various Gopher servers on AOL's menus. You might be in Switzerland one moment and Germany the next. That's the nature of the Net: distance has no meaning in cyberspace.

That's about all there is to lament, however. AOL wraps up Gopher in a fine cloak of colors, offering its Gopher menus in the Web browser window, where everything is familiar and comfortable. If you're used to browsing the Web, you won't have any trouble using Gopher. In fact, some folks are beginning to rediscover Gopher, thanks to some enterprising individuals who are making Gopher content available via the Web.

The Comics Come to the Net

The original Gopher server at the University of Minnesota was established to bring convenience to the Net. Since copies of all the Internet sites' directories were stored on the server, searching was local. No time was spent connecting to and disconnecting from the individual sites during the data searches.

In time, more Gopher servers came along. There are scores of them now, and searching the *servers* has become a task.

Enter *Veronica*, a tool that is a database of the Gophers' directories.

Prior to Veronica, some wag of a programmer created a utility to search FTP sites, and called it Archie. Not to be outdone, another programmer created a Gopherspace search tool and named it Veronica (for the *Archie* comic book character). She was followed shortly by Jughead, another Gopher searcher. Searching for a name for your latest creation? Pick up the nearest literature—Betty and Moose can't be far behind.

To access Veronica, click the Search button in the main Gopher window—the one with a gopher wearing a hard hat. Be warned: Veronica is *not* fast, and AOL has no control over that. It's just that way.

If you know how to use the Web, you already know how to use AOL's Gopher interface. Take a moment to look at Figure 4-14.

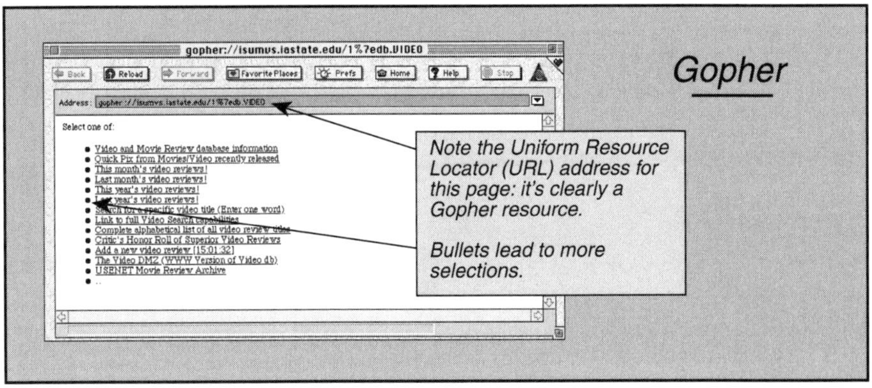
Gopher
Note the Uniform Resource Locator (URL) address for this page: it's clearly a Gopher resource.
Bullets lead to more selections.

Figure 4-14: America Online's Gopher uses the Web's familiar interface.

Like the World Wide Web, the Gopher system invites exploration. It's easy to use, it's one of the Internet's most rewarding resources, and it's always available at keyword: **Gopher**.

FTP

Gopher, newsgroups, and the Web are nifty tools, but what if you want more direct access? What if you want to log on to another machine on the Net, see a directory of its files, and download a few of them? We're talking now about the "engine room" of the Internet, where you access other machines' files as if they were on your own hard drive. FTP, or *File Transfer Protocol*, provides that kind of access; it's how you download files (including programs, sound, sound video, and graphics) from other machines.

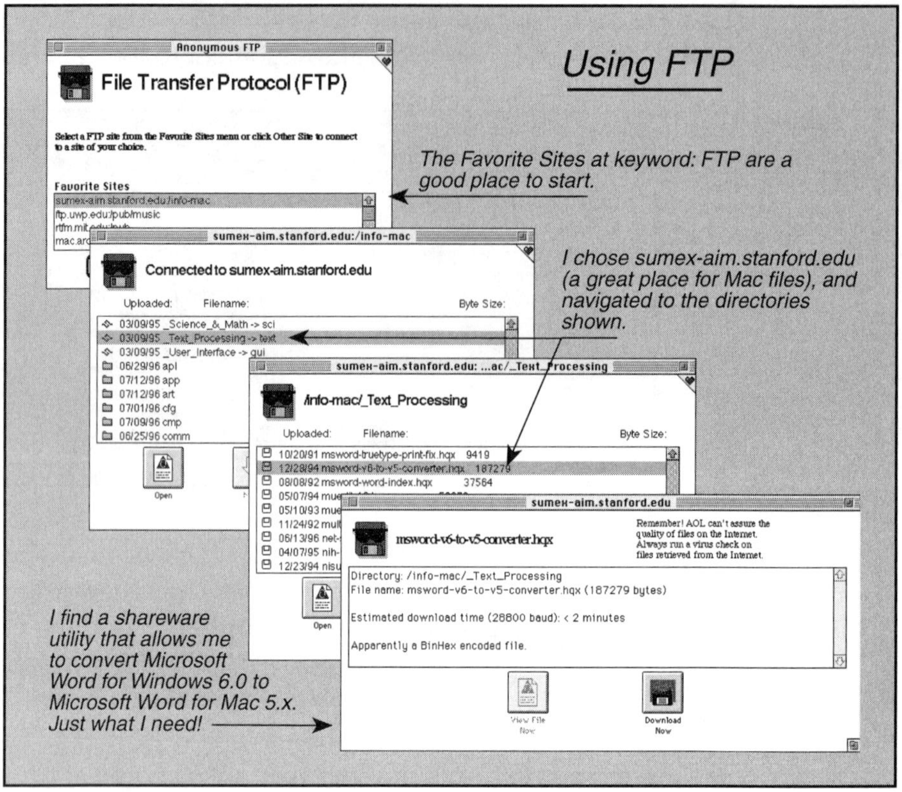
Using FTP
The Favorite Sites at keyword: FTP are a good place to start.
I chose sumex-aim.stanford.edu (a great place for Mac files), and navigated to the directories shown.
I find a shareware utility that allows me to convert Microsoft Word for Windows 6.0 to Microsoft Word for Mac 5.x. Just what I need!
Anonymous FTP
File Transfer Protocol (FTP)
Favorite Sites
sumex-aim.stanford.edu:/info-mac
Connected to sumex-aim.stanford.edu
/info-mac/_Text_Processing
mswrd-v6-to-v5-converter.hqx
Directory: /info-mac/_Text_Processing
File name: msword-v6-to-v5-converter.hqx (187279 bytes)
Estimated download time (28800 baud): < 2 minutes
Apparently a BinHex encoded file.
Download Now

Figure 4-15: Using FTP to download a Mac program that converts Microsoft Word files.

FTP is two things, actually. First, it's a protocol, allowing machines on the Net to exchange data (files) without concern for the type of machine that originated the file, the file's original format, or even the operating systems of the machines involved. FTP is also a *program* that enables FTP. Just as the word *telephone* denotes both a device you hold in your hand and a system for international communications, FTP is both the message and the medium.

The term also is used as both noun ("It's available via FTP") and verb ("FTP to **ftp.aol.com** and look in the pub directory"). It's hard to misuse the term, in other words. Just don't try to make a word out of "FTP" when you say it aloud—always use the initials.

Anonymous FTP

Originally, most FTP sessions occurred between a site and a person at a remote location who had an account at that site. The person would log on by supplying an account name and a password, then conduct the appropriate file activities.

The need soon became apparent, however, for less restrictive access. What if a site wanted to post a file for *anyone* to download? A number of publicly funded agencies required such an arrangement. NASA's space images, as an example, are funded by public money; therefore, it was decided that the public should have access to them.

The solution they came up with was *anonymous FTP*. During an anonymous FTP session, the user logs on to the remote site using the account name "anonymous" (AOL does this for you unless you supply a specific username). The password for anonymous login, typically, is the user's Internet address—a common courtesy so the people at the remote site can determine, if they wish, who is using their system. Again, AOL does this for you unless you supply a specific password.

Operating FTP successfully and acquiring a library of fertile FTP locations (and knowing when to access them) is a skill worthy of pursuing, but it *does* require time to develop. Begin by reading the Help files available at the keyword: **FTP** (and pictured in Figure 4-11), and practice for a while using AOL's "Favorite Sites" pictured in Figure 4-15. If you feel you need more help, post questions on the Internet Connection message boards. AOL's community is always ready to help you learn.

Telnet

Yet one more tool remains for us to discover: Telnet. A number of Internet users require operating-system access to machines on the Net, not for the purpose of transferring files (which is FTP's job) but to run programs on those remote machines. Often these programs are games, but chat applications are common as well; so are databases.

People who require Telnet access to the Internet have specific needs, and most of these people have favorite programs—Telnet clients—that they prefer to use for the task. This isn't a situation where AOL can provide a client for you; Telnet is too idiosyncratic for that.

Instead, AOL provides a "socket" into which you plug your Telnet client. The AOL client—your AOL software—recedes to the background under these circumstances, and the Telnet client assumes command. At AOL's end, signals from your computer are routed directly to the remote computer you're accessing. AOL's host computers remain transparent until your Telnet session concludes.

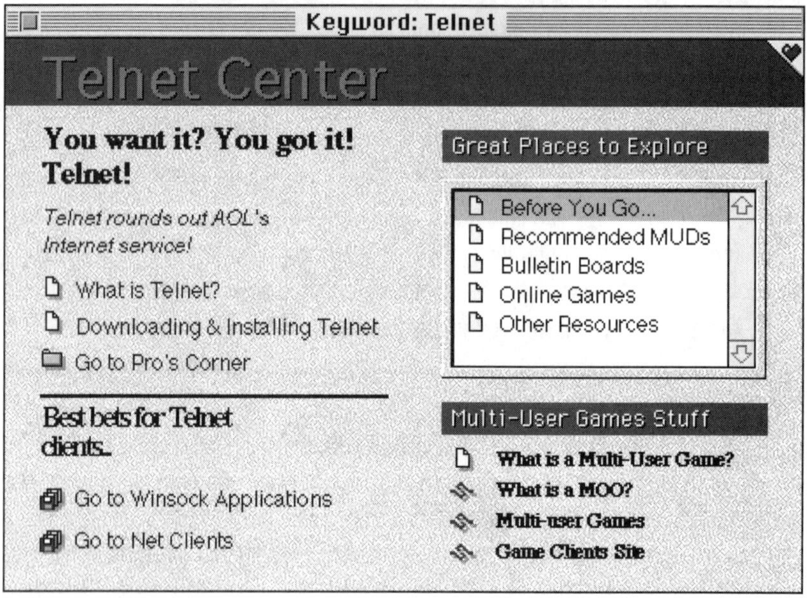
Keyword: Telnet
Telnet Center
You want it? You got it! Telnet!
Telnet rounds out AOL's Internet service!
What is Telnet?
Downloading & Installing Telnet
Go to Pro's Corner
Best bets for Telnet clients.
Go to Winsock Applications
Go to Net Clients
Great Places to Explore
Before You Go...
Recommended MUDs
Bulletin Boards
Online Games
Other Resources
Multi-User Games Stuff
What is a Multi-User Game?
What is a MOO?
Multi-user Games
Game Clients Site

Figure 4-16: Telnet allows you to connect the client of your choosing directly to the Internet.

If you require Telnet access to the Net, use the keyword: **Telnet**. You'll find plenty of information there to get you started. Take the time to review the informational resources pictured in Figure 4-16 if you're not already familiar with this technology.

AnswerMan

Speaking of a community that's eager to help you learn, if you want to learn more about the Internet, use the keyword: **AnswerMan**, and investigate the AnswerMan area (see Figure 4-17). It's intended for newcomers to the Internet who might be feeling a bit overwhelmed by it all. AnswerMan doesn't have all of the answers, but he does have a message board to which he replies (click the Ask AnswerMan Message Boards button). His live appearances are frequent and informative (click the Sunday AnswerMan Chat button for a schedule). AnswerMan Answers provides quick responses to some of the most frequently asked questions from the AnswerMan message boards. Be sure to check it out.

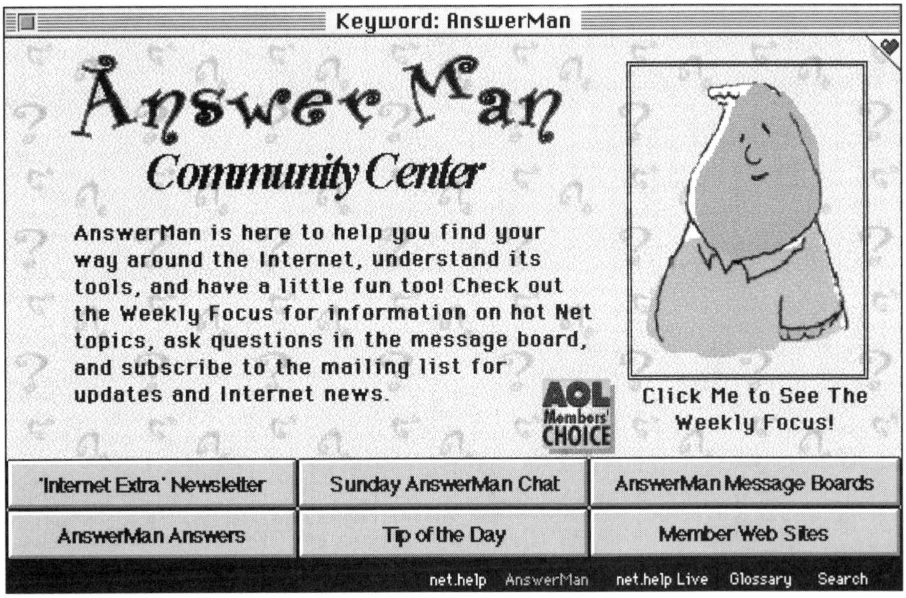
Keyword: AnswerMan
AnswerMan
Community Center
AnswerMan is here to help you find your way around the Internet, understand its tools, and have a little fun too! Check out the Weekly Focus for information on hot Net topics, ask questions in the message board, and subscribe to the mailing list for updates and Internet news.
AOL Members' CHOICE
Click Me to See The Weekly Focus!
'Internet Extra' Newsletter
Sunday AnswerMan Chat
AnswerMan Message Boards
AnswerMan Answers
Tip of the Day
Member Web Sites
net.help
AnswerMan
net.help Live
Glossary
Search

Figure 4-17: Find answers to your Internet questions at keyword: **AnswerMan**.

Moving On

Each Internet resource described on these pages is an existing AOL feature. Others will no doubt come along. That's part of the fun of telecommunications: this is just the beginning, and there's always more to come. Becoming a member of AOL (and exploring the Internet) is a little like planting a fruit tree: there are many rewards (blossoms, bees, fruit, firewood), and each year there's a more bountiful harvest than there was the year before.

It's positively organic. ;-)

In this chapter, we might have temporarily lost our focus. This is a book about America Online, not the Internet, and AOL offers a motherlode of resources for the intrepid electronic explorer. Many of these appear in the form of files: programs, graphics, fonts, sounds, and video ready for transfer to your computer at the click of a mouse. It's remarkably easy to do, and we will discuss all of these file types in the next chapter.

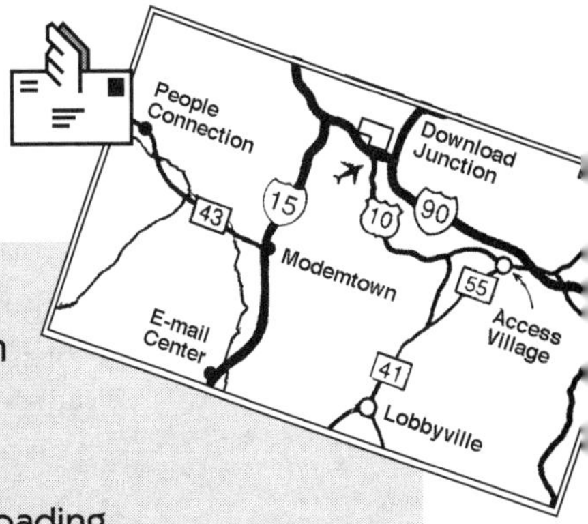
People Connection
Download Junction
15
43
10
90
Modemtown
55
Access Village
E-mail Center
41
Lobbyville

CHAPTER 5

Transferring Files

- What Is Downloading
- A Downloading Session
- Downloading the File
- Multitasking
- Finding Files for Downloading
- File Formats & File Compression
- Download 101
- Uploading Files

A community leader wrote to me the other day. "If I had a nickel for every time I was asked how to download or what a download is," she said, "I would be a rich woman."

Exaggeration, perhaps—it takes 20,000,000 nickels to make a millionaire—but her message is clear: people want to know what this "downloading" business is all about. And, well they should: downloading is one of the top five activities people do online, and more than 100,000 files are available for downloading on AOL, spread across the service like flowers in a meadow. Members graze this meadow, smiling, downloading bouquets of files. People must be on to something here, and those who aren't want to be. A chapter on the subject seems warranted. Here it is.

What Is Downloading?

Simply put, *downloading* is the process of transferring files—for example, transferring a file from AOL's computers to a disk in your computer. Files can be programs, utilities, drivers, fonts, graphics (many of the graphics in this book have been downloaded), sound, animation, and, of course, text. On AOL, downloads don't cost extra money: your normal AOL access charges are in effect whenever you download; you pay nothing additional for this privilege.

And that's it. You may have heard horror stories about downloading, but they probably had something to do with computer viruses or complex downloading protocols. Fortunately, those are things of the past. All of the appropriate files on AOL are checked for viruses before they're made available for downloading, and AOL's software handles the protocols automatically.

Note: This chapter discusses the process of downloading files stored in AOL's libraries. Another form of downloading—FTP, or File Transfer Protocol—has to do with downloading files stored on the Internet, via AOL. There's a considerable difference. File Transfer Protocol is discussed in Chapter 4, "Using the Internet."

A Downloading Session

Perhaps the best way to explain downloading is to download a file for you and explain the process as it's happening. If your computer is nearby, you might want to sign on and follow along.

Finding the File

Before you can download a file, you have to find it. There are lots of ways to find files, but for the purposes of this exercise, we'll go directly to a known location. Later, we'll discuss methods of finding a file when its location is *not* known, or when the name of the file isn't at hand.

Begin by signing on and using the keywords: **Mac Utilities**. Though we'll discuss forums in Chapter 9, "Boards & Forums," it's enough for the moment for you to know that most forums offer libraries, as does this one. Simply stated, a *library* is an online reservoir of files. Some of these files are placed online by the forum's staff; others are uploaded by AOL members (I'll discuss uploading later in this chapter). There's usually a forum staff member who maintains the library, checking files for viruses, clarifying file descriptions, and removing outdated entries.

By now you should see the Software Libraries button in the Macintosh Utilities Forum window. Click it (see Figure 5-1).

Figure 5-1: The Macintosh Utilities Forum is an especially rewarding place to find Mac files for downloading.

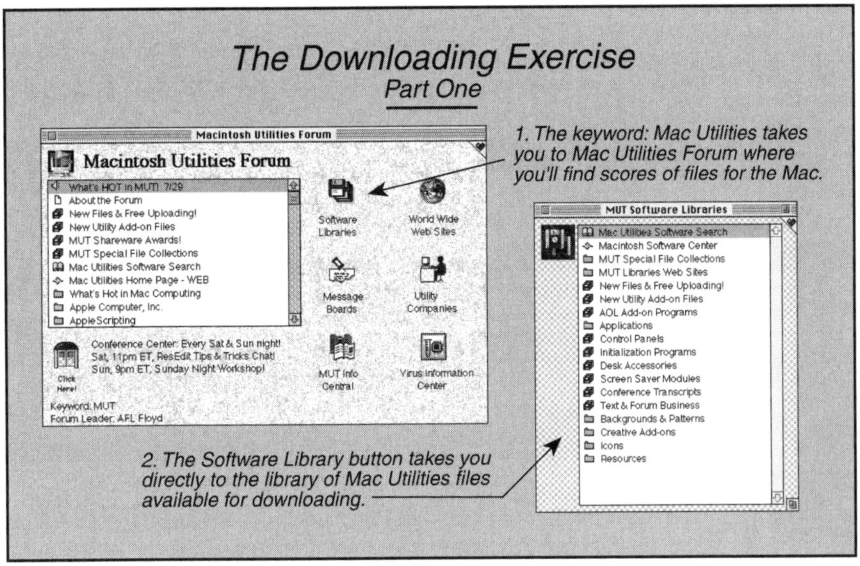
The Downloading Exercise
Part One
Macintosh Utilities Forum
Macintosh Utilities Forum
What's HOT in MUT! 7/29
About the Forum
New Files & Free Uploading!
New Utility Add-on Files
MUT Shareware Awards!
MUT Special File Collections
Mac Utilities Software Search
Mac Utilities Home Page - WEB
What's Hot in Mac Computing
Apple Computer, Inc.
AppleScripting
Software Libraries
World Wide Web Sites
Message Boards
Utility Companies
MUT Info Central
Virus Information Center
Conference Center: Every Sat & Sun night! Sat, 11pm ET, ResEdit Tips & Tricks Chat! Sun, 9pm ET, Sunday Night Workshop!
Click Here!
Keyword: MUT
Forum Leader: AFL Floyd
1. The keyword: Mac Utilities takes you to Mac Utilities Forum where you'll find scores of files for the Mac.
MUT Software Libraries
Mac Utilities Software Search
Macintosh Software Center
MUT Special File Collections
MUT Libraries Web Sites
New Files & Free Uploading!
New Utility Add-on Files
AOL Add-on Programs
Applications
Control Panels
Initialization Programs
Desk Accessories
Screen Saver Modules
Conference Transcripts
Text & Forum Business
Backgrounds & Patterns
Creative Add-ons
Icons
Resources
2. The Software Library button takes you directly to the library of Mac Utilities files available for downloading.

Writing on Water

This exercise is a litany of specifics, and when it comes to the telecommunications industry, describing specifics is like writing on water. By the time you read this, the appearance of the Mac Utilities Forum may have changed, the forum's libraries might have been restructured, and StuffIt Lite 3.5 could have been superseded by a new version.

Assuming this *fait accompli*, I suggest adaptability. A forum of some kind for Macintosh utilities will always exist, and so will its file libraries. StuffIt will probably be with us for a long time, though you might find a later version online when you conduct your search. Tolerate change, and your online life—not to mention your experience with this book—will come a lot easier.

Click the Software Libraries button pictured in Figure 5-1. The Mac Utilities Software Libraries window will appear, offering a variety of categories of files.

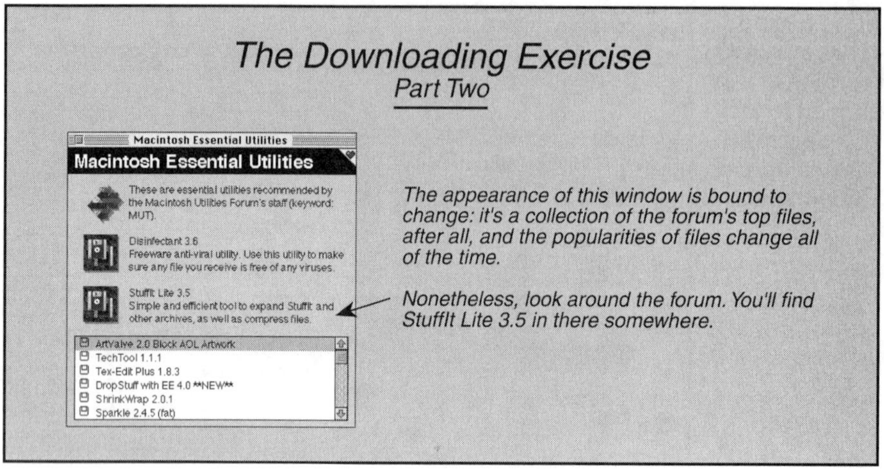
The Downloading Exercise
Part Two
Macintosh Essential Utilities
Macintosh Essential Utilities
These are essential utilities recommended by the Macintosh Utilities Forum's staff (keyword: MUT).
Disinfectant 3.6
Freeware anti-viral utility. Use this utility to make sure any file you receive is free of any viruses.
StuffIt Lite 3.5
Simple and efficient tool to expand StuffIt and other archives, as well as compress files.
ArtValve 2.0 Block AOL Artwork
TechTool 1.1.1
Tex-Edit Plus 1.8.3
DropStuff with EE 4.0 **NEW**
ShrinkWrap 2.0.1
Sparkle 2.4.5 (fat)
The appearance of this window is bound to change: it's a collection of the forum's top files, after all, and the popularities of files change all of the time.
Nonetheless, look around the forum. You'll find StuffIt Lite 3.5 in there somewhere.

Figure 5-2: StuffIt Lite is one of the forum's most popular shareware offerings.

StuffIt

You can't survive long in the downloading environment without some form of compression/decompression software. Compression and decompression are as common to downloading files as stink is to skunks. Though I'll discuss file compression later in this chapter, you're going to need file compression software eventually, and now's a good time to get some. StuffIt is an excellent choice, and since this exercise requires that you download something, we might as well make it something useful.

Downloading the File

StuffIt Lite (see Figure 5-2) is appropriate to my needs. I found it by first selecting the MUT Special File Collections shown in Figure 5-1 and then opening the Macintosh Essential Utilities folder. To download it, I double-click it, then click the Download Now button in the file description window that results. The standard Macintosh file-saving window appears next. Choose a place for StuffIt on your hard disk, then click the Save button. The progress indicator shown in Figure 5-3 appears, estimating the amount of time required to download the file and providing visual indication of the file's progress. When the transfer is finished, the process concludes. It's as easy as that.

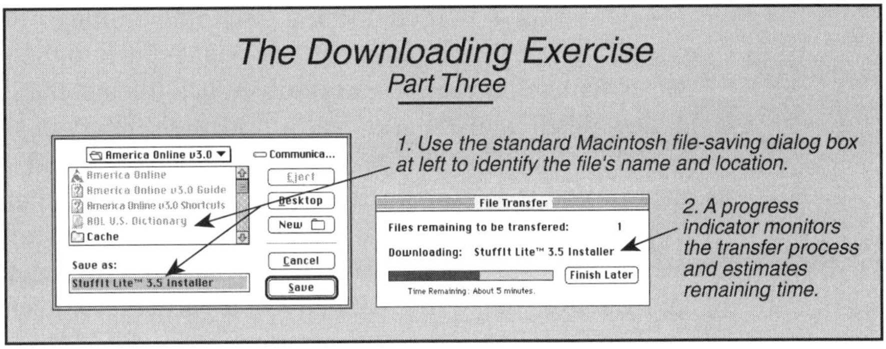
The Downloading Exercise
Part Three
America Online v3.0
Communica...
America Online
America Online v3.0 Guide
America Online v3.0 Shortcuts
AOL U.S. Dictionary
Cache
Eject
Desktop
New
Save as:
StuffIt Lite™ 3.5 Installer
Cancel
Save
1. Use the standard Macintosh file-saving dialog box at left to identify the file's name and location.
File Transfer
Files remaining to be transfered: 1
Downloading: StuffIt Lite™ 3.5 Installer
Finish Later
Time Remaining: About 5 minutes.
2. A progress indicator monitors the transfer process and estimates remaining time.

Figure 5-3: Determine where you want the file to go on your hard disk, then click Save. The remainder of the transfer is automatic.

Filenames & Destinations

Look again at Figure 5-3 and note the proposed filename. If you want to use a filename other than the one proposed, all you have to do is select the name (if it isn't selected already) and start typing. I don't recommend this, unless the proposed filename conflicts with one already on your disk. The file's documentation, for example, might refer to the file by the original name; if you change the name, the reference might be unclear. Also, forum discussions might refer to the file's original name. If you search for an update to the file, you'll need to use its original name. So stick to the original name unless you have a good reason not to.

The **America Online v3.0** folder pictured in Figure 5-3 is the default destination for downloaded files. Some would say that this folder isn't the best place to use: there will no doubt be an update to Version 3.0 some day, and when it comes along you will probably make a new folder for it—something like **America Online v3.5**. When the installation of the update is complete, you might be tempted to delete the old **America Online v3.0** folder, forgetting that you have a number of valuable downloads in there. By the time you remember, it might be too late. The file-saving dialog box in Figure 5-3 allows you to declare any folder on any disk as a destination. Don't hesitate to change the destination.

Sign off now if you've nothing else to do online (the Sign Off command is under the Go To menu). Navigate back to the folder where you downloaded StuffIt, and double-click the installer file you downloaded. StuffIt's installation is routine, with plenty of Help buttons available along the way. When installation is finished, open the "Read Me" file and then run StuffIt. That's the best way to get to know the program, and since this is a book about AOL—not StuffIt—I'll move on to a different subject now. The important thing to mention is that you have downloaded a file from AOL—a particularly useful file—and all you had to do was click a few buttons.

Multitasking

America Online offers three ways to download files: (1) You can simply click the Download Now button and sit in front of your machine like a fossil, watching all the excitement the progress indicator provides; (2) You can queue files for downloading and wait until the end of your online session (or for another part of the day) and download then (this is a function of the Download Manager, which we'll discuss in Chapter 6); or (3) You can do something else with your Mac while the download concludes in the background, like write that letter you owe your mother or pay the bills.

Doing more than one thing at a time with your computer is known as *multitasking*, and it might come as a surprise to you (even many veteran AOL members are ignorant of this feature) to discover that your AOL software offers true multitasking capabilities: start a download, then do something else with your Mac.

Here's how it's done:

- Sign on, locate the file you want to download, and start the downloading process.
- Once the progress indicator appears (pictured in Figure 5-3), you can do whatever you please with the applications on your computer, including the AOL application itself. If you want to read mail or visit a forum, do it. If you want to use another application on your computer, use the pull-down menu in the upper right corner of your screen to either select the application or return to the Finder. AOL will continue downloading in the background in either case.

When the download concludes, AOL will announce that it has completed the task.

With all that said, a few caveats are in order:

- You will notice some degradation in your computer's performance. It's doing double duty after all, and each task gets its little slice of your computer's power.
- Some software doesn't tolerate multitasking very well, especially software that relies heavily on disk activity or your computer's central processing unit. Games are notoriously unsuited to the multitasking environment.
- If you've got lights on your modem, watch them. If the Receive Data (RD) light goes out or flickers badly while you're multitasking, you're asking too much of your system. Let AOL have your system to itself while you stretch a bit or go for a walk. If that won't do, find another task to perform with your computer that isn't quite so demanding.

Multitasking seems a bit magical to me, and at first I didn't trust it. But it works. In three years, I've never had a download go bad or a file become corrupted because of a multitasking problem. In fact, I'm writing this sentence as a download is underway. It's a great way to magnify your potential.

Finding Files for Downloading

Now that you've seen how easy it is to download a file, you probably have come to realize that it isn't downloading that requires your understanding, it's *finding the files* for downloading. AOL offers over 100,000 of them, after all, and like prospecting for gold, the search is 99 percent of the expedition.

Searching through 100,000 files would be a horrendous task were it not for AOL's searchable database of online files. This database contains information on all of the files stored in the computing forums, and it's constantly maintained. Every file in the computing forums' libraries appears in this database within a few hours after it's posted. As you might expect, access to the database requires only a click of your mouse.

Finding Files While You're Online

There are two ways you can find files while you're online: you can search for them or you can browse among them. Searching implies that you know what you're looking for; browsing is a more leisurely activity. Each requires its own strategy.

File Search

You can search at any time, from any place online—you don't have to be in a specific forum to do so. All you have to do is click the disk-and-magnifier button on the toolbar (see Figure 5-4).

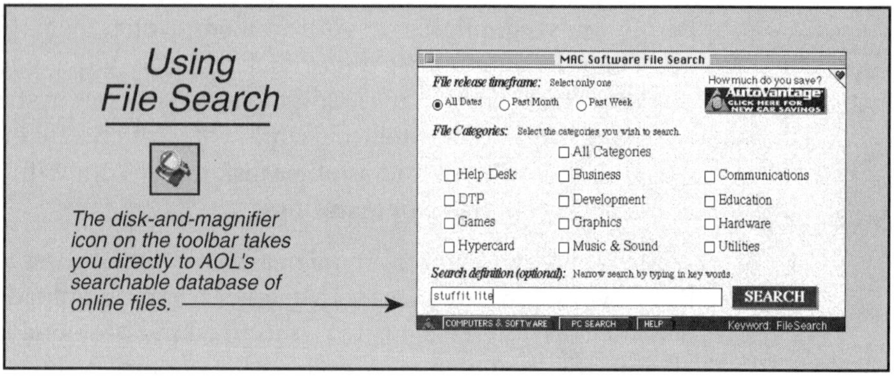
Using
File Search
The disk-and-magnifier icon on the toolbar takes you directly to AOL's searchable database of online files.
MAC Software File Search
File release timeframe: Select only one
All Dates
Past Month
Past Week
How much do you save?
File Categories: Select the categories you wish to search.
All Categories
Help Desk
Business
Communications
DTP
Development
Education
Games
Graphics
Hardware
Hypercard
Music & Sound
Utilities
Search definition (optional): Narrow search by typing in key words.
stuffit lite
SEARCH
COMPUTERS & SOFTWARE
PC SEARCH
HELP
Keyword: FileSearch

Figure 5-4: Using either the disk-and-magnifier button on the toolbar or the keywords: **File Search** takes you directly to a database of files stored on AOL. There you can enter specific criteria to help you find exactly the file you want.

Look again at the Software File Search dialog box pictured in Figure 5-4. Two sets of check boxes are provided: you can specify only those files that have been uploaded recently (the Past Week option is great for finding only new files), or only those files that fit certain criteria.

More important, there's also a text box within the File Search dialog. Here you can specify your own criteria. Words entered here are matched against keywords appearing in the following areas:

- The person who uploaded the file.
- The file's name.
- The subject line.
- Keywords assigned to the file.

There are three special words you can use in a match phrase: AND, OR, and NOT. I might receive dozens of matches to the search phrase "Versailles," most of which would be references to the suburb of Paris or the palace, not to my objective—the Versailles font. The search phrase "Versailles AND font," on the other hand, narrows the search. (The AND modifier is the default, by the way. Whenever more than one word appears in a search phrase, AOL assumes there's an AND between them. Thus the phrase "Versailles AND font" is the same as the phrase "Versailles font.")

Perhaps you want the Utopia font as well as the Versailles font. Here is where the OR modifier comes in. The phrase "Versailles OR Utopia" finds either one.

The NOT modifier narrows the search by excluding material matching the criterion that follows it. The phrase "Versailles NOT France" would provide a listing of all references to Versailles that aren't associated with France.

Combining modifiers can be unclear. The phrase "Versailles OR Utopia AND font" is ambiguous. Do we mean "Versailles, or Utopia and font," or do we mean "Versailles or Utopia, and font"? To clarify, use parentheses. The phrase "(Versailles OR Utopia) AND font" says "look for Versailles or Utopia, excluding everything but fonts from either category." It pays to be specific.

File Descriptions

In my haste to download StuffIt, I neglected to fully explain an important item: the file description. Every file offers one—it's the window with the Download Now and Download Later buttons in it—and you must display this window before you can download the file. Be sure to read these descriptions! Figure 5-5 pictures StuffIt's file description.

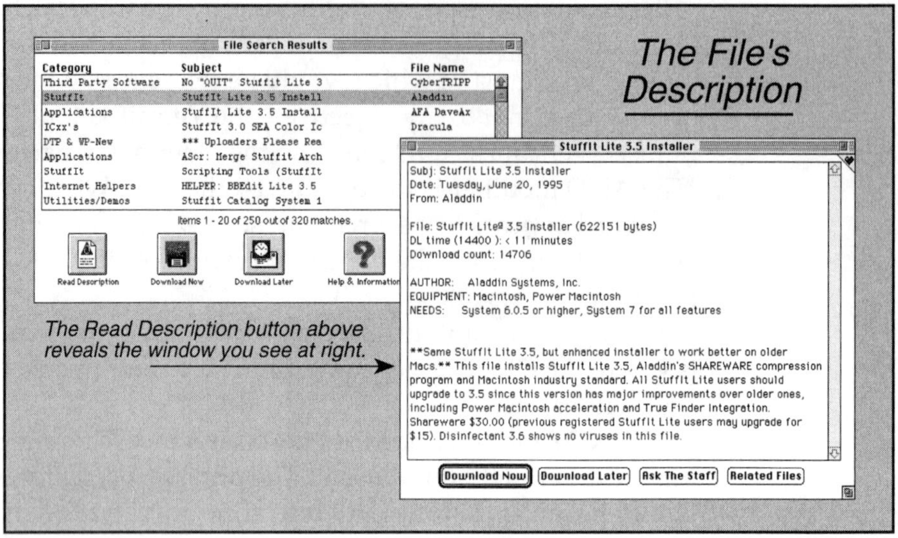
File Search Results
Category
Subject
File Name
Third Party Software
No "QUIT" Stuffit Lite 3
CyberTRIPP
StuffIt
StuffIt Lite 3.5 Install
Aladdin
Applications
StuffIt Lite 3.5 Install
AFA DaveAx
ICxx's
StuffIt 3.0 SEA Color Ic
Dracula
DTP & WP-New
*** Uploaders Please Rea
Applications
AScr: Merge Stuffit Arch
StuffIt
Scripting Tools (StuffIt
Internet Helpers
HELPER: BBEdit Lite 3.5
Utilities/Demos
Stuffit Catalog System 1
Items 1 - 20 of 250 out of 320 matches.
Read Description
Download Now
Download Later
Help & Information
The File's Description
StuffIt Lite 3.5 Installer
Subj: StuffIt Lite 3.5 Installer
Date: Tuesday, June 20, 1995
From: Aladdin
File: StuffIt Lite® 3.5 Installer (622151 bytes)
DL time (14400): < 11 minutes
Download count: 14706
AUTHOR: Aladdin Systems, Inc.
EQUIPMENT: Macintosh, Power Macintosh
NEEDS: System 6.0.5 or higher, System 7 for all features
Same StuffIt Lite 3.5, but enhanced installer to work better on older Macs. This file installs StuffIt Lite 3.5, Aladdin's SHAREWARE compression program and Macintosh industry standard. All StuffIt Lite users should upgrade to 3.5 since this version has major improvements over older ones, including Power Macintosh acceleration and True Finder Integration. Shareware $30.00 (previous registered StuffIt Lite users may upgrade for $15). Disinfectant 3.6 shows no viruses in this file.
Download Now
Download Later
Ask The Staff
Related Files
The Read Description button above reveals the window you see at right.

Figure 5-5: Read file descriptions before you download.

When I click Figure 5-5's Read Description button, AOL provides a complete description of the file. This intermediate step is critical. There are lots of things I need to know about this file before I can decide whether to download it.

Let's look at StuffIt's file description in its entirety (see Figure 5-6).

Figure 5-6:
A wealth of information is found in file descriptions.

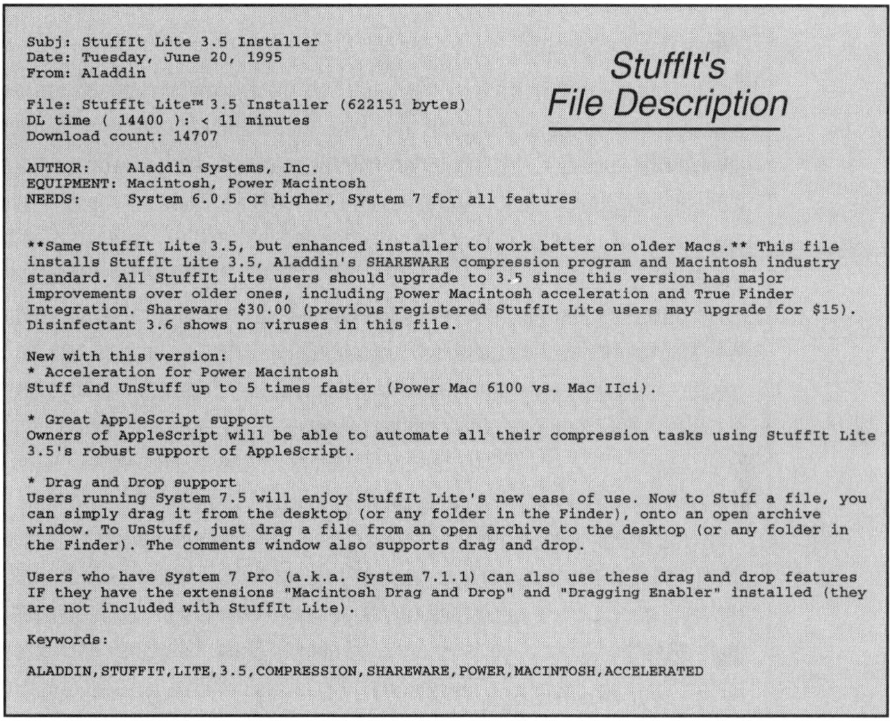
StuffIt's
File Description

Subj: StuffIt Lite 3.5 Installer
Date: Tuesday, June 20, 1995
From: Aladdin

File: StuffIt Lite™ 3.5 Installer (622151 bytes)
DL time (14400): < 11 minutes
Download count: 14707

AUTHOR: Aladdin Systems, Inc.
EQUIPMENT: Macintosh, Power Macintosh
NEEDS: System 6.0.5 or higher, System 7 for all features

Same StuffIt Lite 3.5, but enhanced installer to work better on older Macs. This file installs StuffIt Lite 3.5, Aladdin's SHAREWARE compression program and Macintosh industry standard. All StuffIt Lite users should upgrade to 3.5 since this version has major improvements over older ones, including Power Macintosh acceleration and True Finder Integration. Shareware $30.00 (previous registered StuffIt Lite users may upgrade for $15). Disinfectant 3.6 shows no viruses in this file.

New with this version:
* Acceleration for Power Macintosh
Stuff and UnStuff up to 5 times faster (Power Mac 6100 vs. Mac IIci).

* Great AppleScript support
Owners of AppleScript will be able to automate all their compression tasks using StuffIt Lite 3.5's robust support of AppleScript.

* Drag and Drop support
Users running System 7.5 will enjoy StuffIt Lite's new ease of use. Now to Stuff a file, you can simply drag it from the desktop (or any folder in the Finder), onto an open archive window. To UnStuff, just drag a file from an open archive to the desktop (or any folder in the Finder). The comments window also supports drag and drop.

Users who have System 7 Pro (a.k.a. System 7.1.1) can also use these drag and drop features IF they have the extensions "Macintosh Drag and Drop" and "Dragging Enabler" installed (they are not included with StuffIt Lite).

Keywords:

ALADDIN, STUFFIT, LITE, 3.5, COMPRESSION, SHAREWARE, POWER, MACINTOSH, ACCELERATED

The *Subj, Date, From,* and *File* lines are all searchable criteria. Don't confuse the From line with the AUTHOR line. The From line contains the name of the person who uploaded the file. That person is often a Forum Assistant or another member, not the author as it is in this case.

Note that the File line tells you both the file's name and its size. *File* indicates the actual name of the file as it will download to your machine. This is what you'll see in the Finder after you've downloaded the file.

The *Date* is used when you specify "All Dates," "Past month" or "Past week" in the File Search dialog box.

What Is Shareware?

You might note that StuffIt is *shareware*. There are two major channels for the distribution of computer programs and data. The traditional commercial channel involves the publisher, the distributor, and the retailer—each of whom, in order to make a living, must add a bit to the cost of the product. There's a considerable distance between the creator of the software and the people who purchase and use it.

A software product distributed by the alternative method is called *shareware*. With shareware, there's usually a direct connection between the user and the creator. Shareware programs and data are posted on telecommunications services like AOL, where they can be downloaded whenever we, the users, please. Individuals or user groups also can distribute shareware among themselves without fear of recrimination. As a rule, shareware authors welcome this kind of distribution.

If you download a shareware program, you normally get the complete program—not a "crippled" version. It usually comes with documentation as well. You can try it out for a few weeks before you decide to buy. If you decide to keep it, in most cases the author expects you to send money. Since the money goes directly to the author—no publishers, distributors, or retailers are involved—shareware theoretically can cost much less than commercially distributed software. The author's share is all you pay for shareware, and the author's share is a very small portion of the total cost of the software distributed through commercial channels.

With shareware, there's also a direct channel for communication between user and author. If you have a complaint or a suggestion for improvement, send e-mail to the author. Chances are you'll get a reply. This is a significant feature: to whom do you send mail if you think your car or your refrigerator can be improved? And do you really think anyone will ever reply?

While most shareware authors request financial remuneration, a few simply give their material away (freeware). Others request a postcard from your city or town (postcardware), or a donation to a favored charity.

The shareware system only works if users pay, and payment is voluntary. Sadly, only about 10 percent of the people who use shareware programs actually pay for them. This is undoubtedly the biggest fault in the shareware concept. Shareware can be a boon to us users, but only if we obey the honor code that's implicit in the system. In other words, if you use shareware, pay for it—and encourage others to do the same.

The *download time* (or *DL time)* is AOL's best guess as to how long it will take to download the file. The time is estimated based on the baud rate at which you're connected. If you're connected at 14,400 bps, the estimate is based on that baud rate. This number is only an estimate. If you signed on during a peak-use period (for example, around 9 p.m. Eastern time), this number might be slightly optimistic. If you're signed on at 4 a.m., this number will be pessimistic. I downloaded StuffIt—which AOL estimated to be an 11-minute download—in less than 10 minutes during a mid-morning session at 14,400 bps.

The *Download Count* is a rough indication of the file's popularity. If you're looking for a graphic of a cat, for example, and 40 files match your search criteria, you might let the number of downloads direct you. Often, however, the number of downloads says more about the catchiness of a file's name or description than it does about the nature or quality of its content. Sometimes you have to balance the download count and date to gauge the quality of a file. If something has been online for a year and only has 20 downloads, you can normally assume that it's of limited usefulness. StuffIt Lite 3.5, on the other hand, was uploaded in June of 1995, and by July of this year had already racked up over 14,000 downloads (in addition to the tens of thousands of downloads accumulated by previous versions). It's a pretty safe bet that this is a good program. You'll get a feel for this sort of thing as you peruse and sample the various files available.

The *Equipment* line, if present, indicates any hardware and/or software beyond a basic Mac you'll need to run the file. Sometimes, though, this line is used to indicate what hardware or software the author used to create the file.

The *Needs* line is critical: if your Mac isn't up to the task, or if you need special software, it's nice to know before you download the file. For example, you'll need System 7.0 or later to take advantage of all features in StuffIt Lite 3.5.

Keywords are those that provide matches when you enter your own search criteria. Read these. They offer valuable insight into how best to word your search phrases. For example, by reading the keywords for StuffIt Lite, I see that I could also have found it using the search phrase "Aladdin Compression." It's this versatility that makes AOL's file searches so easy and useful. That's how I knew to specify "StuffIt Lite" when I originally declared my search phrase. Keywords are assigned by the AOL staff to each file.

Note: In this context, a keyword is a word assigned to a shareware file that is used to help categorize and describe it for easy search and retrieval. These keywords are separate from and can't be used by AOL's navigational keyword function (accessed by typing Command-K or by clicking the Keyword button on the toolbar).

The *description* itself is provided by the person who uploaded the file. StuffIt's description, for example, indicates changes since the last update to the application—an important consideration if you have an earlier version.

File descriptions can be saved for later reference. Choose Save from the File menu before you close the description window. America Online will ask where you want to store the description. If you'd like to read it later with a word processor, save it in Text Only format from the File Type menu. Then it can be read offline (after you've saved it to a separate file) with any word processor or the AOL software (just choose Open from AOL's File menu).

Browsing for Files

File Search is not the only way to locate files while you're online. What if you're simply looking for a nice graphic? You don't necessarily know *which* graphic you're looking for, just a graphic.

Here's a real-life situation: The other day I needed a provocative graphic for use as Figure 4-1 in the previous chapter. I had no idea which graphic that would be, so File Search was out—"provocative" isn't a very precise search criterion.

An abyssal reservoir of graphics resides in the Mac Graphic Arts & CAD Forum. Whenever I'm in the mood for something pretty to brighten up my screen, or something intriguing to pique my visual curiosity, this is where I go to browse. (The Mac Graphic Arts & CAD Forum is discussed in Chapter 9, "Boards & Forums.")

I used the keywords: **Mac Graphics**, clicked the Software Libraries button, and began to browse (see Figure 5-7).

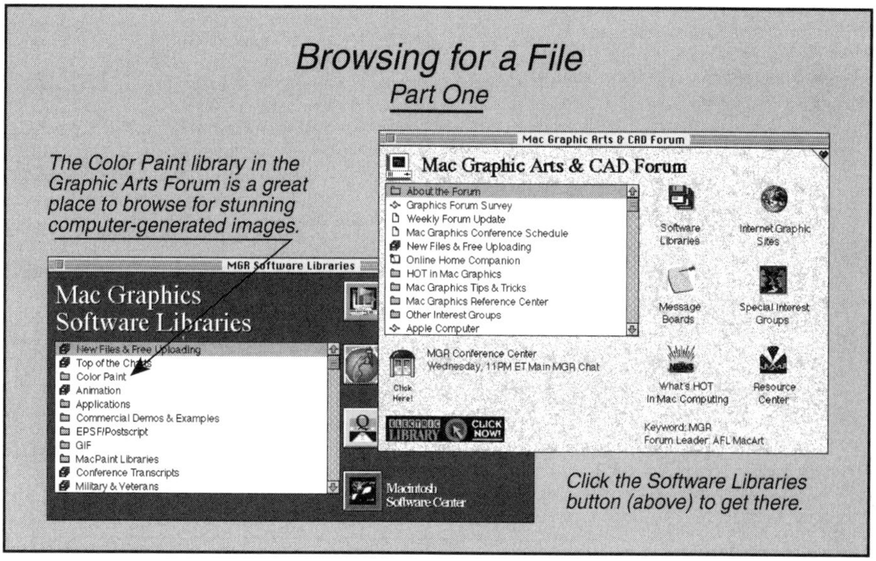
Browsing for a File
Part One
The Color Paint library in the Graphic Arts Forum is a great place to browse for stunning computer-generated images.
Mac Graphic Arts & CAD Forum
Mac Graphic Arts & CAD Forum
About the Forum
Graphics Forum Survey
Weekly Forum Update
Mac Graphics Conference Schedule
New Files & Free Uploading
Online Home Companion
HOT in Mac Graphics
Mac Graphics Tips & Tricks
Mac Graphics Reference Center
Other Interest Groups
Apple Computer
Software Libraries
Internet Graphic Sites
Message Boards
Special Interest Groups
MGR Conference Center
Wednesday, 11PM ET Main MGR Chat
Click Here!
What's HOT In Mac Computing
Resource Center
ELECTRIC LIBRARY
CLICK NOW!
Keyword: MGR
Forum Leader: AFL MacArt
MGR Software Libraries
Mac Graphics Software Libraries
New Files & Free Uploading
Top of the Charts
Color Paint
Animation
Applications
Commercial Demos & Examples
EPSF/Postscript
GIF
MacPaint Libraries
Conference Transcripts
Military & Veterans
Macintosh Software Center
Click the Software Libraries button (above) to get there.

Figure 5-7: The Mac Graphic Arts & CAD Forum at keywords: **Mac Graphics** is a great place to browse for images.

I know from experience that the Mac Graphic libraries contain thousands of particularly sublime images—the kind that make my books look better. I've seen a number of full-color images, many of which have been something of a heady experience, so I chose the Color Paint folder pictured in Figure 5-8. Within that folder, I browsed through many full-color paint images. These decisions are illustrated in Figure 5-8, along with the library listing for "The Internet 1," Jeff Stewart's evocative image of the Internet, which I eventually chose, to use as Figure 4-1.

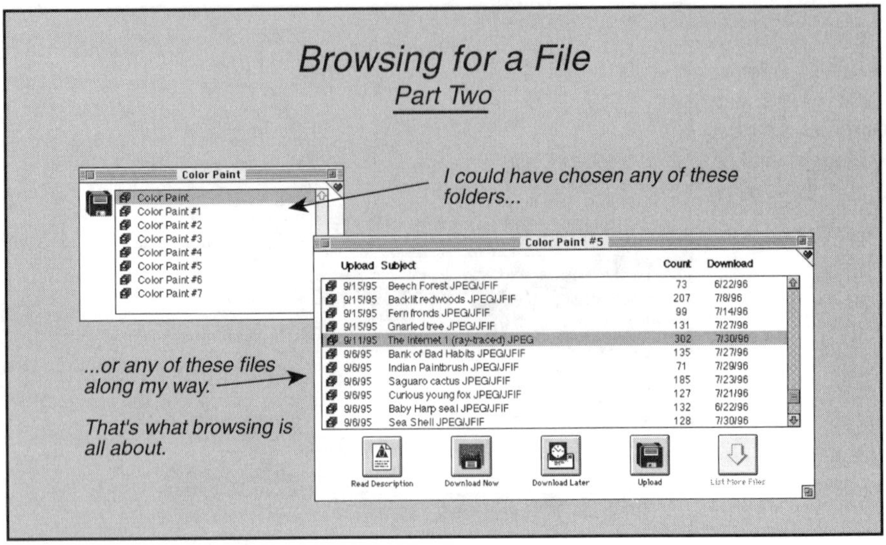
Browsing for a File
Part Two
Color Paint
Color Paint
Color Paint #1
Color Paint #2
Color Paint #3
Color Paint #4
Color Paint #5
Color Paint #6
Color Paint #7
I could have chosen any of these folders...
Color Paint #5
Upload Subject Count Download
9/15/95 Beech Forest JPEG/JFIF 73 6/22/96
9/15/95 Backlit redwoods JPEG/JFIF 207 7/8/96
9/15/95 Fern fronds JPEG/JFIF 99 7/14/96
9/15/95 Gnarled tree JPEG/JFIF 131 7/27/96
9/11/95 The Internet 1 (ray-traced) JPEG 302 7/30/96
9/6/95 Bank of Bad Habits JPEG/JFIF 135 7/27/96
9/6/95 Indian Paintbrush JPEG/JFIF 71 7/29/96
9/6/95 Saguaro cactus JPEG/JFIF 185 7/23/96
9/6/95 Curious young fox JPEG/JFIF 127 7/21/96
9/6/95 Baby Harp seal JPEG/JFIF 132 6/22/96
9/6/95 Sea Shell JPEG/JFIF 128 7/30/96
Read Description
Download Now
Download Later
Upload
List More Files
...or any of these files along my way.
That's what browsing is all about.

Figure 5-8: 24-bit rendered ray tracings are among the most captivating images available online.

Note that I could have chosen any other library or folder along the way. I could have browsed the Mac Graphics & CAD Forum for hours, peeking at thumbnails (see the "Thumbnails" sidebar) and downloading images that caught my eye. Browsing for files is a leisurely pursuit—most browsing is—with plenty of opportunity for detours and new discoveries. Finding files on AOL is like shopping: if you know what you're after, you can go directly to your destination and nab the merchandise; or you can meander, grazing in meadows of opportunity. The choice is yours.

Thumbnails

A feature recently added to the AOL software allows you to view *thumbnails* of graphics files before they're downloaded. This is a boon to members: thumbnails allow us to see a graphic before we spend time downloading it. Thumbnails appear in the top left corner of a graphics file's description window (see Figure 5-9). You can't miss them.

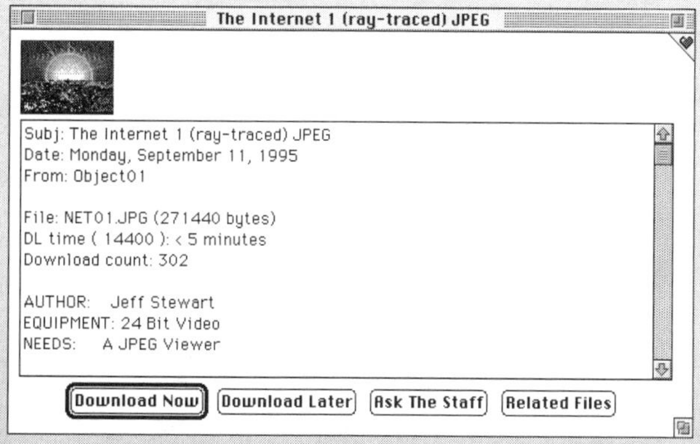
The Internet 1 (ray-traced) JPEG
Subj: The Internet 1 (ray-traced) JPEG
Date: Monday, September 11, 1995
From: Object01
File: NET01.JPG (271440 bytes)
DL time (14400): < 5 minutes
Download count: 302
AUTHOR: Jeff Stewart
EQUIPMENT: 24 Bit Video
NEEDS: A JPEG Viewer
Download Now
Download Later
Ask The Staff
Related Files

Figure 5-9: Most graphics offer thumbnail views so you can preview the graphic before you make the decision to download it. The thumbnail in this illustration is in the upper left corner.

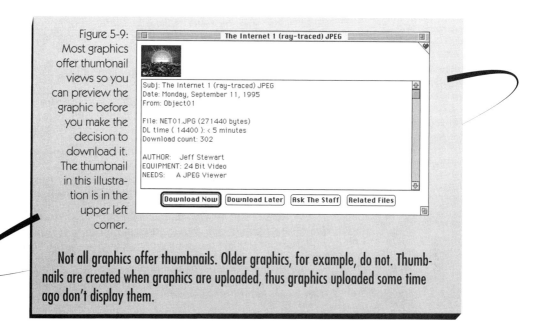

Not all graphics offer thumbnails. Older graphics, for example, do not. Thumbnails are created when graphics are uploaded, thus graphics uploaded some time ago don't display them.

The Graphics Viewer

Your AOL software offers a graphics viewer which allows you to see graphics as they're downloaded. The viewer is especially valuable when there's no thumbnail (see the "Thumbnails" sidebar) available and you're downloading in the dark, so to speak.

Assuming the graphic you're downloading is in the JPG, GIF, or PICT format (more about formats later in this chapter), AOL will display the graphic on your screen as soon as enough of it is received for you to see. (There's a preference available to turn the viewer off, though its default setting is On. Preferences are discussed in Appendix E.)

You don't need to do anything to invoke the viewer: it just appears when it's supposed to. Figure 5-10 shows the viewer in action as Jeff Stewart's graphic is being received.

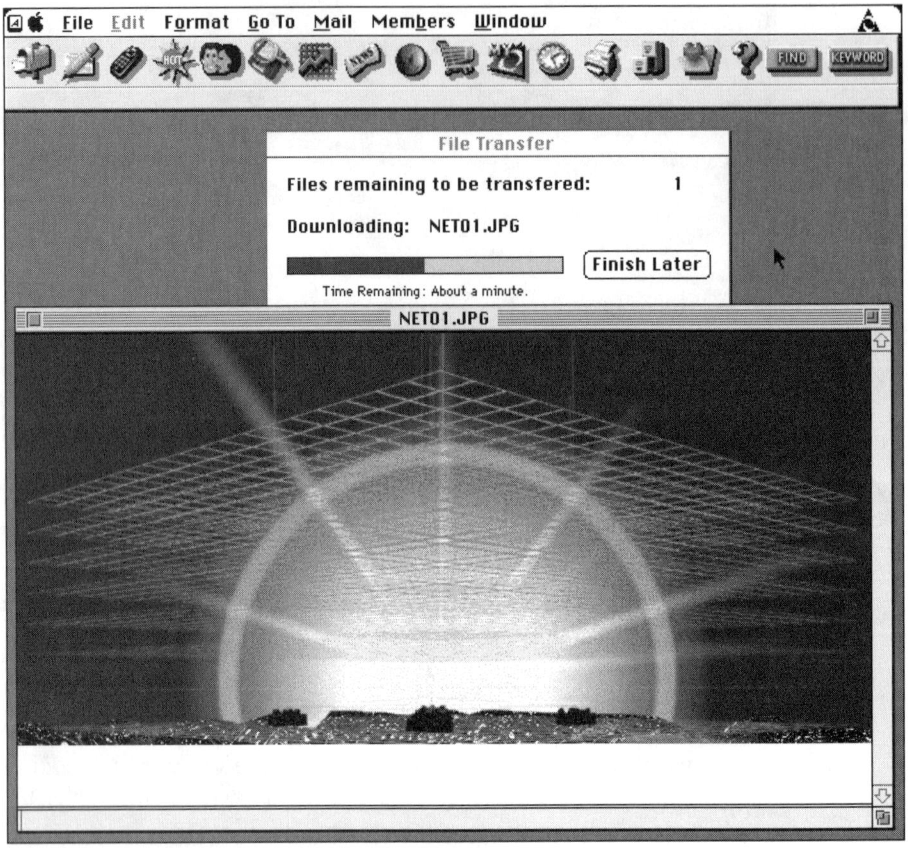

File Edit Format Go To Mail Members Window
FIND
KEYWORD
File Transfer
Files remaining to be transfered: 1
Downloading: NET01.JPG
Finish Later
Time Remaining: About a minute.
NET01.JPG

Figure 5-10: The graphics viewer allows you to see graphics as they're received.

Let's face it: not all graphics are of archival quality. You'll occasionally encounter one that in spite of an acceptable thumbnail isn't worth the time it takes to download it. File descriptions and thumbnails go a long way toward avoiding that potential, but sometimes you just have to see an image full size to pass judgment. That's what the graphics viewer is for. By the time a third of a graphic is received, you'll probably know whether you want it or not. Just keep your eyes on the screen and be ready to click that Cancel button (look for it in Figure 5-10) if you don't like what you see.

Graphics Viewer Trivia

Many regular users aren't aware of it, but AOL's graphics viewer can be used to open existing graphics stored on your hard disk—whether you're online or off—and store them in either the GIF, JPG, or PICT format. In other words, you can not only use your AOL software to download graphics, you can use it to open them whenever you want—online or off.

Aimless Roving

The graphics example I've been using assumes your browsing is focused: I was looking for a graphic when I found that picture—a graphic that was to serve a specific purpose.

Often, browsing is less deliberate. Sometimes you go to a bookstore for a novel; sometimes you go to a bookstore for a book. There's a big difference. Browsing for files is much the same.

If you're browsing for browsing's sake, investigate AOL's Software Center at keywords: **Software Center** (see Figure 5-11). The Software Center is a bookstore of files. As you would expect, it supports browsing of the specific variety, but it also offers a splendid opportunity to browse aimlessly.

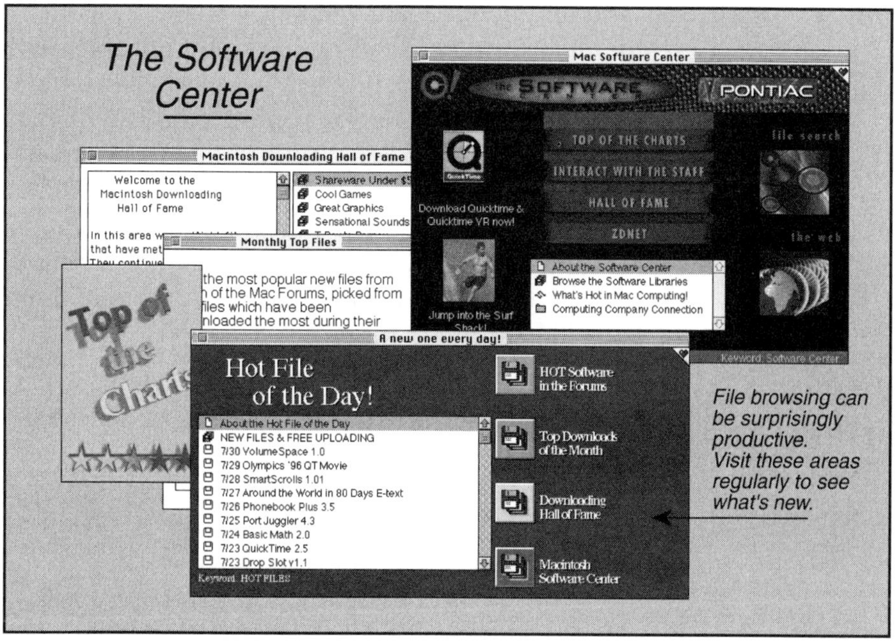
The Software Center
Mac Software Center
PONTIAC
Macintosh Downloading Hall of Fame
Monthly Top Files
A new one every day!
Hot File of the Day!
File browsing can be surprisingly productive. Visit these areas regularly to see what's new.

Figure 5-11: The Software Center is the place to find AOL's best downloading fare.

Look at those categories in Figure 5-11: the Hall of Fame, Top of the Charts, highlighted files—the list goes on, as you can see.

The libraries in the Software Center are updated every week; make it one of the places you visit on a regular basis.

File Formats & File Compression

The number of potential file formats for downloaded files is staggering. Fortunately, some standards and conventions help to organize the confusion.

Filename extensions are the realm of DOS files (files used by IBM-PCs and clones). Nearly every DOS filename consists of up to eight characters, a period, and a three-character filename extension, such as NET01.JPG. Though this is limiting (eight characters is hardly enough for a properly descriptive filename), the three-character extension is particularly useful. All you have to do is look at a DOS file's name to see what kind of file it is. DOS filenames ending in .xls are Excel worksheets, for example. Those ending in .txt are text files and are readable by most word processors and text editors, including the AOL software itself. Those ending in .zip or .sit are files compressed using a file-compression utility (more about these later in this chapter). And those ending in .jpg are graphics files.

This convention is finding its way into the Macintosh community as well, and for good reason: Unlike DOS files, Macintosh filenames don't identify their formats. Though this might not seem significant when you're viewing file icons on the Mac, there are no file icons when you're reading file descriptions online. That's why most online filenames include extensions, even if they're Mac files.

The chart pictured in Figure 5-12 identifies some of the common Macintosh filename extensions and their meanings. Your AOL software is compatible with a surprisingly large number of these formats. It really can open sound and video files, and play them too—assuming you have the hardware for it.

Figure 5-12: Filename extensions for some of the most common Macintosh file formats you'll find online. Those marked with an asterisk can be opened with your AOL software.

Filename Extensions

Textual formats

*TXT	Unformatted ASCII text
MW	MacWrite
DOC	Microsoft Word, WordPerfect

Graphic formats

*TIF	Tagged-image file format
*GIF	Graphic interchange format
*JPG	Joint Photographic Experts Group
*PICT	Macintosh PICT
PAINT	MacPaint (also PNT)
EPS	Encapsulated PostScript

Compressed formats

*SIT	StuffIt (AOL unzips automatically)
SEA	Self-extracting archive
*ZIP	PKZip (primarily IBM-PCs and clones)

Other formats

*SND	Macintosh sound
*AU	Sun workstation audio
MIDI	Musical Instrument Digital Interface
*QT	Macintosh QuickTime (animation)
PM5	PageMaker version 5
XLS	Excel worksheet
XLC	Excel chart

File Compression

Look again at Figure 5-12. Four *compressed* formats are identified there, and they require further explanation.

Why compress files? There are three good reasons: (1) compressed files are much smaller than files that haven't been compressed and thus take significantly less time to download; (2) compressed files require less storage space; and (3) compressed files are often stored in an archive (several files compressed into a single file). Archives are a convenient way of grouping multiple files for storage and downloading.

Amazingly, compressed files can be reduced to as little as 20 percent of the original size; yet when they're decompressed, absolutely no data are lost. I don't know how they do it. Smoke and mirrors, I suppose.

Compression Comparisons
No compression: 21394 bytes
Compressed to 9111 bytes, then decompressed for printing.

Figure 5-13: The original image on the left measures 21,394 bytes. The image on the right was compressed to 9,111 bytes (43 percent of the original), then decompressed for printing. No data were lost; both pictures are identical. (Scanning and retouching by David Palermo.)

What's wrong with compressed files? They're useless until they're *de*compressed. The compressed image in Figure 5-13 couldn't be included in the illustration until it was decompressed. In other words, you must have decompression software before you can use compressed images. That's the bad news. The good news is that you already have decompression software: it's part of the AOL software package installed in your Mac.

StuffIt

StuffIt is responsible for a great deal of the file compression encountered in the Mac environment. StuffIt can compress (or *stuff*, as it's called) a single file or a multitude of files into a single file—an archive. StuffIt archives are identified by the .sit filename extension.

Like all archives, StuffIt archives must be decompressed (unstuffed) before use, and, incredibly, it happens automatically when you use AOL. If compression is done with smoke and mirrors, automatic decompression must be done with smoke and mirrors and an eye of newt. Whatever the technique, it works—and we're the beneficiaries.

When your AOL software downloads a file with .sit in its filename, it makes a note to itself to unstuff the file immediately after you sign off. (You must have this option in effect. It's a preference, and preferences are discussed in Appendix E of this book.) An unstuffed copy of the file appears on your disk after decompression, ready for use.

To Stuff or Not to Stuff

The automatic unstuffing feature can be disabled if you want. Automatic unstuffing might create files in places that you'd rather not have them, such as the America Online 3.0 folder which is the default destination for downloads. To avoid that problem, you can override the automatic unstuffing and do it yourself later. There's a preference available to disable automatic unstuffing, though its default setting is On. (Preferences are discussed in Appendix E.)

There are also preferences available to allow you to configure AOL's software to automatically delete the original file. Though you might want to activate this preference in deference to disk space, I recommend leaving it turned off. Once the download is complete (and once the AOL software has decompressed the file), copy the archive to a floppy and store the floppy somewhere, *then* delete the archive from the disk to which it was downloaded. This strategy provides an archived backup of your downloaded data, ready for recovery should something catastrophic happen to the working copy on your Mac.

America Online not only gives you the unstuffing part of StuffIt, it gives you the stuffing part as well. You can use your AOL software to unstuff any file with the .sit filename extension: just choose Open from AOL's File menu, find the file on your disk, and "open" it . If you want to stuff your own files, follow the directions in Chapter 3 that describe attaching files to e-mail. You can do this while you're offline. It makes no difference who you identify as the e-mail recipient, because after AOL stuffs the file, you simply *don't send the mail* (just close its window and say No when AOL asks you if you want to send it).

You're also welcome to acquire a copy of StuffIt for yourself. It's available online: use the keywords: **File Search**, then search for StuffIt Lite. You'll find a number of files meeting the criterion; be sure you get the latest. StuffIt Lite is shareware. If you like the application, pay the shareware fee and you can use it indefinitely with a clear conscience.

Raymond Lau

StuffIt author Raymond Lau wrote the application in 1987 when he was 16 years old. Ray writes, "A friend, who had both a PC and Mac, asked me one day why, with PackItIII, then standard [for the Mac], you couldn't easily skip files when decompressing like you can with the IBM programs. StuffIt was originally written as a utility for our own use... Its name, as well as its original trash chute icon, was meant as a play on words and images."

Only Ray Lau knows how many shareware copies of StuffIt have been registered, but you can be sure that it's in the tens of thousands. Courtesy of his StuffIt royalties, Ray is now pursuing a Ph.D. in—naturally—computer science.

A more elaborate version of StuffIt—StuffIt Deluxe—is available commercially from Aladdin Systems, Inc. (use the keyword: **Aladdin**). StuffIt Deluxe offers more features and better support, but StuffIt Lite remains available as shareware. It's nice to have the choice. If you're interested in buying the Deluxe commercial version, check out the AOL Marketplace (see Chapter 15, "Buying & Selling," for more information about shopping online).

Compact Pro

This wouldn't be a democracy without competition, and StuffIt's primary shareware competition is *Compact Pro*, by Bill Goodman. Compact Pro archives can span multiple floppies (making it an effective alternative to backup software) and support data encryption (in the versions distributed in North America). If you're going to invest in compression software for the Macintosh, don't forget to include this software in your library.

Self-Extracting Archives

You now know all about compressed files, but there is another type of archive you'll find online: the *self-extracting archive.* Just as the name implies, these are archives that decompress themselves when you run them. A prime example of a self-extracting archive is *Disinfectant,* by John Norstad. Disinfectant is virus-protection freeware, intended to detect (and optionally) remove any computer viruses on your Mac. You should have this program. To locate it online, use the keywords: **File Search**, then the criterion Disinfectant. Once you have it, use it.

Look at the top window in Figure 5-14. I've just downloaded Disinfectant 3.6.sea to a blank floppy disk and you're seeing that disk's window. Note that the filename concludes with the .sea extension. Files with this extension are self-extracting archives. Rather than depend on software on your disk for decompression, .sea files decompress themselves. Disinfectant 3.6.sea was created with Compact Pro; others were created with StuffIt. Normally, AOL's software will automatically decompress .sea files at sign-off. If it doesn't, all you have to do is double-click the .sea file's icon to decompress it manually.

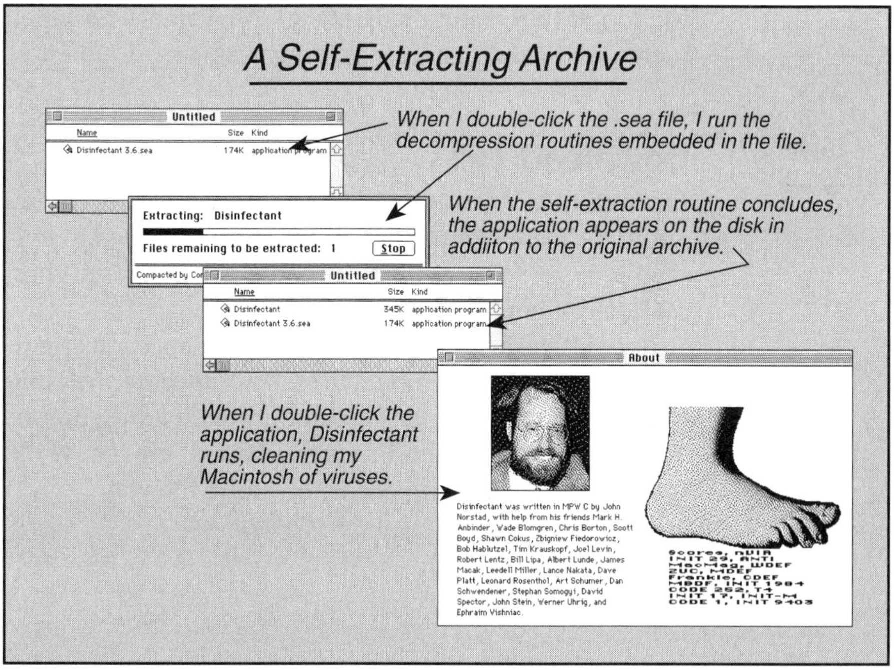
A Self-Extracting Archive
Untitled
Name Size Kind
Disinfectant 3.6.sea 174K application program
When I double-click the .sea file, I run the decompression routines embedded in the file.
Extracting: Disinfectant
Files remaining to be extracted: 1
Stop
Compacted by Co
When the self-extraction routine concludes, the application appears on the disk in addiiton to the original archive.
Untitled
Name Size Kind
Disinfectant 345K application program
Disinfectant 3.6.sea 174K application program
About
When I double-click the application, Disinfectant runs, cleaning my Macintosh of viruses.
Disinfectant was written in MPW C by John Norstad, with help from his friends Mark H. Anbinder, Wade Blomgren, Chris Borton, Scott Boyd, Shawn Cokus, Zbigniew Fiedorowicz, Bob Hablutzel, Tim Krauskopf, Joel Levin, Robert Lentz, Bill Lipa, Albert Lunde, James Macak, Leedell Miller, Lance Nakata, Dave Platt, Leonard Rosenthol, Art Schumer, Dan Schwendener, Stephan Somogyi, David Spector, John Stein, Werner Uhrig, and Ephraim Vishniac.

Figure 5-14: The Disinfectant self-extracting archive decompresses itself when I double-click its icon. The decompression software is embedded in the archive; no local decompression software is required.

Note the two Untitled windows pictured in Figure 5-14. The top one shows a single file—the archive Disinfectant 3.6.sea—on my floppy. After the archive is decompressed, two files appear on the same floppy: the original (compressed) archive and the (decompressed) Disinfectant application. Note the *size* of the files pictured in Figure 5-14. The original archive measures 174k. The decompressed Disinfectant application measures 345k, almost twice the size of its original archive.

PKZip

While StuffIt is the file compression standard for Macintoshes, a program called *PKZip* is the standard for the IBM-PCs and clones. Instead of being stuffed and unstuffed, PKZip files (followed by the .zip extension) are "zipped" and "unzipped." A number of files suitable for use on either platform—graphics, mostly—were originally constructed on PCs and are zipped rather than stuffed. (This is beginning to sound like a recipe for baked turkey: First stuff, then zip the carcass, then bake at 350 degrees for four hours.)

Amazingly, the Mac AOL software can unzip these files automatically for you. If they don't unzip at sign-off, just choose Open from the File menu, find the zipped file on your disk, and double-click its filename.

Download 101

Even with AOL's automation and downloading conveniences, downloading can be confusing. And though I've tried to explain it thoroughly here, some people are better served by another voice. I'm not offended if you're one of them.

If you have any downloading questions, try using the keywords: **Download 101**. Download 101 is AOL's center for downloading questions and answers, and it's rich in downloading tips and techniques. There's also a downloading simulation there that walks you through the process, explaining each step along the way.

download 101
download 101
5 easy steps to a world of software!
1
LESSON 1:
What Is Downloading?
2
LESSON 2:
Where Can I Find Files?
3
LESSON 3:
How Do I Download Files?
4
LESSON 4:
How Do I Use Downloaded Files?
5
LESSON 5:
Troubleshooting, Tips and Tricks.
Keyword: DOWNLOAD101

Figure 5-15: Download 101 is the place to get hands-on downloading experience, free of charge.

Best of all, Download 101 is free. Spend as much time there as you need to become familiar and comfortable with the downloading process. All it costs is your time.

Uploading Files

With all this talk about downloading, it's easy to forget that before a file can be *down*loaded, it first must be *up*loaded. True to its community spirit, AOL depends on its members for most of its files—members like you and me. Uploading isn't the exclusive realm of AOL employees and forum staff, nor is it the realm of the weenies and the dweebs. Most of the files you can download from AOL—I'd guess more than 90 percent—have been uploaded by members, using Macs just like yours.

Earlier I defined downloading as "the process of transferring a file from AOL's computers to a disk on your computer." Uploading is just the reverse: the process of transferring a file from a disk on your computer to a disk on AOL's computers. Once received, it's checked for viruses and the quality of its content, then it's posted. The process rarely takes more than a day. Upload a file on Monday, and you'll probably see it available for downloading Tuesday morning.

The Uploading Process

Begin the uploading process by visiting the forum where your file seems to fit (forums are discussed in Chapter 9, "Boards & Forums"). If it's a graphic, post it in the Graphic Arts Forum. If it's poetry, post it in the Writers' Club. Once you're in the forum, select the library that's the most appropriate place for your file (if there's more than one library in the forum) and click the Upload File button. (Some forums have a button marked Submit a File; use this button if it's available.) Also note that some forums have very specific libraries marked Free Uploading and New Files—send your uploaded files there. Be sure, too, to read any files marked "Read This Before Uploading," or the like. They usually contain information specific to uploading material to that forum.

Recently I uploaded a magazine article to the Writers' Club. When I clicked on the Upload button, I received the Upload File Information form pictured in Figure 5-16. You'll encounter this form every time you upload a file to AOL.

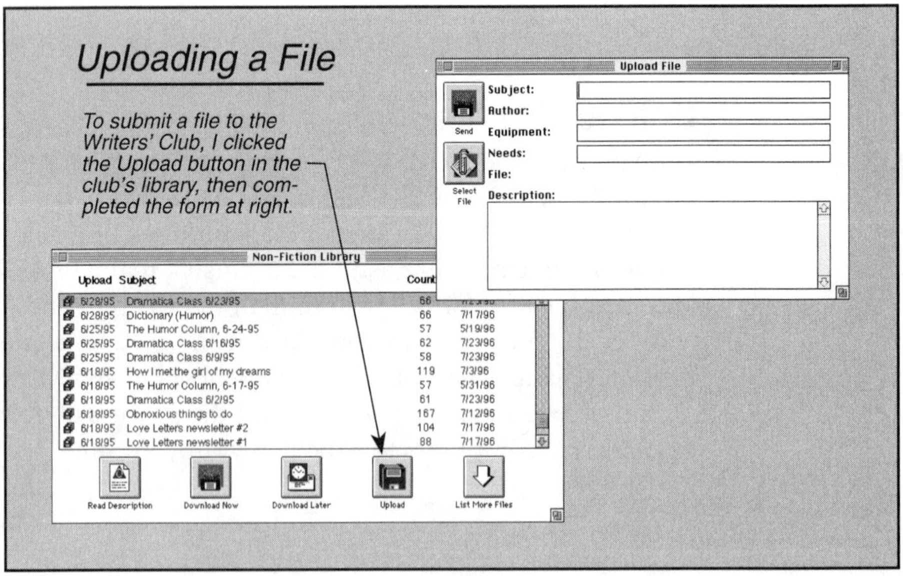

Uploading a File
To submit a file to the Writers' Club, I clicked the Upload button in the club's library, then completed the form at right.
Upload File
Send
Subject:
Author:
Equipment:
Needs:
Select File
File:
Description:
Non-Fiction Library
Upload Subject
Count
6/28/95 Dramatica Class 6/23/95 66
6/28/95 Dictionary (Humor) 66 7/17/96
6/25/95 The Humor Column, 6-24-95 57 5/19/96
6/25/95 Dramatica Class 6/16/95 62 7/23/96
6/25/95 Dramatica Class 6/9/95 58 7/23/96
6/18/95 How I met the girl of my dreams 119 7/3/96
6/18/95 The Humor Column, 6-17-95 57 5/31/96
6/18/95 Dramatica Class 6/2/95 61 7/23/96
6/18/95 Obnoxious things to do 167 7/12/96
6/18/95 Love Letters newsletter #2 104 7/17/96
6/18/95 Love Letters newsletter #1 88 7/17/96
Read Description
Download Now
Download Later
Upload
List More Files

Figure 5-16: You'll be asked to fill out the Upload File information form for every file you upload to America Online.

The Upload File Information Form

All too often, uploaders fail to complete the Upload File information form adequately. This form "sells" your file to other members, and what you have to say about it determines whether a member will take the time to download it. Here are some hints for creating accurate, useful, and compelling descriptions of files you upload.

- The *Subject* field should be descriptive and catchy, in that order. Look at Figure 5-16. Do you see how the subjects are listed there? The subject line is your headline. If you want members to read your story, hook 'em with a really great subject line.
- The *Equipment* line should identify any special equipment required to access the file. A color graphic requires a color Macintosh; Mac SEs and Classics won't do. As mentioned earlier, some people use this line to list what they used to create the file, although this is generally not proper protocol.
- The *Needs* line is where you specify the particular software application or program required to access your file. An Excel worksheet, for example, requires the Excel spreadsheet program.
- The *Description* field is where you get specific. Here you differentiate your file from others that might be similar. If you're submitting an application, you should include the version number. Be specific and persuasive: you're selling your file here. Think about what you would want to read if you were considering downloading the file. Make it sound irresistible.

If you're submitting a number of related files, or if your file is larger than about 50K, compress it (or them) using StuffIt or something equivalent. This saves downloading time, and it's the polite way to offer your material. America Online only accepts StuffIt archives for Macintosh files. As I mentioned before, StuffIt is available online.

Concluding the Uploading Process

America Online's by-now-familiar progress indicator will keep you entertained while the upload is under way, followed by a dialog box announcing your success. The time spent uploading your file will be credited back to you. Though you might not see the credit before you sign off, it will appear soon thereafter.

To check your billing information, use the keyword: **Billing**. A day or so after your upload is completed, you should see a note crediting your account with any time you have spent uploading files. The billing area is free, so you won't be charged for whatever time you spend online checking your account's billing information.

Moving On

It's time for you to get your second wind. Though we've covered a parking lot full of technicalities, there's more.

Much more, in fact. Your AOL software is not only capable of downloading, it's not only capable of downloading multiple files in one session, it's also capable of downloading multiple files in only one *unattended* session—in the middle of the night, if that's when you choose to do your downloading (and you might: system activity is minimal in the middle of the night; files transfer faster). Your AOL software is also capable of conducting all of your mail activities at the same time, so your new mail is already retrieved and waiting for you first thing in the morning. These are the features of Automatic AOL & the Download Manager. We discuss them next.

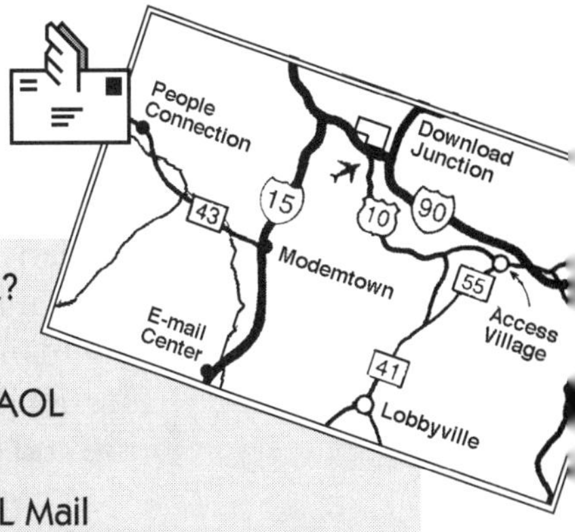
People Connection
Download Junction
43
15
10
90
Modemtown
55
E-mail Center
Access Village
41
Lobbyville

CHAPTER 6

Automatic AOL & the Download Manager

- What Is Automatic AOL?
- Futility Revisited
- Scheduling Automatic AOL Sessions
- Reading Automatic AOL Mail
- The Download Manager

The greatest volume of mail I receive from my *Tour Guide* readers comes in response to this chapter. These people are thrilled. They've discovered AOL's two automation features—Automatic AOL and the Download Manager—and they are dancing rapturously on the virtual sidewalks of the electronic community. If AOL has to deliver your mail with a forklift and you've been reading and responding to it online, you're going to love what this chapter has to say.

There's more: if you're a downloading zealot—if you collect shareware, utilities, fonts, and graphics the way Woody Allen collects troubles—you too will want to read this chapter. Your AOL software can sign on in the middle of the night—to take advantage of minimum online traffic and maximum transfer speeds—and download a queue of files you've scheduled for downloading. It can even resurrect partially downloaded files—files that were interrupted in mid-download when you lost the connection or the cat chewed the phone line in half.

AOL offers solutions to all of these problems: Automatic AOL and the Download Manager.

What Is Automatic AOL?

Automatic AOL is a feature that lets you automate online sessions. At its highest level of automation, Automatic AOL signs on at a predetermined time, downloads all of your incoming e-mail, downloads any files you identified earlier for transfer, and uploads any e-mail you've prepared but not sent. When all of that is completed, Automatic AOL signs off, leaving a note on your screen telling you what happened and when, along with notification of any errors encountered.

Many people use Automatic AOL in a spontaneous fashion, invoking it manually as they work (I just invoked it moments ago, to check my mail while I write this paragraph), or at the conclusion of an online session—sort of an "I'm ready to sign off now: clean everything up for me and sign off" command.

Others—people who conduct business via e-mail and need to check their mailboxes frequently during the day—schedule Automatic AOL to run automatically every hour or half-hour, maintaining an almost continuous connection with AOL and, therefore, with their e-mail community.

There are even a few people who schedule Automatic AOL to occur in the wee hours of the morning, preferring to conduct the majority of their online events when network traffic is light and connect times are minimal. These are people who delight in seeing their e-mail waiting for them when they awaken, sort of like breakfast in bed.

Futility Revisited

In Chapter 3, you sent yourself a letter. Yes, it was an exercise in futility, but you saw e-mail in action. We're about to repeat the exercise, but this time we'll have the computer do it for us. We'll experience not just futility; we'll experience *automated* futility. This is *not* what computing is supposed to be, but it might prove to be enlightening.

- Do not sign on. Rather, run your AOL software and choose Compose Mail from the Mail menu. As you did in Chapter 3, prepare a short message to yourself. Your Compose Mail window should look something like the one pictured in Figure 6-1. (Be sure to put your screen name, *not mine*, in the To: box. You'd be amazed at the amount of mail I receive with "This is a test of Auto AOL" in the message field.)

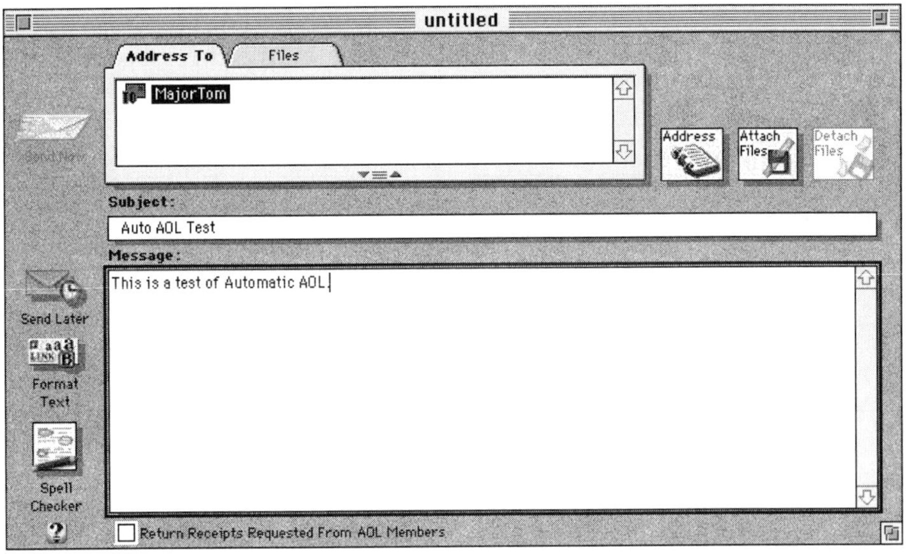
untitled
Address To
Files
MajorTom
Send Now
Address
Attach Files
Detach Files
Subject:
Auto AOL Test
Message:
This is a test of Automatic AOL
Send Later
Format Text
Spell Checker
Return Receipts Requested From AOL Members

Figure 6-1: Compose a message to yourself, using *your* screen name in the To: field.

Note that the Send Now button is dimmed. Since you're not online, this command is not available. Instead, click the Send Later button. Unless you've changed your preferences from the default (preferences are discussed in Appendix E, "Preferences"), AOL will reply with the message pictured in Figure 6-2.

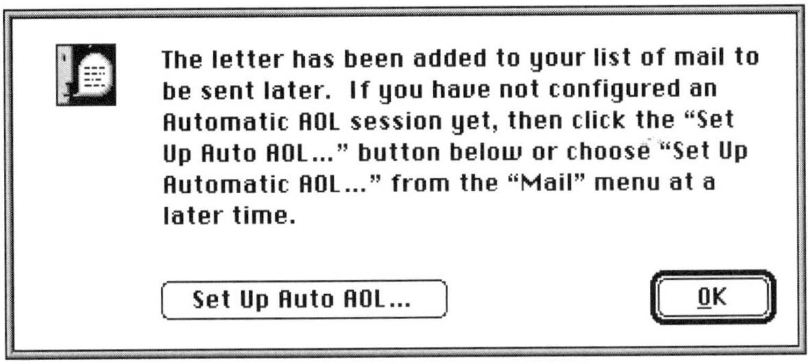
The letter has been added to your list of mail to be sent later. If you have not configured an Automatic AOL session yet, then click the "Set Up Auto AOL..." button below or choose "Set Up Automatic AOL..." from the "Mail" menu at a later time.
Set Up Auto AOL...
OK

Figure 6-2: America Online confirms your request to Send Later.

Note that the dialog box shown in Figure 6-2 points out that if you "...have not configured an Automatic AOL session yet, then you can click the "Set Up Auto AOL..." button below or choose "Set Up Automatic AOL..." from the "Mail" menu at a later time." You can access the Automatic AOL Scheduler Preferences now by clicking the button at the bottom of the window.

The Automatic AOL Scheduler Preferences window will appear (see Figure 6-3), including all the check boxes shown.

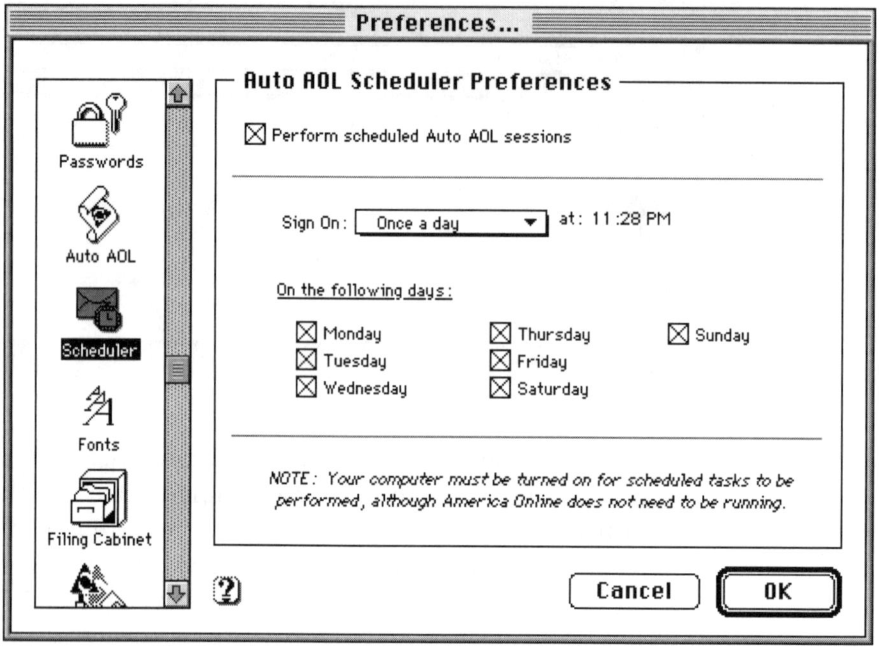
Preferences...
Passwords
Auto AOL
Scheduler
Fonts
Filing Cabinet
Auto AOL Scheduler Preferences
Perform scheduled Auto AOL sessions
Sign On: Once a day
at: 11:28 PM
On the following days:
Monday
Tuesday
Wednesday
Thursday
Friday
Saturday
Sunday
NOTE: Your computer must be turned on for scheduled tasks to be performed, although America Online does not need to be running.
Cancel
OK

Figure 6-3: Configure Automatic AOL in the Scheduler Preferences window.

- Now click the icon marked Auto AOL from the column on the left, and complete the resulting form as pictured in Figure 6-4. Next, click the icon marked Passwords and enter the passwords for the screen names you chose earlier. (Notice that your password isn't displayed as you type: bullets representing each letter in your password appear instead. That's as it should be. You never know who's looking over your shoulder.) Now check the box on the right side if you want your password used only for Automatic AOL, which I advise. Remember, anyone with access to your computer can sign on to your account if you store a password here. When you have completed the Passwords window, click the OK button to save your Automatic AOL preferences.

Walk Me Through

If you're new to Automatic AOL, AOL offers a step-by-step tutorial on the subject. To begin, select "Set Up Automatic AOL..." from the Mail menu. After the Preferences window appears, another window offering help on how to set up Automatic AOL will open. Use the arrows in the lower right-hand corner to navigate through the tutorial. The walk-through guides you through the Automatic AOL setup process with extensive visual and verbal instructions along the way. It will even escort you through your first Automatic AOL session at the end.

If you need help, you can always click the Help icon (the question mark at the bottom) in the Preferences window to invoke it again. If you're an infrequent Automatic AOL user and prone to absentmindedness, this feature always stands ready to serve.

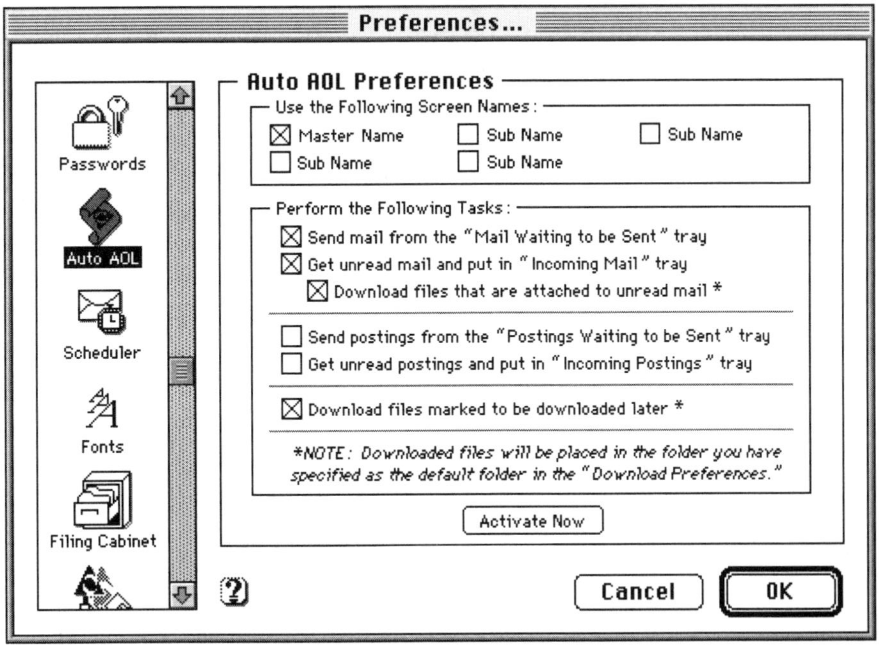
Preferences...
Auto AOL Preferences
Use the Following Screen Names:
Master Name
Sub Name
Sub Name
Sub Name
Sub Name
Perform the Following Tasks:
Send mail from the "Mail Waiting to be Sent" tray
Get unread mail and put in "Incoming Mail" tray
Download files that are attached to unread mail *
Send postings from the "Postings Waiting to be Sent" tray
Get unread postings and put in "Incoming Postings" tray
Download files marked to be downloaded later *
*NOTE: Downloaded files will be placed in the folder you have specified as the default folder in the "Download Preferences."
Activate Now
Passwords
Auto AOL
Scheduler
Fonts
Filing Cabinet
Cancel
OK

Figure 6-4: Complete the Automatic AOL Preferences window.

Back at the Sign-On window, choose Run Automatic AOL from the Mail menu. America Online will respond with the form pictured in Figure 6-5.

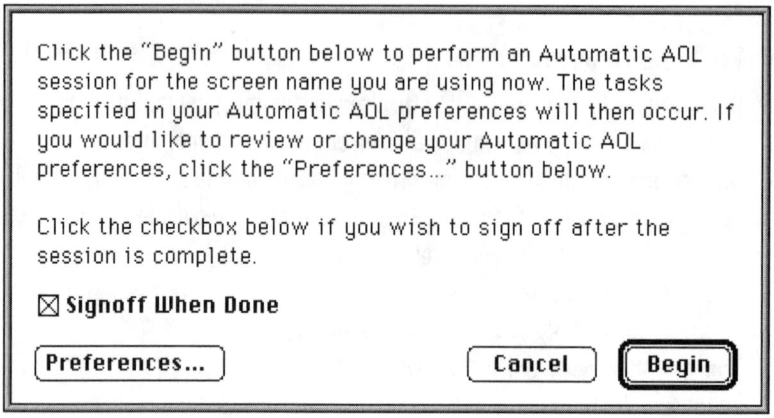
Click the "Begin" button below to perform an Automatic AOL session for the screen name you are using now. The tasks specified in your Automatic AOL preferences will then occur. If you would like to review or change your Automatic AOL preferences, click the "Preferences..." button below.
Click the checkbox below if you wish to sign off after the session is complete.
Signoff When Done
Preferences...
Cancel
Begin

Figure 6-5: If this is your first Automatic AOL session, read these instructions carefully and review your Automatic AOL preferences if you want.

The Signoff When Done feature allows you to run an Automatic AOL session—sending and receiving mail and newsgroup postings, uploading and downloading files—then go offline after the session concludes. This is our intention at the moment. For the purposes of this exercise, be sure the Signoff When Done option is checked, as shown in Figure 6-5.

Click the button marked Begin. America Online takes over (Figure 6-6).

AOL must have had a double espresso on the day that I produced Figure 6-6: this Automatic AOL session has resulted in both an upload and a download. Not only did I send mail to myself, I also received it—all during the same session. This isn't always the case. Sometimes the e-mail system is too busy to turn a piece of mail around and send it back before the session signs off. Don't be surprised if you have to run your Automatic AOL session a second time in order to receive the sent mail in this exercise.

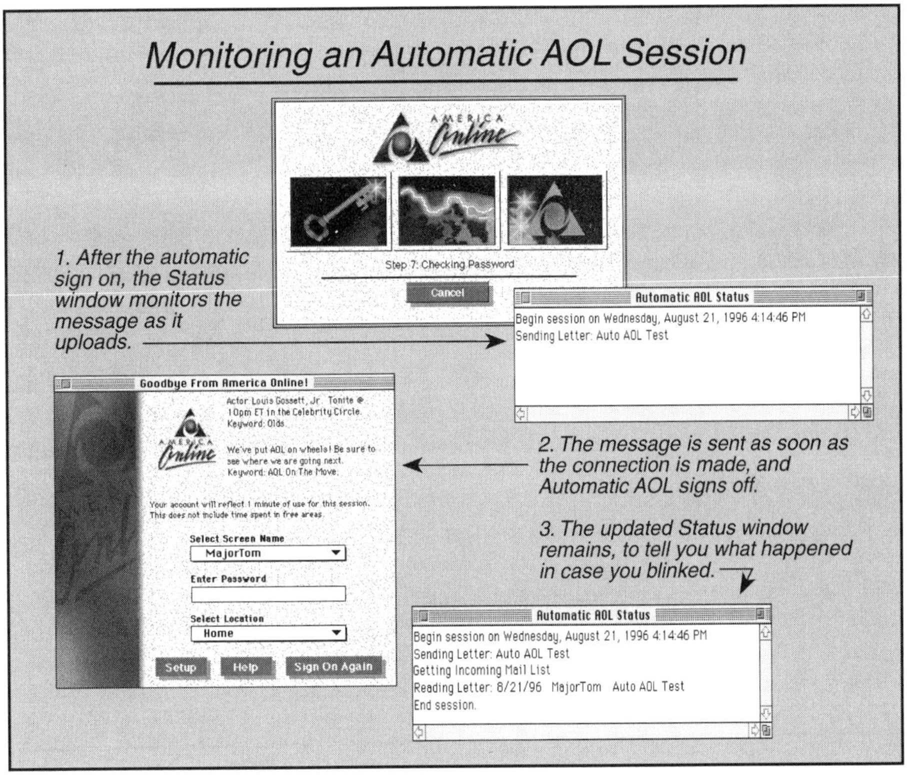
Monitoring an Automatic AOL Session
AMERICA Online
Step 7: Checking Password
Cancel
1. After the automatic sign on, the Status window monitors the message as it uploads.
Automatic AOL Status
Begin session on Wednesday, August 21, 1996 4:14:46 PM
Sending Letter: Auto AOL Test
Goodbye From America Online!
Actor Louis Gossett, Jr. Tonite @ 10pm ET in the Celebrity Circle. Keyword: Olds.
We've put AOL on wheels! Be sure to see where we are going next. Keyword: AOL On The Move.
Your account will reflect 1 minute of use for this session. This does not include time spent in free areas.
Select Screen Name
MajorTom
Enter Password
Select Location
Home
Setup
Help
Sign On Again
2. The message is sent as soon as the connection is made, and Automatic AOL signs off.
3. The updated Status window remains, to tell you what happened in case you blinked.
Automatic AOL Status
Begin session on Wednesday, August 21, 1996 4:14:46 PM
Sending Letter: Auto AOL Test
Getting Incoming Mail List
Reading Letter: 8/21/96 MajorTom Auto AOL Test
End session.

Figure 6-6: The Automatic AOL session signs on, "flashes" your mail to AOL Headquarters in Virginia, and signs off—all in seconds.

Regardless of whether you've had to run a second Automatic AOL session or not, you've got mail, and you need to read it. But you're not online. How do you read mail when you're offline?

Pull down the Mail menu. Choose the Read Offline Mail option, which is always available (see the top portion of Figure 6-7).

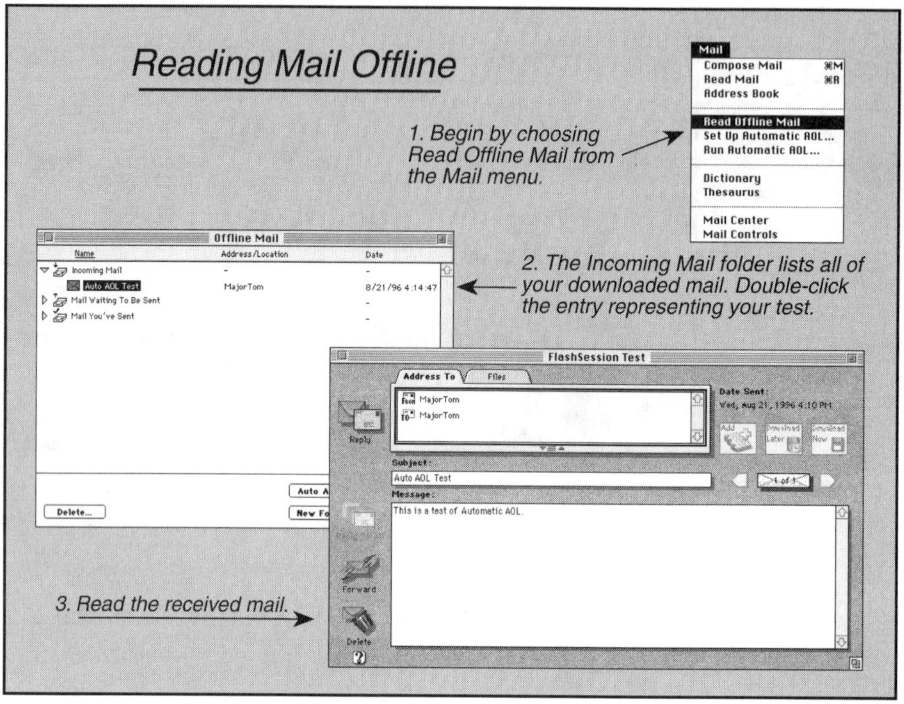
Reading Mail Offline
1. Begin by choosing Read Offline Mail from the Mail menu.
Mail
Compose Mail ⌘M
Read Mail ⌘R
Address Book
Read Offline Mail
Set Up Automatic AOL...
Run Automatic AOL...
Dictionary
Thesaurus
Mail Center
Mail Controls
Offline Mail
Name
Address/Location
Date
Incoming Mail
Auto AOL Test
MajorTom
8/21/96 4:14:47
Mail Waiting To Be Sent
Mail You've Sent
Delete...
2. The Incoming Mail folder lists all of your downloaded mail. Double-click the entry representing your test.
FlashSession Test
Address To
Files
MajorTom
MajorTom
Date Sent:
Wed, Aug 21, 1996 4:10 PM
Reply
Forward
Delete
Subject:
Auto AOL Test
Message:
This is a test of Automatic AOL.
3. Read the received mail.

Figure 6-7: You can read mail offline when it's convenient for you and the clock's not running.

The Offline Mail window will appear (see the middle portion of Figure 6-7). To find the mail you sent yourself, open the folder marked Incoming Mail by selecting it and clicking the Open button, clicking the arrow to the left of the folder, or double-clicking the folder itself. Now double-click the entry representing your test.

A second window will open (Figure 6-7, bottom), containing the text of your test. After you've read it, delete it by clicking the Delete button in the lower left corner.

I'm reminded of a big Mercedes sedan I read about the other day. In an irrational effort to remain the technological leader among automobiles, Mercedes equipped the car with *motorized headrests*! Now *that's* technology. Our exercise was a little like that. We threw technology at a task that was no doubt best left undone. At least we're in good company.

Scheduling Automatic AOL Sessions

You can invoke an Automatic AOL session at any time, whether you're online or off. Alternatively, you can schedule Automatic AOL sessions to occur at predetermined intervals: every day, every hour—whenever you please. Before any session can get under way, however, you have to tell AOL some things it needs to know.

Automatic AOL Session Setup

I can hear it now: it's 4:00 a.m. and El Edwards's voice calls from my computer in the other room. "Tom," he says, "come out here and type in your password!" Bleary-eyed, I stumble to my Mac and type my password. I crawl back into bed and start to drift off when he calls again. "Tom," (is that a smirk in his voice?) "come out here and tell me which screen name to use!" Again, I stumble to the Mac, tripping over the dog, who, rudely awakened, runs yelping into the hall table, knocking over the Waterford crystal vase. I pick up the pieces, hiding those that don't seem to fit together any longer, and Band-Aid the laceration across the dog's nose. I do all this smiling, of course. Always smiling.

Do I make my point? The manual entry of passwords and screen names would defeat the whole purpose of unattended Automatic AOL sessions. These things have to be communicated to the Mac before the first Automatic AOL session begins. Once communicated, they're stored on disk, eliminating the need for re-entering them for each subsequent session.

Selecting Screen Names & Entering Stored Passwords

Many AOL members use more than one screen name. Perhaps more than one member of your family uses the service. Maybe you have an alter ego. Perhaps you're shy, or famous, or reclusive, and you don't want anyone to see your real name on the screen. Whatever the reason, if you use more than one screen name, you have to tell your Mac which of these names to use for Automatic AOL sessions, and if you want the sessions to run unattended, you'll have to enter a password for each screen name.

Selecting names and entering passwords is easy, and once it's done you won't need to do it again unless you want to reconfigure Automatic AOL. I won't linger here, as we've already selected a name and entered a password during the exercise that led off this chapter. Figure 6-8 shows you how to do it.

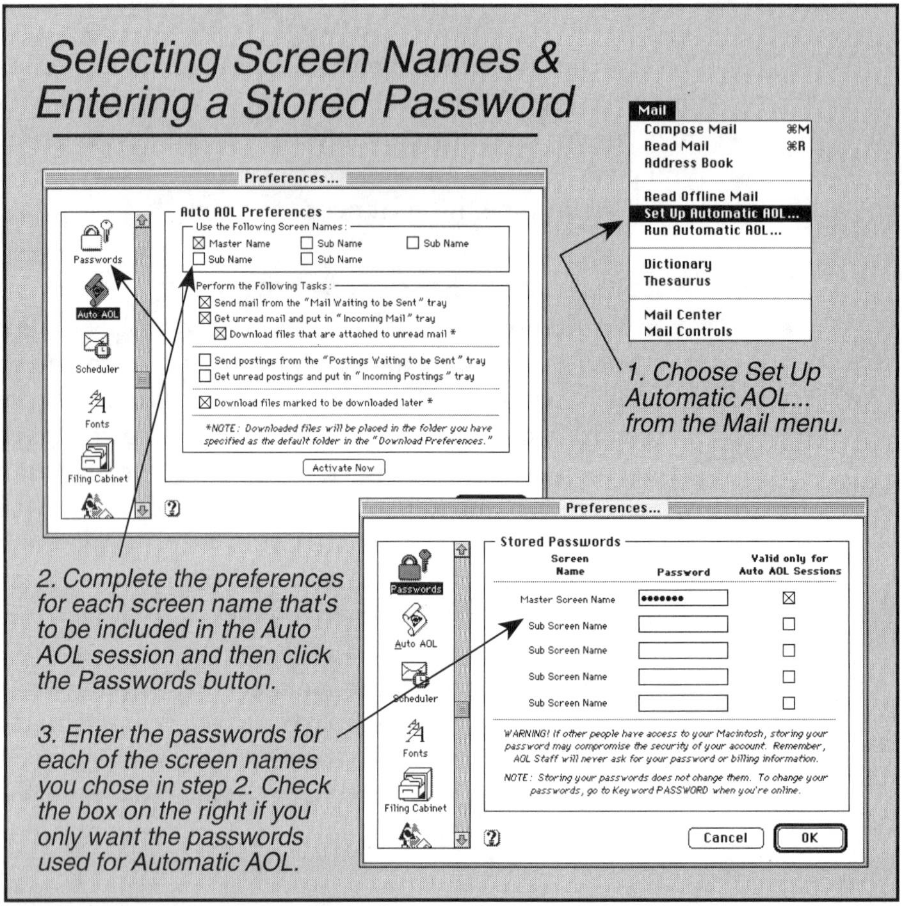
Selecting Screen Names & Entering a Stored Password
Mail
Compose Mail ⌘M
Read Mail ⌘R
Address Book
Read Offline Mail
Set Up Automatic AOL...
Run Automatic AOL...
Dictionary
Thesaurus
Mail Center
Mail Controls
1. Choose Set Up Automatic AOL... from the Mail menu.
Preferences...
Auto AOL Preferences
Use the Following Screen Names:
Master Name
Sub Name
Perform the Following Tasks:
Send mail from the "Mail Waiting to be Sent" tray
Get unread mail and put in "Incoming Mail" tray
Download files that are attached to unread mail *
Send postings from the "Postings Waiting to be Sent" tray
Get unread postings and put in "Incoming Postings" tray
Download files marked to be downloaded later *
*NOTE: Downloaded files will be placed in the folder you have specified as the default folder in the "Download Preferences."
Activate Now
Passwords
Auto AOL
Scheduler
Fonts
Filing Cabinet
2. Complete the preferences for each screen name that's to be included in the Auto AOL session and then click the Passwords button.
3. Enter the passwords for each of the screen names you chose in step 2. Check the box on the right if you only want the passwords used for Automatic AOL.
Stored Passwords
Screen Name
Password
Valid only for Auto AOL Sessions
Master Screen Name
Sub Screen Name
WARNING! If other people have access to your Macintosh, storing your password may compromise the security of your account. Remember, AOL Staff will never ask for your password or billing information.
NOTE: Storing your passwords does not change them. To change your passwords, go to Keyword PASSWORD when you're online.
Cancel
OK

Figure 6-8: The Set Up Automatic AOL... command under the Mail menu takes you to the Preferences window for selecting names and storing passwords.

Though Figure 6-8 illustrates the selection of a single screen name for Automatic AOL only (and the entry of a password for that screen name), the Passwords preference will include all of the screen names you are using for your account, up to the maximum of five. Enter only the passwords for the screen names you want included in your Automatic AOL sessions (if you intend to have Automatic AOL occur while you're away), and check the box for each. Checking the box ensures that the password can only be used for Automatic AOL.

Caution!

There's a minor potential for unauthorized use of your account whenever you store your passwords, even if you store them only for the use of Automatic AOL. I'm getting ahead of myself, but peek ahead at Figure 6-10 and note the check box labeled "Signoff When Done." This check box allows anyone with access to your computer to invoke what's called an *offline* Automatic AOL session, which normally signs on in response to the operator's command, does all of its session activities, then signs off. That last step, however, is omitted if the Signoff When Done box is left unchecked. In effect, this allows anyone with a little AOL savvy to run Automatic AOL on your account, then stay online to do as he or she pleases, for as long as he or she wishes—all without needing to know your password. If there's a potential for this kind of abuse around your machine (and there always is with laptops, which are prime targets for theft), don't store passwords.

Declaring the Download Destination

One more setup task remains before you can start an Automatic AOL session: you must declare a destination for downloaded files. Figure 6-9 illustrates the process and offers a brief glimpse of the Download preferences, a subject we will discuss later in this chapter when we cover the Download Manager.

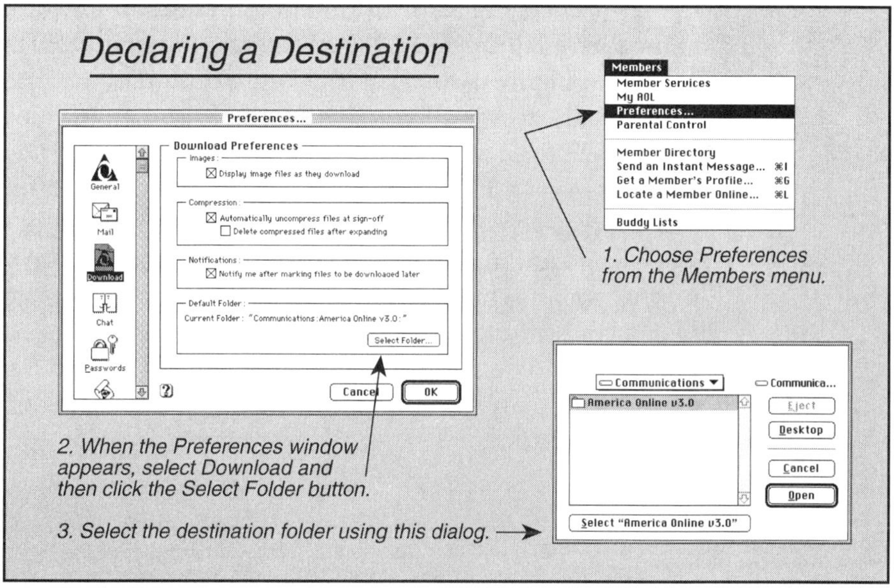
Declaring a Destination
Members
Member Services
My AOL
Preferences...
Parental Control
Member Directory
Send an Instant Message... ⌘I
Get a Member's Profile... ⌘G
Locate a Member Online... ⌘L
Buddy Lists
1. Choose Preferences from the Members menu.
Preferences...
Download Preferences
Images:
Display image files as they download
Compression:
Automatically uncompress files at sign-off
Delete compressed files after expanding
Notifications:
Notify me after marking files to be downloaded later
Default Folder:
Current Folder: "Communications:America Online v3.0:"
Select Folder...
General
Mail
Download
Chat
Passwords
Cancel
OK
2. When the Preferences window appears, select Download and then click the Select Folder button.
Communications
Communica...
America Online v3.0
Eject
Desktop
Cancel
Open
Select "America Online v3.0"
3. Select the destination folder using this dialog.

Figure 6-9: The Download preferences let you specify where you want to save downloaded files. The America Online v3.0 folder is the default.

Attended Automatic AOL Sessions

Now that you've stored your screen names, passwords, and destinations, you're ready to run an Automatic AOL session. The exercise that began this chapter describes an *attended Automatic AOL session*—one that occurs when you issue an Automatic AOL command. Let's examine attended Automatic AOL sessions first.

Many Automatic AOL sessions occur when you're about to wrap up an online session. There's something organic about the flow of an online session: after a couple of months online, you'll glide from one task to another with all the fluidity of warm honey. About the last thing you'll want to do is interrupt your progress with a download or the transmission of a piece of mail. Instead, you can schedule an Automatic AOL session to take care of these things when your session has concluded. More about this in a moment.

Another kind of attended Automatic AOL session occurs when you're offline and want your Mac to sign on, transfer mail and files, and sign off. As you saw during the earlier exercise, the advantage here is speed. Automatic AOL "knows" exactly what it's doing; it wastes no time, it wastes no money, and you don't have to stick around while it's under way.

Offline Attended Automatic AOL Sessions

This is exactly what we did during the earlier exercise in this chapter. You begin an offline Automatic AOL session not by signing on but rather by choosing Run Automatic AOL... from the Mail menu (shown at the top of Figure 6-10). When the resulting window appears (see the bottom of Figure 6-10), click the Begin button.

Normally, this is all you need to do to run an offline attended Automatic AOL session. When you click the Begin button, your Mac signs on, does everything it's been told to do, then signs off. It repeats the process for each of the screen names you've indicated. When the dust settles, an Automatic AOL Status window remains on your screen to inform you of what happened (Figure 6-11). This is more a necessity than a convenience. Without the Automatic AOL Status window, you might have to perform some major sleuthing to find out what happened during an Automatic AOL session, especially one that occurred in your absence.

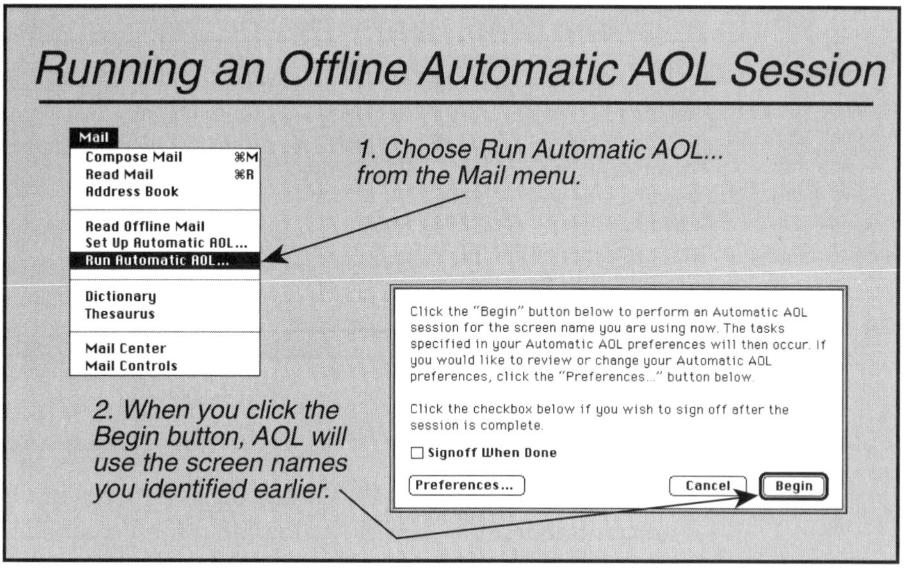
Running an Offline Automatic AOL Session
Mail
Compose Mail ⌘M
Read Mail ⌘R
Address Book
Read Offline Mail
Set Up Automatic AOL...
Run Automatic AOL...
Dictionary
Thesaurus
Mail Center
Mail Controls
1. Choose Run Automatic AOL... from the Mail menu.
Click the "Begin" button below to perform an Automatic AOL session for the screen name you are using now. The tasks specified in your Automatic AOL preferences will then occur. If you would like to review or change your Automatic AOL preferences, click the "Preferences..." button below.
Click the checkbox below if you wish to sign off after the session is complete.
Signoff When Done
Preferences...
Cancel
Begin
2. When you click the Begin button, AOL will use the screen names you identified earlier.

Figure 6-10: Once your screen name and password are stored, a menu selection and a mouse click are all it takes to run an offline attended Automatic AOL session.

Do You Know Who You Are?

There's a bit of a trap waiting for you if you follow the two steps illustrated in Figure 6-10 and aren't paying attention. It's not apparent what screen names AOL will use during the upcoming Automatic AOL session. Review the Scheduler preferences in Figure 6-3, if necessary. Note that AOL will run a session for each name that's selected in the Scheduler preferences, not just the screen name that's currently showing in the Welcome (sign-on) window. Be sure you know which names are selected in your Scheduler preferences before you allow your Automatic AOL sessions to run.

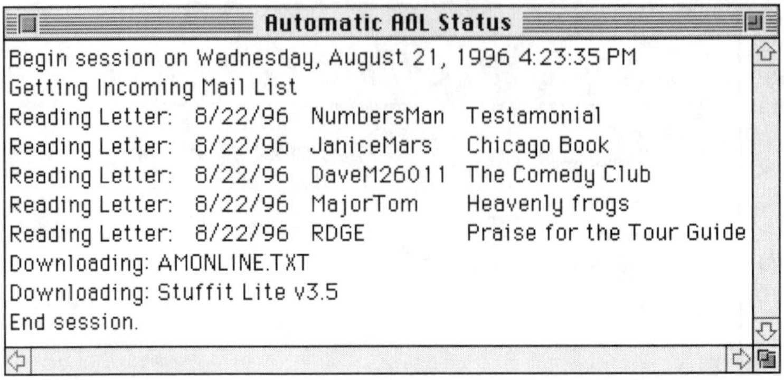
Automatic AOL Status
Begin session on Wednesday, August 21, 1996 4:23:35 PM
Getting Incoming Mail List
Reading Letter: 8/22/96 NumbersMan Testamonial
Reading Letter: 8/22/96 JaniceMars Chicago Book
Reading Letter: 8/22/96 DaveM26011 The Comedy Club
Reading Letter: 8/22/96 MajorTom Heavenly frogs
Reading Letter: 8/22/96 RDGE Praise for the Tour Guide
Downloading: AMONLINE.TXT
Downloading: Stuffit Lite v3.5
End session.

Figure 6-11: The Automatic AOL Status window lets you know what happened during a session, just in case you weren't watching.

Look again at Figure 6-11. I received five pieces of new mail (one with an attached file) and downloaded a file I'd scheduled for download earlier.

It isn't uncommon for only two entries to appear there, representing the start and finish of an Automatic AOL session, with nothing in between. This isn't as meaningless as it might seem. If there was no activity during a session I had scheduled for the middle of the night, I would be aware of that the next morning, and I wouldn't waste time looking for mail or files that weren't there. Of additional benefit is notification of errors. If I incorrectly addressed some mail or if the session was interrupted for some reason, I'd read about it here.

Online Attended Automatic AOL Sessions

Another form of attended Automatic AOL session is the one that occurs at sign-off. During a typical online session, you might visit a forum or two, mark some files for downloading, reply to some mail, and perhaps compose some new mail. Downloads in particular can disrupt the flow of an online session. Sitting at your Mac watching a progress indicator is not the best use of your time. That's why AOL provides sign-off Automatic AOL sessions.

When you've done everything you want to do online, choose Run Automatic AOL... from the Mail menu (rather than selecting Sign Off from the Go To menu—see the top of Figure 6-12), click the Signoff When Done option, then click the Begin button (see the bottom of Figure 6-12). This is one alternative to the Sign Off command; the other is the Download Manager, which I'll discuss later in this chapter. Either one will work if activity remains that doesn't require your involvement.

Note that you can choose either to stay online after the Automatic AOL session concludes (which is the default, as shown in Figure 6-12), or to have the software automatically sign off after your Automatic AOL activities have ended (see Figure 6-13). You will have to specifically activate the Signoff When Done option if it's your preference.

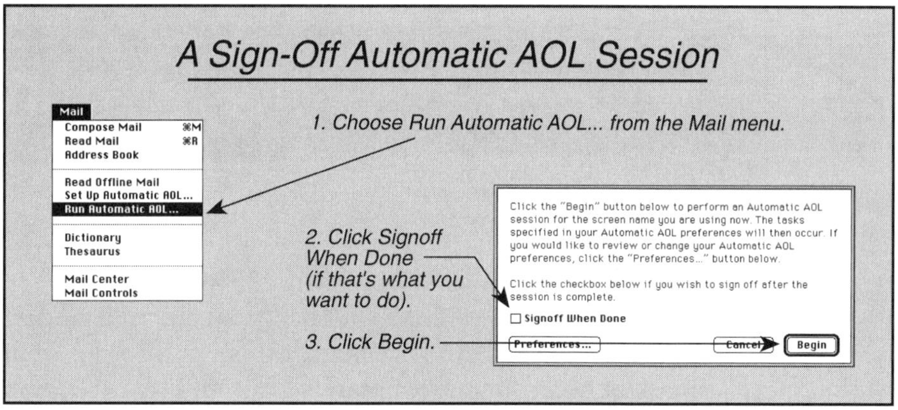
A Sign-Off Automatic AOL Session
Mail
Compose Mail ⌘M
Read Mail ⌘R
Address Book
Read Offline Mail
Set Up Automatic AOL...
Run Automatic AOL...
Dictionary
Thesaurus
Mail Center
Mail Controls
1. Choose Run Automatic AOL... from the Mail menu.
2. Click Signoff When Done (if that's what you want to do).
3. Click Begin.
Click the "Begin" button below to perform an Automatic AOL session for the screen name you are using now. The tasks specified in your Automatic AOL preferences will then occur. If you would like to review or change your Automatic AOL preferences, click the "Preferences..." button below.
Click the checkbox below if you wish to sign off after the session is complete.
Signoff When Done
Preferences...
Cancel
Begin

Figure 6-12: Rather than choose Sign Off from the Go To menu, choose Run Automatic AOL... from the Mail menu. All your queued downloads and mail routines will become a part of the sign-off routine.

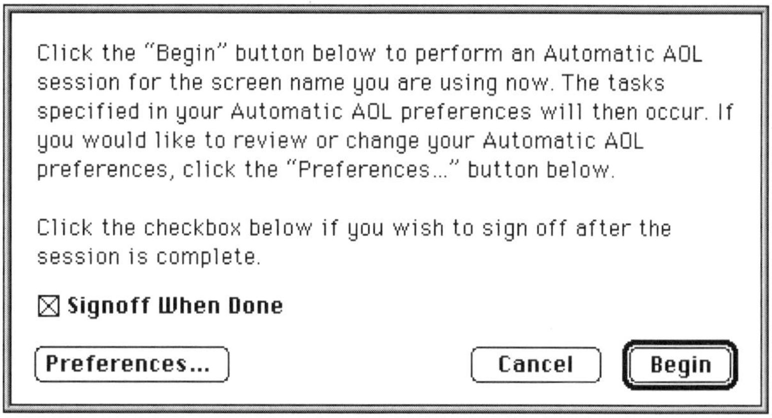
Click the "Begin" button below to perform an Automatic AOL session for the screen name you are using now. The tasks specified in your Automatic AOL preferences will then occur. If you would like to review or change your Automatic AOL preferences, click the "Preferences..." button below.
Click the checkbox below if you wish to sign off after the session is complete.
☒ Signoff When Done
Preferences...
Cancel
Begin

Figure 6-13: Turn on the Signoff When Done option to sign off automatically when an Automatic AOL session concludes.

Where'd That File Go?

Automatic AOL not only receives any mail that AOL is holding for you, it also downloads any files that are attached to that mail. Unfortunately, the destination of those downloads is often obscure and you're forced to scour your hard disk after the Automatic AOL session, looking for the e-mail attachments it has downloaded.

Like all computer programs, AOL only does what it's told. In the case of files attached to e-mail, it defaults to the folder identified by your Download preferences. Though I'll discuss the preferences and the Download Manager later in this chapter, all you have to do to find your files is choose Preferences from your Members menu and select Download from the column on the left (as shown in Figure 6-9). The downloading folder will be plainly identified at the bottom of the resulting window.

Unattended Automatic AOL Sessions

My agent uses e-mail. My publisher uses e-mail. My editor uses e-mail. Indeed, most authors and many others in the book-publishing business work at home, and most manuscripts and related communications are exchanged electronically. There are days when communication sparks across the continent like migrating locusts. Contracts are negotiated, manuscripts are edited, illustrations tweaked—sometimes five or six times a day.

The literary profession isn't unique in its reliance on e-mail. For lawyers, salespeople, brokers, and others who need to send messages—across town, across the country, or around the world—*unattended Automatic AOL sessions* are beyond mere conveniences, they're necessities.

On locust days like these, I instruct Automatic AOL to check for mail every half-hour. This it does, in the background, as reliably as clockwork, regardless of what I'm doing with my computer. There's no need to interrupt my train of thought: Automatic AOL simply signs on, sends queued mail, receives new mail, and signs off. I don't even have to be in the building. That's why they're called "unattended Automatic AOL sessions."

You're not limited to a half-hourly schedule either: you can run unattended Automatic AOL sessions as frequently or as infrequently as you desire. Some people even run them in the predawn hours to take advantage of off-peak hours when traffic is light.

> **Predawn Automatic AOL Tips**
>
> Lots of people run Automatic AOL in the middle of the night. Many of these people are downloading zealots: their download sessions often last for hours. Under these conditions, downloading when system activity is minimal—around 4:00 a.m. Eastern time—makes significant economic sense.
>
> If a 4:00 a.m. Automatic AOL session appeals to you, be sure to leave your computer on with the AOL software running. Don't forget to leave the modem on too (if it's the external variety), but turn off the monitor if you can: monitors (color, especially) consume a lot of power.

Scheduling Unattended Automatic AOL Sessions

In addition to choosing screen names and entering stored passwords, one significant task remains: scheduling the time of day and the days of the week that you want Automatic AOL to conduct its sessions. Figure 6-14 illustrates the procedure.

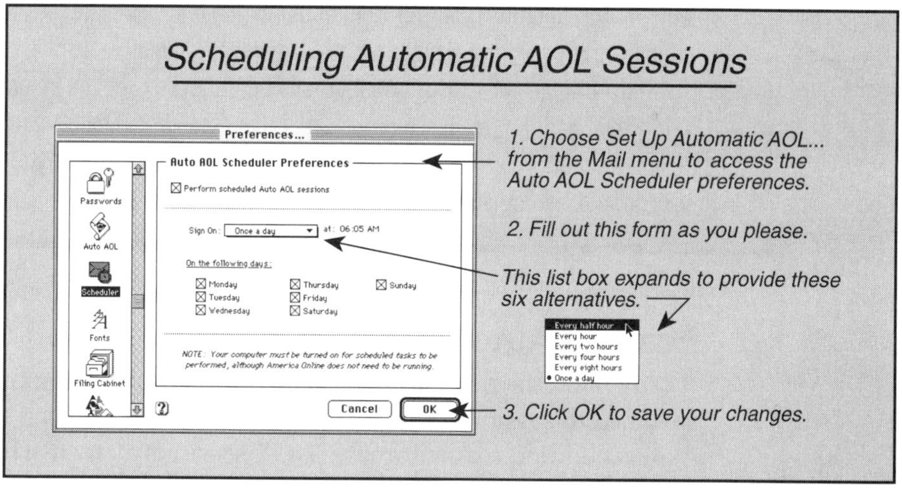
Scheduling Automatic AOL Sessions
Preferences...
Auto AOL Scheduler Preferences
Perform scheduled Auto AOL sessions
Sign On: Once a day at: 06:05 AM
On the following days:
Monday
Tuesday
Wednesday
Thursday
Friday
Saturday
Sunday
NOTE: Your computer must be turned on for scheduled tasks to be performed, although America Online does not need to be running.
Passwords
Auto AOL
Scheduler
Fonts
Filing Cabinet
Cancel
OK
1. Choose Set Up Automatic AOL... from the Mail menu to access the Auto AOL Scheduler preferences.
2. Fill out this form as you please.
This list box expands to provide these six alternatives.
Every half hour
Every hour
Every two hours
Every four hours
Every eight hours
Once a day
3. Click OK to save your changes.

Figure 6-14: The Auto AOL Scheduler Preferences let you declare the days and times you want unattended Automatic AOL sessions to run. Be sure to check the Perform scheduled Auto AOL sessions box (it's easy to neglect) or Automatic AOL won't run.

I've assumed here that you've used the Auto AOL Scheduler Preferences (pictured in Figure 6-14) to check all the activities you want AOL to carry out during a session. Usually you'll want to select all the activities shown in the illustration.

I've also assumed that you have declared the appropriate screen names (and stored passwords) for which you want Automatic AOL to apply. Review Figure 6-8 if you're unsure.

Look again at Figure 6-14. Note that Automatic AOL is scheduled for 5 minutes after the hour. In fact, I can schedule Automatic AOL for any time I like. To change the time, simply click on either the hour display or the minute display with the mouse, and arrows will appear to the left.

Excepting Incoming Files

Just last week, I attempted to send some e-mail to a friend. Attached to the message was a 270K file. Unfortunately, I misspelled his screen name in the To: box of the Compose Mail form. Even more unfortunately, the misspelling meant the mail went to another legitimate AOL screen name—along with the 270K file. Though I resent the mail to the proper person later, the person who was on the receiving end of the misdirected mail was no doubt quite displeased with me if his Automatic AOL session downloaded my file. My error might have cost him 10 minutes or more of connect time.

In other words, to protect yourself from encountering a mistake like the one I inadvertently inflicted on that unsuspecting AOL member, you might want to deactivate the "Download files that are attached to unread mail" option in the Auto AOL Preferences window (see Figure 6-4). "On" is the default; you might want to change that. After all, you can always sign back on to download files, but you can't undo the cost of a lengthy unwanted download once it's done.

Reading Automatic AOL Mail

It only makes sense that AOL lets you read incoming mail from Automatic AOL sessions. What's interesting is that you can read *outgoing* mail scheduled for Automatic AOL sessions as well. This is especially comforting for those of us who suffer from occasional bouts of irresolution. Until it's actually sent, outgoing mail is ours to edit, append, or "wad up and throw away." (Now that I think about it, you can edit, append, or wad up and throw away mail even after it's sent—as long as it's not Internet mail and as long as no one has read it. Refer to Chapter 3, "Electronic Mail & the Personal Filing Cabinet," if you're not familiar with this feature.)

Reading Incoming Mail

Incoming Mail is stored in the Incoming Mail folder in the Offline Mail drawer of your Personal Filing Cabinet. (The Personal Filing Cabinet is discussed in Chapter 3, "Electronic Mail & the Personal Filing Cabinet.") To read Incoming Mail, use the Read Offline Mail command under the Mail menu (or choose Personal Filing Cabinet from the Mail menu), then open the Incoming Mail folder (see Figure 6-15).

Figure 6-15: Reading incoming mail is easy. Because incoming mail is stored on your machine, not AOL's, you can read it when you're offline.

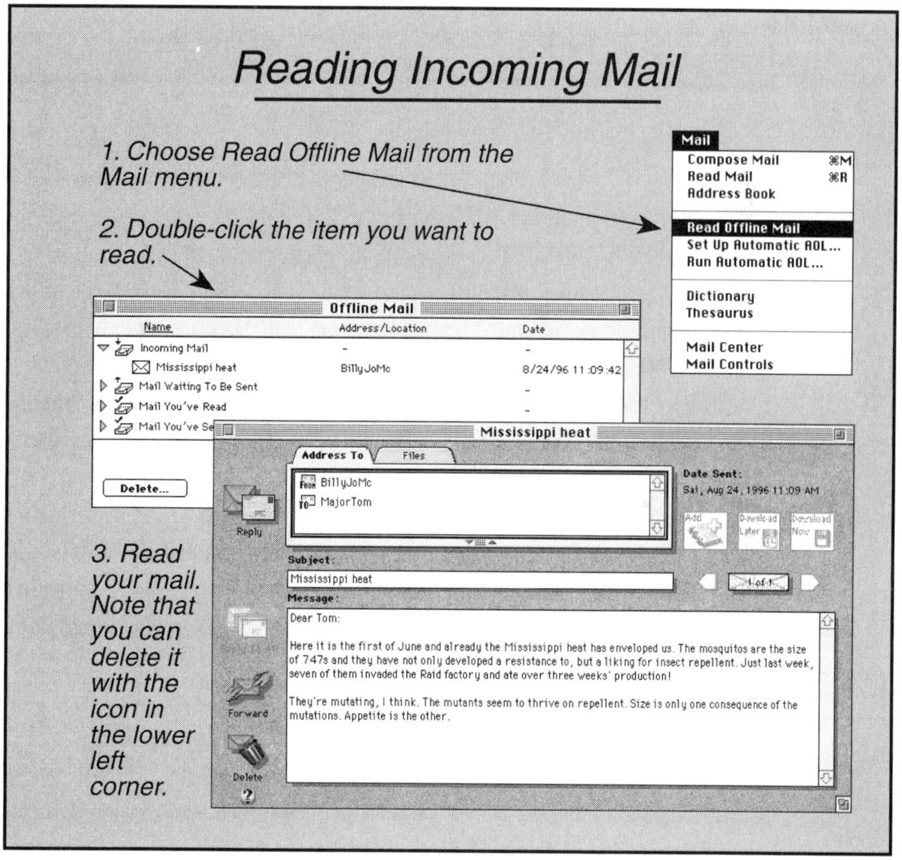
Reading Incoming Mail
1. Choose Read Offline Mail from the Mail menu.
2. Double-click the item you want to read.
3. Read your mail. Note that you can delete it with the icon in the lower left corner.
Mail
Compose Mail ⌘M
Read Mail ⌘R
Address Book
Read Offline Mail
Set Up Automatic AOL...
Run Automatic AOL...
Dictionary
Thesaurus
Mail Center
Mail Controls
Offline Mail
Name
Address/Location
Date
Incoming Mail
Mississippi heat
BillyJoMc
8/24/96 11:09:42
Mail Waiting To Be Sent
Mail You've Read
Delete...
Mississippi heat
Address To
Files
BillyJoMc
MajorTom
Date Sent:
Sat, Aug 24, 1996 11:09 AM
Reply
Forward
Delete
Subject:
Mississippi heat
Message:
Dear Tom:
Here it is the first of June and already the Mississippi heat has enveloped us. The mosquitos are the size of 747s and they have not only developed a resistance to, but a liking for insect repellent. Just last week, seven of them invaded the Raid factory and ate over three weeks' production!
They're mutating, I think. The mutants seem to thrive on repellent. Size is only one consequence of the mutations. Appetite is the other.

Don't confuse the Incoming Mail folder with the Mail You've Read folder which also appears in the Offline Mail drawer of your Personal Filing Cabinet. Mail You've Read stores mail you've already read and chosen to have saved here. The Incoming Mail folder holds only the mail retrieved from an Automatic AOL session. (Again, review Chapter 3 for a thorough explanation of e-mail commands.)

Watch Those Screen Names!

It's important to note that the only mail appearing in the Incoming Mail window is mail addressed to the screen name currently appearing in the window that was onscreen when you issued the command to check your mail. If you've used an Automatic AOL to download mail for more than one screen name, you must change the screen name in the Welcome window (or the Goodbye window, if you've signed on and signed off earlier) to identify incoming mail for each of your screen names. Only then will you find all the mail that came in during the session.

Avoid Clutter

As I mentioned earlier, incoming mail is stored in the Incoming Mail folder in the Offline Mail drawer of your Personal Filing Cabinet. All incoming mail messages are stored there until they're deleted or moved, even after they have been read. This is no place to file your mail. Mail left in this folder continues to appear in the Incoming Mail window, with the oldest at the top. Discovering new mail under these circumstances can be awkward, and you might even miss a piece or two.

Either file incoming mail in your personal mail folders, or delete it after you've read it. Remember also that if you've set your mail preferences to retain copies, all incoming mail will appear in *two* places in your Offline Mail drawer: in the Incoming Mail folder and in the Mail You've Read folder. Be sure to delete both copies if you delete mail, or file one and delete the other.

The Personal Filing Cabinet is discussed in Chapter 3, "Electronic Mail & the Personal Filing Cabinet." Mail preferences are discussed in Appendix E, "Preferences."

Reading Mail Waiting to Be Sent

The Mail Waiting To Be Sent folder stores and allows you to read outgoing mail before you send it. The contents of this folder can be examined either online or off, as long as you've prepared mail for sending with Automatic AOL but haven't sent it yet.

Again, don't confuse this folder with the Mail You've Sent folder. The Mail You've Sent folder is holding mail you've sent and chosen to save a copy of here. The mail Waiting To Be Sent folder holds only mail you've scheduled for delivery but haven't sent yet.

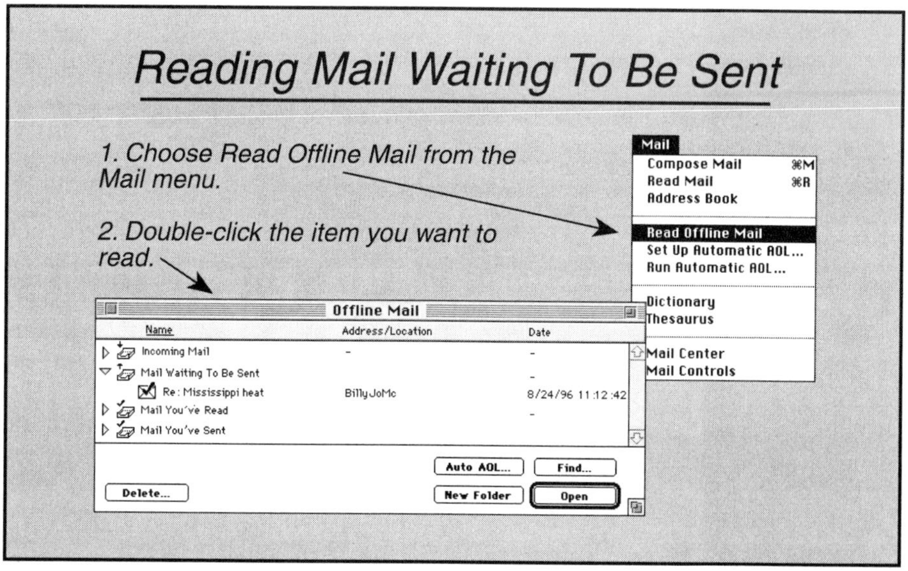
Reading Mail Waiting To Be Sent
1. Choose Read Offline Mail from the Mail menu.
2. Double-click the item you want to read.
Mail
Compose Mail ⌘M
Read Mail ⌘R
Address Book
Read Offline Mail
Set Up Automatic AOL...
Run Automatic AOL...
Dictionary
Thesaurus
Mail Center
Mail Controls
Offline Mail
Name
Address/Location
Date
Incoming Mail
Mail Waiting To Be Sent
Re: Mississippi heat
BillyJoMc
8/24/96 11:12:42
Mail You've Read
Mail You've Sent
Auto AOL...
Find...
Delete...
New Folder
Open

Figure 6-16: The Mail Waiting To Be Sent folder is full only when mail has been scheduled for delivery but hasn't been sent.

The Download Manager

Downloads probably offer more potential than any other AOL feature. There are tens of thousands of files on AOL's hard disks, and every one of them can be downloaded to your computer. There are millions more on the Internet, and many of those are available to you as well. Using the Download Manager, you can establish a queue of files while you're online, reading descriptions and estimating time. When your session is almost over, you then instruct the Download Manager to download the files and sign off—or schedule an Automatic AOL session to download your files for you later, when system activity is less intrusive. Either way, once the process has begun, you can walk away.

Let's watch a typical Download Manager session to see what the screens look like. We'll schedule two files for downloading; then we'll instruct the Download Manager to handle the downloading process and sign off automatically.

Selecting Files for Downloading

Figure 6-17 illustrates the process of selecting a graphic from the VH1 area (at keyword: **VH1**). This is a particularly rewarding area if you're looking for something to download. It's full of graphics, sound, and—of course—video.

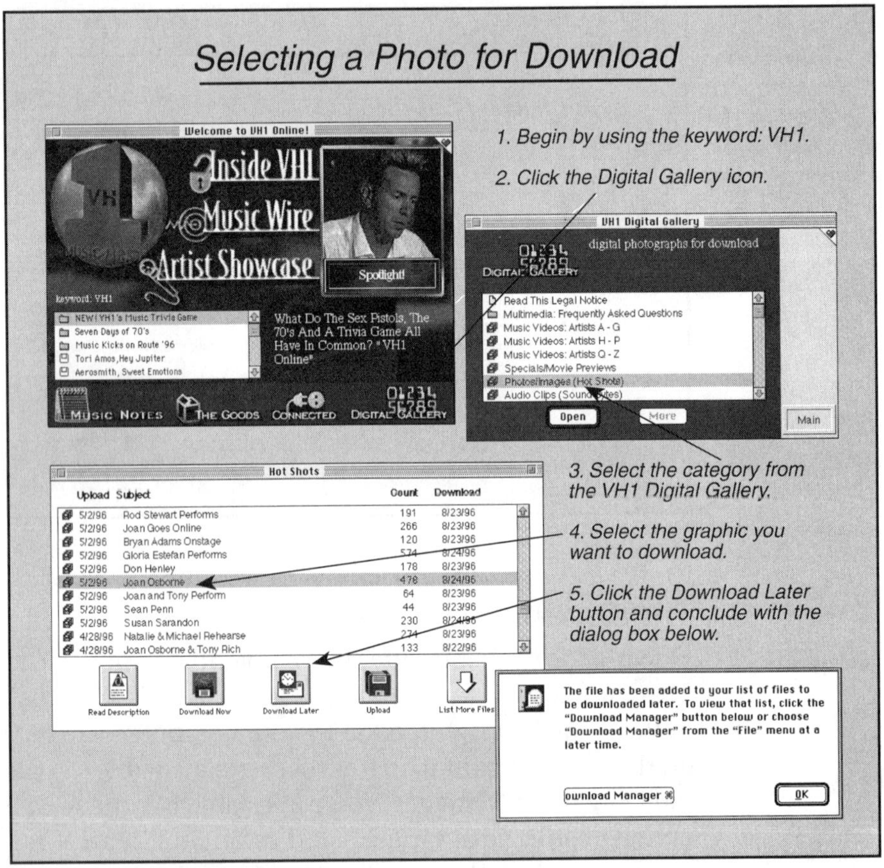
Selecting a Photo for Download
Welcome to VH1 Online!
Inside VH1
Music Wire
Artist Showcase
Spotlight!
keyword: VH1
NEW! VH1's Music Trivia Game
Seven Days of 70's
Music Kicks on Route '96
Tori Amos,Hey Jupiter
Aerosmith, Sweet Emotions
What Do The Sex Pistols, The 70's And A Trivia Game All Have In Common? " VH1 Online"
Music Notes
The Goods
Connected
Digital Gallery
1. Begin by using the keyword: VH1.
2. Click the Digital Gallery icon.
VH1 Digital Gallery
digital photographs for download
Read This Legal Notice
Multimedia: Frequently Asked Questions
Music Videos: Artists A - G
Music Videos: Artists H - P
Music Videos: Artists Q - Z
Specials/Movie Previews
Photos/Images (Hot Shots)
Audio Clips (Sound Bytes)
Open
More
Main
3. Select the category from the VH1 Digital Gallery.
Hot Shots
Upload Subject Count Download
5/2/96 Rod Stewart Performs 191 8/23/96
5/2/96 Joan Goes Online 266 8/23/96
5/2/96 Bryan Adams Onstage 120 8/23/96
5/2/96 Gloria Estefan Performs
5/2/96 Don Henley 178 8/23/96
5/2/96 Joan Osborne 478 8/24/96
5/2/96 Joan and Tony Perform 64 8/23/96
5/2/96 Sean Penn 44 8/23/96
5/2/96 Susan Sarandon 230
4/28/96 Natalie & Michael Rehearse 8/23/96
4/28/96 Joan Osborne & Tony Rich 133 8/22/96
4. Select the graphic you want to download.
5. Click the Download Later button and conclude with the dialog box below.
Read Description
Download Now
Download Later
Upload
List More Files
The file has been added to your list of files to be downloaded later. To view that list, click the "Download Manager" button below or choose "Download Manager" from the "File" menu at a later time.
ownload Manager
OK

Figure 6-17: The last step in selecting a VH1 graphic for delayed downloading is to click the Download Later button, which calls up the dialog box at the bottom of the illustration.

We might as well give the Download Manager more than one thing to do, so let's select another file to add to the download queue. A Mike Keefe political cartoon seems appropriate (see Figure 6-18).

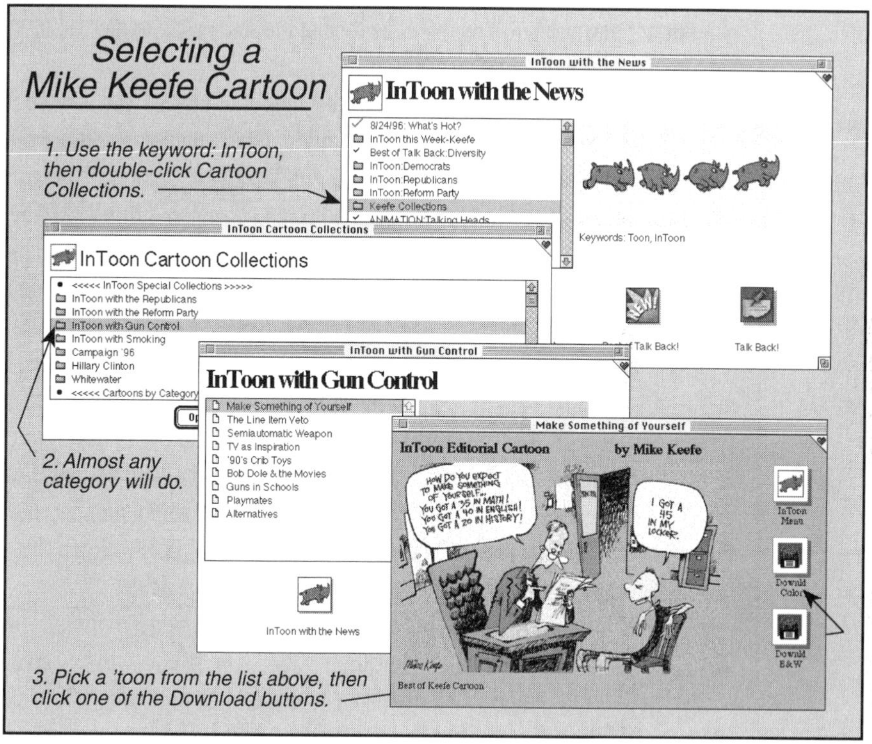
Selecting a Mike Keefe Cartoon
1. Use the keyword: InToon, then double-click Cartoon Collections.
2. Almost any category will do.
3. Pick a 'toon from the list above, then click one of the Download buttons.
InToon with the News
InToon Cartoon Collections
InToon with Gun Control
Make Something of Yourself
InToon Editorial Cartoon
by Mike Keefe

Figure 6-18: Selecting a Mike Keefe cartoon for delayed downloading.

The Control Room

After a couple of hours in the hardware room with Matt Korn (see Chapter 1), my comprehension of things electronic had reached overload. I felt like a tourist inside of a nuclear power plant. You might be feeling the same way, immersed as you are here in AOL's lofty automation features.

Sensing my fatigue, Matt led me to a steel door that opened into a room of contradictory calm and quiet. As I stepped inside, the steel door whooshed shut behind me, latching with the metallic *thunk* of a bank vault. Scores of 21-inch computer monitors lined the room, stacked two and sometimes three high. Seven people scurried about on wheeled chairs, answering incessantly ringing telephones in hushed tones, responding to Instant Messages, and conversing with AOL's online staff working the chat rooms.

This is AOL's control room. Some of its monitors displayed graphical images of AOL's host computer system: webs of interconnections radiating from scores of system processors. Other monitors watched the communications system that connects AOL to the world, displaying, quite graphically, the network of communications links described in Chapter 1. A few text-only monitors tallied the total number of users on the system and the number of logins per minute. The operators watched these seemingly insignificant displays like a driver watches a fuel gauge.

I was reminded of the control room in the movie *The China Syndrome*. The place was alive with drama. I expected the clatter of a klaxon to pierce the air at any minute and Jack Lemmon to emerge from behind a glass wall, proprietary and custodial. I fantasized myself as Michael Douglas, clandestinely taking pictures from beneath a coat folded over my arm. Where's Jane Fonda when I need her?

Running the Download Manager

Eventually, the time will come to reap the harvest. Rather than sign off, choose Download Manager from the File menu. This is a second alternative to the Sign Off command (the first being Run Automatic AOL...—under the Mail menu—described earlier in this chapter). The Run Automatic AOL... command accommodates both delayed mail and downloading activities, but it doesn't offer the control that the Download Manager does. The Download Manager—under the File menu—doesn't send or receive queued mail or newsgroup postings, but it offers access to all the options pictured in Figure 6-19. If you have mail to send and files to download when you sign off, choose Run Automatic AOL... (and configure the Download Manager ahead of time). If you have only files to download, choose the Download Manager.

Figure 6-19: The Download Manager window lists all files scheduled for download.

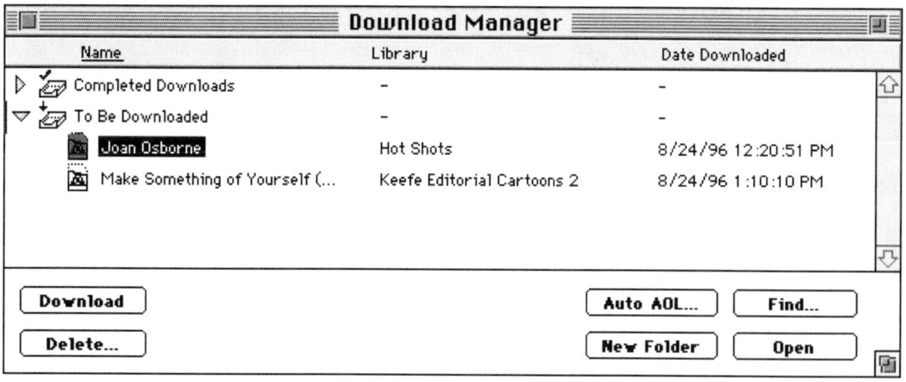
Download Manager
Name
Library
Date Downloaded
Completed Downloads
-
-
To Be Downloaded
-
-
Joan Osborne
Hot Shots
8/24/96 12:20:51 PM
Make Something of Yourself (...
Keefe Editorial Cartoons 2
8/24/96 1:10:10 PM
Download
Delete...
Auto AOL...
Find...
New Folder
Open

Note the folders and buttons in Figure 6-19. This is an impressive array of options. America Online wants you to have complete control over the downloading process, especially now that it's about to begin.

- The *Completed Downloads* folder lets you review your past downloads. There's no value in downloading the same file twice. Though AOL will warn you if you try to download a file you've already downloaded, you can save yourself the trouble by checking this list first.
- The *To Be Downloaded* folder stores your files you've marked to be downloaded later, along with the library they reside in and the date you tagged them for later download.
- The *Download* button begins the download process for the file or files you've selected. We'll use it in a moment.
- The *Delete...* button allows you to remove a file (or two, or three) from the list. Sometimes enthusiasm exceeds resources.
- The *Auto AOL...* button allows you to begin an Automatic AOL session if you have mail you wish sent or received as well.

- The *New Folder* button allows you to organize your Download Manager by creating new folders with your own names. If you have marked a large number of files for download but want to save some to retrieve during another session, you could create a folder titled "Download Next Time" and move files into that folder.
- The *Find...* button lets you search for something among the file names in your Download Manager. This can be useful when you have a large number of completed downloads and are trying to determine if you've already downloaded a file in the past.
- The *Open* button allows you to either open a selected folder, or to view a selected file's description just as you would while browsing a file library by double-clicking its name. Though you probably read the file's description a half-hour ago, chances are you remember nothing about it, now that you've reached the Download Manager window. Lots of things could have happened in the interim. This ability saves a long trip back to the file's original location to review its description.

The Download Preferences, available by selecting Preferences... from the Members menu, determine whether images are displayed while downloading. (See Chapter 5, "Transferring Files," for a discussion of the online graphics viewer.) Options to decompress files upon signing off and to delete compressed files after expanding are also presented here (again, see Chapter 5), as is the ability to change the default download folder. Refer to Appendix E, "Preferences," for a comprehensive discussion of the AOL preference options.

Pick Up Where You Left Off

Occasionally, the downloading process is interrupted. Lightning strikes. A power cord gets tripped over. The phone line develops a stutter. These kinds of things don't happen often, but when they do they always seem to occur when you're 80 percent of the way through a 47-minute download. *Poof!* There goes 35 minutes of connect time.

Don't worry about it. If a file was interrupted during a download, your AOL software makes a note of it and will resume the download queue where you left off the next time you return to the Download Manager.

The downloading process commences when you click the Download button (see Figure 6-20). You can select just one file to download, a series of files (hold down the Shift key while you select them), or an entire folder.

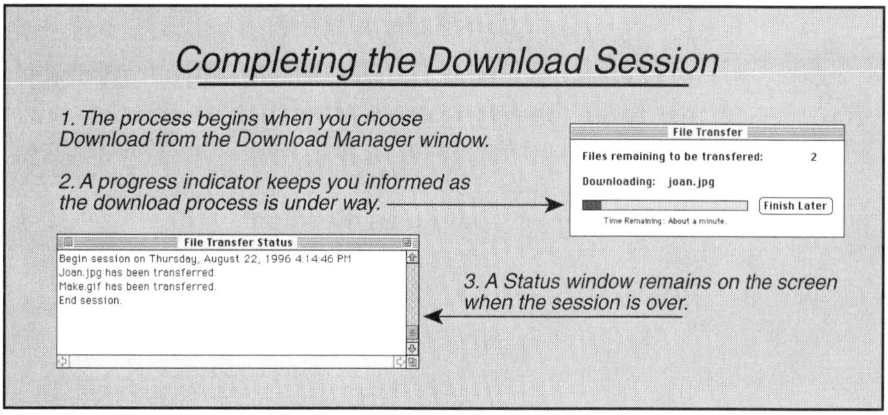
Completing the Download Session
1. The process begins when you choose Download from the Download Manager window.
2. A progress indicator keeps you informed as the download process is under way.
File Transfer
Files remaining to be transfered: 2
Downloading: joan.jpg
Finish Later
Time Remaining: About a minute.
File Transfer Status
Begin session on Thursday, August 22, 1996 4:14:46 PM
Joan.jpg has been transferred.
Make.gif has been transferred.
End session.
3. A Status window remains on the screen when the session is over.

Figure 6-20: The Automatic AOL session ends with a display of the File Transfer Status window.

Suitable for Framing
HOW DO YOU EXPECT TO MAKE SOMETHING OF YOURSELF... YOU GOT A 35 IN MATH! YOU GOT A 40 IN ENGLISH! YOU GOT A 20 IN HISTORY!
I GOT A 45 IN MY LOCKER.
Mike Keefe

Figure 6-21: Tack a couple of downloaded printouts to your wall each day; people will think you're clever, erudite, and urbane.

Moving On

All this time spent talking about Automatic AOL and the Download Manager might make you feel like a real yahoo if you don't use them. Don't worry about it: not all AOL members get enough mail or download enough files to make Automatic AOL and the Download Manager worthwhile. In other words, you've got plenty of company: the yahoos are the majority.

There's a political statement there, I'm sure; but to explore it would hardly be the way to conclude a chapter. Instead, reward yourself for reading this far by turning the page. The "Computing" chapter follows. That's one subject we all have in common, and AOL offers plenty of information on computers. Read on.

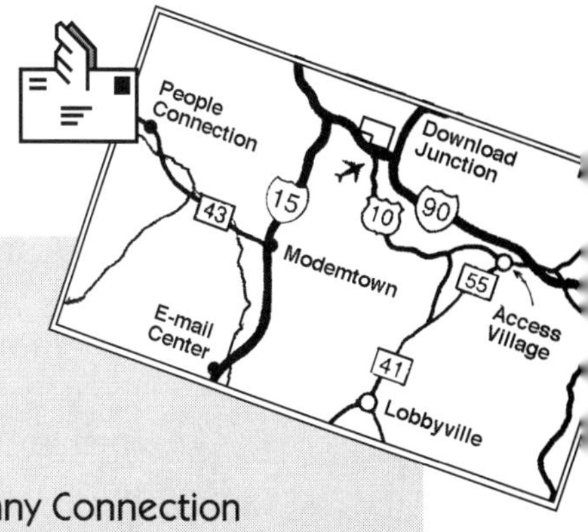
People Connection
Download Junction
15
10
90
43
Modemtown
55
E-mail Center
Access Village
41
Lobbyville

CHAPTER 7

Computing

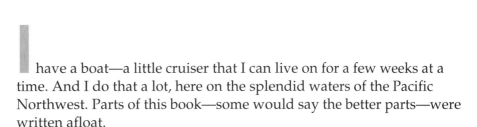

- The Computers & Software Channel
- Live Events
- Computing Media
- The Computing Company Connection
- A Medley of Computing Essentials

I have a boat—a little cruiser that I can live on for a few weeks at a time. And I do that a lot, here on the splendid waters of the Pacific Northwest. Parts of this book—some would say the better parts—were written afloat.

I won't bore you with boat talk, but I got to thinking that it would be nirvana if I could sign on to AOL and find anything and everything to feed my aquatic habit, at no charge other than my normal connect fee. Just think of it: boat stuff, boat advice—even boats themselves—all available online! Elysian waters, indeed.

Boating

If you are also a boating enthusiast, AOL won't disappoint you. Try the keyword: **Boating**. You'll find *Boating* magazine there, the Sailing Forum, newsgroups, World Wide Web sites, and a message board, with ongoing discussions about navigation, tow vehicles, cruising, personal watercraft—the gamut. There are many more boating newsgroups too. Use the keyword: **Newsgroups**, then search using the Search All Newsgroups button. The World Wide Web has recently added a variety of boating sites. Use the keyword: **Web**, then use Webcrawler to search for additional boating subjects (newsgroups and the Web are discussed in Chapter 4, "Using the Internet").

Now if only I could figure out a way to download a nice, 32-foot trawler. . . .

OK, it ain't gonna happen. But my other habit—computing—is amply served in exactly the way I've described. I can get computer programs, drivers, fonts, graphics, sounds, movies, accessories—even the computers themselves—here on AOL. And, with the exception of the hardware, it's all available at nothing more than the cost of my normal connect time and an occasional shareware fee. AOL's computing resources are the consummate carnival—an opiate, a tabernacle, a jubilation for Mac Jedi.

In fact, even if you're not a Mac Jedi, you'll spend a lot of time with AOL's computing resources. There are thousands of files available—fonts and graphics in particular—that will appeal to even the casual Mac user. And if you need help with either your Mac or the software you run on it, AOL is ready to oblige. There are stimulating forums here, ranging from the fundamental to the existential. This place is as rife with opportunity as a sunny Saturday in August, and you can enjoy it any day of the year.

The Computers & Software Channel

Almost everything we'll discuss in this chapter falls under the custody of the Computers & Software Channel (see Figure 7-1). You'll find the Computers & Software Channel listed in the Channels windows, or you can use the keywords: **Computers & Software** to get there.

Computers and Software!!
COMPUTERS & SOFTWARE
the SOFTWARE CENTER
the MULTIMEDIA Zone
Magazine Rack
Support Forums
Family Computing
COMPANY CONNECTION
ZDNet
CONSUMER ELECTRONICS
Lots of good inexpensive software is waiting just a mouse click away.
WHAT'S HOT
marketplace
the web
newswire
AOL CHANNELS
MEMBER SERVICES
FIND
Keyword: Computers & Software

Figure 7-1: The Computers & Software Channel serves as the headwaters for almost everything discussed in this chapter.

The resources offered by this channel are so vast that I've had to divide them up and present them in various chapters of this book. You'll find a discussion of the Computers & Software Channel forums, for example, in Chapter 9, "Boards & Forums." Many of the Computers & Software Channel's Help resources are discussed in Chapter 2, "The Abecedarium."

Remember that you have two ways to reach any destination available on AOL. You can use either menus (in this case, the Computers & Software Channel would be your "top" menu) or keywords. Menus are effective when you're on a discovery mission; keywords get you where you want to go when you know where that place is and want to get there in a hurry.

Although I'll be offering keywords throughout this chapter, remember that you can also get to most of these places via the Computers & Software Channel's main window, pictured in Figure 7-1. You can take the expressway (keywords) and get to a place quickly, or you can use the Computers & Software Channel to explore an alternate route. The best rewards are often found when you travel the back roads.

Live Events

A unique benefit offered by the online community is real-time conferencing. Although this subject is discussed in Chapter 8, "The Community," it warrants special mention here. Perhaps you've noticed already: people who use computers are never shy when the topic of discussion turns to computing. We have more opinions about computers than Andy Rooney has about politics, and Mac evangelists are often especially vocal.

Live computing events occur each week. Many feature celebrities, others feature a computer company representative, and others bring a noted columnist or writer to the stage. Don't confuse these events with one-way media like television or magazines: these are interactive discussions, and you the member are as much a part of them as the guest. Where else could you sit down and chat with Bill Gates or Steve Wozniak?

Keeping up with the schedule of these appearances, however, is like keeping up with a television schedule. We need some kind of "channel listing" of upcoming live events, and it's available in the Computers & Software Channel's Rotunda window (keyword: **Rotunda**), where it's called "Box Office" (see Figure 7-2).

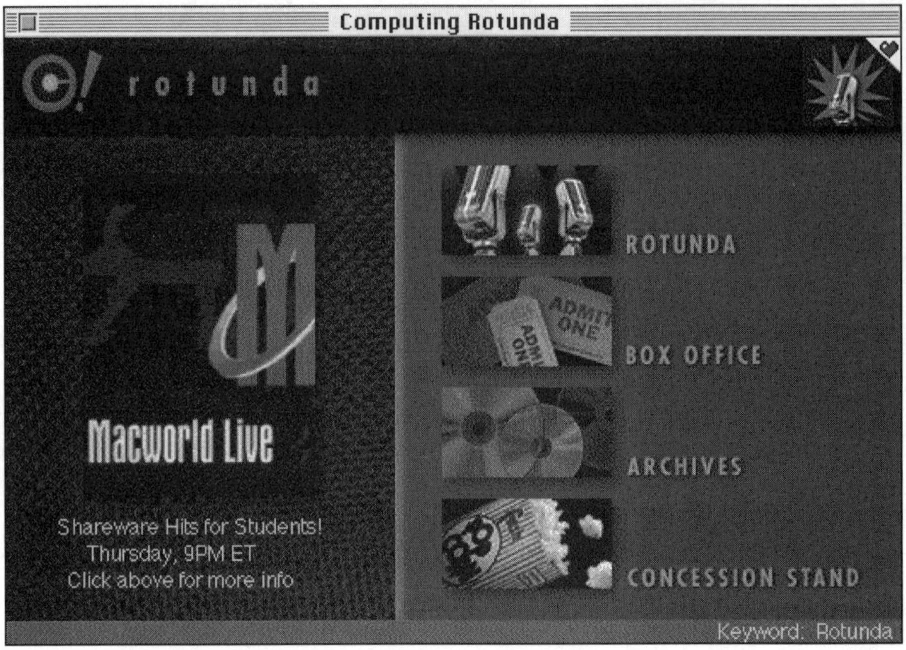
Computing Rotunda
rotunda
Macworld Live
Shareware Hits for Students!
Thursday, 9PM ET
Click above for more info
ROTUNDA
BOX OFFICE
ARCHIVES
CONCESSION STAND
Keyword: Rotunda

Figure 7-2: The Box Office is your guide to upcoming live computing events in the Rotunda.

At Your Doorstep

Just like subscribing to *TV Guide*, you can receive notifications of upcoming live events via e-mail. The people at AOL will send you a notice every week listing all of the events scheduled for the following week, including their start times and keywords.

Unlike *TV Guide*, the service is free. Just send e-mail to the screen name: MailEvents. Ask to be placed on the list of upcoming Computing Rotunda events. They'll take care of the rest.

Computing Media

You simply cannot find a computer magazine that doesn't participate in the online medium in some way. In fact, almost every magazine offers an e-mail address. With magazines, an online presence is a conditioned reflex. Magazines aren't the only computing medium that has discovered the online community—television, radio, newspapers, books: they all offer a presence in some way or other, many on AOL.

Many are computer industry publications, a few of which I'll describe in the paragraphs that follow. For a discussion of online media beyond the computer industry, read Chapter 10, "Staying Informed."

Magazine Rack

If the Computing Forum is a clearinghouse for everything online that relates to computing, the Magazine Rack area is a clearinghouse for all media online that relate to computing (see Figure 7-3). Here's where you'll find all of AOL's online magazines and radio features, plus links to the most popular computing-media Web sites.

The Cobb Group Online
MacUser
Mobile Office
WIRED
HOMEPC
Magazine Rack
ComputerLife
A Guided Tour
Business Week's Computer Room
Cartoons - on Computers & Technology
ChipNet
c|net: the computer network
Cobb Group Online
Communications Week - WEB
Computer America
Computer and Internet Dictionary
Get Answers at the Komando Klinic
HomePC
Read the hot reviews in HomePC
Check Out Speak Out!
Live Events
Webcrawler Search
Keyword: Magazine Rack
Macworld
MULTIMEDIA WORLD
BW
Kim Komando's Komputer Klinic

Figure 7-3: Use the keywords: **Magazine Rack** to access all of the computing media resources from one central location.

Macworld Online

There's so much great media stuff here, it's hard to know where to begin. One thing I know we all have in common is our Macs, so Macworld Online (see Figure 7-4) is probably a good starting point.

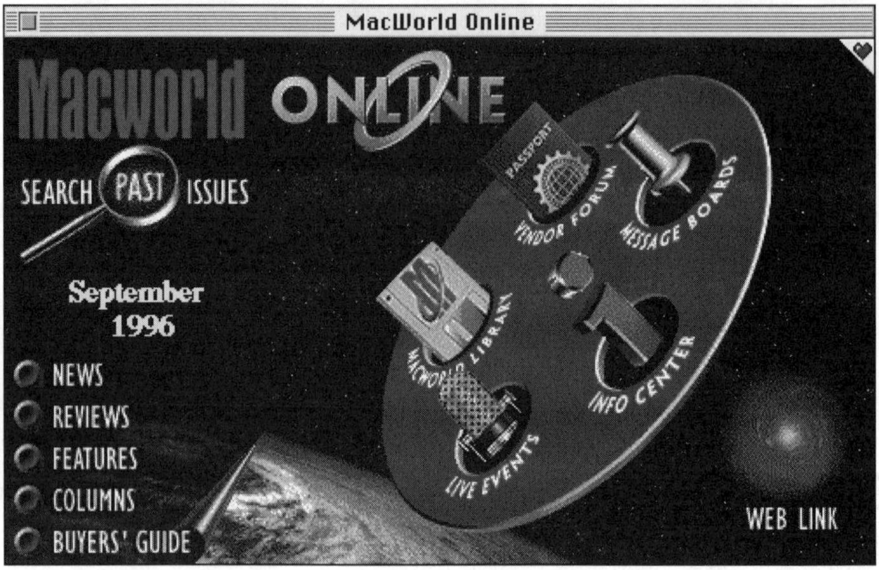
MacWorld Online
Macworld ONLINE
SEARCH PAST ISSUES
September 1996
NEWS
REVIEWS
FEATURES
COLUMNS
BUYERS' GUIDE
PASSPORT
VENDOR FORUM
MESSAGE BOARDS
MACWORLD LIBRARY
INFO CENTER
LIVE EVENTS
WEB LINK

Figure 7-4: Everything but the ads: nearly everything in the current issue of *Macworld* is online, plus past issues, software libraries, and message boards. Use the keyword: **Macworld**.

I visit Macworld Online once a month without fail, and whenever I'm contemplating a purchase—hardware or software—I consult the reviews. Are you interested in all of the latest stuff for the Mac? Search for it via Macworld Online's Search button (look for it near the top of the window in Figure 7-4). Last year I researched high-speed CD-ROM drives. After briefly searching past issues, I discovered that the price of the drive I needed—and eventually purchased—was about to drop. I recently heard that the new "multimedia" CD-ROM drives were available, so once again I consulted the *Macworld* archives (see Figure 7-5).

While past issues are a primary feature of Macworld Online, hundreds of news stories, reviews, and files also are available—all searchable, and all in a form you can use in documents of your own. In addition, Macworld Online offers message boards and live events that put you in touch with *Macworld*'s editorial staff. And a library of files offers indices to past issues, macros, and programs (see Figure 7-6).

Figure 7-5: Searching past issues of *Macworld*, America Online found an article describing "multi-media" CD-ROM drives.

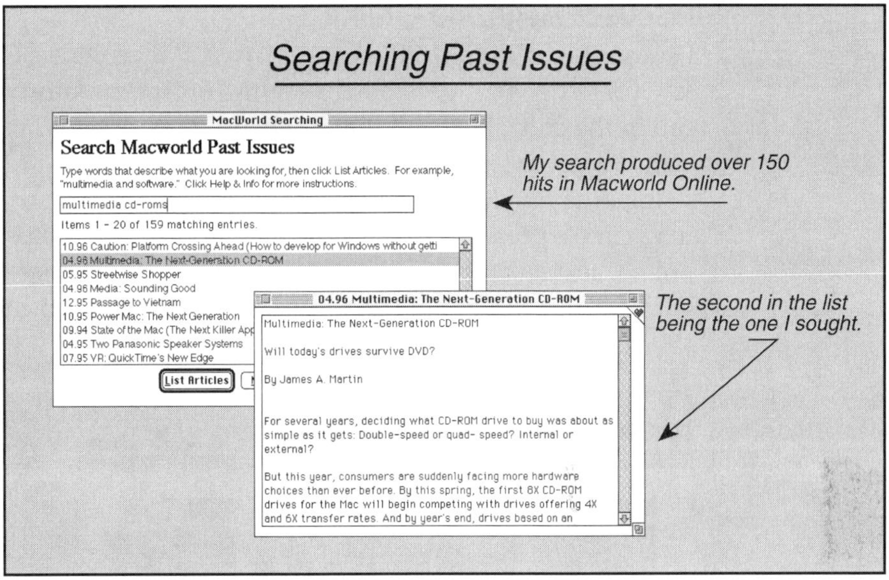
Searching Past Issues
MacWorld Searching
Search Macworld Past Issues
Type words that describe what you are looking for, then click List Articles. For example, "multimedia and software." Click Help & Info for more instructions.
multimedia cd-roms
Items 1 - 20 of 159 matching entries.
10.96 Caution: Platform Crossing Ahead (How to develop for Windows without getti
04.96 Multimedia: The Next-Generation CD-ROM
05.95 Streetwise Shopper
04.96 Media: Sounding Good
12.95 Passage to Vietnam
10.95 Power Mac: The Next Generation
09.94 State of the Mac (The Next Killer App
04.95 Two Panasonic Speaker Systems
07.95 VR: QuickTime's New Edge
List Articles
My search produced over 150 hits in Macworld Online.
04.96 Multimedia: The Next-Generation CD-ROM
Multimedia: The Next-Generation CD-ROM
Will today's drives survive DVD?
By James A. Martin
For several years, deciding what CD-ROM drive to buy was about as simple as it gets: Double-speed or quad- speed? Internal or external?
But this year, consumers are suddenly facing more hardware choices than ever before. By this spring, the first 8X CD-ROM drives for the Mac will begin competing with drives offering 4X and 6X transfer rates. And by year's end, drives based on an
The second in the list being the one I sought.

Figure 7-6: A software library, an info center, a vendor forum, and the *Macworld* Web page, all at keyword: **Macworld**.

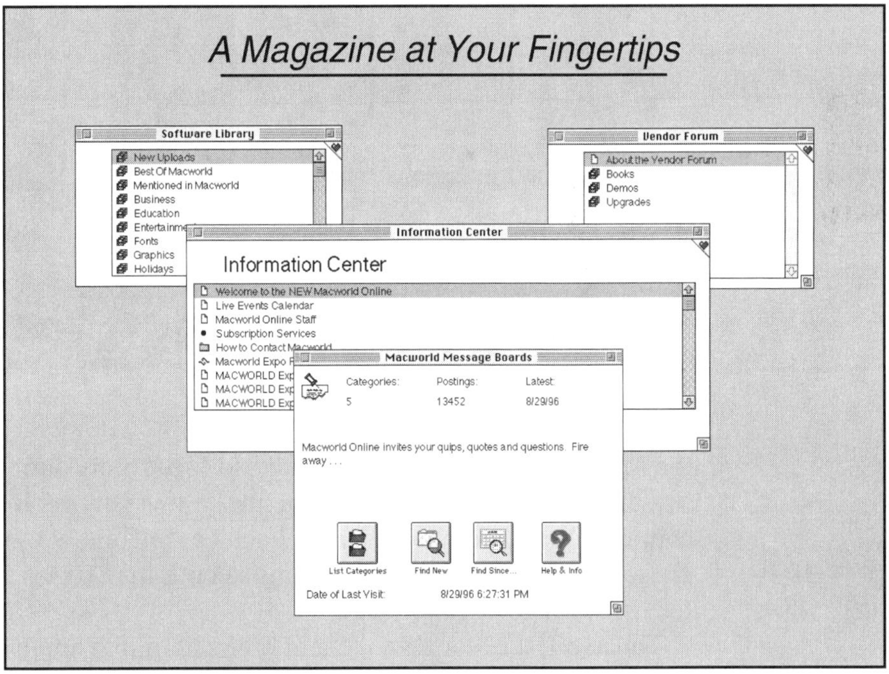
A Magazine at Your Fingertips
Software Library
New Uploads
Best Of Macworld
Mentioned in Macworld
Business
Education
Fonts
Graphics
Holidays
Vendor Forum
About the Vendor Forum
Books
Demos
Upgrades
Information Center
Information Center
Welcome to the NEW Macworld Online
Live Events Calendar
Macworld Online Staff
Subscription Services
Macworld Message Boards
Categories:
Postings:
Latest:
5
13452
8/29/96
Macworld Online invites your quips, quotes and questions. Fire away . . .
List Categories
Find New
Find Since...
Help & Info
Date of Last Visit:
8/29/96 6:27:31 PM

MacUser Magazine Online

I subscribe to both *MacUser* and *Macworld* magazines. Over the past few years I've thought about allowing one of the subscriptions to lapse. But in the end, I realized that I depend on both equally, and I simply didn't want to let go of either one.

Imagine my delight when *MacUser Magazine* appeared online. This magazine's presence is substantial: everything in the printed version is online, and an extensive library of files for Mac users—including games, utilities, sounds, and music—complements the textual material.

MacUser Magazine
MacUser
Info
Feedback
SOFTWARE
MESSAGES
NEWS
EVENTS
MacUser
ABSOLUTE
POWER
MacUserWeb
Now
Utility Of The Month
Read MacUser
Keyword: MacUser
WOW!
Free
CD-ROM!
MacUser
ad index
ZDNet

Figure 7-7: MacUser Magazine Online focuses on information and resources for the Mac user.

Enumerating the features offered by this forum would be redundant: the MacUser Magazine and Macworld forums are similar in design and presentation. Like the print magazines, however, the forums differ in content. Duplication is minimal. Each complements the other. Just as I chose to continue my subscriptions to both magazines, so it is with the forums: you gotta have both.

The MacUser Magazine forum offers a unique and significant feature: a library of programs written by the magazine's staff. There are scores of programs here, including the industry standard MacBench, a performance-measuring utility with a wealth of reporting features (see Figure 7-8).

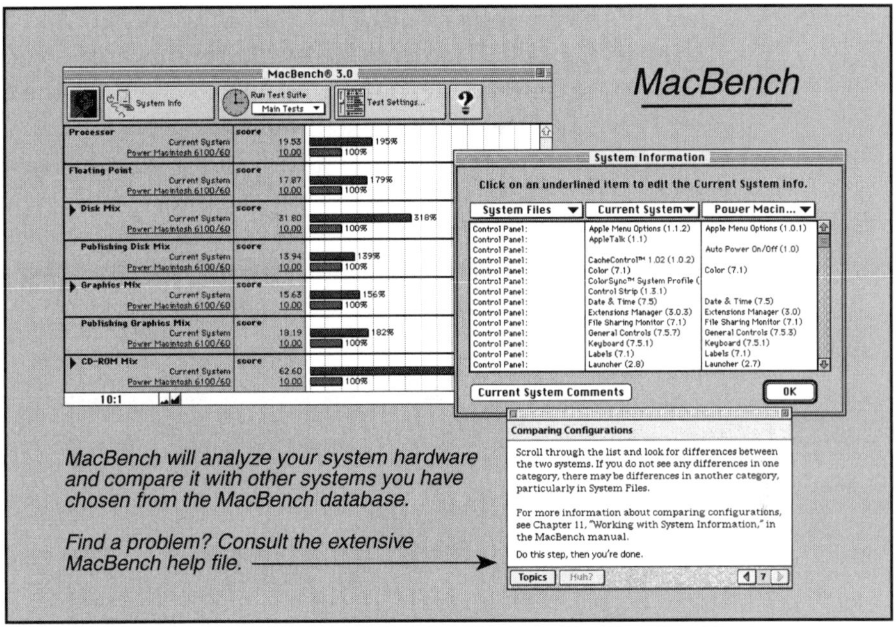
MacBench
MacBench® 3.0
System Information
Click on an underlined item to edit the Current System info.
Current System Comments
OK
Comparing Configurations
Scroll through the list and look for differences between the two systems. If you do not see any differences in one category, there may be differences in another category, particularly in System Files.
For more information about comparing configurations, see Chapter 11, "Working with System Information," in the MacBench manual.
Do this step, then you're done.
Topics
MacBench will analyze your system hardware and compare it with other systems you have chosen from the MacBench database.
Find a problem? Consult the extensive MacBench help file.

Figure 7-8: MacBench can measure the performance of your Mac and find possible problems with your hardware or setup. A review of the program's exhaustive Help file will offer some solutions.

A real-world example best illustrates the value of online support for the computer user. My new PowerMac was acting erratically—one of those nagging problems that left no signature and defied positive identification. I used MacBench to isolate the problem; with the results, I traveled to the Macintosh Utilities forum (keyword: **MUT**) to see if anyone there had a solution.

Sure enough, many others had experienced the same problem. The solution turned out to be replacing my older extensions with the native PowerMac extensions that had been conveniently posted on AOL. I downloaded the extensions, installed them, and improved my computer's performance *by 20 percent* in just a few minutes. This I did at night on a holiday weekend, when no other resources were available (or necessary, as it turned out). I have MacUser Magazine online (and the Mac Utilities forum) to thank for my redemption.

Business Week Online's Computer Room

You know about *Business Week* magazine. It's online, at keyword: **BW**, and there are few that can compare with its immediacy and depth in reporting on current issues. If you're an incorrigible digit-head, you also know that *Business Week* is the first general-interest magazine to break out a separate department to provide weekly bulletins from the world's technology fronts. That was 15 years ago, and now it's all available online. There's no keyword for this area—yet (there might be one by the time you read this). But it's available in the Magazine Rack window, at keywords: **Magazine Rack**.

The Cyberscooter

One of the more eccentric stories available in the Business Week Online Computer Room is about the Cyberscooter: a Neimann-Marcus offering in their 1995 Christmas catalog (see Figure 7-9).

Figure 7-9: The Cyberscooter.

It seems that Motorola Cellular Service has teamed up with underwear maker Joe Boxer to create the Cyberscooter—just the thing for fashion-conscious technology-minded road warriors. The polka-dotted Vespa is equipped with a cellular phone and a digital communicator, allowing simultaneous I-way and byway cruising for the terminally bored. Also included in the deal are a bright yellow "happy face" helmet and antenna flag, 30 pairs of boxer shorts, and your very own page on Joe Boxer's World Wide Web site, all for a trivial $10,000. And you thought this computer stuff was just for dweebs.

An Embarrassment of Riches

The three online computer magazines I've described are only a few of AOL's online computer-oriented publications. Be sure to investigate Home *Office* Computing, *MacHome* Journal, Computer *Life* Online, *FamilyPC* Online, and *WIRED*. Each is available by using the italicized portion of its title above as the keyword.

> **Keyword Tricks**
>
> If you take the time to thumb through Appendix B of this book, you'll see that AOL's list of keywords is epic, and more are being added every day. In fact, almost every keyword has a synonym or two—or three—and those synonyms are typically common-sense words.
>
> Let's say you want to go to the *New York Times* online area. Actually its online name is "@times," but you've forgotten that. Don't fret: try the keywords: **New York**, or **Times**, or **NYC**, or **NYTimes**—they'll all get you there.
>
> This tip doesn't just apply to the *Times*, nor does it just apply to the computer-related online magazines mentioned in the text: it applies to almost every area online. Forget the keyword? Press Command-K, then type in almost anything that describes where you want to go. What's to lose? Even if the keyword doesn't exist, AOL may suggest other keywords that are spelled similarly. The worst that can happen is that you'll get an "Invalid Keyword" error, and no one has failed to recover from that.
>
> Thanks to Sean Stallings (who uses a HAL 9000 for his online travels) for this tip.

The Computing Company Connection

Computer users often need help with hardware or software, which leads us directly into a discussion of the Computing Company Connection. There are a number of ways to solve problems with your computer:

- Worry at the problem, trying solutions as they come to mind. This might take a week.
- Look up the solution in the manual (if you can remember where you put it). This usually takes half a day.

- Call the publisher or manufacturer—which can involve 20 minutes on hold (listening to a bad radio station playing commercials for stores in a city 3,000 miles away) then several days waiting for someone to return your call.
- Or you can sign on to AOL, type in the software publisher's keyword, and post your question. Within 24 hours you will receive not only a response from the vendor you're trying to reach but also helpful advice from fellow users who have experienced the same problem (see Figure 7-10).

Figure 7-10: No waiting on hold: post your question online and read a response at your convenience a few hours later.

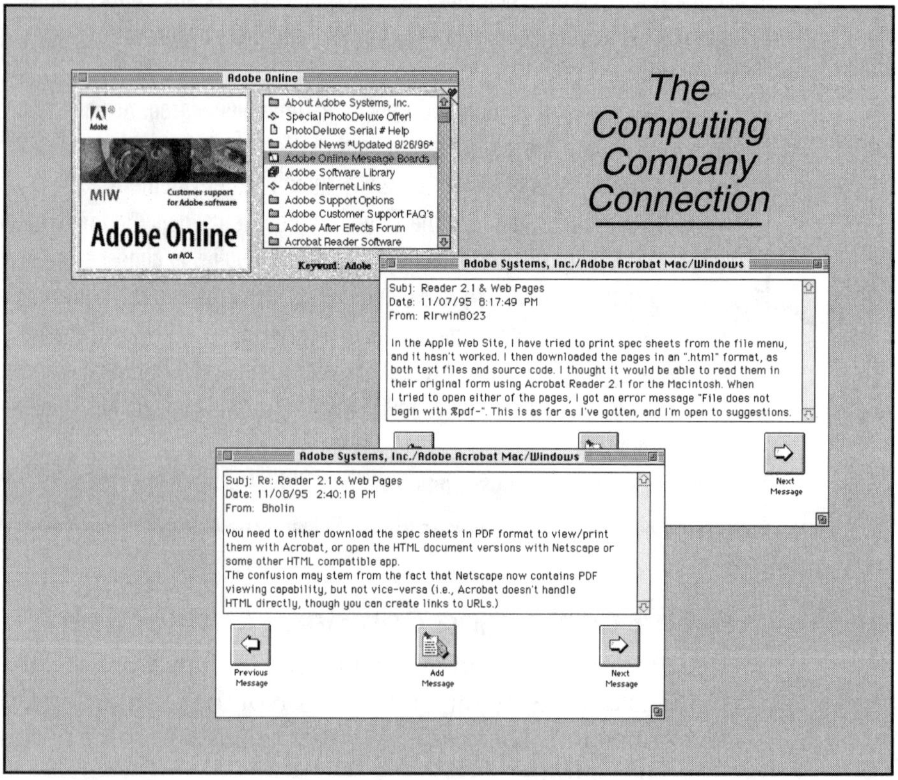
Adobe Online
About Adobe Systems, Inc.
Special PhotoDeluxe Offer!
PhotoDeluxe Serial # Help
Adobe News *Updated 8/26/96*
Adobe Online Message Boards
Adobe Software Library
Adobe Internet Links
Adobe Support Options
Adobe Customer Support FAQ's
Adobe After Effects Forum
Acrobat Reader Software
MIW
Customer support for Adobe software
Adobe Online on AOL
Keyword: Adobe
The Computing Company Connection
Adobe Systems, Inc./Adobe Acrobat Mac/Windows
Subj: Reader 2.1 & Web Pages
Date: 11/07/95 8:17:49 PM
From: RIrwin8023
In the Apple Web Site, I have tried to print spec sheets from the file menu, and it hasn't worked. I then downloaded the pages in an ".html" format, as both text files and source code. I thought it would be able to read them in their original form using Acrobat Reader 2.1 for the Macintosh. When I tried to open either of the pages, I got an error message "File does not begin with %pdf-". This is as far as I've gotten, and I'm open to suggestions.
Next Message
Adobe Systems, Inc./Adobe Acrobat Mac/Windows
Subj: Re: Reader 2.1 & Web Pages
Date: 11/08/95 2:40:18 PM
From: Bholin
You need to either download the spec sheets in PDF format to view/print them with Acrobat, or open the HTML document versions with Netscape or some other HTML compatible app.
The confusion may stem from the fact that Netscape now contains PDF viewing capability, but not vice-versa (i.e., Acrobat doesn't handle HTML directly, though you can create links to URLs.)
Previous Message
Add Message
Next Message

No Place for Vilification

Look again at RIrwin8023's question in Figure 7-10. He identifies the complexity of his problem, including methods he's using to work around it. He resisted the temptation to take out his frustration on the manufacturer. Instead, he is concise, specific, and nonantagonistic.

If we all communicated our problems this courteously—no matter how frustrating and agonizing the problems might be—we'd be more likely to receive prompt, courteous responses like this one. Requesting support—whether it's from the industry or from a peer—is not the proper time to show off our expertise or shower abuse on those who are trying to help us.

Prepare your question in advance, before you sign on. Include the hardware brand name, software version number, system configuration, additional boards—those kinds of things. Spend a few moments checking your message for clarity, brevity, and courtesy. Sign on and post your message only after it has passed this kind of scrutiny. You can prepare a message offline, away from a message board, by choosing New from the File menu (or pressing Command-N). After you have prepared the message, select it all and copy it. Now sign on and find the message board you want, then paste your message into the form used for posting messages on the board. The Select All, Copy, and Paste commands are all under the Edit menu.

The service that provides this help is AOL's *Company Connection* shown in Figure 7-11 (use the keyword: **Company Connection**). Hundreds of vendors currently maintain message boards on AOL, and each vendor checks its board at least once a day. Not only is excellent vendor support found here, but also peer support, libraries of accessories and updates, announcements from the industry, and tips from other users.

Company Connection
COMPANY CONNECTION
Mutual Fund Center
IN THE SPOTLIGHT
COMPANY SUPPORT
DEMO LIBRARY
COMPUTING LIVE
COMPUTING MARKETPLACE
Mustang Software
Metrowerks
company search
the web
FEEDBACK
Keyword: Company Connection

Figure 7-11: The Company Connection is your direct route to hundreds of software and hardware manufacturers.

Software libraries usually round out the company support area online. These libraries boast a variety of programs for downloading, including patches, demo versions, diagnostic tools, and hardware and software drivers—programs that would otherwise only be available directly from software manufacturers.

A Medley of Computing Essentials

I've been a regular visitor to AOL's computing areas for over four years now, and I still haven't seen it all. This place is as vast as Bill Gates's ambition. Though I'm going to describe a number of computing areas on the upcoming pages, the list is by no means comprehensive. Don't confine yourself to those mentioned in this book. Use the keyword: **Computing**, and explore. When it comes to doing things online, a healthy curiosity is as rewarding as a fast modem.

Kim Komando's Komputer Klinic

You might have heard of Kim Komando. You might have seen her on Fox TV or read her columns in *FamilyPC* magazine. She has a couple of books on the shelves and a regular talk radio show too.

Most of all, Kim Komando knows how to answer questions about computers. She does that in plain English, without affectation or embroidery. Moreover, she's accessible: she's willing to help members regardless of how simple their questions might seem. Computerdom needs more Kim Komandos, but at least we have *one* (see Figure 7-12, and use the keyword: **Komando**).

Helping You Take Komand of Your Komputer
Kim Komando's Komputer Klinic
Answer Zone
Downloads
Contests/ Chat
Hot Ideas
Tips
Store
The Net
MAG RACK
FIND
ANSWER ZONE

Figure 7-12: Kim Komando's Komputer Klinic is one of the best places online for straight talk about hardware and software. That's Kim in the lower right corner—proof positive that she is *not* Mr. Science, in spite of rumors to the contrary.

You'll find answers to common questions about buying and upgrading a computer, downloading and uploading, CD-ROMs, scanners, sound and video, memory, networking, and the Internet (be sure to check out her Internet Hot Spots). Naturally, you can submit questions of your own and receive a reply within a couple of days.

You'll also find the highly respected American Computer Exchange—AmCoEx—listing of used computer systems and related equipment pricing. Take a look and you'll know exactly the high, low, and average price paid on just about any piece of computer hardware.

Kim Komando is also one of only two people who actually know the identity of radio's Mr. Science, and apparently she has an in with him, as her area is one of the few places in *any* medium that offers a direct connection to the man who phones in his radio interviews from a telephone booth outside a WalMart store in Medina, Arkansas.

Komando (pronounce it "commando") really *is* Kim's last name, she doesn't wear a pocket protector and she admits to being a blonde.

Family Computing

I'm going to let you in on one of AOL's little secrets: the Family Computing Forum is one of AOL's most popular areas—in fact, it's among the Computers & Software Channel's top five performers. And when it comes to popularity among members, few areas can compare to the Computers & Software Channel.

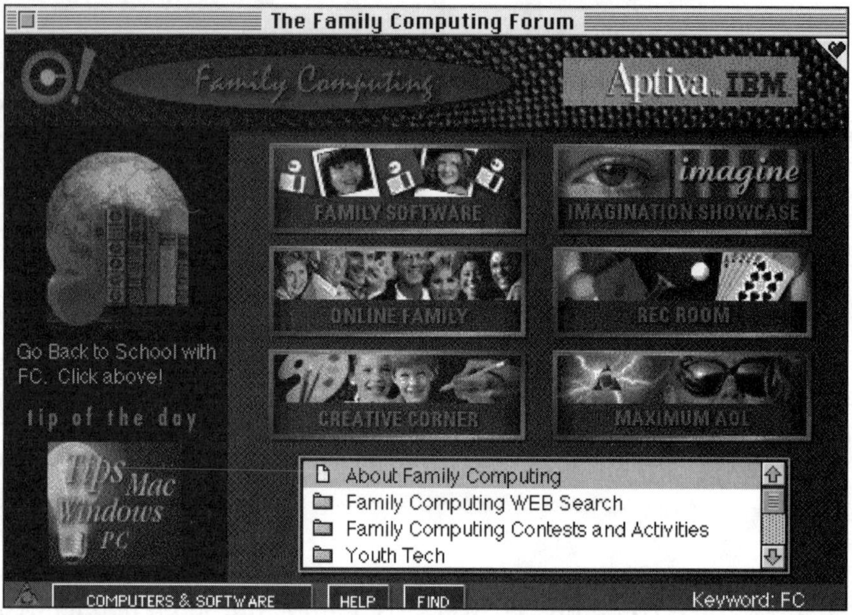
The Family Computing Forum
Family Computing
Aptiva IBM
imagine
FAMILY SOFTWARE
IMAGINATION SHOWCASE
ONLINE FAMILY
REC ROOM
Go Back to School with FC. Click above!
tip of the day
CREATIVE CORNER
MAXIMUM AOL
Tips Mac Windows PC
About Family Computing
Family Computing WEB Search
Family Computing Contests and Activities
Youth Tech
COMPUTERS & SOFTWARE
HELP
FIND
Keyword: FC

Figure 7-13: The Family Computing Forum is one of AOL's worst-kept secrets.

Why is this area so popular? There are a number of theories, but 10 minutes in the forum tells all: people are made to feel welcome here. You'll learn about your computer, in a refreshingly shirtsleeve atmosphere—one where you can take the family and learn about computers together. You'll find pictures of members and their families in the Family Gallery and the "Refrigerator Door," where young artists hang their computer graphic originals. There's a chat room where you can take your grandmother, if you want, without fear of snerts or trolls or phishers offending her (snerts, phishers, and trolls are discussed in Chapter 8, "The Community"). There's a rec room for family game-playing and a Maximum AOL area where family members can go to learn new things about using AOL (probably the best tips area on the service!).

Excellence, it seems, is often discovered in the most unlikely places. The Family Computing Forum is one of them.

Software/Hardtalk With John Dvorak

You probably know who John Dvorak is. You might listen to his *Software/Hardtalk* on public radio stations and Armed Forces Radio, or read his monthly column in *MacUser Magazine*.

Dvorak's Software/Hardtalk area on AOL publishes all of his radio interviews and provides a discussion area for the subjects and issues covered on the program. You'll see some commentary that hasn't appeared in other media. Get all the skinny at keyword: **Dvorak**.

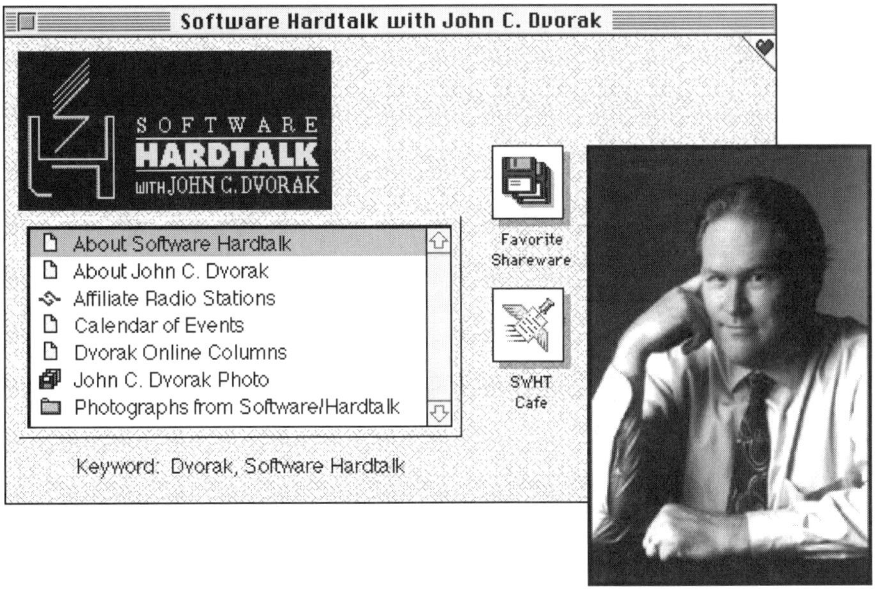
Software Hardtalk with John C. Dvorak
SOFTWARE
HARDTALK
WITH JOHN C. DVORAK
About Software Hardtalk
About John C. Dvorak
Affiliate Radio Stations
Calendar of Events
Dvorak Online Columns
John C. Dvorak Photo
Photographs from Software/Hardtalk
Favorite Shareware
SWHT Cafe
Keyword: Dvorak, Software Hardtalk

Figure 7-14: John C. Dvorak's Software/Hardtalk offers a reprise of his radio broadcasts, commentary, discussions, and frequent live events.

Fonts

Fonts are the chocolate of computing: you can never have enough. To many of AOL's members, fonts are the most tempting downloads AOL offers. They're relatively small (most download in less than a minute at 14.4 kbps) and inexpensive. Most of these fonts are shareware or freeware; the shareware fees rarely exceed $15. Best of all, they enhance your documents with personality and individuality, like icing on a cake. Chocolate icing, of course. Yum.

Mac fonts come in two flavors: TrueType and PostScript (the Desktop & Web Publishing Forum—where you'll find vast libraries of fonts—calls these "Type 1" and "Type 3" fonts respectively). Most general Mac users seem to prefer TrueType, though desktop publishers prefer PostScript. Neither group could ask for much more than these extensive Desktop and Web Publishing Forum offerings. Researching this chapter, I found more than 800 PostScript Mac fonts online. I didn't bother to count the TrueType ones, but there were just as many, or more. In addition, a number of Windows-to-Macintosh font converters were available, which means the entire Windows desktop publishing font library is accessible as well. We're talking about thousands of fonts here. If fonts are chocolate, AOL is the passkey to the Godiva kitchens (Figure 7-15).

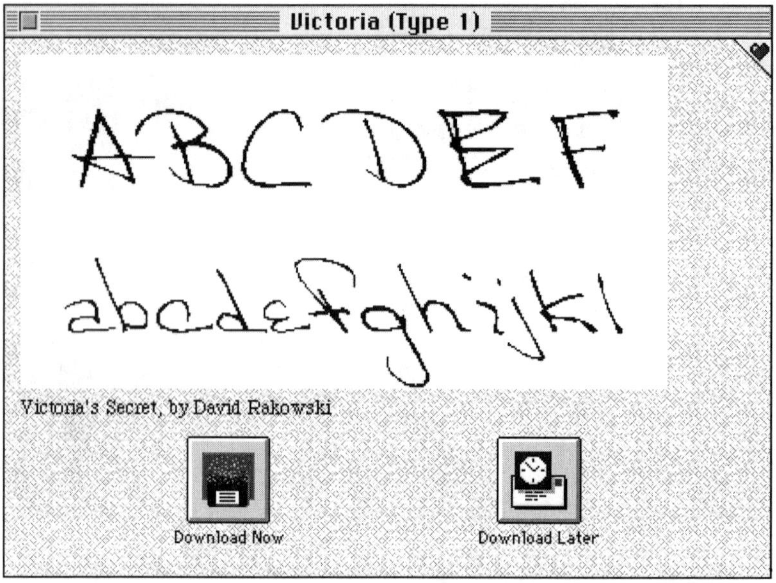
Victoria (Type 1)
ABCDEF
abcdefghijkl
Victoria's Secret, by David Rakowski
Download Now
Download Later

Figure 7-15: The Desktop & Web Publishing Forum (keyword: **DWP**) offers an area where you can see fonts before they're downloaded.

New Product Showcase

The New Product Showcase area at keyword: **NPS** offers information and services you're unlikely to find anywhere else—events, trends, and innovations in the high-technology industry, including multimedia and interactivity. Unlike most other information, the information you receive via the New Product Showcase comes to you directly from the source: from the high-tech manufacturer or service company—in their language, unedited and unfiltered.

Figure 7-16: Events, trends, and innovations at keyword: **NPS**.

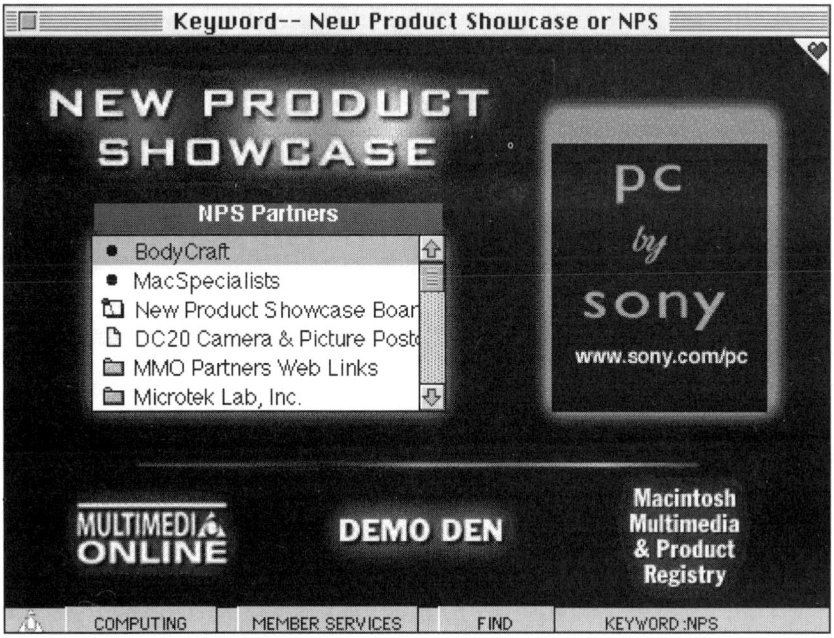
Keyword-- New Product Showcase or NPS
NEW PRODUCT SHOWCASE
NPS Partners
BodyCraft
MacSpecialists
New Product Showcase Boar
DC20 Camera & Picture Post
MMO Partners Web Links
Microtek Lab, Inc.
pc by sony
www.sony.com/pc
MULTIMEDIA ONLINE
DEMO DEN
Macintosh Multimedia & Product Registry
COMPUTING
MEMBER SERVICES
FIND
KEYWORD:NPS

You'll find photos, press kits and demos, transcripts of live press announcements, and comprehensive product directories here—all of the latest stuff in the computing and multimedia industry.

Electronic Frontier Foundation

Out here in the west, it wasn't long ago that we called ourselves a frontier. There were no population centers, no organized form of government. Things ran pretty much according to chance. It was survival of the fittest.

When you stop to think about it, computer-based communication media are becoming the basis of a new form of community. This community—without a single, fixed geographical location—comprises the first settlement in an electronic frontier, not unlike that of the west a couple of hundred years ago.

According to the Electronic Frontier Foundation's charter, "The Electronic Frontier Foundation has been established to help civilize the electronic frontier; to make it truly useful and beneficial not just to a technical elite, but to everyone; and to do this in a way which is in keeping with our society's highest traditions of the free and open flow of information and communication."

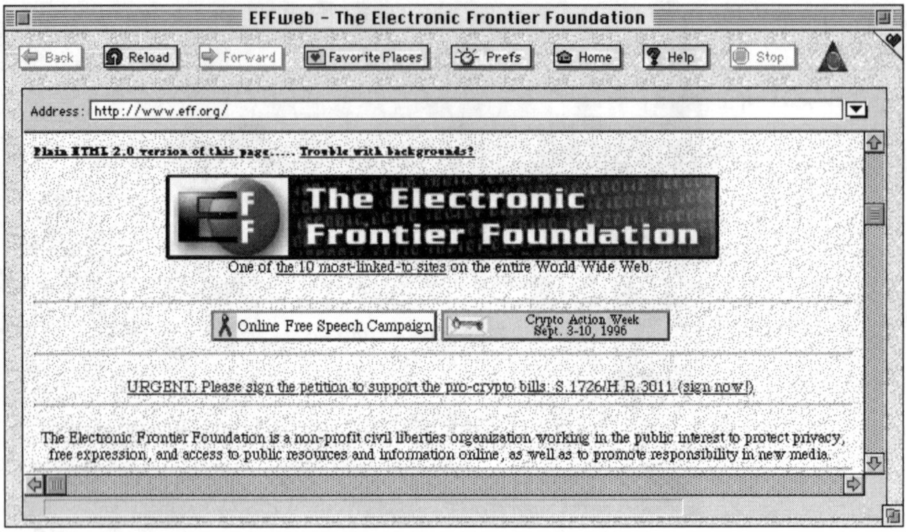
EFFweb - The Electronic Frontier Foundation
Back
Reload
Forward
Favorite Places
Prefs
Home
Help
Stop
Address: http://www.eff.org/
Plain HTML 2.0 version of this page..... Trouble with backgrounds?
The Electronic Frontier Foundation
One of the 10 most-linked-to sites on the entire World Wide Web.
Online Free Speech Campaign
Crypto Action Week Sept. 3-10, 1996
URGENT: Please sign the petition to support the pro-crypto bills: S.1726/H.R.3011 (sign now!)
The Electronic Frontier Foundation is a non-profit civil liberties organization working in the public interest to protect privacy, free expression, and access to public resources and information online, as well as to promote responsibility in new media.

Figure 7-17: The Electronic Frontier Foundation serves as our advocate in the frontier we call cyberspace.

The Electronic Frontier Foundation (at keyword: **Netorgs**) promotes educational activities, lobbies policy makers, advocates civil liberties, and develops new tools to afford telecommunications access for non-technical users. If you're at all interested in the future of our industry as a society, you should be a regular visitor here. Like the wagons on the Oregon Trail, the EFF is blazing new ground every day, and those of us who feel a responsibility for this medium find the EFF to be an effective delegate and a capable paladin.

All the Rest

There's much more for the computer enthusiast online. Craig Crossman's Computer America offers a radio simulcast, and the Programmer University serves up a savory plate of support for computer programmers. CyberLex reports legal developments affecting the computer industry.

There are more, and new computer-related areas are arriving every day. Search the Directory of Services (look under your Go To menu) with the criterion: Computer, for a comprehensive list, and be sure to use the keyword: **New** every couple of days so that you can catch new ones as they arrive.

Moving On

This has been a long chapter steeped in technicalities. Computers are inherently technical, and almost everything discussed in this chapter has been technical as well.

But America Online is much more than technicalities. Many members use it for the community alone: e-mail, chat, kids, and seniors. In fact, community is the heart of AOL. There are millions of wonderful people here. Turn the page. I want you to meet a few of them.

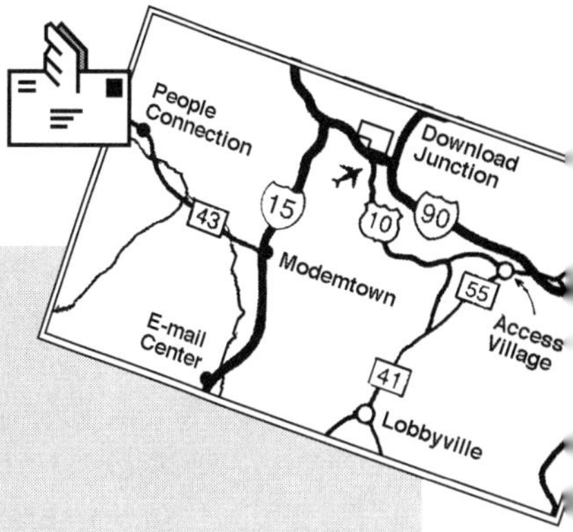

People Connection
Download Junction
43
15
10
90
Modemtown
55
Access Village
E-mail Center
41
Lobbyville

CHAPTER 8

The Community

- People Connection
- The Guidepager
- Chat Room Sounds
- The Auditoriums
- AOL Live!
- Instant Messages
- Buddy Lists
- Kids & Parents
- Seniors
- Women's Issues
- Guttersnipe

For many AOL members, the online community is what it's all about: chat, Instant Messages, games, auditoriums—telecommunicating in real time with real people all around the world. This is a two-way medium; it's a level playing field; it's egalitarian, attainable, and less expensive than cable TV. On the other hand, these very qualities are its greatest weaknesses: parity of access and freedom of expression don't necessarily promote honor and virtue. Thieves and scoundrels find this medium to be just as inviting as do scholars and prophets. Along with brotherhood and beneficence, there be dragons here. It's a community as diverse as America itself, and like America, America Online warrants scrutiny under strong light. Thus, this chapter.

People Connection

I discussed e-mail in Chapter 3, newsgroups and mailing lists in Chapter 4, and I'll discuss message boards in Chapter 9. All of these tools foster dialog between people, but none of the dialogs occur in real time. *People Connection* is the real-time, member-to-member communications headquarters of AOL. I was about to compare People Connection dialogs with telephone conversations, but at People Connection any number of people can be involved, there's rarely a long-distance toll to pay, and many of the people you talk to are strangers—but never for long.

People Connection is the heart of the AOL community. Here is where you make the enduring friendships that keep you coming back, day after day. Here, in a "diner," you can order a short stack and a cup of coffee, and talk over the weekend ahead. You can also sip a brew in a "pub" after a long day on the job. There are "events" here as well, where you can interview eminent guests and hobnob with luminaries.

Doesn't that sound like a community to you? This isn't couch potato entertainment; this is interactive telecommunication—where imagination and participation are contagious, and the concept of community reaches its most eloquent expression.

It sure beats reruns.

A Haven for Shy People

America Online is a haven for shy people. Shy people usually like other people and they're likable themselves; they just don't do well with strangers. Most shy people want to make friends—and all friends were once strangers—but they aren't very adept at doing it.

This is why shy people like AOL. Nobody can see them online; nobody seems to notice if they don't talk much; and if they're uncomfortable, they can always escape when they wish by signing off. Perhaps best of all, if you're a shy person, you can use a *nom de plume* and no one will even know who you are. We're back at the masquerade ball I mentioned in Chapter 2: you can wear the mask of a different screen name and be whatever or whomever you want to be. There's something comforting yet exciting about those possibilities.

Shy people can begin the AOL journey in a "safe" place like a forum (forums are discussed in Chapter 9, "Boards & Forums"), where no one's the wiser when they read a few forum messages or download a file or two. The next step would be to make an online friend and exchange some mail. Regardless of the path taken, it takes some time to work up the courage to venture into People Connection. It invariably means ending up in a room full of strangers, and this is not where shy people feel most comfortable.

The irony is that shy folks love People Connection once they become acquainted with it. It's the perfect outlet for years of pent-up longing for sociability. I'm a shy person. It took me months to work up to People Connection. Yet now it's one of my greatest online rewards. I go there whenever I have time. You will too, once you get the hang of it.

The Lobby

Unlike other areas within AOL, a visit to People Connection requires first passing through the "Lobby." The Lobby is one of AOL's so-called *chat rooms*, where real people communicate in real time. No messages are left here. There are no files to download. America Online's Lobby is similar to the lobby of a hotel: it's an area people pass through, often on their way to some other destination. Every so often, people bump into an acquaintance. Or they just sit there a moment to rest.

If you've never visited People Connection, come along with me and we'll give it a whirl. Click the two-heads icon on the toolbar, choose People Connection from the Main Menu window, or use the keyword: **Lobby**. No matter which method you use, you will soon find yourself in the Lobby (see Figure 8-1).

Figure 8-1: The Lobby screen seems empty just after I enter.

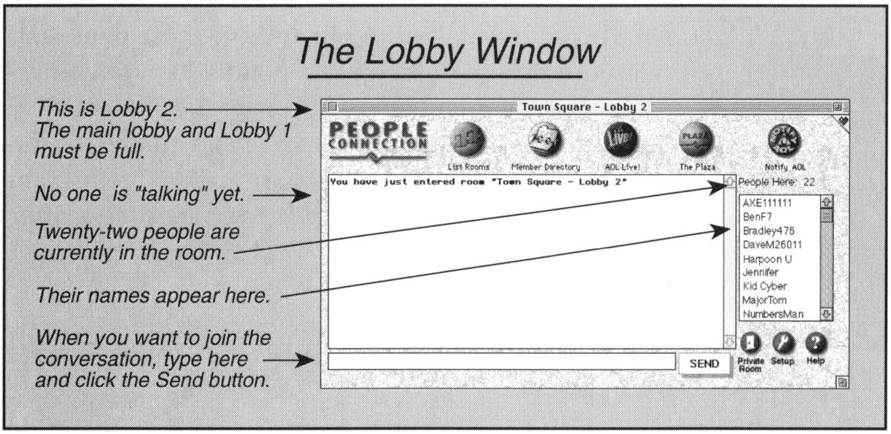
The Lobby Window
This is Lobby 2. The main lobby and Lobby 1 must be full.
No one is "talking" yet.
Twenty-two people are currently in the room.
Their names appear here.
When you want to join the conversation, type here and click the Send button.
Town Square - Lobby 2
PEOPLE CONNECTION
List Rooms
Member Directory
AOL Live!
The Plaza
Notify AOL
You have just entered room "Town Square - Lobby 2"
People Here: 22
AXE111111
BenF7
Bradley476
DaveM26011
Harpoon U
Jennifer
Kid Cyber
MajorTom
NumbersMan
SEND
Private Room
Setup
Help

Note that the message in the chat room window pictured in Figure 8-1 says that you are in Lobby 2. When I entered the Lobby, AOL routed me to Lobby 2. This happens whenever traffic on the system is heavy. When the main lobby reaches capacity (rooms are considered filled when they contain 23 members), AOL places people in the secondary lobby—Lobby 1. It, too, must have filled by the time I arrived, so I was placed in Lobby 2. Note that it was also full to capacity, so new arrivals were being routed into yet another lobby. This isn't uncommon. There are often several dozens of lobbies in operation at any one time.

Have Faith

If you really are following along with me, you've been in a lobby for a couple of minutes now. Your screen is full of chat, some of it indecipherable, some of it scurrilous, and some of it from people just as confounded as you are. Some people find lobby chat to be provocative; other people think it's insipid; still others would say it's simply vulgar. If your first experience in a lobby doesn't pique your interest in AOL's chat rooms, don't give up. Finish this chapter: there are rooms where the conversation is enlightening, urbane, and predictably polite. Read on and I'll tell you how to find them.

Also note that of the 22 people in Lobby 2 at the time, a few of their names appear in the scroll box on the right side of Figure 8-1's window. My preferences are set to arrange these names alphabetically (preferences are discussed in Appendix E, "Preferences"). Your scroll box may list the members in the order they appear.

Finally, note that there is no text in the main (conversation) portion of the window other than the announcement telling me where I am. The only true conversation appearing here occurs after my arrival, and I have just walked in the door. That situation changes the moment I speak (see Figure 8-2).

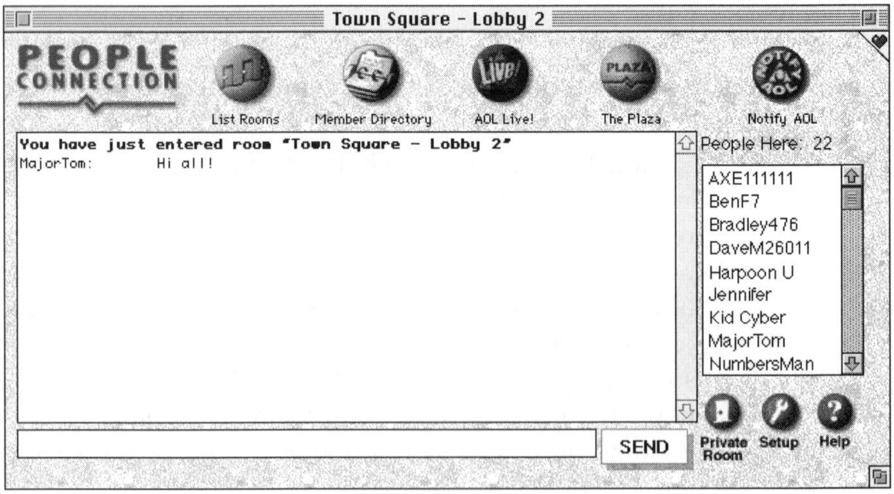

Town Square - Lobby 2
PEOPLE CONNECTION
List Rooms
Member Directory
AOL Live!
The Plaza
Notify AOL
You have just entered room "Town Square - Lobby 2"
MajorTom: Hi all!
People Here: 22
AXE111111
BenF7
Bradley476
DaveM26011
Harpoon U
Jennifer
Kid Cyber
MajorTom
NumbersMan
SEND
Private Room
Setup
Help

Figure 8-2: No matter how shy you're feeling, say hello when you enter a room.

Look again at Figure 8-2. This lobby is active today. People are rushing through it with hardly a pause. By the time I've said hello—a matter of seconds—two more people have arrived. America Online's lobbies are something like a hotel lobby just after a large meeting has let out: people are scurrying everywhere. (This is particularly true during periods of heavy usage. The session pictured occurred on a Sunday morning. America Online is almost always busy on the weekends.)

Password Surfing

You've no doubt seen messages to this effect already, but if you're new to People Connection it's worth repeating here: *no one from AOL's staff will ever, EVER ask you for your password.* I don't mean to imply that other people won't ask you for your password: password thieves are always a problem. I'll discuss the problem of password thieves later in this chapter; but just in case a message pops up on your screen while you're "lobbying" with me asking for your password, simply close its window and forget about it—at least for the time being. You probably won't hear from that person again.

Seconds later, a conversation has begun (see Figure 8-3).

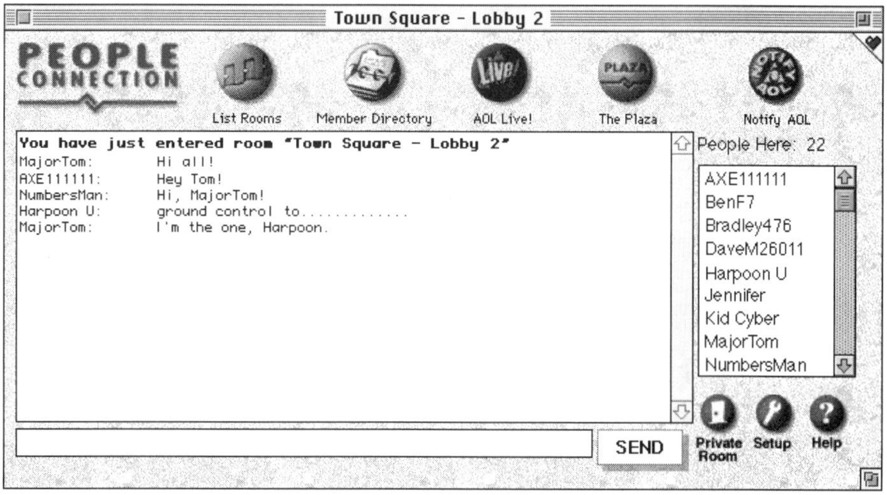
Town Square - Lobby 2
PEOPLE CONNECTION
List Rooms
Member Directory
AOL Live!
The Plaza
Notify AOL
You have just entered room "Town Square - Lobby 2"
MajorTom: Hi all!
AXE111111: Hey Tom!
NumbersMan: Hi, MajorTom!
Harpoon U: ground control to............
MajorTom: I'm the one, Harpoon.
People Here: 22
AXE111111
BenF7
Bradley476
DaveM26011
Harpoon U
Jennifer
Kid Cyber
MajorTom
NumbersMan
SEND
Private Room
Setup
Help

Figure 8-3: Catchy screen names come in handy when you first enter a room.

Though I immediately became involved in a conversation, don't feel obligated to do so yourself. It's perfectly all right to say hello, then just watch for a while. In fact, I recommend it: it gives you a chance to adapt to the pace of the conversation—to get to know who is in the room and what they're like. Lobbies are good for this. They're lobbies, after all. It's perfectly natural for people to sit in a lobby and watch other people.

Lurkers

It's not a very flattering term: *lurker*. It always makes me think of dark alleys and trench coats. In the online context, however, a lurker is one who visits a chat room and chooses not to participate in the conversation. There's nothing wrong with online lurking. I always lurk for a few minutes after I enter a room and say hello, to see who's in the room and to get a feel for the tenor of the conversation. You can lurk online for as long as you want to, but leave the trench coat in the closet.

As is the case with hotel lobbies, however, you won't want to stay in AOL's lobbies indefinitely. Awaiting you are lots of other rooms where conversations are more focused and residents less transitory. These rooms can be great fun; all you have to do is find the one that suits you best.

Kinds of Rooms

People who are new to AOL often have trouble understanding all of the kinds of rooms AOL has to offer. Each type of room serves a different purpose. Entering one without understanding what's inside is a bit like opening meeting room doors in a large hotel: some might welcome you enthusiastically, others might make you feel unwelcome, and still others might be engaged in conversations that are of no interest to you whatsoever.

Public Rooms

If you're still in a lobby, you'll soon discover the List Rooms button at the top left of the lobby's window (review Figure 8-2). This leads to the Public Rooms window pictured in Figure 8-4. Here, you can scan lists of all the public rooms available at the moment, and choose the one that suits you best.

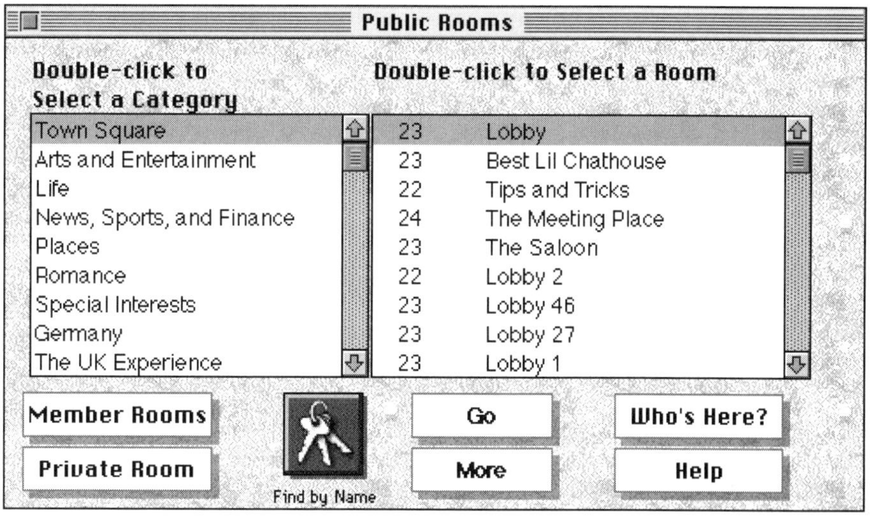
Public Rooms
Double-click to Select a Category
Double-click to Select a Room
Town Square
Arts and Entertainment
Life
News, Sports, and Finance
Places
Romance
Special Interests
Germany
The UK Experience
23 Lobby
23 Best Lil Chathouse
22 Tips and Tricks
24 The Meeting Place
23 The Saloon
22 Lobby 2
23 Lobby 46
23 Lobby 27
23 Lobby 1
Member Rooms
Private Room
Find by Name
Go
More
Who's Here?
Help

Figure 8-4: This Public Rooms list appears whenever you click the List Rooms button in a chat window.

Help's on the Way!

People write to me all of the time, telling me how overwhelmed they once were by all of the activity going on in People Connection. All of those rooms, all of those people, the shorthand—it can be downright intimidating.

Don't let it be. Find out all you can. Read this chapter, of course, but be sure to also click the question mark button in the lower right corner of any People Connection screen. That button leads to People Connection Help (Figure 8-5), where you can learn about any People Connection topic—from shorthands to IMs. This is a great place to meet people. Some would say it's the heart of the online experience. You owe it to yourself to learn all you can about People Connection, and give it a good try.

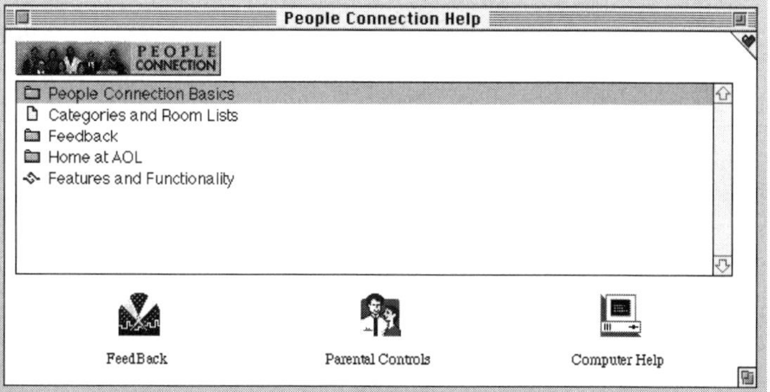
People Connection Help
PEOPLE CONNECTION
People Connection Basics
Categories and Room Lists
Feedback
Home at AOL
Features and Functionality
FeedBack
Parental Controls
Computer Help

Figure 8-5: People Connection Help is only a click of the mouse away.

The rooms appearing in the list box in Figure 8-4 all represent so-called *public* rooms at America Online. Public rooms share a number of common characteristics:

- As you might expect, they're open to the public. Anyone can enter (unless the room is full) and leave whenever they wish.
- Most public rooms are limited to 23 people (there are exceptions, but they're few). I don't know where that number came from, but it's appropriate: conversations in rooms with more than 23 people would be hard to follow, especially if those people were all in a garrulous mood.
- Public rooms are named by AOL employees. Most of them are *self-replicating*: when Lobby 2 fills, for example, Lobby 3 is automatically created.

The Best Seat in the House

The best way to find a "seat" in a self-replicating room is to attempt to enter one that's already full: if you want to enter a lobby, for example, try Lobby 1—even if it's full. AOL will display a message telling you that room is full and ask you if you want to enter another one that's like it. Answer yes. Chances are, someone just walked out of one of the full lobbies and AOL will put you in that person's seat. AOL always tries to find you the best seat in the house if you use this technique.

- Guides visit public rooms occasionally, either to offer assistance or to help keep the peace. (Guides were discussed in Chapter 2, "The Abecedarium.") In addition, some public rooms are hosted by volunteers (known as Hosts) who will welcome you and keep the conversation lively and interesting. Aside from the occasional Guide or Host, however, most public rooms are occupied by members only: there are no staff members present.
- The names of all public rooms are "published" via the windows pictured in Figure 8-4.

To enter a public room, select the category, then scroll the list box shown in Figure 8-4 until you find the room you want, then double-click its name. (Be sure to read the "Best Seat in the House" sidebar to find a good seat.) As soon as you arrive (the chat window on your screen will tell you—review Figure 8-2), be sure to say hello.

To find out more about the people in the room, refer to the scroll box on the right side of the room's window. The screen names of all of the people in the room are listed there. To see the profile of someone else in a room, double-click his or her screen name, then click the Get Info button (see Figure 8-6). Not only will you be able to call up a profile of that person (profiles were discussed in Chapter 2, "The Abecedarium"), but you can send them an Instant Message as well (we'll discuss Instant Messages later in this chapter).

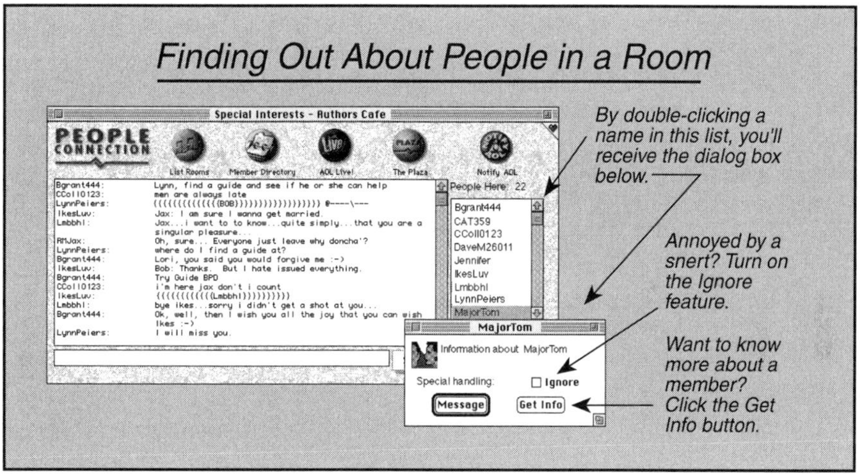
Finding Out About People in a Room
Special Interests - Authors Cafe
PEOPLE CONNECTION
List Rooms
Member Directory
AOL Live!
The Plaza
Notify AOL
People Here: 22
Bgrant444
CAT359
CColl0123
DaveM26011
Jennifer
IkesLuv
Lmbbhl
LynnPeiers
MajorTom
By double-clicking a name in this list, you'll receive the dialog box below.
Annoyed by a snert? Turn on the Ignore feature.
MajorTom
Information about MajorTom
Special handling:
Ignore
Message
Get Info
Want to know more about a member? Click the Get Info button.

Figure 8-6: Double-click any name on a people list to find out more about that individual.

Conference Rooms

While the Authors Cafe illustrated in Figure 8-6 is a public room, the Writers Cafe is a *conference room*. Conference rooms are usually associated with forums (I'll discuss forums in Chapter 9, "Boards & Forums") and are typically accessed through those forums. You can't get to them via the Lobby, and they're not listed when you click the List Rooms button shown in Figure 8-2. Other than that, conference rooms aren't much different than public rooms, but since they require a bit more savvy to find, they're less privy to the kind of harassment I alluded to in the "Special Handling" sidebar.

Refer to Figure 8-7: the Writers Cafe is only available via the Writers Club. You can't get there with Command-L or the two-heads icon on the toolbar; you've got to venture through the Writers Club first—and encounter a friendly prequel about the room—before you get to the Writers Cafe.

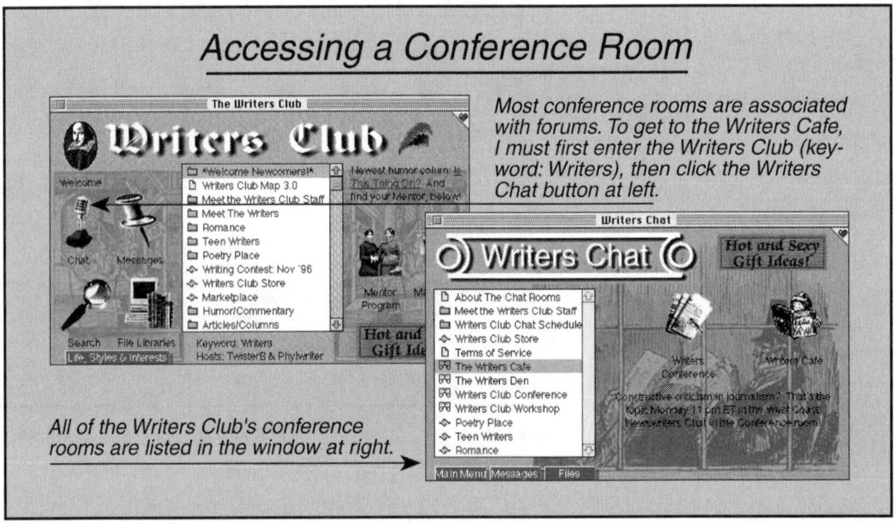
Accessing a Conference Room
Most conference rooms are associated with forums. To get to the Writers Cafe, I must first enter the Writers Club (keyword: Writers), then click the Writers Chat button at left.
All of the Writers Club's conference rooms are listed in the window at right.
The Writers Club
Writers Club
Writers Chat
About The Chat Rooms
Meet the Writers Club Staff
Writers Club Chat Schedule
Writers Club Store
Terms of Service
The Writers Cafe
The Writers Den
Writers Club Conference
Writers Club Workshop
Poetry Place
Teen Writers
Romance

Figure 8-7: You have to travel through a forum to reach most conference rooms.

Because they're associated with forums (the Writers Club is a forum; we'll discuss forums in Chapter 9), and because they're slightly less accessible than public rooms, conference rooms exhibit some characteristics not common in public rooms:

- Most conference rooms can hold more than a public room's maximum of 23 people. Thirty or forty people aren't uncommon. In spite of the crowd, conversations are rarely difficult to follow, due to the use of *protocol* in most conference rooms. (See the "Protocol Rooms" sidebar.)
- You're more likely to find hosts in conference rooms. They're forum hosts—not Guides—and sometimes you can't determine that they're hosts without checking their profiles, but their presence usually makes a room more orderly and focused.
- Conference rooms are often scheduled: forums hold regularly scheduled meetings in their conference rooms during which a host is usually present and the subject matter is carefully regulated. Become familiar with a conference room's schedule before you enter it: you don't want to walk in on a scheduled conference unaware of what you're doing.
- Even during unscheduled times, conference room topics are more focused. I wouldn't expect to find people discussing model airplanes in the Writers Cafe (unless they were writing *books* about model airplanes), and hobbyists wouldn't expect to find me talking about agents and deadlines in their conference rooms either.
- The people in conference rooms are less transitory. People often graze among public rooms, looking for The Perfect Chat like a remote-wielding couch potato seeking The Perfect Channel. Such is not the case with conference rooms. People often stay in conference rooms for hours.

I'm trying to make a subtle point here: if you're attracted by chat but repelled by public rooms, seek out a forum that aligns with an interest of yours and see if it has a conference room. If it does, pop in. You might find yourself coming back again and again.

Protocol Rooms

At times, some conference rooms operate with *protocol*, usually when there is a guest speaker or a specific topic under discussion.

You can usually tell when you've entered a protocol room because you'll be greeted by a message informing you of the protocol. Protocol rooms invariably have a moderator as well, and the moderator's influence on the conversation will be readily apparent. One way or another, it doesn't take long to tell you're in a protocol room: just watch the conversation. Here are some of the conventions you'll see:

Type a question mark (**?**) if you have a question and wait until the moderator calls on you.

Type an exclamation point (**!**) if you have a comment and, again, wait.

Type **GA** (for Go Ahead) or **/end** when you're done with your question or comment. It's also wise to have your material typed and ready to go before you're called on.

Parlor Games

A particular type of protocol room (see the "Protocol Rooms" sidebar) that's dedicated to games is the *Game Parlor*, where mental challenges mingle with casual socializing (use the keyword: **Parlor**, and see Figure 8-8).

Each game has an official host and scorekeeper, and most have a greeter. The greeter will provide you with the host's and scorekeeper's names, and some of the rules. The action is usually fast and erudite but don't let that intimidate you: everyone has a first time, and new visitors are always made to feel comfortable.

Parlor game schedules are always changing; you can see the latest at keyword: **Parlor**.

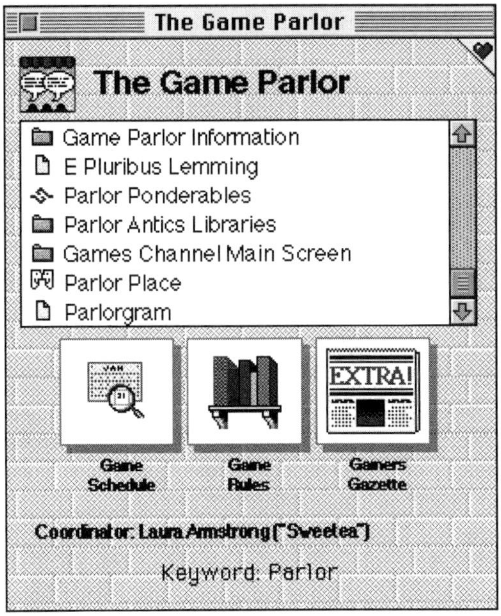
The Game Parlor
The Game Parlor
Game Parlor Information
E Pluribus Lemming
Parlor Ponderables
Parlor Antics Libraries
Games Channel Main Screen
Parlor Place
Parlorgram
EXTRA!
Game Schedule
Game Rules
Gamers Gazette
Coordinator: Laura Armstrong ("Sweetea")
Keyword: Parlor

Figure 8-8: Parlor games are one of the best ways to get to know people online.

Member Rooms

Member rooms are named and created by members. A list of them is available by clicking the Member Rooms button pictured in Figure 8-4. The subject of a member room is entirely up to the member who creates the room and is usually identified by the room's name (see Figure 8-9).

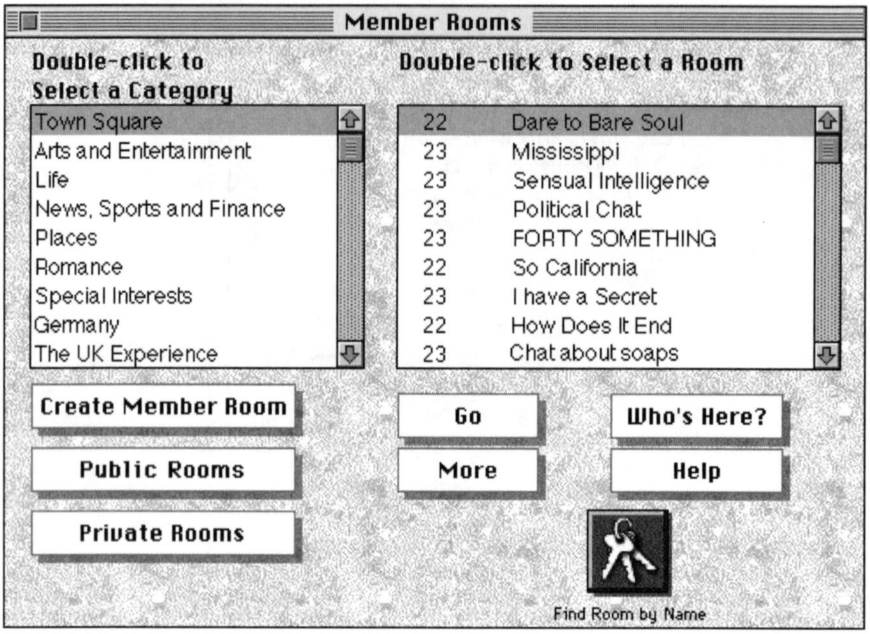
Member Rooms
Double-click to Select a Category
Town Square
Arts and Entertainment
Life
News, Sports and Finance
Places
Romance
Special Interests
Germany
The UK Experience
Double-click to Select a Room
22 Dare to Bare Soul
23 Mississippi
23 Sensual Intelligence
23 Political Chat
23 FORTY SOMETHING
22 So California
23 I have a Secret
22 How Does It End
23 Chat about soaps
Create Member Room
Public Rooms
Private Rooms
Go
More
Who's Here?
Help
Find Room by Name

Figure 8-9: Member room topics vary from the innocuous to the scurrilous.

Note that member rooms are grouped by the same categories as public rooms. Since they're created by members—who aren't obliged to follow any kind of room category rules—member rooms often blur AOL's category distinctions. (Note that the "Mississippi" room pictured in Figure 8-9 really belongs in the Places category, though its popularity hasn't suffered from its misplacement.)

Member rooms share a number of common characteristics:

- Member rooms are open to the public unless they're full.
- Member rooms have a maximum capacity of 23 people and are not self-replicating.

- Member rooms are created and named by members (I'll tell you how in a moment). Member room names must abide by AOL's TOS (Terms of Service—TOS is discussed in Chapter 2, "The Abecedarium"); those with names found to be in violation of TOS are closed by People Connection staff.
- Member rooms are never hosted by staff members, though they *are* often hosted. The hosts in these circumstances are often host "wannabes." I'm not using that term derogatorily: many conference room hosts get started by hosting a member room.
- Member rooms are rarely patrolled by Guides. Guides only enter member rooms when summoned via the Guidepager (see the Guidepager section of this chapter for more).

Figure 8-10 shows the same Member Rooms window that's pictured in Figure 8-9, though in Figure 8-10 the Places category has been selected. Note that the More button is dimmed in Figure 8-10 (all of the Places category rooms are available within the list box on the right); you would have to click Figure 8-9's More button—perhaps more than once—to see all of the rooms in the Town Square category.

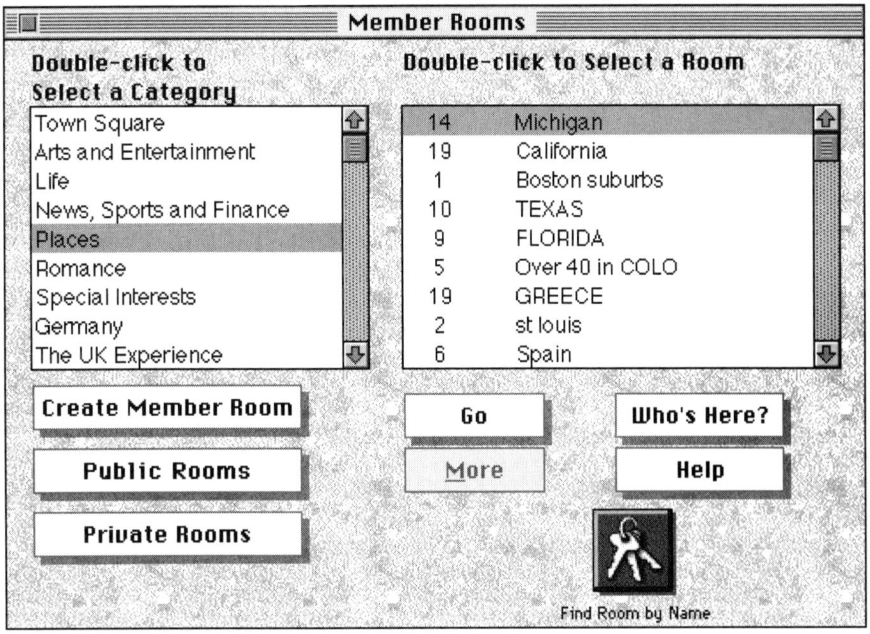
Member Rooms
Double-click to Select a Category
Town Square
Arts and Entertainment
Life
News, Sports and Finance
Places
Romance
Special Interests
Germany
The UK Experience
Double-click to Select a Room
14 Michigan
19 California
1 Boston suburbs
10 TEXAS
9 FLORIDA
5 Over 40 in COLO
19 GREECE
2 st louis
6 Spain
Create Member Room
Public Rooms
Private Rooms
Go
More
Who's Here?
Help
Find Room by Name

Figure 8-10: Member rooms in the Places category.

Anyone can create a member room: just follow the sequence that's described in Figure 8-11.

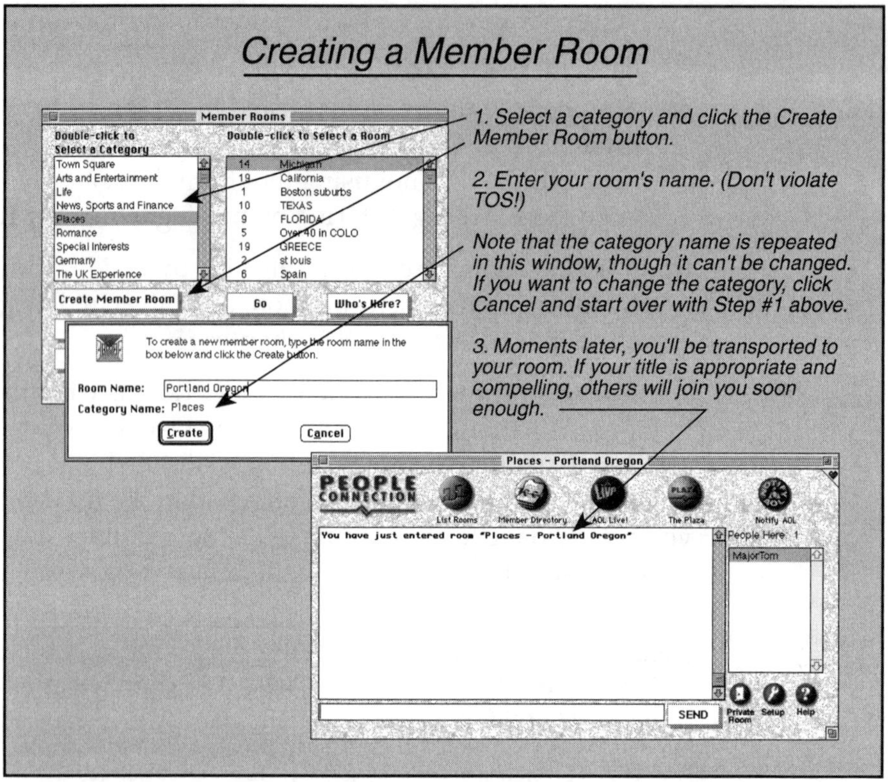
Creating a Member Room
1. Select a category and click the Create Member Room button.
2. Enter your room's name. (Don't violate TOS!)
Note that the category name is repeated in this window, though it can't be changed. If you want to change the category, click Cancel and start over with Step #1 above.
3. Moments later, you'll be transported to your room. If your title is appropriate and compelling, others will join you soon enough.
Member Rooms
Create Member Room
Room Name: Portland Oregon
Category Name: Places
Create
Cancel
Places - Portland Oregon
You have just entered room "Places - Portland Oregon"
SEND

Figure 8-11: Creating a member room of your own amounts to little more than clicking a button.

I hope the picture is coming into focus by now: the content, quality, and integrity of member rooms differ considerably from room to room. Some of the best rooms on the service are found here; so are the worst. I often visit the Portland, Oregon, room: one of our local TV meteorologists hangs out there, and weather is a subject about which Oregonians *always* have an opinion. However, there are other member rooms that are like the dark under the stairs to me: their names usually tell all.

Private Rooms

Like member rooms, private rooms are created by members and can hold 23 people. That, however, is where the similarity ends. Here are the specifics:

- Private rooms are not available to the public. There's no way to see a list of private rooms.
- Since you can't see a list of private rooms, you must know the exact name of a private room in order to enter it. You'll never know about a private room unless you create one of your own or someone invites you into theirs by providing you with its name.
- Private rooms are never patrolled—AOL's Terms of Service, in fact, specifically prohibits AOL staff from monitoring private room conversations (TOS is discussed in Chapter 2, "The Abecedarium").
- You can leave a private room whenever you want to: just click its Close box.

Refer to Figure 8-12. The Private Rooms button pictured there allows you to create or visit a private room. When you click this button, AOL asks you for a room name. If you enter a name and the room already exists, AOL takes you into that room. If it doesn't exist, AOL creates it and takes you there. If you create a room, the only people who can enter it are those who know its name.

Figure 8-12: Private rooms are created in exactly the same fashion as member rooms.

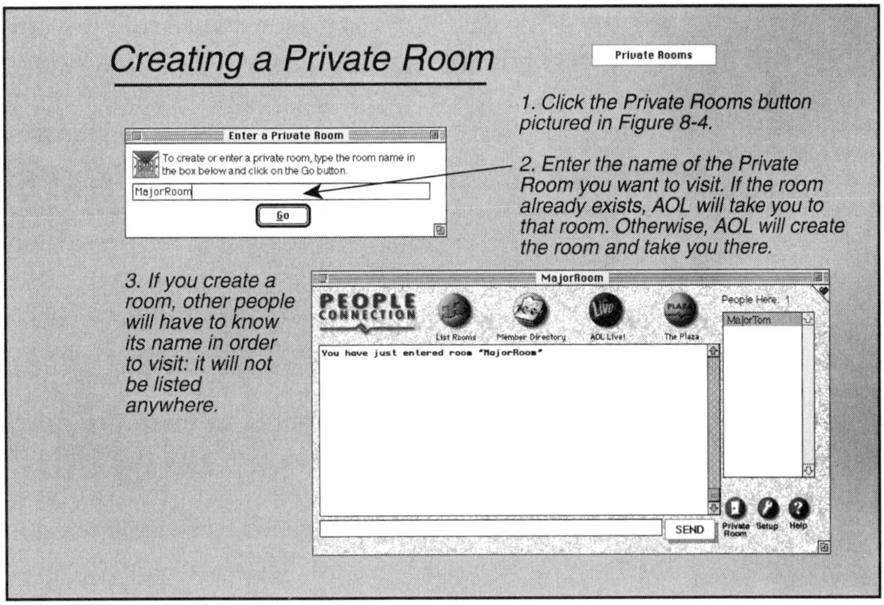
Creating a Private Room
Private Rooms
1. Click the Private Rooms button pictured in Figure 8-4.
Enter a Private Room
To create or enter a private room, type the room name in the box below and click on the Go button.
MajorRoom
Go
2. Enter the name of the Private Room you want to visit. If the room already exists, AOL will take you to that room. Otherwise, AOL will create the room and take you there.
3. If you create a room, other people will have to know its name in order to visit: it will not be listed anywhere.
MajorRoom
PEOPLE CONNECTION
List Rooms
Member Directory
AOL Live!
The Plaza
People Here: 1
MajorTom
You have just entered room "MajorRoom"
SEND
Private Room
Setup
Help

Online Conference Calls

Consider the private room as an alternative to the conference call. We don't tend to think of them that way, but private rooms are essentially mechanisms whereby people from around the country can hold real-time conferences. America Online's private rooms are much less expensive than the phone company's conference calls, and participants can keep a log of the conversation for review once the conference has concluded (for a discussion of logs, see Chapter 10, "Staying Informed"). Conferences are often more productive when participants have to write what they say (makes 'em think before they speak) and vocal inflections don't cloud the issue.

To hold a private room conference call (or to simply meet some friends for a chat in a private room), tell the participants the name of the room and the time you want to meet beforehand, then arrive a few minutes early and create the room. Instruct the participants to enter the Lobby (the two-heads icon on the toolbar gets you there in a hurry) when they sign on, click the Private Room button on the bottom right, then type in the name of your room (keep the name simple). Try it: it's in many ways superior to a conference call—and cheaper to boot.

Using Favorite Places to Get to a Room

I discussed *Favorite Places* in Chapter 4, "Using the Internet," but only in the context of Web pages. In fact, any AOL window with a little heart icon in its upper right corner can be added to your list of Favorite Places. Once a location is added to the list, you can return to it quickly and easily by choosing Favorite Places from the Go To menu or clicking the folder-and-heart button on the toolbar.

With that said, you might notice that most of the rooms we have discussed so far offer Favorite Places hearts on their title bars. The implication, then, is that you can add any room to your Favorite Places list and return to it later with a few clicks of the mouse. Are you fond of the Star Trek Club's "The Bridge" conference room? Add it to your Favorite Places list. The next time you want to go there, call up the list and double-click the entry for The Bridge. You'll bypass the Lobby and the List Rooms windows and be teleported (an appropriate Star Trek term) directly to your destination. It's as if Scotty were handling the controls.

Remember too that Favorite Places are available even when you're offline. If you're offline and want to sign on and visit The Bridge, just call up your Favorite Places list and double-click the entry for The

Bridge. AOL will sign on (and ask you for your password if you haven't stored one—see Chapter 6 for a discussion of stored passwords) and burrow directly to The Bridge. You'll hardly have time to dust off your communicator pin.

Chat Room Tips & Etiquette

It's appropriate that we wrap up the People Connection part of this chapter with a few comments about chat room etiquette and technique:

- Review America Online's Terms of Service (discussed in Chapter 2 and available free at keyword: **TOS**), and get to know terms like *scrolling, impersonation, disruption, polling, chain letters,* and *pyramid schemes* as they pertain to the online environment.
- Don't give your password to anyone, no matter how convincing their argument to the contrary might be. Read about trolls, phishers, and snerts in the "Guttersnipe" section of this chapter for more on this subject.
- Say hello when you arrive in a room. Say goodbye before you leave.
- When you first enter a room (and after saying hello), watch the conversation for a few minutes to see which way the wind is blowing. Only then should you enter into the conversation.
- Don't type in uppercase. That's shouting.
- Speak when spoken to, even if you say nothing more than "I don't know."
- A catchy screen name works wonders. When I enter a room using my business screen name—which isn't catchy at all—I encounter far fewer rejoinders from its inhabitants than I do when I enter using my MajorTom screen name.
- Your screen name should contain a convenient "handle"—ideally your first name. Talking to TLic6865 is like talking to a license plate. "MajorTom" allows people to call me "Major," or "Tom," or "MT."
- Keep a log of your first few chat room visits (logs are discussed in Chapter 10, "Staying Informed"). Review the log offline when the session has concluded. You'll learn a lot about chats this way.

- Get to know *smileys* and *emoticons*. These are the shorthand symbols you'll encounter online such as ROTFL (Rolling On The Floor Laughing), BTW (By the Way), ;-) (a wink: turn your head 90 degrees counterclockwise), and hundreds of others. There are a number of files available for downloading that list them all. Use the keywords: **File Search**, then search with the criterion: Emoticons. I'm fond of the *Unofficial Emoticons Dictionary* by L.L. Drummond. Keyword: **Shorthands** also offers a brief description.
- You might want to see who's in a room before you enter it. A screen name often tells a lot about a person. You can see who's in a room by clicking *once* on any name in the Public Rooms window (review Figure 8-4) or the Member Rooms windows (review Figure 8-10), then clicking the Who's Here? button.
- Learn what to do if you witness a TOS violation.

That last item points us directly toward the subject of the Guidepager: AOL's equivalent of an online 911. Read on.

The Guidepager

Freedom within the online community is threatened by a number of things—legislation, access, resources—but the most insidious and menacing threat to online freedom is abuse of the medium. And abuse, most frequently, appears in chat rooms.

Often the abusers are simply ignorant of the society. Sometimes they're brats on a lark, and a few are vandals, plain and simple. In all cases, the best way to deal with them is to report them, quickly and resolutely. This isn't tattling or hiding behind Mommy's apron; it's an imperative that we should all observe if we want to keep this community a healthy place. Those who would inflict online abuse represent a "social virus" to the online community: the scourge spreads like typhoid if left unchecked.

AOL's Guides are much more than the charitable souls they might seem to be. Think of them as you would think of the police: while they prefer to travel about benevolently assisting people in need, they are also vested with considerable responsibility. Guides can make requests to remove a member from a room, sever a member's access to People Connection for a period, or even terminate an account.

The *Guidepager* is a device used to summon a Guide for help, especially in the event of a TOS violation. The Guidepager is *not* a method of getting general help on AOL: read Chapter 2, "The Abecedarium," for information on that. The Guidepager is available at any time, 24 hours a day, 7 days a week, at the keyword: **Guidepager** or by clicking the Notify AOL button in any chat room window and then clicking the Summon a Guide button (see Figure 8-13).

I Need Help!
I Need Help!
Password
Someone just asked me for my password or credit card number!
Chat
I'm in a chat room and want to report a problem!
Other
I have a problem with...
E-mail - Attached files - Message Boards - Screen Name\Profile - Instant Message

Figure 8-13: Use the Guidepager whenever you witness a violation of AOL's Terms of Service.

Before you use the Guidepager, be sure to note the category and name of the room you are in, the screen name of the member causing the problem, and a brief description of the problem. The Community Action Team Advisor or an on-duty Guide will come to your assistance as soon as possible. Don't abuse this service: sending false or frivolous pages can result in the termination of your account.

Chat Room Sounds

Interestingly, the online medium offers potential for much more than the textual exchange of dialog. In a few years (perhaps less) you will probably command an *avatar*—an online visual presence of yourself—just as you "wear" a screen name now; and when your avatar enters a chat room you will see other members' avatars in the room. Members in the room will likewise see your avatar when you enter, just as they see your screen name when you enter a room now.

It's all very radical, I suppose (and aptly described in the novel *Snow Crash*, by Neal Stephenson), but not inconceivable. In fact, part of this scenario is here now, in the form of *chat room sounds.*

You can broadcast chat room sounds to a room just as you send text; people in the room will hear the sound just as they would read the text. There are a couple of caveats, however:

- Your Mac needs to have its sound turned on and the volume turned up to hear chat room sounds.
- The only people who will hear sounds you send are those using computers equipped to play sounds.
- The person sending the sound and all those who want to hear it must have the sound already installed on their hard disks. America Online doesn't transmit the actual sound file when you send a sound (sending the actual sound itself would take too long using a modem); rather, it sends a *notification* to play the sound. Members' machines will play the sound only if they have the sound on file.
- To broadcast a sound in a chat room, type a line matching the format below, then click the chat window's Send button.
  {S WELCOME}

  Notice that the command above is enclosed in braces {} and that it begins with a capital *S* (a lowercase *s* won't do). There's one (and only one) space after the *S*, then the name of the sound.

Finding & Installing Sounds

Thousands of sounds are available in the Mac Music and Sound Forum (keywords: **Mac Music**). To find them quickly, use the keyword: **FileSearch**, then specify "chat sound" as your search criteria. Remember, sound files are large—usually at least 5K per second—so they may take a while to download. To convert Windows sounds to Mac format, use one of the many utilities available from the Mac Music and Sound Forum. I use "Balthazar," from Craig Marciniak (file search using the criterion: Balthazar), but there are lots of others available.

Once you have downloaded (or converted) a sound file, drag it on top of your System folder. From then on, you can use it in chat situations by following the directions above.

Sound files are great fun, especially in those chat rooms where they're used extensively. LaPub (keyword: **LaPub**) is a good example. More than a room, LaPub is a microcosmic community, complete with its own library of sounds. With a sound card, speakers, and LaPub's library of sounds on your hard disk, a visit to the Pub is reminiscent of the TV series "Cheers," replete with the clinking of glasses and the occasional splat of a pie hitting a face.

Earmuffs

Under some circumstances, chat room sounds can be disruptive. There are both technical and societal reasons for this, but the important thing is that chat room sounds can be turned off if you don't want to hear them. Read Appendix E, "Preferences," for more information.

The Auditoriums

So far, all we've discussed are rooms with a relatively small capacity: 23 persons, for the most part. But what if President Clinton were to make an online appearance? (It has happened.) How about Billy Joel, Oprah Winfrey, Anthony Edwards, or David Bowie? (They all have appeared.)

Such a vehicle exists. In fact, a number of them do. Collectively they're known as AOL's auditoriums, and each one has a name: Cyberplex, Odeon, Globe, Bowl, Coliseum—there are 11 of them in total.

Collectively, AOL's auditoriums can hold up to 55,000 people at a time (see the "Media Melding" sidebar). When you enter, you're assigned a "row" in the auditorium. Each row holds 16 people, and the 16 of you can talk among yourselves all you want: no one else can hear your conversation.

Participating in an Auditorium Event

AOL's auditoriums are significantly different from other chat rooms. They have to be: thousands of people populate the auditoriums—many, many more than a normal chat room's maximum of 23. Here's how it works:

- When you're ready to interact with the people on stage, click the Interact button pictured in Figure 8-14. Your question or comment will be placed in a queue for the moderator's consideration. With audiences numbering in the thousands, not all questions are answered, but the dialog is always engaging, whether you participate or not.

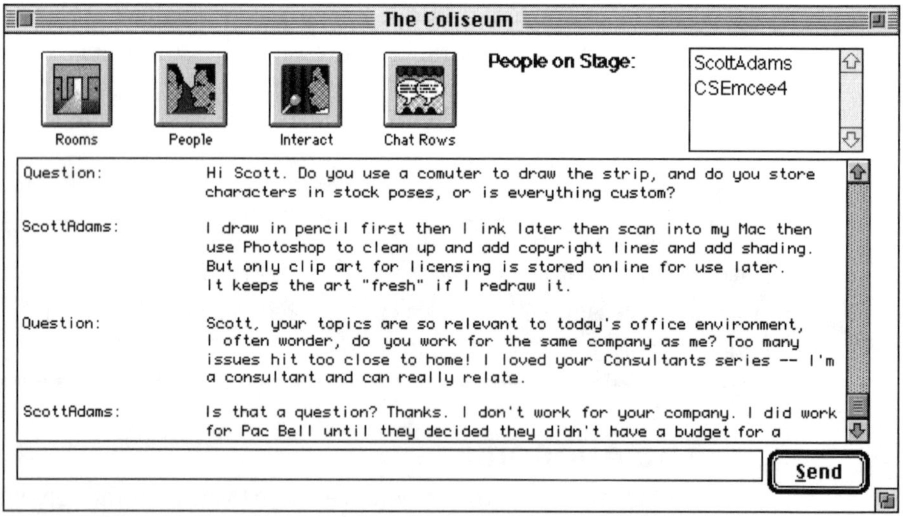
The Coliseum
Rooms
People
Interact
Chat Rows
People on Stage:
ScottAdams
CSEmcee4
Question: Hi Scott. Do you use a comuter to draw the strip, and do you store characters in stock poses, or is everything custom?
ScottAdams: I draw in pencil first then I ink later then scan into my Mac then use Photoshop to clean up and add copyright lines and add shading. But only clip art for licensing is stored online for use later. It keeps the art "fresh" if I redraw it.
Question: Scott, your topics are so relevant to today's office environment, I often wonder, do you work for the same company as me? Too many issues hit too close to home! I loved your Consultants series -- I'm a consultant and can really relate.
ScottAdams: Is that a question? Thanks. I don't work for your company. I did work for Pac Bell until they decided they didn't have a budget for a
Send

Figure 8-14: In the auditoriums with Scott Adams, creator of the "Dilbert" comic strip.

- If you simply type a comment into the lower text box pictured in Figure 8-14 and click the Send button, your comment will appear in the main text box, *but only on the screens of the people in your row.* Comments such as this are easy to recognize: they're preceded by your row number, which appears in parentheses.
- Clicking Figure 8-14's People button will display a listing of the other people in your row. You can send them Instant Messages or view their profiles as if you were in a normal chat room (review Figure 8-6).
- The Chat Rows button shown in Figure 8-14 will produce a listing of all of the rows in use within the auditorium, and the number of people in each one. You can use this button to jump from one row to another, or to find out about people in the auditorium who aren't in your row.

Media Melding

It was a media first: Michael Jackson appearing in a simulcast with America Online and MTV. It also set a record for Auditorium attendance at AOL. In fact, over 16,000 people were "in" the auditorium with Michael Jackson that night, sitting in virtual seats, reading the conversation on their computer monitors while they watched The Man on their television screens. It wasn't the first, nor will it be the last multiple-medium online event: President Clinton's appearance was simulcast on the "Larry King Live" program on CNN, and the cast and crew of "Wings" appeared online while an episode was being taped!

Out of context, 16,000 is a meaningless number. Let's put it in perspective: the previous record for Auditorium attendance was 2,035, set a few months earlier by actress Sandra Bullock. President Clinton drew 1,364 and Anthony Edwards (from NBC's "ER") drew 1,846.

Michael Jackson's auditorium event was, in other words, a Big Deal—probably the biggest online event in the history of the medium. You owe it to yourself to witness at least one of these events. Use the keyword: **Live!** to see the schedule of celebrity appearances. On the appointed evening, use the keyword indicated on the schedule to join the fun.

At the time that I'm writing this, AOL has 11 auditoriums: Odeon, Globe, Rotunda, Bowl, Coliseum, AOLLIVE!, AOL Live Chat Cafe, News Room, International, CyberRap, and Cyberplex. Each can hold up to 5,000 people. There really isn't any difference between them besides their names—they all have the same capacity and they all work the same way. There are 11 of them so that AOL can accommodate simultaneous online events. AOL's auditoriums are similar to the auditoriums in a multiscreen theater: some want to watch *The Rocky Horror Picture Show;* some want to watch *On Golden Pond*. To each his own.

Games Night

Celebrity appearances aren't the only things that happen in AOL's auditoriums. Games are big events as well. Every Saturday night is game night, and gamers turn out by the thousands.

By way of example, I'll pick something familiar. *Wheel Watchers* is a popular offering, based on the syndicated "Wheel of Fortune" TV game show. Three players are selected at random for each of the two preliminary rounds of play, each consisting of two puzzles. Once in play, a puzzle is displayed with asterisks representing the missing letters of the puzzle.

The "spins" of the wheel provide the values for the letters that players guess. If a "7" is spun, its value is 700 points for each time the letter appears in the puzzle. Players with at least 250 points can buy vowels. If you're familiar with the TV game, you're familiar with *Wheel Watchers*.

There are scores of other games: *Lucky 7, Stump the Standup, Roll 'Em, Scrambled Eggs, Hands Up!, 3-in-a-Row, Mixups*—there are more. And this isn't Hollywood: not only does everyone get a good seat in the audience, but, in most games, everyone gets to play!

With all of these luminaries and games appearing online—sometimes over a dozen a day—how do you tell who's appearing, and when, and where? And how can you get there? Read on.

Auditorium Help

People, hosts, guests, etiquette, protocol—they can overwhelm the first-time visitor, I know. Any large gathering is that way.

Fortunately, there's help, and it's available right from the AOL Live! Main Screen. Use the keyword: **Live**, then click the Help button.

AOL Live!

Auditoriums, the Games Night, conference rooms—at any moment (especially in the evenings) scores of them are active. Keeping track of them all would be an unrealistic undertaking, were it not for *AOL Live!*

Simply put, AOL Live! is your *TV Guide* for online events. Want to know what's playing? Use the keyword: **Live** and look over the schedule of Coming Attractions (see Figure 8-15). You can check the schedule according to time of day, or search for a specific guest, room, or time.

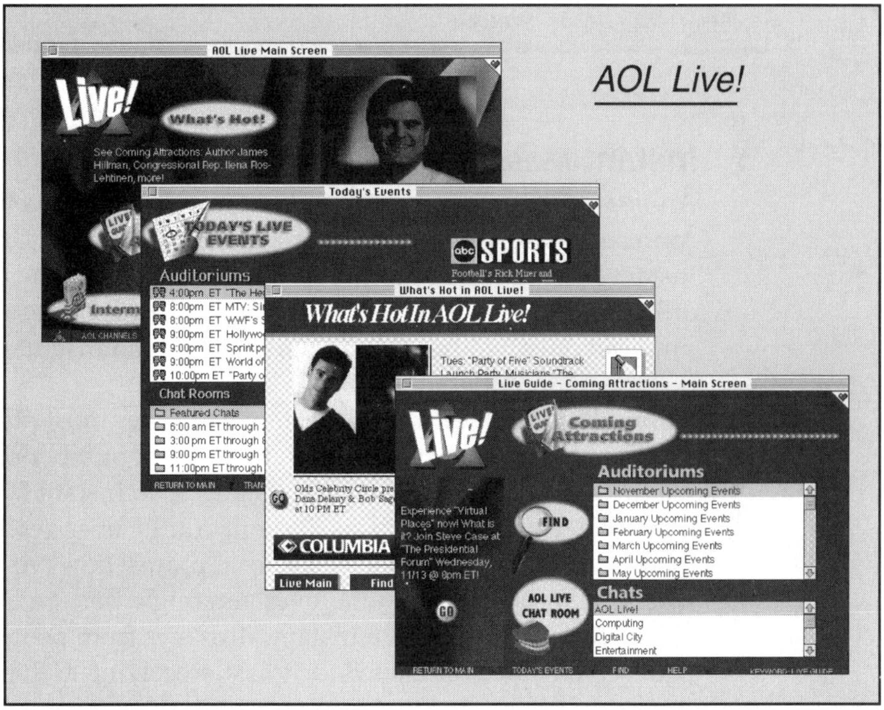

AOL Live!
AOL Live Main Screen
What's Hot!
See Coming Attractions: Author James Hillman, Congressional Rep. Ilena Ros-Lehtinen, more!
Today's Events
TODAY'S LIVE EVENTS
SPORTS
Auditoriums
Chat Rooms
Featured Chats
What's Hot in AOL Live!
What's Hot In AOL Live!
Tues: "Party of Five" Soundtrack
COLUMBIA
Live Main
Find
Live Guide - Coming Attractions - Main Screen
Coming Attractions
Auditoriums
November Upcoming Events
December Upcoming Events
January Upcoming Events
February Upcoming Events
March Upcoming Events
April Upcoming Events
May Upcoming Events
FIND
Experience "Virtual Places" now! What is it? Join Steve Case at "The Presidential Forum" Wednesday, 11/13 @ 9pm ET!
GO
AOL LIVE CHAT ROOM
Chats
AOL Live!
Computing
Digital City
Entertainment

Figure 8-15: Use the keyword: **Live** to see what's happening in AOL's auditoriums and conference rooms.

So how do you get to all of these nifty auditorium events? Here's a tip: you can get to any auditorium, at any time, by using the keyword: **Intermission**, then clicking the Auditorium Entrances button. When auditorium events are advertised (especially on the Welcome screen), you're usually given a keyword that will take you to the forum or sponsor for the event. That's fine—especially if you want to know more about the sponsoring organization—but if you simply want to get there fast, use the **Intermission** keyword.

Express Delivery

Often, online promotions for auditorium events—you'll see them on the Welcome screen all the time—mention the name of the auditorium in which the event is occurring.

When you know an auditorium's name and want to get there as if Scotty beamed you, use the auditorium's name as a keyword, *preceded by an @ sign.* If something is happening in the Odeon at 7:30, for example, wait till 7:30, then use the keyword: **@Odeon**. You'll materialize in the Odeon just like Kirk and Spock on a distant planet, ready for action.

Instant Messages

An *Instant Message* is a message sent to someone else online. Don't confuse Instant Messages with e-mail or chat rooms. Unlike e-mail, Instant Messages work only if both the sender and the recipient are online at the same time. Like chat rooms, Instant Messages occur in real time, but only two people can participate in an Instant Message: there's no "room" for others.

You'll probably encounter Instant Messages most often when you're in a room. It's then, after all, that the greatest number of people know you're online. Under those circumstances, an Instant Message is something like whispering in class, though you'll never get in trouble for it. Instant Messages aren't limited to chat rooms, however: they work whenever you're online, wherever you might be.

You'll also often receive Instant Messages from people who have your screen name on their Buddy List. Receiving an Instant Message from a Buddy is always a welcome intermission.

Earlier in this chapter I suggested a private room as an alternative to conference calls. You might also consider Instant Messages as alternatives to long-distance phone calls. Pam Richardson (formerly my primary contact at Ventana) and I needed to have a number of discussions nearly every day. Unfortunately, Pam, located in North Carolina, was about as far away from Oregon as one can be without being in a different country. Instead of making long-distance telephone calls across the country and four different time zones, we agreed on mutual times to go online, allowing us to "talk" without worrying about the cost. The cost amounted to nothing more than the normal connect-time charge. A conversation we had recently appears in Figure 8-16.

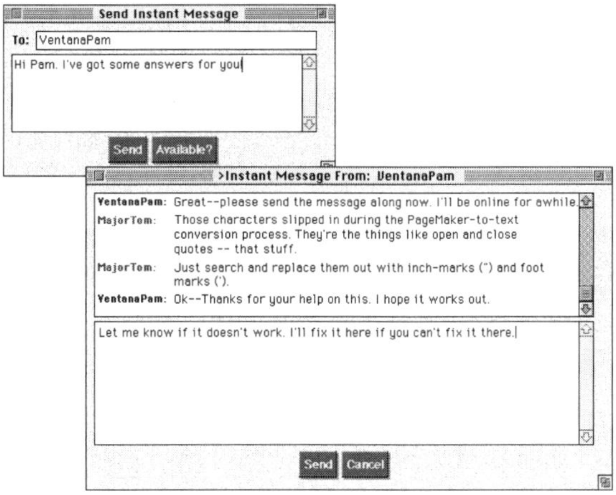
Send Instant Message
To: VentanaPam
Hi Pam. I've got some answers for you
Send
Available?
>Instant Message From: VentanaPam
VentanaPam: Great--please send the message along now. I'll be online for awhile.
MajorTom: Those characters slipped in during the PageMaker-to-text conversion process. They're the things like open and close quotes -- that stuff.
MajorTom: Just search and replace them out with inch-marks (") and foot marks (').
VentanaPam: Ok--Thanks for your help on this. I hope it works out.
Let me know if it doesn't work. I'll fix it here if you can't fix it there.
Send
Cancel

Figure 8-16: The "Instant Message From VentanaPam" window contains a running log of our conversation in the upper text box, along with the response I'm composing in the lower one.

To send an Instant Message, choose Send an Instant Message from the Members menu, or type Command-I. Enter the recipient's screen name and your message, as shown in the upper window of Figure 8-16, and click Send. After that, a running log of the conversation is maintained in the Instant Message window, as pictured in the lower window of Figure 8-16.

Before you send an Instant Message, use the Available? button in the Instant Message window, pictured at the top of Figure 8-16, or the Locate a Member Online command under the Members menu. If the recipient isn't online when you send an Instant Message, AOL tells you, and you'll have to wait for another opportunity. (If a member is not available online, consider sending e-mail instead. Electronic mail is discussed in Chapter 3.)

Available or Locate?

The Available? button in the Send Instant Message window does the same thing as the Locate a Member Online command under the Members menu. I prefer the button. Most of the time, if a member is online you're going to want to say hello, right? If you discover the member online via the Locate command and want to say hello, you have to call up the Send Instant Message dialog box anyway; but in the time it takes to produce that box, you might lose your opportunity.

OK, it's a small matter, and locating members online isn't like locating pike: they aren't liable to disappear in a matter of seconds. Nonetheless, it's one less command to learn, and every time you don't use the Available? button, you'll wish you did.

- Figure 8-16's lower window has been enlarged from the default. Like all of AOL's windows, the Instant Message window can be resized. If you want to change the size of a window permanently, choose Remember Placement from the Window menu after you have sized the window to your satisfaction.
- You cannot send Instant Messages while in a free area, though you can compose them while you're there. America Online closes any open Instant Message windows when you enter a free area, and exits a free area as soon as you attempt to send an Instant Message.
- Use the Available? button in the Send Instant Message window to determine where the intended recipient is before sending an Instant Message. This feature tells you if the recipient is online and, if so, whether he or she can receive Instant Messages. It also tells you if a member is in a chat room, in which case you might want to go to that room rather than send an Instant Message.
- Instant Messages are accompanied by a "tinkerbell" sound (assuming your Mac's sound is turned on), and the Instant Message window will appear on your screen. See the "Ongoing Instant Messages" sidebar for more.

Ongoing Instant Messages

Occasionally, you'll find yourself engaged in an ongoing Instant Message conversation. You might want to do something else online while it's under way—read the postings on a board, for example, or check the weather.

Doing something else online, however, pushes the IM window to the back, and if your IM sounds are disabled, you'll need another method of determining when your correspondent has replied. How can you tell with the IM window in the background?

Easy: before you pursue another task, position the IM window on your screen (it's a window like any other and you can move it by dragging its title bar) so that its title bar will show, even if it's in the background and other windows have come to the front. While you're working on another task, keep your eye on the IM window's title bar. When your friend sends a reply, the > symbol will appear in the IM window's title bar, even if it's in the background. Then it's a simple matter of bringing the IM window to the front and composing your reply.

- You can log Instant Messages (handy for telephone-style Instant Messages such as those I exchanged with Pam) by choosing Log Manager from the File menu. Use the "Instant Message" log option.
- If you don't want to be disturbed by Instant Messages, you can turn them off at any time by sending an Instant Message to "$im_off" (without the quotation marks, with the dollar sign, and always in lowercase). Include a character or two as text for the message; otherwise AOL will respond with a "cannot send empty Instant Message" error. A single character will do. To turn Instant Messages back on, send an Instant Message to "$im_on."

Buddy Lists

Supply and demand: classical economics expounds on the balance between equilibrium and chaos, citing theories and pointing to business graphics that look like the Grand Tetons and apple pies—all very arcane and inscrutable.

It's not that complex at America Online. At AOL, the supply-and-demand theory is simple: if we the members demand it, AOL will supply it. Such is the case with *Buddy Lists*. By mid-1995, the demand from members for Buddy Lists warranted AOL's examination of the matter. Six months later, the feature was available.

What's a Buddy List? The flaw in the Instant Message scenario that we've been discussing is that you have to know if the recipient is online before you can send an Instant Message. The Locate a Member Online command under the Members menu serves the need after a fashion, but what if the person you're trying to locate signs on four seconds after you've tried to locate him or her? What if that person is online when you sign on? Wouldn't it be nice to know that as soon as the "Welcome" greeting is finished?

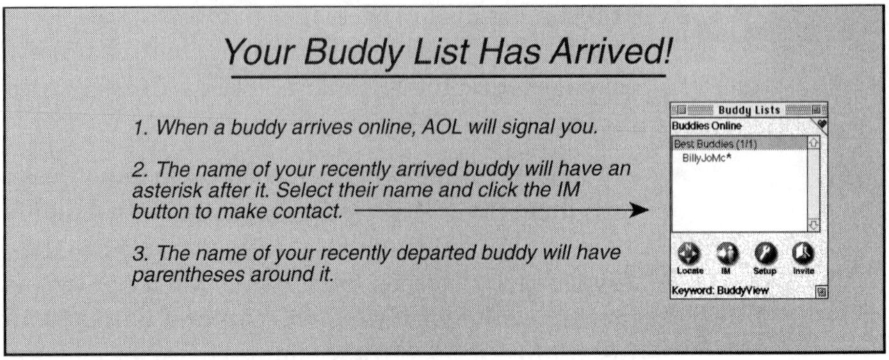
Your Buddy List Has Arrived!
1. When a buddy arrives online, AOL will signal you.
2. The name of your recently arrived buddy will have an asterisk after it. Select their name and click the IM button to make contact.
3. The name of your recently departed buddy will have parentheses around it.
Buddy Lists
Buddies Online
Best Buddies (1/1)
BillyJoMc*
Locate
IM
Setup
Invite
Keyword: BuddyView

Figure 8-17: Once a Buddy List is active, you'll receive automatic notification of a buddy's arrival whenever the buddy signs on.

You're not limited to a single Buddy List. You can have as many of them as you like—for each of your screen names. As MajorTom, I might have a group of buddies on my "Readers" Buddy List, and another group of buddies on my "Business" Buddy List. If I was online doing work, I'd activate my Business list. If I was there to be social, I'd use the Readers list.

You can create Buddy Lists; and you can add, edit, or delete buddies on those lists using the windows pictured in Figure 8-18 (at keyword: **Buddy**). You can also specify those members whose Buddy Lists you want your name to appear on (and those you don't) by using the Buddy List preferences discussed in Appendix E.

Now that you have your list of buddies, what else could you need? A way to invite them to join you in a chat room or a forum, of course. Using the Invite button pictured on the bottom right of Figure 8-17, you can send a special invitation to a whole group of buddies at once. To send an invitation, select either a list of buddies or just one buddy from your Buddy List window and type in a message appropriate to the invitation. Then fill in either the name of the private room you'd like to invite them to or the address (URL) of a forum, chat room, or even a Web site. Anything that has a URL is fair game for an invitation, and any window with a favorite place heart in the upper right corner has a URL. You can obtain a window's URL by clicking the heart, selecting "Copy to clipboard," and pasting it in (favorite places are discussed in more detail in Chapter 4, "Using the Internet").

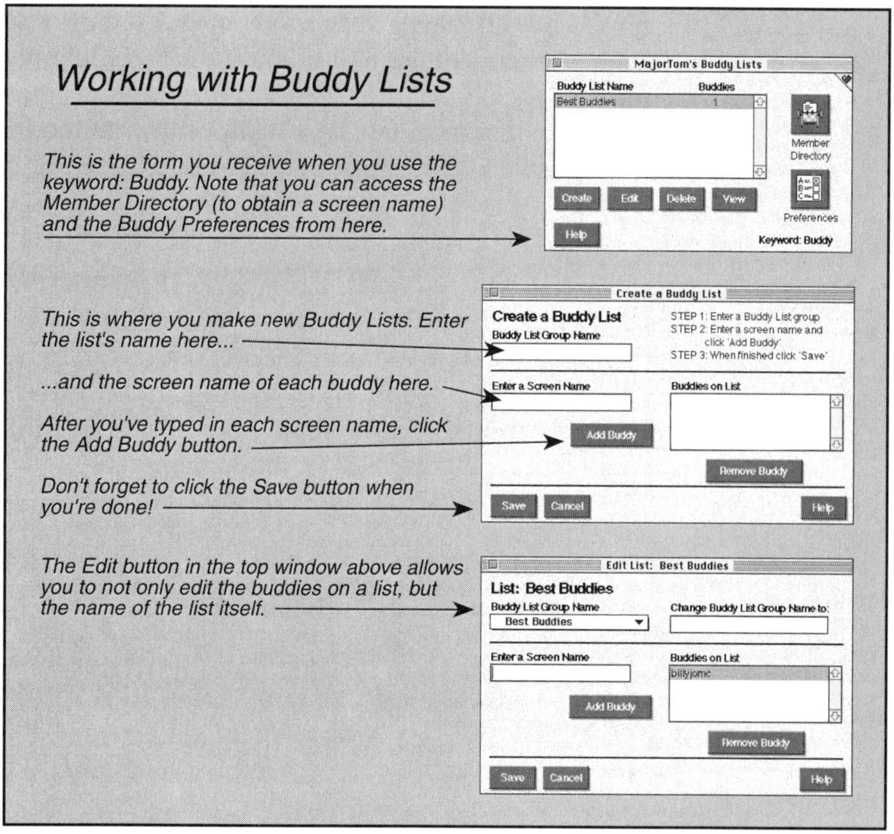
Working with Buddy Lists
This is the form you receive when you use the keyword: Buddy. Note that you can access the Member Directory (to obtain a screen name) and the Buddy Preferences from here.
MajorTom's Buddy Lists
Buddy List Name
Buddies
Best Buddies
1
Member Directory
Preferences
Create
Edit
Delete
View
Help
Keyword: Buddy
This is where you make new Buddy Lists. Enter the list's name here...
...and the screen name of each buddy here.
After you've typed in each screen name, click the Add Buddy button.
Don't forget to click the Save button when you're done!
Create a Buddy List
Create a Buddy List
Buddy List Group Name
STEP 1: Enter a Buddy List group
STEP 2: Enter a screen name and click 'Add Buddy'
STEP 3: When finished click 'Save'
Enter a Screen Name
Buddies on List
Add Buddy
Remove Buddy
Save
Cancel
Help
The Edit button in the top window above allows you to not only edit the buddies on a list, but the name of the list itself.
Edit List: Best Buddies
List: Best Buddies
Buddy List Group Name
Best Buddies
Change Buddy List Group Name to:
Enter a Screen Name
Buddies on List
billyjonic
Add Buddy
Remove Buddy
Save
Cancel
Help

Figure 8-18: Create, add, edit, and delete buddies and Buddy Lists using these routines.

Kids & Parents

In its early years, the online industry was composed almost entirely of adult males. The online services of the 1980s concentrated on computer topics and issues. (AOL was no exception: it was called *Apple Personal Edition* in those days, and was devoted exclusively to users of the Apple computer.) The Internet was up and running then, but military and academic users dominated its use—hardly a forum for kids, or seniors, or even women.

Things have changed. Kids, women, and seniors are the fastest-growing segments of the online community. Probably no other segment of our society adapts as well to computers as our kids do, and kids have no qualms about striking up a new online friendship, uploading original art, or speaking their minds on a topic.

Kids Only

Kids Only (keyword: **Kids**) is a full-fledged channel on AOL. It's AOL's place for kids to interact with each other and to find information appropriate to their age level. Not surprisingly, parents (and other adults) are asked to refrain from posting on the kids' boards or chatting in the rooms, though browsing the channel is a delight for people of all ages (just look at Figure 8-19 for an indication of the wealth of offerings in this area).

Nintendo Power Source
NINTENDO POWER
Cartoon Network
CARTOON NETWORK
KIDS' WB! ONLINE
Click on the Tower!
Check out KBIC!!!
GET BIZZY
MESSAGE CENTER
NICKELODEON
CLUB TALK
WHAT DO YOU THINK?
GAMES
DEMOS
KIDSOFT SUPER STORE
CASTLE EXPLORER
THE DUMP
Try On Our Question of the Week?

Figure 8-19: The visual abundance of Kids Only is apparent even in black and white. What you can't see or hear are the animations or sounds that accompany each of these areas. For that, you'll have to use the keyword: **Kids**, and explore the channel for yourself.

Take Five for Online Safety

I'm lifting these five rules directly from the Kids Only Channel. It's important for kids to realize that people online aren't always who they say they are. These five rules will help kids—of all ages—manage in our community to their greatest benefit:

- Don't give your AOL password to anyone, even your best friend.
- Never tell someone your home address, telephone number, or school name without asking a parent.
- Never say you'll meet someone in person without asking a parent.
- Always tell a parent about any threatening or bad language you see online.
- If someone says something that makes you feel unsafe or uncomfortable, don't just sit there—take charge! Call a Guide (keywords: **KO Help**). If you're in a chat room, leave the room. Or just sign off.

Nickelodeon Online

As you would expect from an organization with a rich visual heritage like TV's *Nickelodeon*, Nickelodeon Online is a hit with kids. Oh sure, there are the *de rigueur* plugs for Nickelodeon shows—popular and colorful events in themselves—but there are also scads of events, message boards, and chat rooms.

Nickelodeon Online - Main Menu
NICKELODEON
Chew on This!
AOL Members' CHOICE
WHAT'S HOT?
Try On Our Question of the Week?
SHOW PLUGS
THE DUMP
CONNICKTION
Smorgasboards

Figure 8-20: Nickelodeon Online is home to much more than a cable TV channel.

The *Blabbatorium* is a huge chat room where Nickelodeon viewers from all over the world discuss TV. *Smorgasboards* is the home of the Game Domain, an area devoted to the fine art of game-playing online—and while we're on the topic of fine art, kids can upload their own drawings in the *Nick Art Room*. And there's *The Dump*, where kids download Nickelodeon sights, sounds, and videos. (I hesitate to mention this, but Nickelodeon Online also offers a free how-to downloading manual titled *How to Take a Dump*. Whatever you might think of the title, it's a great downloading primer, and it will save parents hours of frustrating—and perhaps futile—tutelage.)

What makes Nickelodeon Online a premier area? The attitude and talent of the people who put it together. This is online programming for kids at its best.

KidzBiz Invention Connection

There are few things more encouraging than a kid with an idea. Unfortunately, parents are often ill equipped to deal with such a potential, and out of ignorance, or lack of time, end up quashing it.

In fact, ambition is best shared with peers, and that's what KidzBiz is all about. KidzBiz is where kids can share inventions, ideas, and job and money issues—even fads (see Figure 8-21).

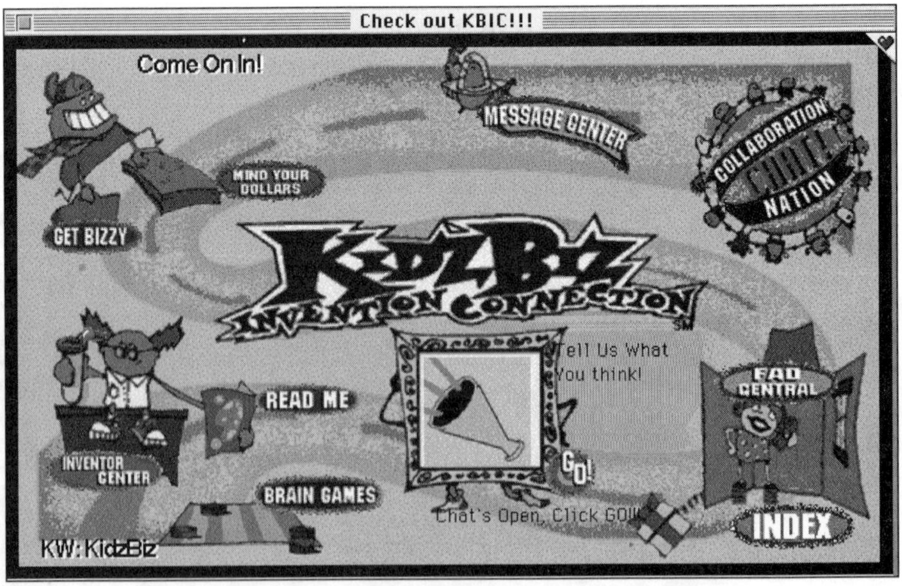
Check out KBIC!!!
Come On In!
MESSAGE CENTER
COLLABORATION NATION
MIND YOUR DOLLARS
GET BIZZY
KidzBiz
INVENTION CONNECTION
Tell Us What You think!
FAD CENTRAL
READ ME
INVENTOR CENTER
GO!
BRAIN GAMES
INDEX
KW: KidzBiz

Figure 8-21: KidzBiz is where creativity and ambition meet: peer support for tomorrow's business and technology leaders. It's all at keyword: **KidzBiz**.

FAD Central

I remember trying to keep up with my daughter's fads when she was a kid. They changed every week, it seems. If only I wudda had KidzBiz FAD Central. Just the other day I found out what a Pog is (and I also found out that they're on their way out—passed me right by!), and the message in Figure 8-22 clarified something I always suspected: expansion team jerseys are poison!

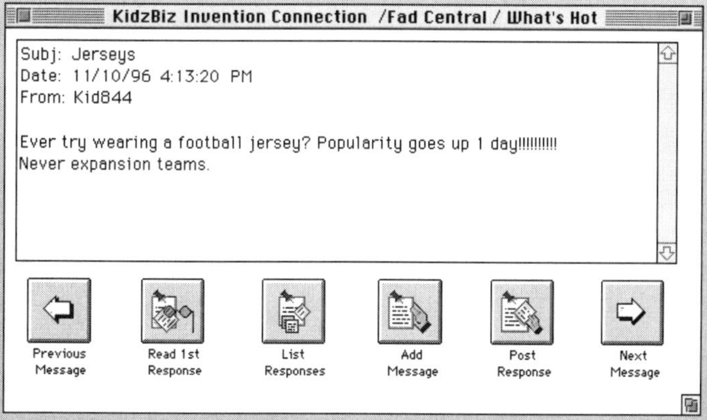
KidzBiz Invention Connection /Fad Central / What's Hot
Subj: Jerseys
Date: 11/10/96 4:13:20 PM
From: Kid844
Ever try wearing a football jersey? Popularity goes up 1 day!!!!!!!!!
Never expansion teams.
Previous Message
Read 1st Response
List Responses
Add Message
Post Response
Next Message

Figure 8-22: A one-day program for success. If only I'd known about football jerseys when I was in school.

Blackberry Creek

There's no better use of this medium than the exchange of kids' artistic creations, and Blackberry Creek exists for that single purpose (see Figure 8-23). Kids love to create, and they love to share their work. At Blackberry Creek, they reach an audience potential of millions.

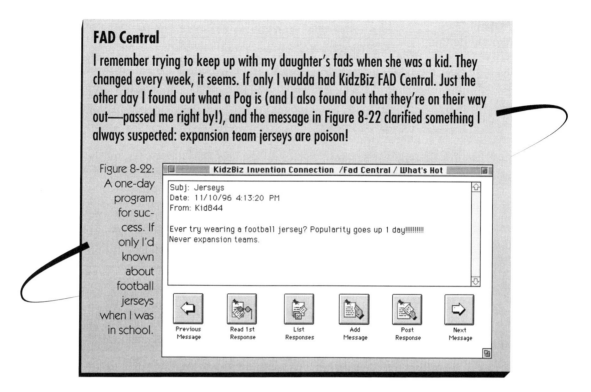

Blackberry Creek
BLACKBERRY CREEK
THE KIDS' CREATIVITY COMMUNITY
NOW SHOWING
Meet The Pickles!
Be A Circus Star and Win!
IT'S HOT! IT'S COOL!
See the best
By Blackberry kids.
SEND US YOUR STUFF!
Stories, drawings
to share? Send here!
Keyword: Blackberry
Clubhouse
Message Boards
Chat Room
The Pixels
Party People
Story Tellers
The Players

Figure 8-23: Blackberry Creek is where kids can post their creations for all to enjoy.

Blackberry Creek isn't just graphics: *Party People* is a trove of party ideas—by kids, for kids (scout leader alert!), *Story Tellers* is a collection of stories by kids, and *The Players* offers scripts for the stage and screen.

Kids Chat

If there's one thing kids like to do even more than exchange their creations, it's exchange their opinions. All kids have opinions about something, and most of them have opinions about everything. And there's no medium better suited for that purpose than America Online.

There are chat rooms all over the Kids Only Channel. Nickelodeon has the Blabbatorium, Warner Brothers has the Chat Shack—there are lots of others. These rooms serve a distinct audience; they're not the same as conference rooms or the rooms in People Connection. A few suggestions and specifics on features, restrictions, and unacceptable behavior:

- Some kids rooms (all of those in Kids Only, for example) are for kids of a specific age. Determine a room's age restrictions before you enter.

- The age restrictions are for participants, not observers. Parents should visit these rooms—to observe the conversations—before their children become participants.
- Most kids rooms are staffed at peak times; some are staffed round the clock. It's not uncommon to find three or four "nicks" (Nickelodeon hosts) in the Blabbatorium, for example, on any weekday afternoon.
- Profanity is not allowed anywhere on America Online. Use of such language in chat rooms and message boards will result in a TOS violation. Using symbols to disguise these words is also a violation.
- Rudeness to a guest, verbally or by behavior, will be considered a room disruption and is subject to TOS review.
- Harassing a staff member or another member in a chat room is not allowed. If someone harasses *you*, do not respond in the same manner. If the harassment appears in the form of an IM, use the Ignore feature (discussed earlier in this chapter) and report the violation to TOS. Don't let one person's rudeness make you behave in the same way.
- Talk of illegal activity is forbidden on America Online.
- *Scrolling* (when a user repeatedly hits the return key so that previous chat room messages move too fast for the users to see) is forbidden. Scrolling is specifically defined as a TOS violation.
- *Polling* (asking a question and requiring all present to post a specific letter, number, or word in response, such as "Type '3' if you love David Bowie.") isn't specifically a TOS violation, but it's a little moronic and always disruptive.
- Before coming to a Kids Chat room, check the calendar. If there is a scheduled event, the room is reserved. You're welcome to join the event in progress, of course, but if you're looking for a social chat, wait until the scheduled event is finished.
- Do not post age/sex checks (requests for room occupants' age and gender) during scheduled events. This disrupts a discussion, is rude to a guest, and makes it difficult to play a game. Ask in Instant Messages if you really can't wait till the event is finished.

There's Much More

I'm only describing a portion of the kids areas available online in this chapter. An exceptional offering of educational resources for students of all ages is described in Chapter 13, "Learning & Culture."

Parental Considerations

Though it occurs throughout the service, harassment and exploitation are particularly obstructive in any kids area. To be effective, AOL must be a place where kids are made to feel welcome: it's their online home, and a home—above all—must always be comfortable.

TOS & Kids

America Online's Terms of Service (TOS is discussed in Chapter 2) clearly define the rules of acceptable online behavior—for all members, including kids. Parents should understand these rules and make sure their children understand them before signing on. In the perspective of TOS and kids it's important to remember that the person who is the master account holder is responsible for all of the users whose screen names are on the account.

An Extra Measure of Security

Here's a nifty little tip from remote Forum Leader Tom Quindry: use the Passwords preference in the Preferences under the Members Menu to store your kids' passwords. The kids won't need a password to sign on—which might be convenient—but more important, they won't be able to see the passwords on the screen, even if they choose the Passwords preference. (Note in Figure 8-24 that stored passwords are displayed as asterisks.)

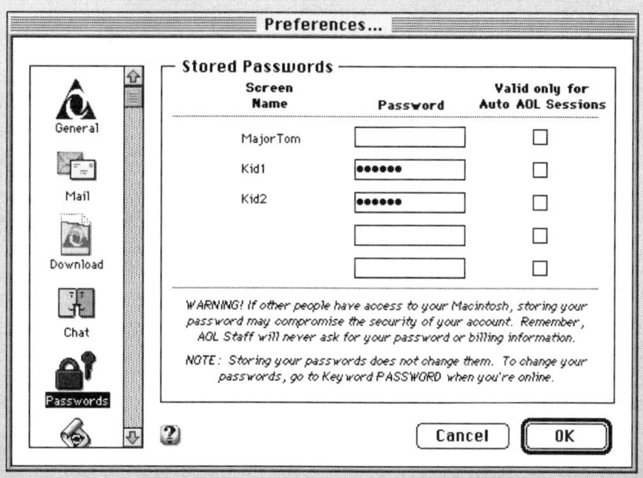
Preferences...
General
Mail
Download
Chat
Passwords
Stored Passwords
Screen Name
Password
Valid only for Auto AOL Sessions
MajorTom
Kid1
Kid2
WARNING! If other people have access to your Macintosh, storing your password may compromise the security of your account. Remember, AOL Staff will never ask for your password or billing information.
NOTE: Storing your passwords does not change them. To change your passwords, go to Keyword PASSWORD when you're online.
Cancel
OK

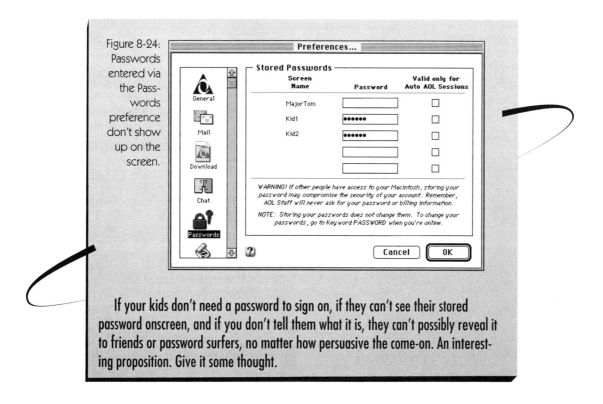

Figure 8-24: Passwords entered via the Passwords preference don't show up on the screen.

If your kids don't need a password to sign on, if they can't see their stored password onscreen, and if you don't tell them what it is, they can't possibly reveal it to friends or password surfers, no matter how persuasive the come-on. An interesting proposition. Give it some thought.

KO Help

When your child witnesses a TOS violation, he or she should be encouraged to use the keywords: **KO Help** and ask a Guide to enter the room where the violation is occurring (see Figure 8-25). KO Help is sort of a Guidepager for kids. It's a bit more kid-friendly, but it carries the same degree of authority as any other Guide online. Not only will the offender be made to understand the significance of TOS enforcement (that's as politely as I can put it), but your child will see what happens when these rules are broken. A witness to a "TOS event" rarely forgets the experience.

GUIDEPAGER FOR KIDS
Guidepager for Kids
Use Guidepager for Kids when you witness a Terms of Service (TOS) violation, such as vulgarity (swearing, crude comments) or harassment, and a Guide is not present. Please click on the 'Get a Guide' button below and a Guide will be along shortly to assist you.
Get a Guide
Report Password Scam
Keyword: KO Help

Figure 8-25: Making AOL a better place for all kids: KO Help is only a keyword away.

Instant Messages & Kids

Instant Messages often arrive unbidden, and when kids are involved these messages are occasionally unwelcome as well. Your child should know how to turn Instant Messages off, a procedure described in the "Instant Messages" section of this chapter.

Online Time

A friend of mine once recounted her horror when she discovered that her daughter had fallen asleep for two hours while making a call to a 900 number. While 900 numbers usually charge by the minute and AOL charges by the hour, AOL's charges can add up quickly when a child—who can hardly be expected to understand the significance of a month of six-hour Saturdays in the KOOL Tree House—is left unattended online. The Kids Only staff suggests you teach your children how to use Automatic AOL for collecting and posting mail (Automatic AOL is discussed in Chapter 6, "Automatic AOL & the Download Manager"). Set limits on the amount of time they are allowed online, in much the same way you limit their television viewing. KOOL should be a fun electronic clubhouse but not a financial burden. America Online cannot be held responsible for charges you might deem excessive.

The Internet & Kids

As I mentioned in Chapter 4, the Internet is a vast superset of AOL, extending around the world. It is, therefore, an environment over which AOL has no control. There is no Internet TOS, and even if there was one, there would be little authority for its enforcement: the Internet is still an anarchy in many ways.

On the other hand, an increasing number of schools are going online via the Internet, and the array of services available there is constantly growing. This is not an appropriate resource for parents to prohibit, though it *is* one to restrain and monitor (we'll discuss that later in this chapter, when we get to "Parental Controls").

By all means, encourage your children to explore the Internet, but do so only after you've explored this section of the book and visited the keywords: **Parental Controls**. Should you become aware of the transmission, use, or viewing of child pornography while on the Net, immediately report it to the National Center for Missing or Exploited Children by calling 1-800-843-5678. The Center has an excellent brochure on this subject titled *Child Safety on the Information Highway* (Figure 8-26). The brochure was written by Lawrence J. Magid, a syndicated columnist for the *Los Angeles Times* and author of a number of books on the subjects of computers and the Internet.

Child Safety on the Information Highway

Figure 8-26: Parents who intend to allow their children to explore the Internet should order this brochure from the National Center for Missing or Exploited Children. Call 1-800-843-5678 to order.

Parent Soup

We discussed Parental Controls in Chapter 2, "The Abecedarium," but have you heard of *Parent Soup*? Being a parent myself, I know all about parent soup: parents never have enough time for the job of parenting; and all parents can use information, advice, and empathy on the subject. Unfortunately, the online community hasn't made the job any easier.

Or has it? Parent Soup is available from the comfort of your own home, at whatever time of day or night you've got a moment. You can drop by to ask a question, talk to other concerned and involved parents, go to a talk by a leading expert, even get some comic relief. You may be in pajamas or in bagged-out sweats, you might even be dressed for a meeting, but wherever you are, whatever you're doing, the real advantage of Parent Soup is that whenever you're ready, someone there is ready to take your question, hear your sigh, boost you up, or just listen—no small thing when you're a parent.

Note that I said "someone there is ready." The implication is that Parent Soup is a live resource. Many parenting issues require answers *now*, not tomorrow or the next day. Parent Soup offers a profusion of resources, but wherever you travel in Parent Soup, you'll see a Help button. When in doubt, just press it and someone there will come running.

Parent Soup is an antidote for parental paranoia—especially the kind that's provoked by the online community. If you're a parent, take the time to get to know what's available. It's at the keywords: **Parent Soup**, of course.

Seniors

I've remarked on the value of online community. The kids are certainly aware of it, and so too are the members of another demographic sector: seniors. Sometimes isolated, occasionally sedentary, but often gregarious—seniors are perfect candidates for the convenience and camaraderie the online medium offers. True to form, two of the most active areas on the service are in the seniors' domain.

The Communities Center

Kids, seniors, women—they're all discussed in this chapter. But how about Hispanics, Native Americans, African Americans, Twentysomethings, Lions, Eagles, Toastmasters, and Jaycees?

There are message boards for each of these communities, and many more. To reach them all, use the keyword: **Communities**.

AARP Online

The American Association of Retired Persons (AARP) is the nation's oldest and largest organization of older Americans, with a membership of more than 33 million. Membership is open to anyone age 50 or older, working or retired. Over one-third of the Association's membership is in the workforce. Whether you're a member of the AARP or not (information about joining is available online), you'll find AARP Online (keyword: **AARP**) a supportive network of people concerned with issues such as caring for parents, grandparenting in the '90s, planning for a sound retirement, re-entering the workforce, and consumer fraud (see Figure 8-27).

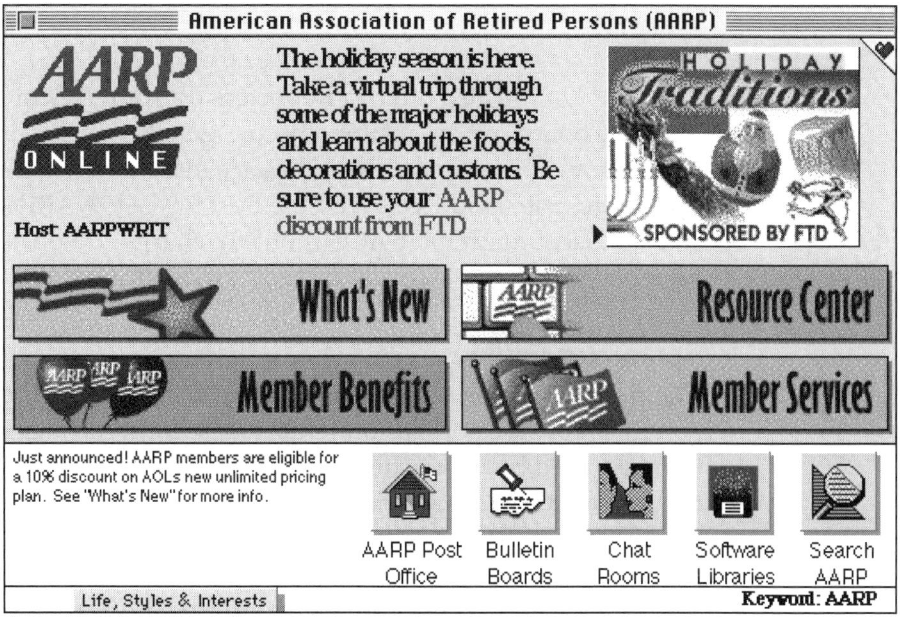
American Association of Retired Persons (AARP)
AARP ONLINE
Host: AARPWRIT
The holiday season is here. Take a virtual trip through some of the major holidays and learn about the foods, decorations and customs. Be sure to use your AARP discount from FTD
HOLIDAY Traditions
SPONSORED BY FTD
What's New
Resource Center
Member Benefits
Member Services
Just announced! AARP members are eligible for a 10% discount on AOLs new unlimited pricing plan. See "What's New" for more info.
AARP Post Office
Bulletin Boards
Chat Rooms
Software Libraries
Search AARP
Life, Styles & Interests
Keyword: AARP

Figure 8-27: AARP Online offers a wealth of research and information.

Of particular interest is the forum's searchable database of senior issues. Through its research center and its magazine, the AARP has developed a wellhead of senior-oriented information over the years. The database puts it all online, and it's available to AARP members and nonmembers alike (see Figure 8-28).

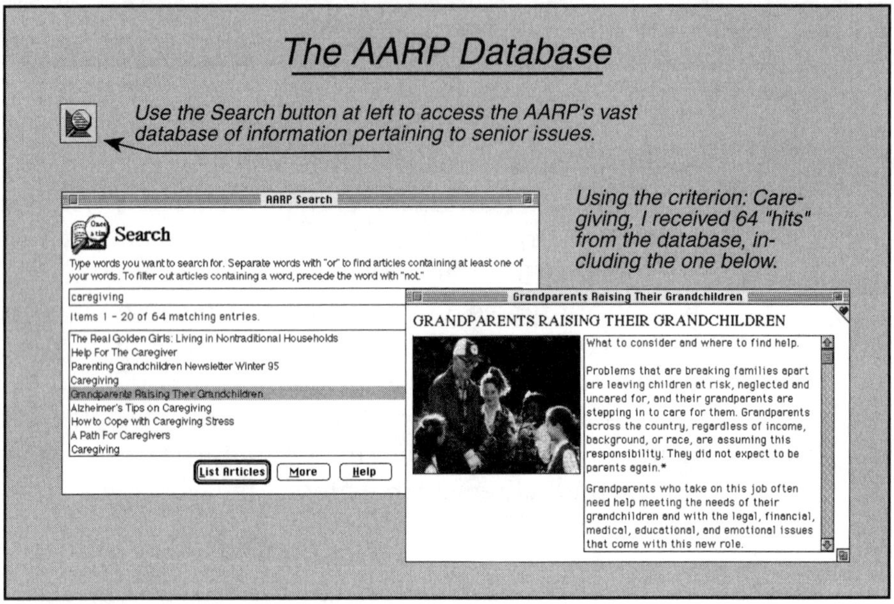
The AARP Database
Use the Search button at left to access the AARP's vast database of information pertaining to senior issues.
Using the criterion: Caregiving, I received 64 "hits" from the database, including the one below.
AARP Search
Search
Type words you want to search for. Separate words with "or" to find articles containing at least one of your words. To filter out articles containing a word, precede the word with "not."
caregiving
Items 1 - 20 of 64 matching entries.
The Real Golden Girls: Living in Nontraditional Households
Help For The Caregiver
Parenting Grandchildren Newsletter Winter 95
Caregiving
Grandparents Raising Their Grandchildren
Alzheimer's Tips on Caregiving
How to Cope with Caregiving Stress
A Path For Caregivers
Caregiving
List Articles
More
Help
Grandparents Raising Their Grandchildren
GRANDPARENTS RAISING THEIR GRANDCHILDREN
What to consider and where to find help.
Problems that are breaking families apart are leaving children at risk, neglected and uncared for, and their grandparents are stepping in to care for them. Grandparents across the country, regardless of income, background, or race, are assuming this responsibility. They did not expect to be parents again.*
Grandparents who take on this job often need help meeting the needs of their grandchildren and with the legal, financial, medical, educational, and emotional issues that come with this new role.

Figure 8-28: The AARP's database of senior issues is a pertinent and extensive resource.

AARP Online also offers a Reporters' Resource Center and a message board, where visitors discuss generational issues, consumer affairs, transitions, finances, and many more topics germane to the senior lifestyle. And I've saved the best for last: AARP members receive a discount on their AOL monthly charge. If you're an AARP member, be sure to take advantage of this offer.

SeniorNet Online

The AARP isn't the only nationwide resource established to serve America's senior population. There's a second one—SeniorNet—that's more focused but every bit as lavish in content as AARP. And fortunately for AOL's senior membership, they're both available online. SeniorNet, the parent organization of SeniorNet Online, grew out of a research project begun in 1986 at the University of San Francisco to determine if computers and telecommunicating could enhance the lives of older adults—in this case, those who are 55 or older.

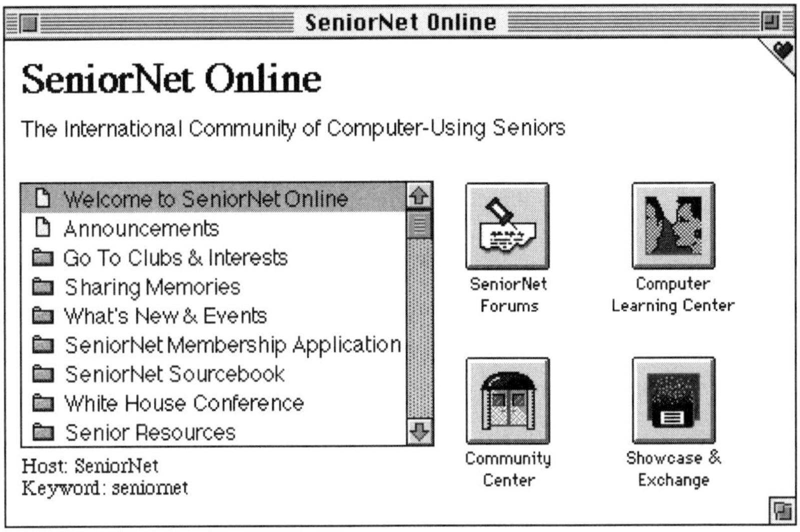
SeniorNet Online
SeniorNet Online
The International Community of Computer-Using Seniors
Welcome to SeniorNet Online
Announcements
Go To Clubs & Interests
Sharing Memories
What's New & Events
SeniorNet Membership Application
SeniorNet Sourcebook
White House Conference
Senior Resources
Host: SeniorNet
Keyword: seniornet
SeniorNet Forums
Computer Learning Center
Community Center
Showcase & Exchange

Figure 8-29: SeniorNet Online is home to thousands of SeniorNet members. Just use the keyword: **seniornet**.

Though access to SeniorNet Online is afforded to any AOL member, those who qualify for and join SeniorNet receive a number of other benefits:

- Unlimited SeniorNet Online access.
- Discounts of 25 to 50 percent on selected magazines and books (including this one).
- Significant discounts on computer hardware and software.
- *Newsline*, SeniorNet's quarterly newsletter, which includes step-by-step computer workshops, computer product reviews, computer tips, and other articles of interest to computer-using seniors.
- Discounted admission to the national SeniorNet conference. The 1993 conference was held in Hawaii.

SeniorNet Online's boards are especially well designed and appropriate for the membership. Topics range from wellness to writing, and hundreds of postings appear every day. When I last visited, more than 75,000 messages were available. This is one of the most active forums on AOL.

The History of the World

Peeking at the SeniorNet libraries the other day, I happened across this gem from history teacher Richard Lederer. Richard has pasted together the following "history" of the world from certifiably genuine student bloopers collected by teachers throughout the United States. Read carefully: you might learn something!

"The inhabitants of ancient Egypt were called mummies. They lived in the Sarah Dessert and traveled by Camelot. The climate of the Sarah is such that the inhabitants have to live elsewhere, so certain areas of the dessert are cultivated by irritation. The Egyptians build the Pyramids in the shape of a huge triangular cube. The Pyramids are a range of mountains between France and Spain.

"Without the Greeks, we wouldn't have history. The Greeks invented three kinds of columns—Corinthian, Doric and Ironic. They also had myths. A myth is a female moth. One myth says that the mother of Achilles dipped him into the River Stynx until it become intolerable.

"Achilles appears in the Iliad, by Homer. Homer also wrote The Oddity, in which Penelope was the last hardship that Ulysses endured on his journey. Actually Homer was not written by Homer but by another man of that name.

"Socrates was a famous Greek teacher who went about giving people advice. They killed him. . . .

"In midevil times, most of the people were aliterate. The greatest writer of the time was Chaucer, who wrote many poems and verses and also wrote literature. Another tale tells of William Tell who shot an arrow through an apple while standing on his son's head.

"The Renaissance was an age in which more individuals felt the value of their human being. Martin Luther was nailed to the church door at Wittenberg for selling papal indulgences. He died a horrible death, being excommunicated by a bull. . . .

"It was an age of great inventions and discoveries. Gutenberg invented the Bible. Sir Walter Raleigh invented cigarettes. Sir Francis Drake circumcised the world with a 100-foot clipper. . . .

"Delegates from the original thirteen states formed the Contented Congress. Thomas Jefferson, a Virgin, and Benjamin Franklin were two singers of the Declaration of Independence. Franklin had gone to Boston carrying all his clothes in his pocket and a loaf of bread under each arm. He invented electricity by rubbing cats backwards and declared, 'A horse divided against itself cannot stand.' Franklin died in 1790 and is still dead."

Surely you know more now than you did a few minutes ago, even though I've cut more than half the article in the interest of brevity. If you want it all, snoop around in the SeniorNet libraries (snoop hard: it's there, under the title "The History of the World"). There's great reading to be found there.

SeniorNet Online also offers the SeniorNet "headquarters," where they've put all the information you want to know about SeniorNet (the club), such as Member Benefits, Member Discounts, and a list of SeniorNet Learning Centers. Naturally, if you're not already a member you can sign up online to join SeniorNet. It's that easy.

Women's Issues

Sitting at your computer, probably in private, it's difficult to imagine the sheer magnitude of the AOL community. There are over five million people here: more people "live" in the AOL community than in the metro areas of San Francisco, Madrid, or Sydney. Every community this size has its share of societal rewards—and problems. AOL is no exception.

Perhaps no segment of AOL's society benefits more from these rewards—and suffers more of the problems—than women. A section on Women's Issues, then, is not only appropriate for this book; it's integral to the understanding of the community. This is a responsibility I don't take lightly.

I'm not a woman, however, nor am I so arrogant as to assume that I can speak on women's behalf. For that purpose I have drafted the perspectives of five women of online significance and vision. They're all active participants in the online community, and they've all been here long enough to have things in proper perspective. Short biographies appear as sidebars; I'm using the women's screen names to identify them.

Future Tense

My interviews with Jennifer, Gwen, Eva, Sue, and Sooze occurred in mid-November of 1995, more than three months before the official launch of the Women's Channel. Buddy Lists weren't available at that time either. For this reason, you won't see much mention of either of these pertinent women's features in their comments. This should in no way be interpreted as a dilution of their message or their lack of awareness.

Screen Names

Any woman who has ventured into People Connection with a gender-specific screen name probably has a shocking tale to tell. Instant Messages overlap on your screen like paper emerging from a hyperactive photocopier. Most of the senders are men, and most are shy and relatively innocent. Some are not.

What's a woman to do? Take a gender-neutral screen name? Avoid People Connection? Cancel her account? All of the women on our panel use gender-specific screen names. Here's why.

Jennifer: "I've always used a primary gender-specific screen name simply because, quite simply, *I'm* gender-specific. <grin> After I'd been on AOL for a few weeks, I considered the idea of having a gender-neutral name, but it seems like 'hiding' or sacrificing my identity in some way. So I didn't, and I'm glad I made that choice. I've met many women who refuse to use a gender-specific screen name because they feel that they will be harassed and/or discriminated against. I've only been harassed while in the People Connection chats (and that is no big deal to me), and rarely (if ever) discriminated against. So I use a gender-specific screen name because I like my name (most names have been a variation on Jennifer) and because I am female. It is just who I am."

Jennifer

Jennifer became an America Online member many years ago—with few expectations; but she found an extraordinary world filled with promise and discovery. In an effort to give something back to the online community, she became a volunteer and consultant. Among the many hats she wears are "dean" of an online private training academy, keyword list compiler, and author of several AOL-related articles, guides, and books. In fact, she is the coauthor of the very book you hold in your hands. She also assists and trains other online community leaders.

EvaS: "I've always used my own name. The only time I didn't was in order to see how different my experience might be were I to sign on and go to a chat room using a man's name. It was interesting. I was ignored. :(. . . I'm a woman and like being one. I like my own name. I've learned how to deal with harassment. I ignore it completely. . . ."

SueBD: "In contrast to some of the rest of you, I do get sick of harassment in chat rooms. Most of the time I deal with it by either not going in there to begin with, or by going in under a gender-neutral name. I have noticed, however, as Eva has, that I get less attention that way.

"Entirely naively, I may have gotten myself into a worse situation than those who 'merely' have female screennames. SueBD was really just my initials when I joined AOL in 1993, but I have discovered since then (to my chagrin) that B & D also stands, in some circles, for bondage and discipline, and suggests all *kinds* of kinky things to some folks. Since doing kinky things is the *last* place I want to be online, I finally resorted to making a pretty blatant statement in my profile. As someone else suggested, it works most of the time. I've toyed with the idea of changing my screenname, but I'm on a billion mailing lists, and everyone online knows me by this name, and it just seems like a big undertaking at this point. Furthermore, SueBD is the top name on my account, and if I delete the whole account to get rid of it I lose my mailing list names, too."

SueBD

SueBD works in the medical profession and in her "spare time" owns and operates the Women's Web Construction Company, doing Web site design, graphics, and consultation regarding online community building (at http://wwcoco.com). She also moderates a medical profession mailing list (mailing lists are discussed in Chapter 4) with over 700 members around the world.

GwenSmith: "Both [my business screen name] and my 'civvie' one . . . are gender-specific. Why? Because I like to feel that I am showing 'me' online, that I am not hiding myself from others. When I started on AOL, I did have a more 'obscure' name, which allowed me to wander around without anyone knowing who I was—in fact (as it's my original log-on) I still have it and use it, now and again. However . . . people can see a gender-specific name and, well, hormones get the best of 'em, I guess. But I am not going to hide myself because they can't control themselves."

Sooze50: "I closed my account and restarted twice, out of paranoia, to get new screen names. If I were giving advice, I'd say, stow your main screen name, never use it, create one suitable changeable alter ego screen name, and use that for actual online activities. That way, you can dump the alternate screen name without going through the bother of canceling the account. My local police suggested I should never use my real name or give my real address. That proved impractical, since I wanted to exchange books and manuscripts with writers I met online. There is something of depth, an opportunity for mind to mind communication, a surprisingly high level of intimacy of thought, that is worth the risk. E-mail cuts across all the boundaries—age, gender, race, religion, location, time of day. It sounds corny, but, since the picture of the earth that was taken from the moon, I think that the biggest opportunity for world peace is going to be world wide communication by e-mail and the Internet. In worrying about the problems, I say, let's not lose sight of the Big Picture."

Self-Defense

Using a gender-specific name, however, eventually provokes an unwanted advance or two. Here's how the members of our panel deal with them:

Jennifer: "I got a lot of these my first year here, and I almost never get them now. I think the biggest reasons are that I don't frequent the same places (People Connection chat rooms), I don't attract that kind of attention anymore, and I know what to do with those who do bother me. There are definitely places online that will bring more unwelcome advances than others, but that shouldn't be a reason to stay away if you want to visit them. Women just need to know that they don't have to respond to all the IMs they get (it *is* OK to close that IM window if you don't want to reply!), how to turn off IMs if necessary, and how to report problems. These days I just ignore the IMs, but if I'm in a particularly talkative mood, I may try to explain to them that asking a woman what she looks like isn't necessary when you are online, and that they have the opportunity to get to know someone from the inside out here. . . .

"Another more 'controversial' way to avoid unwelcome advances is to not call attention to yourself. That means skipping the 'cute' screen names, sticking to basics in your profile, and not giggling and blushing a lot in a chat room. It is similar to walking with confidence down a street when you are worried about muggers. If you act in a strong, self-confident manner online, you will be overlooked more often in favor of those who don't. This doesn't mean you have to act tough at all. Just that you won't take any nonsense."

GwenSmith: "I find if I'm entering a room I haven't been in before, I tend to lurk and get the feel of the area. This often 'comes off' as 'avoiding being cute'—and saves me a lot of trouble! Another thing is to be wary about how much personal information you give out—like addresses and phone numbers, stuff like that. I never list my actual city in my profile (I'll use geographic locales instead), and will usually tell others who ask where I am that I'm 'Near (name a nearby city), CA'. . . ."

GwenSmith

GwenSmith has been an America Online member since spring of 1993, and has seen the system—and herself—grow and change during that time. Gwen works as an online community consultant and spends much of her time online with a very close circle of friends in the Gazebo chat room. She has a Web page at http://members.aol.com/gwensmith.

EvaS: "[The] first line of defense is to ignore unwelcome IMs. If they're salacious, lewd, report them to TOS. In other words, there I am—or, actually, was—hosting The Womens Room in People Connection. And an IM comes in: 'Wanna go private?' I don't answer. I just click the IM box off. . . . Same is true of unwanted e-mail.

"Before I was a host, though, I tried this technique. It would go something like this:

"IM to EvaS: 'Wanna go private?'. . .

"EvaS's reply: 'Hey, I'm old enough to be your grandmother!'

"IM to Eva: 'How old are you?'

"Reply: '52' (which is what I was five years ago;))

"::long pause::

"IM to Eva: 'I like older women!'

"So, with that kind of reply, I decided they weren't going to be put off by my age, that this approach was useless, that most of them are lonely guys of various ages . . . and that every woman who's willing to engage in cybersex looks the same. ;) From then on—and it did take me a couple of months to learn that my response was not working—I simply ignored them."

EvaS

EvaS was one of the founders and the Online Coordinator of the Women's Channel on AOL. She is also the Forum Leader of the Evenings with Eva, a women's issues conference series. In addition, in September of '91, she started The Womens Room, now Womens POV, in People Connection. "I'm really excited by the fact that more and more women are signing on to AOL," Eva says. "What I'd like to see is a true representation of women reflecting the population. Fifty percent women is my goal. And I do think we'll get there someday!"

Sooze50: "I was expecting to meet Stephen Hawking online and argue chaos theory. Virgin me, I knew nothing about 'hot chat.' I ventured innocently into the chat rooms with a feminine screen name . . . and, via IM, immediately met 'Lefty' of Florida who claimed to make 'XXXX videos.' There was also 70 year old Frank from Maryland who was interested in writing 'personal erotica.' I teach testosterone, and consider myself a 'woman of the world,' and I am familiar with the male libido. But I was surprised to find the Electronic Bonejumpers online, so quickly!, so eager to peek up my Cyberskirts, and with so little foreplay! Initially I was frightened by the horny porny guys. I found, however, that simply saying I 'was not interested in that sort of thing' put an end to it. My advice on the handling of this problem is a combination of a sense of humor, caution, and faithful logging. You can always 'forward' to TOS." (**Note:** Logging is discussed in Chapter 10, "Staying Informed." TOS is discussed in Chapter 2, "The Abecedarium.")

Sooze50

Sooze50 is Professor of Biology at Temple University. She has taught courses and written textbooks on biological clocks, the pineal gland, and endocrinology. She is 51, and planning an active future with her retired husband in the Rocky Mountains.

GwenSmith: "Undesired IMs are promptly ignored. If the conversation isn't going to go past 'What are you wearing?,' then what's the point. Of course, if it's vulgar, off it goes to the TOS staff. A couple tips I have passed on to folks include:

"1. Don't bother to IM with a person who won't enter the chat room [you're in]. If they won't enter the room and talk, but want to carry on a conversation with you, then there is probably good reason to be suspicious of their intentions. Usually, I will 'invite' the person to come in and talk, just to see what their response is.

"2. Add something into your profile. Just putting a quick 'No Cybersex' or such in a profile can really help keep people away. A lot of the 'cruisers' check those profiles, and if they see 'No'—well, some of them will actually listen."

The Value of Online Friends

Most of us who have used this medium over time can attest to its greatest reward—finding and making friends online. Of my very few "best friends," I've met two online. Over the years we've shared death, marriage, retirement, and, of course, philosophy. Intellectual and emotional exchange with these people tends to be more intimate and intense than it is with my other good friends. The medium does that.

I have an unfair advantage, however. Scores of readers write to me every day, so I don't have to look very far for opportunities to make online friends. People tend to write to me using their primary account names rather than their alter egos. And I'm a man: few who write to me have ulterior motives. These are advantages few other people have, and for women, soliciting friendships online is an exceptional vulnerability.

Sooze50: "In the beginning, I thought, what the heck can I do with this? As an author, I had talked only to editors and readers. Wouldn't it be fun to be friends with some authors? So, I thought, I'll try to find some. I found them, and some surprises, by searching the AOL Membership Directory. For example, searching Melville produced everybody interested in Herman Melville—and also everyone who lived in the town of Melville. I found Edward (name changed) while searching for the ghost of Moby Dick. He wrote, 'please write anytime' and launched into a discourse on Skylab blowing up. Edward was as scary as Stephen King with the black humor of John Irving. Edward and I wrote over 600,000 (!) Strictly Platonic biting witty words to one another in the course of a year before he got [angry with me] the second, and Final, time. . . . Therein lies the pleasure, and the danger. Because, when Edward disappeared, both the first and the second time, my feelings were hurt . . . we wrote for a long time, and I still miss him."

EvaS: "I have Chronic Fatigue and Immune Dysfunction Syndrome. Being online saved my life. I started a CFS support group, The Womens Room in PC, and so on. To put it yet another way, I found support through finding others with this rotten illness. And I found friends in the support group, people who didn't think I was a malingerer, who knew the illness was/is real. . . . One of the things I've learned about a lot of people online is that they find out new things about themselves. They can try out being more assertive, are less shy. They can speak up more. And all these experiments they try finally do leak over into their offline life. They actually try their wings here, unseen, unheard, and learn to speak out—not only here, but at work and at home."

GwenSmith: "All of my closest (other than my spouse and some long time friends from high school) are from friendships gathered online. . . . Back in [the] halcyon days of '93, I met friends who are *still* here, friends that I have since met offline and who mean a lot to me. We all, I think, have had to make the first step in gaining friends, whether it was from opening up rooms, or from seeing someone else online who seemed like a nice person, and opening up a dialogue. I know that I usually get folks contacting me over hobbies, etc., in my profile, and think the [idea of an] 'extended profile' is a great idea!" (**Note:** No sooner said than done. Read the "Personal Publisher" section in Chapter 2, "The Abecedarium.")

Sooze50: "Here's my best story: My husband joined CompuServe. Which was better? I said, 'Let's try both.' He is sitting in His Home Office, I am sitting in My Home Office. We are separated by a bedroom, bathroom, and laundry room, a long hallway, and an electronic highway. I've been married to this man thirteen years, and my eyeballs popped when his hot poetry burned my screen. . . . I didn't even know the man could rhyme. He's turned out to be a regular e e cummings."

Making Online More Female Friendly

I don't have figures for this, but I'll bet that the fastest-growing segment of the online community is women. If it isn't, I'm sure it will be someday soon. This might be a medium of snakes in the grass, but the grass itself is a verdant meadow of grace and regard.

Like any crop, however, this one benefits from fertilizing. Below, the panel's comments.

Sooze50: "America Online already took the first big step. Free diskettes, easy to use, lots of help. The Best Little Tour Guide in America. :) It may be the 80% of the membership that don't read the Tour Guide that have the most problems, because the Tour Guide tells about Parental Chat Control, etc."

Thank you, Sooze, for the plug. Readers of these pages, however, are poor candidates for Tour Guide sales. :-(Her implied advice, however, is sound: if you haven't read Chapter 2, "The Abecedarium," or the other sections of this chapter, be sure to do so.

EvaS (speaking somewhat as staff): "We can tell them how we handle snerts. We can teach them how we handle snerts. Part of this is what AOL—meaning, the new Women's Channel—will try to do. [We] have been working on a course to teach women how to help themselves deal with the mean streets here. ;)

"Just because you're sitting at home at your very own computer doesn't mean that you won't have to deal [with sexual problems online]. Second thing to get across is that there are ways to deal . . . we've covered a lot of these already. The main one being that we don't have to answer someone who talks to us, either in a chat room, via IM, or e-mail. Click off the IM. Put the jerk on Ignore. Don't answer the e-mail.

"The problem is that most women are taught to speak when spoken to. Men are not as bound by that stricture as women. The other problem is that we're taught, as women, that what happens to us *vis a vis* men is our doing, our fault. So, if a man whistles at us on the street, we wonder if we're wearing clothing that is too provocative, whether we gave some kind of come on, whether we're emitting pheromones of sexual invitation. So, there we are at home, and a man IMs us, asking what we're wearing. . . . We *must* have asked for this in some way. Maybe he's a mind reader, and we've had our sexual desires, needs, thoughts, read. This a blame-the-victim mentality which is very much alive and well. :(

"It's compounded in another way by the new things that are finally happening—successful sexual harassment suits, empowerment of women, and so on. So, she sits there, thinking: 'Why should I have to take this kind of thing?? I didn't ask for it. Who the hell does he think he is?? I'm paying for this damned service and look what happens!! This is s**t and I'm going to tell him a thing or two!'

"Wrong thing to do, of course. And if women can be taught that this is really a large city, that if you're on 42nd St. in NYC, you have to watch it, that you don't have to respond to the guy who's whistling at you, or the equivalent, just because you're female, that you have to ignore the come-ons, etc. And, most important of all, you didn't ask for this.

"We have to direct women to areas online that are safer, more women-friendly already. And there will be a new women's area soon, a big one, that will be that way. Not that women will be protected from snerts, but that it will be women in the majority."

Jennifer: "Female-friendly means many things to me. It means educating our friends, family, colleagues, and passers-by on general online etiquette and matters of consideration. Not just educating women, and not just educating them about women's issues online.

"Being female-friendly also means getting more women online to level out the playing field. AOL is still predominately male, and it can be intimidating to be in the minority. We should encourage the women in our life to use the computer, get online, and discover the opportunities.

"Another aspect of being female friendly is to help women realize that this medium is as much theirs as anyone else's. Personally, I won't pander to self-deprecating jokes some women make about how they don't know how to use AOL or their computers. Too many women are still afraid of the computer, or expect their husband or boyfriend to do all the 'techie' stuff for them. Woman need to understand that it isn't 'unfeminine' to use a computer and to *like* it—it is simply a tool that helps us accomplish things and realize dreams.

"Other things are:

"—Don't assume the owner of a non-gender-specific screen name is male. (It happens a *lot*.)

"—Don't act different around those who you know are female. Take advantage of one of the great benefits of being online and treat everyone equally.

"—Report problems you see happening online. If you don't, no one may.

"—Talk about this subject with others. Not only does it increase awareness, but you may learn more!"

GwenSmith (in summation): "I feel it is up to those of us who are on staff to provide 'female-friendly' content and environments online, and it is up to those of us who are members (all of us) to make sure people know we are here."

Community awareness comes slowly. We tend to explore first, exchange some mail, and maybe visit a room or two. Later, we might develop a few friendships and find a few favorite haunts. Most of us, however, take a year or two before we become of the AOL community as a whole. It's a revelation when we do: AOL is vibrant and diverse, and like any vital community, it requires teamwork to prosper and grow. Gwen, Sue, Jennifer, Eva, and Sooze all endeavor to put back into the community more than they take from it. We should all aspire to their benevolence.

Interesting Places for Women Online

As I write this chapter, a whole new women's area of America Online is under construction. It will probably become a full-fledged Women's Channel, offering expanded women's resources and a place for women to go. Though not exclusively so, this will be a women's space—a "private space," as writer Deborah Tannen calls it—where women's communication will prosper.

The Women's Network

Unlike the Women's Channel, the Women's Network exists now. It's the online equivalent of Tannen's private space and will no doubt remain so even after the Women's Channel is launched. There's a terrific Women-to-Women area, ". . . a place for all of us to communicate about what concerns us, to share our experiences, thoughts and feelings. Only through seriously listening to and reading others' ideas and sharing our own can we widen our views, challenge our assumptions, and find common ground." (Quoting the area's description.) Look also in the Arts & Letters area, the Women's Online Directory, and the Women's News area; and visit the Conference Room every Tuesday from 9:00 to 10:30 p.m.

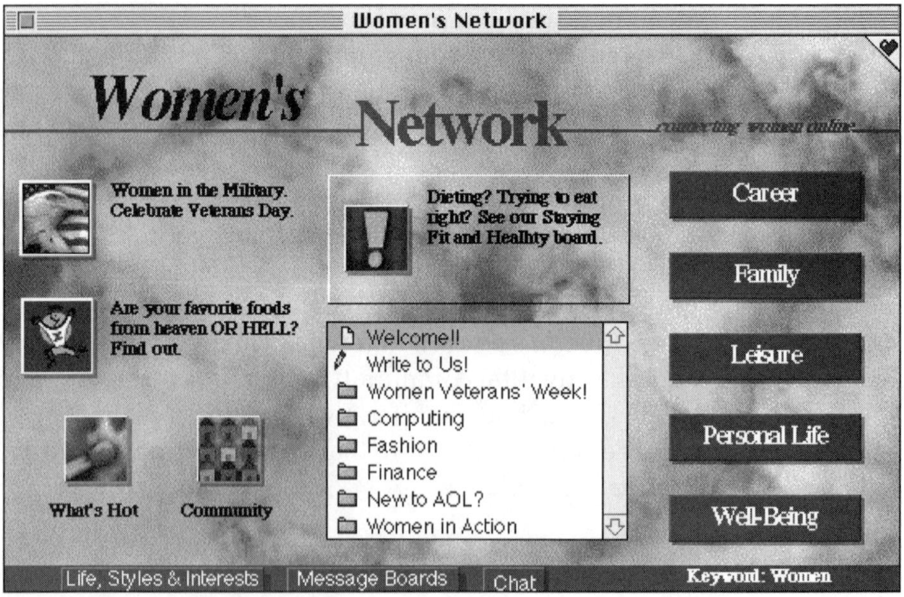
Women's Network
Women's Network
Women in the Military. Celebrate Veterans Day.
Dieting? Trying to eat right? See our Staying Fit and Healhty board.
Are your favorite foods from heaven OR HELL? Find out.
Welcome!!
Write to Us!
Women Veterans' Week!
Computing
Fashion
Finance
New to AOL?
Women in Action
What's Hot
Community
Career
Family
Leisure
Personal Life
Well-Being
Life, Styles & Interests
Message Boards
Chat
Keyword: Women

Figure 8-30: The Women's Network offers women a place to find common ground online. They're available at keyword: **Women**.

NetGirl

Irreverant, perhaps. Outspoken, without a doubt. The *Berkeley Barb* of online, maybe. One thing is for sure: NetGirl doesn't paint with pastels. This is women's online programming with an attitude, and if you're a woman, the attitude is decidedly positive (use the keyword: **NetGirl**, and see Figure 8-31).

Keyword: NetGirl
Dear NetGirl
Personals
Chat Room
Message Boards
NetGirl
AOL Members Choice
Your Guide to Relationships in Cyberspace
MajorTom, have you met NetGirl?
Chat Room & Live Events
NetGirl: AOL Members' Choice
Who Is NetGirl?
NetGirl Message Boards
Personals Message Boards
NetGirl Photo Personals
NetGirl Chat Room
The AT&T College Network
Hey Students: RESEARCH THIS!
NetGirl is here for you.
About Help Search Live Events Newsletter Message Boards Internet Connection

Figure 8-31: If you're a woman, NetGirl "is here to answer your every need" at keyword: **NetGirl**.

The World Wide Web (discussed in Chapter 4, "Using the Internet") is rapidly becoming a primary medium for women's exchange, and true to her name, NetGirl lists hundreds of women's Web resources, and the list is getting longer every day. Click the Resources button.

Unique to the commercial online medium, however, are NetGirl's Personals. These are the alternative-newspaper personals you've seen: people seeking partners, parent to parent, friends seeking friends. That last one is one you might want to investigate: it's organized by region, and it's one of AOL's best methods of finding people—people nearby—for online friendships.

Lifetime Online

Lifetime Television—"Television for Women"—was created by the merger of Daytime and Cable Health Networks in 1984. Since then, Lifetime's original programming has received over 200 awards and Emmys. Lifetime Online is a Web page, and the number of links is not only enormous, it's significant as well: the links represent a compendium of the best women's resources on the Internet.

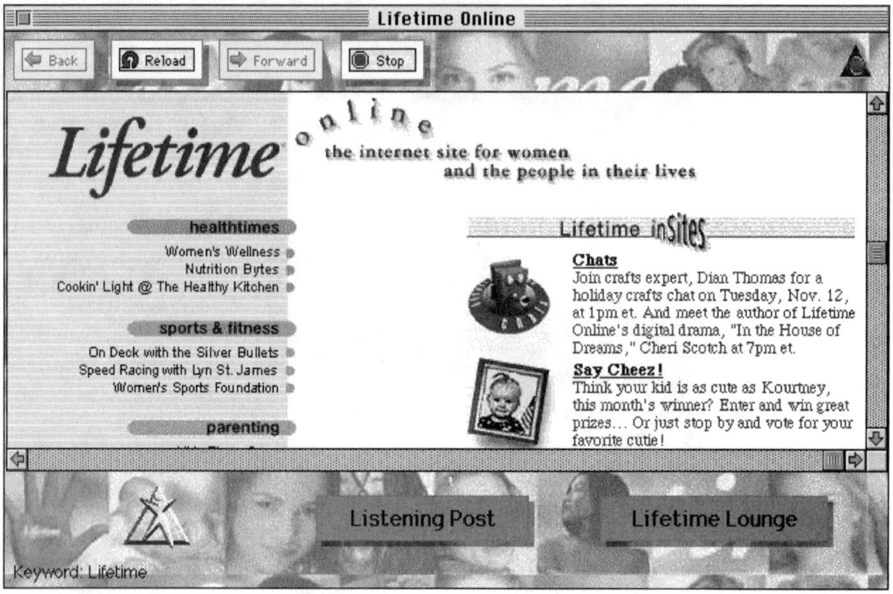
Lifetime Online
Back
Reload
Forward
Stop
Lifetime online
the internet site for women
and the people in their lives
healthtimes
Women's Wellness
Nutrition Bytes
Cookin' Light @ The Healthy Kitchen
sports & fitness
On Deck with the Silver Bullets
Speed Racing with Lyn St. James
Women's Sports Foundation
parenting
Lifetime inSites
Chats
Join crafts expert, Dian Thomas for a holiday crafts chat on Tuesday, Nov. 12, at 1pm et. And meet the author of Lifetime Online's digital drama, "In the House of Dreams," Cheri Scotch at 7pm et.
Say Cheez!
Think your kid is as cute as Kourtney, this month's winner? Enter and win great prizes... Or just stop by and vote for your favorite cutie!
Listening Post
Lifetime Lounge
Keyword: Lifetime

Figure 8-32: Lifetime Online offers in-depth programming information and lots of Web links at keyword: **Lifetime**.

ELLE Online

As a leading women's fashion magazine, *ELLE* continues to break new ground as the first magazine in its category to be featured online. In addition to its fashion and beauty areas, ELLE Online offers an extensive Fitness and Health focus. Look for Susan Blumenthal's comments in ELLE's Health Newsletter—Dr. Blumenthal is the Assistant Surgeon General and U.S. Deputy Assistant Secretary for Women's Health.

Woman's Day Online

With my wife Victoria in medical school and our daughter Sybil long ago on her own, I have become, of necessity and convenience, a homemaker. And in this capacity, I admit to visiting the Woman's Day Online area for homemaking tips and recipes. There's much more, including a superb resource center and message board for breast cancer issues. If you visit and see me there, be sure to say hello.

ELLE Online
ELLE
ONLINE
FASHION
FITNESS/HEALTH
BEAUTY
ATTRACTIONS
TOP MODEL
ELLE & BEYOND
WHAT'S NEW
Download ELLE's sexiest lingerie and swimwear!
SATURN
Resorts Online
RESORTS ONLINE
LIFE, STYLES & INTERESTS
LINKS
MESSAGES
CHAT
FIND
SPONSORS
Keyword: ELLE

Figure 8-33: ELLE Online offers features on fashion, beauty, fitness, and health at keyword: **Elle**.

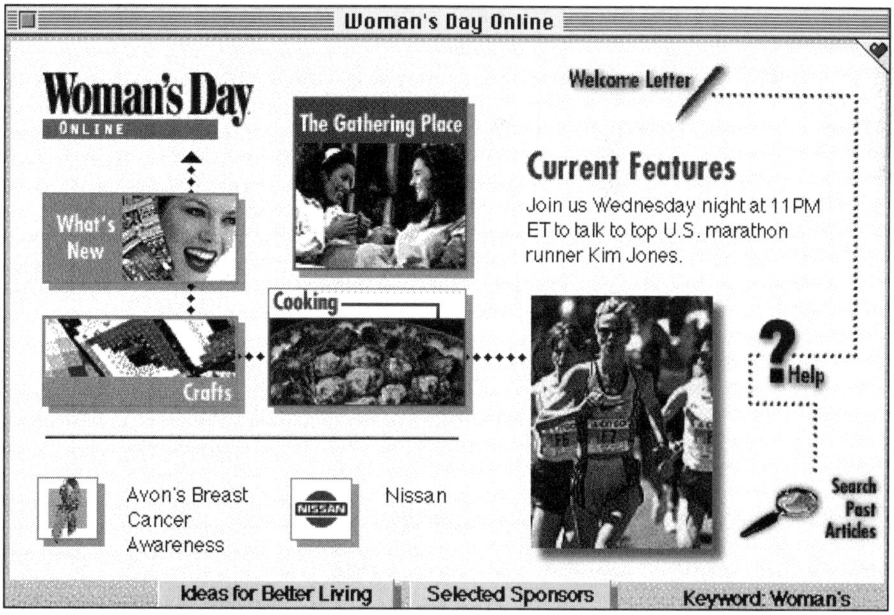
Woman's Day Online
Woman's Day
ONLINE
Welcome Letter
The Gathering Place
Current Features
Join us Wednesday night at 11PM ET to talk to top U.S. marathon runner Kim Jones.
What's New
Cooking
Crafts
Help
Avon's Breast Cancer Awareness
Nissan
Search Past Articles
Ideas for Better Living
Selected Sponsors
Keyword: Woman's

Figure 8-34: For a discussion of practical issues for both sexes, use the keywords: **Woman's Day**.

Guttersnipe

In a community of six million, it should come as no surprise to learn that there are a number of interlopers online. And typical of an industry that embraces acronyms and sobriquets, AOL members fastidiously categorize these gremlins according to the severity of their pestilence.

Trolls

Least sinister are the *trolls.* Trolls dawdle along the information highway, impeding traffic and undermining good will. Trolls enter chat rooms with palaver like "Is anyone horny?" or "Press 3 if you like Spam." They're a bit more loquacious on message boards, but their posts usually disappear when the staff makes its first sweep of the day. Trolls send me e-mail all the time that says, "Did you know your name is in the Tour Guide?" Recondite discourse, that.

Trolls are easy to manage: just ignore them. They're seeking attention, after all, and if it's granted, they have their reward. Trolls are the first category of urchin to Ignore in a chat room (the Ignore button was discussed earlier in this chapter). If a troll sends you e-mail or IMs you, copy his screen name and close his window. He probably won't be back. Use the copied screen name to block yourself from his Buddy List (blocking Buddy Lists is a preference and is discussed in Appendix E, "Preferences") and forget about it. You just passed a ragamuffin on the street; don't break your stride and he won't break his.

Phishers

We're moving up the scavenger's food chain now. *Phishers* are trolls who have graduated from misdemeanors to larceny. Phishers snack on passwords, and they feast on credit card numbers.

The common phisher appears in the form of an unsolicited IM on your screen. The message therein identifies the phisher as a member of AOL's staff. There will be a comment about damaged files at AOL and a request for your password "so that we can reconstruct our database."

More sophisticated phishers will send you an IM or e-mail claiming to be a member of AOL's staff, offering an irresistible discount on an article of merchandise. Who can resist a 28.8 modem for $24.95? The hitch, of course, is that they're not AOL staff, they have no modems, and the conversation will eventually get around to a request for your credit card number.

Other phishers, also masquerading as AOL staff, will ask you to send specific files on your hard disk to them. Though the files might seem benign and the request might seem sanctioned, this is phishing nonetheless. The requested file probably contains your encrypted password—for use by unattended Automatic AOL sessions, for example—and some phishers are sophisticated enough to decipher them.

If you ever receive a message—e-mail or IM—asking for your password, a file, or your credit card number, you can be sure it's a phisher. It is *not* a member of AOL's staff, no matter how eloquent or convincing the request.

FOOLED YOU!

Many phishers use the old "O and L" trick. The word "GUIDE" will be rejected if it appears anywhere within a proposed screen name, but the word "GUlDE" will not (the third character is a lowercase *L*, not an *I*). Thus, you might receive a message from "GUlDE TOM" and think he's an official of some sort. Beware of zeros as well: "A0L Tom" is not a staff member. Though AOL is a blocked sequence for screen names, A-*zero*-L is not.

Phishers should always be reported. Don't close that IM window! Instead, click somewhere within the message, choose Select All from the Edit menu, then choose Copy from the same menu. Write down the phisher's screen name, then use the keyword: **Guidepager**. You'll find your way from there.

The term *phisher* probably originated with the phone freaks of the 1970s and early 1980s—they called themselves "phreaks." They were the first (phirst?) of the breed, and unfortunately this breed is especially prolific. They can be *very* sophisticated: don't be phooled.

Snerts

Trolls troll for attention. Phishers phish for passwords. *Snerts,* however, are virtual voyeurs. Their primary goal is an indiscriminate assault on privacy. They live under tenement stairs where there is no light and an abundance of virulence. There they concoct schemes specifically designed to wreak havoc online, and harassment is their preferred bounty. When they discover a technique that seems especially repulsive, they broadcast it to other snerts (usually via the Internet) and come knocking on AOL's electronic doors.

A small army of AOL technicians vigilantly patrols for snerts (read the "The Guidepager" sidebar in this chapter), but the battle is often an impasse.

Recidivistic Trolls

The word *snert* is an acronym: Sexually Nerdishly Expressive Recidivistic Trolls. Hardcore snerts, however, eschewed sex in the traditional sense of the word a long time ago—if they ever knew about it in the first place. They prefer the online medium for their carnal romps now; they don't have time for the triviality of substantive matters. Perhaps we should be thankful for that: their arrogance suppresses procreation. Snerts may be a vanishing species.

Unfortunately, snerts are as hard to catch as arsonists, and every bit as destructive. When you encounter one, immediately use the keyword: **TOS** (or keyword: **Guidepager** when in a chat room) and report them.

Moving On

There's another form of community: the community of association. You might live in one community, but you might also travel to meet with people with similar interests. My trailerboating community has no specific body of water: I take my boat to waterways all over the northwest, and I meet with other boaters when I do.

Thus, we move from the general to the specific; from the online community to the forums, each a microcommunity of its own—an association of members sharing similar tastes and attitudes. If you have a hobby, a vocation, or a belief, AOL probably has a forum of folks with similar interests. Turn the page to find out.

CHAPTER 9

Boards & Forums

- Message Boards
- Computers & Software Forums
- Community Forums
- Gaming Forums

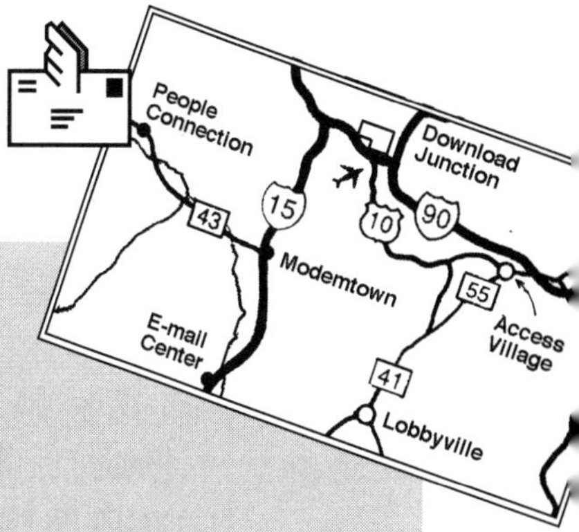
People Connection
Download Junction
15
10
90
43
Modemtown
55
E-mail Center
Access Village
41
Lobbyville

I'm having a semantics problem: in previous editions of the *Tour Guide*, I've called the subjects of this chapter "clubs," but the word *club* implies exclusivity, and that isn't quite right. AOL's attitude toward exclusivity is similar to that of Groucho Marx: in a letter to Hollywood's Friar's Club, Groucho wrote, "Please accept my resignation. I don't care to belong to any club that will have me as a member." Kinda puts exclusivity in its place, don't you think?

I suppose the proper term is *forum.* It has a certain Roman quality to it: Roman forums were public meeting places for sharing ideas and interests. That's close to where we're headed with this chapter. On the other hand, whole Roman cities were laid out with forums as their focus. That's a bit pretentious in this context, but it will have to do.

AOL's forums are where people with a common interest gather to exchange opinions, solicit advice, and hobnob with celebrities. Forums are the *vox populi* of AOL's living room referendum; they're as diverse as Pacific Northwest weather and as abundant as its rain; and if you can't find a forum to your liking, there are always the Internet newsgroups, more than 36,000 of them, and AOL carries nearly every one.

How to Find a Forum

AOL offers hundreds of forums. How can you tell if one exists that addresses your interest in, say, celestial navigation? Here's a methodical approach:

Search the Directory of Services. Use the keywords: **Directory of Services**, then specify your interest. Try a variety of search phrases: if the phrase "celestial navigation" doesn't work, try "navigation." If that doesn't work, try some general or related topics such as "boating" or "flying."

Try using your specific interest as a keyword. Click the Keyword button on the toolbar, then enter **celestial navigation**. If that doesn't work, use keyword search. Click the Keyword button on the toolbar, enter a few words describing your interests, then click the Search button. Again, don't hesitate to experiment.

Perhaps there's a newsgroup on the Internet that matches your interest. Use the keyword: **Newsgroups**, then click the Search All Newsgroups button. This is especially effective if your interest is regional. Be sure to read Chapter 4, "Using the Internet," before you participate.

AOL's forums usually consist of a conference room, where meetings are held and guest appearances are scheduled; a library, where members submit software they find useful, or files of their work—text, graphics, music, video—for others to enjoy; and message boards, where members converse without the boundaries of time or place.

We discussed libraries in Chapter 5, "Transferring Files," and conference rooms in Chapter 8, "The Community." Message boards, however, provide a more direct, more personal, and sometimes more interesting route to the sources than rooms and libraries put together. This chapter, therefore, begins with a discussion of boards and their operation. After that, we'll examine some of the forums themselves.

Message Boards

America Online's message boards are the electronic analog of the familiar cork board and pushpins. Message boards (call them "boards") are especially appropriate to online forums. One of the unique advantages boards offer is convenience: you can drop in any time of the day or night, read the messages, and post your replies.

Most of us visit our favorite boards every time we sign on and anxiously read all the messages posted since the last time we visited. The feeling is remarkably immediate, and withdrawal symptoms set in after about three days' absence. In other words, boards are addictive—but that's part of the fun.

Reading Messages

One of my favorite forums is the Cooking Club (keywords: **Cooking Club**). These folks like their food, and their libraries of recipes range from elegant appetizers to tantalizing desserts. The Cupboard offers articles and reviews of cookbooks and cooking software, and The Kitchen (a chat room, a topic we discussed in Chapter 8) opens each Sunday at 8:00 P.M. eastern time for a cooking class, new recipes, and lively camaraderie. (This is an especially nonthreatening chat room, by the way. If you're new to chat rooms you might try this one first: there's very little aggression among people who spend their Sundays sipping sherry and discussing soufflés.)

Editing the Go To Menu

Once you've found a forum to your liking, you might want to visit it every time you sign on. Rather than navigating a stack of menus or typing a keyword, give the forum a place on your Go To menu. Items at the bottom of the Go To menu are under your control; you can add or delete any one you please. The only requirement is that the item must have a keyword.

Once a place is added, you can go there via its keystroke shortcut: Command-1, Command-2, and so on. This is even easier than using the Favorite Places feature described in Chapter 4, "Using the Internet." Only 10 places can be added to your Go To menu, however, so save these entries for your most frequently visited places.

Let's say you've become an active participant in the Cooking Club. To add it to your Go To menu, follow the procedure illustrated in Figure 9-1.

Figure 9-1: Adding menu items is accommodated via the Edit Go To Menu command.

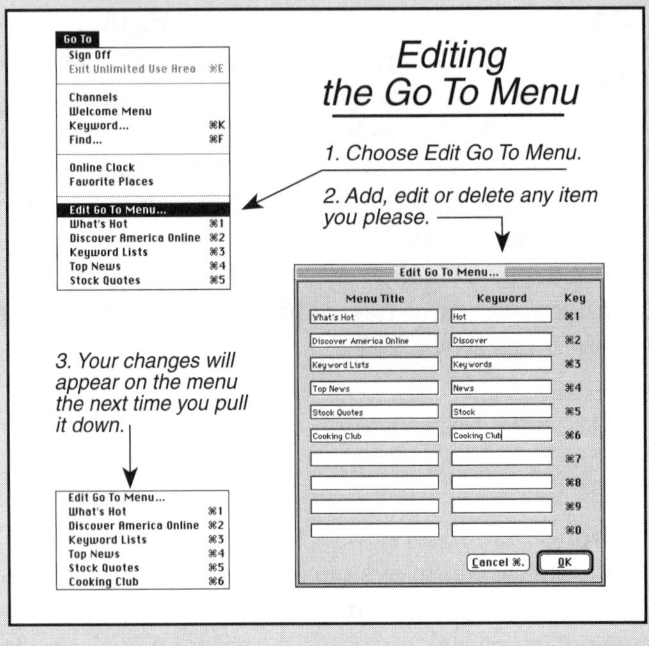
Editing the Go To Menu
1. Choose Edit Go To Menu.
2. Add, edit or delete any item you please.
3. Your changes will appear on the menu the next time you pull it down.
Go To
Sign Off
Exit Unlimited Use Area ⌘E
Channels
Welcome Menu
Keyword... ⌘K
Find... ⌘F
Online Clock
Favorite Places
Edit Go To Menu...
What's Hot ⌘1
Discover America Online ⌘2
Keyword Lists ⌘3
Top News ⌘4
Stock Quotes ⌘5
Edit Go To Menu...
Menu Title
Keyword
Key
What's Hot
Hot
Discover America Online
Discover
Keyword Lists
Keywords
Top News
News
Stock Quotes
Stock
Cooking Club
Cooking Club
Cancel ⌘.
OK
Cooking Club ⌘6

Note that there are 10 positions for you to customize on the Go To menu and that mine only has six positions active. You don't have to have all ten filled if you don't want to, nor do you have to use those that AOL initially provides. You can change any item (select it and type over), or delete items (select the item, then use the backspace key on your keyboard). Changes to the Go To menu are in effect only on the computer used in making them, by the way, and not to any particular screen name. They won't appear when you're using another machine, but they *will* appear when you're using another screen name on the original computer.

Once you have added a forum, all you have to do to get there is choose that forum from the Go To menu or use the Command key equivalent. My Go To menu contains the names of the places I like to check every time I'm online. By choosing each one in order, I never neglect to visit places I'm likely to forget.

But I'm getting ahead of myself. I've chosen this forum because it's an excellent example of message boards. In fact, it has eight of them. Everyone eats food, after all, and most of us aren't shy when it comes to talking about it. For this discussion, we'll examine the Cooking Club's recipe-exchange boards in The AOL Cookbook (see Figure 9-2).

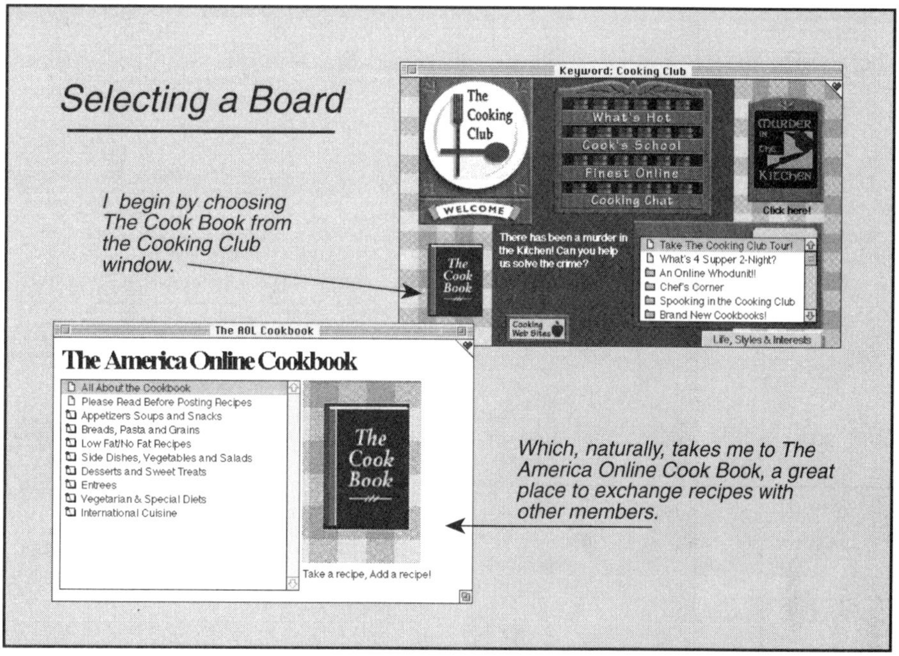
Selecting a Board
Keyword: Cooking Club
The Cooking Club
What's Hot
Cook's School
Finest Online
Cooking Chat
WELCOME
Click here!
I begin by choosing The Cook Book from the Cooking Club window.
The Cook Book
There has been a murder in the Kitchen! Can you help us solve the crime?
Take The Cooking Club Tour!
What's 4 Supper 2-Night?
An Online Whodunit!!
Chef's Corner
Spooking in the Cooking Club
Brand New Cookbooks!
Cooking Web Sites
Life, Styles & Interests
The AOL Cookbook
The America Online Cookbook
All About the Cookbook
Please Read Before Posting Recipes
Appetizers Soups and Snacks
Breads, Pasta and Grains
Low Fat/No Fat Recipes
Side Dishes, Vegetables and Salads
Desserts and Sweet Treats
Entrees
Vegetarian & Special Diets
International Cuisine
Take a recipe, Add a recipe!
Which, naturally, takes me to The America Online Cook Book, a great place to exchange recipes with other members.

Figure 9-2: Type the keywords: **Cooking Club** to open the Cooking Club's main window, then click The Cook Book icon to visit the boards.

Look at Figure 9-3. Note that categories of boards are pictured in the top window. Because this is a complex board—it's a cookbook, after all, and cookbooks are typically large and organizationally complex—a double-click on any one of these categories produces a list of folders representing topics within that category (the center window in Figure 9-3). The Desserts and Sweet Treats category, for example, is further subdivided into more specific topics (Candy and Confections, Ice Cream). Note that these topics are the members' creations: almost every folder was a member's idea. While this is a little anarchistic, it's also democratic; and that's the way message boards should be. If you feel like making a comment that's off the subject, use the Create Topic button to make a new folder for it.

Figure 9-3: The eight categories posted on The Cookbook's recipe board are followed by a number of member topics. Each topic folder contains a number of individual recipes.

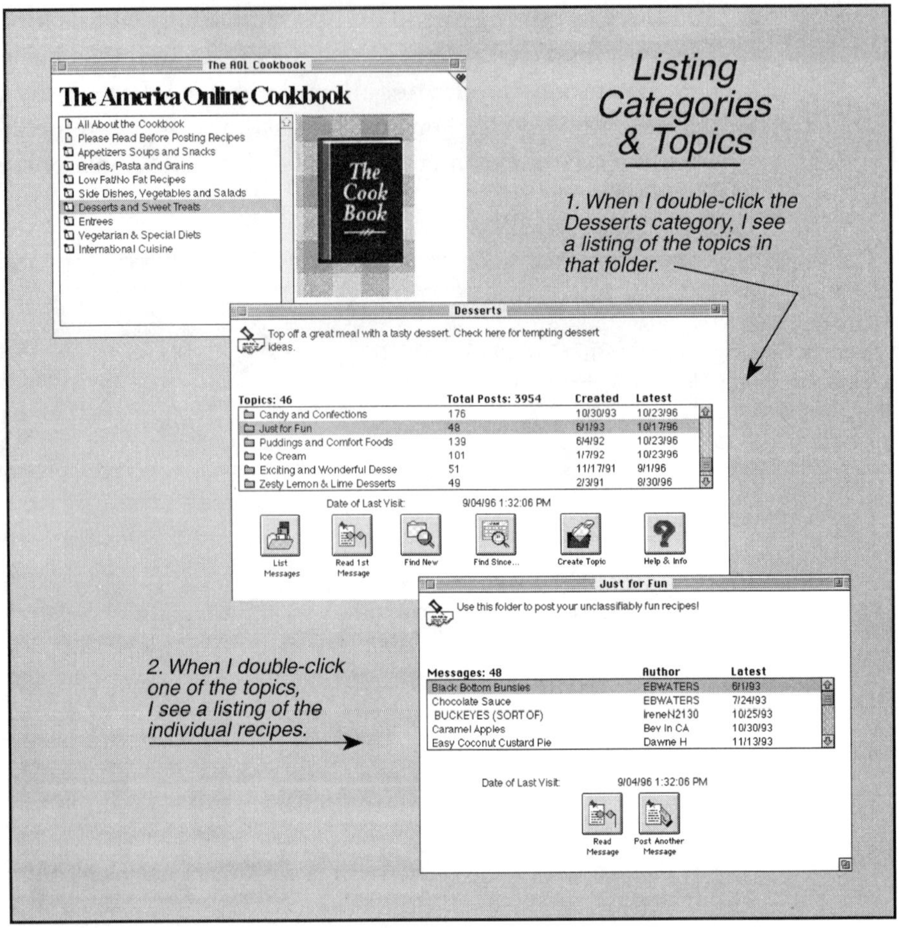
Listing Categories & Topics
1. When I double-click the Desserts category, I see a listing of the topics in that folder.
2. When I double-click one of the topics, I see a listing of the individual recipes.
The AOL Cookbook
The America Online Cookbook
All About the Cookbook
Please Read Before Posting Recipes
Appetizers Soups and Snacks
Breads, Pasta and Grains
Low Fat/No Fat Recipes
Side Dishes, Vegetables and Salads
Desserts and Sweet Treats
Entrees
Vegetarian & Special Diets
International Cuisine
The Cook Book
Desserts
Top off a great meal with a tasty dessert. Check here for tempting dessert ideas.
Topics: 46
Total Posts: 3954
Created
Latest
Candy and Confections 176 10/30/93 10/23/96
Just for Fun 48 6/1/93 10/17/96
Puddings and Comfort Foods 139 6/4/92 10/23/96
Ice Cream 101 1/7/92 10/23/96
Exciting and Wonderful Desse 51 11/17/91 9/1/96
Zesty Lemon & Lime Desserts 49 2/3/91 8/30/96
Date of Last Visit: 9/04/96 1:32:06 PM
List Messages
Read 1st Message
Find New
Find Since...
Create Topic
Help & Info
Just for Fun
Use this folder to post your unclassifiably fun recipes!
Messages: 48
Author
Latest
Black Bottom Bunsies EBWATERS 6/1/93
Chocolate Sauce EBWATERS 7/24/93
BUCKEYES (SORT OF) IreneN2130 10/25/93
Caramel Apples Bev In CA 10/30/93
Easy Coconut Custard Pie Dawne H 11/13/93
Date of Last Visit: 9/04/96 1:32:06 PM
Read Message
Post Another Message

The Creation Issue

No, I'm not going to debate Darwinism. This is a computer book and we're discussing cooking. That's off-subject enough. The Cooking Club offers examples of a board that allows members to create folders. The Create Topic button pictured in Figure 9-3's center window allows you to create a folder on the board, in which you or any other interested member can post a message.

You'll find other boards where there's no Create Topic button. The topics are established by the board's staff; members can't change them.

To allow creation or not to allow creation: the decision is up to the forum's staff. I mention it because I don't want you to expect a Create Topic button on every board you visit.

The bulletin board metaphor is distorted a bit here. Individual messages aren't normally posted on boards; *folders* are posted on boards (the messages themselves are inside the folders). Look again at the center window in Figure 9-3: this board is currently holding almost 4,000 messages. If all 4,000 were posted independently, the board would be a mess. You would never find a thing. The board's nested folders are merely organizational tools intended to help you locate topics of interest to you.

To read the messages placed in a folder, double-click the folder. By double-clicking the Just for Fun topic folder shown in Figure 9-3's center window, we reveal the recipes listed in the Just for Fun window at the bottom of that illustration. Although only five recipes are listed in the window, you can scroll down to view the rest.

To read all the messages in a folder, double-click the first one, then use the Next Message button (see Figure 9-4) to sequentially display the rest.

Figure 9-4: Once you have read the first message in a folder, click the Next Message button to read the remaining messages in the order of their posting.

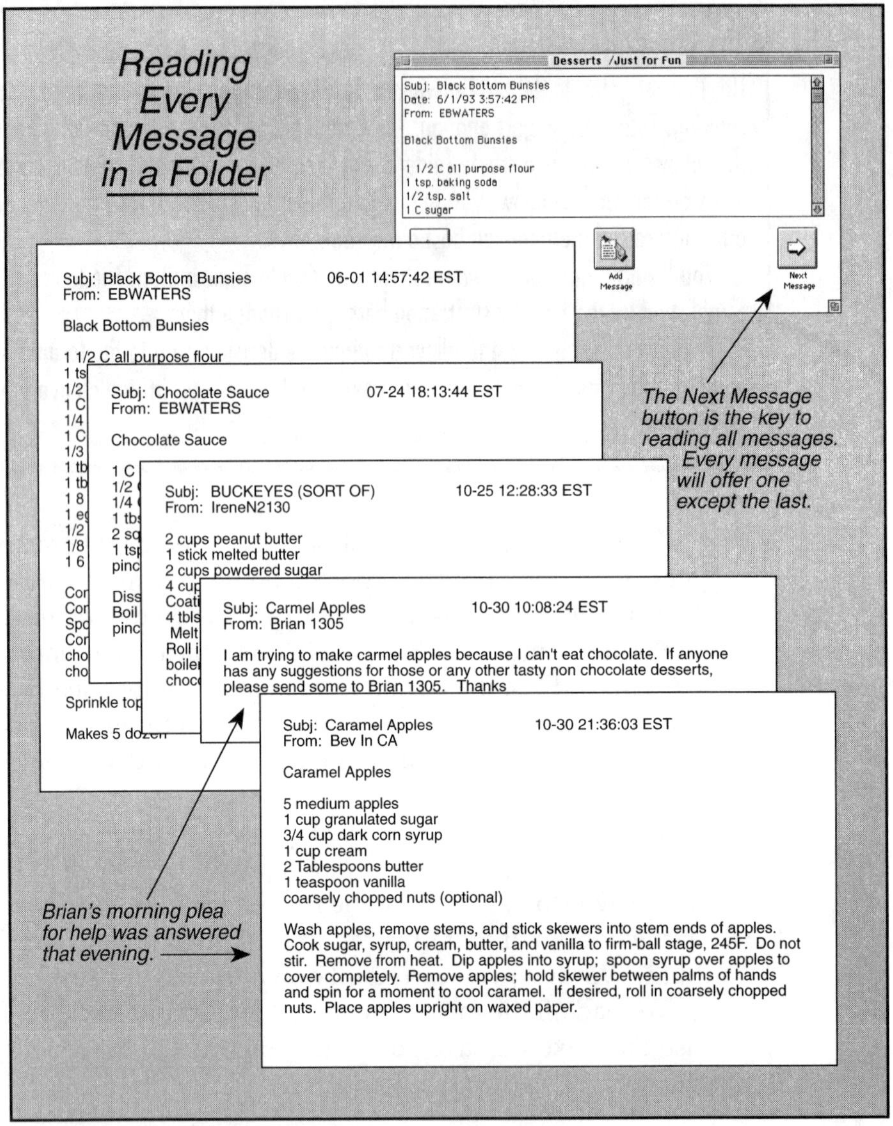
Reading Every Message in a Folder
Desserts /Just for Fun
Subj: Black Bottom Bunsies
Date: 6/1/93 3:57:42 PM
From: EBWATERS
Black Bottom Bunsies
1 1/2 C all purpose flour
1 tsp. baking soda
1/2 tsp. salt
1 C sugar
Add Message
Next Message
The Next Message button is the key to reading all messages. Every message will offer one except the last.
Subj: Black Bottom Bunsies 06-01 14:57:42 EST
From: EBWATERS
Black Bottom Bunsies
1 1/2 C all purpose flour
Sprinkle top
Makes 5 dozen
Subj: Chocolate Sauce 07-24 18:13:44 EST
From: EBWATERS
Chocolate Sauce
Subj: BUCKEYES (SORT OF) 10-25 12:28:33 EST
From: IreneN2130
2 cups peanut butter
1 stick melted butter
2 cups powdered sugar
Subj: Carmel Apples 10-30 10:08:24 EST
From: Brian 1305
I am trying to make carmel apples because I can't eat chocolate. If anyone has any suggestions for those or any other tasty non chocolate desserts, please send some to Brian 1305. Thanks
Subj: Caramel Apples 10-30 21:36:03 EST
From: Bev In CA
Caramel Apples
5 medium apples
1 cup granulated sugar
3/4 cup dark corn syrup
1 cup cream
2 Tablespoons butter
1 teaspoon vanilla
coarsely chopped nuts (optional)
Wash apples, remove stems, and stick skewers into stem ends of apples. Cook sugar, syrup, cream, butter, and vanilla to firm-ball stage, 245F. Do not stir. Remove from heat. Dip apples into syrup; spoon syrup over apples to cover completely. Remove apples; hold skewer between palms of hands and spin for a moment to cool caramel. If desired, roll in coarsely chopped nuts. Place apples upright on waxed paper.
Brian's morning plea for help was answered that evening.

Log Those Messages

Reading messages is one of the most time-consuming activities AOL offers. Rather than read messages online, save a log of them (we'll discuss logs in Chapter 10, "Staying Informed") as they download to your computer. Let them scroll off your screen as fast as they can; don't try to read them while you're online. When you have finished the session, sign off, open the log (choose Open from AOL's File menu), and read it at your leisure. You can always add messages to boards by signing back on again.

Browsing, Finding & Reading Messages

I need to take a side trip here. The verbs *browse, find,* and *read* have particular, unequivocal meanings when it comes to message boards; it's important that you understand how to use them. Think of a public library: you might go to the library simply to pass the time. You walk in and browse, picking up a book here and there as different titles strike your fancy. On another day, you might visit the library with a specific title already in mind, in which case you go straight to the card or electronic files and find that particular book. Regardless of how you come across a book, you eventually want to sit down and read it, page by page.

America Online attaches the same meanings to these verbs. Look again at the Desserts window at the center of Figure 9-3. Six buttons parade across the bottom of the window, representing variations on the three verbs we're discussing.

The List Messages button displays the folder's message subjects, authors, and dates, not the messages themselves (see the Just for Fun window at the bottom of Figure 9-3). Using the List Messages feature is like browsing through the books in a library: the concept is the same for both. The leftmost button (List Messages, in this case) is the default: if you double-click a folder, you'll see the list that appears in the lower window of Figure 9-3.

Clicking the Read 1st Message button produces a window displaying the first message in the folder (see the top window in Figure 9-4).

The Subject Line

As you read through this section, note the role played by a message's subject line. A subject line like "Comment" doesn't illuminate its contents very well. Alternatively, a subject line like "Savory Béarnaise Sauce Recipe" clearly summarizes the content of the message and intrigues the reader. Spend a moment thinking about subject lines when you post your own messages; they're significant.

This might be a board you read often. You might visit it every time you sign on. If you do, you can go right to the Find New button, which displays only those messages posted since you last visited (see Figure 9-5).

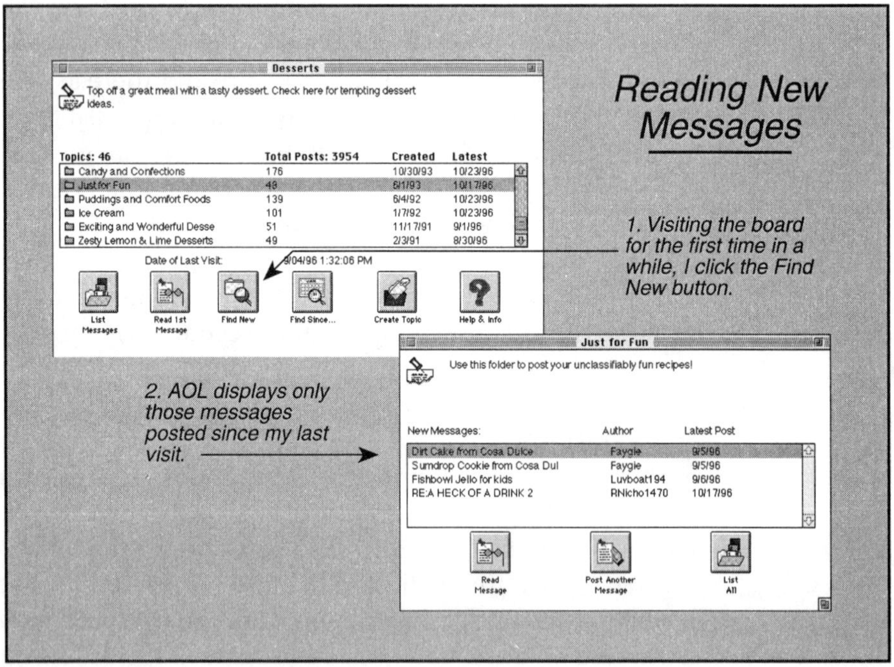
Reading New Messages
1. Visiting the board for the first time in a while, I click the Find New button.
2. AOL displays only those messages posted since my last visit.
Desserts
Top off a great meal with a tasty dessert. Check here for tempting dessert ideas.
Topics: 46
Total Posts: 3954
Created
Latest
Date of Last Visit:
List Messages
Read 1st Message
Find New
Find Since...
Create Topic
Help & Info
Just for Fun
Use this folder to post your unclassifiably fun recipes!
New Messages:
Author
Latest Post
Read Message
Post Another Message
List All

Figure 9-5: Only new messages appear when you click the Find New button. You can read them, add to them, or list all the messages in the folder.

Note the Post Another Message button at the bottom of Figure 9-5. This is how you add messages to the folder. All you need to do is click the button, enter the subject and text of your message, then click Post Another Message to submit your effort. Your message will be added to the folder immediately. I'll discuss this further in a moment.

Your Personal Date

Your personal "date of last visit" is marked the instant you visit a board. This implies two things: (1) No matter how many (or how few) messages you read while visiting a board, none of the messages posted prior to that visit are displayed when you next click the Find New button; and (2) If anyone (including you) posts a message on a board while you're reading, that message will appear when you next click the Find New button.

Note that I'm talking about *boards* here, not folders. If a board contains 600 messages in 24 folders and you read one message in one folder, none of the remaining messages will show up the next time you click the Find New button. In other words, your Date of Last Visit applies to *every* folder on a board, whether or not you actually read every folder during your last visit. It's a significant subtlety, so don't let it trip you up.

Your Date of Last Visit is associated with your screen name, and it's recorded on AOL's hard disks, not yours. Thus your Date of Last Visit reflects the date you last read messages on the board, regardless of the machine you used.

Most boards contain hundreds of messages. No matter how interested in the subject you might be, it's doubtful you'll want to read every message the first time you visit a board. Or maybe you've been away from the board for a few months and don't want to be deluged with all the messages posted since your last visit. These are two of the reasons why AOL provides the Find Since... button (see Figure 9-6).

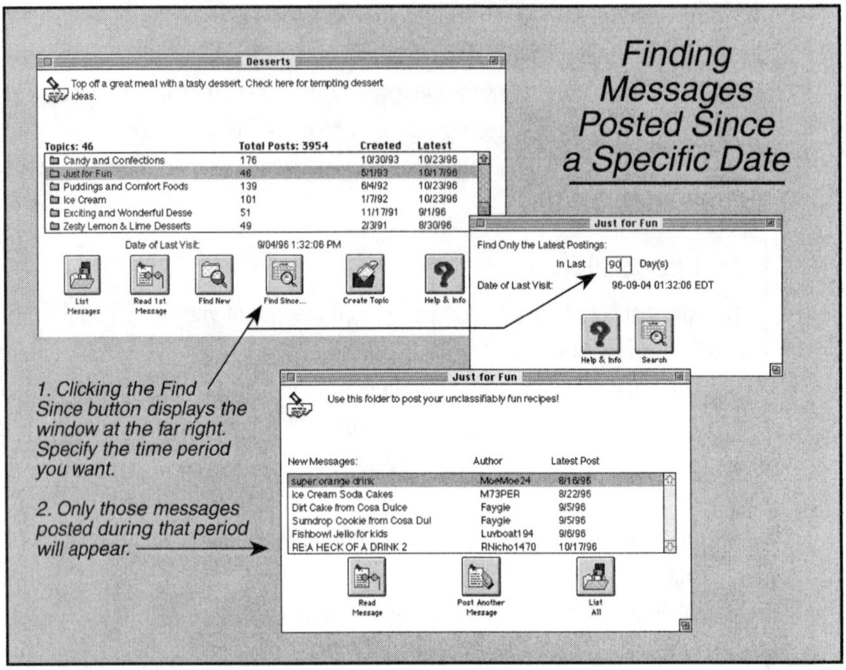
Finding Messages Posted Since a Specific Date
Desserts
Top off a great meal with a tasty dessert. Check here for tempting dessert ideas.
Topics: 46 Total Posts: 3954 Created Latest
Candy and Confections 176 10/30/93 10/23/96
Just for Fun 46 8/1/93 10/17/96
Puddings and Comfort Foods 139 6/4/92 10/23/96
Ice Cream 101 1/7/92 10/23/96
Exciting and Wonderful Desse 51 11/17/91 9/1/96
Zesty Lemon & Lime Desserts 49 2/3/91 8/30/96
Date of Last Visit: 9/04/96 1:32:06 PM
List Messages
Read 1st Message
Find New
Find Since...
Create Topic
Help & Info
Just for Fun
Find Only the Latest Postings:
In Last 90 Day(s)
Date of Last Visit: 96-09-04 01:32:06 EDT
Help & Info
Search
1. Clicking the Find Since button displays the window at the far right. Specify the time period you want.
2. Only those messages posted during that period will appear.
Just for Fun
Use this folder to post your unclassifiably fun recipes!
New Messages: Author Latest Post
super orange drink MoeMoe24 8/16/96
Ice Cream Soda Cakes M73PER 8/22/96
Dirt Cake from Cosa Dulce Faygie 9/5/96
Sumdrop Cookie from Cosa Dul Faygie 9/5/96
Fishbowl Jello for kids Luvboat194 9/6/96
RE:A HECK OF A DRINK 2 RNicho1470 10/17/96
Read Message
Post Another Message
List All

Figure 9-6: The Find Since ... button allows you to specify the extent of a message list.

It took me months to figure out just how the List Messages, Find, and Read buttons work. I hope this little discussion saves you the trouble. Regardless, find a board that interests you and start reading its messages. Start with just one or two folders, read the last week's worth of messages, and become familiar with the subject and the people. When you feel confident, post your own messages. It is at that moment—when you have joined the fray—that message boards start to get really interesting. This is part of the fun; don't deny yourself the opportunity.

Posting Messages

A moment ago, I suggested you post your own messages. It might help if we review that process. There is not much to it: take a look at Figure 9-7.

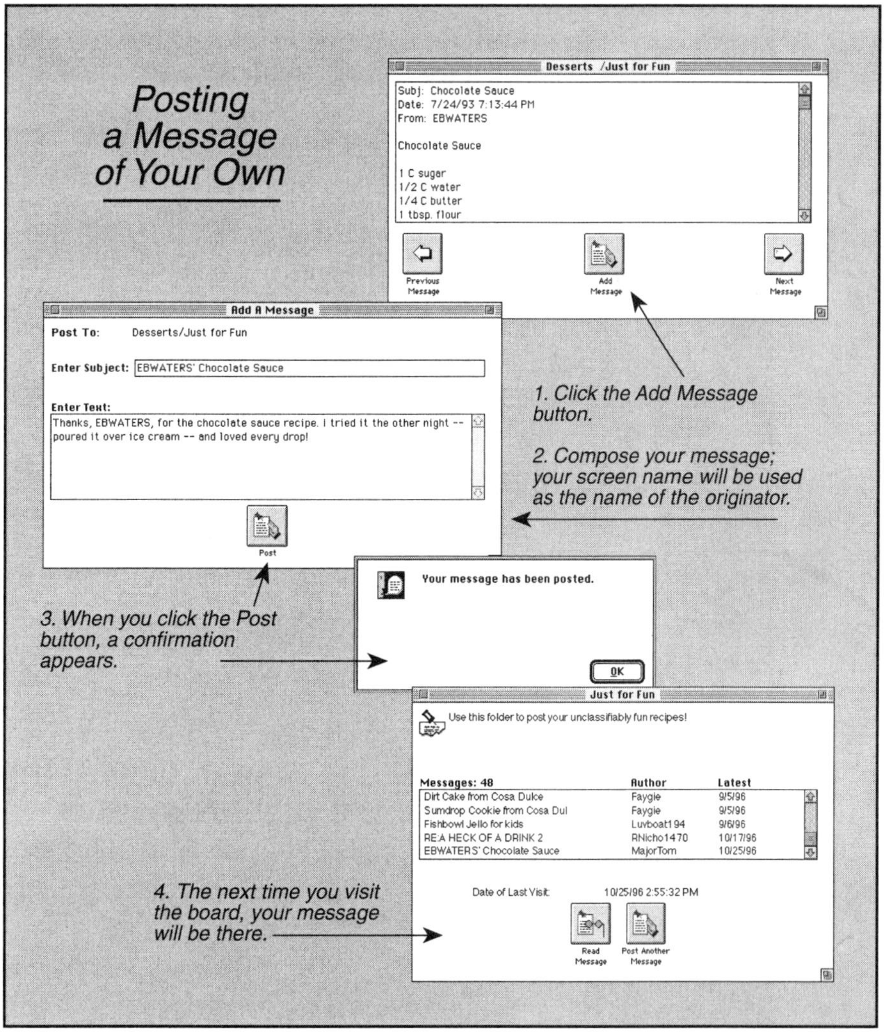
Posting a Message of Your Own
Desserts /Just for Fun
Subj: Chocolate Sauce
Date: 7/24/93 7:13:44 PM
From: EBWATERS
Chocolate Sauce
1 C sugar
1/2 C water
1/4 C butter
1 tbsp. flour
Previous Message
Add Message
Next Message
Add A Message
Post To: Desserts/Just for Fun
Enter Subject: EBWATERS' Chocolate Sauce
Enter Text:
Thanks, EBWATERS, for the chocolate sauce recipe. I tried it the other night -- poured it over ice cream -- and loved every drop!
Post
1. Click the Add Message button.
2. Compose your message; your screen name will be used as the name of the originator.
Your message has been posted.
OK
3. When you click the Post button, a confirmation appears.
Just for Fun
Use this folder to post your unclassifiably fun recipes!
Messages: 48
Author
Latest
Dirt Cake from Cosa Dulce Faygie 9/5/96
Sumdrop Cookie from Cosa Dul Faygie 9/5/96
Fishbowl Jello for kids Luvboat194 9/6/96
RE:A HECK OF A DRINK 2 RNicho1470 10/17/96
EBWATERS' Chocolate Sauce MajorTom 10/25/96
Date of Last Visit: 10/25/96 2:55:32 PM
Read Message
Post Another Message
4. The next time you visit the board, your message will be there.

Figure 9-7: Posting your own message is as simple as clicking a button.

Message Board Etiquette

If you want to be heard, if you want replies to your messages, and if you want to be a responsible online citizen, you should comply with a few rules of telecommunications etiquette. Because Emily Post and Miss Manners haven't yet spoken on the subject, we'd best discuss it here.

- Post messages only when you have something to say, phrase the subject header effectively, and be succinct. The best messages have provocative headers and pithy prose. If your message fills more than a screen of text—if it requires a trip to the scroll bar to read—edit it.
- Stick to the subject. If the folder you're participating in is entitled "Weasels in Wyoming," don't discuss armadillos in Arizona.
- If your message wanders, summarize before responding. You might quote a previous posting (do so in brackets: "When you said <<I really prefer Macintosh>> were you talking about apples or Apples?"). This will help others stick to the topic.
- Don't post chain letters, advertisements, or business offers unless the board was created for it. And never send junk mail to unsuspecting recipients.
- HEY YOU! CAN YOU HEAR ME??!! (Did I get your attention? Did you like the way I did it?) All-caps are distracting, hard to read, and, worse, arrogant. Use all-caps only when you really want to shout (and those occasions should be rare). For emphasis, place asterisks around your text: "I *told* you he was a geek!"
- Do not issue personal attacks, use profanity, or betray a confidence. If criticism is specifically invited, remember that there is no vocal inflection or body language to soften the impact and remove the potential for misinterpretation. E-mail is a better forum for criticism than boards are.
- For the same reason, subtleties, double entendres, and sarcasm are rarely effective.

- Avoid emotional responses. Think before you write. Once you've posted a message, you can't take it back.
- Remember your options. Some replies are better sent as mail than as messages. If you're feeling particularly vitriolic, send mail to the perpetrator. This saves face for both of you.

Posting effective messages is something of an art. Messages like "Me too," or "I don't think so" don't really contribute to a board. Before you post a message, be sure you have something to say, take the time to phrase it effectively, and give it a proper subject header.

Threaded Boards

Some boards offer *message threading*: messages arranged so that you can elect to read responses to a specific message. Compare this with the Read 1st Message command pictured in Figure 9-6. Reading the first message displays the first message on a board with the option to read the remaining messages on the board as well.

Threaded message boards allow you to choose to read only the replies to a specific message. This is especially appropriate where the subject of a particular folder is likely to be broad, and its messages are numerous and varied. To examine a threaded board, let's visit the Pet Care Forum (use the keywords: **Pet Care**). A number of veterinarians from universities and private practices visit this board regularly, some of whom are on the board's staff. If you have pets—dogs, cats, reptiles, birds, even farm animals—this is a forum you will want to visit often (see Figure 9-8). For now, let's look for information about cats. Click the Cats button, then select Cat Message Board.

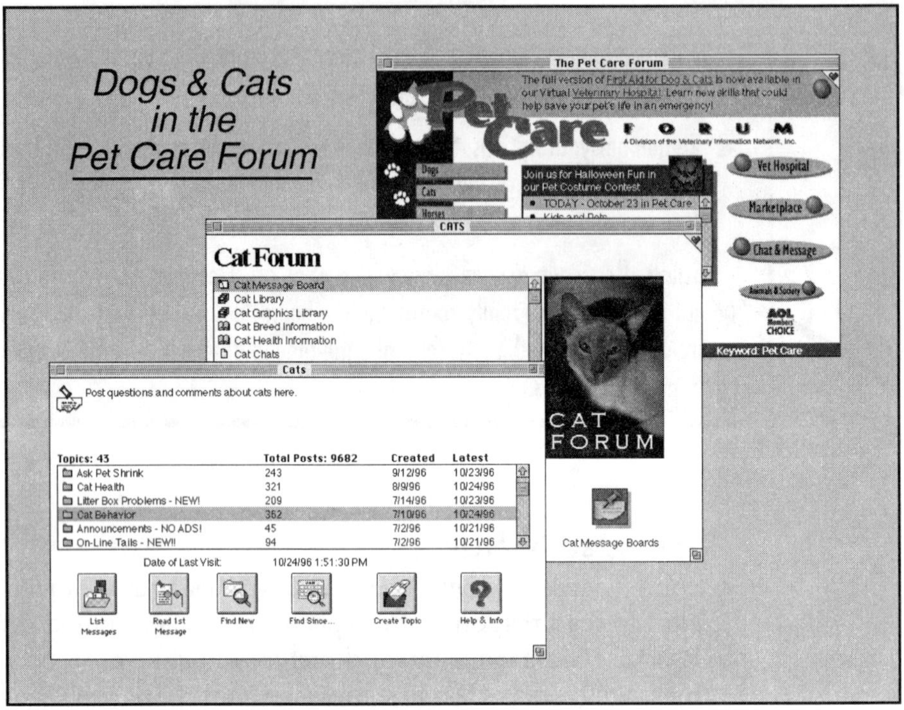
Dogs & Cats
in the
Pet Care Forum
The Pet Care Forum
Pet Care FORUM
Vet Hospital
Marketplace
Chat & Message
Keyword: Pet Care
CATS
Cat Forum
Cat Message Board
Cat Library
Cat Graphics Library
Cat Breed Information
Cat Health Information
Cat Chats
CAT FORUM
Cat Message Boards
Cats
Post questions and comments about cats here.
Topics: 43
Total Posts: 9682
Created
Latest
Ask Pet Shrink 243 9/12/96 10/23/96
Cat Health 321 8/9/96 10/24/96
Litter Box Problems - NEW! 209 7/14/96 10/23/96
Cat Behavior 352 7/10/96 10/24/96
Announcements - NO ADS! 45 7/2/96 10/21/96
On-Line Tails - NEW!! 94 7/2/96 10/21/96
Date of Last Visit: 10/24/96 1:51:30 PM
List Messages
Read 1st Message
Find New
Find Since...
Create Topic
Help & Info

Figure 9-8: The Pet Care Forum offers boards for not only dogs and cats but farm animals, fish—even reptiles.

Until now, threaded boards look just like unthreaded boards. But look what happens when I double-click the folder that's labeled "Cat Behavior" (see Figure 9-9).

Look carefully at Figure 9-9: a Responses column appears, identifying the number of responses that have been posted to any particular message. A new List Responses button appears at the bottom of the window as well.

Now watch what happens when I double-click the "Water Lover" posting (see Figure 9-10).

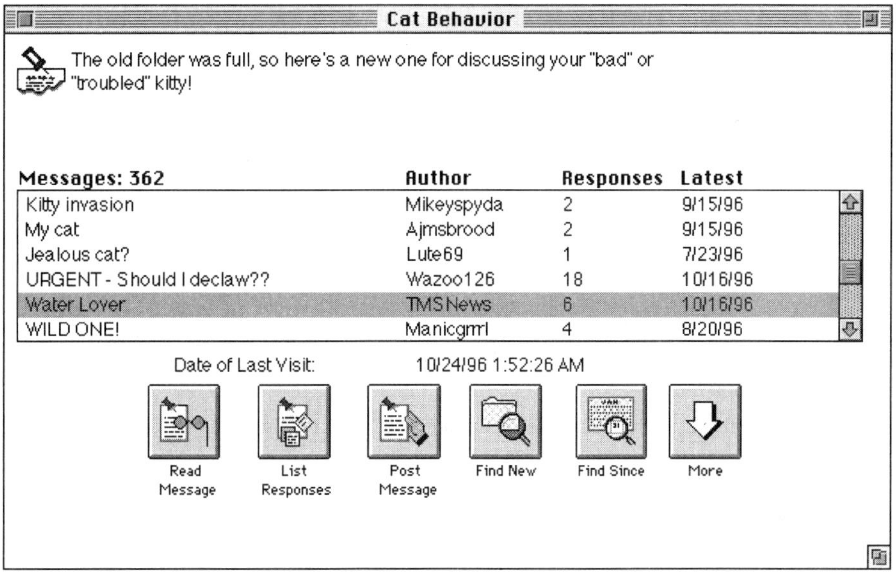
Cat Behavior
The old folder was full, so here's a new one for discussing your "bad" or "troubled" kitty!
Messages: 362
Author
Responses
Latest
Kitty invasion
Mikeyspyda
2
9/15/96
My cat
Ajmsbrood
2
9/15/96
Jealous cat?
Lute69
1
7/23/96
URGENT - Should I declaw??
Wazoo126
18
10/16/96
Water Lover
TMSNews
6
10/16/96
WILD ONE!
Manicgrrl
4
8/20/96
Date of Last Visit:
10/24/96 1:52:26 AM
Read Message
List Responses
Post Message
Find New
Find Since
More

Figure 9-9: Threaded boards offer a Responses column and a List Responses button at the bottom of the window.

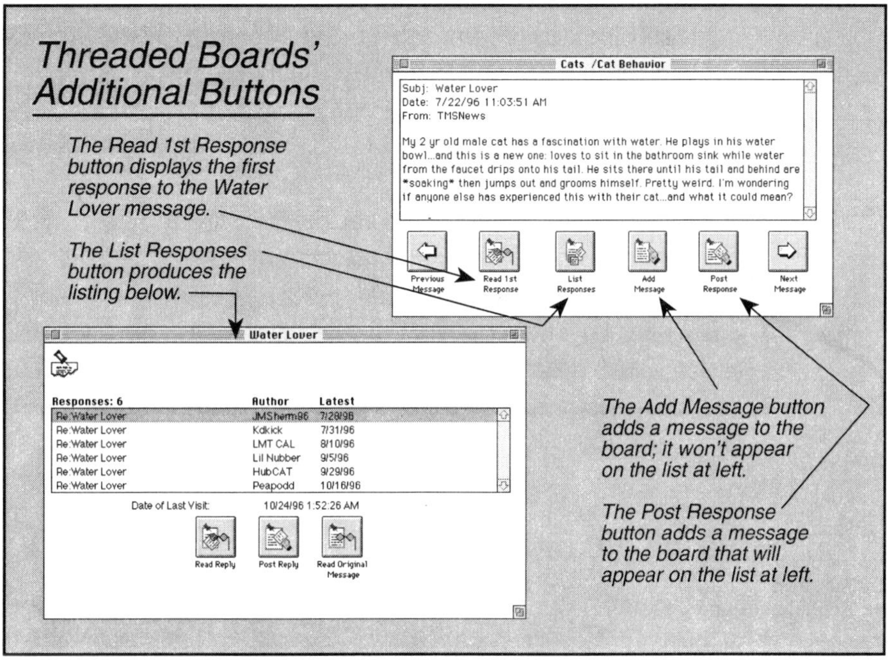
Threaded Boards' Additional Buttons
Cats /Cat Behavior
Subj: Water Lover
Date: 7/22/96 11:03:51 AM
From: TMSNews
My 2 yr old male cat has a fascination with water. He plays in his water bowl...and this is a new one: loves to sit in the bathroom sink while water from the faucet drips onto his tail. He sits there until his tail and behind are *soaking* then jumps out and grooms himself. Pretty weird. I'm wondering if anyone else has experienced this with their cat...and what it could mean?
Previous Message
Read 1st Response
List Responses
Add Message
Post Response
Next Message
The Read 1st Response button displays the first response to the Water Lover message.
The List Responses button produces the listing below.
Water Lover
Responses: 6
Author
Latest
Re:Water Lover
JMSherm96
7/28/96
Re:Water Lover
Kdkick
7/31/96
Re:Water Lover
LMT CAL
8/10/96
Re:Water Lover
Lil Nubber
9/5/96
Re:Water Lover
HubCAT
9/29/96
Re:Water Lover
Peapodd
10/16/96
Date of Last Visit:
10/24/96 1:52:26 AM
Read Reply
Post Reply
Read Original Message
The Add Message button adds a message to the board; it won't appear on the list at left.
The Post Response button adds a message to the board that will appear on the list at left.

Figure 9-10: Note how the list of responses to the "Water Lover" message allows me to post a reply or reread the original message in case I've forgotten a detail.

The Read 1st Response and List Responses buttons are new to the message window, as is the Post Response button. When I click the List Responses button I see a listing of only the responses to the "Water Lover" message. This allows me to stick to the "Water Lover" subject, rather than wander all over the board.

Proper Replies

Be sure you post replies to messages properly. Look again at the upper window in Figure 9-10: two reply buttons appear there—Add Message and Post Response. The Add Message button simply adds a message to the board; the added message is posted independently and not identified as a response to any other message. A message posted via the Post Response button will appear as a response in a list of responses, similar to those pictured in the lower window of Figure 9-10. It's not just a matter of semantics; it's an organizational imperative. Give consideration to your replies on threaded boards: post them where they're most appropriate.

Not all boards are threaded. Some lend themselves to threading, some don't. Some of my favorites aren't threaded, and I'm glad: threading discourages the kind of browsing that favored boards merit. Don't look upon an unthreaded board as old-fashioned or anarchistic. Welcome them and celebrate their diversity.

Hard Hat Area

By the time you read this, message boards may look considerably different than they do here. As of this writing, AOL is working on a new message board system that will offer greater flexibility and accessibility. Development is still in its early stages, however, and I would be doing you a disservice to preview it before its time. Take comfort in the fact that help will be available should you need it.

Computers & Software Forums

Enough of this talk about boards. Before you can participate on a board, you need to visit a forum. There are no membership requirements: you don't need to register when you first enter a forum; you don't have to prove your expertise or anything more than a passing interest. You never know whether you'll like a place until you visit, and visiting AOL's forums requires nothing more than knowledge of how to get there.

Perhaps the busiest forums on AOL are found in the Computers & Software Channel. The computer industry is a moving target, and those who try to keep it in their sights seek information with eagerness that borders on the fanatical. The Computers & Software Channel offers forums for every level of computer enthusiast, from beginners to developers, and these forums are all extremely popular.

The Mac Help Forum

Perhaps there's no better example of a forum for us to discuss than the Mac Help Forum (keywords: **Mac Help**). We all have an interest in AOL, and this is a traditional AOL forum. There's a conference room (open Monday, Tuesday, Thursday, and Friday at 9:30, and Wednesdays from 9:30 to 10:30 P.M. eastern time to provide you with immediate AOL help); libraries of files (Zip Tips, answers to frequently asked questions, a Beginner's Starter Kit, and even an upload/download primer); and a message board (official responses are guaranteed within 24 hours—guaranteed responses are very rare).

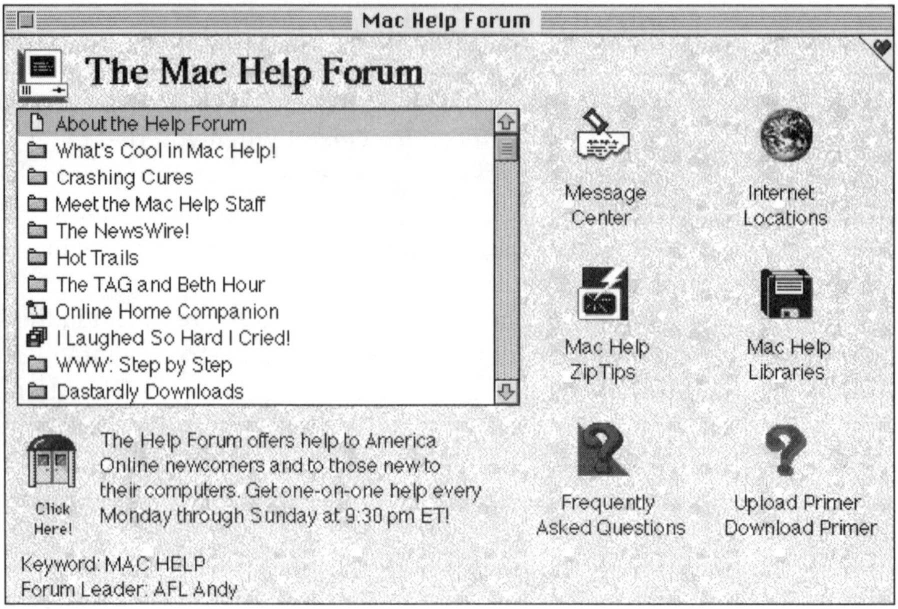
Mac Help Forum
The Mac Help Forum
About the Help Forum
What's Cool in Mac Help!
Crashing Cures
Meet the Mac Help Staff
The NewsWire!
Hot Trails
The TAG and Beth Hour
Online Home Companion
I Laughed So Hard I Cried!
WWW: Step by Step
Dastardly Downloads
Message Center
Internet Locations
Mac Help ZipTips
Mac Help Libraries
Click Here!
The Help Forum offers help to America Online newcomers and to those new to their computers. Get one-on-one help every Monday through Sunday at 9:30 pm ET!
Frequently Asked Questions
Upload Primer Download Primer
Keyword: MAC HELP
Forum Leader: AFL Andy

Figure 9-11: Among all of the things mentioned in the text, note that the Mac Help Forum also offers a primer on uploading and downloading files. It's an invaluable tool for anyone just starting out on AOL—just click the question mark button.

The Macintosh Utilities Forum

Another topic in which we all have an interest is our Macs. Probably the most fertile field for those of us who use the Mac is the Utilities Forum. You can either choose the forum from the main Computers & Software Channel window at keyword: **Computing** (once you get to the Computers & Software window, click the Support Forums button—the Macintosh Utilities Forum is listed in the scroll box on the right as Utilities Forum), or use the keyword: **MUT**.

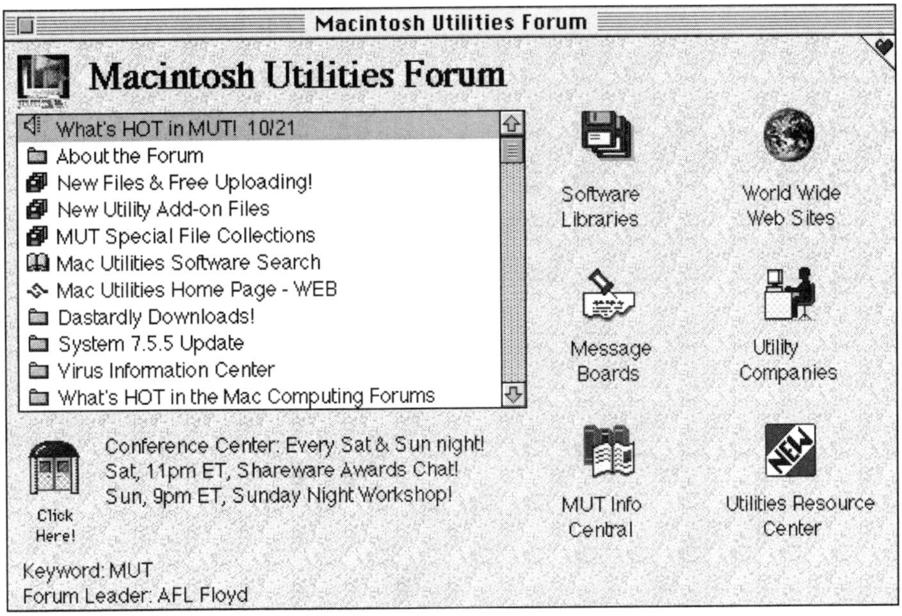
Macintosh Utilities Forum
Macintosh Utilities Forum
What's HOT in MUT! 10/21
About the Forum
New Files & Free Uploading!
New Utility Add-on Files
MUT Special File Collections
Mac Utilities Software Search
Mac Utilities Home Page - WEB
Dastardly Downloads!
System 7.5.5 Update
Virus Information Center
What's HOT in the Mac Computing Forums
Software Libraries
World Wide Web Sites
Message Boards
Utility Companies
Conference Center: Every Sat & Sun night!
Sat, 11pm ET, Shareware Awards Chat!
Sun, 9pm ET, Sunday Night Workshop!
Click Here!
MUT Info Central
Utilities Resource Center
NEW
Keyword: MUT
Forum Leader: AFL Floyd

Figure 9-12: The Macintosh Utilities Forum offers a utility for every need. A bounty among the bountiful.

The Family Computing Forum

This forum (at keyword: **FC**) is exactly what its title promises it to be, with one significant exception, the "Novice Member Playground." The Playground offers a place for you to practice participating on a board and downloading from a library—without connect charges! Look for it in the Maximum AOL area.

The Family Computing Forum
Family Computing
AutoVantage
CLICK HERE FOR NEW CAR SAVINGS
FAMILY SOFTWARE
imagine
IMAGINATION SHOWCASE
Youth Tech
A Fun Place For Today's Youth
Click Graphic to Visit Youth Tech!
ONLINE FAMILY
REC ROOM
tip of the day
CREATIVE CORNER
MAXIMUM AOL
Tips Mac Windows PC
About Family Computing
Dastardly Downloads
The Computing Marketplace
Youth Tech
Members' Choice

Figure 9-13: The Family Computing Forum offers a virtual family room for computer users and a free area where you can practice participating in a board and downloading graphics.

December 28

Throughout this book, I have suggested that you try to time your online events to align with slack time on the network—before 6:00 P.M. eastern time. I say "the network" because the stress is placed more on the communications system between you and AOL than on AOL's host computer system itself. The telecommunications system that knits us all together is vast and difficult to modify. Growth in such a system takes time.

There's another time when the system is stressed: a few days after Christmas. Lots of people receive a computer for Christmas, and most of those computers now include a modem and a free sign-on kit for AOL or one of its competitors. When the relatives have departed and the wrapping paper is disposed of, people set up their new computers and go about the process of signing on for the first time. This is not an insignificant number of people. In fact, AOL's busiest day of the year is invariably December 28th.

Invite the relatives to stay another few days. Go for a sleigh ride. Haul some wood for the fire, but find another day for your AOL journeys. In cyberspace, December 28th is the busiest day of the year.

The Mac Hardware Forum

You just bought a new machine and want to know the best way to use it. Maybe you're interested in upgrading and aren't sure what to buy. Or you have a new printer and want the latest driver for it. The Mac Hardware Forum (keyword: **MHW**) offers all of this and more. The message boards are great for peer support (some would say this is the best support available), and the file libraries offer a treasure trove of utilities and drivers. There's also a resource center, the Virus Information Center, a printer knowledge base, and an expanded conference schedule.

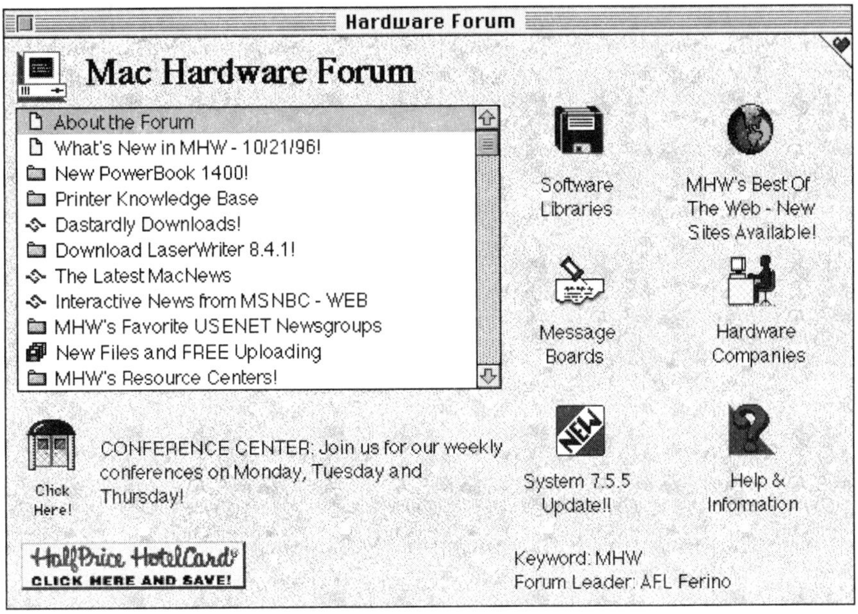
Hardware Forum
Mac Hardware Forum
About the Forum
What's New in MHW - 10/21/96!
New PowerBook 1400!
Printer Knowledge Base
Dastardly Downloads!
Download LaserWriter 8.4.1!
The Latest MacNews
Interactive News from MSNBC - WEB
MHW's Favorite USENET Newsgroups
New Files and FREE Uploading
MHW's Resource Centers!
Software Libraries
MHW's Best Of The Web - New Sites Available!
Message Boards
Hardware Companies
CONFERENCE CENTER: Join us for our weekly conferences on Monday, Tuesday and Thursday!
Click Here!
System 7.5.5 Update!!
Help & Information
HalfPrice HotelCard
CLICK HERE AND SAVE!
Keyword: MHW
Forum Leader: AFL Ferino

Figure 9-14: The Mac Hardware Forum is a great place online for hardware help and support.

The Macintosh Software Center

If there's a Mac Hardware Forum, you would expect a Mac Software Forum. There is one, and it's called the Mac Software Center (keywords: **Software Center**). Macintosh Thunder-Lizard users are fond of the bumper stickers that read "He who dies with the most software wins!" Thunder-Lizard users collect files like baseball cards, and they do most of their collecting here. Every library in the Computers & Software channel is available here, along with several special collections like the Downloading Hall of Fame.

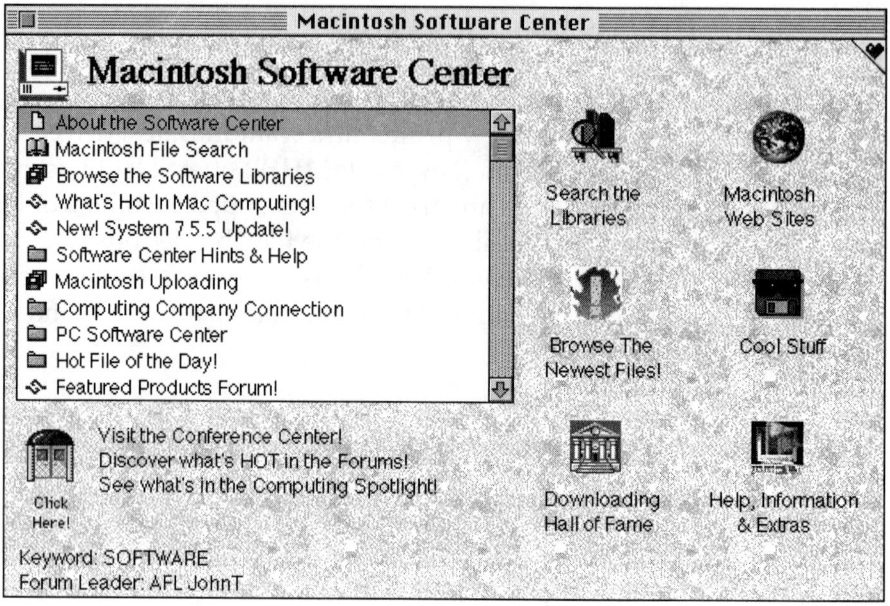
Macintosh Software Center
Macintosh Software Center
About the Software Center
Macintosh File Search
Browse the Software Libraries
What's Hot In Mac Computing!
New! System 7.5.5 Update!
Software Center Hints & Help
Macintosh Uploading
Computing Company Connection
PC Software Center
Hot File of the Day!
Featured Products Forum!
Search the Libraries
Macintosh Web Sites
Browse The Newest Files!
Cool Stuff
Click Here!
Visit the Conference Center!
Discover what's HOT in the Forums!
See what's in the Computing Spotlight!
Downloading Hall of Fame
Help, Information & Extras
Keyword: SOFTWARE
Forum Leader: AFL JohnT

Figure 9-15: The Mac Software Center's libraries offer the best collections of files.

Don't conclude your visit to this forum without investigating the "Hot File of the Day." Everything you need for productive use of your Mac shows up here: compression, word processing, spreadsheet, database, and desktop publishing shareware—something new every day. To find it, look under What's Hot in Mac Computing!

The Multimedia Zone

With the advent of the World Wide Web, desktop video and multimedia have taken on all the importance of oil in Texas. Suddenly, everyone is anxious to hear sounds, watch movies, and publish electronically with their Mac. With the Web as its medium, multimedia is the computing industry's darling of the '90s.

Fortunately, the Multimedia Zone (keywords: **Mac Video**) is prepared to help us get on board. Answers to frequently asked questions, an extensive multimedia library, Desktop Video 101, and many others are all standing by, ready to serve you (see Figure 9-16).

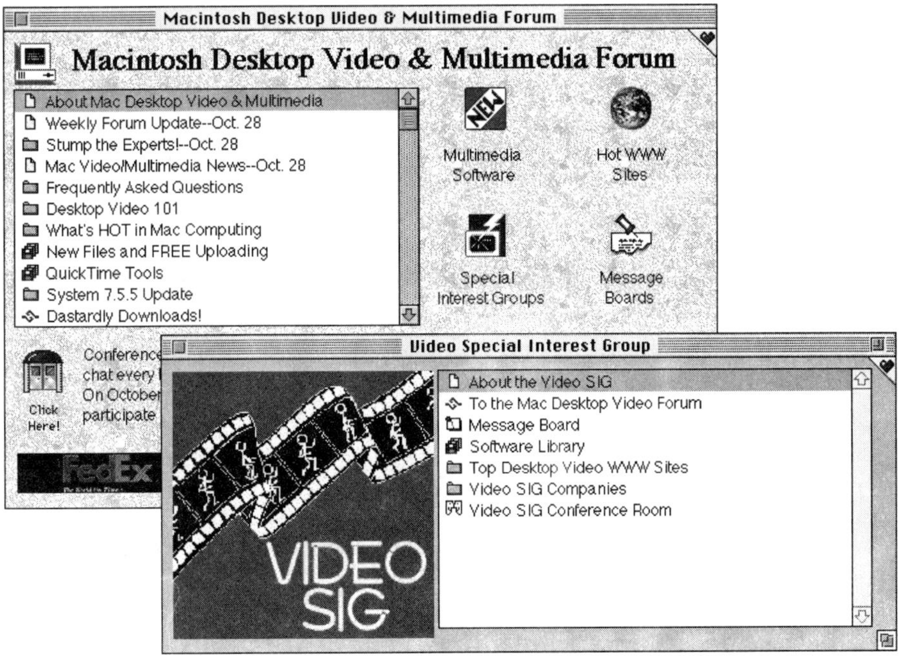
Macintosh Desktop Video & Multimedia Forum
Macintosh Desktop Video & Multimedia Forum
About Mac Desktop Video & Multimedia
Weekly Forum Update--Oct. 28
Stump the Experts!--Oct. 28
Mac Video/Multimedia News--Oct. 28
Frequently Asked Questions
Desktop Video 101
What's HOT in Mac Computing
New Files and FREE Uploading
QuickTime Tools
System 7.5.5 Update
Dastardly Downloads!
Multimedia Software
Hot WWW Sites
Special Interest Groups
Message Boards
Click Here!
Video Special Interest Group
About the Video SIG
To the Mac Desktop Video Forum
Message Board
Software Library
Top Desktop Video WWW Sites
Video SIG Companies
Video SIG Conference Room
VIDEO SIG

Figure 9-16: The Multimedia Zone offers support and motivation for multimedia authors, game players, and electronic publishers.

The Video SIG (SIG stands for Special Interest Group) pictured in Figure 9-16 is particularly valuable for anyone who is considering desktop video. A while back I indicated that peer support is probably the best available, a claim that is easily substantiated by exploring this group's extensive message boards. If you're interested in desktop video, be sure to check out their library's files on the subject.

Finding Leadership Online

If you've ever wondered who's in charge of running the forums, you've probably run into the answer if you spend much time online: the *Forum Leader*. Forum Leaders are responsible for the day-to-day management of the forums in their charge. But forum life online is so busy that each Forum Leader maintains a team of forum assistants and consultants, usually selected from the general membership for their expertise in a given area. The Forum Leader, consultants, and assistants work as a team to provide technical support, answer member inquiries, process file uploads, and help direct forum conferences. You can identify forum personnel quickly by looking for one of these three prefixes on a screen name: AFL (Forum Leader), AFA (Forum Assistant), or AFC (Forum Consultant). (PC prefixes denote Forum Leaders for the PC forums.) Look for these folks when you have a question: they're among the best.

The Mac Graphic Arts & CAD Forum

Imagine having access to tens of thousands of graphics files, with more becoming available every day. Imagine a database of these files, searchable by keywords, author names, and filenames. Imagine special interest groups, help from graphics experts, and a tips and tricks collection describing the secrets it could normally take years to discover. This, of course, is the Mac Graphic Arts & CAD Forum (keyword: **MGR**).

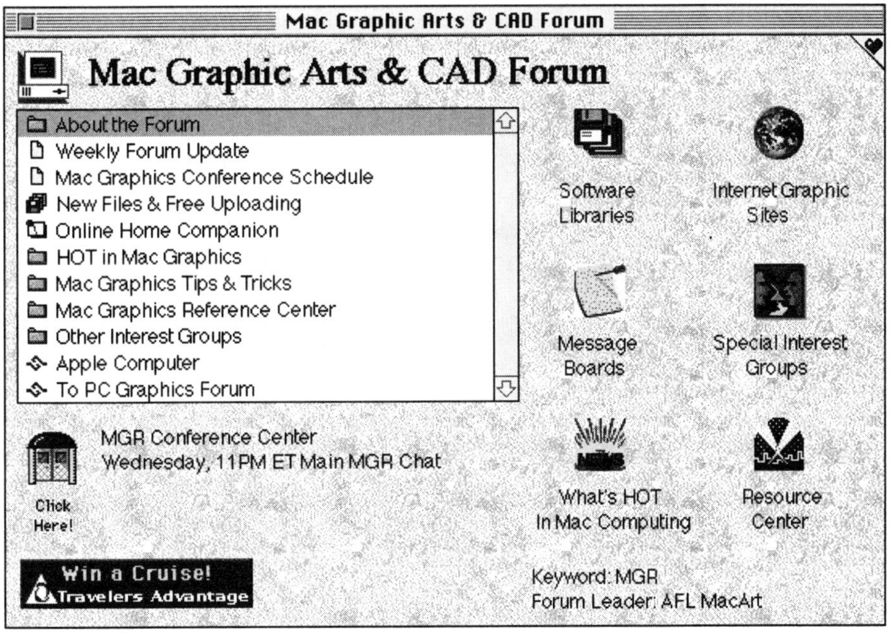
Mac Graphic Arts & CAD Forum
Mac Graphic Arts & CAD Forum
About the Forum
Weekly Forum Update
Mac Graphics Conference Schedule
New Files & Free Uploading
Online Home Companion
HOT in Mac Graphics
Mac Graphics Tips & Tricks
Mac Graphics Reference Center
Other Interest Groups
Apple Computer
To PC Graphics Forum
Software Libraries
Internet Graphic Sites
Message Boards
Special Interest Groups
MGR Conference Center
Wednesday, 11PM ET Main MGR Chat
Click Here!
What's HOT In Mac Computing
Resource Center
Win a Cruise!
Travelers Advantage
Keyword: MGR
Forum Leader: AFL MacArt

Figure 9-17: The Mac Graphic Arts & CAD Forum offers 16 categories of graphics files and utilities, ranging from simple line art to complex PostScript images. In addition, there is a library for the most popular and useful files in the forum.

No Place for Chauvinism

Only half the graphics available online reside in the Mac Graphic Arts & CAD Forum. An equal number await the adventurous in the—dare we say it?—PC Graphics Arts & Animation Forum (keywords: **PC Graphics**, or click the appropriate folder from the list box pictured in Figure 9-17). This sister forum is just as plentiful as the Mac forum, and many of the graphics there are in GIF or JPEG format, meaning they can be viewed and used on almost any Mac with your AOL software. So go ahead, slip into the PC Graphics Arts & Animation Forum. They're up to some pretty interesting stuff over there.

The Mac Developers Forum

Computer programmers range from hobbyists to professionals, and they're both served well by the Mac Developers Forum (keyword: **MDV**). Message boards play a leading role here, as programmers assist programmers with sticky problems and eternal bugs.

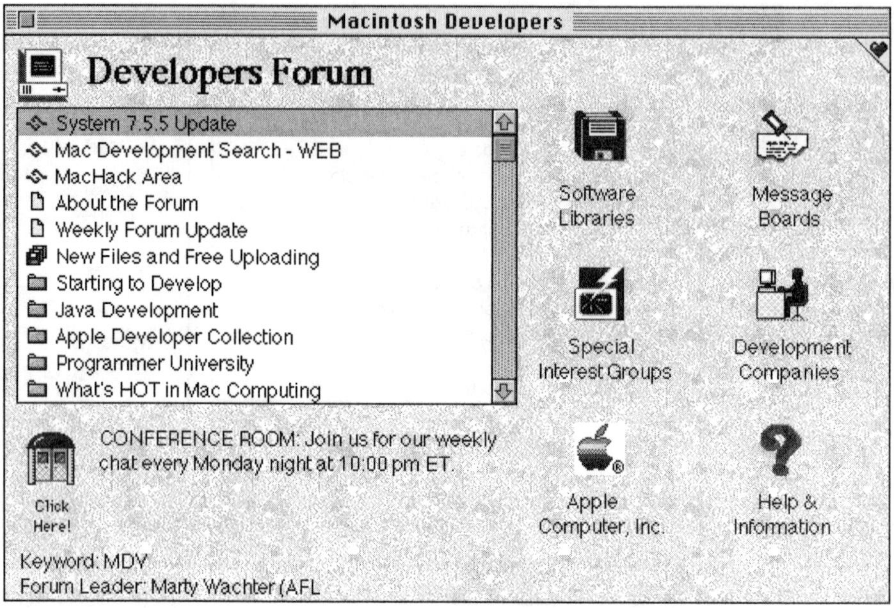
Macintosh Developers
Developers Forum
System 7.5.5 Update
Mac Development Search - WEB
MacHack Area
About the Forum
Weekly Forum Update
New Files and Free Uploading
Starting to Develop
Java Development
Apple Developer Collection
Programmer University
What's HOT in Mac Computing
Software Libraries
Message Boards
Special Interest Groups
Development Companies
CONFERENCE ROOM: Join us for our weekly chat every Monday night at 10:00 pm ET.
Click Here!
Apple Computer, Inc.
Help & Information
Keyword: MDV
Forum Leader: Marty Wachter (AFL

Figure 9-18: The Macintosh Developers Forum offers utilities, examples, and advice for computer programmers—both amateur and professional.

Community Forums

The computing forums represent the category of forums dedicated to the support of a specific subject. There are many, many more, however, ranging from the Adoption Forum to the Writers Club. This forum category, in which the primary subject is *community*, offers resources, debate, and fraternity—the elements that define and support all vital communities, virtual or otherwise.

The Gay & Lesbian Community Forum

If ever there was a community that stood to benefit from the peer support and organized resources that forums provide, it's the Gay and Lesbian Community Forum (keyword: **GLCF**). And if ever there was a sympathetic medium for those activities, it's AOL. We go back to the late 1980s for this one, when the gay and lesbian community operated under the name of GLUE (Gays and Lesbians United Electronically). GLUE quietly operated behind the scenes, making its voice heard to the AOL management team. The effort did not fall upon deaf ears, and the result is the Gay and Lesbian Community Forum as we know it today: comprehensive, compassionate, and supportive not only to the gay and lesbian community but to the transgender and AIDS communities as well. This is one of AOL's most proactive forums, with a membership of staggering proportions and a staff that's as large as AOL itself was back in the days when GLUE was getting underway. With its elegant redesign in the winter of 1995, this forum warrants your investigation regardless of your sexual orientation (see Figure 9-19).

The Gay and Lesbian Community Forum
AOL Members' CHOICE
GLCF
Email Contact GLCF Ask
GLCF - News and Politics
GLCF - Events and Conferences
GLCF - Resource Library
GLCF - Organizations
The GLCF Travel Index
GLCF - Message Boards
NEW
Leather onQ!
GLCF User Manual
Chats
GL CF
Communities
Women's Space. *THE* place online for lesbians!
CARDS JUST FOR YOU!
onQ CITIES
WIN $5,000 Shoppers Advantage
Life, Styles & Interests
Subscribe to Pride Press
Search the GLCF
Keyword: GLCF

Figure 9-19: The Gay and Lesbian Community Forum is one of AOL's largest and most active forums. The benefits are generous and the compassion is sincere—for participants of all predilections.

There is no hostility or insularity here: it's a forum of support and sympathy. As forum member GLCF Wendy puts it:

"Anyone who feels they have no place . . .

"Anyone who feels alone . . .

"Anyone who is scared . . .

"And anyone who feels that no one cares . . .

". . . is welcome here."

Let's look at each of the Forum's features:

- *News & Politics* is where the forum's staff monitors the print, music, and electronic media for developments pertinent to the community. You'll also find the forum's *Pride Press*—a twice-monthly newsletter of exceptional quality and awareness. (Keywords: **GLCF News**)
- *Events & Conferencing* gathers all of the forum's chat and conference rooms (chat rooms are discussed in Chapter 8) in one place, for easy access. You'll find the forum's chat schedule here as well. (Keywords: **GLCF Chat**)
- Text, graphics, and even sounds are available in the *Resource Library*. Look for the Lambda Rising Bookstore here too, with books, music, videos, apparel, and accessories (even refrigerator magnets!) available for purchase. (Keywords: **GLCF Library**)
- *Organizations* offers the Organizations Database, a space for members to contact and receive information about various local and national organizations within the lesbian/gay/bisexual/transgender community. The database is searchable and exceptionally comprehensive. (Keywords: **GLCF Orgs**)
- *Travel* offers a listing of tour operators and cruise companies, and an exclusive connection to the International Gay Travel Association—a network of travel industry professionals dedicated to encouraging and assisting in the promotion of gay and lesbian travel. (Keywords: **GLCF Travel**)
- *Message Boards* gathers the forum's myriad message boards together in one place for easy access. (Keywords: **GLCF Boards**)

There's more to the Gay and Lesbian Community Forum. Read on.

Gaymeland

::dancedancelaughdance:: So begins your introduction to Gaymeland, the GLCF's "Island Oasis of Constant Fun." The heart of Gaymeland is the *Romping Room*, with live interactive "gaymes" every night of the week. In the *Zilla Scrolls* you'll find fake astrology, brainteasers, interactive stories, wisecracks, challenges—anything and everything "Gaymezilla" can come up with for inclusion on a message board. The *National GaymEnquirer* is "more than just your father's newsletter," and the *Library Lagoon* offers a library of sounds used in the Gaymeland conference and chat rooms. There's a healthy irreverence here, served up with disarming wit and charm. Use the keyword: **Gaymeland** and *::dancedancedance::* the night away!

The Positive Living Forum

The Positive Living Forum (keyword: **PLF**) is a place for people to find information and support about HIV and AIDS. It's appropriate for people infected with the virus, and people interested in learning how to avoid the virus, as well as caregivers and family (see Figure 9-20).

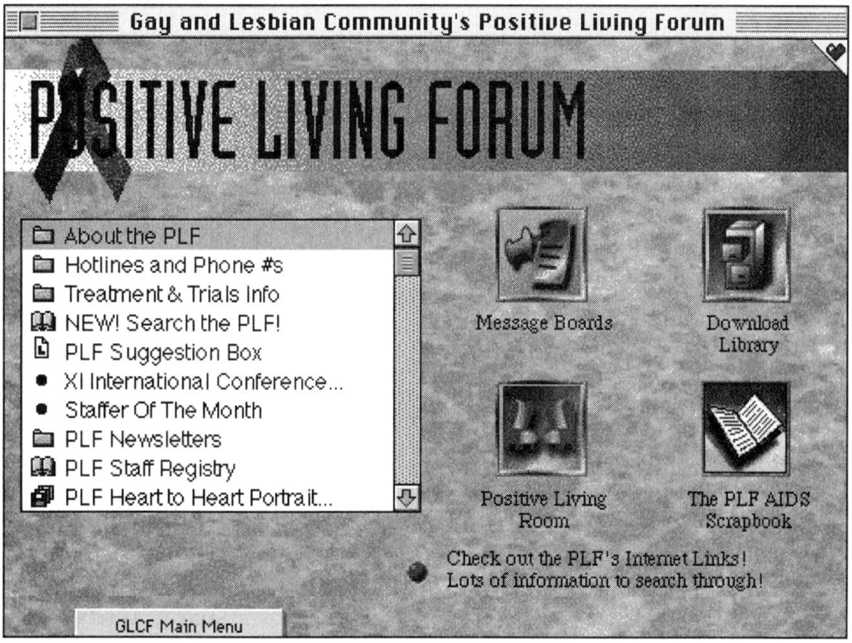
Gay and Lesbian Community's Positive Living Forum
POSITIVE LIVING FORUM
About the PLF
Hotlines and Phone #s
Treatment & Trials Info
NEW! Search the PLF!
PLF Suggestion Box
XI International Conference...
Staffer Of The Month
PLF Newsletters
PLF Staff Registry
PLF Heart to Heart Portrait...
Message Boards
Download Library
Positive Living Room
The PLF AIDS Scrapbook
Check out the PLF's Internet Links!
Lots of information to search through!
GLCF Main Menu

Figure 9-20: The Positive Living Forum offers support and resources for people who need or seek help with HIV and AIDS.

The forum offers a comprehensive resource of AIDS/HIV information, whether it be online articles, file libraries, or folders in message boards. Like the GLCF, the Positive Living Forum's emphasis is on compassion and caring, and its large complement of health care professionals, researchers, and social service workers underscores its benevolent charter.

The Transgender Community Forum

The Transgender Community Forum offers support and provides education and outreach about transgender issues. The forum welcomes the transgendered, transsexuals, transvestites, crossdressers, significant others, family, supportive friends, medical and legal professionals—without regard to race, sexual preference, or lifestyle.

The forum is also a resource for all America Online members. Everyone is welcome to contribute and participate; all viewpoints are welcome. You'll find them at keywords: **GLCF TCF.**

Better Health & Medical Network

Not so many years ago, the common approach to health care was one of repairing the human machine. The primary character was the friendly family doctor, the focus was on symptoms, and the medical profession was a staid and reliable community fixture.

Paralleling technology's move toward integration, today's health care has shifted toward a broader concept of health that includes information, lifestyle, mental health, making informed decisions, the family unit, gender-specific health, alternative medical approaches, health problems of the workplace, stress, learning disorders, and issues focused on specific age groups.

Best of all, health care now recognizes the vital importance of the patient in his or her own health care decisionmaking and healing. Healing no longer means repair of a part but a comprehensive approach to the whole person, a perspective America Online shares and addresses in its Better Health & Medical Network (see Figure 9-21). To get there, just use the keywords: **Better Health**.

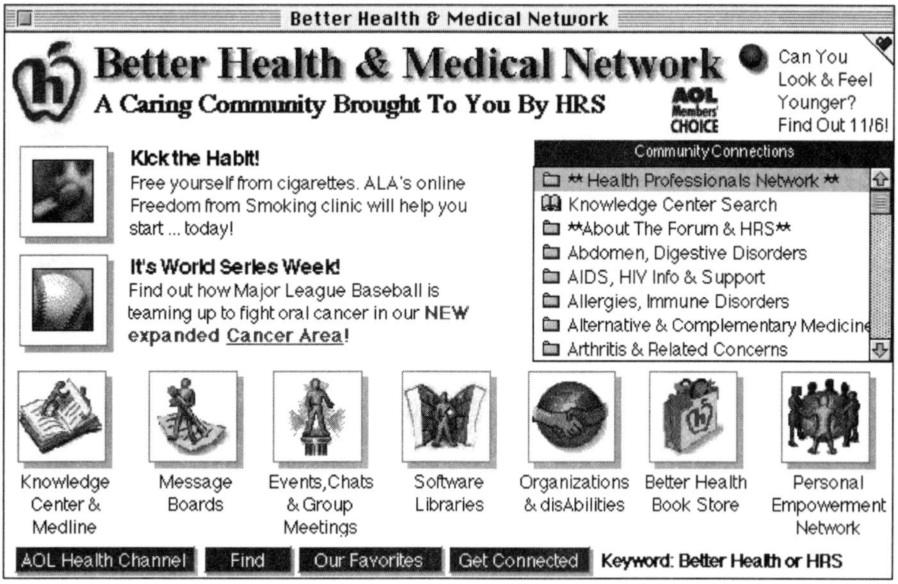
Better Health & Medical Network
Better Health & Medical Network
A Caring Community Brought To You By HRS
AOL Members' CHOICE
Can You Look & Feel Younger? Find Out 11/6!
Kick the Habit!
Free yourself from cigarettes. ALA's online Freedom from Smoking clinic will help you start ... today!
It's World Series Week!
Find out how Major League Baseball is teaming up to fight oral cancer in our NEW expanded Cancer Area!
Community Connections
** Health Professionals Network **
Knowledge Center Search
About The Forum & HRS
Abdomen, Digestive Disorders
AIDS, HIV Info & Support
Allergies, Immune Disorders
Alternative & Complementary Medicine
Arthritis & Related Concerns
Knowledge Center & Medline
Message Boards
Events, Chats & Group Meetings
Software Libraries
Organizations & disAbilities
Better Health Book Store
Personal Empowerment Network
AOL Health Channel
Find
Our Favorites
Get Connected
Keyword: Better Health or HRS

Figure 9-21: The Better Health & Medical Network is your connection to personal health care information, advice, and support groups of people who share your problems or concerns.

The Religion & Beliefs Forum

Here's a singular combination: the newest of all human creations—electronic communication—in concert with perhaps the oldest of all human traditions—religion. (See Figure 9-22.) Actually, the focus of this forum is not entirely old, for the forum is shared equally by long-established religious traditions, relatively young traditions, and modern discussions in ethics and philosophy.

You'll find file libraries and lively message boards on Christianity, Judaism, Buddhism, Hinduism, pagan beliefs, New Age thought, philosophy, Humanism, Islam, and Quakerism, to name just a few. Be sure to check out the religious art exhibits and message boards where religious and ethical dialogs regarding current events and issues take place. You'll find it all at keyword: **Religion**.

Religion & Beliefs
RELIGION & BELIEFS
Follow the news in Israel.
Old Testament Trivia is here!
CHRISTIANITY
JUDAISM
WORLD BELIEFS
SPIRITUAL MOSAIC
ETHICS & VALUES
New! Old Testament Trivia by NTN
Religion & Beliefs Store
Religion & Beliefs Message Boards
Atheism-Agnosticism Forum
Avoid Religious Discrimination
WHAT'S HOT
CHAT
AOL CHANNELS
MEMBER SERVICES
FIND
Keyword: RELIGION

Figure 9-22: The Religion & Beliefs Forum is a place to discuss and learn about the ultimate human question.

The Garden Spot

The Garden Spot is America Online's gardening message and information center (see Figure 9-23). If your fuchsias are faltering, or you want to know exactly how to prune your pear tree, here's where you can find out. The Gardening Message Boards can put you in touch with experts in every area of gardening, from aquatic plant life to weed control.

Of particular value are the regional gardening boards—message centers dedicated to plant health solutions for specific geographic areas of the country. If you need horticultural information fast, the Garden Spot (keyword: **Garden**) is a great place to start.

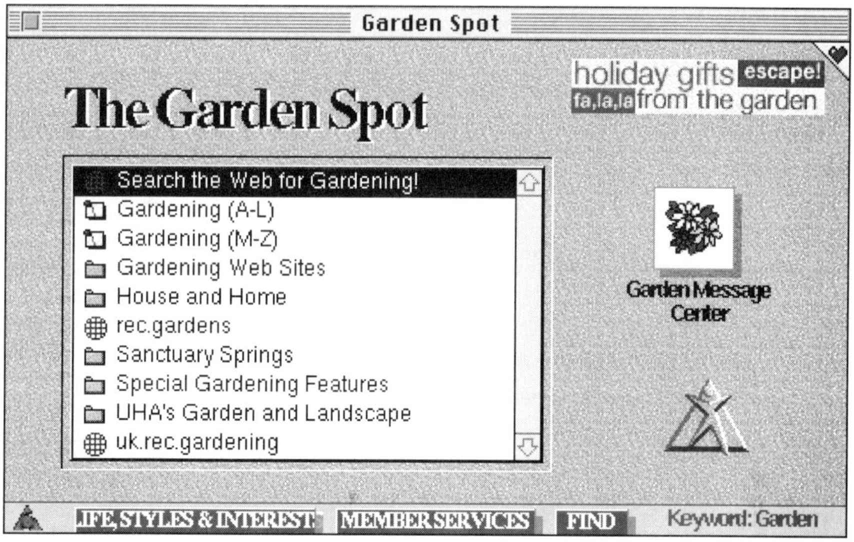
Garden Spot
The Garden Spot
holiday gifts escape!
fa,la,la from the garden
Search the Web for Gardening!
Gardening (A-L)
Gardening (M-Z)
Gardening Web Sites
House and Home
rec.gardens
Sanctuary Springs
Special Gardening Features
UHA's Garden and Landscape
uk.rec.gardening
Garden Message Center
LIFE, STYLES & INTEREST
MEMBER SERVICES
FIND
Keyword: Garden

Figure 9-23: The Garden Spot is your connection to horticultural experts and master gardeners in your own geographical area.

The Genealogy Forum

Genealogical research has taken three great steps forward with the arrival of personal computers: new software has made family tree organization simpler; connection via modem to major genealogical archives has broadened and accelerated information searches; and e-mail facilitates personal communication among family members all over the world.

America Online's Genealogy Forum (see Figure 9-24) represents another step forward for genealogy hobbyists and researchers by combining message centers, file and software archives, live genealogy conferences, and genealogical research guides into one easy-to-find location. The Genealogy Forum is one of AOL's most popular areas, and no wonder: whether you'd like to do a simple surname search or initiate the creation of an extensive family tree, you'll find all the tools and pointers you'll need by typing the keyword: **Roots**.

Genealogy Forum
The Genealogy Forum
Resource Center
Visit the New Improved Resource Center!
Genealogy Chat
Visit One of Our Five Chat Rooms
Genealogy on the Internet
Locate your Genealogy on the Internet
Beginners Start Here
Click here if you are just starting
New Chat Room!
"For Starters" - the new Chat Room for Beginners
MAIN MENU
Member Welcome Center
DearMYRTLE Daily Column
Genealogy Forum NEWS - Dec 96
Message Boards
File Libraries
.New File Uploads.
Genealogy Chat Schedule
Upcoming Forum Special Events
Genealogy Conferences & Events
Genealogy Store
Family Tree Maker Online
AOL Members' CHOICE
LIFE, STYLES & INTERESTS
MEMBER SERVICES
FIND
Keyword: Roots

Figure 9-24: Learn more about your family's history using the Genealogy Forum's tools and archives.

The Writers Club

Writers, often by choice as much as necessity, swim alone and only occasionally come up for air. And when they do, their first breaths fuel the need to find and converse with their peers. America Online, which constantly relies on hundreds of writers, understands this full well and has created a place and structure for writers of all genres and persuasions (see Figure 9-25).

You'll find genre-specific message boards and chats, of course, serving the creative gamut from technical writing to poetry. You'll also find workshops and conferences—49 scheduled when I last looked—for just about every type of writing. And for those whose schedules are staunchly idiorhythmic, the Writer's Cafe is open for conversation 24 hours a day.

Three areas of the Writers Club deserve special mention. The Articles and Columns area provides tips and information for those developing their writing craft. Job announcements may be found via the Writers > Messages > Writer's Market Message Center trail. And, thanks to AOL, you can establish a personal relationship with a published author via the Mentor program. You'll find all of this and much more at keyword: **Writers**.

The Writers Club
Writers Club
Welcome
Chat
Messages
Search
File Libraries
Life, Styles & Interests
Writers Club Map 3.0
Meet the Writers Club Staff
Welcome Newcomers!
Romance
Teen Writers
Poetry Place
Writers Club Store
Marketplace
Humor/Commentary
Articles/Columns
Auditorium
Contests
Keyword: Writers
Hosts: TwisterB & Phylwriter
Hot off the "press"...
FictionMaster for
Windows is here!!
Have Better Sex!
Mailing List
NEED A BOOK ON WRITING? WE'VE GOT ALL THE BEST!

Figure 9-25: Whether you're a beginning writer or a seasoned pro, the Writers Club offers tips, ideas, information, and contacts.

Gaming Forums

It's not difficult to become obsessed with a game: chess, Nintendo, flight simulation—they often consume inordinate amounts of time and cerebral energy. There's rarely any harm in that, of course—in fact, friends are often made in the pursuit. That's where the gaming forums come in: this is where gamers meet gamers, where strategies are discreetly disclosed, and where obsessions feed obsessions. It's all good fun, and it often leads to improved scores. If this sounds like your trump suit, read on.

Flight Simulations Resource Center

Flight simulation is, indeed, a virtual world unto itself, and AOL has provided flight simulation aficionados with a place to meet and exchange hangar talk. The Flight Simulations Resource Center (see Figure 9-26) is where newcomers can find advice on flight simulation software, and experienced virtual pilots can download the latest utilities, sound, scenery, program add-ons, and images.

Are you captivated by the Golden Age of Flight, or is hyperspace your arena? You'll find people here who share your passion—in software-specific flight simulation clubs with themes ranging from the early days of flight to space flight of the distant future. You can even join (or create and operate) your own virtual airline. Just use the keyword: **Flight**.

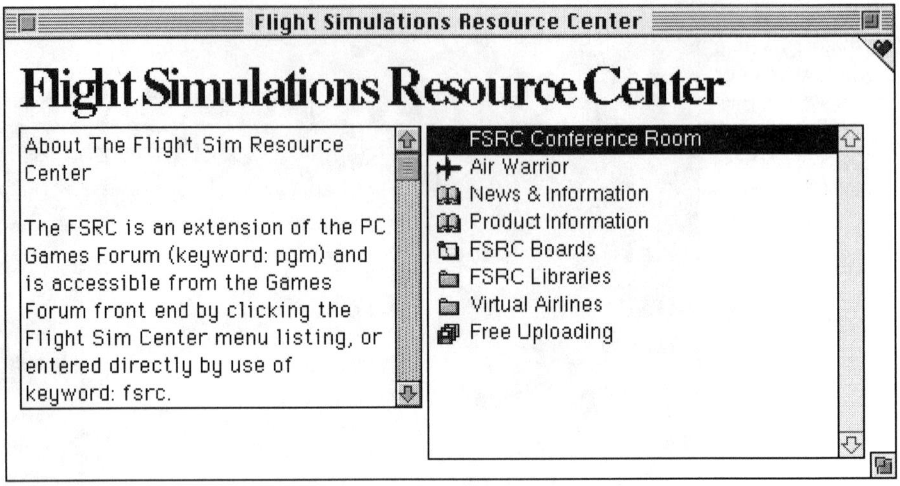
Flight Simulations Resource Center
Flight Simulations Resource Center
About The Flight Sim Resource Center
The FSRC is an extension of the PC Games Forum (keyword: pgm) and is accessible from the Games Forum front end by clicking the Flight Sim Center menu listing, or entered directly by use of keyword: fsrc.
FSRC Conference Room
Air Warrior
News & Information
Product Information
FSRC Boards
FSRC Libraries
Virtual Airlines
Free Uploading

Figure 9-26: If your joystick hand convulses after 10 hours away from the computer; if you practice Immelmans at your nonvirtual desktop while you're supposed to be earning a living; if you race out the front door when the sound of a Pratt & Whitney radial fills the sky, the Flight Simulations Resource Center had better be among your favorite places.

Star Trek Club

The signature phrase of the *Star Trek* television program, "where no one has gone before" is an apt description of the online medium. What better place than AOL, then, for fellow Trekkers to meet and converse.

The Star Trek Club (keyword: **Trek**) features information and meeting areas dedicated to the original TV show, the Star Trek movies, *Star Trek: The Next Generation*, *Star Trek: Deep Space 9*, and *Star Trek: Voyager*. You can join the Star Trek writer's group on The Bridge to help create the continuing saga, or try your hand at Trek trivia in the Trivia Center.

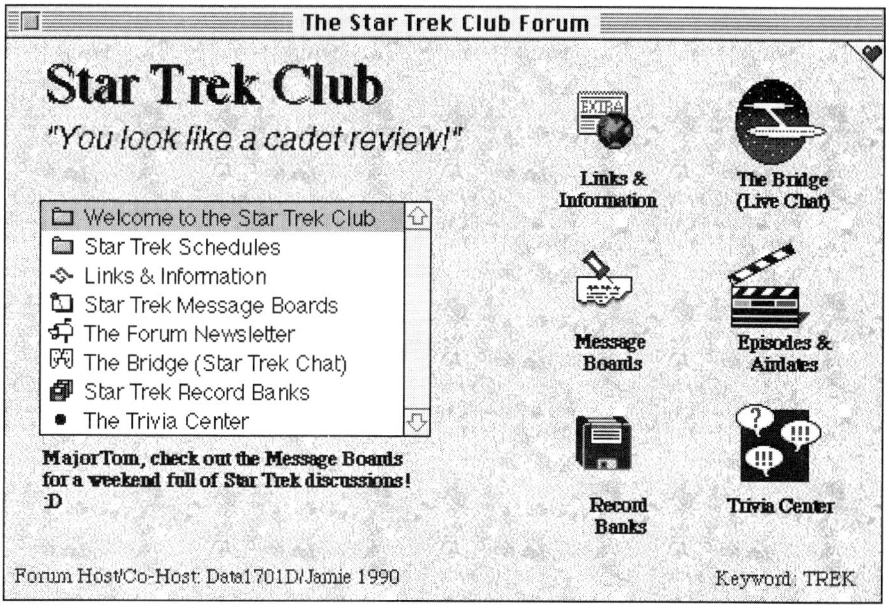
The Star Trek Club Forum
Star Trek Club
"You look like a cadet review!"
Welcome to the Star Trek Club
Star Trek Schedules
Links & Information
Star Trek Message Boards
The Forum Newsletter
The Bridge (Star Trek Chat)
Star Trek Record Banks
The Trivia Center
MajorTom, check out the Message Boards for a weekend full of Star Trek discussions! :D
Links & Information
The Bridge (Live Chat)
Message Boards
Episodes & Airdates
Record Banks
Trivia Center
Forum Host/Co-Host: Data1701D/Jamie 1990
Keyword: TREK

Figure 9-27: The Star Trek Club feeds the Trekkie fancy.

Strategy & WarGames Forum

The very fact that you're reading this book indicates you are a person who enjoys mental activity, the acquisition of information, and problem solving. And that's what the Strategy and WarGames Forum is all about—conversation about games of all types that use strategy and tactics to solve problems (see Figure 9-28). (**Note:** The games themselves are discussed in Chapter 11, "Divertissements.")

Strategy & WarGames Forum
STRATEGY & WAR GAMES
About The Forum
Learn about the different areas in the Strategy & War Games Forum!
Strategy Messaging
Solicit games, discuss strategies and post gaming results!
Chess Forum
Messaging, discussion, file libraries, web links and much more.
Strategy Library
Looking for a specific game file? Or want to upload one? Do it here!
Wargaming Clubs
Ad. Squad Leader, AOL Wargaming, Axis & Allies, Diplomacy, and Lead Eaters Clubs!
Conference Hall
Real-time chat with game players from all over the nation!
Strategy Host: OGF Musashi
Chess Host: OGF Chess
GAMES CHANNEL
FIND
Keyword: STRATEGY

Figure 9-28: Use the keyword: **Strategy** to share your game-playing skills or to start up an e-mail game of your own.

Not surprisingly, this forum is also the home of America Online's Chess Forum, where you can converse with other players, study chess strategies, research game collections from national and international tournaments, review chess books and software, access news reports from the world of professional chess, and read commentary and answers to members' questions from AOL's resident Grand Master Gabriel Sanchez.

All these features clearly make the Chess Forum a valuable resource for chess fans, but there's more. Here you can always find someone to play by posting a message in the Looking for a Game folder. And when you think you're ready to move up to a new level, you'll find tournaments and USCF rated game opportunities to test your knowledge and provoke your creativity. Curious? Just use the keyword: **Strategy**.

Nintendo Power Source

History is filled with dates signifying the beginning of important trends. Some future historian will no doubt note the "then unrecognized" importance of the industrious Mario Brothers. Lest we err by disregarding those energetic little workmen, now familiar to an entire generation, we should remember the ultimate success of a certain singing mouse some fifty-odd years before.

The Nintendo Power Source (see Figure 9-29) is the home of the Nintendo Forum, and while the forum is undeniably an information, message, and chat center for the avid fans of the Marios and other Nintendo home video games, it is also a picture window into the emerging world of recreational virtual reality, a world that is evolving no less rapidly than that of home computers. Whether you're looking for help with your latest game, or looking through the game into the future, you'll find there's much to be learned at keyword: **Nintendo**.

Nintendo Power Source
NINTENDO POWER SOURCE
HQ
Play It Loud
SEARCH
Systems
GAMES
WHAT'S NEW
Keyword(s): Nintendo, NOA

Figure 9-29: You'll find the Nintendo Forum under the Play It Loud button on Nintendo's main screen.

Moving On

As good as AOL is at helping you pursue an interest—a hobby or an avocation—it's even better at keeping you informed. The online medium, after all, doesn't have to wait for "film at 11" or the morning edition. If there's news worth breaking, it's online immediately. Some of AOL's weather maps are never more than 15 minutes old. This could very well be information's ideal medium. Turn the page to see what I mean.

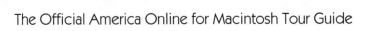

Staying Informed

CHAPTER 10

- The News
- Digital Cities
- Sports
- Weather

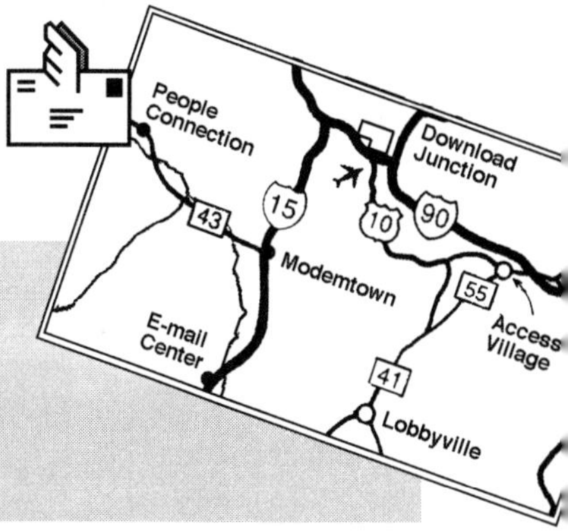
People Connection
Download Junction
43
15
10
90
Modemtown
55
Access Village
E-mail Center
41
Lobbyville

In the beginning of the information age, people got their news from newspapers. At best, newspapers offered the news once a day—a small inconvenience considering the limited expectations of the public in those days. Radio emerged 70 years ago, offering immediate "on-the-scene" coverage. But there were no pictures, and if you weren't listening when the news was broadcast, you missed it. Forty years ago, television brought pictures, but even today you're at the mercy of TV scheduling if you want the latest.

What if you had access to the most up-to-date news and information all the time—exactly when and how you wanted it? What if you could see the pictures and hear the sounds while you're seated in front of your computer? That's the way America Online thinks news should be. And as you can tell from the abundance of opportunity pictured in Figure 10-1, the potential supply is inexhaustible.

The News

AOL's Today's News window, pictured in Figure 10-1, is where most of your informational journeys will begin. The contents of this window are changing continuously, as are the stories to which they lead.

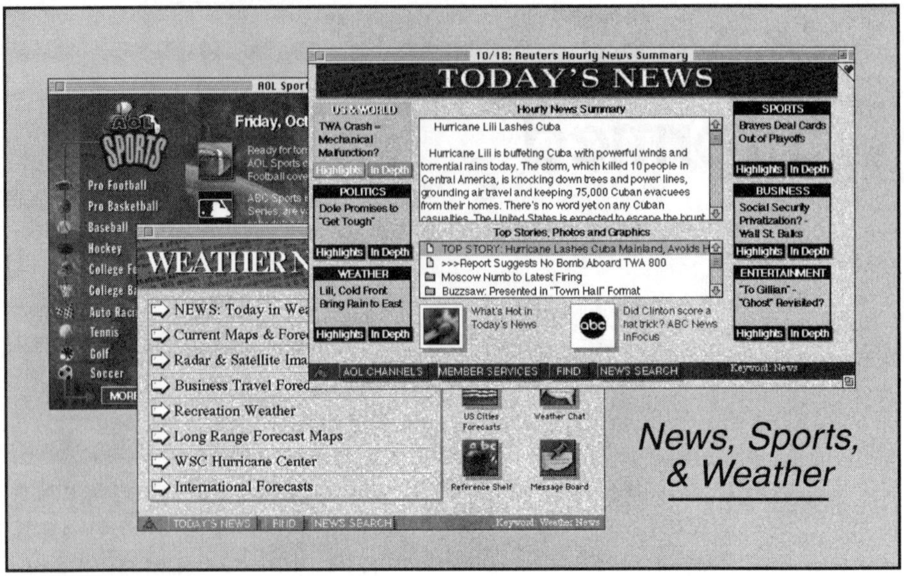
10/18: Reuters Hourly News Summary
TODAY'S NEWS
US & WORLD
TWA Crash – Mechanical Malfunction?
Highlights
In Depth
Hourly News Summary
Hurricane Lili Lashes Cuba
Hurricane Lili is buffeting Cuba with powerful winds and torrential rains today. The storm, which killed 10 people in Central America, is knocking down trees and power lines, grounding air travel and keeping 75,000 Cuban evacuees from their homes. There's no word yet on any Cuban
POLITICS
Dole Promises to "Get Tough"
Top Stories, Photos and Graphics
TOP STORY: Hurricane Lashes Cuba Mainland, Avoids H
>>>Report Suggests No Bomb Aboard TWA 800
Moscow Numb to Latest Firing
Buzzsaw: Presented in "Town Hall" Format
WEATHER
Lili, Cold Front Bring Rain to East
What's Hot in Today's News
Did Clinton score a hat trick? ABC News InFocus
SPORTS
Braves Deal Cards Out of Playoffs
BUSINESS
Social Security Privatization? - Wall St. Balks
ENTERTAINMENT
"To Gillian" - "Ghost" Revisited?
AOL CHANNELS
MEMBER SERVICES
FIND
NEWS SEARCH
Keyword: News
AOL Sports
Friday, Oct
Pro Football
Pro Basketball
Baseball
Hockey
Tennis
Golf
Soccer
WEATHER N
NEWS: Today in We
Current Maps & Fore
Radar & Satellite Ima
Business Travel Forec
Recreation Weather
Long Range Forecast Maps
WSC Hurricane Center
International Forecasts
US Cities Forecasts
Weather Chat
Reference Shelf
Message Board
TODAY'S NEWS
FIND
NEWS SEARCH
Keyword: Weather News
News, Sports, & Weather

Figure 10-1: The keyword: **News**, the keyword: **Sports**, and the keyword: **Weather** connect you with an arsenal of information resources, continually updated and maintained.

The Top Stories

Look again at the Today's News window in Figure 10-1. The list you see in the bottom center of this window, as well as the news summary in the top center window, is always current; it changes as events happen. These are the stories that lead the news; the online "front page." By simply double-clicking a headline, Today's News calls up the complete text of the story.

Some headlines are complex and contain several related story lines. Note the small "folder" icon beside the Moscow listing in Figure 10-1. Double-clicking a line with a folder icon displays a window containing story menus, and often a headline banner and lead story (see Figure 10-2).

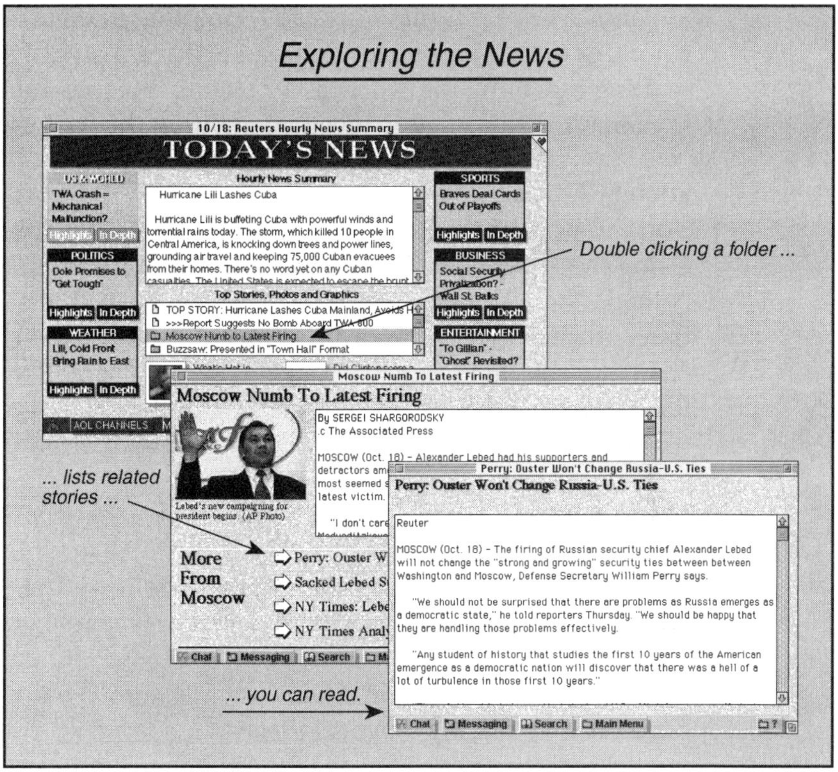
Exploring the News
Double clicking a folder ...
... lists related stories ...
... you can read.

Figure 10-2: Folder icons identify items that include collections of related stories.

Informational Preparedness

You'll want to save some of the material you see, or print it, or specify the scope of your wanderings. Here's how it's done.

Saving Articles

Whenever an article appears on your screen in the frontmost window, it's available to be saved on your hard drive or a floppy disk. To save an article (news or otherwise—I'm talking about *any* article, at any time), just choose Save from the File menu. You'll see a standard Macintosh Save dialog box, where you can assign the article a name and file location.

Articles can be saved as pure text and can be opened with any word processor. (**Hint:** select Text Only from the file type menu at the bottom of the dialog box so that the material you save offers the most compatibility with any software you might use.) You can open any articles saved this way with AOL's software—whether you're online or off—by choosing Open from the File menu.

Some articles may have special formatting in them, such as styles, colors, or even "hyperlinks" to other articles. You can retain this formatting by saving the article as a "Memo." Keep in mind that articles in memo format can only be opened within the AOL software reliably.

Printing Articles

You can print any article that appears in AOL's frontmost window. Using the File menu, choose Print and you'll see your Mac's standard print dialog box. Make any necessary changes to the print configuration and click Print. America Online will print the article to your Mac's currently selected printer. When you print directly like this, you won't have much control over the formatting of the printed page; if you want that kind of control, open the article using your word processor.

Keeping a Log

While articles like those pictured in Figure 10-2 are informative, invaluable, and often fascinating, reading them online is not. I prefer to absorb information like that at my leisure, when the online clock isn't running.

The solution is found in AOL's *Log Manager*. When a log is turned on, all text appearing on your screen is recorded on your disk. You can zip through an online session without delay, letting articles flash across your screen at the tempo of an MTV video. Then, when you've accessed what you need, sign off and review the log. Any word processor will open a log file, as will your AOL software. Just choose Open from the File menu.

Now that I've read the paragraph above, I feel compelled to make a disclaimer: some things offer their own saving routines (World Wide Web pages—discussed in Chapter 4, "Using the Internet"—are a good example); others may have to be copied and pasted into a new document for saving. Generally, the logging feature is used for articles—AOL text files—so that they can be saved for later review.

To start a log: while you're online, choose Log Manager from the File menu. In the Log Manager window, open a System Log by clicking the New Log... button on the right side of the window. America Online will display a standard File | Save dialog box complete with a suggested filename and location (see Figure 10-3). Make any filename/location changes you want, then click Save. From then on, all the text you see onscreen will be saved on your disk.

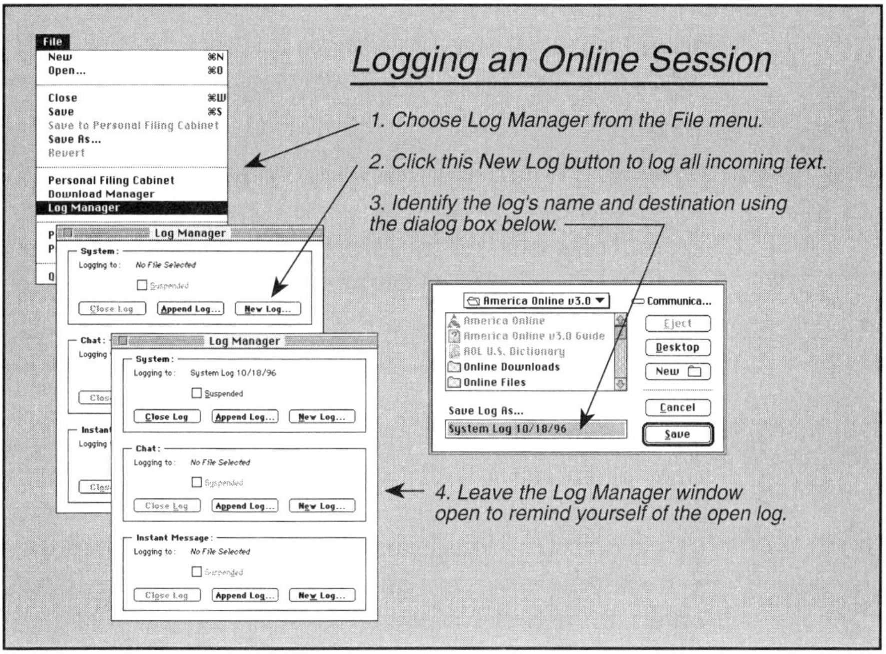
Logging an Online Session
1. Choose Log Manager from the File menu.
2. Click this New Log button to log all incoming text.
3. Identify the log's name and destination using the dialog box below.
4. Leave the Log Manager window open to remind yourself of the open log.
File
New
Open...
Close
Save
Save to Personal Filing Cabinet
Save As...
Revert
Personal Filing Cabinet
Download Manager
Log Manager
Log Manager
System:
Logging to: System Log 10/18/96
Suspended
Close Log
Append Log...
New Log...
Chat:
Logging to: No File Selected
Instant Message:
America Online v3.0
Communica...
America Online
America Online v3.0 Guide
AOL U.S. Dictionary
Online Downloads
Online Files
Eject
Desktop
New
Save Log As...
System Log 10/18/96
Cancel
Save

Figure 10-3: Log files capture and save onscreen activity to disk for later review.

A Few Notes About Logs

- To capture the complete article in your log you must double-click (open) the article's headline while you're online (and while logging is enabled, of course) and allow AOL to finish the transmission of the article to your Mac (be sure it's complete). When the beachball cursor changes back to the arrow cursor, transmission is complete. You don't have to read it online—you don't even have to scroll to the end of it—you just have to receive it in its entirety.
- Log files can be as large as you want them to be, but they can grow quickly if you don't pay attention. Monitor your activity online while a log file is open as you would monitor your fuel gauge while traveling through Death Valley.
- You can always close the log or append an existing one by using the buttons in the Log Manager window (refer again to Figure 10-3). This is handy when you want to turn your log on and off: you can use the Close Log and Append Log... buttons as you would the Pause button on a tape recorder, capturing the

material you want and excluding what you don't want. The Log Manager window works while you're offline as well, so you can start a log even before you sign on. You'll never miss a thing that way.

- If you look carefully at the bottom window in Figure 10-3, you will note three types of logs. The System log is the one that captures articles like those discussed in this chapter; it doesn't capture chats and instant messages (I discussed those in Chapter 8, "The Community").

Searching the News

Look again at the Today's News window pictured at the top of Figure 10-1. In the bottom center of the window there is a button labeled "News Search." This is an extremely powerful tool. It's powerful because it searches not only world news but also news about business, entertainment, sports, and even weather. If you know of a subject that's in the news and you want to know more, click this button.

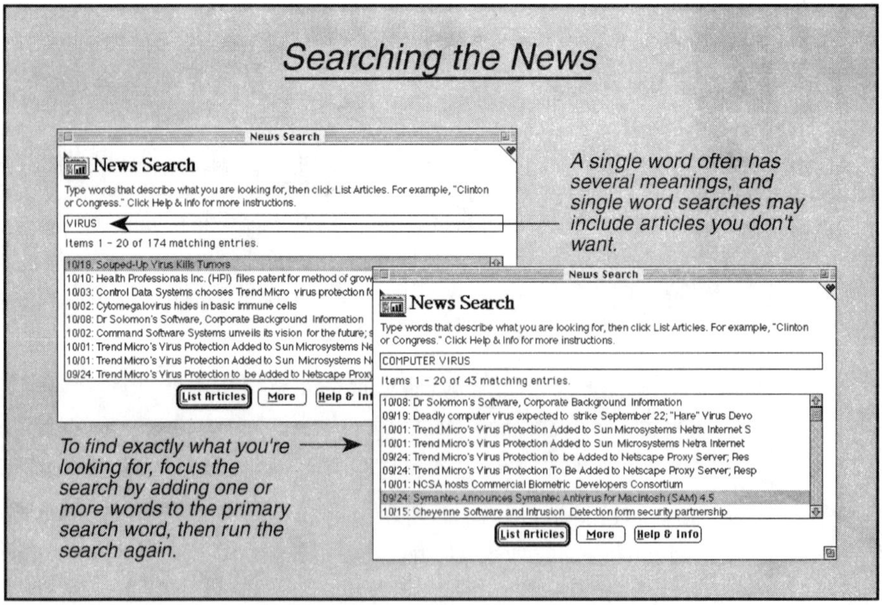
Searching the News
News Search
Type words that describe what you are looking for, then click List Articles. For example, "Clinton or Congress." Click Help & Info for more instructions.
VIRUS
Items 1 - 20 of 174 matching entries.
A single word often has several meanings, and single word searches may include articles you don't want.
COMPUTER VIRUS
Items 1 - 20 of 43 matching entries.
10/08: Dr Solomon's Software, Corporate Background Information
09/19: Deadly computer virus expected to strike September 22; "Hare" Virus Devo
10/01: Trend Micro's Virus Protection Added to Sun Microsystems Netra Internet S
10/01: Trend Micro's Virus Protection Added to Sun Microsystems Netra Internet
09/24: Trend Micro's Virus Protection to be Added to Netscape Proxy Server; Res
09/24: Trend Micro's Virus Protection To Be Added to Netscape Proxy Server; Resp
10/01: NCSA hosts Commercial Biometric Developers Consortium
09/24: Symantec Announces Symantec Antivirus for Macintosh (SAM) 4.5
10/15: Cheyenne Software and Intrusion Detection form security partnership
List Articles
More
Help & Info
To find exactly what you're looking for, focus the search by adding one or more words to the primary search word, then run the search again.

Figure 10-4: Using the criterion: Virus, I receive 174 "hits" in an America Online news search. By specifying Computer Virus, I narrow my search to only 43 hits, including four articles that are exactly what I'm looking for.

Searching for the word *Virus*, AOL found 174 stories in the news, with topics ranging from Australian animal viruses to antibody research. Along the way, AOL even found a story about African National Soccer. Because my true interest was in new computer antivirus programs, I focused my search by using the criterion: Computer Virus. This time AOL's narrowed search produced 43 "hits" (pictured in the lower window of Figure 10-4).

Specifying effective search criteria for AOL's database searches takes a bit of practice and a working knowledge of the so-called Boolean operators—the modifying terms (AND, OR, and NOT) used to clarify a search. If necessary, review the discussion of these modifiers in the File Search section of Chapter 5, starting on page 158.

No Criteria

Here's a little trick you might find revealing: conduct a news search using no criteria whatsoever. Press the spacebar to place nothing more than a space in the criteria field (where the words *Virus* and *Computer Virus* appear in Figure 10-4), then click the List Articles button.

This tells AOL to search for *anything*, and it will find every article in Today's News. Typically, you'll see several thousand of them, which gives you an idea of just how large the Today's News area really is. America Online subscribes to scores of news services. Few news sources are this extensive.

News Sources

We've arrived at your "16th birthday." You know how to operate the machine—how to search for news; how to log, save, and print your selections—and now you're ready to venture forth onto the information highway. What you need now is a road map: something to identify the roadside attractions that America Online has to offer. Let's consider that road map.

U.S. & World News

America Online's top story menus and News Search provide access to every news article on file in the Today's News area—over 47,000 of them on the day I researched for this chapter. If you prefer a more structured approach to your daily news, use the buttons arrayed throughout the Today's News window (review Figure 10-1).

Looking at the "US & World" section, you can see an In Depth button (several of the sections have one), which leads you to an organized presentation of the day's US and World News (see Figure 10-5). Use the keywords: **US News** if you want to access this feature directly.

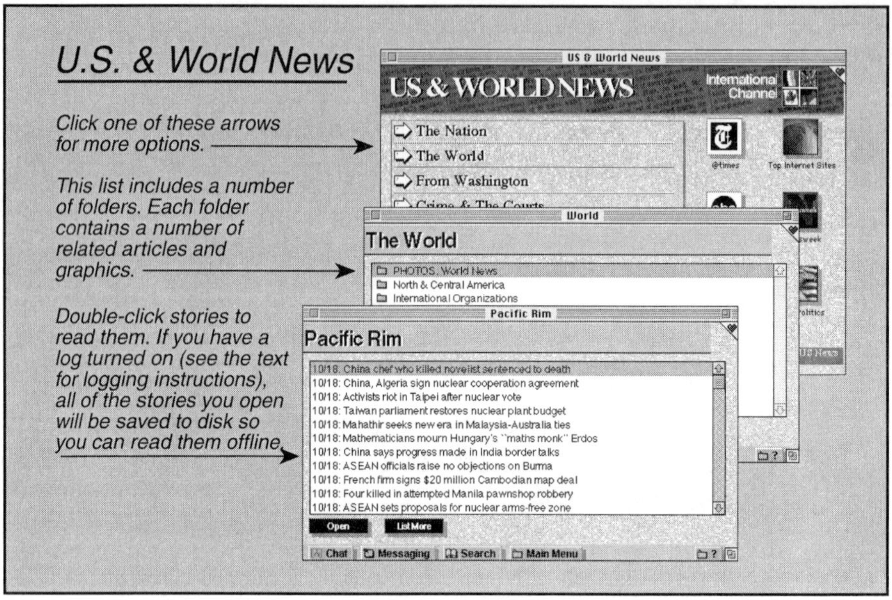
U.S. & World News
Click one of these arrows for more options.
This list includes a number of folders. Each folder contains a number of related articles and graphics.
Double-click stories to read them. If you have a log turned on (see the text for logging instructions), all of the stories you open will be saved to disk so you can read them offline.
US & World News
US & WORLD NEWS
International Channel
The Nation
The World
From Washington
@times
Top Internet Sites
World
The World
PHOTOS, World News
North & Central America
International Organizations
Pacific Rim
Pacific Rim
10/18: China chef who killed novelist sentenced to death
10/18: China, Algeria sign nuclear cooperation agreement
10/18: Activists riot in Taipei after nuclear vote
10/18: Taiwan parliament restores nuclear plant budget
10/18: Mahathir seeks new era in Malaysia-Australia ties
10/18: Mathematicians mourn Hungary's "maths monk" Erdos
10/18: China says progress made in India border talks
10/18: ASEAN officials raise no objections on Burma
10/18: French firm signs $20 million Cambodian map deal
10/18: Four killed in attempted Manila pawnshop robbery
10/18: ASEAN sets proposals for nuclear arms-free zone
Open
List More
Chat
Messaging
Search
Main Menu

Figure 10-5: AOL categorizes US & World News by region. By first selecting the "Pacific Rim" entry in the U.S. & World News category, I'm presented with a list of associated regional news stories.

The six mini-headline windows along the sides of the Today's News window (again, refer to Figure 10-1) are analogous to the sections of your daily newspaper. They're especially useful if you're just browsing the news, with no particular subject in mind. Each also allows you to skim the day's highlights, or pursue the area in greater detail, depending on which button you click.

Business News

Don't confuse Today's Business News with the Personal Finance Channel I'll describe in Chapter 12, "Personal Finance." Like all the other items found in Today's News, the business news offered there is just what its title implies: today's most recent business news from around the world. Other business information, such as investing advice, stock market timing charts, and mutual fund analysis is covered in Chapter 12.

Like the US & World News area, the Business News area brings a coherent structure to an array of news articles. The main Business News window presents a wide array of news categories with stories not only of the day but of the *moment*. You can peruse the Top Business news stories by clicking the arrow buttons on the left side of the Business News window (see Figure 10-6).

Figure 10-6: The Business News section offers multiple categories of news, each containing selected items from the day's key business news stories.

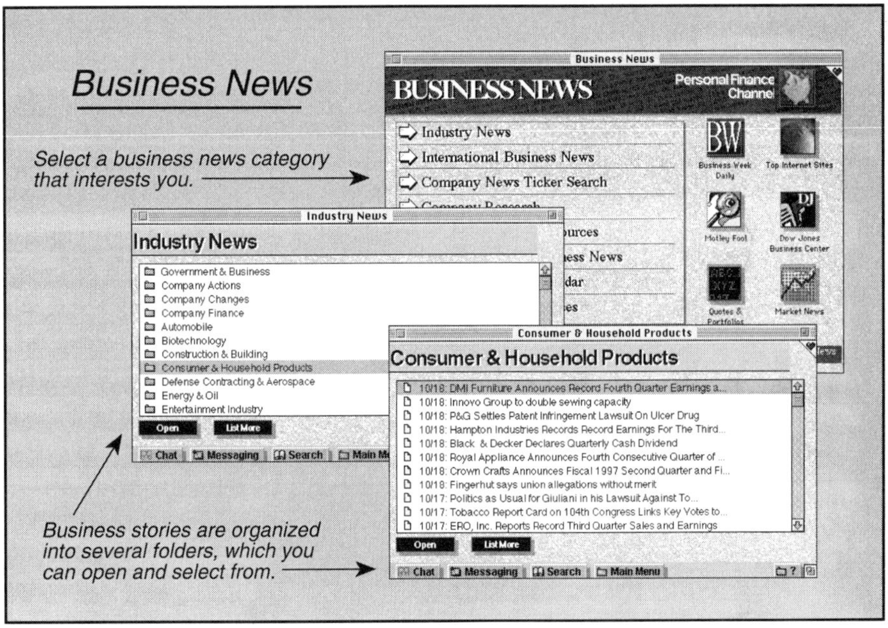
Business News
Select a business news category that interests you.
Business stories are organized into several folders, which you can open and select from.
BUSINESS NEWS
Personal Finance Channel
Industry News
International Business News
Company News Ticker Search
Industry News
Government & Business
Company Actions
Company Changes
Company Finance
Automobile
Biotechnology
Construction & Building
Consumer & Household Products
Defense Contracting & Aerospace
Energy & Oil
Entertainment Industry
Consumer & Household Products
10/18: DMI Furniture Announces Record Fourth Quarter Earnings a...
10/18: Innovo Group to double sewing capacity
10/18: P&G Settles Patent Infringement Lawsuit On Ulcer Drug
10/18: Hampton Industries Records Record Earnings For The Third...
10/18: Black & Decker Declares Quarterly Cash Dividend
10/18: Royal Appliance Announces Fourth Consecutive Quarter of ...
10/18: Crown Crafts Announces Fiscal 1997 Second Quarter and Fi...
10/18: Fingerhut says union allegations without merit
10/17: Politics as Usual for Giuliani in his Lawsuit Against To...
10/17: Tobacco Report Card on 104th Congress Links Key Votes to...
10/17: ERO, Inc. Reports Record Third Quarter Sales and Earnings
Open
List More
Chat
Messaging
Search
Main Menu

Market News

Look again at Figure 10-6. Do you see the button labeled "Market News"? This is another stock market resource offered by AOL (see Figure 10-7); many others are discussed in Chapter 12, "Personal Finance." All the information you expect to see in your newspaper is here, with one significant difference: AOL's stock market information is updated continually during periods of stock market activity.

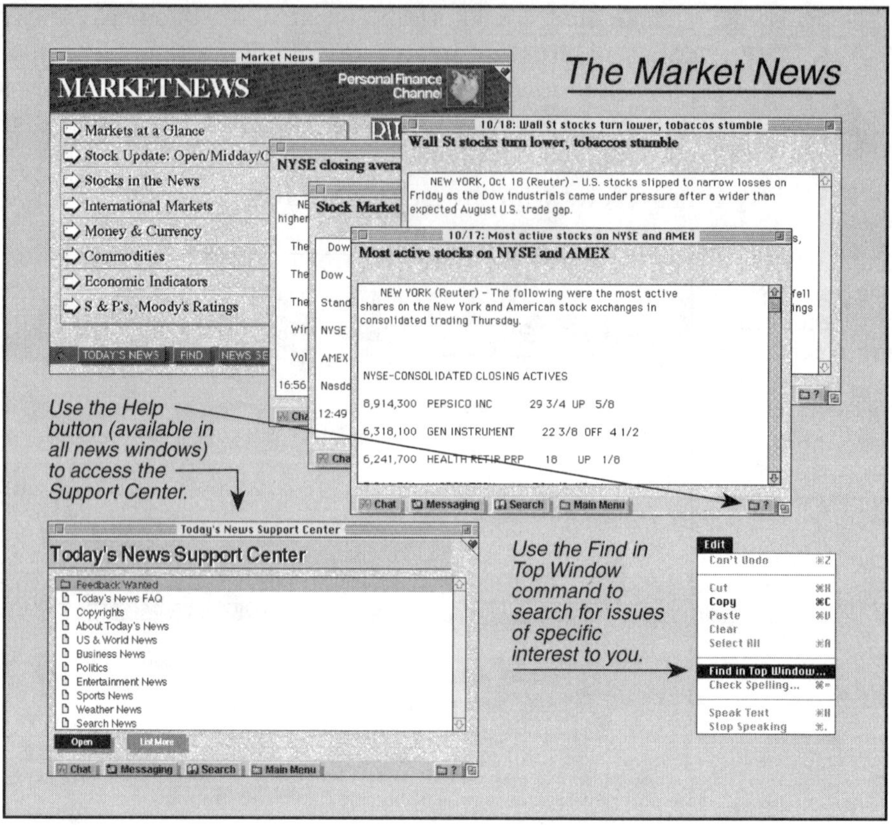
The Market News
Market News
MARKET NEWS
Personal Finance Channel
Markets at a Glance
Stock Update: Open/Midday/C
Stocks in the News
International Markets
Money & Currency
Commodities
Economic Indicators
S & P's, Moody's Ratings
TODAY'S NEWS
FIND
NYSE closing avera
Stock Market
10/18: Wall St stocks turn lower, tobaccos stumble
Wall St stocks turn lower, tobaccos stumble
NEW YORK, Oct 18 (Reuter) - U.S. stocks slipped to narrow losses on Friday as the Dow industrials came under pressure after a wider than expected August U.S. trade gap.
10/17: Most active stocks on NYSE and AMEX
Most active stocks on NYSE and AMEX
NEW YORK (Reuter) - The following were the most active shares on the New York and American stock exchanges in consolidated trading Thursday.
NYSE-CONSOLIDATED CLOSING ACTIVES
8,914,300 PEPSICO INC 29 3/4 UP 5/8
6,318,100 GEN INSTRUMENT 22 3/8 OFF 4 1/2
6,241,700 HEALTH RETIR PRP 18 UP 1/8
Chat
Messaging
Search
Main Menu
Use the Help button (available in all news windows) to access the Support Center.
Today's News Support Center
Today's News Support Center
Feedback Wanted
Today's News FAQ
Copyrights
About Today's News
US & World News
Business News
Politics
Entertainment News
Sports News
Weather News
Search News
Open
List More
Use the Find in Top Window command to search for issues of specific interest to you.
Edit
Can't Undo
Cut
Copy
Paste
Clear
Select All
Find in Top Window...
Check Spelling...
Speak Text
Stop Speaking

Figure 10-7: America Online's Market News rarely trails the NYSE ticker by more than 20 minutes during trading. To get there in a hurry, use the keywords: **Market News**.

People & Entertainment

Can you recall an occasion when you purchased a product and were pleasantly surprised when you got more than you bargained for? If you're interested in news from the entertainment field, signing on to AOL might just be one of those occasions.

I say this because the People & Entertainment section of Today's News offers articles from *Variety*, the preeminent industry magazine that profoundly influences people in the entertainment capitals of our nation. It's posted each day on AOL.

To reach the People & Entertainment area, use the keywords: **Entertainment News**, naturally (see Figure 10-8). In addition to individual stories, AOL carries *Variety*'s front page in a single file.

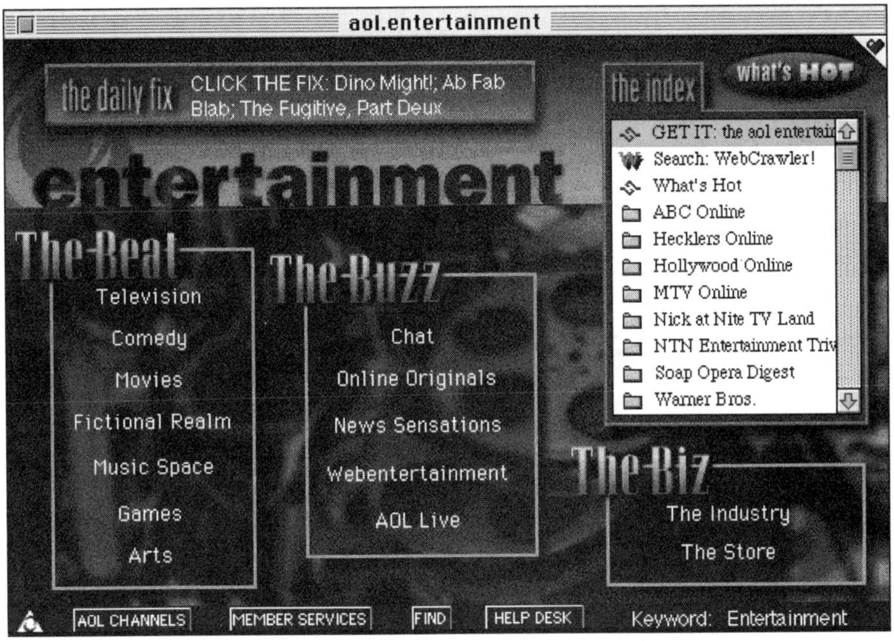
aol.entertainment
the daily fix
CLICK THE FIX: Dino Might!; Ab Fab Blab; The Fugitive, Part Deux
the index
what's HOT
GET IT: the aol entertain
Search: WebCrawler!
What's Hot
ABC Online
Hecklers Online
Hollywood Online
MTV Online
Nick at Nite TV Land
NTN Entertainment Triv
Soap Opera Digest
Warner Bros.
entertainment
The Reel
Television
Comedy
Movies
Fictional Realm
Music Space
Games
Arts
The Buzz
Chat
Online Originals
News Sensations
Webentertainment
AOL Live
The Biz
The Industry
The Store
AOL CHANNELS
MEMBER SERVICES
FIND
HELP DESK
Keyword: Entertainment

Figure 10-8: The Entertainment section of Today's News features news of the entertainment industry, most of which is drawn from *Variety* magazine.

This is one of AOL's best-kept secrets. *Variety* magazine is the entertainment industry's "Bible," and now you know where to find it.

The Newsstand

If the immediacy of Today's News is the online analog to television, the Newsstand compares with the magazine section at the library, the main difference being that it offers a distinctly different, but profoundly significant, journalistic advantage: capacity.

Most magazine readers value the printed medium; but if you're like me, you've given up on filing past issues. After a few months, I just recycle most of my magazines. And all too often, after I dispose of them I decide to review something I saw in an issue that's now gone.

I have good news, periodical patrons: the Newsstand is AOL's answer to the problem of that stack of magazines in the garage, a place where you can read current issues, save articles, download files, and even talk to the editors online. Perhaps best of all, the Newsstand is not only horizontally comprehensive (lots of publications), it's vertically comprehensive as well (most back issues are searchable). Chances are, if you search for a subject of interest, it's there. That's what I mean by the benefits of capacity. To get there, click the Newsstand button in the Channels window, or use the keyword: **Newsstand**.

There's so much great stuff in the Newsstand, it's hard to know where to begin. One thing I know we all have in common—our Macs. So we'll begin our exploration by double-clicking Computing Print & Broadcast from the scroll box pictured in Figure 10-9.

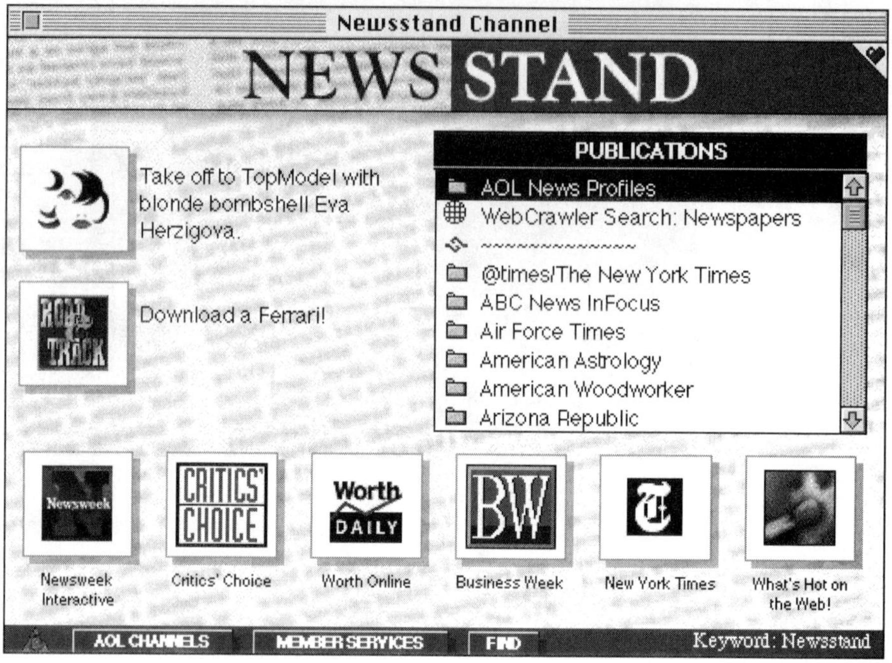
Newsstand Channel
NEWS STAND
Take off to TopModel with blonde bombshell Eva Herzigova.
Download a Ferrari!
PUBLICATIONS
AOL News Profiles
WebCrawler Search: Newspapers
@times/The New York Times
ABC News InFocus
Air Force Times
American Astrology
American Woodworker
Arizona Republic
Newsweek Interactive
Critics' Choice
Worth Online
Business Week
New York Times
What's Hot on the Web!
AOL CHANNELS
MEMBER SERVICES
FIND
Keyword: Newsstand

Figure 10-9: The Newsstand gathers all of AOL's online magazines into one central location—use the keyword: **Newsstand** to get there.

Your Personal News Agent

AOL's Personal News Profiles feature (it appears at the top of The Newsstand list box) is manna for news junkies. Personal News Profiles allow you to specify the kinds of news stories that interest you. Once you've done that, your own personal news "agent" reads every story, looking for the words and phrases you have specified. Those stories that meet your criteria—and the criteria can be quite specific—are then sent to you as e-mail, as soon as the stories become available.

Be sure to take advantage of this feature, but *read the instructions carefully* before you do: left to its own devices, a news agent can find an unimaginable amount of news that can overwhelm your mailbox (not to mention your mind) with everything from the Aaland Islands to zygzyva.

Though we discussed a few of AOL's computer-oriented magazines in Chapter 7, "Computing," there are scores of other entries available from the Newsstand (see Figure 10-10). However you use your computer at home, you'll find these publications have lots to offer.

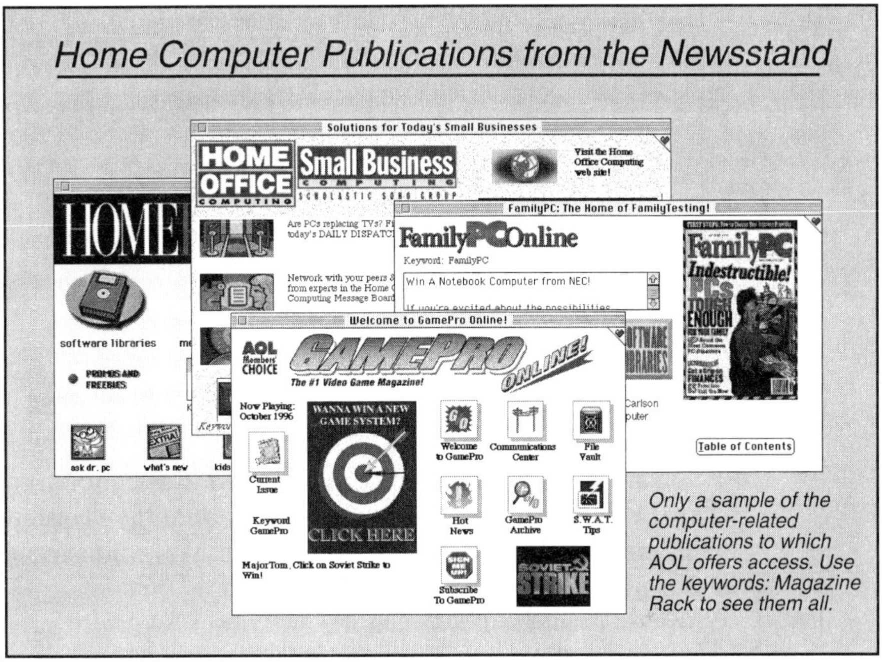
Home Computer Publications from the Newsstand
Solutions for Today's Small Businesses
HOME OFFICE
Small Business
FamilyPC: The Home of FamilyTesting!
FamilyPCOnline
Keyword: FamilyPC
Win A Notebook Computer from NEC!
HOME
software libraries
PROMOS AND FREEBIES
ask dr. pc
what's new
Welcome to GamePro Online!
AOL Members' CHOICE
GAMEPRO ONLINE!
The #1 Video Game Magazine!
Now Playing: October 1996
WANNA WIN A NEW GAME SYSTEM?
CLICK HERE
Current Issue
Keyword GamePro
Welcome to GamePro
Communications Center
File Vault
Hot News
GamePro Archive
S.W.A.T. Tips
Subscribe To GamePro
SOVIET STRIKE
Table of Contents
Only a sample of the computer-related publications to which AOL offers access. Use the keywords: Magazine Rack to see them all.

Figure 10-10: Games, resources, contests, troubleshooting, message boards, hardware and software reviews—diverse features chosen to address the diverse interests of home computer users.

By now you may be wondering if any of your old print media favorites have made the leap to online publication. They probably have: most major magazines are already publishing online, and more are joining the list every week. We'll discuss two of them below.

Business Week

September 7, 1929: Volume 1, Number 1 of *Business Week* magazine appeared on the shelves, just in time to forewarn its readers of "dangerous overheating" in the stock market. On October 29—only a few weeks later—*Business Week*'s prophecy became an infamous entry in the history books, and the Great Depression began.

An auspicious beginning for the world's largest business magazine, which has been pointing the way for business and financial leaders ever since. *Business Week* is available online—not only the domestic edition but international editions as well. And not only the current issue but issues dating back to January 1994.

Beyond news. Intelligence
BusinessWeek ONLINE
Keyword: BW
BusinessWeek
JACK'S ENCORE
Click image for BW Contents
One More Time
GE's Jack Welch is on another crusade. His new goal: Creating a services powerhouse
Life after 6000
Can this market rocket keep climbing? Most of the numbers suggest that it can
Soviet H-Bomb Secrets
Now revealed: Everything from Stalin's role in key decisions to the horrid factory conditions
TALK & CONFERENCES
OFFERS & INFO
SEARCH & DOWNLOADS
HOT PICKS
BW PLUS!
ABOUT BW ONLINE

Figure 10-11: Each Thursday night, Business Week Online uploads all of its domestic and international editions, hours before the magazine hits newsstands on Friday. It's all available at keyword: **BW**.

Naturally, the text and some selected illustrations from the magazine are available online, but you can also attend live conferences with *Business Week* editors and newsmakers. You can learn all about the Best Business Schools (including how to apply, in some cases electronically); browse Business Books Online and order books through the Bookstore; search the Business Week Online Corporate Directory (which lists the names and addresses of *Business Week* 1000 companies and is only available online); and, as you might expect, search the magazine's archives for the electronic text of stories you want to review or might have missed.

How Sweet It Is

In the cover story for the January 8, 1996, issue of *Business Week*, Steve Jobs, cofounder of Apple Computer, was mentioned as an entrepreneur of the year. Anyone who follows Steve's journeys might wonder what qualified him for such a prestigious honor: he has been trying to come up with a second hit (after he left Apple) for a decade, after all. If you've followed Steve's career *very* carefully (or if you read *Business Week*), however, you're aware that in late November of 1995, Steve's company, Pixar Animation Studios, makers of the smash hit movie *Toy Story* (see Figure 10-12), went public with a bang. The stock, priced at 22, zoomed to 49, and Jobs's 80 percent stake was briefly worth $1.1 billion—yes, that's a "b." What's next? His other company, NeXT, is making software for the World Wide Web, and Jobs may have profited from his third public offering by the time you read this.

Figure 10-12: For a brief period in late 1995, Pixar's *Toy Story* put Steve Jobs on the billionaire list. (I found this graphic in Business Week Online's file libraries.)

Business Week Online is a trove of multimedia treasures—indeed, the variety of material offered here is unique in the online medium (and most certainly not available via the printed version of the magazine). Not only will you find audio and video clips but also HTML scripts (for viewing World Wide Web pages associated with *Business Week* stories) and Adobe Acrobat documents, featuring searchable and printable magazine-like presentations, complete with photos and charts. To look them over, use the keyword: **BW**, then click the button labeled Search & Downloads. Look in the Downloads window that appears for file libraries with names like HTML Files and Audio & Video Files.

@times

Business Week isn't the only place for contemporary multimedia, however. @times—the *New York Times* online area—is just as splendid, especially since its redesign in late 1995. If you're like me, and Sunday morning simply isn't Sunday morning to you unless you have a copy of the Sunday *Times*, you're going to gravitate toward @times.

One of the great strengths of the *Times* is its cultural coverage and criticism. For decades, readers have relied on the *Times* critics for guidance in choosing everything from books to videos. Now, with @times, thousands of *Times* reviews—movies, videos, books—are available in one place (see Figure 10-13).

Welcome to The New York Times Online
AOL Members' CHOICE
@times
The New York Times
LATE NEWS: 1 P.M. Update
CAMPAIGN AUDITORIUM: Alex Jones, Monday 8 PM ET
POLITICS '96: Rival Camps in Final Debate Faced Subtle and
WEEK IN REVIEW: A Missing Issue in the Big Race
OP-ED & EDITORIALS: Anthony Lewis, Bob Herbert, A.M. Ros
SCIENCE TIMES: A Direct Link Between Smoking and Lung
HOME & LIVING: Giving Birth to Family Reunions
Today's News
@times Index
Message Boards
Classified Ads
Computers & Technology
Arts & Entertainment
Politics '96

Figure 10-13: @times offers, among other things, the crème de la crème of the *New York Times*: its entertainment and arts features. To get there in a hurry, use the keyword: **@times**.

Look for the *New York Times* Best Seller List here, along with the *Times* weekday book, video, and movie reviews. @times also features the top international and domestic news, business, and sports stories. These stories appear before they're printed in the paper: articles from the next day's newspaper begin appearing after 11 P.M. Sunday through Friday, and after 9 P.M. Saturday.

The New Republic

I'll describe one more venerable publishing giant, but there are many more, especially the special-interest magazines. Be sure to investigate them all at keyword: **Newsstand**.

At the 1994 National Magazines Awards—where the *New Republic* magazine was presented with the General Excellence award—the judges said: ". . . every issue is informed by a muscular intelligence that makes you keep reading no matter how tough or familiar the subject. In a period of intense concern with the direction of American politics and policy . . . the *New Republic* offers lucid analysis, sophisticated reporting, and the zest of a good argument. . . ."

These accolades refer primarily to the *New Republic*'s in-house staff. There are plenty of other contributors to the magazine, including Vice President Gore, Norman Mailer, John Updike, Gail Sheehy, and Naomi Wolf.

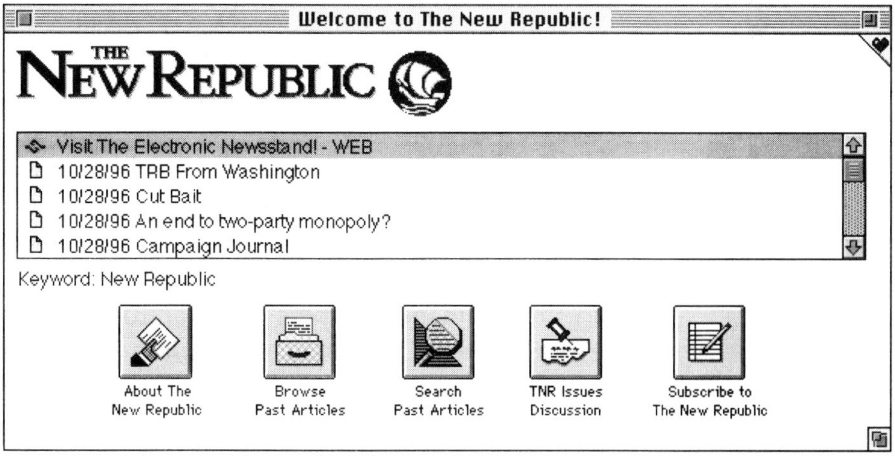
Welcome to The New Republic!
THE NEW REPUBLIC
Visit The Electronic Newsstand! - WEB
10/28/96 TRB From Washington
10/28/96 Cut Bait
10/28/96 An end to two-party monopoly?
10/28/96 Campaign Journal
Keyword: New Republic
About The New Republic
Browse Past Articles
Search Past Articles
TNR Issues Discussion
Subscribe to The New Republic

Figure 10-14: Some of the most sagacious insights into our culture are available when you use the keywords: **New Republic**.

Who reads the *New Republic*? The list is a Who's Who of America: Bill and Hillary Clinton, Les Aspin, Bob Dole, David Geffen, Mitch Kapor, Yo-Yo Ma, Richard Dreyfuss, Ted Koppel, Diane Sawyer, and Rush Limbaugh, among others. You should be reading it too, and you can—not only the current issue but past issues as well—by using the keywords: **New Republic**.

Other Sources

There are scores of online versions of print publications in the Newsstand. Some—such as Bicycling Magazine, Car & Driver, Cycle World, Flying Magazine, and Stereo Review—cater to specific interests. Others—such as American Woodworker, DC Comics Online, Nintendo Power Source, and Popular Photography—cater to the hobbyist. Others serve more general needs. Among the general-interest publications you'll find online are Smithsonian, WIRED (mentioned in Chapter 4, "Using the Internet"), Atlantic Monthly, Worth, and many others that might appeal to you. This place is a quarry of priceless literary nuggets, and you pay nothing extra for access to it.

Digital Cities

Times have changed. Though paper grows on trees, as a society we've discovered that trees don't necessarily grow at the rate at which we use paper. Every form of paper-based media, from catalogs to postcards, has felt the pinch, and the pressure is unrelenting. Just a few months ago, *OMNI* magazine was forced to cease publication due to rises in the cost of paper. Others are following.

The medium that has most painfully felt the increasing cost of paper, however, is the newspaper. Once the parapet of timely information, newspapers are suffering not only from escalating costs but from the superior immediacy of electronic media as well.

On the other hand, newspapers are local. In most markets, their coverage can't be beat. To many communities, losing its newspaper is like losing the community itself.

A savior has emerged, in the form of the online medium. The almost insignificant cost of the medium itself is a boon to financially strapped local news operations, and access is rapidly becoming commonplace. The medium offers a rich blend of not only print and graphics but sound and video as well. And if you please, it can be printed. Reader's choice. It's no wonder that in the past year, over a dozen newspapers in major markets around the country have gone online. In fact, the potential is so rich that AOL has created a new channel for them: Digital Cities. In this section I'll discuss just one, but you should investigate them all. Click the Digital Cities button in the Channel window to find the Digital City nearest you.

Digital City Chicago

When I first visited AOL's headquarters, the staff was particularly optimistic about a newly launched service called Chicago Online. At that time, Chicago Online represented two significant innovations that made the inauguration of the Newsstand auspicious and that today offer a glimpse into the future of online journalism.

First, Chicago Online is a stand-alone municipal communications service—a parochial service, optimized for the people of Chicago, by the people of Chicago. It has its own message boards, chat rooms, news, sports, and weather (plenty of the latter, actually). In a way, Chicago Online is like a local newspaper. The nation has *USA Today* and the *Wall Street Journal*, and Chicago has the *Chicago Tribune*. The nation has AOL and Chicago has Chicago Online. Neither precludes the other. Nearly every community in the country has its own newspaper; we might someday all have our own little online areas as well. After all, local communications channels are as much a part of the community as national ones. America Online knows that, and that's why it tested the waters with Chicago Online (see Figure 10-15).

The test was a success. Chicago Online is now Digital City Chicago. For additional evidence of the potential of this alliance, visit the Digital City Channel, at keywords: **Digital City.**

Digital City Chicago
Chat/Forums
Index
Feedback
What's Hot
DIGITAL CITY
CHICAGO
A service of the Chicago Tribune
Welcome to the new Digital City Chicago, where you'll find news, practical guides and local chat. Click What's Hot.
Crains
Will Walgreen's kick the habit?
Bernardin stops cancer care
Order Bulls vs. Trailblazers
click here to
Bank Online
with
first chicago.online
News
Weather, Traffic
Sports
Entertainment
Visiting Chicago
Community
Marketplace
Keyword: Chicago

Figure 10-15: Digital City Chicago offers a tantalizing glimpse of future telecommunications, as well as a banquet of sustenance for the online appetite.

Digital City Chicago also is a *strategic alliance*. The service is the product of an alliance between the *Chicago Tribune* and AOL. The *Tribune* gains a communications channel that's significantly more bilateral (and less costly) than a daily newspaper, and AOL gets a test bed for another avenue in the electronic community. Perhaps best of all, we all get to observe the formative moments of a new communications medium. Ecologically speaking, the "electronic newspaper" (or something like it) will become increasingly appropriate, and through this alliance two of the most progressive representatives of the electronic and print media are exploring its potential. There's lots of hope here, for all of us.

But enough existentialism. The *Chicago Tribune* is no lightweight when it comes to information, after all. There's a wealth of practical information for us outlanders. Check out Gene Siskel's Flick Picks (as well as reviews by Dave Kehr, Roy Leonard, and Sherman Kaplan). Take a look at Ed Curran's Technogadgets and the Chicago Tribune Cookbook Online. Digital City Chicago isn't a half-hearted experiment in alternative media; it's a mature, expansive, and resourceful communications medium. Give it a half-hour of your time. It will reward you eloquently.

Sports

Back in the old days, football was played in the mud by men in leather helmets, boxing was gloveless and bloody, and families went to baseball games on Sunday afternoons.

Those, of course, were the days before TV and the couch potato. Until recently, sports had become a solitary activity, practiced by supine sluggards in dark living rooms brandishing TV remotes and dissipative bowls of Cheetos.

I'm happy to report that sports have again become interactive, team-oriented activities. Oh, there's still the glow of a cathode-ray tube in the living room on Sunday afternoons, but it's probably displaying AOL now, and the gamester at the controls is enlightened, participatory, and fraternal.

Once again, the nation can be proud of its pastime.

Sports News

The sports fan who clicks the In Depth button in the Sports mini-headline window at the top right of the Today's News main menu (see Figure 10-1, or use the keywords: **Sports News**) enters a sports news area that has few peers (see Figure 10-16).

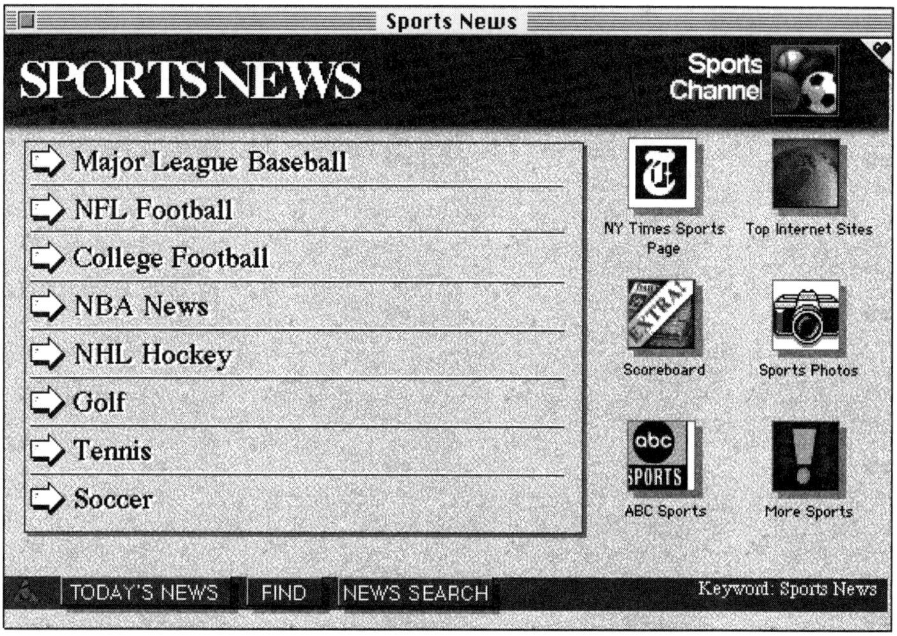
Sports News
SPORTS NEWS
Sports Channel
Major League Baseball
NFL Football
College Football
NBA News
NHL Hockey
Golf
Tennis
Soccer
NY Times Sports Page
Top Internet Sites
Scoreboard
Sports Photos
ABC Sports
More Sports
TODAY'S NEWS
FIND
NEWS SEARCH
Keyword: Sports News

Figure 10-16: Sports News offers not only the top stories but routes to the sports discussion boards, sports scoreboards, and various topical sports news areas as well.

It's not surprising that America Online's Sports News is organized like AOL's other news areas; AOL's method is the fastest way for you, the user, to find what you want. And once you've learned how to look for news in one news channel, you'll find the same information structure in any other channel, whether it be Politics, Business, Sports, life.style, or Weather.

You can browse headlines in the Sports News window, click the category arrows to display stories in other categories, double-click storylines to read stories, and use the button at the right on the Sports News main window to explore stories further. It's really pretty simple.

The Sports Channel

There's a lot more to sports than news, however. Look again at Figure 10-16. The button near the top right is labeled "Sports Channel." This is your pathway to the AOL Sports Channel's main window (see Figure 10-17), where you'll find a broad array of sports information, services, products, message boards, and interest groups. You can also go directly to the Sports Channel from anywhere in AOL by using the keyword: **Sports**.

Once you've arrived at the Sports Channel, AOL makes it just as easy for you to return to the Sports News window.

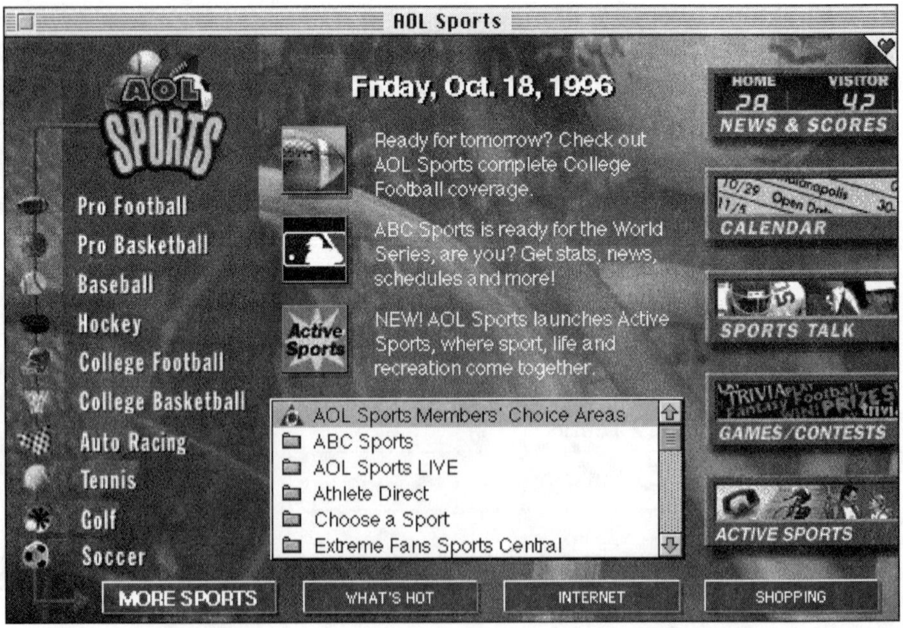
AOL Sports
Friday, Oct. 18, 1996
Ready for tomorrow? Check out AOL Sports complete College Football coverage.
ABC Sports is ready for the World Series, are you? Get stats, news, schedules and more!
NEW! AOL Sports launches Active Sports, where sport, life and recreation come together.
Pro Football
Pro Basketball
Baseball
Hockey
College Football
College Basketball
Auto Racing
Tennis
Golf
Soccer
AOL Sports Members' Choice Areas
ABC Sports
AOL Sports LIVE
Athlete Direct
Choose a Sport
Extreme Fans Sports Central
NEWS & SCORES
CALENDAR
SPORTS TALK
GAMES/CONTESTS
ACTIVE SPORTS
MORE SPORTS
WHAT'S HOT
INTERNET
SHOPPING

Figure 10-17: Use the keyword: **Sports** to access the top level of AOL's Sports Channel.

If you've come to the Sports Channel windows to browse a specific sport, click the sport of your choice from the list at the left of the window to go directly to that sport's area. If you don't see the one you want, just click the More Sports link. Odds are, your game's in here somewhere. On the other hand, if you're not in the mood for browsing and you'd like to explore a specific Sports News story, the best strategy is to use the button in the Sports News window to search. It's just a mouse click away.

So far in this chapter, I've written only about News. The introduction of the Sports Channel has broadened our discussion, and some clarification is in order. To better understand how Sports News is related to the Sports Channel, think of Sports News as a fast-flowing river of information; then think of the Sports Channel as a great lake into which the river pours. But read on. As you'll see, AOL's sports arena is very large indeed.

ABC Sports

If you were AOL and you wanted a sports channel that honored the medium and the members, you probably wouldn't start from scratch. Starting from scratch would necessitate crews of photographers and reporters at all of the key games; libraries of knowledge, images, and videos; and armies of staff members and consultants.

No, if you were AOL and you wanted to do the job properly, you'd seek the largest sports organization in the country and form a partnership with them. You would do what you do best—offer a medium and expertise in its use—and allow your partner to do what it does best: event coverage and analysis. AOL has such a partner, and the partner, of course, is ABC Sports (see Figure 10-18).

ABC Sports Online
abc
SPORTS
All Star Game Tonight! Get All The Info In the OFFICIAL MLB AREA!
WHAT A GAME.
CLICK
QB's Troy Aikman & Dan Marino LIVE 10/22 @ 9PM!
WWOS Online
Span the Globe Online, with Figure Skating & Women's Sports!
ABC MNF
Dan Dierdorf previews the Raiders&Chargers! Click here for more!
College Football
Read Announcer Brian Holloway's Latest From the Pit!
ESPN & ESPNET
Miss the Big Show? No sweat, we GAT IT right here!
TEAM NFL
Inside Scoops, Stats, Breakdowns, Join the OFFICIAL TEAM!
ABC Track
Get Handicapper's Edge Daily only on the ABC Track!
Stuff
Scores
Store
Chat
Inside
Live
ABC SOAPS
ABC NEWS
ABC KIDZ
TEST TUBE
ABC TV

Figure 10-18: ABC Sports is the nation's venerable sports authority, and its partnership with America Online spells nothing but enrichment for the membership.

Depending on the season, ABC Sports offers major league baseball, the National Hockey League, Monday Night Football—even thoroughbred racing! Figure 10-18's All Star Game button, for example, leads to comprehensive background information for the upcoming game, graphics of key players, biographies, statistics—enough data to make any couch potato a savant among supplicants.

The Grandstand

If you enjoy sports, you'll love the Grandstand (use the keyword: **Grandstand**; it's the most effective way of getting there). America Online's homage to the sports enthusiast is current, relevant, and vast (see Figure 10-20). In the interest of sports widows everywhere, however, I suggest moderation. The walls of prehistoric caves the world over are covered with pictographs of smashed keyboards and fractured computer screens. It's not a pretty sight.

Behind the Scenes

For the broadcast of the 1995 Kentucky Derby, ABC used no fewer than 26 cameras, including its unmanned "cablecam" at trackside (the one that races down the backstretch alongside the horses), miniature cameras on the starting gates, and its trademark airborne camera aboard a hovering blimp.

Figure 10-19: One of ABC's 26 cameras at the 1995 Kentucky Derby.

Details such as this are rife in the ABC Sports area (which is where I found the camera information): just look for "Behind the Scenes" buttons.

Figure 10-20: The Grandstand offers something for every sports enthusiast.

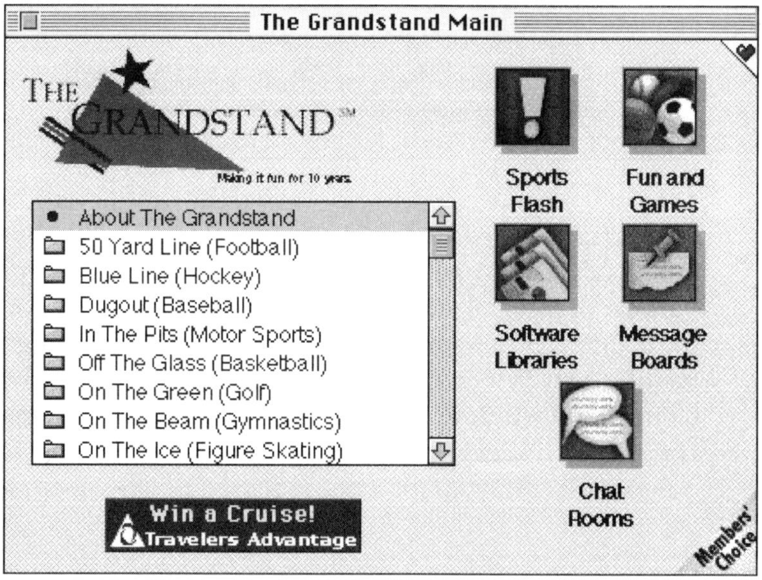
The Grandstand Main
THE GRANDSTAND℠
Making it fun for 10 years.
About The Grandstand
50 Yard Line (Football)
Blue Line (Hockey)
Dugout (Baseball)
In The Pits (Motor Sports)
Off The Glass (Basketball)
On The Green (Golf)
On The Beam (Gymnastics)
On The Ice (Figure Skating)
Sports Flash
Fun and Games
Software Libraries
Message Boards
Chat Rooms
Win a Cruise! Travelers Advantage
Members' Choice

While investigating the Grandstand the other day, I found scores of graphics uploaded to AOL by members and organizations (see Figure 10-21). I even discovered an online club dedicated entirely to baseball cards. It provides news, price polls, and conferences for card collectors throughout the nation.

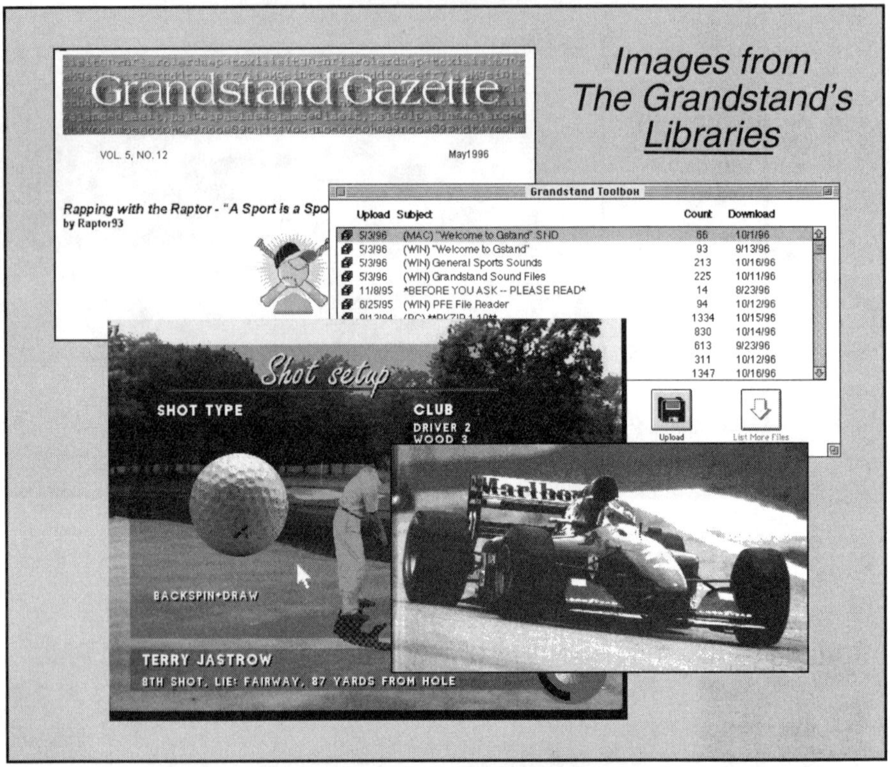
Images from
The Grandstand's
Libraries
Grandstand Gazette
VOL. 5, NO. 12
May1996
Rapping with the Raptor - "A Sport is a Spo
by Raptor93
Grandstand Toolbox
Upload Subject Count Download
5/3/96 (MAC) "Welcome to Gstand" SND 66 10/1/96
5/3/96 (WIN) "Welcome to Gstand" 93 9/13/96
5/3/96 (WIN) General Sports Sounds 213 10/16/96
5/3/96 (WIN) Grandstand Sound Files 225 10/11/96
11/8/95 *BEFORE YOU ASK -- PLEASE READ* 14 8/23/96
6/25/95 (WIN) PFE File Reader 94 10/12/96
Upload
List More Files
Shot setup
SHOT TYPE
CLUB
DRIVER 2
WOOD 3
BACKSPIN+DRAW
TERRY JASTROW
8TH SHOT, LIE: FAIRWAY, 87 YARDS FROM HOLE

Figure 10-21: A quick browse through the Grandstand turns up a picture of a Ferrari 412 T1 uploaded by Nigel Mans, a screen capture from an about-to-be-released golf game from Accolade, the Grandstand Gazette, and the Grandstand Toolbox window, a treasure of downloadable sound and video programs to let you access all that the Sports Channel has to offer.

Sports fans like to talk about their interests with other sports fans. Sports talk is especially rewarding when it's with people who are outside your usual circle of acquaintances—who live, in fact, all over the country. If this sounds appealing, consider visiting the message boards. Just click on the Sports Boards icon on the right side of the Grandstand window, or open the folder of the sport that interests you (see Figure 10-22).

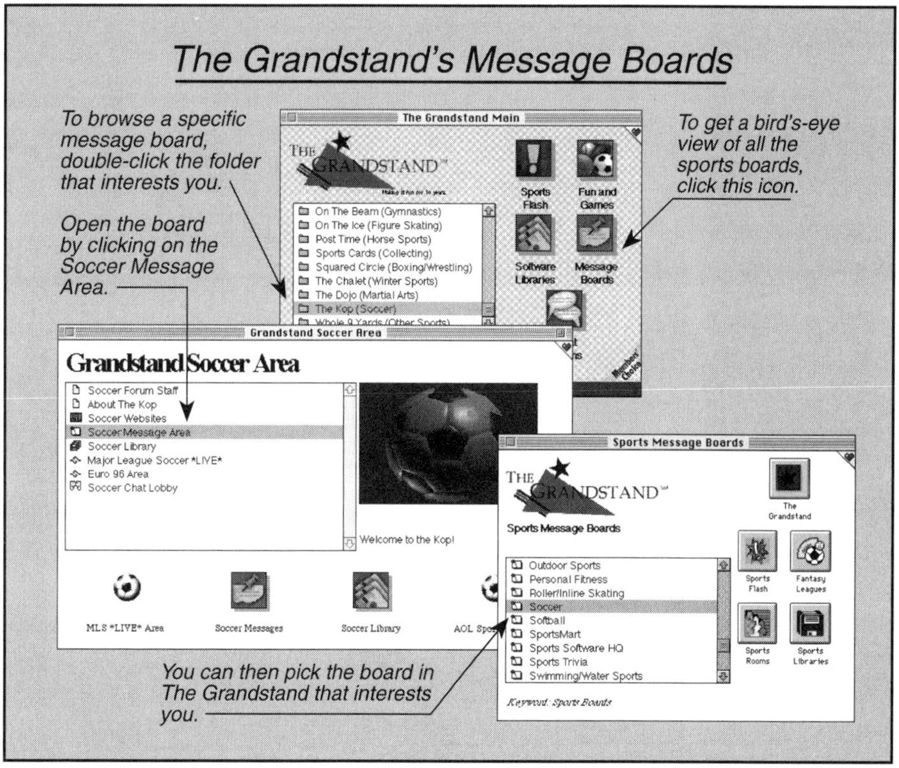
The Grandstand's Message Boards
To browse a specific message board, double-click the folder that interests you.
Open the board by clicking on the Soccer Message Area.
To get a bird's-eye view of all the sports boards, click this icon.
You can then pick the board in The Grandstand that interests you.
The Grandstand Main
On The Beam (Gymnastics)
On The Ice (Figure Skating)
Post Time (Horse Sports)
Sports Cards (Collecting)
Squared Circle (Boxing/Wrestling)
The Chalet (Winter Sports)
The Dojo (Martial Arts)
The Kop (Soccer)
Sports Flash
Fun and Games
Software Libraries
Message Boards
Grandstand Soccer Area
Soccer Forum Staff
About The Kop
Soccer Websites
Soccer Message Area
Soccer Library
Major League Soccer *LIVE*
Euro 96 Area
Soccer Chat Lobby
Welcome to the Kop!
MLS *LIVE* Area
Soccer Messages
Soccer Library
Sports Message Boards
Outdoor Sports
Personal Fitness
Roller/Inline Skating
Soccer
Softball
SportsMart
Sports Software HQ
Sports Trivia
Swimming/Water Sports
The Grandstand
Sports Flash
Fantasy Leagues
Sports Rooms
Sports Libraries
Keyword: Sports Boards

Figure 10-22: Browse your favorite sport's message board or take in all the boards. Either way, you'll find a wealth of information.

Messages on the sports boards are diverse and occasionally unexpected. Consider the thread of messages I found on the hockey board (pictured in Figure 10-23). It's great to see unbridled appreciation.

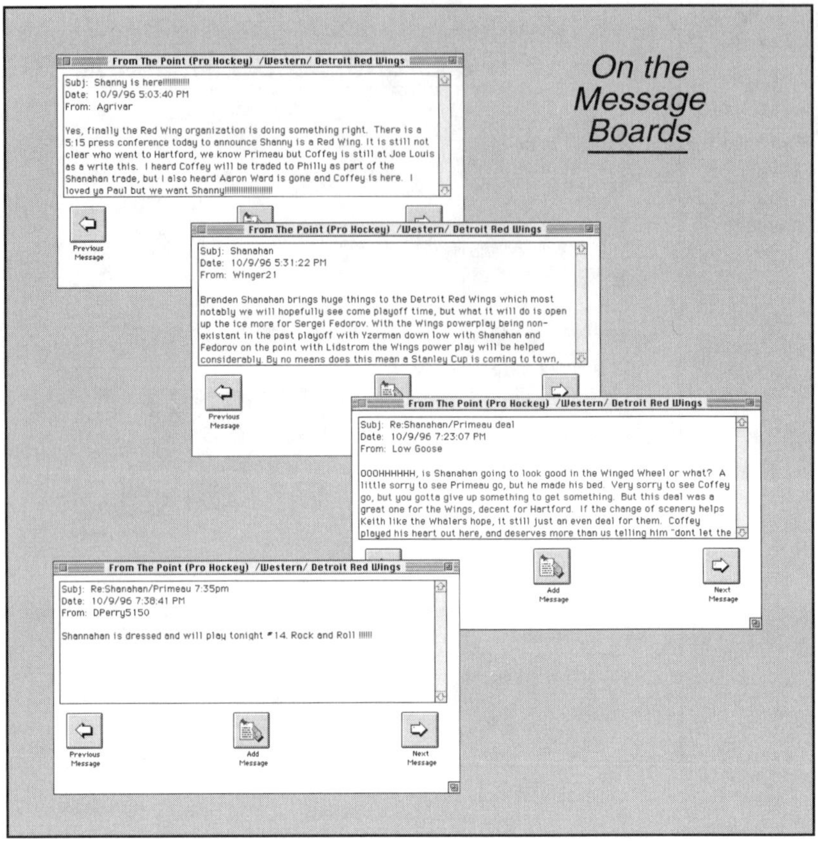
On the Message Boards
From The Point (Pro Hockey) /Western/ Detroit Red Wings
Subj: Shanny is here!!!!!!!!!!!!
Date: 10/9/96 5:03:40 PM
From: Agrivar
Yes, finally the Red Wing organization is doing something right. There is a 5:15 press conference today to announce Shanny is a Red Wing. It is still not clear who went to Hartford, we know Primeau but Coffey is still at Joe Louis as a write this. I heard Coffey will be traded to Philly as part of the Shanahan trade, but I also heard Aaron Ward is gone and Coffey is here. I loved ya Paul but we want Shanny!!!!!!!!!!!!!!!!!!!!
Previous Message
From The Point (Pro Hockey) /Western/ Detroit Red Wings
Subj: Shanahan
Date: 10/9/96 5:31:22 PM
From: Winger21
Brenden Shanahan brings huge things to the Detroit Red Wings which most notably we will hopefully see come playoff time, but what it will do is open up the ice more for Sergei Fedorov. With the Wings powerplay being non-existant in the past playoff with Yzerman down low with Shanahan and Fedorov on the point with Lidstrom the Wings power play will be helped considerably. By no means does this mean a Stanley Cup is coming to town,
Previous Message
From The Point (Pro Hockey) /Western/ Detroit Red Wings
Subj: Re:Shanahan/Primeau deal
Date: 10/9/96 7:23:07 PM
From: Low Goose
OOOHHHHHH, is Shanahan going to look good in the Winged Wheel or what? A little sorry to see Primeau go, but he made his bed. Very sorry to see Coffey go, but you gotta give up something to get something. But this deal was a great one for the Wings, decent for Hartford. If the change of scenery helps Keith like the Whalers hope, it still just an even deal for them. Coffey played his heart out here, and deserves more than us telling him "dont let the
Add Message
Next Message
From The Point (Pro Hockey) /Western/ Detroit Red Wings
Subj: Re:Shanahan/Primeau 7:35pm
Date: 10/9/96 7:38:41 PM
From: DPerry5150
Shannahan is dressed and will play tonight #14. Rock and Roll !!!!!!
Previous Message
Add Message
Next Message

Figure 10-23: A slice of online camaraderie.

Message boards are wonderful things, but it takes some learning to use them effectively. You can find more about using them in Chapter 9, "Boards & Forums."

Perhaps the most interesting aspect of the Grandstand is its assortment of fantasy teams assembled by members—make-believe teams made up of real players in the sport. The Grandstand Fantasy Baseball League (GFBL), for example, is modeled after "Rotisserie League Baseball," as described in the book of the same name by Glen Waggoner (Bantam Books). Team owners (that's us—the members of AOL) draft 23 players from the available talent in the American or National Leagues. The players' actual big-league performances are used in computing the standings of the GFBL team. Standings, stats, newsletters, and other league information items are found in the message and library sections of the GFBL (see Figure 10-24), and members follow them fanatically. Double-click any of the folders in the scroll box of the Grandstand's main window to access the leagues.

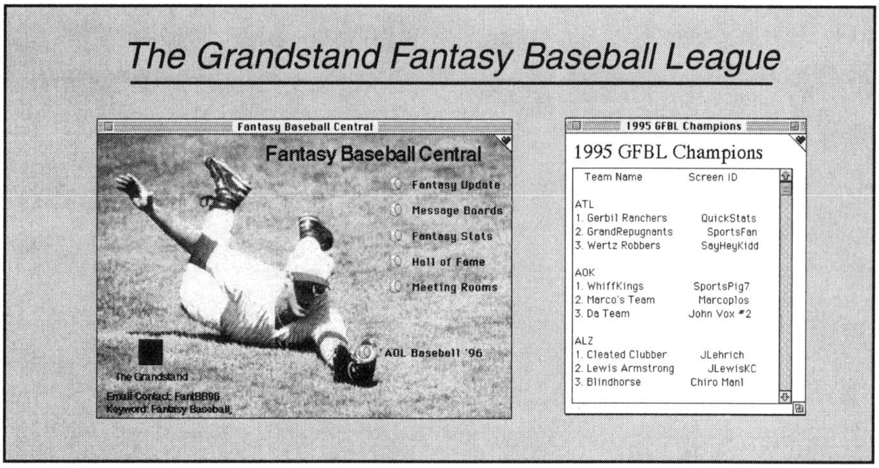
The Grandstand Fantasy Baseball League
Fantasy Baseball Central
Fantasy Update
Message Boards
Fantasy Stats
Hall of Fame
Meeting Rooms
AOL Baseball '96
The Grandstand
1995 GFBL Champions
Team Name Screen ID
ATL
1. Gerbil Ranchers QuickStats
2. GrandRepugnants SportsFan
3. Wertz Robbers SayHeyKidd
AOK
1. WhiffKings SportsPig7
2. Marco's Team Marcoplos
3. Da Team John Vox #2
ALZ
1. Cleated Clubber JLehrich
2. Lewis Armstrong JLewisKC
3. Blindhorse Chiro Man!

Figure 10-24: The GFBL window, and the 1995 GFBL Champions.

Special Coverage

Without the restrictions imposed by commercial broadcast, America Online is free to devote as many resources as necessary to the appropriate coverage of not only the major but the not-so-major sporting events as well. AOL goes beyond the "who and what" to provide in-depth answers to the "why and how" of the U.S. Olympic Festival, U.S. Open Tennis, and Wimbledon, to name a few. You'll find extensive background information from a variety of sources, graphics and sounds, Web pages, and message boards, for a free exchange of knowledge and opinions with other members (see Figure 10-25).

Figure 10-25: The college football games are about to get under way as I prepare this chapter, and look at all of the stuff AOL has to offer!

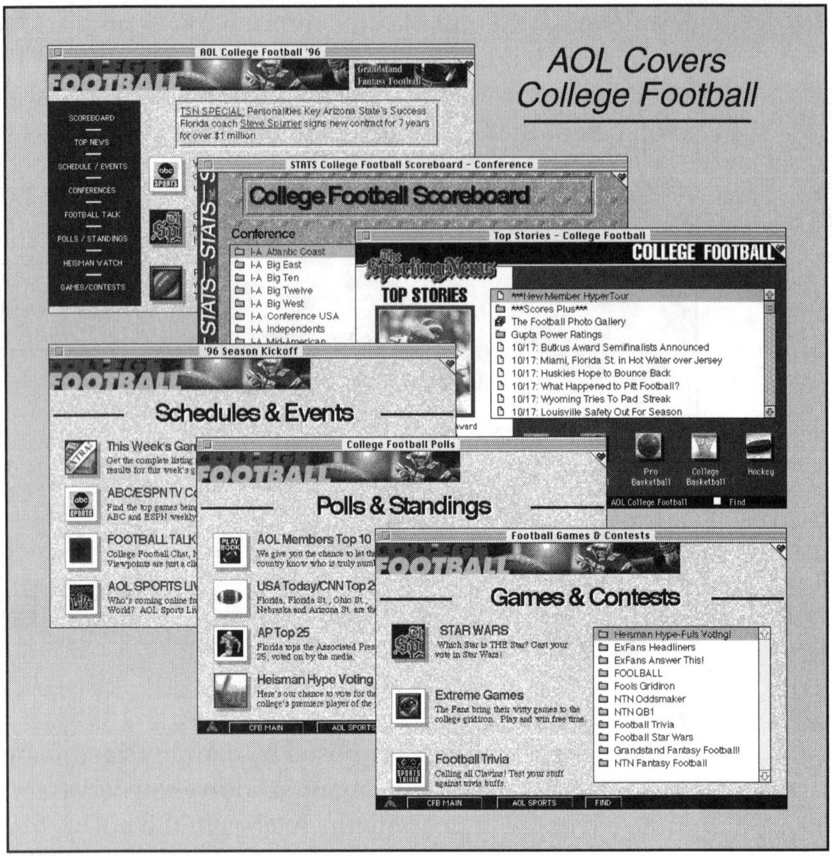
AOL Covers College Football
AOL College Football '96
SCOREBOARD
TOP NEWS
SCHEDULE / EVENTS
CONFERENCES
FOOTBALL TALK
POLLS / STANDINGS
HEISMAN WATCH
GAMES/CONTESTS
TSN SPECIAL: Personalities Key Arizona State's Success
Florida coach Steve Spurrier signs new contract for 7 years for over $1 million
STATS College Football Scoreboard - Conference
College Football Scoreboard
Conference
I-A Atlantic Coast
I-A Big East
I-A Big Ten
I-A Big Twelve
I-A Big West
I-A Conference USA
I-A Independents
Top Stories - College Football
COLLEGE FOOTBALL
TOP STORIES
***New Member HyperTour
Scores Plus
The Football Photo Gallery
Gupta Power Ratings
10/17: Butkus Award Semifinalists Announced
10/17: Miami, Florida St. in Hot Water over Jersey
10/17: Huskies Hope to Bounce Back
10/17: What Happened to Pitt Football?
10/17: Wyoming Tries To Pad Streak
10/17: Louisville Safety Out For Season
Pro Basketball
College Basketball
Hockey
'96 Season Kickoff
Schedules & Events
This Week's Gan
ABC/ESPN TV C
FOOTBALL TALK
AOL SPORTS LI
College Football Polls
Polls & Standings
AOL Members Top 10
USA Today/CNN Top 2
AP Top 25
Heisman Hype Voting
CFB MAIN
AOL SPORTS
Football Games & Contests
Games & Contests
STAR WARS
Which Star is THE Star? Cast your vote in Star Wars!
Extreme Games
Football Trivia
Calling all Clavins! Test your stuff against trivia buffs.
Heisman Hype-Fuls Voting!
ExFans Headliners
ExFans Answer This!
FOOLBALL
Fools Gridiron
NTN Oddsmaker
NTN QB1
Football Trivia
Football Star Wars
Grandstand Fantasy Football!
NTN Fantasy Football
FIND

The Online Pace of Change

The Sports Channel, as well as many other areas on AOL, has undergone significant change during the last few months, so if it's been a while since you visited here, give it a try and see all that's been added. (And don't be surprised if something on your screen looks a little different than it appears in this book—AOL can change quickly. That is, after all, the beauty of this medium.)

Weather

Naturally, AOL is brimming with weather information. This is where the online medium really excels. America Online's weather is not only always up to the minute, it's also graphic and colorful.

The primary Weather window (see Figure 10-26) offers access to the day's weather news (check here before traveling or when the weather is particularly interesting or threatening), forecasts (updated continuously and organized by state), and boards (lots of experts hang out here; post questions freely). It also offers a route to the color weather maps. And that's where the fun begins.

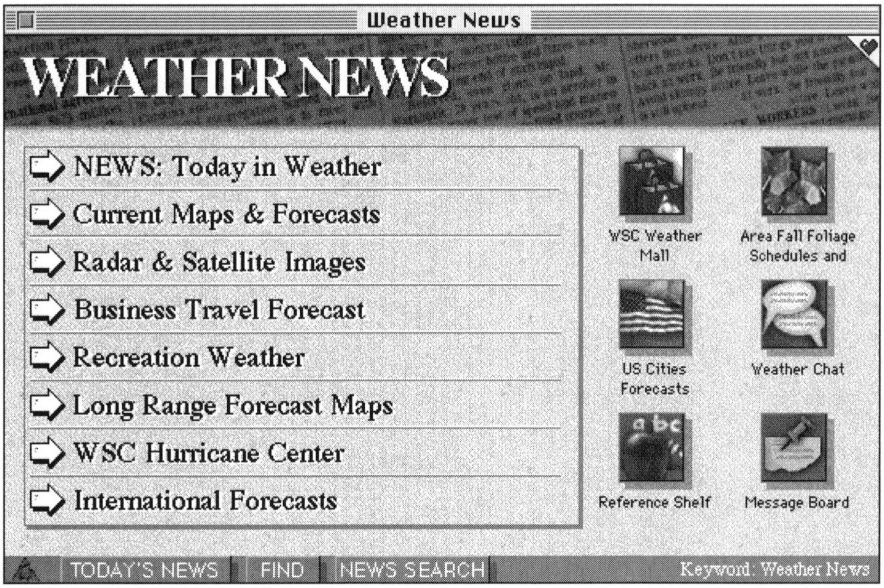
Weather News
WEATHER NEWS
NEWS: Today in Weather
Current Maps & Forecasts
Radar & Satellite Images
Business Travel Forecast
Recreation Weather
Long Range Forecast Maps
WSC Hurricane Center
International Forecasts
WSC Weather Mall
Area Fall Foliage Schedules and
US Cities Forecasts
Weather Chat
Reference Shelf
Message Board
TODAY'S NEWS
FIND
NEWS SEARCH
Keyword: Weather News

Figure 10-26: America Online's primary Weather window offers a wealth of current weather information, including maps.

The maps are from Weather Services Corporation, which provides forecasting and consultation services for *USA Today*, among others. Those colorful weather maps on the back page of *USA Today* are derived from the same data that's available on AOL when you use the keyword: **Weather**.

The precipitation, jet stream, and tropical outlook maps are released between 10 a.m. and 11 a.m. Eastern time each day; the temperature bands for the next day will be available between 6 p.m. and 7 p.m. (see Figure 10-27).

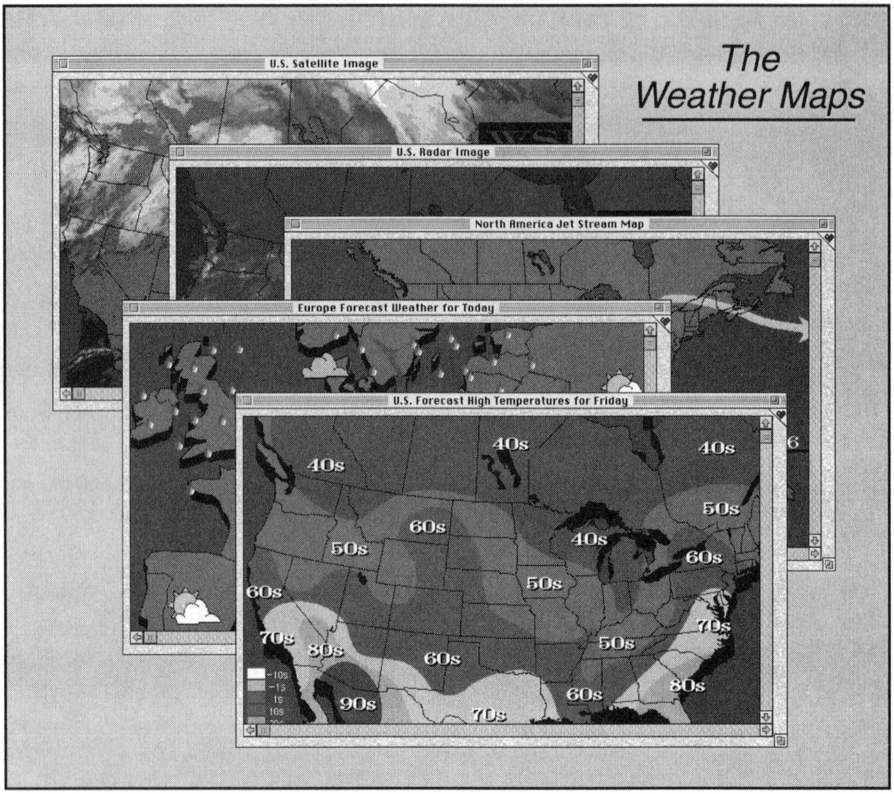
The Weather Maps
U.S. Satellite Image
U.S. Radar Image
North America Jet Stream Map
Europe Forecast Weather for Today
U.S. Forecast High Temperatures for Friday
40s
40s
40s
50s
60s
40s
50s
60s
60s
50s
70s
70s
80s
60s
50s
80s
90s
60s
70s

Figure 10-27: You'll have to imagine it here, but each of these maps is displayed in 16 colors and downloads in less than a minute. To get to them quickly, use the keyword: **Weather** and double-click on Current Maps and Forecasts (or one of the several other weather areas available).

You don't need special software to view these maps: simply double-click any listing, read the description if you wish, then click the Download Now button. If you're using Version 2.5 (or a later version) of the AOL software, the maps will be displayed onscreen as they're downloaded. None of them takes more than a minute to download at 9600 baud; they'll display satisfactorily even if you don't have a color monitor (or printer); and the files are always available for viewing after you've downloaded them (even after you sign off) by choosing Open from the File menu.

Moving On

As I come to the end of this chapter, I see that I've barely scratched the surface of AOL's abundant online resources. After all, we've only explored news, sports, and weather. There is so much more to discover—online games, resources for self-reliance in the health arena, travel information, critics—AOL seems as vast as the Pacific ocean sometimes.

What we need to do is a bit of "channel surfing," much as one might do with a TV remote. I'll bet it won't take much surfing to come upon something that really appeals to you. Turn the page.

CHAPTER 11

Divertissements

- Games
- Entertainment Media
- Travel
- MusicSpace

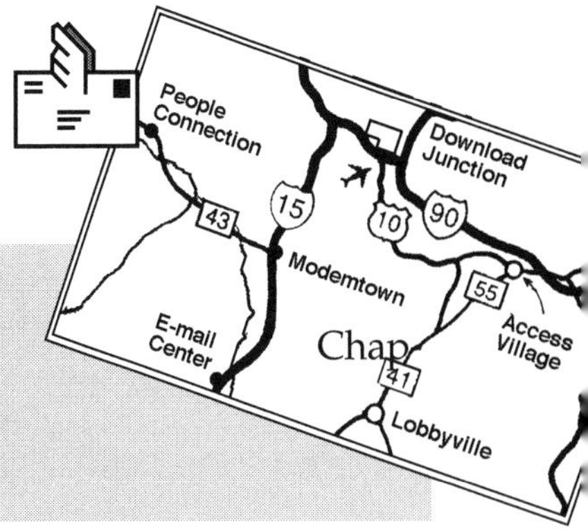
People Connection
Download Junction
Modemtown
E-mail Center
Chap
Access Village
Lobbyville
43
15
10
90
55
41

The outline for this book is posted on the bulletin board here in my office. Having it at my side helps me keep perspective—something that's easy to lose in the midst of a 700-page book project.

This morning, that outline reminds me that so far we've discussed things like the AOL community, the Internet, staying informed, and transferring files. That's all necessary information, but what if we want to have some fun? We're here partly for the fun of it, after all. What's in it for us?

The answer is "plenty." As evidence, I offer this chapter of divertissements: diversions, amusements—places where fun is foremost and duty is disenfranchised. Loosen your tie. Kick off your shoes. Admit intemperance into your life. The night's young.

Games

There's a world of game lovers who find the game-playing arena online to be their hermitage, the place where games are paramount and challenges abound. It's here that knights slay dragons, space voyagers conquer aliens, and residents of the late 20th century scratch their heads in bewilderment. You owe it to yourself to try an online game if you never have: the challenge of playing with remote competitors—unseen and unknown—is unmatched by any other. And if you get hooked, the gaming resources at AOL stand ready to nourish your obsession.

GemStone III

GemStone III is an online fantasy role-playing game. There's no other online experience quite like role-playing; and there's no better way to role-play than with real people with unbounded intellectual stimulation in real time.

GemStone requires no special software other than the AOL software you already have. To play, you sign on, enter the GemStone Forum (keyword: **Gemstone**), then create your own character with the Character Generator to begin your adventure (see Figure 11-1). Don't be fooled into thinking that the text-based nature of the game makes for a limited environment—the sophistication and depth here are mind-numbing. There's great treasure here, not to mention the *real* gems scattered about the game. GemStone is a subculture unto itself, and the sense of community here is very strong.

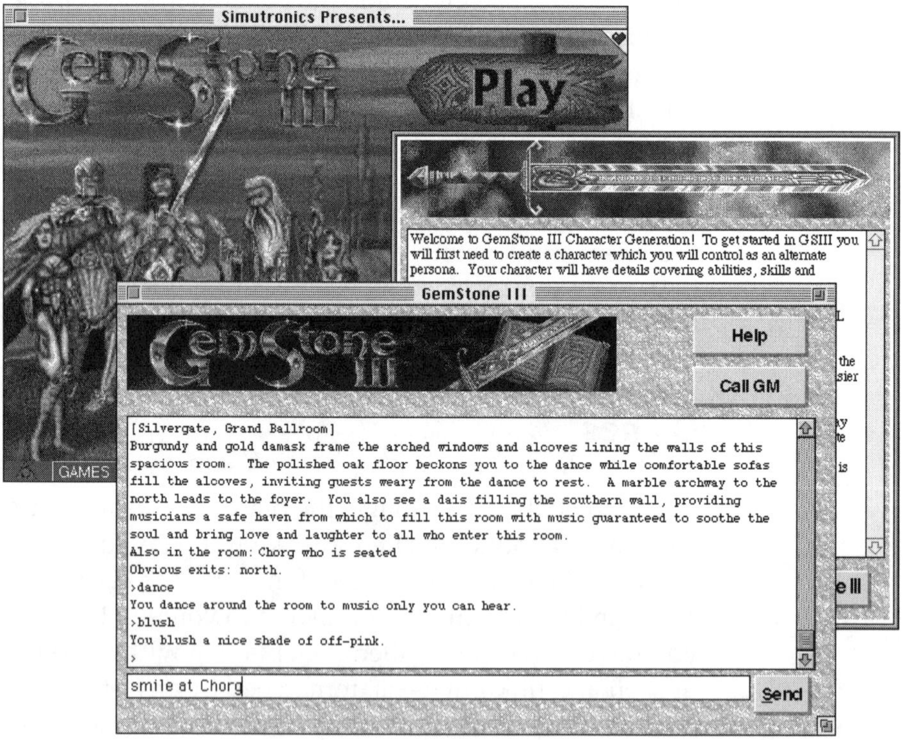
Simutronics Presents...
GemStone III
Play
GAMES
Welcome to GemStone III Character Generation! To get started in GSIII you will first need to create a character which you will control as an alternate persona. Your character will have details covering abilities, skills and
GemStone III
Help
Call GM
[Silvergate, Grand Ballroom]
Burgundy and gold damask frame the arched windows and alcoves lining the walls of this spacious room. The polished oak floor beckons you to the dance while comfortable sofas fill the alcoves, inviting guests weary from the dance to rest. A marble archway to the north leads to the foyer. You also see a dais filling the southern wall, providing musicians a safe haven from which to fill this room with music guaranteed to soothe the soul and bring love and laughter to all who enter this room.
Also in the room: Chorg who is seated
Obvious exits: north.
>dance
You dance around the room to music only you can hear.
>blush
You blush a nice shade of off-pink.
>
smile at Chorg
Send

Figure 11-1: GemStone III greets you with brave adventurers and bounteous treasure.

When I tried out the game, I was a little overwhelmed by its immensity until I happened upon Lord Athanos (a fellow member and adventurer). He kindly showed me some of the ropes (there are a lot of them). He let me follow him around; helped me acquire silver, treasures, and weapons; cast spells upon my character to make it stronger and less vulnerable to the terrible beasts I met along the way; and saved my character's life on more than one occasion. This isn't special treatment: anyone who needs help has only to ask. People are incredibly helpful and congenial here. There are message boards, several libraries, and a chat room where you can relax and get to know other players. Any of these are fertile ground for members new to the game who need help.

GemStone offers a degree of interactivity and realism that entices the new member and challenges the veteran player. Many people join AOL solely to play this game—it's that good. While you may not be quite so fervently committed, you should at least explore the game. It's a remarkable realization of the telecommunications medium.

Brainbuster Trivia

Eggheads of the world, unite! The fact that Brainbuster Trivia is an interactive, online trivia game running around the clock is remarkable enough. But this is the granddaddy of all trivia games, boasting the toughest trivia questions you'll find anywhere on the subjects of history, literature, science, and geography! Where else can you show off all that knowledge you've collected with other players around the world in real time? Best of all, you can win free online time for scoring well in special competition games. You'll find it at the keyword: **BrainBuster** (see Figure 11-2).

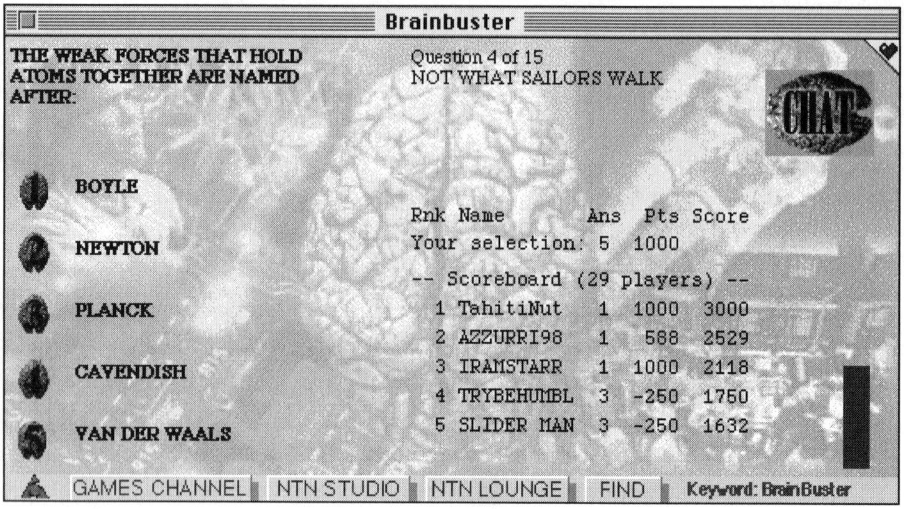

Brainbuster
THE WEAK FORCES THAT HOLD ATOMS TOGETHER ARE NAMED AFTER:
Question 4 of 15
NOT WHAT SAILORS WALK
CHAT
BOYLE
NEWTON
PLANCK
CAVENDISH
VAN DER WAALS
Rnk Name Ans Pts Score
Your selection: 5 1000
-- Scoreboard (29 players) --
1 TahitiNut 1 1000 3000
2 AZZURRI98 1 588 2529
3 IRAMSTARR 1 1000 2118
4 TRYBEHUMBL 3 -250 1750
5 SLIDER MAN 3 -250 1632
GAMES CHANNEL
NTN STUDIO
NTN LOUNGE
FIND
Keyword: BrainBuster

Figure 11-2: Quickly: can you find the right answer to this trivia question? If you can, you should be playing NTN Brainbuster Trivia. (Van Der Waals is the correct answer.)

Like GemStone III, Brainbuster requires no additional software to run. The game is a feature of NTN Games Studio (see Figure 11-3), which features other interactive trivia games like classic Countdown, TV Trivia, and Entertainment Trivia. Keep your eye on these people: more is in the works.

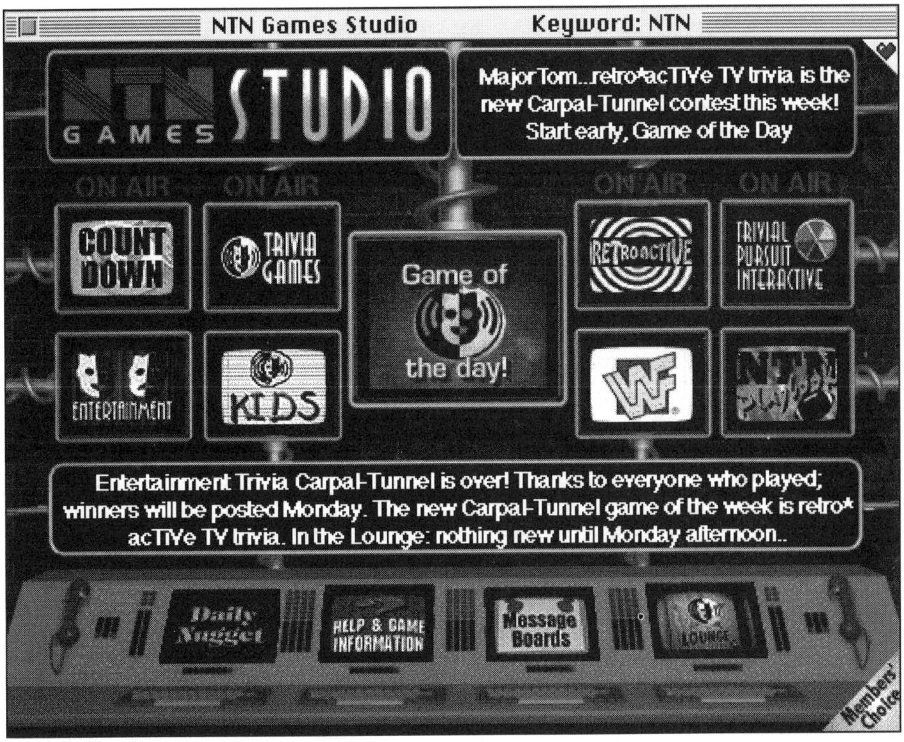
NTN Games Studio
Keyword: NTN
NTN GAMES STUDIO
MajorTom...retro*acTiVe TV trivia is the new Carpal-Tunnel contest this week! Start early, Game of the Day
ON AIR
ON AIR
ON AIR
ON AIR
COUNT DOWN
TRIVIA GAMES
Game of the day!
RETROACTIVE
TRIVIAL PURSUIT INTERACTIVE
ENTERTAINMENT
KIDS
WWF
Entertainment Trivia Carpal-Tunnel is over! Thanks to everyone who played; winners will be posted Monday. The new Carpal-Tunnel game of the week is retro* acTiVe TV trivia. In the Lounge: nothing new until Monday afternoon..
Daily Nugget
HELP & GAME INFORMATION
Message Boards
LOUNGE
Members' Choice

Figure 11-3: NTN Games Studio is host to Brainbuster Trivia (use the keyword: **NTN**). If you like trivia, keep your eye on this keyword. There is more to come.

Online Gaming Forums

You might not believe this, but there is an entire collection of forums dedicated to the pursuit of online gaming that requires nothing more than a fertile imagination. The Online Gaming Forums are a world unto themselves, rich with variety and community. Many of these forums have been on AOL since its inception and continue to attract members with their simplicity and camaraderie. Here you will find simulations, role playing, collectible cards, and free-form gaming, just to name a few. Your entertainment tour would not be complete without a visit to keyword: **Gaming** (see Figure 11-4).

Online Gaming Forums
The Online Gaming Forums
Games Channel Newsletter
OGF News & Info
OGF Posting Guidelines
General Information Board
Collectible Card Games Forum
Colosseum
Free Form Gaming Forum
Game Designers Forum
Gaming Company Support
Gaming Information Exchange
Non-Affiliated Games Forum
Play-By-Mail Forum
Role Playing Gaming Forum
RPGA Network Club - F.O.G.
Simming Forum
Conference Center
Conference Schedule
GameBase
Electronomicon Library
GC Newsletter
OGF Coordinator:
Yvonne Anagnost ("OGFCoordYA")
Keyword: Gaming

Figure 11-4: Free-form, play-by-mail, and role-playing games abound in the Online Gaming Forums.

Of particular interest are a number of play-by-mail games. Play-by-mail allows a group of people around the world to play a game online, using electronic mail and message boards. Games usually require a short amount of actual playing time each week. The cerebral part of the game—planning moves, figuring strategy, assessing opponents—takes place offline, while you're driving a car, falling asleep, or staring at bad television. Perhaps best of all, you don't have to find three other people who have an evening free to play.

The superstar of play-by-mail games is VGA Planets, a science-fiction strategy game of galactic exploration and conquest. It's designed to allow a large number of players of different ages and skill levels to compete. It's not only a game, it's a terrific way to meet people and become involved with the online community.

Contest Area

They say it's not whether you win or lose but how you play the game. In this case, playing is fun but winning can be very rewarding. Contests of every variation, from simple entry-form sweepstakes to full-blown test-your-skills competitions, are available around AOL. Until recently, finding these contests took a fair amount of skill at detective work, and discovery would have been worthy of a prize in and of itself. Now they're all collected in the Contests Area (keyword: **Contest**), they're lots of fun, and the prizes range from token to spectacular (see Figure 11-5).

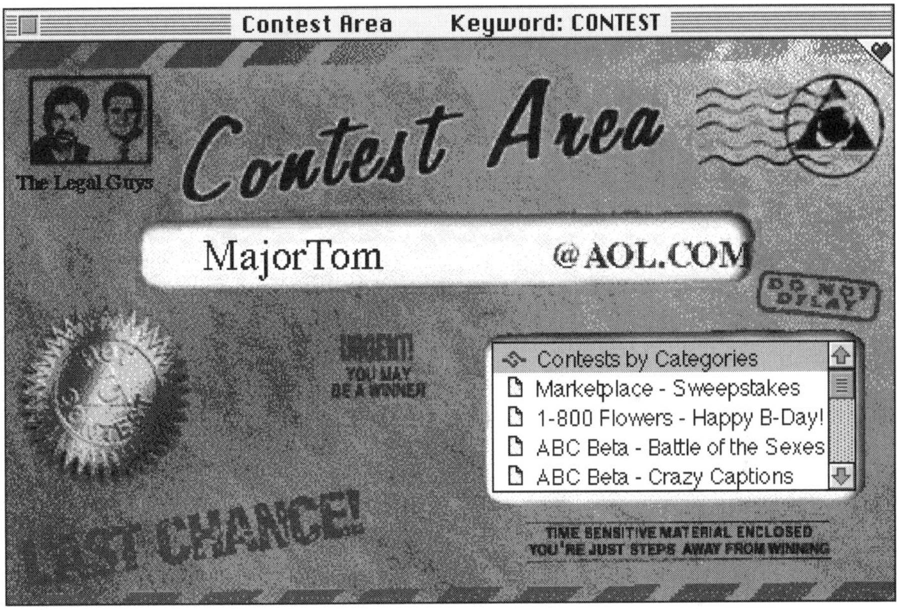
Contest Area Keyword: CONTEST
The Legal Guys
Contest Area
MajorTom
@AOL.COM
DO NOT DELAY
URGENT!
YOU MAY BE A WINNER
Contests by Categories
Marketplace - Sweepstakes
1-800 Flowers - Happy B-Day!
ABC Beta - Battle of the Sexes
ABC Beta - Crazy Captions
LAST CHANCE!
TIME SENSITIVE MATERIAL ENCLOSED
YOU'RE JUST STEPS AWAY FROM WINNING

Figure 11-5: The games and sweepstakes at keyword: **Contest** are fun, plentiful, and surprisingly rewarding.

Here are a few examples. Cindy Adams's Match the Stars awards a weekly prize to a winner who correctly answers star trivia questions—winners are then eligible for a grand prize trip to Rio de Janeiro. In the ABC Beta's Battle of the Sexes contest, the funniest definition of a word from a stereotypical male or female perspective each month wins a T-shirt. The Fly-Fishing Broadcast Network sponsors a weekly amateur writing contest where members submit stories about the "one that got away." Contests come and go, but there are always plenty, and the prizes get better all the time.

Federation

Federation is an adult space fantasy multiplayer game, set within a future scenario of interstellar trade, exploration, and intrigue. You can buy drinks for space princesses, swap tips with hardened traders, and gossip with aliens.

These characters are, of course, other players. That's the first thing you do before you enter the game: devise a character. You can be any sex, race, type, or even any species you want. It is the other players that really make things interesting, as the dynamic of the situation is as unpredictable as a lottery.

Though science fiction in nature, Federation is about commerce, politics, intrigue, power, and money—real-life stuff. There's little reward for violence, thus it's rarely encountered. It's called an "adult" fantasy game (not an "adult fantasy" game) because its emphasis is on pragmatic themes rather than violence and subterfuge. But that doesn't stop it from being fun. Give it a try at keyword: **Federation** (see Figure 11-6).

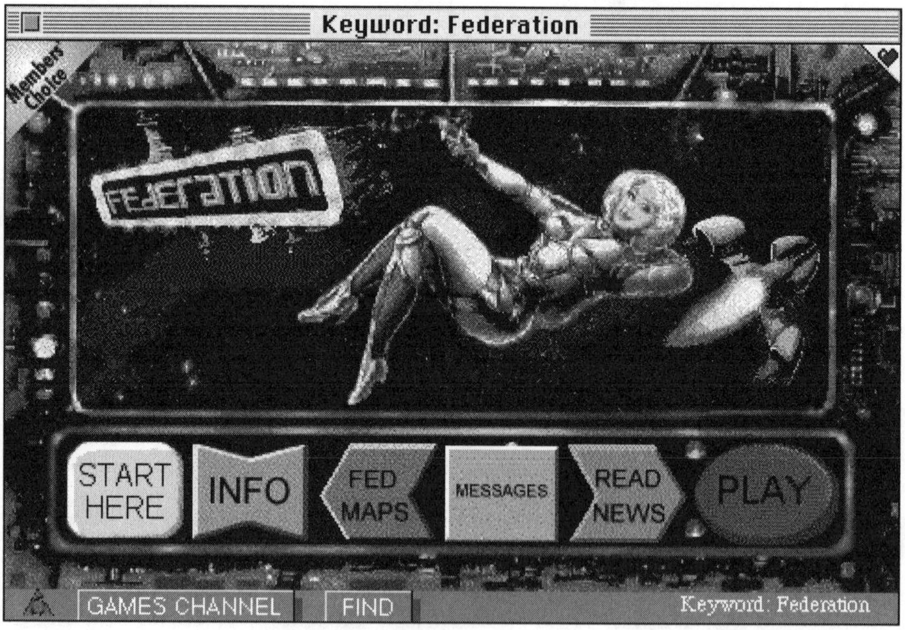
Keyword: Federation
Members' Choice
FEDERATION
START HERE
INFO
FED MAPS
MESSAGES
READ NEWS
PLAY
GAMES CHANNEL
FIND
Keyword: Federation

Figure 11-6: Federation features real-time, multiple-player role playing. You never know who you'll encounter there, or what will be on their minds.

Get Caught!

In less than two years, the World Wide Web has become a focus of online game players. Where else can you meet up with players from all over the world and explore enticing titles like Mr. Edible Starchy Tuberhead, Gigabox, and Hairball? There are more traditional games as well, like Virtual Vegas and Bridge—plus nine electronic gaming magazines and 24 video game companies (numbers that are bound to change by the time you read this).

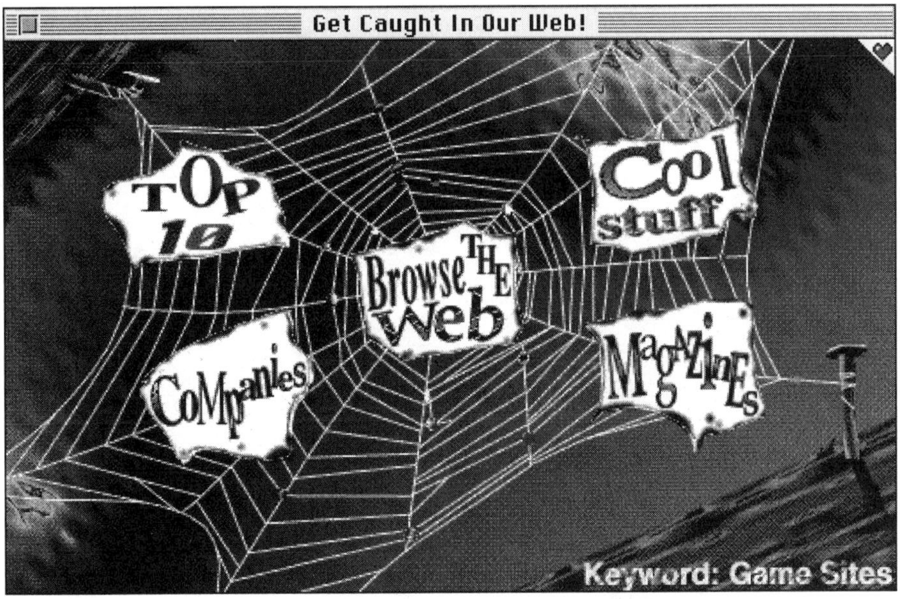
Get Caught In Our Web!
TOP 10
Cool stuff
Browse THE Web
Companies
Magazines
Keyword: Game Sites

Figure 11-7: Get Caught! connects you directly to the most popular gaming sites on the World Wide Web.

All of these goodies are found at keywords: **Game Sites**, where the people at the Games Channel not only provide the connections but also prowl the Web constantly on your behalf, searching for the best games and monitoring new additions.

Chess

As I write this chapter, AOL is working on an ambitious project: constructing an area dedicated to the game of chess. Chess lovers with enlightened Internet connections have long been able to participate in the Internet Chess Club, but participation in the Club required a Telnet connection, and save for the chess board itself, the interface was primarily textual.

The Internet Chess Club, however, is home to tournament players, Masters, International Masters, and even some International Grandmasters. Without these people, a chess area—even a chess area in a community as large as AOL—wouldn't be worthy of an avid chess player's pawn.

As you might expect, AOL has entered into an agreement with the Internet Chess Club and is building a graphical interface for the area that will provide complete access to the Club, including tournament play and chat. To see the results of their labor, use the keyword: **Chess**.

Figure 11-8: A fanciful rendition of a chess board displaying a game between Bobby Fischer and Josef Kupper in 1959. The POV-Ray image was created by David Shrock and is available in full color by using the keywords: **File Search**, then searching with the criterion: Shrock.

Entertainment Media

I've made a number of online friends over the years, and I've developed ongoing philosophical discussions with a few of them. It's my brain food, and I enjoy it.

The other day a friend and I were discussing some of the significant changes in the American lifestyle over the past 100 years. Our conclusion: three major developments have changed that lifestyle forever: (1) the automobile, (2) the computer, and (3) the media.

That last development is the one that brings us to the subject at hand: entertainment. Imagine entertainment when there were no movies, no videos, no television, no magazines, and very few books! What did those people do with their time? They certainly couldn't hang around AOL's Entertainment Channel.

That opportunity, it would appear, is uniquely ours. And it's one you're not going to want to miss. This place is rife with the spangles of technoglitter.

Critics' Choice

Critics' Choice (see Figure 11-9) is actually a multimedia syndicate, specializing in entertainment reviews. You'll find their reviews not only on AOL but in newspapers as well. Their mission is to serve as a provident guide to entertainment—a mission they fulfill admirably. Use the keyword: **Critics**.

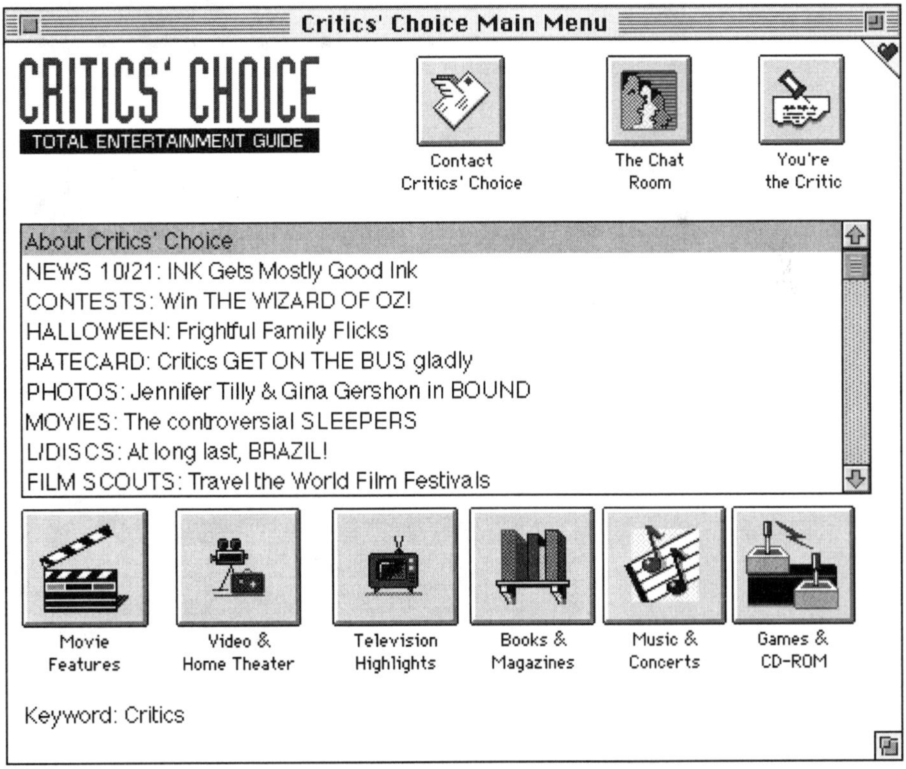
Critics' Choice Main Menu
CRITICS' CHOICE
TOTAL ENTERTAINMENT GUIDE
Contact Critics' Choice
The Chat Room
You're the Critic
About Critics' Choice
NEWS 10/21: INK Gets Mostly Good Ink
CONTESTS: Win THE WIZARD OF OZ!
HALLOWEEN: Frightful Family Flicks
RATECARD: Critics GET ON THE BUS gladly
PHOTOS: Jennifer Tilly & Gina Gershon in BOUND
MOVIES: The controversial SLEEPERS
L/DISCS: At long last, BRAZIL!
FILM SCOUTS: Travel the World Film Festivals
Movie Features
Video & Home Theater
Television Highlights
Books & Magazines
Music & Concerts
Games & CD-ROM
Keyword: Critics

Figure 11-9: Though there are lots of places to find reviews of books, television, videos, and movies online, I prefer Critics' Choice.

A Review of Online Reviews

While Critics' Choice is AOL's sovereign source of media reviews, you'll find a number of others. Hollywood Online (discussed later in this chapter) is one; @times/The New York Times and Digital City Chicago (discussed in Chapter 10, "Staying Informed") are a couple of others.

The Afterwards Cafe (keyword: **Arts**) discusses art, the Atlantic Monthly (keyword: **Atlantic**) reviews a wide variety of media, and SPINonline (keyword: **SPIN**) reviews music. Try each of these services: it's the only way to find the reviewers whose preferences match yours.

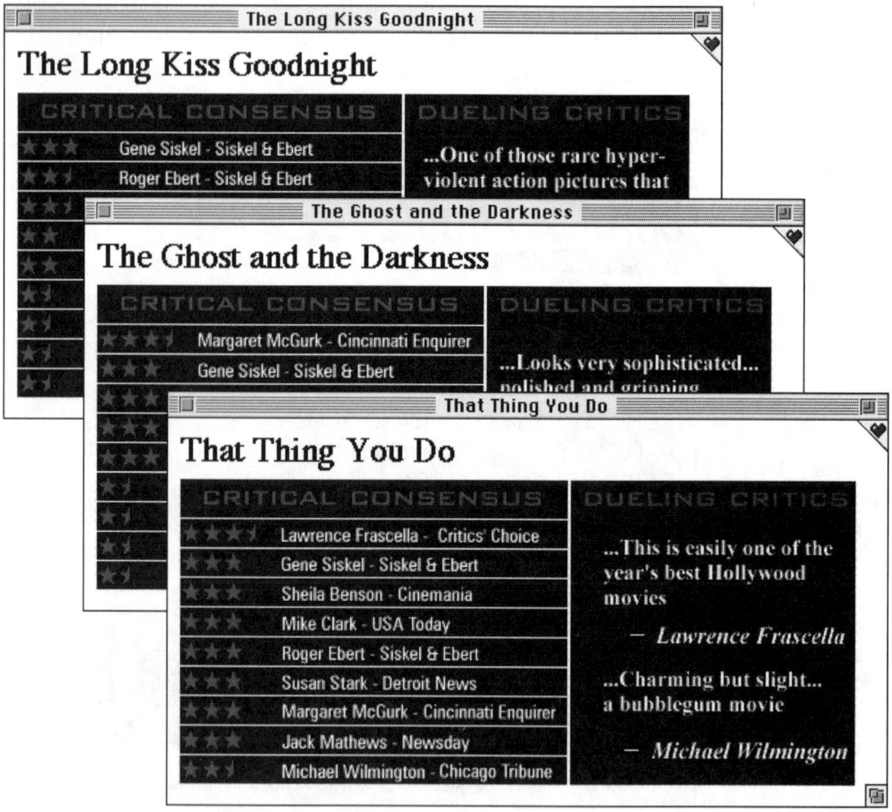
The Long Kiss Goodnight
The Long Kiss Goodnight
CRITICAL CONSENSUS
DUELING CRITICS
Gene Siskel - Siskel & Ebert
Roger Ebert - Siskel & Ebert
...One of those rare hyper-
violent action pictures that
The Ghost and the Darkness
The Ghost and the Darkness
CRITICAL CONSENSUS
DUELING CRITICS
Margaret McGurk - Cincinnati Enquirer
Gene Siskel - Siskel & Ebert
...Looks very sophisticated...
That Thing You Do
That Thing You Do
CRITICAL CONSENSUS
DUELING CRITICS
Lawrence Frascella - Critics' Choice
Gene Siskel - Siskel & Ebert
Sheila Benson - Cinemania
Mike Clark - USA Today
Roger Ebert - Siskel & Ebert
Susan Stark - Detroit News
Margaret McGurk - Cincinnati Enquirer
Jack Mathews - Newsday
Michael Wilmington - Chicago Tribune
...This is easily one of the year's best Hollywood movies
— Lawrence Frascella
...Charming but slight... a bubblegum movie
— Michael Wilmington

Figure 11-10: A sampling of the reviews (and reviewers) available online.

The remainder of Critics' Choice offers consummate, relevant reviews of all of today's media (see Figure 11-11). While you're there, note the Coming Soon feature in the movies section, and the Laserdisc Report in the video section. The television section describes this week's episodes of nearly all shows; the magazine section describes the feature stories of dozens of popular magazines; the music section offers a gift guide; and the games section offers strategies and tips.

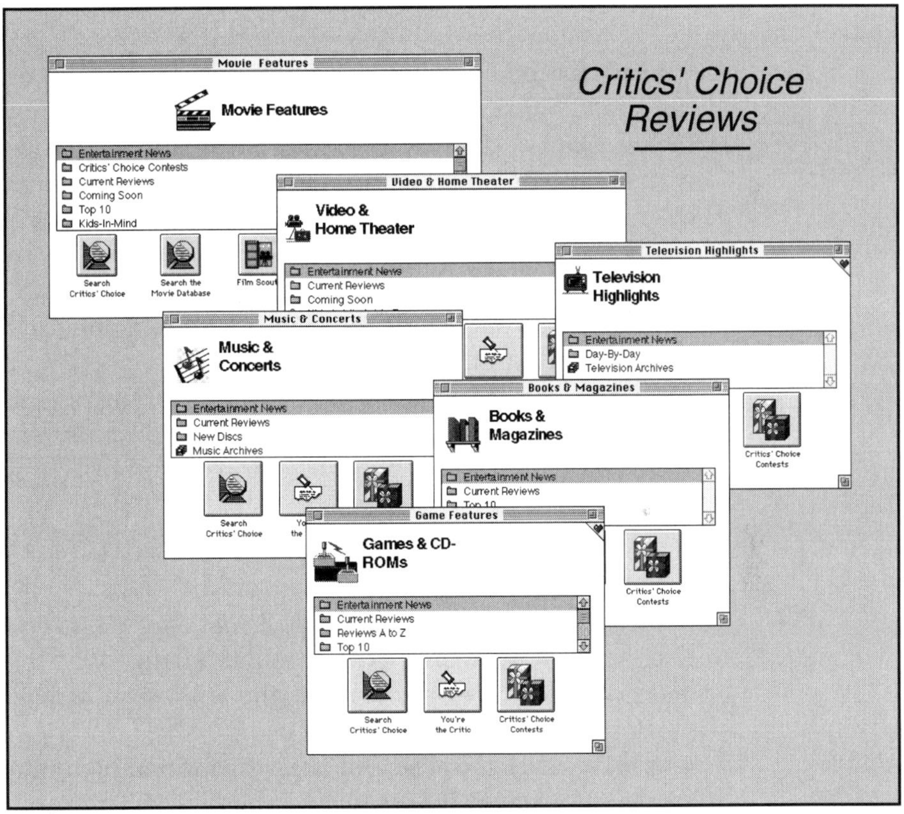
Critics' Choice Reviews
Movie Features
Entertainment News
Critics' Choice Contests
Current Reviews
Coming Soon
Top 10
Kids-In-Mind
Search Critics' Choice
Search the Movie Database
Video & Home Theater
Television Highlights
Day-By-Day
Television Archives
Music & Concerts
New Discs
Music Archives
Books & Magazines
Games & CD-ROMs
Reviews A to Z
You're the Critic
Critics' Choice Contests

Figure 11-11: The contents of Critics' Choice. Nearly every current attraction is reviewed, and all reviews are searchable.

Search Tips

All the reviews in Critics' Choice are searchable—just click any of the search icons pictured in Figure 11-11. Want to see a really great movie? Search for "4STAR." Want to take the kids to a matinee? Search for "MPAAG." Want a review of a Scott Turow novel? Search for "thriller and legal." Search methods are described in "About Critics' Choice—How to Search for Articles," available from the area's main screen.

Don't forget the Critics' Choice video reviews. If you're like me, you can spend hours in a video store and leave with nothing to show for it. Unless I know what I want before I walk in the door, I'm tormented with indecision after 10 minutes of browsing. The video store in my town is about the size of Texas. It's hard to browse in a store the size of Texas. Either you know what you want or you're swallowed by the immensity of it all, wandering aimlessly in a labyrinth of racks and little plastic boxes, where the exits are known only to the pubescent knaves who staff the place.

Critics' Choice is an operative example of the potential of today's online services. Before you buy the popcorn, before you fire up the VCR, before you visit a bookstore or record shop, check out Critics' Choice.

Hollywood Features

In the introduction to her book *Kiss Kiss Bang Bang*, movie critic Pauline Kael wrote, "The words 'Kiss Kiss Bang Bang,' which I saw on an Italian movie poster, are perhaps the briefest statement imaginable of the basic appeal of movies."

A bit harsh, I suppose, but true: the motion picture medium is the art form to which we all have access, thus we all have opinions and we all take fervent interest in its players and its community. Our passion for everything cinematic is evidenced by staggering box-office receipts and the surfeit of Hollywood-oriented features described below.

Hollywood Online

Hollywood Online offers all the things you'd expect from its title: pictures of your favorite stars from the Pictures and Sounds library, cast and production notes in Movie Notes, and discussion on the Movie Talk message board (see Figure 11-12).

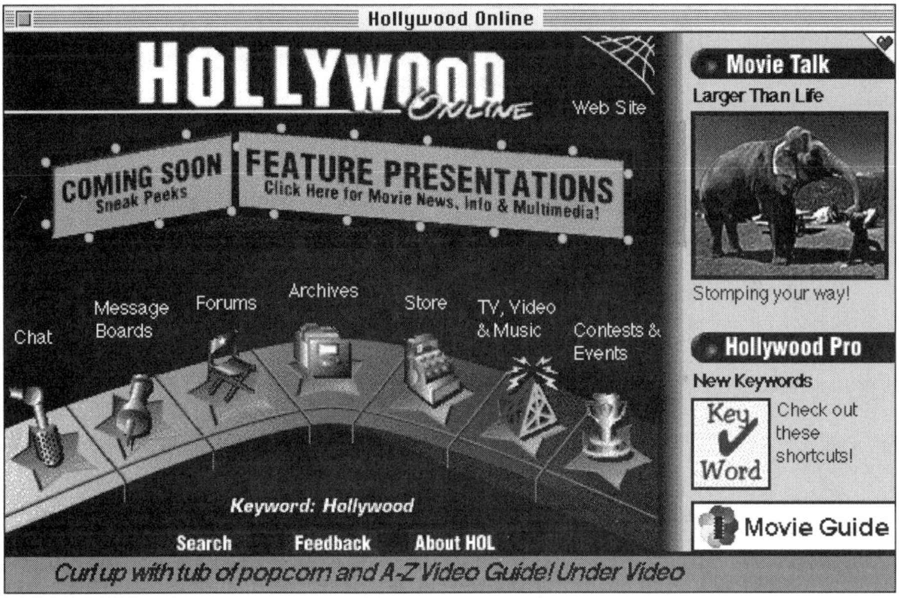
Hollywood Online
HOLLYWOOD
ONLINE
Web Site
COMING SOON
Sneak Peeks
FEATURE PRESENTATIONS
Click Here for Movie News, Info & Multimedia!
Chat
Message Boards
Forums
Archives
Store
TV, Video & Music
Contests & Events
Keyword: Hollywood
Search
Feedback
About HOL
Movie Talk
Larger Than Life
Stomping your way!
Hollywood Pro
New Keywords
Key Word
Check out these shortcuts!
Movie Guide
Curl up with tub of popcorn and A-Z Video Guide! Under Video

Figure 11-12: Hollywood Online (keyword: **Hollywood**) is AOL's window on everything cinematic.

Two other things, however, are worthy of your investigation at Hollywood Online: (1) you can download sneak previews of selected motion pictures before they're released, and (2) multimedia figures heavily in Hollywood Online's contents. Film clips come complete with color, sound, and animation; and interactive "kits" give you a chance to browse a film's contents, allowing you to replay scenes that interest you and skip those that don't.

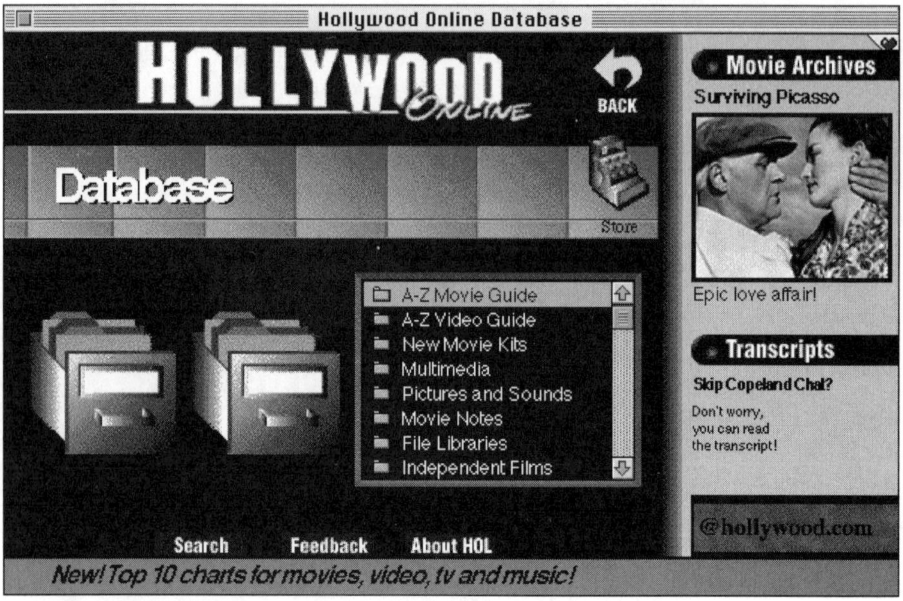
Hollywood Online Database
HOLLYWOOD ONLINE
BACK
Database
Store
Movie Archives
Surviving Picasso
Epic love affair!
A-Z Movie Guide
A-Z Video Guide
New Movie Kits
Multimedia
Pictures and Sounds
Movie Notes
File Libraries
Independent Films
Transcripts
Skip Copeland Chat?
Don't worry, you can read the transcript!
@hollywood.com
Search
Feedback
About HOL
New! Top 10 charts for movies, video, tv and music!

Figure 11-13: The Hollywood Online Database boasts not just reviews and comment, but graphics, sound, and even video.

EXTRA Online

The problem with critics is that their opinions don't always align with ours. The problem with box-office success is that it's the result of all kinds of marketing efforts that have little to do with the movie itself.

Yet the critics and the box office are the two most influential factors in our movie decision-making process. Samuel Goldwyn once said, "Why should people go out and pay good money to see bad films when they can stay at home and see bad television for nothing?" That's the trouble: decisions based on flawed filters can be expensive.

The solution, I believe, is to present the available information (facts, opinions, marketing efforts, and all) and then encourage discussion of it on a wide scale, such as on AOL. EXTRA Online has done just that by making their popular magazine available online and then expanding its usefulness exponentially through "buzz" in active message boards and conferences.

Welcome to EXTRA Online
EXTRA
Microsoft Internet Explorer 3.0
better
Click Here
What's Hot Today
EXTRA Exclusive
Superstar Library
EXTRA Inside
EXTRA's Meeting Hall
EXTRA's Live Chat
Free Newsletter
CLICK HERE
MajorTom, celebrate the 6,000th episode of Y&R Live from the set with an EXTRA Chat on Tues at 9pm ET!
X-FILES Chats: Thursdays 8pm ET
EXTRA's Bikini Madness!
EXTRA Encore!
Keyword: EXTRA
GO TO WB ONLINE
MOVIE SITES
TV SITES
MUSIC SITES

Figure 11-14: EXTRA Online is available at keyword: **EXTRA**.

Books

Two features in the Books area are of particular interest. The first is the bestseller lists (see Figure 11-15), compiled via a recurring survey of national distributors and booksellers and presented in the Book Nook. These lists are an alternative to those that appear in the *New York Times* (discussed in Chapter 10, "Staying Informed"). Compare them: the differences are occasionally enlightening.

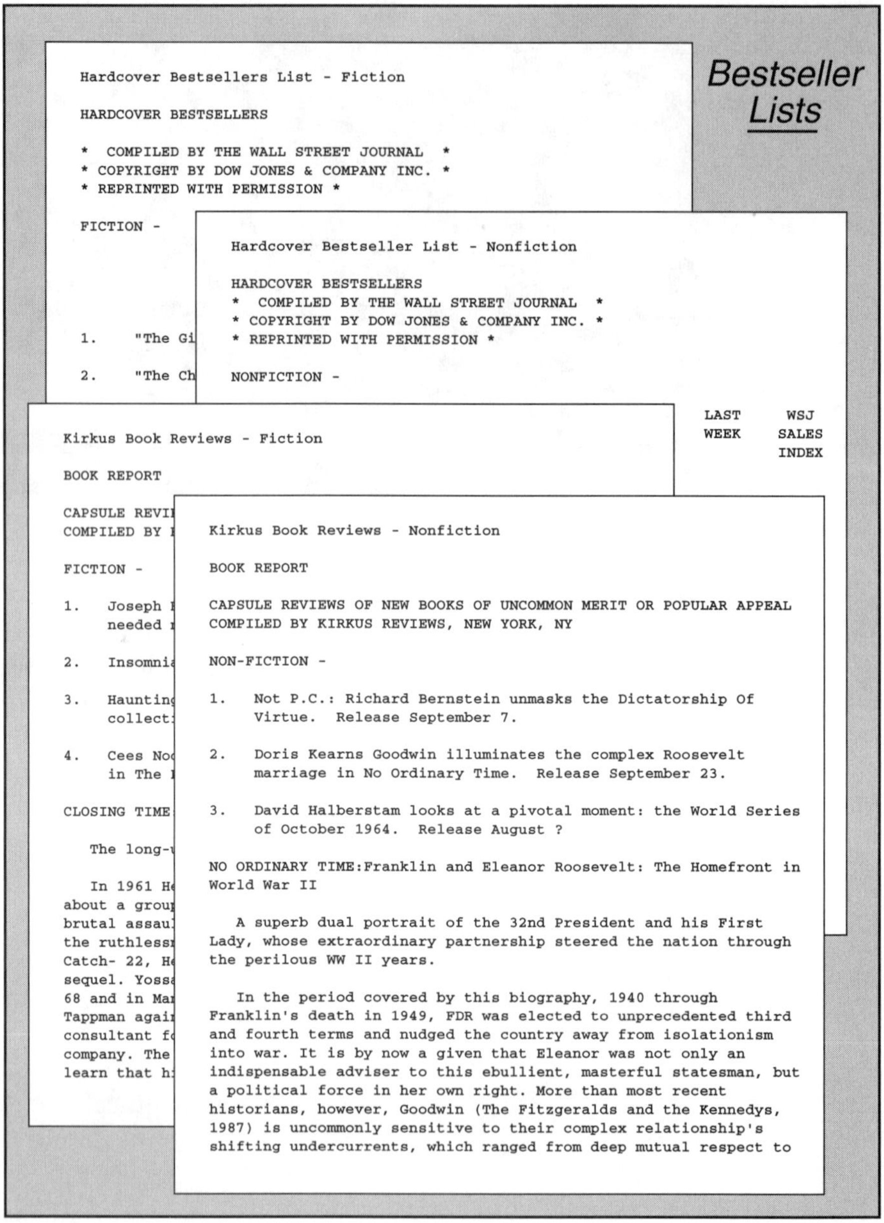
Bestseller Lists
Hardcover Bestsellers List - Fiction
HARDCOVER BESTSELLERS
* COMPILED BY THE WALL STREET JOURNAL *
* COPYRIGHT BY DOW JONES & COMPANY INC. *
* REPRINTED WITH PERMISSION *
FICTION -
1. "The Gi
2. "The Ch
Hardcover Bestseller List - Nonfiction
HARDCOVER BESTSELLERS
* COMPILED BY THE WALL STREET JOURNAL *
* COPYRIGHT BY DOW JONES & COMPANY INC. *
* REPRINTED WITH PERMISSION *
NONFICTION -
LAST WEEK
WSJ SALES INDEX
Kirkus Book Reviews - Fiction
BOOK REPORT
CAPSULE REVI
COMPILED BY
FICTION -
1. Joseph
needed
2. Insomni
3. Hauntin
collect
4. Cees No
in The
CLOSING TIME
The long-
In 1961 H
about a grou
brutal assau
the ruthless
Catch- 22, H
sequel. Yoss
68 and in Ma
Tappman agai
consultant f
company. The
learn that h
Kirkus Book Reviews - Nonfiction
BOOK REPORT
CAPSULE REVIEWS OF NEW BOOKS OF UNCOMMON MERIT OR POPULAR APPEAL
COMPILED BY KIRKUS REVIEWS, NEW YORK, NY
NON-FICTION -
1. Not P.C.: Richard Bernstein unmasks the Dictatorship Of Virtue. Release September 7.
2. Doris Kearns Goodwin illuminates the complex Roosevelt marriage in No Ordinary Time. Release September 23.
3. David Halberstam looks at a pivotal moment: the World Series of October 1964. Release August ?
NO ORDINARY TIME:Franklin and Eleanor Roosevelt: The Homefront in World War II
A superb dual portrait of the 32nd President and his First Lady, whose extraordinary partnership steered the nation through the perilous WW II years.
In the period covered by this biography, 1940 through Franklin's death in 1949, FDR was elected to unprecedented third and fourth terms and nudged the country away from isolationism into war. It is by now a given that Eleanor was not only an indispensable adviser to this ebullient, masterful statesman, but a political force in her own right. More than most recent historians, however, Goodwin (The Fitzgeralds and the Kennedys, 1987) is uncommonly sensitive to their complex relationship's shifting undercurrents, which ranged from deep mutual respect to

Figure 11-15: The bestseller lists and reviews found in the Book Nook. Use the keywords: **Book Nook** to get there quickly.

The second feature is the reviews available in Rogue Print. These are independent reviewers, so the reviews often are more diverse than those appearing in the *Times*. Again, compare for yourself and—if you are truly of the literati—give thanks that AOL offers such alternatives.

Don't forget the Book Bestseller boards (in the Reading Room). This is the place for your review—often the most incisive of all.

Cartoons

Let's take a little survey. What's the first section you read when you pick up the Sunday paper? If you're like me, you read "the funnies" before anything else. Often they're the *only* thing I read, depending on how dreary the world has been that week.

America Online is particularly rich in cartoons, and you don't have to wait until Sunday morning to enjoy them. A number of nationally acclaimed cartoonists contribute to AOL each week. They include the following:

- Scott Adams's comic strip "Dilbert," reaching more than 30 million newspaper readers in 9 countries. "Dilbert" was the first syndicated comic strip to appear online, where fans have initiated more than 30,000 comic downloads monthly and generated over 50,000 e-mail messages. "Dilbert" is at keyword: **Dilbert**.
- The Comic Strip Centennial, where you can learn about the history of one of the very few art forms "born in the U.S.A." This area is presented in cooperation with the Newspaper Features Council in honor of the 100th anniversary of the birth of the comics, and it includes exhibits from the Library of Congress and the U.S. Postal Service (see Figure 11-16).
- The Cartoon Network, with its own forum of 'toons and comments.
- Mike Keefe's InToon with the News political satire cartoons complete with "hot air"—a contest where you fill in the "word balloon" and win prizes.

The Funnies
The Funny Pages
The Funny Pages
Cartoon Network
Mike Keefe Editorial Cartoons
Week 25: Hot Air Balloon - Ear Wax!
Week 25 Contest: Ear Wax!
Post Entry
Prizes!
Week 24 Winner
Fill in the word balloon!! Deadline 10:00 AM EDT, Monday 10/28/96
THE COMIC STRIP CENTENNIAL
DICK TRACY
USA 32
LI'L ABNER
32 USA
WE'LL BE GETTING A NEW "BUNGEE BOSS" SOMETIME TODAY.
HI-I'M-YOUR-NEW-BOSS-LET'S-CHANGE-EVERY-THING-BEFORE-I-GET-REASSIGNED-OOPS-TOO-LATE-GOODBYE.
SPROING
HE WAS LIKE A MENTOR TO ME.
I THINK HE MADE A DIFFERENCE.
INCOMING!

Figure 11-16: Cartoons abound at keyword: **Funnies**. The main screen appears at upper right; then the logo from the Comic Strip Centennial, two postage stamps from the U.S. Postal Service, InToon's Hot Air "fill in the balloon" contest, and "Bungee Boss," a Dilbert strip from Scott Adams.

Visit the Cartoon Forum at keyword: **Cartoons**, for even more 'toons and comment. New cartoons are posted there every week, including those from the AOL membership. This is your chance to get your 'toons published online!

Columnists & Features Online

Columnists & Features Online is the best way to read provocative newspaper columnists and communicate with them online (see Figure 11-17).

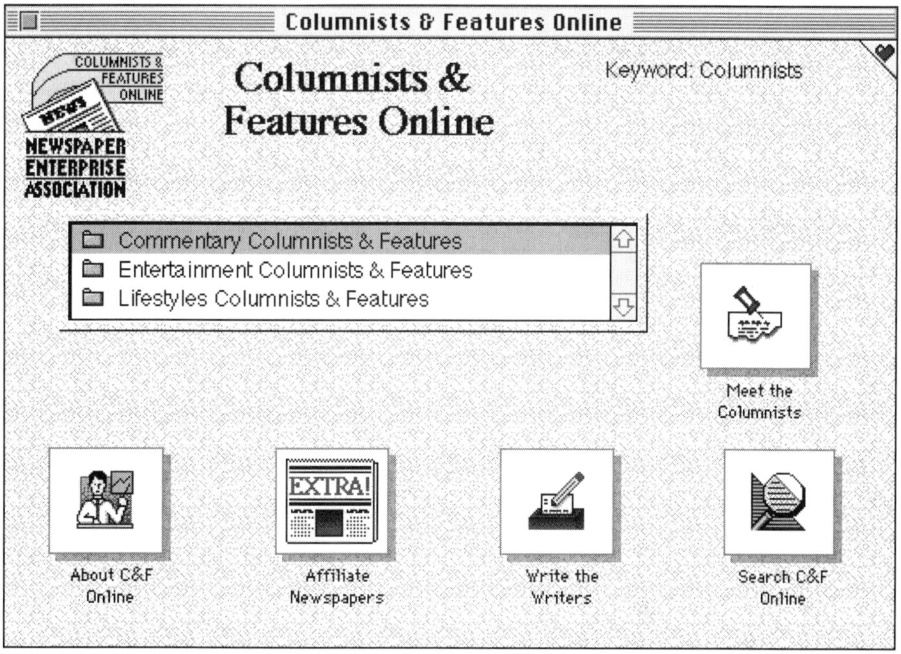
Columnists & Features Online
COLUMNISTS & FEATURES ONLINE
NEWS
NEWSPAPER ENTERPRISE ASSOCIATION
Columnists & Features Online
Keyword: Columnists
Commentary Columnists & Features
Entertainment Columnists & Features
Lifestyles Columnists & Features
Meet the Columnists
EXTRA!
About C&F Online
Affiliate Newspapers
Write the Writers
Search C&F Online

Figure 11-17: Columnists & Features Online offers current material as well as an extensive searchable library. Use the keyword: **Columnists**.

The Newspaper Enterprise Association (NEA) syndicates distinguished writers and political columnists to newspapers nationwide, including the 29 (a number that's sure to grow) featured on AOL (see Figure 11-18).

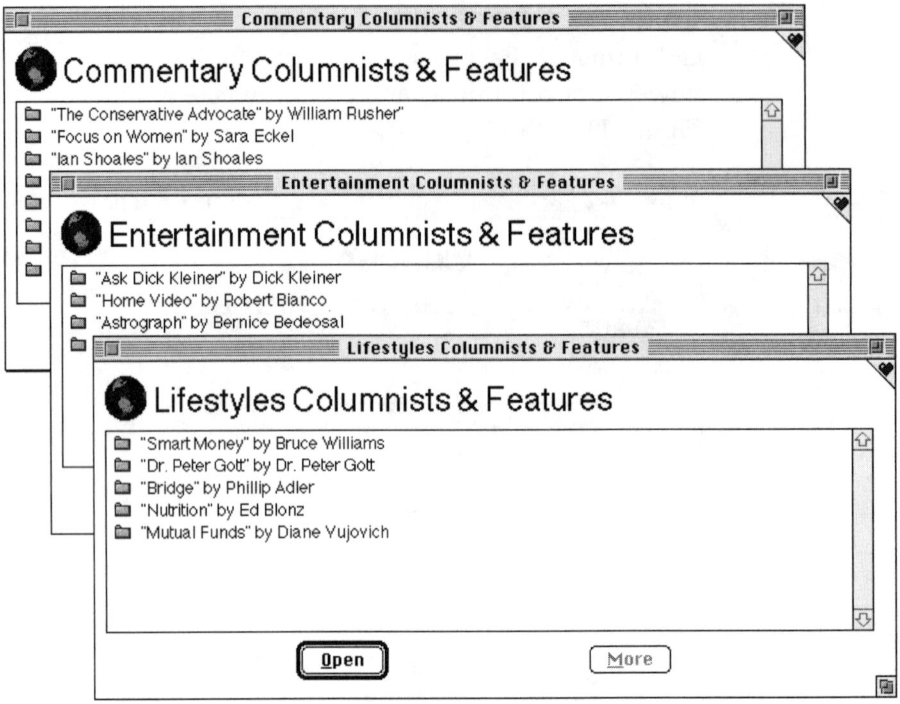
Commentary Columnists & Features
Commentary Columnists & Features
"The Conservative Advocate" by William Rusher"
"Focus on Women" by Sara Eckel
"Ian Shoales" by Ian Shoales
Entertainment Columnists & Features
Entertainment Columnists & Features
"Ask Dick Kleiner" by Dick Kleiner
"Home Video" by Robert Bianco
"Astrograph" by Bernice Bedeosal
Lifestyles Columnists & Features
Lifestyles Columnists & Features
"Smart Money" by Bruce Williams
"Dr. Peter Gott" by Dr. Peter Gott
"Bridge" by Phillip Adler
"Nutrition" by Ed Blonz
"Mutual Funds" by Diane Vujovich
Open
More

Figure 11-18: A sample of the columnists assembled for bilateral discourse via Columnists & Features Online.

The text of each column appears the same day it is released to the newspapers and remains online for a week. After that, past columns are posted in the library. Use standard AOL criteria to search them. Some of the columnists include the following:

- William Rusher, the former publisher of the *National Review* and a popular voice of the American Right. In his column "The Conservative Advocate" Rusher uses a mixture of humor and political commentary to jab and lampoon liberals and the American Left.
- Nat Hentoff, one of the foremost authorities on the First Amendment. Hentoff's column, which appears in the *Washington Post*, examines how legislative decisions affect our basic freedoms to speak, write, think, and assemble.

- George Plagenz, an ordained minister and news veteran who writes "Saints and Sinners," a personal look at family values and spiritual issues.
- Ian Shoales, a popular humor columnist from National Public Radio and the *San Francisco Examiner*, known for his amusing social commentary.
- Joseph Spear, an advocate for the average American, who offers witty, insightful political commentary.
- Robert Bianco, a *Pittsburgh Post-Gazette* journalist who writes "Home Video," up-to-the-minute reviews of home video releases.
- Radio personality Bruce Williams, whose column "Smart Money" gives incisive answers to personal finance questions.
- Dr. Peter Gott, a practicing physician and patients' rights advocate who offers readers free medical advice.
- Astrologer Bernice Bedeosal, the author of "Astrograph." What's in the stars for you? You'll find it in "Astrograph," one of the most popular astrology columns in America.

Horoscopes

Mention of Bernice Bedeosal's "Astrograph" column reminds me that horoscopes play a transcendental role in the Entertainment Channel. Daily horoscopes for each of the astrological signs are posted each week; you're welcome to consult them before you do anything rash. Use the keyword: **Horoscope** to access this area quickly. And if you'd like something a little more specific, stop by the Crystal Ball Forum (keywords: **Crystal Ball**) to see what the tarot cards have to say about the future.

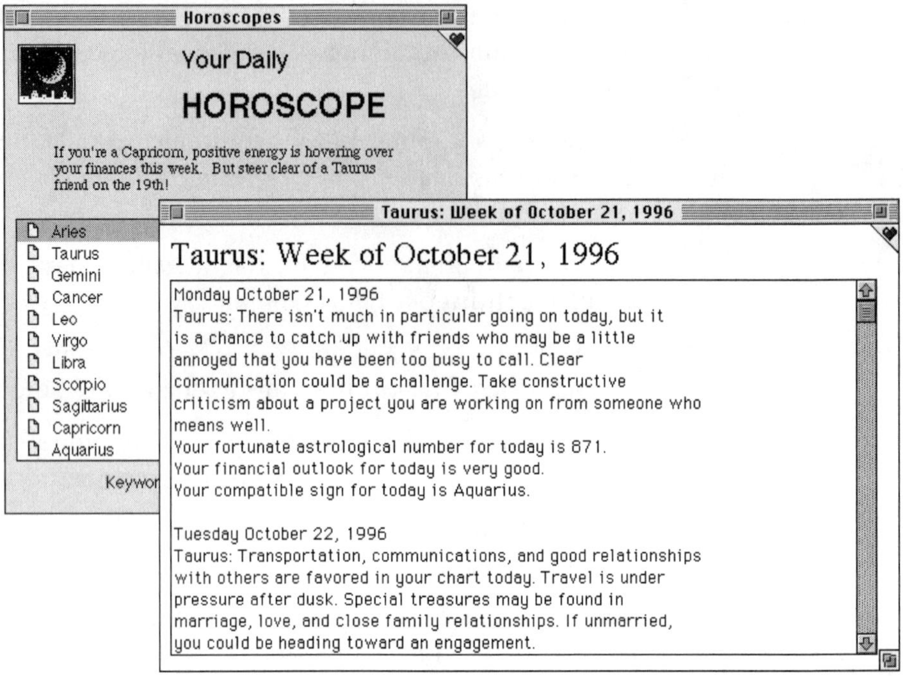
Horoscopes
Your Daily
HOROSCOPE
If you're a Capricorn, positive energy is hovering over your finances this week. But steer clear of a Taurus friend on the 19th!
Aries
Taurus
Gemini
Cancer
Leo
Virgo
Libra
Scorpio
Sagittarius
Capricorn
Aquarius
Taurus: Week of October 21, 1996
Taurus: Week of October 21, 1996
Monday October 21, 1996
Taurus: There isn't much in particular going on today, but it is a chance to catch up with friends who may be a little annoyed that you have been too busy to call. Clear communication could be a challenge. Take constructive criticism about a project you are working on from someone who means well.
Your fortunate astrological number for today is 871.
Your financial outlook for today is very good.
Your compatible sign for today is Aquarius.
Tuesday October 22, 1996
Taurus: Transportation, communications, and good relationships with others are favored in your chart today. Travel is under pressure after dusk. Special treasures may be found in marriage, love, and close family relationships. If unmarried, you could be heading toward an engagement.

Figure 11-19: That's my horoscope you're reading there. Let's see . . . it seems today would be a good day to call my broker (an Aquarius) and buy 871 shares of AOL stock. . . . Or maybe I should consult the cards to be sure.

ABC Online

ABC Online is one of the most dazzling areas available at AOL. A vast reservoir of images, sounds, and videos is available in the libraries, along with pertinent talk and commentary on today's media (see Figure 11-20).

Welcome to ABC Online
Keyword: ABC
abc
ON LINE
Mark your calendars because Oprah's going to be On!...Line! LIVE! Wed., October 23 at 8:00pmET!
CLICK!
AOL Members' CHOICE
STORE
CHAT
STUFF
POSTS
GAMES
AFFILIATE
LIVE
Felicia has a change of heart about Kevin! Catch the action on GH!
The abortion issue: Why isn't anyone talking about it? ABC News InFocus
R U Ready for Some Football? ABC College & MNF are On-Line!
Need a laugh? The ABC Kidzine Joke Book is full of 'em!
It's amore!! That's "love" to you and me - come found out why....
Review the latest episode of "Lois & Clark" in the Critics' Corner!
ABC SOAPS
ABC NEWS
ABC SPORTS
ABC KIDZ
TEST TUBE
ABC TV
Figure 11-20: ABC Online is one of AOL's showcase expositions.

Sports fans will appreciate the depth ABC Sports (discussed in Chapter 10) delivers online, and aficionados of daytime TV will wallow in suds at Soapline Daily (keywords: **ABC Soaps**). And don't neglect ABC Test Tube (keywords: **ABC Beta**), especially the "America Out of Line" feature. A little irreverence is good for all of us.

Entertainment Weekly Online

Entertainment Weekly Online (keyword: **EW**) brings AOL subscribers the full text of *Entertainment Weekly* magazine each week: feature stories and reviews of movies, TV, music, books, videos, and multimedia.

That's the official line, but if you're an *Entertainment Weekly* reader, you know there's much more to the magazine than that. Just this week I dropped in and caught Mary Makarushka's encore piece about Jim Croce. *Rolling Stone* noted that the critics were content to consign him to the status of a likable nonentity, yet Makarushka reminds us of some of his most poignant lyrics—"Time in a Bottle" is still one of my favorite lyrics of all time, and Makarushka agrees. There's insightful, contemporary journalism here.

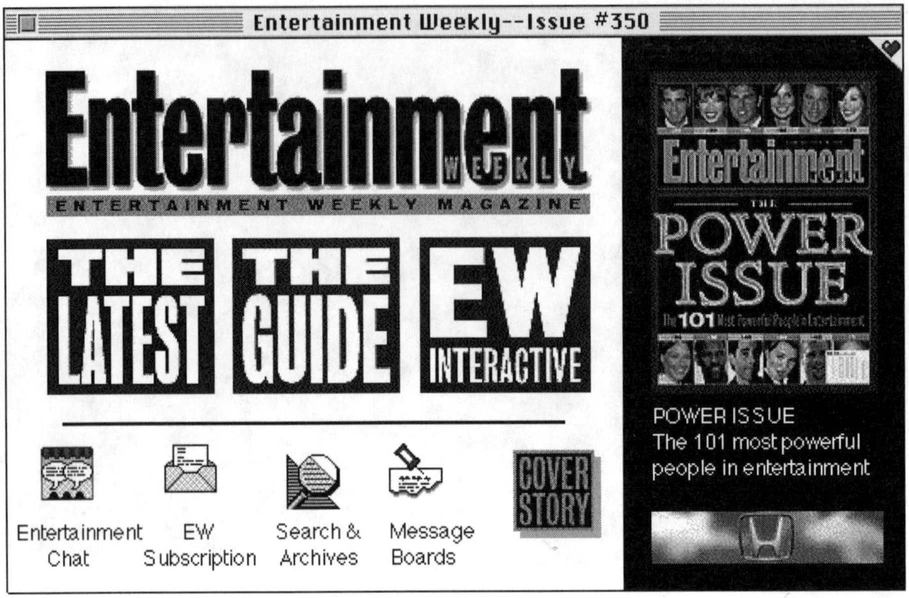
Entertainment Weekly--Issue #350
Entertainment WEEKLY
ENTERTAINMENT WEEKLY MAGAZINE
THE LATEST
THE GUIDE
EW INTERACTIVE
Entertainment Chat
EW Subscription
Search & Archives
Message Boards
COVER STORY
POWER ISSUE
POWER ISSUE
The 101 most powerful people in entertainment

Figure 11-21: Entertainment Weekly Online offers not only the full text of the magazine each week, but you can chat with staffers and participate in guest events. Be sure to check out the notable programs for the week in the TV section every Monday, and parents should avail themselves of their weekly Parents' Guide.

Travel

Who hasn't indulged in an "If I had a million dollars. . ." fantasy? My favorite is travel: South America, the British Isles, a blue-water cruise, the Orient Express. . . . Heck, I'd be happy if someone just gave me a ticket to Tucumcari.

Of course, fantasies require money. That's why they're fantasies. If you want money-optional indulgences, try AOL's Travel Channel (keyword: **Travel**). Not only can you indulge your fantasies here, you can actually fulfill them as well. You can find exceptional travel bargains; book airline, car, and hotel reservations; consult with other travelers before you depart. They say there are only two types of people in the world: those who are on vacation, and those who wish they were. The Travel Channel serves both types.

preview travel

Perhaps one of the most specific advantages offered online is the ability to shop for your own airline reservations. For years, travel agents have peered at computer screens and applied their expertise to interpret cryptic displays for tyro travelers. Now, however, the computer screen is your own; the display is graphical and precise; you can examine the alternatives yourself and make your own decisions; you can even book the reservations from your keyboard.

Changes Ahead

It's frustrating to describe an area that's under construction, especially when it's as integral—both to this book and to AOL—as the airline reservation feature. What am I to do? I can't leave it out.

My best strategy is to be frank and tell you that as I write this, the preview travel feature is in an early phase of development. Consequently, I must omit the system's preliminary screens where you provide your traveler's profile, billing information, and seating, class, meals, airline, home airport, and frequent flyer information. I must also omit the fare information and itinerary verification dialogs. Thus, interpret this section of the book as a glimpse of a far greater whole. If you look carefully at Figures 11-22, 11-23, and 11-24 you'll note that all of the preview travel screens offer Help buttons. Moreover, if you click on the blue column headings within most of preview travel's windows, you receive even more help. This help information is comprehensive and germane. Use it liberally when you have questions.

Itinerary Planning

One of my favorite jaunts is a trip to North Carolina in the summer. They have some delectable cuisine there (to say nothing of the mint juleps); it's a pleasant and friendly place; and the natives talk with a lilt that could melt even Jack Palance's heart. (Did I mention that my publisher is there, too? And that my publisher usually pays for the trip? It's amazing how a travel allowance can make a place seem even more endearing.) Let's use preview travel to see if there's a flight that will get me there.

I begin by entering my departure and destination cities, and my preferred time and date of departure (see Figure 11-22).

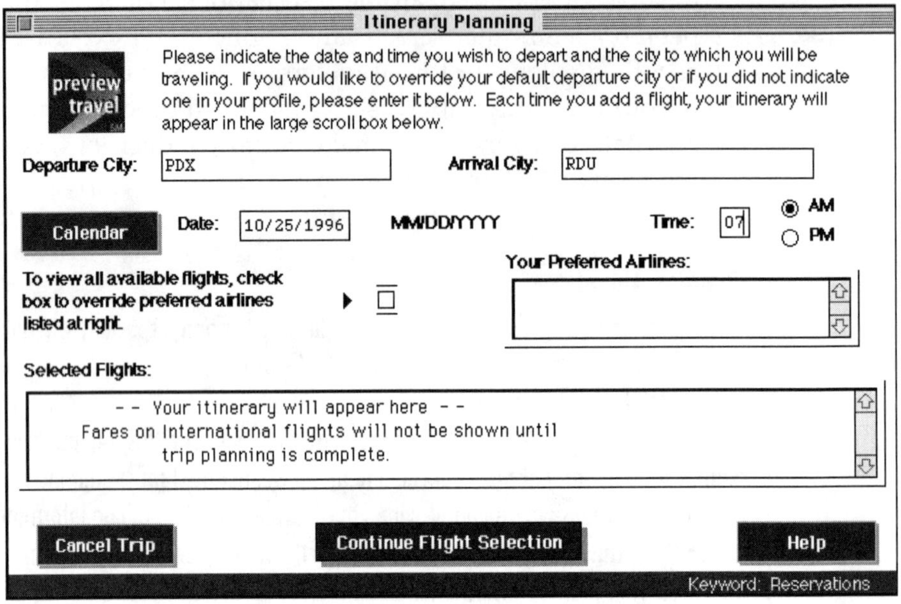
Itinerary Planning
preview travel
Please indicate the date and time you wish to depart and the city to which you will be traveling. If you would like to override your default departure city or if you did not indicate one in your profile, please enter it below. Each time you add a flight, your itinerary will appear in the large scroll box below.
Departure City:
PDX
Arrival City:
RDU
Calendar
Date:
10/25/1996
MM/DD/YYYY
Time:
07
AM
PM
Your Preferred Airlines:
To view all available flights, check box to override preferred airlines listed at right.
Selected Flights:
-- Your itinerary will appear here --
Fares on International flights will not be shown until trip planning is complete.
Cancel Trip
Continue Flight Selection
Help
Keyword: Reservations

Figure 11-22: I begin by identifying where and when I want to travel.

There are three points I should make about Figure 11-22: (1) I didn't have to use the departure and destination codes (PDX, RDU) that you see in the illustration. I could have answered the questions in plain English and preview travel would have determined my need or asked me to clarify my meaning. (2) The Your Preferred Airlines box contains the airlines that I defined earlier, when I indicated my preferences. (3) The Selected Flights list box would contain earlier flights in this itinerary: a departure flight, for example, if I was booking my return.

Once I've entered the information, pictured in Figure 11-22, I click the Continue Flight Selection button.

Flight Selection

The Flight Selection window appears next, displaying the flights preview travel has discovered that meet my travel criteria. To select a flight, all I need to do is double-click it.

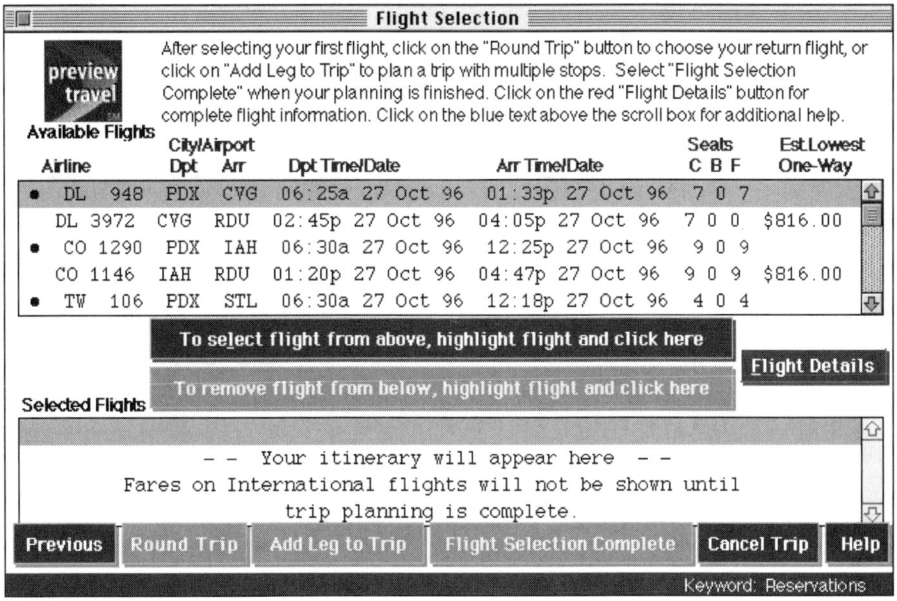
Flight Selection
preview travel
After selecting your first flight, click on the "Round Trip" button to choose your return flight, or click on "Add Leg to Trip" to plan a trip with multiple stops. Select "Flight Selection Complete" when your planning is finished. Click on the red "Flight Details" button for complete flight information. Click on the blue text above the scroll box for additional help.
Available Flights
Airline
City/Airport
Dpt Arr
Dpt Time/Date
Arr Time/Date
Seats
C B F
Est Lowest One-Way
• DL 948 PDX CVG 06:25a 27 Oct 96 01:33p 27 Oct 96 7 0 7
DL 3972 CVG RDU 02:45p 27 Oct 96 04:05p 27 Oct 96 7 0 0 $816.00
• CO 1290 PDX IAH 06:30a 27 Oct 96 12:25p 27 Oct 96 9 0 9
CO 1146 IAH RDU 01:20p 27 Oct 96 04:47p 27 Oct 96 9 0 9 $816.00
• TW 106 PDX STL 06:30a 27 Oct 96 12:18p 27 Oct 96 4 0 4
To select flight from above, highlight flight and click here
Flight Details
To remove flight from below, highlight flight and click here
Selected Flights
- - Your itinerary will appear here - -
Fares on International flights will not be shown until trip planning is complete.
Previous
Round Trip
Add Leg to Trip
Flight Selection Complete
Cancel Trip
Help
Keyword: Reservations

Figure 11-23: To select a flight, double-click it in the Available Flights window.

As Figure 11-23 indicates, approximate fare information would appear in the upper list box along with the flights meeting my criteria. Using this information, I could select a flight for inclusion in the itinerary I'm building below.

The Fare Display

When you've decided upon your departure and return flights—and any others in between—you'll click Figure 11-23's Flight Selection Complete button. This will provoke the Fare Display window appearing in Figure 11-24.

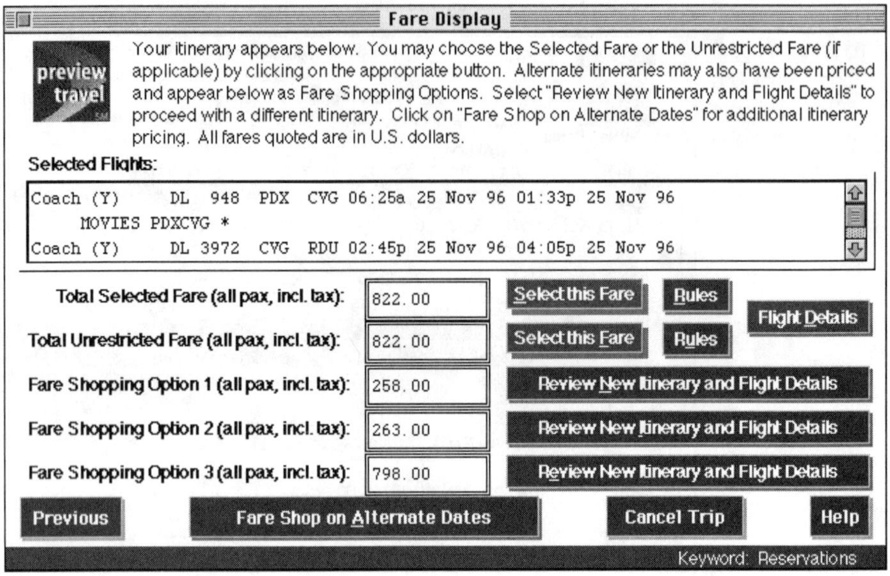
Fare Display
preview travel
Your itinerary appears below. You may choose the Selected Fare or the Unrestricted Fare (if applicable) by clicking on the appropriate button. Alternate itineraries may also have been priced and appear below as Fare Shopping Options. Select "Review New Itinerary and Flight Details" to proceed with a different itinerary. Click on "Fare Shop on Alternate Dates" for additional itinerary pricing. All fares quoted are in U.S. dollars.
Selected Flights:
Coach (Y) DL 948 PDX CVG 06:25a 25 Nov 96 01:33p 25 Nov 96
MOVIES PDXCVG *
Coach (Y) DL 3972 CVG RDU 02:45p 25 Nov 96 04:05p 25 Nov 96
Total Selected Fare (all pax, incl. tax): 822.00
Select this Fare
Rules
Flight Details
Total Unrestricted Fare (all pax, incl. tax): 822.00
Select this Fare
Rules
Fare Shopping Option 1 (all pax, incl. tax): 258.00
Review New Itinerary and Flight Details
Fare Shopping Option 2 (all pax, incl. tax): 263.00
Review New Itinerary and Flight Details
Fare Shopping Option 3 (all pax, incl. tax): 798.00
Review New Itinerary and Flight Details
Previous
Fare Shop on Alternate Dates
Cancel Trip
Help
Keyword: Reservations

Figure 11-24: You can review your trip plan, change it, select a lower fare, or accept via this window.

Note that preview travel looks for less-expensive seats with its Fare Shopping Option on the flights chosen, and reports them (Figure 11-24).

The itinerary process concludes after you complete passenger and billing information. Your ticket is sent by 2nd-day air. It won't be long before you'll be able to reserve a rental car and a hotel room this way too, with confirmations arriving just as quickly.

You don't have to complete the online reservation process. You can always click a Cancel button. No one will tattle if you indulge in a little fantasy travel. It's a great cure for the summertime or wintertime blues; and who knows, maybe you, too, will visit the beautiful Raleigh-Durham-Chapel Hill Triangle area of North Carolina. Sip a mint julep while you're there: there are none better in the South.

The Independent Traveler

As long as we're in a traveling mood, let's check out the Independent Traveler. Articles, message boards, a resource center, and a library offer a wealth of information and tips for the domestic or world traveler (see Figure 11-25).

Are you looking for a romantic hideaway for your getaway weekend? Check the Cruise message board. If you're looking for the best itinerary for your train trip through Europe, check the World Traveler message board. If you're traveling overseas, check out the U.S. State Department Travel Advisories and the Forum's special events with travel experts. In-depth articles cover topics such as "How to find hotel discounts" and "Should I buy trip cancellation insurance?"

Travel plans, perhaps above all else, benefit from peer support. The Independent Traveler is where you can solicit the advice of peers and pros alike. No travel plans are complete until you talk to those who have been there. For this purpose, check the Independent Traveler's message boards. Lots of people travel, and most who do like to talk about it. Their comments are candid and relevant, and because it's a message board, everything is current.

The Independent Traveler
EUROPEAN RAIL PASSES
If you're headed to Europe, trains are a great way to travel around. European trains still retain the romance and convenience long ago lost in American trains. They're fun, romantic, fast, efficient and reasonably priced. A train can take you to the center of town in just about any city or village you might want to visit in Europe. Trains are also considerably less expensive than flying or driving if you're covering any distance.
PACKING TIPS FOR THE INDEPENDENT TRAVELER
In this modern day of worldwide independent travel, steamer trunks are long gone and carry-on luggage has become the preferred baggage of the frequent traveler. Good quality, softsided carry-on bags are lightweight, durable, washable and absorb shock better than hardsided luggage. By carrying your luggage with you on the plane, you save valuable travel time, and you never need to worry about the airline losing your luggage or have it miss the plane. Just have this happen to you once when you're in a hurry and you'll be a carry-on traveler for life.
Choose the Right Bag
BARGAIN BOX: Travel Deals & Discounts
UNITED'S NEW LOW-COST WEST COAST SHUTTLE
The Independent Traveler!
Independent Traveler
(Formerly Travel Forum)
TRAVEL BOARDS
TRAVELER'S RESOURCE CENTER
TRAVEL LIBRARY
EUROPE THROUGH THE BACK DOOR
TRAVEL CAFE
FREQUENTLY ASKED QUESTIONS
TRAVEL STORE
Lonely Planet is Coming!
Click photo by CarlPix474
Bargain Box: "Discover America" Sale!
Thursday - RV Travel! - 9pm ET
Horrors from San Francisco to Salem!

Figure 11-25: The Independent Traveler (keyword: **Traveler**) offers not only expert advice, but also the experience of traveling peers—perhaps the best advice of all.

Travel Corner

Don't confuse The Independent Traveler with the Travel Corner. Though the two serve similar purposes, there's a subtle but significant difference in their focus.

Arnie Weissmann began planning for an around-the-world journey in the early 1980s. To his dismay, he couldn't find information about his destinations. He knew how he was traveling, he knew what his costs were going to be, he knew what to pack and how to dress. But what he needed were friends, chaperones familiar with his destinations who could tell him where to go and what to do when he arrived—how to behave, how to find the good stuff and avoid the bad. He needed what the Travel Corner calls "destination profiles" (see Figure 11-26). The Independent Traveler, in other words, concentrates on planning, transportation, and reservations. The Travel Corner focuses on what to do once you get there. You should become familiar with both.

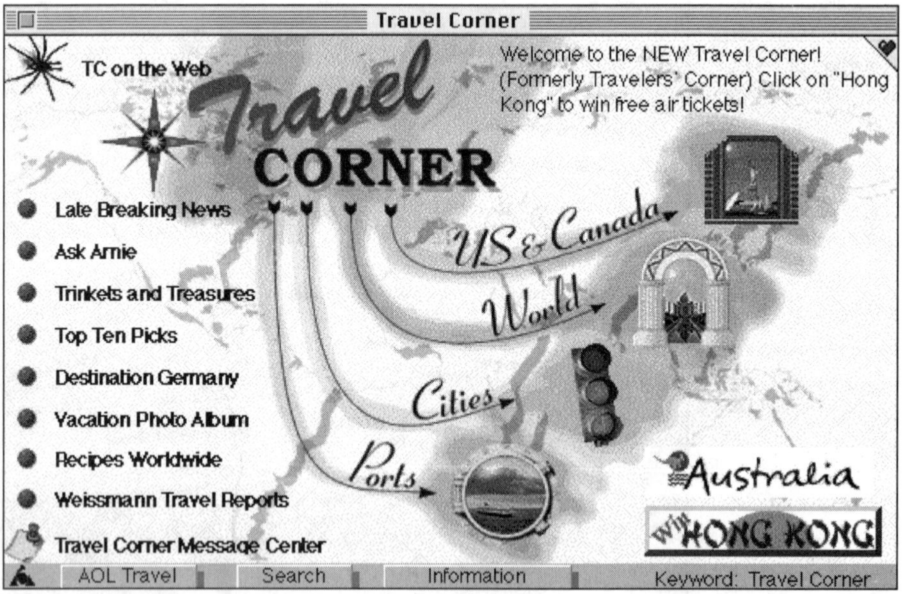
Travel Corner
TC on the Web
Travel
CORNER
Welcome to the NEW Travel Corner! (Formerly Travelers' Corner) Click on "Hong Kong" to win free air tickets!
Late Breaking News
Ask Arnie
Trinkets and Treasures
Top Ten Picks
Destination Germany
Vacation Photo Album
Recipes Worldwide
Weissmann Travel Reports
Travel Corner Message Center
US & Canada
World
Cities
Ports
Australia
HONG KONG
AOL Travel
Search
Information
Keyword: Travel Corner

Figure 11-26: The Travel Corner offers destination information for thousands of locations around the world.

preview travel vacations

With their television and online productions, preview travel is preparing the travel agency of the future. They have the world's largest collection of vacation videos and images, agents on duty seven days a week, and weekly opportunities to win a free vacation. At AOL, they're known as preview travel vacations. To find them, use the keyword: **Vacations**. (See Figure 11-27.)

Go to Preview Travel Vacations
preview travel • vacations
Vacation Offers
Contests & Prizes
Auction House
Our Web Site
Join - it's
Airline Tickets
HOT DEALS!
Travel Update
Multimedia
Hosted by Preview Travel, Inc.
Keyword: VACATIONS
preview travel
WORLDGOLF
Practice your golf while on a perfect vacation! Click here!

Figure 11-27: preview travel vacations offers dozens of competitively priced vacation packages. You can examine the accommodations and fares online—from the world's largest vacation image library—then make the booking, without ever having to leave your keyboard.

preview travel vacations is a full-service travel agency. They not only offer a kaleidoscope of travel images, they not only leverage their extensive media exposure to gather great package deals, but they also make bookings online—including transportation, hotels, and rental cars where appropriate. The human touch isn't ignored either: you can always talk to an agent via their toll-free line when you have specific questions.

Be sure to fill out your vacation profile so that preview travel vacations can contact you when an irresistible deal pops up that fits you perfectly. And don't neglect to enter the drawing for a free vacation: you can't beat that price!

Your Wallet Is Safe at AOL

All this talk about travel agencies, renting cars, and booking airline tickets may make you a little squeamish: "Does my AOL membership obligate me for anything beyond the standard monthly fee and connect charges?" No, not at all. All the additional-expense items I've discussed in this chapter are voluntary—not requisite to membership in AOL. This is the Travel Channel, after all, and most travel is discretionary—and an additional expense.

ExpressNet

ExpressNet from American Express offers a comprehensive online resource for American Express cardholders. Using a password, you can query the status of your American Express account, including all billed and unbilled charges. You can download billing details to your computer for use with Quicken, Managing Your Money for Windows, and Kiplinger's Simply Money software. By providing American Express with your checking account information, you can even pay your American Express bill online!

Welcome to ExpressNet!
ExpressNet
Travel Info & Reservations
Travel Info & Reservations
ExpressNet
Welcome to ExpressNet Shopping
Shopping Services
ExpressNet
Come in and window shop, browse or apply for an American Express Card.
Shop or Browse
How To Buy
Ask About An Order
PRICE GUARANTEE and 2,000 MEMBERSHIP REWARDS BONUS POINTS
Click here to enroll in Membership Rewards
Talk to Us
Apply for a Card
Purchase Gift Cheques
Product of the Week
ExpressNet Main Menu
Travel Channel
Marketplace
Keyword: Amex Shop

Figure 11-28: ExpressNet offers an extensive array of services for American Express cardholders.

ExpressNet members (there's no charge, though you must have an American Express card) also have access to the following:

- The American Express Travel Service for airline, hotel, and car rental reservations.
- The ExpressNet Shopping Service, where every purchase builds bonus miles in the American Express Membership Miles feature.
- A database of the special discounts and value-added offers exclusively available to American Express Cardmembers.

There's more, but you have to have an American Express card to access all of the features ExpressNet has to offer. Naturally, you can apply for a card online—just use the keyword: **ExpressNet**.

Other Travel Services Online

Space limitations simply don't permit me to explore the entirety of the Travel Channel. Still, I'd be remiss if I didn't mention at least some of the other major travel areas offered by AOL. If you've ever thought about taking an ocean cruise, discover Cruise Critic (keywords: **Cruise Critic**), an online cruise guide with in-depth, candid reviews of cruise ships and cruises. You'll find the latest cruise bargains, cruise tips, reviews of more than 100 ships—plus the advice of your fellow AOL cruisers. If you're planning a vacation at a bed and breakfast, the Lanier's Bed & Breakfast area (keywords: **Bed & Breakfast**) is where you'll find everything you need. If you're the outdoors type, then the Outdoor Adventure Online area (keyword: **OAO**) will get you where you want to go. For the bargain-minded, AOL has the Traveler's Advantage area (keywords: **Traveler's Advantage**). And finally, there's complete access to the Internet, where even more travel opportunities and interests await.

Figure 11-29: Just a few of the many other travel areas offered by AOL.

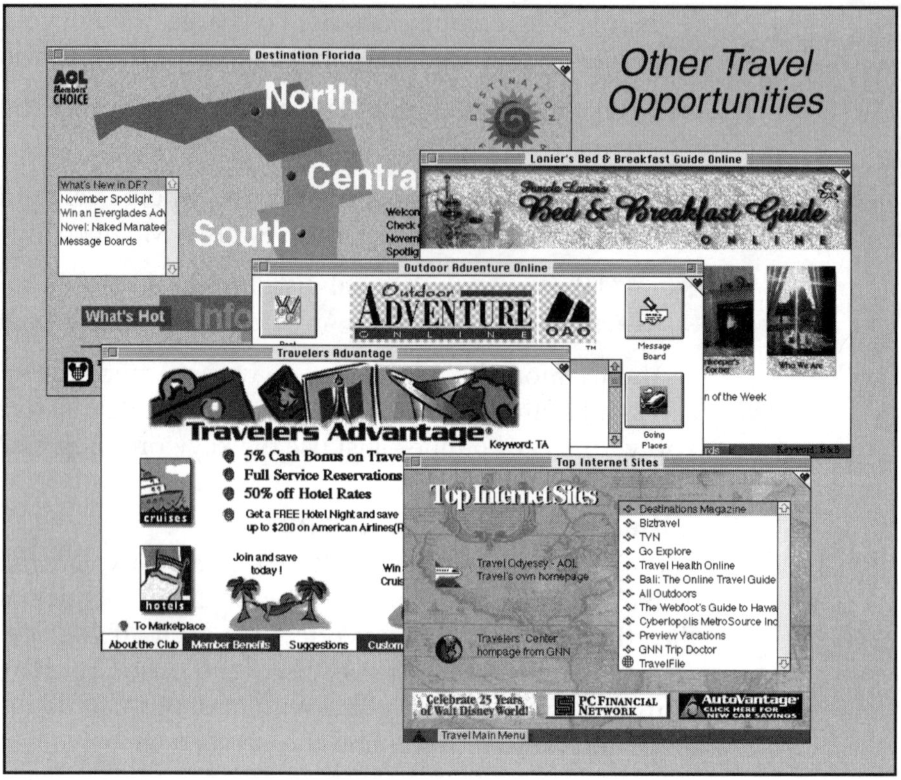
Other Travel Opportunities
Destination Florida
North
Central
South
What's New in DF?
November Spotlight
Message Boards
What's Hot
Lanier's Bed & Breakfast Guide Online
Bed & Breakfast Guide
Outdoor Adventure Online
Outdoor Adventure Online
OAO
Message Board
Going Places
Travelers Advantage
Travelers Advantage
Keyword: TA
5% Cash Bonus on Travel
Full Service Reservations
50% off Hotel Rates
cruises
hotels
Join and save today!
To Marketplace
About the Club
Member Benefits
Suggestions
Top Internet Sites
Top Internet Sites
Travel Odyssey - AOL Travel's own homepage
Travelers' Center hompage from GNN
Destinations Magazine
Biztravel
TVN
Go Explore
Travel Health Online
Bali: The Online Travel Guide
All Outdoors
Preview Vacations
GNN Trip Doctor
TravelFile
Celebrate 25 Years of Walt Disney World!
PC Financial Network
AutoVantage
Travel Main Menu

MusicSpace

We tend to think of the online medium as one that's primarily textual, with a few graphics for window dressing. That perception isn't far off the mark, but the mark is a moving target. The online medium of today bears little resemblance to what we'll be using tomorrow. We are the pioneers. Future generations will remember us as we remember the pony express riders back in the days when mail was carried on horseback.

Perhaps the most profound change will occur in the music business (see the "Thea McCue" sidebar). Music recording technology is already almost exclusively digital; even some musical *instruments* are digital. Digital is the language of computers. It's only a matter of time before digital music and your computer are wedded via the online medium.

Thea McCue

Thea McCue is an Account Coordinator for AOL. Her purview is MusicSpace (described later in this chapter). Like many of AOL's creative staff, her job is not only to manage the day-to-day operation of her area, but to stay an appropriate distance ahead of it as well.

In perhaps five years, when "the bandwidth" opens up and we're all able to connect to AOL at, say, 256 kbps—a megabyte every 10 seconds—Thea foresees a MusicSpace that's considerably different from the one that exists today. "Music producers today are at the mercy of the broadcast media: if radio stations don't play it; if MTV or VH1 doesn't run the video, the music dies." The consumer, in other words, sees and hears new music only after it has passed through the broadcast media's filters—hardly an unbiased selection.

In five years you might be listening to music—perhaps even watching videos—that you've downloaded from Thea's libraries. These libraries will offer all of the new music that's available, not a subset passed through a filter. You'll listen to it when you want and it will be digital quality—the same as CDs today. AOL will keep track of the downloads—just as they do today—and those selections with large download numbers will become hits. Feedback from listener to artist will be direct via message boards and download numbers. You might even furnish your credit card number and have AOL download the entire album to your writeable CD-ROM. Consumer and producer will share a distribution channel that's equitable and immediate.

Music is a personal thing. This scenario will not only complement that intimacy, it will promote it. There are changes ahead, and many of them will be for the better.

In 1969 I camped across from the launch site of Apollo 11, the first rocket to land a man on the moon. The night before launch, the anticipation among the people gathered there was electric. Something big was about to happen and we were all there to see it. AOL's MusicSpace (see Figure 11-30) is like that. It is home to some of the most creative people in mass communications—people drawn to both music and the online medium. They're camped out here, waiting for Something Big. If you want to be there when it happens, visit MusicSpace often.

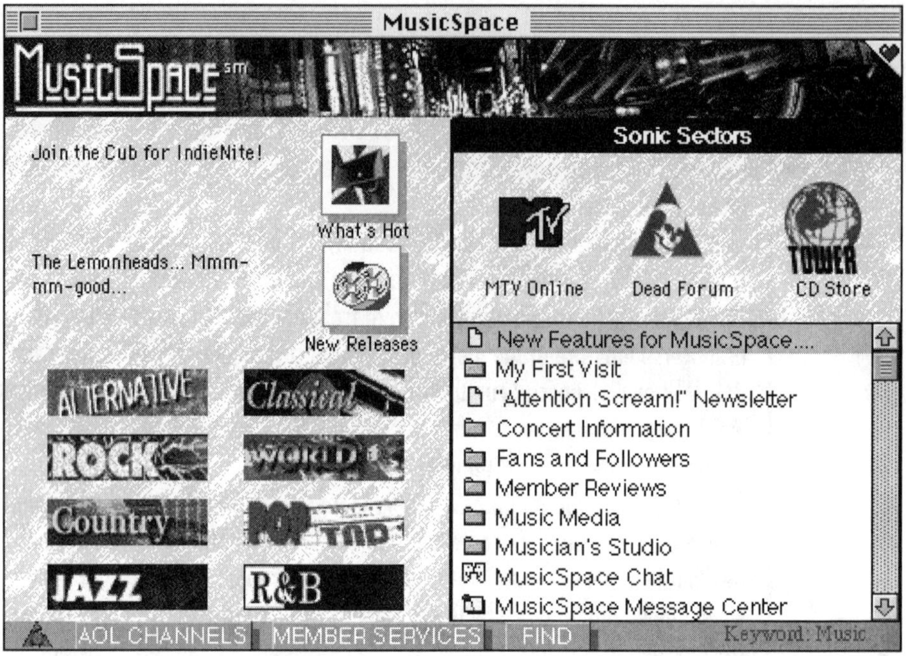
MusicSpace
MusicSpace
Sonic Sectors
Join the Cub for IndieNite!
What's Hot
The Lemonheads... Mmm-mm-good...
New Releases
MTV Online
Dead Forum
CD Store
New Features for MusicSpace....
My First Visit
"Attention Scream!" Newsletter
Concert Information
Fans and Followers
Member Reviews
Music Media
Musician's Studio
MusicSpace Chat
MusicSpace Message Center
AOL CHANNELS
MEMBER SERVICES
FIND
Keyword: Music

Figure 11-30: MusicSpace is the conductor's podium for all things musical on AOL. If you enjoy music—be it classical, hip-hop, or anything in between—use the keyword: **Music** every time you sign on.

MTV

Writing in the *San Francisco Examiner*, Robert Rossney recently referred to AOL as "bringing American commercial culture to the online world as fast as it can." His description of AOL made it sound about as exciting as flat beer by citing areas of the service where you can obtain instructions for making masks from paper plates and throwing block parties.

Obviously, Rossney never visited MTV Online (keyword: **MTV**). This place is about as indicative of American commercial culture as Las Vegas on Halloween. The people at MTV—with screen names like MTVomit, MTVixen, and MTVacuum—love to get "in your face," and the online medium hardly cramps their style (see Figure 11-31).

MTV Main Screen
MTV Music Screen
MTV Online - Head Shop
MTV Online - Tubescan

Figure 11-31: MTV Online is about as reverent as a fraternity house on a Saturday night in June.

Here's a hint: get the map. The list box in the main MTV screen offers an online diagram of the MTV areas and describes what's in each one. How else would you know that you can find an historically significant video every month in the *Buzz Been* section of MTV Past Out, or that Beavis and Butthead hang out at the Head Shop?

With your map in hand, be sure to check out MTV Yack!, the Wavelength, and the Stream Of Consciousnews areas.

Even if you can't make sense of what they're saying, the place flaunts the best Eye Candy that's available online. Be sure your color is turned on!

The Corner Tavern

Anyone who has attended the showing of a good film in a full theater knows that most people prefer their entertainment in the company of other people. We go to the movies not just to see the film, but to see the film in the company of others. We laugh more at sitcoms when we're not alone. We travel to the corner tavern for Monday Night Football so that we can comment to one another while the game is in progress.

It comes as no surprise to the people at AOL, then, to learn that there's a significant coincidence between message board usage and broadcast television. Visit MTV Yak someday while your TV is tuned to the MTV channel, on a weekday, after school has let out. Chances are, the discussion will coincide with the events onscreen. The same can be said of the Melrose Place board—though peak activity might occur just after an episode ends—or, indeed, Monday Night Football. It's a peculiar but quantifiable phenomenon. Someone should write a thesis.

VH1

Shall we mellow the demographic somewhat? On cable, VH1's appeal is to a slightly older market than MTV's, with artists such as Emmylou Harris, Billy Joel, k.d. lang, and Mariah Carey. The same can be said of VH1's online offering (see Figure 11-32).

Digital Gallery
Artist Showcase
Boyz II Men
Bryan Adams
Don Henley
Gloria Estefan
Harry Connick Jr.
Hootie and the Blowfish
Janet Jackson
Artist of the Month
CD SHOP
Inside VH1
Music Wire
Music Wire
Van Halen Released Today! Look For The Surprise Inside Some CD's
Past Music Wire Articles
Melissa Etheridge Baby Shower
---October 22, 1996---
Grammy's Come To The Apple
Beatles Boom
Pat Boone Rocks With Zappa
Music First News
MUSIC NOTES
MAIL BOX
CONNECTED

Figure 11-32: VH1 online spotlights music, of course, and much of it is downloadable. VH1 is a compelling multimedia resource that's available now, at keyword: **VH1**.

VH1 offers all of the chat rooms, message boards, and artist features you would expect from a resource such as this, but two features warrant special mention:

- The *Digital Gallery* offers a spectacular library of video clips and sound samples. Some of the latter are available in digital stereo and, played on the proper equipment, sound every bit as good as a CD. This is a great way to sample material from a new release to see if it's something you want to buy.
- The *Goods* offers a direct connection to Blockbuster Music, so you can buy the music you've read about—perhaps even sampled—without leaving your keyboard!

MusicSpace Message Center

The MusicSpace Message Center is the Big Daddy of all of the message boards on AOL. It's one of the busiest places you'll find anywhere online—it requires a staff of approximately 20 people—and because of its size, there's bound to be a music category that suits your needs (see Figure 11-33).

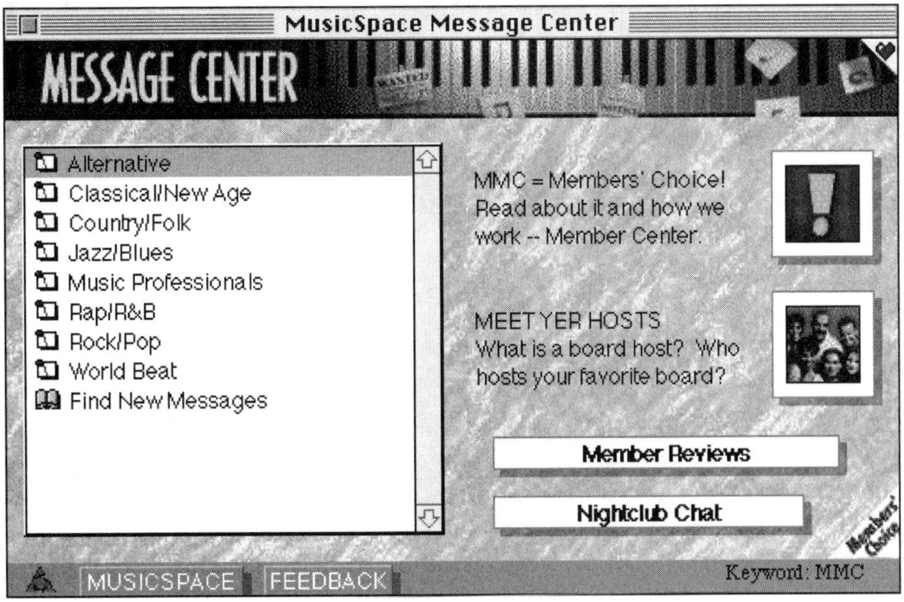
MusicSpace Message Center
MESSAGE CENTER
Alternative
Classical/New Age
Country/Folk
Jazz/Blues
Music Professionals
Rap/R&B
Rock/Pop
World Beat
Find New Messages
MMC = Members' Choice!
Read about it and how we work -- Member Center.
MEET YER HOSTS
What is a board host? Who hosts your favorite board?
Member Reviews
Nightclub Chat
MUSICSPACE
FEEDBACK
Keyword: MMC

Figure 11-33: The MusicSpace Message Center is the place for you to exchange views and queries about music of all forms.

Figure 11-33 hardly does the MusicSpace Message Center justice. Each of the broad categories appearing in the illustration contains scores—sometimes hundreds—of individual folders. The Rock/Pop category, for example, offers over 280 boards, discussing topics from ABBA to Frank Zappa.

The Message Center's success is, most likely, attributable to its attitude. The Center's focus is fans, not the media, and the participants appreciate the lack of industry intrusion. If you like music and you want to talk with others who like music, use the keyword: **MMC**, and become involved with the MusicSpace Message Center.

SPINonline

As you would expect from the people who produce *SPIN* magazine, SPINonline offers creative irreverence and verbal spaghetti. It's all in fun, and every corner of the online medium is exposed along the way. These guys push the envelope (see Figure 11-34).

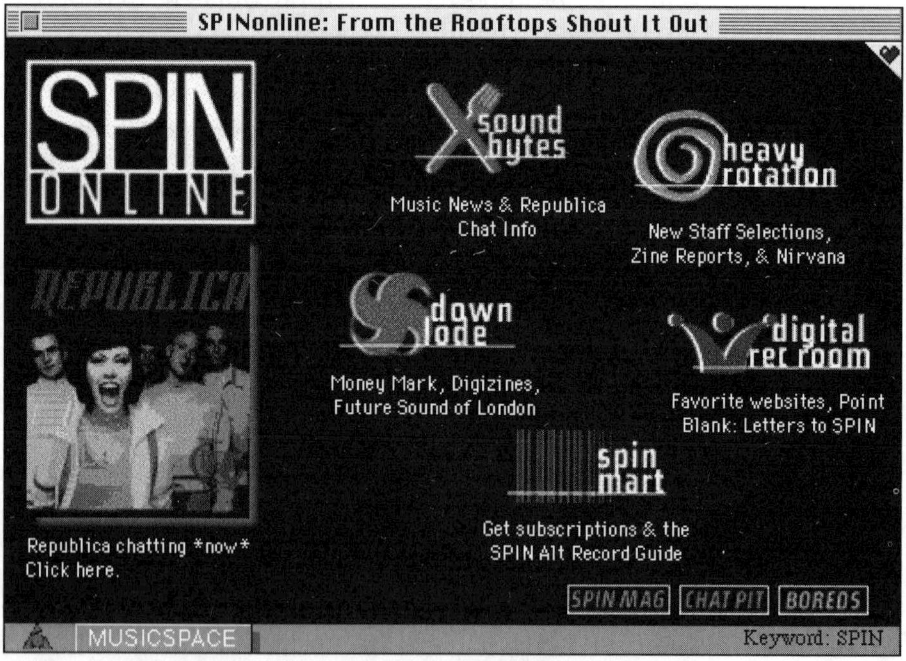
SPINonline: From the Rooftops Shout It Out
SPIN ONLINE
sound bytes
Music News & Republica Chat Info
heavy rotation
New Staff Selections, Zine Reports, & Nirvana
REPUBLICA
down lode
Money Mark, Digizines, Future Sound of London
digital rec room
Favorite websites, Point Blank: Letters to SPIN
spin mart
Get subscriptions & the SPIN Alt Record Guide
Republica chatting *now* Click here.
SPIN MAG
CHAT PIT
BOREDS
MUSICSPACE
Keyword: SPIN

Figure 11-34: The Digital Mosh Pit, the Wasteland, Suspicious Minds, and the SPINonline Garage—they're all waiting to be explored at keyword: **SPIN**.

If you're in a band—even if you're solo—try uploading a sound clip to the SPINonline Garage. The mechanics there review everything received and post the best for everyone else to hear. There's also the SPIN College Radio Network Online. Each week *SPIN* magazine produces a program that airs on more than 300 college radio stations from coast to coast, and SPINonline is where you'll find out about upcoming shows, and meet new artists and your neighborhood college radio programmers.

The Grateful Dead Forum

Have I mentioned my preference for classical music? Stephen King might do his writing while rock and roll plays at 120 decibels, but I write to Mozart. I'm not a purist, however. As an Oregonian and a former "radical" of the '60s, I confess a liking for the Grateful Dead. The Dead were especially fond of Oregon, and they exhibited that fondness with an annual visit to Eugene, a Mecca for Deadheads if there ever was one.

Four years ago, as I was writing the first edition of this book, the Grateful Dead was just another message board in what was then known as the RockLink Forum. It was a crowded board—its messages always numbered around 500—but just a board nonetheless. Two years later when I was updating this book, I discovered that the Dead had a forum of their own. Now I see that they have a newly redesigned forum, complete with psychedelic fractals and a glowing AOL orb (see Figure 11-35). Something peculiar is going on here. This band is older than color TV, yet it comprises one of the most active areas on AOL today.

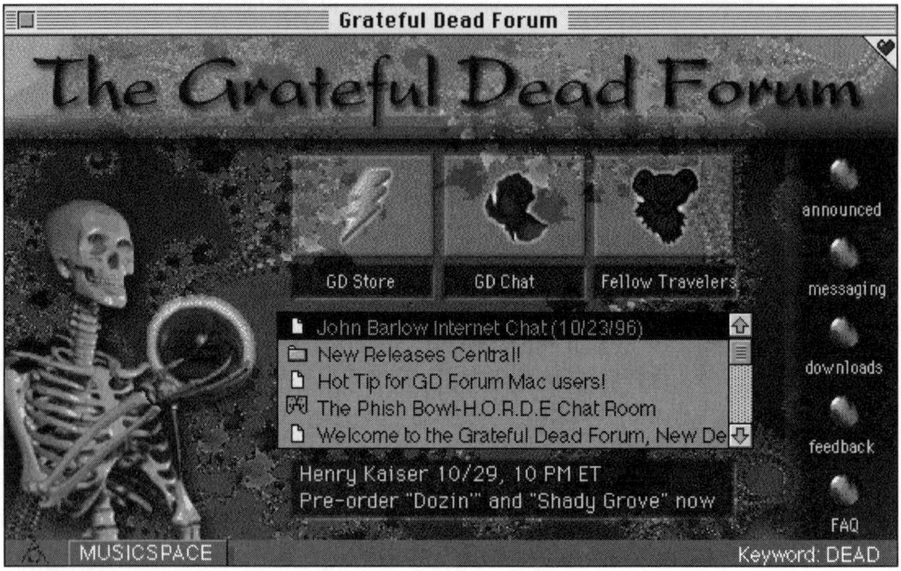
Grateful Dead Forum
The Grateful Dead Forum
GD Store
GD Chat
Fellow Travelers
announced
messaging
downloads
feedback
FAQ
John Barlow Internet Chat (10/23/96)
New Releases Central!
Hot Tip for GD Forum Mac users!
The Phish Bowl-H.O.R.D.E Chat Room
Welcome to the Grateful Dead Forum, New De
Henry Kaiser 10/29, 10 PM ET
Pre-order "Dozin'" and "Shady Grove" now
MUSICSPACE
Keyword: DEAD

Figure 11-35: The Grateful Dead Forum defies rational interpretation

WEB TopStops

AOL's MusicWeb site is a *tour de force* in Web page design. In addition to its changing list of top 10 music sites, AOL also has a number of innovative sites of its own. Look for the "Music Mood Ring," with blue (the blues), red (party music), yellow (mellow, acoustic, profound), pink (bubbly), green (underground), and black (heavy metal). Each of these colors takes you to a Web page that's festooned with links to Web sites from all over the world, with audio and video clips galore. The Music Mood Ring isn't all: AOL has also cooked up the "Browse-O-Matic," where a new recipe for Web sites appears each week, and each of the ingredients is a hyperlink to even more Web sites. The World Wide Web (discussed in Chapter 4, "Using the Internet") is almost overburdened with music resources, but the WEB TopStops brings organization and fun to what could be an overwhelming mire of excess.

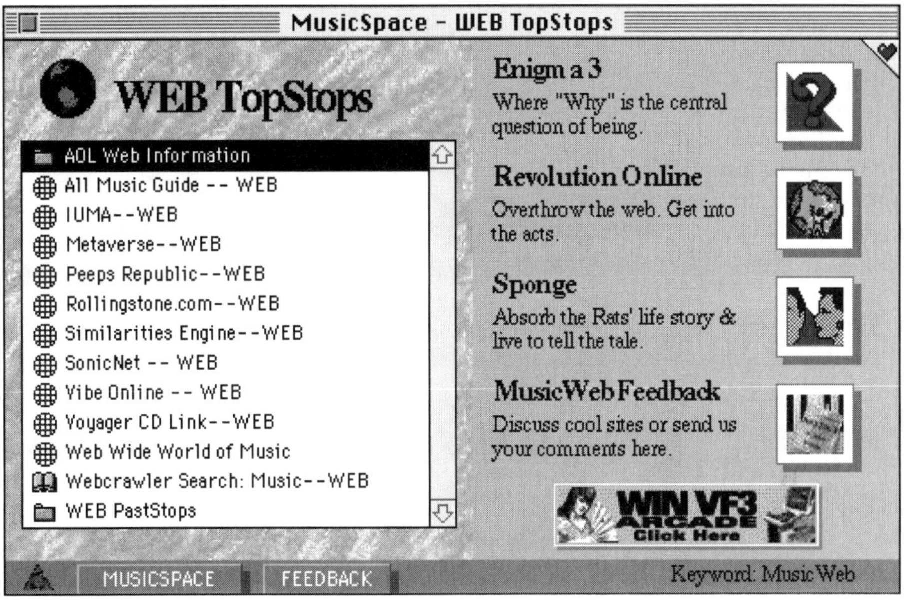
MusicSpace - WEB TopStops
WEB TopStops
AOL Web Information
All Music Guide -- WEB
IUMA--WEB
Metaverse--WEB
Peeps Republic--WEB
Rollingstone.com--WEB
Similarities Engine--WEB
SonicNet -- WEB
Vibe Online -- WEB
Voyager CD Link--WEB
Web Wide World of Music
Webcrawler Search: Music--WEB
WEB PastStops
Enigma 3
Where "Why" is the central question of being.
Revolution Online
Overthrow the web. Get into the acts.
Sponge
Absorb the Rats' life story & live to tell the tale.
MusicWeb Feedback
Discuss cool sites or send us your comments here.
WIN VF3
ARCADE
Click Here
MUSICSPACE
FEEDBACK
Keyword: MusicWeb

Figure 11-36: AOL's WEB TopStops brings order to the chaos of music Web sites at keyword: **MusicWeb**.

Warner/Reprise Online

I saved this one 'til last because it always invokes the image of Porky Pig's head emerging from the old Warner Brothers logo, saying "Th-Th-Th-That's all, folks!" Thus, it seems to fit well at the end of our entertainment media section.

As you would expect, Warner/Reprise online exists to keep fans informed about artists on the Warner/Reprise family of labels, which includes Warner Bros., Reprise, Sire, American Recordings, Giant, Slash, 4AD, Qwest, Luaka Bop, Kinetic Records, the Medicine Label, and Maverick (see Figure 11-37). You'll find music industry news here too, and a kaleidoscope of multimedia files, including an extensive library of videos.

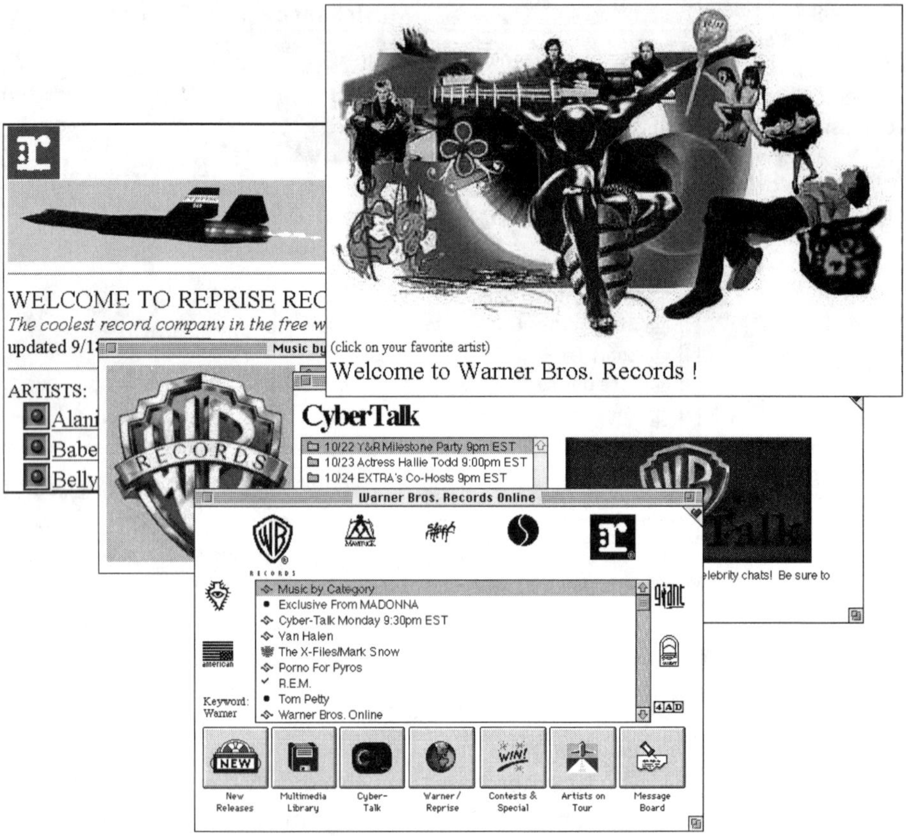
WELCOME TO REPRISE REC
The coolest record company in the free w
updated 9/1
ARTISTS:
Alani
Babe
Belly
Music by
(click on your favorite artist)
Welcome to Warner Bros. Records !
CyberTalk
10/22 Y&R Milestone Party 9pm EST
10/23 Actress Hallie Todd 9:00pm EST
10/24 EXTRA's Co-Hosts 9pm EST
lebrity chats! Be sure to
Warner Bros. Records Online
Music by Category
Exclusive From MADONNA
Cyber-Talk Monday 9:30pm EST
Van Halen
The X-Files/Mark Snow
Porno For Pyros
R.E.M.
Tom Petty
Warner Bros. Online
Keyword: Warner
NEW
WIN!
New Releases
Multimedia Library
Cyber-Talk
Warner / Reprise
Contests & Special
Artists on Tour
Message Board

Figure 11-37: The Warner/Reprise area (keyword: **Warner**) offers news and multimedia files for minstrels, contrapuntists, syncopators, kapellmeisters, and troubadours alike.

I find Warner's CyberTalk, however, to be the area's spectacle among spectacles. CyberTalk is an interactive talk show, occurring every Monday evening at 9:30 (eastern time). The list of guests is impressive: k.d. lang, Vince Neil, Christine McVie, Fleetwood Mac, Elvis Costello, Peter, Paul, and Mary, Van Halen, Arlo Guthrie, Red Hot Chili Peppers, Chaka Khan, Devo—these are just a few of the artists who have appeared. Check the CyberTalk area at keyword: **Warner** for the current schedule. See you Monday nights!

And that—as Porky used to say—is all, folks!

Moving On

From the trivial to the profound—we now make the transition to the world of the Personal Finance Channel. Lots of people subscribe to AOL for financial purposes alone. AOL rewards them with relevant (and current) information, and advice from professionals and fellow investors alike. Grab your checkbook and turn the page.

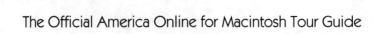

CHAPTER 12

Personal Finance

- Your Personal Stock Portfolio
- Company Research
- Your Business

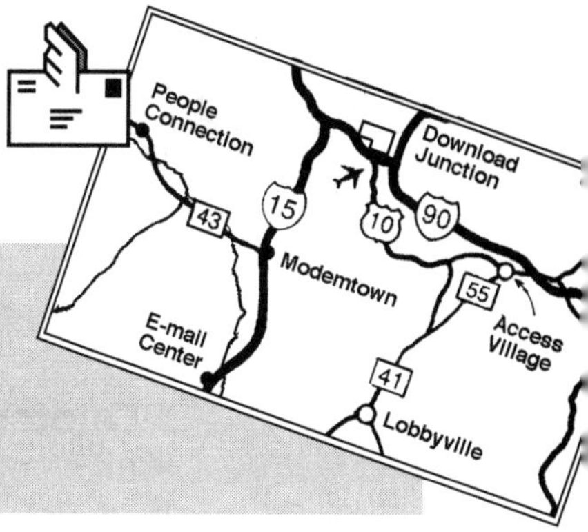
People Connection
Download Junction
15
10
90
43
Modemtown
55
E-mail Center
Access Village
41
Lobbyville

Have you ever seen those little radios that pick up weather reports? I use one every day. It's tuned to the local National Oceanic and Atmospheric Administration (NOAA) station, which broadcasts nothing but the weather, 24 hours a day. These gadgets are the ideal information machine: always current, always available, and nearly free. Now if I could only find a similar source for financial information.

Aha! What about AOL? If ever there was a "machine" for instant financial news, America Online is it. Unlike television or radio, AOL's market information is available whenever you want it: there's no waiting for the 6 o'clock news or suffering through three stories (and four commercials) that you don't want to hear. Unlike newspapers, AOL's financial news is always current. It's not this morning's news; it's this *minute's* news. It's current, it's always available, and it's almost free.

I wonder if Ted Turner knows about this?

Your Personal Stock Portfolio

Let's begin this chapter with a financial exercise. This one is risk-free but nonetheless quite real. A portfolio of investments is a fascinating thing to follow and nourish, even if it's only make-believe. And if you want to add some real punch to it, AOL offers a brokerage service. You can invest real money in real issues and realize real gains (or real losses).

Whether you intend to invest real cash or just funny money, join me as we create a personal portfolio of stocks and securities.

Quotes & Portfolios

Begin the journey by clicking the Personal Finance button on the Channels menu, or by clicking the Keyword button on the toolbar and entering the keyword: **Finance**. America Online responds by transporting you to the Personal Finance department (see Figure 12-1).

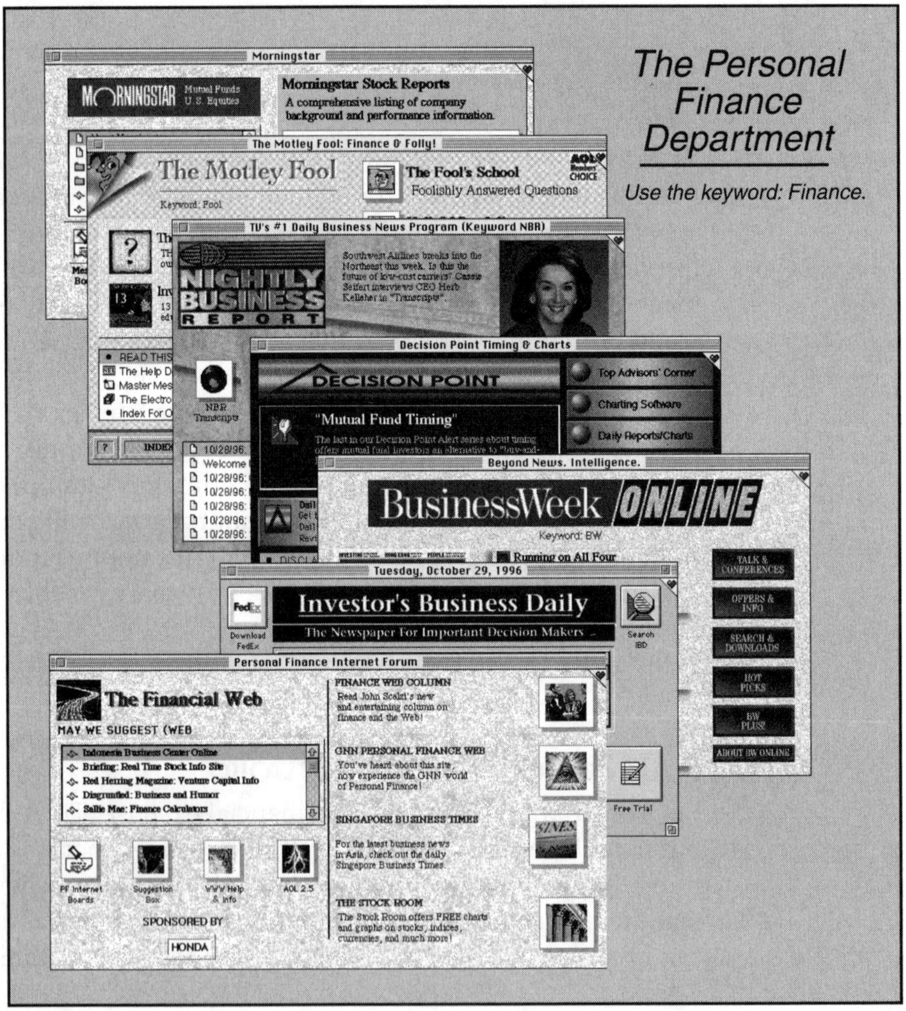
The Personal Finance Department
Use the keyword: Finance.
Morningstar
The Motley Fool: Finance & Folly!
The Motley Fool
The Fool's School
Foolishly Answered Questions
TV's #1 Daily Business News Program (Keyword NBR)
NIGHTLY BUSINESS REPORT
Decision Point Timing & Charts
DECISION POINT
"Mutual Fund Timing"
Top Advisors' Corner
Charting Software
Daily Reports/Charts
Beyond News. Intelligence.
BusinessWeek ONLINE
Keyword: BW
Tuesday, October 29, 1996
Investor's Business Daily
The Newspaper For Important Decision Makers
Personal Finance Internet Forum
The Financial Web
FINANCE WEB COLUMN
GNN PERSONAL FINANCE WEB
SINGAPORE BUSINESS TIMES
THE STOCK ROOM
SPONSORED BY
HONDA

Figure 12-1: America Online might be the perfect financial information machine: it's always current and it's available 24 hours a day.

A wealth (pun intended) of financial information awaits you here, as does opportunity. You not only can seek counsel on your investments; you also can actually buy them here—and maintain a portfolio as well. And the portfolio, for the moment, is our focus. Click the icon labeled Quotes & Portfolios, and let's invest our surplus cash (see Figure 12-2).

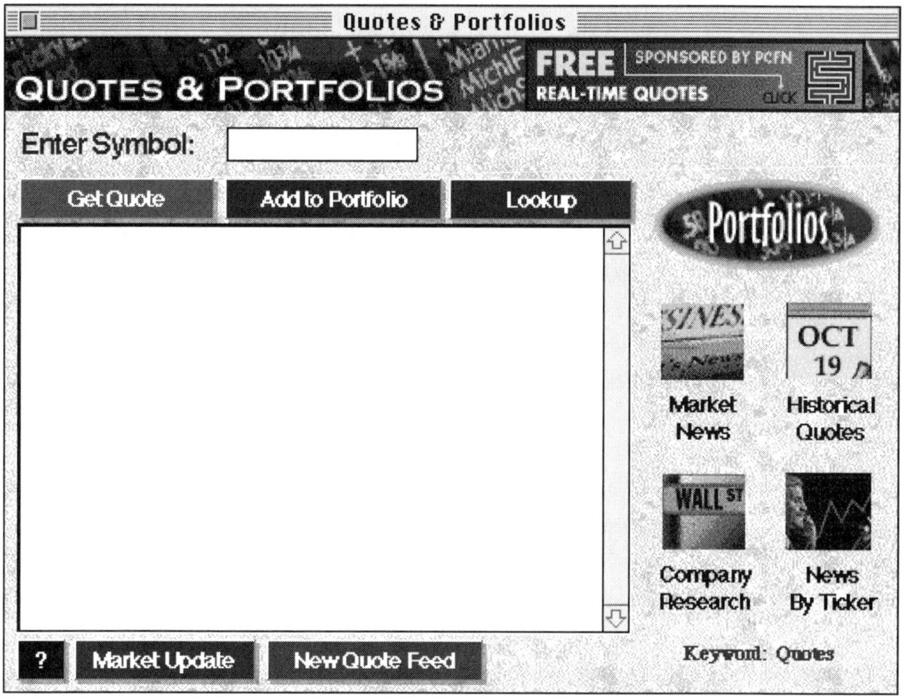
Quotes & Portfolios
QUOTES & PORTFOLIOS
FREE
SPONSORED BY PCFN
REAL-TIME QUOTES
Enter Symbol:
Get Quote
Add to Portfolio
Lookup
Portfolios
OCT
19
Market News
Historical Quotes
Company Research
News By Ticker
?
Market Update
New Quote Feed
Keyword: Quotes

Figure 12-2: The Quotes & Portfolios window allows you to access market news, look up an issue, build a portfolio, and actually buy and sell issues. It's available from the main window of the Personal Finance window, through the jagged-arrow button on the toolbar or the keyword: **Quotes**.

The Quotes & Portfolios section of the Personal Finance Channel is a comprehensive financial information service equaled by few others in the telecommunications industry, and available on AOL without surcharge. The only thing you pay when you're visiting here is your normal connect-time charges. America Online is connected to the financial centers of the world via high-speed data lines, providing financial information that is updated continuously during market hours—usually about 15 minutes behind the action.

Finding a Stock Symbol

America Online is waiting for us to enter a stock symbol. Stock symbols are those abbreviations you see traveling across the Big Board in a stockbroker's office. What shall we buy? Because it's something that we all have in common, let's look up AOL. America Online is a publicly traded issue, after all, so we should offer a reference to it here.

But what's AOL's symbol? Hmmm . . . let's try the Lookup button in the Quotes & Portfolios window, shown in Figure 12-2. When you click that icon and follow the path pictured in Figure 12-3, you discover that AOL is the symbol for America Online.

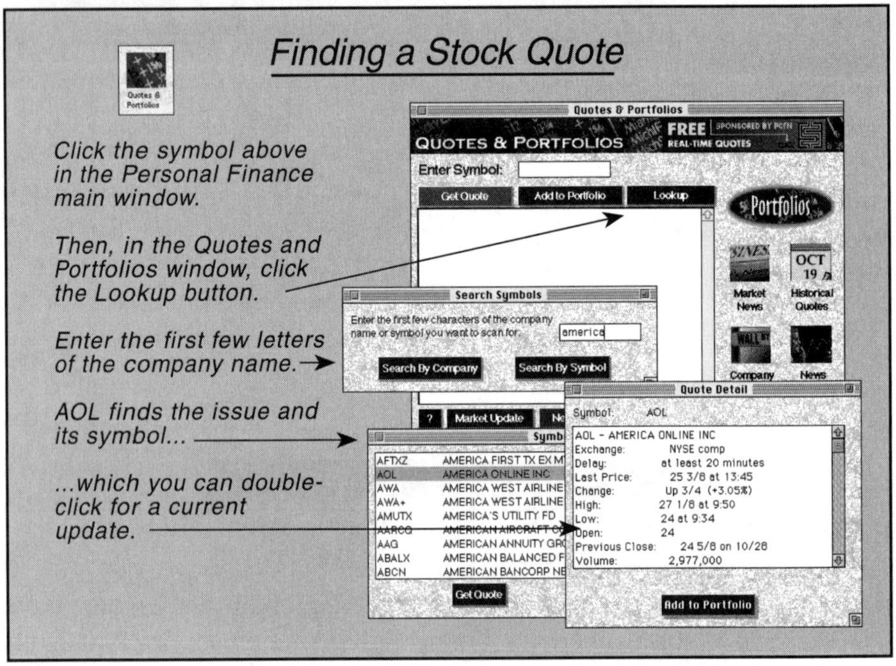
Finding a Stock Quote
Click the symbol above in the Personal Finance main window.
Then, in the Quotes and Portfolios window, click the Lookup button.
Enter the first few letters of the company name.
AOL finds the issue and its symbol...
...which you can double-click for a current update.
Quotes & Portfolios
QUOTES & PORTFOLIOS
FREE
REAL-TIME QUOTES
Enter Symbol:
Get Quote
Add to Portfolio
Lookup
Portfolios
Market News
Historical Quotes
Company
News
Market Update
Search Symbols
Enter the first few characters of the company name or symbol you want to scan for.
america
Search By Company
Search By Symbol
AFTXZ AMERICA FIRST TX EX M
AOL AMERICA ONLINE INC
AWA AMERICA WEST AIRLINE
AWA+ AMERICA WEST AIRLINE
AMUTX AMERICA'S UTILITY FD
AAG AMERICAN ANNUITY GR
ABALX AMERICAN BALANCED F
ABCN AMERICAN BANCORP NE
Get Quote
Quote Detail
Symbol: AOL
AOL - AMERICA ONLINE INC
Exchange: NYSE comp
Delay: at least 20 minutes
Last Price: 25 3/8 at 13:45
Change: Up 3/4 (+3.05%)
High: 27 1/8 at 9:50
Low: 24 at 9:34
Open: 24
Previous Close: 24 5/8 on 10/28
Volume: 2,977,000
Add to Portfolio

Figure 12-3: Don't know the symbol for an issue? Let America Online look it up for you.

Once you have the symbol, enter it into the box as shown in Figure 12-3 and click the Get Quote button (or simply double-click the symbol's line). The results are pictured in Figure 12-3's scroll box.

Building the Portfolio

Note the current price, then click the Add to Portfolio button. America Online responds with the dialog box shown in Figure 12-4.

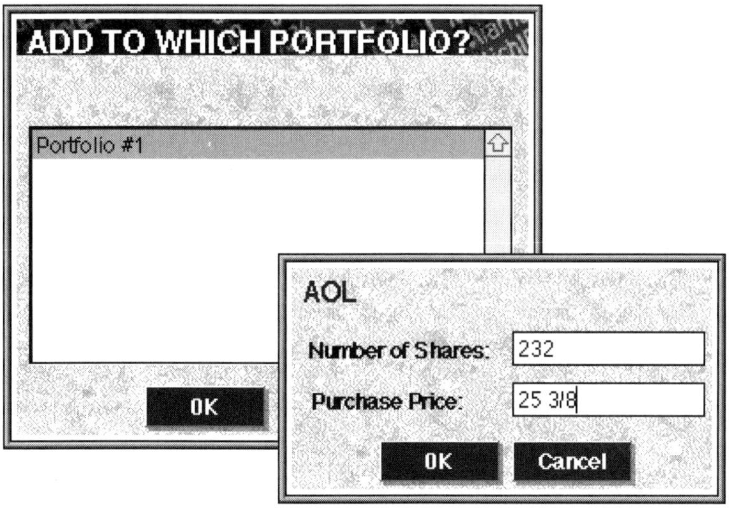
ADD TO WHICH PORTFOLIO?
Portfolio #1
OK
AOL
Number of Shares:
232
Purchase Price:
25 3/8
OK
Cancel

Figure 12-4: Enter the current price and the number of shares you want, then click OK. The "investment" will be added to your portfolio.

Note that you can have more than one portfolio—up to 20, in fact, with as many as 100 issues in each one. You might have to create a portfolio before you can add your "investment" to it; but eventually you'll encounter the windows in Figure 12-4.

Because this is only make-believe, buy as many shares as you like. Don't worry: AOL doesn't share your portfolio with anyone, and you won't be charged any special fees for this exercise; it's a private matter between you and your computer.

To view your portfolio, click the Portfolios button in the Quotes & Portfolios window shown at the top of Figure 12-3, or use the keyword: **Portfolio**. AOL will display the Portfolio Summary window shown in Figure 12-5: double-click the portfolio you want to view.

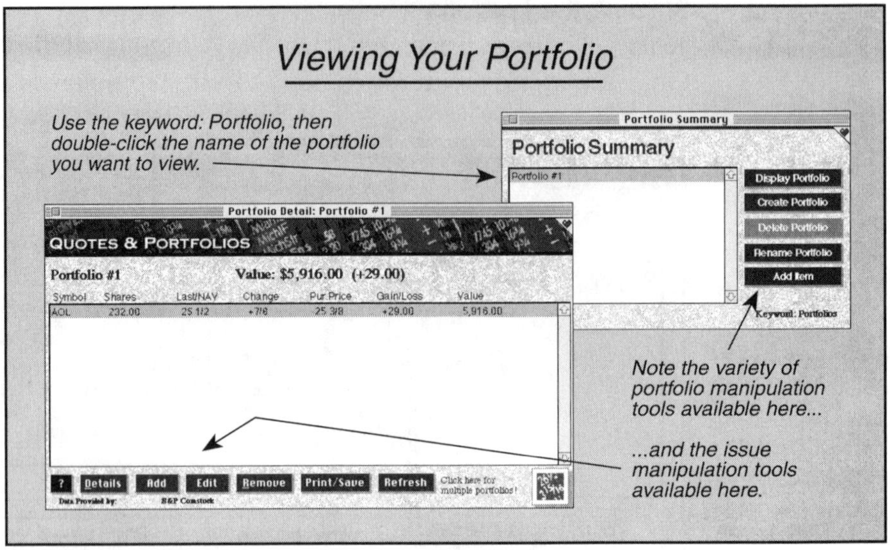
Viewing Your Portfolio
Use the keyword: Portfolio, then double-click the name of the portfolio you want to view.
Portfolio Summary
Portfolio Summary
Display Portfolio
Create Portfolio
Delete Portfolio
Rename Portfolio
Add Item
Keyword: Portfolios
Portfolio Detail: Portfolio #1
QUOTES & PORTFOLIOS
Portfolio #1
Value: $5,916.00 (+29.00)
Note the variety of portfolio manipulation tools available here...
...and the issue manipulation tools available here.
Details
Add
Edit
Remove
Print/Save
Refresh

Figure 12-5: Your portfolio is always available at keyword: **Portfolio.** To make it even easier to access, add it to your list of Favorite Places. (Favorite Places are discussed in Chapter 4.)

Printing & Saving Your Portfolio

The Print/Save button at the bottom of Figure 12-5 prints the data displayed in the Quotes & Portfolios window, as you would expect.

Few people are aware, however, that by clicking the Print/Save button, you can also *save* your portfolio, for advanced analysis by spreadsheet and database programs.

The File | Save command is disabled when the primary Quotes & Portfolios window is displayed, but when you click its Print/Save button, the contents of the window are reformatted (in Courier, for printing) and the Save command is enabled. Your portfolio data will be saved as a text file which many programs—word processing and spreadsheet in particular—can interpret. Microsoft's Excel spreadsheet can even resolve the mixed fractions and decimals in the Last/NAV column. Be sure to choose Text Only in the Save dialog. When you open the file into your spreadsheet, the format will be tab-delimited text (without going into a big discussion of what that is, suffice to say it's an option in almost every spreadsheet).

This is a godsend for those of us who used the portfolio-saving command that was available in earlier versions of the software.

Company Research

You can conduct a significant amount of company research on any one particular issue right from the Quotes & Portfolios Portfolio Detail window: select the issue you want to know more about, then click the Details button. AOL responds with the Stock Quote window illustrated in Figure 12-6.

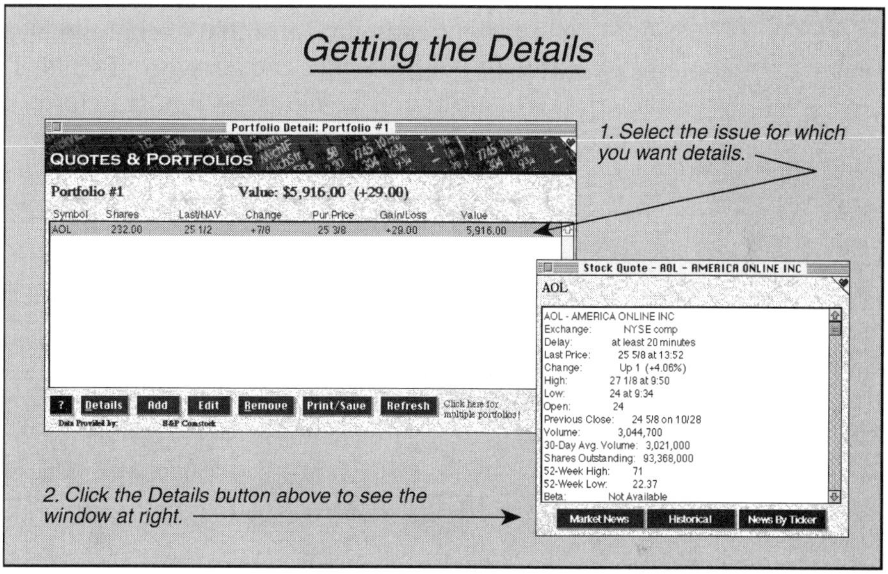
Getting the Details
1. Select the issue for which you want details.
2. Click the Details button above to see the window at right.
Portfolio Detail: Portfolio #1
QUOTES & PORTFOLIOS
Portfolio #1
Value: $5,916.00 (+29.00)
Symbol Shares Last/NAV Change Pur Price Gain/Loss Value
AOL 232.00 25 1/2 +7/8 25 3/8 +29.00 5,916.00
? Details Add Edit Remove Print/Save Refresh
Click here for multiple portfolios!
Data Provided by: S&P Comstock
Stock Quote - AOL - AMERICA ONLINE INC
AOL
AOL - AMERICA ONLINE INC
Exchange: NYSE comp
Delay: at least 20 minutes
Last Price: 25 5/8 at 13:52
Change: Up 1 (+4.06%)
High: 27 1/8 at 9:50
Low: 24 at 9:34
Open: 24
Previous Close: 24 5/8 on 10/28
Volume: 3,044,700
30-Day Avg. Volume: 3,021,000
Shares Outstanding: 93,368,000
52-Week High: 71
52-Week Low: 22.37
Beta: Not Available
Market News
Historical
News By Ticker

Figure 12-6: You can obtain extensive current and historical information about any issue in your portfolio by clicking the Details button.

Two buttons at the bottom of the Stock Quote window shown in Figure 12-6 deserve special mention. Refer to that figure as you read on.

- The News By Ticker button leads to a variety of financial news stories regarding that particular issue. The stories that appear are drawn from Reuters, Knight-Ridder, and the PR Newswire over the past couple of weeks. Read them all and you won't have many unanswered questions about your investment.
- The Historical button calls upon AOL's built-in graphing routines to graph the high-low-open-close (for stocks; a line graph for mutual funds) performance of your investment over time. Be sure to investigate the mini-toolbar in the Graph window: just leave the mouse pointer over any one of them for a moment to see a pop-up tool tip.

The amount of company research that's available directly from the Quotes & Portfolios window is impressive. If you take investing seriously, be sure to investigate what's available—and that includes the Help buttons!

The PC Financial Network

Though you can pretend all you want, eventually you're going to want to make some real investments, and that's what the PC Financial Network is for. To get there, use the keyword: **PCFN**. There's a considerable art download if you've never been here before, and it's worth the wait: this is one of the most handsome areas on the service (see Figure 12-7).

PC Financial Network
PC FINANCIAL NETWORK
MEMBERS' AOL CHOICE
Save on Commissions
Open an Account Now
Try Our Online Demo
Access YOUR ACCOUNT
SPECIAL OFFER
Keyword: PCFN

Figure 12-7: The PC Financial Network. It's here that you can buy and sell investments online.

PC Financial Network (PCFN) is a service of the Pershing Division of Donaldson, Lufkin & Jenrette Securities Corporation, an independent operating subsidiary of the Equitable Life Assurance Society of the United States. Pershing has been a leading provider of brokerage services for more than 50 years and currently handles about 10 percent of the daily volume of the New York Stock Exchange and 8 percent of all listed options trades. With total capital of more than $1 billion and total assets of about $40 billion, Pershing is America's largest online discount brokerage service.

Online investing offers a number of advantages over broker-assisted transactions, and opening an account takes only a few minutes.

- You can buy or sell 24 hours a day via AOL.
- You receive fast, accurate executions. Orders are sent directly to PCFN's computer and then to the markets—all electronically.
- Commissions are significantly lower than you'll find elsewhere. In most cases, the PCFN commissions are even lower than "discount" brokerages. To verify that claim (and set your mind at ease), PCFN offers a "commission calculator," which allows you to see what the commission will be for any particular investment, and then compare that cost to those of other brokerages.
- You can call PCFN day or night to place a trade or ask a question.
- You receive 100 real-time quotes per trade. You also receive 100 real-time quotes when you open an account.
- More than 500 mutual funds are available for trade online.
- You pay no extra monthly or usage fees—only your regular AOL connect-time charges, plus PCFN's low discount commissions.

Trading online is easy and can be fun. To see for yourself, try PCFN's free online demo account. You can "buy and sell" without spending a dime. If the thought of online trading has ever appealed to you, this is the most comprehensive and convenient way to give it a try.

Company Research

Let's see: we talked about managing your portfolio, then we talked about making the investment. Seems a bit out of order, I suppose. Oh well: as long as I'm presenting things from the end to the beginning, let's talk next about the Personal Finance Channel's Company Research area (keywords: **Company Research**, and see Figure 12-8).

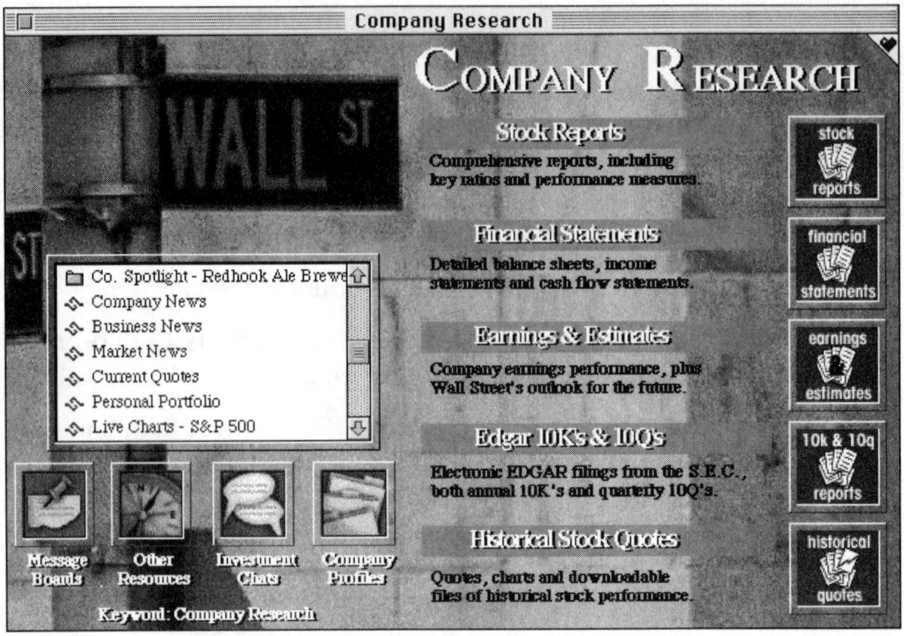
Company Research
COMPANY RESEARCH
Stock Reports
Comprehensive reports, including key ratios and performance measures.
Financial Statements
Detailed balance sheets, income statements and cash flow statements.
Earnings & Estimates
Company earnings performance, plus Wall Street's outlook for the future.
Edgar 10K's & 10Q's
Electronic EDGAR filings from the S.E.C., both annual 10K's and quarterly 10Q's.
Historical Stock Quotes
Quotes, charts and downloadable files of historical stock performance.
stock reports
financial statements
earnings estimates
10k & 10q reports
historical quotes
Co. Spotlight - Redhook Ale Brew
Company News
Business News
Market News
Current Quotes
Personal Portfolio
Live Charts - S&P 500
Message Boards
Other Resources
Investment Chats
Company Profiles
Keyword: Company Research

Figure 12-8: The Company Research area is a harbinger of future online investing.

Easter Egg

"Easter eggs" are tiny secrets hidden within computer programs where they remain hidden for only a few to discover. AOL doesn't have many, but there are a few, and the Company Research screen pictured in Figure 12-8 contains one of them.

Move the tip of your arrow cursor until it points to the top of the triangle inside of the "A" in the "Wall St" sign on the main Company Research screen, then click the mouse button. If it doesn't work the first time, move the mouse a bit and click again—the "hot spot" is small. I won't tell you what happens when you hit it, but you'll know when it does.

Research: it's not a provocative title for a subject, I know, but in fact, this is where the delight is to be found in the Personal Finance Channel. There's no pressure here—no sweaty brow—not if you don't want it. And AOL dedicates an arcade of multimedia catalysts to the purpose. There's no reason why financial research shouldn't be enjoyable as well as informative, and a well-informed investor is more likely to be a successful investor. Successful investors are what Company Research is all about.

The Motley Fool Online

Take financial advice, for example. The image of a stern patriarch comes to mind, humorless and intransigent. But these are the '90s: today's investor was reared on a diet of situation comedies and rock and roll. Musty tweed is as well suited (forgive the pun) to the task as a one-pronged pitchfork. An alternative is requisite, and that alternative is the Motley Fool (keyword: **Fool**).

Perhaps the best way to introduce the Motley Fool is to let the Fools themselves (brothers David and Thomas Gardner) do the talking:

"Once upon a time there was the *Motley Fool*. It was a print publication founded in July of 1993 whose subscription cost $48 a year. The *Motley Fool* had three aims: to inform, to amuse, and to make the reader good money at the same time. It was a literary-cum-investment rag with its own real-money portfolio designed so that any reader could learn from and duplicate it. It was highly Foolish, and there was nothing else quite like it.

"Then one day, the Editors discovered America Online. They started a message board, called 'The Motley Fool.' They answered any question that came their way about anything, and slowly developed a faithful Foolish following. In fact, the Editors soon found themselves spending more time answering questions and talking stocks online than they did in putting their publication together!

"This was perplexing and deeply troubling, and something had to be done about it.

"Just as the Editors prepared to check themselves into a Decyberspacification Center, a nice person who was NOT wearing a white coat came along and offered to start up a new area online, called The Motley Fool Online. The Editors, who were just a couple of kids with the corny old dream of one day making it out of their dusty old town, agreed. Recognizing instantly that their print publication would be rendered obsolete by the advantages of real-time cyberspace, they shut up shop, and sent out tardy refund checks to all of their subscribers.

"The Editors had gotten to know cyberspace quite well by this time, having both racked up budget-busting online bills AND written extensively on the subject. They believed they had come to understand the strengths and weaknesses of the medium, how it could be used well, and how others might abuse it...."

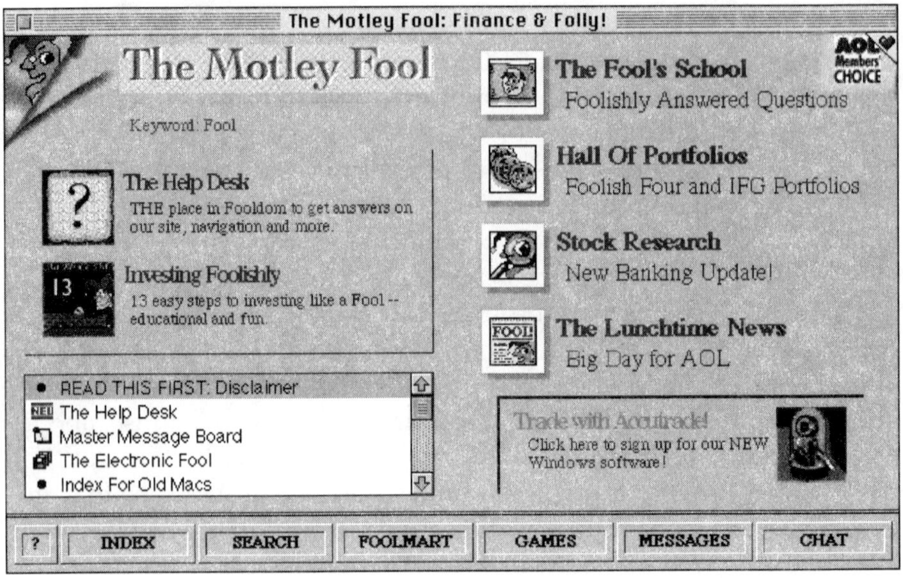

The Motley Fool: Finance & Folly!
The Motley Fool
Keyword: Fool
The Help Desk
THE place in Fooldom to get answers on our site, navigation and more.
Investing Foolishly
13 easy steps to investing like a Fool -- educational and fun.
READ THIS FIRST: Disclaimer
The Help Desk
Master Message Board
The Electronic Fool
Index For Old Macs
The Fool's School
Foolishly Answered Questions
Hall Of Portfolios
Foolish Four and IFG Portfolios
Stock Research
New Banking Update!
The Lunchtime News
Big Day for AOL
Trade with Accutrade!
Click here to sign up for our NEW Windows software!
AOL Members' CHOICE
?
INDEX
SEARCH
FOOLMART
GAMES
MESSAGES
CHAT

Figure 12-9: Come to the Motley Fool for a provocative personal investing perspective.

The Motley Fool is one of AOL's true success stories, and you should wonder why. In addition to their astute observations and advice on the state of the market, the Fools offer the following:

- *An area for learning*. More and more people today are seeking to understand investing—they're learning to do it themselves and in so doing gain a new measure of control over their finances. For no more than the cost of connect charges, the Fool's School offers fun, Foolish, and informative articles on many different aspects of investing. It gets novices up and running, investing for themselves in no time. And for those who want to test their new knowledge, there's always the Monthly Novice Quiz.
- *A fully managed, real-money online portfolio*. The Fool Portfolio is a real-money portfolio, not pie-in-the-sky or make-believe. In the Fool Portfolio, all related costs—including commissions and spreads—are accounted for. There's no hype and nothing ambiguous. If you prefer to learn by watching, here's your classroom.

- *Message boards*. The Motley Fool offers a dynamic exchange on hundreds of message boards; it's dedicated to broader investment approaches in general and scads of individual stocks in particular. The Fools claim that these boards are the best organized and most informative anywhere in cyberspace, and they're probably right.
- *Foolish games*. Fools love games, and the Motley Fool Online offers a few Foolish Games that challenge your mind and offer free online time to the winners. Check out Today's Pitch and Port Folly, via their buttons on the Fool Games screen.

Every online investor should visit the Motley Fool Online regularly. Learning is best accomplished in a supportive, peer-intensive, and *entertaining* environment, and that's exactly what the Fool has to offer.

Morningstar Mutual Funds

I began investing a couple of years ago. I located a broker—Dave is his name—with whom I found mutual trust, and in whom I found a kindred soul. Trading through him has never been stressful.

As I would expect, Dave is extremely knowledgeable about the market—especially mutual funds and bonds, which is where I've done most of my investing. I asked him one day where he got his information. "Morningstar," he said, adding obliquely, "It's an interdictory association." That evening I looked up the meaning of the word "interdictory" and felt that I was right privileged to walk among the ranks of the plutocracy.

Then I browsed around AOL and found Morningstar online, complete with User's Guide and Guided Tour (see Figure 12-10). The plutocracy had come to the proletariat, and the plutocrats didn't even know. Now I read Morningstar just as Dave does. I'm sure I'm a better investor (and a better client) because I do.

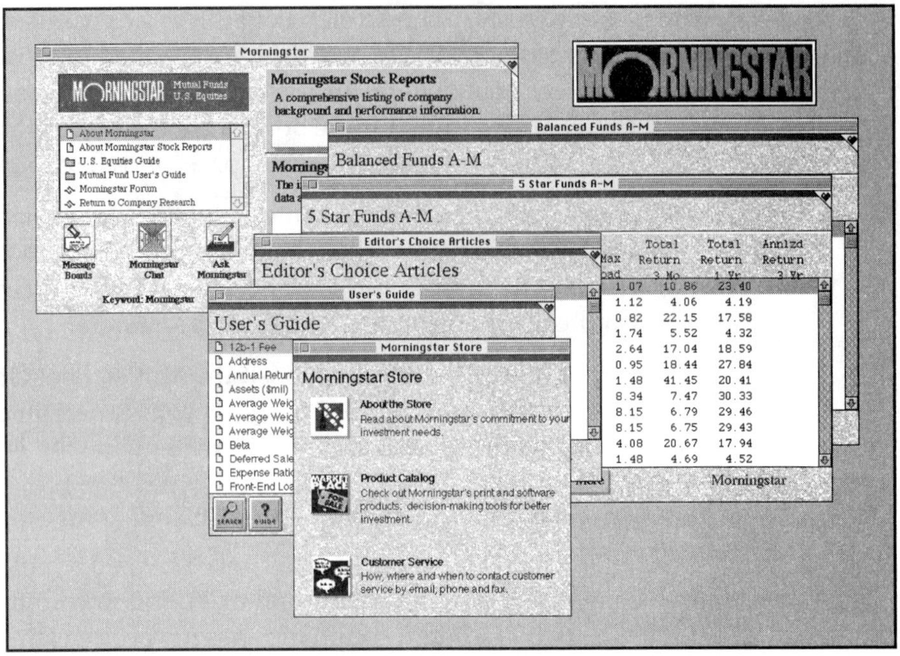
Morningstar
Morningstar Stock Reports
A comprehensive listing of company background and performance information.
Balanced Funds A-M
5 Star Funds A-M
Editor's Choice Articles
User's Guide
Morningstar Store
About the Store
Product Catalog
Customer Service
Message Boards
Morningstar Chat
Ask Morningstar
Keyword: Morningstar

Figure 12-10: Morningstar offers data, publications, and software for analyzing more than 6,000 mutual funds, closed-end funds, variable annuities, variable life, variable universal life, Japanese equities, and American Depository Receipts. Use the keyword: **Morningstar**.

Hoover's Business Resources

Morningstar isn't the only investor's reference available on AOL. If your investing interests exceed the scope of mutual funds and bonds, investigate Hoover's Business Resources (keyword: **Hoovers**). Hoover's collection of searchable databases includes profiles of more than 1,100 of the largest, most influential, and fastest-growing public and private companies in the world. In addition, there are monthly updates on these and 6,200 other major companies. They've even got business rankings from a number of perspectives and industry profiles. The voice is lively and interesting; the data are pertinent to every investor; and the price—free of surcharges to AOL members—is as affordable as old clothes used to be.

The Decision Point Forum

Now we're getting serious. The Decision Point Forum provides a platform and materials to help you learn, refine, and profitably use technical analysis skills and market timing information. You're encouraged to assimilate information and opinions, then arrive at your own conclusions. There are no magic systems here, only aids that help you make your own decisions. And there are plenty of them:

- The *buy/sell signals* generated by the forum's timing models are summarized in the Decision Point Alert, updated every Saturday morning.
- Each market day the forum posts *chart tables* of the 150 stocks and 160 mutual funds being followed. Featured are four proprietary timing models that can help you identify stocks that might be starting a new trend. The forum also offers two-year charts for the stocks and funds in this portfolio.
- There are *message boards*, where you can post questions and exchange ideas with other members about the technical condition of the market and the stocks you own or follow.
- There is a vast collection of *chart libraries* (see Figure 12-11) with files of stock, mutual fund, and market indicator charts. These libraries are updated each week.

Free of Extra Charges

Most commercial online services offer news and finance features similar to those found on AOL. None offers them all, however, and none offers them at the price AOL charges: nothing beyond the normal connect-time charges. This is unique to AOL. In this industry the word "premium" usually translates to "extra charge." You rarely will find an extra charge for any of the services AOL offers. With all the money you save, perhaps you can invest in the stock market or buy a small business. If you do, AOL stands ready to help—at no extra charge, of course.

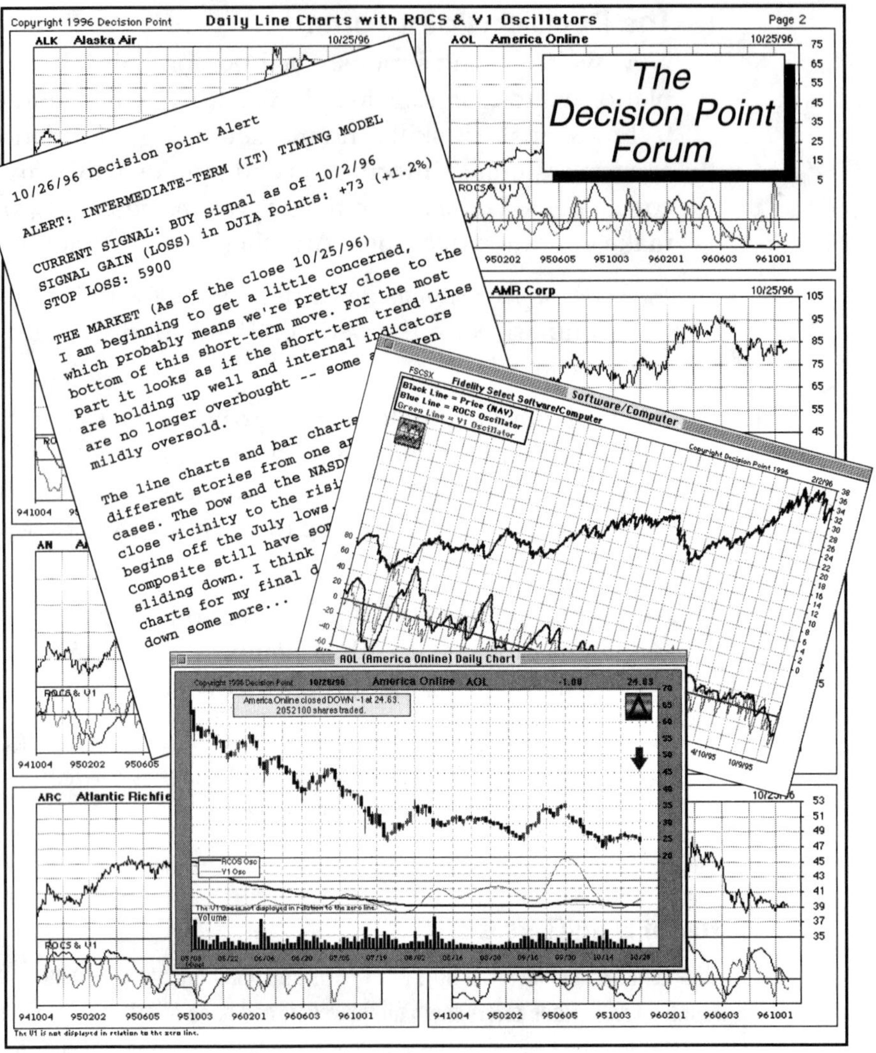
Copyright 1996 Decision Point
Daily Line Charts with ROCS & V1 Oscillators
Page 2
ALK Alaska Air 10/25/96
AOL America Online 10/25/96
The Decision Point Forum
AMR Corp 10/25/96
ARC Atlantic Richfie
10/26/96 Decision Point Alert
ALERT: INTERMEDIATE-TERM (IT) TIMING MODEL
CURRENT SIGNAL: BUY Signal as of 10/2/96
SIGNAL GAIN (LOSS) in DJIA Points: +73 (+1.2%)
STOP LOSS: 5900
THE MARKET (As of the close 10/25/96)
I am beginning to get a little concerned,
which probably means we're pretty close to the
bottom of this short-term move. For the most
part it looks as if the short-term trend lines
are holding up well and internal indicators
are no longer overbought -- some a
mildly oversold.
The line charts and bar charts
different stories from one a
cases. The Dow and the NASD
close vicinity to the risi
begins off the July lows
Composite still have so
sliding down. I think
charts for my final d
down some more...
FSCSX Fidelity Select Software/Computer
Black Line = Price (NAV)
Blue Line = ROCS Oscillator
Green Line = V1 Oscillator
AOL (America Online) Daily Chart
America Online AOL
America Online closed DOWN -1 at 24.63.
2052100 shares traded.
ROCS Osc
V1 Osc
Volume
941004 950202 950605 951003 960201 960603 961001
The V1 is not displayed in relation to the zero line.

Figure 12-11: The Decision Point Forum is the home of America Online's stock market charts. There are hundreds of them here, and they're all available for downloading and viewing with your America Online software at kewords: **Decision Point.**

- A collection of *historical data files* of market indicators and indexes is available for download in the database libraries, allowing you to construct your own charts. These data, too, are updated weekly.

- A collection of *essays and articles* covering various subjects is available in the reading libraries under Instructions & Definitions. Of particular importance is the "Timing Model Documentation"—a thorough explanation of how to use the timing models found elsewhere in the forum.
- The *Top Advisors' Corner* features comments by prominent stock market advisors.
- The *Investor's Resource Center* lists sources of investing information, products, and services.

If you're a serious investor—or if you're considering investments in the stock or mutual funds markets, the Decision Point Forum should be a frequent stop in your AOL journey.

Worth Magazine

No serious investor should conclude an AOL journey without exploring the articles of Worth Online, the electronic version of *Worth* magazine, the magazine of financial intelligence. Here you can download current and past articles written by such Wall Street experts as Peter Lynch, Graef Crystal, Gretchen Morgenson, Bob Clark, Jim Jubak, and John Rothchild. It's available in the main Personal Finance window or by using the keyword: **Worth**.

Chart-O-Matic

The financial market is a moving target. Trying to take aim at it by observing a static chart is like trying to shoot skeet with a cannon: impressive to behold, but hardly nimble enough for the job.

That's why AOL's Chart-O-Matic provides "live" charts for your observation of stock market activity. Choose Live Charts from the list box pictured in Figure 12-8, then pick the issue or the index you want to track. When the chart appears, leave it on your screen: it'll be automatically updated every few minutes (see Figure 12-12).

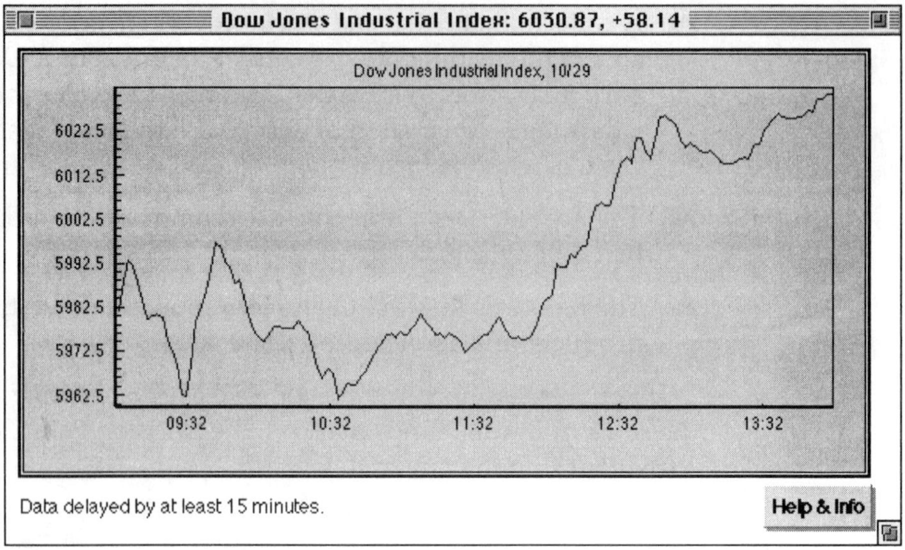
Dow Jones Industrial Index: 6030.87, +58.14
Dow Jones Industrial Index, 10/29
6022.5
6012.5
6002.5
5992.5
5982.5
5972.5
5962.5
09:32
10:32
11:32
12:32
13:32
Data delayed by at least 15 minutes.
Help & Info

Figure 12-12: AOL's Chart-O-Matic live charting feature provides an animated look at stock market activity as it happens, all day long. Use the keywords: **Chart O Matic**.

Your Business

Is "entrepreneurial community" an oxymoron? Your Business (keywords: **Your Business**) doesn't think so. In fact, Your Business exists specifically to promote the entrepreneurial community—an independent and often remote anarchy of unconventionalists in search of community whether they're aware of it or not (see Figure 12-13).

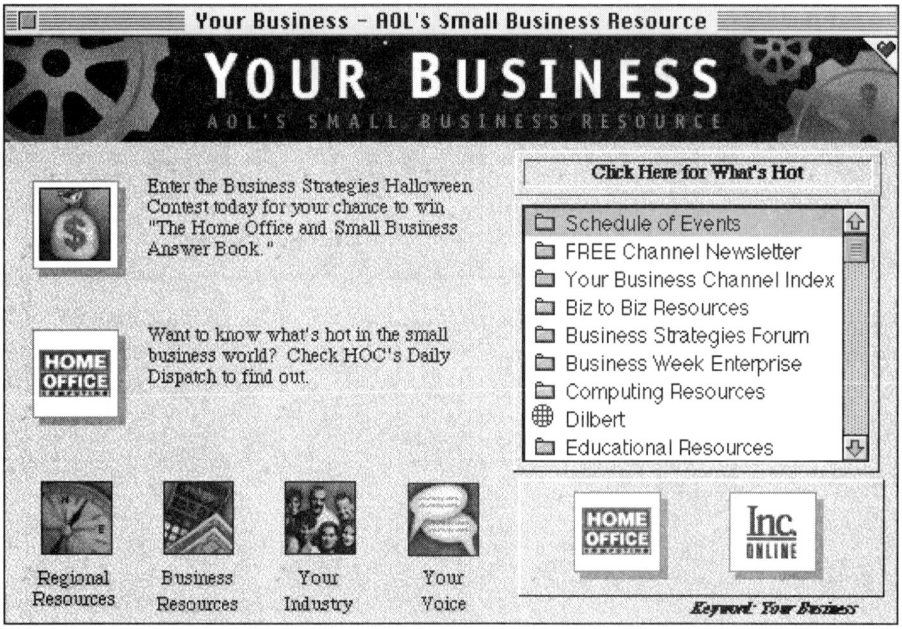
Your Business - AOL's Small Business Resource
YOUR BUSINESS
AOL'S SMALL BUSINESS RESOURCE
Enter the Business Strategies Halloween Contest today for your chance to win "The Home Office and Small Business Answer Book."
Want to know what's hot in the small business world? Check HOC's Daily Dispatch to find out.
HOME OFFICE
Click Here for What's Hot
Schedule of Events
FREE Channel Newsletter
Your Business Channel Index
Biz to Biz Resources
Business Strategies Forum
Business Week Enterprise
Computing Resources
Dilbert
Educational Resources
Regional Resources
Business Resources
Your Industry
Your Voice
HOME OFFICE
Inc. ONLINE
Keyword: Your Business

Figure 12-13: Your Business brings community to a broad range of individuals involved in independent business ventures.

Your Business's service and content are significant (more about that later), but what makes it all work is the diversity of business experience that AOL's members bring to the forum. Your Business welcomes all forms of entrepreneurs: dreamers, consultants, small business owners, and those who work at home. Whether your plans are small or large, a peer group is not only beneficial, it's almost mandatory; and Your Business is where your community makes its home.

The Business Strategies Forum Message Boards

Perhaps nowhere is the spirit of community more active than on the Business Strategies Forum message boards (at keyword: **Strategies**). People all over the country find others working in the same field here, and their discussions enlighten casual readers as effectively as the participants themselves (see Figure 12-14).

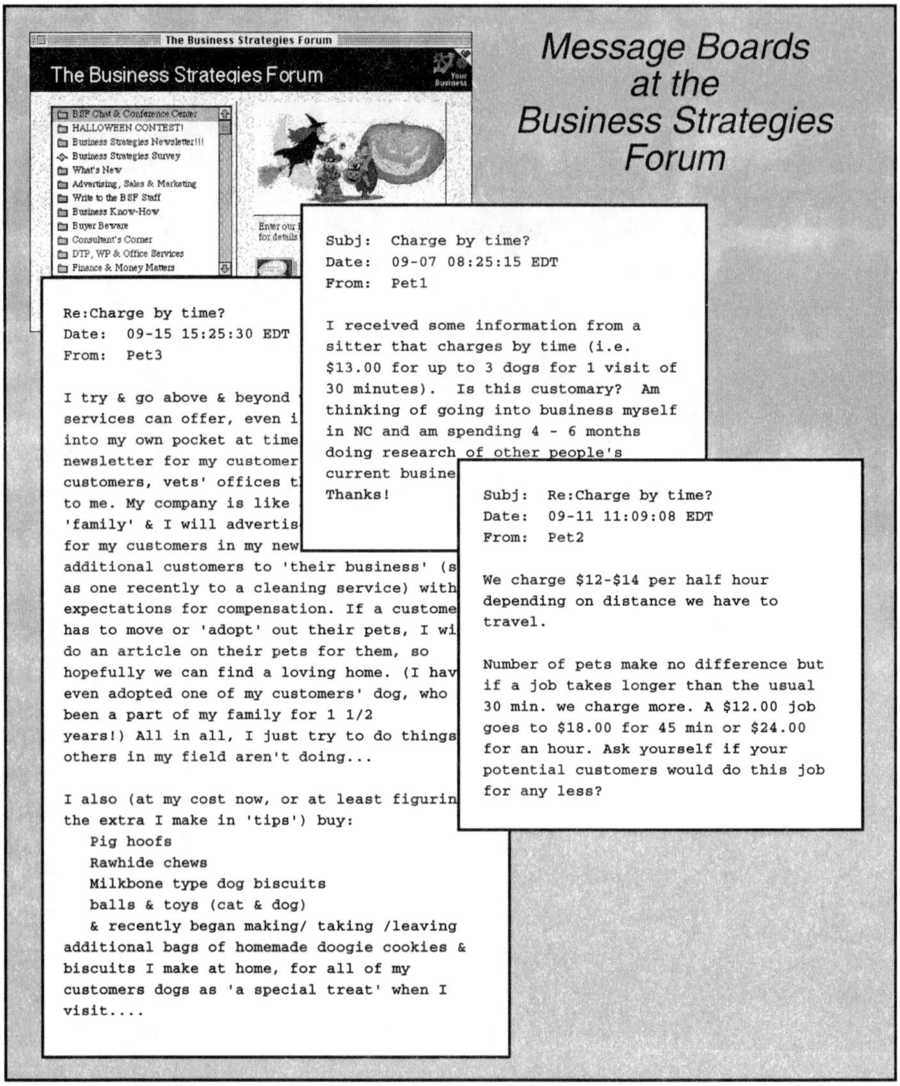

Message Boards at the Business Strategies Forum
The Business Strategies Forum
Subj: Charge by time?
Date: 09-07 08:25:15 EDT
From: Pet1
I received some information from a sitter that charges by time (i.e. $13.00 for up to 3 dogs for 1 visit of 30 minutes). Is this customary? Am thinking of going into business myself in NC and am spending 4 - 6 months doing research of other people's current busine
Thanks!
Re:Charge by time?
Date: 09-15 15:25:30 EDT
From: Pet3
I also (at my cost now, or at least figurin the extra I make in 'tips') buy:
Pig hoofs
Rawhide chews
Milkbone type dog biscuits
balls & toys (cat & dog)
& recently began making/ taking /leaving additional bags of homemade doogie cookies & biscuits I make at home, for all of my customers dogs as 'a special treat' when I visit....
Subj: Re:Charge by time?
Date: 09-11 11:09:08 EDT
From: Pet2
We charge $12-$14 per half hour depending on distance we have to travel.
Number of pets make no difference but if a job takes longer than the usual 30 min. we charge more. A $12.00 job goes to $18.00 for 45 min or $24.00 for an hour. Ask yourself if your potential customers would do this job for any less?

Figure 12-14: The Business Strategies Forum message boards offer peer-to-peer comments and suggestions.

Inc. Online

YB's bedrock, perhaps, is Inc. Online (keyword: **Inc**). *Inc.* magazine has been serving entrepreneurs for years with timely information, relevant and vital to entrepreneurs nationwide. It stands to reason, then, that *Inc.* should have an online presence offering research potential, analysis, entrepreneurial resources, comment, and guests. Inc. Online offers all of that and more; Figure 12-15 offers a snapshot of what it's all about.

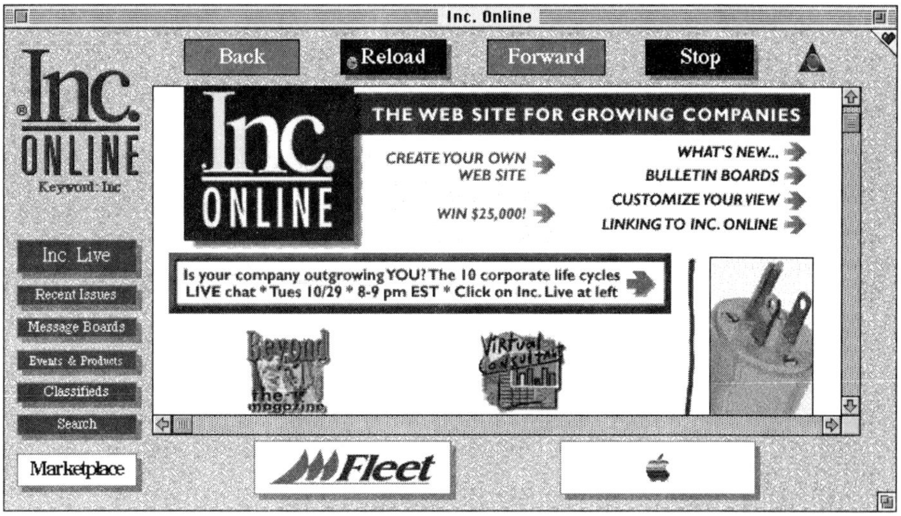
Inc. Online
Back
Reload
Forward
Stop
Inc. ONLINE
Keyword: Inc
THE WEB SITE FOR GROWING COMPANIES
CREATE YOUR OWN WEB SITE
WHAT'S NEW...
BULLETIN BOARDS
CUSTOMIZE YOUR VIEW
WIN $25,000!
LINKING TO INC. ONLINE
Inc. Live
Recent Issues
Message Boards
Events & Products
Classifieds
Search
Is your company outgrowing YOU? The 10 corporate life cycles
LIVE chat * Tues 10/29 * 8-9 pm EST * Click on Inc. Live at left
Marketplace
Fleet

Figure 12-15: Inc. Online offers a fountain of entrepreneurial resources at keyword: **Inc**.

If you're an entrepreneur—or thinking of becoming one—be sure to visit Your Business regularly. This is a field where even minor advantages pay off—directly—and Your Business is an advantage indeed.

Moving On

It's a disservice to the Personal Finance Channel to end this chapter here. There's much more than I've described, and I don't want you to misinterpret my emphasis. I've tried to present the diversity of features offered, not a listing of its best stuff.

Too much time in the Personal Finance Channel, however, can lead to monetary overload. There are plenty of nonmonetary features available on AOL, and we should spend some time examining those. Turn the page and we'll do just that.

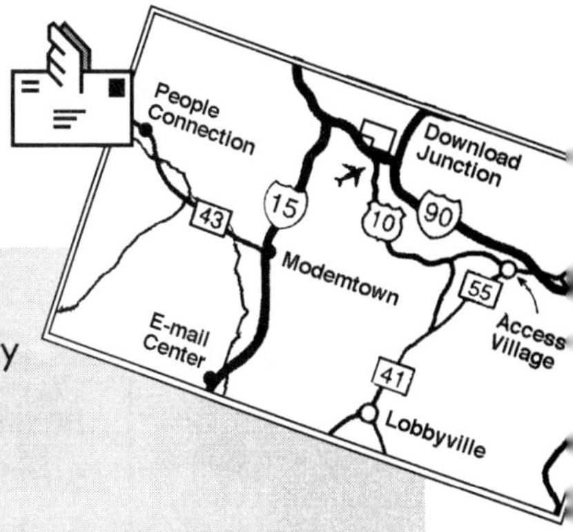

People Connection
Download Junction
43
15
10
90
Modemtown
55
Access Village
E-mail Center
41
Lobbyville

CHAPTER 13

Learning & Culture

- The Online Campus
- The Nature Conservancy Online
- Book Central
- Smithsonian Online
- Scientific American Online
- CultureFinder
- The Odyssey Project
- Kaplan Online
- The Career Center
- The Academic Assistance Center
- College Board Online
- Education for the Teacher
- The Broadcast Media

My dictionary defines the word *inquisitive* as "inclined to investigate; eager for knowledge." While the online medium's chat, e-mail, and files for downloading receive the lion's share of media attention, and while they might be the enticements that lured many of us here in the first place, we soon discover that the true value of the medium is personal enrichment via the pursuit of knowledge. Nothing can compare to the online medium's seemingly limitless variety, hair-trigger immediacy, and extensive multimedia capabilities. If you're "eager for knowledge," the Learning & Culture Channel is your citadel (see Figure 13-1). Use the keyword: **Learning**, or click on the channel's button on the Main Menu.

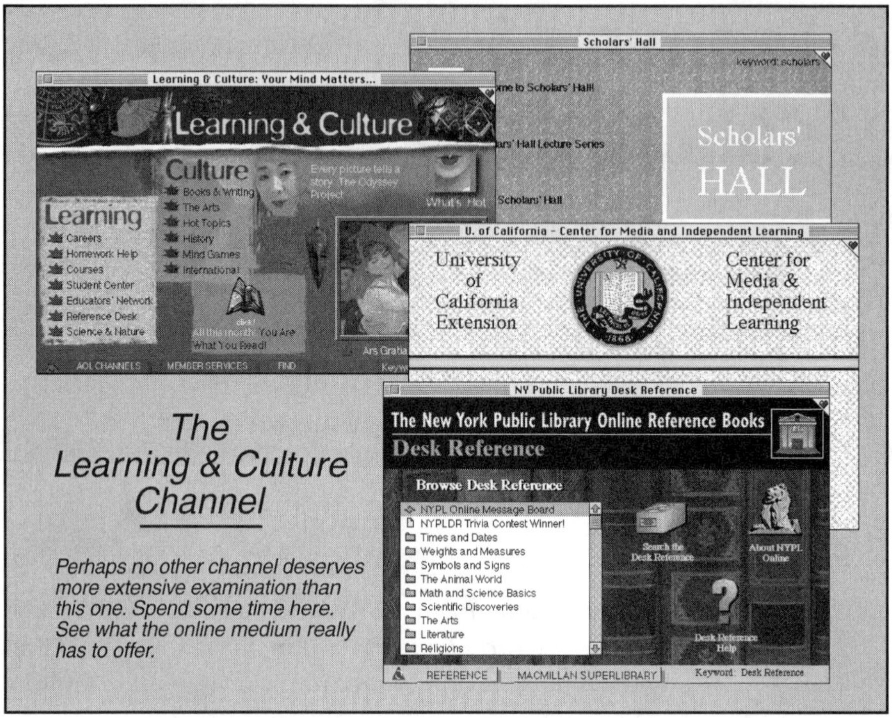
Scholars' Hall
Scholars' HALL
Learning & Culture: Your Mind Matters...
Learning & Culture
Culture
Learning
Careers
Homework Help
Courses
Student Center
Educators' Network
Reference Desk
Science & Nature
Books & Writing
The Arts
Hot Topics
History
Mind Games
International
U. of California - Center for Media and Independent Learning
University of California Extension
Center for Media & Independent Learning
NY Public Library Desk Reference
The New York Public Library Online Reference Books
Desk Reference
Browse Desk Reference
NYPL Online Message Board
NYPLDR Trivia Contest Winner!
Times and Dates
Weights and Measures
Symbols and Signs
The Animal World
Math and Science Basics
Scientific Discoveries
The Arts
Literature
Religions
REFERENCE
MACMILLAN SUPERLIBRARY
Keyword: Desk Reference
The Learning & Culture Channel
Perhaps no other channel deserves more extensive examination than this one. Spend some time here. See what the online medium really has to offer.

Figure 13-1: Alvin Toffler, author of *Future Shock*, once said that ". . . knowledge is the most democratic source of power," referring, perhaps, to its accessibility. The Learning & Culture Channel brings directly to your Mac an infinite resource that can increase your knowledge and, thus, your power. Use the keyword: **Learning** to investigate.

The Online Campus

I used the word "enrichment" earlier. It's a great word. There's a wholesome ring to it. Bread is enriched with vitamins; nitrogen enriches soil; learning enriches us all.

The online campus (keyword: **Campus**) offers a "community enrichment" curriculum, including academic, professional, and special-interest courses. Scores of courses are offered every term—all you have to do is sign up, pay your tuition, and attend.

An example of Online Campus offerings is in order. "Writing the Novel" is an eight-week course covering what you need to know to write a good, publishable novel. A twenty-chapter textbook prepared by the instructor is included (exclusively available to students of this course), as well as access to live question-and-answer conferences, scores of files (including proposals, timelines, character biographies, and recommended books and agents), and a private message board. And for those who wish to pursue their literary potential even further, an eight-week follow-up course is available.

Accreditation

The Online Campus isn't limited to learning exclusively for the purpose of personal enrichment, no matter how honorable an intention that may be. Courses are available for college credit as well, from no less honorable an institution than the University of California, one of the nation's most prestigious communications research centers. The University of California's Center for Media and Independent Learning (CMIL) offers over 150 college, professional, and high school courses in a variety of fields. All courses and instructors are approved by appropriate University of California departments and the University of California at Berkeley Academic Senate. CMIL courses count toward degrees at most institutions of higher education around the country. To find out more, use the keyword: **UCX**.

The class meets (virtually, but in real time) once a week for an hour, and is taught by Lary Crews, author of 3 published mystery novels, 405 published magazine articles, 20 published poems, 2 recorded songs, 1 published short story, 2 produced plays, and 25 radio news documentaries—including one that won an Associated Press award in 1976. Crews is a four-time winner in the Writer's Digest National Writing Competition and is currently writing a new book, a suspense novel. See Figure 13-2.

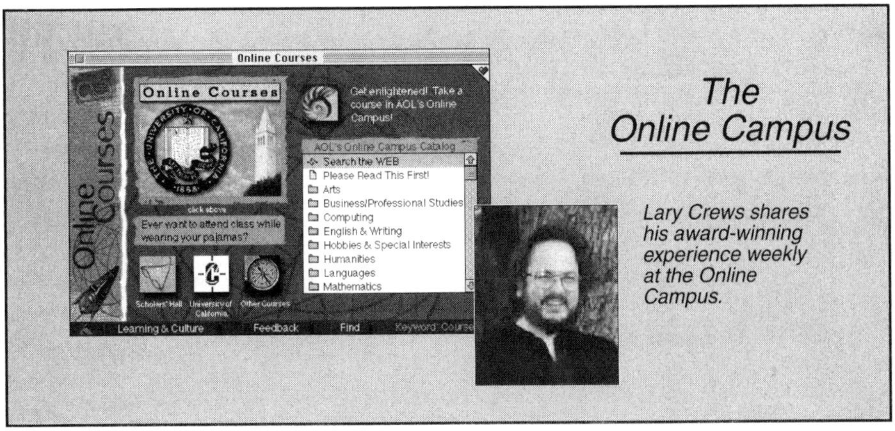
Online Courses
Online Courses
Get enlightened! Take a course in AOL's Online Campus!
AOL's Online Campus Catalog
Search the WEB
Please Read This First!
Arts
Business/Professional Studies
Computing
English & Writing
Hobbies & Special Interests
Humanities
Languages
Mathematics
Ever want to attend class while wearing your pajamas?
Scholars' Hall
University of California
Other Courses
Learning & Culture
Feedback
Find
The Online Campus
Lary Crews shares his award-winning experience weekly at the Online Campus.

Figure 13-2: Real classes, taught by real people: that's the Online Campus.

"Writing the Novel" is but one of many courses offered every term at the Online Campus. Classes are available in the arts, business and professional studies, English and writing, hobbies, the humanities, languages, mathematics, religion and spirituality, and science and nature. The Online Campus also offers the Afterwards Cafe, a hot spot for lively discussions of the arts; the Bull Moose Tavern, where the conversation spins around social and political issues; the Lab, a hangout devoted to discussions of the realms of science and nature; the International Cafe, where you can brush up on your language skills; the Reading Room, where you can join fellow book lovers in discussions of authors, publishers, and favorite works; the Scholars' Hall, where lecture series and graduation ceremonies find a home; and the Teachers' Lounge, where you can hobnob with your instructors after class. Few places offer as much potential for fostering the online community, a community not only of colleagues and companions but one of knowledge as well.

The Nature Conservancy Online

The Nature Conservancy purchased its first parcel of ecologically significant land—60 acres in New York state—in 1951. Since then, acreage under the Conservancy's protection in the United States has increased to 7.9 million, with another 42 million acres in foreign countries. Nearly three-quarters of a million people contribute to the Conservancy's stewardship, and now they have a common resource at the Nature Conservancy Online (use the keyword: **Nature**, and see Figure 13-3).

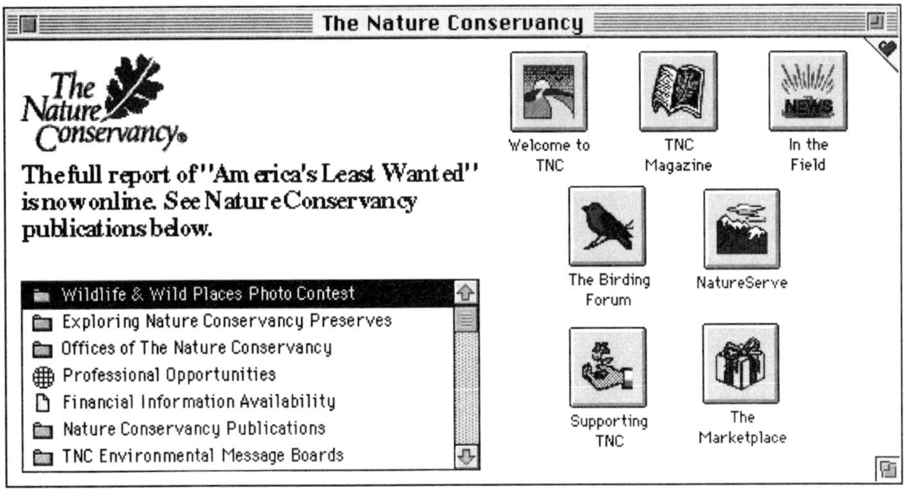
The Nature Conservancy
The Nature Conservancy
The full report of "America's Least Wanted" is now online. See Nature Conservancy publications below.
Wildlife & Wild Places Photo Contest
Exploring Nature Conservancy Preserves
Offices of The Nature Conservancy
Professional Opportunities
Financial Information Availability
Nature Conservancy Publications
TNC Environmental Message Boards
Welcome to TNC
TNC Magazine
In the Field
The Birding Forum
NatureServe
Supporting TNC
The Marketplace

Figure 13-3: The Nature Conservancy uses a science-based, nonconfrontational approach to conservation of the earth's biodiversity.

Book Central

If you thought book lovers were only found in musty libraries with their noses in books, think again. I've found bibliophile nirvana online at Book Central (keyword: **BC**). Book Central recommends and reviews books on just about every topic, as well as offers author biographies. Be sure to stop by the Palladium for special author appearances and other events. My favorite is the By the Book live book trivia game show on Wednesdays and Sunday evenings in the Palladium. And if you're an aspiring writer, there's even an Ask the Agent hour with real agents fielding questions about writing and selling books. A complete schedule of events is available under The Palladium icon (see Figure 13-4).

Welcome to BOOK CENTRAL
Julia Child bakes; Capote remembers
THE BOOKSHELVES
BOOKS & AUTHOR INFO
9 events coming incl. Nora Roberts, "ER"
THE PALLADIUM
LIVE EVENTS
23 groups meeting! Join, or form your own!
CAFE BOOKA
ONLINE READING GROUPS
BEST OF THE WEEK
MESSAGE BOARDS
BOOK CENTRAL
African-American
Arts
Biography
Business
Careers
Child Care
Children's Books
CATEGORIES
AUTHORS
BOOK MARK
Nov. 22
MESSAGE BOARDS
Book talk for all types!
CONTEST
Win book and mug!
BC NEWSLETTER
EARTH'S BIGGEST BOOKSTORE
AMAZON.com Click here
BOOKS & WRITING
SEARCH BC
Keyword: BC

Figure 13-4: Book Central is your guide to books before and after your visit to the bookstore.

Best of all, you can join online reading groups with other members and discuss your favorite books and authors in Cafe Booka. As I write this, Book Central offers over 20 reading groups, including African American, Best Book Ever, Jane Austen, Mystery, Shakespeare, and The Horrible Group (horror).

Book Central is not only fascinating, it's a capital example of the benefits online has to offer a traditionally offline activity.

Smithsonian Online

The Smithsonian Institution in Washington, DC, is probably America's most popular museum. Occupying a significant percentage of the District of Columbia, the Smithsonian is really a collection of 17 museums and galleries, including a zoo. You'll find Smithsonian Online in the main Learning & Culture menu, or simply use the keyword: **Smithsonian** (see Figure 13-5).

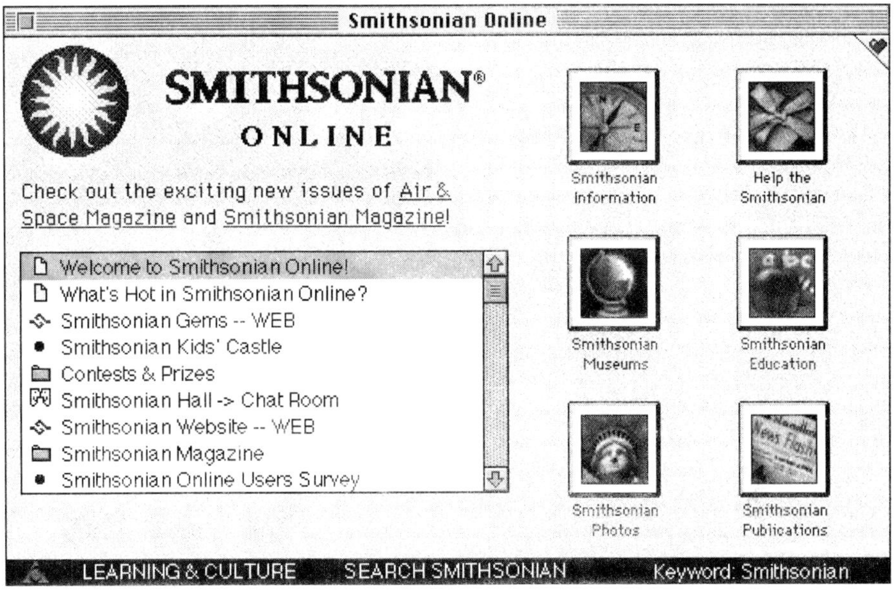
Smithsonian Online
SMITHSONIAN®
ONLINE
Check out the exciting new issues of Air & Space Magazine and Smithsonian Magazine!
Welcome to Smithsonian Online!
What's Hot in Smithsonian Online?
Smithsonian Gems -- WEB
Smithsonian Kids' Castle
Contests & Prizes
Smithsonian Hall -> Chat Room
Smithsonian Website -- WEB
Smithsonian Magazine
Smithsonian Online Users Survey
Smithsonian Information
Help the Smithsonian
Smithsonian Museums
Smithsonian Education
Smithsonian Photos
Smithsonian Publications
LEARNING & CULTURE
SEARCH SMITHSONIAN
Keyword: Smithsonian

Figure 13-5: Smithsonian Online offers round-the-clock electronic access to one of America's most comprehensive resources.

In addition to descriptions, articles, and photos from many of its museums, Smithsonian Online also provides a comprehensive guide for anyone intending to visit the institution—just click the Smithsonian Information button. Making a visit to the Smithsonian is not a casual event; planning is not only recommended, it's essential. And you can do all your pretrip planning using America Online. (See Figure 13-6.)

Figure 13-6: Final flight: the SR-71 Blackbird spy plane touches down on the runway at Dulles International Airport near Washington, DC, having just set a new cross-country speed record on its way to its permanent home at the Smithsonian Institution. The photo is available online and appears here courtesy of the Smithsonian.

The thousands of Smithsonian Photos images are scrupulously indexed; the Smithsonian Education area offers ideas, outlines, and publications for teachers; and the Education Resource Guide catalogs educational materials available from the Smithsonian and several affiliated organizations. This is one of the richest environments available on the service, and it warrants your exploration.

Constant Change

Perhaps you've noticed: telecommunications is not a conservative, tranquil industry. Its waters are about as placid as an Atlantic storm. For this reason, America Online is constantly in a state of change.

Case in point: as I write this, Smithsonian Online has just announced its plans to establish a distinguished-speaker series, including interviews and classes. I can't provide the details yet because they're not available, but don't let omissions like this annoy you. Seek them out and rejoice in their significance: AOL is always improving, and we—AOL's members—are the reason. To stay abreast of the changes, use the keyword: **New**.

Scientific American Online

Quickly now: name every mass communications medium you can think of that's 150 years old. Remember, there was no radio or television 150 years ago, no telephones or C-SPAN, and certainly no Internet or AOL. Newspapers and magazines were *it*, and only one magazine from 150 years ago still survives: *Scientific American* (see Figure 13-7).

Scientific American Online
SCIENTIFIC AMERICAN
WELCOME TO THE ONLINE SERVICE OF THE OLDEST CONTINUOUSLY PUBLISHED MAGAZINE IN AMERICA
SciAm Archives By Topic
New! Connect to SciAm's Web Page!
Back Issues
Send a Letter to the Editors
News for January
Table of Contents
From the Editors
Letters to the Editors
December 1996
Cell Suicide.... Primordial Deuterium and the Big Bang.... The Specter of Biological Weapons.... Daily Life in Ancient Egypt.... Why Freud Isn't Dead.... A Cricket Robot.... Nanophase Materials
Click Here!
SciAm Medical Publications
SciAm Frontiers
More to Explore
Intel recently posted strong 3rd quarter profits; still, Moore's Law posits that the semiconductor maker's future may not be so rosy.
Keyword: SciAm
Message Boards
File Libraries
SciAm Marketplace
Search SciAm

Figure 13-7: Scientific American Online offers the current issue of the magazine online (before it goes on sale at newsstands) and a searchable database of back issues.

Scientific American Online offers the latest from the current issue of *Scientific American* magazine—before it hits the newsstands—and more than a year's worth of back issues; access to the magazine's journalists and fellow readers via the message board; an archive of articles, selected images, and even video clips; the bulletin contents of *Scientific American Medicine* and *Scientific American Surgery*; and abstracts of all *Scientific American* articles published from May 1948 through December 1994. That's quite a résumé of features, and it's all available at keyword: **SciAm**.

CultureFinder

Does the mention of culture sound as appealing as a yogurt and watercress souffle? Even if you are a connoisseur of the fine arts, CultureFinder can help you find answers to those questions about culture you were always afraid to ask. CultureFinder offers a friendly introduction to classical music, opera, theater, and dance for the uninitiated, and then goes on to provide articles, reviews, interviews, and glimpses into the culture kitchen. You can take a taste with the Culture Find of the Week or the StarFinder, which both spotlight a different "find" every week. Or you can gorge yourself with a seven-course buffet by clicking any of the icons pictured in Figure 13-8. You can then top it all off with the CultureQuiz, featuring a not-so-serious trivia question every day. This smorgasbord of culture is yours for the taking at keyword: **CultureFinder** (see Figure 13-8).

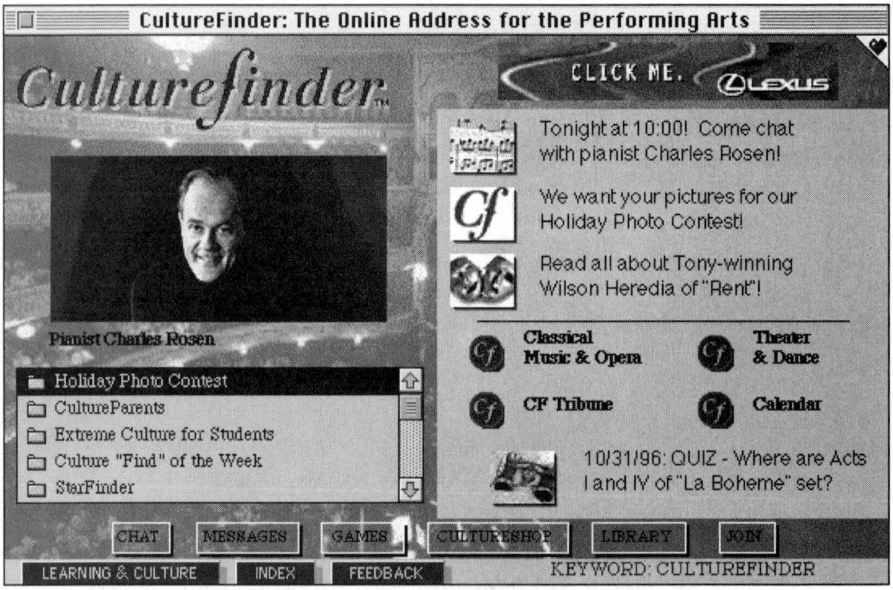
CultureFinder: The Online Address for the Performing Arts
Culturefinder
CLICK ME.
LEXUS
Tonight at 10:00! Come chat with pianist Charles Rosen!
We want your pictures for our Holiday Photo Contest!
Read all about Tony-winning Wilson Heredia of "Rent"!
Pianist Charles Rosen
Classical Music & Opera
Theater & Dance
CF Tribune
Calendar
Holiday Photo Contest
CultureParents
Extreme Culture for Students
Culture "Find" of the Week
StarFinder
10/31/96: QUIZ - Where are Acts I and IV of "La Boheme" set?
CHAT
MESSAGES
GAMES
CULTURESHOP
LIBRARY
JOIN
LEARNING & CULTURE
INDEX
FEEDBACK
KEYWORD: CULTUREFINDER

Figure 13-8: CultureFinder offers a treasury of opinion, arts, and culture at keyword: **CultureFinder**.

The Odyssey Project

Pictures in magazines and newspapers are usually entertaining, especially the really good ones, but the Odyssey Project (keyword: **Odyssey**) puts you right beside the photographer. Not only are the project's pictures majestic and sometimes awe-inspiring—as well they should be, considering the world-class photographers who take them—but you get to listen and watch as these professional adventurers share the "rest of the story" in first-hand sessions. The Odyssey Project (see Figure 13-9) is a window on the pleasures of intensely focused travel, a collection of perspectives on people, cultures, and animals—and a way to scratch the travel itch. It's an experiment with new forms of visual publishing and a community of organizations that encourage us to get out and taste the world for ourselves.

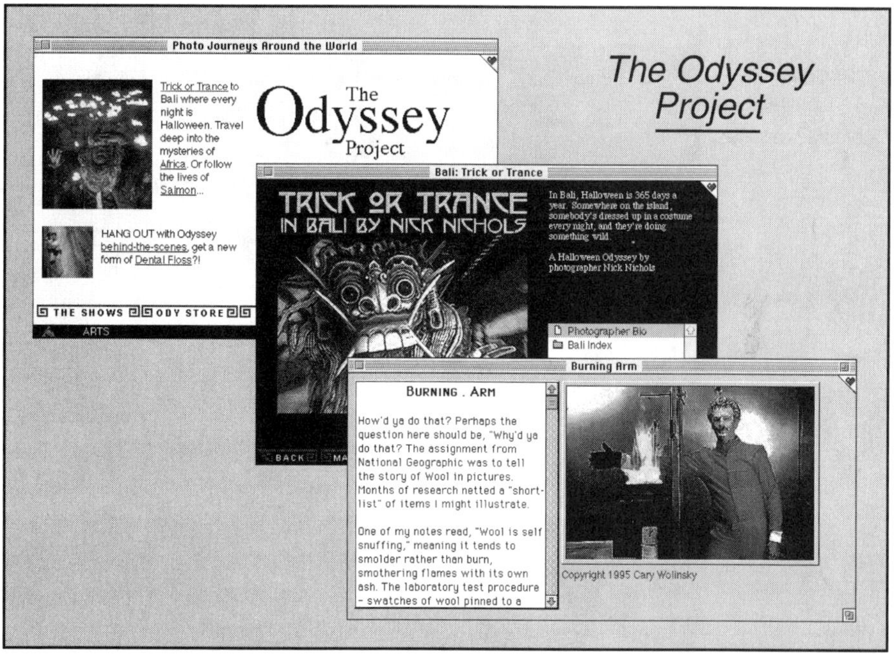

Photo Journeys Around the World
Trick or Trance to Bali where every night is Halloween. Travel deep into the mysteries of Africa. Or follow the lives of Salmon...
The Odyssey Project
HANG OUT with Odyssey behind-the-scenes, get a new form of Dental Floss?!
THE SHOWS
ODY STORE
ARTS
The Odyssey Project
Bali: Trick or Trance
TRICK OR TRANCE IN BALI BY NICK NICHOLS
In Bali, Halloween is 365 days a year. Somewhere on the island, somebody's dressed up in a costume every night, and they're doing something wild.
A Halloween Odyssey by photographer Nick Nichols
Photographer Bio
Bali Index
BACK
Burning Arm
BURNING . ARM
How'd ya do that? Perhaps the question here should be, "Why'd ya do that? The assignment from National Geographic was to tell the story of Wool in pictures. Months of research netted a "short-list" of items I might illustrate.
One of my notes read, "Wool is self snuffing," meaning it tends to smolder rather than burn, smothering flames with its own ash. The laboratory test procedure - swatches of wool pinned to a
Copyright 1995 Cary Wolinsky

Figure 13-9: The Odyssey Project attracts world-class photographic talent, then sits you down with the photographers for a personalized look at their portfolios.

Kaplan Online

Kaplan Online offers courses for over 30 standardized tests, including college admissions exams such as the SAT and ACT; graduate and professional school entrance exams such as the GMAT, GRE, LSAT, and MCAT; professional licensing exams for medicine, nursing, dentistry, and accounting; and specialized exams for foreign students and professionals. The organization has been doing this for 55 years, since young Stanley H. Kaplan first created the test preparation industry in his Brooklyn basement.

Kaplan Online offers sample test questions, examples of how to prepare for the test, a countdown to the test day—even what to do after the test. Best of all, there's no charge. It's all available at keyword: **Kaplan**. (See Figure 13-10.)

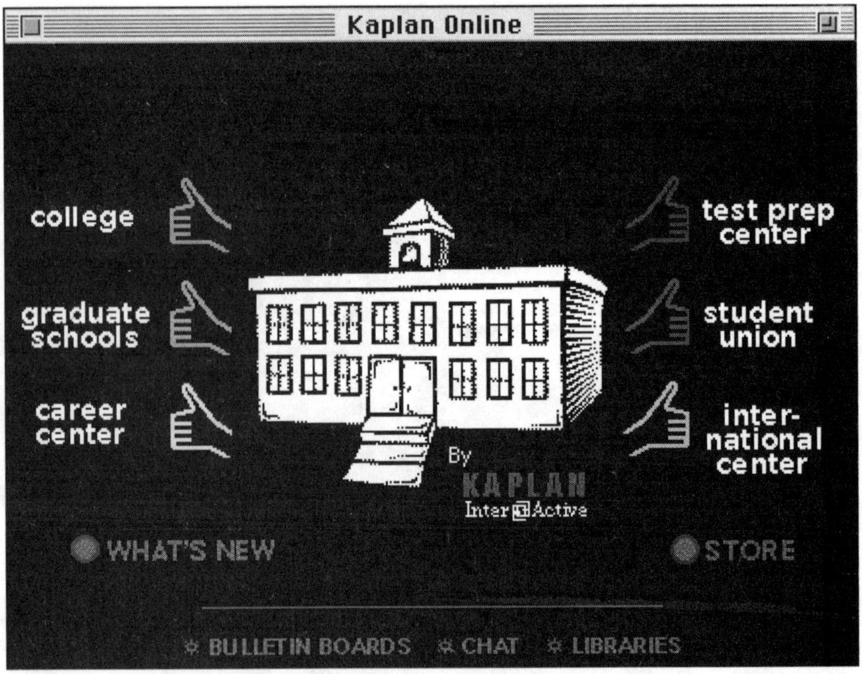
Kaplan Online
college
graduate schools
career center
test prep center
student union
inter-national center
By KAPLAN InterActive
WHAT'S NEW
STORE
BULLETIN BOARDS
CHAT
LIBRARIES

Figure 13-10: Kaplan Online almost gives students an unfair advantage.

Kaplan Online is not limited to test preparation, however, and its recently redesigned windows reflect the rapid changes occurring throughout the education arena. Allow Kaplan to expand your educational perspectives by checking out the Career and International Centers. If you're about to enter college, graduate school, business, law, medicine, or nursing, get to know Kaplan Online.

The Career Center

Let's see, now: we've helped you select a college and even prepare for entry, and now that you've graduated it's time to find a job. We can help with that too, in the form of the Career Center (see Figure 13-11).

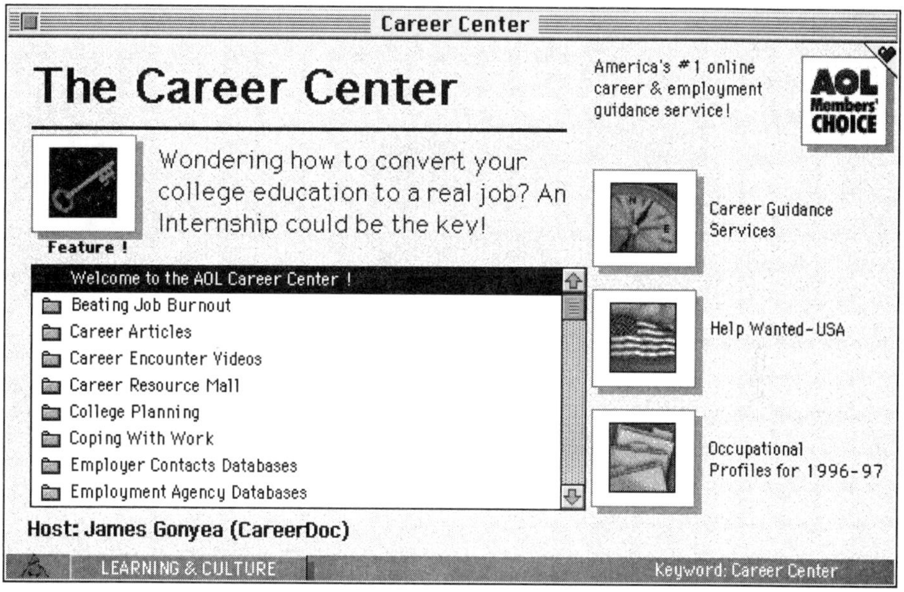
Career Center
The Career Center
America's #1 online career & employment guidance service!
AOL Members' CHOICE
Wondering how to convert your college education to a real job? An Internship could be the key!
Feature !
Welcome to the AOL Career Center !
Beating Job Burnout
Career Articles
Career Encounter Videos
Career Resource Mall
College Planning
Coping With Work
Employer Contacts Databases
Employment Agency Databases
Career Guidance Services
Help Wanted-USA
Occupational Profiles for 1996-97
Host: James Gonyea (CareerDoc)
LEARNING & CULTURE
Keyword: Career Center

Figure 13-11: The Career Center is the first electronic career and employment guidance agency in America.

The Career Center offers career counseling, articles on hiring trends, libraries of résumé and employment letter templates, profiles of those elusive home computing business opportunities, and a database of employer contacts. There's information on over 200 occupations—job descriptions, entrance qualifications, salaries, future prospects, and working conditions—in the occupational profiles database, and help-wanted and employment agency databases as well. You can even list your professional skills in the Career Center's talent database. If you're looking for work, this place is a gold mine of opportunity. Use the keywords: **Career Center**.

The Academic Assistance Center

Perhaps I got ahead of myself. You might not be in the job market yet. Lots of AOL members are still students. For students, the Academic Assistance Center (keyword: **AAC**) offers tutoring, help with homework, or assistance in polishing skills that have become rusty. In particular, this is the place to find teachers—teachers who are online and dedicated to the pursuit of academic goals (see Figure 13-12).

Academic Assistance Center
Academic Assistance Center
Have you used our Educational WebLinks in the "Assistance by Subject" area? They have been carefully researched to provide you with the finest assistance.
Teacher Pager
Tutoring Center
Assistance By Subject
Academic Contests
AAC brings learning to the comfort of your own computer!
AAC Staff Profiles
AAC Info Center
keyword: AAC

Figure 13-12: The Academic Assistance Center is where students can find teachers and other professionals who will help them with their school work.

The Academic Assistance Center is dedicated to helping the student—online, without surcharge. And it's guaranteed: all the message boards mentioned below are closely monitored; if a student posts a message on any of them and doesn't receive a response within 48 hours, AOL credits the student with an hour of free time.

In the Academic Assistance help area, students can find live, real-time help with a general or specific subject area. They can post questions, attend one of many regularly scheduled sessions on a variety of subjects, or sign up for an individual session with one of AOL's instructors.

The Teacher Pager

During the evening, the Teacher Pager is ready to connect a student—any AOL member, actually; people of all ages use this feature—with a teacher, online and live. All you need to do is use the keyword: **TeacherPager**. You'll receive an online form to fill out—in which you identify your question and talk a bit about yourself—and within five minutes, a teacher will reply. More than 500 teachers and professionals are on the Teacher Pager staff. You can't remain in the dark for long with a service such as this.

Homework is one area that's often foremost on a student's mind, and it's what leads most students to the Academic Assistance Center in the first place. Figure 13-13 identifies a few of the subject areas that were active on the Homework Help Message Center when I visited. You can get there by clicking the Assistance By Subject button on the Academic Assistance Center's main screen, then looking for pushpin icons.

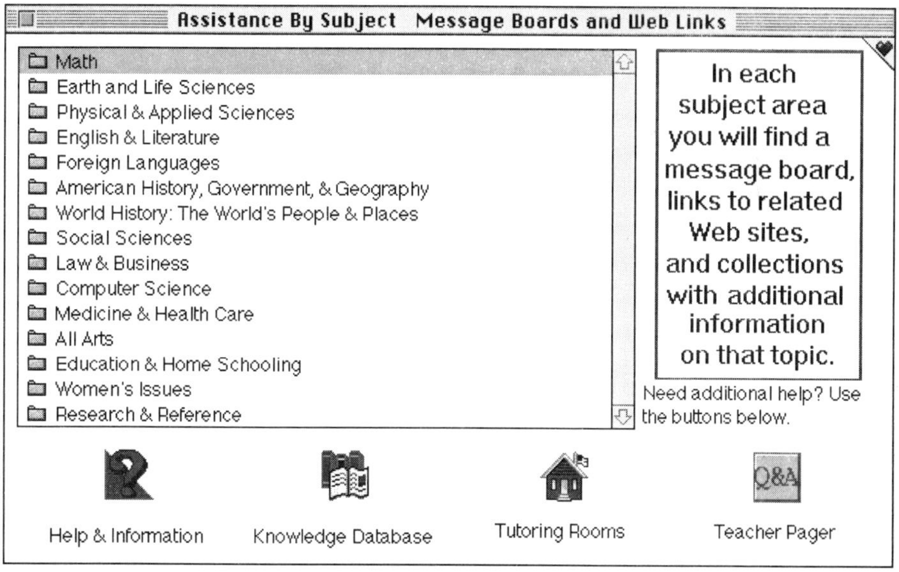
Assistance By Subject Message Boards and Web Links
Math
Earth and Life Sciences
Physical & Applied Sciences
English & Literature
Foreign Languages
American History, Government, & Geography
World History: The World's People & Places
Social Sciences
Law & Business
Computer Science
Medicine & Health Care
All Arts
Education & Home Schooling
Women's Issues
Research & Reference
In each subject area you will find a message board, links to related Web sites, and collections with additional information on that topic.
Need additional help? Use the buttons below.
Help & Information
Knowledge Database
Tutoring Rooms
Q&A
Teacher Pager

Figure 13-13: At the beginning of the academic year, thousands of messages fill the Homework Q & A message board.

College Board Online

Founded in 1900, the College Board is a national, nonprofit association of more than 2,500 institutions and schools, systems, organizations, and agencies serving both higher and secondary education. The College Board assists students moving from high school to college with services that include guidance, admissions, placement, credit by examination, and financial aid. In addition, the board is chartered to sponsor research, provide a forum to discuss common problems of secondary and higher education, and address questions of educational standards.

Which is a mouthful. What it means is that the College Board Online (keywords: **College Board**) is an invaluable service to the student faced with all the college-related questions: Where should I go? How much will it cost? What are the admission requirements? What are my chances of being accepted? (See Figure 13-14.)

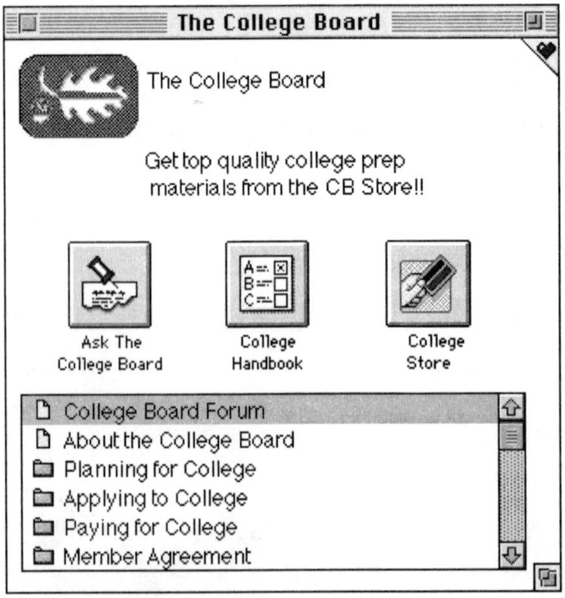
The College Board
The College Board
Get top quality college prep materials from the CB Store!!
Ask The College Board
College Handbook
College Store
College Board Forum
About the College Board
Planning for College
Applying to College
Paying for College
Member Agreement

Figure 13-14: The College Board Online is invaluable for the student contemplating a college education.

Perhaps the best way to introduce the College Board is to play the part of a prospective student and query the College Handbook. The Handbook contains descriptions of more than 3,100 colleges and universities. Information about each school includes majors offered, academic programs, freshman admissions, student life, and athletics. You can search the Handbook either by topic or by college name.

Let's say I'm interested in journalism and black history, and I've decided to pursue the combination of the two as a career. For this, I need an education. Perhaps the College Handbook has the answer (see Figure 13-15).

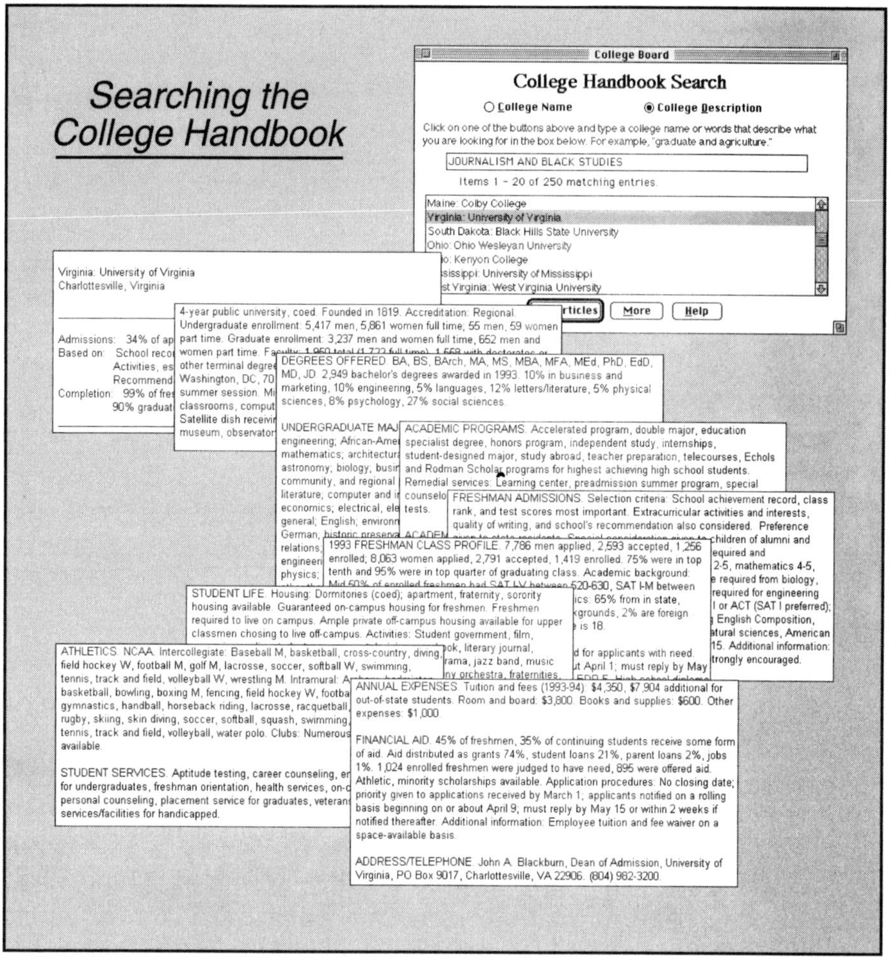
Searching the College Handbook
College Board
College Handbook Search
College Name
College Description
Click on one of the buttons above and type a college name or words that describe what you are looking for in the box below. For example, "graduate and agriculture."
JOURNALISM AND BLACK STUDIES
Items 1 - 20 of 250 matching entries.
Maine: Colby College
Virginia: University of Virginia
South Dakota: Black Hills State University
Ohio: Ohio Wesleyan University
More
Help
Virginia: University of Virginia
Charlottesville, Virginia
4-year public university, coed. Founded in 1819. Accreditation: Regional.
Undergraduate enrollment: 5,417 men, 5,861 women full time; 55 men, 59 women
DEGREES OFFERED: BA, BS, BArch, MA, MS, MBA, MFA, MEd, PhD, EdD, MD, JD. 2,949 bachelor's degrees awarded in 1993. 10% in business and marketing, 10% engineering, 5% languages, 12% letters/literature, 5% physical sciences, 8% psychology, 27% social sciences.
ANNUAL EXPENSES: Tuition and fees (1993-94): $4,350, $7,904 additional for out-of-state students. Room and board: $3,800. Books and supplies: $600. Other expenses: $1,000.
FINANCIAL AID: 45% of freshmen, 35% of continuing students receive some form of aid. Aid distributed as grants 74%, student loans 21%, parent loans 2%, jobs 1%. 1,024 enrolled freshmen were judged to have need, 895 were offered aid. Athletic, minority scholarships available. Application procedures: No closing date; priority given to applications received by March 1; applicants notified on a rolling basis beginning on or about April 9; must reply by May 15 or within 2 weeks if notified thereafter. Additional information: Employee tuition and fee waiver on a space-available basis.
ADDRESS/TELEPHONE: John A. Blackburn, Dean of Admission, University of Virginia, PO Box 9017, Charlottesville, VA 22906. (804) 982-3200.
Figure 13-15: A query of the College Handbook identifies the University of Virginia at Charlottesville, Virginia, as a possible destination for someone interested in studying journalism and black studies.

My search criteria for Figure 13-15 were "journalism" and "black studies." The College Handbook found 250 colleges that matched my criteria, one of which is the University of Virginia at Charlottesville. By selecting the University of Virginia listing, I received all the text that's pictured in Figure 13-15. This is a profusion of information, and it's available for each of the other 249 educational institutions as well.

One thing I notice as I read the UVA admission requirements is that this is one tough school to get into. My credentials will have to be sterling. For this I need help, and for help I turn to the College Board Store (see Figure 13-16).

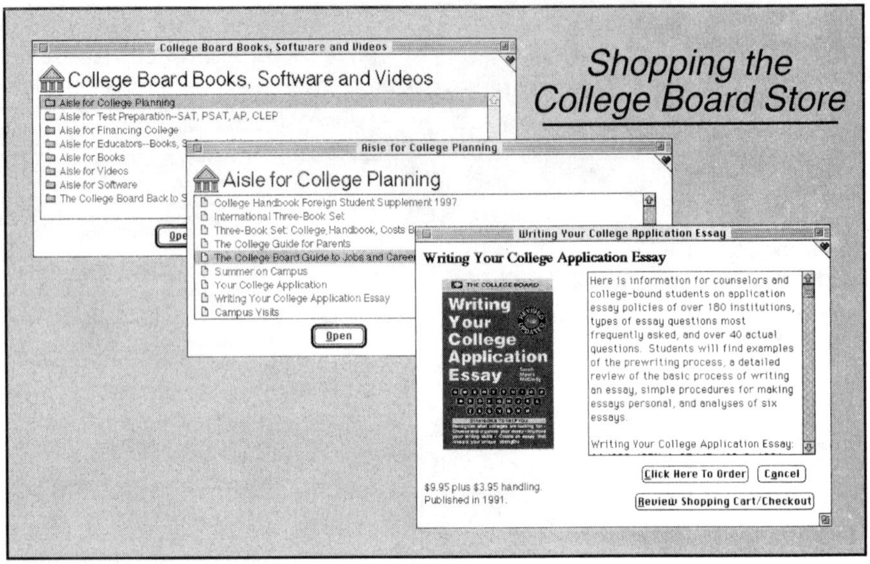
College Board Books, Software and Videos
College Board Books, Software and Videos
Aisle for College Planning
Aisle for Test Preparation--SAT, PSAT, AP, CLEP
Aisle for Financing College
Aisle for Books
Aisle for Videos
Aisle for Software
Shopping the College Board Store
Aisle for College Planning
Aisle for College Planning
College Handbook Foreign Student Supplement 1997
International Three-Book Set
The College Guide for Parents
Summer on Campus
Your College Application
Writing Your College Application Essay
Campus Visits
Open
Writing Your College Application Essay
Writing Your College Application Essay
Writing Your College Application Essay
Here is information for counselors and college-bound students on application essay policies of over 180 institutions, types of essay questions most frequently asked, and over 40 actual questions. Students will find examples of the prewriting process, a detailed review of the basic process of writing an essay, simple procedures for making essays personal, and analyses of six essays.
Writing Your College Application Essay:
$9.95 plus $3.95 handling.
Published in 1991.
Click Here To Order
Cancel
Review Shopping Cart/Checkout
Figure 13-16: The College Board Store offers books, software, and videos—and a wealth of references to assist in college planning.

Education for the Teacher

Education is not an isolated activity. Education involves the transfer of knowledge, and the transfer of knowledge typically begins with a teacher. The people at America Online know that; that's why the Learning & Culture Channel features a number of areas specifically intended for teachers. Four service areas deserve specific mention:

- The Educators' Network (keyword: **TEN**) not only provides information on education, it's also a gathering place where educators can exchange information, ideas, and experiences.
- CNN Newsroom Online is one of America Online's most popular offerings for teachers. CNN (Cable News Network) is the largest news-gathering organization in the world, and CNN Newsroom Online brings the power of CNN to the classroom, complete with ready-to-use outlines and materials for the teacher. You'll find it at keyword: **CNN**.

- The National Education Association (keywords: **NEA Public**) is a teachers' union providing benefits, support, networking, and—through related associations—accreditation for teachers and institutions. NEA Online is an ideal communications vehicle for the association: most teachers have access to a computer, and communication of this sort is best handled quickly, efficiently, and bilaterally.
- The American Federation of Teachers' AFT Plus area (keyword: **AFT**) offers an electronic hub for AFT news, resources, and activities—a place where AFT members can stop by for timely updates on what's happening, current information on major issues, and an exchange of views and ideas.

The Broadcast Media

Although I've already mentioned CNN, there are two other broadcast services that should be of interest to you: National Public Radio Outreach and C-SPAN. An article I once read (from *WIRED* Magazine—see Chapter 4, "Using the Internet") discussed the future of broadcast media and suggested that the era of passive, one-way broadcast communication is rapidly drawing to a close. I agree. Our curiosity seeks an astounding diversity of information, and AOL's broadcast (and magazine) forums are burgeoning answers to that need.

National Public Radio Outreach Online

This is NPR's avenue of communication with educators and listeners alike. Educators will find a wealth of teachers' guides, newsletters, and brochures (found under Ed. Guides & Newsletters) that tie in with NPR programs—not unlike the strategy employed by CNN. The rest of us will find press releases, biographies (and photos) of on-air personalities, programming schedules, and member-station listings (see Figure 13-17).

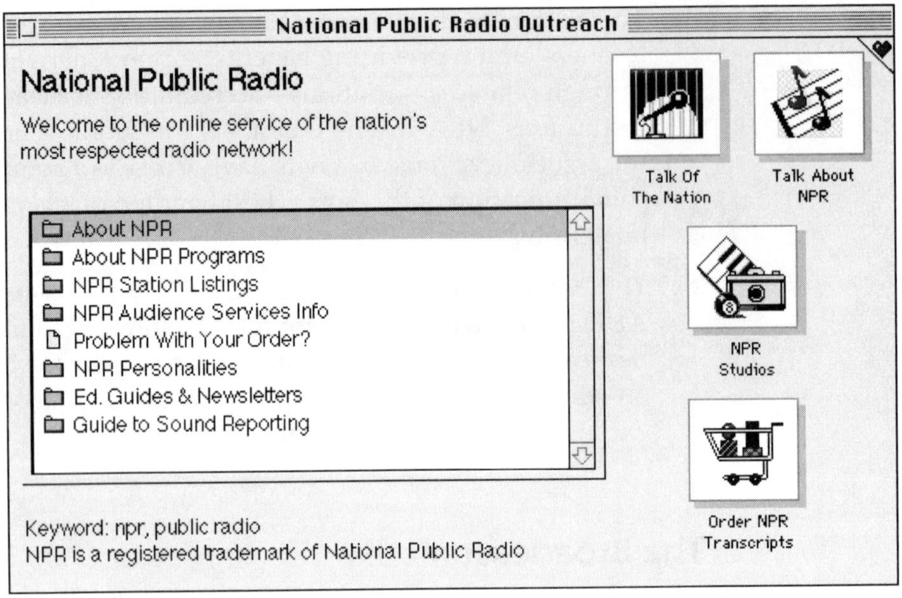
National Public Radio Outreach
National Public Radio
Welcome to the online service of the nation's most respected radio network!
About NPR
About NPR Programs
NPR Station Listings
NPR Audience Services Info
Problem With Your Order?
NPR Personalities
Ed. Guides & Newsletters
Guide to Sound Reporting
Talk Of The Nation
Talk About NPR
NPR Studios
Order NPR Transcripts
Keyword: npr, public radio
NPR is a registered trademark of National Public Radio

Figure 13-17: National Public Radio Outreach Online offers services for educators and listeners alike.

Two items are of particular interest: (1) "Talk About NPR" provides direct access to NPR's listener-feedback loop. You're not only assured that your comment will be read, but you may receive a reply as well. (2) The Audience Services Info area provides information on books, music, and films reviewed on NPR's *All Things Considered, Morning Edition,* and *Talk of the Nation*. Typically, contact information is included for individuals and organizations discussed in program features. The keyword? **NPR**, of course!

C-SPAN Online

Former U.S. House of Representatives Speaker Jim Wright once called C-SPAN (Cable-Satellite Public Affairs Network) "America's Town Hall." Indeed, since 1977, C-SPAN has been providing live, unedited, balanced views of government forums that are unmatched in the broadcast industry. Now C-SPAN Online brings C-SPAN's viewers even closer to cable television's public affairs network (see Figure 13-18).

Perhaps the most significant parts of the online service are its program descriptions and long-range scheduling information: finally, we can tell what's coming up next!

Welcome To C-SPAN Online
C-SPAN
Go to Our Web Site
C-SPAN's Convention Coverage
About C-SPAN
Subscribe to Our NEW E-Mailing List
Message Boards
C-SPAN AUDITORIUMS
Viewer Services
Audio Networks
C-SPAN Today
Online Political Guide - WEB
C-SPAN Interactive
C-SPAN Chat
Download Libraries
C-SPAN Store
Keyword: C-SPAN
A Public Service Created by America's Cable Television Companies
C-SPAN Online
C-SPAN Online - C-SPAN in the Classroom
C-SPAN
In the Classroom
About C-SPAN in the Classroom
1995-96 Equipment-for-Education Grant
Winners: National Scholarship Competition
Subscribe to our e-mailing list
Teachers: Check out our online lesson plans in the lesson plans collection!!
Congressional Calendar
Download Resources
C-SPAN School Bus
Lesson Plans
Write C-SPAN in the Classroom
Share Your Teaching Tips

Figure 13-18: C-SPAN Online offers schedules, feedback, educational services, and a searchable database for its viewers at keyword: **CSPAN**.

Educators who are interested in using C-SPAN as a teaching resource can join the network's free membership support service: C-SPAN in the Classroom. This service offers teaching guides, access to C-SPAN's archives, a toll-free educators' hotline, and special issues of the *C-SPAN Digest*. Together with CNN and NPR, C-SPAN in the Classroom offers a gold mine of current affairs study material that's professionally produced, contemporary, and—not to be forgotten—almost free. I wish my teachers had had access to this material when I was in school.

Moving On

The Learning & Culture Channel is a vast collection of resources: a joint venture by professionals, parents, and students alike. Coupled with America Online's ease of use and graphical interface, it's not only one of the most comprehensive online resources available, it's really fun. Educators will tell you that learning is most effective when it's enjoyable. The Learning & Culture Channel is that kind of experience—enlivening, satisfying, and encouraging to students of every age.

Those who know, however, will assure you that *research* is a significant portion of the education process. And research is rapidly becoming an electronic medium. There's good reason for that. Find out by turning the page.

CHAPTER 14

Reference

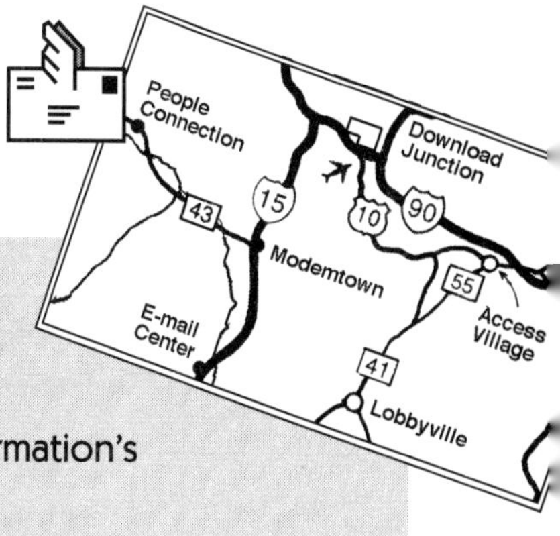

People Connection
Download Junction
43
15
10
90
Modemtown
55
E-mail Center
Access Village
41
Lobbyville

- Compton's NewMedia Forum
- Merriam-Webster
- American Business Information's Business Yellow Pages
- Pro CD's Phone Book on AOL (the White Pages)
- MEDLINE
- Nolo Press Self-Help Law Center
- Resources on the World Wide Web
- Online Databases

If ever there was a message in search of a medium, it's *reference.* The print medium—home to reference works for centuries—is losing its predominance. Large volumes containing thousands of pages are simply too inconvenient, too wasteful of natural resources, and too unwieldy to meet the push-button demands of the electronic information age.

A printed encyclopedia, for example, made sense 60 years ago, but to describe every aspect of today's society—especially today's technological society—a comprehensive encyclopedia would have to fill a room, not a shelf. Even if you had the room, you would hesitate to use the thing: searching—especially cross-referencing—would be too tedious; information would probably be out of date by the time it was printed (and certainly by the time you had it paid for); and the perpetual revisions would make indexing a nightmare.

Forget the printed encyclopedia. Forget the room to house it. Forget the payments and revisions. Turn on your computer, punch up AOL, and click the Reference Desk button on the main menu, or use the keyword: **Reference** (see Figure 14-1). It's all here, it's all topical, it's all affordable. And not a single tree fell to make it possible.

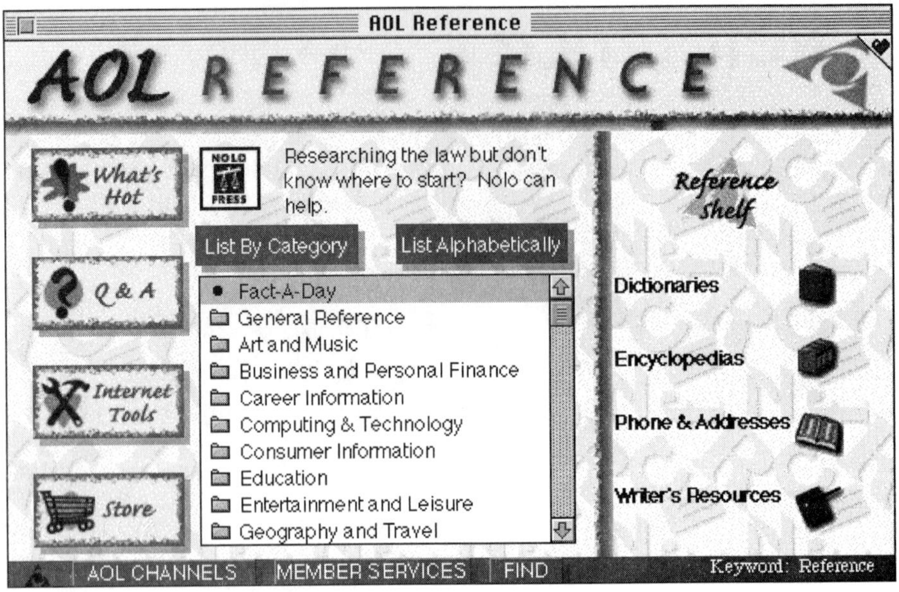
AOL Reference
AOL REFERENCE
What's Hot
Researching the law but don't know where to start? Nolo can help.
List By Category
List Alphabetically
Q & A
Fact-A-Day
General Reference
Art and Music
Business and Personal Finance
Career Information
Computing & Technology
Consumer Information
Education
Entertainment and Leisure
Geography and Travel
Internet Tools
Store
Reference Shelf
Dictionaries
Encyclopedias
Phone & Addresses
Writer's Resources
AOL CHANNELS
MEMBER SERVICES
FIND
Keyword: Reference

Figure 14-1: AOL's Reference window.

Alternative Listings

Look carefully at Figure 14-1. Note the buttons immediately above the list box marked List By Category and List Alphabetically. Normally, this list appears with categories displayed, but if you know which reference work you're looking for, click the List Alphabetically button. *Zip!* Folders containing every reference work available on AOL will appear (an extraordinary number of them), all sorted alphabetically and ready for you to peruse.

Compton's NewMedia Forum

Four years ago, the keyword: **Comptons** brought you a rather plain presentation of *Compton's Encyclopedia*. It was an admirable resource—more than 9,000,000 words; 5,274 full-length articles; 29,322 capsule articles; 63,503 index entries—and won the Critics' Choice award for the best education program, as well as top honors at the 1991 Software Publisher's Association awards ceremony. But it remained primarily textual, a vestige of its print heritage; hardly a sterling example of the online medium.

That, of course, was in the days of 1200 baud modems and black-and-white 9-inch displays. Today, things have changed, including the Compton's NewMedia Forum (see Figure 14-2).

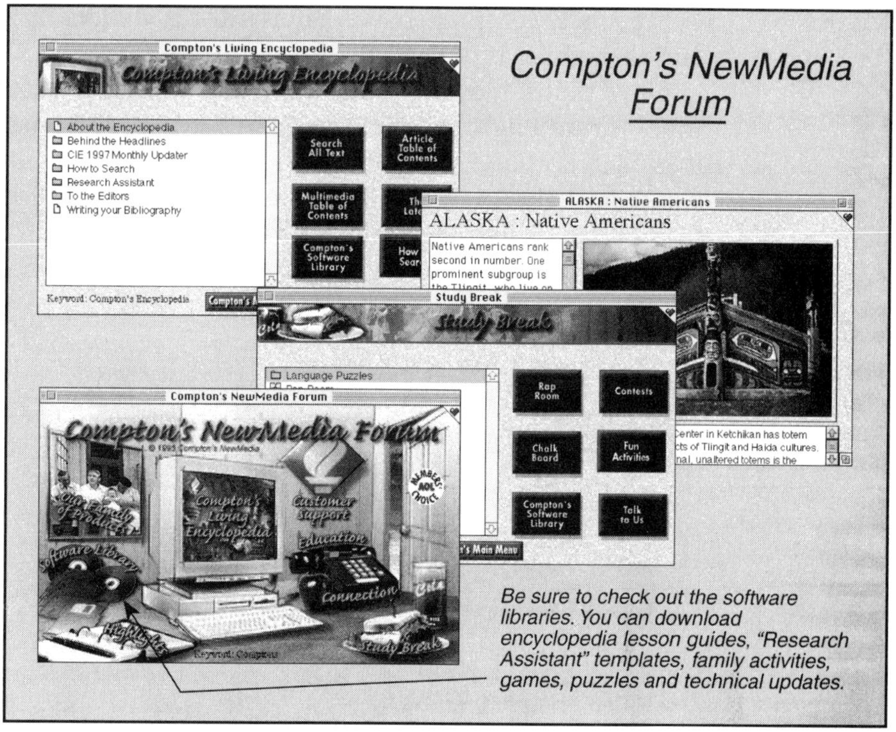
Compton's NewMedia Forum
Compton's Living Encyclopedia
About the Encyclopedia
Behind the Headlines
CIE 1997 Monthly Updater
How to Search
Research Assistant
To the Editors
Writing your Bibliography
Search All Text
Article Table of Contents
Multimedia Table of Contents
Compton's Software Library
Keyword: Compton's Encyclopedia
ALASKA : Native Americans
Native Americans rank second in number. One prominent subgroup is
Study Break
Language Puzzles
Rap Room
Contests
Chalk Board
Fun Activities
Compton's Software Library
Talk to Us
Compton's NewMedia Forum
Be sure to check out the software libraries. You can download encyclopedia lesson guides, "Research Assistant" templates, family activities, games, puzzles and technical updates.

Figure 14-2: Compton's NewMedia Forum offers a newly enhanced multimedia encyclopedia and a growing array of support services.

> **Encyclopedic Potential**
>
> Compton's isn't the only encyclopedia available online. Look also for the Columbia Concise Encyclopedia (keyword: **CCE**), and the Grolier Multimedia Encyclopedia, at keyword: **Grolier**.

At the root of it all is Compton's Living Encyclopedia—an enhanced version of the printed work, and a multimedia extravaganza. The Encyclopedia offers not only text but graphics, sounds, and videos as well. Oh it's a reference work all right, and as a reference work it's exhaustively comprehensive. But it's also a *multimedia* reference work, and that makes it fun as well.

I love trains. I love the sound and smell—and the romance—of trains. I ride a light rail system to town (Metropolitan Area Express [MAX] in Portland, Oregon), and Amtrak's most popular route—the Coast Starlight—passes within a few miles of my house. To test Compton's Living Encyclopedia as an effective resource, I searched for the word "railroad" and was more than gratified with the results (see Figure 14-3).

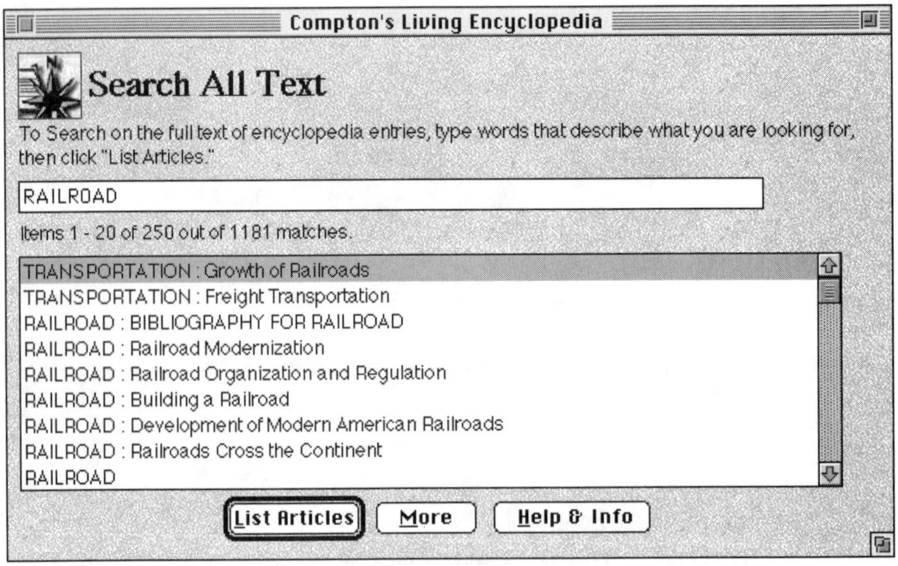
Compton's Living Encyclopedia
Search All Text
To Search on the full text of encyclopedia entries, type words that describe what you are looking for, then click "List Articles."
RAILROAD
Items 1 - 20 of 250 out of 1181 matches.
TRANSPORTATION : Growth of Railroads
TRANSPORTATION : Freight Transportation
RAILROAD : BIBLIOGRAPHY FOR RAILROAD
RAILROAD : Railroad Modernization
RAILROAD : Railroad Organization and Regulation
RAILROAD : Building a Railroad
RAILROAD : Development of Modern American Railroads
RAILROAD : Railroads Cross the Continent
RAILROAD
List Articles
More
Help & Info

Figure 14-3: Over a thousand references to railroads! Elysian Fields for the railnaut.

Notable Passenger Trains

These are the trains I want to travel in someday. The text below is extracted from Compton's Living Encyclopedia, Online Edition, and downloaded from AOL.

- **Blue Train, South Africa**
  Said to be the most luxurious train in the world, the Blue Train makes a leisurely 1,000-mile, 26-hour trip once or twice a week between Pretoria and Cape Town.
- **Coast Starlight, United States**
  Though I've already mentioned this train as Amtrak's most popular, it warrants a second mention here. The Coast Starlight crosses the Cascade Mountains and follows the coastline of California in a 1,400-mile, 33-hour trip between Seattle and Los Angeles. Save your pennies and get a sleeper.
- **Indian Pacific, Australia**
  Another luxury train, the Indian Pacific crosses the Australian continent, from Sydney to Perth, in less than three days.
- **Orient Express, Europe**
  Europe's first transcontinental express, for years unmatched in luxury and comfort. From 1883 to 1977 (with interruptions during WWI and WWII), it ran from Paris to Constantinople (now Istanbul) in Turkey. Short runs are still made over portions of the original route.
- **Rheingold, West Germany**
  One of Europe's finest trains, the Rheingold runs between Amsterdam, the Netherlands, and Basel, Switzerland, following the Rhine River and stopping at such cities as Cologne, Mainz, and Munich.
- **Rossiya, Trans-Siberian Railway**
  The Rossiya runs daily between Moscow and Vladivostok. The trip takes a week. Call your travel agent (better yet, consult the Independent Traveler, discussed in Chapter 11) before you pack: things are changing over there.
- **TGV, France**
  This is the fastest train in the world, cruising at 180 miles per hour and covering the 267 miles between Paris and Lyon in two hours.

Whoa! One hundred and eighty miles an hour! Few cars can reach that speed—in fact, few private aircraft can cruise at 180 miles an hour. But the TGV does it every day, with aplomb, replete with French cuisine and a most eclectic group of passengers.

Merriam-Webster

Forgive my rambling. I got sidetracked, so to speak, when the subject of trains came up. I was talking about antiquated media, and another has just come to our attention: the ubiquitous dictionary. Quickly now: name the first dictionary that comes to mind. Chances are, you said Webster's, and that's just what AOL has to offer (see Figure 14-4).

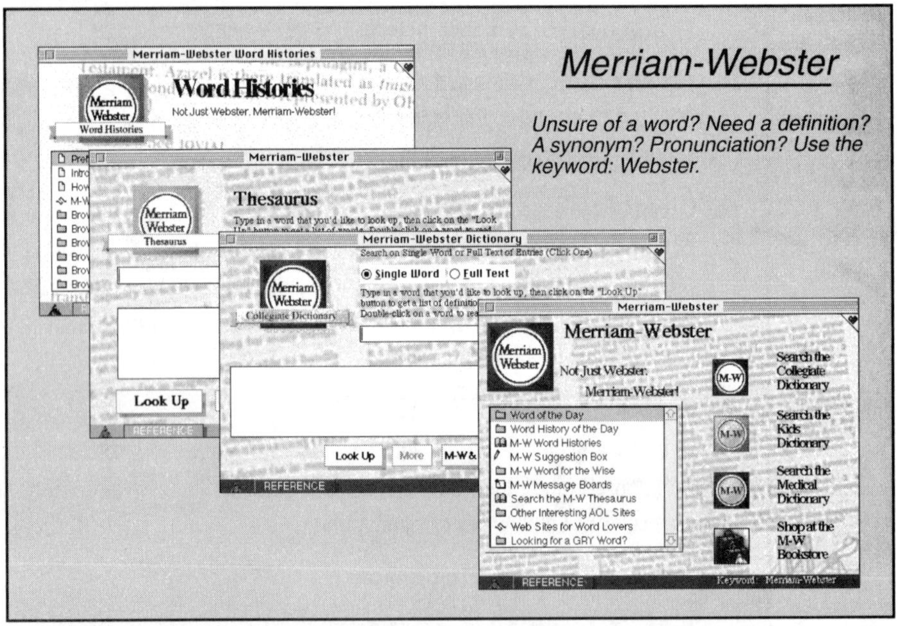
Merriam-Webster
Unsure of a word? Need a definition? A synonym? Pronunciation? Use the keyword: Webster.
Merriam-Webster Word Histories
Word Histories
Not Just Webster. Merriam-Webster!
Merriam-Webster
Thesaurus
Look Up
Merriam-Webster Dictionary
Single Word
Full Text
Collegiate Dictionary
Look Up
More
Merriam-Webster
Not Just Webster. Merriam-Webster!
Word of the Day
Word History of the Day
M-W Word Histories
M-W Suggestion Box
M-W Word for the Wise
M-W Message Boards
Search the M-W Thesaurus
Other Interesting AOL Sites
Web Sites for Word Lovers
Looking for a GRY Word?
Search the Collegiate Dictionary
Search the Kids Dictionary
Search the Medical Dictionary
Shop at the M-W Bookstore
REFERENCE
Keyword: Merriam-Webster

Figure 14-4: Merriam-Webster not only obligingly places its complete dictionary online, it also includes a thesaurus and its delightful Word Histories lexicon.

The dictionary is another message looking for an improved medium, and like the encyclopedia, the dictionary is perfectly served by the machinery of the online medium. So is the thesaurus, which Merriam-Webster also offers online. AOL's machines search Merriam-Webster's references with speed and accuracy, returning not only definitions, pronunciations, and synonyms, but fascinating information about the etymology of words—especially if you choose to consult *Word*

Histories, Merriam-Webster's nutriment for the bibliophile appetite. You'll find all the Merriam-Webster offerings on the Reference Desk's main menu, or use the keywords: **Merriam-Webster**.

American Business Information's Business Yellow Pages

When you want to find a new restaurant, an electrician, the nearest theater, or an odd part for your bicycle, where's the first place you look? Virtually all of us would say the Yellow Pages, that ubiquitous corpus of commerce. Well now there is a worthy alternative to thumbing those familiar pages, and it's free on AOL!

You'll quickly find that AOL's American Yellow Pages offer some significant advantages over traditional printed Yellow Pages. Like AOL's other reference services, its American Yellow Pages are searchable. Whether your quest be common or exotic, you can quickly locate products or services by letting AOL's fingers, rather than yours, do the walking (see Figure 14-5).

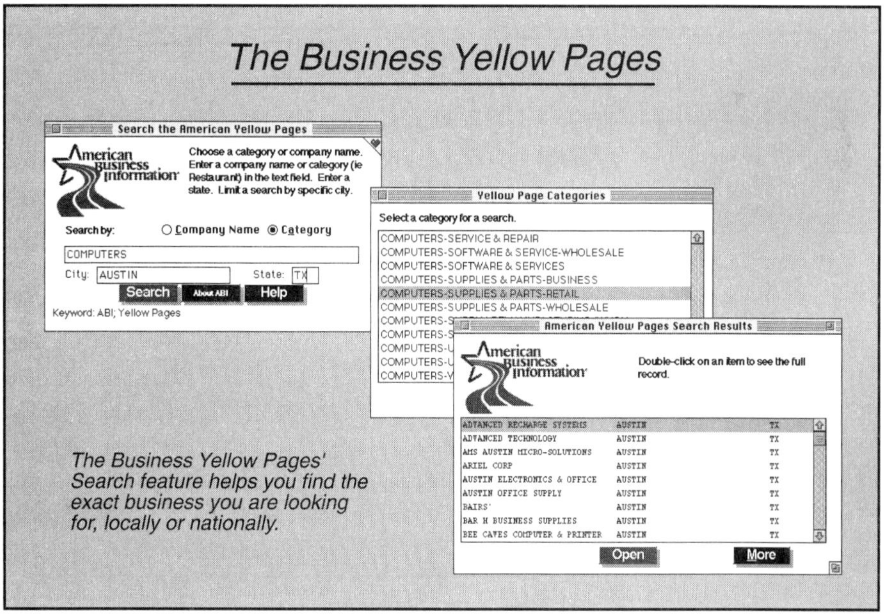
The Business Yellow Pages
Search the American Yellow Pages
American Business Information
Choose a category or company name. Enter a company name or category (ie Restaurant) in the text field. Enter a state. Limit a search by specific city.
Search by: Company Name Category
COMPUTERS
City: AUSTIN State: TX
Search About ABI Help
Keyword: ABI; Yellow Pages
Yellow Page Categories
Select a category for a search.
COMPUTERS-SERVICE & REPAIR
COMPUTERS-SOFTWARE & SERVICE-WHOLESALE
COMPUTERS-SOFTWARE & SERVICES
COMPUTERS-SUPPLIES & PARTS-BUSINESS
COMPUTERS-SUPPLIES & PARTS-RETAIL
COMPUTERS-SUPPLIES & PARTS-WHOLESALE
American Yellow Pages Search Results
Double-click on an item to see the full record.
ADVANCED RECHARGE SYSTEMS AUSTIN TX
ADVANCED TECHNOLOGY AUSTIN TX
AMS AUSTIN MICRO-SOLUTIONS AUSTIN TX
ARIEL CORP AUSTIN TX
AUSTIN ELECTRONICS & OFFICE AUSTIN TX
AUSTIN OFFICE SUPPLY AUSTIN TX
BAIRS' AUSTIN TX
BAR H BUSINESS SUPPLIES AUSTIN TX
BEE CAVES COMPUTER & PRINTER AUSTIN TX
Open More
The Business Yellow Pages' Search feature helps you find the exact business you are looking for, locally or nationally.

Figure 14-5: The American Business Information Yellow Pages, an AOL service that's all business!

Perhaps best of all, AOL's American Yellow Pages include nationwide listings; no longer will your curiosity be limited by the scope of your local telephone book. In just minutes you can locate business sources in the next town, or in Chicago, Bar Harbor, or San Diego. Just click the Yellow Pages entry on the main Reference Desk menu, or use the keywords: **Yellow Pages**.

Pro CD's Phone Book on AOL (the White Pages)

This morning I happened to think of an old friend, a musician from high school days. The last I heard he was in Iowa, but I haven't talked with him in years. I was wondering.

You're already ahead of me. Yes, if AOL offers the Yellow Pages, it must offer white pages too (see Figure 14-6). And like the Yellow Pages, AOL will do the looking for you, whether your goal be a business or residence. You can find the Online White Pages by using the keywords: **White Pages** and then clicking Pro CD. This is not only a viable alternative to long-distance Directory Assistance, it's much less expensive.

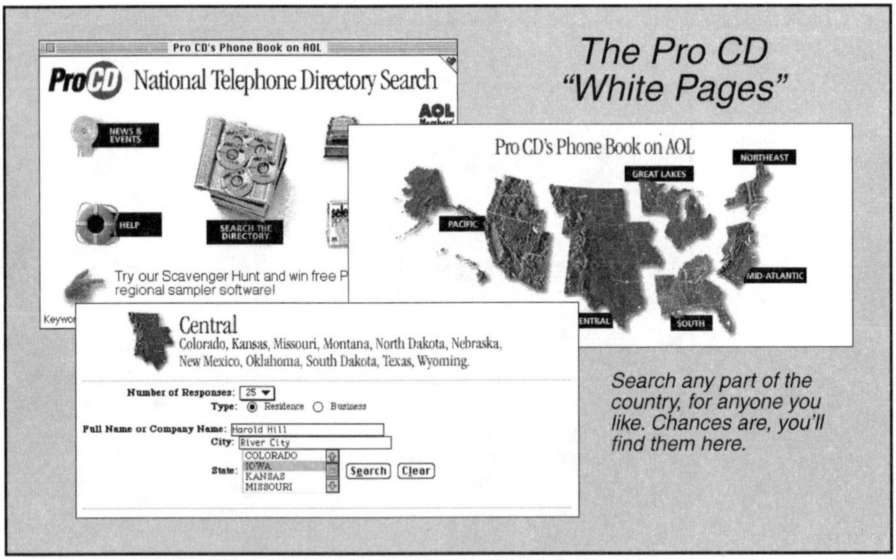

The Pro CD "White Pages"
Pro CD's Phone Book on AOL
National Telephone Directory Search
NEWS & EVENTS
HELP
SEARCH THE DIRECTORY
Try our Scavenger Hunt and win free P
regional sampler software!
Pro CD's Phone Book on AOL
NORTHEAST
GREAT LAKES
PACIFIC
MID-ATLANTIC
SOUTH
Central
Colorado, Kansas, Missouri, Montana, North Dakota, Nebraska, New Mexico, Oklahoma, South Dakota, Texas, Wyoming
Number of Responses: 25
Type: Residence Business
Full Name or Company Name: Harold Hill
City: River City
State: COLORADO IOWA KANSAS MISSOURI
Search Clear
Search any part of the country, for anyone you like. Chances are, you'll find them here.

Figure 14-6: Harold was always a likable fellow; I wonder what he's up to.

MEDLINE

For at least the last hundred years, health care decisions have been solely the province of doctors, modern society's scientific experts on the machinery of the human body. In real life and in countless television and film productions, patients have traditionally played passive rather than active roles in the management of their personal health care and therapy. But as the end of the century approaches, deep and significant changes are afoot in the definition and delivery of complete health care, many of which offer patients greatly increased participation, understanding, and compassion—not to mention renewed status as human beings.

America Online's noteworthy contribution to this trend is found in MEDLINE, an online compendium of medical networks and resources that has been popular with doctors for years but now is available to everyone through AOL. If a single example were to be requested as to the benefits of the online medium, MEDLINE would be an excellent choice.

Access to MEDLINE is gained either via the main Reference Desk menu, or the keyword: **MEDLINE** (see Figure 14-7). The main MEDLINE window leads directly to several incredibly rich areas: MEDLINE's arsenal of search tools, the MEDLINE Message Boards, the Better Health & Medical Network, and the Personal Empowerment Network.

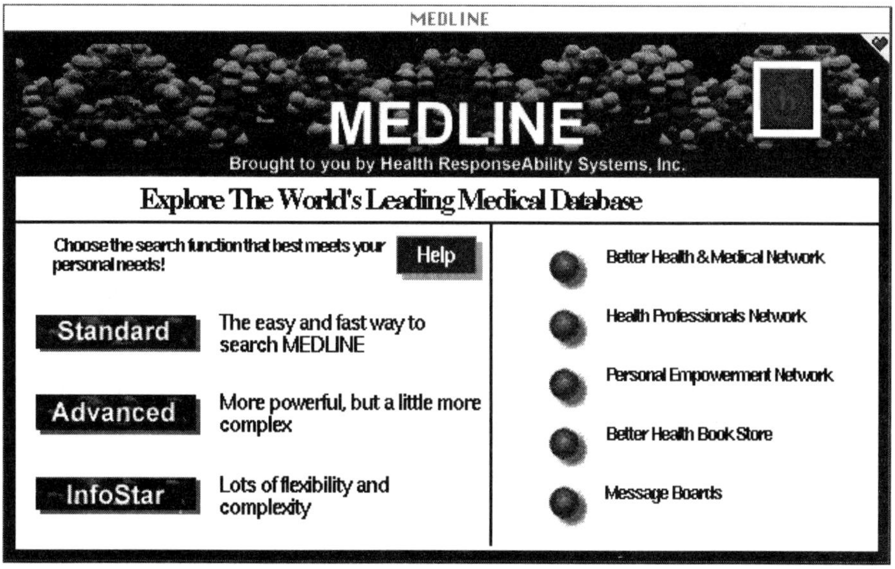
MEDLINE
MEDLINE
Brought to you by Health ResponseAbility Systems, Inc.
Explore The World's Leading Medical Database
Choose the search function that best meets your personal needs!
Help
Standard
The easy and fast way to search MEDLINE
Advanced
More powerful, but a little more complex
InfoStar
Lots of flexibility and complexity
Better Health & Medical Network
Health Professionals Network
Personal Empowerment Network
Better Health Book Store
Message Boards

Figure 14-7: No longer the exclusive province of doctors, MEDLINE is your health information gateway to medical research, organizations, and health-related groups.

MEDLINE Search Tools

By now you are no doubt familiar with AOL's basic search mechanisms, all offering dialog boxes or menus that can help you find exactly what you are looking for. While MEDLINE Searches utilize this same structure, they differ in that they display not one but three different levels of search refinement.

MEDLINE's Standard Search is the one most like other AOL search dialog boxes—with a few enhancements. In addition to a standard search word dialog box, there are check boxes to focus the search (see Figure 14-8).

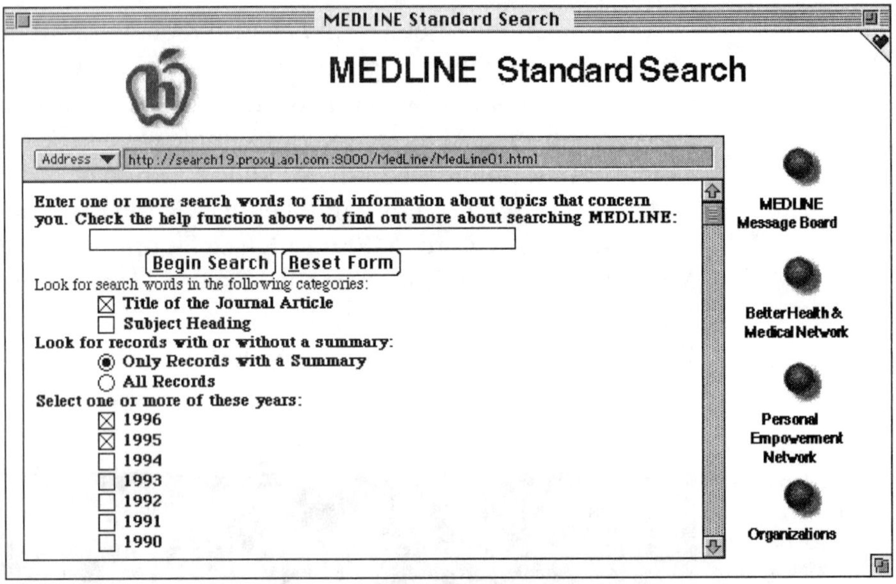
MEDLINE Standard Search
MEDLINE Standard Search
Address
http://search19.proxy.aol.com:8000/MedLine/MedLine01.html
Enter one or more search words to find information about topics that concern you. Check the help function above to find out more about searching MEDLINE:
Begin Search
Reset Form
Look for search words in the following categories:
Title of the Journal Article
Subject Heading
Look for records with or without a summary:
Only Records with a Summary
All Records
Select one or more of these years:
1996
1995
1994
1993
1992
1991
1990
MEDLINE Message Board
Better Health & Medical Network
Personal Empowerment Network
Organizations

Figure 14-8: MEDLINE's Standard Search is the easiest way to begin your medical inquiries.

MEDLINE's Advanced Search adds another level of complexity, including the ability to specify title, summary, subject heading or central concepts, author, and institution (see Figure 14-9).

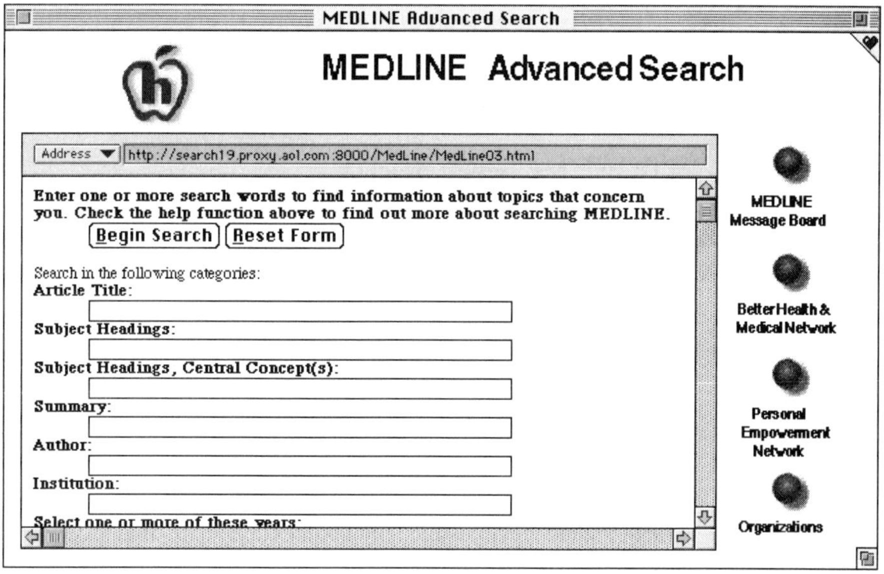
MEDLINE Advanced Search
MEDLINE Advanced Search
Address
http://search19.proxy.aol.com:8000/MedLine/MedLine03.html
Enter one or more search words to find information about topics that concern you. Check the help function above to find out more about searching MEDLINE.
Begin Search
Reset Form
Search in the following categories:
Article Title:
Subject Headings:
Subject Headings, Central Concept(s):
Summary:
Author:
Institution:
MEDLINE Message Board
Better Health & Medical Network
Personal Empowerment Network
Organizations

Figure 14-9: MEDLINE's Advanced Search is appropriate for more experienced users.

MEDLINE's InfoStar Search includes all the features of the Advanced Search, plus MeSH headings, abstracts, volume/issue numbers, title abbreviations, CAS registry numbers, journal title codes, and unique identifiers (see Figure 14-10).

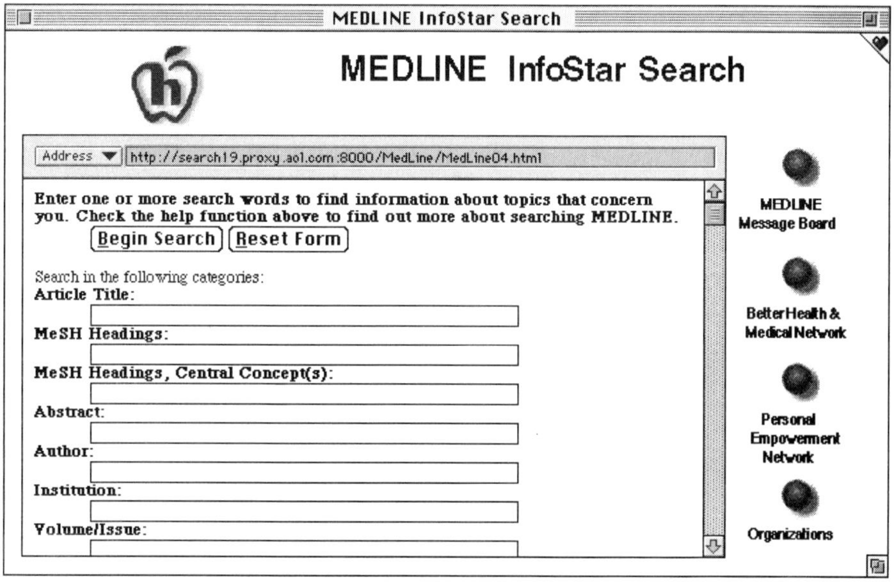
MEDLINE InfoStar Search
MEDLINE InfoStar Search
Address
http://search19.proxy.aol.com:8000/MedLine/MedLine04.html
Enter one or more search words to find information about topics that concern you. Check the help function above to find out more about searching MEDLINE.
Begin Search
Reset Form
Search in the following categories:
Article Title:
MeSH Headings:
MeSH Headings, Central Concept(s):
Abstract:
Author:
Institution:
Volume/Issue:
MEDLINE Message Board
Better Health & Medical Network
Personal Empowerment Network
Organizations

Figure 14-10: InfoStar Search is often used by medical professionals.

MEDLINE's Search array clearly offers search options appropriate to a wide range of user backgrounds, and it's all available at the keyword: **MEDLINE.**

MEDLINE Message Board

Message boards usually conjure a vision of hastily scribbled notes tacked up where everyone can see. And that's a useful concept, both in its simplicity and familiarity. But in regard to the MEDLINE Message Board, such a concept doesn't quite seem to apply; the tone here is more serious, more intense, and sometimes more urgent.

Here you'll find excellent tips on using MEDLINE's Standard, Advanced, and InfoStar searches as well as other information useful to first-time MEDLINE browsers. But most of all you'll find people who are looking for information, who possess knowledge, and who are interested in helping. Look around. If you don't find what you're looking for, choose the MEDLINE Suggestions folder and officially enlist the help of some unseen friends.

Nolo Press Self-Help Law Center

Twenty-five years ago two former Legal Aid lawyers, dissatisfied with the lack of affordable legal information and advice available to the public, began writing understandable, easy-to-use self-help law books. Legal kits, software, and tapes all followed, but the purpose has never changed: to take the mystery out of law and make it accessible to Everyman.

Since they were already involved in print, audio, and video publications, it seemed only natural that Nolo Press would commit to the online medium as well, and they've done just that with their Nolo Press Self-Help Law Center at keywords: **Nolo Press** (see Figure 14-11).

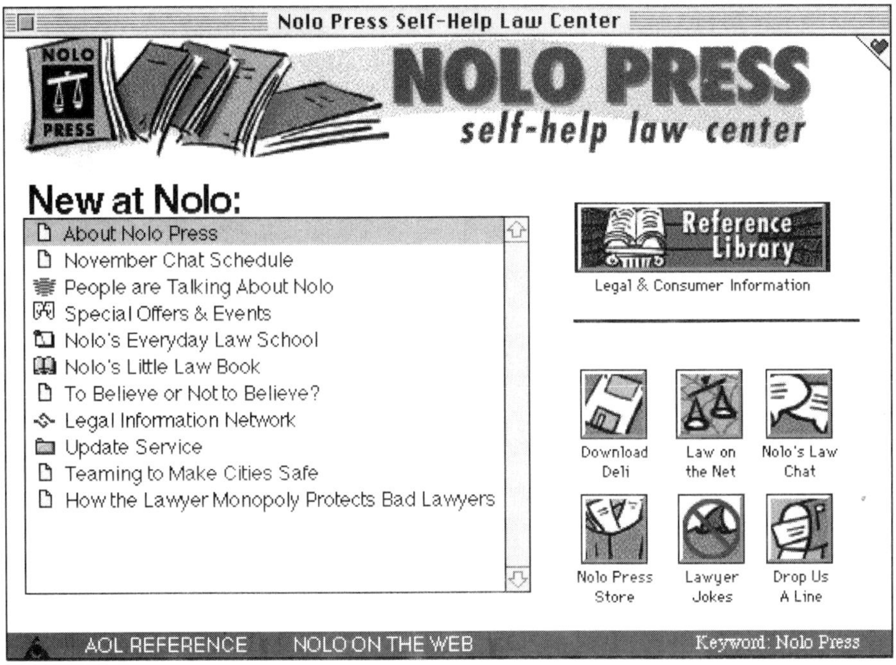
Nolo Press Self-Help Law Center
NOLO PRESS
self-help law center
New at Nolo:
About Nolo Press
November Chat Schedule
People are Talking About Nolo
Special Offers & Events
Nolo's Everyday Law School
Nolo's Little Law Book
To Believe or Not to Believe?
Legal Information Network
Update Service
Teaming to Make Cities Safe
How the Lawyer Monopoly Protects Bad Lawyers
Reference Library
Legal & Consumer Information
Download Deli
Law on the Net
Nolo's Law Chat
Nolo Press Store
Lawyer Jokes
Drop Us A Line
AOL REFERENCE
NOLO ON THE WEB
Keyword: Nolo Press

Figure 14-11: Look to the Nolo Law Center for legal self-help.

Pay particular attention to Nolo's Pocket Guide to Family Law. You'll find chapters dedicated to adoption, alimony, child support, divorce, domestic violence, marriage, property and debt, reproductive rights, rights of unmarried people, and more.

Resources on the World Wide Web

AOL isn't your only source for online reference, and the first people to admit that are the people at America Online. Fortunately, you're not excluded from the remainder of the reference universe. That universe, you see, resides on the World Wide Web (the Web is discussed in Chapter 4, "Using the Internet"), and the Web is an integral feature of the Reference Desk.

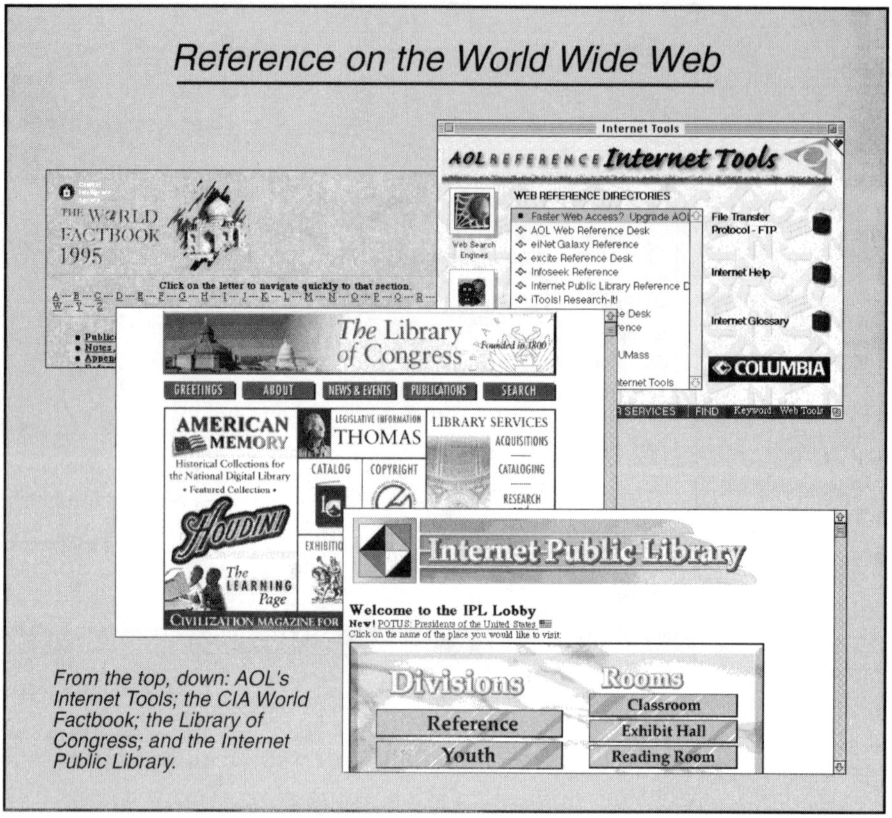
Reference on the World Wide Web
Internet Tools
AOL REFERENCE Internet Tools
WEB REFERENCE DIRECTORIES
Faster Web Access? Upgrade AOL
AOL Web Reference Desk
eiNet Galaxy Reference
excite Reference Desk
Infoseek Reference
Internet Public Library Reference
iTools! Research-It!
File Transfer Protocol - FTP
Internet Help
Internet Glossary
COLUMBIA
THE WORLD FACTBOOK 1995
Click on the letter to navigate quickly to that section.
The Library of Congress
GREETINGS
ABOUT
NEWS & EVENTS
PUBLICATIONS
SEARCH
AMERICAN MEMORY
THOMAS
LIBRARY SERVICES
Internet Public Library
Welcome to the IPL Lobby
Divisions
Rooms
Reference
Youth
Classroom
Exhibit Hall
Reading Room
From the top, down: AOL's Internet Tools; the CIA World Factbook; the Library of Congress; and the Internet Public Library.

Figure 14-12: The World Wide Web is rife with reference resources, and they're all available via the Internet Tools button on the main Reference screen.

This is where reference comes into its own: the reference potential on the Web is worldwide, after all, and the world is a sea of information. Imagine having the Library of Congress, the Internet Public Library, the CIA Factbook, AT&T's 800-number directory, the National Science Foundation, the Smithsonian, NASA, the U.S. Geological Survey, the Rutgers University Law Library, and even a virtual hospital at your fingertips!

One of the best places to begin exploring the reference potential of the Web is with one of AOL's (and community leader REF Jane's) recommended Web reference pages (see Figure 14-13, top). You'll find it listed (along with many others) in the Web Reference Directories list box shown in Figure 14-12. The eiNet Galaxy Reference home page is an encyclopedic inventory of nearly all of the reference sites on the Web, and probably the best jumping-off point for information exploration the Web has to offer.

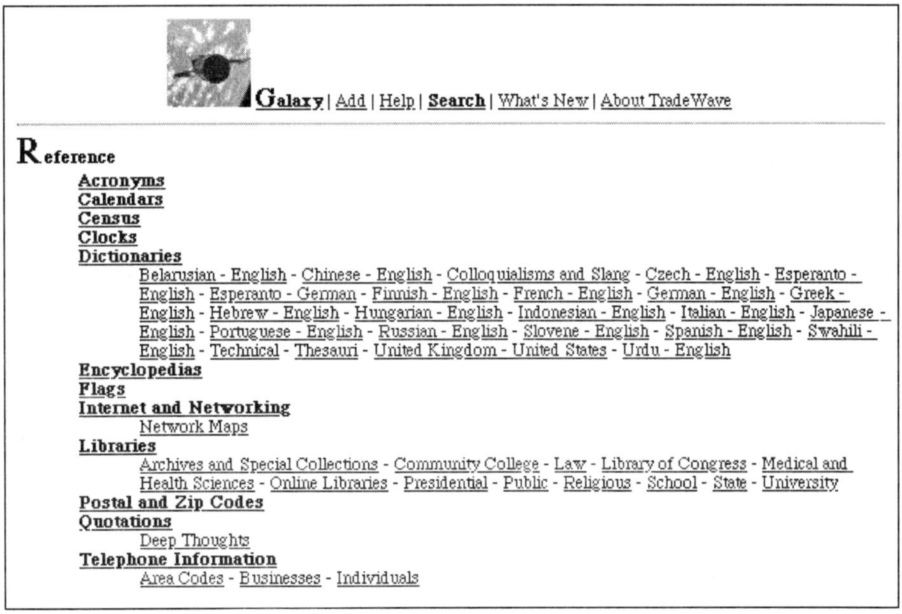
Galaxy | Add | Help | Search | What's New | About TradeWave
Reference
Acronyms
Calendars
Census
Clocks
Dictionaries
Belarusian - English - Chinese - English - Colloquialisms and Slang - Czech - English - Esperanto - English - Esperanto - German - Finnish - English - French - English - German - English - Greek - English - Hebrew - English - Hungarian - English - Indonesian - English - Italian - English - Japanese - English - Portuguese - English - Russian - English - Slovene - English - Spanish - English - Swahili - English - Technical - Thesauri - United Kingdom - United States - Urdu - English
Encyclopedias
Flags
Internet and Networking
Network Maps
Libraries
Archives and Special Collections - Community College - Law - Library of Congress - Medical and Health Sciences - Online Libraries - Presidential - Public - Religious - School - State - University
Postal and Zip Codes
Quotations
Deep Thoughts
Telephone Information
Area Codes - Businesses - Individuals

Figure 14-13: The eiNet Galaxy Reference page on the World Wide Web is an exhaustive listing of the Web's reference links. (Only about a third of the page is pictured here.)

Online Databases

With the fall 1994 release of the Reference Desk, AOL effectively consolidated all its online databases into one place. Whether it's a telephone book or a dictionary of Wall Street terminology, if it's available online, it's available at keyword: **Reference**.

We've explored many of AOL's databases in previous chapters, and others are highly specialized. But two warrant our attention here.

AOL Local Access Numbers

The list of telephone numbers you can use to contact AOL is a prodigious database in itself. America Online is available around the world, after all, and that's a lot of territory (and a lot of access numbers). If you plan to travel with your computer, search this database for a list of access numbers for the localities you'll be visiting. Print the list, pack it with your modem, and take it along. You can access the database from the Reference Desk, or by using the keyword: **Access**.

If you are a frequent traveler, you'll want to read Appendix D, "On the Road." There are lots of tips there for the AOL road warrior.

Software File Search

Speaking of searching, probably the places you'll search most frequently are AOL's own file libraries. Though the Reference Desk area lists Software File Search among the options in the main window's scroll box, you don't have to visit here to conduct a search. You can search AOL's file libraries at any time, from any location, by using the keywords: **File Search**, or by clicking the Find button on the toolbar.

File Search (you might hear it called "Quickfinder"; either term is accurate and the keyword: **Quickfinder**—or just **Quickfind**—works just as well) is AOL's mechanism for searching its list of online files. When you use the keyword, the Software Search dialog box will appear (see Figure 14-14).

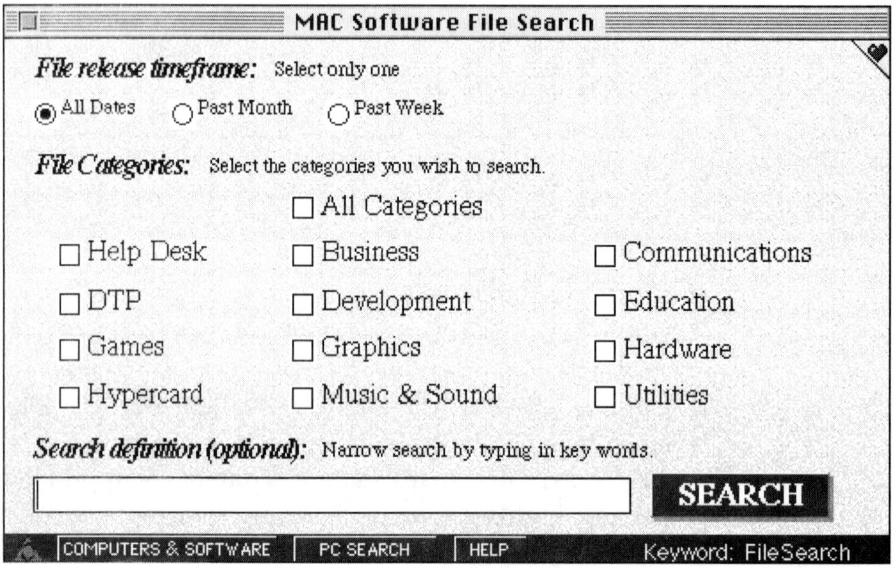
MAC Software File Search
File release timeframe: Select only one
All Dates
Past Month
Past Week
File Categories: Select the categories you wish to search.
All Categories
Help Desk
Business
Communications
DTP
Development
Education
Games
Graphics
Hardware
Hypercard
Music & Sound
Utilities
Search definition (optional): Narrow search by typing in key words.
SEARCH
COMPUTERS & SOFTWARE
PC SEARCH
HELP
Keyword: FileSearch

Figure 14-14: The Software Search dialog box.

Most searches of AOL's online files are successful, but you might encounter situations in which the search fails (no files are found) even though you know there are files online that meet your criteria, or in which the search is too successful (wading through a hundred or more matches is just too much effort).

How Many Files Are Available?

One way of tracking AOL's growth is to periodically check the total number of files available online. When I first joined the service (I'm a "charter member," having first signed on in early 1990), there were fewer than 10,000 files. When I checked today, there were more than 100,000!

How did I determine the number of files available online? It's easy: just leave the Mac Software File Search dialog box empty (as it's pictured in Figure 14-14). Don't check any of the check boxes and don't put any criteria in the text box. Just leave the dialog as it appears when you first summon it, be sure the All Dates button is selected, then click the Search button.

America Online will respond by listing all the files available online and telling you how many there are. With this many files, you won't even want to browse the list, but the total number might be informative. Do this occasionally and watch AOL grow.

Let's say that you need to send a file to a friend who is using a PC rather than a Mac. It's common to compress files before sending them, and your friend uses PKZIP. PKZIP is built into the Windows version of the AOL software, and most online files for PCs are "zipped," as they say, so this isn't uncommon. Unfortunately, you've got a Mac, and Macs usually use the StuffIt compression software, not PKZIP. (StuffIt and PKZIP are discussed in Chapter 5, "Transferring Files.") Needing a Mac utility that will compress a file in the PKZIP format, you sign on and use File Search to locate the utility.

Your first temptation is to simply type the category (or name) of the program you're looking for in the text box, as shown in the top window of Figure 14-15. You don't really want PKZIP itself; it only runs on PCs. You want something that will zip files on the Mac for the PC, so the generic term "PC" is about the best criterion for your purpose.

Figure 14-15: Homing in on a zipping program for the Mac.

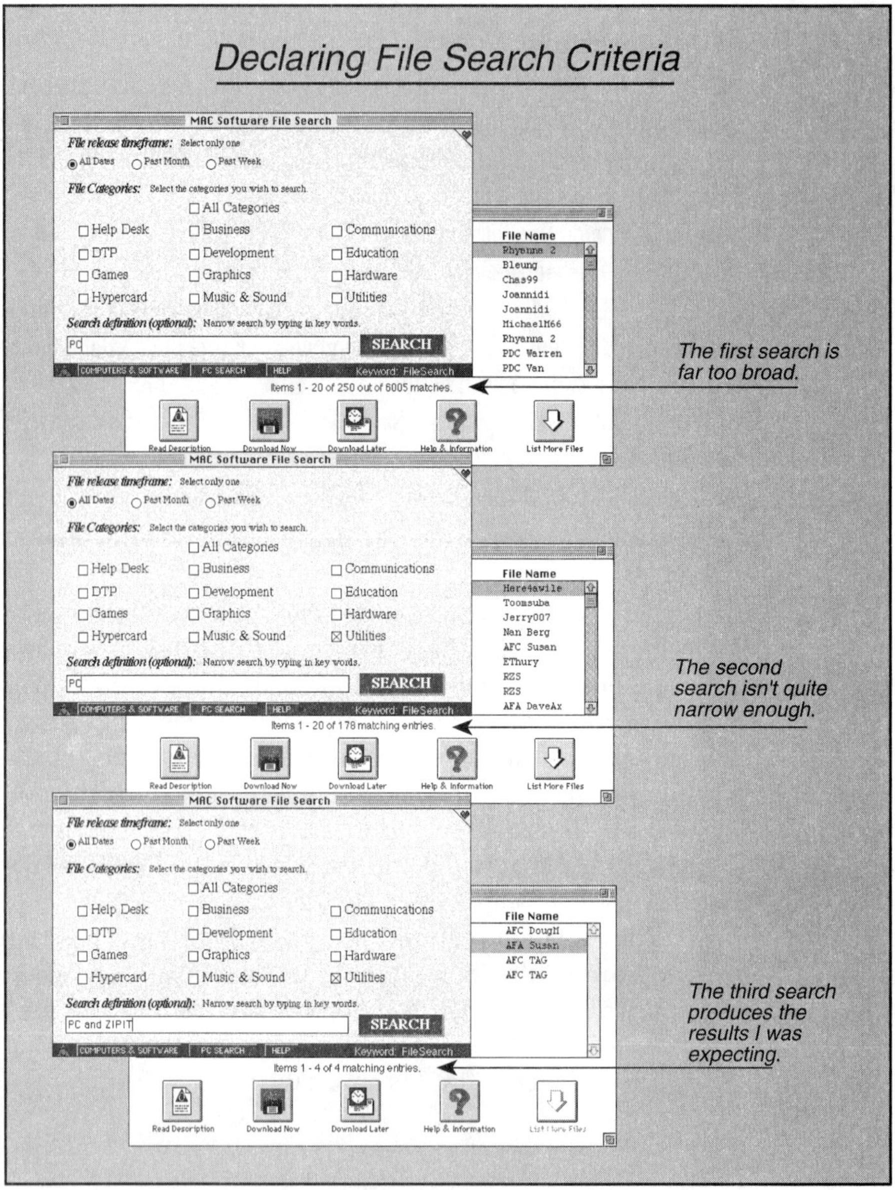
Declaring File Search Criteria
MAC Software File Search
File release timeframe: Select only one
All Dates
Past Month
Past Week
File Categories: Select the categories you wish to search.
All Categories
Help Desk
Business
Communications
DTP
Development
Education
Games
Graphics
Hardware
Hypercard
Music & Sound
Utilities
Search definition (optional): Narrow search by typing in key words.
PC
SEARCH
COMPUTERS & SOFTWARE
PC SEARCH
HELP
Keyword: FileSearch
File Name
Items 1 - 20 of 250 out of 6005 matches.
Read Description
Download Now
Download Later
Help & Information
List More Files
The first search is far too broad.
Items 1 - 20 of 178 matching entries.
The second search isn't quite narrow enough.
PC and ZIPIT
Items 1 - 4 of 4 matching entries.
The third search produces the results I was expecting.

Notice the results of the first search: 6,005 files! Indeed, a few file-searching tips seem in order:

- Use check boxes to narrow your search. It's tempting to ignore the check boxes in the middle of the File Search dialog box. If you do, All Categories is the default condition, even if it's not checked. By specifying a check box (I specified Utilities in the second example in Figure 14-15), my search produced 178 files, hardly a manageable number.
- Narrow your search with *ands*, *ors*, and *nots*. I used an *and* function in the third example pictured in Figure 14-15 and eliminated all the other PC-related files—whatever they were—that cluttered my results. (Be careful: mixing *ands* with *ors* or *nots* can sometimes produce misleading results.)
- Don't specify version numbers. You might have heard that ZipIt 1.4 is the latest version. Searching with the criterion: ZipIt 1.4 would not produce the latest version, ZipIt 1.5.3.
- Criteria are not case-sensitive. Don't worry about uppercase and lowercase when you're typing criteria. America Online doesn't care. It also doesn't care if you make things plural or singular: "PC" works no better or worse than "PCs."
- Use whole words. Abbreviations won't work, nor will wild cards. "ZIP" (for ZipIt) or "ZIP*" (using a wild card) would not be an efficient way to find ZipIt.
- Search specific libraries if File Search fails. Using File Search to find "MajorTom," for example, will fail. Since the only MajorTom file posted online is a graphic, and because it's stored in the Gallery (discussed in Chapter 8, "The Community"), go to the Gallery, and conduct your search there.
- To find the latest files, leave everything blank and specify "Past Week." This finds all the files posted in just the past week.

Moving On

My overview of America Online's Reference Channel has lightly touched on topics representing the diversity of American culture. Yet, curiously, I've not written a single word about what may be the most popular of all American activities, an activity where time is information and information is literally money, an activity with a unique relationship to the online medium: the purchasing and selling of goods and services.

It's not as if America Online has not planned and prepared; indeed, AOL has been toiling in the background, constructing the virtual storefront and painting the virtual front door that you're about to enter. Get ready: "Buying & Selling" is up next.

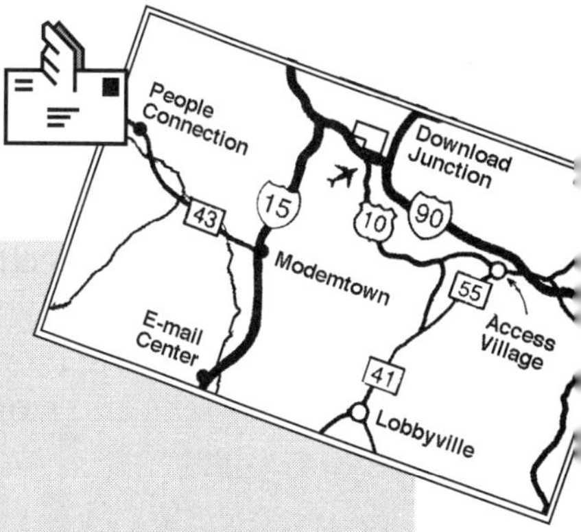
People Connection
Download Junction
Modemtown
E-mail Center
Access Village
Lobbyville
43
15
10
90
55
41

CHAPTER 15

Buying & Selling

- The AOL Store
- 1-800-FLOWERS
- Hallmark Connections
- Eddie Bauer
- One Hanes Place
- OfficeMax Online
- Tower Records
- Health & Vitamin Express
- Shoppers' Advantage
- The Sharper Image
- Classifieds Online
- The FreeShop Online
- KidSoft Super Store
- Omaha Steaks International
- Downtown AOL
- Caffè Starbucks

Ask 10 people what a shopping excursion means to them and you'll probably get 10 different answers. An elder might recall a time when shopping meant a once-a-month trip to "the store," where the selection was meager if there was a selection at all. Someone new to American shores might describe an open-air produce market, a Mediterranean bazaar, or the British post-shopping ritual of high tea. Another might recount stories of quests for unusual or arcane objects, spanning months or even years of browsing in dusty little shops. Globe trotters might speak excitedly of the streets of Paris, Sydney, Amsterdam, Hong Kong, or New York. And any one of these respondents might mention going to the mall, alluding to the social scene as well as the plethora of goods to be found there.

Whether by car, carriage, ferry, or foot, all these shopping destinations have demanded transportation. Today, however, another shopping method is emerging and taking hold—one that offers exotica, style, selection, product information, speed—and above all, the ultimate convenience of home access. I speak, of course, of electronic commerce, and this chapter is your guide to a new generation of shopping, indeed a new definition of buying and selling, that is being written even as you read these words.

Electronic marketing is in its infancy. As you explore, remember that what you will find is important not only for the products and marketing models available now, but also as a prediction of product selection and store location of the future.

The AOL Store

The electronic communication medium is AOL's backyard, so what better place to begin than at the AOL Store (see Figure 15-1). Here you can find clothing, coffee mugs, and other products to let you proclaim your affiliation with AOL, as well as products such as modems, computer accessories, software, and books (like this one) to speed your online navigation and indulge your curiosity. Take a moment to check out the Multimedia Showcase, send an AOL gift certificate to a friend, or download one of AOL's hottest sound tracks. Just use the keywords: **AOL Store**.

The America Online Store
THE America Online store
GIFT CERTIFICATES
SIGN ON A FRIEND
AMERICA ONLINE'S INTERNET
SHOP THE STORE
AOL Store Contest
AOL Book Shop
AOL Hardware Shop
AOL Modem Shop
AOL Software Shop
Customer Service
Apply for the AOL Visa Card - earn FREE time!
Master the Internet!
Featured Product
Keyword: AOL Store

Figure 15-1: Show your pride in America Online! Wear an AOL sweatshirt while you sip coffee from an AOL mug.

1-800-FLOWERS

It's easy to forget that communication is much more than words. No matter the occasion, situation, or location, one of the most pleasant and touching messages you can send is the gift of flowers, a gift made simple by entering the keyword: **Flowers**. (See Figure 15-2.)

You'll find seasonal and holiday suggestions for fresh cut flowers, as well as event and gift items including chocolates, cakes, centerpieces, gift baskets, wreaths, dried flower arrangements, and even a gift reminder service! You'll find it all at keyword: **Flowers**.

Welcome to the World's Favorite Florist!
1-800-FLOWERS
1-800-FLOWERS
MajorTom,
Need a gift for that special somone, old or new? Choose a gift that is simple, yet expressive, of how you feel!
Feature of the Day
A Fresh Approach To Living And Giving
Shop Our Store
Welcome & What's New
Gift Concierge Service
Customer Service
Contests & Promotions
Fresh Thoughts
Flower Talk
Featured Product
Keyword: Flowers
Shopping Cart
Marketplace

Figure 15-2: 1-800-FLOWERS: the world's premier florist and gift shop.

Hallmark Connections

The Marketplace Channel has expanded quite a bit in recent months, and no doubt it will expand even more by the time this book reaches you. AOL has always been at the forefront of online technology, especially in the area of multimedia, so expect to see lots of new areas here. The Hallmark Connections area is a perfect example (see Figure 15-3).

Hallmark Connections
Coffee Lover's Cards
Hallmark
CONNECTIONS
Greeting Cards
What's New
Shop for Cards
Card Chat
How to Shop & Customer Service
Keyword: Hallmark

Figure 15-3: Hallmark Connections—when you care enough to send the very best (but don't want to drive to the store). . . .

How many times has a birthday or anniversary slipped your mind until it was nearly upon you? What do you do? You could stop what you're doing, jump in your car, drive to a store, and get a card, but who has that kind of time these days? Well, Hallmark Connections is here to change all of that.

How would you like to be able to order high-quality, personalized greeting cards without ever leaving home (or work)? Better yet, how would you like to have someone mail those cards for you at the appropriate time? Talk about having a personal secretary!

The area is organized much like a real-world card department in any store you might visit. You can choose from seven departments, ranging from seasonal cards to business greeting cards. Once you've selected a card department, AOL will either ask you to narrow your search a bit further, or show you a list of available cards within your chosen department. Once you select a particular card, you'll be able to see what it actually looks like.

You'll also be able to personalize your card by supplying the recipient's name or other information as indicated, as well as your own closing message and name. The cards will be printed on recycled paper, and your closing message and name will be printed in a scripted font to simulate a signature. Your card will then be mailed to any address in the United States—either within 48 hours of your order or at any time you choose.

Eddie Bauer

Considering its humble beginnings 75 years ago in a small downtown Seattle store, Eddie Bauer has become one of America's most innovative retailers, with over 400 stores in three countries, a CD-ROM, and now, an online presence on AOL (see Figure 15-4).

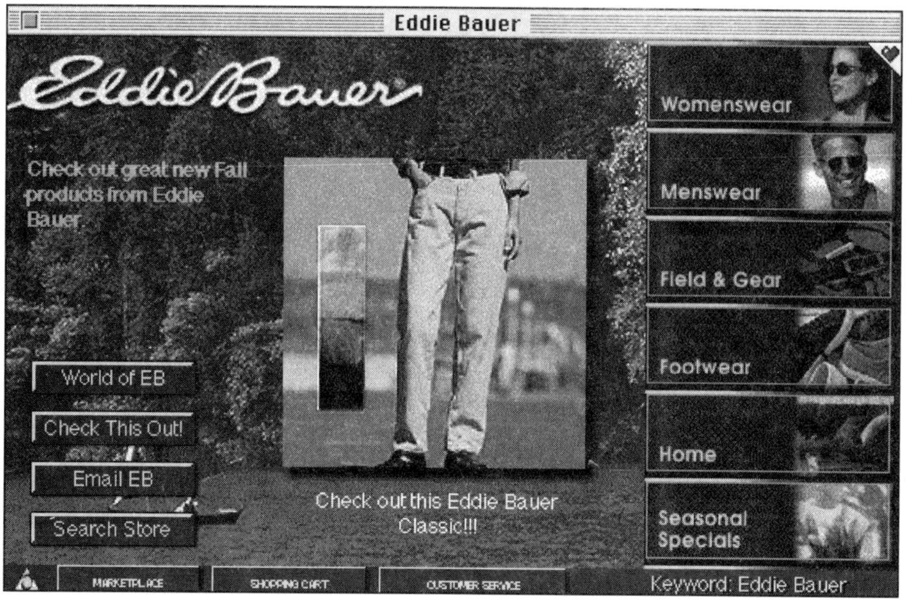
Eddie Bauer
Eddie Bauer
Check out great new Fall products from Eddie Bauer.
World of EB
Check This Out!
Email EB
Search Store
Check out this Eddie Bauer Classic!!!
Womenswear
Menswear
Field & Gear
Footwear
Home
Seasonal Specials
MARKETPLACE
SHOPPING CART
CUSTOMER SERVICE
Keyword: Eddie Bauer

Figure 15-4: The greenest commercial destination online: Eddie Bauer offers clothing, field accessories, products for the home, and the Eddie Bauer/Global ReLeaf Tree Project. Use the keywords: **Eddie Bauer**, of course!

In addition to Eddie Bauer's traditional line of exceptional products with a casual attitude, the keywords: **Eddie Bauer** also take you to the Eddie Bauer/Global ReLeaf Tree Project, a program designed to plant healthy, native trees in eight reforestation sites in North America. All you do is click the order button and Eddie Bauer plants a one- to two-year-old tree on your behalf for each dollar you donate *and* matches your donation!

Eddie Bauer and the Global ReLeaf Tree Project have planted over 300,000 trees to date.

One Hanes Place

One Hanes Place (see Figure 15-5) is also a new addition to AOL. The Main Store at One Hanes Place is stocked with great everyday values on fashion legwear, intimate apparel, and activewear, as well as brand-name basics. You'll save up to 50 percent on Hanes, L'eggs, Bali, Playtex, Hanes Her Way, Champion, Just My Size, and Color Me Natural products.

One Hanes Place
ONE HANES PLACE
What's NEW - NFL Activewear!
Shop the Main Store
Contests & Specials
Search Hanes
Discover Our Store
What's NEW?
Customer Service
Keywords: Hanes, L'eggs, Bali, Playtex, Champion
Slightly Imperfects Up To 40% Off
Featured Product
GREEN BAY
PACKERS

Figure 15-5: The One Hanes Place Main Store and the Olympic Shop "store within a store."

OfficeMax OnLine

So far we've seen interesting stores offering a wide selection of products at the Marketplace, but they've all been, for the most part, in the personal category. Don't worry. There are plenty of places where you can fulfill your practical needs—personal and business—as well.

OfficeMax OnLine is an online concept from one of the nation's largest and fastest-growing operators of high-volume, deep-discount office products superstores. OfficeMax opened its first store in suburban Cleveland, Ohio, on July 5, 1988, and in less than 7 years grew to become one of America's largest specialty retailers, with more than 400 stores in 147 markets in 40 states from coast to coast, including Puerto Rico.

OfficeMax is able to buy in huge quantities and pass the savings on to you. They offer deep discounts on brand-name office products, business machines, electronics, furniture, computer hardware, software, and related products. Plus, everything they sell is backed by their low-price guarantee. And now with OfficeMax OnLine, you can buy their products from your keyboard and your order will be delivered directly to your door (see Figure 15-6).

OfficeMax OnLine
OfficeMax ONLINE
SHOP OUR STORE
CUSTOMER SERVICE
SPECIAL
BUSINESS
FEATURED PRODUCT
Shop Our Store
SHOP OUR STORE
OFFICE
BUSINESS
COMPUTERS, PRINTERS &
OFFICE
PRODUCT SEARCH
OfficeMax ONLINE
FROM YOUR KEYBOARD TO YOUR DOOR!™

Figure 15-6: OfficeMax OnLine—your one-stop office products shopping center.

Tower Records

When Tower Records went online, I went to heaven. I'm a music junkie—CDs are my habit—and without a weekly fix I'm petulant and sullen. Imagine my delight, then, when Tower offered me the ability to shop for music without having to leave my keyboard! (See Figure 15-7.)

Tower Records
1000 top sellers
TOP 1000 HITS
...cheap...overnight...
TUNE FINDER
PULSE!
ONLINE
Sale Rack
Distinctive Gifts
New This Week
@TOWER
Check Out Tower's Top 1000!
Available Overnight!
Van Halen
"Best Of Vol. 1"
Neil Diamond
"In My Lifetime"
Miles Davis/Gil Evans
"Columbia" Box Set
Quick Search
by Artist:
SEARCH
MARKETPLACE
SHOPPING CART
CUSTOMER SERVICE
Keyword: TOWER

Figure 15-7: Tower Records offers sustenance for the musically malnourished.

Perhaps most significantly, the online version of Tower Records provides a search mechanism for finding the music you're after. No more confusion and indecision standing in front of incomprehensibly organized racks of tapes or CDs. At Tower Records Online you can bypass the stacks and quickly search by an artist's (or composer's) name, by an individual song (not just album) title, or by category. And if you're an inveterate browser, you'll find Tower Records's online listings diverse, extensive, easy to understand and follow, and pleasantly accessible.

Here's a fascinating tidbit: Tower Records's offerings aren't limited to music. Be sure to check out the Categories/Other Categories listing. You'll find comedy; TV and radio nostalgia; sound tracks; sound effects; nature sounds; and book, spoken word, self-help, and instructional recordings.

Health & Vitamin Express

Shopping for health care products can be as confusing as a foreign language. Claims and counterclaims, lists of ingredients as long as an IRS "clarification"—I've sometimes left health care stores as bewildered as a hound with hay fever. But with AOL's help, it doesn't have to be that way (see Figure 15-8).

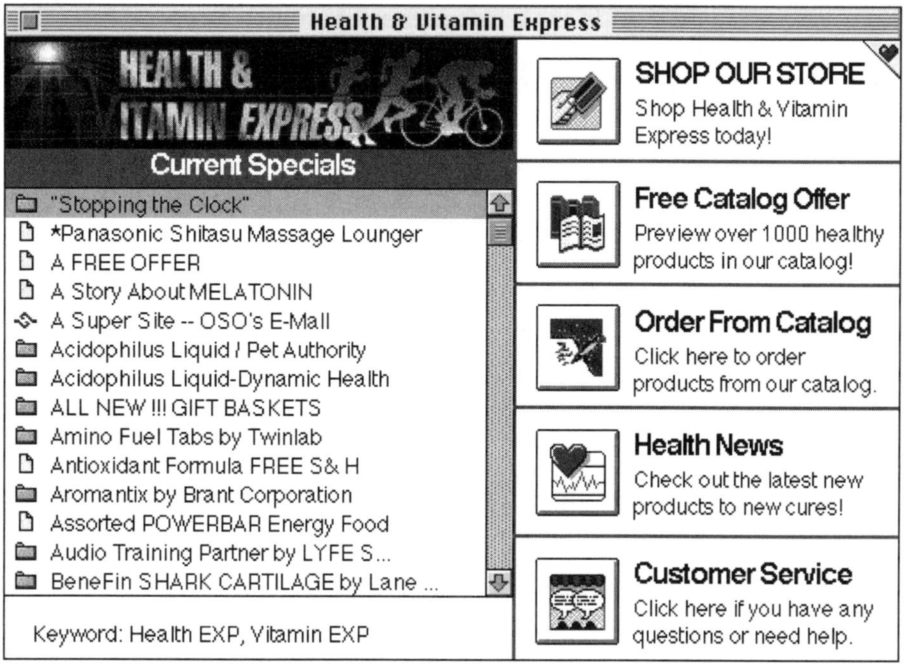
Health & Vitamin Express
HEALTH & VITAMIN EXPRESS
Current Specials
"Stopping the Clock"
*Panasonic Shitasu Massage Lounger
A FREE OFFER
A Story About MELATONIN
A Super Site -- OSO's E-Mall
Acidophilus Liquid / Pet Authority
Acidophilus Liquid-Dynamic Health
ALL NEW !!! GIFT BASKETS
Amino Fuel Tabs by Twinlab
Antioxidant Formula FREE S& H
Aromantix by Brant Corporation
Assorted POWERBAR Energy Food
Audio Training Partner by LYFE S...
BeneFin SHARK CARTILAGE by Lane ...
Keyword: Health EXP, Vitamin EXP
SHOP OUR STORE
Shop Health & Vitamin Express today!
Free Catalog Offer
Preview over 1000 healthy products in our catalog!
Order From Catalog
Click here to order products from our catalog.
Health News
Check out the latest new products to new cures!
Customer Service
Click here if you have any questions or need help.

Figure 15-8: Health & Vitamin Express offers health care products—and consultation too!

The people at Health & Vitamin Express (keywords: **Health EXP**) understand that health care can be complex and confusing, so they offer what any good store should offer: a comprehensive product array, low prices, and good information that's available for free. You can leave a message online and return later for a reply, or call their toll-free hotline for an immediate consultation about your individual needs and the products that can best meet those needs. And once you've determined what you're looking for, chances are very good you'll find it at Health & Vitamin Express at 10 to 15 percent off regular prices.

Shoppers' Advantage

Speaking of browsing, approximately 3.1 million members (more than 1 percent of the United States' population!) browse Shoppers' Advantage on a regular basis. This is a little like the shopping "clubs" that have sprouted up nationwide: you pay a small annual membership fee and you're rewarded with a warehouse full of products, attractively priced, in stock, and ready for shipment. Shoppers' Advantage not only adds the convenience of online shopping (no crowds, no parking lots, no waiting), it guarantees the lowest prices anywhere or it will refund the difference. Now that's a powerful package!

You can browse the store whether or not you're a member of Shoppers' Advantage—a significant advantage over local shopping clubs—and you can enroll online at any time. Look at the benefits Shoppers' Advantage offers:

- Discounts from 10 to 50 percent on all manufacturers' list prices.
- More than 250,000 name-brand products, all in a searchable online database. If a product you're looking for is not on the database, you can contact the Product Research team, and they will try to get it for you.
- Automatic two-year free warranty extension. Even if there is only a three- or six-month manufacturer's warranty, the folks at Shoppers' Advantage will extend the warranty on any product purchased through them to two years, at no cost.
- Merchandise from name-brand manufacturers, including Panasonic, GE, JVC, Nikon, Sony, Pioneer, AT&T, Nintendo, Whirlpool, Quasar, Jordache, Hoover, Pentax, Timex, Memorex, Rayban, Radio Shack, Pierre Cardin, Singer, and Magnavox—an all-star roster of manufacturers.
- The Department Store (click the Shop Our Entire Store button), where browsing—rather than searching—is the order of the day, and the Best Buys section, where the staff posts their best bargains. If you want to compare prices and features for yourself, Shoppers' Advantage can compare as many as 50 similar items at the same time and display the results for your consideration.

- Guaranteed lowest price. If within 30 days of buying something through Shoppers' Advantage you find the same piece of merchandise being sold for a lower price by an authorized dealer, send the staff at Shoppers' Advantage a copy of the ad, and they will send you the difference.
- A money-back membership guarantee. If you are not fully satisfied with Shoppers' Advantage, all you need to do is call its toll-free number to cancel your membership. Your current membership fee will be refunded in full.

The Sharper Image

For many of us, life is not complete without a Sharper Image Catalog. This is the ultimate toy store for children over 20, where technology perfects the art of living, courtesy of hundreds of products, each as compelling as a popsicle in August.

There's a free customer service number (800-344-5555) and a 60-day return guarantee. There's a 60-day price protection plan too: if you see the same product advertised for less, the Sharper Image will refund the difference. Use the keywords: **Sharper Image** for access to products to enhance your life, improve your health, and help the environment.

Figure 15-9: The imperative store for boys, the Sharper Image offers goodies no gizmo lover can resist.

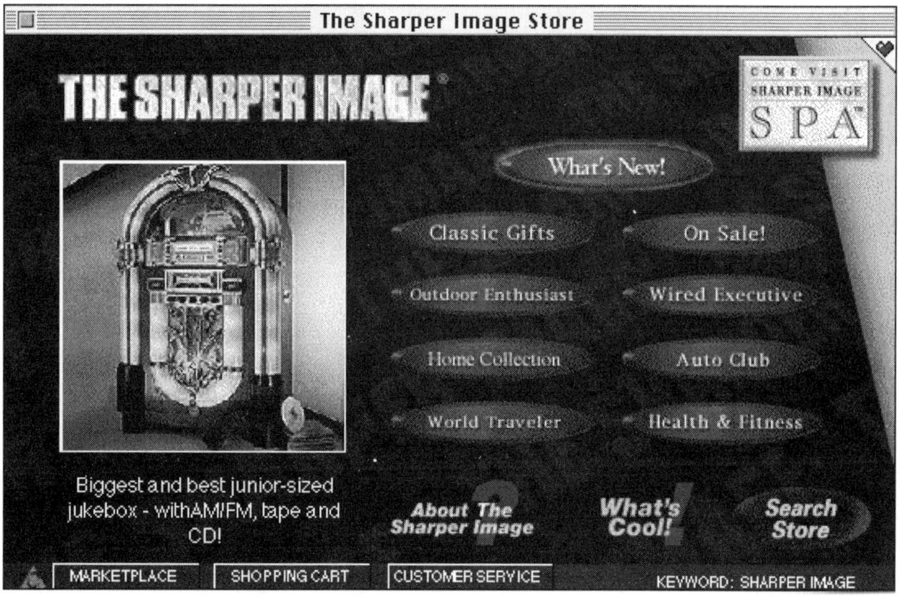
The Sharper Image Store
THE SHARPER IMAGE
COME VISIT SHARPER IMAGE SPA
What's New!
Classic Gifts
On Sale!
Outdoor Enthusiast
Wired Executive
Home Collection
Auto Club
World Traveler
Health & Fitness
Biggest and best junior-sized jukebox - withAM/FM, tape and CD!
About The Sharper Image
What's Cool!
Search Store
MARKETPLACE
SHOPPING CART
CUSTOMER SERVICE
KEYWORD: SHARPER IMAGE

Classifieds Online

This wouldn't be a fully operative communications medium without classified ads, and AOL has them. AOL's Classifieds feature all the product categories you'd expect in any large newspaper, with no paper waste and an ease of accessibility that no newspaper could hope to match (see Figure 15-10). Just select Classifieds Online from the main Marketplace screen, or use the keyword: **Classifieds**.

Classifieds Online
Classifieds
The Classifieds you loved, & much more!
Welcome to AOL Classifieds
SELL IT! New Premier Ad Info
NEW! Premier Ads SEARCH!
DO IT! Premier Ad How-To
TARGET! Identify your category
BUY & SELL! Bulletin Boards
LOOK! Buyer/Seller Cautions
INTERACT! Community Center
View Premier Ads
Select a Subject
-- or --
Select a Region
Search Premier Ads
Place a Premier Ad
Customer Service
AOL Business Directory
MARKETPLACE
CUSTOMER SERVICE
FEEDBACK
Keyword: Classifieds

Figure 15-10: Classifieds Online, where you can buy and sell computers and components, advertise your professional services, search the job postings, and take advantage of business opportunities.

Classifieds Online offers, among other things, a library that adds unique value to the classifieds: ZIP Code and area code directories; UPS, FedEx, and U.S. Mail rate charts; a UPS manifest-printing program; and the complete American Computer Exchange used-computer pricing guide.

The Hard Sell

Browsing the Classifieds Online library the other day, I came across the following excerpt from *Direct-Marketing Firepower*, an intriguing book by Jonathan Mizel. He's describing his friend Joe, who placed an ad on a local bulletin board system—a similar situation (though much more parochial) to AOL's Classifieds Online:

"So he decided this local BBS would be just the place to advertise it (an unneeded hard disk) since they allowed free classifieds for computer items. Joe placed the ad for this item on a Monday. I think he said he was selling it for $120.00. Guess how many responses Joe got by Wednesday. Go on, guess.

"Within 48 hours, Joe had received 220 responses to his little classified ad on a system that was only used by San Francisco technical computer people. The total number of people who are on the system is probably fewer than 5,000. He was freaked out, even mad, because people kept e-mailing him and calling him to get this damn piece of equipment (which, by the way, sold immediately) . . .

"Too bad old Joe didn't have 220 hard drives!"

Joe was advertising on a system with fewer than 5,000 members. America Online has more than 6 million. When I last checked, more than 211,000 classifieds were running, with more coming in every day. There's a portentous potential here.

The FreeShop Online

Everyone loves free stuff. Discovering a free product sample in the mailbox can be almost like Christmas morning. Wouldn't it be nice if we could find out what all the free offers are out there, and even pick and choose among those we want?

Such a service does exist, and you need look no further than AOL's FreeShop Online (see Figure 15-11). Here you'll find hundreds of free product samples, offers, catalogs, videos, and magazines nestled in a database that's much easier to explore and contains much more than your mailbox could ever hold. If you're looking for free stuff, this is a great place to start. Just use the keywords: **Free Shop**

The FreeShop Online
THE FreeShop ONLINE
Check out The FreeShop Online for hot samples and FREE offers!
NEW OFFERS
Choose from many - The New American, Yikes for Tykes, National Audubon, CNI Telecom
ALL OFFERS
OFFERS BY CATEGORY
CUSTOMER SERVICE
SPOTLIGHT OFFER
Keyword: FreeShop
CNI Telecom
Yikes for Tikes
Organic Cotton
New American

Figure 15-11: Looking for all that's free? The FreeShop is the place to be.

KidSoft Super Store

The KidSoft Super Store is the "kids" source for prescreened quality software just for children, with special emphasis on learning software (see Figure 15-12). You'll find software focusing on reading, math, spelling, music, creativity/art, geography, reference, and much more, featuring well-known names such as Mario, Putt-Putt, the Science Sleuths, Dr. Seuss, the Lion King, and Carmen Sandiego. And to make things easy as pie, you can search by age grouping, software title, or category to find descriptions and sample screens. You can get there with the keyword: **KidSoft**.

Club KidSoft
CLUB KIDSOFT
CLUB TALK
WHAT DO YOU THINK?
HIGH VOLTAGE
GAMES
DEMOS
win ARCADE RACING THIS WEEK!!
Cool Stuff!
CONTEST CENTRAL
KIDSOFT SUPER STORE
Keyword: KidSoft
FREE! Club KS Newsletter

Figure 15-12: The KidSoft SuperStore: a software store just for kids.

Omaha Steaks International

Even though rampant change is a given in the online medium, some online discoveries tend to surprise more than others, such as food service businesses in general and Omaha Steaks in particular (see Figure 15-13). Omaha Steaks International's reputation as a premium purveyor of steaks, meats, and other gourmet foods spans 75 years, 8 states, and 28 locations, with its mail order branch claiming an astonishing 44-year history. So at second glance, Omaha Steaks's move to the online arena is a completely natural progression.

Omaha Steaks Online
PREMIUM HEARTLAND QUALITY
OMAHA STEAKS
ONLINE
Receive a FREE gift with any Omaha Steaks Purchase!
Shop our Store
This Week's Specials
What's New
Holiday Gifts
Your Recipes, Our Cookbook
Customer Service
6 (6oz.) Filets, Grand Opening sale, $44.99 Reg. $64.99!
Featured Product

Figure 15-13: From Omaha, Nebraska, and the heart of cattle country direct to your door, Omaha Steaks's internationally recognized meats, seafood, and desserts are available now on AOL!

Omaha Steaks's mission is the delivery of the very best beef, poultry, pork, veal, lamb, seafood, and desserts to your Omaha Steaks table, or to your front door. If your Epicurean interests are creative, you'll also find proven-delicious recipes from the nation's heartland. And don't forget to check out Omaha Steaks's Chocolate Ecstasy Cake and triple-trimmed filet mignons in the Specialties area. Are you hungry now? Just use the keyword: **Steaks**.

Downtown AOL

Are you shopping for something special or out of the ordinary, or maybe looking for a hard-to-find service? Or are you thinking about establishing an online presence for your business? Then be sure to explore Downtown AOL, AOL's fast-growing virtual community of shops and services (see Figure 15-14).

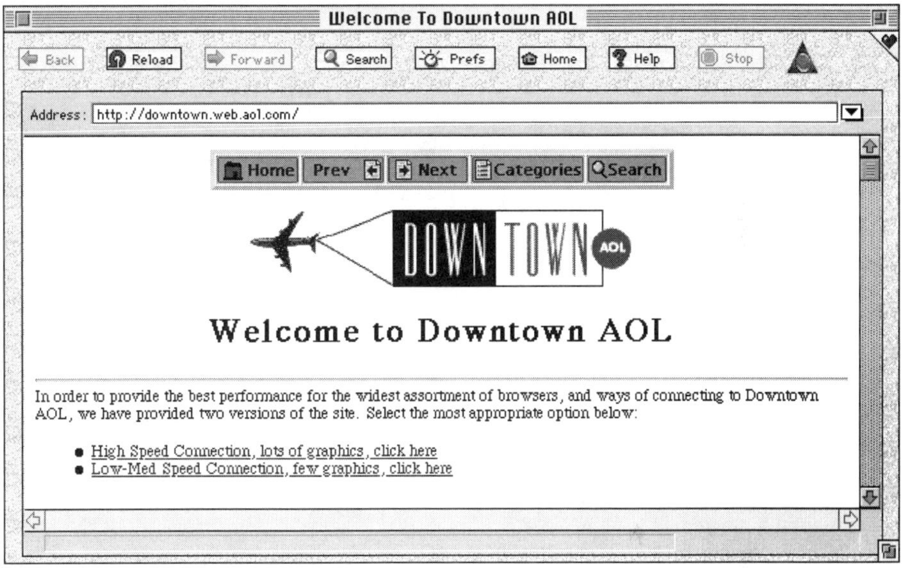
Welcome To Downtown AOL
Back
Reload
Forward
Search
Prefs
Home
Help
Stop
Address: http://downtown.web.aol.com/
Home
Prev
Next
Categories
Search
DOWNTOWN
AOL
Welcome to Downtown AOL
In order to provide the best performance for the widest assortment of browsers, and ways of connecting to Downtown AOL, we have provided two versions of the site. Select the most appropriate option below:
High Speed Connection, lots of graphics, click here
Low-Med Speed Connection, few graphics, click here

Figure 15-14: The virtual businesses of the future are being built right now in Downtown AOL!

Downtown AOL is your gateway to the people, products, networks, businesses, and services that are rushing to establish an economic structure on one of the most vibrant of all online media, the World Wide Web. Customers can use AOL's easy-to-use Web software to quickly and efficiently search for that hard-to-find product or service. Businesses can take advantage of easily updated product descriptions and additions, full-color graphics, and focused links to consumer groups. And everyone benefits! Take an electronic stroll to city center by typing the keywords: **Downtown AOL**.

Caffè Starbucks

After all this talk of shopping, you're probably ready for a good cup of coffee, right? Then you should not be surprised to find that Starbucks, one of the premier suppliers of gourmet coffees, is as close as AOL and the keyword: **Starbucks**. Being a top coffee contender is no mean feat in the northwest, where a request for a "double-skinny-mocha-decaf" is received with utter aplomb. And now you can join in the coffee revolution no matter where you live (see Figure 15-15).

Caffe Starbucks
Caffè Starbucks
COFFEE CHAT
Passion for Coffee
FIND A STORE NEAR YOU
STARBUCKS COFFEE
SHOP STARBUCKS
CARE
CUSTOMER SERVICE

Figure 15-15: Coffee advice, coffee philosophy, coffee cups, even regular coffee deliveries—Starbucks is your one-stop coffee resource!

No discussion of coffee would be complete without mention of the myriad delectables that can transform a superior coffee break into an extraordinary culinary experience. Just click the Sweets and Treats button in the Store itself and unleash your imagination.

Moving On

I've only scratched the surface of the Marketplace. You can select and purchase your groceries and pharmacy products here, and even have them delivered to your door. You can buy discounted books at the Online Bookstore. You can sell your old adding machine in the Classifieds, and you can buy a new one at OfficeMax. Of course, you don't really need an adding machine because you have a computer, but isn't it time for a new one? Computer Express has not only computers but components and software as well.

You've had a glimpse of the Marketplace in the present and, young as it is, I'm sure you've also envisioned its future as well—bright and bristling with potential. But now it's time for some intangible rewards. This book's most popular chapter follows, and if you've read this far, you deserve the pot at the end of the rainbow. It's time for the Ten Best: the ten best tips, the ten best downloads, the ten best ways to meet people online—they're all available at the turn of the page.

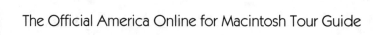

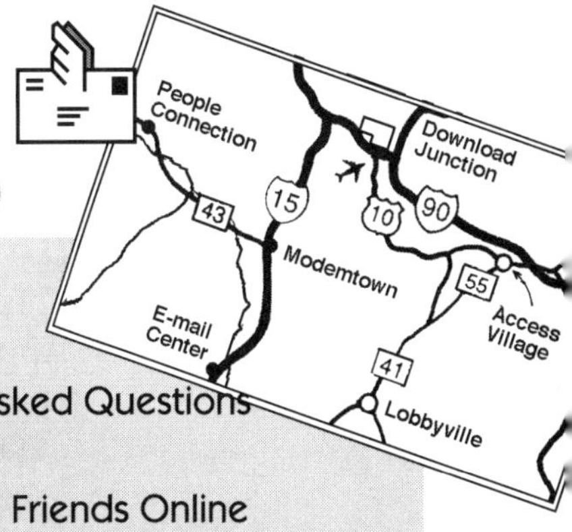
People Connection
Download Junction
15
10
90
43
Modemtown
55
Access Village
E-mail Center
41
Lobbyville

CHAPTER 16

Ten Best

- Ten Best Tips
- Ten Best Downloads
- Ten Most Frequently Asked Questions of Customer Relations
- Ten Best Ways to Make Friends Online
- Ten Best Greenhouse Projects
- Ten Best Tips From Community Leaders

When I was a boy, I believed that if I remained quiet and cooperative all day and all night Christmas Eve, Santa would be especially generous to me. For one 24-hour period every year, I was a model child. I did everything that was asked of me, exactly as requested. I must have been right: nowadays I receive paperweights and paisley ties on Christmas mornings rather than the electric trains and red wagons I received back in the days of deference.

Have you been naughty or nice? You haven't turned to this chapter first, have you? This chapter is a reward for faithful readers only. This is my Ten Best chapter, and I award it only to those who have read all of the preceding 15 chapters. If that's you, read on. . . .

Ten Best Tips

As long as we're discussing honor and privilege, let's begin with my list of the Ten Best Tips for using AOL. Most of these tips are intended to save you time online (so you save money); all of them will make your online activities more efficient and effective; and not a one of them is dishonorable.

1. *Read this book.*
   If you're reading this paragraph in spite of my admonition, at least plan to read the rest of the book eventually—the sooner the better. It's full of insights and techniques—not only mine but those of scores of other members as well. You don't have to be online to use this book. Take it on your next blue-water cruise: people will think you're very erudite, urbane, and jocose.

2. *Use keywords and keyboard shortcuts.*
   This tip is so important that I've included a lengthy appendix—Appendix B—listing all of AOL's keywords. Keywords can save you tons of time. Don't worry about committing them all to memory, just memorize those you use often. (Your most frequently used keywords should be added to your Go To menu, which is explained in Chapter 9, "Boards & Forums.") Keywords take you to locations that normally require navigating menus within menus within menus, and they do it in less than a second. To enter a keyword, click the Keyword button on the toolbar, or press Command-K. To search AOL's list of keywords, press Command-K, provide an approximation of what you're looking for, then click the Search button.

   America Online's keyboard shortcuts are the same or so close to the ones you use on the Mac that only a few require additional thought. A few are unique, and they're worth memorizing: Command-K to enter a keyword; Command-M to compose new mail; Command-F to find a file, place, or member's profile; Command-L to locate a member online; Command-I to send an Instant Message—that's only five. It won't take long to learn them.

3. *Use Command-period and watch for the hollow arrow.*
   Speaking of Command-key combinations, don't forget Command-period. Command-period disconnects sluggish sign-ons, cancels printing, and halts long articles and lists as you receive them online. That's important: sometimes you'll double-click an article icon only to find that you got yourself into a four-minute feed that you don't want to read after all. No problem: press Command-period. The same goes for lists: Command-period stops my list of old mail, for example, which contains hundreds of entries.

   I don't want to give the wrong impression here: Command-period does *not* intervene in situations that produce the beachball cursor (the rotating black-and-white sphere that appears whenever your Mac is receiving data over the modem). The beachball usually means that your computer is waiting for something from AOL's host computers, and if the system is sluggish or for some reason you've become disconnected, the beachball cursor can become quite annoying. This leads us to our next topic of discussion: how to circumvent the beachball cursor.

The hollow arrow cursor is a little-known AOL feature, introduced with Version 2.0. Whenever you see the beachball cursor, try moving it around on the screen. Usually, the beachball will become a hollow arrow when you pass over scroll bars and menu bars. When you're receiving a long list of items, you can start scrolling through that list without having to wait for the beachball to go away. All you have to do is explore a bit: move that beachball around, click your mouse, and watch what happens.

If manipulating screen controls isn't what you want to do, or if nothing happens when you try, it's time to get drastic. The solution? Press Command-Option-Escape. This will produce a dialog asking if you're sure you want to quit America Online. Click OK. This is *absolutely* a last resort. It's called a *force quit*, and it can destabilize your system. It's best to use this only if AOL has locked up, and you have other programs open with material you need to save. Once you execute the force quit, switch to the other program, save your work, then restart your Mac and sign back on to AOL.

4. *Use Automatic AOL, and read and compose mail and newsgroup postings offline.*
The Compose Mail command (Mail menu) works offline as well as on. You can compose all your mail offline while the clock's not running, perfecting every phrase. You can even attach files while you're composing mail offline. When you have finished composing a piece of mail, click the Send Later button at the left of the new mail (Untitled) window. America Online will store it (and any other mail you compose) on your disk for transmission later when you're online via an Automatic AOL session (discussed in Chapter 6).

   Likewise, resist the urge to read new mail online. Rather, wait until you've finished all your other online activity, then choose Run Automatic AOL from the Mail menu. America Online will download all your incoming mail, then sign off. Once you're offline, choose Read Offline Mail from the Mail menu and read your mail at your own pace.

5. *Use Help.*
Read the "Getting Help" sidebar in Chapter 2, and follow the tips there, in the order in which they appear.

6. *Keep track of your time and money.*
   It's easy to lose track of time and money when you're online, but no one—neither you nor AOL—benefits from unexpected charges when the bill arrives. You can always check your current (and previous) month's bill by using the keyword: **Billing** (which is free), and the keyword: **Clock** tells you how long you've been online during any particular session. (It also tells you the current time, accurate to within a second or so. This might be the most accurate clock in the house.)

7. *Log your sessions and save to disk.*
   Don't spend time reading material online that can just as easily be saved and read later while you're offline. Logging is a mechanism that allows you to capture all the text you encounter online without stopping to read it, whether it's text from the encyclopedia, messages on a board, or a discussion in a conference room. Any text that appears on your screen will be saved to a log if you open one before you start your online journey. (See Chapter 10, "Staying Informed," for a discussion of logging procedures.)

   Logging is particularly valuable for new members. Start a log, sign on, and visit a few areas, then sign off. Once you're offline, review the log (use the Open command under the File menu to open logs). You'll learn a lot about AOL when you can review an online session at your leisure.

   Of course, it's not easy to remember to open a log for each session, and sometimes you don't know you're going to run across something you want to save until you're there. Fortunately, all text received on AOL can be saved onto your hard drive for later review offline. Simply go to the File menu and select Save. This causes all the text in the article or message in the frontmost window on your screen to be transferred to any disk drive you specify, where you can have it saved as a plain text file that you can read using AOL or the word processor of your choice. Note that it isn't necessary for you to scroll through the entire article in order to save it. Even though you haven't seen the entire text of the article, your computer has, and everything is saved when you issue the Save command.

8. *Multitask and download when system activity is minimal.*
   Your AOL software can download in the background while you're reading mail, working on a spreadsheet, or using your word processor. If you start a long download—even if it's via an Auto-

matic AOL session—and you have something else to do with your Mac, do it. You can start another program, or do most anything with the AOL software itself: visit a forum, read mail, or chat. Do not, however, engage in any activity that involves *another* download while one's already under way. Even if the AOL software lets you do it, it's uneconomical—it'll slow things down.

Here's another downloading tip: the AOL system—AOL's mainframes and the long-distance carrier in your local area—gets very busy in the evenings and on weekends. Your time on the system is allocated in slices, and these time slices get smaller as the system becomes more active. Your computer spends more of its time waiting in line for data when these time slices get small, yet the clock keeps running regardless.

Whenever you're planning a long download—say, anything over 10 minutes—plan it for the time of day when the system is least active. Typically, that's the morning: the earlier the better. Read about Automatic AOL and the Download Manager in Chapter 6, and use both of them to reduce your download time.

9. *Look for More buttons.*
   Lots of AOL windows include buttons or folders marked More. Don't overlook them. America Online doesn't tie up your system feeding you all 500 matching entries to a database search, for example. Rather, it offers the first 20, then waits to see if you want more. You might want to cancel at that moment, or you might want to see more. When the conditions are appropriate, AOL always offers the More option, but it's only useful if you choose to exercise it. America Online users who ignore the More buttons online never know what they're missing.

10. *Use the Find in Top Window command.*
    The Find in Top Window command under the Edit menu allows you to specify text for the AOL client to find. While searching articles comes immediately to mind, this command is also handy for finding specific elements in long lists (in the File Search Results window, for example) and searching scrolling lists available in AOL's channels (for example, use the keyword: **Reference**, then find Health in the List By Category window). This command can save not only hours of reading but precious online time as well, by "reading" lists and scroll boxes for you.

Ten Best Downloads

This list is hardly objective and is most certainly in no particular order These are just the freeware and shareware products I use, or readers use, most often. I've tested them all; they're all of the highest quality and well suited to their tasks.

To find any of the downloads mentioned, use the keywords: **File Search**, then specify the name of the file—excluding the version number (see the searching tips in Chapter 5, "Transferring Files")—as your search criterion. If you find more than one version of a particular program available, be sure to download the one with the highest version number, since it's the most recent release of that program.

1. *StuffIt*
   StuffIt is offered as a commercial product (StuffIt Deluxe), as shareware (previously StuffIt Classic, now StuffIt Lite), and as an integral feature of your AOL software. (However, using AOL to stuff files that you don't intend to attach to e-mail is a bit awkward.) StuffIt's interface is as easy to learn as they come. StuffIt Lite should be on every Mac user's shelf, especially when you consider the minimal shareware fee. File compression is discussed in Chapter 5, "Transferring Files."

2. *Disinfectant*
   Disinfectant is virus-detection freeware capable of deleting many viruses as well as eliminating them. Disinfectant is one of the best pieces of software—shareware or commercial—ever written, and it's free. Disinfectant is discussed in Chapter 5, "Transferring Files." Use the keyword: **Virus** for more information.

3. *GIFConverter*
   Most of the really spectacular graphics available on AOL are in a format that your AOL software can open and display. Occasionally, however, you might run into one that chokes AOL's software or won't import into your word processing or desktop publishing program. For those occasions, you need a "Swiss Army knife" of a graphics program—one that opens anything (including .GIF, .JPG, .TIF, and .PICT) and saves in formats that are useful to you. That program is GIFConverter, by Kevin Mitchell. Kevin is an AOL member and can answer your questions via the screen name "KevinM17."

4. *Sound Manager*
   If you're fond of chat room sounds, you must have this software. America Online offers hundreds of sounds for use in chat rooms, but they first have to be incorporated into your Mac's system. That's what Sound Manager does (among other things). Chat rooms, chat room sounds, and Sound Manager are described in Chapter 8, "The Community."

5. *Kid's Clicks*
   Kid's Clicks is a free program that amuses and teaches children through colorful screens and animated sounds. The idea is simple—you click on objects in a scene and hear sounds associated with those objects. Kids delight in trying to find all the hidden sounds. The best part is you can make your own scenes and sounds, presenting opportunities for both education and entertainment.

6. *ZTerm*
   ZTerm is widely hailed by shareware fans as not just the best shareware telecommunications/modem program, but perhaps the best modem program regardless of the distribution method. ZTerm allows for a high degree of scripting and customization, something very important when using a telecommunications program for repeating the same boring steps over and over. You won't need it to work with AOL, but you will need it if you want to work with most other telecom packages.

7. *Smileys*
   There are lots of lists of smileys posted online. Use the keywords: **File Search**, then search with the criterion: Smileys. You'll find the Smiley Face DA, a venerable introduction to smiley etiquette; and you'll find the Comprehensive Smiley collection, an enormous smiley anthology along with some other shorthands. With these lists at your side, you can smile with the best of 'em. ;-)

8. *Text-Edit Plus*
   This is the best little text editor around. In fact, if your word processing needs are basic (and 90 percent of most people's seem to be), this is all you may need. I find it especially valuable for searching my files for occurrences of words like "deadline."

9. *RoboWar*
I forgive RoboWar its combative title because it's such a kick. This shareware game allows you to program your own robots using a special scripting language, then send them into the field to battle with other robots—either others of your own making or any of the thousands posted on AOL. To get an idea of this game's popularity, use the keywords: **File Search** and search with the criterion: RoboWar. You'll find the program, of course, but you'll also find all of the robots and tips other players have posted online.

10. *AOLPress*
It used to be that to build a Web site, you had to learn the meanings of terms like HTML, URL, ISMAP, FTP, CGI, PERL, and C. No longer. You have your very own Web site already (see the discussion of My Place in Chapter 2, "The Abecedarium"), and AOLPress is a free Web page "authoring" tool that anyone can use.
Almost everything is done via menus. All you have to do is type the text and decide where your graphics (or sounds or videos) will appear. AOLPress creates the HyperText Markup Language code for you, which you can then upload to AOL and publish on the Web. AOLPress is so easy to use that you probably won't need a manual. (If you do, one's available—though it's not free.)
To find out about AOLPress, use the keyword: **AOLPress**. Note that this is a *keyword,* not a file search criterion.

Ten Most Frequently Asked Questions of Customer Relations

No one knows the nature of the questions asked of AOL's Customer Relations Department better than the Customer Relations Department staff itself; thus I went to them for this section of the book. I was aptly rewarded with the list below. Okay, it's more than 10, but who can fault a Customer Relations Department that offers more than it's asked for?

Huge thanks go to Steve Brannon, who prepared this material.

1. *I just installed AOL. Where do I begin? How do I get help?*
Although not the question most often asked of member services, "How do I get help?" is likely the question asked by our members more often than any other when they run into a problem and want

to know who to call, how to get online information, and so on. In Chapter 2 of this book, the section "Getting Help: a Methodical Approach" addresses this topic.

2. *How do I obtain the latest access number information for AOL?*
America Online is constantly adding new access numbers and new access methods. To discover the latest methods and phone numbers for accessing America Online, use the keyword: **Access**. You will discover information on the AOLNet 800 number, contacting AOL from foreign countries using AOLGlobalnet, how to request a local access phone number, and answers to the most often asked questions about access to AOL.

3. *Can I get information about my account while online?*
To obtain information on charges for using America Online, use the keyword: **Billing**. You can modify your address information, see a summary of your current bill, request a detailed bill, and access the list of frequently asked questions for the billing staff.

4. *I've just witnessed offensive behavior in a chat room; is there someone I can contact?*
We want the America Online community to be a friendly and safe place for our members to visit. Therefore, we enforce the AOL Terms of Service, and take appropriate action when violations are reported to us.

   If you witness chat in a public chat room that violates AOL's Terms of Service, you may contact an AOL Service Guide by using the keyword: **GuidePager**. You may also contact AOL's Terms of Service Staff about any violation by using the "Write to the Community Action Team" icon located in the Terms of Service area (keyword: **TOS**).

   Also, *never reveal your password to anyone*! No one from America Online will *ever* ask you for your password, as a means of identification, as a way to correct a "problem" with your account, or for *any* other purpose.

   Anyone who knows your screen name and password can sign on with your account, and leave you to pay the bill! America Online is very much like a city with millions of residents (members). You wouldn't give your house keys to a stranger you met in a big city, and you shouldn't give your password, or any other account information, to people you meet online.

5. *Where can I find <my favorite subject> online?*
   Lots of questions are along the line of "Is AARP online?" and "I heard that *Consumer Reports* is on AOL—how do I find it?"
   One great way to find if an area you are interested in is on AOL is to use the "Where on AOL do I find . . ." message board in the Members Helping Members section of AOL. This board can be found by entering the keyword: **MHM**; continue on any informative panels until you reach the Members Helping Members message boards. Double-click the "Where on *AOL* do I find . . ." board. Browse for existing questions, or post your own.
   And don't forget the Find button on the toolbar!

6. *I use the menus and the screen panels to move from area to area. Is there a faster way?*
   Yes, there is: use keywords. In addition, you can obtain a list of the latest keywords. Use the keyword: **Keywords**, of course.
   Use the keyword: **New** to discover the latest additions to America Online. By double-clicking one of the items in the NEW list, you'll be taken directly to that new service. If a keyword is available for the new area, it will be displayed on the lower portion of the panel. You can also access the NEW feature by clicking the What's Hot icon on the toolbar at the top of the screen.

7. *How can I determine if my friend has an AOL account? Is he logged on now?*
   For confidentiality reasons, America Online cannot give out personal account information about other members.
   However, many members create a Member Profile containing information such as their name, hobbies, and interests. To check a member's profile, select Get a Member's Profile from the Members menu. If you're not sure of the spelling of their screen name, or if you wish to search by last name or profile, go to the keywords: **Member Directory.**
   You can use AOL's Buddy List feature to receive notification whenever your friends log on. (Buddy lists are discussed in Chapter 8, "The Community.")

8. *I know that AOL provides access to the Internet and the World Wide Web. How can I learn how to use them?*
   Use the keyword: **AnswerMan** and explore what's offered there. If you still have a question after your review of AnswerMan, use the

keyword: **Internet**, then post your question on one of the message boards there. The CyberJockeys who staff those boards are especially helpful.

9. *My Web browser has slowed considerably. What can I do to speed it up?* AOL's browser comes with a "cache." This means that pages you use frequently are stored on your hard disk for fast reloading when you return to them during the same Web session. A large cache setting, however, can slow your machine.

   To adjust the size of your cache, go to the Members menu and select Preferences. Click Web and change the Disk Cache size at the bottom of the window.

10. *What should I know about upgrading and maintaining my AOL software?*
    Member *x* has AOL 2.7 and obtains the upgrades for 3.0. Now what? (Install it.) Will my preferences be retained? (Yes.) Will the old copy of AOL be deleted? (No.)

    Many members don't understand that the upgrade files for AOL for Macintosh 3.0 are not automatically installed. The member must run the installer application (the downloaded upgrade file). Once the new version is installed, the member must next start it (not the old version). Finally, the member should search his/her hard disk and consider erasing any old versions of AOL (we've heard from people who have many, many old copies of AOL on their machine).

11. *I love using e-mail, and I'd like to expand my use. How can I find out more?*

- *Questions that we get routinely are as follows:*
- How can I determine if a friend has an e-mail address?
- How do I establish subaccounts?
- A friend of mine has an Internet address—how do I send mail to it?
- I have a friend on the Internet—what address should I give my friend so that he can send me mail?
- How do I attach a file to my mail?
- What is the least expensive way to send and receive e-mail?

- Can I send mail to several people at once?
- Can I send a copy of my mail without everyone else knowing I sent it?
- I just sent e-mail, can I get it back before the other person reads it?
- If I have to leave while writing a letter, can I save what I'vetyped and continue later?
- I sent mail yesterday, now I'd like to send the same mail to someone else. Do I have to type it all over again?
- Can I prevent my mail from being deleted after a few days?
- Someone sent me an "attached" file. What do I do with it?

Most of these questions are answered at keywords: **Mail Center** or keywords: **Mail Gateway**. If you don't see the answer you need at these two keywords, use the keyword: **Questions** and take it from there.

Ten Best Ways to Make Friends Online

Perhaps above all, AOL is a community. If you're not a part of it, you're missing a wealth of opportunity. Like any community, you're ahead of the game if you know how to break into it. Here's how:

1. *Visit the Members Helping Members message boards.*
   The Members Helping Members message boards (keyword: **MHM**) area is one of the friendliest places online—not only because the people there (they're not staff: most of them are simply members, just like you and me) are so helpful, but also because the area is free. Browse through the boards the first few times you visit; post questions after you've read a number of messages and have a feel for the place. Soon enough, you'll be an expert yourself, helping other new members with your sage advice.

2. *Find a favorite room and hang out there.*
   Chapter 8, "The Community," describes the different kinds of chat rooms that are available online. Look that chapter over, find a room that interests you, and visit it when it's available. You might also find a favorite room by visiting any of AOL's forums (forums are described in Chapter 9, "Boards & Forums").

3. *Post your profile.*
   Don't neglect to post your profile. Use the keyword: **Profile**, or choose My AOL from the Members menu, and then select Create Your Member Profile. Talk about yourself. Make your personality irresistible. People in chat rooms often peek at other occupants' profiles, and if you haven't posted a profile, you're a persona non grata.

4. *Use Personal Publisher to post a Web page.*
   Personal Publisher is the home of the AOL membership's home pages. Home pages incorporate text and graphics—and even sound and video. In less than a year they've become the electronic version of calling cards, and everyone has fun with them. Personal Publisher pages are searchable and available to any AOL member.

   There's lots of online help available, plus Personal Publisher itself at keywords: **Personal Publisher**.

5. *Use an effective screen name.*
   You can use the Edit Screen Names command under the Members menu to add a screen name to your account if the one you're using now isn't very effective in a social situation. People have a hard time relating to a screen name like "Tlich6734," but many find "MajorTom" worthy of notice. If nothing else, include your first name or your nickname in your screen name so people can address you as the friend you want to be.

6. *Search the membership for others with similar interests.*
   Use the keyword: **Directory** to search the Member Directory for others with interests similar to yours. Read their profiles and send them e-mail. You'll be surprised at the number who reply.

7. *Read messages and reply.*
   Find a forum that interests you (see Chapter 9, "Boards & Forums"), go to its message boards, and start reading messages. Eventually, you'll see some that provoke a response. Go ahead, post your comment. It gives you a great sense of purpose the next time you sign on. You'll scramble to that message board to see if anyone responded to your posting.

8. *Post a message soliciting replies.*
   Members Helping Members (keyword: **MHM**; see Chapter 2, "The Abecedarium") is a great place for message posting, but any forum will do. Post a message asking for help or an opinion. People love to help, and everyone has an opinion.

9. *Read newsgroups and reply.*
   This is similar to item 7. Newsgroups (discussed in Chapter 4, "Using the Internet") are similar to forums, only they're not limited to the AOL membership. Anyone with Internet access to newsgroups—tens of millions of people in hundreds of countries—can participate, and most do. I've made friends as far away as Australia this way.

10. *Download a file posted by another member and reply.*
    This goes especially for fonts and graphics. Download a few files (downloading is discussed in Chapter 5, "Transferring Files") and reply to the originator via e-mail. In selecting the graphics for this book, I sent e-mail to dozens of online artists, and every one of them replied within a day or two—most with two or three pages of enthusiastic banter.

Ten Best Greenhouse Projects

I'm starting to feel like an online old-timer. A sea dog. Savant. Guru, even. This is my twelfth year online, my fifth year at AOL. I receive tips from readers almost every day. For four months I was Forum Leader of one of AOL's largest departments—a job from which I had to resign in order to return to my Tour Guide activities.

Perhaps the most significant change I've witnessed has occurred in the past 18 months: commercialism in the online industry. My thesaurus lists mostly disreputable synonyms for the word "commercialism": barbarism, vulgarism, vandalism, philistinism, even artlessness. That's awfully judgmental and it's not what I'm talking about. I'm talking about a commercial online medium similar to the commercial broadcast medium: logos for Chevrolet and Coke, ads for pain relievers, even infomercials. Believe me, it's coming. You've probably seen signs of it already.

As a commercial vehicle, this medium is in its infancy. No one knows exactly how to make effective commercial use of it. What the medium needs is a place where information-age entrepreneurs (infopreneurs?) can experiment with strategies, ideas, and technologies. A place to make mistakes and find solutions. A place to break the rules.

That place exists. It's at AOL, and it's called the *Greenhouse* (keyword: **Greenhouse**). If you want a peek at the future, this is the place to look. To see them all, use the keyword: **Greenhouse**. To see my favorite Greenhouse projects, read on.

1. *The Motley Fool* (keywords: **Motley Fool**) offers investment tips for novices and experts, with an irreverent spin.
2. *Love@AOL* (keyword: **Love@AOL**) lets you look for love in all the right places and get a few tips on offline as well as online romance.
3. *iGOLF* (keyword: **iGOLF**) features timely coverage of golfing events worldwide, interactive golf games, and columns by golfing celebrities.
4. *Better Health and Medical Forum* (keywords: **Better Health**) is a trove of newsworthy health issues, health information updates, and support groups.
5. *NetNoir* (keyword: **NetNoir**) is the community room for the Afrocentric fellowship. Music, sports, and business information abounds.
6. *eGG* (keyword: **eGG**) is a haven for gastronomes, including cookbook reviews, meal planning guides, and special appearances by cooking celebrities.
7. *Health Zone* (keyword: **HealthZone**) offers access to fitness and nutrition experts, diets and fitness support groups, and appearances by celebrity athletes.
8. *Hecklers Online* (keyword: **Hecklers**) offers absolutely nothing of socially redeeming value. It goes the extra mile to be politically incorrect. It's the Monty Python of the online community. If you refuse to be silenced by gatekeepers of monotonous information, heckle here.

9. *About Work* (keywords: **About Work**) is the ultimate career center, where "work" is no longer a dirty word. Get help finding work, enjoying work, and even creating work you can love. Their Work-from-Home Community is a treasure trove, with the kind of advice and resources that can give home-based entrepreneurs a real advantage.
10. *PicturePlace* (keywords: **Picture Place**) makes it fast, easy, and inexpensive to get your pictures scanned. You send the picture (or negative), it's scanned, put in a private area online for you to download, and the original is sent back to you. There are no floppy disks to wait for or additional software required to use your pictures.

Ten Best Tips From the Community Leaders

A visit to AOL's Virginia headquarters is impressive enough: three multistory buildings are packed with staff offices (there must be hundreds of them). And Virginia isn't AOL's only location any longer: there are many others, scattered all over the country.

As is often the case, however, it's what you *can't* see that's most impressive. Thousands of people are employed as *community leaders* (also known as *remote staff*) at AOL: they work from their homes for the most part, managing forums and libraries, answering member mail, and more. I'm sure someone keeps track of all of these people, but I don't—thus my guess as to their number is a wild one at best. I'll bet there are over 5,000.

Working with members day in and day out, these community leaders are probably the most knowledgeable group of AOL users around, so it only makes sense that I would poll them for their ten best tips. In fact, I received hundreds of tips from the leaders. The process of whittling them down to 10 was painful. Someday I should write another book.

Below are their tips, along with their screen names. My thanks to each and every one of the community leaders who participated.

1. *PCA Walt: Know the difference between keywords and search words.* I hear from members all of the time, and one of the most common areas of confusion is the difference between keywords and searching criteria.

A *keyword* is a shortcut to a frequently visited area on AOL. To use a keyword, press Command-K, or click the Keyword button on the toolbar, then type in the keyword. There's a list of them in Appendix B of this book.

Search criteria are words you use to find a specific file in AOL's download libraries. Let's say you're looking for StuffIt Lite. You wouldn't use StuffIt Lite as keywords: it's not an area, it's a file. Instead, you would use the keywords: **File Search**—or click the disk-and-magnifier icon on the toolbar—then use the criterion: StuffIt Lite to find the file.

2. *CJ Daye: Use World Wide Web addresses as keywords.*
   Having a home page on the World Wide Web is tantamount to success in the marketplace, at least if television and print advertising are to be believed. World Wide Web addresses (*URLs*, or *Uniform Resource Locators*) appear on half the print and television ads published today, it seems, with more appearing every day.

   So what do you do if "http://www.hormel.com" appears in a Spam ad in *Bon Appetit*? It's easy: fire up AOL and sign on, then click the Keyword button on the toolbar and enter the URL you saw *as a keyword.* That's all there is to it. It's even easier if someone sends you a URL via e-mail. While you're still online, copy the URL, press Command-K, then paste the URL into the Keyword window. Click the Go button and you're there!

   You have to be signed on to use this tip, and the URL must begin with "http://" (which is often left out of advertising plugs) in order to work.

3. *CJ Jon: Search intelligently.*
   When searching for information on a particular topic, use the wide range of searching resources AOL has to offer. Start your search locally, then branch out to the Internet. Begin by using the Find button on the toolbar. For more detail, the keyword: **Services** allows you to conduct a topical search on areas available on AOL. You might also want to look at keyword: **Reference** for encyclopedias, dictionaries, and so forth. You can also do a keyword search at the keyword box by clicking on the Search button there.

   If the resource you're after is on the Internet, use the keyword: **Webcrawler** and search there. You might also try using the keyword: **Yahoo** to use the Yahoo Web search engine.

4. *PC Tom: Want to search by filename? All I can recommend is just don't do that!!!*
   Using a filename as a criterion for searching is the absolute worst way to conduct a search. Even though filenames are part of the search algorithm, unless you are absolutely sure of the filename for the last version of the program, this doesn't give you a reliable search. When version numbers change, so does the filename.
   Instead, search less specifically. If you're searching for StuffIt Lite, try using "file compression" or "archive" as a search criterion. The whole idea is to avoid version numbers (which change) and specific product names (which are often obtuse: is it "StuffIt Lite" or "Stuff It Lite"?).

5. *CJ Sarah: To leave the unlimited usage area, just pull down your Go To menu and select "Exit Unlimited Usage Area."*
   Members are often caught behind AOL's "free curtain" where keywords don't work, mail can't be sent, and the Internet is off limits. Sure, the clock's not running, but what if you want to get back at it? I've had some people tell me that they turn off their modems to get out of free areas! Sarah's advice is the best there is.

6. *Host CWC: Turn off graphics in online documents.*
   Online graphics such as photos can slow your AOL sessions to a crawl. Turning them off won't keep you from getting new artwork for a new *area* you try to access, but it will keep you from having to sit and wait if there is a picture connected to a particular *article* you are trying to access. In place of the picture, there's a Get Graphic button instead.
   To turn off online graphics, use keywords: **Multimedia Prefs** and adjust the settings as you like.
   This tip applies to the World Wide Web as well. Even with a fast modem, the Web is at best lethargic. To pump a little adrenaline into the Web's bloodstream, turn off its graphics. The Preferences button—which leads you to the Show images option—is in plain view in the Web browser's window. If you encounter a page with graphics you want to see, turn the graphics preference back on, then click the Reload button.

7. *Teacher cc: Use the keyword:* ***Shorthands*** *to find out ways to help you communicate with more than just typed text.*
   Don't know what "ROTFLOL" means? Want to soften what might be interpreted as harsh criticism when it's not really meant that way? In speech, we use vocal intonations and facial expressions, but vocal intonations and facial expressions aren't available via the online medium, thus emotional "shorthands" (or *emoticons*) have been developed. To get a listing of them all, use the keyword: **Shorthands**.

8. *Jennifer: Use your AOL software as a word processor when your needs aren't extensive.*
   Many members aren't aware that their AOL software has a number of features that mimic fancier word processing software. In addition to the size, style, color, and alignment functions under the Format menu, there is the added benefit of a built-in spell checker, thesaurus, and a find feature. For most people, this is all they need in a word processor. If you do take advantage of these extras and wish to save your work, be sure to use the Memo format (the default) when you Save. The Memo format will retain your formatting information.

9. *Phylwriter: Learn about ASCII text!*
   ACSII text (or just plain *text*) allows everyone on all platforms to read your work. If you write (and save) messages in AOL's text editor (that is, by choosing New from the File menu), you can guarantee they are ASCII text if you select "Text Only" from the menu at the bottom of the window when saving it. You can copy and paste from ASCII documents with impunity, and you can attach saved ASCII documents (use the filename extension ".TXT" for best compatibility) to e-mail and rest assured that it will reach its destination with minimal hassle on the recipient's part, regardless of the recipient's choice of computers.

   Remember this: most of the nongraphical material you will encounter online is ASCII text. You can copy and paste it into e-mail documents or new text documents you create by choosing New from the File menu. When you're offline you can review saved text by choosing Open from the File menu, or you can open it with any word processor. ASCII text is as universal and useful as white flour, with no calories and zero grams of fat!

10. *FPC Mary: Use the Address Book to keep track of information about your online friends.*
    Mary uses the Person window of the Address Book to store vital information about her friends, for instance, birth date, spouse's name, or primary interest, *as well as* their name and screen name. It's like having your own personal Rolodex right in the AOL software. Thus, whenever Mary looks up Tom Lichty in her Address Book, she might see "Author of Tour Guide, wife Victoria in medical school" in the Notes field, along with my name and screen name, "MajorTom." Mary can even attach a photo of me by clicking the turned-up page in the lower right-hand corner and then selecting a graphics file from her hard drive. Then, when she writes to me, she can say, "How's Victoria doing in school?" or ask, "Have you lost your tan from the summer yet?" and I'll feel all the more flattered.

Everybody Out of the Bus!

Our tour has concluded. Typical of tours everywhere, ours has been an abridgment, a synopsis of things I find most interesting about AOL. You will find your own favorites, and in so doing discover things that I not only didn't mention but didn't know myself. Moreover, AOL is a moving target: like most online services, AOL is almost fluid—flowing from opportunity to opportunity, conforming to trends and advances, relentlessly expanding to fill new voids. I'll try to keep up, and no doubt there will be another edition of this book someday to describe an even bigger and better AOL than the one we know today.

Meanwhile, this edition has reached its end. While you're waiting for the next one, sign on to AOL and send me some e-mail. Tell me what you want included (or excluded) in the next edition. Tell me what you liked or disliked about this book. Send me logs, files, articles—anything you think might complement *The Official America Online Tour Guide*. I look forward to hearing from you.

—MajorTom

APPENDIX A
Making the Connection

If you have never used America Online—if you have never even installed the software—this appendix is for you. It's written for novices—those who hold disks in their sweaty palms and wonder if they are stalwart enough to connect their Macs to the outside world.

If you *have* used America Online—if you already have an account and a password—read on. I'll tell you when it's appropriate to skip the new member material in this chapter, and what page to turn to.

Most of us think of computers as machines—functional, autonomous, and independent. We've come to accept computing as an isolated activity, and our dialogs with the computer as closed circuits. The only external device we've ever encountered is a printer. Oh, we might personify our Macs. We might give them names and even voices, and we might think of their error messages and dialog boxes as "communication." But we know better.

Computers don't think. Computers don't respond with imagination or indignation or intelligence. They react—to comply with our wishes—only as they have been preprogrammed to do. There are no threats to us here.

Connecting to America Online puts human intelligence at the other end of the line. That's because AOL isn't just a computer complex in Virginia. It's people, and people online expect a dialog. People respond, with innovation and humor.

This is not the familiar, predictable universe we're accustomed to. So why mess with it?

Because there's more to life, that's why. Think of your first car, your first love, your first job—experiences resplendent with reward but not without their share of anxiety. We're talking about discovery here, and while AOL and the Internet may not rank with finding love or starting a career, they do offer exceptionally rewarding opportunities.

Things You'll Need

Let's take inventory here. There are a few things you need before you can connect with America Online. You may already have them, but let's be sure.

The Computer

You need a Mac, of course. It has to be capable of running System 7.1.x (better yet, System 7.5.x or higher), which should already be installed and tested on your machine. A 9600 bps-or-faster modem is also required.

You will need at least 8 megabytes of RAM (random access memory) and 16 megabytes is preferred. You'll also need a hard disk with 15 megabytes of free space—even more if you plan to use the Web browser's cache. (See the sidebar titled "The Fine Print.") You also will need a CD-ROM drive. If you need the software on a medium other than the one you have, call 800-827-6364.

The Fine Print

The minimum required disk space mentioned above is for the installation of the software only. America Online offers a disk-based cache feature for use with the World Wide Web that speeds the presentation of Web pages. The speed gain is so significant that anyone planning to use the Web should also plan to use the cache.

If you do plan to use the cache, assume you will need to allocate at least 5 percent of your hard disk—more if it's available. The World Wide Web and other Internet features are discussed in Chapter 4, "Using the Internet."

Your AOL software also offers a Personal Filing Cabinet, where you can store your electronic mail, and Favorite Places (the Personal Filing Cabinet and e-mail are discussed in Chapter 3; Favorite Places are discussed in Chapter 4). If you intend to use the Personal Filing Cabinet, add another 5MB of hard disk space to the minimum requirement.

In other words, for a full installation, you will need 15MB for the software, 5 percent of your disk's capacity—we'll call it 15MB—for the browser's cache, and 5MB for the Personal Filing Cabinet. That's a total of 35MB—ample room for AOL to roam.

Finally, a monitor capable of displaying 256 colors at a resolution of 640 by 480 or better is required. Your AOL software works with grayscale systems, but the presentation of the service is optimized for 256 colors or better. Refer to your Macintosh manual (or the manual for your video card, if one is installed as an option) for information on how to change the number of colors your system displays.

The Telephone Line

You need access to a telephone line. Your standard residential phone line is fine. A multiline business telephone might be more of a challenge. What's really important is that your telephone plugs into a modular telephone jack (called an *RJ-11* jack, if you care about that sort of thing). It's the one with the square hole—measuring about a quarter-inch—on one side.

Whenever you're online, your telephone is out of commission for normal use. If you try to make a voice call using an extension phone on the same line, it's as if you picked up the phone and someone else was having a conversation—except that you'll *never* want to eavesdrop on an AOL session; the screeching sound that modems make when communicating with each other is about as pleasant as fingernails on a blackboard—and about as intelligible.

The Membership Kit

America Online membership kits come in a number of forms, but they all include four things: this book, the software, a temporary registration number, and a temporary password. The software comes on a CD. Find the software, the registration number, and the password, and set them by your Mac. Keep this chapter nearby as well.

Once you've copied the software, put the original AOL CD-ROM somewhere safe. You never know when you might need it again.

The Modem

A modem (short for *mo*dulator/*dem*odulator) is a device that converts computer data into audible tones that the telephone system can transmit. Modems are required at both ends of the line: AOL has a number of them at their end as well.

Modems are rated according to their data-transmission speed. If you're shopping for a modem, get one rated at 28,800 bps if you can.

Modems rated at 28,800 bps are fast and are capable of extracting every bit of performance AOL has to offer. (If AOL doesn't offer 28,800 bps capability in your area when you read this, be patient. It's probably in the works.) On the other hand, high-speed modems really only strut their stuff when you're browsing the World Wide Web or downloading files (discussed in Chapters 4 and 5, respectively). In other words, a 14,400 baud modem might satisfy your needs if all you really want to do is exchange electronic mail. That's all I have on my laptop, for example. A 14,400 baud modem, however, should be considered the minimum, if you can find one at all.

I prefer modems with speakers and lights. Lights, of course, are only found on external modems, and external modems typically require an available serial port. If you have an internal modem, you won't need an available serial port (and you won't have any lights to watch). My modem has six or seven lights. I don't understand most of them, but they look important. The one marked RD (receiving data) is worth watching when you are transferring a file (I discuss file downloading in Chapter 5). It should stay on almost continuously. If, during a file transfer, your RD light is off more than it's on, you've either got a noisy phone line or the system is extremely busy. Whatever the cause, it's best to halt the file transfer (AOL always leaves a Finish Later button on the screen for that purpose) and resume it another time. That's why I advise buying a modem with lights: if you don't have them, how can you tell what's going on?

If your modem is the external variety, it will need power of some kind. A few older external modems use your ADB (keyboard) port for power, but most use AC power and plug into the wall. Be sure an outlet is available.

Most important, be sure you have the proper cables. For an external modem, you need two cables: one to connect the modem to the Mac and another one to connect the modem to the phone jack. The modem-to-phone-jack cable bundled with many modems rarely exceeds 6 feet. If the distance between your modem and your phone jack exceeds that distance, you can buy an extension cable at a phone, electronics, or hardware store. Extension cables are standardized and are inexpensive.

Check your modem's manual to see if your modem requires a hardware-handshaking (high-speed) cable. If it does, it's essential that you use one, as it will provide a more reliable connection at top speed.

Baud Rates

The term *baud rate* refers to the signaling rate, or the number of times per second the signal changes. Don't confuse the baud rate with *bits per second* (bps)—they're not the same thing. By using modern electronic wizardry, today's modems can transmit 2, 3, or 4 bits with each change of signal, increasing the speed of data transfer considerably. Because it takes 8 bits to make a byte, a modem rated at 28,800 bps can transfer anywhere between 3,600 and 14,400 bytes per second. A *byte* is the amount of data required to describe a single character of text. In other words, a modem with a baud rate of 28,800 should transmit at least 3,600 characters—about 45 lines of text—per second.

Alas, the world is an imperfect place—especially the world of phone lines. If there's static or interference of any kind on the line, data transmission is garbled. And even one misplaced bit can destroy the integrity of an entire file. To address the problem, AOL validates the integrity of received data. In plain English, this means that AOL sends a packet of information (a couple of seconds' worth) to your Mac, then waits for the Mac to say, "I got that, and it's okay," before it sends the next packet. Validation like this means things run a little slower than they would without validation, but it's necessary. We're probably down to a minimum of 3,000 characters per second once we factor in the time it takes to accommodate data validation.

Then there's noise. You've heard it: static on the line. If you think it interferes with voice communication, it's murder on data. Often your Mac says, "That packet was no good—send it again," and AOL complies. The reliability of any particular telephone connection is capricious. Some are better than others. Noise, however, is a definite factor, and packets have to be re-sent once in a while. Now we're probably down to a minimum of 2,900 characters per second on a good telephone line on a good day—which is still over 40 lines of text per second at 28,800 bps.

In other words, a 28,800 bps modem isn't 16 times faster than a 2400 bps model, and a 9600 bps modem isn't 4 times faster than one rated at 2400 bps. On the other hand, a 28,800 bps modem doesn't cost 16 times as much as a 2400 bps model. What I'm trying to say is, in terms of baud per buck, 28,800 is your best buy.

You might also need to make some provision for using your phone on the same line when you're not online. It's less complicated if the modem has a jack for your phone. In that case, you can plug the modem into the wall jack, then plug the phone into the modem. The jacks on the back of the modem should be marked for this. **Note:** You will *not* be able to use your modem and your phone simultaneously: it's one or the other.

If your modem only has a single jack and you want to continue using your phone as well as your modem on the same line, you might also want to invest in a modular splitter, which plugs into the phone jack on your wall, making two jacks out of one. You plug your phone into one of the splitter's jacks and your modem into the other. Plugging both devices into the same jack won't interfere with everyday telephone communications; incoming calls will continue to go to your phone, just as they did before. You should be able to find a splitter at a phone, electronics, or hardware store for less than $3.

If all this sounds like a lot of wires to keep track of and you have trouble plugging in a toaster, don't worry. Most modems come with good instructions, and the components are such that you can't connect anything backward. Just follow the instructions and you'll be all right.

The Money

Before you sign on to AOL for the first time, there's something else you'll need: money. America Online wants to know how you plan to pay the balance on your account each month. Cash won't do. Instead, you can provide a credit card number: VISA, MasterCard, American Express, or the Discover Card are all acceptable. So are certain bank debit cards. Or have your checkbook handy: AOL can have your bank automatically transfer the funds each month if you provide the necessary numbers.

The Screen Name

We're almost ready, but right now I want you to get all other thoughts out of your mind and decide what you want to call yourself. Every AOL member has a unique screen name. Screen names are how AOL tells us apart from each other. You must have one, and it has to be different from everybody else's.

A screen name must consist of from three to ten characters—letters, or letters and numbers. Punctuation and spaces are not acceptable. Millions of people use AOL, and they all have screen names of 10 or fewer characters. Chances are, the screen name you want most is taken, so have a number of alternates ready ahead of time and prepare yourself for disappointment. Hardly anyone ever gets his or her first choice.

Though screen names aren't case-sensitive—you can address mail to majortom or MajorTom or MAJOR TOM, and it will still get to me—they always appear onscreen the way they were first entered. I first entered my screen name, for example, as MajorTom. If you send mail to majortom, I will see MajorTom on the To: line of my incoming mail. I'm MajorTom in chat rooms and Instant Messages as well. Keep this in mind as you enter your screen name for the first time, and capitalize your screen name as you want others to see it.

There's no going back, by the way. Once AOL accepts your initial screen name, it's yours as long as you remain a member. Though your account can have as many as five screen names (to accommodate other people in your family or your alter egos), your initial screen name is the one AOL uses to establish and verify your identity. For this reason, your initial screen name can't be changed. Be prepared with a zinger (and a half-dozen alternates); otherwise, AOL will assign you something like TomLi5437, and you'll forever be known by that name. People have a hard time relating to a name like that.

MajorTom

I worked my way through college as a traffic reporter for an Oregon radio station. I was both reporter and pilot. It was a great job: perfect hours for a student, easy work, and unlimited access to a flashy plane. It didn't pay much, but somehow that wasn't important—not in the halcyon days of bachelorhood.

I hate to date myself, but David Bowie was an ascending force on the music scene in those days. Impertinent, perhaps—a little too androgynous and scandalous for the conservative element of the Nixon era—but definitely a hit-maker. Our station played Bowie. On my first day, the morning show disk jockey switched on his microphone and hailed "Ground Control to Major Tom"—a line from Bowie's Space Oddity—to get my attention. The name stuck. I was known as Major Tom from then on.

When the time came for me to pick my screen name years ago, AOL suggested TomLi5437 and I balked. How about just plain Tom? I asked. It's in use, AOL replied. I tried four others, and AOL continued to remind me of my lack of imagination. In desperation I tried MajorTom, and AOL accepted it. Once an initial screen name is accepted, that's it. I'm MajorTom on AOL now, and I will be forever more.

The Password

Oh yes, you need a password. Without a password, anyone knowing your screen name can log on using your name and have a heyday on your nickel. Passwords must be from four to eight characters in length, and any combination of letters, or letters and numbers, is acceptable. (As is the case with screen names, punctuation and spaces aren't allowed in passwords.) You will enter your password every time you sign on, so choose something easy to remember—something that's not a finger-twister to type. It should be different from your screen name, phone number, Social Security number, address, or real name—something no one else would ever guess, even if they know you well.

A Case for Elaborate Passwords

In his book *The Cuckoo's Egg,* Cliff Stoll describes computer hackers' methods for breaking passwords. Since most computers already have a dictionary on disk—all spelling-checkers use dictionaries—the hackers simply program their computers to try every word in the dictionary as a password. It sounds laborious, but computers don't mind.

Read this carefully: *No one from AOL will ever ask you for your password.* This is another hacker's ruse: lurking in AOL's dark corners, hackers troll for new members. When they spot someone they think is new, they'll send e-mail or an Instant Message (a real-time message that pops onto your screen) masquerading as an AOL employee. They'll say they're verifying billing records, or something like that, and ask for your password—this is referred to as *phishing. Don't reply*! Instead, make a note of the perpetrator's screen name, then use the keyword: **TOS** (it's free) to access the Terms of Service and determine what you should do next.

In other words, I'm making a case for elaborate passwords here. Don't make it personal, don't use your Social Security number, don't write it down, select something that's not in a dictionary, and never ever give out your password to anyone. This is important.

Installing the Software

Don't fret: installing the AOL software is a straightforward process. An installation program does all the work for you.

Insert the CD into your CD-ROM drive. Connect your modem to your Mac and to the phone jack, and turn it on. Refer to your modem's instruction manual if you're not sure how to connect it. The modem doesn't have to be connected in order to install the software, but the assumptions the Installer program makes about your hardware will be more accurate.

Start your Mac and find the AOL software Installer on the CD-ROM. Double-click the Install program's icon to install your software to your hard drive. Eventually, the Installer's Quick Reference Guide will appear (see Figure A-1).

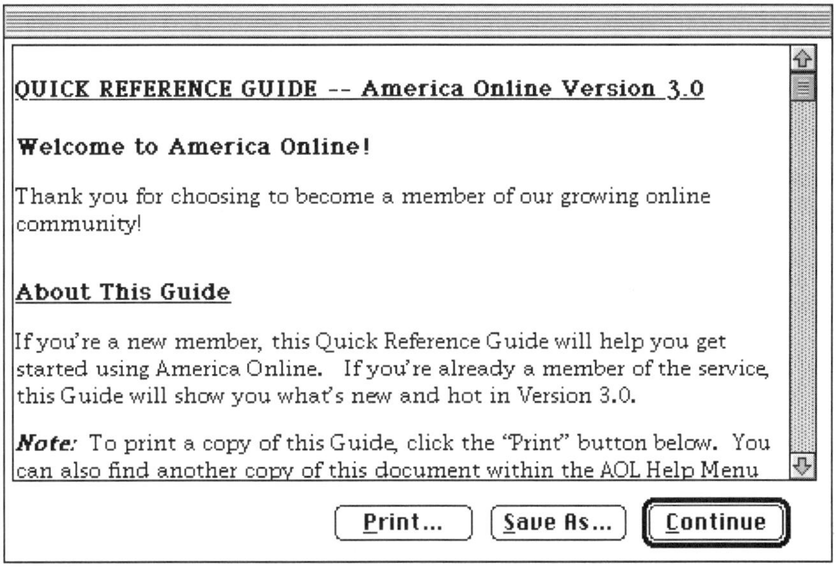
QUICK REFERENCE GUIDE -- America Online Version 3.0
Welcome to America Online!
Thank you for choosing to become a member of our growing online community!
About This Guide
If you're a new member, this Quick Reference Guide will help you get started using America Online. If you're already a member of the service, this Guide will show you what's new and hot in Version 3.0.
Note: To print a copy of this Guide, click the "Print" button below. You can also find another copy of this document within the AOL Help Menu
Print...
Save As...
Continue

Figure A-1: The Installer welcomes you with the Quick Reference Guide.

Once you have read the Quick Reference Guide (which I highly recommend), click the Continue button. The Installer then displays the window pictured in Figure A-2. It asks you where you want to place AOL's folder.

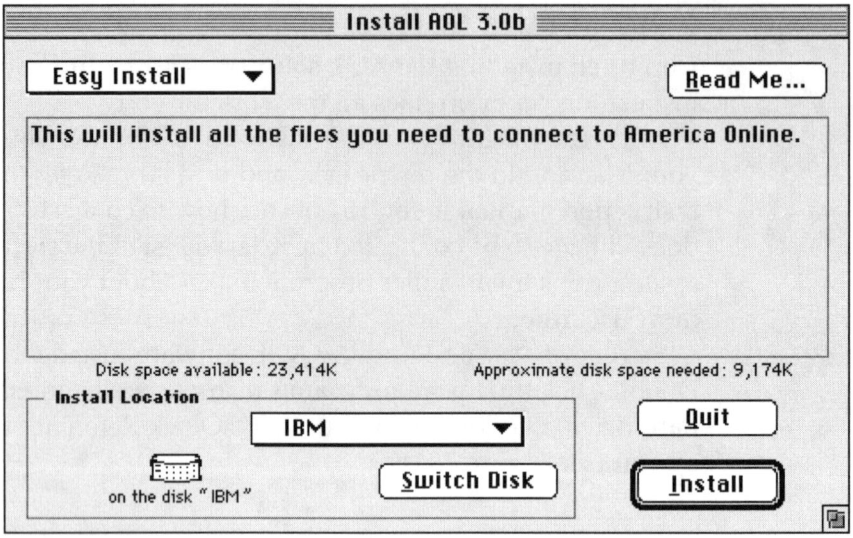
Install AOL 3.0b
Easy Install
Read Me...
This will install all the files you need to connect to America Online.
Disk space available: 23,414K
Approximate disk space needed: 9,174K
Install Location
IBM
on the disk "IBM"
Switch Disk
Quit
Install

Figure A-2: The Installer wants to know which disk will be used to install America Online.

IBM

Eagle-eyed readers will note that the hard disk on my Macintosh is named "IBM." There's a good reason for this: my hard disk *is* an IBM. When I first received my Mac and popped open the case (not a recommended method for getting to know a Mac, but often educational), the striped blue "IBM" logo was the first thing I saw. (It's hard to miss in that context.)

As it turns out, IBM makes hard disks and Apple doesn't. IBM is on Apple's list of suppliers and Apple buys hard disks from any high-quality supplier who offers the right price at the right time. Apparently, IBM's price was right when my Mac was constructed and my Mac has been a mixed-breed computer ever since. It's kind of embarrassing, but it's mine and I'm not about to hide it.

The moral of the story: open the case only when you're prepared for the consequences.

Remember that you're about to install a folder, not a file. You needn't have a folder already prepared for AOL: it makes its own.

Once you click Figure A-2's Install button, you are asked to verify that you'd like to continue the installation. Note that once you click the Continue button, the Installer will automatically quit all open applications in preparation for the restart necessary after the installation process is complete. After that, the Installer does its work. This takes a couple of minutes. As it's working, a "thermometer" keeps you abreast of the Installer's progress (see the center window in Figure A-3). If your membership kit contained two disks, you will be asked to insert the second disk. When the installation process is complete, AOL notifies you that "installation was successful" and you must now restart your computer (bottom window of Figure A-3).

Figure A-3: The installation process is automatic: all you have to do is watch.

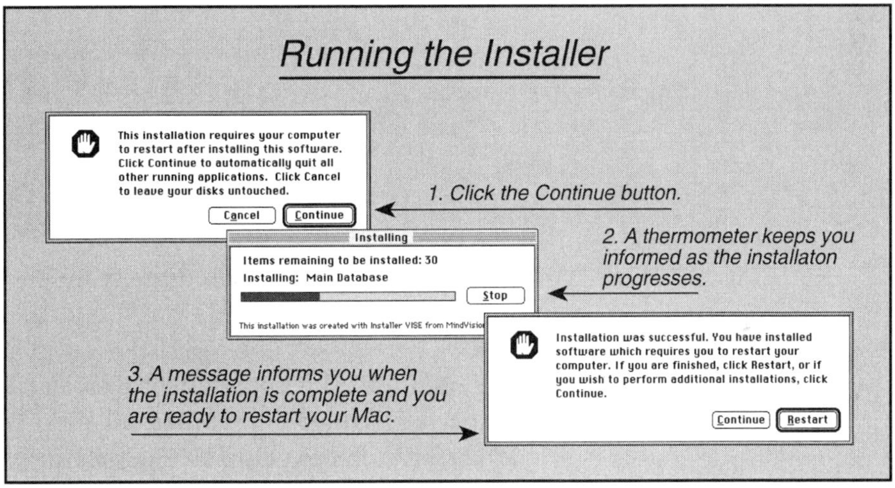
Running the Installer
This installation requires your computer to restart after installing this software. Click Continue to automatically quit all other running applications. Click Cancel to leave your disks untouched.
Cancel
Continue
1. Click the Continue button.
Installing
Items remaining to be installed: 30
Installing: Main Database
Stop
2. A thermometer keeps you informed as the installaton progresses.
Installation was successful. You have installed software which requires you to restart your computer. If you are finished, click Restart, or if you wish to perform additional installations, click Continue.
Continue
Restart
3. A message informs you when the installation is complete and you are ready to restart your Mac.

After you click the Restart button pictured in Figure A-3, your computer will automatically quit the Installer and restart. Once your Mac has completed the restart, take a moment to explore your hard disk. The Installer has created a new folder on the hard drive you specified, containing the AOL application and several other files and folders (see Figure A-4). Note that the folder and its contents equal over 7 megabytes, even though the Installer program is much smaller than that. The secret is file compression. Using a product called StuffIt (described in Chapter 5, "Transferring Files"), the AOL folder's components were compressed (stuffed) before they were placed on the CD-ROM; the compressed files were copied to your hard disk; then the Installer unstuffed them. It's all very logical, I suppose, but it's still magic to me.

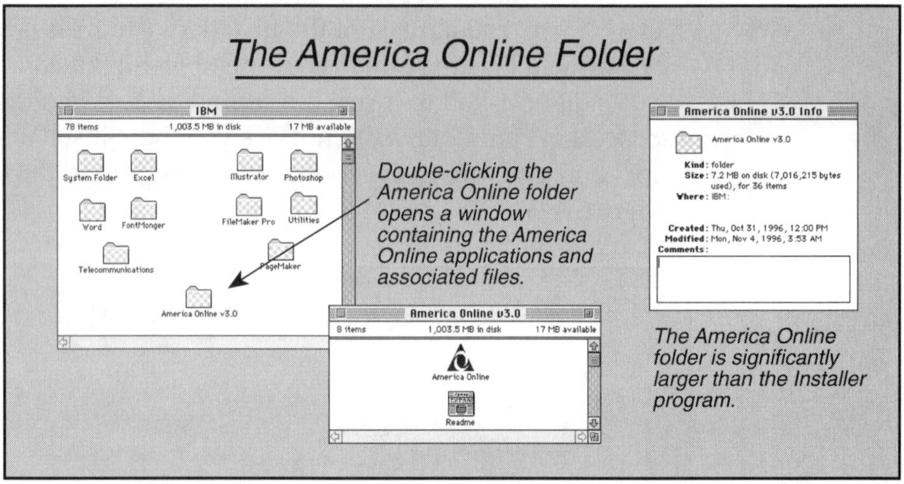
The America Online Folder
IBM
78 items
1,003.5 MB in disk
17 MB available
System Folder
Excel
Illustrator
Photoshop
Word
FontMonger
FileMaker Pro
Utilities
Telecommunications
PageMaker
America Online v3.0
Double-clicking the America Online folder opens a window containing the America Online applications and associated files.
America Online v3.0
8 items
1,003.5 MB in disk
17 MB available
America Online
Readme
America Online v3.0 Info
America Online v3.0
Kind: folder
Size: 7.2 MB on disk (7,016,215 bytes used), for 36 items
Where: IBM:
Created: Thu, Oct 31, 1996, 12:00 PM
Modified: Mon, Nov 4, 1996, 3:53 AM
Comments:
The America Online folder is significantly larger than the Installer program.

Figure A-4: The Installer places on your hard disk a folder containing the America Online software and all of the necessary files and folders.

There. You've done it. You've installed the software, and you're ready to sign on. Eject the CD-ROM and put it in a safe place. Then let's get on with it.

Existing members, note: The upcoming pages discuss finding local phone numbers and declaring a billing method—matters that aren't your concern. Please turn to the "Upgrading" heading on page 546 of this appendix to continue your upgrade.

The Initial Online Session

The initial online session takes about 15 minutes. Be sure you have the time and uninterrupted access to the phone before you begin. You needn't worry about money: though you'll be online for a while, the setup process is accomplished on AOL's dime, not yours. You needn't worry if you make a mistake either; plenty of Cancel buttons are offered during the initial session. If you get cold feet, you can always hang up and start over.

Configuring the Telephone Connection

Before it can successfully make the connection, AOL needs to know a number of things about your telephone. It needs to know whether you have touch-tone or rotary dialing, whether it needs to dial a 9 (or something else) to reach an outside line, and whether a 1 should be dialed before the 800 number. Canadian and international members will need to supply additional information.

Your modem should be connected to the phone line and to your Mac before you begin the initial online session, and everything should be turned on.

You can resize and relocate the AOL window for a neater desktop if you wish—it's just like any other window. Double-click the America Online icon to launch the AOL software. A Welcome screen greets you as soon as the software loads (see Figure A-5).

Welcome to America Online!
We will now take you through a quick and easy set-up and registration process. Before you begin, make sure your modem is turned on and that it is connected to your Macintosh and your phone line.
Cancel
Upgrade
Continue

Figure A-5: This window greets you when you first run the America Online software.

A second screen greets you when you click the Continue button shown in Figure A-5. (This screen is shown at the top of Figure A-6.) Carefully read the list of assumptions presented here. If they describe your situation accurately, click the Continue button. If they don't, click the Special Setup button. Special Setup accommodates dial phones, modem connections to the Macintosh printer port, and members calling from Canadian exchanges.

If you've followed the step above, a third screen will verify your modem's speed and port (see the third screen in Figure A-6). The assumptions displayed here are the result of the installer program's investigation routines. Here's a tip: Even if your modem is Hayes-compatible, select your modem brand and model from the list. Specificity pays under these circumstances.

When you click on the Modem Selection window's OK button, the application dials an 800 number to find a local access number for you. You will be able to monitor the call's progress by watching the window pictured at the bottom of Figure A-6. Once you see the message that says "Connected at XXXXX baud" (the baud rate is determined by the speed of your modem), you can be sure your Mac and modem are communicating properly. You can be sure that your modem and the telephone system are connected as well. If the AOL software found anything amiss prior to this point, it would have notified you and suggested solutions.

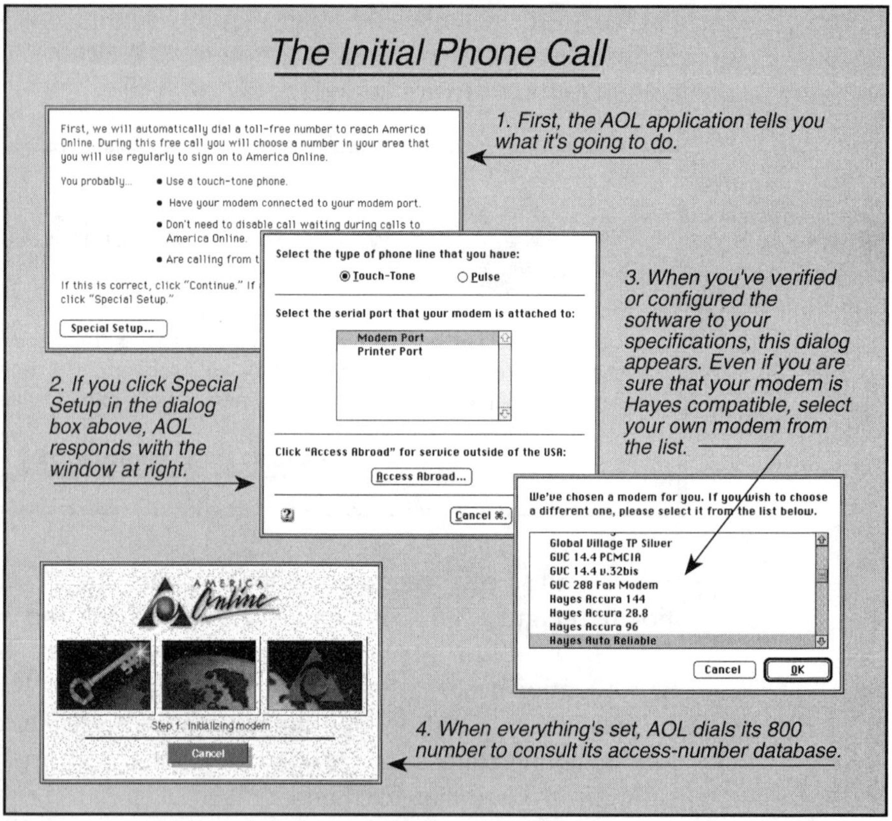
The Initial Phone Call
First, we will automatically dial a toll-free number to reach America Online. During this free call you will choose a number in your area that you will use regularly to sign on to America Online.
You probably...
Use a touch-tone phone.
Have your modem connected to your modem port.
Don't need to disable call waiting during calls to America Online.
Are calling from t
If this is correct, click "Continue." If
click "Special Setup."
Special Setup...
1. First, the AOL application tells you what it's going to do.
Select the type of phone line that you have:
Touch-Tone
Pulse
Select the serial port that your modem is attached to:
Modem Port
Printer Port
Click "Access Abroad" for service outside of the USA:
Access Abroad...
Cancel
2. If you click Special Setup in the dialog box above, AOL responds with the window at right.
3. When you've verified or configured the software to your specifications, this dialog appears. Even if you are sure that your modem is Hayes compatible, select your own modem from the list.
We've chosen a modem for you. If you wish to choose a different one, please select it from the list below.
Global Village TP Silver
GVC 14.4 PCMCIA
GVC 14.4 v.32bis
GVC 288 Fax Modem
Hayes Accura 144
Hayes Accura 28.8
Hayes Accura 96
Hayes Auto Reliable
Cancel
OK
AMERICA Online
Step 1: Initializing modem
Cancel
4. When everything's set, AOL dials its 800 number to consult its access-number database.

Figure A-6: Read these screens carefully; make changes if they're necessary. Take advantage of the opportunity to specify your modem. Once you OK the modem selection, AOL dials an 800 number for the initial connection.

Isolating Connection Errors

Though they rarely do, things can go wrong during the connect process. The problem could be at your end (e.g., the modem or the phone lines), or it could be at AOL's end. You'll know that the problem is at your end if you don't hear a dial tone (assuming your modem has a speaker) before your modem begins dialing. If you hear the dial tone, the dialing sequence, and the screeching sound that modems make when they connect, you'll know everything is okay all the way to the common carrier (long-distance service) you're using. If your connection fails during the initial connect process, don't panic. Wait a few minutes and try again. If it fails a second time, call AOL Technical Support at 800-827-6364.

Selecting Your Local Access Numbers

Now you're connected, and AOL is anxious to say hello. Its initial greeting is friendly, if a bit prosaic (see the top window in Figure A-7). Its singular interest right now is to find some local access numbers for you. To do that, it needs to know where you are. It finds that out by requesting your local area code.

Using your area code, AOL consults its database of local access numbers and produces a list of those nearest you (see the second window in Figure A-7). Look over the list carefully. The phone number at the top of the list isn't necessarily the one closest to you. Also, note the baud rates listed in the third column. You should select any number with a baud rate that's as fast as your modem or faster.

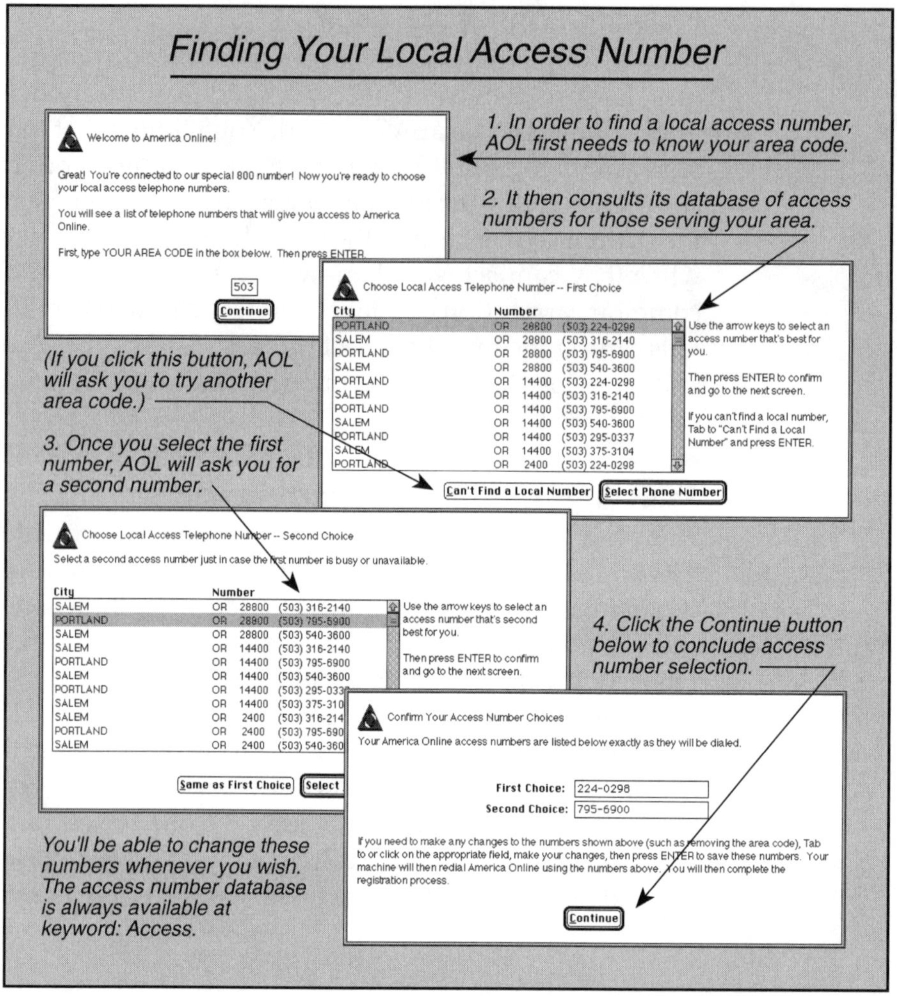
Finding Your Local Access Number
Welcome to America Online!
Great! You're connected to our special 800 number! Now you're ready to choose your local access telephone numbers.
You will see a list of telephone numbers that will give you access to America Online.
First, type YOUR AREA CODE in the box below. Then press ENTER.
503
Continue
1. In order to find a local access number, AOL first needs to know your area code.
2. It then consults its database of access numbers for those serving your area.
Choose Local Access Telephone Number -- First Choice
City
Number
PORTLAND OR 28800 (503) 224-0298
SALEM OR 28800 (503) 316-2140
PORTLAND OR 28800 (503) 795-6900
SALEM OR 28800 (503) 540-3600
PORTLAND OR 14400 (503) 224-0298
SALEM OR 14400 (503) 316-2140
PORTLAND OR 14400 (503) 795-6900
SALEM OR 14400 (503) 540-3600
PORTLAND OR 14400 (503) 295-0337
SALEM OR 14400 (503) 375-3104
PORTLAND OR 2400 (503) 224-0298
Use the arrow keys to select an access number that's best for you.
Then press ENTER to confirm and go to the next screen.
If you can't find a local number, Tab to "Can't Find a Local Number" and press ENTER.
Can't Find a Local Number
Select Phone Number
(If you click this button, AOL will ask you to try another area code.)
3. Once you select the first number, AOL will ask you for a second number.
Choose Local Access Telephone Number -- Second Choice
Select a second access number just in case the first number is busy or unavailable.
City
Number
SALEM OR 28800 (503) 316-2140
PORTLAND OR 28800 (503) 795-6900
SALEM OR 28800 (503) 540-3600
SALEM OR 14400 (503) 316-2140
PORTLAND OR 14400 (503) 795-6900
SALEM OR 14400 (503) 540-3600
PORTLAND OR 14400 (503) 295-033
SALEM OR 14400 (503) 375-310
SALEM OR 2400 (503) 316-214
PORTLAND OR 2400 (503) 795-690
SALEM OR 2400 (503) 540-360
Use the arrow keys to select an access number that's second best for you.
Then press ENTER to confirm and go to the next screen.
Same as First Choice
Select
4. Click the Continue button below to conclude access number selection.
Confirm Your Access Number Choices
Your America Online access numbers are listed below exactly as they will be dialed.
First Choice: 224-0298
Second Choice: 795-6900
If you need to make any changes to the numbers shown above (such as removing the area code), Tab to or click on the appropriate field, make your changes, then press ENTER to save these numbers. Your machine will then redial America Online using the numbers above. You will then complete the registration process.
Continue
You'll be able to change these numbers whenever you wish. The access number database is always available at keyword: Access.

Figure A-7: Using your area code, America Online attempts to select two local numbers for access to the service.

If there isn't a local number listed for your area—that is, if you have to dial a 1 before your access number in order to complete the call—you might have to pay long-distance charges to your telephone company in order to connect to AOL. (There's an alternative: read about "The Other 800 Number" in the sidebar that follows.) Once the initial sign-on process concludes and you're online, use the keyword: **Access** and investigate AOL's database of access numbers on a regular basis. You may find a number there after all.

The Other 800 Number

AOL actually offers two 800 numbers. The first is the one the Setup program consults when it's searching for access numbers in your area. The second 800 number is there to save you money. In order to serve members who live in remote communities, AOL has established this 800 number for access from anywhere in the contiguous United States. While this number isn't exactly toll-free, the charge for its use is considerably less than most long-distance tariffs. If you must dial 1 to reach AOL, sign on and investigate the 800 number at keyword: **Access**.

It's a good idea to have a secondary number as well. A secondary number (if available) is just that: a second number for your modem to call if the first one is busy (which happens rarely) or bogged down with a lot of traffic (which happens more frequently). Interestingly, dozens of modems can use the same number at the same time by splitting their usage into tiny packets. This is all very perplexing to those of us who think of phone numbers as capable of handling one conversation at a time, but it's nonetheless true. There is a limit, however, and when it's reached, AOL tries the second number. The third window in Figure A-7 illustrates the screen used to select this alternate.

Finally, AOL presents the screen confirming your selections, pictured at the bottom of Figure A-7.

The Temporary Registration Number & Password

Assuming you've clicked on the Continue button shown in Figure A-7, your Mac will disconnect from the 800 number and dial your primary local access number you've selected. Once the connection is reestablished, AOL presents the screen shown in Figure A-8. This is where you must enter the temporary registration number and password you received with your startup kit. These are the temporary equivalents of the permanent screen name and password you'll soon establish. Enter the words and numbers carefully; they're usually nonsensical and difficult to type without error.

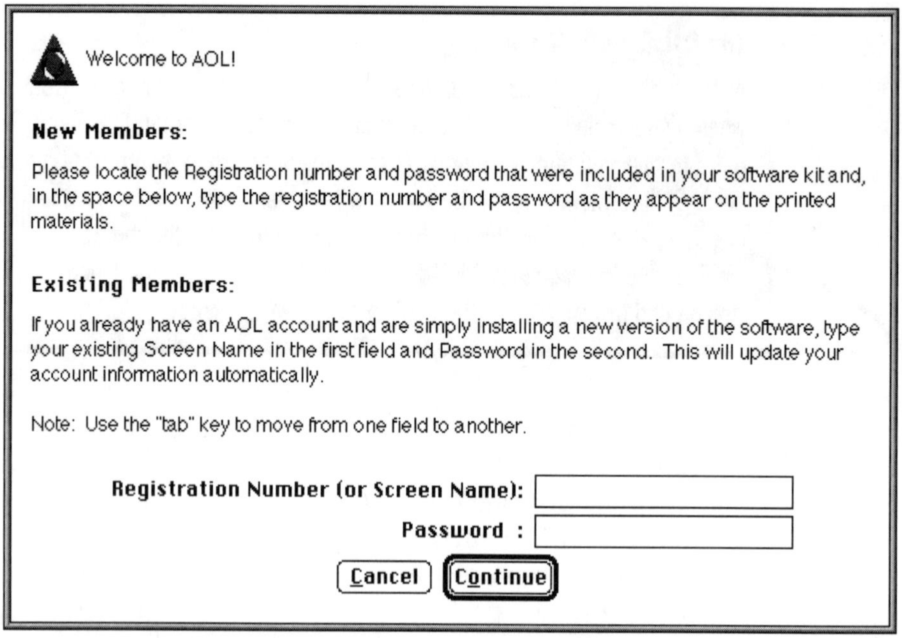
Welcome to AOL!
New Members:
Please locate the Registration number and password that were included in your software kit and, in the space below, type the registration number and password as they appear on the printed materials.
Existing Members:
If you already have an AOL account and are simply installing a new version of the software, type your existing Screen Name in the first field and Password in the second. This will update your account information automatically.
Note: Use the "tab" key to move from one field to another.
Registration Number (or Screen Name):
Password :
Cancel
Continue

Figure A-8: Enter your registration number and password here. Be sure to type them exactly as they appear on your certificate or label.

Your Name & Address

When you click the Continue button shown in Figure A-8, AOL provides directions for using an online form like the one shown in Figure A-9. If you're not familiar with the Mac, you'll want to read the directions carefully. If you've used Mac software before—even a little bit—you already know this stuff. It's traditional Mac protocol.

Once you've read the instructions, click the Continue button, and AOL will ask you for some personal information (see Figure A-9).

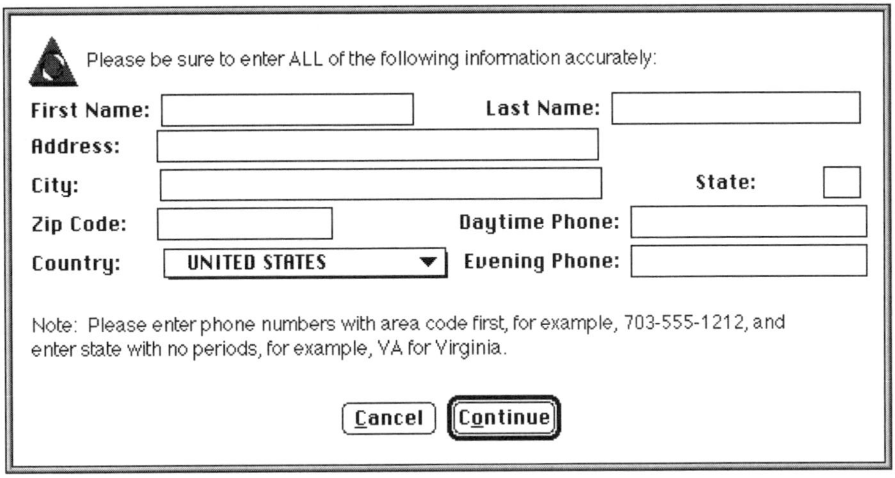
Please be sure to enter ALL of the following information accurately:
First Name:
Last Name:
Address:
City:
State:
Zip Code:
Daytime Phone:
Country:
UNITED STATES
Evening Phone:
Note: Please enter phone numbers with area code first, for example, 703-555-1212, and enter state with no periods, for example, VA for Virginia.
Cancel
Continue

Figure A-9: Provide your name, phone number(s), and address. Be sure to use the telephone number format shown in the illustration.

America Online uses this information to communicate with you offline. Although AOL never bills members directly (we'll discuss money in a moment), and though this information is not available online to other members, the AOL staff occasionally does need to contact you offline, and they use this information to do so. They might want to send you a disk containing an upgrade to the software, or perhaps you've ordered something from them (this book, for example) that needs to be mailed. That's what this information is for.

Your Phone Number

Your phone number becomes an important part of your record at America Online—not because anyone at AOL intends to call you but because AOL's Customer Service Department uses this number to identify you whenever you call. Should you ever need to call, the first question Customer Service will ask is, What's your phone number? It's unique, after all, so Customer Service uses it to look up your records. It's an efficient method, but only if you provide the number accurately during your initial sign-on.

Providing Your Billing Information

Let's be up-front about it: America Online is a business run for profit. In other words, AOL needs to be paid for the service it provides. It offers a number of ways to accomplish this. VISA, MasterCard, and American Express are the preferred methods of payment. The Discover/Novus card also is acceptable. Certain bank debit cards are acceptable as well, though you will have to confirm their acceptability with your financial institution. If none of these work for you, America Online also can arrange to debit your checking account automatically. (There's a fee for this—more than a credit card costs you—so you might want this option to be your last resort.)

When you click the Continue button shown in Figure A-9, another screen appears, identifying AOL's connect-time rates. Read it carefully—you need to know what you're buying and what it's costing you, after all—then move on (see Figure A-10).

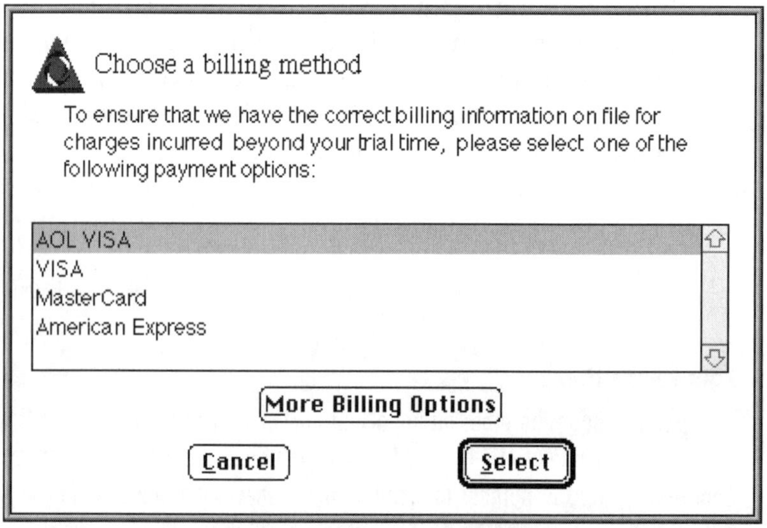
Choose a billing method
To ensure that we have the correct billing information on file for charges incurred beyond your trial time, please select one of the following payment options:
AOL VISA
VISA
MasterCard
American Express
More Billing Options
Cancel
Select

Figure A-10: VISA, MasterCard, and American Express cards are welcome, and the More Billing Options button leads to information about using the Discover/Novus card or debiting your checking account.

Figure A-11 shows an example of the billing information screen that lies under the options pictured in Figure A-10. This is the VISA form, but the forms for the other cards are about the same.

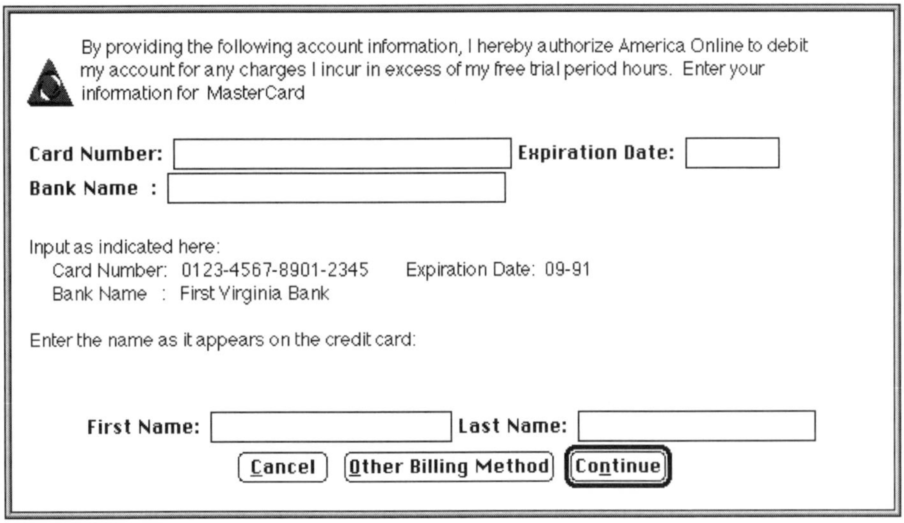
By providing the following account information, I hereby authorize America Online to debit my account for any charges I incur in excess of my free trial period hours. Enter your information for MasterCard
Card Number:
Expiration Date:
Bank Name :
Input as indicated here:
Card Number: 0123-4567-8901-2345
Expiration Date: 09-91
Bank Name : First Virginia Bank
Enter the name as it appears on the credit card:
First Name:
Last Name:
Cancel
Other Billing Method
Continue

Figure A-11: The MasterCard form is about the same as the one for VISA, American Express, or the Discover/Novus card. Use the number formats described.

Choosing a Screen Name & Password

When you click the Continue button shown in Figure A-11, AOL provides a series of screens informing you of the significance of screen names, concluding with the screen name input form pictured at the top of Figure A-12. AOL does not choose a screen name for you—an incentive to have your own choices at hand.

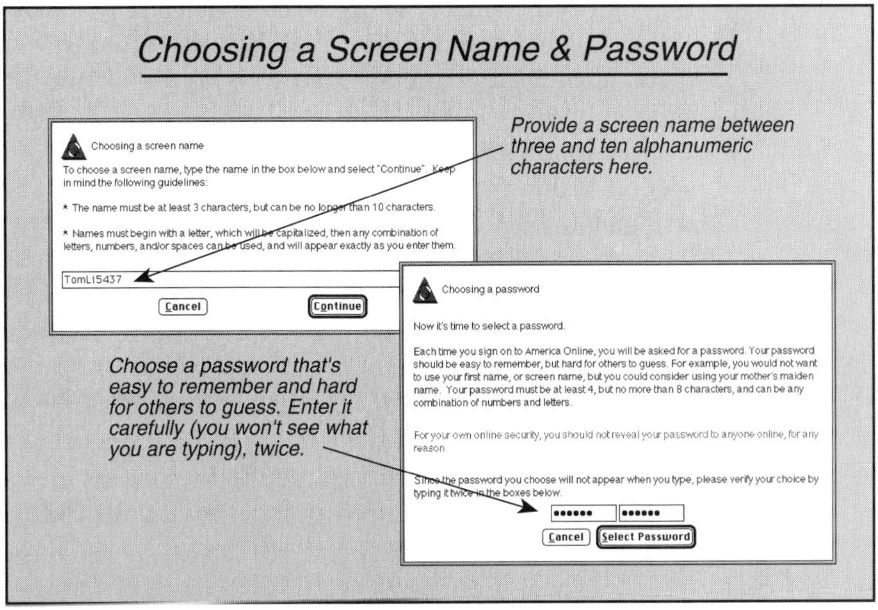
Choosing a Screen Name & Password
Choosing a screen name
To choose a screen name, type the name in the box below and select "Continue". Keep in mind the following guidelines:
* The name must be at least 3 characters, but can be no longer than 10 characters.
* Names must begin with a letter, which will be capitalized, then any combination of letters, numbers, and/or spaces can be used, and will appear exactly as you enter them.
TomLi5437
Cancel
Continue
Provide a screen name between three and ten alphanumeric characters here.
Choose a password that's easy to remember and hard for others to guess. Enter it carefully (you won't see what you are typing), twice.
Choosing a password
Now it's time to select a password.
Each time you sign on to America Online, you will be asked for a password. Your password should be easy to remember, but hard for others to guess. For example, you would not want to use your first name, or screen name, but you could consider using your mother's maiden name. Your password must be at least 4, but no more than 8 characters, and can be any combination of numbers and letters.
For your own online security, you should not reveal your password to anyone online, for any reason.
Since the password you choose will not appear when you type, please verify your choice by typing it twice in the boxes below.
Cancel
Select Password

Figure A-12: Conclude the registration process by entering your screen name and password.

Note that the characters of your password don't appear on your screen as you type them. Substituting asterisks for the letters of your password is a standard security precaution—you never know who's looking over your shoulder. America Online asks you to enter your password twice to be sure you didn't mistype it the first time.

Upgrading

Like all good things, the America Online software is continually improving. You can always download the latest copy of the software online at keyword: **Upgrade**. In fact, you may want to stop in there to verify that you have the latest version of software. You can check to see what version you are currently running by selecting About America Online from the Apple menu.

If you are already an AOL member and you're installing an updated version of the software, here are a couple of tricks that will expedite the process.

Use Your Existing Account Information

Be sure you're signed off and you have quit your AOL software. Do *not* remove the outdated AOL software from your hard disk. The current America Online folder contains a bounty of account and other information that you probably want to retain, such as e-mail and Parental Controls. This information can all be transferred to your new software, *if* you leave the outdated software on your disk until the upgrading process has concluded.

Now follow the steps detailed in the "Installing the Software" section of this appendix, on pages 533 through 536. The Setup program will install the new software in a folder named America Online v3.0. Change the folder name if you wish, but *do not overwrite your existing AOL software.* This implies that you will temporarily have to have enough room on your hard disk for two AOL installations, until you're ready to delete the old one.

Once installed on your hard disk, double-click the AOL icon. When you come to the Welcome screen pictured in Figure A-5, click the Upgrade button. AOL will ask you to locate the older America Online application and then begin copying your e-mail and Parental Controls over to the new software.

Delete Your Old Software

Once you've signed off, use the Finder to delete the old America Online folder. This will free up considerable space on your hard disk and prevent you from accidentally invoking your old software when you next sign on—a common error.

Where to Go From Here

Once you're online, you have the entire AOL universe to explore. The thought is at once enticing and overwhelming. Here's what I suggest: if you're new, spend a half-hour wandering around aimlessly. Click the Keyword button on the toolbar, then enter **Hot** to see what's hot online this month. Use the keyword: **Internet** to find an Internet feature that interests you; then, without any particular agenda, explore that feature and perhaps one other.

During this initial session, don't try to absorb the entire contents of AOL or the Internet. Rather, wander aimlessly, getting a feeling for the nature of the online universe. AOL's interface takes practically no getting used to: just enjoy yourself.

After a half-hour or so, you might want to sign off. Choose Sign off from the Go To menu, and click the Sign Off button on the Exit screen. Once the dust settles, turn to the chapter in this book that describes a feature you just visited. Read that chapter, then sign back on and explore that department again. See if you can find the things I described in the chapter. Spend another half-hour at this.

Now you're on your own. Explore another department if you wish, or turn to Chapter 3, "Electronic Mail & the Personal Filing Cabinet," and learn how to send mail to somebody. You'll probably get a response in a few days. People at AOL are very friendly. It really *is* a community.

APPENDIX B
Keywords

Keywords are the fastest way to get from one place to another on America Online. To go to a specific forum or area, you just click the Keyword button on the toolbar (or press Command-K), and enter its keyword.

Of course, you need to know the keyword before you can enter it. The most current list of keywords is always available by using (what else?) a keyword: **Keywords**. It's a long list, and because of its length, you might have trouble finding the keyword you're after by consulting the list online. (Printing it is an option.)

Allow me to suggest two alternatives: (1) Click the Keyword button on the toolbar, enter a description of what you're after, then click the Search button in the Keyword window (instead of the Go button). This invokes the Directory of Services, a searchable database of services offered by America Online (and it's discussed in Chapter 2, "The Abecedarium"). Because it's searchable, the Directory can be a faster method of locating an online area than reading through the list of keywords. (2) Use the lists of keywords appearing below. They're alphabetical by keyword. They may save you the trouble of printing a list of your own.

Keyword Tips

The three little keyword tips below may be of help to you:

- Like screen names, keywords are neither case-sensitive nor space-sensitive. "directoryofservices" works just as well as "Directory of Services."
- Many of AOL's areas identify their associated keywords in their primary window somewhere. Look for these.

- If you find an area you think you'll visit again often, click the little heart icon on the title bar of that area's window. This will add the location to your list of Favorite Places, where you can organize and access it conveniently. The Favorite Places feature is discussed in Chapter 4, "Using the Internet."

The keyword lists below were compiled by Jennifer Watson (screen name: KEY List) on October 30, 1996. Please e-mail changes or additions to her, as she maintains the lists on a continuing basis. Questions about keywords can also be sent to Jennifer or posted on the message board at keyword: **Keywords**. Thanks, Jennifer!

Entries with asterisks (*) are within free areas. Entries that are platform-dependent (those that are available only to members using specific types of computers) are indicated as such: "GAOL" is Geos AOL (DOS); "MAOL" is Mac AOL; "WAOL" is Windows AOL; and "3.0" refers to version 3.0 of the AOL software for either Mac or Windows.

Alphabetical by Keyword

@ACTIVE SPORTS	Thrive@Active Sports [3.0 only]
@AOL DEAD	AOL Live Auditorium
@AOL LIVE	AOL Live Auditorium
@BOWL	The Bowl Auditorium
@COLISEUM	The Coliseum Auditorium
@CYBER RAP	Cyber Rap Auditorium
@CYBERPLEX	Cyberplex Auditorium
@DOME	AOL Sports Dome Auditorium
@GLOBE	The Globe Auditorium
@INC LIVE	Inc Live Conference Room
@MAINSTAGE	Main Stage Auditorium
@MARKETPLACE	Thrive@Marketplace
@NEWSROOM	The News Room Auditorium
@ODEON	The Odeon Auditorium
@ROTUNDA	Rotunda Auditorium
@THE.MOVIES	@the.movies
@ THE MOVIES	@the.movies
@THENEWSROOM	The News Room Auditorium
@TIMES	@times/The New York Times Online
@TIMES CROSSWORD	The New York Times Crosswords
@TIMES STORE	@times: Store
:)	Grateful Dead Forum
;)	Hecklers Online
;-)	Hecklers Online
;-D	Virtual Christian Humor
<><	Christianity Online
?	Member Services*
1-800-TREKER	800-TREKKER: 24 Hour Sci-Fi Collectibles Hotline
1-800-TREKKER	800-TREKKER: 24 Hour Sci-Fi Collectibles Hotline
1010	A Day in the Life of Cyberspace
17	Seventeen Magazine Online
1995	1995: The Year in Review
20	Twentieth Century Mutual Funds
20/20	ABC News-On-Demand
20TH	Twentieth Century Mutual Funds
21ST	Twentieth Century Mutual Funds
24 HOURS	24 Hours of Democracy Web Site
25 REASONS	Best of America Online Showcase
2MARKET	Marketplace Gift Valet
3-D	3D Forum
3-D RENDERING	3D Forum
3.0 TOUR	3.0 Upgrade Tour* [Platform-dependent]
3A	AAA Online
3D	3D Forum
3D AUDIO	SRS Labs
3D REALMS	Apogee/3D Realms Support Center
3D RENDERING	3D Forum
3D SIG	3D Special Interest Group
3D SOUND	SRS Labs
3D-RENDERING	3D Forum
3DO	The 3DO Company
4DDA ENTRY	Mac Business Forum [MAOL only]
4RESOURCES	AT&T Home Business Resources
4TH	AOL's Independence Day Area [May disappear without notice]
5TH GENERATION	Symantec

60	Amazing Instant Novelist
7 WONDERS	Seven Wonders of the Web
777-FILM	MovieLink
777-FILM ONLINE	MovieLink
7TH	Seventh Level Software
800	AT&T 800 Directory Web Site
800 DIRECTORY	AT&T 800 Directory Web Site
800 FLOWERS	800-Flowers
800-FLOWERS	800-Flowers
800-TREKER	800-TREKKER: 24 Hour Sci-Fi Collectibles Hotline
800-TREKKER	800-TREKKER: 24 Hour Sci-Fi Collectibles Hotline
90210	90210 Wednesdays
90210 WEDNESDAYS	90210 Wednesdays
95 APPLY	AOL for Windows 95 Beta Test Application [3.0 only]
9600	High Speed Access*
9600 ACCESS	High Speed Access*
9600 CENTER	High Speed Access*
99.1	WHFS 99.1 FM
A&B	Simon & Schuster College Online
A'S	Major League Baseball Team: Oakland Athletics
A-LIST	Style Channel
A3	AAA Online
AAA	AAA Online
AAC	Academic Assistance Center
AAFMAA	Army and Air Force Mutual Aid Association
AAII	American Association of Individual Investors
AAPMR	American Academy of Physical Medicine and Rehabilitation
AARDVARK	Aardvark Pet Supplies
AARP	American Association of Retired People
AARP ANNUIT	AARP Annuity Program
AARP ANNUITY	AARP Annuity Program
AARP BANK 1	AARP Credit Card Services
AARP FUND	AARP Investment Program
AARP HART	AARP Auto & Homeowners Program
AARP HARTFORD	AARP Auto & Homeowners Program
AARP LIFE	AARP Life Insurance Program
AARP NY LIFE	AARP Life Insurance Program
AARP PHAR	AARP Pharmacy
AARP PRU	AARP Group Health Insurance
AARP SCUDDER	AARP Investment Program
AATRIX	Aatrix Software, Inc.
ABBATE VIDEO	Abbate Video
ABC	ABC Online
ABC AUDITORIUM	ABC Online Auditorium
ABC AUTO RACING	ABC Sports REV Speedway
ABC BASEBALL	ABC Sports Major League Baseball
ABC BETA	ABC Online: Beta Area
ABC CLASS	The ABC Classroom
ABC CLASSROOM	The ABC Classroom
ABC COLLEGE FOOTBALL	ABC Sports College Football
ABC CROWN	ABC Triple Crown
ABC DAYTIME	ABC Daytime/Soapline
ABC ENTERTAINMENT	ABC Prime Time
ABC EVENTS	ABC Online Auditorium
ABC FIGURE SKATING	ABC Sports Figure Skating
ABC FOOTBALL	ABC Sports College Football
ABC GMA	ABC Good Morning America
ABC GUESTS	ABC Online Auditorium
ABC HELP	ABC Online Help
ABC HOCKEY	ABC Sports Hockey/NHL Online
ABC HORSEING	ABC Horseing
ABC KIDS	ABC Kidzine
ABC KIDZINE	ABC Kidzine
ABC LOVE	ABC Love Online
ABC NEWS	ABC News-On-Demand
ABC NEWS VIEWS	ABC Online: News Views
ABC NHL	ABC Sports Hockey/NHL Online
ABC PRIME TIME	ABC Prime Time
ABC RADIO	ABC Radio
ABC SOAPS	ABC Daytime/Soapline
ABC SPORTS	ABC Sports
ABC SPORTS STORE	ABC Sports Store
ABC STARS	ABC Online: Stars and Shows [3.0 only]
ABC STATION	ABC Online: Stations
ABC STATIONS	ABC Online: Stations
ABC TRACK	ABC Track
ABC TRANSCRIPTS	ABC Online Auditorium
ABC TRIPLE	ABC Triple Crown
ABC TRIPLE CROWN	ABC Triple Crown
ABC VIDEO	ABC Online: Video Store
ABC WOMEN	ABC Sports Women's Sports
ABC WOMEN'S	ABC Sports Women's Sports
ABCCFB	ABC Sports College Football
ABF	Help Desk [Platform-dependent]
ABI	Business Yellow Pages
ABI YELLOW PAGES	Business Yellow Pages
ABM	Adventures by Mail
ABN	All Business Network [Web Site]
ABOUT WORK	About Work
ABOVE THE RIM	NESN: New England Basketball
ACADEMY AWARDS	Academy Awards [May disappear without notice]
ACC	AOL Community Cares
ACC CARING ORGS	ACC: Caring Organizations
ACC CHAT	ACC: Chats
ACC HELP	ACC: Help Yourself & Others
ACCESS	Accessing America Online*

ACCESS ERIC	AskERIC
ACCESS EXCELLENCE	Access Excellence
ACCESS NUMBERS	Accessing America Online*
ACCESS.POINT	access.point
ACCESS SOFTWARE	Access Software
ACCESSPOINT	access.point
ACCOLADE	Accolade, Inc.
ACCORDING	Company Research Message Boards
ACCORDING TO BOB	Company Research Message Boards
ACE VENTURA	EXTRA Online
ACE VENTURE STORE	EXTRA Online
ACER	Acer America Corporation
ACLU	American Civil Liberties Union
ACS	American Cancer Society
ACSNATL	American Cancer Society
ACT	Kaplan Online/SAT, ACT
ACTING	Casting Central
ACTIVE SPORTS	Active Sports
ACTIVISION	Activision
ACTORS	Casting Central
ACTRESSES	Casting Central
ACUBED	America-3: The Women's Team
AD	Athlete Direct [3.0 only]
AD SIG	Advertising Special Interest Group
AD&D	AD&D Neverwinter Nights
ADAMS	Cindy Adams: Queen of Gourmet Gossip
ADD	AD&D Neverwinter Nights
ADDONS	BPS Software
ADOBE	Adobe Center Menu
ADOBE PHOTOSHOP	Adobe Center Menu
ADOPTION	Adoption Forum
ADVANCED	Advanced Software, Inc.
ADVANCED GRAVIS	Advanced Gravis
ADVANCED LOGIC	Advanced Logic Research
ADVENTURE	Outdoor Adventures Online
ADVENTURES BY MAIL	Adventures by Mail
ADVERTISING	Advertising Special Interest Group
ADVERTISING SIG	Advertising Special Interest Group
ADVICE	Advice & Tips
ADVISOR	Top Advisor's Corner
ADVISORS	Top Advisor's Corner
ADVSOFT	Advisor Software
AE	Awakened Eye Special Interest Group
AECSIG	Architects, Engineers and Construction Special Interest Group
AEFD	American Express Financial Direct [3.0 only]
AEN	American Entertainment Network
AF'S SECRET BARGAINS	Arthur Frommer's Secret Bargains
AFFINIFILE	Affinity Microsystems
AFFINITY	Affinity Microsystems
AFGHANISTAN	Afghanistan [3.0 only]
AFRICA	Afrocentric Culture
AFRICAN	Genealogy Forum
AFRICAN AMERICAN	The Exchange: Communities Center
AFRICAN-AMERICAN	Afrocentric Culture
AFROCENTRIC	Afrocentric Culture
AFT	American Federation of Teachers
AFTEREFFECTS	AfterEffects
AFTERWARDS	Afterwards Cafe
AGGIES	AOL College Football '96 [3.0 only]
AGNOSTIC	Atheism-Agnosticism Forum
AGNOSTICISM	Atheism-Agnosticism Forum
AGOL	Assemblies of God Online
AGRICULTURE	NAS Online
AHH	Alternatives: Health & Healing [3.0 only]
AHS	American Hiking Society
AI INC	Hecklers Online: Antagonistic Trivia
AIDS	AIDS and HIV Resource Center
AIDS DAILY	AIDS Daily Summary
AIDS QUILT	GLCF Aids Scrapbook
AIQ	AIQ Systems
AIQ SYSTEMS	AIQ Systems
AIR JORDAN	Jordan [3.0 only]
AIR WARRIOR	Air Warrior [3.0 only]
AIRCRAFT	Flying Magazine
AIRCRAFTS	Flying Magazine
AIRPLANE	Aviation Forum
AIRPORTS	Flying Magazine
AIRSHOWS	Aviation Forum
AKIMBO	FullWrite
AKSOFT	AKSoft [3.0 only]
AL	Extreme Fans: American League
ALA	America Lung Association
ALADDIN	Aladdin Systems, Inc.
ALARM	Consumer Electronics
ALASKA	Digital Cities: Alaska
ALASKA DC	Digital Cities: Alaska
ALASKA DCITY	Digital Cities: Alaska
ALASKA DIGC	Digital Cities: Alaska
ALASKA DIGITAL CITY	Digital Cities: Alaska
ALBANY	Digital Cities: Albany NY
ALBANY DC	Digital Cities: Albany NY
ALBANY DCITY	Digital Cities: Albany NY
ALBANY DIGC	Digital Cities: Albany NY
ALBANY DIGITAL CITY	Digital Cities: Albany NY
ALBANY NY	Digital Cities: Albany NY
ALBUQUERQUE	Digital Cities: Albuquerque/Santa Fe NM
ALBUQUERQUE DC	Digital Cities: Albuquerque/Santa Fe NM

ALBUQUERQUE DCITY	Digital Cities: Albuquerque/Santa Fe NM
ALBUQUERQUE DIGC	Digital Cities: Albuquerque/Santa Fe NM
ALDUS	Adobe Systems Inc.
ALF	American Leadership Forum
ALIENS	Parascope
ALL MY CHILDREN	ABC Daytime/Soapline
ALL STAR	MLB All-Star Ballot
ALLYN & BACON	Simon & Schuster College Online
ALOHA	Apple Aloha for eWorld Alumni
ALPHA TECH	Alpha Software Corporation
ALPT	The Grandstand's Simulation Golf
ALR	Advanced Logic Research
ALTERNATIVE	MusicSpace: Alternative Music Forum
ALTERNATIVE MEDICINE	Alternative Medicine Forum
ALTERNATIVES	Alternatives: Health & Healing [3.0 only]
ALTSYS	Altsys Corporation
ALUMNI	Alumni Hall
ALUMNI HALL	Alumni Hall
ALYSIS	Alysis Software
AM FOCUS	AnswerMan's Weekly Focus
AM GLOSSARY	AnswerMan: Glossary
AMATEUR RADIO	Ham Radio Club
AMBROSIA	Ambrosia Software
AMC	ABC Daytime/Soapline
AMERICA ONLINE STORE	America Online Store
AMERICA OUT OF LINE	ABC Online: America Out Of Line
AMERICA'S CUP	America's Cup
AMERICA3	America3: The Women's Team
AMERICAN AGENDA	ABC News-On-Demand
AMERICAN ART	National Museum of American Art
AMERICAN ASTROLOGY	Astronet
AMERICAN DIABETES	American Diabetes Association
AMERICAN DIALOGUE	American Dialogue
AMERICAN EXPRESS	ExpressNet (American Express)
AMERICAN HISTORY	National Museum of American History
AMERICAN INDIAN	The Exchange: Communities Center
AMERICAN LUNG	American Lung Association
AMERICAN LUNG ASSOC	American Lung Association
AMERICAN WOODWORKER	American Woodworker
AMERICAS CUP	America's Cup 1995
AMERICON	America Online Gaming Conference
AMEX	ExpressNet (American Express)
AMEX ART	ExpressNet Art Download*
AMOR	Love@AOL
AMORE	Love@AOL
AMPHIBIAN	Pet Care Forum
AMPLIFIERS	Stereo Review Online
ANALOG	Fictional Realm
ANDERSEN	Andersen Windows Online
ANDERSEN WINDOWS	Andersen Windows Online
ANDERSON	Andersen Windows Online
ANDERTON	Craig Anderton's Sound Studio & Stage
ANDORRA	Andorra [3.0 only]
ANDY PARGH	Andy Pargh/The Gadget Guru
ANGEL	Religion & Beliefs
ANGELS	Major League Baseball Team: California Angels
ANIMAL	Pet Care Forum
ANIMALS	Pet Care Forum
ANIMATED SOFTWARE	Animated Software
ANIMATION	Graphic Forum [Platform-dependent]
ANIME	Wizard World
ANOTHER CO	Another Company
ANSWERMAN	Answer Man
ANTAG	Hecklers Online: Antagonistic Trivia
ANTAGON	Hecklers Online: Antagonistic Trivia
ANTAGONIST	Hecklers Online: Antagonistic Trivia
ANTAGONIST TRIVIA	Hecklers Online: Antagonistic Trivia
ANTAGONISTIC TRIVIA	Hecklers Online: Antagonistic Trivia
ANTI-AGING	Longevity Magazine Online
ANTI-OXIDANTS	Longevity Magazine Online
ANTIAGING	Longevity Magazine Online
ANTIQUES	The Exchange: Collector's Corner
AOL BEGINNERS	Help Desk [Platform-dependent]
AOL BUSINESS	AOL Enterprise
AOL CANADA	AOL Canada
AOL CARD	AOL Visa Card
AOL CLASSIFIED	AOL Classifieds
AOL CLASSIFIEDS	AOL Classifieds
AOL CRUISE	AOL Member Cruise
AOL DEAD	AOL Live Auditorium
AOL DIAG	AOL Diagnostic Tool [3.0 only]
AOL DINER	Everything Edible!
AOL EDUCATION	America Online Education Initiative
AOL ENTERPRISE	AOL Enterprise
AOL ENTERPRISES	AOL Enterprise
AOL FAMILIES	AOL Families
AOL FULL DISCLOSURE	AOL's Full Disclosure for Investors
AOL GAME FORUMS	Games Channel
AOL GIFT	AOL Gift Certificates
AOL GUARANTEE	AOL Cybershopping Guarantee
AOL HIGHLIGHTS	AOL Highlights Tour
AOL INTERNATIONAL	International Channel
AOL INVESTOR RELATIONS	AOL's Full Disclosure for Investors
AOL ISRAEL	Israel
AOL ISREAL	Israel
AOL LIVE	AOL Live!
AOL MAX	Family Computing Forum: Maximum AOL
AOL MEMBER CRUISE	AOL Member Cruise

AOL MFC	AOL Mutual Fund Center
AOL MOVIES	@the.movies
AOL ON THE MOVE	AOL on the Move [May disappear without notice]
AOL ON TV	AOL on TV (AOL Commercials)
AOL PREVIEW	Upgrade to latest AOL software
AOL PRODUCTS	America Online Store
AOL ROADTRIP	AOL Roadtrips [3.0 only]
AOL SOFTWARE SHOP	AOL Software Shop
AOL SPORTS LIVE	AOL Sports Live
AOL STORE	America Online Store
AOL TIPS	Family Computing Forum: Tip of the Day
AOL VISA	AOL Visa Card
AOL VISA CARD	AOL Visa Card
AOL WORLD	International Channel
AOLGLOBALNET	AOLGLOBALnet International Access*
AOLHA	Apple Aloha for eWorld Alumni
AOLIR	AOL's Full Disclosure for Investors
AOLNET	AOLNET
AOLSEWHERE	AOLsewhere
AOOL	ABC Online: America Out Of Line
AOP	Association of Online Professionals
APDA	Apple Professional Developer's Association [MAOL only]
APOGEE	Apogee/3D Realms Entertainment
APPLE	Apple/Macintosh Forums
APPLE COMPUTER	Apple Computer
APPLE UPDATE	Apple System 7.5 Update
APPLEBIZ	Apple Business Consortium
APPLESCRIPT	AppleScript Special Interest Group
APPLICATIONS	Business/Applications Forum [Platform-dependent]
APPLICATIONS FORUM	Business/Applications Forum [Platform-dependent]
APPMAKER	Bowers Development
APPS	Applications/Business Forum [Platform-dependent]
APRIL	AOL's April Fool Area [May disappear without notice]
APRIL FOOL	AOL's April Fool Area [May disappear without notice]
APRIL FOOLS	AOL's April Fool Area [May disappear without notice]
AQUARIUM	Pet Care Forum
ARCADE	Games Forum [Platform-dependent]
ARCATAPET	Arcata Pet
ARCHAEOLOGY	Archaeology Forum
ARCHITECTURE	Home Magazine Online
ARCHIVE	Archive Photos
ARCHY	Archaeology Forum
ARFA	American Running & Fitness Association
ARGOSY	Argosy
ARIEL	Ariel Publishing
ARIZONA	Arizona Central
ARIZONA CENTRAL	Arizona Central
ARM	AOL's Real Estate Center
ARNIE	Ask Arnie about Travel [3.0 only]
AROUND THE HORN	NESN: New England Baseball
ARSENAL	Arsenal Commmunications
ART	Graphic Forum [Platform-dependent]
ART BELL	Parascope: Art Bell
ART CRIMES	Art Crimes [Web Site]
ARTEMIS	Artemis Software
ARTHUR FROMMER	Arthur Frommer's Secret Bargains
ARTICULATE	Articulate Systems
ARTIFICE	Artifice, Inc.
ARTIST	Artists on America Online
ARTIST GRAPHICS	Artist Graphics
ARTIST'S SPOTLIGHT	Artist's Spotlight
ARTISTS	Artists on America Online
ARTISTS SPOTLIGHT	Artist's Spotlight
ARTS	Afterwards Cafe
ARTSPEAK	The Hub: ArtSpeak
ARUBA	Aruba
ASANTE	Asante Technologies
ASC TECH	Alpha Software Corporation
ASC TS	Alpha Software Corporation
ASCD	Assoc. for Supervisor & Curriculum Development
ASFL	The Grandstand's Simulation Football
ASI	Articulate Systems
ASIAN	The Exchange: Communities Center
ASIMOV	Fictional Realm
ASK AMERICA ONLINE	Member Services*
ASK AOL	Member Services*
ASK ARNIE	Ask Arnie about Travel [3.0 only]
ASK CS	Member Services*
ASK GLORIA	Ask Gloria Steinem
ASK SERENA	Weekly World News
ASK STAFF	Questions*
ASK TODD	The Image Exchange: Ask Todd Art
ASK TODD ART	The Image Exchange: Ask Todd Art
ASKERIC	AskERIC
ASNE	Newspaper Association of America
ASP	Association of Shareware Professionals
ASSASSINS	Assassins
ASSEMBLY	Development Forum [Platform-dependent]
ASSN	Christianity Online: Associations & Interests
ASSN ONLINE PROF	Association of Online Professionals

AST	AST Support Forum
ASTROGRAPH	Astrograph
ASTROLOGY	Astronet
ASTROMATES	Astronet
ASTRONAUTS	Challenger Remembered
ASTRONET	Astronet
ASTRONOMY	Astronomy Club
ASTROS	Major League Baseball Team: Houston Astros
ASYLUM	Snowboarding Online
ASYMETRIX	Asymetrix Corporation
AT	Hecklers Online: Antagonistic Trivia
AT ONCE	atOnce Software
AT TIMES	@times/The New York Times Online
AT&T	AT&T
ATAGONISTS	Hecklers Online: Antagonistic Trivia
ATG	Hecklers Online: Antagonistic Trivia
ATHEISM	Atheism-Agnosticism Forum
ATHEIST	Atheism-Agnosticism Forum
ATHLETE DIRECT	Athlete Direct [3.0 only]
ATHLETICS	Major League Baseball Team: Oakland Athletics
ATL COMM	Digital City Atlanta: Community
ATL FUN	Digital City Atlanta: Fun
ATL MARKET	Digital City Atlanta: Marketplace
ATL NEWS	Digital City Atlanta: News
ATL PEOPLE	Digital City Atlanta: People
ATLANTA	Digital Cities: Atlanta GA
ATLANTA BRAVES	Major League Baseball Team: Atlanta Braves
ATLANTA DIGITAL CITY	Digital Cities: Atlanta GA
ATLANTIC	The Atlantic Monthly Online
ATLANTIC MONTHLY	The Atlantic Monthly Online
ATLANTIC ONLINE	The Atlantic Monthly Online
ATLUS	Atlus Software
ATT	AT&T
ATT WIRELESS	AT&T
ATTICUS	Atticus Software
AUDIO	Stereo Review Online
AUDITORIUM	AOL Live!
AUG	User Group Forum
AUSTIN	Digital Cities: Austin TX
AUSTIN DC	Digital Cities: Austin TX
AUSTIN DCITY	Digital Cities: Austin TX
AUSTIN DIGC	Digital Cities: Austin TX
AUSTIN DIGITAL CITY	Digital Cities: Austin TX
AUSTIN TX	Digital Cities: Austin TX
AUSTRALIA	Australia
AUSTRIA	Austria
AUSTRIAN	Genealogy Forum
AUTO	AutoVantage
AUTO RACING	AOL Auto Racing
AUTO SOUND	Consumer Electronics
AUTOCAD	CAD Resource Center
AUTODESK	Autodesk Resource Center
AUTOEXEC	Tune Up Your PC
AUTOMATE	Affinity Microsystems
AUTOMATION	Affinity Microsystems
AUTOMOBILE	Car/Cycle Selections
AUTOMOTIVE	Car/Cycle Selections
AUTOS	Road & Track Magazine
AUTOSPELL	CompuBridge [3.0 only]
AUTOVANTAGE	AutoVantage
AV	AutoVantage
AV FORUM	Aviation Forum
AVALANCHE	NHL Hockey
AVIATION	Aviation Forum
AVID	Avid Technology
AVID DTV	Avid Technology
AVOCAT	Avocat Systems
AVOCAT SYSTEMS	Avocat Systems
AVON	Avon
AW	About Work
AW CAREER SHIFT	About Work: Career Shift
AW COMPANY LIFE	About Work: Company Life
AW ENTREPRENEURS	About Work: Entrepreneurs
AW FIRST JOBS	About Work: First Jobs
AW OUT-OF-WORK	About Work: Out-Of-Work
AW WORK-FROM-HOME	About Work: Work-From-Home
AWAKE EYE	Awakened Eye Special Interest Group
AWAKENED EYE	Awakened Eye Special Interest Group
AWAY	AOLsewhere
AX GARDENING	Arizona Central: House/Home
AZ ALT	Arizona Central: ALT.
AZ ALT.	Arizona Central: ALT.
AZ ASU	Arizona Central: Sports
AZ AT EASE	Arizona Central: At Ease
AZ BENSON	Arizona Central: Sound Off
AZ BEST	Arizona Central: The Best
AZ BIZ	Arizona Central: Small Business
AZ BUSINESS	Arizona Central: Your Money
AZ CACTUS	Arizona Central: Cactus League (Classifieds)
AZ CALENDARS	Arizona Central: Plan On It
AZ CARDS	Arizona Central: Sports
AZ CAROUSING	Arizona Central: Carousing
AZ CARTOON	Arizona Central: Sound Off
AZ CENTRAL	Arizona Central
AZ COLUMNS	Arizona Central: Sound Off
AZ COMMUNITY	Arizona Central: Your Community
AZ COMPUTERS	Arizona Central: Computers
AZ CONCERTS	Arizona Central: Carousing

AZ COUCHING	Arizona Central: Couching
AZ DESTINATIONS	Arizona Central: Destinations
AZ DIAMONDBACKS	Arizona Central: Sports
AZ DINING	Arizona Central: Dining
AZ EATS	Arizona Central: Dining
AZ EDITORIALS	Arizona Central: Sound Off
AZ ENTERTAINMENT	Arizona Central: At Ease
AZ FILMS	Arizona Central: Films
AZ FUN	Arizona Central: Plan On It
AZ GOLF	Arizona Central: Golf
AZ HIGH SCHOOLS	Arizona Central: Preps
AZ HOME	Arizona Central: House/Home
AZ HOUSE	Arizona Central: House/Home
AZ KTAR	Arizona Central: KTAR Talk Radio
AZ LETTERS	Arizona Central: Sound Off
AZ LIFE	Arizona Central: Your Life
AZ MONEY	Arizona Central: Your Money
AZ MOVIES	Arizona Central: Films
AZ NEWS	Arizona Central: Newsline
AZ NEWSLINE	Arizona Central: Newsline
AZ OPINIONS	Arizona Central: Sound Off
AZ PENELOPE	Arizona Central: Dining
AZ PHOTOS	Arizona Central: Photos
AZ PREPS	Arizona Central: Preps
AZ SCHOOLS	Arizona Central: Schools
AZ SCOREBOARD	Arizona Central: Scoreboard
AZ SCORES	Arizona Central: Scoreboard
AZ SMALL BUSINESS	Arizona Central: Small Business
AZ SOUNDOFF	Arizona Central: Sound Off
AZ SPORTS	Arizona Central: Sports
AZ SPORTS CALENDARS	Arizona Central: Plan On It
AZ SPORTS SCHEDULE	Arizona Central: Plan On It
AZ STARDUST	Arizona Central: Stardust
AZ SUNS	Arizona Central: Sports
AZ THEATER	Arizona Central: Stardust
AZ THEATRE	Arizona Central: Stardust
AZ TRAVEL	Arizona Central: Destinations
AZ TRIPS	Arizona Central: Destinations
AZ TV	Arizona Central: Couching
AZ U OF A	Arizona Central: Sports
AZ VOLUNTEERS	Arizona Central: Volunteers
AZERBAIJAN	Azerbaijan [3.0 only]
B&B	Bed & Breakfast U.S.A.
B5	Babylon 5
BA	Bank of America
BABY	Parent Soup: Baby & Toddler
BABY BOOMER	Baby Boomers Area
BABY BOOMERS	Baby Boomers Area
BABY NAME	Parent Soup: Baby Names
BABY NAMES	Parent Soup: Baby Names
BABYLON	Babylon 5
BABYLON 5	Babylon 5
BACK TO SCHOOL	Back to School [May disappear without notice]
BACKCOUNTRY	Backpacker Magazine
BACKPACKER	Backpacker Magazine
BADGERS	AOL College Football '96 [3.0 only]
BAHA'I	Baha'i Faith Forum
BAHA'I FAITH	Baha'i Faith Forum
BAHAI	Baha'i Faith Forum
BAIR	James Bair Software
BALANCE SHEET	Disclosure's Financial Statements
BALI	One Hanes Place
BALKAN	Balkan Operation Joint Endeavor
BALL	Extreme Fans: Baseball Daily
BALLOON	800-Flowers
BALLOONS	800-Flowers
BALTIMORE ORIOLES	Major League Baseball Team: Baltimore Orioles
BANK	Banking Center
BANK AMERICA	Bank of America
BANK@HOME	Union Bank of California Online [3.0 only]
BANK OF AMERICA	Bank of America
BANK OF STOCKTON	Bank of Stockton [3.0 only]
BANK RATE	BRM Data Center [3.0 only]
BANKING	Banking Center
BANKING CENTER	Banking Center
BANKNOW	BankNOW [3.0 only]
BARGAINS	Checkbook Bargains
BARRONS	Barrons Booknotes
BARTLETT	Bartlett's Quotations
BARTLETT'S	Bartlett's Quotations
BARTLETTS	Bartlett's Quotations
BASEBALL	MLB Baseball
BASEBALL DAILY	Baseball Daily by Extreme Fans
BASEBALL WORKSHOP	Motley Fool: The Fool Dome
BASELINE	Baseline Publishing
BASEVIEW	Baseview Products, Inc.
BASIC	Development Forum [Platform-dependent]
BASKETBALL	NBA Basketball
BASKETBALL TRIVIA	NTN Basketball Trivia
BASS	BASS Tickets
BASS TICKETS	BASS Tickets
BATBOY	Weekly World News
BATMAN	DC Comics Online
BATTLETECH	Multiplayer BattleTech [3.0 only]
BAUMRUCKER	Baumrucker Conference [May disappear without notice]
BAY CITY	Digital Cities: Bay City MI
BAY CITY DC	Digital Cities: Bay City MI

BAY CITY DCITY	Digital Cities: Bay City MI
BAY CITY DIGC	Digital Cities: Bay City MI
BAY CITY MI	Digital Cities: Bay City MI
BAYWATCH FRAGRANCE	Baywatch Fragrance
BB	Extreme Fans: Baseball Daily
BBS	BBS Corner
BBS CORNER	BBS Corner
BC	Book Central
BC BOARDS	Book Central: Message Boards
BC BOOKSHELVES	Book Central: Book and Author Information
BCREEK	Blackberry Creek
BCS	Boston Computer Society
BD	Extreme Fans: Baseball Daily
BEANIE	Pangea Toy Net
BEANIE BOY	Pangea Toy Net
BEARS	Chicago Bears Football Coverage [3.0 only]
BEATCO	Beaty & Company
BEATLES ANTHOLOGY	The ABC Rock & Road Beatles Anthology
BEATY	Company Research Message Boards
BEATY & COMPANY	Beaty & Company
BEAUTIFUL	The World of Beautiful Cooking
BEAUTIFUL COOKING	The World of Beautiful Cooking
BEAUTY	Elle Magazine Online
BEAUTY 911	Style Channel
BEAVERS	Beavers: Canadian Humour With Bite [3.0 only]
BED	Bed & Breakfast U.S.A.
BED & BREAKFAST	Bed & Breakfast U.S.A.
BEE	BeeSoft
BEEPER	Consumer Electronics
BEER	Food & Drink Network
BEESOFT	BeeSoft
BEGINNER	Help Desk [Platform-dependent]
BEGINNERS	Help Desk [Platform-dependent]
BELGIUM	Belgium
BERK SYS WIN	Berkeley Systems
BERKELEY	Berkeley Systems
BERKSYS	Berkeley Systems
BERNIE	Bernie Siegel Online
BEST OF AOL	Best of America Online Showcase
BEST TIPS	Top Tips for AOL
BETA APPLY	Beta Test Application Area [May disappear without notice]
BETHEL	Bethel College and Seminary
BETHESDA	Bethesda Softworks, Inc.
BETHESDA SOFTWORKS	Bethesda Softworks, Inc.
BETHSEDA	Bethesda Softworks, Inc.
BETTER HEALTH	Better Health & Medical Forum
BETTER HEALTH BOOKS	Better Health Bookstore
BETTER LIVING	Ideas for Better Living

BEVERAGES	Everything Edible!
BEVERLY HILLS	90210 Wednesdays
BEVERLY HILLS 90210	90210 Wednesdays
BEYOND	Beyond, Inc.
BI	Gay & Lesbian Community Forum
BI TEEN	GLCF Youth Area
BI YOUTH	GLCF Youth Area
BIBLE	Religion & Beliefs: Christianity
BIC MAG	Bicycling Magazine
BICYCLE	The Bicycle Network
BICYCLING	Bicycling Magazine
BICYCLING MAGAZINE	Bicycling Magazine
BIDDLE	Christianity Online: Brother Biddle
BIG TWIN	Big Twin Online: The All-Harley Magazine
BIGFOOT	Weekly World News
BIKENET	The Bicycle Network
BILLING	Accounts and Billing*
BIOLOGY	Simon & Schuster Online: Biology Dept.
BIOSCAN	OPTIMAS Corporation
BIRD	Pet Care Forum
BIRDING	Birding Selections
BIRDS	Pet Care Forum
BISEXUAL	Gay & Lesbian Community Forum
BISEXUAL TEEN	GLCF Youth Area
BISEXUAL TRIVIA	Gay & Lesbian Community Forum: Gaymeland
BISEXUAL YOUTH	GLCF Youth Area
BIT JUGGLERS	Bit Jugglers
BIZ	The Entertainment Biz
BIZ WEEK	Business Week Online
BIZINSIDER	Herb Greenberg's Business Insider
BK	Burger King College Football
BKG	American Dialogue
BL	Buddy Lists
BLACK	Afrocentric Culture
BLACK AMERICAN	Afrocentric Culture
BLACK HERITAGE	Black History Month [May disappear without notice]
BLACK HISTORY	Black History Month [May disappear without notice]
BLACK VOICES	Orlando Sentinel Online: Black Voices
BLACK-AMERICAN	Afrocentric Culture
BLACK-VOICES	Orlando Sentinel Online: Black Voices
BLACKBERRY	Blackberry Creek
BLACKBERRY CREEK	Blackberry Creek
BLACKHAWKS	NHL Hockey
BLACKS	Afrocentric Culture
BLIND	DisABILITIES Forum
BLIZZARD	Blizzard Fun! [May disappear without notice]
BLIZZARD ENT	Blizzard Entertainment

BLOC DEVELOPMENT	TIGERDirect, Inc.
BLOCKBUSTER	Blockbuster Music's Online Store
BLUE JAYS	Major League Baseball Team: Toronto Blue Jays
BLUE RIBBON	Blue Ribbon Soundworks
BLUEPRINT	Graphsoft, Inc.
BLUES	Blues Chat
BLUES CHAT	Blues Chat
BM	Blockbuster Music's Online Store
BMUG	Berkeley Macintosh Users Group
BMX	The Bicycle Network
BOARDSAILING	Sailing Forum
BOAT	Boating Online
BOATING	Boating Selections
BOATS	The Exchange
BOB BEATY	Company Research Message Boards
BOBB	Company Research Message Boards
BOBSSOFT	Bob's Software [3.0 only]
BODY ELECTRIC	Style Channel
BOFA	Bank of America
BONJOUR	Bonjour Paris [3.0 only]
BONJOUR PARIS	Bonjour Paris [3.0 only]
BOOK	The Book Nook
BOOK BESTSELLERS	Books Area
BOOK CENTRAL	Book Central
BOOK REPORT	The Book Report
BOOKNOOK	The Book Nook
BOOKNOTES	Barrons Booknotes
BOOKS	Books Area
BOOKS & CULTURE	Christian Books & Culture
BOOKS ON BREAK	Just Books!
BOOKSHOP	Mysteries from the Yard
BOOKSTORE	Bookstores on AOL
BOSNIA	Balkan Operation Joint Endeavor
BOSOX	Major League Baseball Team: Boston Red Sox
BOSTON	Digital Cities: Boston MA
BOSTON BRUINS	NESN: New England Hockey
BOSTON CELTICS	NESN: New England Basketball
BOSTON ONLINE	Digital Cities: Boston MA
BOSTON RED SOX	Major League Baseball Team: Boston Red Sox
BOWERS	Bowers Development
BOWL	AOL Live!
BOWL GAME	Fool Bowl
BOWL GAMES	NCAA Football Bowl Info
BOWLING	The Grandstand: Other Sports
BOWLS	NCAA Football Bowl Info
BOXER	Boxer*Jam Gameshows [WAOL only]
BOXER JAM	Boxer*Jam Gameshows [WAOL only]
BOXER*JAM	Boxer*Jam Gameshows [WAOL only]
BOXING	Sports Channel
BOYS	Focus on Family: Breakaway Magazine
BP MARKETPLACE	Backpacker Online's Marketplace
BPS	BPS Software
BPS SOFTWARE	BPS Software
BRAINBUSTER	NTN's Brainbuster Trivia
BRAINSTORM	Brainstorm Products
BRAINSTORMS	Brainstorms Store
BRATS	Overseas Brats
BRAVES	Major League Baseball Team: Atlanta Braves
BRAVOS	Major League Baseball Team: Atlanta Braves
BREAKAWAY	Focus on Family: Breakaway Magazine
BREAKFAST	Bed & Breakfast U.S.A.
BREW	Food & Drink Network
BREWERS	Major League Baseball Team: Milwaukee Brewers
BREWING	Food & Drink Network
BRIDGES	The Hub: Even More Bridges of Madison County
BRINKLEY	ABC News-On-Demand
BRIO	Focus on Family: Brio Magazine
BRITISH	Genealogy Forum
BRO	Christianity Online: Brother Biddle
BROADBAND	AOL's Cable Center
BROADCAST SOFTWARE	Software Unboxed
BROADWAY	Playbill Online
BRODERBUND	Broderbund
BROKEN ARROW	Broken Arrow
BROKER	PC Financial Network: Brokerage Center [3.0 only]
BROKERAGE	PC Financial Network: Brokerage Center [3.0 only]
BRONCOS	Denver Broncos Football Coverage [3.0 only]
BROTHER BIDDLE	Christianity Online: Brother Biddle
BROWSER FIX	AOL 2.6 for Macintosh* [MAOL only]
BRUINS	NHL Hockey
BRUINS HOCKEY	NESN: New England Hockey
BRYAN	Digital Cities: Waco/Temple/Bryan TX
BRYAN DC	Digital Cities: Waco/Temple/Bryan TX
BRYAN DCITY	Digital Cities: Waco/Temple/Bryan TX
BRYAN DIGC	Digital Cities: Waco/Temple/Bryan TX
BRYAN DIGITAL CITY	Digital Cities: Waco/Temple/Bryan TX
BRYAN TX	Digital Cities: Waco/Temple/Bryan TX
BRYCE	MetaTools, Inc.
BS FORUM	Business Strategies Forum
BT	Big Twin Online: The All-Harley Magazine
BUCKEYES	AOL College Football '96 [3.0 only]
BUCS	Major League Baseball Team: Pittsburgh Pirates
BUDDHA	The Buddhism Forum
BUDDHISM	The Buddhism Forum
BUDDHIST	The Buddhism Forum
BUDDIES	Buddy Lists

BUDDY	Buddy Lists
BUDDY LIST	Buddy Lists
BUDDY LISTS	Buddy Lists
BUDDY MAIN	Buddy Lists
BUDDY VIEW	Buddy View
BUFFALO	Digital Cities: Buffalo NY
BUFFALO DC	Digital Cities: Buffalo NY
BUFFALO DCITY	Digital Cities: Buffalo NY
BUFFALO DIGC	Digital Cities: Buffalo NY
BUFFALO DIGITAL CITY	Digital Cities: Buffalo NY
BUFFALO NY	Digital Cities: Buffalo
BUFFALOES	AOL College Football '96 [3.0 only]
BUILDING	HouseNet
BULGARIA	Bulgaria
BULL	Merrill Lynch
BULL MOOSE	Bull Moose Tavern
BUNGIE	Bungie Software
BURGER KING	Burger King College Football
BUS	AOL Roadtrips [3.0 only]
BUSINESS	Business News Area
BUSINESS CENTER	Your Business
BUSINESS FORUM	Applications/Business Forum [Platform-dependent]
BUSINESS INSIDER	The Business Insider
BUSINESS KNOW HOW	Business Strategies Forum
BUSINESS LUNCH	Your Business Lunch
BUSINESS NEWS	Business News area
BUSINESS RANKINGS	Business Rankings
BUSINESS RESOURCES	Hoover's Business Resources
BUSINESS SCHOOL	Kaplan Online or The Princeton Review
BUSINESS SENSE	Business Sense
BUSINESS STRATEGIES	Business Strategies Forum
BUSINESS WEEK	Business Week Online
BUZZSAW	Buzzsaw
BV	Buddy View
BV CHAT	Orlando Sentinel Online: Black Voices' Chat
BV GAY	Black Voices: Ebony Gay & Lesbian
BW	Business Week Online
BW ONLINE	Business Week Online
BW SEARCH	Business Week: Search
BWOL	Motley Fool: The Fool Dome
BYTE	ByteWorks
BYTE BY BYTE	Byte By Byte Corporation
BYTEWORKS	ByteWorks
C	Development Forum [Platform-dependent]
C!	Computers & Software channel [Platform-dependent]
C&S	Computers & Software channel [Platform-dependent]

CA	Crossword America
CABLE	AOL's Cable Center
CABLE MODEM	AOL's Cable Center
CABLE NEWS	New England Cable News
CAD	CAD Resource Center
CADILLAC	Cadillac WWW Home Page
CAFFE STARBUCKS	Caffe Starbucks
CALENDAR	What's Hot in Computing [Platform-dependent]
CALENDAR GIRLS	The Hub: Calendar Girls
CALIFORNIA ANGELS	Major League Baseball Team: California Angels
CALL	Accessing America Online*
CALLISTO	Callisto Corporation
CAMERA	Photography Selections
CAMERAS	Popular Photography Online
CAMEROON	Cameroon
CAMPAIGN 96	The Campaign Trail
CAMPING	Backpacker Magazine
CAMPUS	Online Campus
CAMPUS LIFE	Campus Life Magazine
CAN'T SLEEP	The Late Night Survey
CANADA	AOL Canada
CANADA CHAT	AOL Canada: Chat
CANADIAN	AOL Canada
CANADIENS	NHL Hockey
CANCEL	Cancel Account*
CANCELLED TV SHOWS	Lost & Found TV Shows
CANCER	Cancer Forum
CANCER J SCIAM	Cancer Journal from Scientific American
CANCER JOURNAL	Cancer Journal from Scientific American
CANINE	Hobby Central: Pets & Animals
CANNES	Cannes Film Festival
CANT SLEEP	The Late Night Survey
CANUKS	NHL Hockey
CANVAS	Deneba Software
CAPITAL	Politics
CAPITAL CONNECTION	Politics
CAPITALS	Washington Capitals
CAPS	Washington Capitals
CAPSTONE	Capstone Software
CAR	Car/Cycle Selections
CAR AND DRIVER	Car and Driver Magazine
CAR INFO	AutoVantage: New Car Summary
CAR PHOTOS	Wheels Exchange
CAR SUMMARY	AutoVantage: New Car Summary
CARD	AOL Visa Card
CARDINAL	Cardinal Technologies, Inc.
CARDINALS	Major League Baseball Team: St. Louis Cardinals
CARDS	Hallmark Connections
CAREER	Career Selections

CAREER NEWS	USA Today Industry Watch section
CAREERS	Career Selections
CAROLE 2000	Astronet
CARPENTRY	HouseNet
CARS	Car/Cycle Selections
CARTOON NETWORK	Cartoon Network
CARTOONS	The Cartoons Forum
CASADY	Casady & Greene
CASCOLY	Cascoly Software [3.0 only]
CASINO	RabbitJack's Casino
CASTING	Casting Central
CASTING CENTRAL	Casting Central
CASTING FORUM	Casting Central
CAT	Pet Care Forum
CATHOLIC	Catholic Community
CATHOLIC NEWS	Catholic News Service
CATHOLIC NEWS SERVICE	Catholic News Service
CATHOLIC REPORTER	National Catholic Reporter
CATS	Pet Care Forum
CAVALIERS	AOL College Football '96 [3.0 only]
CB	College Board
CBD	Commerce Business Daily
CC	Computing Company Connection
CC MAG	Christian Computing Magazine
CCB	Chicago Online: Crain's Chicago Business
CCC	Computing Company Connection
CCCS	Consumer Credit Counseling Service of Sacramento
CCDA	Christian Community Development Association
CCE	Columbia Encyclopedia
CCG	Christian College Guide
CCGF	Collectible Card Games Forum
CCI	Christian Camping International
CDN	AOL Canada
CDS	Stereo Review Online
CE	Consumer Electronics
CE SOFTWARE	CE Software
CEC	Christian Education Center
CELEBRITIES	Style Channel
CELEBRITY	The Hub: Celebrity Sightings
CELEBRITY CIRCLE	Oldsmobile/Celebrity Circle
CELEBRITY COOKBOOK	Celebrity Cookbook
CELLULAR	Consumer Electronics
CELLULAR PHONE	Consumer Electronics
CELTICS	NESN: New England Basketball
CELTICS BASKETBALL	NESN: New England Basketball
CENTER STAGE	AOL Live!
CENTRAL	Symantec
CENTRAL POINT	Symantec
CENTURA	Centura Bank [3.0 only]
CENTURY	Twentieth Century Mutual Funds
CENTURY FUNDS	Twentieth Century Mutual Funds
CEP	Council on Economic Priorities
CEREBRAL PALSY	United Cerebral Palsy Association
CF	CultureFinder
CG	Computer Gaming World
CGW	Computer Gaming World
CH	Christian History Magazine
CH PRODUCTS	CH Products
CHALLENGER	Challenger Remembered
CHAMPION	One Hanes Place
CHANGE PASSWORD	Change your password*
CHANGE PROFILE	Edit your member profile
CHANNEL 1	Channel One Network Online
CHANNEL C	CNN Newsroom Online [MAOL only]
CHANNEL ONE	Channel One Network Online
CHANNEL ZERO	The Hub: Channel Zero
CHARITY	access.point
CHARTER	Charter Schools Forum
CHARTER SCHOOL	Charter Schools Forum
CHARTER SCHOOLS	Charter Schools Forum
CHARTOMATIC	Chart-O-Matic: Auto Stock Charting [3.0 only]
CHAT	People Connection Channel
CHEERLEADING	The Grandstand's Cheerleading Area
CHEESECAKE	Eli's Cheesecakes
CHEESECAKES	Eli's Cheesecakes
CHEF	Everything Edible!
CHEF'S CATALOG	Chef's Catalog
CHEFS	Everything Edible!
CHEFS CATALOG	Chef's Catalog
CHENA	Chena Software
CHESS	Strategy & Wargaming Forum
CHICAGO	Chicago Online
CHICAGO CUBS	Major League Baseball Team: Chicago Cubs
CHICAGO ONLINE	Chicago Online
CHICAGO SYMPHONY	Chicago Symphony Orchestra Online
CHICAGO TRIBUNE	Chicago Tribune
CHICO	California State University
CHILD SAFETY	Child Safety Brochure
CHILDREN'S HEALTH	Children's Health Forum
CHILDREN'S SOFTWARE	HomePC Magazine: Children's Software
CHINCHILLA	Pet Care Forum
CHINESE ASTROLOGY	Astronet
CHIP	ChipNet Online
CHIPNET	ChipNet Online
CHOCOLATE	The Health Zone
CHOOSE	MTV Online: Choose or Lose 1996
CHOOSE A SPORT	Choose a Sport on AOL

CHOOSE OR LOSE	MTV Online: Choose or Lose 1996
CHRIST	Christianity Online
CHRISTIAN	Religion & Ethics Forum
CHRISTIAN CAMPING	Christian Camping International
CHRISTIAN COLLEGES	Christian College Guide
CHRISTIAN COMPUTING	Christian Computing Magazine
CHRISTIAN CONNECTION	Christianity Online Chat & Live Events
CHRISTIAN EDUCATION	Christian Education Center
CHRISTIAN FAMILIES	Christianity Online: Marriage/Family Forum
CHRISTIAN FAMILY	Christianity Online: Marriage/Family Forum
CHRISTIAN HISTORY	Christian History Magazine
CHRISTIAN KID	Christianity Online: Kids
CHRISTIAN KIDS	Christianity Online: Kids
CHRISTIAN MAN	Christianity Online: Men
CHRISTIAN MEDIA	Christian Media Source
CHRISTIAN MEN	Christianity Online: Men
CHRISTIAN PRODUCTS	Christian Products Center
CHRISTIAN READER	Christian Reader
CHRISTIAN SINGLES	Christianity Online: Singles
CHRISTIAN STUDENT	Christianity Online: Campus Life's Student Hangout
CHRISTIAN STUDENTS	Christianity Online: Campus Life's Student Hangout
CHRISTIAN WOMAN	Christianity Online: Women
CHRISTIAN WOMEN	Christianity Online: Women
CHRISTIANITY	Christianity Online
CHRISTIANITY TODAY	Christianity Today
CHROL CHAT	Christianity Online Chat & Live Events
CHROL CLASSIFIEDS	Christianity Online Classifieds
CHROL RESOURCES	Christian Resource Center
CHURCH LEADERS	Christianity Online: Church Leaders Network
CHURCH LEADERS NETWORK	Christianity Online: Church Leaders Network
CIGAR	Food & Drink Network
CIGARS	Food & Drink Network
CINCINNATI REDS	Major League Baseball Team: Cincinnati Reds
CINDY	Cindy Adams: Queen of Gourmet Gossip
CINDY ADAMS	Cindy Adams: Queen of Gourmet Gossip
CINEMA	@the.movies
CINEMAN	Movie Review Database
CINEMAN SYNDICATE	Movie Review Database
CIS	Virtual Refugees Forum
CITIBANK	The Apple Citibank Visa Card
CITIZEN	access.point
CITY WEB	City Web
CIVIC	access.point
CIVIL LIBERTIES	American Civil Liberties Union
CIVIL WAR	The Civil War Forum
CJ CONTESTS	CyberJustice Contests
CJNOYESSW	Christopher J. Noyes Software [3.0 only]
CL	Campus Life Magazine
CLARIS	Claris
CLASSES	Online Campus
CLASSICAL	Classical Music Forum
CLASSICAL MUSIC	CultureFinder
CLASSIFIED	AOL Classifieds
CLASSIFIEDS	AOL Classifieds
CLASSIFIEDS ONLINE	AOL Classifieds
CLASSROOM	President's Day [May disappear without notice]
CLEARANCE	The Fragrance Counter: Clearance Counter
CLEVELAND INDIANS	Major League Baseball Team: Cleveland Indians
CLICK HERE	The Hub: Click Here
CLIFE	Computer Life Magazine
CLINTON	White House Forum
CLN	Christianity Online: Church Leaders Network
CLOCK	Time of day and length of time online
CLOTHES	Elle Magazine Online
CLOTHING	Elle Magazine Online
CLS	Christianity Online Classifieds
CLUB KIDSOFT	Club KidSoft
CLUBS	Life, Styles & Interests Channel
CLUBS & INTERNET	Life, Styles & Interests' Top Internet Sites
CM	Christian Ministries Center
CMC	Creative Musician's Coalition
CMIL	University of California Extension
CMS	Christian Media Source
CMT	Coda Music Tech
CN	Christianity Online Newsstand
CNEWS	Christianity Online Newsstand
CNFA	The Grandstand's Simulation Football
CNN	CNN Newsroom Online
CNN GUIDES	CNN Newsroom Online
CNN NEWSROOM	CNN Newsroom Online
CNS	Catholic News Service
CO ASSOCIATIONS	Christianity Online: Associations & Interests
CO CLASSIFIEDS	Christianity Online Classifieds
CO CONTEST	Christianity Online: Contest
CO FAMILIES	Christianity Online: Marriage/Family Forum
CO FAMILY	Christianity Online: Marriage/Family Forum
CO HOLIDAY	Christianity Online: Holidays and COntests
CO HOLIDAYS	Christianity Online: Holidays and COntests
CO INTERESTS	Christianity Online: Associations & Interests
CO KIDS	Christianity Online: Kids
CO LIVE	Christianity Online Chat & Live Events
CO MAN	Christianity Online: Men
CO MEN	Christianity Online: Men
CO NEWS	Christianity Online Newsstand
CO SINGLE	Christianity Online: Singles
CO SINGLES	Christianity Online: Singles

CO STUDENT	Christianity Online: Campus Life's Student Hangout
CO STUDENTS	Christianity Online: Campus Life's Student Hangout
CO TEEN	Christianity Online: Campus Life's Student Hangout
CO TEENS	Christianity Online: Campus Life's Student Hangout
CO WOMAN	Christianity Online: Women
CO WOMEN	Christianity Online: Women
CO YOUTH	Christianity Online: Campus Life's Student Hangout
COBB	The Cobb Group Online
COBB GROUP	The Cobb Group Online
CODA	Coda Music Tech
CODA MUSIC	Coda Music Tech
COINS	The Exchange
COL	Chicago Online
COL BUSINESS	Chicago Online: Business Guide
COL CALENDAR	Chicago Online: Calendar & Almanac
COL CHAT	Chicago Online: Chat
COL EDUCATE	Chicago Online: Education Guide
COL EDUCATION	Chicago Online: Education Guide
COL ENTERTAINMENT	Chicago Tribune: Local Entertainment Guide
COL FILES	Chicago Online: Libraries
COL GOVERNMENT	Chicago Tribune: Election '96
COL GOVT	Chicago Tribune: Election '96
COL LIFESTYLES	Chicago Online: Lifestyles
COL MALL	Chicago Online: Mall
COL MARKETPLACE	Chicago Online: Marketplace
COL MEDIA	Chicago Online: Media Guide
COL NEWS	Chicago Online: News, Business & Weather
COL PLANNER	Chicago Online: Planner
COL SPORTS	Chicago Online: Sports
COL TECH	Chicago Online: Technology Guide
COL TICKET	Chicago Online: Ticketmaster
COL TRAFFIC	Chicago Tribune: Traffic Updates
COL VISITOR	Chicago Online: Visitor Guide
COLISEUM	AOL Live!
COLLECT	Collectibles Online
COLLECT CARDS	Collectible Card Games Forum
COLLECTIBLES	Collectibles Online
COLLECTIBLES ONLINE	Collectibles Online
COLLECTING	Wizard World
COLLECTOR	The Exchange
COLLEGE	College Selections
COLLEGE BOARD	College Board
COLLEGE FOOTBALL	AOL College Football '96 [3.0 only]
COLLEGE HOOPS	Extreme Fans: College Hoops
COLLEGE ONLINE	Simon & Schuster College Online
COLLEGIATE	Merriam-Webster's Collegiate Dictionary
COLLEGIATE DICTIONARY	Merriam-Webster's Collegiate Dictionary
COLOGNE	The Fragrance Counter
COLOR IMAGING	Advanced Color Imaging Forum
COLOR WEATHERMAPS	Main Weather Area
COLORADO ROCKIES	Major League Baseball Team: Colorado Rockies
COLUMBIA	Columbia Encyclopedia
COLUMBIA.NET	Columbia's Health Today
COLUMBIA/HCA	Columbia's Health Today
COLUMBIANET	Columbia's Health Today
COLUMNISTS	Columnists & Features Online
COLUMNS	Columnists & Features Online
COM FED BANK	Commercial Federal Bank [3.0 only]
COMEDY	The Comedy Pub
COMEDY PUB	The Comedy Pub
COMIC STRIP	Comic Strip Centennial
COMICS	Comics Selection
COMMANDO	Kim Komando's Komputer Clinic
COMMERCE	Commerce Bank [3.0 only]
COMMON GROUND	Common Ground Software
COMMUNICATIONS	Communications Forum [Platform-dependent]
COMMUNITIES	The Exchange: Communities Center
COMMUNITY	access.point
COMMUNITY CENTER	Life, Styles & Interests Channel
COMMUNITY UPDATE	Community Update Letter*
COMP SITES	Computing Internet Sites
COMP SPOT	What's Hot in Computing & Software [Platform-dependent]
COMPANIES	Computing Company Connection
COMPANY	Company Research
COMPANY 3DO	The 3DO Company
COMPANY NEWS	Company News
COMPANY PROFILES	Hoover's Handbook of Company Profiles
COMPANY RESEARCH	Company Research
COMPANY UPDATES	Hoover's Company Masterlist
COMPAQ	Compaq
COMPASS	Compass Bank [3.0 only]
COMPOSER	Composer's Coffeehouse
COMPOSER'S	Composer's Coffeehouse
COMPOSERS	Composer's Coffeehouse
COMPTONS	Compton's NewMedia Forum
COMPTONS ENCYCLOPEDIA	Compton's Living Encyclopedia
COMPTONS SOFTWARE	Compton's Software Library
COMPU SCHOOL	CompuSchool
COMPUADD	CompuAdd
COMPUKIDS	Compukids

COMPUSERVE	Virtual Refugees Forum
COMPUSPOOK	Dastardly Downloads [May disappear without notice]
COMPUSTORE	Shopper's Advantage Online
COMPUTER	Computers & Software channel [Platform-dependent]
COMPUTER AMERICA	Craig Crossman's Computer America
COMPUTER FORUM	Computers & Software channel [Platform-dependent]
COMPUTER GAMES	Hecklers Online
COMPUTER GAMING	Computer Gaming World
COMPUTER GAMING WORLD	Computer Gaming World
COMPUTER LAW	CyberLaw/Cyberlex
COMPUTER LIFE	Computer Life Magazine
COMPUTER NEWS	Newsbytes
COMPUTER PERIPHERALS	Computer Peripherals, Inc.
COMPUTER TERMS	Dictionary of Computer Terms
COMPUTING	Computers & Software channel [Platform-dependent]
COMPUTING AND SOFTWARE	Computers & Software channel [Platform-dependent]
COMPUTING DEPT	Computing & Software (Old Style) [MAOL 2.7 or earlier]
COMPUTING FORUMS	Computers & Software channel [Platform-dependent]
COMPUTING LIFESTYLES	Family Computing Forum: Lifestyles & Computing
COMPUTING NEWS	Computing News [MAOL only]
COMPUTING SITES	Computing Internet Sites
COMPUTOON	CompuToon area
CON	Christianity Online: Contest
CONCERTS	MusicSpace: Concerts
CONFERENCE	Computing Forum Chats and Conferences
CONFIG	Tune Up Your PC
CONGRESS	Politics Forum
CONGRESSIONAL	Congressional Quarterly
CONNECTING	Accessing America Online*
CONNECTION	Intel Corporation
CONNECTIX	Connectix
CONSPIRACY	Parascope
CONSUMER	Consumer Reports
CONSUMER ELECTRONICS	Consumer Electronics
CONSUMER REPORTS	Consumer Reports
CONSUMERS	Consumer Reports
CONTACTS	Employer Contacts Database
CONTEST	AOL Contest Area
CONTEST AREA	AOL Contest Area
CONTEST CENTRAL	Family Computing Forum: Contest Central
CONTESTS	AOL Contest Area

COOK	Everything Edible!
COOKBOOK	Celebrity Cookbook
COOKING	Everything Edible!
COOKING CLUB	Cooking Club
COOKS	Everything Edible!
COOPER	JLCooper Electronics
CORBIS	Corbis Media
CORBIS MEDIA	Corbis Media
CORCORAN	Corcoran School of Art
COREL	Corel Special Interest Group
CORELDRAW	Corel Special Interest Group
CORESTATES	Core States Bank & NJ National Bank [3.0 only]
CORKSCREWED	Corkscrewed Online
CORNER	Pro's Corner
CORNHUSKERS	AOL College Football '96 [3.0 only]
CORPORATE PROFILES	Hoover's Handbook of Company Profiles
COSA	AfterEffects
COSTAR	CoStar
COTTONWOOD	Cottonwood Sofware [3.0 only]
COUNTDOWN	NTN Trivia
COUNTRIES	The World
COUNTRY	Country Music Forum
COURSES	Online Courses
COURSEWARE	Electronic Courseware
COURT TV	Court TV's Law Center
COURTROOM TELEVISION	Court TV's Law Center
COURTS	CyberJustice's Courts of Karmic Justice
COW	Christianity Online: Women
COWBOYS	Dallas Cowboys Football Coverage [3.0 only]
COWLES	Cowles/SIMBA Media Information Network
COWLES SIMBA	Cowles/SIMBA Media Information Network
COYOTES	NHL Hockey
CP&B	Computing Print & Broadcast
CPB	Computing Print & Broadcast
CPC	Christian Products Center
CPI	Computer Peripherals, Inc.
CPS	Symantec
CQ	Congressional Quarterly
CR	Christian Reader
CRAFTS	Craft Selections
CRAIG CROSSMAN	Craig Crossman's Computer America
CRAIN'S	Chicago Online: Crain's Chicago Business
CRAIN'S SMALL BIZ	Chicago Online: Crain's Small Business
CRAINS	Chicago Online: Crain's Chicago Business
CRASH	Flight Sim Resource Center
CRAZY HORSE	Rockline Online
CRC	Family Computing: Maximum AOL
CREATE	PC Graphic Creation Station

CREATION	PC Graphic Creation Station
CREDIT	Credit Request Form for connect problems*
CREDIT REQUEST	Credit Request Form for connect problems*
CREED	Religion & Ethics Forum
CRESTAR	Crestar Bank [3.0 only]
CRIMINAL JUSTICE	Simon & Schuster Online: Criminal Justice Dept.
CRIMSON TIDE	AOL College Football '96 [3.0 only]
CRISPY	Pangea Toy Net
CRITIC	Critic's Choice
CRITICS	Critic's Choice
CRITICS CHOICE	Critic's Choice
CROATIA	Croatia
CROSSDRESSER	Transgender Community Forum
CROSSDRESSING	Transgender Community Forum
CROSSMAN	Craig Crossman's Computer America
CROSSWORD	The New York Times Crosswords
CROSSWORDS	The New York Times Crosswords
CRUISE	Cruise Critic
CRUISE CRITIC	Cruise Critic
CRUISE CRITICS	Cruise Critic
CRUISES	Cruise Critic
CRUSADE	Avon's Breast Cancer Awareness Crusade Online
CRYSTAL	Crystal Dynamics
CRYSTAL BALL	The Crystal Ball Forum
CS	AOL Live!
CS HOT	What's Hot in Computing & Software [Platform-dependent]
CSB	Chicago Online: Crain's Small Business
CSLIVE	Member Services*
CSMITH	CyberSmith
CSPAN	C-SPAN
CSPAN BUS	C-SPAN in the Classroom
CSPAN CLASS	C-SPAN in the Classroom
CSPAN CLASSROOM	C-SPAN in the Classroom
CSPAN ONLINE	C-SPAN
CSPAN SCHOOLS	C-SPAN in the Classroom
CSUC	California State University
CT	Christianity Today
CTSOFTWARE	CT Software
CUBBIES	Major League Baseball Team: Chicago Cubs
CUBS	Major League Baseball Team: Chicago Cubs
CULTUREFINDER	CultureFinder
CURRICULUM	Assoc. for Supervisor & Curriculum Development
CUSTOMER SERVICE	Member Services*
CUTTING EDGE	NESN: New England Hockey
CW	Cycle World Online

CWUG	ClarisWorks User Group
CYBER 24	24 Hours in Cyberspace
CYBERCAFE	CyberSmith
CYBERCAMP	Summer Cyber Camp
CYBERJUSTICE	CyberJustice
CYBERLAW	CyberLaw/CyberLex
CYBERLEX	CyberLaw/CyberLex
CYBERLOVE & LAUGHTER	Cyberlove & Laughter
CYBERSALON	Cybersalon
CYBERSERIALS	Cyberserials
CYBERSLIM	The Health Zone
CYBERSMITH	CyberSmith
CYBERSOAP	Cyberserials
CYBERSOAPS	Cyberserials
CYBERSPORTS	The Grandstand's Fantasy & Simulation Leagues
CYBERVIEW	This Week's Best Cyberviews
CYBERVIEWS	This Week's Best Cyberviews
CYBERZINES	Digizine Sites on the Web
CYCLE	Cycle World Online
CYCLE WORLD	Cycle World Online
CYCLING	Cycle World Online
CYMRU	Virtual Wales [3.0 only]
CYRANO	The Hub: Cyrano
CZECH REPUBLIC	Czech Republic
DACEASY	DacEasy, Inc.
DAD	AOL Families
DADS	AOL Families
DAILY	Reference Daily Dose
DAILY FIX	The Daily Fix
DAILY LIVING	Daily Living
DALAI LAMA	Dalai Lama Conference [May disappear without notice]
DALLAS	Digital Cities: Dallas-Ft. Worth TX
DALLAS DIGC	Digital Cities: Dallas-Ft. WorthTX
DALLAS DIGITAL CITY	Digital Cities: Dallas-Ft. Worth TX
DAN HURLEY	Amazing Instant Novelist
DANCE	Dance SelEctions
DANISH	Genealogy Forum
DARK SKIES	Parascope: Dark Skies
DATABASE	Database Support Special Interest Group
DATABASES	Database Support Special Interest Group
DATADESK	Datadesk
DATAPACK	DataPak Software
DATAPAK	DataPak Software
DATAWATCH	Datawatch
DATE	Love@AOL
DATING	Romance Connection
DATING SERVICE	Love@AOL

DATING SERVICES	Love@AOL
DAVE	Dave Letterman's Late Show Online [3.0 only]
DAVID LETTERMAN	Dave Letterman's Late Show Online [3.0 only]
DAVIDSON	Davidson & Associates
DAY ONE	ABC News-On-Demand
DAYNA	Dayna Communications
DAYO	DAYO Software
DAYTIMER	DayTimer Technologies
DAYTON	Digital Cities: Dayton OH
DAYTON DC	Digital Cities: Dayton OH
DAYTON DCITY	Digital Cities: Dayton OH
DAYTON DIGC	Digital Cities: Dayton OH
DAYTON DIGITAL CITY	Digital Cities: Dayton OH
DAYTON OH	Digital Cities: Dayton OH
DC	Digital City or DC Comics
DC ALASKA	Digital Cities: Alaska
DC ALBANY	Digital Cities: Albany NY
DC ALBUQUERQUE	Digital Cities: Albuquerque/Santa Fe NM
DC ATLANTA	Digital Cities: Atlanta GA
DC AUSTIN	Digital Cities: Austin TX
DC BAY CITY	Digital Cities: Bay City MI
DC BRYAN	Digital Cities: Waco/Temple/Bryan TX
DC BUFFALO	Digital Cities: Buffalo NY
DC CHAT	DC Comics Online: Chat Rooms
DC COMICS	DC Comics Online
DC COMICS ONLINE	DC Comics Online
DC DALLAS	Digital Cities: Dallas-Ft. Worth TX
DC DAYTON	Digital Cities: Dayton OH
DC DENVER	Digital Cities: Denver CO
DC DETROIT	Digital Cities: Detroit
DC EL PASO	Digital Cities: El Paso
DC EUGENE	Digital Cities: Eugene
DC EVENT	Digital City: The Event Source
DC FLINT	Digital Cities: Flint
DC FORT WORTH	Digital Cities: Dallas-Ft. Worth
DC FRESNO	Digital Cities: Fresno/Visalia CA
DC FT LAUDERDALE	Digital Cities: Miami-Ft. Lauderdale
DC FT MYERS	Digital Cities: Ft. Myers/Naples FL
DC FUN	Digital City: Entertainment
DC HOTLANTA	Digital Cities: Atlanta
DC HOUSTON	Digital Cities: Houston
DC JOIN	Register as a Digital Citizen
DC LA	Digital Cities: Los Angeles
DC LOS ANGELES	Digital Cities: Los Angeles
DC MARKETPLACE	Digital City: Marketplace
DC MIDWEST	Digital Cities: Midwest
DC MINNEAPOLIS	Digital Cities: Minneapolis-St. Paul
DC NAPLES	Digital Cities: Ft. Myers/Naples FL
DC NEW BEDFORD	Digital Cities: New Bedford Massachusetts
DC NEW ORLEANS	Digital Cities: New Orleans Louisiana
DC NEWPORT NEWS	Digital Cities: Newport News and Norfolk
DC NEWS	Digital City: News/Weather
DC PEOPLE	Digital City: People
DC PHILA	Digital Cities: Philadelphia
DC PHILADELPHIA	Digital Cities: Philadelphia
DC PHILLY	Digital Cities: Philadelphia
DC RENO	Digital Cities: Reno
DC SAGINAW	Digital Cities: Saginaw
DC SAN DIEGO	Digital Cities: San Diego CA
DC SAN FRANCISCO	Digital Cities: San Francisco CA
DC SANTA FE	Digital Cities: Albuquerque/Santa Fe NM
DC SD	Digital Cities: San Diego CA
DC SEATTLE	Digital Cities: Seattle/Tacoma WA
DC SF	Digital Cities: San Francisco CA
DC SOUTH	Digital Cities: South
DC SPORTS	Digital City: Sports
DC ST PAUL	Digital Cities: Minneapolis-St. Paul
DC ST PETERSBURG	Digital Cities: Tampa-St. Petersburg
DC TAMPA	Digital Cities: Tampa-St. Petersburg
DC TEMPLE	Digital Cities: Waco/Temple/Bryan TX
DC TORONTO	Digital Cities: Toronto
DC TULSA	Digital Cities: Tulsa OK
DC VISALIA	Digital Cities: Fresno/Visalia CA
DC WACO	Digital Cities: Waco/Temple/Bryan TX
DC WEB	City Web
DC WEST	Digital Cities: West
DCI CHAT	The Discovery Channel: Chat
DCITY ALASKA	Digital Cities: Alaska
DCITY ALBANY	Digital Cities: Albany NY
DCITY ALBUQUERQUE	Digital Cities: Albuquerque/Santa Fe NM
DCITY AUSTIN	Digital Cities: Austin TX
DCITY BAY CITY	Digital Cities: Bay City MI
DCITY BRYAN	Digital Cities: Waco/Temple/Bryan TX
DCITY BUFFALO	Digital Cities: Buffalo NY
DCITY DAYTON	Digital Cities: Dayton OH
DCITY EL PASO	Digital Cities: El Paso
DCITY EUGENE	Digital Cities: Eugene
DCITY FLINT	Digital Cities: Flint
DCITY FRESNO	Digital Cities: Fresno/Visalia CA
DCITY FT MYERS	Digital Cities: Ft. Myers/Naples FL
DCITY NAPLES	Digital Cities: Ft. Myers/Naples FL
DCITY NATIONAL	Digital City
DCITY NEW BEDFORD	Digital Cities: New Bedford Massachusetts
DCITY NEW ORLEANS	Digital Cities: New Orleans LA
DCITY NEWPORT NEWS	Digital Cities: Newport News and Norfolk
DCITY NORFOLK	Digital Cities: Newport News and Norfolk
DCITY RENO	Digital Cities: Reno
DCITY SAGINAW	Digital Cities: Saginaw

DCITY SANTA FE	Digital Cities: Albuquerque/Santa Fe NM
DCITY TEMPLE	Digital Cities: Waco/Temple/Bryan TX
DCITY TULSA	Digital Cities: Tulsa OK
DCITY VISALIA	Digital Cities: Fresno/Visalia CA
DCITY WACO	Digital Cities: Waco/Temple/Bryan TX
DCL	Dictionary of Cultural Literacy
DCN	Digital City
DCNATIONAL	Digital City
DD	Dial/Data
DEAD	Grateful Dead Forum
DEAD END	The Dead End of the Internet [3.0 only]
DEADLY	Deadly Games
DEAF	Deaf & Hard of Hearing Forum
DEAR DOTTI	Weekly World News
DEBATE	Politics
DEC	Digital Equipment Corporation
DECISION	Decision Point Forum
DECISION 94	The Campaign Trail
DECISION POINT	Decision Point Forum
DECORATING	Home Magazine Online
DEFENSE	Military City Online
DELL	Dell Computer Corporation
DELRINA	Symantec
DELTA	Delta Tao
DELTA POINT	Delta Point
DELTA TAO	Delta Tao
DEMOCRACY	CNN Newsroom Online
DEMOCRAT	Democratic Party Online
DEMOCRATS	Democratic Party Online
DEMS	Democratic Party Online
DENEBA	Deneba Software
DENMARK	Denmark
DENOMINATION	Religion & Ethics Forum
DENVER	Digital Cities: Denver CO
DENVER DIGC	Digital Cities: Denver CO
DENVER DIGITAL CITY	Digital Cities: Denver CO
DEPARTMENT 56	Department 56 Collecting
DEPENDENCY	Dependency and Recovery Issues
DEPIXION	InToon with the News
DEPT 56	Department 56 Collecting
DES	DeskMate
DESIGN	Elle Magazine Online
DESIGN SIG	Design Special Interest Group
DESIGNER	Design Special Interest Group
DESIGNER STUDIO	Style Channel
DESIGNERS	Elle Magazine Online
DESK REFERENCE	NY Public Library Desk Reference
DESKMATE	DeskMate
DESKTOP CINEMA	Desktop Cinema*
DESKTOP PUBLISHING	Desktop and Web Publishing area [Platform-dependent]
DESTINATION EUROPE	Destination Europe
DETROIT	Digital Cities: Detroit
DETROIT DIGC	Digital Cities: Detroit
DETROIT DIGITAL CITY	Digital Cities: Detroit
DETROIT TIGERS	Major League Baseball Team: Detroit Tigers
DEV	Development Forum [Platform-dependent]
DEVELOPER	Development Forum [Platform-dependent]
DEVELOPERS STUDIO	Developers Studio
DEVELOPMENT	Development Forum [Platform-dependent]
DEVELOPMENT FORUM	Development Forum [Platform-dependent]
DEVILS	NHL Hockey
DF	The Daily Fix
DF FOOD	Destination Florida: Restaurants and Nightlife
DF OUT	Destination Florida: Outdoors
DF PARKS	Destination Florida: Attractions
DF ROOMS	Destination Florida: Places to Stay
DF SHOP	Destination Florida: Shopping
DF SPACE	Destination Florida: Kennedy Space Center
DF SPORTS	Destination Florida: Sports
DF TICKET	Destination Florida: Ticketmaster
DG	Heckers Online: Digital Graffiti
DI	Disney Interactive
DIABETES	American Diabetes Association
DIAL	Dial/Data
DIALOGUE	American Dialogue
DIAMOND	Diamond Computer Systems
DIAMOND COMPUTERS	Diamond Computer Systems
DICTIONARY	Dictionary Selections
DIG CITY	Digital City
DIG CITY NATIONAL	Digital City
DIG CITY PHILLY	Digital Cities: Philadelphia
DIG CITY USA	Digital City
DIGC	Digital City
DIGC ALASKA	Digital Cities: Alaska
DIGC ALBANY	Digital Cities: Albany NY
DIGC ALBUQUERQUE	Digital Cities: Albuquerque/Santa Fe NM
DIGC ATLANTA	Digital Cities: Atlanta GA
DIGC AUSTIN	Digital Cities: Austin TX
DIGC BAY CITY	Digital Cities: Bay City MI
DIGC BRYAN	Digital Cities: Waco/Temple/Bryan TX
DIGC BUFFALO	Digital Cities: Buffalo NY
DIGC DAYTON	Digital Cities: Dayton OH
DIGC DENVER	Digital Cities: Denver CO
DIGC DETROIT	Digital Cities: Detroit
DIGC EL PASO	Digital Cities: El Paso
DIGC EUGENE	Digital Cities: Eugene
DIGC FLINT	Digital Cities: Flint

DIGC FRESNO	Digital Cities: Fresno/Visalia CA
DIGC FT LAUDERDALE	Digital Cities: Miami-Ft. Lauderdale
DIGC FT MYERS	Digital Cities: Ft. Myers/Naples FL
DIGC FT WORTH	Digital Cities: Dallas-Ft. Worth
DIGC HOTLANTA	Digital Cities: Atlanta
DIGC HOUSTON	Digital Cities: Houston
DIGC LA	Digital Cities: Los Angeles
DIGC LOS ANGELES	Digital Cities: Los Angeles
DIGC MIAMI	Digital Cities: Miami-Ft. Lauderdale
DIGC MIDWEST	Digital Cities: Midwest
DIGC MINNEAPOLIS	Digital Cities: Minneapolis-St. Paul
DIGC NAPLES	Digital Cities: Ft. Myers/Naples FL
DIGC NEW BEDFORD	Digital Cities: New Bedford Massachusetts
DIGC NEW ORLEANS	Digital Cities: New Orleans LA
DIGC NEWPORT NEWS	Digital Cities: Newport News and Norfolk
DIGC PHILA	Digital Cities: Philadelphia
DIGC PHILADELPHIA	Digital Cities: Philadelphia
DIGC PHILLY	Digital Cities: Philadelphia
DIGC RENO	Digital Cities: Reno
DIGC SAGINAW	Digital Cities: Saginaw
DIGC SAN DIEGO	Digital Cities: San Diego CA
DIGC SAN FRANCISCO	Digital Cities: San Francisco CA
DIGC SANTA FE	Digital Cities: Albuquerque/Santa Fe NM
DIGC SD	Digital Cities: San Diego CA
DIGC SEATTLE	Digital Cities: Seattle/Tacoma WA
DIGC SF	Digital Cities: San Francisco CA
DIGC SOUTH	Digital Cities: South
DIGC ST PAUL	Digital Cities: Minneapolis -St. Paul
DIGC ST PETERSBURG	Digital Cities: Tampa-St. Petersburg
DIGC TACOMA	Digital Cities: Seattle/Tacoma WA
DIGC TAMPA	Digital Cities: Tampa-St. Petersburg
DIGC TEMPLE	Digital Cities: Waco/Temple/Bryan TX
DIGC TORONTO	Digital Cities: Toronto
DIGC TULSA	Digital Cities: Tulsa OK
DIGC VISALIA	Digital Cities: Fresno/Visalia CA
DIGC WACO	Digital Cities: Waco/Temple/Bryan TX
DIGC WEST	Digital Cities: West
DIGITAL	Digital Menu
DIGITAL CITIES	Digital City
DIGITAL CITY	Digital City
DIGITAL CITY ALASKA	Digital Cities: Alaska
DIGITAL CITY ALBANY	Digital Cities: Albany NY
DIGITAL CITY ATLANTA	Digital Cities: Atlanta GA
DIGITAL CITY AUSTIN	Digital Cities: Austin TX
DIGITAL CITY BRYAN	Digital Cities: Waco/Temple/Bryan TX
DIGITAL CITY BUFFALO	Digital Cities: Buffalo NY
DIGITAL CITY DALLAS	Digital Cities: Dallas-Ft. Worth TX
DIGITAL CITY DAYTON	Digital Cities: Dayton OH
DIGITAL CITY DENVER	Digital Cities: Denver CO
DIGITAL CITY DETROIT	Digital Cities: Detroit
DIGITAL CITY EL PASO	Digital Cities: El Paso
DIGITAL CITY EUGENE	Digital Cities: Eugene
DIGITAL CITY FLINT	Digital Cities: Flint
DIGITAL CITY FRESNO	Digital Cities: Fresno/Visalia CA
DIGITAL CITY FT WORTH	Digital Cities: Dallas-Ft. Worth
DIGITAL CITY HOUSTON	Digital Cities: Houston
DIGITAL CITY JOIN	Register as a Digital Citizen
DIGITAL CITY LA	Digital Cities: Los Angeles
DIGITAL CITY MIAMI	Digital Cities: Miami-Ft. Lauderdale
DIGITAL CITY MIDWEST	Digital Cities: Midwest
DIGITAL CITY NAPLES	Digital Cities: Ft. Myers/Naples FL
DIGITAL CITY NATIONAL	Digital City
DIGITAL CITY PHILLY	Digital Cities: Philadelphia
DIGITAL CITY RENO	Digital Cities: Reno
DIGITAL CITY SANTA FE	Digital Cities: Albuquerque/Santa Fe NM
DIGITAL CITY SD	Digital Cities: San Diego CA
DIGITAL CITY SEATTLE	Digital Cities: Seattle/Tacoma WA
DIGITAL CITY SF	Digital Cities: San Francisco CA
DIGITAL CITY SOUTH	Digital Cities: South
DIGITAL CITY ST PAUL	Digital Cities: Minneapolis-St. Paul
DIGITAL CITY TACOMA	Digital Cities: Seattle/Tacoma WA
DIGITAL CITY TAMPA	Digital Cities: Tampa-St. Petersburg
DIGITAL CITY TORONTO	Digital Cities: Toronto
DIGITAL CITY TULSA	Digital Cities: Tulsa OK
DIGITAL CITY US	Digital City
DIGITAL CITY VISALIA	Digital Cities: Fresno/Visalia CA
DIGITAL CITY WACO	Digital Cities: Waco/Temple/Bryan TX
DIGITAL CITY WEST	Digital Cities: West
DIGITAL ECLIPSE	Digital Eclipse
DIGITAL GRAFFITI	Heckers Online: Digital Graffiti
DIGITAL IMAGING	Digital Imaging Resource Center
DIGITAL RESEARCH	Novell Desktop Systems
DIGITAL RESEARCH INC	Novell Desktop Systems
DIGITAL TECH	Digital Technologies
DIGITAL USA	Digital City
DIGIZINES	Digizine Sites on the Web
DILBERT	Dilbert Comics
DILBERT COMICS	Dilbert Comics
DILBOARD	Dilbert Comics
DINE	Everything Edible!
DINE OUT	Dinner On Us Club
DINER	The Web Diner
DINER CREW	The Web Diner
DINING	Everything Edible!
DIR OF SERVICES	Directory of Services
DIR OF SVCS	Directory of Services
DIRECTORY	Member Directory
DIRECTORY OF SERVICES	Directory of Services

DIS	DisABILITIES Forum
DISABILITIES	DisABILITIES Forum
DISABILITY	DisABILITIES Forum
DISCLOSURE	Disclosure Incorporated
DISCOVER	Orientation Express
DISCOVER AOL	Orientation Express
DISCOVERY	The Discovery Channel
DISCOVERY CHAT	The Discovery Channel: Chat
DISCOVERY ED	The Discovery Channel: Education
DISNEY	Disney Services
DISNEY ADVENTURES	Disney Adventures Magazine
DISNEY INTERACTIVE	Disney Interactive
DISNEY JOBS	Disney Jobs
DISNEY MAGAZINE	Disney Adventures Magazine
DISNEY SOFT	Disney Interactive
DISNEY SOFTWARE	Disney Interactive
DISPLAY DOCTOR	SciTech Software
DIVA	Soap Opera Digest
DIVA LA DISH	Soap Opera Digest
DJ	Don Johnston, Inc.
DJBC	Dow Jones Business Center
DL	Dalai Lama [May disappear without notice]
DNC	Democratic Party Online
DO SOMETHING	Do Something!
DOBSON	Focus on the Family
DOCL	Dictionary of Cultural Literacy
DOCTOR WHO	Doctor Who Online
DODGE	Dodge Truck [Web Site]
DODGERS	Major League Baseball Team: Los Angeles Dodgers
DOG	Pet Care Forum
DOGERS	Major League Baseball Team: Los Angeles Dodgers
DOGS	Pet Care Forum
DOLE	Republican National Committee
DOLL	Pangea Toy Network
DOMARK	Domark Software, Inc.
DON JOHNSTON	Don Johnston, Inc.
DON'T CLICK HERE	Don't Click Here [3.0 only]
DONATION	access.point
DONATIONS	access.point
DONKEY	Democratic Party Online
DONT MISS	Directory of Services
DOROTHY	CyberJustice's Oasis of Xaiz
DOS 6	MS-DOS 6.0 Resource Center
DOS 60	MS-DOS 6.0 Resource Center
DOW	Dow Jones Business Center
DOW JONES	Dow Jones Business Center
DOWNLOAD	Software Center [Platform-dependent]
DOWNLOAD 101	Download Help*
DOWNLOAD CREDIT	Credit Request Form for connect problems*
DOWNLOAD GAMES	Download Online Games* [WAOL and GAOL only]
DOWNLOAD HELP	Download Help*
DOWNLOADING	Software Center [Platform-dependent]
DOWNTOWN	Downtown AOL
DOWNTOWN AOL	Downtown AOL
DOWNTOWN MSG	Downtown AOL Message Boards
DP	Decision Point Forum
DPA	Decision Point Forum
DR D	Dr. D Talks About [3.0 only]
DR. D	Dr. D Talks About [3.0 only]
DR. D TALKS	Dr. D Talks About [3.0 only]
DR GAMEWIZ	Dr Gamewiz Online
DR WHO	Doctor Who Online
DRAGONREALMS	DragonRealms
DREALMS	DragonRealms
DRESSAGE	Horse Forum's Dressage MiniForum
DRI	Novell Desktop Systems
DRINK	Everything Edible!
DRIVING	Car and Driver Magazine
DROWNED GOD	Drowned God
DRUG REFERENCE	Consumer Reports Complete Drug Reference Search
DRUM	Drum Magazine
DS	Do Something!
DSC	The Discovery Channel
DSC ED	The Discovery Channel: Education
DSC-ED	The Discovery Channel: Education
DT	Downtown AOL
DT AOL	Downtown AOL
DTP	Desktop and Web Publishing area [Platform-dependent]
DTV	Motley Fool: Desktop Video
DUBLCLICK	Dubl-Click Software
DUCKS	NHL Hockey
DUTCH	Genealogy Forum
DV	DV (Desktop Video) Magazine
DVORAK	Software Hardtalk with John C. Dvorak
DWP	Desktop & Web Publishing [Platform-dependent]
DYNAMIX	Sierra On-Line
DYNAWARE	Dynaware USA
DYNAWARE USA	Dynaware USA
DYNOTECH	DynoTech Software
E!	E! Entertainment Television
E	Entertainment channel
E-ZONE	Your Business
EAGLE	Eagle Home Page

EAGLES	Philadelphia Eagles Football Coverage [3.0 only]
EAGLES ONLINE	Philadelphia Eagles Online
EARL'S GARAGE	Pro's Corner
EARLS GARAGE	Pro's Corner
EARLY ED	Preschool/Early Childhood SIG
EARLY EDUCATION	Preschool/Early Childhood SIG
EARTH	Environmental Forum
EARTHLINK	TBS Network Earth/IBM Project [MAOL and GAOL only]
EASTER	AOL's Easter Area [May disappear without notice]
EASTERN EUROPEAN	Genealogy Forum
EAT	Dinner On Us Club
EAT OUT	Dinner On Us Club
EATS	Good Morning America Recipes
@EATS	THRIVE: @Eats
EATS TALK	Thrive@AOL: Eats Talk
EB STORE	Eddie Bauer
EBBASEBALL	Extreme Fans: Baseball Daily
ECCLESIASTICAL	Religion & Ethics Forum
ECHAT	Entertainment Chat
ECOTOURISM	Backpacker Magazine
ECS	Electronic Courseware
ED ADVISORY	Education Advisory Council Online
ED ANGER	Weekly World News
EDA	Education Advisory Council Online
EDDIE	Eddie Bauer
EDDIE BAUER	Eddie Bauer
EDELSTEIN	Fred Edelstein's Pro Football Insider
EDGAR	Disclosure's EdgarPlus
EDGE	Company Research
EDIT PROFILE	Edit your member profile
EDITOR'S CHOICE	Pictures of the Week
EDITORIAL CARTOONS	InToon with the News
EDITORS CHOICE	Pictures of the Week
EDMARK	Edmark Technologies
EDTECH	Assoc. for Supervisor & Curriculum Development
EDUCATION	Learning & Culture channel
EDUCATION CONNECTION	Compton's Education Connection
EFCF	Extreme Fans: College Football
EFORUM	Environmental Forum
EFPRO-EFPRO	Extreme Fans: Pro Football
EGG	Electronic Gourmet Guide
EGG BASKET	Electronic Gourmet Guide
EGYPT	Egypt
EL PASO	Digital Cities: El Paso
EL PASO DC	Digital Cities: El Paso
EL PASO DCITY	Digital Cities: El Paso
EL PASO DIGC	Digital Cities: El Paso
EL PASO DIGITAL CITY	Digital Cities: El Paso
EL PASO TX	Digital Cities: El Paso
ELECTION HANDBOOK	Student's Election Handbook
ELECTRIC	Electric Image
ELECTRIC IMAGE	Electric Image
ELECTRIC WORD	Digital City San Francisco: The Electric Word
ELECTRONIC PUBLISHING	Desktop & Web Publishing [Platform-dependent]
ELECTRONICS	Andy Pargh/The Gadget Guru
ELEPHANT	Republican National Committee
ELI	Eli's Cheesecakes
ELI CONTEST	Eli's Cheesecakes Contest
ELI'S	Eli's Cheesecakes
ELI'S CHEESECAKES	Eli's Cheesecakes
ELIGIBLE	Love@AOL: Eligible Magazine
ELIGIBLE MAGAZINE	Love@AOL: Eligible Magazine
ELIS CHEESECAKES	Eli's Cheesecakes
ELLE	Elle Magazine Online
ELVIS	Weekly World News
EMAIL	Post Office
EMALL	Orlando Sentinel Online: E-Mall
EMERALD COAST	Emerald Coast
EMERGENCY	Public Safety Center
EMERGENCY RESPONSE	Public Safety Center
EMIGRE	Emigre Fonts
EMMASOFT	EmmaSoft Software Company, Inc.
EMPOWERMENT	Personal Empowerment Network
ENCYCLOPEDIA	Encyclopedias
ENDNOTE	Niles and Associates
ENGINEERING	NAS Online
ENGLISH	Simon & Schuster Online: English Dept.
ENGMTNFOR	English Mountain Software
ENT SPOT	What's Hot in Entertainment
ENTERPRISE	AOL Enterprise
ENTERPRISES	AOL Enterprise
ENTERTAINMENT	Entertainment channel
ENTERTAINMENT CHAT	Entertainment Chat
ENTERTAINMENT NEWS	Entertainment News
ENTERTAINMENT STORE	Entertainment Store
ENTERTAINMENT WEEKLY	Entertainment Weekly
ENTREPRENEUR ZONE	Your Business
ENVIRONMENT	Environment Forum
ENVIRONMENTAL ED	Earth Day/Environment
ENVOY	Motorola
EOL	AOL Enterprise
EPARTNERS	Electronic Partnerships
EPSCONVERTER	Art Age Software

EPUB	Desktop & Web Publishing [Platform-dependent]
EPUBS	Desktop & Web Publishing [Platform-dependent]
EQUIBASE	Horse Racing
EQUINE	Pet Care Forum
EQUIS	Equis International
ER	ER Forum
ERC	Public Safety Center
ERIC	AskERIC
ESC	Educational Software Cooperative
ESH	Electronic Schoolhouse
ESPOT	What's Hot in Entertainment
ETEXT	PDA's Palmtop Paperbacks!
ETHICS	Ethics & Values
ETHICS & VALUES	Ethics & Values
ETRADE	How to use StockLink & Gateway Host
EUGENE	Digital Cities: Eugene
EUGENE DC	Digital Cities: Eugene
EUGENE DCITY	Digital Cities: Eugene
EUGENE DIGC	Digital Cities: Eugene
EUGENE DIGITAL CITY	Digital Cities: Eugene
EUGENE OR	Digital Cities: Eugene
EUN	Electronic University Network
EUROPE	Europe Selections
EVENT	Today's Events in AOL Live!
EVENTS	Today's Events in AOL Live!
EVERYTHING EDIBLE	Everything Edible!
EW	Entertainment Weekly
EWORLD	Apple Aloha for eWorld Alumni
EXAM PREP	Exam Prep Center
EXCELLENCE	Access Excellence
EXCHANGE	The Exchange
EXERCISE	Fitness Forum
EXPERT	Expert Software, Inc.
EXPERTS	Ask the Marketplace Gift Experts
EXPERT PAD	PDA/Palmtop Forum
EXPERT SOFT	Expert Software, Inc.
EXPOS	Major League Baseball Team: Montreal Expos
EXPRESS NET	ExpressNet (American Express)
EXPRESSNET ART	ExpressNet Art Download*
EXTENSIS	Extensis Corporation
EXTRA	EXTRA Online
EXTREME FANS	Extreme Fans: College Hoops
EZ	Your Business
EZINE	PDA's Palmtop Paperbacks!
EZINES	Digizine Sites on the Web
EZONE	Your Business
F2M	Transgender Community Forum
FAB	Fabulous Facts
FABFACTS	Fabulous Facts
FACE	Style Channel
FAITH	Religion & Beliefs
FALCONS	Atlanta Falcons Football Coverage [3.0 only]
FALL TV	Lost & Found TV Shows
FALL TV SHOWS	Lost & Found TV Shows
FAM HOT	What's Hot in AOL Families
FAMILY	Family Areas
FAMILY ALBUM	Family Computing Forum: The Family Room
FAMILY COMPUTING	Family Computing Resource Center
FAMILY FINANCES	MoneyWhiz
FAMILY GAMES	Family Computing Forum: Family Games
FAMILY LIFE	Family Life Magazine Online
FAMILY NEWS	Family Computing Forum: News & Reviews
FAMILY PC	FamilyPC Online
FAMILY RESOURCE	Family Computing Forum: Maximum AOL
FAMILY ROOM	Family Computing Forum: Family Room
FAMILY SHOWCASE	Family Product Showcase
FAMILY TRAVEL	Family Travel Selections
FAMILY TRAVEL NETWORK	Family Travel Network
FANS	Extreme Fans: College Hoops
FANTASY	Fictional Realm
FANTASY BASEBALL	The Grandstand's Fantasy Baseball
FANTASY BASKETBALL	The Grandstand's Fantasy Basketball
FANTASY FOOTBALL	The Grandstand's Fantasy Football
FANTASY HOCKEY	The Grandstand's Fantasy Hockey
FANTASY LEAGUE	The Grandstand's Fantasy & Simulation Leagues
FANTASY LEAGUES	The Grandstand's Fantasy & Simulation Leagues
FAO	F.A.O. Schwarz
FAO SCHWARZ	F.A.O. Schwarz
FARALLON	Farallon
FARM	Pet Care Forum
FARM AID	Official Farm Aid '96 [May disappear without notice]
FARM ANIMAL	Pet Care Forum
FARM ANIMALS	Pet Care Forum
FASHION	Elle Magazine Online
FATHER	AOL Families
FATHERS	AOL Families
FAVE FLICKS	Favorite Flicks!
FAVORITE FLICKS	Favorite Flicks!
FAX	Fax/Paper Mail
FAXMAIL	FaxMail for Windows
FBN	Fly-Fishing Broadcast Network
FC	Family Computing Forum
FC TIPS	Family Computing Forum: Tip of the Day

FCF	Family Computing Forum
FCNBD	First Chicago NBD Online [3.0 only]
FCRC	Family Computing Forum: Maximum AOL
FD	AOL's Full Disclosure for Investors
FDN	Food & Drink Network
FEATURES	Columnists & Features Online
FED	Federation
FEDERATION	Federation
FEDEX	Federal Express Online
FEEDBACK	Member Services*
FELINE	Hobby Central: Pets & Animals
FELISSIMO	Felissimo
FELLINI	La Dolce Vita
FELLOWSHIP	Fellowship of Online Gamers/RPGA Network
FELLOWSHIP HALL	Christianity Online Chat & Live Events
FERNDALE	Ferndale [3.0 only]
FERRET	Pet Care Forum
FFGF	Free-Form Gaming Forum
FICTION	The Atlantic Monthly Online
FICTIONAL REALM	Fictional Realm
FID	Fidelity Online Investments Center
FID AT WORK	Fidelity Online's Working Area
FID BROKER	Fidelity Online's Funds Area
FID FUNDS	Fidelity Online's Funds Area
FID GUIDE	Fidelity Online's Guide Area
FID NEWS	Fidelity Online's Newsworthy Area
FID PLAN	Fidelity Online's Planning Area
FIDELITY	Fidelity Online Investments Center
FIESTA	Hispanic Heritage [3.0 only]
FIESTA BOWL	Fool Bowl
FIFTH	Symantec
FIGHTING IRISH	AOL College Football '96 [3.0 only]
FIGURE SKATING	ABC Sports Figure Skating
FILE	Software Center [Platform-dependent]
FILE SEARCH	Search database of files [Platform-dependent]
FILEMAKER	The Filemaker Pro Resource Center
FILES	Software Center [Platform-dependent]
FILM REVIEW DATABASE	Movie Review Database
FILM REVIEW DB	Movie Review Database
FILM REVIEWS DATABASE	Movie Review Database
FILM STUDIOS	MovieVisions
FILMBALL	Follywood Games
FINANCE	Personal Finance channel
FINANCIAL ASTROLOGY	Astronet
FINANCIAL PLANNING	MoneyWhiz
FINANCIAL STATEMENT	Disclosure's Financial Statements
FINANCIALS	Disclosure's Financial Statements
FIND	Directory of Services
FINLAND	Finland
FIREBALL	Flight Sim Resource Center
FIRST	First Look at Hot New Products
FIRST BYTE	Baumrucker Conference [May disappear without notice]
FIRST CHICAGO ONLINE	First Chicago Online
FIRST LADY	Hillary Rodham Clinton
FIRST LOOK	First Look at Hot New Products
FISCHERGRAFIX	Fischer Grafix & Software [3.0 only]
FISH	Boating Online
FISHING	Boating Online
FITNESS	Fitness Forum
FIX	What's Hot in Entertainment
FLASH	Mad About Music
FLASHCARDS	MarketMaster
FLIGHT	Flight Sim Resource Center
FLIGHT CENTER	Flight Sim Resource Center
FLIGHT SIM	Flight Sim Resource Center
FLIGHT SIMS	Flight Sim Resource Center
FLIGHT SIMULATIONS	Flight Sim Resource Center
FLINT	Digital Cities: Flint
FLINT DC	Digital Cities: Flint
FLINT DCITY	Digital Cities: Flint
FLINT DIGC	Digital Cities: Flint
FLINT DIGITAL CITY	Digital Cities: Flint
FLINT MI	Digital Cities: Flint
FLORIDA	Destination Florida
FLORIDA KEYS	The Florida Keys
FLORIDA MARLINS	Major League Baseball Team: Florida Marlins
FLOWERS	800-Flowers
FLY	Aviation Forum
FLY FISHING	Fly-Fishing Broadcast Network
FLY-FISHING	Fly-Fishing Broadcast Network
FLYERS	NHL Hockey
FLYING	Flying Magazine
FLYING MAG	Flying Magazine
FLYING MAGAZINE	Flying Magazine
FOCUS	Focus Enhancements
FOCUS ENHANCEMENTS	Focus Enhancements
FOF	Focus on the Family [3.0 only]
FOF STORE	Focus on the Family: Online Resource Center
FOG	Fellowship of Online Gamers/RPGA Network
FOLKWAYS	Folklife & Folkways
FOLLYWOOD	Follywood
FONTBANK	FontBank
FOOD	Everything Edible!
FOOD & DRINK	Food & Drink Network
FOOL	The Motley Fool: Finance & Folly
FOOL AERO	Motley Fool: Aero

FOOL AIR	Motley Fool: Airlines
FOOL BIO	Motley Fool: Biotechnology
FOOL BOWL	Fool Bowl
FOOL CHEM	Motley Fool: Chemicals
FOOL CHIPS	Motley Fool: Semiconductors
FOOL DOME	Motley Fool: The Fool Dome
FOOL DTV	Motley Fool: Desktop Video
FOOL FOOD	Motley Fool: Food
FOOL HARD	Motley Fool: Hardware
FOOL HEALTH	Motley Fool: Health
FOOL MART	Motley Fool: FoolMart
FOOL NET	Motley Fool: Networking
FOOL OIL	Motley Fool: Oilfield Services
FOOL PAPER	Motley Fool: Paper & Trees
FOOL RAILS	Motley Fool: Railroads
FOOL REIT	Motley Fool: Real Estate
FOOL REITTO	Motley Fool: Real Estate
FOOL SEM	Motley Fool: Semiconductors
FOOL SOFT	Motley Fool: Software
FOOL SPORTS	Motley Fool: The Fool Dome
FOOL STORE	Motley Fool: FoolMart
FOOL TECH	Motley Fool: Storage Tech
FOOL UTIL	Motley Fool: Utilities
FOOL VID	Motley Fool: Desktop Video
FOOLBALL	Motley Fool: The Fool Dome
FOOLISH	The Motley Fool: Finance & Folly
FOOTBALL	AOL Football
FOREIGN	International Cafe
FORMZ	auto*des*sys, Inc.
FORTE	Forte Technologies
FORTNER	Fortner Research
FORTRAN	Fortner Research
FORUM	Computers & Software channel [Platform-dependent]
FORUM AUD	The Computing Rotunda
FORUM AUDITORIUM	The Computing Rotunda
FORUM ROT	The Computing Rotunda
FORUMS	Computers & Software channel [Platform-dependent]
FOSSIL	Fossil Watches and More
FOSSIL WATCHES	Fossil Watches and More
FOTF	Focus on the Family
FOUND TV	Lost & Found TV Shows
FOUR RESOURCES	AT&T Home Business Resources
FOURTH OF JULY	AOL's Independence Day area [May disappear without notice]
FPF	Mac Featured Products Forum
FRACTAL	Fractal Design
FRACTAL DESIGN	Fractal Design

FRAGRANCE	The Fragrance Counter
FRANCE	International channel
FRANCE & ASSOCIATES	France & Associates
FRANKLIN	Franklin Quest
FRASIER	Frasier Tuesdays
FRASIER TUESDAYS	Frasier Tuesdays
FRATERNITY	Alumni Hall
FREE	Member Services*
FREELANCE	Freelance Artists Special Interest Group
FREEMAIL	FreeMail, Inc.
FREESHOP	The FreeShop Online
FREESHOP ONLINE	The FreeShop Online
FREESOFT	FreeSoft Company
FREETHOUGHT	Freethought Forum
FRENCH OPEN	French Open [May disappear without notice]
FRENCH TEST	France Beta Test* [May disappear without notice]
FREQUENT FLYER	Inside Flyer
FRESNO	Digital Cities: Fresno/Visalia CA
FRESNO CA	Digital Cities: Fresno/Visalia CA
FRESNO DC	Digital Cities: Fresno/Visalia CA
FRESNO DCITY	Digital Cities: Fresno/Visalia CA
FRESNO DIGC	Digital Cities: Fresno/Visalia CA
FRESNO DIGITAL CITY	Digital Cities: Fresno/Visalia CA
FRIDAY AT 4	ABC Online Auditorium
FRIEND	Sign on a friend to AOL*
FRIEND IN FRANCE	France Beta Test* [May disappear without notice]
FROG	The WB Network
FROMMER	Frommer's City Guides
FROMMER'S	Frommer's City Guides
FROMMER'S CITY GUIDES	Frommer's City Guides
FROMMERS	Frommer's City Guides
FROMMERS CITY GUIDES	Frommer's City Guides
FRONTIERS	Scientific American Frontiers
FSRC	Flight Sim Resource Center
FT LAUDERDALE DIGC	Digital Cities: Miami-Ft. Lauderdale
FT MYERS	Digital Cities: Ft. Myers/Naples FL
FT MYERS DC	Digital Cities: Ft. Myers/Naples FL
FT MYERS DCITY	Digital Cities: Ft. Myers/Naples FL
FT MYERS FL	Digital Cities: Ft. Myers/Naples FL
FT MYRES DIGC	Digital Cities: Ft. Myers/Naples FL
FT WORTH	Digital Cities: Dallas-Ft. Worth
FT WORTH DIGC	Digital Cities: Dallas-Ft. Worth
FT WORTH DIGITAL CITY	Digital Cities: Dallas-Ft. Worth
FTN	Family Travel Network
FTP	Internet FTP
FULL DISCLOSURE	AOL's Full Disclosure for Investors
FULLD	AOL's Full Disclosure for Investors

FULLWRITE	FullWrite
FUN	Entertainment channel
FUNB	First Union National Bank [3.0 only]
FUND	Morningstar Mutual Funds
FUNDS	Morningstar Mutual Funds
FUNDWORKS	Fundworks Investors' Center
FUNNIES	The Funny Pages
FURNISHINGS	Home Magazine Online
FURNITURE	Home Magazine Online
FUTURE LABS	Future Labs, Inc.
FUZZY	The Hub: Fuzzy Memories
GADGET	Andy Pargh/The Gadget Guru
GADGET GURU	Andy Pargh/The Gadget Guru
GALACTICOMM	Galacticomm
GALILEO	Galileo Mission to Jupiter [May disappear without notice]
GALLERY	Portrait Gallery
GAME	Games channel
GAME BASE	Game Base
GAME DESIGN	Game Designers Forum
GAME DESIGNER	Game Designers Forum
GAME DESIGNERS	Game Designers Forum
GAME ROOMS	Games Parlor
GAME SITES	WWW Game Sites
GAMEPRO	GamePro Online
GAMES	Games channel
GAMES CHANNEL	Games channel
GAMES DOWNLOAD	Download Online Games* [WAOL and GAOL only]
GAMES & ENTERTAINMENT	Games channel
GAMES FORUM	Games Forum [Platform-dependent]
GAMES PARLOR	Games Parlor
GAMESTER	FamilyPC Online
GAMETEK	Gametek
GAMEWIZ	Dr. Gamewiz Online
GAMEWIZ FILE	Dr Gamewiz: File Libraries
GAMEWIZ INC	Dr Gamewiz Online
GAMING	Online Gaming Forums
GARAGE	Pro's Corner
GARDEN	Gardening Online Selections
GARDENING	Gardening Online Selections
GATEWAY	Gateway 2000, Inc.
GATEWAY 2000	Gateway 2000, Inc.
GATORS	AOL College Football '96 [3.0 only]
GAY	Gay & Lesbian Community Forum
GAY BOARDS	Gay & Lesbian Community Forum Boards
GAY BOOKS	Lambda Rising Bookstore Online
GAY CHAT	Gay & Lesbian Community Forum Events and Conferences
GAY MESSAGE	Gay & Lesbian Community Forum Boards
GAY NEWS	Gay & Lesbian Community Forum News
GAY ORG	Gay & Lesbian Community Forum Organizations
GAY ORGS	Gay & Lesbian Community Forum Organizations
GAY POLITICS	Gay & Lesbian Community Forum News
GAY SOFTWARE	Gay & Lesbian Community Forum Libraries
GAY TRAVEL	Gay & Lesbian Community Forum Travel
GAY TRIVIA	Gay & Lesbian Community Forum: Gaymeland
GAY YOUTH	GLCF Youth Area
GAYME	Gay & Lesbian Community Forum: Gaymeland
GAYMELAND	Gay & Lesbian Community Forum: Gaymeland
GAYMES	Gay & Lesbian Community Forum: Gaymeland
GAZEBO	Transgender Community Forum: Conferences
GAZETTE	CyberJustice's Gazette Online/E-mail
GBL	The Grandstand's Simulation Baseball
GC ACTION	Games Channel: Action
GC CLASSIC	Games Channel: Classic Games
GC CONTESTS	Games Channel: Contests
GC HOT	What's Hot in AOL Games
GC INFO	Games Channel: Gaming Information
GC KNOWLEDGE	Games Channel: Knowledge Games
GC NEWS	Games Channel: News [3.0 only]
GC PERSONA	Games Channel: Persona Games
GC RPG	Games Channel: Role Playing Games
GC SIMULATION	Games Channel: Simulation Games
GC SPORTS	Games Channel: Sports Games
GC STRATEGY	Games Channel: Strategy Games
GCC	GCC Technologies
GCFL	The Grandstand's Simulation Football
GCS	Gaming Company Support
GD STORE	Grateful Dead Forum Store
GDT	GDT Softworks, Inc.
GDT SOFTWORKS	GDT Softworks, Inc.
GEMSTONE	GemStone III
GEMSTONE III	GemStone III
GEN NEXT	Generation Next
GENDER	Transgender Community Forum
GENDER TRIVIA	Gay & Lesbian Community Forum: Gaymeland
GENEALOGY	Genealogy Forum
GENEALOGY CLUB	Genealogy Forum
GENERAL AVIATION	Aviation Forum
GENERAL HOSPITAL	ABC Daytime/Soapline
GENERAL MAGIC	General Magic
GENERAL STORE	Parent Soup: General Store
GENERATION NEXT	Generation Next
GENERATIONS	Generations
GENESIS	Video Games area
GENIE EASY	Astronet
GEO SDK	Geoworks Development

GEOGRAPHIC	Odyssey Project
GEORGE	George Online
GEORGE ONLINE	George Online
GEOWORKS	Geoworks
GERALDO	The Geraldo Show
GERALDO SHOW	The Geraldo Show
GERBIL	Pet Care Forum
GERMANY	International channel
GERTIE	Mercury Center Trivia
GET A LIFE	The Hub: Get A Life
GETTING STARTED	Help Desk [Platform-dependent]
GGL	The Grandstand's Simulation Golf
GH	ABC Daytime/Soapline
GIANTS	Major League Baseball Team: San Francisco Giants
GIF	Graphics Forum [Platform-dependent]
GIF CONVERTER	GIF Converter
GIFT	Marketplace Gift Valet
GIFT CERTIFICATE	AOL Gift Certificates
GIFT EXPERT	Ask the Marketplace Gift Experts
GIFT EXPERTS	Ask the Marketplace Gift Experts
GIFT REMINDER	Gift Reminder
GIFT SERVICE	Marketplace Gift Valet
GIFT SERVICES	Marketplace Gift Valet
GIFT VALET	Marketplace Gift Valet
GIFTED	Gifted Online
GIFTS	800-Flowers
GIGABRAIN	FamilyPC Online
GIGABYTES	The Hub: Gigabytes Island
GIRL STUFF	Style Channel
GIRLS	Focus on Family: Brio Magazine
GIX	Gaming Information Exchange
GLCF	Gay & Lesbian Community Forum
GLCF BOARDS	Gay & Lesbian Community Forum Boards
GLCF CHAT	Gay & Lesbian Community Forum Events and Conferences
GLCF EVENT	Gay & Lesbian Community Forum Events and Conferences
GLCF EVENTS	Gay & Lesbian Community Forum Events and Conferences
GLCF H2H	Gay & Lesbian Community Forum Heart to Heart
GLCF HEART	Gay & Lesbian Community Forum Heart to Heart
GLCF HEART TO HEART	Gay & Lesbian Community Forum Heart to Heart
GLCF LIBRARY	Gay & Lesbian Community Forum Libraries
GLCF NEWS	Gay & Lesbian Community Forum News
GLCF ORG	Gay & Lesbian Community Forum Organizations
GLCF ORGANIZATIONS	Gay & Lesbian Community Forum Organizations
GLCF ORGS	Gay & Lesbian Community Forum Organizations
GLCF QUILT	GLCF Aids Scrapbook
GLCF SOFTWARE	Gay & Lesbian Community Forum Libraries
GLCF TCF	Transgender Community Forum
GLCF TEEN	GLCF Youth Area
GLCF TRAVEL	Gay & Lesbian Community Forum Travel
GLCF WOMAN	GLCF: Women's Space
GLCF WOMEN	GLCF: Women's Space
GLCF YOUTH	GLCF Youth Area
GLENNA	Glenna's Garden: Cancer Support
GLENNA'S GARDEN	Glenna's Garden: Cancer Support
GLOBAL	Global Village Communication
GLOBAL CITIZEN	ExpressNet: Global Citizen [3.0 only]
GLOBAL VILLAGE	Global Village Communication
GLOBALNET	AOLGLOBALnet International Access*
GLOBE	AOL Live!
GLORIA	Ask Gloria Steinem
GLOSSARY	America Online Glossary*
GM	General Motors Web Site
GM'S CORNER	The GM's Corner
GMA	ABC Good Morning America
GMAT	Kaplan Online or The Princeton Review
GMFL	The Grandstand's Simulation Football
GMME	Grolier's Encyclopedia
GMS CORNER	The GM's Corner
GN	GrittyNews
GNN	GNN Best of the Net [3.0 only]
GO SCUBA	Scuba Club
GOALS 200	Goals 2000: National Education Act
GOAT	Pet Care Forum
GODIVA	Godiva Chocolatiers
GOLF	AOL Golf area
GOLF AMERICA	Golfis Forum
GOLF COURSES	Golfis Forum
GOLF DATA	GolfCentral
GOLF INFORMATION	Golfis Forum
GOLF RESORTS	Golfis Forum
GOLFIS	Golfis Forum
GONER TV	Lost & Found TV Shows
GOOD LIFE	Your Good Life
GOOD MORNING AMERICA	ABC Good Morning America
GOP	Republican National Committee
GOPHER	Internet Gopher
GORE	Democratic Party Online
GOSSIP	Entertainment channel
GOURMET	Everything Edible!
GOVERNING	Governing Magazine
GOVERNMENT	AOL Politics
GOVERNMENT RESOURCES	Your Government Resources
GPF	GPF Help [3.0 only]
GPFL	The Grandstand's Simulation Football
GPS	Trimble Navigation, Ltd.

GRADUATE SCHOOL	Kaplan Online or The Princeton Review
GRAFFITI	Heckers Online: Digital Graffiti
GRANDSTAND	The Grandstand
GRANDSTAND TRIVIA	The Grandstand's Sports Trivia
GRAPH SIM	Graphic Simulations
GRAPHCAT	Science Translations
GRAPHIC	Graphic Simulations
GRAPHIC ARTS	Graphic Arts & CAD Forum [Platform-dependent]
GRAPHIC DESIGN	Design Special Interest Group
GRAPHIC SIMULATIONS	Graphic Simulations
GRAPHICS	Graphic Arts & CAD Forum [Platform-dependent]
GRAPHICS FORUM	Graphic Arts & CAD Forum [Platform-dependent]
GRAPHISOFT	Graphisoft
GRAPHSOFT	Graphsoft, Inc.
GRATEFUL DEAD	Grateful Dead Forum
GRAVIS	Advanced Gravis
GRE	Kaplan Online or The Princeton Review
GREAT DEBATE	The Great Debate
GREAT UNSIGNED	The Great Unsigned
GREECE	Greece
GREEK	Genealogy Forum
GREENBERG	Kaplan Online
GREENHOUSE	AOL Greenhouse
GREET ST	Greet Street Greeting Cards
GREET STREET	Greet Street Greeting Cards
GRITTY NEWS	GrittyNews
GROLIER	Grolier's Encyclopedia
GROLIER'S	Grolier's Encyclopedia
GROLIERS	Grolier's Encyclopedia
GROUPWARE	GroupWare Special Interest Group
GRYPHON	Gryphon Software
GRYPHON SOFTWARE	Gryphon Software
GS	WWW Game Sites
GS ARTS	The Grandstand's Martial Arts (The Dojo)
GS AUTO	The Grandstand's Motor Sports (In the Pits)
GS BASEBALL	The Grandstand's Baseball (Dugout)
GS BASKETBALL	The Grandstand's Basketball (Off the Glass)
GS BOXING	The Grandstand's Boxing (Squared Circle)
GS COLLECTING	The Grandstand's Collecting (Sports Cards)
GS FOOTBALL	The Grandstand's Football (50 Yard Line)
GS GOLF	The Grandstand's Golf (On the Green)
GS HOCKEY	The Grandstand's Hockey (Blue Line)
GS HORSE	The Grandstand's Horse Sports & Racing Forum
GS MAG	GS+ Magazine
GS OTHER	The Grandstand's Other Sports (Whole 9 Yards)
GS SIDELINE	The Grandstand's Sideline
GS SOCCER	The Grandstand's Soccer (The Kop)
GS SOFTWARE	The Grandstand's Sports Software Headquarters
GS SPORTS TRIVIA	The Grandstand's Sports Trivia
GS SPORTSMART	The Grandstand's Sports Products (Sportsmart)
GS TRIVIA	The Grandstand's Sports Trivia
GS WINTER	The Grandstand's Winter Sports (The Chalet)
GS WRESTLING	The Grandstand's Wrestling (Squared Circle)
GSC	Graphic Simulations
GSDL	The Grandstand's Simulation Basketball
GSFL	The Grandstand's Simulation Football
GSHL	The Grandstand's Simulation Hockey
GSS	Global Software Suport
GST	GST Technology
GTR	Guitar Special Interest Group
GU	The Great Unsigned
GUAM	Guam
GUARANTEE	AOL Cybershopping Guarantee
GUCCI	Gucci Parfums Counter
GUESS	Guess, Inc.
GUFL	The Grandstand's Simulation Football
GUIDE PAGE	Guide Pager
GUIDE PAGER	Guide Pager
GUINEA PIG	Pet Care Forum
GUITAR	Guitar Special Interest Group
GUITAR SIG	Guitar Special Interest Group
GUNS	The Exchange: Interests & Hobbies
GURU	Andy Pargh/The Gadget Guru
GUY STUFF	Style Channel
GVC	MaxTech Corporation
GWA	The Grandstand's Simulation Wrestling
GWALTNEY	Gwaltney Hams & Turkeys
GWF	The Grandstand's Simulation Wrestling
GWPI	The Hub: Global Worldwide Pictures International, Ltd.
H&C	The Exchange: Home & Careers
H&H	Christianity Online: Holidays and COntests
H2H	Gay & Lesbian Community Forum Heart to Heart
HACHETTE	Hachette Filipacchi Magazines
HACIENDA	Channel One Network Online
HACK	MacHack
HACKER	MacHack
HACKERS	"Hackers" Movie area
HALL OF FAME	Downloading Hall of Fame
HALLMARK	Hallmark Connections
HALLMARK CONNECTIONS	Hallmark Connections

HALLOWEEN	Halloween area [May disappear without notice]
HAM	Ham Radio Club
HAM RADIO	Ham Radio Club
HAMMACHER	Hammacher Schlemmer
HAMMACHER SCHLEMMER	Hammacher Schlemmer
HAMS	Gwaltney Hams & Turkeys
HAMSTER	Pet Care Forum
HANDLE	Add, change or delete screen names
HANDWRITING	Handwriting & You
HANES	One Hanes Place
HAPPY NEW YEAR	Happy New Year area [May disappear without notice]
HAPPY NEW YEARS DAY	Happy New Year area [May disappear without notice]
HARDBALL	Baseball Daily by Extreme Fans
HARDWARE	Hardware Forum [Platform-dependent]
HARDWARE FORUM	Hardware Forum [Platform-dependent]
HARLEY	Big Twin Online: The All-Harley Magazine
HARLEY DAVIDSON	Big Twin Online: The All-Harley Magazine
HASH	Hash, Inc.
HAWKEYES	AOL College Football '96 [3.0 only]
HBS PUB	Harvard Business School Publishing
HDC	hDC Corporation
HDC CORPORATION	hDC Corporation
HEADHUNTER	Motley Fool: Ask the Headhunter
HEADLINES	Today's News channel
HEALTH	Health channel
HEALTH EXP	Health and Vitamin Express
HEALTH EXPRESS	Health and Vitamin Express
HEALTH FOCUS	Health Focus
HEALTH LIVE	Health Speakers and Support Groups
HEALTH MAGAZINE	Health Magazine
HEALTH MAGAZINES	Health Resources
HEALTH REFERENCE	Health Resources
HEALTH RESOURCES	Health Resources
HEALTH TALK	Thrive@AOL: Health Talk
HEALTH TODAY	Columbia's Health Today
HEALTH WEB	Health Web Sites
HEALTH ZONE	The Health Zone
HEART TO HEART	Gay & Lesbian Community Forum Heart to Heart
HEAVEN	The Hub: Heaven
HECKLE	Hecklers Online
HECKLER	Hecklers Online
HECKLER ONLINE	Hecklers Online
HECKLER'S ONLINE	Hecklers Online
HECKLERS	Hecklers Online
HECKLERS CLUBS	Hecklers Online: Clubs
HECKLERS ONLINE	Hecklers Online
HECKLING CLUBS	Hecklers Online: Clubs
HEDGEHOG	People Connection Plaza
HELMETS	Cycle World Online
HELP	Member Services*
HELP DESK	Help Desk [Platform-dependent]
HELP FORUM	Help Desks [Mac or PC]
HELP OKC	Help Heal Oklahoma City
HELP WANTED	Help Wanted Ads
HEM	Home Education Magazine
HERBS	Longevity Magazine Online
HERITAGE	Heritage Foundation
HERITAGE FOUNDATION	Heritage Foundation
HFC	Highlights for Children
HFC CATALOG	Highlights for Children Catalog
HFC STORE	Highlights for Children Catalog
HFM MAGNET WORK	Hachette Filipacchi Magazines
HFS	WHFS 99.1 FM
HH KIDS	Homework Help
HH TEENS	Homework Help for Teens
HICKORY	Hickory Farms
HICKORY FARMS	Hickory Farms
HIGH SPEED	High Speed Access*
HIGHLIGHTS	Highlights for Children
HIGHLIGHTS CATALOG	Highlights for Children Catalog
HIGHLITES	Highlights for Children
HIGHLITES CATALOG	Highlights for Children Catalog
HIGHTS ONLINE	Highlights for Children
HIKER	Backpacker Magazine
HIKING	Backpacker Magazine
HILLARY	Hillary Rodham Clinton
HINDU	The Hinduism Forum
HINDUISM	The Hinduism Forum
HISPANIC	Hispanic Selections
HISPANIC MAGAZINE	HISPANIC Online
HISPANIC ONLINE	HISPANIC Online
HISTORICAL	Company Research
HISTORICAL QUOTES	Historical Stock & Fund Quotes
HISTORY	History Area
HISTORY CHANNEL	The History Channel
HITCHHIKER	The Hub: John the Hitchhiker
HITCHIKER	The Hub: John the Hitchhiker
HITS	Rockline Online
HIV	AIDS and HIV Resource Center
HMCURRENT	Health Magazine's Current area
HMFITNESS	Health Magazine's Fitness area
HMFOOD	Health Magazine's Food area
HMRELATIONSHIPS	Health Magazine's Relationships area
HMREMEDIES	Health Magazine's Remedies area

HO	Hecklers Online
HO CLUBS	Hecklers Online: Clubs
HOB	House of Blues Online [Web Site]
HOBBIES	Life, Styles & Interests channel
HOBBY	Hobby Central
HOBBY CENTRAL	Hobby Central
HOC	Home Office Computing Magazine
HOCKEY	NHL Hockey
HOCKEY TRIVIA	ABC Hockey Trivia
HOF	Downloading Hall of Fame
HOKIES	AOL College Football '96 [3.0 only]
HOL	Hecklers Online
HOL PRO	The Biz!
HOLI	Christianity Online: Holidays and COntests
HOLIDAY	AOL Holiday Central [May disappear without notice]
HOLIDAYS	AOL Holiday Central [May disappear without notice]
HOLIDAYS & HAPPENINGS	Christianity Online: Holidays and COntests
HOLLYWOOD	Hollywood Online
HOLLYWOOD NEWS	Hollywood Online: News
HOLLYWOOD ONLINE	Hollywood Online
HOLLYWOOD PRO	The Biz!
HOLMES	Mysteries from the Yard
HOME	House & Home area
HOME AT AOL	AOL Home Tour [3.0 only]
HOME AUDIO	Consumer Electronics
HOME BANKING	Bank of America
HOME BREW	Food & Drink Network
HOME BREWING	Food & Drink Network
HOME DESIGN	Home Magazine Online
HOME EQUITY LOANS	AOL's Real Estate Center
HOME OFFICE	Home Office Computing Magazine
HOME OWNER	Homeowner's Forum
HOME OWNERS	Homeowner's Forum
HOME PAGE	Personal WWW Publishing area [3.0 only]
HOME PAGE CONTEST	Home Page Contest
HOME PC	HomePC Magazine
HOME REFINANCING	AOL's Real Estate Center
HOME THEATER	Stereo Review Online
HOME VIDEO	Home Video
HOMEOPATHIC REMEDIES	Longevity Magazine Online
HOMER	Homer's Page at The Odyssey Project
HOMESCHOOL	Homeschooling Forum
HOMESCHOOLING	Homeschooling Forum
HOMEWORK	Homework area
HOMEWORK HELP	Homework area
HONG KONG	Hong Kong
HOOPS	NCAA Hoops [May disappear without notice]
HOOPS BOARDS	Extreme Fans: Message Boards
HOOPS TRIVIA	NTN Basketball Trivia
HOOSIERS	AOL College Football '96 [3.0 only]
HOOVER	Hoover's Business Resources
HOOVER'S	Hoover's Business Resources
HOOVERS	Hoover's Business Resources
HOOVERS UPDATES	Hoover's Company Masterlist
HOROSCOPE	Horoscopes
HOROSCOPES	Horoscopes
HORROR	Fictional Realm
HORSE	The Horse Forum
HORSE RACING	The Grandstand: Horse Sports & Racing Forum
HORSE SPORTS	The Grandstand: Horse Sports & Racing Forum
HORSES	The Horse Forum
HOSPITALITY	Hospitality Services
HOSPITALITY SERVICES	Hospitality Services
HOT	What's Hot This Month Showcase
HOT AIR	Global Challenger Balloon Race
HOT BUTTON	The Hub: The Hot Button
HOT CHAT	Entertainment Chat
HOT ENT	What's Hot in Entertainment
HOT ENTERTAINMENT	What's Hot in Entertainment
HOT FILES	Hot Mac Files of the Day
HOT GAMES	What's Hot in AOL Games
HOT HEALTH	What's Hot in Health
HOT MAC	What's Hot in Mac Computing
HOT NET	What's Hot on the Internet
HOT NEWS	Hot News
HOT PC	What's Hot in PC Computing
HOT REF	Hot Reference
HOT REFERENCE	Hot Reference
HOT SOFTWARE	Hot Mac Software
HOT SPORTS	What's Hot in Sports
HOT SPOT	MTV Online: Hot Spot
HOT TODAY	What's Hot Today!
HOT TOPICS	Hot Topics
HOT TRAVEL	What's Hot in Travel
HOTBED	Love@AOL: Hotbed
HOTLANTA	Digital Cities: Atlanta
HOTLINE	Member Services*
HOUSE	Home Magazine Online
HOUSE OF BLUES	House of Blues Online [Web Site]
HOUSENET	HouseNet
HOUSTON	Digital Cities: Houston
HOUSTON ASTROS	Major League Baseball Team: Houston Astros
HOUSTON DIGC	Digital Cities: Houston
HOUSTON DIGITAL CITY	Digital Cities: Houston
HOW TO	Top Tips for AOL
HOWDY	AOL Howdy [3.0 only]

HP	Hewlett-Packard
HP FAX	Hewlett-Packard: Fax Products
HP FILES	Hewlett-Packard: Support Information Files
HP HOME	Hewlett-Packard: Home Products Information
HP MULTI	Hewlett-Packard: Multifunction Products
HP PLOT	Hewlett-Packard: Plotter Products
HP PRN	Hewlett-Packard: Printer Products
HP SCAN	Hewlett-Packard: Scanner Products
HP SCSI	Hewlett-Packard: SCSI Products
HP SERVER	Hewlett-Packard: Server Products
HP STORE	Hewlett-Packard: Information Storage Products
HP VECTRA	Hewlett-Packard: Vectra Products
HQ	Company Research
HQFAX	HTF Consulting
HRS	Better Health & Medical Forum
HSC	MetaTools, Inc.
HSC SOFTWARE	MetaTools, Inc.
HTML	Web Page Toolkit
HTML HELP	The Web Diner
HTS	Home Team Sports
HTTP	What Is HTTP?
HUB	The Hub
HUB CHAT	The Hub: Chat
HUB CONTENTS	The Hub: Index
HUB INDEX	The Hub: Index
HUGHES	Hughes Financial Services
HUM	Virtual Christian Humor
HUMAN SEXUALITY	Simon & Schuster Online: Human Sexuality Dept.
HUMANISM	Humanism-Unitarianism Forum
HUMOR	The Comedy Pub
HUNGARY	Hungary
HUNT	AOL Treasure Hunt
HURLEY	Amazing Instant Novelist
HURRICANE	Tropical Storm and Hurricane Info
HURRICANES	AOL College Football '96 [3.0 only]
HYPERCARD	Mac HyperCard & Scripting Forum
HYPERSTUDIO	Roger Wagner Publishing
HYPR	Hypractv8 with Thomas Dolby
HYW	Hundred Years War
HZ	The Health Zone
I_LINE	ABC Online: iLINE Indie Films
IA	Warner Bros. Insomniacs Asylum
IBD	Investor's Business Daily
IBIZ	InBusiness
IBM	IBM Forum
IBM OS2	OS/2 Forum
IBVA	IBVA Technologies
IBVA TECH	IBVA Technologies
IC	Computing Company Connection

IC HILITES	IC Hilites
IC STORE	Internet Connection Store
ICC	Internet Chess Club
ICELAND	Iceland
ICF	Investors' Exchange
ICS	Internet Connection Store
ICTLEP	Transgender Community Forum: Organizations
IDEAS	The Atlantic Monthly Online
IDEAS FOR BETTER LIVING	Ideas for Better Living
IDITAROD	Iditarod Trail Sled Dog Race
IE	Investors' Exchange
IES	Online Campus
IFGE	Transgender Community Forum: Organizations
IFR	Flying Magazine
IG	Intelligent Gamer Online
IG ONLINE	Intelligent Gamer Online
IGOLF	iGolf
IGOLF HISTORY	iGolf History
IGS	Internet Graphics
IGUANA	Pet Care Forum
IHRSA	The Health Zone
IIN	New Product Showcase
ILINE	ABC Online: iLINE Indie Films
ILLINI	AOL College Football '96 [3.0 only]
ILLUSTRATOR	Mac Graphics Illustrator Special Interest Group
IMAGE	Image Exchange
IMAGE EXCHANGE	Image Exchange
IMAGINATION	Family Computing: Creative Works by Members
IMAGINATION NETWORK	INNsider's Forum
IMAGING	Advanced Color Imaging Forum
IMH	Issues in Mental Health
IMMIGRATION	Genealogy Forum
IMPROV	The IMPROVisation Online
IMPROVISATION	The IMPROVisation Online
IN	Investors' Network
INBIZ	InBusiness
INBOARD	Boating Online
INBUSINESS	InBusiness
INC.	Inc. Magazine
INC	Inc. Magazine
INC. MAGAZINE	Inc. Magazine
INC MAGAZINE	Inc. Magazine
INC. ONLINE	Inc. Magazine
INC ONLINE	Inc. Magazine
INCOME STATEMENT	Disclosure's Financial Statements
INCORPORATE	Incorporate now!
INCORPORATE NOW	Incorporate now!
INDEPENDENCE DAY	AOL's Independence Day area [May disappear without notice]

INDIA	India [3.0 only]
INDIANS	Major League Baseball Team: Cleveland Indians
INDIE	ABC Online: iLINE Indie Films
INDIE MOVIES	Hollywood Online: Independent Films
INDIEFILM	ABC Online: iLINE Indie Films
INDUSTRIES	Your Industry
INDUSTRY CONNECTION	Computing Company Connection
INDUSTRY PROFILES	Hoover's Industry Profiles
INDY	Indianapolis 500
INDY 500	Indianapolis 500
INET CHAT	Internet Chat
INET EMAIL	Internet E-mail
INET EXCHANGE	Internet Exchange
INET MAGAZINES	Internet Computing Magazines
INET MAGS	Internet Computing Magazines
INET ORGS	Internet Organizations
INFINITI	Infiniti Online
INFINITI ONLINE	Infiniti Online
INFODEPOT	Chena Software
INFORMATIK	Informatik Inc.
INFORMATION	Member Services*
INFORMATION PROVIDER	Information Provider Resource Center
INFORMATION PROVIDERS	Information Provider Resource Center
INFORMED PARENT	Princeton Review Informed Parent
INLINE	Inline Design
INLINE SOFTWARE	Inline Design
INN	INNsider's Forum
INNOSYS	InnoSys, Inc.
INSIDE	Industry Insider or The Cobb Group Online
INSIDE FLYER	Inside Flyer
INSIDE MEDIA	Cowles/SIMBA Media Information Network
INSIDER	Industry Insider
INSIGNIA	Insignia Solutions
INSIGNIA SOLUTION	Insignia Solutions
INSOMNIACS	Warner Bros. Insomniacs Asylum
INSOMNIACS ASYLUM	Warner Bros. Insomniacs Asylum
INSTANT ARTIST	Print Artist Special Interest Group
INSTANT ARTIST1	Print Artist Special Interest Group
INSTANT NOVELIST	Amazing Instant Novelist
INSULATION	Owens Corning
INSURANCE	MoneyWhiz
INTEL	Intel Corporation
INTEL INSIDE	Intel Corporation
INTELLIGENT GAMER	Intelligent Gamer Online
INTERACTIVE ASTROLOGY	Astronet
INTERACTIVE ED	Online Courses
INTERACTIVE EDUCATION	Online Courses
INTERCON	InterCon Systems Corporation

INTEREST	Life, Styles & Interests channel
INTERFAITH	Interfaith Forum
INTERIOR DESIGN	Home Magazine Online
INTERNATIONAL	International channel
INTERNATIONAL CAFE	International Cafe
INTERNATIONAL LOVE	Passport to Love
INTERNATIONAL US	International channel
INTERNET	Internet Connection channel
INTERNET BIZ	InBusiness
INTERNET CENTER	Internet Connection channel
INTERNET CHAT	Internet Chat
INTERNET CONNECTION	Internet Connection channel
INTERNET EMAIL	Internet E-mail
INTERNET EXCHANGE	Internet Exchange
INTERNET GRAPHICS	Internet Graphic Sites
INTERNET MAGAZINES	Internet Computing Magazines
INTERNET MAGS	Internet Computing Magazines
INTERNET NEWS	Internet Newsstand
INTERNET NEWSSTAND	Internet Newsstand
INTERNET ORGS	Internet Organizations
INTERNET.ORGS	Internet Organizations
INTERNET QUESTIONS	Internet Questions*
INTERNET SOFTWARE	Internet Software
INTERNET STORE	Internet Connection Store
INTERPLAY	Interplay
INTL	International channel
INTL LOVE	Passport to Love
INTL NEWSTAND	International Newsstand [3.0 only]
INTL TRIVIA	AOL International Trivia
INTOON	InToon with the News
INTREK	InTrek
INTUIT	Intuit, Inc.
INVEST	Investors' Network
INVESTING	Investors' Network
INVESTMENT	Investors' Network
INVESTMENT LINGO	Investment Lingo
INVESTMENTS	Investors' Network
INVESTOR	Investors' Network
INVESTOR RELATIONS	AOL's Full Disclosure for Investors
INVESTOR'S BUSINESS	Investor's Business Daily
INVESTOR'S DAILY	Investor's Business Daily
INVESTOR'S NETWORK	Investors' Network
INVESTORS	Investors' Network
INVESTORS BUSINESS	Investor's Business Daily
INVESTORS DAILY	Investor's Business Daily
INVESTORS NETWORK	Investors' Network
IOMEGA	Iomega Corporation
IOTW	Pictures of the Week
IP	Information Provider Resource Center

IPA	Advanced Color Imaging Forum
IPO CENTRAL	IPO Central
IQ	Wizard World
IR	AOL's Full Disclosure for Investors
IRELAND	Ireland
IRISH	Genealogy Forum
IS	Family Computing: Creative Works by Members
ISCNI	Institute for the Study of Contact with Non Human Intelligence
ISDN	ISDN SIG
ISIS	ISIS International
ISIS INTERNATIONAL	ISIS International
ISKI	iSKI
ISLAM	Islamic Resources
ISLAMIC	Islamic Resources
ISLAND	Island Graphics Corporation
ISLAND GRAPHICS	Island Graphics Corporation
ISLANDERS	NHL Hockey
ISRAEL	Israel
ISREAL	Israel
ISREAL ELECTIONS	Jewish Israeli Elections
ISSUES	AOL Politics
ITALIAN	Genealogy Forum
ITALIAN FOOD	Mama's Cucina by Ragu
ITALY	Italy
IVILLAGE	Parent Soup
JAPAN	International channel
JASC	JASC, Inc.
JAYHAWKS	AOL College Football '96 [3.0 only]
JAYS	Major League Baseball Team: Toronto Blue Jays
JAZZ	Jazz Music Forum
JAZZFEST	House of Blues Online [Web Site]
JCOL	Jewish.COMMunity
JCP	JCPenney
JCPENNEY	JCPenney
JENNY FLAME	The Comedy Pub
JET	Aviation Forum
JEWISH	Jewish.COMMunity
JEWISH ARTS	Jewish Arts
JEWISH BOARDS	Jewish Message Boards
JEWISH CHAT	Jewish Chat Room
JEWISH COMMUNITY	Jewish.COMMunity
JEWISH DOWNLOADS	Jewish File Downloads
JEWISH EDUCATION	Jewish Education
JEWISH ELECTIONS	Jewish Israeli Elections
JEWISH FOOD	Jewish Food
JEWISH HOLIDAY	Jewish Holidays
JEWISH HOLIDAYS	Jewish Holidays
JEWISH MATCHMAKER	Jewish Singles
JEWISH NEWS	Jewish News
JEWISH SINGLES	Jewish Singles
JEWISH STORE	Jewish Store
JEWISH YOUTH	Jewish Youth
JIM	Motley Fool's Rogue
JIM'S BRAIN	Motley Fool's Rogue
JL COOPER	JLCooper Electronics
JOB	MoneyWhiz
JOBS	Help Wanted Ads
JOEL SIEGEL	ABC Good Morning America
JOHN GRAY	Men Are From Mars
JOHN NABER	John Naber [May disappear without notice]
JOIN DC	Register as a Digital Citizen
JOIN DIGITAL CITY	Register as a Digital Citizen
JOKES	Jokes! Etc.
JPEG	Graphics Forum [Platform-dependent]
JPEGVIEW	JPEGView
JPG	Graphics Forum [Platform-dependent]
JUDAISM	Judaism Forum
JUDGMENT	CyberJustice's Record Your Judgment
JULY 4TH	AOL's Independence Day area [May disappear without notice]
JUPITER	Galileo Mission to Jupiter [May disappear without notice]
JUST DO IT	Computer Life Magazine
JUSTINTIME	Just-In-Time Computing Services
KAAL TV	ABC Online: KAAL-TV in Rochester, MN
KABC TV	ABC Online: KABC-TV in Los Angeles, CA
KAIT TV	ABC Online: KAIT-TV in Jonesboro, AR
KAKE TV	ABC Online: KAKE-TV in Wichita, KS
KANSAS CITY ROYALS	Major League Baseball Team: Kansas City Royals
KAPLAN	Kaplan Online
KAPLAN SUPPORT	Kaplan InterActive Software Support
KARATE	The Grandstand's Martial Arts (The Dojo)
KARROS	Eric Karros Kronikles
KASAN	Kasanjian Research
KASANJIAN	Kasanjian Research
KAUFMANN	The Kaufmann Fund
KAZAKHSTAN	Kazakhstan
KEEFE	InToon with the News
KEEPER	Internet Usenet Newsgroup area
KENNEDY SPACE	Challenger Remembered
KENNEDY SPACE CENTER	Challenger Remembered
KENNEHORA	CyberJustice's Kennehora Junction
KENNEHORA JUNCTION	CyberJustice's Kennehora Junction
KENS GUIDE	The Hub: Ken's Guide to the Bible
KENSINGTON	Kensington Microware, Ltd.
KENT MARSH	Kent*Marsh

KESMAI	Air Warrior
KESQ TV	ABC Online: KESQ-TV in Palm Springs, CA
KEWL GRAFFITI	gRaFfItI
KEYWORD	Keyword List Area
KEYWORD LIST	Keyword List Area
KEYWORDS	Keyword List Area
KEZI TV	ABC Online: KEZI-TV in Eugene, OR
KFSN TV	ABC Online: KFSN-TV in Fresno, CA
KGO	KGO-San Francisco Newstalk AM 810
KGO TV	ABC Online: KGO-TV in San Francisco, CA
KGTV TV	ABC Online: KGTV-TV in San Diego, CA
KGUN TV	ABC Online: KGUN-TV in Tucson, AZ
KHBS TV	ABC Online: KHBS/KHOG TV in Fort Smith, AR
KID DESK	Edmark Technologies
KID MOVIES	Hollywood Online: Kids Corner
KID SPORTS	New England Cable Network: Sports for Kids
KID TRAVEL	Family Travel Network
KIDCARE	KidCare
KIDS	Kids Only channel
KIDS CHOICE	Nickelodeon: Kids' Choice Awards
KIDS DICTIONARY	Merriam-Webster's Kids Dictionary
KIDS ONLY	Kids Only channel
KIDS OUT	Kids Out: London's Family Events Guide
KIDS PAGE	Kids' Guide Pager
KIDS PAGER	Kids' Guide Pager
KIDS QUEST	The Quest CD-ROM Companion to AOL's Kids Only channel
KIDS WB	Kids' Warner Brothers Online
KIDS' WB	Kids' Warner Brothers Online
KIDS WEB	Kid's Top Internet Sites
KIDSBIZ	KidsBiz
KIDSOFT	Club KidSoft
KIDSOFT STORE	KidSoft Superstore
KIDZ BIZ	Kidz Biz
KIDZINE	ABC Kidzine
KIFI TV	ABC Online: KIFI-TV in Idaho Falls, ID
KING	Martin Luther King
KING OF THE BEACH	AVP Pro Beach Volleyball
KINGS	NHL Hockey
KIP	Block Financial Software Support
KIPLINGER	Block Financial Software Support
KIRSHNER	Simon & Schuster College Online
KITCHEN	Everything Edible!
KIVETCH	CyberJustice's Worry, Complain & Sob
KIVI TV	ABC Online: KIVI-TV in Boise, ID
KMBC TV	ABC Online: KMBC-TV in Kansas City, MO
KMGH TV	ABC Online: KMGH-TV in Denver, CO
KMIZ TV	ABC Online: KMIZ-TV in Columbia, MO
KNITTING	Needlecrafts/Sewing Center

KNOWLEDGE BASE	Microsoft Knowledge Base
KNTV TV	ABC Online: KNTV-TV in San Jose, CA
KNXV TV	ABC Online: KNXV-TV in Phoenix, AZ
KO	Kids Only Channel
KO CHAT	Kids Only: Chat Rooms
KO HELP	Kids' Guide Pager
KOAT TV	ABC Online: KOAT-TV in Albuquerque, NM
KOB	AVP Pro Beach Volleyball
KOCO TV	ABC Online: KOCO-TV in Oklahoma, OK
KODAK	Kodak Photography Forum
KODAK WEB	Kodak Web Site [3.0 only]
KODE TV	ABC Online: KODE-TV in Joplin, MO
KOMANDO	Kim Komando's Komputer Clinic
KOMPUTER CLINIC	Kim Komando's Komputer Clinic
KOMPUTER TUTOR	Kim Komando's Komputer Clinic
KONSPIRACY	The Hub: Konspiracy Korner
KOREA	Korea
KPT	MetaTools, Inc.
KPT BRYCE	MetaTools, Inc.
KQTV TV	ABC Online: KQTV-TV in St. Joseph, MO
KR	Kasanjian Research
KRAMER	Astronet
KRANK	MTV Online: Krank
KTBS TV	ABC Online: KTBS-TV in Shreveport, LA
KTKA TV	ABC Online: KTKA-TV in Topeka, KS
KTRK TV	ABC Online: KTRK-TV in Houston, TX
KTVX TV	ABC Online: KTVX-TV in Salt Lake City, UT
KTXS TV	ABC Online: KTXS-TV in Abilene, TX
KURZWEIL	Kurzweil Music Systems
KVIA TV	ABC Online: KVIA-TV in El Paso, TX
KVUE TV	ABC Online: KVUE-TV in Austin, TX
KWM WEB	Korean War Memorial Home Page
L AND C	Lois & Clark
L & C	Lois & Clark
L&C HOT	What's Hot in Learning & Culture
L&C STORE	Learning & Culture Store
L'EGGS	One Hanes Place
LA COMM	Digital City Los Angeles: Community
LA DIGC	Digital Cities: Los Angeles
LA DIGITAL CITY	Digital Cities: Los Angeles
LA DOLCE VITA	La Dolce Vita
LA JAVA	L.A. Java
LA NEWS	Digital City Los Angeles: News & Weather
LA PEOPLE	Digital City Los Angeles: People
LA TOUR	Digital City Los Angeles: City Tour
LA WEATHER	Digital City Los Angeles: News & Weather
LACROSSE	The Lacrosse Forum
LAMBDA	Lambda Rising Bookstore Online
LAMBDA RISING	Lambda Rising Bookstore Online

LAMDA	Gay & Lesbian Community Forum
LANDSCAPING	Home Magazine Online
LANGUAGE	International Languages
LANGUAGE SYS	Fortner Research
LANGUAGES	International Cafe
LANIER	Lanier Family Travel Guides
LANIER FAMILY TRAVEL	Lanier Family Travel Guides
LAPIS	Focus Enhancements
LAPTOP	PowerBook Resource Center
LAPUB	LaPub
LAREDO	Laredo National Bank [3.0 only]
LATE NIGHT SURVEY	The Late Night Survey
LATE SHOW	Dave Letterman's Late Show Online [3.0 only]
LATE SHOW ONLINE	Dave Letterman's Late Show Online [3.0 only]
LATINA	HISPANIC Online
LATINO	HISPANIC Online
LATINONET	LatinoNet Registration
LATVIA	Latvia
LAUGH	The Comedy Pub
LAW	Court TV's Law Center
LAW CENTER	Court TV's Law Center
LAW NET	Nolo Press: Law on the Net
LAW SCHOOL	Kaplan Online or The Princeton Review
LAWRENCE	Lawrence Productions
LAX	The Lacrosse Forum
LC HOT	What's Hot in Learning & Culture
LEADER	Leader Technologies
LEADER TECH	Leader Technologies
LEADER TECHNOLOGIES	Leader Technologies
LEADERS NETWORK	Christianity Online: Church Leaders Network
LEADERSHIP	Leadership Journal
LEADERSHIP JOURNAL	Leadership Journal
LEADING EDGE	Leading Edge
LEARN	Learning & Culture channel
LEARNING	Learning & Culture channel
LEARNING AND REFERENCE	Learning & Culture channel
LEARNING CENTER	Learning & Culture channel
LEARNING & CULTURE HOT	What's Hot in Learning & Culture
LEARNING & REFERENCE	Learning & Culture channel
LEATHER	Leather onQ
LEGAL	Online Legal Areas
LEGAL PAD	The Legal Pad
LEGAL SIG	Legal Information Network
LINN SOFTWARE	Linn Software
LIONS	Detroit Lions Football Coverage [3.0 only]
LISTINGS	TV Quest
LISTSERV	Internet Mailing Lists
LITERACY	Adult Literacy & Education Forum
LIVE	AOL Live!
LIVE!	AOL Live!
LIVE PICTURE	Live Picture, Inc.
LIVE SPORTS	AOL Sports Live
LIVE@THRIVE	Thrive@AOL: Chat and Auditorium Events
LIVE TONIGHT	AOL Live!
LIZARD	Pet Care Forum
LJ	Leadership Journal
LLAMA	Pet Care Forum
LNB	Laredo National Bank [3.0 only]
LOCAL NEWSPAPERS	Newspapers Selection
LOCALNEWS	Newspapers Selection
LOCALS	CyberJustice's Meet The Locals
LOGICODE	Logicode Technology, Inc.
LOIS AND CLARK	Lois & Clark
LOIS & CLARK	Lois & Clark
LOL	The Comedy Pub
LONGEVITY	Longevity Magazine Online
LONGHORNS	AOL College Football '96 [3.0 only]
LOOKING GLASS	Looking Glass [3.0 only]
LOS ANGELES	Digital Cities: Los Angeles
LOS ANGELES DIGC	Digital Cities: Los Angeles
LOS ANGELES DODGERS	Major League Baseball Team: Los Angeles Dodgers
LOSE	MTV Online: Choose or Lose 1996
LOST TV	Lost & Found TV Shows
LOST TV SHOWS	Lost & Found TV Shows
LOTTERY	Lotteries
LOVE	Love@AOL
LOVE@AOL	Love@AOL
LOVE AT AOL	Love@AOL
LOVE MOM	I Love My Mom Because... [May disappear without notice]
LOVE ONLINE	ABC Love Online
LOVE SHACK	The Love Shack
LOVER	Love@AOL
LSAT	Kaplan Online or The Princeton Review
LSI	Life, Styles & Interests channel
LUCAS	LucasArts Games
LUCAS ARTS	LucasArts Games
LUNCH	Your Business Lunch
LUST	Love@AOL
LUV	ABC Love Online
LUXEMBOURG	Luxembourg
LYNCH	Merrill Lynch
LYNX	Virtual Airlines
LYNX AIRWAYS	Virtual Airlines
M AND T BANK	Manufacturers & Traders Trust Company [3.0 only]

M'S	Major League Baseball Team: Seattle Mariners
M1	ABC Online: Murder One Show
M2F	Transgender Community Forum
MAC	Apple/Macintosh Forums
MAC ALPT	The Grandstand's Simulation Golf
MAC ART	Graphic Art & CAD Forum [MAOL only]
MAC BIBLE	The Macintosh Bible/Peachpit Forum
MAC BUSINESS	Macintosh Business & Home Office Forum
MAC CAT	Mac Cats
MAC CATS	Mac Cats
MAC CHATS	Mac Computing Forums: Chats and Conferences
MAC COMMUNICATION	Mac Communications and Networking Forum
MAC COMMUNICATIONS	Mac Communications and Networking Forum
MAC COMPUTING	Apple/Macintosh Forums
MAC CONFERENCE	Mac Computing Forums: Chats and Conferences
MAC CONFERENCES	Mac Computing Forums: Chats and Conferences
MAC DESKTOP	Mac Desktop Publishing/WP Forum
MAC DEVELOPMENT	Macintosh Developers Forum
MAC DOWNLOADING	Mac Software Center
MAC DTP	Mac Desktop Publishing/WP Forum
MAC EDUCATION	Mac Education & Technology Forum
MAC ESSENTIALS	Macintosh Essential Utilities
MAC FAQ	Mac Utilities FAQ Resource Center
MAC FORUM NEWS	Mac Forum Newsletters
MAC GAME	Mac Games Forum
MAC GAMES	Mac Games Forum
MAC GRAPHICS	Mac Graphic Art & CAD Forum
MAC HARDWARE	Mac Hardware Forum
MAC HELP	Help Desk [Platform-dependent]
MAC HOME	Mac Home Journal
MAC HOME JOURNAL	Mac Home Journal
MAC HOT	What's Hot in Mac Computing
MAC HYPERCARD	Mac HyperCard & Scripting Forum
MAC LIBRARIES	Mac Software Center
MAC MULTIMEDIA	Mac Desktop Video & Multimedia Forum
MAC MUSIC	Mac Music & Sound Forum
MAC NEWS	Mac Computing News & Newsletters
MAC O/S	Mac Operating Systems Forum
MAC OPERATING SYSTEMS	Mac Operating Systems Forum
MAC OS	Mac Operating Systems Forum
MAC PROGRAMMING	Macintosh Developers Forum
MAC SOFTWARE	Mac Software Center
MAC SOFTWARE CENTER	Mac Software Center
MAC SOUND	Mac Music & Sound Forum
MAC SPEAKERZ	True Image Audio
MAC SPOTLIGHT	In the Mac Spotlight
MAC SUMMER	Mac Computing Forums: Summer [May disappear without notice]
MAC TELECOM	Mac Communications and Networking Forum
MAC TELECOMM	Mac Communications and Networking Forum
MAC TIPS	Family Computing Forum: Tip of the Day
MAC TODAY	Mac Today Magazine
MAC UTILITIES	Mac Utilities Forum
MAC VIRUS	Mac Virus Information Center
MAC WORD PROCESSING	Mac Desktop Publishing/WP Forum
MACHACK	MacHack
MACHINERY	American Woodworker: Tool Reviews
MACINTOSH	Apple/Macintosh Forums
MACINTOSH BIBLE	The Macintosh Bible/Peachpit Forum
MACMILLAN	MacMillan Information SuperLibrary
MACRO	Affinity Microsystems
MACROMEDIA	MacroMedia, Inc.
MACROMIND	MacroMedia, Inc.
MACROS	Affinity Microsystems
MACSCITECH	MacSciTech SIG
MACTIVITY	Mactivity '95 Forum
MACUSER	MacUser Magazine
MACWORLD	MacWorld Magazine
MAD	DC Comics Online
MAD ABOUT	Mad About You Fan Forum
MAD ABOUT YOU	Mad About You Fan Forum
MAD ABOUT YOU SUNDAYS	Mad About You Fan Forum
MAD MAGAZINE	DC Comics Online
MAD WORLD	Today's News: It's a Mad, Mad World... Dispatches from the Wires
MADA	MacApp Developers Association
MAGAZINE RACK	Computing Magazine Rack [3.0 only]
MAGAZINES	The Newsstand
MAGIC LINK	Sony Magic Link
MAGICK	Pagan Religions & Occult Sciences
MAGICKAL	Pagan Religions & Occult Sciences
MAGNET	Hachette Filipacchi Magazines
MAGNETO	Hachette Filipacchi Magazines
MAIL	Post Office
MAIL CENTER	Mail Center
MAIL CONTROLS	Mail Controls
MAIL GATEWAY	Mail Gateway
MAILING LIST	Business Yellow Pages
MAILING LISTS	Internet Mailing Lists
MAINSTAY	Mainstay
MAKEOVER	Style Channel
MAKEUP	Style Channel
MALAWI	Malawi
MALL	Marketplace channel

MALTA	City Guide to Malta
MAM	Mad About Music
MAMA	Mama's Cucina by Ragu
MAMA'S CUCINA	Mama's Cucina by Ragu
MANAGER	Manager's Network
MANAGER'S NETWORK	Manager's Network
MANAGERS	Manager's Network
MANAGING	Manager's Network
MANGA	Wizard World
MANHATTAN GRAPHICS	Manhattan Graphics
MANTICORE	Image Exchange: Gallery of the Mousepad
MAPLE LEAFS	NHL Hockey
MARATHON	Marine Corps Marathon [May disappear without notice]
MARCO	Motorola
MARINE	Boating Online
MARINE CORPS MARATHON	Marine Corps Marathon [May disappear without notice]
MARINERS	Major League Baseball Team: Seattle Mariners
MARKET	MarketMaster
MARKET NEWS	Market News area
MARKET PLACE	Marketplace department
MARKETING PREFERENCES	Marketing Preferences*
MARKETING PREFS	Marketing Preferences*
MARKETPLACE	Marketplace channel
MARKETS	Market News area
MARLINS	Major League Baseball Team: Florida Marlins
MARQUETTE	Marquette Banks [3.0 only]
MARRIAGE	Marriage Partnership Magazine
MARRIAGE PARTNERSHIP	Marriage Partnership Magazine
MARS	Men Are From Mars
MARTIAL ARTS	Hobby Central: Martial Arts
MARTIN	Martin Luther King
MARTIN LUTHER	Martin Luther King
MARTIN LUTHER KING	Martin Luther King
MARTINSEN	Martinsen's Software
MARVEL	Marvel Online [3.0 only]
MASS	Massachusetts Governor's Forum
MASS.	Massachusetts Governor's Forum
MASSACHUSETTS	Massachusetts Governor's Forum
MASSAGE	Longevity Magazine Online
MASTERLIST	Hoover's Company MasterList
MATCHMAKER	Love@AOL
MATCHMAKING	Love@AOL
MATH	NAS Online
MATHEMATICS	Simon & Schuster Online: Mathematics Dept.
MATT	Matt Williams' Hot Corner
MATT WILLIAMS	Matt Williams' Hot Corner
MAW	Martial Arts Network
MAW NETWORK	Martial Arts Network
MAX AOL	Family Computing Forum: Maximum AOL
MAXIMUM AOL	Family Computing Forum: Maximum AOL
MAXIS	Maxis
MAXTECH	MaxTech Corporation
MAY	Mad About You Fan Forum
MBS	Macintosh Business & Home Office Forum
MC	Military City Online
MC ADS	Mercury Center Advertising
MC COMMUNICATION	Mercury Center Communication
MC ENTERTAINMENT	Mercury Center Entertainment area
MC LIBRARY	Mercury Center Newspaper Library
MC LIVING	Mercury Center Bay Area Living area
MC MARKET	Mercury Center Advertising
MC NEW	San Jose Mercury News [GAOL only]
MC NEWS	Mercury Center in the News area
MC SPORTS	Mercury Center Sports area
MC TRIVIA	Mercury Center Trivia
MCAFEE	McAfee Associates
MCAT	Kaplan Online or The Princeton Review
MCDONALD'S	McFamily Community
MCFAMILY	McFamily Community
MCINTIRE	University of Virginia Alumni/McIntire School of Commerce
MCINTIRE ALUMNI	University of Virginia Alumni/McIntire School of Commerce
MCL	Mystic Color Labs
MCM	Mac Communications and Networking Forum
MCO	Military City Online
MCO BASES	Military City Online Worldwide Military Installations Database
MCO COMM	Military City Online Communications
MCO HQ	Military City Online Headquarters
MCO SHOP	Military City Online Shop
MCO TOUR	Military City Online Tour
MDP	Mac Desktop Publishing/WP Forum
MDV	Macintosh Developers Forum
MEANWHILE	The Hub: Meanwhile
MECC	MECC
MED	Mac Education & Technology Forum
MEDIA	Cowles/SIMBA Media Information Network
MEDIA CENTER	Library Media Center SIG
MEDIA INFORMATION	Cowles/SIMBA Media Information Network
MEDICAL DICTIONARY	Merriam-Webster's Medical Dictionary
MEDICAL SCHOOL	Kaplan Online or The Princeton Review
MEDICINE	Health Channel

MEDLINE	Medline
MEDLINSW	Medlin Accounting Shareware
MEGA NEWS	FamilyPC Online
MEGAZINE	FamilyPC Online
MEGAZONE	FamilyPC Online
MELLON	Mellon Bank [3.0 only]
MELROSE	Melrose Mondays
MELROSE MONDAYS	Melrose Mondays
MEMBER DIRECTORY	Member Directory
MEMBER PROFILE	Edit your member profile
MEMBER SERVICES	Member Services*
MEMBER SURVEY	Member Survey
MEMBERS	Member Directory
MEMBERS' RIDES	Wheels Exchange
MEMBERS RIDES	Wheels Exchange
MEMORIAL DAY	Memorial Day 1996 [May disappear without notice]
MEN	The Exchange: Communities Center
MEN ARE FROM MARS	Men Are From Mars
MEN'S HEALTH	Men's Health Forum
MENS' HEALTH WEB	Men's Health Internet Sites
MENTAL HEALTH	Mental Health Forum
MENTAL HEALTH WEB	Mental Health Web Sites
MER	Merrill Lynch
MERRIAM	Merriam-Webster Dictionary
MERRIAM-WEBSTER	Merriam-Webster Dictionary
MERRILL	Merrill Lynch
MERRILL LYNCH	Merrill Lynch
MES	Messiah College
MESSAGE PAD	Newton Resource Center
MESSIAH	Messiah College
MET HOME	Metropolitan Home
METAPHYSICS	Religion & Ethics Forum
METATOOLS	MetaTools, Inc.
METRICOM	Metricom, Inc.
METROPOLITAN HOME	Metropolitan Home
METROWERKS	Metrowerks
METS	Major League Baseball Team: New York Mets
METZ	Metz
MEXICO	Mexico
MF	The Motley Fool: Finance & Folly
MFACTORY	mFactory Inc.
MFC	AOL Mutual Fund Center
MFC 95	AOL Mutual Fund Center
MFOOL	The Motley Fool: Finance & Folly
MFTY	Mysteries from the Yard
MGM	Mac Games Forum
MGR	Mac Graphic Art & CAD Forum
MGX	Micrografx, Inc.
MHC	Mac HyperCard & Scripting Forum
MHJ	Mac Home Journal
MHM	Members Helping Members message board*
MHS	Mac HyperCard & Scripting Forum
MHW	Mac Hardware Forum
MIAMI	Digital Cities: Miami-Ft. Lauderdale
MIAMI COMM	Digital City Miami: Community
MIAMI DIGC	Digital Cities: Miami-Ft. Lauderdale
MIAMI DIGITAL CITY	Digital Cities: Miami-Ft. Lauderdale
MIAMI NEWS	Digital City Miami: News & Weather
MIAMI PEOPLE	Digital City Miami: People
MIAMI TOUR	Digital City Miami: City Tour
MIAMI WEATHER	Digital City Miami: News & Weather
MICE	Pet Care Forum
MICHAEL JORDAN	Jordan [3.0 only]
MICHIGAN	Michigan Governor's Forum
MICHIGAN GOVERNOR	Michigan Governor's Forum
MICHIGAN J FROG	The WB Network
MICRO J	Micro J Systems, Inc.
MICROFRONTIER	MicroFrontier, Ltd.
MICROGRAFX	Micrografx, Inc.
MICROMAT	MicroMat Computer Systems
MICROPROSE	MicroProse
MICROSEEDS	Microseeds Publishing, Inc.
MICROSOFT	Microsoft Resource Center
MIDI	Music & Sound Forum [Platform-dependent]
MIDWEST	Digital Cities: Midwest
MIDWEST DIGC	Digital Cities: Midwest
MIDWEST DIGITAL CITY	Digital Cities: Midwest
MIGHTY DUCKS	NHL Hockey
MIKE KEEFE	InToon with the News
MILESTONE	DC Comics Online
MILITARY	Military and Vets Club
MILITARY CITY	Military City Online
MILITARY CITY ONLINE	Military City Online
MILWAUKEE BREWERS	Major League Baseball Team: Milwaukee Brewers
MIN	Minirth Meier New Life Clinics
MIND AND BODY	Your Mind & Body Online
MIND & BODY	Your Mind & Body Online
MINDSCAPE	Mindscape
MINICAD	Graphsoft, Inc.
MINIRTH MEIER	Minirth Meier New Life Clinics
MINNEAPOLIS	Digital Cities: Minneapolis-St. Paul
MINNEAPOLIS DIGC	Digital Cities: Minneapolis-St. Paul
MINNESOTA TWINS	Major League Baseball Team: Minnesota Twins
MIRABELLA	Mirabella Magazine
MIRABELLA ONLINE	Mirabella Magazine
MIRROR	Mirror Technologies
MISST-U	CyberJustice: Misst-U & The 7 Pillars of Wisdom

MIX CITICORP	Citicorp Mortgage [3.0 only]
MIX CMBA	California Mortgage Bankers Association [3.0 only]
MIX DATA TRACK	Data Track Systems, Inc. [3.0 only]
MIX GENESIS	Genesis 2000 [3.0 only]
MIXSTAR	Mixstar Mortgage Information Exchange
MJ	Jordan [3.0 only]
ML	Merrill Lynch
MLB	ABC Sports Major League Baseball
MLK	Martin Luther King
MLPF&S	Merrill Lynch
MLS	AOL's Real Estate Center
MLS LIVE	The Grandstand's Major League Soccer
MM	PC Multimedia Forum
MM SHOWCASE	Multimedia Showcase*
MMC	Music Message Center
MME	Grolier's Encyclopedia
MMM	Mac Desktop Video & Multimedia Forum
MMNLC	Minirth Meier New Life Clinics
MMS	Mac Music & Sound Forum
MMS TOOL	Sound & Midi Resource Center
MMW	PC World Multimedia Edition
MMZONE	Multimedia Zone [3.0 only]
MO	Moms Online
MOBILE	Mobile Office Online
MOBILEMEDIA	MobileMedia
MODELS	Elle Magazine Online
MODELS! MODELS!	Style Channel
MODEM	High Speed Access*
MODEM HELP	High Speed Access*
MODEM SHOP	AOL Modem Shop
MODERN LIVES	The Hub: Modern Lives
MODERN ROCK	WHFS 99.1 FM
MODUS	Modus Operandi
MODUS OPERANDI	Modus Operandi
MOM	AOL Families
MOMS	AOL Families
MOMS ONLINE	Moms Online
MONEY	Personal Finance channel
MONEYWHIZ	MoneyWhiz
MONOLITH	The Hub: Monolith
MONSTER ISLAND	Adventures by Mail
MONTESSORI	Montessori Schools
MONTESSORI SCHOOLS	Montessori Schools
MONTREAL EXPOS	Major League Baseball Team: Montreal Expos
MOO	Gateway 2000, Inc.
MOONSTONE	Moonstone Mountaineering
MORGAN DAVIS	Morgan Davis Group
MORNINGSTAR	Morningstar Mutual Funds
MORPH	Gryphon Software
MORTGAGE	AOL's Real Estate Center
MORTGAGE RATES	AOL's Real Estate Center
MORTGAGES	AOL's Real Estate Center
MOS	Mac Operating Systems Forum
MOS UPDATE	Apple System 7.5 Update
MOSIAC	Spiritual Mosiac
MOTHER	AOL Families
MOTHER'S DAY	Mother's Day area [May disappear without notice]
MOTHERS	AOL Families
MOTHERS DAY	Mother's Day area [May disappear without notice]
MOTLEY	The Motley Fool: Finance & Folly
MOTLEY FOOL	The Motley Fool: Finance & Folly
MOTORCYCLE	Car/Cycle Selections
MOTORCYCLES	Car/Cycle Selections
MOTORCYCLING	Cycle World Online
MOTOROLA	Motorola
MOTORSPORT	Motorsport '95 Online
MOTORSPORTS	Motorsport '95 Online
MOTU	Mark of the Unicorn
MOUNTAIN	iSKI
MOUNTAIN BIKE	Bicycling Magazine
MOUNTAINEERS	AOL College Football '96 [3.0 only]
MOUSE	Pet Care Forum
MOUSEPAD	Image Exchange: Gallery of the Mousepad
MOVIE	@the.movies
MOVIE FORUMS	Movie Forums area
MOVIE GUIDE	Hollywood Online: A-Z Movie Guide
MOVIE REVIEW DATABASE	Movie Review Database
MOVIE REVIEW DB	Movie Review Database
MOVIE REVIEWS	Movie Reviews
MOVIE REVIEWS DATABASE	Movie Review Database
MOVIELINK	MovieLink
MOVIES	@the.movies
MOVIES WEB	Movies on the Web
MOVIEVISIONS	MovieVisions
MP	Multimedia Preferences
MPBT	Multiplayer BattleTech [3.0 only]
MR SCIENCE	Kim Komando's Komputer Clinic
MRD	Movie Review Database
MRTECINC	M & R Technologies, Inc.
MS BIZ	Your Business
MS DOS 6	MS-DOS 6.0 Resource Center
MS DOS 60	MS-DOS 6.0 Resource Center
MS SUPPORT	Microsoft Resource Center
MS WORKS	Microsoft Works Resource Center
MSA	Management Science Associates

MSBC	Your Business
MSCOPE	Standard & Poor's Marketscope
MSKB	Microsoft Knowledge Base
MSTATION	Bentley Systems, Inc.
MT	iSKI
MTC	Mac Communications and Networking Forum
MTROPOLIS	mFactory Inc.
MTV	MTV Online
MTV NEWS	MTV News
MU	CyberJustice: Misst-U & The 7 Pillars of Wisdom
MUCHMUSIC	MuchMusic Online
MUCHMUSIC ONLINE	MuchMusic Online
MUG	America Online Store
MULTIMEDIA	Multimedia menu
MULTIMEDIA PREFS	Multimedia Preferences
MULTIMEDIA WORLD	PC World Multimedia Edition
MULTIMEDIA ZONE	Multimedia Zone [3.0 only]
MULTIPLE SCLEROSIS	Multiple Sclerosis Forum
MURDER 1	ABC Online: Murder One Show
MURDER ONE	ABC Online: Murder One Show
MUSEUM	Smithsonian Online
MUSEUMS	Smithsonian Online
MUSIC	MusicSpace
MUSIC AND SOUND FORUM	Music and Sound Forum [Platform-dependent]
MUSIC FORUM	Music and Sound Forum [Platform-dependent]
MUSIC MEDIA	Music Media
MUSIC NEWS	MTV Online: News
MUSIC PROMO	MusicSpace Events
MUSIC & SOUND	Music and Sound Forum [Platform-dependent]
MUSIC TALK	MusicSpace Communications
MUSIC WEB	MusicSpace WEB TopStops
MUSICSPACE	MusicSpace
MUSTANG	Mustang Software
MUSTANG SOFTWARE	Mustang Software
MUT	Mac Utilities Forum
MUT AWARD	Mac Shareware Awards [MAOL only]
MUT AWARDS	Mac Shareware Awards [MAOL only]
MUTUAL FUND	AOL Mutual Fund Center
MUTUAL FUND 95	AOL Mutual Fund Center
MUTUAL FUND CENTER	AOL Mutual Fund Center
MUTUAL FUNDS	AOL Mutual Fund Center
MVD	Mac Desktop Video & Multimedia Forum
MVT	Mac Utilities Forum
MW DICTIONARY	Merriam-Webster's Collegiate Dictionary
MW EXPO	MacWorld Expo
MY PLACE	My Place (for FTP sites)
MYOB	Best! Ware
MYSTERIES	Mysteries from the Yard
MYSTERIES FROM THE YARD	Mysteries from the Yard
MYSTERY	Fictional Realm
MZ	Multimedia Zone [3.0 only]
N MARIANA ISLANDS	Northern Mariana Islands
N&V	USA Weekend: News & Views
NAA	Newspaper Association of America
NABER	John Naber [May disappear without notice]
NAEA	NAEA Tax Channel
NAESP	NAESP Web Link
NAGF	Non-Affiliated Gamers Forum
NAME	Add, change, or delete screen names
NAMES	Add, change, or delete screen names
NAMI	National Alliance of Mentally Ill
NAN	Nick at Nite
NAPC	Employment Agency Database
NAPLES	Digital Cities: Ft. Myers/Naples FL
NAPLES DC	Digital Cities: Ft. Myers/Naples FL
NAPLES DCITY	Digital Cities: Ft. Myers/Naples FL
NAPLES DIGC	Digital Cities: Ft. Myers/Naples FL
NAPLES DIGITAL CITY	Digital Cities: Ft. Myers/Naples FL
NAPLES FL	Digital Cities: Ft. Myers/Naples FL
NAQP	National Association of Quick Printers area
NAREE	AOL's Real Estate Center
NAS	NAS Online
NASA	Galileo Mission to Jupiter [May disappear without notice]
NASCAR	AOL Auto Racing
NATIONAL GEOGRAPHIC	Odyssey Project
NATIONAL PARENTING	The National Parenting Center
NATIVE AMERICAN	The Exchange: Communities Center
NATURE	The Nature Conservancy
NAVIGATE	Top Tips for AOL
NAVISOFT	Navisoft
NBA DRAFT	1995 NBA Draft
NBC	NBC... NOT!
NBR	The Nightly Business Report: Making $ense of It All
NBR REPORT	The Nightly Business Report: NBR Online Report
NC8	News Channel 8
NCAA	NCAA Hoops [May disappear without notice]
NCLEX	Kaplan Online
NCR	National Catholic Reporter
NCT	Next Century Technologies
NEA	Accessing the NEA Public Forum*
NEA ONLINE	Accessing the NEA Public Forum*

NEA PUBLIC	National Education Association Public Forum
NEC	NEC Technologies
NEC TECH	NEC Technologies
NECN	New England Cable News
NEIGHBORHOODS	Neighborhoods, USA
NEIGHBORHOODS, USA	Neighborhoods, USA
NEOLOGIC	NeoLogic
NESN	New England Sports Network
NESN BASEBALL	NESN: New England Baseball
NESN BASKETBALL	NESN: New England Basketball
NESN FOOTBALL	NESN: New England Football
NESN HOCKEY	NESN: New England Hockey
NESN OUTDOORS	NESN: New England Outdoors
NESN SPORT CIRCUIT	New England Sports Network
NESN SPORTS	New England Sports Network
NESSIE	Weekly World News
NET	Internet Connection channel
.NET	.net: the internet magazine [3.0 only]
NET BOOKS	Internet Connection Store
NET CHAT	Internet Chat
NET EXCHANGE	Internet Exchange
NET EXPERT	Pro's Corner
NET HEAD JED	CyberSmith
NET HEAD RED	CyberSmith
NET HELP	net.help
NET LIBRARY	Internet Software
NET NEWS	Internet Newsstand
'NET NEWS	Internet Newsstand
NET_NOIR	NetNoir
NET_NOIRE	NetNoir
NET ORGS	Internet Organizations
NET SOFTWARE	Internet Software
NET STORE	Internet Connection Store
NET SUGGESTIONS	Internet Suggestions
NETGIRL	NetGirl
NETGIRL PERSONALS	NetGirl: Personals
NETHERLANDS	Netherlands
NETNOIR	NetNoir
NETNOIRE	NetNoir
NETORGS	Net.Orgs
NETSCAPE	Netscape [3.0 only]
NETWORKING	Communications/Telecom/Networking Forum [Platform-dependent]
NETWORKING FORUM	Communications/Telecom/Networking Forum [Platform-dependent]
NETWORKS EXPO	New Product Showcase
NEVERWINTER	AD&D Neverwinter Nights
NEW	New Features & Services
NEW AGE	Religion & Ethics Forum
NEW AOL	Newest Version of AOL Software [Platform-dependent]
NEW AUTO	AutoVantage: New Car Summary
NEW BEDFORD	Digital Cities: New Bedford Massachusetts
NEW BEDFORD DC	Digital Cities: New Bedford Massachusetts
NEW BEDFORD DCITY	Digital Cities: New Bedford Massachusetts
NEW BEDFORD DIGC	Digital Cities: New Bedford Massachusetts
NEW BEDFORD MA	Digital Cities: New Bedford Massachusetts
NEW CAR	AutoVantage: New Car Summary
NEW ENGLAND	Genealogy Forum
NEW ENGLAND BASEBALL	NESN: New England Baseball
NEW ENGLAND CABLE	New England Cable News
NEW ENGLAND CABLE NEWS	New England Cable News
NEW ENGLAND FOOTBALL	NESN: New England Football
NEW ENGLAND HOCKEY	NESN: New England Hockey
NEW ENGLAND NEWS	New England Cable News
NEW ENGLAND OUTDOORS	NESN: New England Outdoors
NEW ENGLAND PATRIOTS	NESN: New England Football
NEW ENGLAND SPORTS	New England Sports Network
NEW ERA	Tactic Software
NEW FILM	New Movie Releases
NEW FILMS	New Movie Releases
NEW GUINEA	Papua New Guinea
NEW INTERESTS	New Interests
NEW LIFE	Minirth Meier New Life Clinics
NEW MEMBER	Orientation Express (New Member Area)
NEW MEMBERS	Orientation Express (New Member Area)
NEW MOVIE	New Movie Releases
NEW MOVIE RELEASES	New Movie Releases
NEW MOVIES	New Movie Releases
NEW ORLEANS	Digital Cities: New Orleans Louisiana
NEW ORLEANS DC	Digital Cities: New Orleans Louisiana
NEW ORLEANS DCITY	Digital Cities: New Orleans Louisiana
NEW ORLEANS DIGC	Digital Cities: New Orleans Louisiana
NEW ORLEANS LA	Digital Cities: New Orleans Louisiana
NEW PRICING	New Pricing*
NEW PRODUCT	New Product News
NEW PRODUCT SHOWCASE	New Product Showcase
NEW PRODUCTS	New Product News
NEW RELEASES	New Movie Releases
NEW REPUBLIC	The New Republic Magazine
NEW TEK	New Tek
NEW TV SEASON	Lost & Found TV Shows
NEW WORLD	New World Computing
NEW YEAR	Have a Healthy New Year!
NEW YEAR DAY	Happy New Year area [May disappear without notice]
NEW YEARS	Happy New Years area [May disappear without notice]

NEW YORK	@times/The New York Times Online
NEW YORK CITY	@times/The New York Times Online
NEW YORK METS	Major League Baseball Team: New York Mets
NEW YORK TIMES	@times/The New York Times Online
NEW YORK YANKEES	Major League Baseball Team: New York Yankees
NEW ZEALAND	New Zealand
NEWBIE	Orientation Express (New Member Area)
NEWPORT NEWS DC	Digital Cities: Newport News and Norfolk
NEWPORT NEWS DCITY	Digital Cities: Newport News and Norfolk
NEWPORT NEWS DIGC	Digital Cities: Newport News and Norfolk
NEWPORT NEWS VA	Digital Cities: Newport News and Norfolk
NEWS	Today's News channel
NEWS 8	News Channel 8
NEWS AND FINANCE	Today's News channel
NEWS CHANNEL	News Channel 8
NEWS CHANNEL 8	News Channel 8
NEWS & FINANCE	Today's News channel
NEWS LIBRARY	Mercury Center Newspaper Library
NEWS PROFILES	News Profiles
NEWS QUIZ	Chicago Tribune: News Quiz
NEWS & REVIEWS	Family Computing Forum: News & Reviews
NEWS ROOM	Today's News channel
NEWS SEARCH	Search News Articles
NEWS SENSATIONS	News Sensations
NEWS TEXT	Today's News channel
NEWS VIEWS	ABC Online: News Views
NEWS & VIEWS	USA Weekend: News & Views
NEWS WATCH	Search News Articles
NEWS/SPORTS/MONEY	Today's News channel
NEWSBYTES	Newsbytes
NEWSCIENCE	New Science Products, Inc.
NEWSGRIEF	NewsGrief
NEWSGROUP	Internet Usenet Newsgroup area
NEWSGROUPS	Internet Usenet Newsgroup area
NEWSLETTER	Games & Entertainment Newsletter
NEWSLETTERS	Genealogy Forum
NEWSLINK	Today's News channel
NEWSPAPER	Newspapers selection
NEWSPAPER LIBRARY	Mercury Center Newspaper Library
NEWSPAPERS	Newspapers selection
NEWSSTAND	The Newsstand
NEWSWEEK	Newsweek Magazine
NEWSWIRE	Newswire [3.0 only]
NEWTON	Newton Resource Center
NEWTON BOOK	PDA/Palmtop Forum
NEXT	Generation Next
NFL	Team NFL [3.0 only]
NFL DRAFT	NFL Draft
NG	Newsgrief

NGLTF	Nation Gay & Lesbian Task Force
NGS	Odyssey Project
NGUIDES	CNN Newsroom Online
NHL	NHL Online
NICK	Nickelodeon Selections
NICK AT NITE	Nick at Nite
NICK @ NITE	Nick at Nite
NICKELODEON	Nickelodeon Online
NIGERIA	Nigeria
NIGHTLINE	ABC News-On-Demand
NIKON	Nikon Electronic Imaging
NILES	Niles and Associates
NINTENDO	Nintendo Power Source
NINTENDO POWER SOURCE	Nintendo Power Source
NISSAN	Nissan Online
NISUS	Nisus Software
NITTANY LIONS	AOL College Football '96 [3.0 only]
NMAA	National Museum of American Art
NMAH	National Museum of American History
NMSS	National Multiple Sclerosis Society
NNFY	National Network for Youth
NNY	National Network for Youth
NO HANDS	Common Ground Software
NO HANDS SOFTWARE	Common Ground Software
NOA	Nintendo Power Source
NOIR-NET	NetNoir
NOIRE_NET	NetNoir
NOIRENET	NetNoir
NOLO	Nolo Press' Self-Help Law Center
NOLO PRESS	Nolo Press' Self-Help Law Center
NOMADIC	Nomadic Computing Discussion SIG
NON PROFIT NETWORK	access.point: Nonprofit Professionals Network
NONPROFIT	access.point: Nonprofit Professionals Network
NORFOLK	Digital Cities: Newport News and Norfolk
NORFOLK DCITY	Digital Cities: Newport News and Norfolk
NORFOLK DIGC	Digital Cities: Newport News and Norfolk
NORTON	Symantec
NORWAY	Norway
NORWEGIAN	Genealogy Forum
NOT NBC	NBC... NOT!
NOT-FOR-PROFIT	access.point
NOTEBOOK	PowerBook Resource Center
NOVEL	Amazing Instant Novelist
NOVELIST	Amazing Instant Novelist
NOVELL	Novell Desktop Systems
NOW	Now Software
NOW PLAYING	Directory of Services
NPC	The National Parenting Center
NPCA	America's National Parks

NPN	access.point: Nonprofit Professionals Network
NPR	National Public Radio Outreach
NPS	New Product Showcase
NSS	National Space Society
NTN	NTN Trivia
NTN BASKETBALL TRIVIA	NTN Basketball Trivia
NTN HOCKEY TRIVIA	ABC Hockey Trivia
NTN HOOPS TRIVIA	NTN Basketball Trivia
NTN PLAYBOOK	NTN Playbook
NTN TRIVIA	NTN Trivia-"
NUBASE	Tactic Software
NUL	National Urban League
NUMBERS	Accessing America Online*
NURSING	Kaplan Online
NUTRITION	Nutrition Forum
NVN	Newspaper Association of America
NW	Newsweek Magazine
NWFL	The Grandstand's Simulation Football
NWN	AD&D Neverwinter Nights
NY PUBLIC LIBRARY	NY Public Library Desk Reference
NY TIMES	@times/The New York Times Online
NYC	@times/The New York Times Online
NYNEX	@times/The New York Times Online
NYT	@times/The New York Times Online
NYT CROSSWORDS	The New York Times Crosswords
NYT STORE	@times Store
NYTCROSSWORD	The New York Times Crosswords
O.J.	O.J. Simpson Trial [May disappear without notice]
O.J. SIMPSON	O.J. Simpson Trial [May disappear without notice]
O'S	Major League Baseball Team: Baltimore Orioles
OADD	AD&D Neverwinter Nights
OAKLAND A'S	Major League Baseball Team: Oakland Athletics
OAKLAND ATHLETICS	Major League Baseball Team: Oakland Athletics
OAO	Outdoor Adventures Online
OB	iSKI
OBJECT FACTORY	Object Factory
OC	Owens Corning
OCTOBERFEST	Oktoberfest: German Heritage Month [3.0 only]
ODEON	AOL Live!
ODONNELL	Rosie O'Donnell Online
ODY	The Odyssey Project
ODYSSEY	The Odyssey Project
ODYSSEY PROJECT	The Odyssey Project
OFFICE	OfficeMax Online
OFFICEMAX	OfficeMax Online
OFL	The Grandstand's Simulation Football
OGF	Online Gaming Forums
OI	The Online Investor
OILERS	Houston Oilers Football Coverage [3.0 only]
OJ	Court TV's Law Center
OKC	Help Heal Oklahoma City
OKTOBERFEST	Oktoberfest: German Heritage Month [3.0 only]
OLD DOMINION	Virginia Forum
OLD FAVES	Favorite Flicks
OLDS	Oldsmobile/Celebrity Circle
OLDSMOBILE	Oldsmobile/Celebrity Circle
OLDUVAI	Olduvai Software, Inc.
OLI	The Online Investor
OLTL	ABC Daytime/Soapline
OLYMPIC	Olympic Festival Online
OLYMPIC FESTIVAL	Olympic Festival Online
OLYMPIC SHOP	The Olympic Shop
OLYMPIC STORE	The Olympic Shop
OLYMPICS	Olympic Festival Online
OMAHA	Omaha Steaks
OMAHA STEAKS	Omaha Steaks
OMEGA	Omega Research
OMNI	OMNI Magazine Online
OMNI GO	Hewlett-Packard Omni Go 100
OMNI MAGAZINE	OMNI Magazine Online
OMNI ONLINE	OMNI Magazine Online
ON	ON Technology
ON HOOPS	On Hoops Basketball (Web Page)
ON THE MOVE	AOL on the Move [May disappear without notice]
ONE LIFE TO LIVE	ABC Daytime/Soapline
ONE SOURCE	Columbia's Health Today
ONE WORLD	Preview Travel [3.0 only]
ONE WORLD TRAVEL	Preview Travel [3.0 only]
ONLINE CLOCK	Time of day and length of time online
ONLINE DRIVE	NTN Fantasy Baseball: Online Drive [3.0 only]
ONLINE FAMILY	Family Computing Forum: Online Family
ONLINE GAMING	Online Gaming Forums
ONLINE INVESTOR	The Online Investor
ONLINE ORIGINALS	Online Originals
ONLINE PSYCH	Psych Online
ONQ LEATHER	Leather onQ
ONYX	Onyx Technology
OP	Opinion Place
OPCODE	Opcode Systems, Inc.
OPCODE SYSTEMS	Opcode Systems, Inc.
OPEN	U.S. Tennis Open
OPERA	Afterwards Cafe
OPINION PLACE	Opinion Place

OPP	Other People's Problems
OPRAH	Get Movin' With Oprah
OPTIMA	Optima Technology
OPTIMAGE	Philips Media OptImage
OPTIMAS	OPTIMAS Corporation
ORANGE	Nickelodeon Online
ORANGE BOWL	Fool Bowl
ORANGEMEN	AOL College Football '96 [3.0 only]
ORGANIZATIONS	The Exchange: Communities Center
ORIENTATION	Orientation Express (New Member Area)
ORIENTATION EXPRESS	Orientation Express (New Member Area)
ORIGIN	Origin Systems
ORIGIN SYSTEMS	Origin Systems
ORIGINALS	Online Originals
ORIOLES	Major League Baseball Team: Baltimore Orioles
ORLANDO	Orlando Sentinel Online
ORLANDO SENTINEL	Orlando Sentinel Online
OS TWO	OS/2 Forum
OS2	OS/2 Forum
OSCAR	Academy Awards [May disappear without notice]
OSCARS	Academy Awards [May disappear without notice]
OSI	Origin Systems
OSKAR'S	Oskar's Magazine
OSKARS	Oskar's Magazine
OSO	Orlando Sentinel Online
OSO AUTO	Orlando Sentinel Online: Autos
OSO BASEBALL	Orlando Sentinel Online: Baseball
OSO BEACH	Orlando Sentinel Online: Beach
OSO BEACHES	Orlando Sentinel Online: Beach
OSO BLACK	Orlando Sentinel Online: Black Voices
OSO BUSINESS	Orlando Sentinel Online: Business
OSO CHAT	Orlando Sentinel Online: Chat
OSO CLASSIFIED	Orlando Sentinel Online: Classified Ads
OSO CLASSIFIEDS	Orlando Sentinel Online: Classified Ads
OSO COLLEGE FB	Orlando Sentinel Online: College Football
OSO COLLEGE FOOTBALL	Orlando Sentinel Online: College Football
OSO DOWNLOAD	Orlando Sentinel Online: Download Libraries
OSO E-MALL	Orlando Sentinel Online: E-Mall
OSO EMALL	Orlando Sentinel Online: E-Mall
OSO ENTERTAIN	Orlando Sentinel Online: Entertainment
OSO GOVERNMENT	Orlando Sentinel Online: Government
OSO HOMES	Orlando Sentinel Online: Homes
OSO JOBS	Orlando Sentinel Online: Jobs
OSO LIVING	Orlando Sentinel Online: Living
OSO MAGIC	Orlando Sentinel Online: Magic
OSO MAGIC MAG	Orlando Sentinel Online: Magic
OSO MALL	Orlando Sentinel Online: E-Mall
OSO MERCHANDISE	Orlando Sentinel Online: Merchandise
OSO MOVIES	Orlando Sentinel Online: Movies
OSO NET	Orlando Sentinel Online: OSOnet
OSO PHOTOS	Orlando Sentinel Online: Photos
OSO POLITICS	Orlando Sentinel Online: Government
OSO PREDATORS	Orlando Sentinel Online: Predators
OSO REAL ESTATE	Orlando Sentinel Online: Classified Real Estate
OSO RELIGION	Orlando Sentinel Online: Religion News
OSO SERVICE	Orlando Sentinel Online: Services
OSO SERVICES	Orlando Sentinel Online: Services
OSO SOUND OFF	Orlando Sentinel Online: Sound Off
OSO SPACE	Orlando Sentinel Online: Space
OSO SPORTS	Orlando Sentinel Online: Sports
OSO STORM	Orlando Sentinel Online: Hurricane Survival Guide
OSO THEME PARK	Orlando Sentinel Online: Theme Parks
OSO TO DO	Orlando Sentinel Online: Things To Do
OSO TOP	Orlando Sentinel Online: Top Stories
OSO TRANS	Orlando Sentinel Online: Transportation
OSO WANT ADS	Orlando Sentinel Online: Jobs
OSO WEATHER	Orlando Sentinel Online: Weather
OSOSOFT	OsoSoft
OSTRICH	Pet Care Forum
OTHER NEWS	The Hub: The Other News
OTHER PEOPLES PROBLEMS	Other People's Problems
OTR	Over The Rainbow: Travel News for Gay Men & Lesbians
OUR WORLD	Today's News channel
OUTAGE	System Outage Information
OUTBOARD	Boating Online
OUTDOOR	Outdoor Adventures Online
OUTDOOR ADVENTURE	Outdoor Adventures Online
OUTDOOR FUN	The Exchange: Outdoor Fun
OUTDOOR GEAR	Backpacker Magazine
OUTDOORS	The Exchange
OUTEREDGE	OuterEdge [3.0 only]
OVER THE RAINBOW	Over The Rainbow: Travel News for Gay Men & Lesbians
OWENS CORNING	Owens Corning
P6	Intel Corporation
PACEMARK	PaceMark Technologies, Inc.
PACKER	Packer Software
PADRES	Major League Baseball Team: San Diego Padres
PAGAN	Pagan Religions & Occult Sciences
PAGE	Page Sender
PAGEBOOK	Pager Address Book [3.0 only]
PAGER	Consumer Electronics
PALM	Palm Computing
PALM COMPUTING	Palm Computing
PALMTOP	PDA/Palmtop Forum

PANASONIC	Andy Pargh/The Gadget Guru
PANGEA	Pangea Toy Net
PANGEA TOY NET	Pangea Toy Net
PANTHERS	Carolina Panthers Football Coverage [3.0 only]
PAP	Applications Forum
PAPER MAIL	Fax/Paper Mail
PAPERPORT	Visioneer
PAPUA	Papua New Guinea
PAPUA NEW GUINEA	Papua New Guinea
PAPYRUS	Sierra Online
PAPZRAZZI	La Dolce Vita
PARADOX	DC Comics Online
PARASCOPE	Parascope
PARENT	AOL Families
PARENT ADVICE	Princeton Review Informed Parent
PARENT SOUP	Parent Soup
PARENT SOUP CHAT	Parent Soup: Chat
PARENT SOUP LOCAL INFO	Parent Soup: Local Information
PARENT'S SOUP	Parent Soup
PARENTAL CONTROL	Parental Controls*
PARENTAL GUIDANCE	Princeton Review Informed Parent
PARENTING	AOL Families
PARENTS	AOL Families
PARENTS SOUP	Parent Soup
PARGH	Andy Pargh/The Gadget Guru
PARKS	America's National Parks
PARLOR	Games Parlor
PARROT	Pet Care Forum
PARROT KEY	Parrot Key: Tropical Rock Forum
PARSONS	Parsons Technology
PARTY GIRL	Style channel
PASSION	Love@AOL
PASSOVER	Jewish Holidays
PASSPORT	Passport Selections
PASSPORT DESIGNS	Passport Designs
PASSPORT NEWS	Passport Newsletter
PASSPORT NEWSLETTER	Passport Newsletter
PASSPORT NL	Passport Newsletter
PASSPORT TO LOVE	Passport to Love
PASSWORD	Change your password*
PASTA	Mama's Cucina by Ragu
PAT O	The Pat O'Brien Report
PAT O'BRIEN	The Pat O'Brien Report
PAT OBRIEN	The Pat O'Brien Report
PATERNO	Paterno Imports
PAUL FREDERICK	Paul Frederick MenStyle
PAUL HARVEY	ABC Radio
PBM	Play-By-Mail Forum
PBM CLUBS	Play-By-Mail Clubs & Messaging
PC	People Connection channel
PC ANIMATION	PC Graphics Forum
PC APPLICATIONS	PC Applications Forum
PC APPLICATIONS FORUM	PC Applications Forum
PC APS	PC Applications Forum
PC AUD	AOL Live!
PC BEGINNERS	PC Help Desk
PC BG	PC Help Desk
PC CATALOG	PC Today
PC CHAT	PC Computing Forums: Chats and Conferences
PC CHATS	PC Computing Forums: Chats and Conferences
PC CONFERENCE	PC Computing Forums: Chats and Conferences
PC CONFERENCES	PC Computing Forums: Chats and Conferences
PC DATA	PC Data
PC DESKMATE	DeskMate
PC DEV	Developers Forum [Platform-dependent]
PC DEVELOPMENT	Developers Forum [Platform-dependent]
PC DEVELOPMENT FORUM	Developers Forum [Platform-dependent]
PC DM	DeskMate
PC FINANCIAL	PC Financial Network
PC FINANCIAL NETWORK	PC Financial Network
PC FORUMS	Computers & Software channel [Platform-dependent]
PC FORUMS HOT	What's Hot in PC Computing
PC GAMES	PC Games Forum
PC GRAPHICS	PC Graphics Forum
PC GRAPHICS FORUM	PC Graphics Forum
PC HARDWARE	PC Hardware Forum
PC HARDWARE FORUM	PC Hardware Forum
PC HELP	PC Help Desk
PC HOT	What's Hot in PC Computing
PC MUSIC FORUM	PC Music and Sound Forum
PC PC	Personal Computer Peripherals
PC PLAZA	People Connection Plaza
PC SECURITY	Computers & Software channel [Platform-dependent]
PC SOFTWARE	PC Software Center
PC SOUND	PC Music and Sound Forum
PC SOUND FORUM	PC Music and Sound Forum
PC STUDIO	PC Studio
PC TELECOM	PC Telecom/Networking Forum
PC TELECOM FORUM	PC Telecom/Networking Forum
PC TODAY	PC Today
PC TOOL	PC Virtual Toolbox

PC WORLD	PCWorld Online
PC WORLD ONLINE	PCWorld Online
PC-LINK HOTLINE	Credit Request Form for connect problems
PCFN	PC Financial Network
PCM	PC Telecom/Networking Forum
PCMU	PC Music and Sound Forum
PCMUSIC	PC Music and Sound Forum
PCS	MobileMedia
PCW NETSCAPE	PC World: Netscape [3.0 only]
PCW ONLINE	PCWorld Online
PD	Dinner On Us Club
PDA	PDA/Palmtop Forum
PDA DEV	PDA Development SIG
PDA DEV SIG	PDA Development SIG
PDA FORUM	PDA/Palmtop Forum
PDA SHOP	PDA Forum: PDA Shop
PDV	Developers Forum [Platform-dependent]
PEACHPIT	The Macintosh Bible/Peachpit Forum
PEACHTREE	Peachtree Software
PEANUTS	Virgin's Virtual Valley
PEAPOD	Peapod Online
PEN	Personal Empowerment Network
PEN PAL	Edmark Technologies
PENGUINS	NHL Hockey
PENPAL	Digital City Pen Pals
PENPALS	Digital City Pen Pals
PENTIUM	Intel Corporation
PEOPLE	People Connection channel
PEOPLE CONNECTION	People Connection channel
PEREGRINE	Pictorius, Inc.
PERFUME	The Fragrance Counter
PERISCOPE	Parascope
PERSON OF THE WEEK	ABC News-On-Demand
PERSONAL CHOICES	Personal Choices area
PERSONAL CREATIONS	Personal Creations: Unique Personalized Gifts
PERSONAL EMPOWERMENT	Personal Empowerment Network
PERSONAL FINANCE	Personal Finance channel
PERSONAL PUBLISHER 2	Personal Publisher 2 Preview [3.0 only]
PERSUASION	Religion & Ethics Forum
PERU	Peru [3.0 only]
PET	Pet Care Forum
PET CARE	Pet Care Forum
PETER JENNINGS	ABC News-On-Demand
PETER NORTON	Symantec
PETITIONS	Accessing America Online*
PETS	Pet Care Forum
PETS AND ANIMALS	Hobby Central: Pets & Animals
PETS & ANIMALS	Hobby Central: Pets & Animals
PF	Personal Finance channel
PF SOFTWARE	Personal Finance Software Center
PF WEB	Personal Finance [Web Site]
PFSS	Personal Finance Software Support
PGM	PC Games Forum
PGR	PC Graphics Forum
PH	Simon & Schuster College Online
PHIL MARKET	Digital City Philadelphia: Classifieds
PHIL TOUR	Digital City Philadelphia: City Tour
PHILA DIGITAL CITY	Digital Cities: Philadelphia
PHILADELPHIA	Digital Cities: Philadelphia
PHILADELPHIA DIGC	Digital Cities: Philadelphia
PHILADELPHIA EAGLES	Philadelphia Eagles Online
PHILANTHROPY	access.point
PHILIPPINES	Philippines
PHILLIES	Major League Baseball Team: Philadelphia Phillies
PHILLY DIG CITY	Digital Cities: Philadelphia
PHILLY DIGITAL CITY	Digital Cities: Philadelphia
PHILOSOPHY	Religion & Ethics Forum
PHOENIX	Arizona Central
PHONE BOOK	Phone Directories
PHONE DIRECTORY	Phone Directories
PHONE HELP	Local access numbers*
PHONE NUMBER	Accessing America Online*
PHONE NUMBERS	Accessing America Online*
PHONES	Accessing America Online*
PHOTO	Photography area
PHOTO FOCUS	Graphics and Photo Focus area
PHOTODEX	Photodex
PHOTOGRAPHY	Photography area
PHOTOS	Popular Photography Online
PHOTOSHOP	Photoshop SIG
PHS	Practical Homeschooling
PHW	PC Hardware Forum
PHYS ED	Simon & Schuster Online: Health, Phys. Ed. & Rec. Dept.
PHYSICALLY DISABLED	DisABILITIES Forum
PIC	PictureWeb & PicturePlace
PICTORIUS	Pictorius, Inc.
PICTUREPLACE	PictureWeb & PicturePlace
PICTURES	Pictures of the World
PICTUREWEB	PictureWeb & PicturePlace
PIERIAN	Pierian Spring Software
PIERIAN SP	Pierian Spring Software
PIG	Pet Care Forum
PIGS	Pet Care Forum
PIK	Pik a Program, Inc.
PILOTS	Flying Magazine
PIN	AOL Families

PINK TRIANGLE	Gay & Lesbian Community Forum
PIPE	Food & Drink Network
PIPES	Food & Drink Network
PIRATES	Major League Baseball Team: Pittsburgh Pirates
PITTSBURGH PIRATES	Major League Baseball Team: Pittsburgh Pirates
PIXEL	Pixel Resources
PIXEL RESOURCES	Pixel Resources
PKWARE	PKWare, Inc.
PLACES	P.L.A.C.E.S. Interest Group
PLACES RATED	Places Rated Almanac
PLACES RATED ALMANAC	Places Rated Almanac
PLANET EALING	Planet Ealing [3.0 only]
PLANET OUT	Planet Out
PLANETOUT	PlanetOut
PLANNING	MoneyWhiz
PLANS	American Woodworker
PLANTS	800-Flowers
PLASTIC SURGERY	Longevity Magazine Online
PLAY	Entertainment channel
PLAY KEYWORD	Preview Vacations' Travel Update
PLAY-BY-MAIL	Play-By-Mail Forum
PLAYBILL	Playbill Online
PLAYER	Viewer Resource Center
PLAYERS	Viewer Resource Center
PLAYMATES	Pangea Toy Network: ToyBuzz
PLAYTEX	One Hanes Place
PLAYWELL	U.S. Golf Society Online
PLF	The Positive Living Forum
PLF QUILT	GLCF Aids Scrapbook
PLUS	Plus ATM Network
PMM	PC Multimedia Forum
PMU	PC Music and Sound Forum
PNO	PlaNetOut
POETRY	Afterwards Cafe
POG	KidzBiz' POG Area
POGS	KidzBiz' POG Area
POLAND	Poland
POLICY REVIEW	Heritage Foundation
POLITICAL SCIENCE	Simon & Schuster Online: Political Science Dept.
POLITICS	Politics area
POLLS	CyberJustice's Arch of Public Opinion Polls
PONY	Pet Care Forum
POP	Popular Music Forum
POP MUSIC	Popular Music Forum
POP PHOTO	Popular Photography Online
POPE	Catholic Community
POPULAR PHOTOGRAPHY	Popular Photography Online
PORK	Pork Online
PORT FOLLY	The Motley Fool: Port Folly
PORTABLE	Mobile Office Online
PORTABLE COMPUTING	Mobile Office Online
PORTFOLIO	Your Stock Portfolio
PORTUGAL	Portugal
POSITIVE LIVING	The Positive Living Forum
POST OFFICE	Post Office
POSTAL STAMPS	Comic Strip Centennial
POSTCARDS	Virtual Post Card Center
POV	3D Forum
POWER BOATS	Boating Online
POWER EQUIPMENT	American Woodworker: Tool Reviews
POWERBOOK	PowerBook Resource Center
POWERMAC	PowerMac Resource Center
POWERPC	PowerMac Resource Center
POWERTOOL	American Woodworker: Tool Reviews
POWERTOOLS	American Woodworker: Tool Reviews
PP	Personal WWW Publishing area [3.0 only]
PPI	Practical Peripherals, Inc.
PPL	Passport to Love
PR	The Princeton Review Online
PRACTICAL PERIPHERALS	Practical Peripherals, Inc.
PRAIRIE	Prairie Group
PRAIRIE SOFT	Prairie Group
PRAYER NET	The Prayer Network
PREFERRED MAIL	Preferred Mail*
PREMIER	Dinner On Us Club
PREMIER DINING	Dinner On Us Club
PRENTICE HALL	Simon & Schuster College Online
PRESCHOOL	Preschool/Early Childhood SIG
PRESENTING	Presenting... on AOL [3.0 only]
PRESIDENT	President's Day [May disappear without notice]
PRESIDENT 96	President '96
PRESIDENTIAL	President's Day [May disappear without notice]
PRESS	AOL Press Release Library
PRESS RELEASE	AOL Press Release Library
PREVIEW VACATIONS	Preview Vacations
PRICE	Price Online
PRICE ONLINE	Price Online
PRIDE	Gay & Lesbian Community Forum
PRIDE 96	Gay Pride Festival '96 [May disappear without notice]
PRIMASOFT	PrimaSoft PC, Inc.
PRIME HOST	PrimeHost
PRIMESTAR	Andy Pargh/The Gadget Guru
PRIN	Principians Online
PRINCETON	The Princeton Review Online
PRINCETON REVIEW	The Princeton Review Online
PRINCIPALS	National Principals Center Web link
PRINO	Principians Online

PRINT ARTIST	Print Artist Special Interest Group
PRINTER	Mac Printer Knowledge Base
PRINTERS	Mac Printer Knowledge Base
PRO BOWL	1996 Pro Bowl
PRO'S	Pro's Corner
PRO'S CORNER	Pro's Corner
PROCD	ProCD National Telephone Directory Search
PRODIGY	Virtual Refugees Forum
PRODIGY REFUGEES	Virtual Refugees Forum
PRODUCT REVIEWS	Family Computing Forum: News & Reviews
PRODUCTIVITY	Applications/Business/Productivity Forum [Platform-dependent]
PRODUCTIVITY FORUM	Applications/Business/Productivity Forum [Platform-dependent]
PROFILE	Edit your member profile
PROGRAMMER U	Programmer University
PROGRAMMING	Development Forum [Platform-dependent]
PROGRAPH	Pictorius, Inc.
PROS	Pro's Corner
PROS CORNER	Pro's Corner
PROUD	Gay & Lesbian Community Forum
PROVUE	ProVUE Development
PS	Parascope
PSA	PSA Software
PSC	Public Safety Center
PSCP	Parascope
PSION	Psion
PSP	JASC, Inc.
PSYCH ONLINE	Psych Online
PSYCHOLOGY	Psychology Forum
PTC	PC Telecom/Networking Forum
PU	Programmer University
PUB	The Comedy Pub
PUBLIC POLICY	Politics area
PUBLIC RADIO	National Public Radio Outreach
PUBLIC SAFETY	Public Safety Center
PUBLISHERS	Computing Company Connection
PUERTO RICO	Puerto Rico
PUR	PUR Drinking Water Systems
PUZZLE	The Puzzle Zone [3.0 only]
QATAR	Qatar
QB1	NTN's QB1
QMMS	Mac Music & Sound Forum
QMODEM	Mustang Software
QOTD	Grandstand's Sport Trivia Question of the Day
QQP	Quantum Quality Productions
QUALIFYR	Consumer Mortgage Information Net
QUALITAS	Qualitas
QUALITY	The Health Zone

QUARK	Quark, Inc.
QUE	PC Studio
QUEEN	Royalty Online [3.0 only]
QUEER	Gay & Lesbian Community Forum
QUES DICTIONARY	Computer and Internet Dictionary
QUEST	Adventures by Mail
QUEST TEST	Quest Test [3.0 only]
QUESTION	One Stop Infoshop*
QUESTIONS	One Stop Infoshop*
QUICK	Marketplace Quick Gifts
QUICK FIND	Search database of files [Platform-dependent]
QUICK FINDER	Search database of files [Platform-dependent]
QUICK GIFTS	Marketplace Quick Gifts
QUICK PRINTERS	National Association of Quick Printers area
QUICKTIME	Mac Desktop Video & Multimedia Forum
QUIKJUSTICE	CyberJustice's Reward & Punishment
QUILT	Quilting Forum
QUILTERS	Quilting Forum
QUILTING	Quilting Forum
QUOTATION	Bartlett's Quotations
QUOTATIONS	Bartlett's Quotations
QUOTE	StockLink: Quotes & Portfolios area
QUOTES	StockLink: Quotes & Portfolios area
QUOTES PLUS	Quotes Plus
R&B	R&B Music Forum
R&R	ABC Online: Rock & Road
R&T	Road & Track Magazine
RABBIT	Pet Care Forum
RABBITJACK'S CASINO	RabbitJack's Casino
RABBITJACKS CASINO	RabbitJack's Casino
RACING	Wheels
RADIO	Entertainment's Radio Forum
RADIO FORUM	Entertainment's Radio Forum
RADIUS	Radius, Inc.
RAGU	Mama's Cucina by Ragu
RAILROADING	The Exchange
RAINBOW	Lambda Rising Bookstore Online
RALPH Z	UniverseCentral.Com
RALPH ZERBONIA	UniverseCentral.Com
RAM DOUBLER	Connectix Corporation
RANGERS	Major League Baseball Team: Texas Rangers
RANKINGS	Business Rankings
RASTEROPS	Truevision
RATITE	Pet Care Forum
RAW	World Wrestling Federation
RAY	Ray Dream
RAY DREAM	Ray Dream
RAY TRACE	3D Forum
RAZORBACKS	AOL College Football '96 [3.0 only]

RBO	Ringling Online
RC	Christian Resource Center
RCA	Andy Pargh/The Gadget Guru
RDI	Free-Form Gaming Forum
REACH	Reach!
REACTOR	Reactor
READ USA	Online Bookstore
READING ROOM	The Reading Room
REAL DEAL	Real Deals on AOL
REAL ESTATE	Real Estate Selections
REAL LIFE	MoneyWhiz
REC CENTER	Entertainment channel
RECIPES	Woman's Day Online
RECORD	Tower Records
RECORDS	Tower Records
RECREATION	Entertainment channel
RECREATION CENTER	Entertainment channel
RED RAIDERS	AOL College Football '96 [3.0 only]
RED SOX	NESN: New England Baseball
RED SOX BASEBALL	NESN: New England Baseball
RED WINGS	NHL Hockey
RED ZONE	NESN: New England Football
REDGATE	New Product Showcase
REDS	Major League Baseball Team: Cincinnati Reds
REDSKINS	Washington Redskins [3.0 only]
REEBOK	Reach!
REF HOT	Hot Reference
REF NEWS	Reference Desk Newsletter
REFERENCE	Reference Desk channel
REFERENCE DESK	Reference Desk channel
REFERENCE HELP	Reference Desk: Help
REGISTER	Online Campus
REI	REI Recreation Equipment, Inc.
REIT	Motley Fool: Real Estate
RELIGION NEWS	Religion News Update
RELIGIONS	Religion & Ethics Forum
REMINDER	Gift Reminder
REMODELING	Home Magazine Online
REN	Transgender Community Forum: Organizations
RENAISSANCE	Transgender Community Forum: Organizations
RENDERING	3D Forum
RENO	Digital Cities: Reno
RENO DC	Digital Cities: Reno
RENO DCITY	Digital Cities: Reno
RENO DIGC	Digital Cities: Reno
RENO DIGITAL CITY	Digital Cities: Reno
RENO NV	Digital Cities: Reno
REPRISE	Warner/Reprise Records Online
REPTILE	Pet Care Forum
REPTILES	Pet Care Forum
REPUBLICAN	Republican National Committee
REPUBLICANS	Republican National Committee
RESEARCH	Academic Assistance Center
RESERVATION	Preview Travel [3.0 only]
RESERVATIONS	Preview Travel [3.0 only]
RESNOVA	ResNova Software
RESNOVA SOFTWARE	ResNova Software
RESTAURANT	Everything Edible!
RESTAURANTS	Everything Edible!
RETIREMENT	MoneyWhiz
REV	ABC Sports' REV Speedway
REV SPEEDWAY	ABC Sports' REV Speedway
REV WAR	Revolutionary War Forum
REVIEW	1995: The Year in Review
REVIEWS	Family Computing Forum: News & Reviews
REVOLUTIONARY WAR	Revolutionary War Forum
REWARD TOWN	Reward Town
RICK STEVES	Europe Through the Back Door
RICKI LAKE	The Ricki Lake Show
RICOCHET	Metricom, Inc.
RINGLING	Ringling Online
RINGLING BROS	Ringling Online
RINGLING ONLINE	Ringling Online
RKWEST	RK West Consulting
RL	MoneyWhiz
RNC	Republican National Committee
RNU	Religion News Update
ROACH	Hecklers Online
ROAD	Road & Track Magazine
ROAD TO COLLEGE	Road to College
ROAD & TRACK	Road & Track Magazine
ROADTRIP	AOL Roadtrips [3.0 only]
ROADTRIPS	AOL Roadtrips [3.0 only]
ROCK	Rock Music Forum
ROCK AND ROLL	Rock and Roll Hall of Fame
ROCK N ROLL	Rock and Roll Hall of Fame
ROCK & ROAD	ABC Online: Rock & Road
ROCK & ROLL	Rock and Roll Hall of Fame
ROCKIES	Major League Baseball Team: Colorado Rockies
ROCKLINE	Rockline Online
ROCKLINK	RockNet Information & Web Link
ROCKNET	RockNet Information & Web Link
RODEO	Rodeo MiniForum
ROGER CLEMENS	Roger Clemens's Playoff Baseball Journal
ROGER WAGNER	Roger Wagner Publishing
ROGUE	Motley Fool's Rogue
ROLAND	Roland Corporation U.S.
ROLE PLAYING	Role-Playing Forum

ROLLERSKATING	The Grandstand: Other Sports
ROMANCE	Romance Channel
ROMANCE GROUP	Writer's Club: Romance Writers & Readers
ROMANCE STORE	Romance Store
ROOFING	Owens Corning
ROOTS	Genealogy Forum
ROSE BOWL	Fool Bowl
ROSES	800-Flowers
ROSH HASHANA	Jewish New Year area
ROSIE	Rosie O'Donnell Online
ROSIE ODONNELL	Rosie O'Donnell Online
ROTUNDA	The Computing Rotunda
ROYALS	Major League Baseball Team: Kansas City Royals
ROYALTY	Royalty Online [3.0 only]
ROYALTY FORUM	Royalty Forum
RPG	Role-Playing Forum
RPGA	Fellowship of Online Gamers/RPGA Network
RPGA NETWORK	Fellowship of Online Gamers/RPGA Network
RPM	RPM Worldwide Entertainment & Travel
RPM TRAVEL	RPM Worldwide Entertainment & Travel
RR	ABC Online: Rock & Road
RSFL	The Grandstand's Simulation Football
RSG	Manhattan Graphics
RSP	RSP Funding Focus
RT	AOL Roadtrips [3.0 only]
RUBBERMAID	Andy Pargh/The Gadget Guru
RUN	AOL Sports: Running
RUNES	Spiritual Mosiac
RUNNER'S WORLD	Runner's World
RUNNERS WORLD	Runner's World
RUNNING	AOL Sports: Running
RUSSIA	Russia
RW	Runner's World
RX	Health and Vitamin Express
RYOBI	Ryobi
S.F. GIANTS	Major League Baseball Team: San Francisco Giants
S&S	Simon & Schuster College Online
SA	Shopper's Advantage Online
SA MED	Scientific American Medical Publications
SABRES	NHL Hockey
SAF	Scientific American Frontiers
SAFETY	Public Safety Center
SAGINAW	Digital Cities: Saginaw
SAGINAW DC	Digital Cities: Saginaw
SAGINAW DCITY	Digital Cities: Saginaw
SAGINAW DIGC	Digital Cities: Saginaw
SAGINAW MI	Digital Cities: Saginaw
SAILING	Boating Selections

SAN DIEGO	Digital Cities: San Diego CA
SAN DIEGO DIGC	Digital Cities: San Diego CA
SAN DIEGO PADRES	Major League Baseball Team: San Diego Padres
SAN FRAN	Major League Baseball Team: San Francisco Giants
SAN FRANCISCO	Digital Cities: San Francisco CA
SAN FRANCISCO DIGC	Digital Cities: San Francisco CA
SAN JOSE	Mercury Center
SAN MARINO	San Marino [3.0 only]
SANTA FE	Digital Cities: Albuquerque/Santa Fe NM
SANTA FE DC	Digital Cities: Albuquerque/Santa Fe NM
SANTA FE DCITY	Digital Cities: Albuquerque/Santa Fe NM
SANTA FE DIGC	Digital Cities: Albuquerque/Santa Fe NM
SANTA FE DIGITAL CITY	Digital Cities: Albuquerque/Santa Fe NM
SANWA	Sanwa Bank California [3.0 only]
SAT	Kaplan Online or The Princeton Review
SATAN	Weekly World News
SATELLITES	Entertainment's Radio Forum
SATIRE	Soundbites Online
SAUCE	Mama's Cucina by Ragu
SB	Star Chasers CD-ROM
SBA	Small Business Administration
SBC	Your Business
SCAN	Digital Imaging Resource Center
SCANDINAVIAN	Genealogy Forum
SCANNERS	Digital Imaging Resource Center
SCAVENGER	AOL Treasure Hunt
SCAVENGER HUNT	AOL Treasure Hunt
SCENTS	Style channel
SCHEDULE	What's Hot in Computing [Platform-dependent]
SCHOLAR'S HALL	Scholars' Hall
SCHOLARS	Scholars' Hall
SCHOLARS HALL	Scholars' Hall
SCHOLARS' HALL	Scholars' Hall
SCHOLARSHIP	RSP Funding Focus
SCHOLARSHIPS	RSP Funding Focus
SCHOLASTIC	Scholastic Network Preview Area
SCHOOL	Back to School [May disappear without notice]
SCHOOL MATCH	School Match [3.0 only]
SCHOOLHOUSE	Electronic Schoolhouse
SCI AM	Scientific American
SCI FI	Fictional Realm
SCI-FI	Fictional Realm
SCIENCE	Scientific American
SCIENCE FICTION	Fictional Realm
SCIENTIFIC	Scientific American
SCIENTIFIC AMERICAN	Scientific American
SCIFI CHANNEL	The Sci-Fi Channel
SCITECH	SciTech Software

SCOOP	Newsgroup Scoop
SCOPE	Parascope
SCOREBOARD	Sports Scoreboard
SCORPIA	Scorpia's Lair
SCORPIA'S LAIR	Scorpia's Lair
SCORPIAS LAIR	Scorpia's Lair
SCOT	Genealogy Forum
SCOTCH	Genealogy Forum
SCOUNDREL	Military City Online: Villains of Fact & Fiction
SCOUNDRELS	Military City Online: Villains of Fact & Fiction
SCOUTING	Scouting Forum
SCOUTS	Scouting Forum
SCRAPBOOK	Member Scrapbook
SCREAM	MusicSpace Events
SCREEN NAME	Add, change, or delete screen names
SCREEN NAMES	Add, change, or delete screen names
SCRIPT	Affinity Microsystems
SCRIPTING	Affinity Microsystems
SCRIPTS	Affinity Microsystems
SCUBA	Scuba Club
SCUDDER	Scudder Funds Online
SD	Digital Cities: San Diego CA
SD COMM	Digital City San Diego: Community
SD DIGC	Digital Cities: San Diego CA
SD DIGITAL CITY	Digital Cities: San Diego CA
SD NEWS	Digital City San Diego: News & Weather
SD PEOPLE	Digital City San Diego: People
SD TOUR	Digital City San Diego: City Tour
SD WEATHER	Digital City San Diego: News & Weather
SDD	SciTech Software
SEARCH	Software Center [Platform-dependent]
SEARCH AOL LIVE	Search AOL Live
SEARCH NEWS	Search News articles
SEATTLE	Digital Cities: Seattle/Tacoma WA
SEATTLE DIGC	Digital Cities: Seattle/Tacoma WA
SEATTLE DIGITAL CITY	Digital Cities: Seattle/Tacoma WA
SEATTLE MARINERS	Major League Baseball Team: Seattle Mariners
SECOND SIGHT	FreeSoft Company
SECRET BARGAINS	Arthur Frommer's Secret Bargains
SECT	Religion & Ethics Forum
SECURITY	Consumer Electronics
SEGA	Video Games area
SELF HELP	Self Help area
SELF-HELP	Self-Help area
SEM	Motley Fool: Semiconductors
SEMINOLES	AOL College Football '96 [3.0 only]
SENATORS	NHL Hockey
SEND PAGE	Page Sender
SENEGAL	Senegal [3.0 only]
SENIOR	SeniorNet
SENIOR FRIENDS	Columbia's Health Today
SENSATIONS	News Sensations
SEQUENTIAL	Sequential Software, Inc.
SERIALS	Cyberserials
SERIUS	Serius
SERVENET	SERVEnet
SERVICE	Member Services*
SERVICES	Directory of Services
SERVICES DIRECTORY	Directory of Services
SEVEN WONDERS	Seven Wonders of the Web
SEVENTEEN	Seventeen Magazine Online
SEVENTH	Seventh Level Software
SEW	Needlecrafts/Sewing Center
SEWING	Woman's Day Online
SEX	THRIVE@AOL
SEX TALK	Thrive@AOL: Sex Talk
SEYCHELLES	Seychelles [3.0 only]
SF	Fictional Realm or San Francisco
SF COMM	Digital City San Francisco: Community
SF DIGC	Digital Cities: San Francisco CA
SF DIGITAL CITY	Digital Cities: San Francisco CA
SF NEWS	Digital City San Francisco: News & Weather
SF PEOPLE	Digital City San Francisco: People
SF TOUR	Digital City San Francisco: City Tour
SF WEATHER	Digital City San Francisco: News & Weather
SFNB	Security First National Bank [3.0 only]
SHADOW	Traffic Center
SHADOW BROADCASTING	Traffic Center
SHADOW TRAFFIC	Traffic Center
SHAPE TALK	Thrive@AOL: Shape Talk
SHAREWARE	Software Center [Platform-dependent]
SHAREWARE SOLUTIONS	Shareware Solutions
SHARKS	NHL Hockey
SHARPER IMAGE	The Sharper Image
SHAWN	Shawn Green's Journal
SHAWN GREEN	Shawn Green's Journal
SHEEP	Pet Care Forum
SHERLOCK	Mysteries from the Yard
SHERLOCK HOLMES	Mysteries from the Yard
SHIFT	Shift Magazine
SHIP CRITIC	Cruise Critic
SHIP CRITICS	Cruise Critic
SHOPPERS ADVANTAGE	Shopper's Advantage Online
SHOPPING	Marketplace channel
SHOPPING AND TRAVEL	Travel channel
SHOPPING & TRAVEL	Travel channel
SHORTHAND	Online Shorthands

SHORTHANDS	Online Shorthands
SHOW TIMES	MovieLink
SHOWBIZ INFO	Showbiz News & Info
SHOWBIZ NEWS	Showbiz News & Info
SHOWS	AOL Live!
SHUTTLE	Challenger Remembered
SI	Smithsonian Online
SIAF	Shareware Industry Awards Foundation
SIC	Shareware Industry Awards Foundation
SIDESHOW	Weekly World News
SIDING	Owens Corning
SIERRA	Sierra On-Line
SIERRA LEONE	Sierra Leone [3.0 only]
SIESTA	Siesta Software
SIFS	Computers & Software channel [Platform-dependent]
SIGHTINGS	Sightings Online
SIGNUP	Online Campus
SIGS	Computers & Software channel [Platform-dependent]
SILLY PUTTY	The Physics of Silly Putty
SIM	Simming Forum
SIMBA	Cowles/SIMBA Media Information Network
SIMI WINERY	Simi Winery
SIMMING	Simming Forum
SIMON	Simon & Schuster College Online
SIMON & SCHUSTER	Simon & Schuster College Online
SIMS	Simming Forum
SIMULATION AUTO	The Grandstand's Simulation Auto Racing
SIMULATION BASEBALL	The Grandstand's Simulation Baseball
SIMULATION BASKETBALL	The Grandstand's Simulation Basketball
SIMULATION FOOTBALL	The Grandstand's Simulation Football
SIMULATION GOLF	The Grandstand's Simulation Golf
SIMULATION HOCKEY	The Grandstand's Simulation Hockey
SIMULATION LEAGUES	The Grandstand's Fantasy & Simulation Leagues
SIMULATION WRESTLING	The Grandstand's Simulation Wrestling
SIMULATIONS	Graphic Simulations
SIMULATOR	Games Forum [Platform-dependent]
SIN	Religion & Beliefs
SINGAPORE	Singapore
SISTORE	The Sharper Image
SIXTY	Amazing Instant Novelist
SKI	AOL Skiing
SKI CONDITIONS	Ski Reports
SKI REPORTS	Ski Reports
SKI WEATHER	Ski Reports
SKI ZONE	The Ski Zone
SKIING	iSKI
SKY DIVING	Aviation Forum
SKYLINE	Virtual Airlines
SKYLINE AIRWAYS	Virtual Airlines
SLIME	Nickelodeon Online
SLOVAKIA	Slovakia [3.0 only]
SLOVENIA	Slovenia [3.0 only]
SM	Smithsonian Magazine
SMALL BUSINESS	Your Business
SMART WATCHING	The ABC Classroom
SMARTMOUTHS	Smart Mouths
SMITHFIELD	Gwaltney Hams & Turkeys
SMITHSONIAN	Smithsonian Online
SMITHSONIAN MAGAZINE	Smithsonian Magazine
SML	Sony Magic Link
SN LIBRARIES	Scholastic Libraries
SN LIT GAME	Bookwoman's Literature Game
SN SPACE	Space and Astronomy
SNAKE	Pet Care Forum
SNGUESTS	Scholastic Network: Special Guests
SNLITGAME	Bookwoman's Literature Game [K-6]
SNOWBOARDING	Snowboarding Online
SOAP DIGEST	Soap Opera Digest
SOAPLINE	ABC Daytime/Soapline
SOCIAL SCIENCE	NAS Online
SOCIAL WORK	Simon & Schuster Online: Social Work Dept.
SOCIOLOGY	Simon & Schuster Online: Sociology Dept.
SOD	Soap Opera Digest
SOFT SHOP	AOL Software Shop
SOFTARC	SoftArc
SOFTDISK	Softdisk Superstore
SOFTLOGIK	SoftLogik
SOFTWARE	Software Center [Platform-dependent]
SOFTWARE CENTER	Software Center [Platform-dependent]
SOFTWARE COMPANIES	Computing Company Connection
SOFTWARE DIRECTORY	Software Center [Platform-dependent]
SOFTWARE HARDTALK	Software Hardtalk with John C. Dvorak
SOFTWARE HELP	Software Center [Platform-dependent]
SOFTWARE LIBRARIES	Software Center [Platform-dependent]
SOFTWARE LIBRARY	Software Center [Platform-dependent]
SOFTWARE PUBLISHERS	Computing Company Connection
SOFTWARE SHOP	AOL Software Shop
SOFTWARE SUPPORT	Personal Finance Software Support
SOFTWARE TOOLWORKS	Mindscape
SOFTWARE UNBOXED	Software Unboxed
SOFTWORD	Softword Technical
SOHO	Home Office Computing Magazine
SOL	Snowboarding Online
SOLIII	Sol III Play-by-Email Game
SOLOMON ISLANDS	Solomon Islands [3.0 only]
SOMALIA	Somalia [3.0 only]

SONY	Sony Magic Link
SOONERS	AOL College Football '96 [3.0 only]
SOPHCIR	Sophisticated Circuits
SORORITY	Alumni Hall
SOS	Wall Street SOS Forum
SOUND	Stereo Review Online
SOUND ROOM	Sound Room*
SOUNDBITES	Soundbites Online
SOURCERER	The Hub: Sourcerer
SOUTH	Digital Cities: South
SOUTH AFRICA	South Africa
SOUTH DIGC	Digital Cities: South
SOUTH DIGITAL CITY	Digital Cities: South
SOUTHEAST	Digital Cities: South
SPA	Longevity Magazine Online
SPACE	National Space Society
SPACE COAST	Florida's Space Coast
SPACE SHUTTLE	Challenger Remembered
SPACEY	The Hub: Space
SPAIN	Spain
SPAM UPDATE	Mail Spam Update
SPAS	Longevity Magazine Online
SPC	Software Publishing Corporation
SPEAKERS	Stereo Review Online
SPECIAL INTERESTS	Life, Styles & Interests channel
SPECTRUM	Spectrum HoloByte
SPECULAR	Specular International
SPEEDBOATS	Boating Online
SPEEDWAY	ABC Sports' REV Speedway
SPIDER	Spider Island Software
SPIDER ISLAND	Spider Island Software
SPIDERMAN	Marvel Online [3.0 only]
SPIDERWEB	Spiderweb Software
SPIN	Spin Online
SPIN ONLINE	Spin Online
SPINNING	Needlecrafts/Sewing Center
SPIRITUAL	Spiritual Mosaic
SPOOFS	TV Spoofs
SPORTING NEWS	The Sporting News
SPORTS	Sports channel
SPORTS ARCHIVE	AOL Sports Archive
SPORTS BOARDS	The Grandstand's Sports Boards
SPORTS CHAT	The Grandstand's Chat Rooms
SPORTS CIRCUIT	New England Sports Network
SPORTS EVENTS	AOL Sports Live
SPORTS HOT	What's Hot in Sports
SPORTS LIBRARIES	The Grandstand's Libraries
SPORTS LINK	Sports channel
SPORTS LIVE	AOL Sports Live
SPORTS NEWS	Sport News
SPORTS ROOMS	The Grandstand's Chat Rooms
SPOTLIGHT	AOL Live! Spotlight
SPRING	Computing Spring Fling [May disappear without notice]
SPRINT	Sprint Annual Report (Old)
SRS	SRS Labs -or- Transgender Community Forum
SRS LABS	SRS Labs
SSI	Strategic Simulations
SSS	Craig Anderton's Sound Studio & Stage
SSS NEWS	Sound, Studio, Stage News
SSSI	SSSi
ST. LOUIS CARDINALS	Major League Baseball Team: St. Louis Cardinals
ST PAUL	Digital Cities: Minneapolis - St. Paul
ST PAUL DIGC	Digital Cities: Minneapolis - St. Paul
ST PAUL DIGITAL CITY	Digital Cities: Minneapolis - St. Paul
ST PETERSBURG	Digital Cities: Tampa - St. Petersburg
ST PETERSBURG DIGC	Digital Cities: Tampa - St. Petersburg
STAC	STAC Electronics
STAFF	Staff Development SIG
STAMPS	The Exchange
STANFORD	AOL College Football '96 [3.0 only]
STAR	Star Chasers CD-ROM
STAR TREK	Star Trek Club
STAR WARS	Star Wars Sim Forum
STAR WARS SIM	Star Wars Sim Forum
STARBUCKS	Caffe Starbucks
STARFISH	Starfish Software
STARPLAY	Starplay Productions
STARS	Galileo Mission to Jupiter [May disappear without notice]
STARS AND SHOWS	ABC Online: Stars and Shows [3.0 only]
STARTER	Help Desk [Platform-dependent]
STATS	Pro Sports Center by STATS, Inc.
STATS BASKETBALL	Pro Basketball Center by STATS, Inc.
STATS CFB	STATS College Football
STATS FB	STATS Pro Football
STATS HOOPS	Pro Basketball Center by STATS, Inc.

STATS, INC.	Pro Sports Center by STATS, Inc.
STATS INC	Pro Sports Center by STATS, Inc.
STATS INC.	Pro Sports Center by STATS, Inc.
STATS, INC	Pro Sports Center by STATS, Inc.
STD	Sexually Transmitted Diseases Forum
STEAKS	Omaha Steaks
STEREO	Stereo Review Online
STEREO EQUIPMENT	Stereo Review Online
STEREO REVIEW	Stereo Review Online
STEVE CASE	Community Updates from Steve Case*
STF	STF Technologies
STF TECHNOLOGIES	STF Technologies
STOCK	StockLink: Quotes & Portfolios area
STOCK CHARTS	Decision Point Forum
STOCK PORTFOLIO	Your Stock Portfolio
STOCK QUOTES	StockLink: Quotes & Portfolios area
STOCK REPORTS	Stock Reports
STOCK TIMING	Decision Point Forum
STOCKLINK	StockLink: Quotes & Portfolios area
STOCKS	StockLink: Quotes & Portfolios area
STORE	Marketplace channel
STORES	Marketplace channel
STRAIGHT DOPE	Straight Dope
STRANGE	Parascope
STRATA	Strata, Inc.
STRATEGIC	Strategic Simulations
STRATEGIES	Business Strategies Forum
STRATEGY	Strategy & Wargaming Forum
STRIKE-A-MATCH	Boxer*Jam Gameshows [WAOL only]
STUDENT	The Princeton Review Online
STUDENT ACCESS	The Princeton Review Online
STUDIO	MusicSpace Studio
STUDIOWARE	Roger Wagner Publishing
STUDY	Study Skills Service
STUDY BREAK	Compton's Study Break
STUDY SKILLS	Study Skills Service
STUFFIT	Aladdin Systems, Inc.
STUMP	The Computing Rotunda
STW	Mindscape
STYL*E	Style channel
STYLE	Style channel
STYLE 911	Style channel
STYLE CHANNEL	Style channel
SUCK	suck.com [Web site] [3.0 only]
SUGGEST	Suggestion boxes*
SUGGESTION	Suggestion boxes*
SUIT	Style channel
SUMMER MOVIES	New Movie Releases
SUMMER SLAM	World Wrestling Federation
SUN DEVILS	AOL College Football '96 [3.0 only]
SUNAIR	Virtual Airlines
SUNAIR EXPRESS	Virtual Airlines
SUNBURST	Sunburst Communications
SUNSET	Sunset Magazine
SUNSET MAGAZINE	Sunset Magazine
SUPERBOWL	Super Bowl XXX Online
SUPERCARD	SuperCard Scripting Center
SUPERDISK	Alysis Software
SUPERLIBRARY	MacMillan Information SuperLibrary
SUPERMAC	Radius, Inc.
SUPERMAN	Superman Selections
SUPERSTARS	World Wrestling Federation
SUPERSTORE	Softdisk Superstore
SUPPORT	Member Services*
SURF	SurfLink
SURF SHACK	The Surf Shack
SURFBOARD	SurfLink
SURFER	SurfLink
SURFERS	SurfLink
SURFING	SurfLink
SURFLINK	SurfLink
SURNAMES	Genealogy Forum
SURVIVAL	Survival [3.0 only]
SURVIVAL WORLD	Survival World [3.0 only]
SURVIVOR	Survivor Software
SURVIVOR SOFTWARE	Survivor Software
SUSAN	The Hub: Susan
SWEDEN	Sweden
SWEDISH	Genealogy Forum
SWEETHEART	Omaha Steaks Offer
SWIMMING	The Grandstand: Other Sports
SWISS	Genealogy Forum
SWITZERLAND	Switzerland
SYMANTEC	Symantec
SYNEX	Synex
SYSOP	Member Services*
SYSTEM 7	Mac Operating Systems Forum
SYSTEM 7.0	Mac Operating Systems Forum

SYSTEM 7.1	Mac Operating Systems Forum
SYSTEM 71	Mac Operating Systems Forum
SYSTEM RESPONSE	System Response Report Area*
T SHIRT	America Online Store
T TALK	Teachers' Forum
TA	Traveler's Advantage
TA FOOTRACE	Trans-America Footrace
TAC	Top Advisor's Corner
TACKY	The Ultimate Tacky Page
TACOMA	Digital Cities: Seattle/Tacoma WA
TACOMA DIGC	Digital Cities: Seattle/Tacoma WA
TACOMA DIGITAL CITY	Digital Cities: Seattle/Tacoma WA
TACTIC	Tactic Software
TAIWAN	Taiwan
TAKE 2	Take 2 Interactive Software
TAKE 2 INC	Take 2 Interactive Software
TAL	Turner Adventure Learning
TALENT	Talent Bank
TALK	People Connection channel
TALK SHOW	Future Labs, Inc.
TAMPA	Digital Cities: Tampa-St. Petersburg
TAMPA COMM	Digital City Tampa: Community
TAMPA DIGC	Digital Cities: Tampa-St. Petersburg
TAMPA DIGITAL CITY	Digital Cities: Tampa-St. Petersburg
TAMPA NEWS	Digital City Tampa: News & Weather
TAMPA PEOPLE	Digital City Tampa: People
TAMPA WEATHER	Digital City Tampa: News & Weather
TAO	Travel America Online
TAROT	The Crystal Ball Forum
TARTAN	Tartan Software
TAX	Tax Forum
TAX CHANNEL	NAEA Tax Channel
TAX FORUM	Tax Forum
TAXCUT	Block Financial Software Support
TAXES	Computing Tax Corner or Tax Forum
TAXI	TAXI Information and Web Link
TAXLOGIC	Taxlogic
TAY	Taylor University
TAYJEESOFT	TayJee Software
TAYLOR UNIVERSITY	Taylor University
TBIBM	TBS Network Earth/IBM Project [MAOL and GAOL only]
TCF	Transgender Community Forum
TCW	Today's Christian Woman
TEACHER	The Educator's Network
TEACHER PAGER	Teacher Pager
TEACHER'S LOUNGE	Teachers' Lounge
TEACHERS	The Educator's Network
TEACHERS' LOUNGE	Teachers' Lounge
TEACHERS LOUNGE	Teachers' Lounge
TEAM	Team Concepts
TEAM CONCEPTS	Team Concepts
TEAM NFL	Team NFL [3.0 only]
TECH HELP LIVE	Member Services*
TECH LIVE	Member Services*
TECHNOLOGY	Computers & Software channel [Platform-dependent]
TECHNOLOGY WORKS	Technology Works
TECHNOTORIUM	@times/The New York Times Online
TECHWORKS	Technology Works
TEEN	Teen Selections
TEEN HANGOUT	Teen Scene
TEEN SCENE	Teen Selections
TEENS	Teen Selections
TEENWRITER	Writers Club: Teen Writers Area
TEENWRITERS	Writers Club: Teen Writers Area
TEENWRITING	Writers Club: Teen Writers Area
TEKNOSYS	Teknosys Works
TEKTRONIX	Tektronix
TELECOM	Communications/Telecom/Networking Forum [Platform-dependent]
TELECOM FORUM	Communications/Telecom/Networking Forum [Platform-dependent]
TELECOMMUNICATIONS	Communications/Telecom/Networking Forum [Platform-dependent]
TELEPHONE	Phone Directories
TELEPHONE NUMBERS	Phone Directories
TELEPORT	Global Village Communication
TELESCAN	Telescan Users Group Forum
TELEVISION	TV Main Screen
TELLURIDE	Telluride Film Festival
TELNET	Telnet [3.0 only]
TEMPLE	Digital Cities: Waco/Temple/Bryan TX
TEMPLE DC	Digital Cities: Waco/Temple/Bryan TX
TEMPLE DCITY	Digital Cities: Waco/Temple/Bryan TX
TEMPLE DIGC	Digital Cities: Waco/Temple/Bryan TX
TEMPLE TX	Digital Cities: Waco/Temple/Bryan TX
TEMPO	Affinity Microsystems
TEMPO II	Affinity Microsystems
TEMPO II PLUS	Affinity Microsystems
TEN	The Educator's Network
TENNIS	AOL Tennis
TERMS	Terms of Service*
TERMS OF SERVICE	Terms of Service*
TEST DAY	The Princeton Review Online
TEST PREP	Kaplan Online

TEST TUBE	ABC Online: Test Tube
TEXAS INSTRUMENTS	Texas Instrument
TEXAS RANGERS	Major League Baseball Team: Texas Rangers
TG	Transgender Community Forum
TGCOPS	Transgender Community Forum: Organizations
TGLAW	Transgender Community Forum: Organizations
TGS	Pictorius, Inc.
THE BIZ	The Biz!
THE DAILY FIX	The Daily Fix
THE DEAD	Grateful Dead Forum
THE ELECTRIC WORD	Digital City San Francisco: The Electric Word
THE ENTREPRENEUR ZONE	Your Business
THE EXCHANGE	The Exchange
THE FLORIDA KEYS	The Florida Keys
THE GRANDSTAND	The Grandstand
THE HUB	The Hub
THE HUB INDEX	The Hub: Index
THE INDUSTRY	The Industry: Entertainment News
THE KEYS	The Florida Keys
THE LAB	The Lab
THE LATE SHOW	Dave Letterman's Late Show Online [3.0 only]
THE LIMIT	The Limit Software
THE MALL	Marketplace channel
THE MOVIES	@the.movies
THE NATURE CONSERVANCY	The Nature Conservancy
THE NEW REPUBLIC	The New Republic Magazine
THE ODYSSEY PROJECT	The Odyssey Project
THE POST OFFICE	Post Office
THE SPORTING NEWS	The Sporting News
THE TOY NET	Pangea Toy Net
THE WALL	Vietnam Veterans Memorial Wall
THE WB NETWORK	The WB Network
THE WHITE HOUSE	White House Forum
THE WORLD	The World
THE ZONE	Your Business
THEATER	Playbill Online
THEATRE	Playbill Online
THESAURUS	Merriam-Webster's Thesaurus
THIRTIES	The Exchange: Communities Center
THREE SIXTY	Three-Sixty Software
THREEDO	The 3DO Company
THRIVE	Thrive@AOL
THRIVE@EATS	Thrive@AOL: Eats
THRIVE EXPERTS	Thrive@AOL: Experts Grouping
THRIVE MARKETPLACE	Thrive@AOL: Marketplace
THRIVE@SEX	Thrive@AOL: Sex
THRIVE@SHAPE	Thrive@AOL: Shape
THRIVE TALK	Thrive@AOL: Thrive Message Boards & Chat
THRUSTMASTER	Thrustmaster

TI	Texas Instruments
TIA	True Image Audio
TICF	Investors' Exchange
TICKET	Ticketmaster
TICKETMASTER	Ticketmaster
TIES	Woman's Day Online
TIGER	TIGERDirect, Inc.
TIGERDIRECT	TIGERDirect, Inc.
TIGERS	Major League Baseball Team: Detroit Tigers
TIME	Time Message Boards
TIME DAILY	TIME Message Boards
TIMECAPSULE	CyberJustice's Istorian's Time Capsule
TIMES	@times/The New York Times Online
TIMES ART	@times: Museums & Galleries
TIMES ARTS	@times: Art & Entertainment Guide
TIMES BOOKS	@times: Books of The Times
TIMES DINING	@times: Dining Out & Nightlife
TIMES FILM	@times: Film
TIMES LEISURE	@times: Arts & Leisure
TIMES MOVIES	@times: Film
TIMES MUSIC	@times: Music & Dance
TIMES NEWS	@times/The New York Times Online
TIMES REGION	@times: The New York Region
TIMES SPORTS	@times: Sports News
TIMES STORE	@times: Store
TIMES STORIES	@times: Page One-Top Stories
TIMES THEATER	@times: Theater
TIMESLIPS	Timeslips Corporation
TIMEWORKS	GST Technology
TIMEX	Andy Pargh/The Gadget Guru
TIP	Family Computing Forum: Tip of the Day
TIPS	Advice & Tips
TITF	What's Hot in Computing [Platform-dependent]
TL	Travel & Leisure Magazine
TLC	The Learning Channel
TLC ED	The Discovery Channel: Education
TLC-ED	The Discovery Channel: Education
TMS	TV Quest or TMS Peripherals
TNC	The Nature Conservancy
TNEWS	Teachers' Newsstand
TNG	Star Trek Club
TNPC	The National Parenting Center
TNR	The New Republic Magazine
TO MARKET	Marketplace Gift Valet
TO NETSCAPE	Netscape
TODAY PITCH	The Motley Fool: Finance & Folly
TODAY'S OTHER	The Hub: Today's Other News
TODAYS NEWS	Today's News channel
TODAYS PITCH	The Motley Fool: Finance & Folly

TODD ART	The Image Exchange: Ask Todd Art
TODDLER	Parent Soup: Baby & Toddler
TOLL FREE	AT&T 800 Directory (WWW site)
TOM SNYDER	Tom Snyder Productions
TONY AWARDS	Playbill Online: Tony Awards Central
TONYS	Playbill Online: Tony Awards Central
TOOL	American Woodworker: Tool Reviews
TOOLKIT	Web Page Toolkit
TOOLS	American Woodworker: Tool Reviews
TOOLWORKS	Mindscape
TOON	InToon with the News
TOONS	Cartoon Network
TOONZ	InToon with the News
TOP ADVISOR	Top Advisor's Corner
TOP ADVISORS	Top Advisor's Corner
TOP COMP SITES	Top Computing Internet Sites
TOP COMPANY SITES	Companies on the Internet
TOP COMPUTING SITES	Top Computing Internet Sites
TOP MODEL	TopModel Online
TOP NEWS	Today's News channel
TOP TIPS	Top Tips for AOL
TOPS	Transgender Community Forum: Organizations
TORONTO	Digital Cities: Toronto
TORONTO BLUE JAYS	Major League Baseball Team: Toronto Blue Jays
TORONTO DIGC	Digital Cities: Toronto
TORONTO DIGITAL CITY	Digital Cities: Toronto
TOS	Terms of Service*
TOS ADVISOR	Terms of Service*
TOTN	National Public Radio Outreach
TOUR	AOL Highlights Tour
TOUR CHAMPIONSHIP	iGolf: Tour Championship
TOUR DE FRANCE	Bicycling Magazine: Tour de France Coverage
TOUR DE FROG	Bicycling Magazine: Tour de France Coverage
TOUR GUIDE	America Online Store
TOWER	Tower Records
TOWER RECORDS	Tower Records
TOWN	Reward Town
TOY	Pangea Toy Net
TOY NET	Pangea Toy Net
TOYBUZZ	Pangea Toy Network: ToyBuzz
TOYS	The Exchange: Collector's Corner
TPI	Trivial Pursuit Interactive
TPN	The Prayer Network
TRACK	Road & Track Magazine
TRADEPLUS	How to Use StockLink & Gateway Host
TRAFFIC	Traffic Center
TRAIL GUIDES	Backpacker Magazine
TRAILHEADS	MECC
TRAILS	Backpacker Magazine

TRAINING	Career Development Training
TRANS	Transgender Community Forum
TRANSCRIPT	AOL Live! Event Transcripts
TRANSCRIPTS	AOL Live! Event Transcripts
TRANSGENDER	Transgender Community Forum
TRANSGENDER TEEN	GLCF Youth Area
TRANSGENDER YOUTH	GLCF Youth Area
TRANSPORTATION	NAS Online
TRANSSEXUAL	Transgender Community Forum
TRANSVESTITE	Transgender Community Forum
TRAVEL	Travel channel
TRAVEL ADVISORIES	U.S. State Department Travel Advisories
TRAVEL ALABAMA	Travel Alabama
TRAVEL AMERICA	Travel America Online
TRAVEL AMERICA ONLINE	Travel America Online
TRAVEL ARIZONA	Travel Arizona
TRAVEL CALIFORNIA	Travel California
TRAVEL COLORADO	Travel Colorado
TRAVEL CONNECTICUT	Travel Connecticut
TRAVEL FLORIDA	Travel Florida
TRAVEL FORUM	Travel Forum
TRAVEL HAWAII	Travel Hawaii
TRAVEL HOLIDAY	Travel Holiday Magazine
TRAVEL KANSAS	Travel Kansas
TRAVEL KENTUCKY	Travel Kentucky
TRAVEL & LEISURE	Travel & Leisure Magazine
TRAVEL MAINE	Travel Maine
TRAVEL MASSACHUSETTS	Travel Massachusetts
TRAVEL MINNESOTA	Travel Minnesota
TRAVEL NEW HAMPSHIRE	Travel New Hampshire
TRAVEL NEW YORK	Travel New York
TRAVEL NORTH DAKOTA	Travel North Dakota
TRAVEL OHIO	Travel Ohio
TRAVEL PICKS	What's Hot in Travel
TRAVEL RHODE ISLAND	Travel Rhode Island
TRAVEL TEXAS	Travel Texas
TRAVEL UPDATE	Travel Update
TRAVEL UTAH	Travel Utah
TRAVEL VERMONT	Travel Vermont
TRAVEL WASHINGTON DC	Travel Washington D.C.
TRAVELER	Travel Forum
TRAVELERS ADVANTAGE	Traveler's Advantage
TRAVELERS CORNER	Traveler's Corner
TREASURE	AOL Treasure Hunt
TREASURE HUNT	AOL Treasure Hunt
TREASURES	Tell a Story
TREK	Star Trek Club
TREKER	800-TREKKER: 24 Hour Sci-Fi Collectibles Hotline
TREKKER	800-TREKKER: 24 Hour Sci-Fi Collectibles Hotline

TRENDS	Elle Magazine Online
TRENDSETTER	Trendsetter Software
TRIANGLE	Gay & Lesbian Community Forum
TRIB	Chicago Tribune
TRIB ADS	Chicago Online: Classifieds
TRIB CLASSIFIED	Chicago Online: Classifieds
TRIB COLUMNISTS	Chicago Online: Columnists
TRIB SPORTS	Chicago Tribune: Sports Area
TRIBE	Major League Baseball Team: Cleveland Indians
TRIBUNE	Chicago Tribune
TRIESS	Transgender Community Forum: Organizations
TRIMBLE	Trimble Navigation, Ltd.
TRIPLE A	AAA Online
TRIPLE CROWN	ABC Triple Crown
TRIVIA	Trivia Forum
TRIVIA FORUM	Trivia Forum
TRIVIAL PURSUIT	Trivial Pursuit Interactive
TROJANS	AOL College Football '96 [3.0 only]
TROPICAL STORM	Tropical Storm and Hurricane Info
TRUE IMAGE AUDIO	True Image Audio
TRUE TALES	True Tales of the Internet
TS	Trendsetter Software
TSENG	Tseng
TSN	The Sporting News
TSP	Tom Snyder Productions
TSR	TSR Online
TSR ONLINE	TSR Online
TT	ABC Online: Test Tube
TULSA	Digital Cities: Tulsa OK
TULSA DC	Digital Cities: Tulsa OK
TULSA DCITY	Digital Cities: Tulsa OK
TULSA DIGC	Digital Cities: Tulsa OK
TULSA DIGITAL CITY	Digital Cities: Tulsa OK
TULSA OK	Digital Cities: Tulsa OK
TUNE UP	Tune Up Your PC
TUNE UP YOUR PC	Tune Up Your PC
TURKEY	Turkey
TURKMENISTAN	Turkmenistan [3.0 only]
TURNER VISION	Andy Pargh/The Gadget Guru
TURTLE	Pet Care Forum
TURTLE BEACH	Turtle Beach Systems
TURTLE SYS	Turtle Beach Systems
TUTORING	Academic Assistance Center
TV	Main TV Screen
TV GOSSIP	TV Shows Gossip
TV GUIDE	TV Quest
TV LISTINGS	TV Quest
TV NETWORKS	TV Networks area
TV PEOPLE	TV People
TV SHOWS	TV Shows
TV SOURCE	TV Quest
TV SPOOFS	TV Spoofs
TV VIEWERS	TV Viewers Forum
TWENTIES	The Exchange: Communities Center
TWENTIETH	Twentieth Century Mutual Funds
TWENTIETH CENTURY	Twentieth Century Mutual Funds
TWENTIETH-CENTURY	Twentieth Century Mutual Funds
TWI	Time Warner Interactive
TWO MARKET	Marketplace Gift Valet
UA	Unlimited Adventures
UCAL	University of California Extension
UCPA	United Cerebral Palsy Association, Inc.
UCX	University of California Extension
UFC	Ultimate Fighting Championships
UFO	Institute for the Study of Contact with Non-Human Intelligence
UFOS	Institute for the Study of Contact with Non-Human Intelligence
UGF	User Group Forum
UHA	Homeowner's Forum
UKRAINE	Ukraine
ULTIMATE	Ultimate Fighting Championships
ULTRALIGHTS	Aviation Forum
UNDIES	Style channel
UNION	Union Bank of California [3.0 only]
UNIQUE	Best of America Online showcase
UNITARIAN	Humanism-Unitarianism Forum
UNITARIANISM	Humanism-Unitarianism Forum
UNITARIUM	Religion & Ethics Forum
UNITED KINGDOM	United Kingdom
UNIVBE	SciTech Software
UNIVERSE	UniverseCentral.Com
UNIVERSE CENTRAL	UniverseCentral.Com
UNIVERSITIES	Electronic University Network
UNIVERSITY	Electronic University Network
UNLIMITED ADVENTURES	Unlimited Adventures
UNPROFOR	Balkan Operation Joint Endeavor
UNSIGNED	The Great Unsigned
UPDATE ADD	AD&D Neverwinter Nights
UPDATES	Hoover's Company Masterlist
UPGRADE	Upgrade to the latest version of AOL*
URBAN	Urban Legends
URBAN LEAGUE	National Urban League
US GAZETTEER	U.S. Census Information Web Page [3.0 only]
US MAIL	Fax/Paper Mail
US NEWS	U.S. & World News area
USA	USA Weekend
USA WEEKEND	USA Weekend

USEFUL THINGS	The Hub: Useful Things
USELESS THINGS	The Hub: Useless Things
USENET	Internet Usenet Newsgroup area
USER GROUP	User Group Forum
USER GROUPS	User Group Forum
USER NAME	Add, change, or delete screen names
USERLAND	Userland
USFSA	United States Figure Skating Association
USPS	United States Postal Service
USROBOTICS	U.S. Robotics
UTAH	Utah Forum
UTAH FORUM	Utah Forum
UZBEKISTAN	Uzbekistan
VA	Virginia Forum
VA.	Virginia Forum
VAA	Virtual Airlines
VACATION	Preview Vacations
VACATIONS	Preview Vacations
VALET	Marketplace Gift Valet
VALLEY	Virgin's Virtual Valley
VALUES	Ethics & Values
VAMPIRE	Weekly World News
VAN	AOL Roadtrips [3.0 only]
VANGUARD	Vanguard Online
VANGUARD ONLINE	Vanguard Online
VAS	Virtual Airlines
VB	Visual Basic area
VCOMMS	Vanguard Online: Communications
VDISC	Videodiscovery
VEGAN	Cooking Club: Vegetarians Online
VEGETARIAN	Cooking Club
VENTANA	Ventana Communications
VERONICA	Internet Gopher
VERSATILE	Versatile Software Solutions, Inc.
VERTIGO	DC Comics Online
VERTISOFT	Vertisoft
VETERANS	Military and Vets Club
VETS	Military and Vets Club
VETS CLUB	Military and Vets Club
VFR	Flying Magazine
VFUNDS	Vanguard Online: Mutual Funds Campus
VG	Vanguard Online
VGA PLANETS	VGA Planets
VGAP	VGA Planets
VGS	Video Games area
VH	Virtual Christian Humor
VH1	VH1 Online
VIDEO GAME	Video Games area
VIDEO MAG	Video Selections
VIDEO MAGAZINE	Video Magazine
VIDEO ONLINE	Video Magazine
VIDEO SIG	Video SIG
VIDEO TOASTER	New Tek
VIDEO TOOLKIT	Abbate Video
VIDEO ZONE	PC Multimedia's Video
VIDEODISC	Videodiscovery
VIDEODISCOVERY	Videodiscovery
VIDEOS	Home Video
VIDI	VIDI
VIENNA	Computing Print & Broadcast
VIETNAM	Vietnam Veterans Memorial Wall
VIEWER	Viewer Resource Center
VIEWERS	Viewer Resource Center
VIEWPOINT	Viewpoint DataLabs
VILLAGE	Village Software
VILLAGE SOFTWARE	Village Software
VILLAIN	Military City Online: Villains of Fact & Fiction
VILLAINS	Military City Online: Villains of Fact & Fiction
VIP	Style channel
VIREX	Datawatch
VIRGIN	Virgin Records or Virgin Sound & Vision
VIRGIN RECORDS	Virgin Records
VIRGINIA	Virginia Forum
VIRGINIA FORUM	Virginia Forum
VIRTUAL AIRLINES	Virtual Airlines
VIRTUAL HUMOR	Virtual Christian Humor
VIRTUAL REALITY	Virtual Reality Resource Center
VIRTUAL REFUGEE	Virtual Refugees Forum
VIRTUAL REFUGEES	Virtual Refugees Forum
VIRTUAL TORCH	Virtual Torch Relay
VIRTUAL TOYS	Pangea Toy Net
VIRTUAL VALLEY	Virgin's Virtual Valley
VIRTUS	Virtus Corp.
VIRUS	Virus Information Center SIG
VIRUS2	Virus Letter*
VIS HELP	PC Help Forum: Visual Help
VISA	AOL Visa Card
VISA CARD	AOL Visa Card
VISALIA	Digital Cities: Fresno/Visalia CA
VISALIA CA	Digital Cities: Fresno/Visalia CA
VISALIA DC	Digital Cities: Fresno/Visalia CA
VISALIA DIGC	Digital Cities: Fresno/Visalia CA
VISALIA DIGITAL CITY	Digital Cities: Fresno/Visalia CA
VISION VIDEO	Vision Video
VISIONARY	Visionary Software
VISIONEER	Visioneer
VISUAL BASIC	Visual Basic Area
VISUAL HELP	PC Help Forum: Visual Help

VITAMIN EXP	Health and Vitamin Express
VITAMIN EXPRESS	Health and Vitamin Express
VITAMINS	Longevity Magazine Online
VNEWS	Vanguard Online: Vanguard News
VOICE	Your Voice
VOLLEYBALL	AVP Pro Beach Volleyball
VOLUNTEER	access.point
VOLUNTEERS	access.point
VOTE AMERICA	Vote America
VOYAGER	The Voyager Company
VOYETRA	Voyetra Technologies
VR	Virtual Reality Resource Center
VRLI	Virtual Reality Labs, Inc.
VSTATS	Vanguard Fund Information
VSTRATEGY	Vanguard Online: Planning & Strategy
VTOYS	Pangea Toy Net
VV	Vision Video
WACO	Digital Cities: Waco/Temple/Bryan TX
WACO DC	Digital Cities: Waco/Temple/Bryan TX
WACO DCITY	Digital Cities: Waco/Temple/Bryan TX
WACO DIGC	Digital Cities: Waco/Temple/Bryan TX
WACO DIGITAL CITY	Digital Cities: Waco/Temple/Bryan TX
WACO TX	Digital Cities: Waco/Temple/Bryan TX
WAHL	Andy Pargh/The Gadget Guru
WAIS	Internet Gopher
WALES	Virtual Wales [3.0 only]
WALKTHROUGH	Virtus Corp.
WALL	Vietnam Veterans Memorial Wall
WALL STREET WORDS	Wall Street Words
WALLPAPER	Windows Wallpaper & Paint Center
WALMART	Motley Fool: FoolMart
WAND TV	ABC Online: WAND-TV in Decatur, IL
WAR	Military City Online
WARNER	Warner/Reprise Records Online
WARNER BROS. STORE	Warner Bros. Studio Store
WARNER BROS STORE	Warner Bros. Studio Store
WARNER BROS. STU STO	Warner Bros. Studio Store
WARNER MUSIC	Warner/Reprise Records Online
WARNER STORE	Warner Bros. Studio Store
WASH PERSONALS	Digital City Washington: Personals
WASHINGTON	Politics Forum
WASHINGTON WEB	City Web
WATE TV	ABC Online: WATE-TV in Knoxville, TN
WATER	Boating Online
WB	The WB Network
WB STORE	Warner Bros. Studio Store
WBAY TV	ABC Online: WBAY-TV in Green Bay, WI
WBNET	The WB Network
WBRC TV	ABC Online: WBRC-TV in Birmingham, AL
WBRZ TV	ABC Online: WBRZ-TV in Baton Rouge, LA
WC CHAT	Writer's Club: Chat Rooms
WCN	World Crisis Network
WCRG	Writer's Club: Romance Writers & Readers
WCVB TV	ABC Online: WCVB-TV in Boston, MA
WD	Woman's Day Online
WD KITCHEN	Woman's Day Kitchen
WDC	Western Digital
WDHN TV	ABC Online: WDHN-TV in Dothan, AL
WDIO TV	ABC Online: WDIO-TV in Duluth, MN
WDTN TV	ABC Online: WDTN-TV in Dayton, OH
WEAR TV	ABC Online: WEAR-TV in Pensacola, FL
WEATHER	Weather
WEATHER MALL	WSC Weather Mall
WEATHER MAPS	Color Weather Maps
WEAVING	Needlecrafts/Sewing Center
WEB	World Wide Web
WEB ART	Web Page Clip Art Creation Center
WEB BIZ	The Web Diner
WEB COMEDY	Hecklers Online
WEB DINER	The Web Diner
WEB ENT	webentertainment
WEB ENTERTAINMENT	webentertainment
WEB HELP	The Web Diner
WEB HUMOR	Hecklers Online
WEB MAKEOVER	Web Makeover
WEB PAGE	Web Page Toolkit
WEB PAGE TOOLKIT	Web Page Toolkit
WEB PUB	Web Publishing SIG
WEB PUBLISH	Web Publishing SIG
WEB PUBLISHING	Web Publishing SIG
WEB RESEARCH	Reference: Web Research
WEB REVIEW	Web Review [3.0 only]
WEB TOOLS	Reference: Web Research
WEB UNIVERSITY	Web University
WEBCRAWLER	World Wide Web
WEBD	The Web Diner
WEBSITE	The Web Diner
WEBSOURCE	Websource
WEBSTER	Merriam-Webster Dictionary
WEDDING	Wedding Workshop
WEDNESDAYS	90210 Wednesdays
WEEKLY READER	Weekly Reader News
WEEKLY WORLD NEWS	Weekly World News
WEIGAND	Weigand Report
WEIRD	Parascope
WEIRD SISTERS	The Hub: Weird Sisters
WEISSMANN	Traveler's Corner
WELCOME TO PLANET EARTH	Astronet

WELLNESS	Longevity Magazine Online
WELLS FARGO	Wells Fargo Bank [3.0 only]
WELSH	Genealogy Forum
WEST	Digital Cities: West
WEST DIGC	Digital Cities: West
WESTERN DIGITAL	Western Digital
WESTERN EUROPEAN	Genealogy Forum
WESTWOOD	Westwood Studios
WESTWOOD STUDIOS	Westwood Studios
WF	Wells Fargo Bank [3.0 only]
WFAA TV	ABC Online: WFAA-TV in Dallas/Ft. Worth, TX
WFTV TV	ABC Online: WFTV-TV in Orlando, FL
WGGB TV	ABC Online: WGGB-TV in Springfield, MA
WGTU TV	ABC Online: WGTU/WGTQ-TV in Traverse City, MI
WHALERS	NHL Hockey
WHALEZ	Tartan Software
WHAT I$ IT	What Is It? Contest [May disappear without notice]
WHAT IS IT	What Is It? Contest [May disappear without notice]
WHAT'S HOT IN HEALTH	What's Hot in Health
WHATEVER	What's Hot This Month Showcase
WHATS HOT	What's Hot This Month Showcase
WHEELS	Wheels
WHEELS EXCHANGE	Wheels Exchange
WHFS	WHFS 99.1 FM
WHITE HOUSE	White House Forum
WHITE PAGES	ProCD National Telephone Directory Search
WHOI TV	ABC Online: WHOI-TV in Peoria-Bloomington, IL
WHTM TV	ABC Online: WHTM-TV in Harrisburg, PA
WICCA	Pagan Religions & Occult Sciences
WICS	Women in Community Service
WIDE WORLD OF SPORTS	ABC Online: Wide World of Sports
WIERD	Parascope
WILDCAT	Mustang Software
WILDCAT BBS	Mustang Software
WILDERNESS	Backpacker Magazine
WIMBLEDON	Wimbledon [May disappear without notice]
WIN	Windows Forum
WIN 500	Windows Shareware 500
WIN 95	Windows Forum
WIN FORUM	Windows Forum
WIN MAG	Windows Magazine
WIN NEWS	Windows News area
WIN NT	Windows NT Resource Center
WINDHAM	Windham Hill
WINDHAM HILL	Windham Hill
WINDOWS	Windows Services
WINDOWS 500	Windows Shareware 500
WINDOWS 95	Windows Forum
WINDOWS FORUM	Windows Forum
WINDOWS MAG	Windows Magazine
WINDOWS MAGAZINE	Windows Magazine
WINDOWS NT	Windows NT Resource Center
WINDOWS TIPS	Family Computing Forum: Tip of the Day
WINDSURFING	Sailing Forum
WINE	Food & Drink Network
WINERIES	Food & Drink Network
WINERY	Food & Drink Network
WINIMAGE	Gilles Vollant Software
WINNER	AOL Contest area
WINNER'S CIRCLE	ABC Track
WINSOCK	Winsock Central [WAOL only]
WIRED	Wired Magazine
WIRELESS	Wireless Communication
WISE GUYS	Hecklers Online
WIXT TV	ABC Online: WIXT-TV in Syracuse, NY
WIZARD	Wizard World
WIZARD WORLD	Wizard World
WJBF TV	ABC Online: WJBF-TV in Augusta, GA
WJCL TV	ABC Online: WJCL-TV in Savannah, GA
WKBW TV	ABC Online: WKBW-TV in Buffalo, NY
WKRC TV	ABC Online: WKRC-TV in Cincinnati, OH
WKRN TV	ABC Online: WKRN-TV in Nashville, TN
WLOS TV	ABC Online: WLOS-TV in Asheville, NC
WLOX TV	ABC Online: WLOX-TV in Biloxi, MS
WLS	WLS Chicago
WMBB TV	ABC Online: WMBB-TV in Panama, FL
WMDT TV	ABC Online: WMDT-TV in Salisbury, MD
WMUR TV	ABC Online: WMUR-TV in Manchester, NH
WNEP TV	ABC Online: WNEP-TV in Scranton/W-B, PA
WOKR TV	ABC Online: WOKR-TV in Rochester, NY
WOLFF BOOKS	Internet Connection Store
WOLO TV	ABC Online: WOLO-TV in Columbia, SC
WOLVERINES	AOL College Football '96 [3.0 only]
WOMAN	Woman's Day Online
WOMAN BOARDS	Women's Interests: Message Boards
WOMAN COLLECTIONS	Women's Interests: Arts and Letters
WOMAN NEWS	Women's Interests: News
WOMAN VOICES	Women's Interests: Organizations
WOMAN'S DAY	Woman's Day Online
WOMANS DAY	Woman's Day Online
WOMEN	Women's Interests
WOMEN CLASS	Women's Interests: Educational Opportunities
WOMEN MAIN	Women's Interests
WOMEN ONLY	Consumer Reports Complete Drug Reference Search

WOMEN ROUND	Women's Interests: Community
WOMEN SPOTLIGHT	Women's Interests
WOMEN WEB	Women's Interests: Web Sites
WOMEN'S HEALTH	Women's Health Forum
WOMEN'S HEALTH WEB	Women's Health Internet Sites
WOMENS	Women's Interests
WOMENS HEALTH	Women's Health Forum
WOMENS SPACE	GLCF: Women's Space
WOMENS SPORTS	Women's Sports World
WOOD	American Woodworker
WOODSTOCK	Woodstock Online
WOODWORKER	American Woodworker
WOODWORKING	American Woodworker
WORD	Christianity Online: Word Publishing
WORD HISTORIES	Word Histories
WORD PERFECT	Word Perfect Support Center
WORD PROCESSING	Mac Desktop Publishing/WP Forum
WORK	About Work
WORKING	Working Software
WORKOUTS	Longevity Magazine Online
WORKSHOP	Family Computing Forum: Life's Workshop
WORLD	The World
WORLD BELIEFS	World Beliefs
WORLD CRISIS	World Crisis Network
WORLD MUSIC	World Music Forum
WORLD NEWS	U.S. & World News area
WORLD WIDE WEB	World Wide Web
WORLDVIEW	Fodor's Worldview
WORRY	CyberJustice's Worry Free Zone
WORTH	Worth Magazine Online
WORTH MAGAZINE	Worth Magazine Online
WORTH ONLINE	Worth Magazine Online
WORTH PORTFOLIO	Worth Magazine Online Portfolio
WOTV TV	ABC Online: WOTV-TV in Battle Creek, MI
WPBF TV	ABC Online: WPBF-TV in West Palm Beach, FL
WPDE TV	ABC Online: WPDE-TV in Myrtle Beach, SC
WPTA TV	ABC Online: WPTA-TV in Fort Wayne, IN
WQAD TV	ABC Online: WQAD-TV in Moline, IL
WQOW TV	ABC Online: WQOW-TV in Eau Claire, WI
WRD	Christianity Online: Word Publishing
WRESTLING	World Wrestling Federation
WRITE	Writer's Club Chat Rooms
WRITE TO OUR STAFF	Questions*
WRITE TO STAFF	Questions*
WRITER	Writer's Club
WRITER'S	Writer's Club
WRITER'S CLUB	Writer's Club
WRITERS	Writer's Club
WRITERS CLUB	Writer's Club
WRITERS CLUB CHAT	Writer's Club: Chat Rooms
WRITING	Writer's Club
WRTV TV	ABC Online: WRTV in Indianapolis, IN
WS	GLCF: Women's Space
WSB TV	ABC Online: WSB-TV in Atlanta, GA
WSF	Women's Sports World
WSJV TV	ABC Online: WSJV-TV in South Bend, IN
WSW	Wall Street Words
WSYX TV	ABC Online: WSYX-TV in Columbus, OH
WTEN TV	ABC Online: WTEN-TV in Albany, NY
WTNH TV	ABC Online: WTNH-TV in Nashville, TN
WTOK TV	ABC Online: WTOK-TV in Meridan, MS
WTVC TV	ABC Online: WTVC-TV in Chattanooga, TN
WTVQ TV	ABC Online: WTVQ-TV in Lexington, KY
WVII TV	ABC Online: WVII-TV in Bangor, ME
WWF	World Wrestling Federation
WWIR	Washington Week in Review magazine
WWN	Weekly World News
WWOS	ABC Online: Wide World of Sports
WWW	World Wide Web
WWWARDROBE	Style channel
WXOW TV	ABC Online: WXOW-TV in LaCrescent, MN
WZZM TV	ABC Online: WZZM-TV in Grand Rapids, MI
X FILES	X Files Forums
X FILES SIM	X Files Sim Forum
XAOS	Xaos Tools
XAOS TOOLS	Xaos Tools
XCMD	XCMD SIG
XCMD SIG	XCMD SIG
XCON	Christianity Online: Contest
XF FRIDAYS	X Files Fridays
XOL	Christianity Online
XWORDS	Crossword America
YACHTING	Sailing Forum
YACHTS	Boating Online
YAMAHA	Yamaha XG
YAMAHA XG	Yamaha XG
YANKEES	Major League Baseball Team: New York Yankees
YANKS	Major League Baseball Team: New York Yankees
YAVIASA	The Hub: You Are Very Intelligent and Somewhat Artsy
YB	Your Business
YBERSMITH	CyberSmith
YC	Your Church Magazine
YEAR	1995: The Year in Review
YEAR IN REVIEW	1995: The Year in Review
YELLOW JACKETS	AOL College Football '96 [3.0 only]
YELLOW PAGES	Business Yellow Pages
YIR	1995: The Year in Review

YM	MoneyWhiz
YMB	Your Mind & Body Online
YOUNG CHEFS	Young Chefs
YOUNGNESS	Longevity Magazine Online
YOUR BIZ	Your Business
YOUR BUSINESS	Your Business
YOUR BUSINESS LUNCH	Your Business Lunch
YOUR CHOICE	ABC News-On-Demand
YOUR CHURCH	Your Church Magazine
YOUR MIND AND BODY	Your Mind & Body Online
YOUR MIND & BODY	Your Mind & Body Online
YOUR MOMMA	Computing Print & Broadcast
YOUR MONEY	MoneyWhiz
YOUR SPORTS	NESN: New England Outdoors
YOUR TOONS	Cartoon collection
YOUTH	Youth Tech
YOUTH SERVICE AMERICA	SERVEnet
YOUTH TECH	Youth Tech
YOUTHFUL	Longevity Magazine Online
YOUTHNET	National Network for Youth
YOYO	Yoyodyne Entertainment
YOYO GAMES	Yoyodyne Entertainment: Games
YOYODYNE	Yoyodyne Entertainment
YSA	SERVEnet
YT	Youth Tech
YUBBA	Today's Events in AOL Live!
YUGOSLAVIA	Balkan Operation Joint Endeavor
Z	The Health Zone
<Z>	The Health Zone
ZAGAT	Zagat Restaurant/Hotel/Resort/Spa Surveys
ZAGATS	Zagat Restaurant/Hotel/Resort/Spa Surveys
ZD	ZDNet
ZDNET	ZDNet
ZEDCOR	Zedcor, Inc.
ZELOS	Zelos
ZEN	ChipNet Online: ZENtertainment
ZENTERTAINMENT	ChipNet Online: ZENtertainment
ZEOS	Zeos International Ltd.
ZIFF	ZDNet
ZIMA	Zima
ZIMA TALK	Zima Events
ZIP CODE	Zip Code Directory [3.0 only]
ZIP CODE DIRECTORY	Zip Code Directory [3.0 only]
ZIP CODES	Zip Code Directory [3.0 only]
ZIPSERVER	ZipServer
ZODIAC	Astronet
ZON	Zondervan Publishing House
ZONDERVAN	Zondervan Publishing House
ZONE	Your Business
ZONED	The Health Zone
ZONIE	The Health Zone
ZOO	America's Favorite Zoos and Aquariums
ZOOM T	Zoom Telephonics, Inc.
ZOOM TELEPHONICS	Zoom Telephonics
ZP	Zondervan Publishing House
ZPAY	ZPAY Payroll Systems, Inc.
ZROCK	ABC Online: Z-Rock

APPENDIX C

Locations, Modems & CCL Files

America Online's client software is not only user-friendly, it's modem-friendly as well. The first time you sign on to America Online, the software asks you several questions as part of the initial installation process. Your answers supply such things as modem speed and type, and allow AOL to determine local access telephone numbers to use, and so on. This information automatically configures your America Online software to connect effortlessly. However, you may need to modify this information if, for example, you change your location, upgrade your modem, or discover that your nonstandard modem needs special configuration. This appendix will show you how to create and save multiple setups and how to modify your configuration. It also covers modem files and CCL scripts as they relate to successful America Online connection.

Locations

Your America Online software allows you to create and store multiple sets of network setup and connection information. These sets of information are known as "locations," and while they are handy for folks who move from location to location, they also are very useful for those who like to stay put. You can store configurations for different connection speeds as well as access numbers for various locations.

Think of locations as coats. If you live in a temperate region of the country, you may only own one light-weight windbreaker. On the other hand, if you call a more diverse climate your home, you may collect an entire wardrobe of coats to meet a variety of weather conditions. Locations are no different: they allow you to successfully step out into the world of America Online, regardless of where you are, what time it is, or what you wish to accomplish. Best of all, creating and choosing your location before signing on is easier than purchasing a closet full of coats and deciding which one to wear.

New locations are simple to create. Launch the America Online software and, instead of signing on as you normally would, select New Location from the Location pop-up menu at the bottom of the Welcome (sign-on) window. In the new window that appears, enter your information (described below in "Changing Your Location"). When you're finished, save your new location by clicking the Save button in the lower right-hand corner of the window. When you're prompted to name the location, choose a title that reflects the function of the new information, such as "Ann Arbor" (for a different city or town) or "14,400 Access" (for a different connection speed). To use the location you've just created, simply select it from the pop-up menu in your Welcome window. The next time you sign on, your software will use the setup information in the selected location.

Changing Your Location

To create or modify locations, you need to change your network options. Creation is simple, as described above in this appendix. To modify a setup, choose the location you wish to change from the pop-up menu in the Welcome (sign-on) window and then click the Setup button. In both creating and editing a setup, your software displays the Location window with a number of options (see Figure C-1). Be sure to note your current settings in case you need to return to them. You can use this screen to change any number of options, all described below.

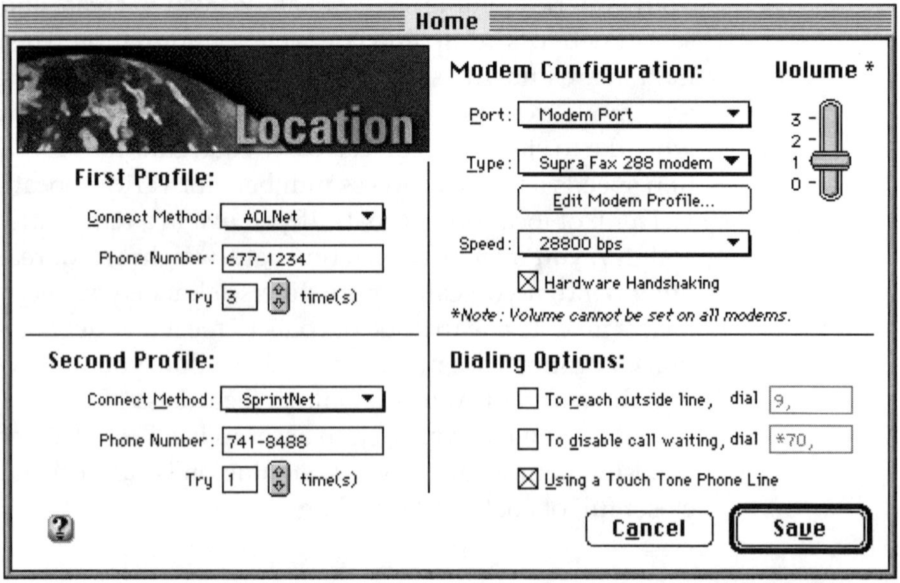
Home
Location
First Profile:
Connect Method: AOLNet
Phone Number: 677-1234
Try 3 time(s)
Second Profile:
Connect Method: SprintNet
Phone Number: 741-8488
Try 1 time(s)
Modem Configuration:
Volume *
Port: Modem Port
Type: Supra Fax 288 modem
Edit Modem Profile...
Speed: 28800 bps
Hardware Handshaking
*Note: Volume cannot be set on all modems.
Dialing Options:
To reach outside line, dial 9,
To disable call waiting, dial *70,
Using a Touch Tone Phone Line
Cancel
Save

Figure C-1: Working offline, click the Setup button in the Welcome (sign-on) window to access your Location Setup information.

Below, we'll look at each one of the variables pictured in Figure C-1.

Connect Method

This pop-up menu is used to select which phone carrier handles your calls from the local access node to America Online's host computers. AOLNet is AOL's private network of telephone lines across the country. Use AOLNet whenever you can. SprintNet is the most widely used third-party carrier for America Online in the United States. There might be a few others, depending on your location. You can use the Network pop-up menu to select the appropriate network as specified for your access number. (The keyword: **Access**—available only when you're online—lists all of AOL's access numbers and the appropriate network carrier.) TCP connections are detailed later in this appendix.

Phone Number

This field contains the phone number your America Online software uses to connect with the host computer. You'll notice that this field and the associated Connect Method field are shown twice in the window. AOL automatically uses the second set of information if the first try with the primary information is unsuccessful. This allows you to set up an alternate access number for your AOL software to dial if the primary number is busy or unavailable. Note also that you can tell AOL how many times you'd like it to try each of the numbers, using the small field below each phone number. You can decrease or increase the number of tries with the small arrows to the right of the field, or just by typing in a new number.

You will need to change your phone numbers if you've moved to a new area, if you're on the road, or if you just want to try a different local access number. You can find local access numbers online via the keyword: **Access**. If there is only one number for your area, use that as both primary and alternate number so the AOL software will redial it automatically if the number is busy on the first try. If you don't want AOL to dial a second number, leave the alternate number field empty.

Tip: In some areas you may need to dial an area code, even for a local call. If you normally need to do this when you place voice calls, you will need to do it when you call America Online access as well.

Note: Remember, any long-distance charges you incur reaching the America Online access number are your responsibility. They're not included as a part of your monthly America Online fee. If you have to dial the number 1 before you can reach AOL's nearest access number, you're no doubt incurring long-distance charges.

Port

This tells the software where to look for the modem's physical connection to your computer, with the default being the modem port. If you want to use a modem connected to your Mac's printer port rather than the modem port, use the Port pop-up menu to make your selection. If you have and use a Geoport or a modem card in a PCMCIA slot, the options "Geoport" or "PC Card Slot" should appear.

Type

This pop-up menu allows you to designate the type of modem you are using, enabling proper setup for connection to America Online. If your modem is not listed, you can use a generic modem (such as Hayes Basic for 2400 baud and below or Hayes Extended for faster speeds) or use a custom modem file (described below in "Modem Files").

Tip: If you have problems connecting, or if your modem refuses to initialize correctly, try one of the Hayes modem types (even if your modem is not a Hayes brand). Frequently, they work when others won't.

Speed

You'll most likely only need to change this if you get a new modem with a speed different than your usual modem, or if you're currently using a local access node that doesn't take full advantage of your modem's speed. For instance, you may use a local access number that can only handle 2400 bps. But if you later switch to a different number that can serve 28.8 kbps modems and you have a 28.8 kbps modem, you need to change the Speed setting your America Online software uses. Use the Speed pop-up menu to change the speed to the highest setting your modem and node can handle.

Hardware Handshaking

This check box is used to turn the hardware handshaking features of your modem on or off. Most modems require hardware handshaking these days. Hardware handshaking is necessary to fully utilize modem speeds over 9600 bauds. Consult your modem manual to see if your modem supports hardware handshaking. Some older Macintosh modem cables cannot support hardware handshaking; if you are experiencing problems with this option enabled, turn it off.

Volume

There are times when you want that noisy modem to be quiet, or when you need to hear it better to troubleshoot a problem. You can increase, decrease, and even turn off the volume of your modem for these times. Altering the volume does not affect your modem's performance, as the volume only applies to what we hear, not America Online. Note that not all modems support the ability to change the volume; if your modem falls into this category, see the "Solving Common Modem Problems" section later in this appendix for information on how you may be able to disable your modem speaker.

Outside Line Prefix

Some telephone systems, particularly those in hotels, offices, and schools, require that you dial a 9 or some other prefix to get an outside line. Enter the number you want America Online to dial; then enter a comma. The comma tells the modem to wait two seconds before dialing the next number. If it takes longer than two seconds for your phone system to access an outside line and generate a dial tone, you might want to add a second comma just to be sure. Note that the America Online software already has entered a 9 for you in the appropriate field. To use this prefix whenever you dial America Online, all you have to do is click this check box.

Disable Call Waiting

When you're connected to America Online and someone tries to call you, he or she would normally get a busy signal. If you have Call Waiting, however, the caller hears a normal ring, and your modem hears the beep that ordinarily lets you know you have a call waiting. As you can imagine, this tends to confuse your Mac (not to mention the host computers). Call Waiting, which is a convenience for voice communications, is an interference for telecommunications and will disconnect your modem from America Online. If you use Call Waiting, you can (and should) temporarily disable it (on most phone systems, by entering a code such as 1170, or *70,) before dialing America Online. Be sure to include the comma after the string of numbers: it tells the modem to wait two seconds before dialing the next number. Note that the America Online software has already entered *70 for you in the appropriate field. To configure your software to turn off Call Waiting whenever you dial America Online (but not any other time), all you have to do is click this check box. When you're finished using AOL, however, you may need to enter the same code from your phone handset to turn Call Waiting back on (or you may start to wonder why everyone is getting busy signals). If you aren't sure what numbers you should enter to disable Call Waiting, check with your local telephone company or look in the front section of your local phone directory, under Call Waiting.

Phone Type

Touch-tone phones are standard equipment today in most homes and hotels. However, there are still a few local phone exchanges (or homes) that do not support tone dialing; they use pulse dialing instead. If your America Online software seems to be having trouble when first dialing the local access number, disable the touch-tone phone option.

Once you've customized your location setup, be sure to save your changes. To save, click the Save button in the lower right-hand corner of the window. Once saved, you can use your new location by selecting it from your Location pop-up menu on your Welcome window before initiating your connection.

Tip: If you use both 14,400 and 28,800 baud access to connect to AOL, set up a location for each along with the appropriate numbers and even modem files, if necessary. This will allow you to choose between 14,400 and 28,800 baud connection before signing on at the click of the mouse.

TCP Connections

America Online also provides access to the service through TCP/IP, which is a communications format for transferring data over the Internet. To sign on with a TCP/IP connection, you must first have a TCP/IP connection from an Internet service provider to your computer. You can download a listing of public access Internet providers by using the keywords: **File Search**, then searching for PDIAL. To use TCP/IP with America Online, install the software your Internet provider recommends for your connection and then simply create a new Location and choose TCP for your connect method, leaving the phone numbers blank.

You can also connect to America Online through a SLIP or PPP connection (a modem-based TCP/IP connection). To connect through SLIP or PPP, you need a program such as Free PPP, which is available online by clicking the disk-and-magnifier icon on the toolbar, then searching for Free PPP. If you have a local area network (LAN), ask your system administrator if you have TCP/IP capabilities.

AOLGLOBALnet Connections

AOLGLOBALnet is America Online's international access network. Access through AOLGLOBALnet carries an additional surcharge and offers high-speed local connections around the world. To use AOLGLOBALnet, download and install the special CCL file from keyword: **AOLGLOBALnet**. More information on using America Online outside of the United States is available at keyword: **AOLsewhere**.

Modem Files

For the majority of members, America Online has made it unnecessary to worry about such things as data bits, stop bits, or parity. All your connection information is collected when you initially run America Online. Should you need to change your modem setup for any reason, follow the steps below:

- Select the location from the Location pop-up menu containing the modem file you wish to update.
- Click the Setup button at the bottom of the Welcome (sign-on) window.
- Click the Edit Modem Profile button.

The Edit Modem Profile window will appear. America Online has taken the extra step of allowing you to customize your modem setup should you need to. If you use a modem that's not included in AOL's preconfigured modem settings, you may need to create a custom modem file. A modem file is simply information that allows your modem and the AOL software to work together smoothly. It tells the modem how to set itself up for dialing out, how to place a call, and how to behave once it is connected. Fortunately, you hardly ever need to alter your modem file, but the option is available on those rare occasions when it is necessary. In these cases, a number of simple solutions are available:

- If you are able to sign on, drop by the free Tech Help Live area online (use the keywords: **Tech Live** and click on the Tech Support Live icon), available weekdays and weekends. An America Online representative will guide you through the process of configuring the software for your modem.
- If you are unable to sign on, call America Online Technical Support at 1-800-827-6364. Like the Tech Help Live area, this service is available seven days a week, and the representatives can offer considerable guidance.
- If you are unable to sign on to America Online but you can sign on to other services, you can access the same Modem Drivers library described above through the America Online Technical Support BBS. Just dial 1-800-827-5808 with a standard telecommunications program (such as ZTerm, available online). Your settings should be: 8 data bits, no parity, 1 stop bit. You can access the BBS at modem speeds up to 14,400 bps. Complete instructions for dialing the BBS and using the Terminal program are available under AOL's Help menu.
- If you are an advanced user, you can create a custom modem file suited to your own needs. Please note that even if you are an expert telecommunicator, you are advised that before making changes you should consult your modem's manual or technical support line for the features you can enable or disable. If you'd like to give this option a go, read on.

Customizing Your Modem File

To customize your modem file, follow the steps below:

- Working offline, click the Setup button in the Welcome window (make sure you have the correct location chosen from the Location drop-down menu).
- Click the Edit Modem Profile button in the Location Setup window.
- Verify that the modem noted at the top of the window is the one you wish to customize. If it is not, click Cancel and select the appropriate modem type from the pop-up menu or just use the Generic (Hayes-compatible) modem.

Figure C-2: America Online offers built-in editors to customize a modem file.

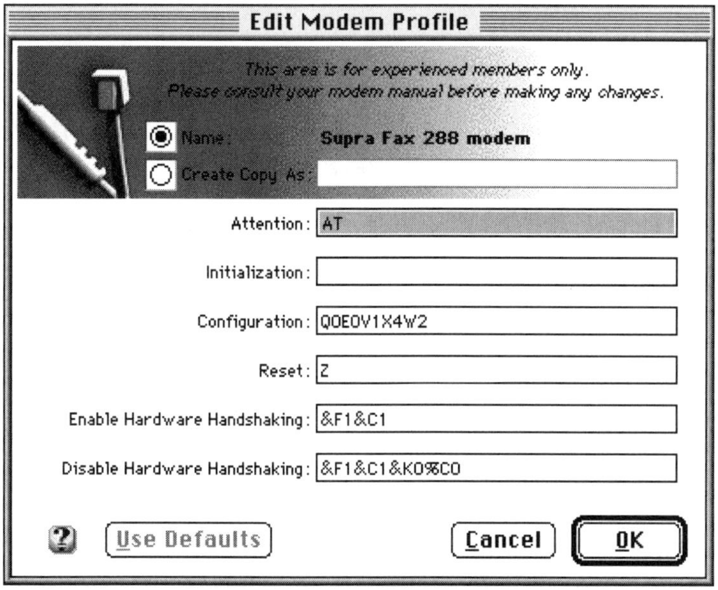
Edit Modem Profile
This area is for experienced members only.
Please consult your modem manual before making any changes.
Name:
Supra Fax 288 modem
Create Copy As:
Attention:
AT
Initialization:
Configuration:
Q0E0V1X4W2
Reset:
Z
Enable Hardware Handshaking:
&F1&C1
Disable Hardware Handshaking:
&F1&C1&K0%C0
Use Defaults
Cancel
OK

You can now edit the modem profile according to your modem manufacturer's instructions. If those instructions aren't available, use the table below. These are the most common modem setup strings.

Parameter	Setting	Usual Command
Data Compression	On	%C1
Error Correction	On	&Q5
Flow Control Hardware - Request to Send/Clear to Send	(RTS/CTS)	&K3
Local Echo	On	E1
Verbose Responses Word responses	V1	
Extended Result Codes Respond to dial tone and busy signal	X1 or X4 (preferably X4)	DCD
Track the state of data carrier from the remote modem	&C1	DTR
Monitor	DTR	&D2

When complete, click the OK button, then Save to save your location file to your hard disk. Your Custom Modem Profile will now be available from the modem type pop-up menu in the location setup window.

Solving Common Modem Problems

Here are some common modem problems and solutions:

Modem Won't Dial

America Online's software requires certain commands to connect properly to the host computer. To verify that these commands are included, click Edit Modem Profile in the Location Setup area and check the command strings. You may want to try adding "ATQ0V1E0" to your Configuration or Initialization String, if something similar isn't already included.

Modem Dials but Won't Connect

If your connection fails at some point between the high-pitched carrier tone and the Welcome window, or if it fails after the first thing you try to do online, the culprits probably are flow control (XON/XOFF), data compression, or error-correction protocols. Make sure that these are disabled. Adding "AT&F" to the beginning of the Initialization String and adding "^M" to the very end should do the trick.

Modem Disconnects on Call Waiting

Sudden disconnections also can be caused by Call Waiting. The click that indicates a call is waiting on the line sounds like a "break" (disconnect immediately) signal to the modem, which obligingly hangs up. If this is a problem, you should disable Call Waiting when you connect to America Online. You can disable it offline by selecting your location in the pop-up menu at the bottom of the Welcome (sign-on) window, clicking the Setup button, and clicking in the check box marked "To disable call waiting, dial." The input field to the right of this line contains the pulse code to disable Call Waiting, which also works for touch-tone users in most areas. In some areas, you may need to change the default of 1170, to *70, for touch-tone use. Include a comma after the code: it tells the modem to wait two seconds before dialing the next number. If you aren't sure what numbers you should enter to disable Call Waiting, check with your local telephone company or look in the front section of your local phone book, under Call Waiting. Remember that once you're done on AOL, you may need to manually re-enable Call Waiting.

Modem Disconnects Frequently

If you have problems with line noise (static on your phone line while signed on to America Online), the result may be file-transfer errors, strange characters on the screen, or occasional disconnections from America Online. One step you can take to cut down on line noise is to set your modem temporarily to a lower baud rate. Try the speed one step down from your current setting. You also can try another local access number (if available).

Another common cause of frequent disconnects is a phone cord with a bad connector (or jack) on one or both ends, or a faulty wall jack. If you hear lots of static when you're talking on the phone, odds are the same amount of static (line noise) is present when you use America Online. Check with your telephone company or an electrician to find out what can be done to improve your line quality.

Modem Speaker Stays On

To disable your modem speaker, click on Edit Modem Profile in the Location Setup area, and add M0 (the letter M and zero) to the Configuration String. If there are already characters present, add M0 at the end.

Alternatively, M1 will enable the speaker until a connection is made, and M2 will keep the speaker turned on after a connection has been established.

CCL Files

The dysfunctionally curious will note the various network files in the Online Files folder—these are known as CCL files. Normally, you won't need to worry about this, but to satisfy your curiosity, here is a brief description of CCLs and what they are all about.

A CCL file (Communication Control Language) is a modem "script" that allows your modem to talk to certain communication systems. Your America Online software comes with CCLs for networks like AOLNet, SprintNet, and Tymnet enabling them to work with America Online. CCL scripts are written in a programming language and can be modified with a simple text editor. The CCLs come preconfigured and already in place; you needn't do anything to take advantage of these, other than verify that the appropriate CCL for your access number is selected in the Connect Method pop-up menu in the Location Setup screen. Additionally, it is unlikely you will need to alter a CCL script; modem files can handle virtually all your needs. There may be times, however, when the connection process is too complicated for a modem file. If you find that a modified or custom modem file does not solve your problems, contact America Online Technical Support for further details.

APPENDIX D
On the Road

Your access to America Online need not end where your wanderlust begins. Whether you travel across the country or use a notebook Mac at work and at home, America Online is only a phone call away. This appendix gives you tips for calling America Online while traveling, finding local access numbers, and signing on using a computer other than your own.

Using America Online on the Road

Using America Online when you are traveling is easy with these few preparations and helpful hints:

- Inexpensive kits are available that help in setting up your modem when traveling. It's also a good idea to travel with an extra length of standard phone line with modular (RJ-11) jacks on each end, and a phone splitter. These items are available at many phone and electronics stores.
- If you're going to be staying in a hotel, ask for a "computer-ready" room: one with an extra phone jack for your modem (some hotels also use phones that have a special "data port" jack built into the side of the unit). If the hotel doesn't have phones set up for computer users, you can usually remove the phone cable from its phone jack and connect your modem cable. However, since many hotels use digital lines and private branch exchanges (PBXs), these jacks are often powered. Connecting your modem to one may toast your modem, and could damage your laptop as well. Line checkers are available from many electronics dealers.

- If you need to dial a long-distance access number and do not want to pay the hotel's long-distance charges or accrue charges on a friend's phone bill, you can use your calling card. Edit your location's network setup (detailed in Appendix C) by inserting the following in the Phone Number field:

  <Long-distance carrier number, if needed> + 0 + <area code> + <access number> + ,,,,, + <calling card number> + PIN (personal identification number, which may be optional)

  For example: 10333-0-313-665-2900,,,,,12312312341234#

  Those five commas cause AOL to wait 10 seconds while your long-distance carrier comes on the line and asks for your calling card number.

  Note that your long-distance carrier number may be needed to override the default carrier for the phone you are calling from: AT&T is 10288, MCI is 10222, and Sprint is 10333. Call Waiting may cause problems here, so disable it if you are having difficulties. Also, be sure you've got the required prefix to access an outside line entered in the "Use the following prefix..." box.

- Use America Online to back up your work while you're traveling. Send mail to yourself and attach the file you want to save. If you need to restore the file, you can read the mail and download the saved file. If you lose your work while you're on the road, or even after you return, you'll have a backup waiting online when you get home.

- In your travels, you may find yourself using America Online in places where sounds could be disruptive to others around you, such as a friend's guest room or a waiting room. In these situations, you can disable your America Online sounds (check your General Preferences under the Members menu) or turn your modem speaker off (refer to Appendix C, "Locations, Modems & CCL Files," or check your modem manual).

- Look up the local access numbers (by using the keyword: **Access**) for the area you'll be visiting. Do this before you leave: it's much easier. Create individual locations (discussed in Appendix C) for your most frequent destinations, and name them appropriately.

Now when you need to sign on you can simply select your location, say, Work, Branch Office, Home, or Cottage, through the Setup button on the Welcome (sign-on) window, and you're ready to go!

- If there is no local access number available in your area, you can access America Online anywhere in the United States, Puerto Rico, and the U.S. Virgin Islands by using a special 800 number. The number is 1-800-716-0023 and it does carry a surcharge for use. More information is available at keyword: **AOLnet**.

General help with signing on is available in the America Online Software under the Help menu.

Finding Local Access Numbers Offline

If you discover you need a new access number while you're on the road but you are unable to get online to search the number directory, you aren't alone. Many others have traveled down this path before, and a variety of options have opened up:

- Sign on with the NewLocal# option in the Select Screen Name pop-up menu on the welcome (sign-on) window. With this option enabled, America Online will call a toll-free number automatically and give you a list of access numbers to choose from.
- Call America Online's Customer Service Hotline at 1-800-827-6364 (within the United States) or 1-703-893-6288 (from Canada or overseas), between 6 a.m. and 4 a.m. eastern time seven days a week.
- Phone the carrier network if you do not want to use AOLnet: Tymnet can be reached at 1-800-336-0149; SprintNet at 1-800-877-5045 ext. 5, and SprintNet's automatic access number listings at 1-800-473-7983.
- If you have a fax modem or access to a fax machine, call America Online's FAXLink service at 1-800-827-5551 and ask that a list of access numbers be faxed to you. An automated voice menu will guide you through the choices.
- Connect to America Online's Technical Support BBS at 1-800-827-5808 with a standard telecommunications program. Your settings should be: 8 data bits, no parity, 1 stop bit. You can access the BBS

at modem speeds up to 14,400 bps. Complete instructions for dialing the BBS are available from AOL Guide. Select AOL Guide from the Balloon Help menu and look for the heading "Where else can I get offline help?"

- If you're within the United States, you can connect to SprintNet's Local Access Numbers Directory with a standard telecommunications program. To access, simply dial any SprintNet node directly and, once connected, type **@D** and press the Return key twice. At the @ prompt, type **c mail** and press Return, then type **PHONES** for the username and **PHONES** again for the password. You can look up any local SprintNet number available.

Signing On as a Guest

In your travels you are likely to visit others who have America Online on their computers. While your screen names won't appear in their software, you can still use their machine to sign on with your account. Just select the "Guest" screen name from the pop-up menu on the Welcome (sign-on) window and then click the Sign On button. (The "Guest" name option always appears in the list of screen names, no matter whose machine you're using or what kind of computer it is.) The software will dial the local access number and connect to America Online.

After you've made the connection, you'll see a dialog box that asks for a screen name and the password. Enter your screen name and password. America Online will connect using your account. Charges you accrue during the session (other than long-distance charges, if any) will be billed to your account rather than your friend's.

Note: Your password and your screen name will not be stored on the computer you're using to sign on as a guest. They will remain secure.

Note: Data such as your Address Book and Automatic AOL information is stored locally in your America Online software rather than on AOL's machines. As a result, you will not be able to see this information when signed on as a Guest on another computer. You are also unable to edit your screen names while signed on as a Guest.

To sign off from a Guest session, simply choose Sign Off from the Go To menu as you normally would.

AOL Abroad

If you travel out of the country and want to continue accessing America Online, don't leave home without visiting keyword: **AOLsewhere** first. The AOLsewhere area online provides access to AOLGLOBALnet international access numbers, technical support, international Web sites, the travel channel, and even a message board where you can network with other travelers. For information on connecting with AOLGLOBALnet access numbers, see Appendix C, and read the directions in the AOLGLOBALnet area carefully (you can get there quickly with keyword: **AOLGLOBALnet**).

APPENDIX E

Preferences

Like all good software, America Online offers the opportunity to configure the client to your liking via a group of user preferences. What if you work in a crowded office and don't want to hear sounds like "You've got mail!" broadcast for all to hear? What if you get tired of typing in your password every time you sign on? Why does AOL close your Compose Mail window after you've sent mail?

All of these things—and a number of others—are covered by AOL's member preferences. Preferences can be set online or off, so you can access them any time your software is running.

Begin by choosing Preferences from the Members menu. You don't have to be online to do this. (You can also access your Preferences via the My AOL icon on the toolbar, but the Members | Preferences path is quicker.) Fourteen categories of preferences will appear in the form of fourteen icons along the left side of the window. You will need to scroll down to access all categories (see Figure E-1).

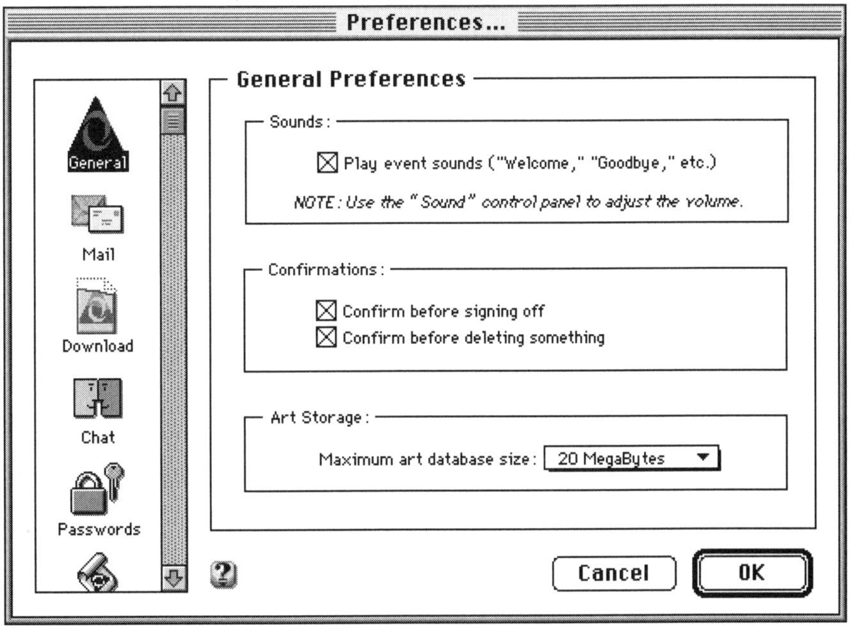

Preferences...
General
Mail
Download
Chat
Passwords
General Preferences
Sounds :
Play event sounds ("Welcome," "Goodbye," etc.)
NOTE : Use the "Sound" control panel to adjust the volume.
Confirmations :
Confirm before signing off
Confirm before deleting something
Art Storage :
Maximum art database size : 20 MegaBytes
Cancel
OK

Figure E-1: Fourteen categories of preferences are available through this window. Click on any one of them to make changes.

On the pages that follow, we will examine these preferences individually.

General Preferences

Here's where you have control over sounds, confirmations, and the size of your art database (see Figure E-1).

- *Play event sounds* activates the sounds like "Welcome" when you sign on, and "You've got mail!" when mail is waiting for you. Other sounds are controlled from within their own preference category, including chat sounds and text-to-speech. If you don't want to hear event sounds, turn this control off. (On is the default.)
- *Confirm before signing off* displays the "Are sure you want to sign off" dialog box when you select Sign Off from the Go To menu. It's a good idea to leave this one turned on, however, in case you accidentally hit Command-Q (for Quit), which signs you off before it quits. Left on, this command interrupts that potential accident. (On is the default.)
- *Confirm before deleting something* gives you the option of enabling or disabling the confirmation notice when deleting something, such as mail (online or offline), files in your Download Manager, favorite places, or entries in your Address Book. Unless you delete items frequently, it is best to keep this on in case you accidentally select the wrong item to delete. (On is the default.)
- *Maximum art database size* controls the amount of disk space allocated for graphics that adorn the windows you see online. If you visit a lot of places—exploratory journeys are notorious for this—your online art database can become huge. This not only squanders disk space; it also slows down AOL's performance. Twenty megabytes is about right, if you have that amount of hard-disk space to spare. Use a smaller setting if you don't, or the unlimited setting if size is no object. (The default is 20 megabytes.)

Mail Preferences

Electronic mail is an important part of America Online (e-mail is discussed in Chapter 3, "Electronic Mail & the Personal Filing Cabinet"). Here are the preferences that apply to your e-mail.

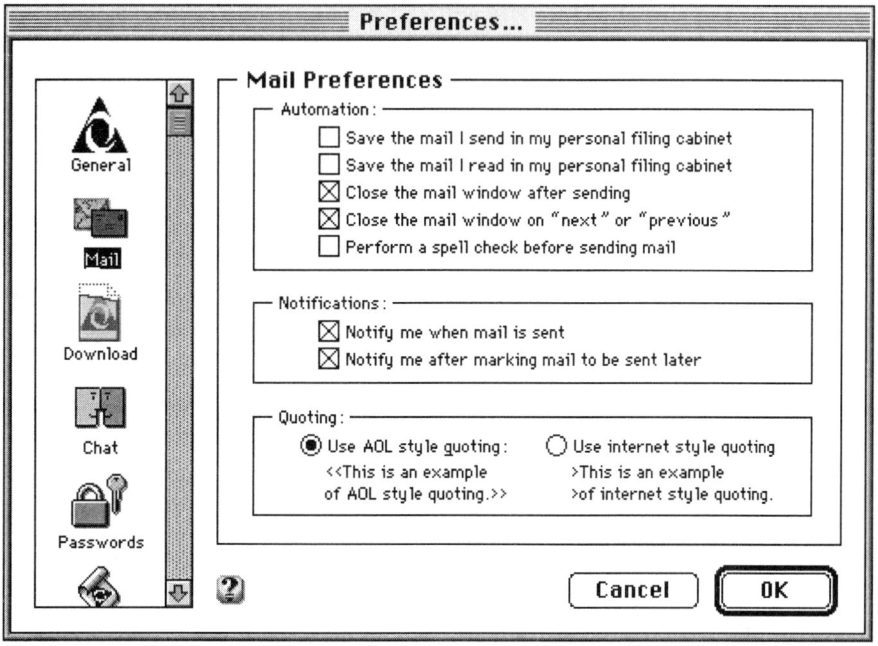
Preferences...
General
Mail
Download
Chat
Passwords
Mail Preferences
Automation:
Save the mail I send in my personal filing cabinet
Save the mail I read in my personal filing cabinet
Close the mail window after sending
Close the mail window on "next" or "previous"
Perform a spell check before sending mail
Notifications:
Notify me when mail is sent
Notify me after marking mail to be sent later
Quoting:
Use AOL style quoting:
<<This is an example
of AOL style quoting.>>
Use internet style quoting
>This is an example
>of internet style quoting.
Cancel
OK

Figure E-2: The Mail Preferences offer control over mail sent and received.

- *Save the mail I send in my personal filing cabinet* (the Personal Filing Cabinet is discussed in Chapter 3, "Electronic Mail & the Personal Filing Cabinet") keeps a copy on your hard disk of the mail you send. This is useful if you want to keep a permanent record of your mail. **Note:** The Sent Mail button available when reading new mail accesses the mail that AOL holds for you on their hard disks in Virginia. This is a courtesy, and the amount of mail held there is subject to change. Only your Personal Filing Cabinet is capable of automatically storing your mail indefinitely. (The default is Off.)

- *Save the mail I read in my personal filing cabinet* keeps a copy of the mail you have read on your hard disk. Be careful: under certain conditions this can balloon the size of your Personal Filing Cabinet on your hard disk. If you subscribe to Internet mailing lists, for example, your Personal Filing Cabinet could grow in size very quickly. (The default is Off.)
- *Close the mail window after sending* will close an e-mail window after you've sent the mail to the recipient. If you would like to keep a document you've already sent open on your screen, turn this preference off. (The default is On.)
- *Close the mail window on "next" or "previous"* will close an e-mail window after you click the right (next) or left (previous) arrow; these arrows are located at the top of the mail window when you're scrolling through your mail messages. This prevents leaving a "bread crumb" trail of open windows across your screen. If you want these windows to stay open, turn the preference off. (The default is On.)
- *Perform a spell check before sending mail* will check your mail's text for spelling, grammar, and punctuation errors before it is sent. If you aren't a good speller or want to be sure that mail goes out looking its very best, enable this preference. (The default is Off.)
- *Notify me when mail is sent* gives you a dialog box after your mail has been sent. If you send a lot of mail, you may prefer to turn this preference off. (The default is On.)
- *Notify me after marking mail to be sent later* also gives you a dialog box, this time after you click the Send Later button on a piece of mail. Again, if you send a lot of mail, you may prefer to turn this preference off. (The default is On.)
- *Use AOL style quoting* and *Use Internet style quoting* allow you to toggle between AOL's style of quoting text (<< and >> around the text) and the Internet's style (> in front of each line only). If you frequently send e-mail across the Internet, you may prefer to change this preference accordingly. (The default is AOL style.)

Download Preferences

If you do much downloading, you should (1) use the Download Manager, and (2) examine these preferences. (Downloading is discussed in Chapter 5; the Download Manager is discussed in Chapter 6.)

Figure E-3: The Download Preferences dialog box provides control over your downloading configuration.

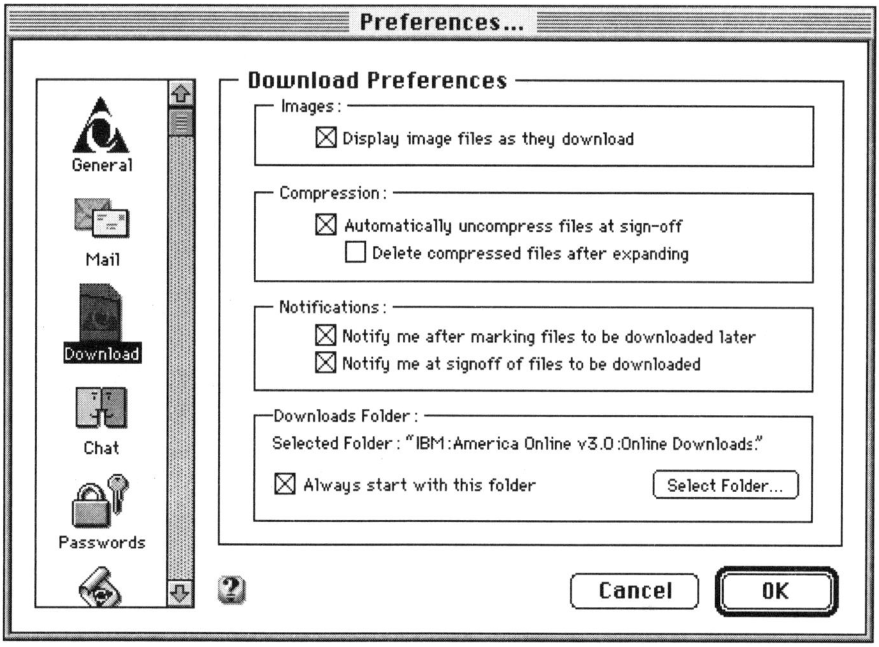
Preferences...
General
Mail
Download
Chat
Passwords
Download Preferences
Images:
Display image files as they download
Compression:
Automatically uncompress files at sign-off
Delete compressed files after expanding
Notifications:
Notify me after marking files to be downloaded later
Notify me at signoff of files to be downloaded
Downloads Folder:
Selected Folder: "IBM:America Online v3.0:Online Downloads:"
Always start with this folder
Select Folder...
Cancel
OK

- *Display image files as they download* allows you to view most graphics as they're downloaded. Viewing them online allows you to abort the download if you don't like (or need) what you see. It's best to leave this preference on unless your Mac is very low on memory or very slow. (On is the default.)
- *Automatically uncompress files at sign-off* uses AOL's built-in version of StuffIt (StuffIt is discussed in Chapter 5, "Transferring Files") to uncompress any stuffed files you have downloaded. AOL automatically unstuffs these files when you sign off. If you would prefer that these files not be unstuffed, turn this preference off. (On is the default.)
- *Delete compressed files after expanding* removes the archive from your disk after it's decompressed. Since many of us prefer to store the archive as a form of backup, this option defaults to the off condition.

- *Notify me after marking files to be downloaded later* causes the dialog box pictured in Figure E-4 to appear whenever you add a file to your queue of files to be downloaded.

The file has been added to your list of files to be downloaded later. To view that list, click the "Download Manager" button below or choose "Download Manager" from the "File" menu at a later time.
Download Manager
OK

Figure E-4: AOL displays this dialog box whenever you add a file to your download queue. If you don't want to bother with it, turn the appropriate preference off.

- *Notify me at signoff of files to be downloaded* will prompt the software to notify you when you have files in your download manager upon signing-off. Again, this reminder can be a nuisance or a nicety, depending on how often you use your Download Manager. (The default is On.)

  This dialog box is a convenience if you like to visit the Download Manager every time you add a file to its list. It's an annoyance if you do not. If it annoys you, turn the preference off. (The default is On.)

- *Default folder* allows you to declare a destination folder other than the Online Downloads folder, which is the default. **Note:** All the files in a single Download Manager session must be downloaded to the same folder.
- *Always start with this folder* tells the software to always open to the default folder you've selected when downloading a file. You can have the file download to another folder by navigating to it in the Save dialog box, but AOL will start in your default folder for the first download of your session when this preference is enabled. If you prefer not to have the software start in your default folder, disable this preference. (The default is On.)

Chat Preferences

If you're fond of chat rooms, look these preferences over carefully. Chat rooms are discussed in Chapter 8, "The Community."

- *Play chat sounds sent by other members* activates member-sent sounds in chat rooms. Some chat rooms are especially sound-oriented. Try LaPub for an example. These people love to laugh out loud and slap one another on the back—quite aurally. To hear these sounds, you must have them installed on your machine and you must leave this preference turned on. (For more about chat room sounds, read Chapter 8, "The Community.") (On is the default.)

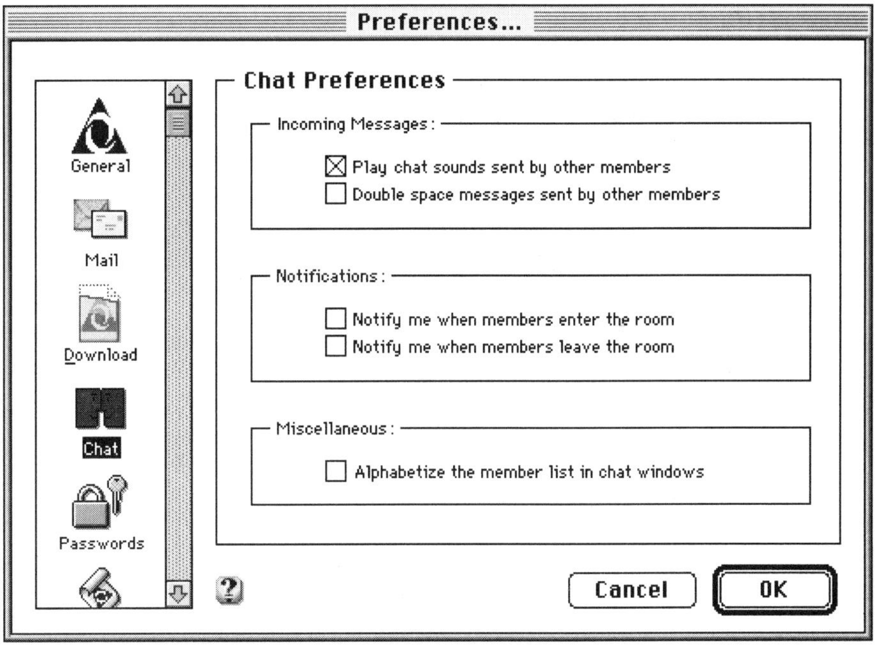
Preferences...
General
Mail
Download
Chat
Passwords
Chat Preferences
Incoming Messages:
Play chat sounds sent by other members
Double space messages sent by other members
Notifications:
Notify me when members enter the room
Notify me when members leave the room
Miscellaneous:
Alphabetize the member list in chat windows
Cancel
OK

Figure E-5: The Chat Preferences provide control over your chat room environment.

- *Double space messages sent by other members* just makes them easier to read. It also halves the amount of conversation that's displayed on your screen at any one time. It's a compromise, but the decision is yours. (The default is Off.)

- *Notify me when members enter the room* causes the "OnlineHost" to place a line in your chat room window announcing the entrance of every arriving member. Host and Guides love this feature, and it's helpful for all of us when we're in a room that doesn't have a lot of comings and goings. If the members in a room are transitory—as people in lobbies, for instance, tend to be—you will probably want to leave this preference off. (The default is Off.)
- *Notify me when members leave the room* is the same as the preference described earlier, except the notification is provided when the member leaves, rather than arrives in, the room. Again, it's helpful for Hosts and Guides. (The default is Off.)
- *Alphabetize the member list in chat windows* offers you the choice of viewing the member list (the little scroll box of member names in the upper right corner of chat windows) in alphabetical order or in the order in which members arrive in the chat room. If you want to watch comings and goings (and the Notify preferences are turned off), leave this preference turned off. If you tend to refer to the list often—perhaps to look up the profiles of or send Instant Messages to other members in the room—alphabetizing it may help. (The default is Off.)

Passwords Preferences

Passwords keep other people from using your account when you're not around. Once a password is stored, anyone using that machine can sign on and spend hours online, at your expense.

On the other hand, there are those of us for whom that potential simply doesn't exist. Perhaps you lock your computer when you're away, or the other people in your office or home are trustworthy beyond reproach. I sign on 5 or 10 times a day, and my computer is in my studio, which is sanctified ground. Typing my password 5 or 10 times a day is not only unnecessary, it's counterproductive. For this reason, I store my password (Figure E-6) and never have to type it in.

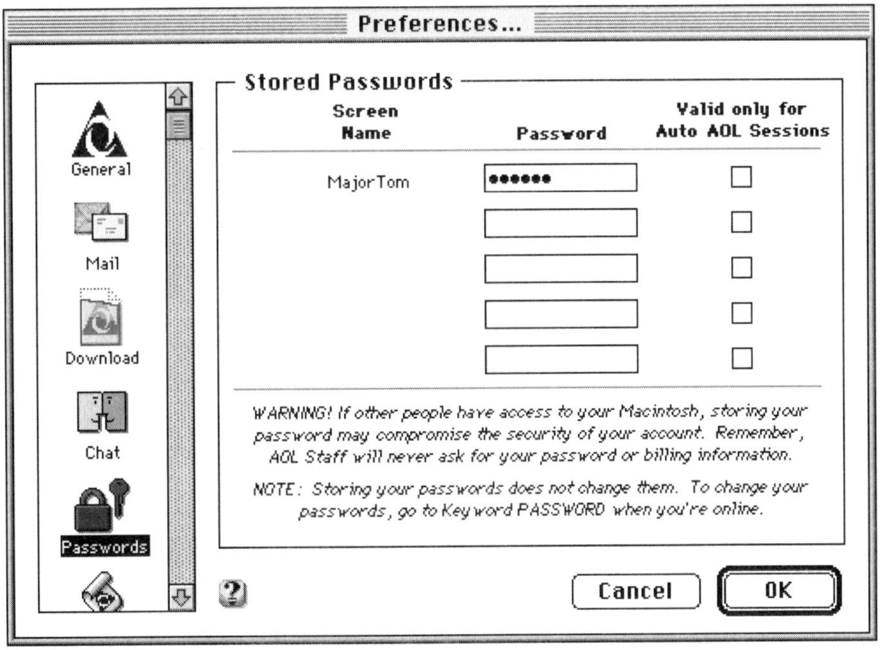
Preferences...
General
Mail
Download
Chat
Passwords
Stored Passwords
Screen Name
Password
Valid only for Auto AOL Sessions
MajorTom
••••••
WARNING! If other people have access to your Macintosh, storing your password may compromise the security of your account. Remember, AOL Staff will never ask for your password or billing information.
NOTE: Storing your passwords does not change them. To change your passwords, go to Keyword PASSWORD when you're online.
Cancel
OK

Figure E-6: You can't read my stored password. AOL displays only bullets. The password, nonetheless, is there, and I don't have to type it in when I sign on.

- *Valid only for Auto AOL Sessions* instructs the software to use the password only for an Auto AOL session. Be sure to enable this if you only use the stored password for Auto AOL. (The default is Off.)

Use the stored password option with care! AOL shows no pity when members call with unexpected bills run up by fellow office workers or members of the family. If there's a possibility that someone might access your account while you're away, don't utilize this feature. Finally, *never, ever, ever* use the stored password feature on a laptop installation. If someone is low enough to make off with your portable, they will undoubtedly be happy to run up a large AOL bill at your expense. (The default is Off.)

Auto AOL Preferences

These preferences pertain to Auto AOL, the feature that allows you to automatically send and receive mail and newsgroup postings, as well as download files you have marked for later retrieval. Auto AOL is discussed in Chapter 6, "Automatic AOL & the Download Manager."

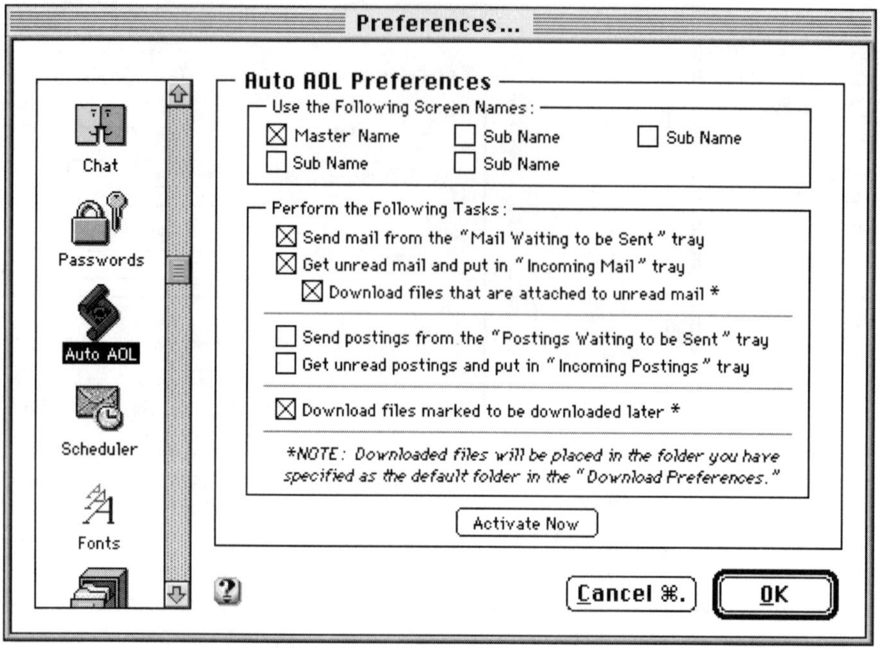
Preferences...
Chat
Passwords
Auto AOL
Scheduler
Fonts
Auto AOL Preferences
Use the Following Screen Names:
Master Name
Sub Name
Sub Name
Sub Name
Sub Name
Perform the Following Tasks:
Send mail from the "Mail Waiting to be Sent" tray
Get unread mail and put in "Incoming Mail" tray
Download files that are attached to unread mail *
Send postings from the "Postings Waiting to be Sent" tray
Get unread postings and put in "Incoming Postings" tray
Download files marked to be downloaded later *
*NOTE: Downloaded files will be placed in the folder you have specified as the default folder in the "Download Preferences."
Activate Now
Cancel ⌘.
OK

Figure E-7: The Auto AOL Preferences allow you to set up the automatic transmission and retrieval feature.

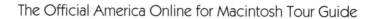

- *Use the Following Screen Names...* allows you to select the screen names you want Auto AOL to use. (The default is Off.)

- *Send mail from the "Mail Waiting to be Sent" tray* instructs Auto AOL to send all mail marked to be sent later for the screen names you selected at the top. (The default is On.)

- *Get unread mail and put in "Incoming Mail" tray* directs Auto AOL to read and save all new mail and file it in the "Incoming Mail" folder within your Personal Filing Cabinet. Again, only mail sent to the screen names you've designated for Auto AOL will be retrieved. (The default is On.)

- *Download files that are attached to unread mail* instructs Auto AOL to download all files that are encountered while reading your new mail. You may wish to disable this preference if you prefer to check first to be sure the file is one you want. **Note:** All downloaded files will be placed in the folder you specified in your Download Preferences. (The default is On.)

- *Send postings from the "Postings Waiting to be Sent" tray* instructs Auto AOL to send all newsgroup postings marked to be posted later for the screen names you selected at the top. (The default is Off.)

- *Get unread postings and put in "Incoming Postings" tray* directs Auto AOL to read and save all new newsgroup postings from your selected newsgroups and file them in the "Incoming Postings" folder within your Personal Filing Cabinet. (The default is Off.)

- *Download files marked to be downloaded later* tells Auto AOL to download all files you have marked in your Download Manager. Note: Again, all downloaded files will be placed in the folder you specified in your Download Preferences. (The default is On.)

Auto AOL Scheduler Preferences

The Auto AOL Scheduler is an important part of the Auto AOL feature (Auto AOL is discussed in Chapter 6, "Automatic AOL & the Download Manager"). Here are the preferences that apply to your scheduler.

- *Perform scheduled Auto AOL sessions* tells the software to turn on the Auto AOL feature and run it on the days and times you set. You must have this preference enabled to use Auto AOL. (The default is Off.)

- *Sign On:* allows you to set the frequency at which you want Auto AOL to sign on and perform its operations. Once a day is usually enough for most folks. **Note:** Your Mac must be turned on in order for Auto AOL to sign on. (The default is every half hour.)

- *On the following days:* tells Auto AOL which days of the week you'd like it to run. (The default is each day.)

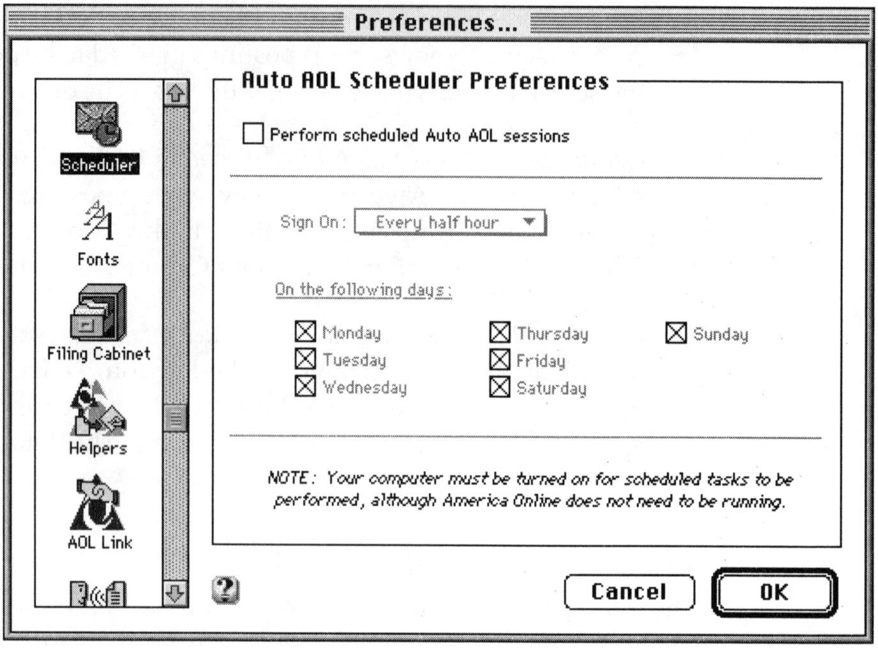
Preferences...
Auto AOL Scheduler Preferences
Perform scheduled Auto AOL sessions
Sign On: Every half hour
On the following days:
Monday
Tuesday
Wednesday
Thursday
Friday
Saturday
Sunday
NOTE: Your computer must be turned on for scheduled tasks to be performed, although America Online does not need to be running.
Scheduler
Fonts
Filing Cabinet
Helpers
AOL Link
Cancel
OK

Figure E-8: The Scheduler Preferences allow you to set times and days for Auto AOL sessions.

Font Preferences

The Fonts Preferences allow you to change your preference for the font and size of type you see in online text articles, in chat and conference rooms, and in your mail (see Figure E-9). For example, if you have difficulty reading online text, you might be more comfortable with a larger size, or even a different font. You can select any font and size you have installed on your Mac. The font you select as your mail font will be seen when you compose and receive mail, but the formatting preferences of other members who send you mail will control the display you see when you receive their mail.

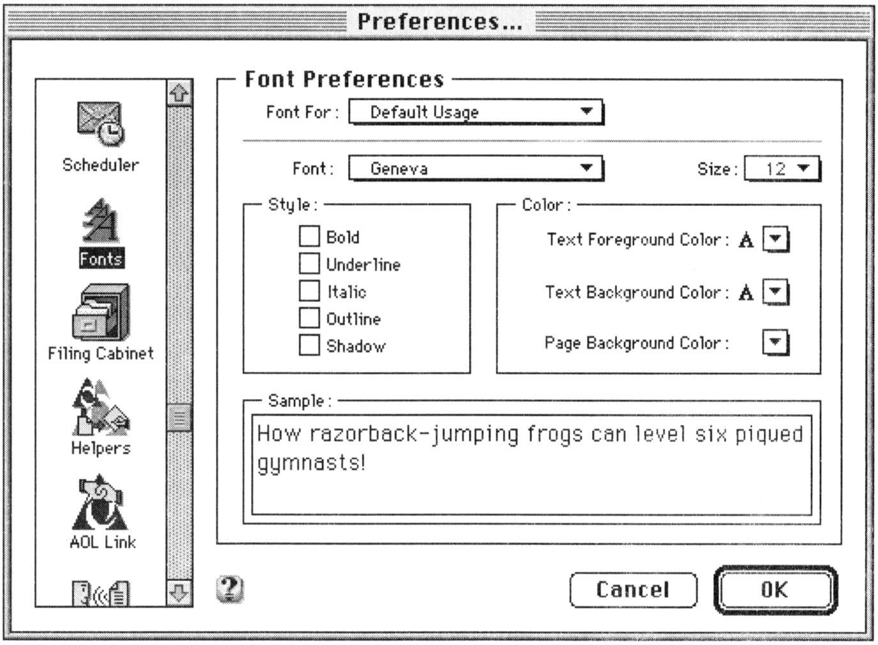
Preferences...
Scheduler
Fonts
Filing Cabinet
Helpers
AOL Link
Font Preferences
Font For: Default Usage
Font: Geneva
Size: 12
Style:
Bold
Underline
Italic
Outline
Shadow
Color:
Text Foreground Color:
Text Background Color:
Page Background Color:
Sample:
How razorback-jumping frogs can level six piqued gymnasts!
Cancel
OK

Figure E-9: The Font Preferences allow you to control the font and size of online text.

- *Font For:* allows you to set the font for different areas of the system, such as mail, chat, and conference rooms, or general text such as that found in online articles (default usage). Change this only if you want your default usage font to be different from your mail font or from your chat font. (The default is default usage.)

- *Font:* sets the font you'd like to use for the usage you've determined above. Again, any font installed on your Mac will be available for you to select here. (The default is Geneva.)

- *Size:* sets the size you'd like to see your online text displayed in, ranging from 9 (quite small) to 24 (very large). (The default is 12.)

- *Style:* changes the text style to bold, underline, italic, outline, or shadow, or any combination. I advise against using any style that will make your text difficult to read. (The default is Off.)

- *Color:* sets the colors that online text (foreground and background) as well as the page background are displayed in. If the standard black on white doesn't suit you, experiment with this preference to find a combination that does. The Sample at the bottom of the window will help you in choosing the best colors. (The default is black on white.)

Personal Filing Cabinet Preferences

The Personal Filing Cabinet (PFC) organizes your Favorite Places, e-mail, and newsgroup postings, among other things. As it stores some important items, preferences are provided to protect against accidental deletion. Other preferences control its size and organization (see Figure E-10).

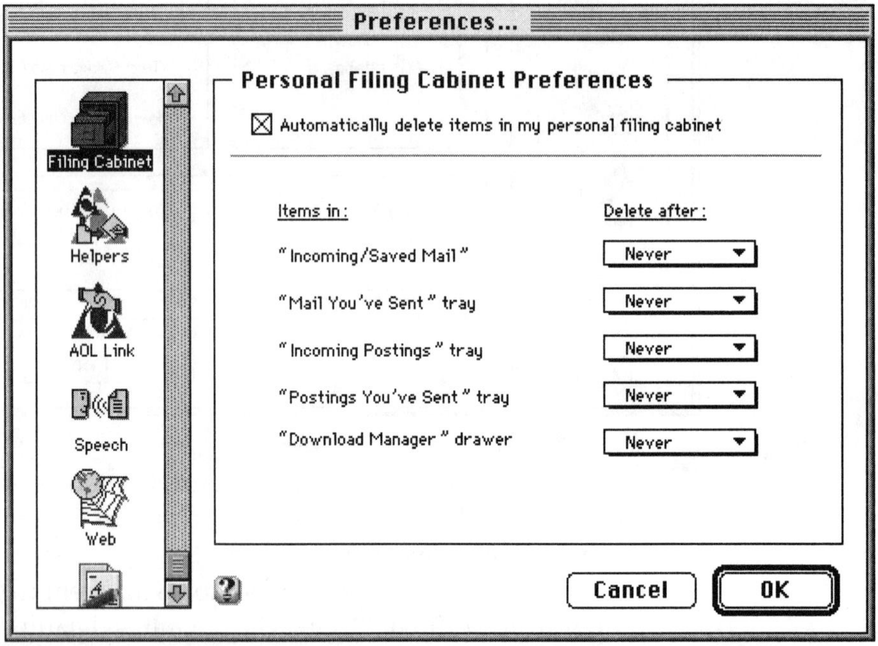
Preferences...
Filing Cabinet
Helpers
AOL Link
Speech
Web
Personal Filing Cabinet Preferences
Automatically delete items in my personal filing cabinet
Items in:
Delete after:
"Incoming/Saved Mail"
"Mail You've Sent" tray
"Incoming Postings" tray
"Postings You've Sent" tray
"Download Manager" drawer
Never
Never
Never
Never
Never
Cancel
OK

Figure E-10: The Personal Filing Cabinet Preferences allow you to control deletion of items in your Personal Filing Cabinet.

- *Automatically delete items in my personal filing cabinet* gives you the option of enabling or disabling automatic deletion of items in your Personal Filing Cabinet, which are determined by the options below it. Unless you frequently add items to your Personal Filing Cabinet or have very limited hard-disk space, you will probably prefer not to remove items automatically. (The default setting is Off.)
- *Items in:/Delete after:* allows you to set the deletion date for various items stored in your Personal Filing Cabinet. Options range from one week to one year, several points in between, or simply never. (The default is never.)

Helpers Preferences

The Helpers allow you to modify and expand the support for Web pages and other multimedia files (see Figure E-11).

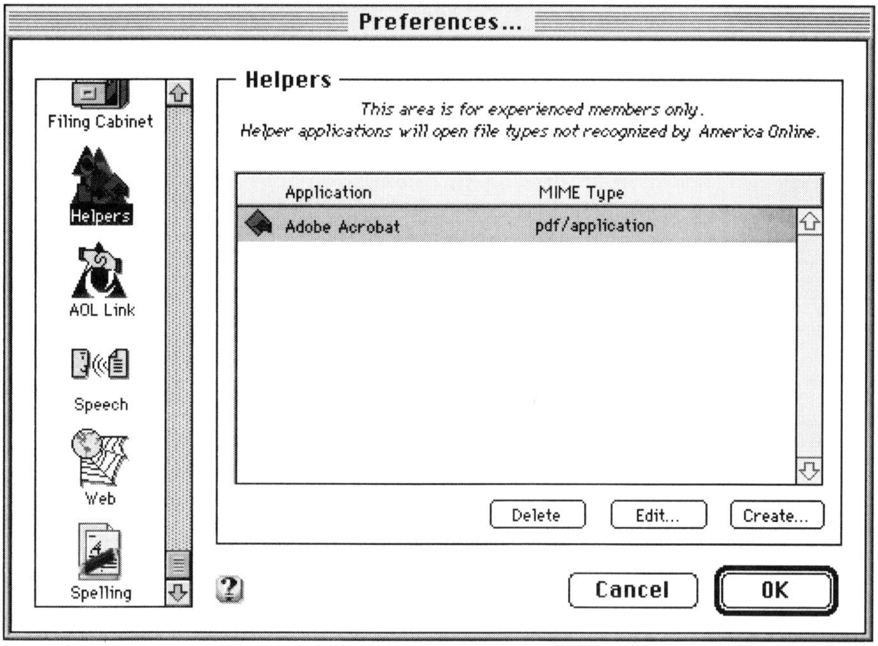
Preferences...
Filing Cabinet
Helpers
AOL Link
Speech
Web
Spelling
Helpers
This area is for experienced members only.
Helper applications will open file types not recognized by America Online.
Application
MIME Type
Adobe Acrobat
pdf/application
Delete
Edit...
Create...
Cancel
OK

Figure E-11: Helpers provide control over opening and viewing information with special multimedia data.

Some pages contain special encoded data for graphic or sound formats. AOL decodes most of this special information automatically, but you have the option of using a separate application to view or open it. To use a separate application, just modify an existing setting or create a new one by clicking on the Create... button and filling in the required information. You can also set the browser to recognize other types of data and open the appropriate software to decode it. For example, the Adobe page at http://www.adobe.com/ suggests configuring your browser for PDF (Portable Document Format) use. You can do this by creating a new setting, typing **application/pdf** as the MIME type, **PDF** as the suffix (extension), and the name of your application that reads PDF files (such as **Adobe Acrobat**) for the application name (see Figure E-12). Then when you click on a hyperlink to a PDF file, the browser will download the file and automatically launch your application to open and view the file. Note that you can also use a Helper to open files that even AOL would normally open if you prefer to use an application other than AOL by enabling the preference at the bottom of the window. (The default is Off.)

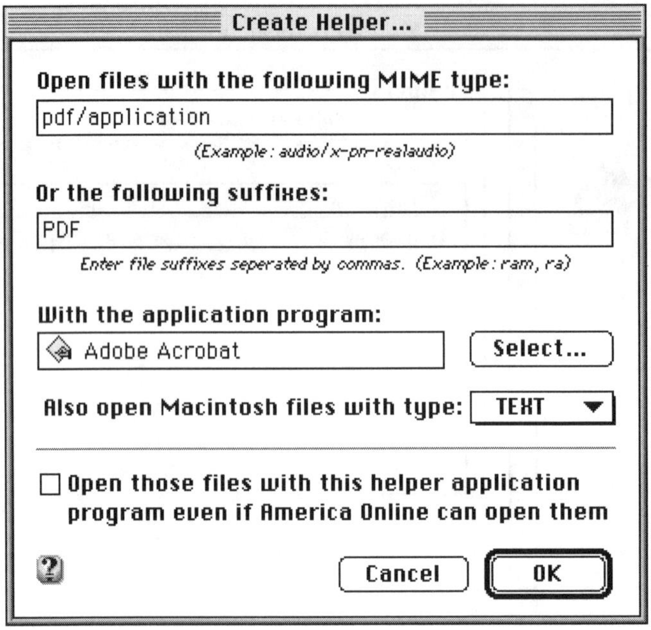
Create Helper...
Open files with the following MIME type:
pdf/application
(Example: audio/x-pn-realaudio)
Or the following suffixes:
PDF
Enter file suffixes seperated by commas. (Example: ram, ra)
With the application program:
Adobe Acrobat
Select...
Also open Macintosh files with type:
TEXT
Open those files with this helper application program even if America Online can open them
Cancel
OK

Figure E-12: Setting up AOL to recognize PDF files and open Adobe Acrobat to view them.

AOL Link Preferences

AOL Link gives you the ability to use other Internet applications (such as Netscape) over the AOL connection (see Figure E-13). It also allows you to configure AOL Link if you use an Internet Service Provider (see TCP Connections in Appendix C, "Locations, Modems & CCL Files").

Use AOL Link when connecting with a modem will check to make sure your Mac is configured to use AOL Link. If it is not configured, AOL will modify your TCP control panel and you will be prompted to restart your computer. This preference enables you to immediately sign on and have AOL Link ready to use with other Internet applications through the AOL connection. If you use an Internet Service Provider, you will want to disable this preference. (The default is On.)

For example, if you prefer to use the Netscape browser, you first make sure your automatic AOL Link preference is enabled, then download Netscape at keyword: **Netscape**, decompress and open it, sign on to AOL, and then use Netscape to access the Internet through your AOL connection. If you encounter a problem, make sure you have a control panel named "MacTCP" or "TCP/IP" installed and active. If you have no control panel for TCP/IP, you will need to contact America Online Technical Support at 1-800-827-5808. With the proper control panel installed and active, you can use other applications, for example Filemaker Pro, through the AOL connection to network with someone who is running the same program, similarly configured, on their computer.

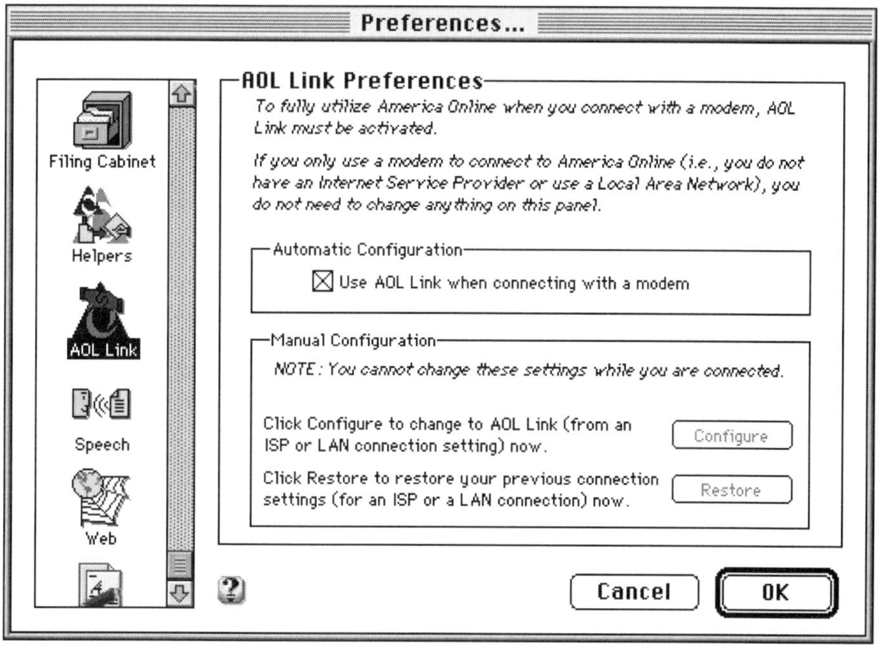
Preferences...
Filing Cabinet
Helpers
AOL Link
Speech
Web
AOL Link Preferences
To fully utilize America Online when you connect with a modem, AOL Link must be activated.
If you only use a modem to connect to America Online (i.e., you do not have an Internet Service Provider or use a Local Area Network), you do not need to change anything on this panel.
Automatic Configuration
Use AOL Link when connecting with a modem
Manual Configuration
NOTE: You cannot change these settings while you are connected.
Click Configure to change to AOL Link (from an ISP or LAN connection setting) now.
Configure
Click Restore to restore your previous connection settings (for an ISP or a LAN connection) now.
Restore
Cancel
OK

Figure E-13: The AOL Link Preferences allow you to configure and restore settings to use other Internet applications through AOL.

Manual Configuration allows you to configure or restore your settings as needed. This comes in handy if you don't want AOL to automatically configure AOL Link for you, (which is necessary if you use an Internet Service Provider) but you still want to use AOL Link at times. **Note:** If you are using the TCP/IP control panel, you can create and save different connection settings to aid in toggling between AOL (with AOL Link) and your Internet Service Provider.

Speech Preferences

Yes, AOL will even speak for you! By converting text to speech and using the Mac's built-in speech manager, AOL can read online text for you. This is particularly useful if you find it difficult to read online text, or if you need to look away from the computer for more than a few minutes. I like to use it in a situation where I am in a chat room with a friend who has to temporarily leave the keyboard. While my friend is "afk" (away from keyboard), I can be doing something else without watching the screen because I'll "hear" them when they return. If you enable speech, be sure your sound is turned up using the Sound control panel. **Note:** Enabling speech only applies to your software; other members will not hear spoken text unless they also enable their speech feature (and at this time, only Mac members have this option).

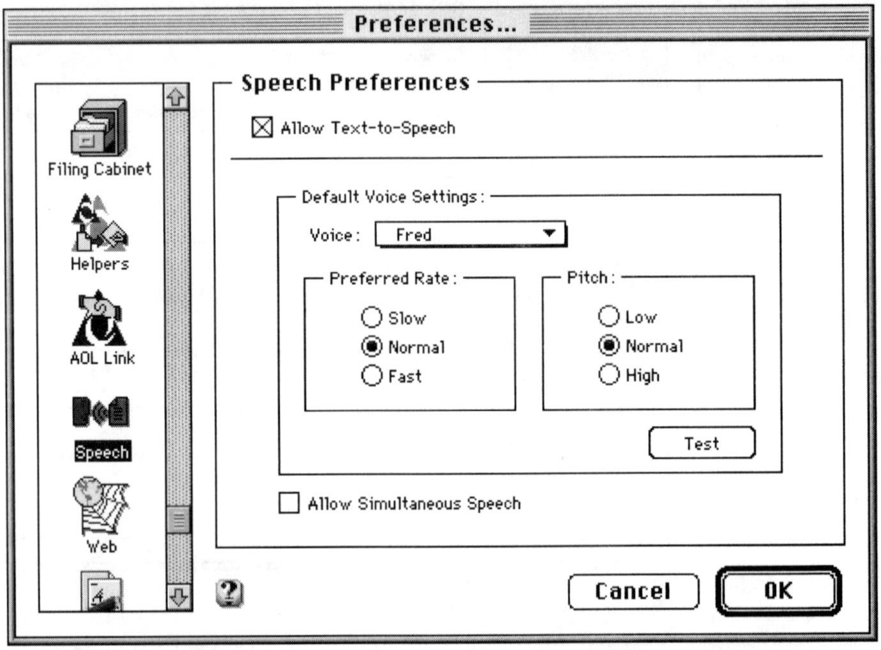
Preferences...
Filing Cabinet
Helpers
AOL Link
Speech
Web
Speech Preferences
Allow Text-to-Speech
Default Voice Settings:
Voice:
Fred
Preferred Rate:
Slow
Normal
Fast
Pitch:
Low
Normal
High
Test
Allow Simultaneous Speech
Cancel
OK

Figure E-14: The Speech Preferences allow you to configure your text-to-speech options.

- *Allow Text-to-Speech simply turns on the speech option.* (The default is On.)
- *Voice: lets you select any voice you have installed on your Mac.* The voices range from serious to downright silly. Have fun experimenting with them by using the Test button at the bottom. My favorite is Deranged; listen to it and you'll know why. (The default is Fred.)
- *Preferred Rate: allows you to select the rate at which text is spoken.* Most likely you will prefer the normal setting, but a particular voice may need to be slowed down or speeded up. (The default is Normal.)

- *Pitch: simply changes the voice's pitch.* You can change the "gender" of a voice this way, as well as configure it to come across clearer through your speaker. (The default is Normal.)

- *Allow Simultaneous Speech lets you hear text from multiple sources at once.* For example, you could have AOL speak the text of an article while you're sitting in a chat room and you would also hear the members of the chat speaking. (The default is Normal.)

Web Preferences

The Microsoft Internet Explorer Web browser may be fully integrated into your AOL software, but it retains enough unique features to qualify as the stand-alone application that it is. Like all good software, it can be configured to your liking (see Figure E-15). Keep in mind that these preferences should be set before you enter the Web, and that like most of AOL's preferences, you can set them whether you're online or off.

The interface for these preferences is currently under development, as is the number of preferences for which you'll be provided control. There are a few, however, that are bound to stay and therefore warrant mention here.

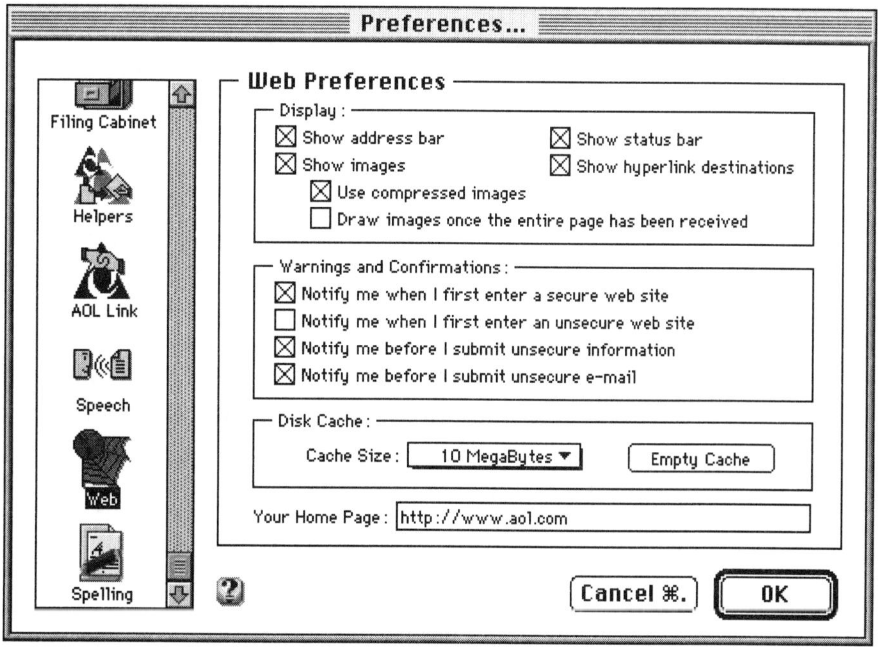
Preferences...
Filing Cabinet
Helpers
AOL Link
Speech
Web
Spelling
Web Preferences
Display :
Show address bar
Show status bar
Show images
Show hyperlink destinations
Use compressed images
Draw images once the entire page has been received
Warnings and Confirmations :
Notify me when I first enter a secure web site
Notify me when I first enter an unsecure web site
Notify me before I submit unsecure information
Notify me before I submit unsecure e-mail
Disk Cache :
Cache Size :
10 MegaBytes
Empty Cache
Your Home Page :
http://www.aol.com
Cancel ⌘.
OK

Figure E-15: The Web Preferences window provides control over your browser window's display.

- *Show address bar* gives you the URL address at the top of the window for the Web page you are on. This is useful if you want to double-check to see if you are where you meant to be, but it isn't necessary. You may disable this option if you'd prefer more room in your browser window. (The default setting is On.)
- *Show images* gives you the option of turning off images (graphics) in Web pages. If you prefer speed over scenery, disable this preference and you will see a framed text placeholder (or a generic picture of geometric shapes, if there is no text associated with the graphic) wherever a graphic would have appeared. (The default setting is On.)
- *Use compressed images* gives you a choice in how you'd like to view (or not view) the graphics in Web pages. If you prefer quicker access, choose compressed images. If you'd like to see the Web in its full glory (and you don't mind waiting a little longer), disable this preference. (The default is On.)
- *Draw images once the entire page has been received* delays adding the images to a Web page until after all information has been received. This may allow you to read text or choose hyperlinks without being held up waiting for an image to load. (The default setting is Off.)
- *Show status bar* displays a bar at the bottom of the browser window with information on the page as it is being received as well as a "thermometer" showing how much has been received. Keep this preference enabled if you like to keep abreast of the page's progress. (The default setting is On.)
- *Show hyperlink destinations* presents the URL addresses for links when your cursor moves over the words/phrases (hypertext) or buttons (hypergraphics) that lead to them. The destination address appears in the lower left-hand corner of the status bar at the bottom of the browser window. This serves as an added clue that there is another link available from a Web page, as well as identifying the destination of the link. **Note:** You must have the status bar preference enabled to view hyperlink destinations. (The default setting is On.)
- *Notify me when I first enter a secure web site* displays a dialog box informing you when a Web page will encrypt your data before transmitting it across the Internet. This is particularly useful to

know if you intend to purchase any products or services over the Web. (The default is On.)

- *Notify me when I first enter an unsecure web site* also displays a dialog box, this time informing you when a Web site does not take steps to secure any data you may wish to transmit. This is generally useful only if you frequent secured Web sites and wish to know when one is not. (The default is Off.)
- *Notify me before I submit unsecure information* displays a dialog box asking you to verify that the information you are about to send is not secured. This is important to know if you are about to send your credit card or other personal information. (The default is On.)
- *Notify me before I submit unsecure e-mail* also displays a dialog box, this time informing you that the e-mail you are about to send is not secured. This can be helpful to have as e-mail is often the place for transactions and love letters to your favorite web geek. Note that this preference only applies to web-based e-mail—your regular e-mail is always secure. (The default is On.)
- *Disk Cache*: The browser's cache holds the most recent pages and graphics you've accessed from the World Wide Web. There's a great value here: if, for example, you visit a page that you've visited recently, the browser will find the page in its cache—on your hard disk—and retrieve it from there, rather than taking the time to go "out on the Web" for the information. Local access is *much* faster. The browser's preferences allow you to control this feature, or disable it entirely. The following controls are available:
    - The *Cache Size* control allows you to set the amount of hard-disk space you want to allocate for the cache. Start with the default if you have that amount of space to spare. If you frequently visit a number of different sites, this number might be too low—something you'll know when frequently visited sites' pages have to be downloaded each time they're visited. If you only visit a site or two on a regular basis, try decreasing this value. (The default is 10 megabytes.)
    - The *Empty Cache* control will remove all pages that have been saved on your hard disk. You may wish to do this if you want to revisit those pages and have them update with new information, or if your browser has become extremely slow.

- *Your Home Page* allows you to designate the page you'd like to start at when you first enter the Web. Change this to another URL address if you'd like to begin at that page instead. (The default setting is the address for AOL's own Web site.)

Spelling Preferences

The built-in spell checker is a convenient feature that allows you to check the spelling, grammar, and punctuation of your text in both documents and e-mail (the spell checker is discussed in Chapter 3, "Electronic Mail & the Personal Filing Cabinet"). The spell checker is available under the Edit menu when you have a document open, or from within a new mail window when you select Compose Mail from the Mail menu.

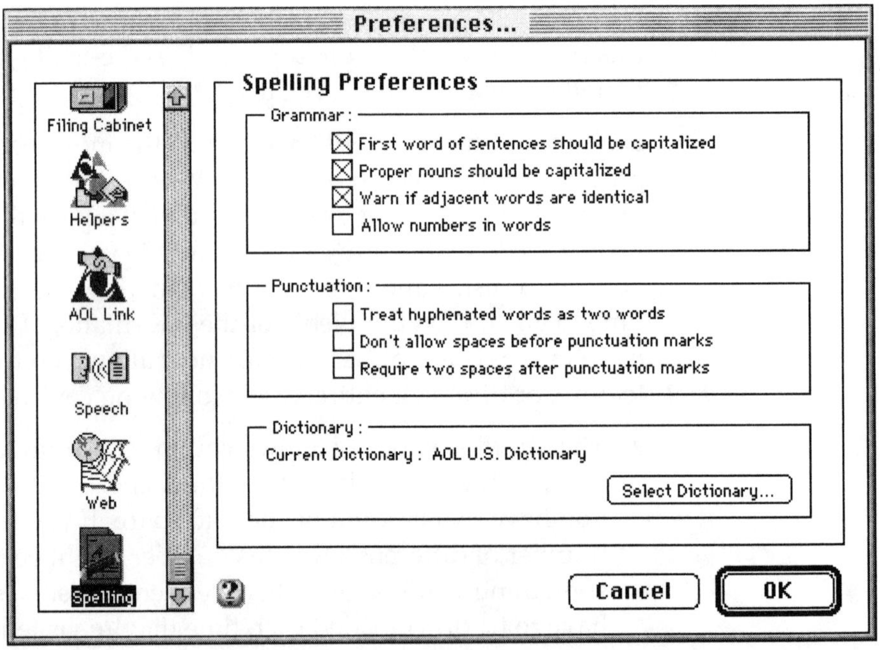
Preferences...
Filing Cabinet
Helpers
AOL Link
Speech
Web
Spelling
Spelling Preferences
Grammar:
First word of sentences should be capitalized
Proper nouns should be capitalized
Warn if adjacent words are identical
Allow numbers in words
Punctuation:
Treat hyphenated words as two words
Don't allow spaces before punctuation marks
Require two spaces after punctuation marks
Dictionary:
Current Dictionary: AOL U.S. Dictionary
Select Dictionary...
Cancel
OK

Figure E-16: Spelling Preferences provide control over AOL's built-in spell checker.

- *First word of sentences should be capitalized* will change the initial letter of the first word in a sentence to a capital letter if it is lowercase. (The default is On.)

- *Proper nouns should be capitalized* will change the initial letter of a proper noun to a capital letter if it is lowercase. (The default is On.)

- *Warn if adjacent words are identical* will inform you when it finds a word used twice in a row. (The default is On.)
- *Allow numbers in words* will not alert you to a word if there is a number in it. (The default is Off.)
- *Treat hyphenated words as two words* will check the hyphenated word as if there were a space in place of the hyphen. This is a good preference to enable if you use a lot of hyphenated words that aren't found in a dictionary. For example, with this preference disabled, the checker will stop on Anderson-Watson when it would otherwise be skipped. (The default is Off.)
- *Don't allow spaces before punctuation marks* will alert you to spaces used before punctuation marks, which are generally a no-no. You may want to leave this off if you use "smilies" such as :-) in your e-mail, so that the spell checker doesn't alert you to the spaces that in most cases precede them. (The default is Off.)
- *Require two spaces after punctuation marks* will not alert you if there are two spaces after punctuation marks. According to my friend Robin Williams, author of *The Mac Is Not a Typewriter*, you should only use one space after punctuation, including periods. Two spaces are only used on typewriters, or when a typewriter (monospaced) font is used. So this preference is best left off. (The default is Off.)
- *Dictionary:* allows you to select the dictionary to be used when checking spelling. The U.S. Dictionary is the only available dictionary at this time, but more may become available later.

Buddy List Preferences

Buddy Lists are a convenient feature that allow you to keep a list of friends or colleagues and then find out if they are online at the click of a button (Buddy Lists are discussed in Chapter 8, "The Community"). Equally convenient are the controls AOL gives you to set up this feature to suit your needs. You cannot access Buddy List Preferences from the Preferences dialog, and you can't access them unless you're online. Instead, select Buddy Lists from the Members menu, or use the keyword: **Buddy**, and click the Preferences button.

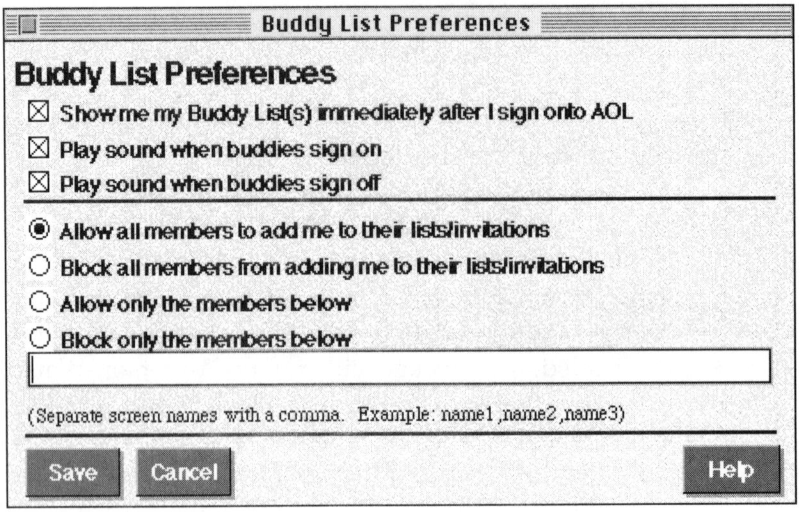
Buddy List Preferences
Buddy List Preferences
Show me my Buddy List(s) immediately after I sign onto AOL
Play sound when buddies sign on
Play sound when buddies sign off
Allow all members to add me to their lists/invitations
Block all members from adding me to their lists/invitations
Allow only the members below
Block only the members below
(Separate screen names with a comma. Example: name1,name2,name3)
Save
Cancel
Help

Figure E-17: Buddy List Preferences provide control over AOL's Buddy Lists feature.

- *Show me my Buddy List(s) immediately after I sign onto AOL* displays your Buddy Lists automatically, when you first connect to America Online. If this preference is off, you will have to issue the Buddy List command (from the Members menu) before AOL will monitor the comings and goings of your buddies for you. If you use Buddy Lists often, you may wish to turn this preference on. (The default setting is On.)
- *Play sound when buddies sign on* gives you an aural alert any time someone in one of your buddy lists logs on to AOL. This keeps you from having to constantly check the Buddy List window.
- *Play sound when buddies sign off* is exactly the opposite, noisily notifying you that one of your buddies has taken off.

The next four Buddy List preferences determine who can add *your* screen name to *their* Buddy List. You may select only one of the four.

- *Allow all members to add me to their lists/invitations* lets any other AOL member put your name in their Buddy List as well as invite you to a room or place online.
- *Block all members from adding me to their lists/invitations* prevents anyone from listing your screen name.

- *Allow only the members below* allows you to enter into the text box a specific group of people who have your permission to list your name.
- *Block only the members below* prevents a specific group of people from listing your name.

These preferences are offered to protect the privacy of members who would rather not be Buddy Listed. Use them as you see fit.

Explore these preferences. Alter every one of them and live with the changes for a week. You may discover something you didn't know about yourself!

Glossary

This glossary was prepared by Jennifer Watson (screen name: Jennifer) and George Louie (screen name: NumbersMan), America Online community leaders (to whom I express my heartfelt thanks for a job very well done). It's updated regularly and posted online. To find it, use the keyword: KEYWORDS and open the Learn More About AOL folder, or use the keyword: FileSearch, then search with the criterion: VirtualLingo.

800 number—AOL provides an 800 number, at a modest hourly rate, to members who are without local access numbers. To use this number, you must have WAOL 2.5 (or higher) or MAOL 2.5.1 (or higher). If you have a version below 3.0 of either software, you may need the AOLnet CCL file available at keyword: AOLNET. Additional information on this number can be found at keyword: AOLNet. See also *access number* and *AOLnet*.

$im_off/$im_on—These are the commands for ignoring Instant Messages (IMs). Sending an IM to the screen name $im_off will block incoming IMs. Conversely, sending an IM to $im_on will allow you to receive IMs again. When using these commands to turn IMs off or on, type only in lowercase letters exactly as shown. To initiate the command, either type some text in the message box and send the IM (by clicking on the Send button) or simply click on the Available? button. You will receive confirmation in the form of an AOL dialog box when either turning IMs on or off. If members try to send you an IM or use the Available? button on the IM window, they will be told that <your screen name> cannot currently receive Instant Messages. Note that IMs cannot be turned off for specific individuals—it is all or nothing. See also *IM*; contrast *Ignore* and *parental chat controls*.

<< and **>>**—These symbols are used to quote text and often used in e-mail and posts. Members using WAOL 2.5 or higher, or MAOL 3.0 or higher, can get automatic quoting simply by selecting and copying a block of text in an e-mail, and then clicking Reply. See also *e-mail* and *post*.

//roll—The command for rolling dice. When entered in a chat or conference room, AOL's host computer will return a random result for two six-sided dice to the room. For example:

```
OnlineHost : NumbersMan rolled 2 6-sided dice:   2  4
```

The command can also be used to roll other types and quantities of dice. The full syntax of the command is //roll -diceXX -sidesYYY (where XX is 0-15 and YYY is 0-999). Be sure to include the spaces. It is considered rude to roll dice in Lobbies or other public chat areas (with the exception of the Red Dragon Inn, sims, and other special game rooms). This command is often used when role-playing or in lieu of drawing straws. See also *chat rooms, OnlineHost,* and *sim.*

/ga—This is common shorthand for go ahead, often used during conferences with protocol. See *protocol.*

abbreviations—These are acronyms for common online phrases used in chat, IMs, and e-mail. Examples include LOL (laughing out loud) and BRB (be right back). See also *chat* and *shorthands;* contrast with *body language* and *emoticons.*

access number—A phone number (usually local) your modem uses to access America Online. To find an access number online, go to keyword: ACCESS or AOLNET. If you aren't signed on to AOL, there are a number of ways to get access numbers:

- Sign on with the New Local# (WAOL or MAOL 3.0) or Get Local# (MAOL 2.7 and lower) option in the Set Up & Sign On window.
- Delete all your numbers in Setup; AOL will automatically call the 800 number and let you choose from the list of access numbers.
- Phone the network: Call SprintNet at 1-800-877-5045, ext. 5 or SprintNet's automatic access number listings at 1-800-473-7983; call Tymnet at 1-800-336-0149, ext 2.
- Dial up SprintNet's Local Access Numbers Directory: Using a general telecommunications program, you can call in to a SprintNet node directly. Once connected, type **@D** and hit the Enter key twice. At the @ prompt given, type **c mail** and hit Enter, then type **PHONES** for the username and PHONES again for the password. You can look up any local SprintNet number available.

- Call America Online's Customer Service Hotline at 1-800-827-6364 (within U.S.A.) or 1-703-893-6288 (from Canada or overseas), open 24 hours a day, seven days a week.
- Call AOL's FAXLink service at 1-800-827-5551 and request a list of access numbers be faxed to you. An automated voice menu will guide you through the choices.
- Dial up AOL's Customer Service BBS with a standard telecommunications program at 1-800-827-5808 [settings: 8 data bits, no parity, 1 stop bit, up to 14.4K].

If you don't have a local access number, read the information in the Access Number area (keyword: ACCESS) on how to obtain one. See also *800 number, AOLnet, SprintNet, Tymnet,* and *node.*

address—There are two types of addresses you'll hear about on AOL and the Internet. The first is an e-mail address, which allows you to send an e-mail to anyone on AOL, the Internet, and just about any other online service. You can look up addresses for AOL members at keyword: MEMBERS, and addresses for Internet denizens at various places on the WWW (World Wide Web). The second is a location address for information on AOL or the WWW, which is better known as a URL. An example of an address on AOL is aol://1722:keyword, which takes you to the Ultimate Keyword List area when entered into the keyword window. On the Web, the address http://members.aol.com/jennifer/ will take you to Jennifer's home page. See also *e-mail, e-mail address, Internet, URL,* and *WWW.*

Address Book—An AOL software feature that allows you to store screen names for easy access. Your Address Book may be created, edited, or used through the Address Book icon available when composing mail. You can also create or edit it with the Edit Address Book option under your Mail menu. On WAOL and MAOL 2.7 and below, you will need to specify an individual or group name in the first field and the screen name(s) of the account(s) in the second field. To use the names in your Address Book when composing mail, be sure your cursor is in either the To: box or the CC: box, and then click on the Address Book icon. You can then select the name(s) you'd like to have your e-mail addressed to. On MAOL 3.0, click the Person or Group icon to add a new entry—note that you can include a photo (or graphic) on the second page of any entry (click the dog-eared corner to get there). To use the names in your Address Book, be sure to select Compose Mail from the Mail menu first and then click on the Address Book icon. See also *e-mail* and *screen name.*

afk—Common shorthand for "away from keyboard." It's most often used in chat and IMs when it's necessary to leave the keyboard for an extended length of time. There are few reasons for going "afk" that are valid, but taking your pet hamster out for a walk is one of them. Upon return, "bak" is used, meaning "back at keyboard." See also *shorthands, abbreviations,* and *chat;* contrast with *body language* and *emoticons.*

Alt key—A special function key on the PC keyboard. Usually located near the spacebar, you'll find the letters *Alt* printed on it. Holding down the Alt key while another key is pressed will often activate a special function. For example, Alt + H will bring up the Help section under WAOL and GAOL. (**Note**: Some Macintosh keyboards also have a key labeled "Alt," but this is primarily for use when operating a PC emulator on the Mac and is otherwise defined as the Option Key.) See also *Control key, Command key,* and *Option Key.*

America Online, Incorporated (AOL)—The nation's leading online service, headquartered in Virginia. Formerly known as Quantum Computer Services and founded in 1985, AOL has grown rapidly in both size and scope. AOL has over seven million members and hundreds of alliances with major companies. America Online's stock exchange symbol is AOL. To contact AOL headquarters call 1-703-448-8700, or use 1-800-827-6364 to speak to a representative. See also *AOL;* contrast *CompuServe, eWorld, Microsoft Network,* and *Prodigy.*

analog—Information composed of continuous and varying levels of intensity, such as sound and light. Much of the information in the natural world is analog while those man-made, such as from computers, are digital. For example, the sound of your significant other asking you politely and sensitively to get off AOL for the tenth time is analog. Yet if you were to convert that information to a computer sound file, it would become digital. Contrast with *digital.*

AOL—Abbreviation for America Online, Inc. Occasionally abbreviated as AO. See also *America Online, Incorporated.*

AOLiversary—A date celebrated yearly on which a member first became an active on America Online. Considered an accurate yardstick by some to determine their state of addiction. See *AOLoholic.*

AOLnet—America Online's own packet-switching network that provides members with up to 28,800 bps local access numbers. To use this network, you must have WAOL 2.5 (or higher), or MAOL 2.5.1 (or higher). If you have a version below 3.0 of either software, you may need the AOLnet CCL file available at keyword: AOLNET. AOLnet numbers are located across the country. For members who do not have a local access number, there is also an 800 number that is more affordable than most long-distance fees. To find AOLnet local access numbers, go to keyword: AOLNET. See also *800 number, packet-switching network,* and *access number;* contrast with *SprintNet* and *Tymnet.*

AOLoholic—A member of AOL who begins to display any of the following behaviors: spending most of their free time online; thinking about AOL even when offline (evidenced by the addition of shorthands to non-AOL writings); attempting to bring all their friends and family online; and/or thinking AOL is the best invention since the wheel. A 12-step plan is in development. Many, but not all, AOLoholics go on to become community leaders. See also *community leader* and *member.*

ARC—Short for archive, this is an older compression utility that was the PC standard prior to ZIP. This utility will compress one file, or multiple files, into a file (called an archive), which will make for shorter transferring while uploading or downloading. Some older files online are still packaged in the ARC format. See also *archive, file, file compression, PKZip,* and *StuffIt.*

archive—1. A file that has been compressed smaller with file compression software. See also *file, file compression, ARC, PKZip,* and *StuffIt.* 2. A file that contains message board postings that may be of value, but have been removed from a message board due to their age, inactivity of topic, or lack of message board space. These messages are usually bundled into one document, and placed in a file library for retrieval later. See also *file* and *library.*

article—A text document intended to be read online, but may be printed or saved for later examination offline. Usually articles are less than 25k, as anything larger would probably scroll off the top of your window. Note that with GAOL only 8k of an article may be read at one time, with excess usually scrolling off the top; use your log feature to capture the entire article if this happens. In version 3.0 of the AOL software, article size is unlimited. See also *document*; contrast with *file*.

asbestos—A flame retardant. Used as a modifier to anything intended to protect one from flames. For example, "donning asbestos underwear." This is usually used just before saying something that is expected to produce flames. Contrary to popular belief, hamsters are not flame-retardant, and system slowdowns can be attributed to the increased number of flames. See also *flame*.

ASCII—Acronym for American Standard for Computer Information Interchange (or American Standard Code for Information Interchange). ASCII is the numeric code used to represent computer characters on computers around the world. Because only seven bits are used in ASCII, there are no more than 128 (2^7) characters in the standard ASCII set. Variations of ASCII often extend the available characters by using an 8-bit means of identifying characters and thus may represent as many as 256 characters. The standard ASCII code set consists of 128 characters ranging from 0 to 127. America Online supports characters 28-127 in chat areas, IMs, and message boards. Pronounced "ask-key." See also *ASCII text*.

ASCII art—Pictures created with no more than the 128 ASCII characters. ASCII art can be humorous, entertaining, or serious. It is popular in some chat rooms. Some members find it disruptive when large ASCII art is displayed in a chat room, so you are advised to ask before scrolling it. See also *ASCII* and *ASCII text*.

ASCII text—Characters represented as ASCII. Sometimes called "plain text"; this is compatible with all platforms represented on AOL. See also *ASCII*.

Ask the Staff button—See *Comment to Staff button*.

asynchronous—Data communication via modem of the start-stop variety where characters do not need to be transmitted constantly. Each character is transmitted as a discrete unit with its own start bit and one or more stop bits. AOL is asynchronous. See also *synchronous*.

attached file—A file that hitches a ride with e-mail. Be the file text, sound, or pictures of your hamster Bruno, it is said to be attached if it has been included with the e-mail for separate downloading by the recipient (whether addressed directly, carbon copied, or blind carbon copied). E-mail that is forwarded will retain any attached files as well. Files are usually attached because the information that they contain is either too long to be sent in the body of regular e-mail or is impossible to send via e-mail, such as with software programs. Multiple files may be attached by compressing the files into one archive and attaching the archive to the piece of e-mail with the Attach File icon. See also *archive*, *download*, *e-mail*, and *file*.

auditorium—Auditoriums are specially equipped online "rooms" that allow large groups of AOL members to meet in a structured setting. Currently, there are several auditoriums: AOL Live, The Bowl, The Coliseum, Cyberplex, CyberRap, The Globe, International, News Room, and The Odeon (for special and general events); Rotunda (for computing-related topics or computing company representatives); and Tech Live (for questions and help on AOL—this is in the free area). The auditoriums are divided into two parts: the stage, where the emcee and the guest speaker(s) are located, and the chat rows, where the audience is located. Upon entering an auditorium, a user is assigned to one of the chat rows, consisting of up to 15 other audience members. Audience members in the same row may talk to each other without being heard by those on stage or by those in other rows. Nothing said in the audience can be normally heard by anyone on stage, although anything said on stage can be broadcast and heard by everyone in the audience. The OnlineHost will broadcast important information throughout the conference. The emcee moderates the conference and will broadcast more specific information. You can tell the difference between what is said on stage and what is said in your chat row because what is said in your chat row is preceded by a row number. More information on auditoriums can be found at keyword: LIVE. See also *emcee*, *OnlineHost*, *The Coliseum*, *Rotunda*, and *Tech Help Live*; contrast with *chat rooms* and *conference room*.

Automatic AOL—An automated feature that can send and receive your e-mail and files, as well as receive newsgroup postings. Also known as FlashSessions on WAOL and MAOL 2.7 (and lower). Auto AOL can be set up to run at any time, including while you are online. It is accessible under your Mail menu. See also *e-mail*, *file*, *flashmail*, and *newsgroups*.

bandwidth—A measure of the amount of information that can flow through a given point at any given time. Technically, bandwidth is the difference, in Hertz (Hz), between the highest and lowest frequencies of a transmission channel. However, as typically used, it more often refers the amount of data that can be sent through a given communications circuit. To use a popular analogy, a low bandwidth is a two-lane road while a high bandwidth is a six-lane superhighway.

bash—A get-together or party of AOL members in a particular area. Members who attend are often referred to as bashees, and popular bashes are the Big Apple Bash (in NYC) and the Texas Bash. Information on bashes can usually be found in The Quantum Que, a community message board available at keyword: QUE.

basher—A particularly vile form of snert. A basher will usually target a certain group and harass them for the basher's pleasure. This usually takes place in a People Connection chat room dedicated to that group, but may also occur in conference rooms. See also *snert*, *People Connection*, *chat rooms*, and *conference room*.

baud rate—A unit for measuring the speed of data transmission. Technically baud rates refer to the number of times the communications line changes states each second. Strictly speaking, baud and bits per second (bps) are not identical measurements, but most non-technical people use the terms interchangeably. See also *bps*.

BBS (Bulletin Board System)—A system offering information that can be accessed via computer, modem, and phone lines. While that definition technically includes AOL, BBSes are typically much smaller in size and scope. Most BBSes maintain message boards and file libraries and some feature Internet access, newsfeeds, and online games. For more information online, go to keyword: BBS. BBSes are sometimes abbreviated as simply "board," and should not be confused with message boards on AOL. Contrast with *message board*.

Bertelsmann, AG—A German media company which has joined forces with America Online and developed an AOL-based online service for members living in Germany. This new service, currently called "AOL Germany," launched on November 28, 1995. Local access is available at speeds of up to 28.8 bps in over 25 cities today and growing quickly.

beta test—A period in a new product or service's development designed to discover problems (or "bugs") prior to its release to the general public. AOL often selects members to beta test its new software. If you are interested in beta testing AOL software, you may be able to apply at keyword: BETA APPLY. Hamsters are notoriously bad beta testers; the bugs distract their attention. See also *bug*.

blind carbon copy (bcc)—A feature of the AOL e-mail system that allows you to send e-mail to a member or members without anyone other than you being aware of it. To blind carbon copy, simply place parentheses around the screen name(s). For example, (JoeShmo) or (JoeShmo, HughHamstr). MAOL 3.0 users can use the small pop-up menu to change an address to BCC. GAOL users will need to use two parentheses, as in ((JoeShmo)) or ((JoeShmo, HughHamstr)). When a blind carbon copy is made, it is said to be bcc'ed. See also *e-mail*; contrast with *carbon copy*.

board—An abbreviated reference to a message board or bulletin board service (BBS). See also *message board* and *BBS*.

body language—An online expression of physical movement and nonverbal emotions through text. Two popular methods have developed on AOL: colons (:::yawning:::) and brackets (<yawning and trying to stay awake for 10 straight hours in front of a monitor>). See also *chat*; contrast with *abbreviations*, *emoticons*, and *shorthands*.

bounce—v. Something that is returned, such as e-mail. For example, e-mail sent to receipients outside of AOL may bounce and never make it to its intended destination, especially if it was not addressed correctly. Sometimes users who are punted will refer to themselves as bounced. See also *e-mail* and *punt*.

bps (bits per second)—A method of measuring data transmission speed. Currently, 1200 through 28,800 bps are supported on AOL (see keyword: AOLNET for more information). See also *baud*.

brb—Common shorthand for "be right back." It is used by AOL members when participating in chat/conference rooms or talking in IMs (Instant Messages). See also *shorthands, abbreviations,* and *chat*; contrast with *body language* and *emoticons*.

browse—To casually explore rather than examine in detail. Typically used in reference to message boards and file libraries. Browsing information online without a specific target is one prominent trait of an budding AOLoholic. Contrast *search*.

browser—A way of accessing the World Wide Web. On MAOL 3.0 and WAOL 2.5 and higher, this is an integrated component of the software. On MAOL 2.6 and 2.7, it is a separate piece of software. See also *favorite place, Internet, hot list, page, Personal Filing Cabinet, site,* and *WWW*.

btw—Common shorthand for "by the way." It is used in IMs, chat/conference rooms, e-mail and message postings. See also *shorthands, abbreviations,* and *chat*; contrast with *body language* and *emoticons*.

buddy—A friend or family member who has an AOL membership and has been added to your Buddy List. See also *Buddy List*.

Buddy List—A special list that stores your "buddies" (screen names of friends, family members, co-workers, etc.) and informs you when they sign on or off AOL. You add (or remove) buddies yourself, and can define several groups of buddies as you like. The Buddy List is a feature of the WAOL and MAOL 3.0 software. See also *buddy* and *invitation*.

bug—A problem or glitch in a product, be it software or hardware. A bug may be referred to jokingly as a "feature." You can report a problem with AOL software or services by going to keyword: QUESTIONS and clicking on Report a Problem. See also *GPF*.

bulletin board—See *message board* and *BBS*.

carbon copy (cc)—A feature of the AOL e-mail system that allows you to address e-mail to a member for whom the e-mail is not directly intended or is of secondary interest. The primary addressee(s) are aware that the copy was made, similar to the carbon copy convention used in business correspondence. As such, the members carbon copied are not usually expected to reply. When a carbon copy is made, it is said to be cc'ed. Also known as a courtesy copy. See also *e-mail*, contrast with *blind carbon copy*.

CCL (Communication Control Language)—A script that allows you to control your modem. CCL scripts are most useful when the connection process is more complicated than can be handled by a modem file. For example, if your modem needs certain commands every time a connection is established, you can use or write a CCL script to automate this process. America Online uses standard CCLs and modem files to control your modem; in other words, you shouldn't need to worry about CCLs when connecting to AOL. See also *modem file*.

Center Stage—See *auditorium*.

channel—This is the broadest category of information into which America Online divides its material. Also known as department. At this writing, these are the channels for the different areas online:

C! Computers and Software
Digital City
Entertainment
Games
Health & Fitness
The Hub
International
Internet Connection
Kids Only
Learning & Culture
Life, Styles & Interests
Marketplace
MusicSpace
Newsstand
Today's News

People Connection
Reference Desk
Sports
Style Channel
Travel
Member Services (unlimited use area)

chat—To engage in real-time communications with other members. AOL members that are online at the same time may chat with each other in a number of ways: Instant Messages (IMs), chat/conference rooms, and auditoriums. Chatting provides immediate feedback from others; detailed discussions are better suited towards message boards and lengthy personal issues are best dealt with in e-mail if a member isn't currently online. See also *IM, chat room, conference rooms* and *auditorium*, contrast with *message board* and *e-mail*.

chat rooms—Online areas where members may meet to communicate and interact with others. There are two kinds of chat areas—public and private. Public chat areas can be found in the People Connection area (keyword: PEOPLE) or in the many forums around AOL (see keyword: AOL LIVE for schedules). Public rooms may either be officially sanctioned rooms or member-created rooms (which are listed separately). All public rooms are governed by AOL's Terms of Service (TOS) and are open to anyone interested. Private chat rooms are available from most chat areas and are open only to those who create them or know their names and meeting times. All chat rooms accommodate at least 23 members, while some of the chat areas in forums other than People Connection may hold up to 48 members. Those chat rooms that can be created by members (both public and private) must have names with no more than 20 characters, beginning with a letter, and containing no punctuation. Beware that Stratus hamsters have been known to escape and surprise unsuspecting members in chat rooms. See also *private room, chat, host, Guide, TOS* and *People Connection*; contrast *auditorium* and *conference room*.

chat sounds—Sounds may be played and broadcast to others in chat areas by typing:

```
{S <sound>}
```

and sending it to the chat area. Be sure to type it exactly as shown and insert the exact name of the sound you wish to play where <sound> appears in the example. For example, {S Welcome} will play AOL's Welcome sound in a chat area. New sounds can be found online by searching the libraries. To install sounds into your AOL software for playing, you'll need a sound utility (also found in the libraries online). Keep in mind that other members will need to have the same sound installed in their AOL software to hear it when played. Sounds should be used sparingly so as not to disturb conversations or awaken slumbering hamsters. Please note also that GAOL users cannot hear chat sounds, nor can those without sound capabilities. See also *chat rooms* and *library*.

CIS—Short for CompuServe Information Service. May also be abbreviated as CI$. See also *CompuServe*; contrast with *AOL*, *eWorld*, *Microsoft Network*, and *Prodigy*.

client—A computer that requests information from another. On AOL, you are the client and the Stratus is the host. Contrast *host (1)*.

close box—The small box in the upper-left corner of your window. Clicking on this box closes the window on the Mac and gives you the option on the PC. Not to be confused with a shoe box, boom box, or even clothes box. See also *window*; contrast *zoom box*.

club—See *forum*.

Coliseum, The—See *auditorium*.

Command key—A special function key on the Mac. Usually located near the spacebar, you'll find printed on it either an open Apple symbol or a clover-leaf symbol (or both). Holding down the Command key while another key is pressed will often activate a special function. Also known as the Open-Apple key. See also *Control key*, *Option key*, and *Alt key*.

Comment to Staff button—A button available in file libraries that takes you to the Download Info Center, which offers a great deal of information about libraries and allows you to send a note to the managers of the library. Note that it doesn't send a note to the uploader, only the library managers (often a forum leader or assistant). Note that this is labeled "Ask The Staff" on WAOL and GAOL. The Download Info Center is also available directly at keyword: INFO CENTER. See also *download* and *library*.

community leader—AOL members who help in the various forums and areas. They usually work from their homes not AOL headquarters, hence they have been called "remote staff" in the past. Often these are Guides, Hosts, Forum leaders/assistants/consultants, etc. With partners, the community leaders are usually those who do not work on the premises of the partner's offline physical location, whereas those partner employees who do are known as corporate staff. See also *Guide, host, partner,* and *uniform*; contrast *corporate staff* and *in-house*.

compression—See *file compression*.

CompuServe (CIS)—A large, established commercial online service similar to America Online. While CompuServe Information Service (CIS) has more databases available, their service is priced higher and is less user-friendly than AOL. CIS is owned by H&R Block. May be referred to as "CIS" or "CI$" in shorthand during chat. Contrast with *America Online, Incorporated, eWorld, Microsoft Network,* and *Prodigy*.

conference room—A specific kind of chat area found in forums all around AOL where members can meet, hold conferences, and interact in real-time. Conference rooms can hold up to 23 or 48 members at any one time (depending on location), and are located outside of the People Connection. Currently, there are over 400 public conference rooms with more being added all the time. Often special events are held in these rooms, and a protocol system may be used to make them proceed smoothly. Hosts or moderators often facilitate the discussions and conferences here. Hamster sightings are less frequent in these rooms. See also *host, moderator,* and *protocol*; contrast *chat rooms* and *auditorium*.

Control key—A special function key, usually located on the bottom row of keys, you'll find printed on it either "Ctrl" or "Control." Holding down the Control key while another key is pressed will often activate a special function. (Note: Some Macintosh keyboards also have a key labeled "Control," but this is primarily for use when operating a PC emulator on the Mac.) See also *Command key*, *Option key*, *Alt key*, and *Open-Apple key*.

corporate staff—Members who are usually company or partner (information provider) employees and work at the corporate offices of the company. In-house AOL, Inc., staff is often referred to in this manner as well. See also *in-house* and *partner*; contrast with *community leader*.

cracker—One who violates security. Coined by hackers in the 1980s in defense against the growing assumption that all hackers are malevolent. A password scammer is a cracker. See also *password scammer*; contrast *hacker*, *phisher*, and *snert*.

cross-post—vi. To make the same message in several folders, message boards, or newsgroups. Overuse of this is bad netiquette, and may result in having your posts hidden (if on AOL) or your mailbox barraged with flaming e-mail (if on the Internet). See also *flame*, *newsgroups*, *post*, and *Spam*.

CS Live—See *Tech Help Live*.

Customer Relations—America Online's Customer Relations Hotline is open 24 hours a day, seven days a week. You can reach them at 1-800-827-6364. See also *Tech Help Live*.

cyberpunk—First used to designate a body of speculative fiction literature focusing on marginalized people in technologically enhanced cultural "systems." Within the last few years, the mass media has used this term to categorize the denizens of cyberspace. Cyberpunks are known to cruise the information landscapes with alacrity, or lacking that, eagerness.

cyberspace—An infinite world created by our computer networks. Cyberspace is no less real than the real world—people are born, grow, learn, fall in love, and die in cyberspace. These effects may or may not be carried over into the physical world. America Online is an example of cyberspace created through interaction between the energies of the members, community leaders, staff, and computers. See also *online community*.

daemon—An automatic program that performs a maintenance function on AOL. For example, a board daemon may run at 3 in the morning and clean up old posts on a message board. Rumored to stand for "Disk And Execution MONitor."

database—A collection of information, stored and organized for easy searching. A database can refer to something as simple as a well-sorted filing cabinet, but today most databases reside on computers because they offer better access. Databases are located all over AOL, with prominent examples being the Member Directory (keyword: MEMBER DIRECTORY) and the Directory of Services (keyword: SERVICES). See AOL's Reference Desk (keyword: REFERENCE) for a large collection of databases. See also *Directory of Services*, *Member Directory*, and *searchable*.

Delete—An AOL e-mail system feature that allows you to permanently remove a piece of mail from any and all of your mailboxes. To use, simply select and highlight the piece of mail you wish to delete (from either your new mail, read mail, or sent mail) and click on the Delete button at the bottom of the window. The mail will be permanently deleted and cannot be retrieved. Mail you have deleted without reading first will appear as "(deleted)" in the Status box of the sender. The Delete feature is useful for removing unneeded mail from your Old Mail box. Do not confuse this feature with the Unsend option, which will remove mail you've sent from the recipient's mailbox. See also *e-mail* and *Status*; contrast *Unsend*.

demoware (demonstration software)—These are often full-featured versions of commercial software, with the exception being that the Save or Print features are often disabled. Some demos are only functional for certain periods of time. Like shareware, demonstration software is a great way to try before you buy. Contrast *freeware*, *public domain*, and *shareware*.

department—See *channel.*

digital—Information that is represented by discrete states. Most information in the real world is not digital, but must be converted into this form to be used by computers. The converse is also true; digital information normally needs to be converted into analog information before people can use it. An example of this would be AOL chat sounds, which are stored as digital information, but must be converted into their analog equivalents before they are actually heard by us. Contrast with *analog*.

Directory of Services—A searchable database that allows AOL members to quickly locate AOL's available services. This is available at keyword: SERVICES. See also *database* and *searchable.*

document—An information file, usually relating specific details on a topic. On AOL, these can be in the form of articles (which are read-only), or modifiable documents, usually created with the New (Memo) menu command within AOL. See also *article* and *file.*

DOD—Abbreviation for Download On Demand, a method of receiving artwork updates that was used prior to progressive artwork downloading, still used on MAOL 2.7 and WAOL 2.5 and lower. AOL was rather unique in that as it grew and new areas were added, the custom artwork associated with new services and areas was added on the fly. When you enter an area that includes new artwork, such as a logo or icon, it was automatically downloaded and stored on your computer. Once you visited an area, you never had to wait for the artwork to download again. Similarly, if you never entered a new area with artwork updates, you did not need to wait for the DODs. The difference between DOD and Smart Art (progressive artwork downloading) is that your computer is tied up while the download is in progress and you do not see the artwork until the download has completed with DOD. Contrast *Smart Art* and *UDO.*

domain—In Internet addresses, usually everything to the right of the @ symbol is referred to as the domain. For example, the domain name for AOL member addresses is aol.com. See also *address, e-mail, e-mail address*, and *Internet.*

DOS—Abbreviation for Disk Operating System, also called PC DOS or MS DOS (Microsoft). DOS is the most widely used operating system for IBM PCs and compatibles. Pronounced "dahss." Contrast *OS/2*, *system*, and *Windows*.

download—The transfer of information stored on a remote computer to a storage device on your personal computer. This information can come from AOL via its file libraries, or from other AOL members via attached files in e-mail. Usually, downloads are files intended for review once you're offline. You download graphics and sounds, for instance. Download is used both as a noun and a verb. For example, you might download a graphic file to your hard drive, where you store your latest downloads. Hamsters have been known to defect via downloads. See also *archive, attached file, download count, download manager, FileGrabber*, and *library*.

download count—The download count (often abbreviated "Cnt" in a library window) refers to the number of times that file has been downloaded. This is often used as a gauge of the file's popularity. While this may not be too significant for a new upload, it is a good indication of the popularity of files that have been around for a while. For example, the file Stuffit Expander in the Macintosh Computers & Software channel has over 23,000 downloads. Often, however, the number of downloads is more reflective of the appeal of a file's name or description rather than of its content. Note that a newly uploaded file will always have a download count of 1, even though it hasn't been downloaded yet. So to divine the true number of downloads, always subtract one from the total. Also, if the system is slow, the download count visible at the top level of the library may not update immediately. See also *file, library*, and *download*.

download manager—An AOL software feature that allows you to keep a queue of files to download at a later time. You can even set up your software to automatically sign off when your download session is complete. You can schedule your software to sign on and grab files listed in the queue at times you specify. See also download and file. See also *Automatic AOL* and *Personal Filing Cabinet*.

e-mail—Short for electronic mail. One of the most popular features of online services, e-mail allows you to send private communications electronically from one person to another. No wasted paper, leaky pens, or terrible-tasting envelope glue involved! E-mail is usually much faster and easier to send than ordinary mail; the shortcomings are that not everyone has an e-mail address to write to and your mail resides in electronic form on a computer system, although e-mail is considered as private and inviolable as regular U.S. Mail. With AOL's e-mail system, mail can be sent directly to scores of people, carbon copied, blind carbon copied, forwarded, and even include attached files. E-mail can also be sent (and forwarded) to any other service that has an Internet address. On 3.0, there is no limit to the size of mail that can be sent and received. On WAOL and MAOL below 3.0, mail can be sent and received up to 32k. GAOL can send mail up to 8k in size and receive mail up to 32k (through 8k chunks). Your screen name's mailbox is limited to 550 pieces of mail at any one time, including both read and unread mail. Unread mail will remain in your New Mail box for four weeks after the date it was sent and mail you have read remains in your Old Mail box for three days. If the amount of mail in your mail box exceed 550 pieces, AOL will start to delete excess mail, starting with read mail—AOL will not delete any of your unread mail, however. These limits almost never present a problem for even frequent AOL users, however. See also *attached file, blind carbon copy, carbon copy, Delete, e-mail address, flashmail, gateway, Ignore, Keep As New, mailbomb, massmail, Personal Filing Cabinet, return receipt,* and *Status;* contrast *snail mail, message,* and *IM.*

e-mail address—A cyberspace mailbox. On AOL, your e-mail address is simply your screen name; for folks outside of AOL, your address is yourscreenname@aol.com. For example, if our friend Sharon wants to e-mail us from her Internet account, she can reach us as jennifer@aol.com or numbersman@aol.com. For mail outgoing from AOL, check out the Mail Gateway area (keyword: MAIL GATEWAY) for more information. See also *address, e-mail,* and *screen name.*

Easter egg—A hidden surprise in software often left in at the whim of the programmers. Both Macintosh and Windows applications have Easter eggs. There are also some Easter eggs scattered around AOL, but be forewarned they come and go as quickly as chocolate bunnies on Easter Sunday. We do know that you can find one at keyword: EDGE on 3.0—check out the letter *A.*

echo—A rare AOL system bug that rapidly repeats a person's chat over and over in a chat or conference room. Also known as a system scroll. If this occurs, you should leave the room immediately and page a Guide using keyword: GUIDEPAGER.

emcee—A member who has been trained to moderate and host events held in auditoriums. See also *auditorium;* contrast with *host* and *moderator*.

emoticons—Symbols consisting of characters found on any keyboard that are used to give and gain insight on emotional states. For example, the symbol :) is a smile—just tilt your head to the left and you'll see the : (eyes) and the) (smile). The online community has invented countless variations to bring plain text to life and you'll see emoticons used everywhere from chat rooms to e-mail. Emoticons, like emotions, are more popular in "face-to-face" chat and some consider them unprofessional or overly cute. Regardless, they are one of the best methods of effective communication online. Emoticons may also be referred to as smileys, and collectively with other chat devices as shorthands. A brief list is available at keyword: SHORTHANDS. See also *shorthands* and *chat;* contrast with *abbreviations* and *body language*.

encryption—The manipulation of data in order to prevent any but the intended recipient from reading that data. There are many types of data encryption, and they are the basis of network security.

ET (EST or EDT)—Abbreviation for Eastern Time. Most times are given in this format as AOL is headquartered in this time zone. MAOL users can change this default time zone through their Preferences under the Members menu.

eWorld—Apple Computer's now defunct online service. Based on AOL's client system, eWorld had stylized graphics, extensive Apple support, and "ZMac George" (our own NumbersMan in his eWorld incarnation). eWorld opened to the public on June 20, 1994, and closed only a year and a half later. Contrast with *AOL, CompuServe, Microsoft Network*, and *Prodigy*.

FAQ—Short for Frequently Asked Questions. FAQs may take the form of an informational file containing questions and answers to common concerns/issues. These are used to answer questions that are brought up often in message boards or discussions. These files may be stored online in an article or archived in a file library. See also *message board* and *library*.

favorite place—1. On WAOL 2.5 and MAOL 3.0 and higher, this refers to a feature that allows you to "mark" AOL and WWW places you'd like to return to later. These favorite places are stored in your Personal Filing Cabinet. Any WWW site can be made a favorite place, as well as any AOL window with a little heart in the upper right hand corner of the window. See also *Personal Filing Cabinet*.
2. On MAOL 2.7 and lower and GAOL, a favorite place is one of the user-definable locations at the bottom of the Go To menu. You can edit this with the Edit Favorite Places option.

fax (facsimile)—A technique for sending graphical images (such as text or pictures) over phone lines. While faxes are usually sent and received with a stand-alone fax machine, faxes may also be sent to or from computers using fax software and a modem. In the past you could send a fax through AOL for a fee at keyword: FAX, but AOL has discontinued this service. Contrast with *e-mail* and *snail mail*.

file—Any amount of information that is grouped together as one unit. On AOL, a file can be anything from text to sounds and can be transferred to and from your computer via AOL. Collections of files are available in libraries for downloading, and files may be attached to e-mail. See also *download*, *library*, and *software file*; contrast with *article*.

file compression—A programming technique by which many files can be reduced in size. Files are usually compressed so that they take up less storage space, can be transferred more quickly, and/or can be bundled with others. Files must be decompressed before they can be used, but the AOL software can be set to automatically decompress most files (check your Preferences). See also *file* and *download*.

file library—See *library*.

File Transfer Protocol—See *FTP*.

FileGrabber—A piece of software built into WAOL and MAOL that will automatically decode encoded data (also known as "binaries"), such as that found in some newsgroups. Besides making sure that your newsgroup preferences are set to allow you to decode files, you don't need to do anything to use it—FileGrabber will automatically detect encoded data and ask you if you want to download the file. For more information, see the aol.newsgroups.help.binaries newsgroup. See also *download, file, Internet,* and *newsgroups*.

filename extensions—These are usually three-character codes found suffixing a filename, and are primarily used for PC files. A comprehensive list would take several pages, but here are some common extensions:

Text/Word Processor formats:

DOC	Microsoft Word document
HLP	Help file
HTM	HyperText Markup Language (WWW) format
HTX	HyperText document
LF	Line Feeds added to text format
LET	Letter file, as to a friend (i.e., FRIEND.LET)
LOG	America Online log file, usually text
MW	MacWrite document
RTF	Rich Text Format
SAM	Ami Professional document
TXT	Unformatted ASCII Text
WS	WordStar document
WP (or WPD)	WordPerfect document

Graphic formats:

BMP	OS/2 or Windows Bitmap
EPS	Encapsulated PostScript
GIF	Graphics Interchange Format
JPG	Joint Photographic Experts Group (JPEG)
MAC	MacPaint (also PNT)
PIC	Macintosh PICT
PCX	Zsoft Paintbrush
TIF	Tagged Image File Format (TIFF)
WPG	WordPerfect Graphic

Compressed formats:

SIT	StuffIt (MacAOL 2.x can unstuff this automatically)
ZIP	PKZip (PC/GEOS, WAOL, and Mac AOL 2.1 or later can unstuff this automatically)
ARC	Abbreviation for ARChive; similar to PKZip (PC/GEOS and WAOL can unstuff this automatically)
SEA	Self Extracting Archive

Other formats:

BAT	Batch file; executable file; DOS
BIN	Binary program file; often a subdirectory name
BMK	Windows Bookmark file; references Help segment
COM	Executable program file; DOS
DAT	Data file or subdirectory with data files
DBF	DBase file
DLL	Dynamic Link Library; program files recognized by Windows
EXE	PC executable file, can be a self-extracting archive
GRP	Windows Program Group
INI	Initialization file for Windows and other applications
MAC	Macro
MOV	QuickTime movie
MPG	MPEG animation
PM4	PageMaker version 4.x file
SLK	SYLK file
SYS	Device driver or System file
WAV	Windows sound file
XLC	Excel chart
XLS	Excel worksheet

flame—Made popular on the Internet, this means to chat, post messages, or send e-mail about something that is considered inflammatory by other members, and may cause fires among those who read and respond to it. "Flaming" may spark a lively debate when selectively and appropriately used. More often, it will cause misunderstandings and divided parties. Harassment and vulgarity are not allowed on

America Online, and if you see this occurring, you may report the occurrence at keyword: TOS. See also *asbestos, chat, message board, e-mail,* and *TOS.*

flashmail—This is a feature of the AOL software that allows you to save your outgoing e-mail to your hard disk to send at a later time, or save your incoming e-mail so you can look at it later, online or offline. These e-mails are stored in your flashbox, and the outgoing files are sent with flashsessions. Note: On MAOL 3.0, the term "flashmail" is no longer used and "flashsessions" are now "Automatic AOL sessions." See also *Automatic AOL* and *e-mail.*

folder—Groupings of messages by topic within message boards are termed "folders" on America Online. In most message boards, you may create a folder. Folder names are limited to 28 characters. See also *message* and *message board.*

form—A window for an area online—usually comprising a text field, a list box (scrollable), and one or more icons. Often special artwork will be placed in the form as well, as in a logo. Examples of forms include Star Trek Club (keyword: TREK), MTV Online (keyword: MTV), and the Mac Games Forum (keyword: MGM). See also *icon* and *window.*

forum—A place online where members with similar interests may find valuable information, exchange ideas, share files, and get help on a particular area of interest. Forums (also known simply as areas or clubs) are found everywhere online, represent almost every interest under the sun, and usually offer message boards, articles, chat rooms, and libraries, all organized and accessible by a keyword. Forums are moderated by forum hosts or forum leaders. For example, in the Macintosh Computers & Software channel, each forum has a forum leader (denoted by AFL at the beginning of their screen name), and is assisted by Forum Assistants (denoted by AFA) and often assisted even further by Forum Consultants (denoted by AFC). See also *form* and *keyword.*

freeware—A file that is completely free and often made available in libraries of online services like AOL for downloading. Unlike public domain files, you are not able to modify it and the author retains the copyright. Since the author or programmer usually posts freeware and the user downloads it, distribution is direct and nearly without cost. Users are generally encouraged to make copies and give them to friends, even post them on other services. Check the file's documentation for limits on use and distribution. VirtuaLingo is freeware—you are encouraged to pass this along to anyone who may be interested, but please do not modify or incorporate it into another work without permission. See also *file, shareware,* and *public domain.*

FTP—Abbreviation for File Transfer Protocol. A method of transferring files to and from a computer that is connected to the Internet. AOL offers FTP access via the keyword: FTP, as well as personal FTP sites at keyword: MY PLACE. See also *Internet, WWW,* and *home page*; contrast *library.*

Fwd:—Short for "forward," as in forwarding e-mail to someone. See also *e-mail.*

gateway—A link to another service, such as the Internet, a game (Gemstone III), or a service (STATS, Inc.). Gateways allow members to access these independent services through AOL. Used as both a noun and a verb. It is also rumored that the celestial gateway to Heaven is hidden somewhere online. See also *Internet.*

GAOL—The PC platform's DOS version of the AOL client software, based on the GeoWorks graphical operating system. The current version is 1.5a, although a special 2.0 version exists for GEOS users. AOL has no plans to continue upgrading this software, but members may continue using the current versions. May also be referred to as PC/GEOS, PCAO, or GEOS. Contrast with *MAOL* and *WAOL.*

GIF (Graphics Interchange Format)—A type of graphic file that can be read by most platforms; the electronic version of photographs. The GIF standard was developed by CompuServe as a standard for sharing graphical information across platforms (any with graphical display abilities). GIFs can be viewed with your AOL software or with GIF viewer utilities, which are located at keyword: VIEWERS. Member GIFs are also located in the Portrait Gallery (keyword: GALLERY). To view a Mac GIF on a PC you may need to strip off the Macintosh header with an application called AOMAC2PC. This utility is located in the Viewer Resource Center. The g in GIF should not be pronounced like the brand of peanut butter, but rather like "gift." (Yes, we know others claim otherwise, but if it were to be pronounced like "JIF," it would have been spelled that way.)

Gopher—A feature of the Internet that allows you to browse huge amounts of information. The terms implies that it will "go-pher" you to retrieve information. It also refers to the way in which you "tunnel" through the various menus, much like a gopher would. See also *WAIS* and *Internet*; contrast *newsgroups* and *WWW*.

GPF—Abbreviation for General Protection Fault. If you get a GPF error, it means that Windows (or a Windows application) has attempted to access memory that has not been allocated for use. GPFs are the scourge of WAOL members everywhere. If you experience a GPF while using WAOL, write down the exact error message, then go to keyword: GPF HELP for assistance. [Note: As you may have guessed, GPFs occur only on PCs with Microsoft Windows installed.] See also *bug*.

GUI—Graphical User Interface. Some examples of GUIs include the Mac Operating System, OS/2, and Windows. See also *OS, system, OS/2,* and *Windows*.

Guide—Experienced AOL member who has been specially chosen and trained to help other members enjoy their time online. All on-duty Guides wear their "uniforms"—the letters "Guide" followed by a space and a two-or-three letter suffix in all caps. If you would like to apply to become a Guide, send a request to the screen name "GuideApply" or ask a Guide for a copy of the application. Applicants must be at least 18 years of age, have an account that has been active six months or more, and be a member in good standing (no TOS or billing problems). To offer a compliment or lodge a complaint against a Guide, send e-mail to "Guide MGR." See also *Guide Pager, Lobby,* and *uniform*; contrast *host* and *moderator*.

Guide Pager—A feature of AOL that allows you to page a Guide when there is a problem in a chat or conference room, or when someone is requesting your password (a big no-no). Simply go to keyword: GUIDEPAGER, and you will be presented with a simple form to complete regarding the problem. Kids have a special Guide Pager of their own at keyword: KIDS PAGER. If a Guide is unavailable, you may report the offending text at keyword: TOS or through the button on your chat window. See also *Guide* and *TOS*.

gullible—Anyone who believes there are really hamsters on AOL. But seriously, the hamsters scattered throughout this glossary are just pranksters. The authors take no responsibility for their actions. We really don't know how they get in here.

hacker—Not to be confused with hamsters, hackers are self-taught computer gurus who take an unholy delight in discovering the well-hidden secrets of computer systems. Blighted by a bad reputation of late, hackers do not necessarily denote those who intend harm or damage. There are those, however, who feed upon the pain inflicted by viruses. See also *password scammer, phisher,* and *virus*.

hamster—Unbeknownst to most users, AOL's host computers are actually powered by these small, efficient creatures with large cheek pouches. They are notorious for being temperamental workers. When things slow down or troubles mount online, it is a sure sign that an AOL employee forgot to feed the hamsters. See also *host* and *Stratus*.

handle—An outdated term for your electronic nom de plume, or screen name. See also *e-mail address* and *screen name*.

header—The information at the top (or bottom) of e-mail received from the Internet and contains, among other things, the message originator, date, and time. Headers can also be found in newsgroup postings. See also *e-mail, Internet,* and *newsgroups*.

help room—Online room where members can go to get live help with the AOL software/system as well as assistance in finding things online. There are two types of help rooms: Guide-staffed and Tech Live. The Guide-staffed rooms are located in the People Connection | Public Rooms area (keyword: PEOPLE). On weekdays, there is a generic help room, AOL Help, open from 3 PM to 6 PM ET, with platform-specific rooms open from 6 PM to 3 AM ET. On weekends, the generic help room opens at noon, with the platform-specific rooms open from 3 PM to 3 AM. For more information on the Tech Live help rooms, see *Tech Help Live*. See also *Guide*, and *MHM*.

home page—1. The first page in a World Wide Web site.
2. Your own page on the WWW. Every member on AOL can now create their own home page—see keyword: MY HOME PAGE for more information.
3. The page you go to when you first enter the WWW.
See also *browser, favorite place, hot list, page, site, URL,* and *WWW.*

host—1. The AOL computer system, affectionately referred to as the Stratus (which is actually an outdated term, but it is particularly tenacious). See also *Stratus.*
2. An AOL member who facilitates discussion in chat rooms. These are usually chat-fluent, personable individuals with particular expertise in a topic. You can find hosts all over the system, and they will often be wearing "uniforms"—letters in front of their names (usually in all caps) to designate the forum they host for. See also *Guide, chat rooms, conference rooms,* and *uniform.*

hot chat—A safe, euphemistic term that means to chat about (read "flirt") and engage in the popular online dance of human attraction and consummation. Virtually, of course. And usually in private rooms or IMs. Unfortunately, hamsters are prone to this activity, but usually only on Monday, Wednesdays, and Fridays in the early morning hours, for reasons man has yet to fathom.

hot list—On MAOL 2.6 and 2.7 with the WWW browser, this is a place for storing your favorite WWW site addresses. See also *browser, page, site, URL,* and *WWW.*

icon—A graphic image of a recognizable thing or action that leads to somewhere or initiates a process. For example, the icons in the Compose Mail window may lead you to the Address Book, allow you to attach a file, send the mail, or look up help. Icons are activated by clicking on them with a mouse; some may even be used with keyboard shortcuts. See also *keyboard shortcuts.*

Ignore—1. Chat blinders; a way of blocking a member's chat from your view in a chat/conference room window. Ignore is most useful when the chat of another member becomes disruptive in the chat room. Note that the Ignore button does not block or ignore IMs from a member—it only blocks the text from your own view in a chat or conference room. To ignore a member's chat on MAOL 2.7 or lower and GAOL, click on the People icon, highlight the screen name of the person you wish to ignore, and click on the Ignore button. To ignore chat on WAOL and MAOL 3.0, double-click on the member's screen name from the list of member names in the upper right hand corner of the Chat room window. You will be presented with a dialog box that offers an option to ignore the selected member's text. Ignore can be confirmed on all platforms by either checking for the words "Ignored" next to the screen name in question in the People in this Room window, or by selecting their name and checking to see if the Ignore check box is enabled. Once ignored, a member's chat can be reinstated through the same process. See *$im_off/$im_on* for instructions on ignoring IMs.
2. An AOL e-mail system feature that allows you to ignore mail in your New Mail box, causing it to be moved to your Old Mail box without having to read it first. To use, simply select and highlight the piece of mail you wish to ignore in your New Mail box and then click on the Ignore button at the bottom of the window. Mail you have ignored without reading first will appear as (ignored) in the Status box. See also *e-mail* and *Status*.

IM (Instant Message)—AOL's equivalent of passing notes to another person during a meeting, as opposed to speaking up in the room (chat) or writing out a letter or memo (e-mail). Instant Messages (IMs) may be exchanged between two AOL members signed on at the same time and are useful for conducting conversations when a chat room isn't appropriate, available, or practical. To initiate an IM conversation, select Send Instant Message from the Member menu or use the keyboard shortcuts listed below, enter the recipient's screen name and a message, and finally send the IM by clicking on Send or using the keyboard shortcuts. If your intended victim is currently online, they will receive the IM within seconds. IMs may be exchanged at any time and from any part of the service, although IMs may not be sent when you are in the free area or when you are uploading a file. On both the Mac and Windows versions of AOL, IMs are similar to a mini-chat room, but with a larger chat buffer. On GAOL, messages are displayed one at a time, with no continuous log kept onscreen. IMs can be logged with the Instant Message Log available in MAOL and WAOL, and with the System Log in GAOL. IMs may be ignored (see $im_off/$im_on). It is also possible to send an IM to yourself, and this is often used as a therapy exercise for recovering AOLoholics. IM is used as a noun ("I have too many IMs!") or a verb ("I'm IMing with him now."). See also *IMsect*.

Keyboard shortcuts for IMs:
- MAOL:
  - Command + I—to bring up a new IM window
  - Command + Return -or- Enter—to send the IM
- WAOL:
  - Ctrl + I—to bring up a new IM window
  - Ctrl + Enter—to send the IM
- GAOL:
  - Ctrl + I—to bring up a new IM window
  - Tab to Send button then Enter—to send the IM

IMsect—An annoying Instant Message (IM). These are usually from someone who insists on IMing you when you're busy, or when you've indicated you'd rather not talk in IMs. If this happens, you have the option of turning your IMs off completely (see *$im_off/$im_on* for directions). If someone persists in IMing you even though you've politely asked them to stop, this may be considered harassment and you should report it via keyword: TOS. See also *IM*.

in-house—Used to describe those employees that actually work at AOL's Virginia-based headquarters or one of the other satellite offices. May also be referred to as corporate staff. This is contrasted with community leaders, many of whom are actually volunteers and work from their homes. See also *community leader* and *corporate staff*.

insertion point—The blinking vertical line in a document marking the place where text is being edited. The insertion point may be navigated through a document with either the mouse or the arrow keys. Also called a cursor.

interactive—Having the ability to act on each another. AOL is interactive in the sense that you can send information and, based upon that, have information sent back (and vice versa). The chat rooms are an excellent example.

Internet—The mother of all networks is not an online service itself, but rather serves to interconnect computer systems and networks all over the world. The Internet, originally operated by the National Science Foundation (NSF), is now managed by private companies (one of which is AOL). AOL features the Internet Connection channel, which includes access to e-mail service to and from Internet addresses, Usenet newsgroups, Gopher & WAIS databases, FTP, and the World Wide Web. Telnet access is now available with version 3.0 of the AOL software. AOL has even provided "CyberJockeys" who rove among the areas helping members out (they wear "CJ" in front of their screen names). To receive mail through the Internet gateway, you need to give others your Internet mailing address, which consists of your AOL screen name (without any blank spaces) followed by the "@" symbol and "aol.com" (i.e., jennifer@aol.com). To obtain more information about the Internet, use the keyword: INTERNET to go to the Internet Connection. For information about TCP/IP access to America Online, see TCP/IP. See also *address, browser, domain, FTP, gateway, Gopher, header, IRC, newsgroups, page, site, URL*, and *WAIS*.

invitation—A request by another member to join a chat or visit an area on AOL, made possible by a special feature of the software available on WAOL and MAOL 3.0. To invite someone, add them to your Buddy List, select their name, and click the Invite button. You will then be prompted to fill in the information regarding the Invite. Note that you may need the address (or URL) of an area in order to invite someone to it. See also *address, buddy, Buddy List*, and *URL*.

IRC (Internet Relay Chat)—The Internet protocol for chat, allowing one to converse with others connected to the Internet in real-time. While similar to AOL chat rooms, there are many differences—AOL's chat rooms are more intuitive and user-friendly, while IRC chats offer greater control over the environment. See also *Internet*; contrast *chat rooms*.

IP (Information Provider)—See *partner*.

ISDN—Abbreviation for Integrated Services Digital Networks. ISDN is a relatively new type of access offered by local telephone companies. You can use an ISDN to connect to other networks at speeds as high as 64,000 bps (single-channel). AOL is expected to support ISDN at some point in the future. See also *TCP/IP*; contrast *packet-switching network*.

Keep As New—An AOL e-mail system feature that allows you to keep mail in your New Mail box, even after you've read or ignored it. To use, simply select and highlight the piece of mail you wish to keep (in either your New Mail or Old Mail list [a.k.a. Mail You Have Read list]) and then click on the Keep As New button at the bottom of the window. Returning read mail to your New Mail box with the Keep As New button will not change the time and date that appears in the Status box of the sender. See also *e-mail*.

keyboard shortcuts—The AOL software provides us with keyboard command equivalents for menu selections. For example, rather than selecting Send Instant Message from the menu, you could type **Ctrl + I** on the PC (WAOL or GAOL), or **Command + I** on the Mac. For a complete list of these keyboard shortcuts, see the Keyboard Shortcuts Chart included as a supplement to the VirtuaLingo Glossary.

keyword—1. A fast way to move around within America Online. For example, you can "beam" directly to the Star Trek Forum by using the keyword: TREK. To use a keyword, type either **Command + K** on the Mac or **Ctrl+ K** on the PC, and then the keyword, followed by the Return or Enter key. Keywords are communicated to others in a standard format: Keyword: NAME. The name of the keyword is shown in all caps to distinguish it from other words around it, but it does not need to be entered that way. Currently, there are over 6000 public keywords. An updated list of all public keywords is available at keyword: KEYWORD. There is also a book listing all the keywords now in stores—it is titled *AOL Keywords* and was authored by yours truly (Jennifer Watson).

2. A single word you feel is likely to be included in any database on a particular subject. A key word is usually a word that comes as close as possible to describing the topic or piece of information you are looking for. Several of AOL's software libraries, mainly those in the Computers & Software channel, can be searched for with key words.

lamer—A colloquial term for someone who follows others blindly without really having a grasp on the situation. Used frequently within the hacker culture. See also *hacker*.

library—An area online in which files may be uploaded and downloaded. The files may be of any type: text, graphics, software, sounds, and so forth. These files can be downloaded from AOL's host computer to your personal computer's hard disk or floppy disk. Some libraries are searchable, while others must be browsed. You may also upload a file that may interest others to a library. A library is the best way to share large files with other AOL members. To search libraries available for your platform, go to keyword: FILESEARCH. See also *file, download, upload, search,* and *browse*; contrast *FTP*.

line noise—Extraneous noise on telephone lines that is often heard as clicks or static. While line noise is usually only a nuisance to voice communications, it means trouble for data being transmitted through modems. If you are having problems remaining connected, it may be the result of line noise. Signing off, redialing, and getting a new connection will often help this problem.

link—A pointer to another place that takes you there when you activate it (usually by clicking on it). AOL has literally millions of links that crisscross the service, but they can't compare to the links on the WWW (often called "hyperlinks"), which can cross continents without you knowing it. See also *address, browser, favorite place, hot list, page, site, URL,* and *WWW*.

listserv—An automated mailing list distribution system that allows a group of e-mail addresses to receive (and often send) e-mail to one another as a group. You can subscribe to a listserv mailing list as a member of AOL. More information and a database of available mailing lists are available at keyword: LISTSERV. See also *e-mail* and *mailing list*.

Lobby—Often seeming more like the Grand Central Station of AOL rather than a sedate hotel foyer, the Lobby is the default chat room of the People Connection. When you first enter the People Connection, you will most likely enter a Lobby where any other number of members are also gathered. Some prefer the bustling atmosphere of the Lobby, while others use it as a waystation for other rooms in the People Connection. There will usually be a Guide present in the main Lobby at all times. If the main Lobby is full (with a maximum of 23 members at any one time), additional Lobbies will be created, and suffixed with 1, 2, 3, and so on. To get to the Lobby, go to keyword: LOBBY. Stop by on a chilly night for a warm mug of cocoa, but beware of pie fights and desk burnings. See also *chat, chat rooms,* and *Guide.*

LOL—Shorthand for "Laughing Out Loud," often used in chat areas and Instant Messages. Another variation is ROFL, for "Rolling On Floor Laughing." See also *shorthands, abbreviations,* and *chat*; contrast with *body language* and *emoticons.*

lurk—To sit in a chat room or read a message board, yet contribute little or nothing at all. Hamsters are known lurkers. See also *chat* or *conference room.*

MAOL—The Apple Macintosh version of the AOL client software. The current version is 3.0. May also be referred to as Mac AOL. Contrast with GAOL and WAOL.

macro—A "recording" of keystrokes or mouse movements/clicks on a computer that allows you to automate a task. Macros are usually created with shareware and commercial software and can be initiated with a single key. They may contain something as simple as your signature for an e-mail note or a complex sequence that opens an application, converts the data, saves it in a special format, and shuts your computer down. Online, macros are most useful for sending large amounts of text to a chat area or for automating tasks such as archiving a message board or saving e-mail. Unfortunately, only Mac and Windows users can run macros; the GAOL environment doesn't allow macro use.

mail controls—A set of preferences that enable the master account holder to control who you receive mail from. It can be set for one or all screen names on the account. Changes can be made by the master account holder at any time. To access controls, go to keyword: MAIL CONTROLS. You can also block junk mail from your e-mailbox at keyword: PREFERRED MAIL. See also *e-mail*.

mailbomb—n. What you have when one person sends you an excessive amount of e-mail, usually done in retaliation for a perceived wrong. This is a serious offense, as it not only inconveniences you but occupies mail system resources. If you receive a mailbomb, you can report it at keyword: TOS. See also *e-mail, snert,* and *TOS*.

mailing list—A group of e-mail addresses that receive e-mail on a regular basis about a topic they have a mutual interest in. Mailing lists can be as simple as a few friends' addresses that you often e-mail, or as complex as a daily digest of news delivered to the e-mailboxes of millions of addresses. See also *address, e-mail,* and *listserv*.

massmail—v. The act of sending a piece of e-mail to a large number of members. Also used as a noun. See also *e-mail, carbon copy* and *blind carbon copy*.

megabyte—1,048,576 bytes of data.

member—An AOL subscriber. The term "member" is embraced because AOLers are members of the online community. There are currently over seven million members on AOL. See also *online community*.

Member Directory—The database of AOL member screen names that have profiles. To be included in this database, a member need only to create a Member Profile. Note that profiles for deleted members are purged periodically, therefore it's possible to have a Member Profile for a deleted screen name. You can search for any string in a profile. Wildcard characters and Boolean expressions also may be utilized in search strings. The Member Directory is located at keyword: MEMBERS. See also *member, Member Profile, database,* and *searchable*.

Member Profile—A voluntary online information document that describes oneself. Name, address information, birthday, sex, marital status, hobbies, computers used, occupation, and a personal quote may be provided. This is located at keyword: MEMBERS or PROFILE. See also *member* and *Member Directory.*

message—A note posted on a message board for other members to read. Message titles are limited to 30 characters. Message text sizes have practical limits on each of the platforms—note that GAOL users can only read 5095 bytes of text in a message (with any additional text scrolling off the top); MAOL and WAOL can read any message in its entirety. A maximum of 500 messages may be contained in a folder, with some containing considerably less. A message may also be referred to as a post. See also *message board.*

message board—An area where members can post messages to exchange information, ask a question, or reply to another message. All AOL members are welcome and encouraged to post messages in message boards (or boards). Because messages are a popular means of communication online, message boards are organized with folders, wherein a number of messages on a specific subject (threads) are contained in sequential order. A maximum of 50 folders may be created in one message board, with some boards having lower limits of 30 or 20 folders. While you can usually create a new folder for your topic, you should try to find an existing topic folder for your related message before creating a new one. There are two kinds of message boards in use on AOL right now: regular and response-threaded. Message boards may be grouped together in a Message Center to provide organization and hierarchy. Message boards are occasionally called bulletin boards. See also *cross-post, folder, message, Message Center, Spam,* and *thread.*

message board pointer—An automatic place-marker for message boards. AOL keeps track of the areas you have visited by date, allowing you to pick up where you left off upon your return. Once you've visited a message board, clicking on the Find New button will show you only the new messages that have been posted since your last visit. The pointers are updated each time you return. These pointers stay in effect for 60 days after your last visit.

Message Center—A collection of message boards in one convenient area. For example, the 12 message boards in BikeNet (keyword: BIKENET) are organized into one Message Center. See also *message board.*

MHM (Members Helping Members)—A message board in the free area where America Online members can assist and get assistance from other members. Located at keyword: MHM.

Microsoft Network—A relatively new online service that debuted the summer of 1995 and now has over 1,500,000 users. It is the third-largest network in the nation. Often abbreviated as MSN. See also *America Online, CompuServe, eWorld,* and *Prodigy.*

modem—An acronym for modulator/demodulator. This is the device that translates the signals coming from your computer into a form that can be transmitted over standard telephone lines. A modem also translates incoming signals into a form that your computer can understand. Two modems, one for each computer, are needed for any data communications over telephone lines. Your modem speaks to a modem at AOL through a network of telephone lines provided by AOLnet, SprintNet, or Tymnet, for example.

modem file—An information file that stores your modem settings for connecting to AOL. As modems differ, you often need to use a modem file configured specifically for your modem. Luckily, AOL offers over 100 standard modem files you can select from in the Setup window. If you cannot find a modem file for your modem, you can call AOL Customer Service, try the Modem Help area (keyword: MODEM HELP) or edit your modem file. See also *CCL.*

moderator—Typically a host who facilitates a discussion during a conference. The moderator usually manages protocol, if used. See also *host, conference room,* and *protocol.*

MorF—Acronym for Male or Female. To ask another member their sex. This happens frequently in Lobbies and chat rooms in the People Connection, but it is considered ill-mannered by most seasoned onliners. BorG (Boy or Girl?) is another manifestation of this virus that seems to infect some members. See also *Lobby, chat rooms,* and *People Connection.*

MSN—See *Microsoft Network.*

Net—Abbreviation for the Internet. See *Internet.*

Netiquette—Net manners. Cyberspace is a subculture with norms and rules of conduct all its own—understanding of these will often make your online life more enjoyable and allow you to move through more smoothly. Online etiquette includes such things as proper capitalization (don't use all caps unless you mean to shout). Basically, the most important rule to keep in mind is one we learned offline and in kindergarten of all places: Do unto others as you'd have them do unto you (a.k.a. The Golden Rule). See keyword: SHORTHANDS for a primer in AOL etiquette.

network—A data communications system that interconnects computer systems at various different sites. AOL could be considered a network.

Network News—AOL maintenance broadcasts and feedback that are displayed in a small window when transmitted. Network News can be enabled or disabled with the AOL software (select Preferences under the Members menu).

newbie—Affectionate term for a new member (under six months). The New Member Lounge in the People Connection is a popular haunt for the newly initiated. Good places for the new member to visit are keywords: DISCOVER AOL, TOP TIPS, KEYWORDS, and TOUR. Contrast *wannabe.*

newsgroups—Internet's version of a public message board. Available on AOL at keyword: NEWSGROUPS. See also *FileGrabber, header,* and *Internet;* contrast *FTP, Gopher, WAIS,* and *WWW.*

node—A single computer or device accessible via a phone number and used by one or more persons to connect to a telecommunications network, such as AOL. Everyone signs on to AOL via a node, which is usually local to them and doesn't involve long-distance charges. Sometimes a bad connection is the result of a busy node, and can be corrected by trying a new node. See also *packet-switching network, 800 number, access number, AOLnet, SprintNet,* and *Tymnet.*

offline—The condition of a computer that is unconnected.

online—The condition of a computer when it is connected to another machine via modem.

online community—A group of people bound together by their shared interest or characteristic of interacting with other computer users through online services, BBSes, or networks. Because of the pioneer aspects of an online community, established onliners will welcome newcomers and educate them freely, in most cases. On AOL, elaborate conventions, legends, and etiquette systems have developed within the community. See also *cyberspace*.

OnlineHost—The screen name of AOL's host computer used to send information and usually seen in chat rooms, conference rooms, and auditoriums. The OnlineHost screen name may signal when a member enters or leaves the room. On all platforms, the OnlineHost screen name will give you the result of dice rolled. See also *chat rooms, conference room, auditorium,* and *//roll*.

Open-Apple key—See *Command key*.

OS (operating system)—The software that is used to control the basic functions of a computer. Operating systems are generally responsible for allocation and control of a computer's resources. Some common operating systems are: System 7, MS-DOS, UNIX, and OS/2. See also *DOS*, *system*, *UNIX*, and *Windows*.

Option key—A special function key commonly found on Mac keyboards. Usually located on the bottom row of keys and labelled Option. Holding down the Option key while another key is pressed will often activate a special function.

OS/2—IBM's 32-bit operating system that offers a Macintosh-like interface for IBM PC and compatible machines. The current release of OS/2 is called OS/2 Warp and runs Windows 3.1, DOS, and OS/2 specific applications. See also *OS, DOS,* and *Windows*.

P*—Shorthand for Prodigy Service. See also *Prodigy*.

packet-switching network (PSN)—An electronic network that enables you to access a remote online service by dialing a local phone number. Information going to and from your computer is segmented into "packets" and given an address. The packets are then sent through the network to their destination much as a letter travels through the postal system, only much faster. AOL uses a variety of PSNs to supply local nodes (local telephone numbers) for members' access. Also see *access number, node, AOLnet, SprintNet,* and *Tymnet*; contrast *ISDN*.

page—A document on the World Wide Web, presented in the browser window. WWW pages can contain any combination of links, text, graphics, sounds, or videos. A set of pages is often referred to as a site. See also *browser, favorite place, home page, hot list, link, site, URL,* and *WWW.*

palmtop—See *PDA*.

parental chat controls—Parental Control enables the master account holder to restrict access to certain areas and features on AOL (such as blocking IMs and rooms). It can be set for one or all screen names on the account; once Parental Control is set for a particular screen name, it is active each time that screen name signs on. Changes can be made by the master account holder at any time. To access controls, go to keyword: PARENTAL CONTROL. Contrast *$im_off/$im_on* and *Ignore.*

parity—A method of error correction at the character level that is used in sending information via modems. Error correction occurs less frequently now—every 1,024 characters isn't rare—so parity is almost a thing of the past.

partner—A person or party supplying material for use on AOL's services and/or responsible for the content of an area on America Online's services. Also known as an information provider or IP. See also *corporate staff* and *community leader.*

password—Your secret four-to-eight character code word that you use to secure your account. Because password security is so important, we've included a number of password-creation tips and reminders below. Please read these and pass these along to your friends (and enemies). See also *phish*.

- Your password should be as long as possible (use all eight characters, if you can).
- Your password should not include any word found in your profile, any of your names (or your spouse's/kid's names), or anything commonly found in a dictionary.
- Your password should be a combination of letters and numbers.
- Try using the first letter of each word in an eight-word sentence.
- Or, use a word that is easy to remember and insert numbers into it such as SU8M3ER. (Important: Do *not* use any passwords you have ever seen used as examples.)
- Change your password often (use keyword: PASSWORD).

password scammer—See *phish*.

PC/GEOS—See *GAOL*.

PC-Link—A discontinued service for PC users that utilized a Deskmate-style interface with special support areas provided by the Tandy Corporation. PC-Link was phased out in late 1994. Abbreviated PCL. See also *AOL* and *Q-Link*.

PDA—Short for Personal Digital Assistant. A hand-held computer that performs a variety of tasks, including personal information management. PDAs are gaining in popularity and variety, although AOL is only officially supported on the Zoomer (Casio Z7000/Tandy Z-PDA/AST Gridpad 2390), the Sharp PT9000, the Sony Magic Link, and the Motorola Envoy. The Zoomer, Magic Link, and Envoy versions of AOL only allow you to access a limited number of features. PT9000 allows almost complete access, and it can be run on the Zoomer. For those with an HP100LX, HP200LX, or other DOS-based palmtop with CGA capability, a work-around with GAOL 1.6 is possible. Wider PDA access to AOL is expected in the future, including the Apple Newton. If you can't wait for regular AOL access on the Newton, a shareware program called Aloha allows you to access your AOL e-mail. For more information, check out the PDA Forum at keyword: PDA. PDAs may also be referred to as palmtops.

People Connection (PC)—The AOL channel dedicated to real-time chat. Many different rooms can be found here: Lobbies, officially-sanctioned rooms, member-created rooms, private rooms, the AOL Live area, and PC Plaza. You can access this area with keyword: PEOPLE. Feel free to surf PC, but please obey hamster crossing signs. See also *channel* and *chat rooms*; contrast *conference room*.

Personal Filing Cabinet—On MAOL 3.0 or WAOL 2.5 and higher, this is a special feature of the AOL software that organizes your mail, files, newsgroups postings, and favorite places. Note that everything in your Personal Filing Cabinet is stored on your hard disk. You can set your Filing Cabinet preferences by opening Preferences from the Members menu and selecting Personal Filing Cabinet. This feature is not currently available for those on MAOL 2.7 and lower or GAOL. See also *e-mail, favorite place, file,* and *newsgroups*.

phish—v. The act of tricking members into revealing their passwords, credit card numbers, or other personal information. Phishers will often disguise themselves as AOL staff, but remember that AOL staff will *never ever* ask you for your password or credit card information while you are online. They may also ask you to send certain files to them, or do something that seems odd to you. Phishers should always be reported to AOL so they don't continue to prey on other, less-knowledgeable members. If you get an IM from them, save the IM and then report them at keyword: GUIDEPAGER immediately. See also *hacker* and *password*

PKZip—A compression utility for PCs to compress one file, or multiple files, into a smaller file (called an archive), which will make for shorter up/downloading. The latest version is 2.04g. WAOL 2.5 and MAOL 2.6 (and higher) can automatically decompress 2.04 ZIP archives. See *also archive, download, file, file compression, ARC,* and *StuffIt*.

phisher—One who phishes. See also *cracker, hacker,* and *snert*.

polling—v. The act of requesting information from everyone in a chat room. For example, a member may write "Everyone here who is cool press 1," and the chat room will scroll with 1's for several minutes. This is considered disruptive and shouldn't be done in a public room. See also *chat rooms*.

post— 1. v. The act of putting something online, usually into a message board or newsgroup.
2. n. A message in a message board or newsgroup. See also *message board* and *message*; contrast *upload*.

postmaster—The person responsible for taking care of e-mail problems, answering queries about users, and other e-mail related work at a site. AOL's postmaster can be reached at, you guessed it, screen name "Postmaster." You can also reach other postmasters by simply adding the @ symbol and the domain name you wish to reach, such as postmaster@gnn.com. See also *domain* and *e-mail*.

private—adj. The state of being in a private room. It is considered taboo by some members to be "seen" in a private room because this is often the communication channel of choice for "hot chatters." In reality, however, private rooms are a convenient way to meet with someone when IMs would get in the way. If you are private and another member does a search for your screen name, they will be told that <screen name> is online, but in a private room. See also *private room* and *hot chat*; contrast *chat rooms* and *conference room*.

private room—A chat room that is created by a member via an option in People Connection where the name is not public knowledge. Private room names have the same restrictions as chat room names: they may only contain up to 20 characters, must begin with a letter, and cannot contain punctuation. Some commonly named private rooms are rumored to be open 24 hours a day; AOLoholics have been known to make a hobby out of finding these hidden rooms. If you happen to stumble into a private room already occupied by other members, proper etiquette calls for you to stay silent for a few minutes to catch any interesting tidbits, and then disappear as silently as you entered. (In fact, etiquette also calls for you to sign off immediately to avoid irate "hot chatters.") See also *chat rooms* and *hot chat*; contrast *conference room* and *auditorium*.

Prodigy—An information service founded as a joint venture between IBM and Sears. In the past it was one of the larger competitors that AOL faced, but it has been steadily losing ground over the years. For those members who defected from Prodigy to AOL, there is a Virtual Refugees Forum online (keyword: PRODIGY). See also *P**; contrast *America Online, CompuServe, eWorld,* and *Microsoft Network.*

profile—AOL allows each screen name to have an informational file (a profile) attached to it. A profile tells a bit about who you are, where you live, what your interests are—anything you want others to know about you. A profile can be created or updated at keyword: PROFILE. You can only modify the profile of the screen name you are currently signed on under, and each screen name has a unique profile. To read another member's profile, press Ctrl+ G (Command + G on the Mac), enter their screen name and hit Enter. Not all members have profiles. You may search profiles through the Member Directory. A little-known AOL fact is that a Member Directory search reveals that over 250 hamsters are lurking among profiles. See also *member, Member Directory,* and *screen name.*

protocol—A system used in conference rooms to keep order and facilitate a discussion. When you have a question, you type **?**, when you have a comment, you type **!** and when you are finished, you type **/ga**. A queue of those waiting with questions and answers is displayed at regular points throughout the conference, and members will be invited to speak by the moderator or host. It is considered impolite and a breach of protocol to speak out of turn. See also *conference room, host,* and *moderator.*

public domain—A file that's completely free, uncopyrighted, and typically posted on services like AOL for distribution (via downloading) directly to the user. Since the producer (or programmer) usually posts this and the user downloads it, distribution is direct and nearly without cost. Users are generally encouraged to make copies and give them to friends—even post them on other services. Often little, or no, documentation is available for it, though. Contrast *freeware* and *shareware.*

punt—The act of being disconnected from AOL, often as a result of difficulties at AOL or interference on your node (such as line noise). Used as a noun or verb. See also *bounce, node,* and *line noise.*

punt pillows—Virtual pillows given, via chat or IMs, to cushion the posterior of a member who was punted. Often depicted as () () () () or [] [] [] [] (the harder, concrete variety). See also *chat, IM,* and *punt.*

'puter—An affectionate abbreviation for one's computer; often employed by enthusiasts and AOLoholics.

Q-Link—A discontinued service for Commodore 64 and 128 users. See also *America Online* and *PC-Link.*

quoting—To include parts of an original message in a reply. One or two greater-than characters (>) is the standard method for setting off a quote from the rest of the message. They are usually placed to the left of the sentence, followed by a space, but may also be placed on the right as well. For example:

```
> Wow! That s great! How did you come by it?  (Internet-style)
>> Wow! That s great! How did you come by it?
>> Wow! That s great! How did you come by it? <<
<< Wow! That s great! How did you come by it? >>
```

MAOL 3.0 and WAOL 2.5 and higher members can quote text automatically in e-mail by first selecting it, then copying it (Ctrl + C on the PC, or Command + C on the Mac), and then clicking on Reply. See also >> *and* <<.

Re:—Short for regarding or reply. See also *e-mail* and *message.*

release—v. To make something available to the general public, such as a file in a file library. See also *file* and *library.*

remote staff—See *community leader.*

return receipt—A feature available with the MAOL software that returns a piece of e-mail acknowledging that mail you sent to another AOL member (or members) has been received. To enable this function, you must check the Return Receipt box on the e-mail window before it is sent. Once the e-mail has been read by the member(s) it was addressed to (including those carbon copied and blind carbon copied), mail with the date and time it was read will be automatically generated and returned to the sender immediately. One note is sent for each member that reads the mail. If you check return receipt on a letter that is carbon copied to 100 people, 100 notes will trickle in as each addressee reads the mail. In general, return receipts are unnecessary as the Status feature can be used to determine when any piece of mail was read. Return receipts are most useful when you need to be immediately informed that the mail was read, usually so you can contact that person as soon as possible. Return receipts should be used sparingly as they can clutter up your mailbox. See also *e-mail, carbon copy, blind carbon copy,* and *Status.*

revolving door—A chat or conference room has a revolving door when members are quickly moving in and out of the room. Lobbies and many popular chat rooms in the People Connection will often have revolving doors. See also *chat rooms, conference room,* and *Lobby.*

Road Trip—An AOL feature, available for MAOL 3.0 or WAOL 2.5 (or higher) members, which allows you to create tours of the WWW and AOL, and then present these to others. For more information, see keyword: ROAD TRIP. See also *WWW.*

Rotunda—An auditorium that features conferences with companies or areas in the Computers & Software channel. Accessible via keyword: ROTUNDA. See also *auditorium.*

savvy—To be knowledgeable or perceptive at something. Often seen as computer-savvy or online-savvy. Contrast *newbie* and *wannabe.*

screen name—The names, pseudonyms more often than not, that identify AOL members online. Screen names may contain no fewer than three and no more than 10 characters, must be unique, and cannot contain vulgarity or vulgar references. Also, some combinations of letters are reserved for community leaders (such as Guide or Host). Screen names may not start with a number. Any one account may have up to five screen names, to accommodate family members or alter egos, and each can have its own unique password. Either way, you cannot delete the original screen name you set up the account with, and the person that establishes the original screen name and account is responsible for all charges incurred by all five screen names. To add or delete your screen name, go to keyword: NAMES. Note that when you add a new screen name, it will be automatically blocked from entering Member Rooms in the People Connection. To disable this block, you will need to switch to the master screen name and use the Parental Control (keyword: PARENTAL CONTROL). See also *address, e-mail address, member*, and *uniform.*

scroll—1. Refers to the movement of incoming text and other information on your computer screen. See *scroll bar.*
2. The act of repeatedly typing similar words on screen, or spacing out the letters of a word. For example, if a member typed the word "hello" seven times in a row, with returns between each, this would be scrolling. So would be hitting Return after each letter of a word. Polling also causes scrolling. Scrolling is prohibited in AOL's Terms of Service, and you may be given a warning for this if observed by a Guide or Host. Go to keyword: TOS for more information. See also *polling.*

scroll bar—The bar on the right hand side of a window that allows you to move the contents up and down, or on the bottom of a window for moving things to the left or right. The area on the scroll bar between the up and down arrows is shaded if there is more information than fits in the window, or white if the entire content of the window is already visible. See also *scroll (1).*

search—Typically used in association with libraries and other searchable databases, the term "search" refers to a specific exploration of files or entries themselves, rather than a causal examination done line by line. See also *searchable, database, file*, and *library*; contrast *browse.*

searchable—A collection of logically related records or database files that serve as a single central reference; a searchable database accepts input and yields all matching entries containing that character string. The Members Directory is an example of a searchable database. See also *search, database, Directory of Services*, and *Members Directory.*

self-extracting archive—A compressed file that contains instructions to automatically decompress itself when opened; the software that decompressed it originally is not needed. On the Mac, these files can be decompressed simply by double-clicking on the icon. Self-extracting archive files are usually identifiable by the .SEA extension. On the PC, these are often identified by an .EXE extension. See also *file compression* and *StuffIt.*

server—A provider of resources, such as a file server. AOL uses many different kinds of servers, as do several of their partners, such as Gemstone III.

shareware—A fully functional file that is distributed with the promise of try before you buy. Made available with the downloader's good conscience in mind, the authors of shareware ask that if you continue to use their product, you pay the fee requested in their documentation. Shareware is often made available in libraries of online services like AOL for downloading or is distributed via CD-ROM collections. There are shareware programs of exceptional quality and many are often comparable to commercially distributed software. There are a great number of variations of the shareware theme such as demoware, which is often fully functional except for printing or saving functions or is only functional for a short period of time; postcardware, which requests a postcard sent to the author; contributionware, and so on. See also *file*; contrast *demoware, freeware*, and *public domain*.

shorthands—The collective term for the many emoticons and abbreviations used during chat. These devices were developed by members over time to give information on the writer's emotional state when ASCII text only is available. A brief list of these is available at keyword: SHORTHANDS. See also *emoticons, abbreviations*, and *chat*; contrast with *body language*.

sig—Short for signature. A block of text that some folks include at the end of their newsgroup postings and/or e-mail. You can designate a sig for your own newsgroup postings through your newsgroup preferences. See also *newsgroups* and *post*.

sign-on kit—The free software, registration codes, and directions for creating a new AOL account. There are a number of ways to obtain sign-on kits. Online, go to keyword: FRIEND and follow the directions there to have kit sent via snail mail. Offline, you can always find a free offer card in a magazine, particularly those magazines that have online forums like *MacUser* magazine. You may also find the sign-on kits themselves bundled with commercial software, modems, and computers. Sign-on kits can also be ordered via phone (1-800-827-6364, ext. 7776). Of course, you can always purchase *The Official America Online Membership Kit & Tour Guide* from your local bookstore; a sign-on kit is included in the back of the book. If you simply need new AOL software but not an entirely new account, you can download the latest software for your platform at keyword: UPGRADE or use the AOL Support BBS (see the *access number* entry for information regarding the AOL Support BBS). If you need to download MAOL 2.7, use keyword: GET 27.

sim—Short for simulation. A sim is a free-form game where participants role play in various scenarios. Sims are generally held in a chat or conference room, and may have rules associated with them. Check out the Simming Forum at keyword: SIM. See also *//roll, chat rooms,* and *conference room.*

simulchat—A chat held simultaneously with a radio call-in broadcast. Online chat participants listen to the broadcast and discuss the same topics being discussed on the air. The radio broadcast takes questions and comments from the online chat as well as from callers. Simulchats are organized through the Digital City Chicago Online (keyword: CHICAGO), and Craig Crossman's Computer America (keyword: CROSSMAN). See also *chat.*

site—A specific place on the Internet, usually a set of pages on the World Wide Web. See also *address, link, page, URL,* and *WWW.*

Smart Art—A capability of the AOL 3.0 software that downloads system art to your computer progressively as you watch. You can stop the art download at any time by clicking a button or closing the window. Smart Art is a significant advantage over the old DOD style of art download, which forced you to wait for new artwork when you opened a window that required it. Contrast *download, DOD,* and *UDO.*

smileys—See *shorthands* and *emoticons.*

snail mail—Mail that is sent via the U.S. Postal Service. Not meant as derogatory, but to point out the difference between nearly instantaneous e-mail versus the delivery of tangible packages. Despite its relative slowness, snail mail will be used until matter transfer becomes possible. See also *e-mail.*

snert—Acronym for Sexually Nerdishly Expressive Recidivistic Trolls. A member who is disruptive or annoying. Contrast *cracker, hacker, phisher,* and *troll.*

software file—A file available in an AOL software library. Often, a software file online is actually multiple files (a program, its documentation, etc.) that are compressed together for shorter uploading or downloading. Every file posted online for download must meet AOL's Terms of Service standards and be checked for functionality and viruses. See also *archive, file, file compression, library, TOS, virus, ARC, PKZip*, and *StuffIt*.

sounds—See *chat sounds*.

Spam—1. n. A luncheon meat produced by the Hormel Foods Corporation. Spam is frequently the butt of many online jokes originally due to Monty Python's use of Spam as the topic of some of their skits. Lately, Spam jokes have taken on a life of their own online and you may see many references to it. There is even a newsgroup dedicated to Spam, as well as at least one WWW site. Fortunately, hamsters consider Spam a delicacy.
2. v. To barrage a message board, newsgroup, or e-mail address with inappropriate, irrelevant, or simply numerous copies of the same post (as in cross-posting). Not only is this annoying, but it is exceedingly bad Netiquette. Members who spam will often have their posts removed (if in an AOL message board) or find their mailbox full of e-mail from angry onliners (if in a newsgroup). See also *cross-post, e-mail address, message board*, and *newsgroups*; contrast with *flame*.

SprintNet—Formerly known as Telenet, SprintNet is a packet-switching network that provides members with 1200, 2400, 9600, 14,400 and 28,800 bps local access numbers to America Online. SprintNet networks are owned and operated by US Sprint. To find SprintNet local access numbers, go to keyword: ACCESS or call 1-800-877-5045, ext. 5. See also *packet-switching network* and *access number*; contrast with *AOLnet* and *Tymnet*.

Status (of e-mail)—An AOL feature that allows you to check whether e-mail has been read yet and, if read, when. The status for an e-mail message will be either (not yet read), (ignored), (deleted) or will show the precise date and time when the mail was read. Status information includes recipients who were carbon copied (and even those who were blind carbon copied, if you were the sender). To check the current status of e-mail on the Mac platform, select and highlight the piece of mail you are interested in (either in the New Mail, Mail You Have Read, or Mail you have sent window) and then click on the Status button at the bottom of the window. On the PC platform, first choose the Check Mail You've Sent option from the Mail menu, select and highlight the piece of mail, and then click on the Show Status button on the bottom of the window. See also *e-mail, carbon copy, blind carbon copy,* and *return receipt.*

Stratus—AOL's host computer is known as the Stratus and is actually a collection of computers manufactured by outside companies, including the Stratus Corporation. These days AOL utilizes other types of computers for specific purposes, but Stratus continues to indicate the collective group of computing power. The Stratus features a fault-tolerant system. This is achieved through redundant multiple processors, disks and memory banks. The Stratus runs 365 days a year, 24 hours a day, and it's backed up by a standby diesel generator in case the power fails. See also *host (1)* and *hamster.*

StuffIt—A popular compression program for the Apple Macintosh currently published by Aladdin Software and written by Raymond Lau. StuffIt is the standard method of compressing Mac files for uploading to AOL's file libraries. With StuffIt, it's possible to combine several files into one archive which is a convenient way of transferring several files at once. StuffIt files, also called archives, are often recognizable by the .SIT extension to the file name. A file that has been compressed with StuffIt is said to be stuffed. Files compressed with StuffIt can be automatically unstuffed when downloaded from Mac AOL or when opened using the Mac AOL software. StuffIt is currently distributed both as a shareware product, StuffIt Lite, and a commercial product, StuffIt Deluxe. Programs to extract stuffed files are free and exist both for the IBM and Mac. See also *archive, file compression, self-extracting archive, download,* and *shareware*; contrast *ARC* and *PKZip.*

surf—To cruise in search of information not readily evident in the hope of discovering something new. Usually paired with another word to describe the type of information being sought. Examples are room surfing and keyword surfing. The joy of surfing is only interrupted by the occasional bump when you forget to stop at the hamster crossing signs distributed randomly around AOL. See also *password scammer.*

synchronous—Data communication technique in which bits are transmitted and received at a fixed rate. Used to transmit large blocks of data over special communications lines. Much more complex than asynchronous communication, this technique has little application for most personal computer users. See also *asynchronous*.

sysop—Abbreviation for system operator. The individual who operates and maintains a computer service—usually including a message board, a library or collection of libraries, and a chat room. Forum leaders are sometimes referred to as sysops, although that term isn't favored by many on AOL. Pronounced "sis-op." See also *forum, host,* and *uniform*.

system—Short for operating system, this refers to the software that controls the basic operations of a computer. System can also refer to the collection of components that have a functional existence when combined. Some examples of this include your computer system, the telephone system, or the AOL system. See also *OS, OS/2,* and *Windows*.

TCP/IP—Acronym for Transmission Control Protocol/Internet Protocol. The protocol language that Internet machines use to communicate. WAOL 2.5 and MAOL 2.6 and higher allow you to sign on via TCP/IP, and you can use other TCP/IP-capable applications through MAOL 3.0 at the same time. See also *Internet*.

Tech Help Live—Previously known as CS Live, this is a free area where you can ask questions of AOL staff live. The Tech Help Live is open from 7 AM to 2:45 AM eastern time, seven days a week. Here you can get live help from experienced Customer Relations staff working in-house at AOL headquarters or remotely. This service is available in the Unlimited Use (free) area through keyword: TECH LIVE. See also *Customer Relations*.

Telnet—An Internet protocol that lets you connect to another computer without hanging up your modem and dialing again, using the connection you've already established with your local provider. Bulletin boards, online stores, and multiuser games are just some of the things you can tap into using Telnet. Telnet is available on AOL at keyword: TELNET. See also *Internet*.

thread—In general terms, a discussion that travels along the same subject line. More specifically, a thread refers a group of posts in a message board under the same subject and (hopefully) topic. See also *message board*.

thwapp—v. To hit someone upside their screen name; a virtual slap. For example you may be ::thwapped:: for requesting an age/sex check in a chat room.

timeout—1. What happens when you've got two computers connected online and one gets tired of waiting for the other (i.e., when the hourglass [PC] or beachball [Mac] cursor comes up and the host fails to respond). You can report problems with frequent timeouts at keyword: SYSTEM RESPONSE.
2. The result of remaining idle for a certain amount of time while signed on to AOL. This timeout time is usually 30 minutes, but may vary with different modems. In this case, AOL's computers are tired of waiting for you. It's also protection against staying signed on all night when an AOLoholic falls asleep at the keyboard.

title bar—The portion of a window where the name of the window is displayed. On the Mac the title bar also may include the close box and the zoom box. See also *close box, window*, and *zoom box*.

toast—Something totally ruined or unuseable. For example, "Well, that file is toast." Also used as a verb.

TOS—Short for America Online's Terms of Service—the terms of agreement everyone agrees to when registering for and becoming a member of America Online. These terms apply to all accounts on the service(s). You can read these terms at keyword: TOS (in the free area), or by going to keyword: PC STUDIO and clicking on Terms of Service. Also included are avenues of reporting TOS violations to AOL. See *TOSAdvisor* and *TOS warning*.

TOSAdvisor—In days of olde, this was the screen name to which all TOS violations observed by members were sent to. These days, if you feel something violates TOS, you should go to keyword: TOS to report it. The Terms of Service Staff area can also be reached at keyword: PC

STUDIO | Terms of Service/Parental Controls | Write to Terms of Service Staff. Note that there is no longer a screen name TOSAdvisor. See *TOS* and *TOS warning.*

TOSsable—The state of being likely to receive a TOS warning. For example, a TOSsable word is one which a TOS warning could be given to if typed online. See *TOS* and *TOS warning*.

TOS warning—An onscreen warning given by a trained Guide or Host for violating AOL's Terms of Service. These warnings are reported to AOL, who takes action (or not, depending on the severity of the breach). See *TOS*.

Tour Guide—Short for *The Official America Online Membership Kit & Tour Guide* by Tom Lichty (which a version of this glossary appears in). A wonderful, light-hearted introduction to AOL for the uninitiated. It has been known to teach AOL veterans a thing or two <ahem>. Includes a membership kit at the back of the book. A version without the sign-on kit or free hours can be ordered online at keyword: TOUR GUIDE.

trojan horse—A destructive program that is disguised within a seemingly useful program. For example, a recent trojan horse was a file called AOLGOLD, which claimed to be a new version of AOL but actually corrupted files if it was executed. A trojan horse is only activated by running the program. If you receive a file attached to e-mail from a sender that you are not familiar with, you are advised not to download it. If you ever receive a file you believe could cause problems, forward it to screen name TOSEmail1 and explain your concerns. Contrast *virus*.

troll—An online wanderer who often leaves a wake of disgruntled members before crawling back under his or her rock. It is unclear why trolls find AOL a popular watering hole, but it could be because they consider hamsters a delicacy. Contrast *cracker, hacker, password scammer*, and *snert*.

Tymnet—A packet-switching network that provides members with 1200 and 2400 bps local access numbers to America Online. Tymnet networks are owned and operated by BT Tymnet. To find Tymnet local access numbers, go to keyword: ACCESS or call 1-800-336-0149. See also *packet-switching network* and *access number*; contrast with *AOLnet* and *SprintNet*.

typo—1. A typographical error.
2. A dialect that many onliners have mastered with the advent of keyboards and late nights.

UDO—An older method of receiving updates to the AOL software. Upon signing-on to AOL, the UDO sends all the necessary updates to your computer before you can do anything else. Rumor has it UDO stands for Unavoidable Delay Obstacle, but we haven't been able to verify it. Contrast *DOD* and *Smart Art*.

uniform—The screen name that's often worn by a staff member, either in-house or remote (community leader), when working online. The screen name usually consists of an identifiable prefix and a personal name or initials. Uniforms aren't usually worn when the member is off duty. See also *Guide*, *host*, and *screen name*. Some current uniforms include:

AFL	Apple/Mac Forum Leader
AFA	Apple/Mac Forum Assistant
AFC	Apple/Mac Forum Consultant
AOLive	AOL Live leader
CJ	CyberJockey
CNR	CNN News Room leader
CSS	Company Support leader
FCA/FCC	Family Computing leader
Guide	General system guide
GWRep	GeoWorks Representative
GWS	GameWiz Staff
HOST	People Connection host
IC	Computing Company Connection
MCC	Manufacturers Corner staff (Consumer Electronics)
NPR	National Public Radio Outreach leader
NWN	Neverwinter Night leader

OnQ	onQ Forum leader
PC	PC Forum Leader
PCA	PC Forum Assistant
PCC	PC Forum Consultant
PCW	PC World Online
REF	Reference Desk host
QRJ	RabbitJack's Casino leader
AOLTech	Tech Live representative (in-house)
TLA	Tech Live Advisor (community leader)
VGS	Video Game Systems leader

UNIX—An easy-to-use operating system developed by Ken Thompson, Dennis Ritchie, and coworkers at Bell Laboratories. Since it also has superior capabilities as a program development system, UNIX should become even more widely used in the future. AOL does not currently have software for the UNIX platform. See also *OS*; contrast *DOS*, *Windows*, and *system*.

Unsend—An AOL e-mail system feature that allows you to retrieve mail that has been sent but not yet read. To use, simply select and highlight the piece of mail you wish to unsend from the Check Mail You've Sent window and click on the Unsend button at the bottom of the window. The mail will be permanently deleted and cannot be retrieved. Note that only mail sent to other AOL members can be unsent or retrieved; Internet e-mail cannot be retrieved. See also *e-mail*.

upload—1. v. The transfer of information from a storage device on your computer to a remote computer, such as AOL's host computer. This information may be uploaded to one of AOL's file libraries or it may be uploaded with a piece of e-mail as an attached file. Generally, any file over 16k (with the exception of text files) should be compressed before uploading to make the transfer faster and save money. Approved compression formats are ZIP, ARC, SIT, and SEAs. Important note: When uploading to AOL file libraries, be sure that the library you wish to upload to is the last one that you've opened after clicking on the Upload button; there is a bug that sends your file to the last opened library, regardless of whether it was the one you initially clicked on the Upload button in or not. See also *file, file compression,* and *library*; contrast with *download*.
2. n. The file or information that is sent or uploaded.

urban legend—A story, which may have once started with a kernel of truth, that has become embroidered and retold until it has passed into the realm of myth. It is an interesting phenomenon that has spread to the Internet and AOL. You may come across several urban legends, such as the $250 Neiman-Marcus Cookie Recipe or the Get Well Cards for the Sick Kid. But never mistake hamsters for legends—we've really seen 'em. Use keyword: URBAN LEGENDS for more fun.

URL—An address for an Internet resource, such as a World Wide Web page or an FTP site. URL stands for Uniform Resource Locator. You can use a URL address to go to a WWW site by entering it directly into the WWW browser, or by typing it into the AOL keyword box (on WAOL 2.5 and MAOL 2.6 or higher). There is no list of URL addresses as they are constantly changing and growing. AOL's home page URL is http://www.blue.aol.com. See also *address, browser, favorite place, hot list, page, site,* and *WWW.*

Usenet—See *newsgroup.*

virus—Computer software that has the ability to attach itself to other software or files, does so without the permission or knowledge of the user, and is generally designed with one intent—to propagate itself. It *may* also be intentionally destructive, however not all virus damage is intentional. Some benign viruses suffer from having been poorly written and have been known to cause damage as well. Virus prevention software and information may be found at keyword: VIRUS. Contrast *trojan horse.*

WAIS—(Wide Area Information Server) A database that allows you to search through huge amounts of information on the Internet, similar in some respects to a Gopher. WAIS databases are now widespread through the Internet. See also *Gopher* and *Internet*; contrast *FTP, newsgroups,* and *WWW.*

wannabe—Someone who aspires to something. Wannabes are often spotted by their obvious enthusiasm, or their frustration at not being able to acquire a skill. Most wannabes are self-proclaimed, and are considered a stage above newbies. For example, "He's a Guide wannabe." See keyword: WANNABE. Contrast *newbie.*

WAOL—The PC platform's Windows version of the AOL client software. The current version is 3.0. (You can look up your revision number by selecting About America Online from the Help menu and then pressing Ctrl + R). Contrast with *MAOL* and *GAOL*.

Web— See *WWW*.

weeding—(Yes, that's weeding as in a garden of bliss.) An online wedding. Often held in the People Connection chat rooms like Romance Connection or in the LaPub. Nuptial announcements and well-wishes can often be found in The Que message board at keyword: QUE.

window—A portion of the computer screen in which related information is contained, usually with a graphical border to distinguish it from the rest of the screen. Especially important in graphic user interfaces, windows may generally be moved, resized, closed, or brought to the foreground or sent to the background. Some common AOL windows include the chat room window, e-mail windows, and IM windows.

Windows—A graphical extension to the DOS operating system used on IBM PCs and compatibles. Developed by Microsoft, the Windows environment offers drop-down menus, multitasking, and mouse-oriented operation. See also *DOS*, *system*, and *UNIX*.

WWW (Web)—Abbreviation for World Wide Web. One of the more popular aspects of the Internet, this is actually an overarching term for the many hypertext documents that are linked together via a special protocol called HyperText Transfer Protocol (or HTTP). WWW information is accessed through a WWW browser, which is available with WAOL 2.5 or MAOL 2.6 (or higher). You use URL addresses to get to various WWW sites, or pages, much like you use keywords on AOL. See also *browser*, *favorite place*, *home page*, *hot list*, *Internet*, *page*, *site*, and *URL*.

ZIP—See *PKZip*.

zoom box—The zoom box is the small box in the upper-right corner of the window. Clicking on the zoom box will cause a reduced window to zoom up to fill the entire screen; clicking on the zoom box of a maximized window will cause it to zoom down to its reduced size. Compare with *close box*.

Index

B

C

E

F

G

H

J

K

L

M

Q

R

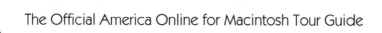

T

U

V

W

X

Y

Z

VENTANA

News Junkies Internet 500

$24.99, 464 pages, illustrated, part #: 461-8

Quench your thirst for news with this comprehensive listing of the best and most useful news sites and sources on the Web. Includes business, international, sports, weather, law, finance, entertainment, politics and more. Plus rated reviews of site strengths, weaknesses, design and navigational properties.

News Junkies
Internet 500
The Top 500 Essential Sites for News
For Mac & Windows
VENTANA

WITH CD-ROM
Internet
Business 500
The Top 500 Essential Sites for Business
For Mac & Windows
Fully hyperlinked text on CD-ROM
VENTANA

Internet Business 500

$29.95, 488 pages, illustrated, part #: 287-9

This authoritative list of the most useful, most valuable online resources for business is also the most current list, regularly updated on the Internet. The companion CD-ROM features a hypertext version of the entire book, linked to updates on Ventana Online.

WITH CD-ROM
Walking the
World Wide Web
Your Personal Guide to the Best of the Web
For Mac & Windows
PLUS! NETSCAPE NAVIGATOR™
Shannon R Turlington
VENTANA

Walking the World Wide Web, Second Edition

$39.95, 800 pages, illustrated, part #: 298-4

Updated and expanded, this bestseller now features 500 listings and an extensive index of servers, arranged by subject. This groundbreaking title includes a CD-ROM enhanced with Ventana's exclusive WebWalker technology; Netscape Navigator; and a hypertext version of the book. Updated online components make it the richest resource available for web travelers.

VENTANA

WITH CD-ROM
3D Studio MAX
Creating Hollywood-Style Special Effects
f/x
Jon A. Bell
Features 24 pages of full color!
VENTANA

3D Studio MAX f/x

$49.99, 552 pages, illustrated, part #: 427-8

Create Hollywood-style special effects! Plunge into 3D animation with step-by-step instructions for lighting, camera movements, optical effects, texture maps, storyboarding, cinematography, editing and much more. The companion CD-ROM features free plug-ins, all the tutorials from the book, 300+ original texture maps and animations.

WITH CD-ROM
Microsoft
SoftImage|3D
Professional Techniques
Comprehensive Guide to Modeling, Animation & Rendering
Andrew Reese
Stephanie Reese
VENTANA

Microsoft SoftImage|3D Professional Techniques

$69.99, 524 pages, illustrated, part #: 499-5

Create intuitive, visually rich 3D images with this award-winning technology. Follow the structured tutorial to master modeling, animation and rendering, and to increase your 3D productivity. The CD-ROM features tutorials, sample scenes, textures, scripts, shaders, images and animations.

WITH CD-ROM
LightWave 3D 5
Character Animation
f/x
Advanced Tips, Tools & Technique
Doug Kelly
VENTANA

LightWave 3D 5 Character Animation f/x

$69.99, 700 pages, illustrated, part #: 532-0

Master the fine—and lucrative—art of 3D character animation. Traditional animators and computer graphic artists alike will discover everything they need to know: lighting, motion, caricature, composition, rendering ... right down to work-flow strategies. The CD-ROM features a collection of the most popular LightWave plug-ins, scripts, storyboards, finished animations, models and much more.